FOREIGN RELATIONS LAW

E. Allan Farnsworth

On January 31, 2005, Aspen Publishers lost a great author, colleague, and friend with the death of E. Allan Farnsworth, the Alfred McCormack Professor of Law at Columbia Law School and author of the seminal student treatise, Contracts, Fourth Edition, by Aspen Publishers.

FOREIGN RELATIONS LAW

Cases and Materials

Second Edition

Curtis A. Bradley
Professor of Law
Duke University School of Law

Jack L. Goldsmith
Professor of Law
Harvard Law School

ASPEN

PUBLISHERS

111 Eighth Avenue, New York, NY 10011
http://lawschool.aspenpublishers.com

© 2006 Aspen Publishers, Inc.
a Wolters Kluwer business
http://lawschool.aspenpublishers.com

Printed in the United States of America.

1 2 3 4 5 6 7 8 9 0

ISBN 0-7355-5783-7

Library of Congress Cataloging-in-Publication Data

Bradley, Curtis A.
  Foreign relations law : cases and materials/Curtis A. Bradley, Jack L. Goldsmith.—
2nd ed.
          p. cm.
    Includes index.
    ISBN 0-7355-5783-7
    1. United States—Foreign relations—Law and legislation. I. Goldsmith, Jack L.
  II. Title.

KF4651.A4B73 2006
342.73′0412—dc22

2005035423

About Aspen Publishers

Aspen Publishers, headquartered in New York City, is a leading information provider for attorneys, business professionals, and law students. Written by preeminent authorities, our products consist of analytical and practical information covering both U.S. and international topics. We publish in the full range of formats, including updated manuals, books, periodicals, CDs, and online products.

Our proprietary content is complemented by 2,500 legal databases, containing over 11 million documents, available through our Loislaw division. Aspen Publishers also offers a wide range of topical legal and business databases linked to Loislaw's primary material. Our mission is to provide accurate, timely, and authoritative content in easily accessible formats, supported by unmatched customer care.

To order any Aspen Publishers title, go to *http://lawschool.aspenpublishers.com* or call 1-800-638-8437.

To reinstate your manual update service, call 1-800-638-8437.

For more information on Loislaw products, go to *www.loislaw.com* or call 1-800-364-2512.

For Customer Care issues, e-mail *CustomerCare@aspenpublishers.com*; call 1-800-234-1660; or fax 1-800-901-9075.

Aspen Publishers
a Wolters Kluwer business

To Kathy, David, and Liana

—Curtis A. Bradley

To Leslie, Jack, and Will

—Jack L. Goldsmith

Summary of Contents

Contents

Preface

This casebook examines the constitutional and statutory law that regulates the conduct of U.S. foreign relations. The topics covered include the distribution of foreign relations authority between the three federal branches, the relationship between the federal government and the states in regulating foreign relations, and the status of international law in U.S. courts. In addition to including excerpts of the major Supreme Court decisions in this area (and some lower court decisions that we thought would be helpful for teaching purposes), we have included a variety of non-case materials, including historical documents; excerpts of statutes, treaties, and Executive Branch pronouncements; and detailed notes and questions.

One of our goals in the book is to give students a sense of the rich history associated with foreign relations law. History is especially important in this field because much of the content of U.S. foreign relations law has developed in response to, and thus can best be understood in light of, discrete historical events. Historical research also has played a significant role in foreign relations scholarship. As a result, much of the first chapter is devoted to history, and we sketch the historical origins of all of the major foreign relations doctrines as they are presented.

Despite these historical materials, the focus of the book is on contemporary controversies, such as debates over the validity of executive agreements, the nature and limits on the war power, the scope of the treaty power, the legitimacy of international human rights litigation, and the propriety of judicial deference to the Executive Branch. In addition to describing the positions taken on these issues by institutional actors, we have attempted to give students some exposure to the extensive academic debates on these topics. We have avoided, however, including long excerpts of law review articles, which, in our experience, are not the best vehicle for teaching. Instead, we have attempted to weave the relevant academic arguments into the notes and questions that follow each set of cases and materials.

Without advocating any particular approach to constitutional interpretation, we also attempt to get students to focus closely on the text of the Constitution, a practice that we believe will be useful to them as lawyers. In addition, we emphasize issues of constitutional structure, especially federalism and separation of powers. Regardless of one's views about the legal relevance of these structural principles to foreign relations (a matter of some debate), we believe it is important to understand these principles at least for their *political* significance. A related theme of the book concerns "legal process" questions about the relative competence of various institutional actors to conduct U.S. foreign relations, questions that overlap with work that has been done in the political science area.

The casebook also emphasizes continuities and discontinuities between foreign relations law and "mainstream" constitutional law, statutory law, and federal jurisdiction issues. Indeed, we believe that many important constitutional law and federal courts doctrines — such as the political question doctrine, federal common law, and dormant preemption — have some of their most interesting applications in the foreign relations context. As a result, it is our hope that the book will appeal not only to students interested in international studies, but also to students interested in domestic constitutional and jurisdictional issues. We also hope that domestic law scholars will be tempted by this book to teach a course in foreign relations law.

Foreign relations law is a fast-changing field, and this second edition contains a significant amount of new material. Among other things, we have included excerpts of recent Supreme Court decisions relating to foreign relations law such as *Sosa v. Alvarez-Machain* (concerning law of nations claims under the Alien Tort Statute), *Hamdi v. Rumsfeld* (concerning the U.S. military detention of a U.S. citizen as an "enemy combatant" in the war on terrorism), *Republic of Austria v. Altmann* (concerning retroactive application of the Foreign Sovereign Immunities Act), and *American Insurance Association v. Garamendi* (concerning the preemption of state law based on sole executive agreements). As with the first edition, we have included a significant amount of material relating to issues posed by the post-September 11 war on terrorism. These issues are raised and addressed where relevant in each chapter, and we have also created a section in the war powers chapter (Chapter 4) specifically devoted to the war on terrorism. In addition to containing updated material throughout the book, this second edition reflects two substantial changes from the first edition. First, we have eliminated what was Chapter 9, on foreign sovereign immunity, and moved those materials to two places: Chapter 2, which covers the role of courts in foreign relations, and Chapter 7, which covers both customary international law and international human rights litigation. We believe that this change will make it easier to teach the sovereign immunity materials by integrating them better with related topics. Second, we have largely rewritten Chapter 4, on war powers. In part this is a reflection of the many interesting issues and developments that have arisen in the war on terrorism. It is also a reflection of additional work that we have both done in this area since the publication of the first edition, and the lessons that we have learned from teaching these materials in a number of classes.

Although (and indeed because) we have participated as scholars in many of the debates implicated by the cases and materials in this book, we have tried hard to present the issues and questions in a balanced manner. We welcome feedback on this and any other aspect of the casebook.

Curtis A. Bradley
Jack L. Goldsmith
December 2005

Acknowledgments

Many people and institutions have helped us in creating this casebook. In preparing the first edition, we benefited greatly from the assistance of the law librarians at the Universities of Virginia and Chicago and from financial and other support from our deans at those schools. We received similarly helpful support from our current law schools, Duke and Harvard, in preparing the second edition. The following individuals provided us with helpful comments and suggestions on drafts of the first edition: Roger Alford, David Bederman, Joe Dellapenna, Martin Flaherty, Ryan Goodman, Jill Hasday, Caleb Nelson, David Sloss, Peter Spiro, Paul Stephan, Geof Stone, Phillip Trimble, Adrian Vermeule, and Andrew Vollmer. Jide Nzelibe, Eric Posner, Michael Pyle, and Michael Ramsey provided helpful comments on the second edition. In preparing both editions of this casebook, we benefited enormously from our interactions with our students. Many of the changes in the second edition are reflections of lessons learned in the classroom. Finally, we would like to thank our able research assistants for their work on the first edition: Elizabeth Amory, Michael Bell, Jared Berg, Bryan Dayton, Megan Davidson, Colin McNary, Mark Mosier, Cynthia Orchard, David Scott, Kendal Sibley, and David Zetoony.

We also should mention that, since the publication of the first edition, we have both worked in the Executive Branch. Professor Goldsmith served as both Special Counsel to the General Counsel at the Department of Defense and as Assistant Attorney General in the Justice Department's Office of Legal Counsel, and Professor Bradley served as Counselor on International Law in the State Department. We both benefited greatly from these experiences and, to the extent that the information is not confidential, we have attempted to incorporate what we have learned into this casebook.

Finally, we thank the copyright holders who kindly granted us permission to reprint excerpts from the following materials:

Roger P. Alford, Misusing International Sources to Interpret the Constitution, 98 Am. J. Int'l L. 57 (2004). Copyright © 2004 by the American Society of International Law. Reprinted with permission of the American Society of International Law.

David P. Currie, The Constitution in Congress: The Federalist Period, 1789-1801 (1997). Copyright © 1997 by The University of Chicago. Reprinted with permission of The University of Chicago Press.

Louis Henkin, U.S. Ratification of Human Rights Conventions: The Ghost of Senator Bricker, 89 Am. J. Int'l L. 341 (1995). Copyright © 1995 by the American Society of International Law. Reprinted with permission of the American Society of International Law.

Robert Kagan, A Twilight Struggle: American Power and Nicaragua, 1977-1990 (1996). Copyright © 1996 by Robert Kagan. Reprinted with permission of Robert Kagan.

Gerald L. Neuman, The Uses of International Law in Constitutional Interpretation, 98 Am. J. Int'l L. 82 (2004). Copyright © 2004 by the American Society of International Law. Reprinted with permission of the American Society of International law.

Editorial Notice

In editing the cases and other materials in this book, we have used ellipses to indicate deletions and brackets to indicate additions. We have not generally signified the deletion of citations or footnotes, and we have not used ellipses at the end of the excerpted material. We have retained citations within the excerpted material only when we thought the citations served a pedagogical purpose or when the citations were needed to identify the source of a quotation.

Overview of International Law and Institutions

Because U.S. foreign relations law often intersects with international law, students may find it useful to acquaint themselves at the outset of this course with the basic sources of international law and some of the most important international institutions. The following is a brief overview.*

1. Sources of International Law

International law can be divided into two categories: public international law and private international law. Traditionally, public international law regulated the interactions between nations, such as the laws of war and the treatment of diplomats. Since the mid-twentieth century, it also has regulated to some extent the way nations treat their own citizens. Private international law, by contrast, encompasses issues relating to transactions and disputes between private parties, such as international commercial standards, international choice of law rules, and the standards for enforcing foreign judgments. References in this course to international law are primarily references to public international law.

There are two principal sources of public international law: treaties and customary international law. Treaties are, quite simply, binding agreements among nations. All such agreements are referred to as "treaties" under international law, regardless of what they are called under each nation's domestic law. By contrast, under U.S. domestic law, "treaties" refers only to the international agreements concluded by the President with the advice and consent of two-thirds of the Senate and does not include "executive agreements" made by the President alone or with a majority approval of Congress.

There are both "bilateral" treaties (between two nations) and "multilateral" treaties (among multiple nations). Typical bilateral treaties include extradition agreements, Friendship, Commerce, and Navigation treaties, and Bilateral Investment Treaties. Multilateral treaties — some of which resemble international legislation in their scope and detail — cover a wide range of subjects, including international trade, the environment, and human rights.

Customary international law results from the general practices and beliefs of nations. By most accounts, customary international law forms only after nations have consistently followed a particular practice out of a sense of legal obligation. It is also commonly accepted that nations that persistently object to an emerging customary international law rule are not bound by it, as long as they do so before the rule becomes settled. Nations that remain silent, however, may become bound by the rule, even if they did not expressly support it. Silence, in other words, is considered a form of implicit acceptance.

Treaties and customary international law have essentially equal weight under international law. As a result, if there is a conflict between these two sources of international law, the later of the two will be controlling. International and domestic adjudicators will likely attempt to reconcile these two sources, however, if that is

* For more extensive discussions, see, for example, Restatement (Third) of the Foreign Relations Law of the United States §§101-103 (1987); David J. Bederman, *International Law Frameworks* (2001); and Mark W. Janis, *An Introduction to International Law* (4th ed. 2003).

reasonably possible. Although it is not uncommon for treaties to supersede customary international law, there are relatively few examples in which customary international law has superseded a treaty.

Before the twentieth century, customary international law was the principal source of international law. Subjects regulated by customary international law included maritime law, the privileges and immunities of diplomats, and the standards for neutrality during wartime. Although customary international law continues to play an important role today, its importance has been eclipsed to some extent by the rise of multilateral treaties, which now regulate many areas previously regulated by customary international law.

Some customary international law rules are said to constitute "*jus cogens*" or "peremptory" norms. A *jus cogens* norm is, according to one widely accepted definition, "a norm accepted and recognized by the international community of States as a whole as a norm from which no derogation is permitted and which can be modified only by a subsequent norm of general international law having the same character."* These norms transcend requirements of national consent, such that nations are not allowed to opt out of them, even by treaty. Norms frequently described as *jus cogens* norms are the prohibitions (now contained in treaties) on genocide, slavery, and torture.

2. International Institutions

The United Nations was established at the end of World War II, pursuant to the United Nations Charter, a multilateral treaty. Today, 191 nations — essentially all the nations in the world — are parties to the Charter and thus members of the United Nations. The purposes of the United Nations, according to the Charter, are to maintain international peace and security; develop friendly relations among nations; achieve international cooperation in solving economic, social, cultural, and humanitarian problems, and in promoting respect for human rights and fundamental freedoms; and to be a center for harmonizing the actions of nations in attaining these ends.

The central deliberative organ of the United Nations is the General Assembly, which is made up of representatives of all the member nations. The General Assembly is an important forum for discussion and negotiation, but it does not have the power to make binding international law. Instead, it conducts studies and issues non-binding resolutions and recommendations reflecting the views of its members.

The principal enforcement arm of the United Nations is the Security Council. The Council is made up of representatives from fifteen nations. Five nations (China, France, Russia, the United Kingdom, and the United States) have permanent seats on the Council, as well as a veto power over the Council's decisions. The other ten seats on the Council are filled by representatives of other nations elected by the General Assembly. Under the United Nations Charter, the Council is given "primary responsibility for the maintenance of international peace and security." To address any threat to the peace, breach of the peace, or act of aggression, "the Council may call upon the members of the United Nations to apply" measures not involving the use of armed force, such as economic sanctions. If the Council determines that such non-military measures are inadequate, it may authorize "such action by air, sea, or land forces as may be necessary to maintain or restore

---

* Vienna Convention on the Law of Treaties, art. 53, May 23, 1969, 1155 U.N.T.S. 331.

international peace and security." The Charter obligates each member to "accept and carry out the decisions of the Security Council."

Another component of the United Nations system is the International Court of Justice (also sometimes referred to as the "World Court"), which is based in The Hague, in the Netherlands. There are fifteen judges on the Court and they are elected to staggered nine-year terms. The Court has jurisdiction over two types of cases: contentious cases and cases seeking an advisory opinion. In contentious cases, only nations may appear as parties. In cases seeking advisory opinions, certain international organizations may also be parties. To be a party to a contentious case before the International Court of Justice, a nation must ordinarily be a party to the Statute of the International Court of Justice (a multilateral treaty) and have consented to the Court's jurisdiction. Consent to jurisdiction can be given in several ways: a special agreement between the parties to submit their dispute to the Court; a jurisdictional clause in a treaty to which both nations are parties; or a general declaration accepting the compulsory jurisdiction of the Court.

In addition to the United Nations system, there are a variety of international institutions established to administer particular treaty regimes. A prominent example is the World Trade Organization (WTO), which was established in 1995 to administer the General Agreement on Tariffs and Trade and related agreements. The WTO has its own dispute settlement body, which adjudicates trade disputes between member nations. To enforce its decisions, the dispute settlement body can authorize the prevailing party to impose trade sanctions on the losing party. Another example is the International Criminal Court, based in The Hague, which has jurisdiction to try and punish certain international offenses, such as genocide.

Finally, there are regional international institutions, the most prominent of which is the European Union (EU). The EU currently is made up of twenty-five member countries. The EU has a number of constitutive organs, including a European Parliament, which is elected by individuals in the member countries; a Council of the European Union, which has representatives from the member governments; and a European Commission (an executive body). It also has a European Court of Justice, based in Luxembourg, which interprets and applies the treaty commitments of the Union. Although not part of the EU system, there is also a European Court of Human Rights, based in Strasbourg, France, which interprets and applies the European Convention for the Protection of Human Rights and Fundamental Freedoms (which has been ratified by over forty countries). The decisions of both the Court of Justice and the Court of Human Rights are binding on the member countries.

FOREIGN RELATIONS LAW

1

Introduction: Historical and Conceptual Foundations

This chapter introduces some of the recurring themes of the casebook. Section A does so in the context of describing the historical origins of the Constitution's foreign relations provisions. Section B then analyzes the constitutional issues implicated by the United States' first foreign relations crisis after ratification of the Constitution — the 1793 Neutrality Controversy. Finally, Section C examines some of the conceptual issues that arise in identifying the sources of the federal government's foreign relations powers.

A. CONSTITUTIONAL BACKGROUND

An understanding of history is often useful for understanding legal doctrine. It is particularly useful when studying foreign relations law. The Constitution was written against the background of, and was designed in part to redress, concrete foreign relations problems that arose in the pre-constitutional period. In addition, constitutional text does not specifically address many practical issues concerning the allocation and proper exercise of foreign relations powers. Often, therefore, the Founders' original understanding is consulted to flesh out and clarify the textual provisions. As we shall see, however, the original understanding of these provisions is sometimes unclear or unknowable.

Post-Founding history is also relevant to foreign relations law. Because of the relative lack of textual guidance, the details of constitutional foreign relations law have been developed through a process of trial and error in discrete historical contexts. When courts decide foreign relations law cases, they often consider this history. Moreover, because of various limitations on judicial review in the foreign relations context, courts have played a relatively modest role in developing and regulating foreign relations law. As a result, much of the law in this area has emerged in political practice outside the purview of courts; to understand the law, one must understand the historical practices out of which it emerges. Furthermore, the world has changed a great deal since the Founding. The United States has gone from a new and relatively weak nation to the world's only superpower, and the international threats and challenges it faces today are substantially different from those it faced in the late 1700s. As we shall see, the constitutional law of foreign relations has developed to meet the evolving challenges of international relations.

For all of these reasons, history is important and is emphasized throughout this casebook. This section presents materials relating to the historical background of the Constitution's foreign relations provisions.

1. Declaration of Independence

In the spring of 1774, representatives of the British colonies in America met in the First Continental Congress for the purpose of responding to British sanctions (known as the "Intolerable Acts") that were themselves responses to earlier acts of colonial defiance. In October 1774, Congress petitioned the King to redress grievances, agreed on sanctions, and agreed to meet the following year. The Second Continental Congress convened in May 1775, approximately three weeks after fighting had broken out between the British and the Americans at Lexington and Concord. It was not until June of 1776, however, that a consensus formed in favor of independence. At this point, it was clear to all involved that the financial, political, and military support of continental European countries would be crucial in achieving victory over the British. And this, in turn, raised questions about the proper conduct of foreign relations and the requirements of international law. Richard Henry Lee, the delegate from Virginia who introduced the resolution of independence, maintained that "[n]o state in Europe will either [enter into treaties] or Trade with us so long as we consider ourselves Subjects of [Great Britain]." He later added: "It is not choice then but necessity which calls for Independence, as the only means by which foreign allies can be obtained." *See* Bradford Perkins, The Creation of a Republican Empire, 1776-1865, 1 Cambridge History of American Foreign Relations 19 (1993). On June 11, 1776, the Continental Congress chose committees to draft a declaration of independence, prepare a plan of confederation, and draft a model commercial treaty. Independence, union, and foreign relations were thus viewed as inextricably related.

But where did the power to conduct foreign relations for the United States rest — with the Continental Congress or the States? No written governmental compact bound the States together or defined the Continental Congress's powers. And the Declaration of Independence itself was unclear as to whether the United States was a nation or a confederate union of thirteen States. On the one hand, its famous first sentence begins: "When in the Course of human events, it becomes necessary for *one people* to dissolve the political bands which have connected them with another...." On the other hand, the document is entitled "The unanimous Declaration of *the Thirteen united States* of America."* And its closing paragraph provides:

> We, therefore, the Representatives of the united States of America, in General Congress, Assembled, appealing to the Supreme Judge of the world for the rectitude of our intentions, do, in the Name, and by Authority of the good People of these Colonies, solemnly publish and declare, That these United Colonies are, and of Right ought to be Free and Independent States; that they are Absolved from all Allegiance to the British Crown, and that all political connection between them and the State of Great Britain, is and ought to be totally dissolved; and that as Free and Independent States,

---

* Thomas Jefferson's original draft, later changed by Congress, read: "A Declaration of the Representatives of the United States of America, in General Congress assembled." *See* 1 The Papers of Thomas Jefferson 423 (Julian P. Boyd ed., 1950).

they have full Power to levy War, conclude Peace, contract Alliances, establish Commerce, and to do all other Acts and Things which Independent States may of right do.

1 The Papers of Thomas Jefferson 432 (Julian P. Boyd ed., 1950).

Moreover, some state constitutions during this period contemplated state foreign relations powers. Article 18 of New York's April 20, 1777, constitution provided that "the governor shall . . . by virtue of his office, be general and commander-in-chief of all the militia, and admiral of the navy of this State. . . ." Similarly, Article 26 of the South Carolina Constitution of 1776 stated that "the president and commander-in-chief [of South Carolina]" would have the power "to make war or peace, or enter into any final treaty" only with the "consent of the general assembly and legislative council." In addition, several states negotiated directly with European nations for loans, arms, clothing, and the like — in direct competition with, and to the great annoyance and disadvantage of, the Continental Congress's official representative and treaty negotiator, Benjamin Franklin. *See* Letter from Benjamin Franklin to the Committee of Foreign Affairs, in 3 Francis Wharton, The Revolutionary Diplomatic Correspondence of the United States 186, 192 (1889).

Despite these suggestions of residual foreign relations powers in the individual former colonies, the Continental Congress conducted foreign relations for the United States. The Continental Congress agreed on a model commercial treaty (the so-called Plan of 1776) in the fall of 1776 and sent a delegation, led by Franklin, to France. The French Foreign Minister, Vergennes, received this delegation, and after much hesitation (having to do with uncertainty about the outcome of the Revolutionary War), the United States and France signed two treaties — of alliance, and of commerce — in Paris on February 6, 1778. (These treaties would be at the center of the Neutrality Controversy, discussed below in Section B.) These treaties constituted the first official recognition of the United States as an independent nation. The Continental Congress ratified these treaties on May 4, 1778. The Continental Congress also authorized several other treaty delegations prior to the ratification of the Articles of Confederation, but no additional treaties were concluded during this period.

[handwritten margin note: 1778 U.S. ? France sign treaties]

On the source of the United States foreign relations power during this period, Justice Chase made the following comments in Ware v. Hylton, 3 U.S. 199, 231-32 (1796):

> It has been enquired what powers Congress possessed from the first meeting, in September 1774, until the ratification of the articles of confederation, on the 1st of March, 1781? It appears to me, that the powers of Congress, during that whole period, were derived from the people they represented, expressly given, through the medium of their State Conventions, or State Legislatures; or that after they were exercised they were impliedly ratified by the acquiescence and obedience of the people. . . . The powers of Congress originated from necessity, and arose out of, and were only limited by, events or, in other words, they were revolutionary in their very nature. Their extent depended on the exigencies and necessities of public affairs. It was absolutely and indispensably necessary that Congress should possess the power of conducting the war against Great Britain, and therefore if not expressly given by all, (as it was by some of the States) I do not hesitate to say, that Congress did rightfully possess such power. The authority to make war, of necessity implies the power to make peace; or the war must be perpetual. I entertain this general idea, that the several States retained all internal sovereignty; and that Congress properly possessed the great rights of external sovereignty: Among others, the right to make treaties of commerce and alliance; as with France on the 6th of February 1778.

[handwritten margin note: opinion that power derived from people]

For similar sentiments, see Penhallow v. Doane, 3 U.S. 54, 80-81 (1795) (Paterson, J.); Chisholm v. Georgia, 2 U.S. 419, 470 (1793) (Jay, C.J.).

2. Articles of Confederation

The Continental Congress adopted the Articles of Confederation in November 1777 and submitted them to the States, which approved them in March 1781. The Articles ostensibly gave broad foreign relations power to "the united states in congress assembled." Among other things, the Continental Congress was given the "sole and exclusive power of determining on peace and war," "of sending and receiving ambassadors," and of "entering into treaties and alliances." In addition, the individual states were expressly prohibited from engaging in certain foreign relations activities without Congress's consent, such as sending and receiving ambassadors, entering into treaties, engaging in war, and keeping troops or vessels of war in time of peace. Despite these provisions, by the time of the Constitutional Convention in 1787, there was widespread agreement that the structure and powers of the national government under the Articles of Confederation were insufficient with respect to the management of foreign relations.

The following excerpt summarizes the operation and weaknesses of the United States' foreign relations machinery under the Articles of Confederation:

Bradford Perkins, The Creation of a Republican Empire, 1776-1865

1 Cambridge History of American Foreign Relations 54-59 (1993)

The Continental Congress, legitimized only by the willingness of states to send delegates, had no power of coercion over them. Seeking to improve things, Congress proposed, and in 1781 the states approved, Articles of Confederation, but the remedy failed to create an effective national government. The approved text failed to capitalize "united states," thus emphasizing the continued sovereignty of the parts. Almost all decisions, even in areas where Congress nominally had power, required the concurrence of nine of the thirteen states. Amendments, several times proposed in an effort to improve the system, could be — and were — blocked by a single state's negative....

The state-oriented thrust of the Articles of Confederation was underlined by the absence of an executive branch. Congress, working sometimes through committees, did all the governing in what was "in effect parliamentary government without a prime minister." The committee system worked badly because there were so many that no congressman could give adequate attention to any one of them, because they competed for influence and because the steady turnover of membership prevented continuity. The Committee of Secret Correspondence and its successor, the Committee for Foreign Affairs, never gained full control of diplomacy, had no staff to manage correspondence and records, and met only intermittently....

In 1781 Congress established a Department of Foreign Affairs, made up of a secretary and four employees, but it kept the department on a very short leash.... Flaws in the diplomatic machinery reflected the central weakness of the Articles of Confederation. The nation did not command respect abroad and had

states retained power so U.S couldn't coerce anything

little ability to develop any. As Jefferson, Franklin's successor at Paris, observed in 1784, Americans were "the lowest and most obscure of the diplomatic tribe." Because the states retained so much power, the government at Philadelphia could not raise revenue, could not bargain effectively, could not assure other nations that any agreements it made would actually be observed by the states, could not develop a unified commercial policy to extort concessions from other countries, could not maintain an effective military or naval force.

The effects of this weakness were pervasive. Leaders in Vermont went so far as to weigh the comparative advantages of a Canadian connection against an American one. Spanish authorities in Louisiana intrigued with Indian tribes and American settlers in territory disputed by Spain and the United States. Canadian officials maintained as much influence as they could over tribes south of the Great Lakes, although, contrary to American belief, they did not urge the Indians to make war on the United States. British garrisons remained in a string of posts stretching from Lake Champlain to Lake Superior, London using as justification the fact that the Congress had been unable to induce the states to carry out promises made in the Treaty of Paris regarding Tory property and the payment of prewar debts. "If we are now to pay the debts due to British merchants," Virginians were alleged to ask, "what have we been fighting for all this time?"

Most important of all was commerce. Looking back, James Madison wrote in 1789, "our trade . . . entirely contradicted the advantages expected from the Revolution, no new channels being opened with other European nations, and the British channels being narrowed by a refusal of the most natural and valuable one to the U.S." Various envoys, most notably Jefferson in France, sought to negotiate the lowering of trade barriers, but they had little to bargain with — Congress could not threaten to close trade, or tax it — and accomplished little. . . .

American powerlessness meant that London had a free hand. Lord Sheffield, an influential advocate of sternness toward the ex-colonies' commerce, justified it in part on the ground that "America cannot retaliate. It will not be an easy matter to bring the American States to act as a nation. They are not to be feared as such by us." An Order in Council issued in 1783 to regulate the direct trade across the Atlantic was not illiberal, and, as the British hoped, that trade soon regained prewar levels. But another Order in Council closed the British West Indies to American vessels, depriving shipowners, exporters, and farmers of traditional business. John Adams, the first American minister to Britain, totally failed in his efforts to improve matters. Although Americans read all of this as a sign of British malevolence, it really reflected nothing more than an understanding of American weakness.

Within only a few years of the euphoric confirmation of independence, these problems came to cloud the skies. So, too, did internal problems, varying from state to state, often centering around the broad issues of liberty and order, property and persons, liberalism and conservatism. . . .

Nevertheless, a good case can be made for the primacy of concerns over American weakness in the world. "Nothing contributed more directly to the calling of the 1787 Constitutional Convention," Walter LaFeber writes, "than did the spreading belief that under the Articles of Confederation Congress could not effectively and safely conduct foreign policy." The Annapolis Convention of 1786, which itself failed to accomplish anything but issued the call for the successful meeting of the next year, was convened specifically to consider the sad condition of American trade. If there was comparatively little discussion at Philadelphia of diplomatic and even military matters, it was because almost everyone agreed that the mechanisms of foreign policy had to be changed. They agreed, too, that American diplomacy had to be further armed for controversies with other nations. Differences were almost always over detail, and far-reaching changes were not so much debated as assumed.

Essentially, no matter how devoted to the rights of states, the delegates at Philadelphia believed that the central government must be made strong enough to command the respect of foreign nations. From Paris, Jefferson pithily summarized the opinion of those who opposed centralized government: "I wish to see our states made one as to all foreign, and several as to all domestic matters." Despite deep concern about standing armies, seen as potential instruments of tyranny, there was general agreement that the national government must be given war powers, both to deter possible enemies and to fight wars effectively.

Similarly, it was recognized that the thirteen states could not, acting individually, extort commercial concessions from other nations. Thus, despite fears that the interests of some states might be sacrificed by a national legislature, Congress was given the power to create policies that might compel Great Britain and others to relax some of their restrictions on American trade. Finally, it was agreed that, if the United States were to bargain effectively, the national government must not only have the power to conclude treaties but to compel states to observe them.

This by no means suggests that the framers of the Constitution wanted or expected the United States to plunge deeply into traditional diplomacy. Even strong nationalists like Madison and Alexander Hamilton thought that the United States should never have more than five or six missions abroad. Others wanted fewer. Some even suggested that none would be needed; other nations should be required to send envoys to America whenever there was anything to negotiate. Such attitudes showed that "the delegates assumed that diplomatic negotiations *per se* would be rare, that foreign relations would be commercial in nature, and that treaties would be few." The creation of a nation with power to defend itself and to bargain commercially, primarily by legislation, would, the delegates thought, be sufficient to transform the scene.

The following excerpt further highlights some of the foreign policy issues faced by the United States during the Articles of Confederation period:

Jack N. Rakove, Making Foreign Policy — The View from 1787

Foreign Policy and the Constitution 1-3 (Robert A. Goldwin & Robert A. Licht eds., 1990)

Foreign affairs loomed far larger in the movement that led to the writing of the Constitution than many scholars have been prepared to recognize....[B]efore 1787 it was the inability of the existing Continental Congress to frame and implement adequate foreign policies that evoked the most telling criticisms of the "imbecility" of the Articles of Confederation. Well into 1786 most efforts to amend the Articles were designed primarily to enable Congress to act effectively in the one area — the realm of foreign relations — where its responsibility was presumably least subject to question.

The essential foreign policy agenda of the newly independent republic emerged within a year of the conclusion of the Treaty of Paris, which recognized that the United States had indeed attained "among the powers of the earth, the separate and equal station" to which they were entitled by various authorities. Three issues posed serious challenges to the national welfare.

First, Britain's refusal to open either the West Indies or the home islands to American shipping, coupled with the flooding of American markets with British ships carrying British goods, raised fundamental issues of commercial policy. The obvious strategy for the United States to pursue was to close its own harbors to British goods until Britain opened imperial ports to American ships. But since Congress had no authority to regulate either interstate or foreign commerce — unless it could conclude a treaty that Britain had no incentive to negotiate — retaliation required the adoption of identical restrictions by all the states. This proved impracticable.

A second issue arose from the refusal of particular states to comply with provisions of the peace treaty concerning the legal rights of private creditors, British subjects, and refugee loyalists who hoped to sue for the recovery of either prewar debts or confiscated property. Britain seized upon noncompliance with these articles as a pretext to retain control of its forts along the frontier — and thus to maintain its influence over hostile Indian nations in western New York and the lands above the Ohio River. This jeopardized congressional plans for settling the national domain, but again Congress could not compel the states to abide by the treaty.

Western expansion was also involved in the third major issue of postwar foreign policy, which stemmed from a Spanish decision of 1784 to close New Orleans and the lower Mississippi River to American navigation. A Union that could not secure American access to the Gulf of Mexico might also lose the allegiance of the mass of settlers surging across the Appalachian chain from the east. Without independent sources of revenue, Congress lacked the means to project American power into the interior. But more than that, the sectional dimensions of the Mississippi question exposed the fragility of the American union, since southern leaders were far more committed to expansion into the Southwest than their counterparts in the North. The explosive potential of this became evident in 1786, when Secretary of Foreign Affairs John Jay (of New York) proposed that Congress abjure its claim to the Mississippi navigation in order to secure the commercial treaty he was then seeking to negotiate with Spain. Jay's request provoked a sharply sectional conflict within Congress, fueling speculation that the union might soon devolve into two or three regional confederacies.

3. United States Constitution

It is against this background that the foreign relations provisions of the United States Constitution were drafted. You should now read the entire Constitution in Appendix A. Pay particular attention to the following provisions: Article I, §1, cl. 1; Article I, §8, cls. 1, 3, 4, 10-16, 18; Article I, §9, cls. 5-6; Article I, §10, cls. 1-3; Article II, §1, cl. 1; Article II, §2, cls. 1-2; Article III, §§1-2; Article VI, §2; and Amendment X.

What follows are excerpts from *The Federalist Papers* concerning the weaknesses of the national government under the Articles of Confederation and the virtues of the foreign relations provisions of the new Constitution. *The Federalist Papers* consist of 85 newspaper essays written by Alexander Hamilton, John Jay, and James Madison during the 1787-1788 deliberations over the proposed U.S. Constitution.

These essays reflect the opinions of three prominent proponents of the Constitution attempting to persuade others to support ratification. They are not definitive accounts of the original understanding of the Constitution's foreign relations provisions, but they have been influential in subsequent debates about these provisions. We include them here to provide a sense of the foreign relations concerns of the Founders and some of their justifications for the Constitution's foreign relations provisions. As we study specific constitutional issues throughout the casebook, we will examine the historical background of the pertinent constitutional provisions in more detail.

To convince ratification of the constitution

Federalist No. 3 (Jay)

It is of high importance to the peace of America that she observe the laws of nations towards all [powers with whom she has treaties and other relations], and to me it appears evident that this will be more perfectly and punctually done by one national government than it could be either by thirteen separate States or by three or four distinct confederacies. . . .

Because, under the national government, treaties and articles of treaties, as well as the laws of nations, will always be expounded in one sense and executed in the same manner, — whereas adjudications on the same points and questions, in thirteen States, or in three or four confederacies, will not always accord or be consistent; and that, as well from the variety of independent courts and judges appointed by different and independent governments, as from the different local laws and interests which may affect and influence them. The wisdom of the convention, in committing such questions to the jurisdiction and judgment of courts appointed by and responsible only to one national government, cannot be too much commended.

Federalist No. 4 (Jay)

Leave America divided into thirteen or, if you please, into three or four independent governments — what armies could they raise and pay — what fleets could they ever hope to have? If one was attacked, would the others fly to its succor, and spend their blood and money in its defense? Would there be no danger of their being flattered into neutrality by its specious promises, or seduced by a too great fondness for peace to decline hazarding their tranquillity and present safety for the sake of neighbors, of whom perhaps they have been jealous, and whose importance they are content to see diminished? Although such conduct would not be wise, it would, nevertheless, be natural.

But whatever may be our situation, whether firmly united under one national government, or split into a number of confederacies, certain it is, that foreign nations will know and view it exactly as it is; and they will act toward us accordingly. If they see that our national government is efficient and well administered, our trade prudently regulated, our militia properly organized and disciplined, our resources and finances discreetly managed, our credit re-established, our people free, contented, and united, they will be much more disposed to cultivate our friendship than provoke our resentment. If, on the other hand, they find us either destitute of an effectual government (each State doing right or wrong, as to its rulers may seem convenient), or split into three or four independent and probably discordant republics or confederacies, one inclining to Britain, another to France, and a third to Spain, and perhaps played off against each other by the three, what a poor, pitiful figure will America make in their eyes!

Federalist No. 11 (Hamilton)

The importance of the Union, in a commercial light, is one of those points about which there is least room to entertain a difference of opinion . . . This applies as well to our intercourse with foreign countries as with each other. . . .

　　If we continue united, we may counteract a policy so unfriendly to our prosperity in a variety of ways. By prohibitory regulations, extending, at the same time, throughout the States, we may oblige foreign countries to bid against each other, for the privileges of our markets. This assertion will not appear chimerical to those who are able to appreciate the importance of the markets of three millions of people — increasing in rapid progression, for the most part exclusively addicted to agriculture, and likely from local circumstances to remain so — to any manufacturing nation; and the immense difference there would be to the trade and navigation of such a nation, between a direct communication in its own ships, and an indirect conveyance of its products and returns, to and from America, in the ships of another country. Suppose, for instance, we had a government in America, capable of excluding Great Britain (with whom we have at present no treaty of commerce) from all our ports; what would be the probable operation of this step upon her politics? Would it not enable us to negotiate, with the fairest prospect of success, for commercial privileges of the most valuable and extensive kind, in the dominions of that kingdom?

Federalist No. 15 (Hamilton)

We may indeed with propriety be said to have reached almost the last stage of national humiliation. There is scarcely any thing that can wound the pride or degrade the character of an independent nation which we do not experience. Are there engagements to the performance of which we are held by every tie respectable among men? These are the subjects of constant and unblushing violation. Do we owe debts to foreigners and to our own citizens contracted in a time of imminent peril for the preservation of our political existence? These remain without any proper or satisfactory provision for their discharge. Have we valuable territories and important posts in the possession of a foreign power which, by express stipulations, ought long since to have been surrendered? These are still retained, to the prejudice of our interests, not less than of our rights. Are we in a condition to resent or to repel the aggression? We have neither troops, nor treasury, nor government. Are we even in a condition to remonstrate with dignity? The just imputations on our own faith, in respect to the same treaty, ought first to be removed. Are we entitled by nature and compact to a free participation in the navigation of the Mississippi? Spain excludes us from it. Is public credit an indispensable resource in time of public danger? We seem to have abandoned its cause as desperate and irretrievable. Is commerce of importance to national wealth? Ours is at the lowest point of declension. Is respectability in the eyes of foreign powers a safeguard against foreign encroachments? The imbecility of our government even forbids them to treat with us. Our ambassadors abroad are the mere pageants of mimic sovereignty.

Federalist No. 42 (Madison)

The *second* class of powers, lodged in the general government, consist of those which regulate the intercourse with foreign nations, to wit: to make treaties; to send and receive ambassadors, other public ministers, and consuls; to define and punish piracies and felonies committed on the high seas, and offenses against the law of nations; to regulate foreign commerce. . . .

This class of powers forms an obvious and essential branch of the federal administration. If we are to be one nation in any respect, it clearly ought to be in respect to other nations.

The powers to make treaties and to send and receive ambassadors, speak their own propriety. . . .

The power to define and punish piracies and felonies committed on the high seas, and offenses against the law of nations, belongs with equal propriety to the general government, and is a still greater improvement on the articles of Confederation. These articles contain no provision for the case of offenses against the law of nations; and consequently leave it in the power of any indiscreet member to embroil the Confederacy with foreign nations.

Federalist No. 75 (Hamilton)

However proper or safe it may be in governments where the executive magistrate is an hereditary monarch, to commit to him the entire power of making treaties, it would be utterly unsafe and improper to intrust that power to an elective magistrate of four years' duration. . . . An avaricious man might be tempted to betray the interests of the state to the acquisition of wealth. An ambitious man might make his own aggrandizement, by the aid of a foreign power, the price of his treachery to his constituents. . . .

To have intrusted the power of making treaties to the Senate alone, would have been to relinquish the benefits of the constitutional agency of the President in the conduct of foreign negotiations. It is true that the Senate would, in that case, have the option of employing him in this capacity, but they would also have the option of letting it alone, and pique or cabal might induce the latter rather than the former. Besides this, the ministerial servant of the Senate could not be expected to enjoy the confidence and respect of foreign powers in the same degree with the constitutional representatives of the nation, and, of course, would not be able to act with an equal degree of weight or efficacy. While the Union would, from this cause, lose a considerable advantage in the management of its external concerns, the people would lose the additional security which would result from the co-operation of the executive. . . .

The fluctuating and, taking its future increase into the account, the multitudinous composition of [the House of Representatives], forbid us to expect in it those qualities which are essential to the proper execution of such a trust. Accurate and comprehensive knowledge of foreign politics; a steady and systematic adherence to the same views; a nice and uniform sensibility to national character; decision, *secrecy*, and dispatch, are incompatible with the genius of a body so variable and so numerous. The very complication of the business, by introducing a necessity of the concurrence of so many different bodies, would of itself afford a solid objection.

Federalist No. 80 (Hamilton)

It seems scarcely to admit of controversy, that the judiciary authority of the Union ought to extend to these several descriptions of cases: . . . 4th, to all those which involve the PEACE of the CONFEDERACY, whether they relate to the intercourse between the United States and foreign nations, or to that between the States themselves; . . .

The fourth point rests on this plain proposition, that the peace of the WHOLE ought not to be left at the disposal of a PART. The Union will undoubtedly be answerable to foreign powers for the conduct of its members. And the responsibility for an injury ought ever to be accompanied with the faculty of preventing it. As the denial or perversion of justice by the sentences of courts, as well as in any other manner, is with reason classed among the just causes of war, it will follow that the federal judiciary ought to have cognizance of all causes in which the citizens of other countries are concerned.

Notes and Questions

1. Based on the above excerpts, what were the structural weaknesses of the Articles of Confederation with respect to the conduct of foreign relations? How were these problems addressed in the Constitution?

2. What was the purpose of the Declaration of Independence? To whom was it addressed? Why did it refer in its opening paragraph to the "opinions of mankind"? Why did its closing paragraph refer to the foreign relations powers of the colonies? What was the relationship between the Declaration and international law? For a discussion of the last question, see David Armitage, *The Declaration of Independence and International Law*, 59 Wm. & Mary Q. 1 (2002); *see also* Eugene Kontorovich, *Disrespecting the "Opinions of Mankind"*, 8 Green Bag 2d 261, 265 (2005) (arguing that "the Declaration was written to *shape* the opinions of mankind; it did not contemplate being influenced by them").

3. According to the text of the Constitution, what foreign relations powers are assigned to Congress? To the President? To the federal courts? What role, if any, can states play in foreign relations? What are the states prohibited from doing? What status do treaties have in the U.S. legal system? What status does the "law of nations" have? Does the Tenth Amendment have any relevance to foreign relations issues?

4. Edward Corwin famously observed that the Constitution "is an invitation to struggle for the privilege of directing American foreign policy." Edward S. Corwin, The President: Office and Powers 1787-1984, at 201 (Randall Bland et al. eds., 5th rev. ed. 1984). In what ways does the text of the U.S. Constitution regulate this struggle? In what ways does it invite the struggle? Is it desirable that the foreign relations powers of the three federal branches, and the states, be clearly defined, or are there virtues to uncertainty with respect to such powers?

5. Do foreign relations powers inhere in sovereignty? If so, which foreign relations powers? Where was the locus of this sovereignty in 1776? During the Articles of Confederation period? If the U.S. Constitution had not allocated foreign relations powers to the national government, would the national government nevertheless possess them? Which ones?

6. For additional discussion of the United States' conduct of foreign relations during the revolutionary period, see Samuel Flagg Bemis, The Diplomacy of the American Revolution (1935); Perkins, 1 Cambridge History of American Foreign Relations, *supra*; Julius W. Pratt, A History of United States Foreign Policy 39-53 (1955). For additional discussion of the foreign relations difficulties under the Articles of Confederation, see Richard B. Morris, The Forging of the Federal Union, 1781-1789 (1987); Jack N. Rakove, The Beginnings of National Politics: An Interpretive History of the Continental Congress (1979); Frederick W. Marks III, Independence on Trial: Foreign Affairs and the Making of the Constitution (1973).

B. NEUTRALITY CONTROVERSY OF 1793

In 1789, the same year the United States began operating under its new Constitution, a violent revolution was initiated in France. The spillover from this revolution led to the first great crisis in the U.S. constitutional law of foreign relations. Central to the controversy were the treaties that the United States had entered into with France in 1778, described above. Among other things, these treaties required the United States to help protect French possessions in the Americas (such as the French West Indies), allowed French warships and privateers to bring prizes into U.S. ports, and disallowed the use by France's enemies of U.S. ports for outfitting privateers and selling prizes. When revolutionary France declared war on Great Britain, Spain, and Holland (France was already at war with Austria and Prussia) following the execution of Louis XVI in early 1793, the French-U.S. treaties raised the prospect that the United States might be drawn into the war on the side of the French. President Washington, however, was determined to avoid entanglement in the European war. As Washington explained to Gouverneur Morris, the U.S. Minister to France, it would be "unwise . . . in the extreme to involve ourselves in the contests of European Nations, where our weight could be but small; tho' the loss to ourselves would be certain." Letter from George Washington to Gouverneur Morris, March 25, 1793, in 32 The Writings of George Washington 402 (John C. Fitzpatrick ed., 1939).

Washington's cabinet debated what the President should do — consistent with international law and the U.S. Constitution — to stay out of the European conflict. The cabinet first considered whether to call Congress into special session, and it decided not to do so. It then considered whether the President should issue a proclamation to prevent U.S. citizens from participating in the war, and whether such a proclamation should contain a declaration of U.S. neutrality. Secretary of State Thomas Jefferson initially argued that the President had no authority to issue a formal declaration of neutrality, because (as he later recounted to Madison) that would amount to "a declaration there should be no war, to which the Executive was not competent." Letter from Thomas Jefferson to James Madison, June 23, 1793, in 26 The Papers of Thomas Jefferson 346 (John Catanzariti ed., 1995). The

[handwritten: Debate as to wether president had power to declare neutrality]

cabinet, including Jefferson, ultimately agreed to issue a proclamation of neutrality, but, perhaps in response to Jefferson's concerns, the proclamation did not use the word "neutrality." The following is an excerpt of the proclamation:

Proclamation of Neutrality, April 22, 1793

32 The Writings of George Washington 430-31
(John C. Fitzpatrick ed., 1939)

Whereas it appears that a state of war exists between Austria, Prussia, Sardinia, Great Britain, and the United Netherlands, on the one part, and France on the other; and the duty and interest of the United States require, that they should with sincerity and good faith adopt and pursue a conduct friendly and impartial toward the belligerent powers:

I have therefore thought fit by these presents, to declare the disposition of the United States to observe the conduct aforesaid towards those powers respectively; and to exhort and warn the citizens of the United States carefully to avoid all acts and proceedings whatsoever, which may in any manner tend to contravene such disposition.

And I do hereby also make known, that whosoever of the citizens of the United States shall render himself liable to punishment or forfeiture under the law of nations, by committing, aiding or abetting hostilities against any of the said powers, or by carrying to any of them, those articles which are deemed contraband by the modern usage of nations, will not receive the protection of the United States against such punishment or forfeiture; and further that I have given instructions to those officers to whom it belongs, to cause prosecutions to be instituted against all persons, who shall, within the cognizance of the Courts of the United States, violate the law of nations, with respect to the powers at war, or any of them.

The Neutrality Proclamation was controversial for two reasons: it was not authorized by Congress, and it was construed by some as a repudiation of U.S. treaty obligations to France. As James Madison wrote to Jefferson on June 19, 1793:

[handwritten: 2 issues!]

> The proclamation was in truth a most unfortunate error. It wounds the National honor, by seeming to disregard to stipulated duties to France.... And it seems to violate the forms & spirit of the Constitution, by making the executive Magistrate the organ of the disposition, the duty & interest of the Nation in relation to war & peace, subjects appropriated to other departments of the Government.

Letter from James Madison to Thomas Jefferson, June 19, 1793, in 15 The Papers of James Madison 33 (Thomas A. Mason et al. eds., 1985).

When criticisms of this sort began to be made in public, Hamilton was moved to defend the Neutrality Proclamation in seven newspaper articles under the pseudonym "Pacificus." Hamilton's defense, and in particular his conception of presidential power, alarmed Jefferson, who urged his friend Madison to respond: "Nobody answers him, & his doctrine will therefore be taken for confessed. For god's sake, my dear Sir, take up your pen, select the most striking heresies, and cut him to pieces in the face of the public." Letter from Thomas Jefferson to James Madison, July 7, 1793, in 26 The Papers of Thomas Jefferson, *supra*, at 444. After some initial reluctance, Madison answered Hamilton in five newspaper articles under the pseudonym "Helvidius." The Pacificus-Helvidius debate is among the most celebrated arguments in U.S. constitutional history. The themes in this debate — the nature and scope of presidential power, the separation of federal powers in foreign relations, and the proper methods of constitutional interpretation — recur throughout this casebook.

"Pacificus" No. 1

15 The Papers of Alexander Hamilton 33-43
(Harold C. Syrett & Jacob E. Cooke eds., 1969)

It will not be disputed that the management of the affairs of this country with foreign nations is confided to the Government of the [United States]. . . .

The inquiry then is — what department of the government of the [United States] is the proper one to make a declaration of Neutrality, in the cases in which the engagements of the Nation permit and its interests require such a declaration.

A correct and well-informed mind will discern at once that it can belong neither to the Legislative nor Judicial Department and of course must belong to the Executive.

The Legislative Department is not the organ of intercourse between the [United States] and foreign Nations. It is charged neither with making nor interpreting Treaties. It is therefore not naturally that Organ of the Government which is to pronounce the existing condition of the Nation, with regard to foreign Powers, or to admonish the Citizens of their obligations and duties as founded upon that condition of things. Still less is it charged with enforcing the execution and observance of these obligations and those duties.

It is equally obvious that the act in question is foreign to the Judiciary Department of the Government. The province of that Department is to decide litigations in particular cases. It is indeed charged with the interpretation of treaties; but it exercises this function only in the litigated cases; that is where contending parties bring before it a specific controversy. It has no concern with pronouncing upon the external political relations of Treaties between Government and Government. This position is too plain to need being insisted upon.

It must then of necessity belong to the Executive Department to exercise the function in Question, when a proper case for the exercise of it occurs.

It appears to be connected with that department in various capacities, as the organ of intercourse between the Nation and foreign Nations — as the interpreter of the National Treaties in those cases in which the Judiciary is not competent, that is in the cases between Government and Government — as that Power, which is charged with the Execution of the Laws, of which Treaties form a part — as that Power which is charged with the command and application of the Public Force. . . .

The second Article of the Constitution of the [United States], section 1st, establishes this general Proposition, That "The EXECUTIVE POWER shall be vested in a President of the United States of America."

The same article in a succeeding Section proceeds to designate particular cases of Executive Power. It declares among other things that the President shall be Commander in Chief of the army and navy of the [United States] and of the Militia of the several states when called into the actual service of the [United States] that he shall have power by and with the advice of the senate to make treaties; that it shall

"Pacificus" - Hamilton argue why the power was with the Pres. to declare neutrality

be his duty to receive ambassadors and other public Ministers and to take care that the laws be faithfully executed.

It would not consist with the rules of sound construction to consider this enumeration of particular authorities as derogating from the more comprehensive grant contained in the general clause, further than as it may be coupled with express restrictions or qualifications; as in regard to the co-operation of the Senate in the appointment of Officers and the making of treaties; which are qualifications of the general executive powers of appointing officers and making treaties: Because the difficulty of a complete and perfect specification of all the cases of Executive authority would naturally dictate the use of general terms — and would render it improbable that a specification of certain particulars was designed as a substitute for those terms, when antecedently used. The different mode of expression employed in the constitution in regard to the two powers the Legislative and the Executive serves to confirm this inference. In the article which grants the legislative powers of the [Government] the expressions are — "All Legislative powers herein granted shall be vested in a Congress of the [United States]," in that which grants the Executive Power the expressions are, as already quoted "The EXECUTIVE POWER shall be vested in a President of the [United States] of America."

The enumeration ought rather therefore to be considered as intended by way of greater caution, to specify and regulate the principal articles implied in the definition of Executive Power; leaving the rest to flow from the general grant of that power, interpreted in conformity to other parts of the Constitution, and to the principles of free government.

The general doctrine then of our constitution is, that the EXECUTIVE POWER of the Nation is vested in the President; subject only to the exceptions and qualifications which are expressed in the instrument.

Two of these have been already noticed — the participation of the Senate in the appointment of Officers and the making of Treaties. A third remains to be mentioned; the right of the Legislature "to declare war and grant letters of marque and reprisal."

With these exceptions the EXECUTIVE POWER of the Union is completely lodged in the President....

And since upon general principles for reasons already given, the issuing of a proclamation of neutrality is merely an Executive Act; since also the general Executive Power of the Union is vested in the President, the conclusion is, that the step, which has been taken by him, is liable to no just exception on the score of authority.

It may be observed that this Inference would be just if the power of declaring war had not been vested in the Legislature, but that this power naturally includes the right of judging whether the Nation is under obligations to make war or not.

The answer to this is, that however true it may be, that the right of the Legislature to declare war includes the right of judging whether the Nation be under obligations to make War or not — it will not follow that the Executive is in any case excluded from a similar right of Judgment, in the execution of its own functions.

If the Legislature have a right to make war on the one hand — it is on the other the duty of the Executive to preserve Peace till war is declared; and in fulfilling that duty, it must necessarily possess a right of judging what is the nature of the obligations which the treaties of the Country impose on the Government; and when in pursuance of this right it has concluded that there is nothing in them inconsistent with a state of neutrality, it becomes both its province and its duty to enforce the laws incident to that state of the Nation. The Executive is charged with the execution of all laws, the laws of Nations as well as the Municipal law, which recognizes and adopts those laws. It is consequently bound, by faithfully executing the laws of neutrality, when that is the state of the Nation, to avoid giving a cause of war to foreign Powers. . . .

It deserves to be remarked, that as the participation of the senate in the making of Treaties and the power of the Legislature to declare war are exceptions out of the general "Executive Power" vested in the President, they are to be construed strictly — and ought to be extended no further than is essential to their execution.

While therefore the legislature can alone declare war, can alone actually transfer the nation from a state of Peace to a state of War — it belongs to the "Executive Power," to do whatever else the laws of Nations, cooperating with the Treaties of the Country enjoin, in the intercourse of the [United States] with foreign Powers.

"Helvidius" Nos. 1, 2

15 The Papers of James Madison 70-72, 81-84
(Thomas A. Mason et al. eds., 1985)

Let us examine [the doctrine being propounded by Pacificus].

In the general distribution of powers, we find that of declaring war expressly vested in the Congress, where every other legislative power is declared to be vested, and without any other qualifications than what is common to every other legislative act. The constitutional idea of this power would seem then clearly to be, that it is of a legislative and not an executive nature.

This conclusion becomes irresistible, when it is recollected, that the constitution cannot be supposed to have placed either any power legislative in its nature, entirely among executive powers, or any power executive in its nature, entirely among legislative powers, without charging the constitution, with that kind of intermixture and consolidation of different powers, which would violate a fundamental principle in the organization of free governments. If it were not unnecessary to enlarge on this topic here, it could be shown, that the constitution was originally vindicated, and has been constantly expounded, with a disavowal of any such intermixture.

The power of treaties is vested jointly in the President and in the Senate, which is a branch of the legislature. From this arrangement merely, there can be no inference that would necessarily exclude the power from the executive class: since the senate is joined with the President in another power, that of appointing to offices, which as far as relate to executive offices at least, is considered as of an executive nature. Yet on the other hand, there are sufficient indications that the power of treaties is regarded by the constitution as materially different from mere executive power, and as having more affinity to the legislative than to the executive character. . . .

But the conclusive circumstance is, that treaties when formed according to the constitutional mode, are confessedly to have the force and operation of laws, and are to be a rule for the courts in controversies between man and man, as much as any other laws. They are even emphatically declared by the constitution to be "the supreme law of the land."

So far the argument from the constitution is precisely in opposition to the doctrine. As little will be gained in its favour from a comparison of the two powers, with those particularly vested in the president alone.

As there are but few, it will be most satisfactory to review them one by one.

> The president shall be commander in chief of the army and navy of the United States, and of the militia when called into the actual service of the United States.

There can be no relation worth examining between this power and the general power of making treaties. And instead of being analogous to the power of declaring war, it affords a striking illustration of the incompatibility of the two powers in the same hands. Those who are to conduct a war cannot in the nature of things, be proper or safe judges, whether a war ought to be commenced, continued, or concluded. They are barred from the latter functions by a great principle in free government, analogous to that which separates the sword from the purse, or the power of executing from the power of enacting laws....

Thus it appears that by whatever standard we try this doctrine, it must be condemned as no less vicious in theory than it would be dangerous in practice. It is countenanced neither by the writers on law; nor by the nature of the powers themselves; nor by any general arrangements or particular expressions, or plausible analogies, to be found in the constitution.

Whence then can the writer have borrowed it?

There is but one answer to this question.

The power of making treaties and the power of declaring war, are royal prerogatives in the British government, and are accordingly treated as Executive prerogatives by British commentators....

Leaving however to the leisure of the reader deductions which the author having omitted might not choose to own, I proceed to the examination of one, with which that liberty cannot be taken.

> However true it may be, (says he) that the right of the legislature to declare war includes the right of judging whether the legislature be under obligations to make war or not, it will not follow that the executive is in any case excluded from a similar right of judging in the execution of its own functions.

...A concurrent authority in two independent departments, to perform the same function with respect to the same thing, would be as awkward in practice, as it is unnatural in theory.

If the legislature and executive have both a right to judge of the obligations to make war or not, it must sometimes happen, though not at present, that they will judge differently. The executive may proceed to consider the question today, may determine that the United States are not bound to take part in a war, and in the execution of its functions proclaim that declaration to all the world. Tomorrow the legislature may follow in the consideration of the same subject, may determine that the obligations impose war on the United States, and in the execution of its functions, enter into a constitutional declaration, expressly contradicting the constitutional proclamation.

In what light does this present the constitution to the people who established it? In what light would it present to the world, a nation, thus speaking, through two different organs, equally constitutional and authentic, two opposite languages, on the same subject and under the same existing circumstances?

But it is not with the legislative rights alone that this doctrine interferes. The rights of the judiciary may be equally invaded. For it is clear that if a right declared by the constitution to be legislative, and actually vested by it in the legislature, leaves, notwithstanding, a similar right in the executive whenever a case for exercising it occurs, in the course of its functions: a right declared to be judiciary and vested in that department may, on the same principle, be assumed and exercised by the executive in the course of its functions: and it is evident that occasions and pretexts for the latter interference may be as frequent as for the former. So again the judiciary department may find equal occasions in the execution of its functions, for usurping the authorities of the executive: and the legislature for stepping into the jurisdiction of both. And thus all the powers of government, of which a partition is so carefully made among the several branches, would be thrown into absolute hotchpot, and exposed to a general scramble.

Another important issue that arose as a result of the French Revolution was whether and how to recognize the ambassador from the revolutionary French government, Edmond Charles Genet. Washington's cabinet worried about the possibility of rival ambassadors if a successor to Louis XVI sent his own representative. The cabinet also was concerned that an unqualified reception of Genet would constitute acceptance of the validity of the French-American treaties. Despite these concerns, Washington ultimately decided to receive Genet without qualification as the representative of France — an exercise of discretion that everyone agreed fell within the President's Article II power to "receive Ambassadors and other public Ministers."

Genet proved to be a major thorn in Washington's side, and a significant challenge to America's neutrality policy. When Genet arrived in the United States, he began to commission and arm privateers, manned by American sailors, to capture prizes on behalf of France.* He also began establishing French prize courts on U.S. soil to oversee the condemnation and sale of captured prize vessels. Genet claimed that his actions were consistent with the French-American treaties. But the British protested, arguing that these activities violated American neutrality and the law of nations.

This controversy presented Washington's cabinet with a number of technical questions under international law. Could the French, consistent with U.S. neutrality, invoke the treaties to justify using American ports for war preparation? Could the French set up prize courts in U.S. territory? Could the warring parties recruit seamen in the United States? Could Americans sell ships to the belligerents? How far at sea could the United States prevent hostilities between the belligerent powers? Were U.S. ships that carried the property of one belligerent immune from capture by the other belligerent?

Washington's cabinet eventually decided that these and related questions could best be addressed by the Justices of the Supreme Court. On July 12, 1793, the cabinet agreed to send "letters . . . to the Judges of the Supreme court of the US requesting their attendance . . . to give their advice on certain matters of public concern which will be referred to them by the President." Cabinet Opinion on

---

* A "privateer" is a private ship authorized by a government during wartime to attack and capture enemy vessels. A "prize" is an enemy ship and its cargo captured at sea during time of war. In effect, Genet was recruiting Americans on American soil for the purpose of attacking British shipping under French authorization.

Consulting the Supreme Court, in 26 The Papers of Thomas Jefferson 485 (John Catanzariti ed., 1995). The cabinet further agreed to inform the ambassadors from Great Britain and France that "the Executive of the US desirous of having done what shall be strictly conformable to the treaties of the US and the laws respecting the said cases has determined to refer the questions arising therein to persons learned in the laws." *Id.* at 484. On July 18, 1793, Jefferson sent the following letter to the Supreme Court, along with a list of 29 questions:

> The war which has taken place among the powers of Europe produces frequent transactions within our ports and limits, on which questions arise of considerable difficulty, and of greater importance to the peace of the US. These questions depend for their solution on the construction of our treaties, on the laws of nature and nations, and on the laws of the land; and are often presented under circumstances which do not give a cognisance of them to the tribunals of the country. Yet their decision is so little analogous to the ordinary functions of the Executive as to occasion much embarrassment and difficulty to them. The President therefore would be much relieved if he found himself free to refer questions of this description to the opinions of the Judges of the Supreme Court of the US whose knowledge of the subject would secure us against errors dangerous to the peace of the US and their authority insure the respect of all parties. He has therefore asked the attendance of such of the judges as could be collected in time for the occasion, to know, in the first place, their opinion, Whether the public may, with propriety, be availed of their advice on these questions? and if they may, to present, for their advice, the abstract questions which have already occurred, or may soon occur, from which they will themselves strike out such as any circumstances might, in their opinion, forbid them to pronounce on.

Letter to the Justices of the Supreme Court, July 18, 1793, in 26 The Papers of Thomas Jefferson, *supra*, at 520.

On August 8, 1793, Chief Justice Jay and the Associate Justices responded to the President as follows:

> We have considered the previous question stated in a letter written by your direction to us by the Secretary of State on the 18th of last month, [regarding] the lines of separation drawn by the Constitution between the three departments of the government. These being in certain respects checks upon each other, and our being judges of a court in the last resort, are considerations which afford strong arguments against the propriety of our extra-judicially deciding the questions alluded to, especially as the power given by the Constitution to the President, of calling on the heads of departments for opinions, seems to have been purposely as well as expressly united to the executive departments.
>
> We exceedingly regret every event that may cause embarrassment to your administration, but we derive consolation from the reflection that your judgment will discern what is right, and that your usual prudence, decision, and firmness will surmount every obstacle to the preservation of the rights, peace, and dignity of the United States.

Chief Justice Jay and Associate Justices to President Washington, Aug. 8, 1793, in 3 The Correspondence and Public Papers of John Jay 488-89 (Henry P. Johnston ed., 1891).

In response to the Justices' letter, Washington's cabinet prepared its own set of "regulations" reflecting its answers to the international law questions it had addressed to the Justices. These guidelines were needed in part to guide the Executive Branch in its prosecution of Americans who had engaged in privateering on behalf of the French in violation of the Neutrality Proclamation. One of the first such prosecutions was against Gideon Henfield, a U.S. citizen and the prize master of the French-commissioned ship *Citoyen Genet*. Henfield was arrested when *Citoyen Genet* brought a captured British prize into port at Philadelphia.

The prosecution of Henfield exacerbated the controversy sparked by the Neutrality Proclamation itself. Article I, §8 of the Constitution empowered Congress rather than the President to "define and punish...Offenses against the Law of Nations." Congress had not exercised this power with respect to neutrality. It thus seemed to many that the President was exercising a power that the Constitution gave to Congress. As John Marshall explained in his biography of George Washington:

> [The Republican newspapers] universally asked, "What law had been offended, and under what statute was the indictment supported? Were the American people already prepared to give to a proclamation the force of a legislative act, and to subject themselves to the will of the executive? But if they were already sunk to such a state of degradation, were they to be punished for violating a proclamation which had not been published when the offence was committed?"

5 John Marshall, The Life of George Washington 359 (1807).

At about the same time as Henfield's arrest, Chief Justice John Jay delivered a famous grand jury charge for the circuit court in Virginia. The charge was not delivered to the actual grand jury considering Henfield's case, but it was designed to state the law with respect to all offenders of the Neutrality Proclamation.

Grand Jury Charge of John Jay

Circuit Court for the District of Virginia, May 22, 1793 Reprinted in
United States v. Henfield, 11 F. Cas. 1099,1100-05 (C.C.D. Pa. 1793)

Gentlemen of the Grand Jury....

That you may perceive more clearly the extent and objects of your inquiries, it may be proper to observe, that the laws of the United States admit of being classed under three heads of descriptions. 1st. All treaties made under the authority of the United States. 2d. The laws of nations. 3dly. The constitution, and statutes of the United States.

Treaties between independent nations, are contracts or bargains which derive all their force and obligation from mutual consent and agreement; and consequently, when once fairly made and properly concluded, cannot be altered or annulled by one of the parties, without the consent and concurrence of the other. Wide is the difference between treaties and statutes — we may negotiate and make contracts with other nations, but we can neither legislate for them, nor they for us; we may repeal or alter our statutes, but no nation can have authority to vacate or modify treaties at discretion. Treaties, therefore, necessarily become the supreme law of the land, and so they are very properly declared to be by the sixth article of the constitution. Whenever doubts and questions arise relative to the validity, operation or construction of treaties, or of any articles in them, those doubts and questions must be settled according to the maxims and principles of the laws of nations applicable to the case. The peace, prosperity, and reputation of the United States, will always greatly depend on their fidelity to their engagements; and every virtuous citizen (for every citizen is a party to them) will concur in observing and executing them with honour and good faith; ...

As to the laws of nations — they are those laws by which nations are bound to regulate their conduct towards each other, both in peace and war. Providence has been pleased to place the United States among the nations of the earth, and therefore, all those duties, as well as rights, which spring from the relation of nation to nation, have devolved upon us. ... On this occasion, it is proper to observe to you, gentlemen, that various circumstances and considerations now unite in urging the people of the United States to be particularly exact and circumspect in observing the obligation of treaties, and the laws of nations, which, as has been already remarked, form a very important part of the laws of our nation. I allude to the facts and injunctions specified in the president's late proclamation; [Jay then repeats the words of the Neutrality Proclamation.]

By this proclamation, authentic and official information is given to the citizens of the United States: — That war actually exists between the nations mentioned in it: That they are to observe a conduct friendly and impartial towards the belligerent powers: That offenders will not be protected, but on the contrary, prosecuted and punished. ... The proclamation is exactly consistent with and declaratory of the conduct enjoined by the law of nations. It is worthy of remark that we are at peace with all these belligerent powers not only negatively in having war with none of them, but also in a more positive and particular sense by treaties with four of them. ...

From the observations which have been made, this conclusion appears to result, viz.: That the United States are in a state of neutrality relative to all the powers at war, and that it is their duty, their interest, and their disposition to maintain it: that, therefore, they who commit, aid, or abet hostilities against these powers, or either of them, offend against the laws of the United States, and ought to be punished; and consequently, that it is your duty, gentlemen, to inquire into and present all such of these offences, as you shall find to have been committed within this district. What acts amount to committing or aiding, or abetting hostilities, must be determined by the laws and approved practice of nations, and by the treaties and other laws of the United States relative to such cases. ...

On the third branch of the laws of the United States, viz: their constitution and statutes, I shall be concise. Here, also, one great unerring principle, viz: the will of the people, will take the lead. The people of the United States ... have ordained and established [a national government] which is specified in their great and general compact or constitution — a compact deliberately formed, maturely considered, and solemnly adopted and ratified by them. ... The statutes of the United States, constitutionally made, derive their obligation from the same source, and must bind accordingly. ... Most essentially, therefore, is it the duty and interest of us all, that the laws be observed, and irresistibly executed.

Justice Wilson gave a similar, though more verbose, charge to Henfield's grand jury. *See Henfield*, 11 F. Cas. at 1105-15.

Henfield and several other defendants were ultimately acquitted in trials for alleged violations of the Neutrality Proclamation. There are a number of possible reasons for the acquittals, including a concern that the defendants had not received sufficient notice that their conduct was criminal, a pro-French bias among the jurors, and a belief that federal criminal law should come from Congress rather than the Executive. Whatever the reasons, Washington asked Congress at its next session to provide a statutory basis for prosecuting violations of the law of nations concerning neutrality. The following is an excerpt of the statute Congress enacted:

Neutrality Act of 1794

Ch. 50, 1 Stat. 381 (1794)

An Act in addition to the act for the punishment of certain crimes against the United States.

Sec. 1. *Be it enacted and declared by the Senate and House of Representatives of the United States of America in Congress assembled*, That if any citizen of the United States shall, within the territory or jurisdiction of the same, accept and exercise a commission to serve a foreign prince or state in war by land or sea, the person so offending shall be deemed guilty of a high misdemeanor, and shall be fined not more than two thousand dollars, and shall be imprisoned not exceeding three years....

Sec. 8. *And be it further enacted and declared*, That it shall be lawful for the President of the United States, or such other person as he shall have empowered for that purpose, to employ such part of the land or naval forces of the United States or of the militia thereof, as shall be necessary to compel any foreign ship or vessel to depart the United States, in all cases in which, by the laws of nations or the treaties of the United States, they ought not to remain within the United States.

Ambassador Genet continued to defy U.S. authorities concerning American neutrality throughout the summer of 1793. He also engaged in other mischief, including making a request to Attorney General Randolph to prosecute Chief Justice Jay and Senator Rufus King for libel and organizing various plots to spark revolution in Louisiana, Florida, and Canada. Washington, on the unanimous recommendation of his cabinet, sought and received Genet's recall. Instead of returning to France (where he likely would have been executed), Genet chose to settle down as a farmer in New York, where he subsequently married the governor's daughter.

Notes and Questions

1. What was the constitutional basis for Washington's Neutrality Proclamation? Who has the better of the debate on this issue, Pacificus or Helvidius? Whose argument is more faithful to constitutional text? When constitutional text is silent about the locus of a foreign relations power (such as the power to proclaim neutrality), what interpretive principles should one use? Original understanding? Constitutional structure? Policy?

2. Hamilton (Pacificus) articulates several justifications for the President's power to proclaim neutrality: (a) that the President has the power to proclaim neutrality by virtue of the Vesting Clause in Article II, which states that "[t]he executive Power shall be vested in a President of the United States of America"; (b) that the President's power to proclaim neutrality flows from his duty in Article II to "take Care that the Laws be faithfully executed"; and (c) that the text and structure of the Constitution make the President the "organ of intercourse between

the United States and foreign nations." All three of these arguments recur throughout this casebook in connection with assertions of presidential power in foreign relations.

3. Is Hamilton's theory of the Vesting Clause of Article II persuasive? What explains the difference in wording between the Vesting Clause in Article I and the Vesting Clause in Article II? For a modern defense and elaboration of Hamilton's theory, see Saikrishna B. Prakash & Michael D. Ramsey, *The Executive Power over Foreign Affairs*, 111 Yale L.J. 231 (2001). For a critique of the theory, see Curtis A. Bradley & Martin S. Flaherty, *Executive Power Essentialism and Foreign Affairs*, 102 Mich. L. Rev. 545 (2004).

4. Does the President's duty to "take Care that the Laws be faithfully executed" provide an independent basis for the Neutrality Proclamation, as Hamilton argues? Does this duty include a power to *interpret* the laws? What laws? Do "the Laws" include the law of nations? Isn't Congress, rather than the President, given the constitutional power to define and punish offenses against the law of nations?

5. Is it true that the President is the "organ of intercourse" between the United States and foreign nations? If so, what is the precise constitutional basis for this role? What is entailed by this role? How does this role relate to Congress's many foreign relations powers?

6. Pacificus and Helvidius disagree about whether a "concurrent authority" between the President and Congress in certain foreign relations contexts is constitutionally justified and practically necessary. This too is an issue that will recur throughout this casebook. Who has the better of this argument?

7. What is the status of the law of nations (referred to today as "customary international law") in the U.S. constitutional system? Unlike treaties, the law of nations is not mentioned in the Supremacy Clause or in Article III. The only mention of the term is in Article I, which gives Congress the power to define and punish offenses against the law of nations. And yet many of the documents reproduced in this chapter suggest that the law of nations is part of U.S. law. For example, John Jay states in *Federalist No. 3* that under the Constitution, the law of nations, like treaties, will "always be expounded in one sense and executed in the same manner." Hamilton states as Pacificus that the law of nations is part of the "law of the land," and argues that the President has a duty to "take care" that the law of nations is faithfully executed. And Jay's grand jury charge states that the law of nations "form[s] a very important part of the laws of our nation." Do these statements mean that the law of nations, or customary international law, is part of U.S. *federal* law? Could the law of nations have been part of "the laws of our nation" or the "law of the land" without being federal law? Why is the domestic legal status of the law of nations important? Why do you think the Constitution only mentions the law of nations in Article I? We explore these issues in detail in Chapter 7.

8. What does the Pacificus-Helvidius debate suggest about the "original meaning" of the Constitution's assignment of foreign relations powers? Can a study of Founding history provide concrete answers to contemporary foreign relations law disputes? Consider these observations by Professor Rakove:

> [D]isputes over the scope of the foreign policy powers of the executive and legislative branches are virtually coeval with the Republic. The early (not to say immediate) emergence of the divergent positions that we associate with Hamilton and Madison seems to suggest that there is something illusory (or delusory) about attempting to recover some pristine, unsullied original meaning of the relevant clauses of the Constitution. Perhaps

the best one can do is to recover the range of considerations, not entirely consistent, that led the framers to vest substantial authority over foreign relations in the legislature while providing the president with a degree of independence that might, over time, evolve into a capacity for the initiation and direction of foreign policy.

Jack N. Rakove, Making Foreign Policy — The View from 1787, in Foreign Policy and the Constitution 17 (Robert A. Goldwin & Robert A. Licht eds., 1990). Do you agree? Will statements from the Founding always be too abstract, or too contested, to be helpful in resolving modern disputes? Does the relevance of Founding history vary depending on the particular foreign relations law controversy? Even if Founding history does provide concrete answers, why should it be binding hundreds of years later, when the nation, and the foreign relations issues it faces, are dramatically different? On the other hand, are modern foreign relations issues in fact dramatically different from the ones faced by the United States early in its history? Keep these questions in mind as you study the materials in subsequent chapters.

9. Why do you think Jefferson, who was a lawyer, wanted the Justices of the Supreme Court to answer the questions about international law? Why did he not simply ask the Attorney General? Why did the Justices not answer Jefferson's questions? Why would it have been "extra-judicial[]" for them to do so? Because the questions were "political"? Or because, in the words of Pacificus, a federal court may decide legal questions only "where contending parties bring before it a specific controversy"? In answering these questions, consider two facts. First, Washington and Hamilton frequently consulted Chief Justice Jay in private about legal matters relating to the Neutrality Controversy; and Jay offered his legal opinion to them in private (including writing a draft of the Neutrality Proclamation itself). Second, the Supreme Court addressed and resolved questions about the meaning of the French-American treaties and related law of nations issues in live cases and controversies presented to it. *See, e.g.*, Glass v. The Sloop Betsey, 3 U.S. (3 Dall.) 6 (1794) (ordering French prize restored to its owners after concluding that France had no right to erect prize courts in the United States).

Whatever its true motivation, the Justices' letter to Jefferson is often cited as a precedent for a variety of judicial "nonjusticiability" doctrines, including the "case or controversy" requirement, the related prohibition on advisory opinions, the standing doctrine, and the ripeness and mootness doctrines. We discuss these doctrines in Chapter 2. On the historical background and significance of the letter from the Justices, see Stewart Jay, Most Humble Servants: The Advisory Role of Early Judges (1997).

10. The controversy sparked by *Henfield's Case* — whether a U.S. citizen could be prosecuted for a non-statutory, common law crime — was later resolved in United States v. Hudson & Goodwin, 11 U.S. 32 (1812), in which the Supreme Court declared that it had "long been settled in public opinion" that there is no federal common law of crimes. *See also* United States v. Coolidge, 14 U.S. 415 (1816) (declining to overturn *Hudson & Goodwin*). We return to this issue, as it relates to the domestic legal status of customary international law, in Chapter 7.

11. What was the constitutional basis for Congress's neutrality statute? Is it more or less clear than the President's power to declare neutrality? Which branch of government is most competent to determine U.S. neutrality policy — Congress or the President? Which branch is more responsive to the wishes of the electorate? Was it constitutional for Congress, in Section 8 of the neutrality statute, to delegate military authority to the President? Did the President already have the authority that Congress was purporting to delegate? We consider the respective powers of Congress and the President concerning the use of military force in Chapter 4.

12. For more detailed accounts of the Neutrality Controversy and the constitutional debates it generated, see David P. Currie, The Constitution in Congress: The Federalist Period, 1789-1801, at 174-82 (1997); Stanley Elkins & Eric McKitrick, The Age of Federalism: The Early American Republic, 1788-1800, at 330-54 (1993); Jay, Most Humble Servants, *supra*, at 117-48. For additional discussion of the neutrality prosecutions, see Stewart Jay, *Origins of Federal Common Law: Part One*, U. Pa. L. Rev. 1003, 1048-53 (1985); Robert C. Palmer, *The Federal Common Law of Crime*, 4 Law and Hist. Rev. 267, 286-99 (1986). For additional discussion of the Pacificus-Helvidius debate, see William R. Casto, *Pacificus and Helvidius Reconsidered*, 28 N. Ky. L. Rev. 612 (2001).

C. NATURE OF U.S. FOREIGN RELATIONS AUTHORITY

The Constitution expressly assigns certain foreign relations powers to the national government, such as the power to enter into treaties (assigned to the President and Senate) and the power to declare war (assigned to Congress). As the Neutrality Controversy demonstrates, however, some foreign relations powers do not have a clear basis in constitutional text. This raises a number of important questions:

> Where . . . is the power to recognize other states or governments; to maintain or rupture diplomatic relations; to open consulates in other countries and permit foreign governments to establish consulates in the United States; to acquire or cede territory; to grant or withhold foreign aid; to proclaim a Monroe Doctrine, an Open-Door Policy, or a Reagan Doctrine; indeed to determine all the attitudes and carry out all the details in the myriads of relationships with other nations that are 'the foreign policy' and 'the foreign relations' of the United States? The power to make treaties is granted, but where is the power to break, denounce, or terminate them? The power to declare war is there, but where is the power to make peace, to proclaim neutrality in the wars of others, or to recognize or deny rights to belligerents or insurgents, or to address the consequences of the United Nations Charter and other international agreements regulating war? Congress can enact laws to define and punish violations of international law, but where is the power to assert U.S. rights or carry out its obligations under international law, to help make new international law, or to disregard or violate law that has been made? Congress can regulate commerce with foreign nations, but where is the power to make other laws relating to U.S. foreign relations — to regulate immigration or the status and rights of aliens, or activities of citizens abroad? These "missing" powers, and a host of others, were clearly intended for, and have always been exercised by, the federal government, but where does the Constitution say that it shall be so?

Louis Henkin, Foreign Affairs and the United States Constitution 14-15 (2d ed. 1996). Keep these questions in mind as you read the following decisions.

Ex Parte Merryman

(Circuit Court, D. Md. 1861) 17 F. Cas. 144 (No. 9,487)

[On April 19, 1861, pro-secession mobs in Baltimore attempted to prevent Union troops from passing through the city on their way to guard Washington, D.C., and

[margin note: can pres command a susp. of the writ of habeaus corpus?]

two soldiers and twelve civilians were killed in the resulting conflict. On April 27, President Lincoln authorized the commanding general of the U.S. army to suspend the writ of habeas corpus if there was resistance "at any point or in the vicinity of any military line which is now or which shall be used between the city of Philadelphia and the city of Washington." On May 25, a military commander at Fort McHenry arrested John Merryman, a Maryland resident suspected of aiding the Confederacy following the Baltimore riot. Merryman petitioned Chief Justice Taney, riding circuit in Baltimore, for a writ of habeas corpus. Taney issued the writ, but the military ignored it because of Lincoln's April 27 order. Taney then wrote the following opinion.]

TANEY, CIRCUIT JUSTICE. . . .

[margin note: also to delegate auth to military officer]

As the case comes before me, therefore, I understand that the president not only claims the right to suspend the writ of habeas corpus himself, at his discretion, but to delegate that discretionary power to a military officer, and to leave it to him to determine whether he will or will not obey judicial process that may be served upon him. . . .

The clause of the constitution, which authorizes the suspension of the privilege of the writ of habeas corpus, is in the 9th section of the first article. This article is devoted to the legislative department of the United States, and has not the slightest reference to the executive department. . . .

[margin note: Exec. is Art II. Nothing in this gives power]

It is the second article of the constitution that provides for the organization of the executive department, enumerates the powers conferred on it, and prescribes its duties. And if the high power over the liberty of the citizen now claimed, was intended to be conferred on the president, it would undoubtedly be found in plain words in this article; but there is not a word in it that can furnish the slightest ground to justify the exercise of the power. . . .

The only power . . . the president possesses, where the "life, liberty or property" of a private citizen is concerned, is the power and duty prescribed in the third section of the second article, which requires "that he shall take care that the laws shall be faithfully executed." He is not authorized to execute them himself, or through agents or officers, civil or military, appointed by himself, but he is to take care that they be faithfully carried into execution, as they are expounded and adjudged by the co-ordinate branch of the government to which that duty is assigned by the constitution. . . .

With such provisions in the constitution, expressed in language too clear to be misunderstood by any one, I can see no ground whatever for supposing that the president, in any emergency, or in any state of things, can authorize the suspension of the privileges of the writ of habeas corpus, or the arrest of a citizen, except in aid of the judicial power. He certainly does not faithfully execute the laws, if he takes upon himself legislative power, by suspending the writ of habeas corpus, and the judicial power also, by arresting and imprisoning a person without due process of law.

Nor can any argument be drawn from the nature of sovereignty, or the necessity of government, for self-defence in times of tumult and danger. The government of the United States is one of delegated and limited powers; it derives its existence and authority altogether from the constitution, and neither of its branches, executive, legislative or judicial, can exercise any of the powers of government beyond those specified and granted; for the tenth article of the amendments to the constitution, in express terms, provides that "the powers not delegated to the United States by the constitution, nor prohibited by it to the states, are reserved to the states, respectively, or to the people."

[Merryman was subsequently released on bail and was never tried on the charges for which he was indicted.]   Not in pres. power

Chinese Exclusion Case (Chae Chan Ping v. United States)

130 U.S. 581 (1889)

[An 1888 federal statute prohibited Chinese laborers from reentering the United   2 issues
States under certain circumstances. This case presented two issues: First, did the statute violate treaties between the United States and China? Second, did Congress have the authority to enact the statute? We examine the first question in Chapter 6 in the materials on the last-in-time rule. The portion of the opinion excerpted below addresses the second question.]

JUSTICE FIELD delivered the opinion of the court. . . .

There being nothing in the treaties between China and the United States to impair the validity of the act of Congress of October 1, 1888, was it on any other ground beyond the competency of Congress to pass it? If so, it must be because it was not within the power of Congress to prohibit Chinese laborers who had at the time departed from the United States, or should subsequently depart, from returning to the United States. Those laborers are not citizens of the United States; they are aliens. That the government of the United States, through the action of the legislative department, can exclude aliens from its territory is a proposition which we do not think open to controversy. Jurisdiction over its own territory to that extent is an incident of every independent nation. It is a part of its independence. If it could not exclude aliens it would be to that extent subject to the control of another power. As said by this court in the case of The Exchange, 7 Cranch, 116, 136, speaking by Chief Justice Marshall: "The jurisdiction of the nation within its own territory is necessarily exclusive and absolute. It is susceptible of no limitation not imposed by itself. Any restriction upon it, deriving validity from an external source, would imply a diminution of its sovereignty to the extent of the restriction, and an investment of that sovereignty to the same extent in that power which could impose such restriction. All exceptions, therefore, to the full and complete power of a nation within its own territories, must be traced up to the consent of the nation itself. They can flow from no other legitimate source."

While under our Constitution and form of government the great mass of local matters is controlled by local authorities, the United States, in their relation to foreign countries and their subjects or citizens are one nation, invested with powers which belong to independent nations, the exercise of which can be invoked for the maintenance of its absolute independence and security throughout its entire territory. The powers to declare war, make treaties, suppress insurrection, repel invasion, regulate foreign commerce, secure republican governments to the States, and admit subjects of other nations to citizenship, are all sovereign powers, restricted in their exercise only by the Constitution itself and considerations of public policy and justice which control, more or less, the conduct of all civilized nations. . . .

The control of local matters being left to local authorities, and national matters being entrusted to the government of the Union, the problem of free institutions existing over a widely extended country, having different climates and varied interests, has been happily solved. For local interests the several States of the Union exist, but for national purposes, embracing our relations with foreign nations, we are but one people, one nation, one power.

To preserve its independence, and give security against foreign aggression and encroachment, is the highest duty of every nation, and to attain these ends nearly all other considerations are to be subordinated. It matters not in what form such aggression and encroachment come, whether from the foreign nation acting in its national character or from vast hordes of its people crowding in upon us. The government, possessing the powers which are to be exercised for protection and security, is clothed with authority to determine the occasion on which the powers shall be called forth; and its determination, so far as the subjects affected are concerned, are necessarily conclusive upon all its departments and officers. If, therefore, the government of the United States, through its legislative department, considers the presence of foreigners of a different race in this country, who will not assimilate with us, to be dangerous to its peace and security, their exclusion is not to be stayed because at the time there are no actual hostilities with the nation of which the foreigners are subjects. The existence of war would render the necessity of the proceeding only more obvious and pressing. The same necessity, in a less pressing degree, may arise when war does not exist, and the same authority which adjudges the necessity in one case must also determine it in the other. In both cases its determination is conclusive upon the judiciary. If the government of the country of which the foreigners excluded are subjects is dissatisfied with this action it can make complaint to the executive head of our government, or resort to any other measure which, in its judgment, its interests or dignity may demand; and there lies its only remedy....

The power of exclusion of foreigners being an incident of sovereignty belonging to the government of the United States, as a part of those sovereign powers delegated by the Constitution, the right to its exercise at any time when, in the judgment of the government, the interests of the country require it, cannot be granted away or restrained on behalf of any one.

congress has the power in war or peace

Carter v. Carter Coal Co.

298 U.S. 238 (1936)

[This case involved a challenge to a 1935 federal statute that provided for the establishment of minimum prices and collective bargaining in the coal industry. In addition to holding that the statute exceeded Congress's authority under the Commerce Clause, the Court rejected the claim that the statute could be upheld on the basis of a "general federal power, thought to exist, apart from the specific grants of the Constitution."]

MR. JUSTICE SUTHERLAND delivered the opinion of the court....

The ruling and firmly established principle is that the powers which the general government may exercise are only those specifically enumerated in the Constitution, and such implied powers as are necessary and proper to carry into effect the enumerated powers....

The proposition, often advanced and as often discredited, that the power of the federal government inherently extends to purposes affecting the nation as a whole with which the states severally cannot deal or cannot adequately deal, and the related notion that Congress, entirely apart from those powers delegated by the Constitution, may enact laws to promote the general welfare, have never been accepted but always definitely rejected by this court. Mr. Justice Story, as early as 1816, laid down the cardinal rule, which has ever since been followed—that the general government "can claim no powers which are not granted to it by the Constitution, and the powers actually granted, must be such as are expressly given, or given by necessary implication." Martin v. Hunter's Lessee, 1 Wheat. 304, 326....

The general rule with regard to the respective powers of the national and the state governments under the Constitution, is not in doubt. The states were before the Constitution; and, consequently, their legislative powers antedated the Constitution. Those who framed and those who adopted that instrument meant to carve from the general mass of legislative powers, then possessed by the states, only such portions as it was thought wise to confer upon the federal government; and in order that there should be no uncertainty in respect of what was taken and what was left, the national powers of legislation were not aggregated but enumerated—with the result that what was not embraced by the enumeration remained vested in the states without change or impairment.... [S]ince every addition to the national legislative power to some extent detracts from or invades the power of the states, it is of vital moment that, in order to preserve the fixed balance intended by the Constitution, the powers of the general government be not so extended as to embrace any not within the express terms of the several grants or the implications necessarily to be drawn there from. It is no longer open to question that the general government, unlike the states, possesses no *inherent* power in respect of the internal affairs of the states; and emphatically not with regard to legislation. The question in respect of the inherent power of that government as to the external affairs of the nation and in the field of international law is a wholly different matter which it is not necessary now to consider.

United States v. Curtiss-Wright Export Corp.

299 U.S. 304 (1936)

[On May 28, 1934, Congress enacted a joint resolution that provided that, if the President found that a prohibition on arms sales to the countries fighting in the Chaco war between Bolivia and Paraguay would promote regional peace, and the President made a proclamation to that effect, such arms sales would be illegal. The President made such a proclamation. Subsequently, four officers of the Curtiss-Wright Export Corporation, along with the corporation and two affiliates, were indicted for conspiring to sell aircraft machine guns to Bolivia, in violation of the joint resolution and proclamation. The defendants challenged their indictment on the ground that the joint resolution had unconstitutionally delegated legislative power to the President.]

Pres decides if sales of arms should be illegal

MR. JUSTICE SUTHERLAND delivered the opinion of the court....

Whether, if the Joint Resolution had related solely to internal affairs it would be open to the challenge that it constituted an unlawful delegation of legislative power to the Executive, we find it unnecessary to determine. The whole aim of the resolution is to affect a situation entirely external to the United States, and falling within the category of foreign affairs. The determination which we are called to make, therefore, is whether the Joint Resolution, as applied to that situation, is vulnerable to attack under the rule that forbids a delegation of the law-making power. In other

if internal it would be invalid, but this is external

words, assuming (but not deciding) that the challenged delegation, if it were confined to internal affairs, would be invalid, may it nevertheless be sustained on the ground that its exclusive aim is to afford a remedy for a hurtful condition within foreign territory?

It will contribute to the elucidation of the question if we first consider the differences between the powers of the federal government in respect of foreign or external affairs and those in respect of domestic or internal affairs. That there are differences between them, and that these differences are fundamental, may not be doubted.

enumerat. articles? n&p clause applies to internal power

The two classes of powers are different, both in respect of their origin and their nature. The broad statement that the federal government can exercise no powers except those specifically enumerated in the Constitution, and such implied powers as are necessary and proper to carry into effect the enumerated powers, is categorically true only in respect of our internal affairs. In that field, the primary purpose of the Constitution was to carve from the general mass of legislative powers *then possessed by the states* such portions as it was thought desirable to vest in the federal government, *leaving those not* included in the enumeration still in the states. Carter v. Carter Coal Co., 298 U.S. 238, 294. That this doctrine applies only to powers which the states had, is self evident. And since the states severally never possessed international powers, such powers could not have been carved from the mass of state powers but obviously were transmitted to the United States from some other source. During the colonial period, those powers were possessed exclusively by and were entirely under the control of the Crown. By the Declaration of Independence, "the Representatives of the United States of America" declared the United [not the several] Colonies to be free and independent states, and as such to have "full Power to levy War, conclude Peace, contract Alliances, establish Commerce and to do all other Acts and Things which Independent States may of right do."

As a result of the separation from Great Britain by the colonies acting as a unit, the powers of external sovereignty passed from the Crown not to the colonies severally, but to the colonies in their collective and corporate capacity as the United States of America. Even before the Declaration, the colonies were a unit in foreign affairs, acting through a common agency — namely the Continental Congress, composed of delegates from the thirteen colonies. That agency exercised the powers of war and peace, raised an army, created a navy, and finally adopted the Declaration of Independence. Rulers come and go; governments end and forms of government change; but sovereignty survives. A political society cannot endure without a supreme will somewhere. Sovereignty is never held in suspense. When, therefore, the external sovereignty of Great Britain in respect of the colonies ceased, it immediately passed to the Union. *See* Penhallow v. Doane, 3 Dall. 54, 80-81. That fact was given practical application almost at once. The treaty of peace, made on September 23, 1783, was concluded between his Brittanic Majesty and the "United States of America." . . .

The Union existed before the Constitution, which was ordained and established among other things to form "a more perfect Union." Prior to that event, it is clear that the Union, declared by the Articles of Confederation to be "perpetual," was the sole possessor of external sovereignty and in the Union it remained without change save in so far as the Constitution in express terms qualified its exercise. The Framers' Convention was called and exerted its powers upon the irrefutable postulate that though the states were several their people in respect of foreign affairs were one. Compare The Chinese Exclusion Case, 130 U.S. 581, 604, 606. In that convention, the entire absence of state power to deal with those affairs was thus forcefully stated by Rufus King:

> The states were not "sovereigns" in the sense contended for by some. They did not possess the peculiar features of sovereignty, — they could not make war, nor peace, nor alliances, nor treaties. Considering them as political beings, they were dumb, for they could not speak to any foreign sovereign whatever. They were deaf, for they could not hear any propositions from such sovereign. They had not even the organs or faculties of defence or offence, for they could not of themselves raise troops, or equip vessels, for war.

5 Elliott's Debates 212.

It results that the investment of the federal government with the powers of external sovereignty did not depend upon the affirmative grants of the Constitution. The powers to declare and wage war, to conclude peace, to make treaties, to maintain diplomatic relations with other sovereignties, if they had never been mentioned in the Constitution, would have vested in the federal government as necessary concomitants of nationality. Neither the Constitution nor the laws passed in pursuance of it have any force in foreign territory unless in respect of our own citizens; and operations of the nation in such territory must be governed by treaties, international understandings and compacts, and the principles of international law. As a member of the family of nations, the right and power of the United States in that field are equal to the right and power of the other members of the international family. Otherwise, the United States is not completely sovereign. The power to acquire territory by discovery and occupation (Jones v. United States, 137 U.S. 202, 212), the power to expel undesirable aliens (Fong Yue Ting v. United States, 149 U.S. 698, 705 et seq.), the power to make such international agreements as do not constitute treaties in the constitutional sense (Altman & Co. v. United States, 224 U.S. 583, 600-601), none of which is expressly affirmed by the Constitution, nevertheless exist as inherently inseparable from the conception of nationality. This the court recognized, and in each of the cases cited found the warrant for its conclusions not in the provisions of the Constitution, but in the law of nations.

In Burnet v. Brooks, 288 U.S. 378, 396, we said, "As a nation with all the attributes of sovereignty, the United States is vested with all the powers of government necessary to maintain an effective control of international relations." Cf. Carter v. Carter Coal Co., supra.

Not only, as we have shown, is the federal power over external affairs in origin and essential character different from that over internal affairs, but participation in the exercise of the power is significantly limited. In this vast external realm, with its important, complicated, delicate and manifold problems, the President alone has the power to speak or listen as a representative of the nation. He *makes* treaties with the advice and consent of the Senate; but he alone negotiates. Into the field of negotiation the Senate cannot intrude; and Congress itself is powerless to invade it. As Marshall said in his great argument of March 7, 1800, in the House of Representatives, "The President is the sole organ of the nation in its external relations, and its sole representative with foreign nations." Annals, 6th Cong., col. 613. . . .

It is important to bear in mind that we are here dealing not alone with an authority vested in the President by an exertion of legislative power, but with such an authority plus the very delicate, plenary and exclusive power of the President as the sole organ of the federal government in the field of international relations — a power which does not require as a basis for its exercise an act of Congress, but which, of course, like every other governmental power, must be exercised in subordination to the applicable provisions of the Constitution. It is quite apparent that if, in the maintenance of our international relations, embarrassment — perhaps serious embarrassment — is to be avoided and success for our aims achieved, congressional legislation which is to be made effective through negotiation and inquiry within the international field must often accord to the President a degree of discretion and freedom from statutory restriction which would not be admissible were domestic affairs alone involved. Moreover, he, not Congress, has the better opportunity of knowing the conditions which prevail in foreign countries, and especially is this true in time of war. He has his confidential sources of information. He has his agents in the form of diplomatic, consular and other officials. Secrecy in respect of information gathered by them may be highly necessary, and the premature disclosure of it productive of harmful results. . . .

When the President is to be authorized by legislation to act in respect of a matter intended to affect a situation in foreign territory, the legislator properly bears in mind the important consideration that the form of the President's action — or, indeed, whether he shall act at all — may well depend, among other things, upon the nature of the confidential information which he has or may thereafter receive, or upon the effect which his action may have upon our foreign relations. This consideration, in connection with what we have already said on the subject, discloses the unwisdom of requiring Congress in this field of governmental power to lay down narrowly definite standards by which the President is to be governed. . . .

In the light of the foregoing observations, it is evident that this court should not be in haste to apply a general rule which will have the effect of condemning legislation like that under review as constituting an unlawful delegation of legislative power. The principles which justify such legislation find overwhelming support in the unbroken legislative practice which has prevailed almost from the inception of the national government to the present day. . . .

Practically every volume of the United States Statutes contains one or more acts or joint resolutions of Congress authorizing action by the President in respect of subjects affecting foreign relations, which either leave the exercise of the power to his unrestricted judgment, or provide a standard far more general than that which has always been considered requisite with regard to domestic affairs. . . .

The result of holding that the joint resolution here under attack is void and unenforceable as constituting an unlawful delegation of legislative power would be to stamp this multitude of comparable acts and resolutions as likewise invalid. And while this court may not, and should not, hesitate to declare acts of Congress, however many times repeated, to be unconstitutional if beyond all rational doubt it finds them to be so, an impressive array of legislation such as we have just set forth, enacted by nearly every Congress from the beginning of our national existence to the present day, must be given unusual weight in the process of reaching a correct determination of the problem. A legislative practice such as we have here, evidenced not by only occasional instances, but marked by the movement of a steady stream for a century and a half of time, goes a long way in the direction of proving the presence of unassailable ground for the constitutionality of the practice, to be found in the origin and history of the power involved, or in its nature, or in both combined. . . .

The uniform, long-continued and undisputed legislative practice just disclosed rests upon an admissible view of the Constitution which, even if the practice found far less support in principle than we think it does, we should not feel at liberty at this late day to disturb.

We deem it unnecessary to consider, *seriatim*, the several clauses which are said to evidence the unconstitutionality of the Joint Resolution as involving an unlawful delegation of legislative power. It is enough to summarize by saying that, both upon principle and in accordance with precedent, we conclude there is sufficient warrant for the broad discretion vested in the President to determine whether the enforcement of the statute will have a beneficial effect upon the reestablishment of peace in the affected countries; whether he shall make proclamation to bring the resolution into operation; whether and when the resolution shall cease to operate and to make proclamation accordingly; and to prescribe limitations and exceptions to which the enforcement of the resolution shall be subject. Legislation can give president such a broad power

Notes and Questions

1. There are at least three theories concerning the source of the federal government's foreign relations powers. The first theory is that the federal government has only the foreign relations powers delegated to it in the Constitution. This delegated powers theory is expressed by Justice Taney in *Merryman*. As made clear in *Carter Coal Co.*, this is also the theory of governmental power that has long been applied to the national government's exercise of *domestic* power. Under this theory, the federal government would not necessarily be limited to the foreign affairs powers specifically mentioned in the Constitution. It might also possess powers that could be *implied* from the specific grants and from other constitutional provisions (such as the Necessary and Proper Clause, the Executive Power Clause, and the Take Care Clause). *Cf.* The Legal Tender Cases, 79 U.S. 457, 534 (1870) ("[I]t is not indispensable to the existence of any power claimed for the Federal government that it can be found specified in the words of the Constitution, or clearly and directly traceable to some one of the specified powers. Its existence may be deduced fairly from more than one of the substantive powers expressly defined, or from them all combined.").

The second theory — embraced in *The Chinese Exclusion Case* — is that foreign relations powers inhere in the "sovereignty" that is implicitly vested by the Constitution in the national government. *See also* Fong Yue Ting v. United States, 149 U.S. 698, 711 (1893) ("The United States are a sovereign and independent nation, and are vested *by the Constitution* with the entire control of international relations, and with all the powers of government necessary to maintain that control and to make it effective.") (emphasis added). The third theory — articulated in *Curtiss-Wright* — also postulates that foreign relations powers inhere in U.S. national sovereignty, but this theory relies on an extra-constitutional source for these sovereignty-based powers, such as the British Crown or international law.

What practical differences are there, if any, between these theories? Consider this assessment from one of the most prominent foreign relations law commentators of the early twentieth century, in which he contrasts the first and third theories:

> Unquestionably the enumerated powers relating to foreign affairs, either by implication or combination, will permit Congress to pass practically any laws properly within that field. Consequently in practice this theory of congressional power differs little from the theory that congressional power can be deduced from national sovereignty in foreign affairs. . . . The difficulty of the sovereignty theory, however, lies in the fact that

a recognition of congressional sovereignty in foreign affairs would seem to exempt Congress from constitutional limitations arising from individual rights, states' rights and the separation of powers in this field. Sovereignty is not only plentitude of power, but also absence of limitation.

Quincy Wright, The Control of American Foreign Relations 134 n.13 (1922). Do you agree with this assessment?

2. *Carter Coal* and *Curtiss-Wright* were both written, within a span of six months, by Justice Sutherland. Taken together, the decisions stand for the proposition that federal power with respect to domestic affairs derives from the Constitution and is subject to constitutional limitation, while federal power with respect to foreign affairs has an extra-constitutional source and is subject to significantly weaker constitutional constraints. Justice Sutherland had articulated a version of this theory of federal sovereignty in 1910 while a Republican senator from Utah. *See* George Sutherland, *The Internal and External Powers of the National Government*, 191 N. Am. Rev. 373 (1910). Ten years later he published a revised version of the theory. *See* George Sutherland, Constitutional Power and World Affairs (1919). In *Curtiss-Wright*, Justice Sutherland was, as one commentator puts it, "in the happy position of being able to give [his] writings and speeches the status of law." David M. Levitan, *The Foreign Relations Power: An Analysis of Mr. Justice Sutherland's Theory*, 55 Yale L.J. 467, 476 (1946). Why would Sutherland, one of the conservative "Four Horsemen" known for "strict construction" of the Constitution and abhorrence of broad federal power in the context of New Deal legislation, indulge such a broad view of federal power in the foreign relations context? For a discussion of this question, see G. Edward White, *The Transformation of the Constitutional Regime of Foreign Relations*, 85 Va. L. Rev. 1 (1999).

3. Does Sutherland's distinction between constitutional powers in the domestic and external realms make sense? How can courts tell whether a case raises an issue of domestic or external power? Couldn't *Curtiss-Wright* itself be characterized as a domestic case because it involved attempted sales by an American company and its U.S. citizen officers? Couldn't *Merryman* be characterized as a foreign relations case because it involved the exercise of military control over insurgents in the context of the Civil War? In our increasingly globalized world, is the domestic/foreign distinction a tenable basis for such important differences in constitutional doctrine?

4. How tenable is the Court's claim in *Curtiss-Wright* that the foreign relations powers of the federal government are derived from a source other than the U.S. Constitution? Is this claim consistent with the historical materials we considered above in Section A? With the idea of a limited national government regulated by a written Constitution? With the actual allocation of foreign relations powers in the Constitution itself? With the Court's assertion that presidential power in foreign affairs, "like every other governmental power, must be exercised in subordination to the applicable provisions of the Constitution"? If the national government does have extra-constitutional foreign relations powers, what are they?

For criticism of the Court's assertion of extra-constitutional foreign relations powers, see, for example, Harold Hongju Koh, The National Security Constitution 94 (1990) (summarizing the "withering criticism" of this aspect of *Curtiss-Wright*); Louis Henkin, Foreign Affairs and the United States Constitution 19-20 (2d ed. 1996) (stating that the notion that "the new United States government was to have major powers outside the Constitution is not intimated in the Constitution itself, in the records of the Convention, in the Federalist Papers, or in contemporary debates"); Michael D. Ramsey, *The Myth of Extraconstitutional Foreign Affairs Power*, 42 Wm. & Mary L. Rev. 379 (2000) (arguing that the Founders of the Constitution did not envision extra-constitutional foreign affairs powers). But *see* Bradford R. Clark, *Federal Common Law: A Structural Reinterpretation*, 144 U. Pa. L. Rev. 1245, 1296-97 (1996) (relying on the *Curtiss-Wright* theory); Richard B. Morris, *The Forging of the Union Reconsidered: A Historical Refutation of State Sovereignty over Seabeds*, 74 Colum. L. Rev. 1056, 1060-68 (1974) (defending the *Curtiss-Wright* theory on historical grounds).

In a historically detailed article, Professor Sarah Cleveland argues that "Sutherland's method of invoking inherent plenary power was entirely familiar to Supreme Court jurisprudence and derived directly from late-nineteenth-century judicial decisions addressing Indians, aliens, and territorial expansion. Sutherland's theory drew extensively from views of dual federalism, sovereignty, and the territorial scope of constitutional power that the Court articulated in a series of decisions in these areas between 1886 and 1910." Sarah H. Cleveland, *Powers Inherent in Sovereignty: Indians, Aliens, Territories, and the Nineteenth Century Origins of Plenary Power over Foreign Affairs*, 81 Tex. L. Rev. 1, 7 (2002). Professor Cleveland also argues, however, that the inherent powers doctrine (a) "cannot be vindicated as originalism" because it "was not accepted at the nation's inception"; (b) is unsupported by the Constitution's text and structure; (c) "cannot be defended on doctrinal grounds, since most of the late-nineteenth-century doctrines from which the theory derives have long since been abandoned in other jurisprudential contexts"; and (d) "[cannot] be defended as modernism" since "[t]he doctrine's origins instead lie in a peculiarly unattractive, late-nineteenth-century nationalist and racist view of American society and federal power." *Id.* at 14.

5. Despite academic criticism of the decision, the Supreme Court continues to cite and quote from *Curtiss-Wright* approvingly. In a recent Indian law decision, the Supreme Court referred favorably to the extraconstitutional theory of foreign affairs powers espoused in *Curtiss-Wright*, stating:

> Moreover, "at least during the first century of America's national existence ... Indian affairs were more an aspect of military and foreign policy than a subject of domestic or municipal law." Insofar as that is so, Congress' legislative authority would rest in part, not upon "affirmative grants of the Constitution," but upon the Constitution's adoption of preconstitutional powers necessarily inherent in any Federal Government, namely powers that this Court has described as "necessary concomitants of nationality." United States v. Curtiss-Wright Export Corp., 299 U.S. 304, 315-322 (1936)....

United States v. Lara, 541 U.S. 193, 201 (2004). And, in a recent decision concerning a federal criminal prosecution relating to the evasion of Canadian liquor taxes, the Court quoted from *Curtiss-Wright* for the proposition that "the Executive is 'the sole organ of the federal government in the field of international relations.'" Pasquantino v. United States, 125 S. Ct. 1766, 1779 (2005).

6. What are the implications of the Court's suggestion in *Curtiss-Wright* that international law notions of sovereignty are the source of the U.S. foreign relations power? International law might dictate that nationhood requires, for example, the ability to engage in international relations and make treaties. But does it also specify the particular allocation of foreign relations power *within* a sovereign — for example, between political branches, or between national and sub-national governments? If international law notions of sovereignty provide the source for the national government's foreign relations powers, do they also provide limitations? For example, if nations are prohibited from engaging in certain acts, such as waging aggressive war, does this mean that the U.S. government lacks the constitutional power to do so? In other words, does the Constitution require that the national government act as a *lawful sovereign*?

7. The issue in *The Chinese Exclusion Case* concerned Congress's power to exclude aliens. Nevertheless, the Court perceived the need to assert that, "For local interests the several States of the Union exist, but for national purposes, embracing our relations with foreign nations, we are but one people, one nation, one power." Similarly, the issue in *Curtiss-Wright* was whether Congress's statutory delegation of certain arms embargo powers to the President was constitutional. And yet the Court talks a great deal about the power of states in foreign affairs. Why are these federalism issues relevant to the scope of federal foreign relations powers?

8. President Lincoln implicitly responded to *Merryman* in his famous July 4, 1861, message to a special session of Congress:

> [T]he legality and propriety of [suspending the writ of habeas corpus] are questioned; and the attention of the country has been called to the proposition that one who is sworn to "take care that the laws be faithfully executed," should not himself violate them.... The whole of the laws which were required to be faithfully executed, were being resisted, and failing of execution, in nearly one-third of the States. Must they be allowed to finally fail of execution, even had it been perfectly clear, that by the use of the means necessary to their execution, some single law, made in such extreme tenderness of the citizen's liberty, that practically, it relieves more of the guilty, than of the innocent, should, to a very limited extent, be violated? To state the question more directly, are all the laws, but one, to go unexecuted, and the government itself go to pieces, lest that one be violated? Even in such a case, would not the official oath be broken, if the government should be overthrown, when it was believed that disregarding the single law, would tend to preserve it?

Message to Congress in Special Session of July 4, 1861, in 4 The Collected Works of Abraham Lincoln 421, 429-30 (Roy P. Basler ed., 1953). Can constitutional limitations — relating either to constitutional structure or to individual rights — be suspended in a national emergency? Which ones? For how long? And who decides — the President, the Congress, or the courts? These issues, which have renewed contemporary relevance in light of the September 11, 2001, terrorist attacks on the United States, are explored in detail in other parts of the casebook. Note that Lincoln went on in his message to argue that, in any event, the suspension of the writ of habeas corpus was constitutional:

> The provision of the Constitution that "The privilege of the writ of habeas corpus, shall not be suspended unless when, in cases of rebellion or invasion, the public safety may require it," is equivalent to a provision — is a provision — that such privilege may be suspended when, in cases of rebellion, or invasion, the public safety does require it. It was decided that we have a case of rebellion, and that the public safety does require the qualified suspension of the privilege of the writ which was authorized to be made. Now it is insisted that Congress, and not the Executive, is vested with this power. But the Constitution itself, is silent as to which, or who, is to exercise the power; and as the provision was plainly made for a dangerous emergency, it cannot be believed the framers of the instrument intended, that in every case, the danger should run its course, until Congress could be called together; the very assembling of which might be prevented, as was intended in this case, by the rebellion.

Id. at 430-31. We shall return to this issue of who has the power to suspend the writ of habeas corpus as well. For now, note that all of the Justices in Hamdi v. Rumsfeld, 124 S. Ct. 2633 (2004), which concerned the detention of a U.S. citizen "enemy combatant" in the war on terrorism, appeared to assume that only Congress could suspend the writ of habeas corpus.

9. The significance of *Curtiss-Wright* was debated in the course of the Iran-Contra affair. That affair, in a nutshell, involved National Security Council officials in the Reagan Administration skirting congressional prohibitions (known as the Boland Amendments) on the expenditure of U.S. funds in support of rebel forces in Nicaragua (known as the "Contras"). These NSC activities caused a national scandal when it became known that profits from secret arms sales to Iran were being used to help finance the Contras. In his testimony before Congress, Colonel Oliver North invoked *Curtiss-Wright* as a justification for ignoring the Boland Amendments. The final congressional report contained a majority report and a minority report, and these reports articulated differing views of the implications of *Curtiss-Wright*. The majority report stated:

> [One] does not have to be a proponent of an imperial Congress to see that [*Curtiss-Wright*] has little application to the situation here. We are not confronted with a situation where the President is claiming inherent constitutional authority in the absence of an Act of Congress. Instead, to succeed on this argument the Administration must claim it retains authority to proceed in derogation of an Act of Congress — and not just any act, at that. Here, Congress relied on its traditional authority over appropriations, the "power of the purse," to specify that no funds were to be expended by certain entities in a certain fashion.... While each branch of our Government undoubtedly has primacy in certain spheres, none can function in secret disregard of the others in any sphere.

Report of the Congressional Committees Investigating the Iran-Contra Affair, S. Rep. No. 100-216, H. Rep. No. 100-433 (1987), at 406 (majority report). The minority report stated:

> [The] Constitution gives the President some power to act on his own in foreign affairs. What kinds of activities are set side for him? The most obvious — other than the Commander-in-Chief power and others explicitly listed in Article II — is the one named in *Curtiss-Wright*: The President is the "sole organ" of the government in foreign affairs.... [Congress] may not use its control over appropriations, including salaries, to prevent the executive or judiciary from fulfilling Constitutionally mandated obligations. The implications of the Boland amendments is obvious. If any part of the amendments would have used Congress's control over salaries to prohibit executive actions that Congress may not prohibit directly, the amendments would be just as unconstitutional as if they had dealt with the subject directly.

Id. at 473, 476 (minority report). How do the views in these reports compare with the Pacificus-Helvidius debate? Which view is more persuasive? We consider additional implications of *Curtiss-Wright* for presidential power in foreign affairs, and for presidential-congressional relations, in Chapter 3.

10. Scholars disagree about the original source of the federal government's foreign relations powers. For the view that the states retained powers of "external sovereignty" in the post-revolutionary period, and that the United States acquired these powers through the Articles of Confederation and the Constitution rather than from Great Britain, see Levitan, The Foreign Relations Power, *supra,* at 478-90; Claude H. Van Tyne, *Sovereignty in the American Revolution: An Historical*

Study, 12 Am. Hist. Rev. 529 (1907). *See also* Charles A. Lofgren, *United States v. Curtiss-Wright Export Corporation: An Historical Reassessment*, 83 Yale L.J. 1, 29-30 (1973) ("Far from supporting the contention that external sovereignty devolved on the federal government ultimately from Great Britain and hence has an extra-constitutional base, Sutherland's historical evidence and judicial precedents suggest the opposite: Federal power in foreign affairs rests on explicit and implicit constitutional grants and derives from the ordinary constitutive authority."). For the view that the states never possessed foreign relations powers, see Morris, The Forging of the Federal Union, *supra*; Curtis Putnam Nettels, *The Origins of the Union and of the States*, 72 Proceedings Mass. Hist. Soc'y 68 (1957-1960). For an account that emphasizes the uncertainties associated with this issue, see Jack P. Greene, Peripheries and Center: Constitutional Development in the Extended Politics of the British Empire and the United States, 1607-1788, at 153-80 (1986).

2

Courts and Foreign Relations

This chapter considers the role of U.S. courts, especially the federal courts, in foreign relations cases. It begins by briefly describing the subject matter jurisdiction of the federal courts and some of the "justiciability" limitations on the exercise of this jurisdiction. It then considers in more detail the political question doctrine, a justiciability limitation that has had particular relevance in the area of foreign relations. The chapter then examines the sovereign immunity enjoyed by foreign nations when they are sued in U.S. courts. Next, it considers the act of state doctrine, which limits the circumstances under which U.S. courts will examine the validity of foreign government acts. Finally, the chapter considers the various forms of deference that courts give to the Executive Branch in the area of foreign relations.

A. JURISDICTION OVER FOREIGN RELATIONS CASES

As discussed in Chapter 1, the constitutional Founders viewed the lack of a meaningful national judiciary as one of the central defects of the Articles of Confederation. The establishment of such a judiciary was important, they explained, for U.S. foreign relations. In *Federalist No. 80*, for example, Alexander Hamilton argued that a national judiciary was needed in order to ensure adequate enforcement of treaty obligations, as well as uniformity in treaty interpretations. He also expressed concern that state courts might be biased against foreign citizens. Noting that "the denial or perversion of justice by the sentence of courts, as well as in any other manner, is with reason classed among the just causes of war," he argued that "it will follow that the federal judiciary ought to have cognizance of all causes in which the citizens of other countries are concerned." Hamilton further argued in *Federalist No. 81* that there should be federal court jurisdiction — indeed, Supreme Court jurisdiction — over cases involving ambassadors and other representatives of foreign nations, both in order to reduce international friction and "out of respect to the sovereignties [these individuals] represent."

Article III of the Constitution addresses these and other foreign affairs concerns in a variety of ways. It provides that the "judicial Power of the United States, shall be vested in one supreme Court, and in such inferior Courts as the Congress may from time to time ordain and establish." It further provides that this judicial power shall extend to various enumerated "Cases" and "Controversies." Some of these cases and controversies have an obvious relationship to foreign affairs. Among other things, the federal courts are allowed under Article III to hear cases arising under treaties, cases affecting ambassadors, admiralty cases, and suits between U.S. citizens and foreign citizens.

By its terms, Article III does not require the creation of any federal courts other than the Supreme Court. In addition, Article III has not been construed as requiring that Congress give the federal courts all the judicial power authorized by Article III. Congress did, of course, establish lower federal courts, and it granted them jurisdiction to hear various cases and controversies. Congress has never given the federal courts the power, however, to hear all the cases and controversies covered by Article III. And it is well settled that, except for the Supreme Court's exercise of its original jurisdiction (which is narrow in scope), the federal courts may not exercise jurisdiction over a case or controversy unless that jurisdiction is authorized both by Article III and by a congressional grant of jurisdiction. (Select jurisdictional statutes are printed at the end of the casebook, in Appendix B.)

The two most important categories of Article III jurisdiction are *federal question jurisdiction* (cases "arising under this Constitution, the Laws of the United States, and Treaties") and *diversity jurisdiction* (controversies between parties of diverse citizenship). Congress has granted the federal courts jurisdiction in both of these categories, but its statutory grants have been construed to be substantially narrower than the bounds of Article III. For example, Article III federal question jurisdiction may extend to any case in which there is a federal law "ingredient." *See* Osborn v. Bank of the United States, 22 U.S. (9 Wheat.) 738, 823 (1824). The federal question jurisdiction statute (28 U.S.C. §1331), by contrast, is subject to a well-pleaded complaint rule: The federal law issue must appear on the face of the plaintiff's well-pleaded complaint and cannot arise merely by way of defense. *See* Louisville & Nashville Railroad v. Mottley, 211 U.S. 149, 152 (1908).

With respect to the diversity jurisdiction statute (28 U.S.C. §1332), the most important limitation is the requirement of complete diversity: ordinarily, no plaintiff can share citizenship with any defendant, even if the other parties are diverse. *See* Strawbridge v. Curtiss, 7 U.S. (3 Cranch) 267, 267-68 (1806). The diversity statute also requires that the amount in controversy exceed a certain amount, currently $75,000. Defendants are allowed to remove to federal court suits brought against them in state court if the suit could have originally been filed in federal court, except that a case may not be removed on the basis of diversity jurisdiction if one or more of the defendants is a citizen of the state in which the suit is brought. *See* 28 U.S.C. §1441(b). (Other jurisdictional statutes relating to foreign affairs, such as the Alien Tort Statute and the Foreign Sovereign Immunities Act, are discussed elsewhere in the casebook.)

As the text of Article III suggests, and as the Supreme Court confirmed early in U.S. history, a suit between two foreign citizens does not satisfy even the minimal diversity requirements of Article III. *See* Mossman v. Higginson, 4 U.S. (4 Dall.) 12, 14 (1800); Hodgson v. Bowerbank, 9 U.S. (5 Cranch) 303, 304 (1809). As a result, to be heard in the federal courts, such suits must fall within some other category of Article III jurisdiction — for example, "Cases . . . arising under . . . the Laws of the United States." There are uncertainties, however, regarding the scope of this "arising under" jurisdiction as it relates to foreign affairs. For example, do the "Laws of the United States" include customary international law? If so, is customary international law also part of "the Laws of the United States which shall be made in Pursuance [of the Constitution]" referred to in Article VI of the Constitution? Do cases that do not involve international law but nevertheless implicate foreign affairs involve "federal common law," such that these cases arise under the laws of the United States? These and other jurisdictional questions are addressed in subsequent materials, especially the materials in Chapter 5 on the "federal common law of foreign relations," and in Chapter 7 on the status of customary international law in the U.S. legal system.

B. JUSTICIABILITY: STANDING, RIPENESS, MOOTNESS

As noted above, Article III allows for the exercise of federal judicial power over "cases" and "controversies." The Supreme Court has construed these terms as imposing certain "justiciability" limitations on the exercise of federal court jurisdiction. This section considers some of these limitations.

Raines v. Byrd
521 U.S. 811 (1997)

[The Line Item Veto Act of 1996 provided that the President could "cancel" items in appropriations bills after signing them into law. The Act further provided that "any member of Congress" could bring a lawsuit challenging the constitutionality of the Act. Four senators and two representatives who voted against the Act brought this lawsuit to challenge the Act's constitutionality.]

CHIEF JUSTICE REHNQUIST delivered the opinion of the Court.

The District Court for the District of Columbia declared the Line Item Veto Act unconstitutional. On this direct appeal, we hold that appellees lack standing to bring this suit, and therefore direct that the judgment of the District Court be vacated and the complaint dismissed . . . .

II

Under Article III, §2, of the Constitution, the federal courts have jurisdiction over this dispute between appellants and appellees only if it is a "case" or "controversy." . . .

One element of the case-or-controversy requirement is that appellees, based on their complaint, must establish that they have standing to sue. The standing inquiry focuses on whether the plaintiff is the proper party to bring this suit, although that inquiry "often turns on the nature and source of the claim asserted," Warth v. Seldin, 422 U.S. 490, 500 (1975). To meet the standing requirements of Article III, "[a] plaintiff must allege *personal injury* fairly traceable to the defendant's allegedly unlawful conduct and likely to be redressed by the requested relief." Allen v. Wright, 468 U.S. 737, 751 (1984) (emphasis added). . . .

We have also stressed that the alleged injury must be legally and judicially cognizable. This requires, among other things, that the plaintiff have suffered "an invasion of a legally protected interest which is . . . concrete and particularized," Lujan [v. Defenders of Wildlife, 504 U.S. 555, 560 (1992)], and that the dispute is "traditionally thought to be capable of resolution through the judicial process," Flast v. Cohen, 392 U.S. 83, 97 (1968).

We have always insisted on strict compliance with this jurisdictional standing requirement.... And our standing inquiry has been especially rigorous when reaching the merits of the dispute would force us to decide whether an action taken by one of the other two branches of the Federal Government was unconstitutional.... In the light of this overriding and time-honored concern about keeping the Judiciary's power within its proper constitutional sphere, we must put aside the natural urge to proceed directly to the merits of this important dispute and to "settle" it for the sake of convenience and efficiency. Instead, we must carefully inquire as to whether appellees have met their burden of establishing that their claimed injury is personal, particularized, concrete, and otherwise judicially cognizable.

III

We have never had occasion to rule on the question of legislative standing presented here. In Powell v. McCormack, 395 U.S. 486, 496, 512-514 (1969), we held that a Member of Congress' constitutional challenge to his exclusion from the House of Representatives (and his consequent loss of salary) presented an Article III case or controversy. But *Powell* does not help appellees. First, appellees have not been singled out for specially unfavorable treatment as opposed to other Members of their respective bodies. Their claim is that the Act causes a type of institutional injury (the diminution of legislative power), which necessarily damages all Members of Congress and both Houses of Congress equally. Second, appellees do not claim that they have been deprived of something to which they *personally* are entitled — such as their seats as Members of Congress after their constituents had elected *them*. Rather, appellees' claim of standing is based on a loss of political power, not loss of any private right, which would make the injury more concrete. Unlike the injury claimed by Congressman Adam Clayton Powell, the injury claimed by the Members of Congress here is not claimed in any private capacity but solely because they are Members of Congress. If one of the Members were to retire tomorrow, he would no longer have a claim; the claim would be possessed by his successor instead. The claimed injury thus runs (in a sense) with the Member's seat, a seat which the Member holds (it may quite arguably be said) as trustee for his constituents, not as a prerogative of personal power.

The one case in which we have upheld standing for legislators (albeit *state* legislators) claiming an institutional injury is Coleman v. Miller, 307 U.S. 433 (1939). Appellees, relying heavily on this case, claim that they, like the state legislators in *Coleman*, "have a plain, direct and adequate interest in maintaining the effectiveness of their votes," *id.*, at 438, sufficient to establish standing. In *Coleman*, 20 of Kansas' 40 State Senators voted not to ratify the proposed "Child Labor Amendment" to the Federal Constitution. With the vote deadlocked 20 to 20, the amendment ordinarily would not have been ratified. However, the State's Lieutenant Governor, the presiding officer of the State Senate, cast a deciding vote in favor of the amendment, and it was deemed ratified (after the State House of Representatives voted to ratify it). The 20 State Senators who had voted against the amendment, joined by a 21st State Senator and three State House Members, filed an action in the Kansas Supreme Court seeking a writ of mandamus that would compel the appropriate state officials to recognize that the legislature had not in fact ratified the amendment. That court held that the members of the legislature had standing to bring their mandamus action, but ruled against them on the merits.

This Court affirmed. By a vote of 5-4, we held that the members of the legislature had standing. In explaining our holding, we repeatedly emphasized that if these legislators (who were suing as a bloc) were correct on the merits, then their votes not to ratify the amendment were deprived of all validity:

> Here, the plaintiffs include twenty senators, whose votes against ratification have been *overridden and virtually held for naught* although if they are right in their contentions *their votes would have been sufficient to defeat ratification.* We think that these senators have a plain, direct, and adequate interest in maintaining the effectiveness of their votes.

Id., at 438 (emphasis added).

> [T]he twenty senators were not only qualified to vote on the question of ratification but *their* votes, if the Lieutenant Governor were excluded as not being a part of the legislature for that purpose, *would have been decisive in defeating the ratifying resolution.*

Id., at 441 (emphasis added).

> [W]e find no departure from principle in recognizing in the instant case that *at least the twenty senators whose votes,* if their contention were sustained, *would have been sufficient to defeat the resolution* ratifying the proposed constitutional amendment, have an interest in the controversy which, treated by the state court as a basis for entertaining and deciding the federal questions, is sufficient to give the Court jurisdiction to review that decision.

Id., at 446 (emphasis added).

It is obvious, then, that our holding in *Coleman* stands (at most) for the proposition that legislators whose votes would have been sufficient to defeat (or enact) a specific legislative Act have standing to sue if that legislative action goes into effect (or does not go into effect), on the ground that their votes have been completely nullified.

It should be equally obvious that appellees' claim does not fall within our holding in *Coleman*, as thus understood. They have not alleged that they voted for a specific bill, that there were sufficient votes to pass the bill, and that the bill was nonetheless deemed defeated. In the vote on the [Line Item Veto] Act, their votes were given full effect. They simply lost that vote. Nor can they allege that the Act will nullify their votes in the future in the same way that the votes of the *Coleman* legislators had been nullified. In the future, a majority of Senators and Congressmen can pass or reject appropriations bills; the Act has no effect on this process. In addition, a majority of Senators and Congressmen can vote to repeal the Act, or to exempt a given appropriations bill (or a given provision in an appropriations bill) from the Act; again, the Act has no effect on this process. *Coleman* thus provides little meaningful precedent for appellees' argument.

Nevertheless, appellees rely heavily on our statement in *Coleman* that the Kansas senators had "a plain, direct, and adequate interest in maintaining the effectiveness of their votes." Appellees claim that this statement applies to them because their votes on future appropriations bills (assuming a majority of Congress does not decide to exempt those bills from the Act) will be less "effective" than before, and that the "meaning" and "integrity" of their vote has changed. The argument goes as follows. Before the Act, Members of Congress could be sure that when they voted for, and Congress passed, an appropriations bill that included funds for Project X, one of two things would happen: (i) the bill would become law and all of the projects listed in the bill would go into effect, or (ii) the bill would not become law and none of the projects listed in the bill would go into effect. Either way, a vote for the appropriations bill meant a vote for a package of projects that were inextricably linked. After the Act, however, a vote for an appropriations bill that includes Project X means something different. Now, in addition to the two possibilities listed above, there is a third option: The bill will become law and then the President will "cancel" Project X.

Even taking appellees at their word about the change in the "meaning" and "effectiveness" of their vote for appropriations bills which are subject to the Act, we think their argument pulls *Coleman* too far from its moorings. Appellees' use of the word "effectiveness" to link their argument to *Coleman* stretches the word far beyond the sense in which the *Coleman* opinion used it. There is a vast difference between the level of vote nullification at issue in *Coleman* and the abstract dilution of institutional legislative power that is alleged here. To uphold standing here would require a drastic extension of *Coleman*. We are unwilling to take that step.

Not only do appellees lack support from precedent, but historical practice appears to cut against them as well. It is evident from several episodes in our history that in analogous confrontations between one or both Houses of Congress and the Executive Branch, no suit was brought on the basis of claimed injury to official authority or power....

There would be nothing irrational about a system which granted standing in these cases; some European constitutional courts operate under one or another variant of such a regime. But it is obviously not the regime that has obtained under our Constitution to date. Our regime contemplates a more restricted role for Article III courts.

JUSTICE SOUTER, concurring in the judgment, with whom JUSTICE GINSBURG joins, concurring....

Because it is fairly debatable whether appellees' injury is sufficiently personal and concrete to give them standing, it behooves us to resolve the question under more general separation-of-powers principles underlying our standing requirements. *See* Allen v. Wright, 468 U.S. 737, 752 (1984); United States v. Richardson, 418 U.S. 166, 188-197 (1974) (Powell, J., concurring). While "our constitutional structure [does not] require . . . that the Judicial Branch shrink from a confrontation with the other two coequal branches," Valley Forge Christian College [v. Americans United for Separation of Church and State, Inc., 454 U.S. 464, 474 (1982)], we have cautioned that respect for the separation of powers requires the Judicial Branch to exercise restraint in deciding constitutional issues by resolving those implicating the powers of the three branches of Government as a "last resort," see *ibid*. The counsel of restraint in this case begins with the fact that a dispute involving only officials, and the official interests of those, who serve in the branches of the National Government lies far from the model of the traditional common-law cause of action at the conceptual core of the case-or-controversy requirement. Although the contest here is not formally between the political branches (since Congress passed the bill augmenting Presidential power and the President signed it), it is in substance an interbranch controversy about calibrating the legislative and executive powers, as well as an intrabranch dispute between segments of Congress itself. Intervention in such a controversy would risk damaging the public confidence that is vital to the functioning of the Judicial Branch, by embroiling the federal courts in a power contest nearly at the height of its political tension.

While it is true that a suit challenging the constitutionality of this Act brought by a party from outside the Federal Government would also involve the Court in resolving the dispute over the allocation of power between the political branches, it would expose the Judicial Branch to a lesser risk. Deciding a suit to vindicate an interest outside the Government raises no specter of judicial readiness to enlist on one side of a political tug-of-war, since "the propriety of such action by a federal court has been recognized since Marbury v. Madison, 1 Cranch 137 (1803)." *Valley Forge Christian College, supra*, at 473-474. And just as the presence of a party beyond the Government places the Judiciary at some remove from the political forces, the need to await injury to such a plaintiff allows the courts some greater separation in the time between the political resolution and the judicial review....

The virtue of waiting for a private suit is only confirmed by the certainty that another suit can come to us. The parties agree, and I see no reason to question, that if the President "cancels" a conventional spending or tax provision pursuant to the Act, the putative beneficiaries of that provision will likely suffer a cognizable injury and thereby have standing under Article III.... While the Court has declined to lower standing requirements simply because no one would otherwise be able to litigate a claim, the certainty of a plaintiff who obviously would have standing to bring a suit to court after the politics had at least subsided from a full boil is a good reason to resolve doubts about standing against the plaintiff invoking an official interest.

Notes and Questions

1. As noted in *Raines*, the Supreme Court has held that Article III imposes three requirements for standing: The plaintiff must have suffered (or be likely to suffer) a concrete injury; the injury must be fairly traceable to the conduct of the defendant; and it must be likely that the injury will be redressed by a favorable decision. *See, e.g.*, Lujan v. Defenders of Wildlife, 504 U.S. 555, 560-61 (1992). The Court also has imposed certain "prudential" limitations on standing, which, for example, generally preclude taxpayer challenges to government expenditures, attempts to litigate the rights of persons not before the court, and the presentation of generalized grievances common to the public at large. These prudential limitations are not constitutionally mandated, however, so they can be overridden by Congress. *See, e.g.*, Federal Election Commission v. Akins, 524 U.S. 11, 20 (1998).

2. What is the holding of *Raines*? Did the plaintiffs lack standing because they alleged an institutional injury as opposed to a personal or private injury? Because their votes were diluted rather than "completely nullified"? Both? Would a member of Congress whose vote was completely nullified have standing to raise an institutional, as opposed to personal, injury? Under what circumstances will a legislator's vote be completely nullified?

3. *Raines* is an important decision for foreign relations law because many of the issues in this area involve disputes between the federal political branches. In limiting "legislative standing," *Raines* makes it more difficult for such disputes to be heard by the courts. Why was it significant in *Raines* that the dispute was between the political branches rather than between a private person and the government? What does Justice Souter's concurrence suggest? Do suits between the political branches present special separation of powers issues beyond the usual "case or controversy" limitation of Article III?

4. In answering these questions, consider Clinton v. City of New York, 524 U.S. 417 (1998), decided one year after *Raines*, which held the Line Item Veto Act unconstitutional. The lawsuit in *Clinton* was brought by the City of New York and related parties who alleged an injury resulting from President Clinton's cancellation, pursuant to the Line Item Veto Act, of a federal statutory waiver of the federal government's right to recoup certain Medicaid-related taxes. The Court held that the plaintiffs had standing because they "alleged a 'personal stake' in having an actual injury redressed, rather than an 'institutional injury' that is 'abstract and widely dispersed.'" 524 U.S. at 430 (quoting *Raines*, 521 U.S. at 830). Why does respect for separation of powers preclude the Court from considering the constitutionality of the Line Item Veto Act when the suit is brought by members of Congress, but not when it is brought by other parties? Didn't the Court waste a year, and a lot of judicial resources, by not deciding the issue on the merits in *Raines*? Consider these questions again after you have read the materials on the political question doctrine in the next section.

5. What is the relationship between the standing requirement and the prohibition on advisory opinions invoked in the letter from the Justices discussed in Chapter 1? Recall that the Justices reasoned that "the lines of separation drawn by the Constitution between the three departments of the government" precluded them from "extra-judicially deciding the questions" presented to them. Is this the same logic underlying standing? *See* Valley Forge Christian College v. Americans United for Separation, 454 U.S. 464, 472 (1982) (standing doctrine "tends to assure that the legal questions presented to the court will be resolved, not in the rarified atmosphere of a debating society, but in a concrete factual context conducive to a realistic appreciation of the consequences of judicial action"); Lujan v. Defenders of Wildlife, 504 U.S. 555, 598 n.4 (1992) (Blackmun, J., dissenting) ("The purpose of the standing doctrine is to ensure that courts do not render advisory opinions rather than resolve genuine controversies between adverse parties."); Ronald J. Krotoszynski, Jr., *Constitutional Flares: On Judges, Legislatures, and Dialogue*, 83 Minn. L. Rev. 1, 32 (1998) ("If a federal court renders a judgment in a case in which the plaintiff lacks standing, then it has authored an advisory opinion. Indeed, such an opinion would fall squarely within the prohibition of The Correspondence of the Justices.").

6. A standing issue that sometimes arises in foreign affairs cases is the ability of *foreign nations* to sue in U.S. courts. It is well accepted that foreign nations have standing to sue in U.S. courts when they (a) are suing private parties, and (b) are seeking to protect their own interests. *See, e.g.*, Principality of Monaco v. Mississippi, 292 U.S. 313, 324 n.2 (1934) ("There is no question but that foreign States may sue private parties in the federal courts."). Although foreign nations may also have standing to sue state or federal government defendants, such suits may be barred on other grounds, such as sovereign immunity, lack of a private right of action, or the political question doctrine. *See, e.g.*, Breard v. Greene, 523 U.S. 371, 377 (1998) (holding that suit by Paraguay against Virginia state officials was barred because of the lack of a private right of action in the relevant treaty, and suggesting that the suit was also barred by Virginia's sovereign immunity). One standing issue that has arisen recently is the ability of foreign governments to sue in U.S. courts on behalf of their citizens. *See, e.g.*, Estados Unidos Mexicanos v. DeCoster, 229 F.3d 332 (1st Cir. 2000) (holding that Mexico lacked "parens patriae" standing to bring discrimination claims on behalf of its nationals). Finally, it is not uncommon for foreign nations to file *amicus curiae* briefs in foreign affairs cases expressing their views about the case. The weight, if any, that courts should give to such briefs is an issue considered in other sections of the casebook.

7. Standing concerns the proper *party* to bring a lawsuit. Two related justiciability doctrines — ripeness and mootness — concern the proper *timing* of federal court adjudication. The ripeness doctrine ensures that courts do not review an issue prematurely at a point when the alleged injury is still speculative. To be ripe, the alleged harm must ordinarily be "immediate" or "imminent" rather than merely "distant" or "speculative." *See, e.g.*, Poe v. Ullman, 367 U.S. 497 (1961) (plurality). As this test shows, the ripeness inquiry is related to standing, and the two inquiries often overlap. The mootness doctrine is also about timing, and is also related to standing. As one commentator has famously noted, mootness is "the doctrine of standing set in a time frame: The requisite personal interest that must exist at the commencement of the litigation (standing) must continue throughout its existence (mootness)." Henry P. Monaghan, *Constitutional Adjudication: The Who and When*, 82 Yale L.J. 1363, 1384 (1973). A case that is ripe when filed will ordinarily be dismissed as moot if it is not still ripe at the time of the decision. *See* DeFunis v. Odegaard, 416 U.S. 312, 316 (1974). The Supreme Court has held, however, that a case that would otherwise be moot can be heard if the issue raised is capable of repetition yet evades judicial review. *See, e.g.*, First National Bank of Boston v. Bellotti, 435 U.S. 765, 774 (1978) (election restrictions); Roe v. Wade, 410 U.S. 113, 125 (1973) (abortion restrictions). Also, a defendant's voluntary cessation of challenged activity ordinarily will not moot a case, because the defendant simply could resume the activity after the case was dismissed. *See* United States v. W.T. Grant Co., 345 U.S. 629, 632 (1953).

8. Note that, because the justiciability limitations discussed in this section are derived from Article III, which regulates the jurisdiction and structure of the *federal courts*, they are not binding on state courts. As a result, state courts sometimes hear cases that are not justiciable in the federal courts. *See, e.g.*, Asarco, Inc. v. Kadish, 490 U.S. 605, 617 (1989) (state courts are not obligated to adhere to federal limitations on standing).

9. For discussions of *Raines*, see Neal Devins & Michael A. Fitts, *The Triumph of Timing: Raines v. Byrd and the Modern Supreme Court's Attempt to Control Constitutional Confrontations*, 86 Geo. L.J. 351 (1997); David J. Weiner, Note, *The New Law of Legislative Standing*, 54 Stan. L. Rev. 205 (2001); and Note, *Standing in the Way of Separation of Powers: The Consequences of* Raines v. Byrd, 112 Harv. L. Rev. 1741 (1999).

C. POLITICAL QUESTION DOCTRINE

The Supreme Court's opinion in Marbury v. Madison, 5 U.S. (1 Cranch) 137 (1803), is famous for announcing the doctrine of constitutional judicial review. In that opinion, Chief Justice Marshall states that it is "emphatically the province and duty of the judicial department to say what the law is," *id.* at 177, and he suggests that for every violation of a vested legal right, there should be a legal remedy. He also suggests, however, that not all disputes are susceptible to judicial resolution. In particular, Marshall states that some government actions are "mere political act[s]" that are not "examinable in a court of justice." *Id.* at 164-65. The materials below address the relevance of this "political question doctrine" to cases implicating foreign affairs.

Baker v. Carr

369 U.S. 186 (1962)

MR. JUSTICE BRENNAN delivered the opinion of the Court.

This civil action was brought under 42 U.S.C. §§1983 and 1988 to redress the alleged deprivation of federal constitutional rights. The complaint, alleging that by means of a 1901 statute of Tennessee apportioning the members of the General Assembly among the State's 95 counties, "these plaintiffs and others similarly situated, are denied the equal protection of the laws accorded them by the Fourteenth Amendment to the Constitution of the United States by virtue of the debasement of their votes," was dismissed by a three-judge court convened under 28 U.S.C. §2281 in the Middle District of Tennessee. The court held that it lacked jurisdiction of the subject matter and also that no claim was stated upon which relief could be granted. We noted probable jurisdiction of the appeal. We hold that the dismissal was error, and remand the cause to the District Court for trial and further proceedings consistent with this opinion . . . .

Our discussion, even at the price of extending this opinion, requires review of a number of political question cases, in order to expose the attributes of the doctrine — attributes which, in various settings, diverge, combine, appear, and disappear in seeming disorderliness. Since that review is undertaken solely to demonstrate that neither singly nor collectively do these cases support a conclusion that this apportionment case is nonjusticiable, we of course do not explore their implications in other contexts. That review reveals that in the Guaranty Clause cases and in the other "political question" cases, it is the relationship between the judiciary and the coordinate branches of the Federal Government, and not the federal judiciary's relationship to the States, which gives rise to the "political question."

We have said that "In determining whether a question falls within [the political question] category, the appropriateness under our system of government of attributing finality to the action of the political departments and also the lack of satisfactory criteria for a judicial determination are dominant considerations." Coleman v. Miller, 307 U.S. 433, 454-455. The nonjusticiability of a political question is primarily a function of the separation of powers. Much confusion results from the capacity of the "political question" label to obscure the need for case-by-case inquiry. Deciding whether a matter has in any measure been committed by the Constitution to another branch of government, or whether the action of that branch exceeds whatever authority has been committed, is itself a delicate exercise in constitutional interpretation, and is a responsibility of this Court as ultimate interpreter of the Constitution. To demonstrate this requires no less than to analyze representative cases and to infer from them the analytical threads that make up the political question doctrine. We shall then show that none of those threads catches this case.

Foreign relations: There are sweeping statements to the effect that all questions touching foreign relations are political questions.[31] Not only does resolution of such issues frequently turn on standards that defy judicial application, or involve

---

31. E.g., "The conduct of the foreign relations of our Government is committed by the Constitution to the Executive and Legislative — 'the political' — Departments of the Government, and the propriety of what may be done in the exercise of this political power is not subject to judicial inquiry or decision." Oetjen v. Central Leather Co., 246 U.S. 297, 302.

the exercise of a discretion demonstrably committed to the executive or legislature; but many such questions uniquely demand single-voiced statement of the Government's views. Yet it is error to suppose that every case or controversy which touches foreign relations lies beyond judicial cognizance. Our cases in this field seem invariably to show a discriminating analysis of the particular question posed, in terms of the history of its management by the political branches, of its susceptibility to judicial handling in the light of its nature and posture in the specific case, and of the possible consequences of judicial action. For example, though a court will not ordinarily inquire whether a treaty has been terminated, since on that question "governmental action . . . must be regarded as of controlling importance," if there has been no conclusive "governmental action" then a court can construe a treaty and may find it provides the answer. Though a court will not undertake to construe a treaty in a manner inconsistent with a subsequent federal statute, no similar hesitancy obtains if the asserted clash is with state law.

While recognition of foreign governments so strongly defies judicial treatment that without executive recognition a foreign state has been called "a republic of whose existence we know nothing," and the judiciary ordinarily follows the executive as to which nation has sovereignty over disputed territory, once sovereignty over an area is politically determined and declared, courts may examine the resulting status and decide independently whether a statute applies to that area. Similarly, recognition of belligerency abroad is an executive responsibility, but if the executive proclamations fall short of an explicit answer, a court may construe them seeking, for example, to determine whether the situation is such that statutes designed to assure American neutrality have become operative. Still again, though it is the executive that determines a person's status as representative of a foreign government, the executive's statements will be construed where necessary to determine the court's jurisdiction. Similar judicial action in the absence of a recognizedly authoritative executive declaration occurs in cases involving the immunity from seizure of vessels owned by friendly foreign governments. Compare Ex parte Peru, 318 U.S. 578, with Mexico v. Hoffman, 324 U.S. 30, 34-35.

Dates of duration of hostilities: Though it has been stated broadly that "the power which declared the necessity is the power to declare its cessation, and what the cessation requires," here too analysis reveals isolable reasons for the presence of political questions, underlying this Court's refusal to review the political departments' determination of when or whether a war has ended. Dominant is the need for finality in the political determination . . . .

It is apparent that several formulations which vary slightly according to the settings in which the questions arise may describe a political question, although each has one or more elements which identify it as essentially a function of the separation of powers. Prominent on the surface of any case held to involve a political question is found a textually demonstrable constitutional commitment of the issue to a coordinate political department; or a lack of judicially discoverable and manageable standards for resolving it; or the impossibility of deciding without an initial policy determination of a kind clearly for nonjudicial discretion; or the impossibility of a court's undertaking independent resolution without expressing lack of the respect due coordinate branches of government; or an unusual need for unquestioning adherence to a political decision already made; or the potentiality of embarrassment from multifarious pronouncements by various departments on one question.

Goldwater v. Carter

444 U.S. 996 (1979)

[As part of the process of recognizing the People's Republic of China, President Jimmy Carter announced that he planned to terminate the U.S. mutual defense treaty with Taiwan, pursuant to a provision in the treaty that allowed either party to withdraw from the treaty after giving a year's notice. In response, eight senators and sixteen members of the House of Representatives sued for declaratory and injunctive relief to prevent Carter from terminating the treaty. The federal district court held that the notice of termination was ineffective absent either a manifestation of the consent of the Senate to such termination by a two-thirds vote, or an approving majority vote by both houses of Congress. The court of appeals reversed, ruling on the merits that the President had the power to terminate the treaty. Without issuing a majority opinion, the Supreme Court granted *certiorari*, vacated the lower court judgment, and remanded the case with directions to dismiss the complaint.]

MR. JUSTICE POWELL, concurring.

Although I agree with the result reached by the Court, I would dismiss the complaint as not ripe for judicial review.

I

This Court has recognized that an issue should not be decided if it is not ripe for judicial review. Prudential considerations persuade me that a dispute between Congress and the President is not ready for judicial review unless and until each branch has taken action asserting its constitutional authority. Differences between the President and the Congress are commonplace under our system. The differences should, and almost invariably do, turn on political rather than legal considerations. The Judicial Branch should not decide issues affecting the allocation of power between the President and Congress until the political branches reach a constitutional impasse. Otherwise, we would encourage small groups or even individual Members of Congress to seek judicial resolution of issues before the normal political process has the opportunity to resolve the conflict.

In this case, a few Members of Congress claim that the President's action in terminating the treaty with Taiwan has deprived them of their constitutional role with respect to a change in the supreme law of the land. Congress has taken no official action. In the present posture of this case, we do not know whether there ever will be an actual confrontation between the Legislative and Executive Branches. Although the Senate has considered a resolution declaring that Senate approval is necessary for the termination of any mutual defense treaty, no final vote has been taken on the resolution. Moreover, it is unclear whether the resolution would have retroactive effect. It cannot be said that either the Senate or the House has rejected the President's claim. If the Congress chooses not to confront the President, it is not our task to do so. I therefore concur in the dismissal of this case.

II

Mr. Justice Rehnquist suggests, however, that the issue presented by this case is a nonjusticiable political question which can never be considered by this Court. I cannot agree. In my view, reliance upon the political-question doctrine is inconsistent with our precedents. As set forth in the seminal case of Baker v. Carr, 369

U.S. 186, 217 (1962), the doctrine incorporates three inquiries: (i) Does the issue involve resolution of questions committed by the text of the Constitution to a coordinate branch of Government? (ii) Would resolution of the question demand that a court move beyond areas of judicial expertise? (iii) Do prudential considerations counsel against judicial intervention? In my opinion the answer to each of these inquiries would require us to decide this case if it were ready for review.

First, the existence of "a textually demonstrable constitutional commitment of the issue to a coordinate political department," *ibid.*, turns on an examination of the constitutional provisions governing the exercise of the power in question. Powell v. McCormack, 395 U.S. 486, 519 (1969). No constitutional provision explicitly confers upon the President the power to terminate treaties. Further, Art. II, §2, of the Constitution authorizes the President to make treaties with the advice and consent of the Senate. Article VI provides that treaties shall be a part of the supreme law of the land. These provisions add support to the view that the text of the Constitution does not unquestionably commit the power to terminate treaties to the President alone.

Second, there is no "lack of judicially discoverable and manageable standards for resolving" this case; nor is a decision impossible "without an initial policy determination of a kind clearly for nonjudicial discretion." Baker v. Carr, *supra*, at 217. We are asked to decide whether the President may terminate a treaty under the Constitution without congressional approval. Resolution of the question may not be easy, but it only requires us to apply normal principles of interpretation to the constitutional provisions at issue. *See* Powell v. McCormack, *supra*, at 548-549. The present case involves neither review of the President's activities as Commander in Chief nor impermissible interference in the field of foreign affairs. Such a case would arise if we were asked to decide, for example, whether a treaty required the President to order troops into a foreign country. But "it is error to suppose that every case or controversy which touches foreign relations lies beyond judicial cognizance." Baker v. Carr, *supra*, at 211. This case "touches" foreign relations, but the question presented to us concerns only the constitutional division of power between Congress and the President.

A simple hypothetical demonstrates the confusion that I find inherent in Mr. Justice Rehnquist's opinion concurring in the judgment. Assume that the President signed a mutual defense treaty with a foreign country and announced that it would go into effect despite its rejection by the Senate. Under Mr. Justice Rehnquist's analysis that situation would present a political question even though Art. II, §2, clearly would resolve the dispute. Although the answer to the hypothetical case seems self-evident because it demands textual rather than interstitial analysis, the nature of the legal issue presented is no different from the issue presented in the case before us. In both cases, the Court would interpret the Constitution to decide whether congressional approval is necessary to give a Presidential decision on the validity of a treaty the force of law. Such an inquiry demands no special competence or information beyond the reach of the Judiciary. *Cf.* Chicago & Southern Air Lines v. Waterman S.S. Corp., 333 U.S. 103, 111 (1948).[1]

---

1. The Court has recognized that, in the area of foreign policy, Congress may leave the President with wide discretion that otherwise might run afoul of the nondelegation doctrine. United States v. Curtiss-Wright Export Corp., 299 U.S. 304 (1936). As stated in that case, "the President alone has the power to speak or listen as a representative of the Nation. He *makes* treaties with the advice and consent of the Senate; but he alone negotiates." *Id.*, at 319 (emphasis in original). Resolution of this case would interfere with neither the President's ability to negotiate treaties nor his duty to execute their

Finally, the political-question doctrine rests in part on prudential concerns calling for mutual respect among the three branches of Government. Thus, the Judicial Branch should avoid "the potentiality of embarrassment [that would result] from multifarious pronouncements by various departments on one question." Similarly, the doctrine restrains judicial action where there is an "unusual need for unquestioning adherence to a political decision already made." Baker v. Carr, *supra*, at 217.

If this case were ripe for judicial review, none of these prudential considerations would be present. Interpretation of the Constitution does not imply lack of respect for a coordinate branch. Powell v. McCormack, *supra*, at 548. If the President and the Congress had reached irreconcilable positions, final disposition of the question presented by this case would eliminate, rather than create, multiple constitutional interpretations. The specter of the Federal Government brought to a halt because of the mutual intransigence of the President and the Congress would require this Court to provide a resolution pursuant to our duty " 'to say what the law is.' " United States v. Nixon, 418 U.S. 683, 703 (1974), quoting Marbury v. Madison, 1 Cranch 137, 177 (1803)....

MR. JUSTICE STEWART, with whom THE CHIEF JUSTICE, MR. JUSTICE STEWART, and MR. JUSTICE STEVENS join, concurring in the judgment.

I am of the view that the basic question presented by the petitioners in this case is "political" and therefore nonjusticiable because it involves the authority of the President in the conduct of our country's foreign relations and the extent to which the Senate or the Congress is authorized to negate the action of the President. In Coleman v. Miller, 307 U.S. 433 (1939), a case in which members of the Kansas Legislature brought an action attacking a vote of the State Senate in favor of the ratification of the Child Labor Amendment, Mr. Chief Justice Hughes wrote in what is referred to as the "Opinion of the Court":

> We think that ... the question of the efficacy of ratifications by state legislatures, in the light of previous rejection or attempted withdrawal, should be regarded as a political question pertaining to the political departments, with the ultimate authority in the Congress in the exercise of its control over the promulgation of the adoption of the Amendment.
>
> The precise question as now raised is whether, when the legislature of the State, as we have found, has actually ratified the proposed amendment, the Court should restrain the state officers from certifying the ratification to the Secretary of State, because of an earlier rejection, and thus prevent the question from coming before the political departments. We find no basis in either Constitution or statute for such judicial action. Article V, speaking solely of ratification, contains no provision as to rejection....

Id., at 450.

Thus, Mr. Chief Justice Hughes' opinion concluded that "Congress in controlling the promulgation of the adoption of a constitutional amendment has the final determination of the question whether by lapse of time its proposal of the amendment had lost its vitality prior to the required ratifications."

I believe it follows *a fortiori* from *Coleman* that the controversy in the instant case is a nonjusticiable political dispute that should be left for resolution by the

---

provisions. We are merely being asked to decide whether a treaty, which cannot be ratified without Senate approval, continues in effect until the Senate or perhaps the Congress takes further action.

Executive and Legislative Branches of the Government. Here, while the Constitution is express as to the manner in which the Senate shall participate in the ratification of a treaty, it is silent as to that body's participation in the abrogation of a treaty. In this respect the case is directly analogous to *Coleman, supra*. . . . In light of the absence of any constitutional provision governing the termination of a treaty, and the fact that different termination procedures may be appropriate for different treaties, the instant case in my view also "must surely be controlled by political standards."

I think that the justifications for concluding that the question here is political in nature are even more compelling than in *Coleman* because it involves foreign relations — specifically a treaty commitment to use military force in the defense of a foreign government if attacked. In United States v. Curtiss-Wright Corp., 299 U.S. 304 (1936), this Court said:

> Whether, if the Joint Resolution had related solely to internal affairs it would be open to the challenge that it constituted an unlawful delegation of legislative power to the Executive, we find it unnecessary to determine. The whole aim of the resolution is to affect a situation entirely external to the United States, and falling within the category of foreign affairs. . . .

Id., at 315.

The present case differs in several important respects from Youngstown Sheet & Tube Co. v. Sawyer, 343 U.S. 579 (1952), cited by petitioners as authority both for reaching the merits of this dispute and for reversing the Court of Appeals. In *Youngstown*, private litigants brought a suit contesting the President's authority under his war powers to seize the Nation's steel industry, an action of profound and demonstrable domestic impact. Here, by contrast, we are asked to settle a dispute between coequal branches of our Government, each of which has resources available to protect and assert its interests, resources not available to private litigants outside the judicial forum. Moreover, as in *Curtiss-Wright*, the effect of this action, as far as we can tell, is "entirely external to the United States, and [falls] within the category of foreign affairs." Finally, as already noted, the situation presented here is closely akin to that presented in *Coleman*, where the Constitution spoke only to the procedure for ratification of an amendment, not to its rejection.

Having decided that the question presented in this action is nonjusticiable, I believe that the appropriate disposition is for this Court to vacate the decision of the Court of Appeals and remand with instructions for the District Court to dismiss the complaint. This procedure derives support from our practice in disposing of moot actions in federal courts.[2] For more than 30 years, we have instructed lower courts to vacate any decision on the merits of an action that has become moot prior to a resolution of the case in this Court. United States v. Munsingwear, Inc., 340 U.S. 36 (1950). The Court has required such decisions to be vacated in order to "prevent a judgment, unreviewable because of mootness, from spawning any legal consequences." *Id.*, at 41. It is even more imperative that this Court invoke this procedure to ensure that resolution of a "political question," which should not have been decided by a lower court, does not "spawn any legal consequences." An Art. III court's resolution of a question that is "political" in character can create far more disruption among the three coequal branches of Government than the resolution of a question presented in a moot controversy. Since the political nature of the

2. This Court, of course, may not prohibit state courts from deciding political questions, any more than it may prohibit them from deciding questions that are moot, so long as they do not trench upon exclusively federal questions of foreign policy. Zschernig v. Miller, 389 U.S. 429, 441 (1968).

questions presented should have precluded the lower courts from considering or deciding the merits of the controversy, the prior proceedings in the federal courts must be vacated, and the complaint dismissed ....

MR. JUSTICE BRENNAN, dissenting.

I respectfully dissent from the order directing the District Court to dismiss this case, and would affirm the judgment of the Court of Appeals insofar as it rests upon the President's well-established authority to recognize, and withdraw recognition from, foreign governments.

In stating that this case presents a nonjusticiable "political question," Mr. Justice Rehnquist, in my view, profoundly misapprehends the political-question principle as it applies to matters of foreign relations. Properly understood, the political-question doctrine restrains courts from reviewing an exercise of foreign policy judgment by the coordinate political branch to which authority to make that judgment has been "constitutional[ly] commit[ted]." Baker v. Carr, 369 U.S. 186, 211-213, 217 (1962). But the doctrine does not pertain when a court is faced with the *antecedent* question whether a particular branch has been constitutionally designated as the repository of political decisionmaking power. *Cf.* Powell v. McCormack, 395 U.S. 486, 519-521 (1969). The issue of decisionmaking authority must be resolved as a matter of constitutional law, not political discretion; accordingly, it falls within the competence of the courts.

The constitutional question raised here is prudently answered in narrow terms. Abrogation of the defense treaty with Taiwan was a necessary incident to Executive recognition of the Peking Government, because the defense treaty was predicated upon the now-abandoned view that the Taiwan Government was the only legitimate political authority in China. Our cases firmly establish that the Constitution commits to the President alone the power to recognize, and withdraw recognition from, foreign regimes. *See* Banco Nacional de Cuba v. Sabbatino, 376 U.S. 398, 410 (1964); Baker v. Carr, *supra*, at 212; United States v. Pink, 315 U.S. 203, 228-230 (1942). That mandate being clear, our judicial inquiry into the treaty rupture can go no further.

Notes and Questions

1. Prior to *Baker v. Carr*, the Supreme Court followed a largely categorical approach in its application of the political question doctrine to foreign affairs cases. Under this approach, courts did not use a multifactored balancing test but rather treated certain well-defined foreign relations decisions by the political branches as final and binding. A good example is Jones v. United States, 137 U.S. 202 (1890). The defendant in *Jones* was prosecuted for committing murder on a Caribbean island that the President had proclaimed, pursuant to an Act of Congress, to be within the jurisdiction of the United States. The defendant argued that the Act of Congress authorizing this presidential assertion of jurisdiction was unconstitutional because it was an attempt by Congress to regulate land outside of U.S. control. The Supreme Court concluded that the question of sovereignty over the island was by its nature a "political question":

> Who is the sovereign, *de jure or de facto,* of a territory is not a judicial, but a political question, the determination of which by the legislative and executive departments of

any government conclusively binds the judges, as well as all other officers, citizens and subjects of that government. This principle has always been upheld by this court, and has been affirmed under a great variety of circumstances . . . .

All courts of justice are bound to take judicial notice of the territorial extent of the jurisdiction exercised by the government whose laws they administer, or of its recognition or denial of the sovereignty of a foreign power, as appearing from the public acts of the legislature and executive, although those acts are not formally put in evidence, nor in accord with the pleadings.

Id. at 212-14. For other examples of such categorical reasoning, see Doe v. Braden, 57 U.S. (16 How.) 635, 657 (1853) (ratification power of foreign government a political question); Williams v. Suffolk Ins. Co., 38 U.S. 415, 420 (1839) (sovereignty of foreign nation a political question); Foster v. Neilson, 27 U.S. (2 Pet.) 253, 308-13 (1829) (territorial boundary determination a political question); and United States v. Palmer, 16 U.S. (3 Wheat.) 610, 633-34 (1818) (recognition of new government a political question). *See generally* Edwin D. Dickinson, *International Political Questions in the National Courts*, 19 Am. J. Int'l L. 157 (1925).

2. How does the Court's conception of the political question doctrine in *Baker* differ from the categorical approach described in Note 1? What role does *Baker* envision for federal courts — an active or passive one? What does it mean for courts to perform a "discriminating analysis" of the "possible consequences of judicial action"? How do courts know when issues demand a "single-voiced statement of the Government's views," or when "multifarious pronouncements" will cause "embarrassment"? What information and expertise would courts need to answer these questions? To what extent should courts defer to Executive Branch representations in answering these questions? Do you see any tension between the aims of the political question doctrine and the judicial tests designed to achieve those aims? Consider the following description of the current state of the doctrine:

No branch of the law of justiciability is in such disarray as the doctrine of the "political question." . . . Even those who accept the existence of the doctrine recognize that there is no workable definition of characteristics that distinguish political questions from justiciable questions, and that the category of political questions is "more amenable to description by infinite itemization than by generalization."

Charles Alan Wright & Mary Kay Kane, Law of Federal Courts 85 (6th ed. 2002). Is that a fair assessment?

3. As Professor Louis Henkin has argued, in many cases in which courts have labeled issues "political questions," they are really saying that a political branch — often the Executive Branch — has the constitutional authority to resolve the issue in a way that is dispositive for the courts. In these cases, courts do not remain agnostic about the issue; rather, they treat as valid a political branch's resolution of it. *See generally* Louis Henkin, *Is There a "Political Question" Doctrine?*, 85 Yale L.J. 597 (1976). As discussed below in Section D, a good example is the way in which courts treated Executive Branch suggestions of foreign sovereign immunity as dispositive prior to the adoption of the Foreign Sovereign Immunities Act. The first factor referred to by the Court in *Baker v. Carr* — "a textually demonstrable constitutional commitment of the issue to a coordinate political department" — appears to concern this type of dispositive political branch authority. Nevertheless, some foreign affairs actions are treated as nonjusticiable in the sense that courts will not express a view about their validity, and some of the other *Baker v. Carr* factors seem relevant to that issue of nonjusticiability. To take an example that we will consider in

Chapter 4, a number of courts held that the validity of the Vietnam War (under the U.S. Constitution and international law) was a nonjusticiable political question, without holding that the war was valid. Similarly, in the *Goldwater* decision excerpted above, the Rehnquist plurality was not arguing that President Carter's treaty termination was constitutionally valid; rather, it was arguing that the Court should not decide the validity of the termination. Do you see the difference between saying that a political branch has the authority to dispositively resolve an issue and saying that the issue is not justiciable? On the other hand, if courts refuse to overturn a political branch action because its validity raises a nonjusticiable political question, how is that different from treating the action as constitutionally valid?

4. The political question doctrine is today only rarely applied in domestic cases. For examples, see Vieth v. Jubelirer, 541 U.S. 267 (2004) (plurality) (dispute concerning alleged political gerrymandering of congressional districts), and Nixon v. United States, 506 U.S. 224 (1993) (challenge to Senate impeachment procedure). In foreign affairs cases, however, the doctrine continues to be applied with some frequency. Why do you think this is so? Is the duty of the courts to "say what the law is," referred to in Marbury v. Madison, any less in foreign affairs cases? As discussed in Chapter 4, the political question doctrine has been applied with particular frequency in cases that involve challenges to U.S. military activities. *See, e.g.,* Doe v. Bush, 323 F.3d 133 (1st Cir. 2003); Campbell v. Clinton, 203 F.3d 19 (D.C. Cir. 2000); Aktepe v. United States, 105 F.3d 1400 (11th Cir. 1997); Lowry v. Reagan, 676 F. Supp. 333 (D.D.C. 1987). In some sense, *Goldwater* itself could be viewed as a military case, because it involved a defense treaty. But the political question doctrine has not been limited to the military context. Nor has it been limited to disputes between the federal political branches. Should it be limited in these ways?

5. An illustration of the potential breadth of the political question doctrine is the Eleventh Circuit's decision in Made in the USA Foundation v. United States, 242 F.3d 1300 (11th Cir. 2001). In that case, a trade group challenged the constitutionality of the North American Free Trade Agreement (NAFTA), which was concluded as a "congressional-executive agreement" — that is, it was negotiated by the President and then approved by a majority of both houses of Congress. The trade group argued that NAFTA was a "treaty" within the meaning of Article II, Section 2 of the Constitution, and thus required two-thirds Senate consent in order to be validly ratified by the United States. (We consider the merits of this argument in Chapter 6.) The Eleventh Circuit began its opinion by noting that "certain international agreements may well require Senate ratification as treaties through the constitutionally-mandated procedures of Art. II, §2." *Id.* at 1302. Nevertheless, the court declined to adjudicate the trade group's challenge to NAFTA, concluding that, at least in this context, "the issue of what kinds of agreements require Senate ratification pursuant to the Art. II, §2 procedures presents a nonjusticiable political question." *Id.* at 1319. In reaching this conclusion, the court applied the factors listed in *Baker*, and it also relied heavily on Justice Rehnquist's and Justice Powell's opinions in *Goldwater*. Are there any relevant differences between this case and *Goldwater*?

The breadth of the political question doctrine is also illustrated by several decisions from the U.S. District Court for the District of New Jersey, in which the court relied on the doctrine to bar adjudication of claims against German and other companies concerning their use of slave labor during World War II. *See* Frumkin v. JA Jones, Inc., 129 F. Supp. 2d 370 (D.N.J. 2001); Iwanowa v. Ford Motor Co., 67 F. Supp. 2d 424 (D.N.J. 1999); Burger-Fischer v. Degussa AG, 65 F. Supp. 2d 248

(D.N.J. 1999). Unlike *Goldwater* and *Made in the USA Foundation*, these cases involved claims for individual relief rather than separation of powers challenges. Nevertheless, the judges in these cases determined that the claims should not be adjudicated because such adjudication would unduly interfere with the political branches' conduct of U.S. foreign relations. *See also* Joo v. Japan, 413 F.3d 45 (D.C. Cir. 2005) (claims against Japan relating to World War II held to pose non-judicial political questions). For a discussion of whether the political question doctrine should be applied in cases such as these that concern international human rights standards, see K. Lee Boyd, *Are Human Rights Political Questions?*, 53 Rutgers L. Rev. 277 (2001). For an argument that institutional competence considerations warrant broad application of the political question doctrine in foreign affairs cases, see Jide Nzelibe, *The Uniqueness of Foreign Affairs*, 89 Iowa L. Rev. 941 (2004).

6. Does application of the political question doctrine constitute an abdication of the judicial function of deciding cases? Are foreign affairs issues appreciably more difficult for courts to resolve than domestic issues? Are there more nonjudicial mechanisms available for resolving foreign affairs disputes than for resolving domestic disputes? Is it possible to draw a bright line today between foreign and domestic issues?

7. Why, according to Justice Rehnquist's plurality opinion in *Goldwater*, is the issue of treaty termination political? What is Justice Powell's response? In Justice Rehnquist correct in stating in footnote two of his plurality opinion that state courts are not prohibited from deciding political questions? Could a state court decide whether the President has the unilateral authority to terminate a treaty?

8. Justice Powell supported dismissal in *Goldwater* on the ground that the case was not "ripe for judicial review." What does Justice Powell mean by ripeness in this context? What difference is there between Justice Powell's ripeness basis for dismissal and the plurality's political question basis? What difference is there between the ripeness requirement and the limitations on legislative standing imposed in *Raines*?

9. Both Justice Rehnquist's and Justice Powell's opinions in *Goldwater* assume that, at least generally, the political branches have adequate tools with which to resolve constitutional foreign affairs issues outside the courts. Is this assumption valid? How do we know whether the Senate, for example, has sufficient leverage to protect its constitutional interests?

10. What is the overall significance of *Goldwater* regarding the termination of U.S. treaty commitments? Do the separate opinions yield a holding on this issue? Does *Goldwater* effectively mean that the President can terminate U.S. treaties with impunity? (The power of treaty termination is discussed more fully in Chapter 6.)

11. A more recent treaty termination case is Kucinich v. Bush, 236 F. Supp. 2d 1 (D.D.C. 2002). In that case, 32 members of the House of Representatives brought suit in federal district court against President Bush and other Executive Branch officials, challenging the Bush Administration's decision to withdraw from the Anti-Ballistic Missile (ABM) Treaty. The ABM Treaty, which was ratified by the United States and the Soviet Union in 1972, strictly limited the number and location of anti-ballistic missile systems that could be deployed by each country. The House members argued that because the Constitution classifies treaties, like federal statutes, as the "supreme law of the land," the President does not have the authority to terminate a treaty without congressional consent, just as he cannot terminate a statute without congressional consent. In dismissing the suit, the court concluded that the House members lacked standing under *Raines*. The court also held that the case raised a nonjusticiable political question, for reasons similar to those articulated by Justice Rehnquist in *Goldwater*.

12. In *Goldwater*, the plaintiffs were seeking injunctive and declaratory relief. Should the requested remedy affect whether an issue is held to be a political question? For example, should courts be more willing to adjudicate foreign affairs cases involving claims for damages than foreign affairs cases involving claims for equitable relief? Compare Ramirez de Arellano v. Weinberger, 745 F.2d 1500 (D.C. Cir. 1984) (en banc) (applying political question doctrine to injunctive claim based on Takings Clause) with Langenegger v. United States, 756 F.2d 1565 (Fed. Cir. 1985) (declining to apply political question doctrine to monetary compensation claim based on Takings Clause). *See also* Koohi v. United States, 976 F.2d 1328, 1332 (9th Cir. 1992) ("A key element in our conclusion that the plaintiffs' action is justiciable is the fact that the plaintiffs seek only damages for their injuries."). For discussion of this issue, see John M. Hillebrecht, *Foreign Affairs Cases and Political Question Analysis*: Chaser Shipping v. United States, 23 Stan. J. Int'l L. 665 (1987).

13. In Japan Whaling Ass'n v. American Cetacean Society, 478 U.S. 221 (1986), the Supreme Court considered a challenge by wildlife groups to the Secretary of Commerce's decision not to certify Japan for statutory sanctions designed to protect whales, despite Japan's violation of an international whaling quota. A majority of the Court concluded that the Executive had not acted contrary to the relevant statutes. The Court rejected the argument, however, that the case posed a nonjusticiable political question. The Court explained: "As *Baker* plainly held . . . the courts have the authority to construe treaties and executive agreements, and it goes without saying that interpreting congressional legislation is a recurring and accepted task for the federal courts. It is also evident that the challenge to the Secretary's decision not to certify Japan for harvesting whales in excess of [the international] quotas presents a purely legal question of statutory interpretation."

Does this decision stand for the proposition that courts cannot invoke the political question doctrine to avoid the interpretation of foreign relations statutes? That the political question doctrine is inapplicable to nonconstitutional claims? For better or worse, although the political question doctrine is most likely to be applied in foreign affairs cases that involve constitutional challenges, it is sometimes applied in cases involving statutory, international, or other non-constitutional claims, especially if the cases concern war or military affairs. *See, e.g.*, United States v. Martinez, 904 F.2d 601 (11th Cir. 1990) (challenge to government's placement of an item on list subject to the Arms Export Control Act); Smith v. Reagan, 844 F.2d 195 (4th Cir. 1988) (suit to have U.S. prisoners of the Vietnam War declared to be in captivity and subject to the terms of the Hostage Act); Schneider v. Kissinger, 310 F. Supp. 2d 251 (D.D.C. 2004) (Alien Tort Statute and other claims against U.S. officials concerning their alleged involvement in an attempted coup in Chile in 1970); Iwanowa v. Ford Motor Co., 67 F. Supp. 2d 424 (D.N.J. 1999) (Alien Tort Statute and other claims against private companies for use of forced labor during World War II). Nevertheless, consistent with *Japan Whaling*, courts often decline to apply the political question doctrine in nonconstitutional cases. They do, however, frequently give deference to the views of the Executive Branch concerning the meaning of foreign affairs statutes and the content of international law, as discussed below in Section G. (Indeed, the Court in *Japan Whaling* gave deference to the Executive's interpretation of the sanctions statutes at issue there.)

14. For a recent decision considering the scope of the political question doctrine in the area of foreign relations, see Alperin v. Vatican Bank, 405 F.3d

727 (9th Cir. 2005). That case involved a class action suit brought by Holocaust survivors against the Vatican Bank for allegedly obtaining stolen property from a puppet regime established by the Nazis in Yugoslavia during World War II, and for allegedly assisting the regime in its war objectives by profiting from its use of slave labor and by helping members of the regime escape punishment for war crimes. In a 2-1 decision, the court held that, although the political question doctrine barred the plaintiffs' war objectives claims, it did not bar their property claims. Applying the factors from *Baker v. Carr*, the court stated:

> We conclude that the claims for conversion, unjust enrichment, restitution, and an accounting with respect to lost and looted property are not committed to the political branches.... Recovery for lost and looted property, however, stands in stark contrast to the broad allegations tied to the Vatican Bank's alleged assistance to the war objectives of the [puppet regime], including the slave labor claims, which essentially call on us to make a retroactive political judgment as to the conduct of war.... Such judgment calls are, by nature, political questions.

In concluding that the property claims were not barred by the political question doctrine, the court noted, among other things, that they had not been the subject of any treaty or executive agreement, and that, despite protests from the Vatican, the State Department had not expressed a view about the case. The court made clear, however, that it was not holding that the plaintiffs' property claims would survive dismissal on other grounds:

> Given the passage of time, the generality of the allegations, the question of the applicability of the Foreign Sovereign Immunities Act. Intricacies of the alleged claims, the class certification issues, whether the plaintiffs have a cognizable legal claim, and a myriad of other procedural and jurisdictional hurdles, the Holocaust Survivors may indeed face an uphill battle in pursuing their claims.

In arguing that the entire case should have been dismissed under the political question doctrine, the dissenting judge argued that the political question doctrine encompasses "*all* matters that fall by their constitutional DNA into this sphere [of controversies between nations], whether the political branches have done anything about them or not." He also complained that

> What the majority has unintentionally accomplished in embracing this case is nothing less than the creation without legislation of a World Court, an international tribunal with breathtaking and limitless jurisdiction to entertain the World's failures, no matter where they happen, when they happen, to whom they happen, the identity of the wrong-doer, and the sovereignty of one of the parties. The consequences of this holding are overwhelming.

Should U.S. courts be open to hearing politically sensitive international claims such as the ones at issue in this case? Is the political question doctrine the proper vehicle for ensuring that such claims do not unduly interfere with the conduct of U.S. foreign relations? What inferences, if any, should courts draw from the failure of the Executive Branch to express a view about a case such as this one?

15. Other doctrines may also render certain foreign affairs issues nonjusticiable. Consider, for example, Tenet v. Doe, 125 S. Ct. 1230 (2005). There, the Supreme Court held that purported Cold War spies could not sue the U.S. government to enforce obligations under a secret espionage agreement. Reaffirming a Civil War-era decision, Totten v. United States, 92 U.S. 105 (1876), the Court explained:

The state secrets privilege and the more frequent use of *in camera* judicial proceedings simply cannot provide the absolute protection we found necessary in enunciating the *Totten* rule. The possibility that a suit may proceed and an espionage relationship may be revealed, if the state secrets privilege is found not to apply, is unacceptable.... Forcing the Government to litigate these claims would also make it vulnerable to "graymail," *i.e.*, individual lawsuits brought to induce the CIA to settle a case (or prevent its filing) out of fear that any effort to litigate the action would reveal classified information that may undermine ongoing covert operations. And requiring the Government to invoke the [state secrets] privilege on a case-by-case basis risks the perception that it is either confirming or denying relationships with individual plaintiffs.

Are these arguments persuasive?

16. For additional discussion of the role of the political question doctrine in foreign affairs cases, see Thomas M. Franck, Political Questions/Judicial Answers (1992); Michael J. Glennon, *Foreign Affairs and the Political Question Doctrine*, 83 Am. J. Int'l L. 814 (1989); Jack L. Goldsmith, *The New Formalism in United States Foreign Relations Law*, 70 U. Colo. L. Rev. 1395 (1999); Louis Henkin, *Is There a "Political Question" Doctrine?*, 85 Yale L.J. 597 (1976); Michael E. Tigar, *Judicial Review, the "Political Question Doctrine," and Foreign Relations*, 17 UCLA L. Rev. 1135 (1970). For more general discussions of the political question doctrine, see Rachel E. Barkow, *More Supreme Than Court? The Fall of the Political Question Doctrine and the Rise of Judicial Supremacy*, 102 Colum. L. Rev. 237 (2002); J. Peter Mulhern, *In Defense of the Political Question Doctrine*, 137 U. Pa. L. Rev. 97 (1988); Martin H. Redish, *Judicial Review and the "Political Question,"* 79 Nw. U. L. Rev. 1031 (1985); Fritz W. Scharpf, *Judicial Review and the Political Question: A Functional Analysis*, 75 Yale L.J. 517 (1966). *See also* Alexander M. Bickel, *The Supreme Court, 1960 Term—Foreword: The Passive Virtues*, 75 Harv. L. Rev. 40 (1961).

D. FOREIGN SOVEREIGN IMMUNITY

1. Background and Overview of the Foreign Sovereign Immunities Act

Verlinden B.V. v. Central Bank of Nigeria

461 U.S. 480 (1983)

[In 1975, Verlinden, B.V., a Dutch corporation, entered into a contract with the Federal Republic of Nigeria to provide it with 240,000 metric tons of cement. The parties agreed that the contract would be governed by Dutch law and that disputes would be resolved by arbitration under the auspices of the International Chamber of Commerce in Paris. Under the contract, the Nigerian government was obligated to establish an irrevocable, confirmed letter of credit through a bank in Amsterdam. Instead, the government's instrumentality, the Central Bank of Nigeria, established an unconfirmed letter of credit through a bank in New York.

Meanwhile, the ports of Nigeria became clogged with hundreds of ships carrying cement, sent by numerous other cement suppliers with whom Nigeria also had entered into contracts. Central Bank then unilaterally directed its correspondent banks, including the New York bank, to adopt a series of amendments to all letters of credit issued in connection with the cement contracts. Central Bank also directly notified the suppliers that payment would be made only for those shipments approved by Central Bank two months before their arrival in Nigerian waters.

Verlinden subsequently sued Central Bank in the U.S. District Court for the Southern District of New York, alleging that Central Bank's actions constituted an anticipatory breach of the letter of credit. Verlinden alleged jurisdiction under the Foreign Sovereign Immunities Act (FSIA). The bank moved to dismiss for, among other reasons, lack of subject-matter and personal jurisdiction. The district court dismissed the complaint, finding no applicable exception to immunity. The court of appeals affirmed, holding that the FSIA exceeded the scope of federal court jurisdiction allowed under Article III of the Constitution.]

CHIEF JUSTICE BURGER delivered the opinion of the Court....

For more than a century and a half, the United States generally granted foreign sovereigns complete immunity from suit in the courts of this country. In The Schooner Exchange v. M'Faddon, 7 Cranch 116 (1812), Chief Justice Marshall concluded that, while the jurisdiction of a nation within its own territory "is susceptible of no limitation not imposed by itself," the United States had impliedly waived jurisdiction over certain activities of foreign sovereigns. Although the narrow holding of *The Schooner Exchange* was only that the courts of the United States lack jurisdiction over an armed ship of a foreign state found in our port, that opinion came to be regarded as extending virtually absolute immunity to foreign sovereigns.

As *The Schooner Exchange* made clear, however, foreign sovereign immunity is a matter of grace and comity on the part of the United States, and not a restriction imposed by the Constitution. Accordingly, this Court consistently has deferred to the decisions of the political branches — in particular, those of the Executive Branch — on whether to take jurisdiction over actions against foreign sovereigns and their instrumentalities. *See, e.g.*, Ex parte Peru, 318 U.S. 578, 586-590 (1943); Mexico v. Hoffman, 324 U.S. 30, 33-36 (1945).

Until 1952, the State Department ordinarily requested immunity in all actions against friendly foreign sovereigns. But in the so-called Tate Letter, the State Department announced its adoption of the "restrictive" theory of foreign sovereign immunity. Under this theory, immunity is confined to suits involving the foreign sovereign's public acts, and does not extend to cases arising out of a foreign state's strictly commercial acts.

The restrictive theory was not initially enacted into law, however, and its application proved troublesome. As in the past, initial responsibility for deciding questions of sovereign immunity fell primarily upon the Executive acting through the State Department, and the courts abided by "suggestions of immunity" from the State Department. As a consequence, foreign nations often placed diplomatic pressure on the State Department in seeking immunity. On occasion, political considerations led to suggestions of immunity in cases where immunity would not have been available under the restrictive theory.

An additional complication was posed by the fact that foreign nations did not always make requests to the State Department. In such cases, the responsibility fell to the courts to determine whether sovereign immunity existed, generally by reference to prior State Department decisions. Thus, sovereign immunity determinations were made in two different branches, subject to a variety of factors, sometimes including diplomatic considerations. Not surprisingly, the governing standards were neither clear nor uniformly applied.

In 1976, Congress passed the Foreign Sovereign Immunities Act in order to free the Government from the case-by-case diplomatic pressures, to clarify the governing standards, and to "[assure] litigants that...decisions are made on purely legal grounds and under procedures that insure due process," H.R. Rep. No. 94-1487, p. 7 (1976). To accomplish these objectives, the Act contains a comprehensive set of legal standards governing claims of immunity in every civil action against a foreign state or its political subdivisions, agencies, or instrumentalities.

For the most part, the Act codifies, as a matter of federal law, the restrictive theory of sovereign immunity. A foreign state is normally immune from the jurisdiction of federal and state courts, 28 U.S.C. §1604, subject to a set of exceptions specified in §§1605 and 1607. Those exceptions include actions in which the foreign state has explicitly or impliedly waived its immunity, §1605(a)(1), and actions based upon commercial activities of the foreign sovereign carried on in the United States or causing a direct effect in the United States, §1605(a)(2).[11] When one of these or the other specified exceptions applies, "the foreign state shall be liable in the same manner and to the same extent as a private individual under like circumstances," §1606.[12]

The Act expressly provides that its standards control in "the courts of the United States and of the States," §1604, and thus clearly contemplates that such suits may be brought in either federal or state courts. However, "[in] view of the potential sensitivity of actions against foreign states and the importance of developing a uniform body of law in this area," H.R. Rep. No. 94-1487, *supra*, at 32, the Act guarantees foreign states the right to remove any civil action from a state court to a federal court, §1441(d). The Act also provides that any claim permitted under the Act may be brought from the outset in federal court, §1330(a).[13] If one of the specified exceptions to sovereign immunity applies, a federal district court may exercise subject-matter jurisdiction under §1330(a); but if the claim does not fall within one of the exceptions, federal courts lack subject-matter jurisdiction.[14] In such a case, the foreign state is also ensured immunity from the jurisdiction of state courts by §1604....

[T]he core question presented by this case [is] whether Congress exceeded the scope of Art. III of the Constitution by granting federal courts subject-matter jurisdiction over certain civil actions by foreign plaintiffs against foreign sovereigns where the rule of decision may be provided by state law.

This Court's cases firmly establish that Congress may not expand the jurisdiction of the federal courts beyond the bounds established by the Constitution. Within Art. III of the Constitution, we find two sources authorizing the grant of jurisdiction in the Foreign Sovereign Immunities Act: the Diversity Clause and the

11. The Act also contains exceptions for certain actions "in which rights in property taken in violation of international law are in issue," §1605(a)(3); actions involving rights in real estate and in inherited and gift property located in the United States, §1605(a)(4); actions for certain noncommercial torts within the United States, §1605(a)(5); certain actions involving maritime liens, §1605(b); and certain counterclaims, §1607.

12. Section 1606 somewhat modifies this standard of liability with respect to punitive damages and wrongful-death actions.

13. "[To] encourage the bringing of actions against foreign states in Federal courts," H.R. Rep. No. 94-1487, p. 13 (1976), the Act specifies that federal district courts shall have original jurisdiction "without regard to amount in controversy." §1330(a).

14. In such a situation, the federal court will also lack personal jurisdiction.

"Arising Under" Clause.[17] The Diversity Clause, which provides that the judicial power extends to controversies between "a State, or the Citizens thereof, and foreign States," covers actions by citizens of States. Yet diversity jurisdiction is not sufficiently broad to support a grant of jurisdiction over actions by foreign plaintiffs, since a foreign plaintiff is not "a State, or [a] [Citizen] thereof." *See* Mossman v. Higginson, 4 Dall. 12 (1800). We conclude, however, that the "Arising Under" Clause of Art. III provides an appropriate basis for the statutory grant of subject-matter jurisdiction to actions by foreign plaintiffs under the Act.

The controlling decision on the scope of Art. III "arising under" jurisdiction is Chief Justice Marshall's opinion for the Court in Osborn v. Bank of United States, 9 Wheat. 738 (1824). In *Osborn*, the Court upheld the constitutionality of a statute that granted the Bank of the United States the right to sue in federal court on causes of action based upon state law. There, the Court concluded that the "judicial department may receive . . . the power of construing every . . . law" that "the Legislature may constitutionally make." The rule was laid down that

> it [is] a sufficient foundation for jurisdiction, that the title or right set up by the party, may be defeated by one construction of the constitution or [laws] of the United States, and sustained by the opposite construction.

Osborn thus reflects a broad conception of "arising under" jurisdiction, according to which Congress may confer on the federal courts jurisdiction over any case or controversy that might call for the application of federal law. The breadth of that conclusion has been questioned. It has been observed that, taken at its broadest, *Osborn* might be read as permitting "assertion of original federal jurisdiction on the remote possibility of presentation of a federal question." Textile Workers v. Lincoln Mills, 353 U.S. 448, 482 (1957) (Frankfurter, J., dissenting). We need not now resolve that issue or decide the precise boundaries of Art. III jurisdiction, however, since the present case does not involve a mere speculative possibility that a federal question may arise at some point in the proceeding. Rather, a suit against a foreign state under this Act necessarily raises questions of substantive federal law at the very outset, and hence clearly "arises under" federal law, as that term is used in Art. III.

By reason of its authority over foreign commerce and foreign relations, Congress has the undisputed power to decide, as a matter of federal law, whether and under what circumstances foreign nations should be amenable to suit in the United States. Actions against foreign sovereigns in our courts raise sensitive issues concerning the foreign relations of the United States, and the primacy of federal concerns is evident. *See, e.g.,* Banco Nacional de Cuba v. Sabbatino, 376 U.S. 398, 423-425 (1964); Zschernig v. Miller, 389 U.S. 429, 440-441 (1968).

To promote these federal interests, Congress exercised its Art. I powers[19] by enacting a statute comprehensively regulating the amenability of foreign nations to suit in the United States. The statute must be applied by the district courts in every action against a foreign sovereign, since subject-matter jurisdiction in any such

---

17. In view of our conclusion that proper actions by foreign plaintiffs under the Foreign Sovereign Immunities Act are within Art. III "arising under" jurisdiction, we need not consider petitioner's alternative argument that the Act is constitutional as an aspect of so-called "protective jurisdiction." [The concept of protective jurisdiction is discussed briefly in Chapter 5, in connection with the federal common law of foreign relations doctrine — EDS.]

19. In enacting the legislation, Congress relied specifically on its powers to prescribe the jurisdiction of federal courts, Art. I, §8, cl. 9; to define offenses against the "Law of Nations," Art. I, §8, cl. 10; to regulate commerce with foreign nations, Art. I, §8, cl. 3; and to make all laws necessary and proper to execute the Government's powers, Art. I, §8, cl. 18.

action depends on the existence of one of the specified exceptions to foreign sovereign immunity, 28 U.S.C. §1330(a). At the threshold of every action in a district court against a foreign state, therefore, the court must satisfy itself that one of the exceptions applies — and in doing so it must apply the detailed federal law standards set forth in the Act. Accordingly, an action against a foreign sovereign arises under federal law, for purposes of Art. III jurisdiction.

In reaching a contrary conclusion, the Court of Appeals relied heavily upon decisions construing 28 U.S.C. §1331, the statute which grants district courts general federal-question jurisdiction over any case that "arises under" the laws of the United States. The court placed particular emphasis on the so-called "well-pleaded complaint" rule, which provides, for purposes of *statutory* "arising under" jurisdiction, that the federal question must appear on the face of a well-pleaded complaint and may not enter in anticipation of a defense. In the view of the Court of Appeals, the question of foreign sovereign immunity in this case arose solely as a defense, and not on the face of Verlinden's well-pleaded complaint.

Although the language of §1331 parallels that of the "Arising Under" Clause of Art. III, this Court never has held that statutory "arising under" jurisdiction is identical to Art. III "arising under" jurisdiction.... Art. III "arising under" jurisdiction is broader than federal-question jurisdiction under §1331, and the Court of Appeals' heavy reliance on decisions construing that statute was misplaced.

In rejecting "arising under" jurisdiction, the Court of Appeals also noted that 28 U.S.C. §1330 is a jurisdictional provision. Because of this, the court felt its conclusion compelled by prior cases in which this Court has rejected congressional attempts to confer jurisdiction on federal courts simply by enacting jurisdictional statutes....

From these cases, the Court of Appeals apparently concluded that a jurisdictional statute can never constitute the federal law under which the action arises, for Art. III purposes. Yet the statutes at issue in these prior cases sought to do nothing more than grant jurisdiction over a particular class of cases....

In contrast, in enacting the Foreign Sovereign Immunities Act, Congress expressly exercised its power to regulate foreign commerce, along with other specified Art. I powers. As the House Report clearly indicates, the primary purpose of the Act was to "[set] forth comprehensive rules governing sovereign immunity," H.R. Rep. No. 94-1487, p. 12 (1976); the jurisdictional provisions of the Act are simply one part of this comprehensive scheme. The Act thus does not merely concern access to the federal courts. Rather, it governs the types of actions for which foreign sovereigns may be held liable in a court in the United States, federal or state. The Act codifies the standards governing foreign sovereign immunity as an aspect of substantive federal law; and applying those standards will generally require interpretation of numerous points of federal law. Finally, if a court determines that none of the exceptions to sovereign immunity applies, the plaintiff will be barred from raising his claim in any court in the United States — manifestly, "the title or right set up by the party, may be defeated by one construction of the...laws of the United States, and sustained by the opposite construction." Osborn v. Bank of United States, 9 Wheat., at 822. That the inquiry into foreign sovereign immunity is labeled under the Act as a matter of jurisdiction does not affect the constitutionality of Congress' action in granting federal courts jurisdiction over cases calling for application of this comprehensive regulatory statute.

Congress, pursuant to its unquestioned Art. I powers, has enacted a broad statutory framework governing assertions of foreign sovereign immunity. In so doing, Congress deliberately sought to channel cases against foreign sovereigns away from the state courts and into federal courts, thereby reducing the potential for a multiplicity of conflicting results among the courts of the 50 States. The resulting jurisdictional grant is within the bounds of Art. III, since every action against a foreign sovereign necessarily involves application of a body of substantive federal law, and accordingly "arises under" federal law, within the meaning of Art. III.

Republic of Austria v. Altmann

541 U.S. 677 (2004)

[This case involved a suit by a U.S. citizen against Austria and an Austrian government-owned art gallery, pursuant to Section 1605(a)(3) of the FSIA, which allows claims for the taking of property in violation of international law, when the property is owned or operated by an agency or instrumentality of the foreign state and the agency or instrumentality is engaged in a commercial activity in the United States. The plaintiff alleged that the Nazis had stolen six paintings from her uncle in the late 1930s and had subsequently sold three of them to the gallery. She also alleged that the gallery had unlawfully retained possession of the paintings by falsely stating in 1948 that her uncle's wife had donated the paintings to the gallery. The U.S. Court of Appeals for the Ninth Circuit held that the FSIA applied to this suit because Austria could not reasonably have expected to receive absolute immunity for its alleged conduct. The court noted, among other things, that the State Department had issued a letter in 1949 stating that the policy of the Executive Branch was to "relieve American courts from any restraint upon the exercise of their jurisdiction to pass upon the validity of the acts of Nazi officials."]

JUSTICE STEVENS delivered the opinion of the Court....
    [The Court begins by summarizing the pre-FSIA history of foreign sovereign immunity in the United States, including the *Schooner Exchange* decision, the State Department's official embrace of the restrictive theory of immunity in the Tate Letter in 1952, and the subsequent politicization of the process for making immunity determinations.]
    In 1976 Congress sought to remedy these problems [with the Tate Letter process] by enacting the FSIA, a comprehensive statute containing a "set of legal standards governing claims of immunity in every civil action against a foreign state or its political subdivisions, agencies, or instrumentalities." The Act "codifies, as a matter of federal law, the restrictive theory of sovereign immunity," and transfers primary responsibility for immunity determinations from the Executive to the Judicial Branch. The preamble states that "henceforth" both federal and state courts should decide claims of sovereign immunity in conformity with the Act's principles. 28 U.S.C. §1602....
    In [Landgraf v. USI Film Products, Inc., 511 U.S. 244 (1994)], we considered whether §102 of the Civil Rights Act of 1991, which permits a party to seek compensatory and punitive damages for certain types of intentional employment discrimination, and to demand a jury trial if such damages are sought, applied to an

employment discrimination case that was pending on appeal when the statute was enacted. The issue forced us to confront the "'apparent tension'" between our rule that "'a court is to apply the law in effect at the time it renders its decision,'" 511 U.S., at 264, and the seemingly contrary "axiom that '[r]etroactivity is not favored in the law'" and thus that "'congressional enactments . . . will not be construed to have retroactive effect unless their language requires this result,'" 511 U.S., at 264.

Acknowledging that, in most cases, the antiretroactivity presumption is just that—a presumption, rather than a constitutional command—we examined the rationales that support it. We noted, for example, that "[t]he Legislature's . . . responsivity to political pressures poses a risk that it may be tempted to use retroactive legislation as a means of retribution against unpopular groups or individuals," *Landgraf,* 511 U.S., at 266, and that retroactive statutes may upset settled expectations by "'tak[ing] away or impair[ing] vested rights acquired under existing laws, or creat[ing] a new obligation, impos[ing] a new duty, or attach[ing] a new disability, in respect to transactions or considerations already past,'" *id.,* at 269. We further observed that these antiretroactivity concerns are most pressing in cases involving "new provisions affecting contractual or property rights, matters in which predictability and stability are of prime importance." 511 U.S., at 271.

In contrast, we sanctioned the application to all pending and future cases of "intervening" statutes that merely "confe[r] or ous[t] jurisdiction." *Id.,* at 274. Such application, we stated, "usually takes away no substantive right but simply changes the tribunal that is to hear the case." *Ibid.* (internal quotation marks omitted). Similarly, the "diminished reliance interests in matters of procedure" permit courts to apply changes in procedural rules "in suits arising before [the rules'] enactment without raising concerns about retroactivity." *Id.,* at 275.

Balancing these competing concerns, we described the presumption against retroactive application in the following terms:

> When a case implicates a federal statute enacted after the events in suit, the court's first task is to determine whether Congress has expressly prescribed the statute's proper reach. If Congress has done so, of course, there is no need to resort to judicial default rules. When, however, the statute contains no such express command the court must determine whether the new statute would have retroactive effect, *i.e.,* whether it would impair rights a party possessed when he acted, increase a party's liability for past conduct, or impose new duties with respect to transactions already completed. If the statute would operate retroactively, our traditional presumption teaches that it does not govern absent clear congressional intent favoring such a result. *Id.,* at 280.

Though seemingly comprehensive, this inquiry does not provide a clear answer in this case. Although the FSIA's preamble suggests that it applies to preenactment conduct, that statement by itself falls short of an "expres[s] prescri[ption of] the statute's proper reach." Under *Landgraf,* therefore, it is appropriate to ask whether the Act affects substantive rights (and thus would be impermissibly retroactive if applied to preenactment conduct) or addresses only matters of procedure (and thus may be applied to all pending cases regardless of when the underlying conduct occurred). But the FSIA defies such categorization. To begin with, none of the three examples of retroactivity mentioned in the above quotation fits the FSIA's clarification of the law of sovereign immunity. Prior to 1976 foreign states had a justifiable expectation that, as a matter of comity, United States courts would grant them immunity for their public acts (provided the State Department did not recommend otherwise), but they had no "right" to such immunity. Moreover, the FSIA merely opens United States courts to plaintiffs with pre-existing claims against foreign states; the Act neither "increase[s those states'] liability for past conduct" nor "impose[s] new duties with respect to transactions already completed." 511 U.S., at 280. Thus, the Act does not at first appear to "operate retroactively" within the meaning of the *Landgraf* default rule.

That preliminary conclusion, however, creates some tension with our observation in *Verlinden* that the FSIA is not simply a jurisdictional statute "concern[ing] access to the federal courts" but a codification of "the standards governing foreign sovereign immunity as an aspect of *substantive* federal law." 461 U.S., at 496-497 (emphasis added). Moreover, we noted in *Verlinden* that in any suit against a foreign sovereign, "the plaintiff will be barred from raising his claim in *any* court in the United States" unless one of the FSIA's exceptions applies, *id.*, at 497 (emphasis added), and we have stated elsewhere that statutes that "*creat[e]* jurisdiction" where none otherwise exists "spea[k] not just to the power of a particular court but to the substantive rights of the parties as well," Hughes Aircraft Co. v. United States ex rel. Schumer, 520 U.S. 939, 951 (1997) (emphasis in original). Such statutes, we continued, "even though phrased in 'jurisdictional' terms, [are] as much subject to our presumption against retroactivity as any other[s]." *Ibid.*

Thus, *Landgraf*'s default rule does not definitively resolve this case. In our view, however, *Landgraf*'s antiretroactivity presumption, while not strictly confined to cases involving private rights, is most helpful in that context. The aim of the presumption is to avoid unnecessary *post hoc* changes to legal rules on which parties relied in shaping their primary conduct. But the principal purpose of foreign sovereign immunity has never been to permit foreign states and their instrumentalities to shape their conduct in reliance on the promise of future immunity from suit in United States courts. Rather, such immunity reflects current political realities and relationships, and aims to give foreign states and their instrumentalities some *present* "protection from the inconvenience of suit as a gesture of comity." Dole Food Co. v. Patrickson, 538 U.S. 468, 479 (2003). Throughout history, courts have resolved questions of foreign sovereign immunity by deferring to the "decisions of the political branches . . . on whether to take jurisdiction." *Verlinden,* 461 U.S., at 486. In this *sui generis* context, we think it more appropriate, absent contraindications, to defer to the most recent such decision — namely, the FSIA — than to presume that decision *inapplicable* merely because it postdates the conduct in question.[16]

This leaves only the question whether anything in the FSIA or the circumstances surrounding its enactment suggests that we should not apply it to petitioners' 1948 actions. Not only do we answer this question in the negative, but we find clear evidence that Congress intended the Act to apply to preenactment conduct.

To begin with, the preamble of the FSIA expresses Congress' understanding that the Act would apply to all postenactment claims of sovereign immunity. That section provides:

> *Claims* of foreign states to immunity should *henceforth* be decided by courts of the United States and of the States in conformity with the principles set forth in this chapter. 28 U.S.C. §1602 (emphasis added).

---

16. Between 1952 and 1976 courts and the State Department similarly presumed that the Tate Letter was applicable even in disputes concerning conduct that predated the letter. *See, e.g.,* National City Bank of N.Y. v. Republic of China, 348 U.S. 356, 364, 99 L. Ed. 389, 75 S. Ct. 423 (1955) (assuming, in dicta, that the Tate Letter would govern the sovereign immunity analysis in a dispute concerning treasury notes purchased in 1920 and 1947-1948).

Though perhaps not sufficient to satisfy *Landgraf*'s "express command" requirement, 511 U.S., at 280, this language is unambiguous: Immunity "claims"—not actions protected by immunity, but assertions of immunity to suits arising from those actions—are the relevant conduct regulated by the Act; those claims are "henceforth" to be decided by the courts....

The FSIA's overall structure strongly supports this conclusion. Many of the Act's provisions unquestionably apply to cases arising out of conduct that occurred before 1976. In Dole Food Co. v. Patrickson, 538 U.S. 468 (2003), for example, we held that whether an entity qualifies as an "instrumentality" of a "foreign state" for purposes of the FSIA's grant of immunity depends on the relationship between the entity and the state at the time suit is brought rather than when the conduct occurred. In addition, *Verlinden*, which upheld against constitutional challenge 28 U.S.C. §1330's grant of subject-matter jurisdiction, involved a dispute over a contract that predated the Act. And there has never been any doubt that the Act's procedural provisions relating to venue, removal, execution, and attachment apply to all pending cases. Thus, the FSIA's preamble indicates that it applies "henceforth," and its body includes numerous provisions that unquestionably apply to claims based on pre-1976 conduct. In this context, it would be anomalous to presume that an isolated provision (such as the expropriation exception on which respondent relies) is of purely prospective application absent any statutory language to that effect.

Finally, applying the FSIA to all pending cases regardless of when the underlying conduct occurred is most consistent with two of the Act's principal purposes: clarifying the rules that judges should apply in resolving sovereign immunity claims and eliminating political participation in the resolution of such claims. We have recognized that, to accomplish these purposes, Congress established a comprehensive framework for resolving any claim of sovereign immunity....

We do not endorse the reasoning of the Court of Appeals. Indeed, we think it engaged in precisely the kind of detailed historical inquiry that the FSIA's clear guidelines were intended to obviate. Nevertheless, we affirm the panel's judgment because the Act, freed from *Landgraf*'s antiretroactivity presumption, clearly applies to conduct, like petitioners' alleged wrongdoing, that occurred prior to 1976 and, for that matter, prior to 1952 when the State Department adopted the restrictive theory of sovereign immunity.[19]

We conclude by emphasizing the narrowness of this holding. To begin with, although the District Court and Court of Appeals determined that §1605(a)(3) covers this case, we declined to review that determination. Nor do we have occasion to comment on the application of the so-called "act of state" doctrine to petitioners' alleged wrongdoing....*

Finally, while we reject the United States' recommendation to bar application of the FSIA to claims based on pre-enactment conduct, nothing in our holding prevents the State Department from filing statements of interest suggesting that courts decline to exercise jurisdiction in particular cases implicating foreign sovereign immunity. The issue now before us, to which the Brief for United States as *Amicus Curiae* is addressed, concerns interpretation of the FSIA's reach—a "pure

---

19. Petitioners suggest that the latter date is important because it marked the first shift in foreign states' expectations concerning the scope of their immunity. Whether or not the date would be significant to a *Landgraf*-type analysis of foreign states' settled expectations at various times prior to the FSIA's enactment, it is of no relevance in this case given our rationale for finding the Act applicable to preenactment conduct.

* [The act of state doctrine is discussed below in Section E.—Eds.]

question of statutory construction . . . well within the province of the Judiciary." INS v. Cardoza-Fonseca, 480 U.S. 421, 446, 448 (1987). While the United States' views on such an issue are of considerable interest to the Court, they merit no special deference. In contrast, should the State Department choose to express its opinion on the implications of exercising jurisdiction over *particular* petitioners in connection with *their* alleged conduct, that opinion might well be entitled to deference as the considered judgment of the Executive on a particular question of foreign policy.[23] We express no opinion on the question whether such deference should be granted in cases covered by the FSIA. . . .

[Justice Breyer issued a concurrence, joined by Justice Souter. Among other things, he disagreed with the dissent's claim that reliance interests might provide a reason for declining to apply the FSIA retroactively to the conduct at issue in this case, stating:

> [C]ontrary to the dissent's contention, neither "reliance" nor "expectation" can justify nonretroactivity here. Does the dissent mean by "reliance" and "expectation" something real, *i.e.* an expropriating nation's actual reliance at the time of taking that other nations will continue to protect it from future lawsuits by continuing to apply the same sovereign immunity doctrine? Such actual reliance could not possibly exist in fact. What taking in violation of international norms is likely to have been influenced, not by politics or revolution, but by knowledge of, or speculation about, the likely future shape of America's law of foreign sovereign immunity? To suggest any such possibility, in respect to the expropriations carried out by the Nazi or Communist regimes, or any other such as I am aware, would approach the realm of fantasy. While the matter is less clear in respect to less dramatic, more individualized, takings, I still find any actual reliance difficult to imagine.

Justice Breyer also noted that "statutes of limitation, personal jurisdiction and venue requirements, and the doctrine of *forum non conveniens* will limit the number of suits brought in American courts." In addition, he stated (more strongly than the majority), that "the United States may enter a statement of interest counseling dismissal."]

[Justice Kennedy issued a dissent, joined by Chief Justice Rehnquist and Justice Thomas. He argued that, even though the FSIA is a jurisdictional statute, it is subject to the presumption against retroactivity because it creates jurisdiction where none existed before. He also argued that there was no clear statement in the FSIA requiring retroactive effect, noting, for example, that the statement in the FSIA that it shall apply "henceforth" "says no more than that the principles immediately apply from the point of the Act's effective date on." As a result, he argued that "our cases require that we consider the character of the statute, and of the rights and liabilities it creates, to determine if its application will impose retroactive

---

23. Mislabeling this observation a "constitutional conclusion," the dissent suggests that permitting the Executive to comment on a party's assertion of sovereign immunity will result in "[u]ncertain prospective application of our foreign sovereign immunity law." We do not hold, however, that executive intervention could or would trump considered application of the FSIA's more neutral principles; we merely note that the Executive's views on questions within its area of expertise merit greater deference than its opinions regarding the scope of a congressional enactment. Furthermore, we fail to understand how our holding, which requires that courts apply the FSIA's sovereign immunity rules in *all* cases, somehow injects greater uncertainty into sovereign immunity law than the dissent's approach, which would require, for cases concerning pre-1976 conduct, case-by-case analysis of the status of that law at the time of the offending conduct — including analysis of the existence or nonexistence of any State Department statements on the subject.

effect on the parties. If it does, we must refuse to apply it in that manner." In this respect, Justice Kennedy noted that

> in 1948 foreign sovereigns, and all other litigants, understood foreign sovereign immunity law to support three valid expectations. (1) Nations could expect that a baseline rule of sovereign immunity would apply. (2) They could expect that if the Executive made a statement on the issue of sovereign immunity that would be controlling. And (3), they could expect that they would be able to petition the Executive for intervention on their behalf.

This understanding, he further noted, continued after the issuance of the Tate Letter:

> The Tate Letter did announce the policy of restrictive foreign sovereign immunity, and this was an important doctrinal development. The policy, however, was within the second expectation that the Executive could shape the framework for foreign sovereign immunity. Under the second category, a foreign sovereign would have expected its immunity to be controlled by such a statement.

Thus, Justice Kennedy argued, "to measure a foreign sovereign's expectation of liability for conduct committed in 1948, the Court should apply the three discussed, interlocking principles of law, which the parties then expected." He also criticized the majority more generally for "open[ing] foreign nations worldwide to vast and potential liability for expropriation claims in regards to conduct that occurred generations ago, including claims that have been the subject of international negotiation and agreement." Finally, Justice Kennedy argued that the majority's (and Justice Breyer's) invitation to the Executive to intervene on a case-by-case basis in FSIA cases implicated difficult questions of Executive power and judicial independence, and threatened to undermine the FSIA's central purpose of transferring immunity decisions away from the Executive so that they could be decided without political influence by the courts.]

Notes and Questions

1. As discussed in *Verlinden*, the adoption of foreign sovereign immunity by U.S. courts is often traced to the Supreme Court's decision in The Schooner Exchange v. McFaddon, 11 U.S. (7 Cranch) 116 (1812). In *Schooner Exchange*, the Court recognized the immunity of foreign sovereign warships from the jurisdiction of U.S. courts, referring to "a principle of public law" — presumably customary international law — whereby" national ships of war, entering the port of a friendly power open for their reception, are to be considered as exempted by the consent of that power from its jurisdiction." Over time, courts extended sovereign immunity to other foreign government ships, then to other foreign government property, and then to any suit against a foreign nation. During the nineteenth century, this immunity was considered by the United States and other nations to be essentially absolute — if the defendant qualified as a foreign sovereign, then it would have immunity for all of its acts, even those that were purely commercial in nature. By the early twentieth century, however, a number of nations began moving away from an absolute approach to immunity towards a restrictive approach. Under the restrictive approach, foreign sovereigns are entitled to immunity for public or sovereign acts, but not for private or commercial acts. What do you think accounts for this shift away from the absolute approach? *See* Gamal Moursi Badr,

State Immunity: An Analytical and Prognostic View (1984); Joseph M. Sweeney, The International Law of Sovereign Immunity (State Dept. 1963).

2. In 1952, in a letter to the Justice Department, the State Department formally announced that it would in all cases follow the restrictive theory of immunity. *See* Letter from Jack B. Tate, Acting Legal Adviser, U.S. Dept. or State, to Acting U.S. Attorney General Philip B. Perlman (May 19, 1952), reprinted in 26 Dept. State Bull. 984, 985 (1952). The letter cites a number of reasons for this policy, including the worldwide trend toward adoption of the restrictive theory and the "widespread and increasing practice on the part of governments of engaging in commercial activities." After the issuance of the Tate Letter, foreign states sued in U.S. courts could seek relief in either of two ways. They could request immunity directly from the State Department, usually by submitting a diplomatic note. If the Department agreed that the foreign state should receive immunity, the Department would send a "Suggestion of Immunity" to the Attorney General with a request that it be transmitted to the court, and courts generally treated these suggestions as binding. Alternatively, foreign states could request immunity directly from the court, in which case the court would have to decide how to distinguish between sovereign and commercial acts, albeit often by reference to prior State Department determinations. This regime, under which the State Department made some immunity determinations and the courts made others, did not always produce consistent decisions. *Compare* Victory Transport, Inc. v. Comisaria General de Abastecimientos y Transportes, 336 F.2d 354 (2d Cir. 1964) (court concludes, without input from State Department, that ship chartered by Spanish government was engaged in commercial activity and thus not entitled to immunity) *with* Isbrandtsen Tankers v. President of India, 446 F.2d 1198, 1200-01 (2d Cir. 1971) (granting immunity in factually similar suit brought against Indian government because, although the court was inclined to "find that the actions of the Indian government were . . . purely private commercial decisions," the State Department had determined otherwise).

Inconsistency in result was not the only problem with the Tate Letter regime. Other perceived inadequacies included the following:

> From a legal standpoint, if the [State] Department applies the restrictive principle in a given case, it is in the awkward position of a political institution trying to apply a legal standard to litigation already before the courts. Moreover, it does not have the machinery to take evidence, to hear witnesses, to afford appellate review.
>
> From a foreign relations standpoint, the initiative is often left to the foreign state. The foreign state chooses which sovereign immunity determinations it will leave to the courts, and which it will take to the State Department. The foreign state also decides when it will attempt to exert diplomatic influences, thereby making it more difficult for the State Department to apply the Tate letter criteria.
>
> From the standpoint of the private litigant, considerable uncertainty results. A private party who deals with a foreign government entity cannot be certain that his legal dispute with a foreign state will not be decided on the basis of nonlegal considerations through the foreign government's intercession with the Department of State.

H.R. Rep. No. 94-1487, at 8-9 (1976). For criticisms of the Tate Letter regime, see, for example, Monroe Leigh, *Sovereign Immunity — The Case of the "Imias,"* 68 Am. J. Int'l L. 280 (1974); and Andreas F. Lowenfeld, *Litigating a Sovereign Immunity Claim — The Haiti Case,* 49 N.Y.U. L. Rev. 377 (1974).

3. In 1976, after years of discussion and debate, Congress enacted the Foreign Sovereign Immunities Act (FSIA), 28 U.S.C. §§1330, 1602-11, the current text of which is printed in Appendix C of this casebook. The House Report on the bill that became the FSIA states that the bill "would codify the so-called 'restrictive' principle of sovereign immunity, as presently recognized in international law." The structure of the statute is described in *Verlinden*. As the Court explains, issues of personal jurisdiction, subject matter jurisdiction, and immunity from suit are intertwined in the FSIA. If proper service is made on a foreign state defendant, personal jurisdiction exists with respect to any claim for which there is federal subject matter jurisdiction. Federal subject matter jurisdiction exists "as to any claim for relief in personam with respect to which the foreign state is not entitled to immunity." 28 U.S.C. §1330(a). And the FSIA in turn specifies various exceptions to sovereign immunity. Under this structure, a court must determine whether the foreign state defendant is immune from suit in order to determine whether the court has personal and subject matter jurisdiction. If the court finds that the defendant is immune, the court lacks personal and subject matter jurisdiction. Conversely, if the court finds that there is an exception to immunity, and that proper service has been made, the court automatically has personal and subject matter jurisdiction (assuming no violation of due process requirements). *See generally* Working Group of the American Bar Association, *Reforming the Foreign Sovereign Immunities Act*, 40 Colum. J. Transnat'l L. 489, 500-06 (2002) (discussing the FSIA's structure).

   4. What was the potential Article III problem in *Verlinden*? What law applied to the suit? Was there diversity jurisdiction? On what basis does the Supreme Court find federal court jurisdiction? Is the Court's jurisdictional analysis mere bootstrapping? Do you think Congress intended to confer federal court jurisdiction over suits such as this one?

   The Supreme Court has not determined the precise bounds of Article III "arising under" jurisdiction. In one decision from the early 1800s, the Court suggested that this jurisdiction might extend to any case in which there is even a potential federal law question, regardless of whether the federal law question is actually litigated. *See* Osborn v. Bank of the United States, 22 U.S. (9 Wheat.) 738 (1824). As the Court notes in *Verlinden*, the reasoning of *Osborn* has been questioned by some judges and commentators, and it is not clear that the modern Supreme Court would construe Article III as broadly as the *Osborn* reasoning might allow. How was the Court in *Verlinden* able to avoid determining the scope of Article III?

   Whatever the bounds of Article III's arising under jurisdiction, it is well established that Congress's grant of federal statutory jurisdiction cannot by itself serve as the federal law question for purposes of this jurisdiction. *See, e.g.*, Mesa v. California, 489 U.S. 121, 136-37 (1989). Indeed, if this were enough for federal question jurisdiction, there would be no limit on Congress's ability to confer jurisdiction on the federal courts. Do you see why? Did the Supreme Court in *Verlinden* ignore this rule? What are the implications of the Supreme Court's statement in *Verlinden* that immunity under the FSIA concerns "substantive" federal law? Is that description of immunity consistent with the Court's description of it in *Altmann*?

   5. What justifications does the majority give in *Altmann* for concluding that the FSIA applies to conduct predating the FSIA's enactment? To conduct predating the Tate Letter? Does retroactive application of the statute threaten to undermine settled expectations concerning immunity from suit, as the dissent argues? After *Altmann*, what limitations are there on suits against foreign sovereigns for conduct that occurred many years ago? Are these limitations sufficient to prevent FSIA litigation from undermining U.S. foreign relations?

6. What are the implications of the majority's statement in *Altmann* that, "should the State Department choose to express its opinion on the implications of exercising jurisdiction over *particular* petitioners in connection with *their* alleged conduct, that opinion might well be entitled to deference as the considered judgment of the Executive on a particular question of foreign policy"? Why does the majority then immediately state that, "We express no opinion on the question whether such deference should be granted in cases covered by the FSIA"? Should the Executive Branch have the ability to affect the exercise of federal court jurisdiction in the case-specific manner suggested by the majority (and even more strongly suggested by Justice Breyer)? Why did the majority not defer to the Executive Branch's views in *Altmann* itself, in which the Executive (in a brief signed by both the Justice Department and the State Department) argued that the FSIA should not be interpreted to apply to expropriations of property that occurred before the FSIA's enactment because, among other things, such retroactive application of the statute would cause foreign relations problems?

7. In the nineteenth century and early twentieth century, although courts sometimes considered the views of the Executive Branch in making sovereign immunity determinations, they did not feel obligated to accept those views. They deferred to the Executive Branch's decisions as to which governments should be recognized, but they felt free to make their own determinations regarding sovereign immunity. Consider, for example, the *Pesaro* litigation in the 1920s, which involved claims against an Italian government-owned steamship relating to its transportation of commercial cargo. The district court in that litigation solicited the views of the State Department, which argued that government-owned merchant vessels employed in commerce "should not be regarded as entitled to the immunities accorded public vessels of war." *See* The Pesaro, 277 F. 473 (S.D.N.Y. 1921). Although the district court did not treat the State Department's views as binding, it agreed with the State Department and held that the Italian ship was not entitled to immunity. Subsequently, this decision was vacated for reasons unrelated to the court's immunity analysis and reconsidered by a different district court judge. The new judge granted immunity based on his reading of prior sovereign immunity decisions, making no mention of the State Department's views. *See* The Pesaro, 13 F.2d 468 (S.D.N.Y. 1926). The Supreme Court affirmed, holding that merchant ships owned and operated by a foreign government have the same immunity as a government warship. *See* Berizzi Bros. Co. v. Steamship Pesaro, 271 U.S. 562 (1926).

This changed starting in the late 1930s. In Compania Espanola de Navegacion Maritima, S.A. v. The Navemar, 303 U.S. 68, 74 (1938), the Supreme Court suggested for the first time that Executive Branch suggestions of immunity were binding on the courts. Subsequently, in Ex parte Peru, 318 U.S. 578 (1943), and Mexico v. Hoffman, 324 U.S. 30 (1945), the Court made clear that, if the Executive Branch expressed its views regarding whether immunity should be granted, courts were bound to accept those views. Thus, the Court stated in *Hoffman* that "[i]t is therefore not for the courts to deny an immunity which our government has seen fit to allow, or to allow an immunity on new grounds which the government has not seen fit to recognize." 324 U.S. at 35. Under this regime, "if the Executive announced a national policy in regard to immunity generally, or for the particular case, that policy was law for the courts and binding upon them, regardless of what international law might say about it." Louis Henkin, Foreign Affairs and the United States Constitution 56 (2d ed. 1996). Why do you think courts adopted this approach? Is this approach consistent with the separation of powers structure of the Constitution, which assigns legislative power to Congress and adjudicatory power to the federal courts?

One of the purposes of the FSIA, according to its legislative history, was "to transfer the determination of sovereign immunity from the executive branch to the judicial branch, thereby reducing the foreign policy implications of immunity determinations and assuring litigants that these often crucial decisions are made on purely legal grounds and under procedures that insure due process." H.R. Rep. No. 94-1487, at 7. Is the Court's suggestion in *Altmann* of case-specific deference to the Executive Branch inconsistent with that purpose? Does it invite a revival of the pre-FSIA regime of Executive determinations of immunity? In any event, as we will see in Chapter 7, vestiges of the pre-FSIA regime remain in suits against foreign heads of state, which courts generally have found not to be covered by the FSIA.

8. The FSIA applies only to suits against "foreign states." "Foreign state" is defined to include not only the state itself but also "a political subdivision of a foreign state or an agency or instrumentality of a foreign state." *See* 28 U.S.C. §1603. The FSIA provides a definition of agencies or instrumentalities of foreign states, which includes, but is not limited to, corporations that have a majority of their shares owned by a foreign state. In Dole Food Co. v. Patrickson, 538 U.S. 468 (2003), the Supreme Court held that instrumentality status under the FSIA is to be determined based on the facts that exist at the time of the suit rather than at the time of the conduct in question. The Court reasoned, among other things, that foreign sovereign immunity "is not meant to avoid chilling foreign states or their instrumentalities in the conduct of their business but to give foreign states and their instrumentalities some protection from the inconvenience of suit as a gesture of comity between the United States and other sovereigns." What is the relationship between the Court's holding in *Dole* and its holding in *Altmann*?

9. Because of the holding in *Dole,* retroactive application of the FSIA may not always benefit plaintiffs. Consider Abrams v. Societe Nationale des Chemins de fer Francais, 389 F.3d 61 (2d Cir. 2004), which involved a suit by Holocaust victims and their heirs against a French government-owned railroad for allegedly having transported thousands of civilians to Nazi death and slave labor camps during World War II. The plaintiffs in this case argued against retroactive application of the FSIA, because, at the time of the events, the railroad was organized as a separate entity from the French government and thus might not have had immunity. Based on *Altmann,* however, the Second Circuit held that the suit was governed by the FSIA. The court reasoned that, "[w]hile [the French railroad] was predominately owned by civilians during World War II, it is now wholly-owned by the French government and . . . is an 'agent' or 'instrumentality' of France under the FSIA," and that, under *Dole* and *Altmann,* "its prior incarnation as a private entity does not bar the [FSIA's] retroactive application." The court also concluded that there was no applicable exception to immunity in that case.

10. In Argentine Republic v. Amerada Hess Shipping Corp., 488 U.S. 428, 443 (1989), the Supreme Court held that the FSIA provides the exclusive basis for U.S. court jurisdiction over suits against foreign states. In that case, Argentine military aircraft had bombed and destroyed an oil tanker in international waters during the 1982 Falkland Islands war between Great Britain and Argentina. The owner of the tanker and the company that had chartered it—both Liberian corporations—brought suit against Argentina in a New York federal court seeking compensation for the loss of the ship and its fuel. They alleged that Argentina's attack on the neutral tanker violated international law, and they argued that federal courts had jurisdiction over the suit pursuant to the Alien Tort Statute, 28 U.S.C. §1350, which provides that the federal district courts "shall have original jurisdiction of any civil action by an alien for a tort only, committed in violation of the law of nations or a treaty of the United States." (We will consider the Alien Tort Statute extensively in Chapter 7.) The Supreme Court ordered dismissal of the suit, reasoning that "the text and structure of the FSIA demonstrate Congress' intention that the FSIA be the sole basis for obtaining jurisdiction over a foreign state in our courts." The Court also concluded that there were no applicable exceptions to immunity in that case.

11. For discussions of the history of foreign sovereign immunity in the United States, see Gary B. Born, International Civil Litigation in United States Courts 199-210 (3d ed. 1996); and Theodore R. Giuttari, The American Law of Sovereign Immunity (1970); *see also* G. Edward White, *The Transformation of the Constitutional Regime of Foreign Relations*, 85 Va. L. Rev. 1, 134-45 (1999) (discussing the treatment of foreign sovereign immunity by U.S. courts in the 1930s and 1940s). For discussions of the FSIA and its origins, see Joseph W. Dellapenna, Suing Foreign Governments and Their Corporations (2d ed. 2003); Mark B. Feldman, *The United States Foreign Sovereign Immunities Act of 1976 in Perspective: A Founder's View*, 35 Int'l & Comp. L.Q. 302 (1986); Robert B. von Mehren, *The Foreign Sovereign Immunities Act of 1976*, 17 Colum. J. Transnat'l L. 33 (1978); and Frederic Alan Weber, *The Foreign Sovereign Immunities Act of 1976: Its Origins, Meaning, and Effect*, 3 Yale J. World Pub. Ord. 1 (1976).

2. Exceptions to Immunity

Saudi Arabia v. Nelson

507 U.S. 349 (1993)

JUSTICE SOUTER delivered the opinion of the Court....

Because this case comes to us on a motion to dismiss the complaint, we assume that we have truthful factual allegations before us, though many of those allegations are subject to dispute. Petitioner Kingdom of Saudi Arabia owns and operates petitioner King Faisal Specialist Hospital in Riyadh, as well as petitioner Royspec Purchasing Services, the hospital's corporate purchasing agent in the United States. The Hospital Corporation of America, Ltd. (HCA), an independent corporation existing under the laws of the Cayman Islands, recruits Americans for employment at the hospital under an agreement signed with Saudi Arabia in 1973.

In its recruitment effort, HCA placed an advertisement in a trade periodical seeking applications for a position as a monitoring systems engineer at the hospital. The advertisement drew the attention of respondent Scott Nelson in September 1983, while Nelson was in the United States. After interviewing for the position in Saudi Arabia, Nelson returned to the United States, where he signed an employment contract with the hospital, satisfied personnel processing requirements, and attended an orientation session that HCA conducted for hospital employees. In the course of that program, HCA identified Royspec as the point of contact in the United States for family members who might wish to reach Nelson in an emergency.

In December 1983, Nelson went to Saudi Arabia and began work at the hospital, monitoring all "facilities, equipment, utilities and maintenance systems to insure the safety of patients, hospital staff, and others." He did his job without significant incident until March 1984, when he discovered safety defects in the hospital's oxygen and nitrous oxide lines that posed fire hazards and otherwise endangered patients' lives. Over a period of several months, Nelson repeatedly advised hospital officials of the safety defects and reported the defects to a Saudi Government commission as well. Hospital officials instructed Nelson to ignore the problems.

The hospital's response to Nelson's reports changed, however, on September 27, 1984, when certain hospital employees summoned him to the hospital's security office where agents of the Saudi Government arrested him.[1] The agents transported Nelson to a jail cell, in which they "shackled, tortured and beat" him, and kept him four days without food. Although Nelson did not understand Arabic, government agents forced him to sign a statement written in that language, the content of which he did not know; a hospital employee who was supposed to act as Nelson's interpreter advised him to sign "anything" the agents gave him to avoid further beatings. Two days later, government agents transferred Nelson to the Al Sijan Prison "to await trial on unknown charges."

At the prison, Nelson was confined in an overcrowded cell area infested with rats, where he had to fight other prisoners for food and from which he was taken only once a week for fresh air and exercise. Although police interrogators repeatedly questioned him in Arabic, Nelson did not learn the nature of the charges, if any, against him. For several days, the Saudi Government failed to advise Nelson's family of his whereabouts, though a Saudi official eventually told Nelson's wife, respondent Vivian Nelson, that he could arrange for her husband' release if she provided sexual favors.

Although officials from the United States Embassy visited Nelson twice during his detention, they concluded that his allegations of Saudi mistreatment were "not credible" and made no protest to Saudi authorities. It was only at the personal request of a United States Senator that the Saudi Government released Nelson, 39 days after his arrest, on November 5, 1984. Seven days later, after failing to convince him to return to work at the hospital, the Saudi Government allowed Nelson to leave the country.

In 1988, Nelson and his wife filed this action against petitioners in the United States District Court for the Southern District of Florida seeking damages for personal injury. The Nelsons' complaint sets out 16 causes of action, which fall into three categories. Counts II through VII and counts X, XI, XIV, and XV allege that petitioners committed various intentional torts, including battery, unlawful detainment, wrongful arrest and imprisonment, false imprisonment, inhuman torture, disruption of normal family life, and infliction of mental anguish. Counts I, IX, and XIII charge petitioners with negligently failing to warn Nelson of otherwise undisclosed dangers of his employment, namely, that if he attempted to report safety hazards the hospital would likely retaliate against him and the Saudi Government might detain and physically abuse him without legal cause. Finally, counts VIII, XII,

---

1. Petitioners assert that the Saudi Government arrested Nelson because he had falsely represented to the hospital that he had received a degree from the Massachusetts Institute of Technology and had provided the hospital with a forged diploma to verify his claim. The Nelsons concede these misrepresentations, but dispute that they occasioned Scott Nelson's arrest.

and XVI allege that Vivian Nelson sustained derivative injury resulting from petitioners' actions. Presumably because the employment contract provided that Saudi
courts would have exclusive jurisdiction over claims for breach of contract, the
Nelsons raised no such matters.

[The trial court dismissed for lack of subject-matter jurisdiction under the
FSIA, the court of appeals reversed, and the Supreme Court granted certiorari.]

The Foreign Sovereign Immunities Act "provides the sole basis for obtaining
jurisdiction over a foreign state in the courts of this country." Argentine Republic v.
Amerada Hess Shipping Corp., 488 U.S. 428, 443 (1989). Under the Act, a foreign
state is presumptively immune from the jurisdiction of United States courts; unless
a specified exception applies, a federal court lacks subject-matter jurisdiction over a
claim against a foreign state.

Only one such exception is said to apply here. The first clause of §1605(a)(2) of
the Act provides that a foreign state shall not be immune from the jurisdiction of
United States courts in any case "in which the action is based upon a commercial
activity carried on in the United States by the foreign state." The Act defines such
activity as "commercial activity carried on by such state and having substantial
contact with the United States," §1603(e), and provides that a commercial activity
may be "either a regular course of commercial conduct or a particular commercial
transaction or act," the "commercial character of [which] shall be determined by
reference to" its "nature," rather than its "purpose," §1603(d).

There is no dispute here that Saudi Arabia, the hospital, and Royspec all qualify
as "foreign state[s]" within the meaning of the Act. For there to be jurisdiction in
this case, therefore, the Nelsons' action must be "based upon" some "commercial
activity" by petitioners that had "substantial contact" with the United States within
the meaning of the Act. Because we conclude that the suit is not based upon any
commercial activity by petitioners, we need not reach the issue of substantial contact with the United States.

We begin our analysis by identifying the particular conduct on which the
Nelsons' action is "based" for purposes of the Act. . . . Although the Act contains
no definition of the phrase "based upon," and the relatively sparse legislative
history offers no assistance, guidance is hardly necessary. In denoting conduct
that forms the "basis," or "foundation," for a claim, see Black's Law Dictionary
151 (6th ed. 1990) (defining "base"); Random House Dictionary 172 (2d ed. 1987)
(same); Webster's Third New International Dictionary 180, 181 (1976) (defining
"base" and "based"), the phrase is read most naturally to mean those elements of a
claim that, if proven, would entitle a plaintiff to relief under his theory of the
case . . . .

What the natural meaning of the phrase "based upon" suggests, the context
confirms. Earlier, we noted that §1605(a)(2) contains two clauses following the one
at issue here. The second allows for jurisdiction where a suit "is based . . . upon an
act performed in the United States in connection with a commercial activity of the
foreign state elsewhere," and the third speaks in like terms, allowing for jurisdiction where an action "is based . . . upon an act outside the territory of the United
States in connection with a commercial activity of the foreign state elsewhere and
that act causes a direct effect in the United States." Distinctions among descriptions juxtaposed against each other are naturally understood to be significant, . . . and Congress manifestly understood there to be a difference between a
suit "based upon" commercial activity and one "based upon" acts performed "in
connection with" such activity. The only reasonable reading of the former term

calls for something more than a mere connection with, or relation to, commercial activity.[4]

In this case, the Nelsons have alleged that petitioners recruited Scott Nelson for work at the hospital, signed an employment contract with him, and subsequently employed him. While these activities led to the conduct that eventually injured the Nelsons, they are not the basis for the Nelsons' suit. Even taking each of the Nelsons' allegations about Scott Nelson's recruitment and employment as true, those facts alone entitle the Nelsons to nothing under their theory of the case. The Nelsons have not, after all, alleged breach of contract, but personal injuries caused by petitioners' intentional wrongs and by petitioners' negligent failure to warn Scott Nelson that they might commit those wrongs. Those torts, and not the arguably commercial activities that preceded their commission, form the basis for the Nelsons' suit.

Petitioners' tortious conduct itself fails to qualify as "commercial activity" within the meaning of the Act . . . . We have seen already that the Act defines "commercial activity" as "either a regular course of commercial conduct or a particular commercial transaction or act," and provides that "the commercial character of an activity shall be determined by reference to the nature of the course of conduct or particular transaction or act, rather than by reference to its purpose." 28 U.S.C. §1603(d). If this is a definition, it is one distinguished only by its diffidence; as we observed in our most recent case on the subject, it "leaves the critical term 'commercial' largely undefined." Republic of Argentina v. Weltover, Inc., 504 U.S. 607, 612 (1992) . . . . We do not, however, have the option to throw up our hands. The term has to be given some interpretation, and congressional diffidence necessarily results in judicial responsibility to determine what a "commercial activity" is for purposes of the Act.

We took up the task just last Term in *Weltover, supra*, which involved Argentina's unilateral refinancing of bonds it had issued under a plan to stabilize its currency. Bondholders sued Argentina in federal court, asserting jurisdiction under the third clause of §1605(a)(2). In the course of holding the refinancing to be a commercial activity for purposes of the Act, we observed that the statute "largely codifies the so called 'restrictive' theory of foreign sovereign immunity first endorsed by the State Department in 1952." 504 U.S., at 612. We accordingly held that the meaning of "commercial" for purposes of the Act must be the meaning Congress understood the restrictive theory to require at the time it passed the statute. *See Weltover, supra,* at 612-613.

Under the restrictive, as opposed to the "absolute," theory of foreign sovereign immunity, a state is immune from the jurisdiction of foreign courts as to its sovereign or public acts (jure imperii), but not as to those that are private or commercial in character (jure gestionis). We explained in *Weltover, supra,* at 614, that a state engages in commercial activity under the restrictive theory where it exercises "only those powers that can also be exercised by private citizens," as distinct from those "powers peculiar to sovereigns." Put differently, a foreign state engages in commercial activity for purposes of the restrictive theory only where it acts "in the manner of a private player within" the market. 504 U. S., at 614; *see* Restatement

---

4. We do not mean to suggest that the first clause of §1605(a)(2) necessarily requires that each and every element of a claim be commercial activity by a foreign state, and we do not address the case where a claim consists of both commercial and sovereign elements. We do conclude, however, that where a claim rests entirely upon activities sovereign in character, as here, jurisdiction will not exist under that clause regardless of any connection the sovereign acts may have with commercial activity.

(Third) of the Foreign Relations Law of the United States §451 (1987) ("Under international law, a state or state instrumentality is immune from the jurisdiction of the courts of another state, except with respect to claims arising out of activities of the kind that may be carried on by private persons").

We emphasized in *Weltover* that whether a state acts "in the manner of" a private party is a question of behavior, not motivation:

> [B]ecause the Act provides that the commercial character of an act is to be determined by reference to its "nature" rather than its "purpose," the question is not whether the foreign government is acting with a profit motive or instead with the aim of fulfilling uniquely sovereign objectives. Rather, the issue is whether the particular actions that the foreign state performs (whatever the motive behind them) are the *type* of actions by which a private party engages in "trade and traffic or commerce." *Weltover, supra,* at 614 (citations omitted) (emphasis in original).

We did not ignore the difficulty of distinguishing "'purpose' (i.e., the *reason* why the foreign state engages in the activity) from 'nature' (i.e., the outward form of the conduct that the foreign state performs or agrees to perform)," but recognized that the Act "unmistakably commands" us to observe the distinction. 504 U. S., at 617 (emphasis in original). Because Argentina had merely dealt in the bond market in the manner of a private player, we held, its refinancing of the bonds qualified as a commercial activity for purposes of the Act despite the apparent governmental motivation. *Ibid.*

Unlike Argentina's activities that we considered in *Weltover*, the intentional conduct alleged here (the Saudi Government's wrongful arrest, imprisonment, and torture of Nelson) could not qualify as commercial under the restrictive theory. The conduct boils down to abuse of the power of its police by the Saudi Government, and however monstrous such abuse undoubtedly may be, a foreign state's exercise of the power of its police has long been understood for purposes of the restrictive theory as peculiarly sovereign in nature . . . . Exercise of the powers of police and penal officers is not the sort of action by which private parties can engage in commerce . . . .

The Nelsons and their amici urge us to give significance to their assertion that the Saudi Government subjected Nelson to the abuse alleged as retaliation for his persistence in reporting hospital safety violations, and argue that the character of the mistreatment was consequently commercial. One amicus, indeed, goes so far as to suggest that the Saudi Government "often uses detention and torture to resolve commercial disputes." But this argument does not alter the fact that the powers allegedly abused were those of police and penal officers. In any event, the argument is off the point, for it goes to purpose, the very fact the Act renders irrelevant to the question of an activity's commercial character. Whatever may have been the Saudi Government's motivation for its allegedly abusive treatment of Nelson, it remains the case that the Nelsons' action is based upon a sovereign activity immune from the subject-matter jurisdiction of United States courts under the Act.

In addition to the intentionally tortious conduct, the Nelsons claim a separate basis for recovery in petitioners' failure to warn Scott Nelson of the hidden dangers associated with his employment. The Nelsons allege that, at the time petitioners recruited Scott Nelson and thereafter, they failed to warn him of the possibility of severe retaliatory action if he attempted to disclose any safety hazards he might discover on the job. In other words, petitioners bore a duty to warn of their own propensity for tortious conduct. But this is merely a semantic ploy. For aught we can see, a plaintiff could recast virtually any claim of intentional tort committed by sovereign act as a claim of failure to warn, simply by charging the defendant with an obligation to announce its own tortious propensity before indulging it. To give jurisdictional significance to this feint of language would effectively thwart the Act's manifest purpose to codify the restrictive theory of foreign sovereign immunity....

JUSTICE WHITE, with whom JUSTICE BLACKMUN joins, concurring in the judgment.

The majority concludes that petitioners enjoy sovereign immunity because respondents' action is not "based upon a commercial activity." I disagree. I nonetheless concur in the judgment because in my view the commercial conduct upon which respondents base their complaint was not "carried on in the United States."...

To run and operate a hospital, even a public hospital, is to engage in a commercial enterprise. The majority never concedes this point, but it does not deny it either, and to my mind the matter is self-evident. By the same token, warning an employee when he blows the whistle and taking retaliatory action, such as harassment, involuntary transfer, discharge, or other tortious behavior, although not prototypical commercial acts, are certainly well within the bounds of commercial activity. The House and Senate Reports accompanying the legislation virtually compel this conclusion, explaining as they do that "a foreign government's...employment or engagement of laborers, clerical staff or marketing agents...would be among those included within" the definition of commercial activity. H.R. Rep. No. 94-1487, p. 16 (1976) (House Report); S. Rep. No. 94-1310, p. 16 (1976) (Senate Report). Nelson alleges that petitioners harmed him in the course of engaging in their commercial enterprise, as a direct result of their commercial acts. His claim, in other words, is "based upon commercial activity."

Indeed, I am somewhat at a loss as to what exactly the majority believes petitioners have done that a private employer could not. As countless cases attest, retaliation for whistle-blowing is not a practice foreign to the marketplace. Congress passed a statute in response to such behavior, see Whistleblower Protection Act of 1989, 5 U.S.C. §1213 et seq. (1988 ed., Supp. III), as have numerous States. On occasion, private employers also have been known to retaliate by enlisting the help of police officers to falsely arrest employees.... More generally, private parties have been held liable for conspiring with public authorities to effectuate an arrest,...and for using private security personnel for the same purposes....

Therefore, had the hospital retaliated against Nelson by hiring thugs to do the job, I assume the majority—no longer able to describe this conduct as "a foreign state's exercise of the power of its police"—would consent to calling it "commercial." For, in such circumstances, the state-run hospital would be operating as any private participant in the marketplace and respondents' action would be based on the operation by Saudi Arabia's agents of a commercial business.

At the heart of the majority's conclusion, in other words, is the fact that the hospital in this case chose to call in government security forces. I find this fixation on the intervention of police officers, and the ensuing characterization of the conduct as "peculiarly sovereign in nature," to be misguided. To begin, it fails to capture respondents' complaint in full. Far from being directed solely at the activities of the Saudi police, it alleges that agents of the hospital summoned Nelson to its security office because he reported safety concerns and that the hospital played a part in the subsequent beating and imprisonment. Without more, that type of behavior hardly qualifies as sovereign. Thus, even assuming for the sake of argument that the role of the official police somehow affected the nature of petitioners' conduct, the claim cannot be said to "rest entirely upon activities sovereign in character." At the very least it "consists of both commercial and sovereign elements," thereby presenting the specific question the majority chooses to elude. The majority's single-minded focus on the exercise of police power, while certainly simplifying the case, thus hardly does it justice.

Reliance on the fact that Nelson's employer enlisted the help of public rather than private security personnel is also at odds with Congress' intent. The purpose of the commercial exception being to prevent foreign states from taking refuge behind their sovereignty when they act as market participants, it seems to me that this is precisely the type of distinction we should seek to avoid. Because both the hospital and the police are agents of the state, the case in my mind turns on whether the sovereign is acting in a commercial capacity, not on whether it resorts to thugs or government officers to carry on its business. That, when the hospital calls in security to get even with a whistle-blower, it comes clothed in police apparel says more about the state-owned nature of the commercial enterprise than about the noncommercial nature of its tortious conduct. . . .

Contrary to the majority's suggestion, this conclusion does not involve inquiring into the purpose of the conduct. Matters would be different, I suppose, if Nelson had been recruited to work in the Saudi police force and, having reported safety violations, suffered retributive punishment, for there the Saudi authorities would be engaged in distinctly sovereign activities. The same would be true if Nelson was a mere tourist in Saudi Arabia and had been summarily expelled by order of immigration officials. In this instance, however, the state-owned hospital was engaged in ordinary commercial business. . . .

Nevertheless, I reach the same conclusion as the majority because petitioners' commercial activity was not "carried on in the United States." The Act defines such conduct as "commercial activity . . . having substantial contact with the United States." 28 U.S.C. §1603(e). Respondents point to the hospital's recruitment efforts in the United States, including advertising in the American media, and the signing of the employment contract in Miami. As I earlier noted, while these may very well qualify as commercial activity in the United States, they do not constitute the commercial activity upon which respondents' action is based. Conversely, petitioners' commercial conduct in Saudi Arabia, though constituting the basis of the Nelsons' suit, lacks a sufficient nexus to the United States. Neither the hospital's employment practices, nor its disciplinary procedures, has any apparent connection to this country. On that basis, I agree that the Act does not grant the Nelsons access to our courts.

JUSTICE KENNEDY, with whom JUSTICE BLACKMUN and JUSTICE STEVENS join as to Parts I-B and II, concurring in part and dissenting in part.

I join all of the Court's opinion except the last paragraph of Part II, where, with almost no explanation, the Court rules that, like the intentional tort claim, the claims based on negligent failure to warn are outside the subject-matter jurisdiction of the federal courts. These claims stand on a much different footing from the intentional tort claims for purposes of the Foreign Sovereign Immunities Act (FSIA). In my view, they ought to be remanded to the District Court for further consideration. . . .

[T]he Nelsons' claims alleging that the hospital, the Kingdom, and Royspec were negligent in failing during their recruitment of Nelson to warn him of foreseeable dangers are based upon commercial activity having substantial contact with the United States. As such, they are within the commercial activity exception and the jurisdiction of the federal courts. Unlike the intentional tort counts of the complaint, the failure to warn counts do not complain of a police beating in Saudi Arabia; rather, they complain of a negligent omission made during the recruiting of a hospital employee in the United States. To obtain relief, the Nelsons would be obliged to prove that the hospital's recruiting agent did not tell Nelson about the foreseeable hazards of his prospective employment in Saudi Arabia. Under the Court's test, this omission is what the negligence counts are "based upon."

Omission of important information during employee recruiting is commercial activity as we have described it. It seems plain that recruiting employees is an activity undertaken by private hospitals in the normal course of business. Locating and hiring employees implicates no power unique to the sovereign. In explaining the terms and conditions of employment, including the risks and rewards of a particular job, a governmental entity acts in "the manner of a private player within" the commercial marketplace. Under the FSIA, as a result, it must satisfy the same general duties of care that apply to private actors under state law. If a private company with operations in Saudi Arabia would be obliged in the course of its recruiting activities subject to state law to tell a prospective employee about the risk of arbitrary arrest and torture by Saudi authorities, then so would King Faisal Specialist Hospital.

The recruiting activity alleged in the failure to warn counts of the complaint also satisfies the final requirement for invoking the commercial activity exception: that the claims be based upon commercial activity "having substantial contact with the United States." 28 U.S.C. §1603(e). Nelson's recruitment was performed by Hospital Corporation of America, Ltd. (HCA), a wholly owned subsidiary of a United States corporation, which, for a period of at least 16 years beginning in 1973, acted as the Kingdom of Saudi Arabia's exclusive agent for recruiting employees for the hospital. HCA in the regular course of its business seeks employees for the hospital in the American labor market. HCA advertised in an American magazine, seeking applicants for the position Nelson later filled. Nelson saw the ad in the United States and contacted HCA in Tennessee. After an interview in Saudi Arabia, Nelson returned to Florida, where he signed an employment contract and underwent personnel processing and application procedures. Before leaving to take his job at the hospital, Nelson attended an orientation session conducted by HCA in Tennessee for new employees. These activities have more than substantial contact with the United States; most of them were "carried on in the United States." 28 U.S.C. §1605(a)(2). In alleging that the petitioners neglected during these activities to tell him what they were bound to under state law, Nelson meets all of the statutory requirements for invoking federal jurisdiction under the commercial activity exception....

Having met the jurisdictional prerequisites of the FSIA, the Nelsons' failure to warn claims should survive petitioners' motion under Federal Rule of Civil Procedure 12(b)(1) to dismiss for want of subject-matter jurisdiction. Yet instead of remanding these claims to the District Court for further proceedings, the majority dismisses them in a single short paragraph. This is peculiar, since the Court suggests no reason to question the conclusion that the failure to warn claims are based on commercial activity having substantial contact with the United States; indeed,

the Court does not purport to analyze these claims in light of the statutory requirements for jurisdiction.

The Court's summary treatment may stem from doubts about the underlying
validity of the negligence cause of action. The Court dismisses the claims because it
fears that if it did not, "a plaintiff could recast virtually any claim of intentional tort
committed by a sovereign act as a claim of failure to warn, simply by charging the
defendant with an obligation to announce its own tortious propensity before indulging it." In the majority's view, "to give jurisdictional significance to this feint of
language would effectively thwart the Act's manifest purpose to codify the restrictive theory of foreign sovereign immunity." These doubts, however, are not relevant to the analytical task at hand.

The FSIA states that with respect to any claim against a foreign sovereign that
falls within the statutory exceptions to immunity listed in §1605, "the foreign state
shall be liable in the same manner and to the same extent as a private individual
under like circumstances." 28 U.S.C. §1606. The Act incorporates state law and "was
not intended to affect the substantive law determining the liability of a foreign state."
First Nat. City Bank v. Banco Para el Comercio Exterior de Cuba, 462 U.S. 611, 620
(1983). If the governing state law, which has not yet been determined, would permit
an injured person to plead and prove a tortious wrong for failure to warn against a
private defendant under facts similar to those in this case, we have no authority under
the FSIA to ordain otherwise for those suing a sovereign entity. "Where state law
provides a rule of liability governing private individuals, the FSIA requires the
application of that rule to foreign states in like circumstances." *Id.*, at 622, n.11 . . . .

As a matter of substantive tort law, it is not a novel proposition or a play on
words to describe with precision the conduct upon which various causes of action
are based or to recognize that a single injury can arise from multiple causes, each of
which constitutes an actionable wrong . . . .

We need not determine, however, that on remand the Nelsons will succeed on
their failure to warn claims. Quite apart from potential problems of state tort law
that might bar recovery, the Nelsons appear to face an obstacle based upon the
former adjudication of their related lawsuit against Saudi Arabia's recruiting agent,
HCA. The District Court dismissed that suit, which raised an identical failure to
warn claim, not only as time barred, but also on the merits. That decision was
affirmed on appeal, . . . and may be entitled to preclusive effect with respect to
the Nelsons' similar claims against the sovereign defendants, whose recruitment
of Nelson took place almost entirely through HCA . . . .

But the question of claim preclusion, like the substantive validity under state
law of the Nelsons' negligence cause of action, has not yet been litigated and is
outside the proper sphere of our review . . . . That a remand to the District Court
may be of no avail to the Nelsons is irrelevant to our task here; if the jurisdictional
requirements of the FSIA are met, the case must be remanded to the trial court for
further proceedings. In my view, the FSIA conferred subject-matter jurisdiction on
the District Court to entertain the failure to warn claims, and with all respect, I
dissent from the Court's refusal to remand them.

Notes and Questions

1. As made clear in Section 1604 of the FSIA, absent an international agreement allowing for suit, foreign states are immune from the jurisdiction of U.S.

courts unless one of the FSIA's exceptions is satisfied. Section 1605(a) sets forth seven general exceptions to immunity, including exceptions for waiver, commercial activity, takings of property in violation of international law, noncommercial torts, and suits against state sponsors of terrorism. There are also additional exceptions in §1605 relating to admiralty law and in §1607 relating to counterclaims.

2. Under the FSIA's waiver exception, a foreign state is not immune from suit if it "has waived its immunity either explicitly or by implication." 28 U.S.C. §1605(a)(1). Explicit waivers of immunity, such as a waiver in a treaty or contract, present relatively few problems. Such waiver provisions are commonly included in the legal documents when a foreign state borrows money from a bank or purchases goods or services from a sophisticated company. But what constitutes a waiver "by implication"? The legislative history of the FSIA states as follows:

> With respect to implicit waivers, the courts have found such waivers in cases where a foreign state has agreed to arbitration in another country or where a foreign state has agreed that the law of particular country should govern a contract. An implicit waiver would also include a situation where a foreign state has filed a responsive pleading in an action without raising the defense of foreign sovereign immunity. H.R. Rep. No. 94-1487, at 18.

What does this statement suggest about the scope of the implicit waiver exception? In general, courts have construed the FSIA's implicit waiver exception narrowly, limiting it to situations in which the foreign state defendant has indicated a willingness to be sued in U.S. courts. The selection of U.S. law to govern a contract is generally treated as a waiver of FSIA immunity. *See, e.g.*, Eckert Int'l, Inc. v. Fiji, 32 F.3d 77 (4th Cir. 1994). But a selection of foreign law is generally not viewed as a waiver. *See, e.g.*, Maritime Int'l Nominees Establishment v. Republic of Guinea, 693 F.2d 1094, 1102 n.13 (D.C. Cir. 1982). Nor does a foreign state's waiver of immunity in its own courts typically constitute a waiver of immunity in U.S. courts. *See, e.g.*, Corzo v. Banco Cent. De Reserva del Peru, 243 F.3d 519, 523 (9th Cir. 2001). *See also* Blaxland v. Commonwealth Director of Public Prosecutions, 323 F.3d 1198 (9th Cir. 2003) (use of U.S. extradition procedures held not to constitute a waiver because the extradition process was political rather than judicial).

3. The "commercial activity" exception, 18 U.S.C. §1605(a)(2), is one of the most litigated provisions of the FSIA. It provides that "a foreign state shall not be immune from the jurisdiction" of a U.S. court in any case:

> in which the action is based upon a commercial activity carried on in the United States by the foreign state; or upon an act performed in the United States in connection with a commercial activity of the foreign state elsewhere; or upon an act outside the territory of the United States in connection with a commercial activity of the foreign state elsewhere and that act causes a direct effect in the United States.

Section 1605(a)(2) thus can be satisfied by any one of three independent nexus requirements, and each nexus requirement uses the term "commercial activity." Section 1605(d), in turn, defines "commercial activity" to mean "either a regular course of commercial conduct or a particular commercial transaction or act," and adds that the "commercial character of an activity shall be determined by reference to the nature of the course of conduct or particular transaction or act, rather than by reference to its purpose."

The Supreme Court first interpreted the meaning of "commercial activity" in Republic of Argentina v. Weltover, Inc., 504 U.S. 607 (1992). In *Weltover*, foreign corporate holders of previously issued Argentine bonds declined to accept Argentina's attempted rescheduling of the maturity dates of the bonds, and sued Argentina to obtain payment. The Supreme Court held that the issuance of the bonds was a "commercial activity" and that the suit fell within the third clause of §1605(a)(2). As the Court recounts in *Nelson*, the Court in *Weltover*, drawing on §1605(d)'s definition of "commercial activity," reasoned that the commercial nature of an activity was to be determined by its nature rather than its purpose, and that a foreign state's activity is commercial when the foreign state acts "not as regulator of a market, but in the manner of a private player within it." Is the nature of an activity completely separate from its purpose? Can the nature of an activity be affected by who is doing it? How helpful is the *Weltover* "private player" test? For decisions applying that test, see, for example, Globe Nuclear Services & Supply GNSS, Ltd. v. AO Technsabexport, 376 F.3d 282 (4th Cir. 2004) (agreement to supply uranium hexafluoride that was extracted from nuclear weapons held to be commercial activity because "[t]he entrance into a contract to supply a private party with uranium hexafluoride is the very type of action by which private parties engage in 'trade and traffic or commerce'"), and Beg v. Islamic Republic of Pakistan, 353 F.3d 1323 (11th Cir. 2003) (expropriation of property held not to be a commercial activity because "private actors are not allowed to engage in 'takings' in the manner that governments are").

4. The plaintiffs in *Nelson* sued under the first clause of §1605(a)(2). Why did the Court in *Nelson* conclude that the suit was not "based upon" a commercial activity? What activities, according to the majority, was the plaintiffs' suit based upon? Why did the majority characterize false imprisonment and torture as "exercise of the powers of [Saudi Arabian] police" rather than (per Justice White's suggestion) as an activity, like retaliation for whistleblowing, that private entities sometimes engage in? Does the majority, in contravention of *Weltover*, improperly look to the purpose, as opposed to the nature, of the activity? Why didn't the plaintiffs in *Nelson* sue for breach of Mr. Nelson's employment contract, which would have made their case seem more commercial?

5. Why did the majority in *Nelson* reject the failure to warn claim? Note that the suit was dismissed on the pleadings, so the Court was supposed to presume the correctness of the plaintiffs' allegations. Nevertheless, did the Court implicitly make some judgments about Mr. Nelson's credibility? In any event, was the majority right that the failure to warn claim was just a "semantic ploy"? Is it relevant to your resolution of these questions that the Nelsons had already brought a failure to warn claim against the agent, HCA, and that claim had been dismissed by the trial court on the merits? What do you think of Justice Kennedy's analysis of this issue?

6. The third clause of §1605(a)(2) creates an exception to immunity when "an act outside the territory of the United States in connection with a commercial activity of the foreign state elsewhere and that act causes a direct effect in the United States." Why didn't the plaintiffs in *Nelson* sue under that clause? *Cf.* Berkovitz v. Islamic Republic of Iran, 735 F.2d 329, 332 (9th Cir. 1984) (emotional suffering of family members held not to be a direct effect of tortious conduct abroad).

The Court in *Weltover* addressed the meaning of "direct effect" in the third clause of §1605(a)(2) and held that Argentina's unilateral rescheduling of its bonds satisfied this requirement because New York was a place of payment and Argentina had in fact made some interest payments on the bonds in New York. The Court concluded that "[b]ecause New York was thus the place of performance for Argentina's ultimate contractual obligations, the rescheduling of those obligations necessarily had a 'direct effect' in the United States: Money that was supposed to have been delivered to a New York bank for deposit was not forthcoming." The Court also rejected Argentina's argument that the "direct effect" requirement could not be satisfied where the plaintiffs are all foreign corporations with no other connections to the United States, reasoning that "[w]e expressly stated in *Verlinden* that the FSIA permits 'a foreign plaintiff to sue a foreign sovereign in the courts of the United States, provided the substantive requirements of the Act are satisfied.'" Courts are divided over how broadly to apply the *Weltover* test for "direct effects," with some requiring a "legally significant act" in the United States (such as failure to make a payment specified in the contract to be made in the United States), but others rejecting such a requirement. *See* Keller v. Central Bank of Nigeria, 277 F.3d 811, 817-18 (6th Cir. 2002) (describing division of authority).

7. Another exception to immunity under the FSIA is the so-called "noncommercial tort" exception. This exception removes immunity in any case, not otherwise covered by the commercial activity exception, "in which money damages are sought against a foreign state for personal injury or death, or damage to or loss of property, occurring in the United States and caused by the tortious act or omission of that foreign state or of any official or employee of that foreign state while acting within the scope of his office or employment." 28 U.S.C. §1605(a)(5). The plain language of the noncommercial tort exception requires that the injury or damage occur in the United States and thus by its terms excludes most foreign torts. Moreover, most courts to address the issue have also required that the tortious act or omission occur in the United States. *See, e.g.,* Persinger v. Islamic Republic of Iran, 729 F.2d 835, 842 (D.C. Cir. 1984). The Restatement (Third) of Foreign Relations Law, by contrast, has construed the noncommercial tort exception to apply whenever the injury occurs in the United States, "regardless of where the act or omission causing the injury took place." Restatement (Third) of the Foreign Relations Law of the United States §454, cmt. e (1987). Why is the noncommercial tort exception so much narrower in its territorial application than the commercial activity exception?

8. The noncommercial tort exception does not apply to all torts. In particular, it does not apply to "any claim based upon the exercise or performance or the failure to exercise or perform a discretionary function regardless of whether the discretion be abused." In addition, it does not apply to "any claim arising out of malicious prosecution, abuse of process, libel, slander, misrepresentation, deceit, or interference with contract rights." 28 U.S.C. §1605(a)(5)(B). Why do you think Congress imposed these additional limitations on the noncommercial tort exception?

9. What is the relationship between the immunities conferred by the FSIA and international law? As we have seen, the FSIA purported to codify the restrictive theory of immunity that prevailed in the twentieth century under customary international law. To what extent does it do so? To what extent do its exceptions to immunity go further than what was contemplated by the restrictive theory?

In addition to this general relationship with international law, one of the FSIA's exceptions to immunity refers specifically to international law. Section 1605(a)(3) of the FSIA states that a foreign state is not entitled to immunity with respect to claims:

> in which rights in property taken in violation of international law are in issue and that property or any property exchanged for such property is present in the United States in connection with a commercial activity carried on in the United States by the foreign

state; or that property or any property exchanged for such property is owned or operated by an agency or instrumentality of the foreign state and that agency or instrumentality is engaged in a commercial activity in the United States.

This exception has been invoked in a number of recent cases, including the *Altmann* case excerpted above (although the Supreme Court addressed only the issue of the FSIA's retroactivity and did not address the scope of this particular exception). In applying this exception, should courts look to modern international law concerning the taking of property, or the international law that was in effect at the time of the taking?

10. Foreign sovereign immunity is not the only type of immunity available for foreign officials. Foreign diplomats, consular officials, U.N. representatives and invitees, and international organizations also have certain immunities from criminal and civil liability.

Diplomatic and consular immunities were historically regulated by customary international law, but they are now codified in two treaties — the Vienna Convention on Diplomatic Relations ("Diplomatic Convention"), and the Vienna Convention on Consular Relations ("Consular Convention") — both of which the United States has ratified. Under these treaties, the nation that sends the diplomat or consular official is referred to as the "sending State," and the nation that receives the diplomat or consular official is referred to as the "receiving State."

Diplomatic agents have broad immunity from both criminal and civil jurisdiction. They are not subject to "any form of arrest or detention." Diplomatic Convention, art. 29. In addition, they have absolute immunity from the criminal jurisdiction of the receiving State. *Id.*, art. 31(1). Furthermore, they have immunity from civil and administrative proceedings, with exceptions for certain actions related to immovable property, succession, and non-official commercial activities. *Id.* Consular immunity is more qualified. Consular officials are not liable to arrest or detention "except in the case of a grave crime and pursuant to a decision by the competent judicial authority." Consular Convention, art. 41(1). They have immunity from criminal and civil jurisdiction, but only "in respect of acts performed in the exercise of consular functions." *Id.*, art. 43(1). Even this immunity does not apply with respect to civil actions for certain contract and tort claims where the consular official was not acting expressly in a public capacity. *Id.*, art. 43(2).

In addition to these individual immunities, diplomatic and consular properties are protected against interference by the receiving state. Although these properties are not, contrary to popular belief, treated as part of the sending state's territory, they are considered "inviolable" by the receiving state. For diplomatic missions, this means that they cannot be entered by officials of the receiving State "except with the consent of the head of the mission." Diplomatic Convention, art. 22(1). In addition, the receiving State has a duty "to take all appropriate steps to protect the premises of the mission against any intrusion or damage and to prevent any disturbance of the peace of the mission or impairment of its dignity." *Id.*, art. 22(2). For consular premises, officials of the receiving State cannot enter "that part of the consular premises which is used exclusively for the purpose of the work of the consular post except with the consent of the head of the consular post or of his designee or of the head of the diplomatic mission of the sending State." Consular Convention, art. 31(2). Consent is assumed, however, "in the case of fire or other disaster requiring prompt protective action." *Id.* As with diplomatic missions, the receiving State has a duty "to take all appropriate steps to protect the consular premises against any intrusion or damage and to prevent any disturbance of the peace of the consular post or impairment of its dignity." *Id.*, art. 31(3).

Despite these limitations on its jurisdiction, the receiving state may at any time declare a member of a diplomatic mission or consulate to be *persona non grata*. Once a person is declared *persona non grata*, the sending State must either recall the person or terminate his or her official functions. *See* Diplomatic Convention, art. 9(1); Consular Convention, art. 23(1).

Congress has further clarified the scope and domestic status of diplomatic immunity in the 1978 Diplomatic Relations Act, 22 U.S.C. §§254a-254e. This Act, among other things, authorizes the President, "on the basis of reciprocity and under such terms and conditions as he may determine, [to] specify privileges and immunities for the mission, the members of the mission, their families, and the diplomatic couriers which result in more favorable treatment or less favorable treatment than is provided under the Vienna Convention." *Id.*, §254c. It also provides that "[a]ny action or proceeding brought against an individual who is entitled to immunity with respect to such action or proceeding under the Vienna Convention on Diplomatic Relations . . . shall be dismissed," and that "[s]uch immunity may be established upon motion or suggestion by or on behalf of the individual, or as otherwise permitted by law or applicable rules of procedure." *Id.*, §254d.

Representatives of members of the United Nations and official invitees to the United Nations are also entitled to certain immunities. Under the 1947 Agreement Between the United Nations and the United States of America Regarding the Headquarters of the United Nations, also known as the "UN Headquarters Agreement," representatives of member states "shall, whether residing inside or outside the headquarters district, be entitled in the territory of the United States to the same privileges and immunities . . . as it accords to diplomatic envoys accredited to it." UN Headquarters Agreement, art. V, §15(4). The 1946 Convention on Privileges and Immunities of the United Nations states more specifically that representatives of member states shall "enjoy the following privileges and immunities: (a) immunity from personal arrest or detention . . . ; (b) inviolability for all papers and documents; . . . (g) such other privileges, immunities and facilities not inconsistent [with] the foregoing as diplomatic envoys enjoy." UN Convention, art. IV, §11. The UN Headquarters Agreement also prohibits the imposition of any impediments to transit to or from the headquarters district (a defined area around the United Nations headquarters) by a variety of individuals, including representatives of the UN members as well as "other persons invited to the headquarters district by the United Nations." UN Headquarters Agreement, art. IV, §11.

International organizations also have immunities from suit in U.S. courts. Under the 1945 International Organizations Immunities Act, 22 U.S.C. §§288-288f-4, international organizations "shall enjoy the same immunity from suit and every form of judicial process as is enjoyed by foreign governments, except to the extent that such organizations may expressly waive their immunity for the purpose of any proceedings or by the terms of any contract." *Id.*, §288a(b). The Act defines "international organization" as "a public international organization in which the United States participates pursuant to any treaty or under the authority of any Act of Congress authorizing such participation or making an appropriation for such participation, and which shall have been designated by the President through appropriate Executive order as being entitled to enjoy the privileges, exemptions, and immunities herein provided." *Id.*, §288. The President, however, is authorized "at any time to revoke the designation of any international organization under this section" "if in his judgment such action should be justified by reason of the abuse by an international organization or its officers and employees of the privileges, exemptions, and immunities herein provided or for any other reason." *Id.*

11. Why is it important to give diplomats and consular officials immunity? Why is it important to treat diplomatic premises as inviolable? If the United States fails to respect diplomatic immunity or inviolability, what consequences is it likely to suffer abroad? What degree of immunity is needed to ensure the effective functioning of diplomatic missions and consulates? Do the reasons for diplomatic and consular immunity explain immunity for U.N. representatives and international organizations? What different reasons might there be for immunity in this latter context?

12. The American public and press are often surprised to learn that diplomats have absolute immunity from criminal prosecution, even for egregious crimes. In 1997, for example, a diplomat from the Republic of Georgia was involved in a fatal car crash in Washington, D.C., and many were shocked to learn that he was immune from prosecution in the United States. In an unusual development, the Republic of Georgia decided to waive the diplomat's immunity from prosecution in that case, and the diplomat pleaded guilty to involuntary manslaughter. Absent such a waiver, however, the only "remedy" would have been to declare the diplomat *persona non grata* and order him to leave the country.

13. Both the Diplomatic Convention and the Consular Convention make clear that the immunity of diplomats and consular officials can be waived by the sending state, as long as the waiver is "express." *See* Diplomatic Convention, art. 32; Consular Convention, art. 45. Why is the sending state allowed to waive immunity? Does a waiver of diplomatic immunity with respect to criminal prosecution also constitute a waiver of immunity with respect to civil liability for the same conduct? In the case described above regarding the Georgian diplomat, the court concluded that there was no waiver of civil liability. *See* Knab v. Republic of Georgia, 1998 U.S. Dist. LEXIS 8820 (D.D.C. 1998). The court noted, among other things, that the Diplomatic Convention confers criminal and civil immunity separately and with different scopes, and that the U.S. State Department had expressed the view that the diplomat's civil immunity remained intact. Is this persuasive? Note that diplomats and consular officials are deemed to waive their immunity with respect to counterclaims if they bring suit in a U.S. court. *See* Diplomatic Convention, art. 32(3); Consular Convention, art. 42(3).

14. Although diplomats have absolute immunity from criminal prosecution, their immunity from civil suits is subject to several exceptions. One of these exceptions is for "an action relating to any professional or commercial activity exercised by the diplomatic agent in the receiving State outside his official functions." How does this exception compare with the commercial activity exception in the Foreign Sovereign Immunities Act? To date, courts have read the diplomatic immunity exception much more narrowly, such that it applies only to the conduct of a trade or business, and not to commercial relationships that are incidental to daily life. *See, e.g.,* Tabion v. Mufti, 73 F.3d 535 (4th Cir. 1996); Logan v. Dupuis, 990 F. Supp. 26 (D.D.C. 1997). Why do you think courts have read this exception so narrowly? Should diplomats have broader immunity from civil suits than foreign governments?

15. What deference should courts give to the views of the Executive Branch in determining whether a defendant is protected by diplomatic immunity? Courts generally treat as conclusive State Department certifications of a diplomat's status. *See, e.g.,* Abdulaziz v. Metropolitan Dade County, 741 F.3d 1328, 1331 (11th Cir.

1984). Courts give substantial but not dispositive weight to Executive Branch constructions of the Vienna Conventions. *See, e.g., Tabion,* 73 F.3d at 538. And, while courts give weight to the Executive Branch's views about whether immunity should be granted in a particular case, they do not typically treat those views as binding. *See, e.g., Knab,* 1998 U.S. Dist. LEXIS at *10 ("Although the Court is not obliged to defer to the State Department's opinion, it finds [the State Department's letter to the court] useful evidence.").

These deference issues were implicated in United States v. Al-Hamdi, 356 F. 3d 564 (4th Cir. 2004). In that case, Al-Hamdi, the son of a Yemeni diplomat, appealed his conviction for possessing a firearm as a non-immigrant alien on the ground that he was entitled to diplomatic immunity. Article 37.1 of the Vienna Convention on Diplomatic Immunities provides that "members of the family of a diplomatic agent forming part of his household shall . . . enjoy the privileges and immunities" conferred on diplomats themselves. The Diplomatic Relations Act, which made the Vienna Convention applicable to the United States, provides that the phrase "members of the family" means the "members of the family of a member of a mission . . . who form part of his or her household." 22 U.S.C. §254a(2)(A). Despite these provisions, the State Department certified that Al-Hamdi, who was twenty-five years old at the time of his arrest, lost his diplomatic immunity in November 1998 when he turned twenty-one. The State Department based its certification on a Circular Diplomatic Note that it had issued, of which the Yemeni government had notice, which interpreted the phrase "members of the family" as set forth in the Vienna Convention and the Diplomatic Relations Act to not include children over the age of twenty-one. The Fourth Circuit agreed with the State Department that Al-Hamdi lacked immunity. The court first satisfied itself that the State Department's certification was not based on an impermissible interpretation of the Vienna Convention. After giving "substantial deference" to the State Department's interpretation of the Vienna Convention, and after noting that a receiving state always has had "broad discretion to classify diplomats," the court concluded that the State Department's interpretation was reasonable and, as a result, was binding on the court.

16. For additional discussion of diplomatic and consular immunity, see Restatement (Third) of the Foreign Relations Law of the United States §§464-66 (1987); Eileen Denza, Diplomatic Law: Commentary on the Vienna Convention on Diplomatic Relations (2d ed. 1998); Linda S. Frey & Marsha L. Frey, The History of Diplomatic Immunity (1999); Charles J. Lewis, State and Diplomatic Immunity (3d ed. 1990); Satow's Guide to Diplomatic Practice (5th ed. 1979); and Biswanath Sen, A Diplomat's Handbook of International Law and Practice (3d rev. ed. 1988).

17. The immunity doctrines discussed in this Section play an important, though complicated, role in human rights litigation in U.S. courts, especially in suits against individual state officials and nations determined by the Executive Branch to be state sponsors of terrorism. We discuss the role of immunity doctrines in these cases in Chapter 7.

E. ACT OF STATE DOCTRINE

We now turn to the act of state doctrine, a common law doctrine that limits the circumstances under which U.S. courts will examine the validity of foreign government acts. The act of state doctrine has its roots in early decisions granting foreign governments and their leaders immunity from suit. *See, e.g.*, The Schooner Exchange v. McFaddon, 11 U.S. (7 Cranch) 116 (1812); Hatch v. Baez, 7 Hun. 596 (N.Y. Sup. Ct. 1876). The first U.S. Supreme Court decision that clearly relied on the act of state doctrine was Underhill v. Hernandez, 168 U.S. 250 (1897). In that case, Underhill, an American citizen, had been living in Bolivar, Venezuela, where he had constructed a waterworks system for the city and was carrying on a machinery repair business. A revolutionary army seized control of the city and, for a time, the commander of the army refused to let Underhill leave, in an effort to coerce Underhill to operate the waterworks system and continue his repair business. Underhill eventually was allowed to leave, and he subsequently sued the commander in a U.S. federal court, seeking damages for the detention. In the meantime, the U.S. government recognized the revolutionary government as the legitimate government of Venezuela. In affirming a dismissal of Underhill's suit, the Supreme Court stated:

> Every sovereign State is bound to respect the independence of every other sovereign State, and the courts of one country will not sit in judgment on the acts of the government of another done within its own territory. Redress of grievances by reason of such acts must be obtained through the means open to be availed of by sovereign powers as between themselves.

Id. at 252.

The Supreme Court reaffirmed this doctrine in a number of decisions in the early 1900s. *See, e.g.*, American Banana Co. v. United Fruit Co., 213 U.S. 347, 357-58 (1909) (holding that actions of Costa Rican government in allegedly evicting company from property in Costa Rica could not be challenged because "a seizure by a state is not a thing that can be complained of elsewhere in the courts"); Oetjen v. Central Leather Co., 246 U.S. 297, 303-04 (1918) (explaining that the act of state doctrine "rests at last upon the highest considerations of international comity and expediency," and holding that an expropriation by the Mexican government "is not subject to reexamination and modification by the courts of this country"); Ricaud v. American Metal Co., 246 U.S. 304, 309-10 (1918) (stating that Mexico's expropriation of U.S. citizen's property could not be questioned in a U.S. court because "the act within its own boundaries of one sovereign State cannot become the subject of reexamination and modification in the courts of another").

1. The *Sabbatino* Decision

The Supreme Court's most important decision concerning the act of state doctrine is Banco Nacional de Cuba v. Sabbatino, excerpted below. In reading *Sabbatino*, it is important to keep in mind the historical context. The decision was issued in 1964, during the height of the Cold War. The relations between the United States and Cuba were extremely strained. Fidel Castro's Communist government had assumed power in Cuba in 1959 and, shortly thereafter, proceeded to expropriate U.S. property. The United States supported the attempted invasion of Cuba at the Bay of Pigs in 1961, and it imposed a trade embargo against Cuba in 1962. The Cuban missile crisis also occurred in 1962, during which the United States Navy blocked Soviet ships from reaching Cuba in order to compel the Soviet Union to remove nuclear missiles that it had placed there. This was also a time during which the customary international law rules of state responsibility, especially rules relating to the expropriation of foreign citizen property, were being challenged by Communist and newly independent developing countries.

Banco Nacional de Cuba v. Sabbatino

376 U.S. 398 (1964)

[Farr Whitlock, a U.S. commodities broker, contracted to purchase sugar from a subsidiary of a Cuban company, C.A.V. The sugar was to be shipped to Farr Whitlock's customer in Morocco, and Farr was to pay for it in New York upon presentation of the shipping documents and a sight draft (an instrument that it could present for payment by its customer's bank upon tendering the bill of lading to the customer).

The stock in C.A.V. was owned principally by U.S. residents. In response to a reduction in the United States' sugar quota for Cuba (by President Eisenhower, exercising power delegated to him from Congress), the Cuban government adopted a law allowing it to expropriate property in which U.S. nationals had an interest. The government subsequently expropriated C.A.V.'s property.

To obtain the release of the shipment of C.A.V.'s seized sugar (and have it shipped to its customer in Morocco), Farr Whitlock entered into a payment agreement with a Cuban government bank (Banco Exterior). However, after having the sugar shipped to its customer, receiving the shipping documents from the Cuban entity, and tendering them to the customer and receiving payment from the customer, Farr Whitlock received a claim from C.A.V. for the proceeds of the sale of the sugar. It also received a promise from C.A.V. to indemnify it for any losses as long as it did not turn the money over to Cuba.

A New York court then appointed Sabbatino as a Temporary Receiver of C.A.V.'s New York assets, and enjoined Farr Whitlock from disposing of the proceeds from its sale of the sugar. Following this, pursuant to court order, Farr Whitlock turned the proceeds over to Sabbatino. An assignee of Banco Exterior — Banco Nacional de Cuba — then brought suit against Sabbatino in the federal district court for the Southern District of New York, seeking to recover on the contract/bills of lading. Banco Nacional alleged that Farr Whitlock had unlawfully converted its property. As a defense, Farr Whitlock claimed that the expropriation violated international law and that title to the sugar therefore had not validly passed to Cuba. Both the district court and court of appeals agreed with this argument, declining to apply the act of state doctrine.]

MR. JUSTICE HARLAN delivered the opinion of the Court....

IV

...[The Court discusses *Underhill* and the subsequent act of state decisions, including *Oetjen* and *Ricaud*, and notes that "[n]one of this Court's subsequent cases in which the act of state doctrine was directly or peripherally involved manifest any retreat from *Underhill*."]

In deciding the present case the Court of Appeals relied in part upon an exception to the unqualified teachings of *Underhill*, *Oetjen*, and *Ricaud* which that court had earlier indicated. In Bernstein v. Van Heyghen Freres Societe Anonyme, 163 F.2d 246, suit was brought to recover from an assignee property allegedly taken, in effect, by the Nazi Government because plaintiff was Jewish. Recognizing the odious nature of this act of state, the court, through Judge Learned Hand, nonetheless refused to consider it invalid on that ground. Rather, it looked to see if the Executive had acted in any manner that would indicate that United States Courts should refuse to give effect to such a foreign decree. Finding no such evidence, the court sustained dismissal of the complaint. In a later case involving similar facts the same court again assumed examination of the German acts improper, Bernstein v. N. V. Nederlandsche-Amerikaansche Stoomvaart-Maatschappij, 173 F.2d 71, but, quite evidently following the implications of Judge Hand's opinion in the earlier case, amended its mandate to permit evidence of alleged invalidity, 210 F.2d 375, subsequent to receipt by plaintiff's attorney of a letter from the Acting Legal Adviser to the State Department written for the purpose of relieving the court from any constraint upon the exercise of its jurisdiction to pass on that question.

This Court has never had occasion to pass upon the so-called *Bernstein* exception, nor need it do so now. For whatever ambiguity may be thought to exist in the two letters from State Department officials on which the Court of Appeals relied,[19] is now removed by the position which the Executive has taken in this Court on the act of state claim; respondents do not indeed contest the view that these letters were intended to reflect no more than the Department's then wish not to make any statement bearing on this litigation.

The outcome of this case, therefore, turns upon whether any of the contentions urged by respondents against the application of the act of state doctrine in the premises is acceptable: (1) that the doctrine does not apply to acts of state which violate international law, as is claimed to be the case here; (2) that the doctrine is inapplicable unless the Executive specifically interposes it in a particular case; and (3) that, in any event, the doctrine may not be invoked by a foreign government plaintiff in our courts.

V

Preliminarily, we discuss the foundations on which we deem the act of state doctrine to rest, and more particularly the question of whether state or federal law governs its application in a federal diversity case.[20]

---

19. Abram Chayes, the Legal Adviser to the State Department, wrote on October 18, 1961, in answer to an inquiry regarding the position of the Department by Mr. John Laylin, attorney for *amici*:

> The Department of State has not, in the *Bahia de Nipe* case or elsewhere, done anything inconsistent with the position taken on the Cuban nationalizations by Secretary Herter. Whether or not these nationalizations will in the future be given effect in the United States is, of course, for the courts to determine. Since the *Sabbatino* case and other similar cases are at present before the courts, any comments on this question by the Department of State would be out of place at this time. As you yourself point out, statements by the executive branch are highly susceptible of misconstruction.

A letter dated November 14, 1961, from George Ball, Under Secretary for Economic Affairs, responded to a similar inquiry by the same attorney:

> I have carefully considered your letter and have discussed it with the Legal Adviser. Our conclusion, in which the Secretary concurs, is that the Department should not comment on matters pending before the courts.

20. Although the complaint in this case alleged both diversity and federal question jurisdiction, the Court of Appeals reached jurisdiction only on the former ground. We need not decide, for reasons appearing hereafter, whether federal question jurisdiction also existed.

We do not believe that this doctrine is compelled either by the inherent nature of sovereign authority, as some of the earlier decisions seem to imply, or by some principle of international law. If a transaction takes place in one jurisdiction and the forum is in another, the forum does not by dismissing an action or by applying its own law purport to divest the first jurisdiction of its territorial sovereignty; it merely declines to adjudicate or makes applicable its own law to parties or property before it. The refusal of one country to enforce the penal laws of another is a typical example of an instance when a court will not entertain a cause of action arising in another jurisdiction. While historic notions of sovereign authority do bear upon the wisdom of employing the act of state doctrine, they do not dictate its existence.

That international law does not require application of the doctrine is evidenced by the practice of nations. Most of the countries rendering decisions on the subject fail to follow the rule rigidly. No international arbitral or judicial decision discovered suggests that international law prescribes recognition of sovereign acts of foreign governments, and apparently no claim has ever been raised before an international tribunal that failure to apply the act of state doctrine constitutes a breach of international obligation. If international law does not prescribe use of the doctrine, neither does it forbid application of the rule even if it is claimed that the act of state in question violated international law. The traditional view of international law is that it establishes substantive principles for determining whether one country has wronged another. Because of its peculiar nation-to-nation character the usual method for an individual to seek relief is to exhaust local remedies and then repair to the executive authorities of his own state to persuade them to champion his claim in diplomacy or before an international tribunal. Although it is, of course, true that United States courts apply international law as a part of our own in appropriate circumstances, Ware v. Hylton, 3 Dall. 199, 281; The Nereide, 9 Cranch 388, 423; The Paquete Habana, 175 U.S. 677, 700, the public law of nations can hardly dictate to a country which is in theory wronged how to treat that wrong within its domestic borders.

Despite the broad statement in *Oetjen* that "The conduct of the foreign relations of our Government is committed by the Constitution to the Executive and Legislative . . . Departments," it cannot of course be thought that "every case or controversy which touches foreign relations lies beyond judicial cognizance." Baker v. Carr, 369 U.S. 186, 211. The text of the Constitution does not require the act of state doctrine; it does not irrevocably remove from the judiciary the capacity to review the validity of foreign acts of state.

The act of state doctrine does, however, have "constitutional" underpinnings. It arises out of the basic relationships between branches of government in a system of separation of powers. It concerns the competency of dissimilar institutions to make and implement particular kinds of decisions in the area of international relations. The doctrine as formulated in past decisions expresses the strong sense of the Judicial Branch that its engagement in the task of passing on the validity of foreign acts of state may hinder rather than further this country's pursuit of goals both for itself and for the community of nations as a whole in the international sphere. Many commentators disagree with this view; they have striven by means of distinguishing and limiting past decisions and by advancing various considerations of policy to stimulate a narrowing of the apparent scope of the rule. Whatever considerations are thought to predominate, it is plain that the problems involved are uniquely federal in nature. If federal authority, in this instance

and those that adhere to a free enterprise system. It is difficult to imagine the courts of this country embarking on adjudication in an area which touches more sensitively the practical and ideological goals of the various members of the community of nations.[34]

The possible adverse consequences of a conclusion to the contrary ... is highlighted by contrasting the practices of the political branch with the limitations of the judicial process in matters of this kind. Following an expropriation of any significance, the Executive engages in diplomacy aimed to assure that United States citizens who are harmed are compensated fairly. Representing all claimants of this country, it will often be able, either by bilateral or multilateral talks, by submission to the United Nations, or by the employment of economic and political sanctions, to achieve some degree of general redress. Judicial determinations of invalidity of title can, on the other hand, have only an occasional impact, since they depend on the fortuitous circumstance of the property in question being brought into this country. Such decisions would, if the acts involved were declared invalid, often be likely to give offense to the expropriating country; since the concept of territorial sovereignty is so deep seated, any state may resent the refusal of the courts of another sovereign to accord validity to acts within its territorial borders. Piecemeal dispositions of this sort involving the probability of affront to another state could seriously interfere with negotiations being carried on by the Executive Branch and might prevent or render less favorable the terms of an agreement that could otherwise be reached. Relations with third countries which have engaged in similar expropriations would not be immune from effect.

The dangers of such adjudication are present regardless of whether the State Department has, as it did in this case, asserted that the relevant act violated international law. If the Executive Branch has undertaken negotiations with an expropriating country, but has refrained from claims of violation of the law of nations, a determination to that effect by a court might be regarded as a serious insult, while a finding of compliance with international law would greatly strengthen the bargaining hand of the other state with consequent detriment to American interests.

Even if the State Department has proclaimed the impropriety of the expropriation, the stamp of approval of its view by a judicial tribunal, however impartial, might increase any affront and the judicial decision might occur at a time, almost always well after the taking, when such an impact would be contrary to our national interest. Considerably more serious and far-reaching consequences would flow from a judicial finding that international law standards had been met if that determination flew in the face of a State Department proclamation to the contrary. When articulating principles of international law in its relations with other states, the Executive Branch speaks not only as an interpreter of generally accepted and traditional rules, as would the courts, but also as an advocate of standards it believes desirable for the community of nations and protective of national concerns. In short, whatever way the matter is cut, the possibility of conflict between the Judicial and Executive Branches could hardly be avoided....

Against the force of such considerations, we find respondents' countervailing arguments quite unpersuasive. Their basic contention is that United States courts could make a significant contribution to the growth of international law,

---

34. There are, of course, areas of international law in which consensus as to standards is greater and which do not represent a battleground for conflicting ideologies. This decision in no way intimates that the courts of this country are broadly foreclosed from considering questions of international law.

a contribution whose importance, it is said, would be magnified by the relative paucity of decisional law by international bodies. But given the fluidity of present world conditions, the effectiveness of such a patchwork approach toward the formulation of an acceptable body of law concerning state responsibility for expropriations is, to say the least, highly conjectural. Moreover, it rests upon the sanguine presupposition that the decisions of the courts of the world's major capital exporting country and principal exponent of the free enterprise system would be accepted as disinterested expressions of sound legal principle by those adhering to widely different ideologies ....

It is suggested that if the act of state doctrine is applicable to violations of international law, it should only be so when the Executive Branch expressly stipulates that it does not wish the courts to pass on the question of validity. We should be slow to reject the representations of the Government that such a reversal of the *Bernstein* principle would work serious inroads on the maximum effectiveness of United States diplomacy. Often the State Department will wish to refrain from taking an official position, particularly at a moment that would be dictated by the development of private litigation but might be inopportune diplomatically. Adverse domestic consequences might flow from an official stand which could be assuaged, if at all, only by revealing matters best kept secret. Of course, a relevant consideration for the State Department would be the position contemplated in the court to hear the case. It is highly questionable whether the examination of validity by the judiciary should depend on an educated guess by the Executive as to probable result and, at any rate, should a prediction be wrong, the Executive might be embarrassed in its dealings with other countries. We do not now pass on the *Bernstein* exception, but even if it were deemed valid, its suggested extension is unwarranted.

However offensive to the public policy of this country and its constituent States an expropriation of this kind may be, we conclude that both the national interest and progress toward the goal of establishing the rule of law among nations are best served by maintaining intact the act of state doctrine in this realm of its application ....

MR. JUSTICE WHITE, dissenting.

I am dismayed that the Court has, with one broad stroke, declared the ascertainment and application of international law beyond the competence of the courts of the United States in a large and important category of cases. I am also disappointed in the Court's declaration that the acts of a sovereign state with regard to the property of aliens within its borders are beyond the reach of international law in the courts of this country. However clearly established that law may be, a sovereign may violate it with impunity, except insofar as the political branches of the government may provide a remedy. This backward-looking doctrine, never before declared in this Court, is carried a disconcerting step further: not only are the courts powerless to question acts of state proscribed by international law but they are likewise powerless to refuse to adjudicate the claim founded upon a foreign law; they must render judgment and thereby validate the lawless act. Since the Court expressly extends its ruling to all acts of state expropriating property, however clearly inconsistent with the international community, all discriminatory expropriations of the property of aliens, as for example the taking of properties of persons belonging to certain races, religions or nationalities, are entitled to automatic validation in the courts of the United States. No other civilized country has found such a rigid rule necessary for the survival of the executive branch of its government; the executive of no other government seems to require such insulation from international law adjudications in its courts; and no other judiciary is apparently so incompetent to ascertain and apply international law....

I start with what I thought to be unassailable propositions: that our courts are obliged to determine controversies on their merits, in accordance with the applicable law; and that part of the law American courts are bound to administer is international law.

... The doctrine that the law of nations is a part of the law of the land, originally formulated in England and brought to America as part of our legal heritage, is reflected in the debates during the Constitutional Convention and in the Constitution itself. This Court has time and again effectuated the clear understanding of the Framers, as embodied in the Constitution, by applying the law of nations to resolve cases and controversies. As stated in The Paquete Habana, 175 U.S. 677, 700, "international law is part of our law, and must be ascertained and administered by the courts of justice of appropriate jurisdiction, as often as questions of right depending upon it are duly presented for their determination." Principles of international law have been applied in our courts to resolve controversies not merely because they provide a convenient rule for decision but because they represent a consensus among civilized nations on the proper ordering of relations between nations and the citizens thereof....

The reasons for nonreview, based as they are on traditional concepts of territorial sovereignty, lose much of their force when the foreign act of state is shown to be a violation of international law. All legitimate exercises of sovereign power, whether territorial or otherwise, should be exercised consistently with rules of international law, including those rules which mark the bounds of lawful state action against aliens or their property located within the territorial confines of the foreign state.... [T]o refuse inquiry into the question of whether norms of the international community have been contravened by the act of state under review would seem to deny the existence or purport of such norms, a view that seems inconsistent with the role of international law in ordering the relations between nations. Finally, the impartial application of international law would not only be an affirmation of the existence and binding effect of international rules of order, but also a refutation of the notion that this body of law consists of no more than the divergent and parochial views of the capital importing and exporting nations, the socialist and free-enterprise nations....

There remains for consideration the relationship between the act of state doctrine and the power of the executive over matters touching upon the foreign affairs of the Nation....

Without doubt political matters in the realm of foreign affairs are within the exclusive domain of the Executive Branch, as, for example, issues for which there are no available standards or which are textually committed by the Constitution to the executive.[20] But this is far from saying that the Constitution vests in the executive exclusive absolute control of foreign affairs or that the validity of a foreign act of

20. These issues include whether a foreign state exists or is recognized by the United States, Gelston v. Hoyt, 3 Wheat. 246; The Sapphire, 11 Wall. 164, 168; the status that a foreign state or its representatives shall have in this country (sovereign immunity), Ex parte Muir, 254 U.S. 522; Ex parte Peru, 318 U.S. 578; the territorial boundaries of a foreign state, Jones v. United States, 137 U.S. 202; and the authorization of its representatives for state-to-state negotiation, Ex parte Hitz, 111 U.S. 766; In re Baiz, 135 U.S. 403.

state is necessarily a political question. International law, as well as a treaty or executive agreement, see United States v. Pink, 315 U.S. 203, provides an ascertainable standard for adjudicating the validity of some foreign acts, and courts are competent to apply this body of law, notwithstanding that there may be some cases where comity dictates giving effect to the foreign act because it is not clearly condemned under generally accepted principles of international law. And it cannot be contended that the Constitution allocates this area to the exclusive jurisdiction of the executive, for the judicial power is expressly extended by that document to controversies between aliens and citizens or States, aliens and aliens, and foreign states and American citizens or States.

Notes and Questions

1. Prior to *Sabbatino*, the Supreme Court had indicated that the act of state doctrine was derived from principles of international law and international comity. Is that the way the Court conceives of the doctrine in *Sabbatino*? If not, what, according to the Court, is the source of the doctrine? Why does the Court in *Sabbatino* conceive of the doctrine in this way? For a thoughtful consideration of these and other questions relating to the decision, see Louis Henkin, *The Foreign Affairs Power of the Federal Courts:* Sabbatino, 64 Colum. L. Rev. 805 (1964).

2. One could describe the holding of *Sabbatino* in choice-of-law terms. Normally, in determining title to property, choice of law principles would call for applying the law of the place where the property was located. In *Sabbatino*, this presumably would mean applying the Cuban law that existed at the time of the sale of the sugar, including the Cuban expropriation decree. Courts often decline to apply foreign law, however, if it offends some fundamental public policy of the forum. *See* Restatement (Second) of Conflict of Laws §90 (1971). In *Sabbatino*, the respondents argued that Cuba had violated customary international law in expropriating the sugar, and that it would therefore violate public policy to give legal effect to the expropriation. Why does the Court reject such a public policy limitation? *See also* Anne-Marie Burley, *Law Among Liberal States: Liberal Internationalism and the Act of State Doctrine*, 92 Colum. L. Rev. 1907, 1931-36 (1992) (describing the support by academic commentators and corporate lawyers before *Sabbatino* for a public policy limitation on the act of state doctrine and how, "[a]ccording to conventional wisdom, the act of state doctrine was . . . transformed [by *Sabbatino*] from a conflicts rule, directing a court to apply a foreign law under specified conditions, to a doctrine of judicial restraint or abstention, requiring a court confronting a foreign act of state to refrain from adjudicating the validity of the act").

3. U.S. courts also commonly decline to enforce the penal and revenue laws of other nations. *See, e.g.*, Attorney General of Canada v. R.J. Reynolds Tobacco Holdings, Inc., 268 F.3d 103 (2d Cir. 2001); United States v. Boots, 80 F.3d 580 (1st Cir. 1996); Her Majesty the Queen, 597 F.2d 1161 (9th Cir. 1979); *see also* The Antelope, 23 U.S. (1 Wheat.) 66, 123 (1825) ("The Courts of no country execute the penal laws of another . . . ."). Learned Hand described the justifications for this limitation as follows:

> Even in the case of ordinary municipal liabilities, a court will not recognize those arising in a foreign state, if they run counter to the "settled public policy" of its own. Thus a scrutiny of the liability is necessarily always in reserve, and the possibility

that it will be found not to accord with the policy of the domestic state. This is not a troublesome or delicate inquiry when the question arises between private persons, but it takes on quite another face when it concerns the relations between the foreign state and its own citizens or even those who may be temporarily within its borders. To pass upon the provisions for the public order of another state is, or at any rate should be, beyond the powers of a court; it involves the relations between the states themselves, with which courts are incompetent to deal, and which are entrusted to other authorities. It may commit the domestic state to a position which would seriously embarrass its neighbor. Revenue laws fall within the same reasoning; they affect a state in matters as vital to its existence as its criminal laws. No court ought to undertake an inquiry which it cannot prosecute without determining whether those laws are consonant with its own notions of what is proper.

Moore v. Mitchell, 30 F.3d 600, 604 (2d Cir. 1929) (Hand, J., concurring); *see also* Banco Nacional de Cuba v. Sabbatino, 376 U.S. 398, 437 (1964) (noting the "desire to avoid embarrassing another state by scrutinizing its penal and revenue laws"). Courts also have reasoned that this limitation is consistent with separation of powers principles, because, if the judiciary enforced foreign penal and revenue laws, it would "risk[] being drawn into issues and disputes of foreign relations policy that are better assigned to — and better handled by — the political branches of the government." *Attorney General of Canada*, 268 F.3d at 114. This analysis resembles the analysis underlying the act of state doctrine. But if courts can properly decline to apply a foreign nation's penal and revenue laws, why can't they also decline to apply a foreign nation's expropriation laws? To put it differently, why do sovereignty and separation of powers considerations require abstention in the first situation and preclude abstention in the second? On the other hand, are the justifications for not applying foreign penal and revenue laws persuasive? For an argument that the bar on applying the penal, revenue, and other public laws of foreign nations should be reconsidered "because cooperation in the enforcement of public law would be mutually beneficial," see William S. Dodge, *Breaking the Public Law Taboo*, 43 Harv. Int'l L.J. 161, 163 (2002). *See also* European Community v. Japan Tobacco, Inc., 355 F.3d 123 (2d Cir. 2003) (concluding that the 2001 Patriot Act, which among other things amended the Racketeer Influenced Corrupt Organizations Act (RICO) to include terrorism-related offenses as predicate acts, did not show a clear intent by Congress to abrogate the revenue rule); Republic of Honduras v. Philip Morris Cos., 341 F.3d 1253 (11th Cir. 2003) (same).

In Pasquantino v. United States, 125 S. Ct. 1766 (2005), the Supreme Court held that the revenue rule did not preclude an interpretation of the federal criminal wire fraud statute as applying to a scheme to evade Canadian liquor taxes. In an opinion by Justice Thomas, the Court explained that "[t]he present prosecution is unlike the[] classic examples of actions traditionally barred by the revenue rule. It is not a suit that recovers a foreign tax liability, like a suit to enforce a judgment. This is a criminal prosecution brought by the United States in its sovereign capacity to punish domestic criminal conduct." The Court also reasoned that the prosecution "poses little risk of causing the principal evil against which the revenue rule was traditionally thought to guard: judicial evaluation of the policy-laden enactments of other sovereigns." Among other things, the Court noted that it could "assume that by electing to bring this prosecution, the Executive has assessed this prosecution's impact on this Nation's relationship with Canada, and concluded that it poses little danger of causing international friction." Are these arguments persuasive? To establish a violation of the wire fraud statute, the government must show that the object of the fraud was money or property "in the victim's hands," Cleveland v. United States, 531 U.S. 12, 26 (2000). In applying this requirement to wire fraud prosecutions based on evasion of foreign tax laws, will courts need to assess whether the foreign government had a lawful right to collect the taxes? If so, isn't that exactly what the revenue rule was designed to avoid? When a federal prosecutor brings a wire fraud case, is it fair to assume that the Executive Branch has taken the foreign relations implications of the case into account?

4. The Cuban bank's claim in *Sabbatino* (for conversion of bills of lading) was not governed by federal law. Normally, under the *Erie* doctrine, the choice-of-law principles in such a case would be decided by the law of the state in which the federal court sits. *See* Klaxon Co. v. Stentor Elec. Mfg. Co., 313 U.S. 487 (1941). In *Sabbatino*, however, the Court holds that the act of state doctrine is a rule of federal common law that displaces the state choice of law rule. What justifications does the Court give for this holding? What are the implications of this holding? Does *Sabbatino* authorize the creation of federal common law rules to govern other foreign affairs issues? (We consider this issue further in Chapters 5 and 7.)

5. In the domestic context, the Supreme Court has created a number of abstention doctrines designed to promote comity between the federal and state judicial systems. *See, e.g.,* Colorado River Water Conservation District v. United States, 424 U.S. 800 (1976) (federal courts should sometimes abstain in favor of pending state court proceedings); Younger v. Harris, 401 U.S. 37 (1971) (federal courts should ordinarily abstain from enjoining pending state court criminal proceedings); Railroad Commission of Texas v. Pullman Co., 312 U.S. 496 (1941) (federal courts should sometimes abstain from deciding uncertain questions of state law). Many courts and commentators have described the act of state doctrine as an *international* abstention doctrine, designed to promote comity among nations. Is this description consistent with the Court's characterization of the doctrine in *Sabbatino*? In any event, do courts applying the act of state doctrine really abstain from making a decision? Note that, in W.S. Kirkpatrick & Co. v. Environmental Tectonics Corp., Int'l, 493 U.S. 400 (1990), excerpted below, the Supreme Court stated that "[t]he act of state doctrine is not some vague doctrine of abstention but a '*principle of decision* binding on federal and state courts alike.'" *Id.* at 406 (quoting *Sabbatino, supra*, at 427).

6. The court of appeals in *Sabbatino*, in declining to apply the act of state doctrine, relied heavily on the letters quoted in footnote 19 of the Supreme Court's opinion, stating that, although the letters "are somewhat ambiguous, perhaps intentionally so[,] . . . they express a belief on the part of those responsible for the conduct of our foreign affairs that the courts here should decide the status here of Cuban decrees." 307 F.2d 845, 858 (2d Cir. 1962). Did the court of appeals misconstrue these letters? Note that the Justice and State Departments submitted an *amicus curiae* brief to the Supreme Court in *Sabbatino* urging the Court to apply the act of state doctrine. Among other things, the brief argued that "executive diplomatic action may be seriously impeded or embarrassed by American judicial decisions which undertake, in domestic lawsuits, to pass upon the validity of foreign acts." The brief also disputed the court of appeals' finding that the Executive Branch had supported judicial resolution of the expropriation issue. The letters referred to by the court of appeals, the brief argued, were mere refusals to comment, not an endorsement of the litigation. Finally, the brief argued that Executive Branch approval of the litigation should not be inferred from mere Executive Branch silence. (The issue of whether courts should defer to the Executive Branch in applying the act of state doctrine is explored in more detail in the materials below.) Why do you think that, at least in the Supreme Court, the Executive Branch opposed U.S. court adjudication of the validity of Cuba's expropriation?

7. As Justice White notes in dissent, the Court had stated in prior decisions that international law is part of U.S. law. *See, e.g.*, The Paquete Habana, 175 U.S. 677, 700 (1900). Does the Court in *Sabbatino* reject that proposition? If not, how does it justify its refusal to apply customary international law principles governing the expropriation of foreign citizen property? We consider this issue further in Chapter 7. Note that courts have held that a government's confiscation, within its territory, of the property of *its own citizens* does not violate customary international law. *See, e.g.*, FOGADE v. ENB Revocable Trust, 263 F.3d 1274 (11th Cir. 2001); Bank Tejarat v. Varsho-Saz, 723 F. Supp. 516, 520 (C.D. Cal. 1989); F. Palicio y Compania v. Brush, 256 F. Supp. 481, 487 (S.D.N.Y. 1966).

8. In a portion of its opinion not excerpted above, the Court in *Sabbatino* rejected the respondents' argument that, because the United States had broken off diplomatic relations with Cuba, Cuba should be denied access to U.S. courts. As the Court noted, the general rule is that foreign governments and their officials may bring civil suits in U.S. courts. *See, e.g.*, The Sapphire, 78 U.S. 164, 167 (1870). Foreign governments are not allowed to sue in U.S. courts, however, if they are not "recognized" by the United States. As discussed above in the political question materials, "recognition" is determined by the Executive Branch. However, a decision by the Executive Branch to cut off diplomatic relations with a government does not, by itself, constitute a decision not to recognize the government. *See, e.g.*, National Petrochemical Co. of Iran v. The M/T Stolt Sheaf, 860 F.2d 551 (2d Cir. 1988) (termination of diplomatic relations with Iran did not deprive the Iranian government of access to U.S. courts). For a general discussion of the rights of foreign governments in the United States, see Lori Fisler Damrosch, *Foreign States and the Constitution*, 73 Va. L. Rev. 483 (1987).

9. In response to *Sabbatino*, Congress enacted the Hickenlooper Amendment to the Foreign Assistance Act of 1964 (also called the "Second Hickenlooper Amendment"), which provides as follows:

> Notwithstanding any other provision of law, no court in the United States shall decline on the ground of the federal act of state doctrine to make a determination on the merits giving effect to the principles of international law in a case in which a claim of title or other right to property is asserted by any party including a foreign state (or a party claiming through such state) based upon (or traced through) a confiscation or other taking after January 1, 1959, by an act of that state in violation of the principles of international law, including the principles of compensation and the other standards set out in this subsection: Provided, That this subparagraph shall not be applicable (1) in any case in which an act of a foreign state is not contrary to international law or with respect to a claim of title or other right to property acquired pursuant to an irrevocable letter of credit of not more than 180 days duration issued in good faith prior to the time of the confiscation or other taking, or (2) in any case with respect to which the President determines that application of the act of state doctrine is required in that particular case by the foreign policy interests of the United States and a suggestion to this effect is filed on his behalf in that case with the court.

22 U.S.C. §2370(e)(2).

This statute was applied retroactively to the *Sabbatino* case and, as a result, Cuba's claim was ultimately dismissed. *See* 383 F.2d 166 (2d Cir. 1967). Since then, some courts have interpreted the statute narrowly, such that it applies only when (a) there are claims of *title to property* (rather than mere breach of contract claims), and (b) the property or its proceeds is presently *located in the United States*. *See, e.g.*, Compania de Gas de Nuevo Laredo, S.A. v. Entex, Inc., 686 F.2d 322 (5th Cir. 1982); Banco Nacional de Cuba v. First National City Bank of New York, 431 F.2d 394 (2d Cir. 1970), *rev'd on other grounds*, 406 U.S. 759 (1972); Banco Nacional de Cuba v. Farr, 383 F.2d 166 (2d Cir. 1967). But *cf.* West v. Bancomer, S.N.C, 807 F.2d 820, 829-30 (9th Cir. 1987) (holding that Second Hickenlooper Amendment applies to expropriation of certificates of deposit regardless of their "intangible" or "contractual" nature); Ramirez de Arellano v. Weinberger, 745 F.2d 1500, 1541 n.180 (D.C. Cir. 1984) ("It may be that a primary purpose of the statute was to prevent invocation of the act of state doctrine when property expropriated in a foreign country subsequently makes its way into the United States, but this was not the *sole* situation in which the amendment was to be activated."), *vacated and remanded*, 471 U.S. 1113 (1985).

Are these limitations supported by the language of the statute? Why do you think courts have interpreted the statute narrowly? With or without these limitations, is the statute constitutional? For an affirmative answer, see Banco Nacional de Cuba v. Farr, 383 F.2d 166 (2d Cir. 1967). The Second Hickenlooper Amendment is not the only statutory restriction imposed by Congress on the act of state doctrine. In the controversial Helms-Burton Act, enacted in 1996, Congress authorized lawsuits against individuals or companies trafficking in property confiscated by Cuba from U.S. citizens, and it expressly precluded application of the act of state doctrine to these lawsuits. *See* 22 U.S.C. §6082(a)(6). (This Act allows the President to suspend these lawsuit provisions for six-month terms, and to date presidents have repeatedly done so.) *See also* 9 U.S.C. §15 (act of state doctrine is inapplicable to enforcement of arbitration agreements and awards).

10. The act of state doctrine has been criticized by a number of scholars because, among other things, it reduces the opportunities for U.S. courts to apply customary international law. *See, e.g.*, Michael J. Bazyler, *Abolishing the Act of State Doctrine*, 134 U. Pa. L. Rev. 325 (1986); Harold Hongju Koh, *Transnational Public Law Litigation*, 100 Yale L.J. 2347, 2362-64 (1991). As we shall see in Chapter 7, however, the *Sabbatino* decision is sometimes invoked to support the argument that customary international law has the status in U.S. courts of supreme federal law. Can you see how the decision might be used in this way?

For a more general critique of the Court's reasoning in *Sabbatino*, consider the following comments by Professor Louis Henkin:

> As a principle of the Law of American Foreign Relations, rooted in enlightened United States foreign policy, there is much to be said for Act of State, perhaps also for its application in *Sabbatino*. As constitutional law, as a reflection of the role of the federal judiciary in the application of a national policy, the Court's opinion seems torn by conflicting compulsions which it did not clearly resolve. It favored the classic Act of State doctrine but could not accept the original rationale that it was required by international law or comity. Compelled to seek a basis for the doctrine in domestic law it could not accept a rationale which would release the states from the doctrine and leave an issue important to American foreign affairs to the vagaries and idiosyncrasies of the many states. Seeking a federal basis for the doctrine in supreme federal law, it could not readily find authorization for it from Congress. And the Court was reluctant to make the doctrine depend on authorization or approval of the Executive, lest the courts be, or seem, subject to political dictation from the Department of State. And so, without fully exploring the constitutional difficulties, the Court asserted an

independent judicial power to establish Act of State as supreme federal common law—apparently solely because it relates to American foreign affairs, which are "intrinsically federal," and the needs of which courts are competent to determine. The Court also rested the classic doctrine on this new foundation without explaining why its traditional scope and traditional limitations conform to the needs of American foreign policy today, or why new limitations might not now be consonant with United States policy or the needs of international order.

Louis Henkin, *The Foreign Affairs Power of the Federal Courts*: Sabbatino, 64 Colum. L. Rev. 805, 830-31 (1964). Does Henkin accurately describe the "conflicting compulsions" in the Court's opinion? What are the "constitutional difficulties" that Henkin adverts to?

For other general discussions of the act of state doctrine, see, for example, Anne-Marie Burley, *Law Among Liberal States: Liberal Internationalism and the Act of State Doctrine*, 92 Colum. L. Rev. 1907 (1992); Daniel C. K. Chow, *Rethinking the Act of State Doctrine: An Analysis in Terms of Jurisdiction to Prescribe*, 62 Wash. L. Rev. 397 (1987); Joseph W. Dellapenna, *Deciphering the Act of State Doctrine*, 35 Vill. L. Rev. 1 (1990); Malvina Halberstam, Sabbatino *Resurrected: The Act of State Doctrine in the Revised Restatement of U.S. Foreign Relations Law*, 79 Am. J. Int'l L. 68 (1985); Louis Henkin, *Act of State Today: Recollections in Tranquility*, 6 Colum. J. Transnat'l L. 175 (1967); Michael D. Ramsey, *Acts of State and Foreign Sovereign Obligations*, 39 Harv. Int'l L.J. 1 (1998); Note, *Rehabilitation and Exoneration of the Act of State Doctrine*, 12 N.Y.U. J. Int'l L. & Pol. 599 (1980); and Comment, *The Act of State Doctrine: A History of Judicial Limitations and Exceptions*, 18 Harv. Int'l L.J. 677 (1977).

2. Limitations and Exceptions

W.S. Kirkpatrick & Co. v. Environmental Tectonics Corp.

493 U.S. 400 (1990)

[Harry Carpenter, the Chairman of the Board and Chief Executive Officer of W.S. Kirkpatrick & Co. (Kirkpatrick), paid a bribe to a Nigerian citizen, Benson Akindele, to secure a contract for the construction of an aeromedical center in Nigeria. Although bribery is illegal under Nigerian law, the bribe was successful and the contract was awarded to Kirkpatrick's wholly owned subsidiary, W.S. Kirkpatrick & Co., International (Kirkpatrick International). Environmental Tectonics Corp. (ETC), an unsuccessful bidder for the Nigerian contract, learned of the bribe and alerted U.S. officials. Carpenter and Kirkpatrick were indicted for violating the Foreign Corrupt Practices Act and pleaded guilty. ETC then sued Carpenter, Akindele, and the Kirkpatrick companies under the Racketeer Influenced and Corrupt Organizations Act, the Robinson-Patman Act, and the New Jersey Anti-Racketeering Act. The defendants moved to dismiss the complaint under Rule 12(b)(6) of the Federal Rules of Civil Procedure on the ground that the action was barred by the act of state doctrine.]

JUSTICE SCALIA delivered the opinion of the Court....

The District Court, having requested and received a letter expressing the views of the legal adviser to the United States Department of State as to the applicability of the act of state doctrine, treated the motion as one for summary judgment under Rule 56 of the Federal Rules of Civil Procedure and granted the motion. The

District Court concluded that the act of state doctrine applies "if the inquiry presented for judicial determination includes the motivation of a sovereign act which would result in embarrassment to the sovereign or constitute interference in the conduct of foreign policy of the United States." Applying that principle to the facts at hand, the court held that respondent's suit had to be dismissed because in order to prevail respondent would have to show that "the defendants or certain of them intended to wrongfully influence the decision to award the Nigerian Contract by payment of a bribe, that the Government of Nigeria, its officials or other representatives knew of the offered consideration for awarding the Nigerian Contract to Kirkpatrick, that the bribe was actually received or anticipated and that 'but for' the payment or anticipation of the payment of the bribe, ETC would have been awarded the Nigerian Contract."

The Court of Appeals for the Third Circuit reversed. Although agreeing with the District Court that "the award of a military procurement contract can be, in certain circumstances, a sufficiently formal expression of a government's public interests to trigger application" of the act of state doctrine, it found application of the doctrine unwarranted on the facts of this case. The Court of Appeals found particularly persuasive the letter to the District Court from the legal adviser to the Department of State, which had stated that in the opinion of the Department judicial inquiry into the purpose behind the act of a foreign sovereign would not produce the "unique embarrassment, and the particular interference with the conduct of foreign affairs, that may result from the judicial determination that a foreign sovereign's acts are invalid." The Court of Appeals acknowledged that "the Department's legal conclusions as to the reach of the act of state doctrine are not controlling on the courts," but concluded that "the Department's factual assessment of whether fulfillment of its responsibilities will be prejudiced by the course of civil litigation is entitled to substantial respect." In light of the Department's view that the interests of the Executive Branch would not be harmed by prosecution of the action, the Court of Appeals held that Kirkpatrick had not met its burden of showing that the case should not go forward; accordingly, it reversed the judgment of the District Court and remanded the case for trial....

II

This Court's description of the jurisprudential foundation for the act of state doctrine has undergone some evolution over the years. We once viewed the doctrine as an expression of international law, resting upon "the highest considerations of international comity and expediency," Oetjen v. Central Leather Co., 246 U.S. 297, 303-304 (1918). We have more recently described it, however, as a consequence of domestic separation of powers, reflecting "the strong sense of the Judicial Branch that its engagement in the task of passing on the validity of foreign acts of state may hinder" the conduct of foreign affairs, Banco Nacional de Cuba v. Sabbatino, 376 U.S. 398, 423 (1964). Some Justices have suggested possible exceptions to application of the doctrine, where one or both of the foregoing policies would seemingly not be served: an exception, for example, for acts of state that consist of commercial transactions, since neither modern international comity nor the current position of our Executive Branch accorded sovereign immunity to such acts, see Alfred Dunhill of London, Inc. v. Republic of Cuba, 425 U.S. 682, 695-706 (1976) (opinion of White, J.); or an exception for cases in which the Executive Branch has represented that it has no objection to denying validity to the foreign sovereign act, since then the courts would be impeding no foreign policy goals, see First National City Bank v. Banco Nacional de Cuba, 406 U.S. 759, 768-770 (1972) (opinion of Rehnquist, J.).

The parties have argued at length about the applicability of these possible exceptions, and, more generally, about whether the purpose of the act of state doctrine would be furthered by its application in this case. We find it unnecessary, however, to pursue those inquiries, since the factual predicate for application of the act of state doctrine does not exist. Nothing in the present suit requires the Court to declare invalid, and thus ineffective as "a rule of decision for the courts of this country," Ricaud v. American Metal Co., 246 U.S. 304, 310 (1918), the official act of a foreign sovereign.

In every case in which we have held the act of state doctrine applicable, the relief sought or the defense interposed would have required a court in the United States to declare invalid the official act of a foreign sovereign performed within its own territory. In Underhill v. Hernandez, 168 U.S. 250, 254 (1897), holding the defendant's detention of the plaintiff to be tortious would have required denying legal effect to "acts of a military commander representing the authority of the revolutionary party as government, which afterwards succeeded and was recognized by the United States." In Oetjen v. Central Leather Co., *supra*, and in Ricaud v. American Metal Co., *supra*, denying title to the party who claimed through purchase from Mexico would have required declaring that government's prior seizure of the property, within its own territory, legally ineffective. In *Sabbatino*, upholding the defendant's claim to the funds would have required a holding that Cuba's expropriation of goods located in Havana was null and void. In the present case, by contrast, neither the claim nor any asserted defense requires a determination that Nigeria's contract with Kirkpatrick International was, or was not, effective.

Petitioners point out, however, that the facts necessary to establish respondent's claim will also establish that the contract was unlawful. Specifically, they note that in order to prevail respondent must prove that petitioner Kirkpatrick made, and Nigerian officials received, payments that violate Nigerian law, which would, they assert, support a finding that the contract is invalid under Nigerian law. Assuming that to be true, it still does not suffice. The act of state doctrine is not some vague doctrine of abstention but a "*principle of decision* binding on federal and state courts alike." *Sabbatino, supra* at 427 (emphasis added). As we said in *Ricaud*, "the act within its own boundaries of one sovereign State . . . becomes . . . a rule of decision for the courts of this country." Act of state issues only arise when a court *must decide* — that is, when the outcome of the case turns upon — the effect of official action by a foreign sovereign. When that question is not in the case, neither is the act of state doctrine. That is the situation here. Regardless of what the court's factual findings may suggest as to the legality of the Nigerian contract, its legality is simply not a question to be decided in the present suit, and there is thus no occasion to apply the rule of decision that the act of state doctrine requires . . . .

Petitioners insist, however, that the policies underlying our act of state cases — international comity, respect for the sovereignty of foreign nations on their own territory, and the avoidance of embarrassment to the Executive Branch in its conduct of foreign relations — are implicated in the present case because, as the District Court found, a determination that Nigerian officials demanded and accepted a bribe "would impugn or question the nobility of a foreign nation's motivations," and would "result in embarrassment to the sovereign or constitute interference in the conduct of foreign policy of the United States." The United States, as *amicus curiae*, favors the same approach to the act of state doctrine, though disagreeing with petitioners as to the outcome it produces in the present case. We should not, the United States urges, "attach dispositive significance to the fact that this suit involves only the 'motivation' for, rather than the 'validity' of, a foreign sovereign act," and should eschew "any rigid formula for the resolution of act of state cases generally." In some future case, perhaps, "litigation . . . based on alleged corruption in the award of contracts or other commercially oriented activities of foreign governments could sufficiently touch on 'national nerves' that the act of state doctrine or related principles of abstention would appropriately be found to bar the suit," and we should therefore resolve this case on the narrowest possible ground, viz., that the letter from the legal adviser to the District Court gives sufficient indication that, "in the setting of this case," the act of state doctrine poses no bar to adjudication.

These urgings are deceptively similar to what we said in *Sabbatino*, where we observed that sometimes, even though the validity of the act of a foreign sovereign within its own territory is called into question, the policies underlying the act of state doctrine may not justify its application. We suggested that a sort of balancing approach could be applied — the balance shifting against application of the doctrine, for example, if the government that committed the "challenged act of state" is no longer in existence. But what is appropriate in order to avoid unquestioning judicial acceptance of the acts of foreign sovereigns is not similarly appropriate for the quite opposite purpose of expanding judicial incapacities where such acts are not directly (or even indirectly) involved. It is one thing to suggest, as we have, that the policies underlying the act of state doctrine should be considered in deciding whether, despite the doctrine's technical availability, it should nonetheless not be invoked; it is something quite different to suggest that those underlying policies are a doctrine unto themselves, justifying expansion of the act of state doctrine (or, as the United States puts it, unspecified "related principles of abstention") into new and uncharted fields.

The short of the matter is this: Courts in the United States have the power, and ordinarily the obligation, to decide cases and controversies properly presented to them. The act of state doctrine does not establish an exception for cases and controversies that may embarrass foreign governments, but merely requires that, in the process of deciding, the acts of foreign sovereigns taken within their own jurisdictions shall be deemed valid. That doctrine has no application to the present case because the validity of no foreign sovereign act is at issue.

Notes and Questions

1. What limitation, precisely, does the *Kirkpatrick* decision place on the act of state doctrine? After *Kirkpatrick*, is it ever appropriate for courts to engage in case-by-case balancing in deciding whether to apply the act of state doctrine? If so, when? Note that, since *Kirkpatrick*, a number of courts have concluded that even when the requirements for the act of state doctrine are technically satisfied, the doctrine need not be applied if the foreign relations and other concerns underlying the doctrine are not implicated. *See, e.g.*, Bigio v. Coca-Cola Co., 239 F.3d 440 (2d Cir. 2000); Grupo Protexa, S.A. v. All American Marine Slip, 20 F.3d 1224 (3d Cir. 1994). Are these decisions consistent with *Kirkpatrick*? Should courts be making these foreign relations judgments?

2. In *Kirkpatrick*, the Justice and State Departments filed an *amicus curiae* brief with the Supreme Court arguing that the act of state doctrine should not be applied in that case. The analysis suggested in the brief, however, was substantially different from that adopted by the Supreme Court. The brief argued that, in deciding whether to apply the act of state doctrine, courts should consider a variety of "comity" factors, avoid any absolute distinction between validity and motivation, and give substantial deference to the Executive Branch's views regarding "whether foreign policy concerns, together with considerations made relevant by other components of the act of state doctrine, require that the court give effect to the act of a foreign state." Why did the Court reject that approach?

3. The Supreme Court has indicated that only official, public acts qualify as "acts of state" for purposes of the act of state doctrine. Thus, in Alfred Dunhill of London, Inc. v. Republic of Cuba, 425 U.S. 682 (1976), the Court refused to give effect to a repudiation of a quasi-contract obligation, noting that "[n]o statute, decree, order, or resolution of the Cuban Government itself was offered in evidence indicating that Cuba had repudiated its obligations in general or any class thereof or that it had as a sovereign matter determined to confiscate the amounts due." *Id.* at 695. How formal must the government act be in order to qualify as an act of state? If government officials engage in *illegal* activities, can those activities constitute acts of state? *Compare* Republic of the Philippines v. Marcos, 818 F.2d 1473, 1483 (9th Cir. 1987) ("Since the act of state doctrine prohibits inquiry into the legality of official governmental acts, such acts surely cannot be official only if they are legal."), *opinion withdrawn*, 832 F.2d 1110 (9th Cir. 1987), *with* Sharon v. Time, Inc., 599 F. Supp. 538, 544 (S.D.N.Y. 1984) ("The actions of an official acting outside the scope of his authority as an agent of the state are simply not acts of state. In no sense are such acts designed to give effect to a State's public interests."). *See generally* Lynn E. Parseghian, Note, *Defining the "Public Act" Requirement in the Act of State Doctrine*, 58 U. Chi. L. Rev. 1151 (1991).

4. Another limitation on the act of state doctrine is that it covers only acts by a foreign government taken within its own territory. What is the basis for this limitation? Does this territorial restriction still make sense today in this era of globalization? Note that this limitation can pose some difficult "situs" questions, especially in cases involving intangible property, such as intellectual property and debt obligations. For debt cases, courts often find that the situs is the agreed-upon place of payment. *See, e.g.*, Braka v. Bancomer, S.N.C., 762 F.2d 222 (2d Cir. 1985); Allied Bank Int'l v. Banco Credito Agricola de Cartago, 757 F.2d 516 (2d Cir. 1985); Garcia v. Chase Manhattan Bank, N.A., 735 F.2d 645 (2d Cir. 1984); Perez v. Chase Manhattan Bank, N.A., 463 N.E.2d 5 (N.Y. 1984). *See generally* Margaret E. Tahyar, Note, *The Act of State Doctrine: Resolving Debt Situs Confusion*, 86 Colum. L. Rev. 594 (1986).

5. What is the relationship between the act of state doctrine and foreign sovereign immunity? What are the similarities and differences between their underlying policies? What respective roles do they serve in foreign relations cases? Note that the FSIA's legislative history states that the FSIA "in no way affects existing law on the extent to which, if at all, the 'act of state' doctrine may be applicable." H.R. Rep. No. 94-1487, at 20.

6. As discussed in Section D, one of the most important exceptions to sovereign immunity under the FSIA is the exception for commercial activity. Should a similar exception apply to the act of state doctrine? In the *Dunhill* case, cited above in Note 3, four Justices argued for a commercial activity exception to the act of state doctrine, whereby courts could adjudicate the validity of "purely commercial" acts by foreign governments. To date, courts have not adopted such an exception, although they sometimes consider the commercial character of a foreign government act in deciding whether the policies of the doctrine are implicated in a particular case. *See, e.g.*, Honduras Aircraft Registry Ltd. v. Government of Honduras, 129 F.3d 543, 550 (11th Cir. 1997) ("[T]here is no commercial exception to the act of state doctrine as there is under the [Foreign Sovereign Immunities Act]. The factors to be considered, as recited in *Kirkpatrick*, may sometimes overlap with the FSIA commercial exception, but a commercial exception alone is not enough."). For discussion of whether there should be a commercial activity exception to the act of state doctrine, see Michael D. Ramsey, *Acts of State and Foreign Sovereign Obligations*, 39 Harv. Int'l L.J. 1 (1998); Jonathan M. Wight, *An Evaluation of the Commercial Activities Exception to the Act of State Doctrine*, 19 Dayton L. Rev. 1265 (1994); Russ Schlossbach, Note, *Arguably Commercial, Ergo Adjudicable?: The Validity of a Commercial Activity Exception to the Act of State Doctrine*, 18 B.U. Int'l L.J. 139 (2000).

7. There is also an exception in the FSIA for counterclaims. Even before the FSIA was enacted, the Supreme Court had recognized a counterclaim exception to foreign sovereign immunity, *See* National City Bank of New York v. Republic of China, 348 U.S. 356, 363 (1955). The Court in *Sabbatino*, however, in a portion of the opinion not excerpted above, rejected a counterclaim exception to the act of state doctrine. The Court reasoned that (a) foreign governments could attempt to get around this exception by assigning their claims; (b) if the exception applied to assignees it could undermine the security of titles; (c) the exception would encourage claimants to engage in self-help remedies in an effort to cause the foreign government to become the plaintiff; and (d) the act of state doctrine rests on different policies than foreign sovereign immunity. *See* 376 U.S. at 437-39. Are these points persuasive? In First National City Bank v. Banco Nacional de Cuba, 406 U.S. 759 (1972), the State Department supported a counterclaim exception to the doctrine, but only Justice Douglas clearly accepted such an exception (although Justices Rehnquist, Burger, and White also appeared sympathetic to such an exception).

8. In *Sabbatino*, the Court stated that the act of state doctrine should be applied "in the absence of a treaty or other unambiguous agreement regarding controlling legal principles." The Court also stated that "the greater the degree of codification or consensus concerning a particular area of international law, the more appropriate it is for the judiciary to render decisions regarding it." Consistent with these statements, courts generally have not applied the act of state doctrine to bar treaty claims. *See, e.g.*, Kalamazoo Spice Extraction Co. v. Provisional Military Government of Socialist Ethiopia, 729 F.2d 422 (6th Cir. 1984); American Int'l Group, Inc. v. Islamic Republic of Iran, 493 F. Supp. 522 (D.D.C. 1980), *vacated on other grounds*, 657 F.2d 430 (D.C. Cir. 1981); *see also* Ramirez de Arellano v. Weinberger, 745 F.2d 1500, 1540 (D.C. Cir. 1984) ("[T]he doctrine was never intended to apply when an applicable bilateral treaty governs the legal merits of the controversy."), *vacated and remanded*, 471 U.S. 1113 (1985). *But cf.* Callejo v. Bancomer, S.A., 764 F.2d 1101 (5th Cir. 1985) (suggesting that act of state doctrine might bar some treaty claims). Should some *customary international law* claims be exempt from the act of state doctrine? What if there is a high degree of international consensus regarding the customary international law rule? What if the rule is considered a *jus cogens* norm?

9. The Court in *Sabbatino* reserved judgment on the existence of a "*Bernstein*" exception to the act of state doctrine, whereby courts would decline to apply the act of state doctrine when informed by the Executive Branch that it had no objection to the litigation. (The Second Circuit had endorsed such an exception prior to *Sabbatino* in Bernstein v. N. V. Nederlandsche-Amerikaansche, 210 F.2d 375 (2d Cir. 1954), a case involving an expropriation of property by the Nazis.) In the *City Bank* decision, cited above in Note 7, three Justices (Rehnquist, Burger, and White) argued for a *Bernstein* exception. They reasoned that:

> The act of state doctrine, as reflected in the cases culminating in *Sabbatino*, is a judicially accepted limitation on the normal adjudicative processes of the courts, springing from the thoroughly sound principle that on occasion individual litigants may have to forgo decision on the merits of their claims because the involvement of the courts in such a decision might frustrate the conduct of the Nation's foreign policy. It would be wholly illogical to insist that such a rule, fashioned because of fear that adjudication would interfere with the conduct of foreign relations, be applied in the face of an assurance from that branch of the Federal Government that conducts foreign relations that such a result would not obtain.

In splintered opinions, however, the other six Justices in *City Bank* rejected a *Bernstein* exception. Justice Powell, for example, stated in a concurrence that "the reasoning of *Sabbatino* implicitly rejects that exception" and that he "would be uncomfortable with a doctrine which would require the judiciary to receive the Executive's permission before invoking its jurisdiction." More colorfully, Justice Douglas stated in a concurrence that courts should not become "a mere errand boy for the Executive Branch which may choose to pick some people's chestnuts from the fire, but not others'." And Justice Brennan argued in a four-Justice dissent that avoidance of embarrassment of the Executive Branch in foreign relations is only one of the policies underlying the act of state doctrine and that the other policies are still served when the State Department indicates that it does not oppose the litigation. Justice Brennan further observed that, "As six members of this Court recognize today, the reasoning of that case is clear that the representations of the Department of State are entitled to weight for the light they shed on the permutation and combination of factors underlying the act of state doctrine. But they cannot be determinative." Although the lower federal courts have not applied a *Bernstein* exception since *City Bank*, they do continue to give some weight (but not conclusive weight) to the views of the Executive Branch in deciding whether to apply the act of state doctrine. *See, e.g.*, Environmental Tectonics v. W.S. Kirkpatrick, Inc., 847 F.2d 1052, 1062 (3d Cir. 1988), *aff'd on other grounds*, 493 U.S. 400 (1990); Kalamazoo Spice Extraction Co. v. Provisional Military Gov't of Socialist Ethiopia, 729 F.2d 422, 427-28 (6th Cir. 1984). Is such deference warranted? For a discussion of this issue, see Curtis A. Bradley, Chevron *Deference and Foreign Affairs*, 86 Va. L. Rev. 649, 716-21 (2000).

F. INTERNATIONAL COMITY

Ungaro-Benages v. Dresdner Bank AG

379 F.3d 1227 (11th Cir. 2004)

[The plaintiff, Ursula Ungaro-Benages, sued Dresdner Bank and Deutsche Bank, alleging that during the Nazi regime in Germany the two banks stole her family's interest in a manufacturing company. The district court dismissed the case on multiple grounds, including the political question doctrine and international comity, while also rejecting the defendants' act of state doctrine defense.]

KRAVITCH, CIRCUIT JUDGE....

In the 1990s, class-action lawsuits against the German government and private German companies [arising from Nazi-era expropriations and related issues] increased dramatically in American courts, which caused considerable concern in Germany. In an effort to stem American litigation, the German government sought to enter into an international agreement with the United States to remove this litigation to an alternative forum based in Germany.

In 2000, President Clinton entered into an agreement with the German government ("the Foundation Agreement") aimed at achieving a "legal peace."[4] See Agreement concerning the Foundation "Remembrance, Responsibility and the Future," July 17, 2000, U.S.-F.R.G., 39 I.L.M. 1298. In the agreement, the German government agreed to establish a private foundation, the Foundation "Remembrance, Responsibility, and the Future" ("the Foundation"), to hear claims brought by victims of the Nazi regime. The Foundation is funded by voluntary contributions from the German government and German companies. Both the United States government and the German government argue that this fund offers compensation to victims of the Nazi regime that would not be available through traditional litigation.

In return, the United States agreed to encourage its courts and state governments to respect the Foundation as the exclusive forum for claims from the National Socialist era. The agreement, however, did not suspend or transfer lawsuits in American courts to Germany. Instead, the United States promised to file a Statement of Interest in any lawsuit dealing with WWII restitution or reparations.[6] The statement would inform United States courts that it is in the foreign policy interests of the United States for the case to be dismissed on any valid legal ground but would not suggest that the agreement itself provides an independent legal basis for dismissal....

The plaintiff argues that the [Foundation Agreement] does not cover her suit because the relevant transactions took place before World War II, but the treaty's scope includes any actions committed during the National Socialist era. Article 1 states:

> The parties agree that the Foundation 'Remembrance, Responsibility and the Future' covers, and that it would be in their interests for the Foundation to be the exclusive remedy and forum for the resolution of, *all claims that have been or may be asserted against German companies arising from the National Socialist era* and World War II.

Foundation Agreement, art. I, para. 1. Furthermore, the agreement explicitly covers property claims. In Annex B, the United States government agreed to submit a statement of interest to federal courts announcing that the Foundation is the preferred forum for "the resolution of all asserted claims against German companies arising from their involvement in the National Socialist era and World War II, including without limitation those relating to ... damage to or *loss of property, includ-*

4. The agreement was concluded by the President without ratification by either 2/3 of the Senate or a majority vote of Congress.
6. The United States filed such a statement in this case, both before the district court and before this court.

ing banking assets and insurance policies." Foundation Agreement, Annex B, para. 1 (emphasis added).

The Foundation Agreement, however, does not provide the substantive law to resolve the case before us because it neither settles the outstanding claim nor directs that all claims be transferred to the Foundation's settlement procedures. Rather, the United States simply promises to announce that such a transfer is in the United States' national interests. In Annex B, the United States government is obliged to inform domestic courts that its policy interests "favor dismissal on any valid legal ground," but "does not suggest that its policy interests concerning the Foundation in themselves provide an independent legal basis for dismissal." Foundation Agreement, Annex B, para. 7. Thus, by its own terms, the agreement does not provide a basis to dismiss or suspend litigation against German companies stemming from their actions during the National Socialist era.

Because the Foundation Agreement firmly establishes that issues related to litigation against German corporations from the National Socialist era are governed by federal law, but does not provide any substantive principles by which to adjudicate this case, we must examine federal law not based in treaty to resolve the issues presented here. . . .

[The court declined to uphold dismissal of the case under the political question doctrine, reasoning that "[a]djudication of the present claim would not interfere with the executive's handling of foreign relations or show a lack of respect to the executive's power in foreign affairs." It then turned to consider the doctrine of international comity.]

International comity reflects "the extent to which the law of one nation, as put in force within its territory, whether by executive order, by legislative act, or by judicial decree, shall be allowed to operate within the dominion of another nation." Hilton v. Guyot, 159 U.S. 113, 163 (1895). It is an abstention doctrine: A federal court has jurisdiction but defers to the judgment of an alternative forum. Turner Entm't Co. v. Degeto Film, 25 F.3d 1512, 1518 (11th Cir. 1994).[13] International comity serves as a guide to federal courts where "the issues to be resolved are entangled in international relations." In re Maxwell Communication Corp., 93 F.3d 1036, 1047 (2d Cir. 1996). The district court dismissed this case on international comity grounds in favor of resolution at the Foundation because the Foundation is a specialized system, supported by the United States government and the international community, for addressing Nazi era claims. The district court further considered that all of the relevant transactions leading to this suit took place in Germany and, thus, Germany was the most appropriate forum state for the resolution of these claims.

The doctrine of international comity can be applied retrospectively or prospectively. When applied retrospectively, domestic courts consider whether to respect the judgment of a foreign tribunal or to defer to parallel foreign proceedings. *See, e.g.,* Finanz AG Zurich v. Banco Economico S.A., 192 F.3d 240 (2d Cir. 1999) (affording comity in deference to concurrent foreign bankruptcy proceedings); Turner Entm't, 25 F.3d at 1514 (staying domestic legal proceedings to defer to concurrent German proceedings on the merits of the dispute); *see also* Canadian

13. Abstention doctrines are prudential doctrines and this court is not obligated under American statutory law to defer to foreign courts. *Turner Entm't,* 25 F.3d at 1518 ("Federal courts have a 'virtually unflagging obligation' to exercise the jurisdiction conferred upon them. Nevertheless, in some private international disputes the prudent and just action for a federal court is to abstain from the exercise of jurisdiction.") (internal citations omitted).

Southern Ry. v. Gebhard, 109 U.S. 527 (1883) (dismissing the claims of American railroad bond holders in favor of Canadian legislation and legal proceedings aimed at reorganizing the railroad's corporate structure).

When applied prospectively, domestic courts consider whether to dismiss or stay a domestic action based on the interests of our government, the foreign government and the international community in resolving the dispute in a foreign forum. *See* Bi v. Union Carbide Chems. & Plastics Co., 984 F.2d 582 (2d Cir. 1993) (dismissing the claims of Indian nationals injured by a chemical plant explosion in Bhopal based on Indian legislation granting the Indian government exclusive standing to represent all victims); *see also* Jota v. Texaco, 157 F.3d 153 (2d Cir. 1998) (considering whether to dismiss proceedings related to environmental damage in Equador based on Equador's interest in foreign or domestic resolution and holding dismissal on grounds of forum non conveniens and comity erroneous); Pravin Banker Assocs. v. Banco Popular Del Peru., 109 F.3d 850 (2d Cir. 1997) (considering whether to stay proceedings brought by an American holder of Peruvian debt while Peru attempted to renegotiate its commercial debt under the Brady Plan).

The analysis for both forms of international comity embody similar concerns with foreign governments' interests, fair procedures, and American public policy, but they emphasize different issues. When applied retrospectively, federal courts evaluate three factors: (1) whether the foreign court was competent and used "proceedings consistent with civilized jurisprudence," (2) whether the judgment was rendered by fraud, and (3) whether the foreign judgment was prejudicial because it violated American public policy notions of what is decent and just. Courts also consider whether the central issue in dispute is a matter of foreign law and whether there is a prospect of conflicting judgments.

Applied prospectively, federal courts evaluate several factors, including the strength of the United States' interest in using a foreign forum, the strength of the foreign governments' interests, and the adequacy of the alternative forum. Our determination of the adequacy of the alternative forum is informed by *forum non conveniens* analysis. *See* Jota, 157 F.3d at 161 (noting that forum non conveniens analysis on the adequacy of the foreign forum is equally pertinent to international comity analysis); *see also* Ford v. Brown, 319 F.3d 1302, 1304 n.3 [Republic of Austria v. Altmann, 124 S. Ct. 2240 2255 (2004)] (finding that the international comity analysis and the forum non conveniens calculus were intertwined).

Here, we decide to abstain based on the strength of our government's interests in using the Foundation, the strength of the German government's interests, and the adequacy of the Foundation as an alternative forum. The United States government has consistently supported the Foundation as the exclusive forum for the resolution of litigation against German corporations related to their acts during the National Socialist era. The President entered into negotiations with the German government and determined that the interests of American citizens, on the whole, would be best served by establishing the Foundation Agreement.[14] The agreement offers monetary compensation to nationals who were used as slave labor and were victims of insurance fraud as well as those deprived of their property. The fund to provide this compensation was established with the expectation

---

14. Even if the governments had not engaged in negotiations on this issue, the executive's statements of national interest in issues affecting our foreign relations are entitled to deference. See Altmann, 124 S. Ct. at 2255.

that all such American litigation against German corporations would be resolved at the Foundation. In creating a comprehensive compensatory scheme for all remaining victims of the Nazi era, the Foundation Agreement may end up favoring the monetary interests of some American victims more than others. International agreements, however, often favor some domestic interests over others, and the President has the constitutional authority to settle the international claims of American citizens, even if the claimants would prefer litigation in American courts. Likewise, the German government has a significant interest in having the Foundation be the exclusive forum for these claims in its efforts to achieve lasting legal peace with the international community.

Furthermore, the Foundation is an adequate alternative forum. The tribunal has a speciality in the relevant post-war law and has relaxed standards of proof to ease the burden for the potential plaintiffs to obtain compensation. The Foundation offers victims of the Nazi era an adequate remedy, even if the Foundation cannot provide as substantial an award as American courts. *See* Piper Aircraft Co. v. Reyno, 454 U.S. 235, 254 (1981) (noting that a forum can be adequate even where there is the potential for a smaller damage award).

The plaintiff maintains that the forum does not provide her with a remedy because her claims are barred under the Foundation Agreement. Our reading of the Foundation Agreement, however, does not lead us to the conclusion that her claims necessarily would be barred. Annex A of the agreement specifically addresses claims of deprivation of property by German companies based on discrimination. That provision provides that the plaintiff's claims would be barred if her family could have received compensation under the German restitution laws. The plaintiff is free to argue to the Foundation, just as she has argued to this court, that her claims should not be barred because the defendant banks prevented her family from pursuing their property claims after the war. The Foundation is in just as good a position as this court to consider the allegedly fraudulent acts by the defendant banks and is likely to be far more familiar than this court with German law on the relevant issues.

Moreover, if we did not abstain on international comity grounds, we would have to address whether the plaintiff's claim is barred under American law based on the statute of limitations. The plaintiff's grandmother, from whom the plaintiff's claim is derivative, began proceedings to recover her family's assets in 1950 but then failed to pursue her claim. The district court, applying German law, found that the plaintiff's claim was time barred. We do not reach the issue because we defer to the Foundation, but note the plaintiff faces similar hurdles in federal court to those she would face at the Foundation.

We recognize that the plaintiff would prefer to pursue her claim in federal court. She is an American citizen, and even though her claim is derivative of her grandmother, we give particular attention to her choice of forum. On balance, however, we find that the strength of the interests held by the American government and the German government outweigh the plaintiff's preference. In doing so, we note that American and German governments have entered into extensive negotiations over this subject and those negotiations affect thousands of other victims of the Nazi regime. While we do not use the Foundation Agreement as an independent legal basis to dismiss this case, we must take the governments' ongoing interests in settling claims from the National Socialist era and World War II into account in our international comity analysis. We further note that all of the relevant events implicated in this litigation took place in Germany and will involve issues of German law. Finally, the plaintiff has an alternative forum, established in part by the United States government, where she can seek redress.

Notes and Questions

1. International comity is a multi-faceted doctrine. At the most abstract level, international comity refers to the respect that U.S. courts give to the laws, acts, and decisions of foreign countries. As the Supreme Court famously stated (in a case involving an attempt to enforce a foreign judgment in a U.S. court):

> "Comity," in the legal sense, is neither a matter of absolute obligation, on the one hand, nor of mere courtesy and good will, upon the other. But it is the recognition which one nation allows within its territory to the legislative, executive, or judicial acts of another nation, having due regard both to international duty and convenience, and to the rights of its own citizens or of other persons who are under the protection of its laws.

Hilton v. Guyot, 159 U.S. 113, 163-64 (1895). *See also* Societe Nationale Industrielle Aerospatiale v. United States District Court, 482 U.S. 522, 543 n.27 (1987) ("Comity refers to the spirit of cooperation in which a domestic tribunal approaches the resolution of cases touching the laws and interests of other sovereign states."); Hartford Fire Ins. Co. v. California, 509 U.S. 764 (1993) (Scalia, J., dissenting) (defining "the comity of courts" as a decision by a court in one country to decline jurisdiction "over matters more appropriately adjudged elsewhere"). International comity arises in a variety of contexts, including the recognition and enforcement of foreign judgments, the stay or dismissal of U.S. litigation because of similar litigation already pending in a foreign country, international anti-suit injunctions, and the stay or dismissal of U.S. litigation because of a determination that the case is best brought in a foreign or international or related forum, regardless of whether proceedings have actually begun there. Below we consider each of these situations.

2. Although the Constitution's Full Faith and Credit clause requires each U.S. state to recognize and enforce the judgments of other states, see U.S. Const. art. IV, §1, U.S. courts are not under any constitutional, federal statutory, or treaty obligation to recognize or enforce foreign judgments. As early as 1895, however, the Supreme Court held that foreign judgments are generally enforceable as a matter of common law "comity," subject to a "reciprocity" requirement whereby the foreign government would have to enforce similar U.S. judgments. *See* Hilton v. Guyot, 159 U.S. 113 (1895). Today, enforcement of foreign judgments is generally viewed as governed by state law (either under state common law or state codifications of the Uniform Foreign Money Judgments Recognition Act, 13 U.L.A. 261 (1986 & Supp.)). Under most of these state laws, courts will presumptively recognize and enforce foreign judgments, even in the absence of reciprocity, as long as the foreign court had jurisdiction, the foreign proceedings were procedurally fair, and enforcement does not offend a fundamental public policy. As a result, foreign judgments are often recognized and enforced in the United States, although these judgments receive somewhat less respect in U.S. courts than the judgments of sister states. For cases in which U.S. courts have declined to enforce foreign judgments because of public policy concerns, see, for example, Matusevitch v. Telnikoff, 877 F. Supp. 1 (D.D.C. 1995) (declining to enforce libel judgment from England because doing so would, in light of the lower speech protections in England, violate

public policy); Bachchan v. India Abroad Publications, Inc., 585 N.Y.S.2d 661 (N.Y. Sup. Ct. 1992) (similar). Is it appropriate for U.S. courts to scrutinize foreign judgments in this way? Might such scrutiny undermine U.S. foreign relations?

3. Sometimes courts defer out of comity not to foreign judgments, but rather to foreign judicial proceedings. In such cases, U.S. courts may decide to stay or dismiss litigation in the United States when similar or related litigation is pending in a foreign country. *See, e.g.*, Zurich v. Banco Economico, S.A., 192 F.3d 240 (2d Cir. 1999); Turner Entertainment Co. v. Degeto Film GmbH, 25 F.3d 1512 (11th Cir. 1994); *cf.* Seguros del Estado, S.A. v. Sci. Games, Inc., 262 F.3d 1164 (11th Cir. 2001) (declining to stay U.S. suit out of deference to foreign proceeding because the foreign suit involved materially different issues, documents, and parties). Courts disagree about the precise standards for this sort of "international abstention," with some courts holding that it is appropriate only in exceptional circumstances and other courts holding that there is broad discretion to avoid such duplicative litigation. *See Turner*, 25 F.3d at 1518 (describing differing approaches).

Occasionally U.S. courts will do essentially the opposite of international abstention: they will issue a so-called "anti-suit" injunction to prevent persons or entities subject to their personal jurisdiction from pursuing litigation in foreign tribunals. *See, e.g.*, Laker Airways Ltd. v. Sabena, Belgian World Airlines, 731 F.2d 909 (D.C. Cir. 1984). As with stays in the face of foreign proceedings, courts disagree about the precise standards for issuing anti-suit injunctions, with some courts holding that they are appropriate whenever there is a duplication of parties and issues and the prosecution of simultaneous proceedings would frustrate the speedy and efficient determination of the case, and other courts focusing more narrowly on whether the foreign action imperils the jurisdiction of the forum court or threatens some strong national policy. *See* Quaak v. Klynveld Peat Marwick Goerdeler Bedrijfsrevisoren, 361 F.3d 11, 17-19 (1st Cir. 2004) (describing differing approaches). Considerations of comity are viewed as favoring a stay of U.S. litigation in the face of foreign parallel proceedings, and as weighing against the issuance of an anti-suit injunction that would stop a foreign proceeding.

In both situations, international comity is viewed as favoring foreign over U.S. litigation. Does this make sense? Isn't comity a two-way street? Should U.S. court reliance on comity depend on whether the foreign nation in question gives comity to U.S. proceedings?

4. International comity can involve respect not only for foreign judicial proceedings, but also for foreign laws. Consider, for example, Bi v. Union Carbide Chemical and Plastics Co., 984 F. 2d 582 (2d Cir. 1993). The issue in *Bi* was whether U.S. courts should defer to an Indian statute that gave the Indian government exclusive standing to represent the victims of the Bhopal toxic tort disaster in India in a suit against a U.S. company and its Indian subsidiary. Pursuant to this statute, the Indian government had earlier brought suit in Indian courts to resolve the Bhopal matter, and had reached a comprehensive settlement approved by the Indian Supreme Court. The suit in *Bi* was an attempt by plaintiffs unhappy with the Indian settlement to litigate their claims in the United States. The *Bi* court, characterizing the issue as one "involving comity among nations," rejected the suit. Relying in part on the fact that India was a democratic nation, and in part on the logic of the act of state doctrine, the court reasoned:

> To grant the victims of the Bhopal disaster, most of whom are citizens of India, access to our courts when India has set up what it believes to be the most effective method of

dealing with a difficult problem would frustrate India's efforts .... [W]ere we to pass on the validity of India's response to a disaster that occurred within its borders, it would disrupt our relations with the country and frustrate the efforts of the international community to develop methods to deal with problems of this magnitude in the future.

Id. at 586. Why should an Indian statute rather than U.S. law determine the scope of jurisdiction in U.S. federal courts in cases involving the behavior of U.S. corporations? Why does it matter to the court that India is a democracy? Is the act of state doctrine relevant here?

   5. Considerations of comity can also arise when courts are asked to abstain not in the face of a foreign judicial proceeding or law, but rather in the face of some alternate foreign or international effort to resolve issues related to the litigation. For example, in Pravin Banker Assocs. v. Banco Popular Del Peru, 109 F.3d 850 (2d Cir. 1997), a Peruvian bank that had defaulted on loans from American financial institutions sought to stay enforcement proceedings in the United States while it attempted to restructure its commercial debt under a plan worked out by U.S. Treasury Secretary Nicholas Brady. The court stated that "[u]nder the principles of international comity, United States courts ordinarily refuse to review acts of foreign governments and defer to proceedings taking place in foreign countries, allowing those acts and proceedings to have extraterritorial effect in the United States," but emphasized that international comity "remains a rule of 'practice, convenience, and expediency' rather than of law." *Id.* at 854. It noted that there were two competing U.S. government policy interests in the case: foreign debt resolution under the Brady plan, and ensuring the enforceability of valid debts. Because the district court had previously granted a six-month stay (thus serving to some degree the first interest), the court of appeals concluded (in agreement with the district court) that a further stay would unduly prejudice the second interest. The court did not expressly consider Peru's interest, or the adequacy of the alternative forum. But it did note that granting a stay would have "converted what the United States intended to be voluntary and open-ended negotiations between Peru and its creditors into the equivalent of a judicially-enforced bankruptcy proceeding, for it would, in effect, have prohibited the exercise of legal rights outside of the negotiations." *Id.* at 855. For somewhat similar reasoning, see Bodner v. Banque Paribas, 114 F. Supp. 2d 117, 129-30 (E.D.N.Y. 2000) (declining to defer under international comity to independent commissions formed by the French government to study and propose solutions to Holocaust-era atrocities, reasoning that the suit would not impede the commissions' work, and that in any event the commissions were too informal and did not provide "a conflicting judicial, legislative, or executive act to which this Court could reasonably defer").

   6. In what ways does *Ungaro-Benages* extend the international comity doctrine beyond the decisions described in the above Notes? Why is it appropriate for a U.S. court to dismiss a case brought by a U.S. citizen, over which the court has jurisdiction, in favor of a private, non-U.S., non-judicial claims settlement mechanism that might not provide the plaintiff with relief? Why is the Foundation an adequate alternative forum? Is it true, as the court maintains, that the private German Foundation "is in just as good a position as this court to consider the allegedly fraudulent acts by the defendant banks"? Why does it matter that "all of the relevant events implicated in this litigation took place in Germany and will involve issues of German law"?

   7. In *Ungaro-Benages* the governmental interest analysis was relatively straightforward, since both countries evinced a clear preference for the Foundation in the agreement setting it up. What would happen, however, if there were no such evidence of the governments' relative interests? How would the court decide? Does a court have competence to make such decisions in the absence of express guidance from the governments themselves?

8. More generally, what role did the Foundation Agreement play in the court's decision to abstain in *Ungaro-Benages*? Did the Foundation Agreement impose any *legal* obligations to dismiss the suit? Does it matter that the President entered into this international agreement with Germany on his own authority, without the consent of either the Senate or Congress? As we will learn in Chapter 6, the Supreme Court has recognized presidential authority to enter into so-called "executive agreements" of this sort, and courts have traditionally deferred to such agreements when they require dismissal of suits in U.S. courts in favor of foreign forums. The Foundation Agreement, however, does not compel dismissal in favor of a foreign forum; rather, it simply compels the Executive Branch to urge courts to so dismiss. The Executive Branch did file a "Statement of Interest" in the *Ungaro-Benages* case that stated that the "President of the United States concluded that it would be in the foreign policy interests of the United States for the Foundation to be the exclusive forum and remedy for the resolution of all asserted claims against German companies arising from their involvement in the Nazi era and World War II." Should courts defer to such presidential suggestions in this context? Would the result in the case have been different if the Executive Branch had not suggested dismissal? Would it have been different if Germany had, without U.S. cooperation or pressure, unilaterally established the Foundation to resolve Nazi expropriation claims?

9. The court's application of comity in *Ungaro-Benages* is similar to the forum non conveniens doctrine. Under the forum non conveniens doctrine as applied by federal courts, district courts have discretion to dismiss a case if they determine that there is an adequate alternate forum and various private and public interest factors weigh in favor of adjudicating the case in that forum. *See* Piper Aircraft Co. v. Reyno, 454 U.S. 235 (1981). In determining whether an alternate forum is "adequate," courts look primarily at whether the forum would have jurisdiction to hear the dispute and the ability to provide a remedy. Ordinarily, an alternate forum will not be considered inadequate merely because its laws or procedures are less favorable to the plaintiff than those of the United States. The private interest factors to be considered in the forum non conveniens analysis include "the 'relative ease of access to sources of proof; availability of compulsory process for attendance of unwilling, and the cost of obtaining attendance of willing, witnesses; possibility of view of premises, if view would be appropriate to the action; and all other practical problems that make trial of a case easy, expeditious and inexpensive.'" *Id.* at 241 n.6 (quoting Gulf Oil Corp. v. Gilbert, 330 U.S. 501, 508 (1947)). The public interest factors include "the administrative difficulties flowing from court congestion; the 'local interest in having localized controversies decided at home'; the interest in having the trial of a diversity case in a forum that is at home with the law that must govern the action; the avoidance of unnecessary problems in conflict of laws, or in the application of foreign law; and the unfairness of burdening citizens in an unrelated forum with jury duty." *Id.* In considering these factors, courts apply a presumption in favor of the plaintiff's choice of forum, although less of a presumption is given when the plaintiff is a foreign citizen. *See id.* at 256.

The court in *Ungaro*-Benages states that its determination of the adequacy of the alternative forum is "informed by *forum non conveniens* analysis," but otherwise it treats the prospective application of comity as a separate doctrine from forum non conveniens. Why didn't the court simply apply the forum non conveniens doctrine? How does the court's application of comity differ from the forum non conveniens doctrine? Does it makes sense to have both a comity doctrine like the one applied by the court and a forum non conveniens doctrine?

10. The court in *Ungaro-Benages* describes international comity as an "abstention" doctrine. That is, under the court's approach to comity, U.S. courts are to abstain from exercising their jurisdiction over certain international cases out of deference to, among other things, foreign government interests and proceedings (or potential proceedings). There are a number of *domestic* abstention doctrines, pursuant to which federal courts will abstain from adjudicating an issue or a case in favor of pending or future litigation in state court. *See generally* Richard H. Fallon, Jr., Daniel J. Meltzer & David L. Shapiro, Hart & Wechsler's The Federal Courts and the Federal System 1186-1229 (5th ed. 2003). Although domestic abstention doctrines are extraordinarily complex, the following three factors are usually involved:

> First, the plaintiff claims that a provision of state law is invalid by reason of federal law, whether by constitutional invalidity, or federal preemption, or the like. Second, the state legal provision is ambiguous in terms of the allegedly superseding federal provision; that is, the state provision is susceptible of being construed or applied in a way that would not run afoul of federal law. Third, the legal issue thus posed already has arisen in a pending state proceeding or would so arise in a state proceeding if the legal controversy went forward in the normal course of events.

Fleming James, Jr., Geoffrey C. Hazard, Jr., & John Leubsdorf, Civil Procedure §2.29 at 149-50 (5th ed. 2001). How, if at all, do the justifications for domestic abstention — having to do with federal courts trying to avoid resolving sensitive federal questions out of respect to the state court system — translate into the international arena?

11. To what extent should U.S. courts give comity to the decisions of international tribunals? The Supreme Court was faced with this issue in Medellin v. Dretke, 125 S. Ct. 2088 (2005). That case concerned the effect in the U.S. legal system of a decision of the International Court of Justice (ICJ), Case Concerning Avena and Other Mexican Nationals (Mexico v. United States) (2003). In *Avena*, the ICJ had ordered the United States to provide review and reconsideration of the convictions and sentences of 51 Mexican nationals on death row throughout the United States. In its decision, the ICJ found that state authorities in the United States had violated the Vienna Convention on Consular Relations (a multilateral treaty that the United States has been a party to since 1969) by failing to advise the Mexican nationals that they had the right to have their consulate notified of their arrest and to seek assistance from their consulate. The ICJ also interpreted the consular notice provision in the Vienna Convention as conferring individually enforceable rights, as it had done in an earlier in an earlier decision involving violations of the Vienna Convention with respect to German nationals, LaGrand Case (Federal Republic of Germany v. United States) (2001).

Jose Medellin, one of the Mexican nationals covered by *Avena*, filed a habeas corpus action in a federal court in Texas based on the Vienna Convention violation, but both the district court and the U.S. Court of Appeals for the Fifth Circuit denied relief. The Supreme Court granted certiorari on two issues:

> 1. In a case brought by a Mexican national whose rights were adjudicated in the *Avena* Judgment, must a court in the United States apply as the rule of decision, notwith-

standing any inconsistent United States precedent, the *Avena* holding that the United States courts must review and reconsider the national's conviction and sentence, without resort to procedural default doctrines?

2. In a case brought by a foreign national of a State party of the Vienna Convention, should a court in the United States give effect to the *LaGrand* and *Avena* Judgments as a matter of international judicial comity and in the interest of uniform treaty interpretation?

After the Court agreed to hear *Medellin*, President Bush sent a memorandum to the Attorney General stating that the United States would comply with the *Avena* decision by "having State courts given effect to the decision in accordance with general principles of comity in cases filed by the 51 Mexican nationals addressed in that decision." The Executive Branch stated in its brief to the Supreme Court, however, that it disagreed with the ICJ's conclusion that the Vienna Convention itself created individually enforceable rights, and it also argued that the *Avena* decision did not have direct effect in the U.S. legal system. The Supreme Court subsequently heard oral argument in the case, and then issued a per curiam decision dismissing the writ of certiorari in the case as improvidently granted. The Court noted that there were a number of jurisdictional and procedural issues that could preclude Medellin from obtaining the federal habeas corpus relief that he was seeking, and the Court noted "the possibility that the Texas courts will provide Medellin with the review he seeks pursuant to the *Avena* judgment and the President's memorandum, and the potential for review in this Court once the Texas courts have heard and decided Medellin's pending action."

Four Justices dissented from the per curiam decision. Justice O'Connor, in a dissent joined by Justices Stevens, Souter, and Breyer, argued that the case should have been remanded to the Fifth Circuit. With respect to whether the *Avena* decision should be enforced as a matter of comity, they noted that "[t]hat question can only be answered by holding up the *Avena* interpretation of the treaty against the domestic court's own conclusions, and then deciding how and to what extent the two should be reconciled." In addition, while acknowledging that U.S. courts normally give "considerable weight" to the Executive's construction of a treaty, they stated that "a treaty's meaning is not beyond debate once the Executive has interpreted it." In response, Justices Ginsburg and Scalia argued in a concurrence that the dissent's conception of the comity issue was inconsistent with the usual U.S. approach to enforcement of foreign judgments. Citing *Hilton v. Guyot*, they noted that "[i]t is the long-recognized general rule that, when a judgment binds or is respected as a matter of comity, a 'let's see if we agree' approach is out of order."

What, if anything, does the *Medellin* decision suggest about whether U.S. courts should give comity to ICJ decisions? Assuming such decisions should be given comity, should they be treated like foreign court judgments? What should a U.S. court do if, as in *Medellin*, the Executive Branch disagrees with the reasoning of the ICJ? Does comity entail respect only for the ICJ's judgment, or also for its reasoning? What should U.S. courts do when confronted with violations of the Vienna Convention rights of individuals not covered by the *Avena* judgment?

In addition to arguing that the ICJ decision should be enforced as a matter of comity, Medellin had argued that the decision should be given direct effect in U.S. courts because the United States had agreed by treaty to allow the ICJ to resolve disputes under the Vienna Convention, and had agreed in the United Nations Charter to comply with ICJ decisions to which it was a party. None of the various opinions in *Medellin* expressed a view about how that issue should be resolved, although Justice O'Connor's dissent noted the conflicting positions of Medellin and the Executive Branch on this issue and observed that "[r]easonable jurists can vigorously disagree about whether and what legal effect ICJ decisions have in our domestic courts." In Chapter 6, we consider the constitutional issues that might be posed by giving direct effect to international decisions in U.S. courts. Another issue lurking in *Medellin* was the legal effect of the President's memorandum concerning enforcement of the ICJ's decision in the state courts. We consider the effect of that memorandum in the materials on Executive Branch preemption in Chapter 5.

12. Scholars disagree about the usefulness of having a general doctrine of international comity. For example, Professor Joel Paul has argued that comity is too vague a standard and is inconsistent with the duty of courts to interpret and apply their own sovereign's will rather than the interests of foreign sovereigns. *See* Joel R. Paul, *Comity in International Law*, 32 Harv. Int'l L.J. 1 (1991). Similarly, Professor Michael Ramsey has argued that the comity concept is overly vague, and he contends that the doctrine is a substitution for, rather than an aid to, analysis. *See* Michael D. Ramsey, *Escaping "International Comity,"* 83 Iowa L. Rev. 893 (1998). By contrast, while acknowledging that comity is an amorphous concept, Professor Anne-Marie Slaughter maintains that interactions between courts of different nations is necessary, and increasingly common, in our globalized world, and that considerations of comity are useful in addressing these relations. *See* Anne-Marie Slaughter, *Court to Court*, 92 Am. J. Int'l L. 708 (1998); *see also* Molly Warner Lien, *The Cooperative and Integrative Models of International Judicial Comity: Two Illustrations Using Transnational Discovery and Breard Scenarios*, 50 Cath. U. L. Rev. 591 (2001) (building on Slaughter's approach).

13. Considerations of international comity arise in connection with a number of additional topics in this casebook, including the federal common law of foreign relations (Chapter 5), delegation of authority to international adjudicatory bodies (Chapter 6), and extraterritorial application of U.S. law (Chapter 8). Comity is also relevant to various aspects of international litigation that are not considered in detail in this casebook, such as personal jurisdiction, international discovery, the enforcement of forum selection clauses, the issuance of injunctions against foreign litigation, and the enforcement of foreign judgments. *See generally* Gary B. Born, International Civil Litigation in United States Courts (3d ed. 1996) (addressing these topics in detail).

G. JUDICIAL DEFERENCE TO THE EXECUTIVE BRANCH

Courts often give deference to the views of the Executive Branch when deciding foreign relations cases. As the materials below illustrate, the strength of this deference and the justifications for it vary depending on the issues before the court.

Mingtai Fire & Marine Ins. Co. v. United Parcel Service
177 F.3d 1142 (9th Cir. 1999)

O'SCANNLAIN, CIRCUIT JUDGE:
    We must determine whether adherence to the Warsaw Convention by the People's Republic of China also binds Taiwan . . . .

Mingtai Fire & Marine Insurance Co., Ltd. ("Mingtai"), insured a package, shipped by Gemtronics Corp. from Taipei, Taiwan to San Jose, California, which was lost en route by United Parcel Service, the air carrier. Mingtai alleged that the lost package contained computer chips worth $83,454.80 and brought suit against United Parcel Service and United Parcel International, Inc. (collectively "UPS"), in the Northern District of California alleging, *inter alia*, loss of cargo under the [Warsaw] Convention....

UPS answered that the Convention did not apply, and that its air carrier liability was therefore limited to the $100 released value provided by the air waybill. Upon the parties' cross-motions for summary judgment, the district court so held, concluding that Taiwan, which is not a signatory to the Convention, was not bound by the People's Republic of China's ("China") adherence to the Convention. The district court therefore upheld the limitation on liability provided by the air waybill, and entered summary judgment in Mingtai's favor in the amount of $100.

Mingtai appeals....

The Convention only applies to shipments between territories of signatories, otherwise referred to as "High Contracting Parties." The parties do not dispute that Taiwan is *not* a High Contracting Party, nor that China *is* a High Contracting Party. Thus, the sole question presented is whether China's status as a High Contracting Party is sufficient to bind Taiwan to the terms of the Convention.

China signed the Convention with the declaration that the Convention "shall of course apply to the entire Chinese territory including Taiwan." Mingtai's argument on appeal largely consists of the assertion that the United States' recognition of China and derecognition of Taiwan require this court to honor China's declaration that its adherence to the Convention binds Taiwan. The parties agree that the question of Taiwan's status, that is, whether derecognition rendered Taiwan bound by China's adherence to international agreements, is a question for the political branches, rather than the judiciary. The parties merely dispute what the political branches have determined Taiwan's status to be....

The determination of whether China's adherence to the Convention binds Taiwan conflates two distinct areas of foreign relations: the effects of foreign sovereign recognition, and the status of treaties. It is axiomatic that "the conduct of foreign relations is committed by the Constitution to the political departments of the Federal Government; [and] that the propriety of the exercise of that power is not open to judicial review." United States v. Pink, 315 U.S. 203, 222-23 (1942); *accord* Oetjen v. Central Leather Co., 246 U.S. 297, 302 (1918); *see also* Taiwan v. United States Dist. Ct. for the N. Dist. of Cal., 128 F.3d 712, 718 (9th Cir. 1997) (recognizing "the 'primacy of the Executive in the conduct of foreign relations' and the Executive Branch's lead role in foreign policy") (quoting First Nat'l City Bank v. Banco Nacional de Cuba, 406 U.S. 759, 767 (1972)). Thus, the Supreme Court has repeatedly held that the Constitution commits to the Executive Branch alone the authority to recognize, and to withdraw recognition from, foreign regimes. *See, e.g.*, Banco Nacional de Cuba v. Sabbatino, 376 U.S. 398, 410 (1964) ("Political recognition is exclusively a function of the Executive."). "[R]ecognition of a foreign sovereign conclusively binds the courts," *Pink*, 315 U.S. at 223, because determining "[w]ho is the sovereign, *de jure* or *de facto*, of a territory is not a judicial, but a political question," Jones v. United States, 137 U.S. 202, 212 (1890). Thus, whether China is the sovereign, *de jure* or *de facto*, of the territory of Taiwan is a political question, and "[o]bjections to the underlying policy as well as objections to recognition are to be addressed to the political department and not to the courts." *Pink*, 315 U.S. at 229.

Similarly, "governmental action ... must be regarded as of controlling importance" in determining the status of treaties. Baker v. Carr, 369 U.S. 186, 212 (1962) (quoting Terlinden v. Ames, 184 U.S. 270, 285 (1902)); *see also* Then v. Melendez, 92 F.3d 851, 854 (9th Cir. 1996) (recognizing that whether a treaty remains in force after a change in the sovereign status of one of the signatories is a political question). Thus, courts answer questions regarding the status of treaties following a change in the sovereign status of one of the relevant entities by deferring to the political branches' understanding of the resulting obligations.... Similarly here, we look to the statements and actions of the "political departments" in order to answer whether, following recognition of China and derecognition of Taiwan, China's adherence to the Warsaw Convention binds Taiwan....

As this court has noted, "[w]hen the United States established relations with [China] in 1979, it severed diplomatic relations with Taiwan." Taiwan v. United States Dist. Ct., 128 F.3d at 714. However, the President's Memorandum effecting this change acknowledged that, despite the termination of diplomatic relations with Taiwan, the United States still wished to maintain "commercial, cultural and other relations with the people of Taiwan without official government representation and without diplomatic relations." Thus, the President's Memorandum directed that "[e]xisting international agreements and arrangements in force between the United States and Taiwan shall continue in force...."

Congress, in turn, formalized this continuing relationship by enacting the Taiwan Relations Act, 22 U.S.C. §§3301-3316 ("Act"), "to provide a structure for 'the continuation of commercial, cultural, and other relations between the people of the United States and the people on Taiwan.'" Taiwan v. United States Dist. Ct., 128 F.3d at 714 (quoting 22 U.S.C. §3301(a)(2)). The Act provides that:

> [t]he absence of diplomatic relations or recognition shall not affect the application of the laws of the United States with respect to Taiwan, and the laws of the United States shall apply with respect to Taiwan in the manner that the laws of the United States applied with respect to Taiwan prior to [derecognition].

22 U.S.C. §3303(a).

The Act further provides that "[w]henever the laws of the United States refer or relate to foreign countries, nations, states, governments, or similar entities, such terms shall include and such laws shall apply with respect to Taiwan," 22 U.S.C. §3303(b)(1), and that:

> [f]or all purposes, including actions in any court in the United States, the Congress approves the continuation in force of all treaties and other international agreements, including multilateral conventions, entered into by the United States and the governing authorities on Taiwan recognized by the United States as the Republic of China prior to January 1, 1979....

22 U.S.C. §3303(c).

These provisions, and the Act generally, strongly imply that, despite the absence of official relations, the United States continues to deal separately with Taiwan. With the passage of the Act, the United States not only continued in force its treaties with Taiwan that antedated derecognition; it also gave no indication that existing or future agreements with the newly recognized China would be binding upon Taiwan.

The State Department's publication *Treaties in Force* makes explicit what is implicit in the Act. *Treaties in Force* contains sections listing bilateral treaties with various countries. There are separate sections listing the bilateral treaties between (1) the United States and "China" and (2) the United States and "China (Taiwan)." These sections list numerous treaties in force between the United States and "China" that are not listed as treaties in force between the United States and "China (Taiwan)." . . .

More specific to the question presented here, "China" is listed as a signatory to the Warsaw Convention, while "China (Taiwan)" is not. This listing of "China" does not appear to encompass Taiwan, because (as noted previously) where both China and Taiwan are signatories to a treaty, *Treaties in Force* so indicates. For example, "China" is listed as a signatory to a different aviation treaty — the "Convention on offenses and certain other acts committed on board aircraft." A note to the "China" listing for that treaty states that "[t]he Taiwan authorities have also adhered to this convention." There would be little reason to note Taiwan's adherence if the Executive considered China's adherence to a treaty binding upon Taiwan.

We need not, however, merely rely upon the implications of the Act and the statements in and structure of *Treaties in Force*. Instead, we have the benefit of the Executive's express position on the issue presented. In an amicus brief and at oral argument, the United States made plain its position that China's adherence to the Convention does not bind Taiwan. In Taiwan v. United States District Court, we were similarly presented with a question concerning Taiwan's status, regarding which the United States filed a brief as amicus curiae. We noted that the United States' position was "entitled to substantial deference in light of the 'primacy of the Executive in the conduct of foreign relations' and the Executive Branch's lead role in foreign policy," and thus held in accordance with that position. Similarly here, the United States' position is entitled to deference.

While Mingtai argues that the district court violated separation of powers by rejecting its position, it instead would be an intrusion into the political sphere for this court to rule in Mingtai's favor and effectively to hold, contrary to every indication of executive and legislative intent, that Taiwan has tacitly been recognized by the United States as a party to any treaty signed by China. We will not do so. We caution, however, that we do not independently determine the status of Taiwan; instead, we merely recognize and defer to the political departments' position that Taiwan is not bound by China's adherence to the Warsaw Convention.

Gonzalez v. Reno

212 F.3d 1338 (11th Cir. 2000)

[In November 1999, Florida fishermen found a six-year-old Cuban boy, Elian Gonzalez, drifting at sea off the coast of Florida. The boat carrying Elian, his mother, and eleven others from Cuba had capsized two days earlier, and his mother had died. The Immigration and Naturalization Service (INS) took custody of Elian and then paroled him into the custody of his Miami uncle, Lazaro Gonzalez. Lazaro later sought political asylum on Elian's behalf, stating that Elian was "afraid to return to Cuba" and had a well-founded fear of persecution there. Elian's father in Cuba, Juan Miguel Gonzalez, disagreed. In a letter to the INS, he argued that Elian could not speak for himself and he urged the INS to return Elian to his custody. After meeting with both Juan Miguel and Lazaro, the INS rejected Elian's asylum applications as legally void. Citing the custom that parents generally speak for their children, and finding that no circumstance in this case warranted a departure from that custom, the INS concluded that Elian lacked the capacity to file personally for asylum against the wish of his sole surviving parent. By and through Lazaro as his next friend, Elian then filed a complaint in federal district court seeking to compel the INS to consider the merits of his asylum applications. He alleged that the refusal to consider his applications violated 8 U.S.C. §1158, which provides that "[a]ny alien . . . may apply for asylum," as well as the Fifth Amendment Due Process Clause. The district court rejected both claims and dismissed his complaint.]

EDMONDSON, CIRCUIT JUDGE . . . .

II

Plaintiff contends that the district court erred in rejecting his statutory claim based on 8 U.S.C. §1158. Section 1158 provides that "[a]ny alien . . . may apply for asylum." 8 U.S.C. §1158(a)(1). Plaintiff says that, because he is "[a]ny alien," he may apply for asylum. Plaintiff insists that, by the applications signed and submitted by himself and Lazaro, he, in fact, did apply for asylum within the meaning of section 1158. In addition, Plaintiff argues that the summary rejection by the INS of his applications as invalid violated the intent of Congress as set out in the statute.

The INS responds that section 1158 is silent about the validity of asylum applications filed on behalf of a six-year-old child, by the child himself and a nonparental relative, against the wishes of the child's parent. The INS argues that, because the statute does not spell out how a young child files for asylum, the INS was free to adopt a policy requiring, in these circumstances, that any asylum claim on Plaintiff's behalf be filed by Plaintiff's father. As such, the INS urges that the rejection of Plaintiff's purported asylum applications as legally void was lawful. According to the INS, because the applications had no legal effect, Plaintiff never applied at all within the meaning of the statute.

Guided by well-established principles of statutory construction, judicial restraint, and deference to executive agencies, we accept that the rejection by the INS of Plaintiff's applications as invalid did not violate section 1158.

A.

Our consideration of Plaintiff's statutory claim must begin with an examination of the scope of the statute itself. Chevron, U.S.A., Inc. v. Natural Resources Defense Council, Inc., 467 U.S. 837 (1984); see also INS v. Aguirre-Aguirre, 526 U.S. 415 (1999) (instructing that analysis set out in *Chevron* is applicable to immigration statutes) . . . . In *Chevron*, the Supreme Court explained: "First, always, is the question whether Congress has directly spoken to the precise question at issue. If the intent of Congress is clear, that is the end of the matter; for the court, as well as the agency, must give effect to the unambiguously expressed intent of Congress." We turn, therefore, to the plain language of the statute.

Section 1158 provides, in pertinent part:

> *Any alien* who is physically present in the United States or who arrives in the United States (whether or not at a designated port of arrival and including an alien who is

brought to the United States after having been interdicted in international or United States waters), irrespective of such alien's status, *may apply for asylum* in accordance with this section or, where applicable, section 1225(b) of this title.

8 U.S.C. §1158(a)(1) (emphasis added). Section 1158 is neither vague nor ambiguous. The statute means exactly what it says: "[a]ny alien . . . may apply for asylum." That "[a]ny alien" includes Plaintiff seems apparent. *See* 8 U.S.C. §1101(a)(3) (defining "alien" as "any person not a citizen or national of the United States"). . . . Section 1158, therefore, plainly would permit Plaintiff to apply for asylum.

When an alien does apply for asylum within the meaning of the statute, the INS—according to the statute itself and INS regulations—must consider the merits of the alien's asylum claim. *See* 8 U.S.C. §1158(d)(1) ("The Attorney General *shall* establish a procedure for the consideration of asylum applications filed under subsection (a) of this section.") (emphasis added); 8 C.F.R. §208.9(a) (requiring INS to "adjudicate the claim of each asylum applicant whose application is complete"). The important legal question in this case, therefore, is not whether Plaintiff *may* apply for asylum; that a six-year-old is eligible to apply for asylum is clear. The ultimate inquiry, instead, is whether a six-year-old child *has* applied for asylum within the meaning of the statute when he, or a non-parental relative on his behalf, signs and submits a purported application against the express wishes of the child's parent.

About this question, more important than what Congress said in section 1158 is what Congress left unsaid. In reading statutes, we consider not only the words Congress used, but the spaces between those words. Section 1158 is silent on the precise question at issue in this case. Although section 1158 gives "any alien" the right to "apply for asylum," the statute does not command how an alien applies for asylum. The statute includes no definition of the term "apply." The statute does not set out procedures for the proper filing of an asylum application. Furthermore, the statute does not identify the necessary contents of a valid asylum application. In short, although the statute requires the existence of some application procedure so that aliens may apply for asylum, section 1158 says nothing about the particulars of that procedure.

B.

Because the statute is silent on the issue, Congress has left a gap in the statutory scheme. From that gap springs executive discretion.[10] As a matter of law, it is not for the courts, but for the executive agency charged with enforcing the statute

10. This case is about the *discretion* of the executive branch to make policy, not about ministerial enforcement of the "law" by executive officials. It has been suggested that the precise policy adopted by the INS in this case was required by "law." That characterization of this case, however, is inaccurate. As we have explained, when the INS made its pertinent policy, the preexisting law said nothing about the validity of Plaintiff's asylum applications.

Instead, Congress just provided that "[a]ny alien" may apply for asylum and left the details of the application process to the discretion of the INS. The INS, in its discretion, decided to require six-year-old children—who arrive unaccompanied in the United States from Cuba—to act in immigration matters only through (absent special circumstances) their parents in Cuba. The INS could have shaped its policy in a different fashion, perhaps allowing relatives (for example, those within the fourth degree of relationship) in the United States to act for such children. But it did not, and we cannot. That choice was the sole prerogative of the executive branch. According to the principles set out in *Chevron*, we can only disturb that choice if it is unreasonable. *See Chevron*, 104 S. Ct. at 2793. . . .

(here, the INS), to choose how to fill such gaps.[11] *See Chevron*, 104 S. Ct. at 2793. Moreover, the authority of the executive branch to fill gaps is especially great in the context of immigration policy.[12] *See Aguirre-Aguirre*, 119 S. Ct. at 1445. Our proper review of the exercise by the executive branch of its discretion to fill gaps, therefore, must be very limited.

That the courts owe some deference to executive policy does not mean that the executive branch has unbridled discretion in creating and in implementing policy. Executive agencies must comply with the procedural requirements imposed by statute. Agencies must respect their own procedural rules and regulations. And the policy selected by the agency must be a reasonable one in the light of the statutory scheme. *Chevron*, 104 S. Ct. at 2782. To this end, the courts retain the authority to check agency policymaking for procedural compliance and for arbitrariness. But the courts cannot properly reexamine the wisdom of an agency-promulgated policy.

In this case, because the law — particularly section 1158 — is silent about the validity of Plaintiff's purported asylum applications, it fell to the INS to make a discretionary policy choice. The INS, exercising its gap-filling discretion, determined these things: (1) six-year-old children lack the capacity to sign and to submit personally an application for asylum; (2) instead, six-year-old children must be represented by an adult in immigration matters; (3) absent special circumstances, the only proper adult to represent a six-year-old child is the child's parent, even when the parent is not in this country; and, (4) that the parent lives in a communist-totalitarian state (such as Cuba), in and of itself, does not constitute a special circumstance requiring the selection of a non-parental representative. Our duty is to decide whether this policy might be a reasonable one in the light of the statutory scheme. *See Chevron*, 104 S. Ct. at 2782 . . . .

We accept that the INS policy at issue here comes within the range of reasonable choices . . . .

We have not the slightest illusion about the INS's choices: the choices — about policy and about application of the policy — that the INS made in this case are choices about which reasonable people can disagree. Still, the choices were not

---

11. When a statute is ambiguous or silent on the pertinent issue, it ordinarily is for the judicial branch to construe the statute. *See generally* Marbury v. Madison, 5 U.S. (1 Cranch) 137, 177 (1803) ("It is emphatically the province and duty of the judicial department to say what the law is."). But the ordinary rule does not always apply: where Congress has indicated that gaps in the statutory scheme should be filled in by officers of the executive branch (a political branch accountable to the people and fit for making policy judgments), then the gaps should not be filled in by federal judges. Where Congress has committed the enforcement of a statute to a particular executive agency, Congress has sufficiently indicated its intent that statutory gaps be filled by the executive agency. And the Supreme Court has directed that, for such statutes, if "Congress has not directly addressed the precise question at issue, the court does not simply impose its own construction on the statute . . . . Rather, if the statute is silent . . . the question for the court is whether the agency's answer is based on a permissible construction of the statute." *Chevron*, 104 S. Ct. at 2782.

12. The authority of the executive branch in immigration matters stems from the primacy of the President and other executive officials (such as the INS) in matters touching upon foreign affairs. *See Aguirre-Aguirre*, 119 S. Ct. at 1445. Respect for the authority of the executive branch in foreign affairs is a well-established theme in our law. *See* United States v. Curtiss-Wright Export Corp., 299 U.S. 304 (1936) (recognizing "the very delicate, plenary and exclusive power of the President as the sole organ of the federal government in the field of international relations"). And the judicial respect for executive authority in matters touching upon foreign relations is even greater where the presidential power has been affirmed in an act of Congress. *See* Youngstown Sheet & Tube Co. v. Sawyer, 343 U.S. 579 (1952) (Jackson, J., concurring) ("When the President acts pursuant to an express or implied authorization of Congress, his authority is at its maximum, for it includes all that he possesses in his own right plus all that Congress can delegate.").

unreasonable, not capricious and not arbitrary, but were reasoned and reasonable. The INS's considerable discretion was not abused.

United States v. Lombera-Camorlinga

206 F.3d 882 (9th Cir. 2000)

SCHROEDER, CIRCUIT JUDGE:

Article 36 of the Vienna Convention on Consular Relations, April 24, 1963, 21 U.S.T. 77, provides that law enforcement officials "shall inform" arrested foreign nationals of their right to notification of their consulates. A panel of this court held that Article 36 creates an individual right that is enforceable in the courts of the United States. Reversing the ruling of the district court, the panel further held that a defendant's post-arrest statements made before being advised of this right are inadmissible in a subsequent criminal prosecution, provided the defendant can show prejudice from the lack of notification.

We voted to accept en banc review of the case to consider whether the suppression of evidence is an appropriate remedy for violation of the Vienna Convention. We now hold that it is not, for there is nothing in the language or operation of the treaty provision to suggest Article 36 was intended to create an exclusionary rule with protections similar to those announced by the United States Supreme Court three years later in Miranda v. Arizona, 384 U.S. 436 (1966). In reaching this decision, we give some weight to the State Department's interpretation of the treaty, set forth in a letter originally submitted in conjunction with similar litigation currently pending in the First Circuit.... We do not decide whether the treaty creates individual rights that are judicially enforceable in other ways.

The underlying facts are not in dispute. Jose Lombera-Camorlinga, a citizen of Mexico, was arrested at the Calexico, California port of entry when 39.3 kilograms of marijuana were found in his vehicle. Before questioning Lombera-Camorlinga, officers advised him of his Miranda rights but did not inform him of any rights under the Vienna Convention, nor did they contact the Mexican consular post. Lombera-Camorlinga subsequently made self-incriminating statements.

After his indictment on charges of importation of marijuana and possession of marijuana with intent to distribute, Lombera-Camorlinga moved for suppression of his post-arrest statements on the ground that they were obtained in violation of Article 36 of the Vienna Convention. The district court denied the motion, and Lombera-Camorlinga entered a conditional guilty plea and appealed his subsequent conviction. On appeal, a panel of this court held that the district court erred in denying the motion to suppress without first making a determination of prejudice. In so doing, the panel held that (1) the Vienna Convention creates judicially enforceable individual rights, and (2) suppression may serve as a remedy for the violation of these rights if the foreign national can demonstrate prejudice. A majority of the active, nonrecused judges of this court voted to rehear the case en banc. Our en banc review was aided by the excellent quality of oral argument on behalf of both the appellee and appellant.

The Vienna Convention is a 79-article, multilateral treaty to which both the United States and Mexico are signatories. It was negotiated in 1963 and ratified by the United States in 1969, thereby becoming the supreme law of the land. See U.S. Const. art. VI, cl. 2. Its provisions cover a number of issues that require consular intervention or notification, including the death of a foreign national, the necessity of appointing a guardian or a trustee for a foreign national who is also a minor, the crash of a foreign airplane or the wreck of a foreign boat, and the arrest or detention of a consular officer. Article 36 deals with what a member state must do when a foreign national is arrested. It provides, in relevant part:

> 1. With a view to facilitating the exercise of consular functions relating to nationals of the sending State: . . . .
>
>> (b) if he so requests, the competent authorities of the receiving State shall, without delay, inform the consular post of the sending State if, within its consular district, a national of that State is arrested or committed to prison or to custody pending trial or is detained in any other manner. Any communication addressed to the consular post by the person arrested, in prison, custody or detention shall also be forwarded by the said authorities without delay. The said authorities shall inform the person concerned without delay of his rights under this sub-paragraph.

The panel held that in addition to creating obligations between nations, Article 36 creates individual rights enforceable in the courts of the United States. The panel looked primarily to the plain language of the provision, which states that the foreign national is to be informed of "his rights" under that section. Also lending some support to this view is the fact that the contact with the foreign consulate is required only if the foreign national requests it. Domestic law enforcement authorities thus have no obligation to the foreign consulate unless the foreign national himself triggers one. This implies that the provision exists for the protection of the foreign national.

The Supreme Court has treated the issue of whether the provision creates any judicially enforceable rights as an open question, stating in Breard v. Greene, 523 U.S. 371, 376 (1998), that the Vienna Convention "arguably" creates individual rights. Our own court has on at least two occasions, in a different but related context, recognized a judicially enforceable right to request consular notification in deportation proceedings. In those cases, however, the Department of Justice had embodied the Vienna Convention provisions in a corresponding INS regulation, 8 C.F.R. §242.2(e), and we relied on that regulation in reaching our decisions. We had no occasion to hold that the violation of the treaty alone was sufficient to permit a foreign national to overturn a deportation.

On a general level, the Supreme Court has recognized that treaties can in some circumstances create individually enforceable rights. *See* United States v. Alvarez-Machain, 504 U.S. 655, 659-60 (1992). The leading example is United States v. Rauscher, 119 U.S. 407 (1886), holding that through the provisions of an extradition treaty, the requirement of specialty — permitting prosecution only for the crime on which extradition was based — could serve as a defense to an attempted prosecution for another crime. The Court's reasoning in *Rauscher* relied on the specific provisions of the particular extradition treaty invoked as a defense. In *Alvarez-Machain* the Court considered the extradition treaty between the United States and Mexico, which establishes an orderly process for transferring individuals from one country to the other for criminal prosecution. The Court held that because the treaty failed to expressly prohibit U.S. law enforcement from circumventing this process and abducting Mexican citizens in order to force them to stand trial in the United States, such conduct could not serve as a defense to jurisdiction.

Whether or not treaty violations can provide the basis for particular claims or defenses thus appears to depend upon the particular treaty and claim involved.

The government argues strenuously that Article 36 creates no judicially enforceable individual rights of any kind....

We need not decide whether to accept the government's argument that Article 36 creates no individually enforceable rights, however. We agree with the government's alternative position that assuming that some judicial remedies are available for the violation of Article 36, the exclusion in a criminal prosecution of evidence obtained as the result of post-arrest interrogation is not among them.

In arguing that the statements should be suppressed, appellants urge us to make the unwarranted assumption that the treaty was intended to serve the same purposes as *Miranda* in enforcing the rights to counsel and against self-incrimination in the post-arrest context. Yet, the treaty does not link the required consular notification in any way to the commencement of police interrogation. Nor does the treaty, as *Miranda* does, require law enforcement officials to cease interrogation once the arrestee invokes his right. Furthermore, while the rights to counsel and against self-incrimination are secured under the Fifth and Sixth Amendments to our own Constitution and are essential to our criminal justice system, they are by no means universally recognized or enforced. There is no reason to think the drafters of the Vienna Convention had these uniquely American rights in mind, especially given the fact that even the United States Supreme Court did not require Fifth and Sixth Amendment post-arrest warnings until it decided *Miranda* in 1966, three years after the treaty was drafted....

While the panel was provided with "scant authority" on this issue, the State Department has now spoken, and has expressed its opinion that suppression is an inappropriate remedy. In Factor v. Laubenheimer, 290 U.S. 276 (1933), the Supreme Court stated that in resolving doubts about interpretation, "the construction of a treaty by the political department of the government, while not conclusive upon courts called upon to construe it, is nevertheless of weight." *Id.* at 295. *See also* El Al Israel Airlines, Ltd. v. Tsui Yuan Tseng, 525 U.S. 155 (1999) ("Respect is ordinarily due the reasonable views of the Executive Branch concerning the meaning of an international treaty."); Kolovrat v. Oregon, 366 U.S. 187, 194 (1961) ("While courts interpret treaties for themselves, the meaning given them by the departments of government particularly charged with their negotiation and enforcement is given great weight."). It is true that courts tend to give less weight to an executive branch position adopted in the course of litigation, as is the case here, than to an interpretation made in diplomatic relations with other countries. *See* Restatement (Third) of Foreign Relations §326 reporters' note 2. Given that the Vienna Convention is silent—and therefore ambiguous, at best—on whether or not suppression is an appropriate remedy, however, the State Department's opinion that it is not deserves at least some deference.

Equally important, the State Department's position is well-supported. The State Department indicates that it has historically enforced the Vienna Convention itself, investigating reports of violations and apologizing to foreign governments and working with domestic law enforcement to prevent future violations when necessary. The addition of a judicial enforcement mechanism contains the possibility for conflict between the respective powers of the executive and judicial branches. Moreover, the fact that the State Department is willing to and in fact does work directly with law enforcement to ensure compliance detracts in this instance from the traditional justification for the exclusionary rule: that it is the only available method of controlling police misconduct.

The State Department also points out that no other signatories to the Vienna Convention have permitted suppression under similar circumstances, and that two (Italy and Australia) have specifically rejected it.... By refusing to adopt an exclusionary rule, we thus promote harmony in the interpretation of an international agreement. *See* Restatement (Third) of Foreign Relations §325 cmt. d ("Treaties that lay down rules to be enforced by the parties through their internal courts or administrative agencies should be construed so as to achieve uniformity of result despite differences between national legal systems.")....

BOOCHEVER, CIRCUIT JUDGE, with whom JUDGES JAMES R. BROWNING and THOMAS join, dissenting.

The majority opinion purports to avoid deciding whether Article 36 of the Vienna Convention creates individually enforceable rights to consular notification. "[A]ssuming that some judicial remedies are available for the violation of Article 36," the majority nevertheless leaves as the only current form of enforcement the State Department's self-described practice of "investigating reports of violations and apologizing to foreign governments, and working with domestic law enforcement to prevent further violations when necessary." This is equivalent to securing enforcement by a toothless, clawless lion. Defendants who actually have been prejudiced by the failure to be notified of their Article 36 rights may suffer imprisonment and other punishments to which they would not have been subjected had their rights been observed. Such an interpretation of the treaty hardly conforms to the due process principles embodied in the United States Constitution. We should not so interpret the treaty....

THOMAS, CIRCUIT JUDGE, with whom JUDGES JAMES R. BROWNING and BOOCHEVER join in full, and with whom JUDGE WARDLAW joins with respect to Section II, dissenting:

I respectfully dissent from the majority's conclusion that the exclusionary rule is not the appropriate method by which a private right to consular notification should be enforced in the United States. I also respectfully disagree with the majority's holding that deference should be paid to an agency's litigating position....

The question then is whether it is appropriate to apply the exclusionary rule to confessions obtained in violation of the Vienna Convention. In construing a treaty, we look to its plain words. *See* United States v. Alvarez-Machain, 504 U.S. 655, 663 (1992). The Treaty provides that if a prisoner "so requests, the competent authorities of the receiving State shall, without delay, inform the consular post of the sending State if, within its consular district, a national of that State is arrested or committed to prison or to custody pending trial or is detained in any other manner." Vienna Convention, Article 36(1). It further provides that "[t]he said authorities shall inform the person concerned without delay of his rights under this subparagraph." All parties, including the United States, agree that this language requires United States law enforcement officials to inform an arrested foreign national of the right to have his or her national consul informed of the arrest. The Supremacy Clause makes treaties, such as the one at bar, "the supreme Law of the Land," binding "the Judges in every State."...

The majority quite properly does not opine as to what remedies [other than exclusion of evidence] are available for enforcement of the right to consular notification. However, if one peeks behind the curtain, other alternatives are not attractive, nor are they consistent with the Treaty. In fact, the only options readily apparent are private damage actions, or an acknowledgment that the Treaty created a private right without any remedy at all. The Treaty does not provide expressly for private damage actions. Rather, the plain words of the Treaty provide that the notification right "shall be exercised," not that failure to notify should be compensated. Thus, the Treaty would not seem to contemplate private damage actions, and it would not be sound judicial policy to conjure a legal theory that would expose individual officers to liability for breaches of international treaties. The decision on whether to attach individual liability for such violations should be left to Congress.

That the right to consular notification may be a right without a remedy is also inconsistent with the Treaty's command that the right "be exercised in conformity with the laws and regulations" of the arresting state. Our law of criminal procedure is not merely aspirational; when a procedural right has been established, it is enforced. Thus, alternative readings of what enforcement mechanism might exist under our laws simply do not make sense, either textually or in the context of how our criminal procedural laws are administered. . . .

I must respectfully also part company from the majority in its holding that we must defer to an agency's litigating position. The Supreme Court has rejected such deference. *See, e.g.,* Bowen v. Georgetown Univ. Hosp., 488 U.S. 204, 212 (1988). So have we. *See, e.g.,* Resource Invs., Inc. v. U.S. Army Corps of Eng'rs, 151 F.3d 1162, 1165 (9th Cir. 1998). There is a sound basis for this rule. As the Supreme Court has explained, "Congress has delegated to the administrative official and not to appellate counsel the responsibility for elaborating and enforcing statutory commands." Investment Co. Inst. v. Camp, 401 U.S. 617, 628 (1971). Administrative agency constructions of governing statutes, or in this case a treaty, performed outside the adversary system are properly worthy of deference. However, agency positions developed in response to a lawsuit are not of the same character: they are specifically tailored to help obtain a favorable outcome in a pending controversy in which the agency is involved. Although we must certainly consider the persuasive force of the agency's argument, it is just that. The arguments advanced by an agency in litigation ought to rise or fall on their own weight.

Deference in this case is especially inappropriate because it is given to the agency's litigation position in entirely separate litigation in another circuit. The reasoning of the Department of State has proved persuasive; we need not adopt a special rule deferring to its assertions as a matter of law. I respectfully suggest that we gravely err in creating such a rule.

Notes and Questions

1. As these materials indicate, it is very common for courts to give deference to the views of the Executive Branch in cases perceived as implicating foreign affairs. *See also, e.g.,* Jama v. Immigration & Customs Enforcement, 125 S. Ct. 694, 704 (2005) (referring to the Court's "customary policy of deference to the President in matters of foreign affairs"). Why is this so? Should courts defer in these cases even on pure questions of law — for example, the meaning of a foreign affairs statute or a treaty? If so, how can this deference be reconciled with what is, according to *Marbury v. Madison,* "the province and duty of the judicial department to say what the law is"?

2. "Deference" can take a variety of forms, ranging from respectful considera-tion to conclusive weight. What sort of deference did the courts apply in the above cases? What were the justifications for this deference? What effect, if any, did the deference have on the outcome of the cases? How does the deference in these cases compare with the proposed *Bernstein* exception to the act of state doctrine, dis-cussed above in the act of state doctrine materials? Keep these questions in mind as we consider the Executive Branch's influence (or lack thereof) on other areas of foreign relations law throughout the casebook.

3. What is the relationship between the various deference doctrines and the political question doctrine? Are "political questions" in the foreign affairs context simply examples of absolute deference to the Executive Branch? Do the deference doctrines reduce the need for the political question doctrine, by making it less likely that courts will unduly interfere with foreign policy?

4. As noted in *Mingtai*, the Executive Branch has long received absolute defer-ence in its determinations regarding the status and proper representatives of for-eign nations. Does this deference follow from the Executive Branch's Article II powers? Or are these issues simply nonjusticiable under the *Baker v. Carr* factors? In *Mingtai*, Congress and the Executive Branch had taken similar positions regard-ing the status of Taiwan. What would the court have done if they had taken different positions?

5. As noted in *Lombera-Camorlinga*, the Supreme Court has stated that, although not conclusive, the views of the Executive Branch concerning the mean-ing of a treaty are entitled to "great weight." *See, e.g.*, United States v. Stuart, 489 U.S. 353, 369 (1989); Sumitomo Shoji America, Inc. v. Avagliano, 457 U.S. 176, 184-85 (1982); Kolovrat v. Oregon, 366 U.S. 187, 194 (1961). At times, the Court has used somewhat different terms to describe this deference, but it is not clear that the Court has intended these terms to reflect a different standard. *See, e.g.*, El Al Israel Airlines v. Tsui Yuan Tseng, 525 U.S. 155, 168 (1999) ("[r]espect"); Factor v. Laubenheimer, 290 U.S. 276, 295 (1933) ("of weight"). This deference may have a significant effect on the outcome of treaty decisions. After studying numerous treaty cases, Professor David Bederman has observed that judicial deference to the Executive Branch may be "the single best predictor of interpretive outcomes in American treaty cases." David J. Bederman, *Revivalist Canons and Treaty Inter-pretation*, 41 UCLA L. Rev. 953 (1994). What are the justifications for this treaty deference? Do these justifications apply to Executive Branch interpretations of customary international law? *See* Restatement (Third) of the Foreign Relations Law of the United States, §112, cmt. c (1987) ("Courts give particular weight to the position taken by the United States Government on questions of international law because it is deemed desirable that so far as possible the United States speak with one voice on such matters. The views of the United States Government, more-over, are also state practice, creating or modifying international law.").

One court usefully explained the justifications for treaty deference as follows:

> Because the Executive Branch is involved directly in negotiating treaties, it is well situated to assist the court in determining what the parties intended when they agreed on a particular provision. Moreover, treaties normally carry significant foreign policy implications, matters peculiarly within the purview of the political branches of our government. A court should minimize intrusion in the conduct of foreign affairs by adopting the interpretation suggested by the Executive Branch whenever it can fairly do so. Finally, the Executive Branch generally has administrative authority over the implementation of international agreements. As in the case of domestic legislation, a

court should generally give great weight to the interpretations of agencies charged with implementation of treaties because such agencies may possess significant expertise in the relevant subject matter.

Coplin v. United States, 6 Cl. Ct. 115 (1984) (Kozinski, C.J.), *rev'd on other grounds*, 761 F.2d 688 (Fed. Cir. 1985).

6. Deference to the Executive Branch in foreign relations cases can be analogized to the deference courts give to administrative agencies concerning the meaning of the federal statutes they administer. This administrative agency deference is often referred to as "*Chevron* deference," after the Supreme Court's decision in Chevron, U.S.A., Inc. v. Natural Resources Defense Council, Inc., 467 U.S. 837 (1984). Under *Chevron* deference, courts first examine whether Congress has clearly spoken to the issue before the court. If so, courts will simply apply the statute and not defer to the agency's interpretation. If the statute is ambiguous or does not address the issue, however, courts will defer to the agency's interpretation unless it is unreasonable. This deference is based on the theory that, in charging the administrative agency with administering the statute, Congress may have delegated authority to the agency to fill in gaps and resolve ambiguities in the statute. What are some of the similarities and differences between foreign affairs deference and *Chevron* deference? To what extent do these types of deference overlap? For a consideration of these and related issues, see Curtis A. Bradley, Chevron *Deference and Foreign Affairs*, 86 Va. L. Rev. 649 (2000). *See also* Kevin M. Stack, *The Statutory President*, 90 Iowa L. Rev. 539 (2005); Oren Eisner, Note, *Extending* Chevron *Deference to Presidential Interpretations of Ambiguities in Foreign Affairs and National Security Statutes Delegating Lawmaking Power to the President*, 86 Cornell L. Rev. 411 (2001).

In United States v. Mead Corp., 533 U.S. 218 (2001), the Supreme Court limited *Chevron* deference to situations in which it is "apparent . . . that Congress would expect the agency to be able to speak with the force of law when it addresses ambiguity in the statute or fills a space in the enacted law," and the Court explained that a "very good indicator of delegation meriting *Chevron* treatment" is a congressional authorization to engage in notice-and-comment rulemaking or formal adjudication. *Cf.* Barnhart v. Walton, 535 U.S. 212, 222 (2002) ("In this case, the interstitial nature of the legal question, the related expertise of the Agency, the importance of the question to administration of the statute, the complexity of that administration, and the careful consideration the Agency has given the question over a long period of time all indicate that *Chevron* provides the appropriate legal lens through which to view the legality of the Agency interpretation here at issue."). To what extent should the limitation in *Mead* affect foreign affairs deference?

The Court in *Mead* noted that, when an agency interpretation is not entitled to *Chevron* deference (e.g., because the process by which it is adopted is too informal), it may be entitled to a lesser form of deference, known as "*Skidmore* deference" after a pre-*Chevron* decision, Skidmore v. Swift & Co., 323 U.S. 134 (1944). Under *Skidmore* deference, "[t]he weight [accorded to an administrative] judgment in a particular case will depend upon the thoroughness evident in its consideration, the validity of its reasoning, its consistency with earlier and later pronouncements, and all those factors which give it power to persuade, if lacking power to control." For an argument that, for treaty interpretation, *Skidmore* deference is preferable to *Chevron* deference, see Evan Criddle, Scholarship Comment, Chevron *Deference and Treaty Interpretation*, 112 Yale L.J. 1927 (2003).

7. Sometimes, *Chevron* deference will be directly applicable in the foreign affairs area. In particular, when an Executive Branch agency is interpreting a foreign affairs-related statute that it is charged with administering, it may be entitled to *Chevron* deference. We saw this, for example, in *Gonzales*. In addition, the Supreme Court accorded *Chevron* deference to the views of the Executive Branch concerning the meaning of the sanctions statutes at issue in the *Japan Whaling* case discussed above in Note 13 of Section C. Should the foreign affairs nature of the statute be considered in the deference analysis in these situations? One possibility is that deference is heightened or triggered more easily in this context, because the Executive Branch will be able to claim both *Chevron* deference and general foreign affairs deference. Perhaps this is what the Supreme Court had in mind when it stated, in connection with an Executive Branch interpretation of an immigration statute, that "judicial deference to the Executive Branch [under *Chevron*] is especially appropriate in the immigration context where officials 'exercise especially sensitive political functions that implicate questions of foreign relations.'" INS v. Aguirre-Aguirre, 526 U.S. 415, 425 (1999) (quoting INS v. Abudu, 485 U.S. 94, 110 (1988)). *See also* Abourezk v. Reagan, 785 F.2d 1043, 1063 (D.C. Cir. 1986) (Bork, J., dissenting) ("This principle of [*Chevron*] deference applies with special force where the subject of that analysis is a delegation to the Executive of authority to make and implement decisions relating to the conduct of foreign affairs.").

8. To receive deference, what form must the Executive Branch's position take? Must the position be formulated prior to the litigation? Is an *amicus curiae* brief sufficient? What if the Executive Branch's position is inconsistent with an earlier Executive Branch position? Under *Chevron*, Executive Branch litigating positions are not entitled to deference if they are "wholly unsupported by regulations, rulings, or administrative practice." Bowen v. Georgetown Univ. Hosp., 488 U.S. 204, 212 (1988); *accord* Smiley v. Citibank, 517 U.S. 735, 741 (1996). Should a similar limitation apply to foreign affairs deference? Note that, even under *Chevron*, the Executive Branch may receive deference notwithstanding a change in position on an issue. *See Smiley*, 417 U.S. at 742.

9. In two recent decisions—the *Altmann* decision concerning retroactivity of the FSIA (excerpted above in Section D), and *Sosa v. Alvarez-Machain*, which concerned the scope of the Alien Tort Statute (and which is excerpted in Chapter 7)—the Supreme Court noted that it may be appropriate for courts to give case-specific deference to the views of the Executive Branch concerning the foreign relations impact of adjudicating particular disputes. Is it appropriate, when a court has jurisdiction over a case and the plaintiff has a potentially valid legal claim, to dismiss the case because of the Executive Branch's foreign relations concerns? Is such case-specific deference consistent with the separation of powers structure of the federal government? Is there a danger that it could unduly politicize judicial decisionmaking?

10. On what foreign affairs-related issues should courts *not* defer to the Executive Branch? Why did the Supreme Court decline to defer to the Executive's view about the non-retroactive scope of the FSIA's takings of property exception in *Altmann* (excerpted above in Section D)? Why did a majority of the Justices in *City Bank* (discussed in the notes in Section D) decline to endorse a *Bernstein* exception to the act of state doctrine whereby courts could decline to apply the doctrine when informed by the Executive that it did not object to adjudication of the foreign government act? Why did the Supreme Court decline to defer to the Executive's suggested approach to the act of state doctrine in *Kirkpatrick* (excerpted above in Section E)?

11. For academic commentary arguing that courts should play a more active and independent role in foreign relations cases, see, for example, Thomas M. Franck, Political Questions/Judicial Answers: Does the Rule of Law Apply to Foreign Affairs? (1992); K. Lee Boyd, *Universal Jurisdiction and Structural Reasonableness*, 40 Tex. Int'l L.J. 1 (2004); and Jonathan I. Charney, *Judicial Deference in Foreign Relations*, 83 Am. J. Int'l L. 805 (1989). For commentary that is more skeptical about judicial involvement in foreign relations cases, see, for example, John Yoo, *Federal Courts as Weapons of Foreign Policy: The Case of the Helms-Burton Act*, 20 Hastings Int'l & Comp. L. Rev. 747 (1997). *Cf.* Louis Henkin, *The Foreign Affairs Power of the Federal Courts*: Sabbatino, 64 Colum. L. Rev. 805, 826 (1964) ("Inevitably, the courts tend to establish rules of more-or-less general applicability, which can only relate to the needs of foreign policy grossly, and on the basis of assumptions and generalizations hardly consonant with flexibility, currentness, and consistency.").

3

Congress and the President in Foreign Relations

This chapter considers the basic foreign relations powers of Congress and the President. Sections A and B provide an overview of the specific foreign relations powers conferred in Articles I and II of the Constitution. Section C then discusses the relationship between Congress and the President in the exercise of their constitutional foreign relations powers. Aspects of this relationship relating to the exercise of war powers will be addressed separately in Chapter 4.

Constitutional text does not explicitly address many important issues concerning the foreign relations authority of the federal political branches. As Professor Harold Koh has noted:

> One cannot read the Constitution without being struck by its astonishing brevity regarding the allocation of foreign affairs authority among the branches. Nowhere does the Constitution use the words "foreign affairs" or "national security." Instead, it creates a Congress, president, and federal judiciary and vests in them powers, some of which principally affect foreign affairs. Only occasionally does it explicitly condition one branch's exercise of a foreign affairs power upon another's, as in its grants to the President of the powers, with the Senate's advice and consent, to make treaties and appoint ambassadors. More frequently, the document grants clearly related powers to separate institutions, without ever specifying the relationship between those powers, as for example, with Congress's power to declare war and the President's power as commander-in-chief. Most often, the text simply says nothing about who controls certain domains as, for example, the exercise of international emergency powers or the conduct of covert action.

Harold Hongju Koh, The National Security Constitution: Sharing Power after the Iran-Contra Affair 67 (1990). Because of these constitutional gaps and silences, Professor Edward Corwin famously noted that "the Constitution, considered only for its affirmative grants of power capable of affecting the issue, is an invitation to struggle for the privilege of directing American foreign policy." Edward S. Corwin, The President: Office and Powers 1787-1984, at 201 (Randall Bland et al. eds., 5th ed. 1984).

Notwithstanding these quotations from Koh and Corwin, do the text and structure of the Constitution offer some guidance about the scope of Congress's and the President's foreign relations powers? When the text and structure do not provide sufficient guidance, how should the Constitution's allocation of foreign affairs authority be determined? To what extent should Founding history be consulted? What weight should be given to the historic practices of the political branches?

What weight should be given to functional considerations relating to the effective conduct of U.S. foreign relations? And what role, if any, should courts play in making this determination? Keep these questions in mind as you read the materials that follow.

A. SOURCES OF CONGRESSIONAL POWER

Article I of the Constitution confers on Congress numerous powers relating to the conduct of foreign relations. In addition, the Supreme Court has recognized other congressional foreign relations powers not specifically enumerated in the constitutional text. The decisions and notes below discuss some of Congress's most frequently exercised foreign relations powers — the power to make appropriations, the power to regulate foreign commerce, the power to define and punish offenses against the law of nations, the power to make laws that are necessary and proper to carry into execution other governmental powers, the implied power to regulate immigration, and, more controversially, the "inherent" sovereign power to regulate foreign affairs. Before reading these materials, read carefully Article I, Section 8 of the U.S. Constitution, in Appendix A.

Buttfield v. Stranahan

192 U.S. 470 (1904)

[In this case, the Court considered the constitutionality of the Tea Inspection Act ("Act"), 29 Stat. 604 (1897). The Act required qualified examiners to inspect shipments of tea at U.S. ports of entry to ensure conformity with standards set by a board of tea inspectors, a body of experts selected by and answerable to the Secretary of the Treasury. On January 20, 1902, the plaintiff's firm imported tea into the port of New York. The examiner rejected the tea as "inferior" in quality, both in taste and in flavor. The plaintiff appealed the decision to the board of general appraisers, the Act's appellate body, which affirmed the examiner's decision on March 12, 1902. The following November, the collector of the port of New York denied the plaintiff's requests to repossess the tea and export it out of the United States. Instead, the collector of the port destroyed the tea in accordance with the Act, which only allowed a six-month window for exportation of tea judged inferior upon final reexamination. The plaintiff then sued the collector of the port in a New York state trial court, seeking to recover damages for the seizure, removal, and destruction of the tea. The case was removed to federal court, where the judge directed a verdict in favor of the collector of the port, stating that the "only question was as to the constitutionality of the statute under which the defendant, as collector of the port, acted." The plaintiff then appealed to the Supreme Court.]

MR. JUSTICE WHITE . . . delivered the opinion of the Court. . . .

The power to regulate commerce with foreign nations is expressly conferred upon Congress, and, being an enumerated power, is complete in itself, acknowledging no limitations other than those prescribed in the Constitution. Whatever difference of opinion, if any, may have existed or does exist concerning the limitations of the power, resulting from other provisions of the Constitution, so far as interstate commerce is concerned, it is not to be doubted that from the beginning Congress has exercised a plenary power in respect to the exclusion of merchandise brought from foreign countries; not alone directly by the enactment of embargo statutes, but indirectly, as a necessary result of provisions contained in tariff legislation. It has also, in other than tariff legislation, exerted a police power over foreign commerce by provisions which in and of themselves amounted to the assertion of the right to exclude merchandise at discretion. This is illustrated by statutory provisions which have been in force for more than fifty years, regulating the degree of strength of drugs, medicines, and chemicals entitled to admission into the United States and excluding such as did not equal the standards adopted.

The power to regulate foreign commerce is certainly as efficacious as that to regulate commerce with the Indian tribes. And this last power was referred to in United States v. 43 Gallons of Whiskey, 93 U.S. 194, as exclusive and absolute, and was declared to be "as broad and as free from restrictions as that to regulate commerce with foreign nations." In that case it was held that it was competent for Congress to extend the prohibition against the unlicensed introduction and sale of spirituous liquors in the Indian country to territory in proximity to that occupied by the Indians, thus restricting commerce with them. We entertain no doubt that it was competent for Congress, by statute, under the power to regulate foreign commerce, to establish standards and provide that no right should exist to import teas from foreign countries into the United States, unless such teas should be equal to the standards.

As a result of the complete power of Congress over foreign commerce, it necessarily follows that no individual has a vested right to trade with foreign nations which is so broad in character as to limit and restrict the power of Congress to determine what articles of merchandise may be imported into this country and the terms upon which a right to import may be exercised. This being true, it results that a statute which restrains the introduction of particular goods into the United States from considerations of public policy does not violate the due process clause of the Constitution.

That the [Tea Inspection Act] was not an exercise by Congress of purely arbitrary power is evident from the terms of the law, and a consideration of the circumstances which led to its enactment.... *was not an arbitrary law*

[The Court concludes that the Act did not excessively delegate authority to Executive Branch officials, and that the procedures used by the Executive Branch officials did not violate due process.] *congress had power*

United States v. Arjona

120 U.S. 479 (1887) *counterfeiting columbian Bank Notes in U.S.*

[Ramon Arjona was prosecuted for attempting to counterfeit the official bank notes of a state in Colombia, in violation of a federal statute "to prevent and punish the counterfeiting within the United States of notes, bonds, and other securities of foreign governments."]

MR. CHIEF JUSTICE WAITE delivered the opinion of the Court....

Congress has power to make all laws which shall be necessary and proper to carry into execution the powers vested by the constitution in the government of the United States, (article 1, §8, cl. 18;) and the Government of the United States has

Necessary & Proper clause

been vested exclusively with the power of representing the nation in all its inter-course with foreign countries. It alone can "regulate commerce with foreign nations," (article 1, §8, cl. 3;) make treaties and appoint ambassadors and other public ministers and consuls, (article 2, §2, cl. 2.) A state is expressly prohibited from entering into any "treaty, alliance, or confederation." Article 1, §10, cl. 1. Thus all official intercourse between a state and foreign nations is prevented, and exclusive authority for that purpose given to the United States. The national gov-ernment is in this way made responsible to foreign nations for all violations by the United States of their international obligations, and because of this congress is expressly authorized "to define and punish . . . offenses against the law of nations." Article 1, §8, cl. 10.

The law of nations requires every national government to use "due diligence" to prevent a wrong being done within its own dominion to another nation with which it is at peace, or to the people thereof; and because of this, the obligation of one nation to punish those who, within its own jurisdiction, counterfeit the money of another nation has long been recognized. Vattel in his Law of Nations, . . . uses this language: "From the principles thus laid down, it is easy to conclude that, if one nation counterfeits the money of another, or if she allows and protects false coiners who presume to do it, she does that nation an injury." . . .

This rule was established for the protection of nations in their intercourse with each other. If there were no such intercourse, it would be a matter of no special moment to one nation that its money was counterfeited in another. Its own people could not be defrauded if the false coin did not come among them, and its own sovereignty would not be violated if the counterfeit could not under any circum-stances be made to take the place of the true money. But national intercourse includes commercial intercourse between the people of different nations. It is as much the duty of a nation to protect such an intercourse as it is any other, and that is what Vattel meant when he said: "For the same reason that sovereigns are obliged to protect commerce, they are obliged to support this custom;" "namely, *exchange*, or the traffic or bankers, by means of which a merchant remits immense sums from one end of the world to the other," "by good laws, in which every merchant, whether citizen or foreigner, may find security." . . .

No nation can be more interested in this question than the United States. Their money is practically composed of treasury notes or certificates issued by them-selves, or of bank-bills issued by banks created under their authority and subject to their control. Their own securities, and those of the states, the cities, and the public corporations, whose interests abroad they alone have the power to guard against foreign national neglect, are found on sale in the principal money markets of Europe. If these securities, whether national, municipal, or corporate, are forged and counterfeited with impunity at the places where they are sold, it is easy to see that a great wrong will be done to the United States and their people. Any uncer-tainty about the genuineness of the security necessarily depreciates its value as a merchantable commodity, and against this international comity requires that national protection shall, as far as possible, be afforded. If there is neglect in that, the United States may, with propriety, call on the proper government to provide for the punishment of such an offense, and thus punishment of such an offense, and thus a fear of the consequences of wrong-doing. A refusal may not, perhaps, furnish sufficient cause for war; but it would certainly give just ground of complaint, and thus disturb that harmony between the governments which each is bound to cultivate and promote.

But if the United States can require this of another, that other may require it of them, because international obligations are of necessity reciprocal in their nature. The right, if it exists at all, is given by the law of nations, and what is law for one is, under the same circumstances, law for the other. A right secured by the law of nations to a nation, or its people, is one the United States, as the representatives of this nation, are bound to protect. Consequently, a law which is necessary and proper to afford this protection is one that congress may enact, because it is one that is needed to carry into execution a power conferred by the constitution on the government of the United States exclusively. There is no authority in the United States to require the passage and enforcement of such a law by the states. Therefore, the United States must have the power to pass it and enforce it themselves, or be unable to perform a duty which they may owe to another nation, and which the law of nations has imposed on them as part of their international obligations. This, however, does not prevent a state from providing for the punishment of the same thing, for here, as in the case of counterfeiting the coin of the United States, the act may be an offense against the authority of a state as well as that of the United States....

It remains only to consider those questions which present the point whether, in enacting a statute to define and punish an offense against the law of nations, it is necessary, in order "to define" the offense, that it be declared in the statute itself to be "an offense against the law of nations." This statute defines the offense, and if the thing made punishable is one which the United States are required by their international obligations to use due diligence to prevent, it is an offense against the law of nations. Such being the case, there is no more need of declaring in the statute that it is such an offense than there would be in any other criminal statute to declare that it was enacted to carry into execution any other particular power vested by the constitution or its people by counterfeiting its money, United States. Whether the offense as defined is an offense against the law of nations depends on the thing done, not on any declaration to that effect by congress. As has already been seen, it was incumbent on the United States as a nation to use due diligence to prevent any injury to another nation or its people by counterfeiting its money or its public or *quasi* public securities. This statute was enacted as a means to that end; that is to say, as a means of performing a duty which had been cast on the United States by the law of nations, and it was clearly appropriate legislation for that purpose. Upon its face, therefore, it defines an offense against the law of nations as clearly as if congress had in express terms so declared.

Fong Yue Ting v. United States

149 U.S. 698 (1893)

[In the *Chinese Exclusion Case*, excerpted in Chapter 1, the Supreme Court upheld the constitutionality of an 1888 Act of Congress that excluded certain Chinese laborers from reentering the United States. In 1892, Congress enacted a statute entitled "An act to prohibit the coming of Chinese persons into the United States." Section 6 of this statute required *deportation* of Chinese laborers in the United States unless they obtained a certificate from the Collector of the Internal Revenue demonstrating that they had entered the United States before 1892. To avoid deportation, a Chinese laborer without a certificate was required to show good cause and to present "at least one credible white witness" who would verify his residency prior to 1892. Section 7 of the statute directed the Secretary of the Treasury to issue rules and regulations implementing the statute.

This case involved three writs of habeas corpus filed by Chinese laborers arrested and held by the marshal of the district for not having certificates of residence under the 1892 Act. The plaintiffs argued that Congress lacked the power to deport them, and that the deportation in any event violated the Due Process Clause of the Fifth Amendment. The circuit court dismissed the writs of habeas corpus.]

MR. JUSTICE GRAY . . . delivered the opinion of the court . . . .

"It is an accepted maxim of international law that every sovereign nation has the power, as inherent in sovereignty, and essential to self-preservation, to forbid the entrance of foreigners within its dominions, or to admit them only in such cases and upon such conditions as it may see fit to prescribe. In the United States this power is vested in the national government, to which the constitution has committed the entire control of international relations, in peace as well as in war. It belongs to the political department of the government, and may be exercised either through treaties made by the president and senate or through statutes enacted by congress." [Nishimura Ekiu v. United States, 142 U.S. 651, 659 (1892).]

The right of a nation to expel or deport foreigners who have not been naturalized, or taken any steps towards becoming citizens of the country, rests upon the same grounds, and is as absolute and unqualified, as the right to prohibit and prevent their entrance into the country . . . .

The statements of leading commentators on the law of nations are to the same effect . . . .

The right to exclude or to expel all aliens, or any class of aliens, absolutely or upon certain conditions, in war or in peace, being an inherent and inalienable right of every sovereign and independent nation, essential to its safety, its independence, and its welfare, the question now before the court is whether the manner in which congress has exercised this right in sections 6 and 7 of the act of 1892 is consistent with the Constitution.

The United States are a sovereign and independent nation, and are vested by the Constitution with the entire control of international relations, and with all the powers of government necessary to maintain that control, and to make it effective. The only government of this country which other nations recognize or treat with is the government of the Union, and the only American flag known throughout the world is the flag of the United States . . . .

In exercising the great power which the people of the United States, by establishing a written Constitution as the supreme and paramount law, have vested in this court, of determining, whenever the question is properly brought before it, whether the acts of the legislature or of the executive are consistent with the Constitution, it behooves the court to be careful that it does not undertake to pass upon political questions, the final decision of which has been committed by the Constitution to the other departments of the government . . . .

The power to exclude or to expel aliens, being a power affecting international relations, is vested in the political departments of the government, and is to be regulated by treaty or by act of Congress, and to be executed by the executive authority according to the regulations so established, except so far the judicial department has been authorized by treaty or by statute, or is required by the paramount law of the Constitution, to intervene . . . .

The power to exclude aliens, and the power to expel them, rest upon one foundation, are derived from one source, are supported by the same reasons, and are in truth but parts of one and the same power.

The power of Congress, therefore, to expel, like the power to exclude, aliens, or any specified class of aliens, from the country, may be exercised entirely through executive officers; or Congress may call in the aid of the judiciary to ascertain any contested facts on which an alien's right to be in the country has been made by Congress to depend.

Congress, having the right, as it may see fit, to expel aliens of a particular class, or to permit them to remain, has undoubtedly the right to provide a system of registration and identification of the members of that class within the country, and to take all proper means to carry out the system which it provides....

Chinese laborers...like all other aliens residing in the United States for a shorter or longer time, are entitled, so long as they are permitted by the government of the United States to remain in the country, to the safeguards of the Constitution, and to the protection of the laws, in regard to their rights of person and of property, and to their civil and criminal responsibility. But they continue to be aliens, having taken no steps towards becoming citizens, and incapable of becoming such under the naturalization laws; and therefore remain subject to the power of Congress to expel them, or to order them to be removed and deported from the country, whenever, in its judgment, their removal is necessary or expedient for the public interest....

The question whether, and upon what conditions, these aliens shall be permitted to remain within the United States being one to be determined by the political departments of the government, the judicial department cannot properly express an opinion upon the wisdom, the policy, or the justice of the measures enacted by Congress in the exercise of the powers confided to it by the Constitution over this subject....

Upon careful consideration of the subject, the only conclusion which appears to us to be consistent with the principles of international law, with the Constitution and laws of the United States, and with the previous decisions of this court, is that in each of [the three cases] the judgment of the circuit court dismissing the writ of habeas corpus is right, and must be affirmed.

MR. JUSTICE BREWER, dissenting....

[W]hatever rights a resident alien might have in any other nation, here he is within the express protection of the Constitution, especially in respect to those guaranties which are declared in the original amendments. It has been repeated so often as to become axiomatic that this government is one of enumerated and delegated powers; and, as declared in article 10 of the amendments, "the powers not delegated to the United States by the constitution, nor prohibited by it to the states, are reserved to the states, respectively, or to the people."

It is said that the power here asserted is inherent in sovereignty. This doctrine of powers inherent in sovereignty is one both indefinite and dangerous. Where are the limits to such powers to be found, and by whom are they to be pronounced? Is it within legislative capacity to declare the limits? If so, then the mere assertion of an inherent power creates it, and despotism exists. May the courts establish the boundaries? Whence do they obtain the authority for this? Shall they look to the practices of other nations to ascertain the limits? The governments of other nations have elastic powers. Ours are fixed and bounded by a written constitution. The expulsion of a race may be within the inherent powers of a despotism. History, before the adoption of this Constitution, was not destitute of examples of the exercise of such a power; and its framers were familiar with history, and wisely, and it seems to me, they gave to this government no general power to banish. Banishment may be resorted to as punishment for crime; but among the powers reserved to the people, and not delegated to the government, is that of determining whether whole classes in our midst shall, for no crime but that of their race and birthplace, be driven from our territory.

Whatever may be true as to exclusion, — and as to that see *Chinese Exclusion* . . . — I deny that there is any arbitrary and unrestrained power to banish residents, even resident aliens. What, it may be asked, is the reason for any difference? The answer is obvious. The Constitution has no extraterritorial effect, and those who have not come lawfully within our territory cannot claim any protection from its provisions; and it may be that the national government, having full control of all matters relating to other nations, has the power to build, as it were, a Chinese wall around our borders, and absolutely forbid aliens to enter. But the Constitution has potency everywhere within the limits of our territory, and the powers which the national government may exercise within such limits are those, and only those, given to it by that instrument. Now, the power to remove resident aliens is, confessedly, not expressed. Even if it be among the powers implied, yet still it can be exercised only in subordination to the limitations and restrictions imposed by the Constitution.

MR. JUSTICE FIELD, dissenting . . . .

I had the honor to be the organ of the court in announcing [the opinion in the *Chinese Exclusion Case*]. I still adhere to the views there expressed, in all particulars; but between legislation for the exclusion of Chinese persons, — that is, to prevent them from entering the country, — and legislation for the deportation of those who have acquired a residence in the country under a treaty with China, there is a wide and essential difference. The power of the government to exclude foreigners from this country, — that is, to prevent them from entering it, — whenever the public interests, in its judgment, require such exclusion, has been repeatedly asserted by the legislative and executive departments of our government, and never denied; but its power to deport from the country persons lawfully domiciled therein by its consent, and engaged in the ordinary pursuits of life, has never been asserted by the legislative or executive departments, except for crime, or as an act of war, in view of existing or anticipated hostilities, unless the alien act of 1798 can be considered as recognizing that doctrine . . . .

. . . Aliens from countries at peace with us, domiciled within our country by its consent, are entitled to all the guaranties for the protection of their persons and property which are secured to native-born citizens. The moment any human being from a country at peace with us comes within the jurisdiction of the United States, with their consent, — and such consent will always be implied when not expressly withheld, and, in the case of the Chinese laborers before us, was, in terms, given by the treaty referred to, — he becomes subject to all their laws, is amenable to their punishment, and entitled to their protection. Arbitrary and despotic power can no more be exercised over them, with reference to their persons and property, than over the persons and property of native-born citizens. They differ only from citizens in that they cannot vote, or hold any public office. As men having our common humanity, they are protected by all the guaranties of the Constitution. To hold that they are subject to any different law, or are less protected in any particular, than other persons, is, in my judgment, to ignore the teachings of our history, the practice of our government, and the language of our Constitution . . . .

The government of the United States is one of limited and delegated powers. It takes nothing from the usages or the former action of European governments, nor does it take any power by any supposed inherent sovereignty. There is a great deal of confusion in the use of the word "sovereignty" by law writers. Sovereignty or supreme power is in this country vested in the people, and only in the people. By them certain sovereign powers have been delegated to the government of the United States, and other sovereign powers reserved to the states or to themselves. This is not a matter of inference and argument, but is the express declaration of the Tenth Amendment to the constitution, passed to avoid any misinterpretation of the powers of the general government. That amendment declares that "The powers not delegated to the United States by the Constitution, nor prohibited by it to the States, are reserved to the States, respectively, or to the people." When, therefore, power is exercised by Congress, authority for it must be found in express terms in the Constitution, or in the means necessary or proper for the execution of the power expressed. If it cannot be thus found, it does not exist . . . .

MR. CHIEF JUSTICE FULLER, dissenting . . . .

If the protection of the Constitution extends to Chinese laborers who are lawfully within, and entitled to remain in, the United States, under previous treaties and laws, then the question whether this act of Congress, so far as it relates to them, is in conflict with that instrument, is a judicial question, and its determination belongs to the judicial department.

However reluctant courts may be to pass upon the constitutionality of legislative acts, it is of the very essence of judicial duty to do so, when the discharge of that duty is properly invoked . . . .

The argument is that friendly aliens, who have lawfully acquired a domicile in this country, are entitled to avail themselves of the safeguards of the Constitution only while permitted to remain, and that the power to expel them, and the manner of its exercise, are unaffected by that instrument. It is difficult to see how this can be so, in view of the operation of the power upon the existing rights of individuals; and to say that the residence of the alien, when invited and secured by treaties and laws, is held in subordination to the exertion against him, as an alien, of the absolute and unqualified power asserted, is to import a condition not recognized by the fundamental law. Conceding that the exercise of the power to exclude is committed to the political department, and that the denial of entrance is not necessarily the subject of judicial cognizance, the exercise of the power to expel, the manner in which the right to remain may be terminated, rests on different ground, since limitations exist or are imposed upon the deprivation of that which has been lawfully acquired. And while the general government is invested, in respect of foreign countries and their subjects or citizens, with the powers necessary to the maintenance of its absolute independence and security throughout its entire territory, it cannot, in virtue of any delegated power, or power implied therefrom, of a supposed inherent sovereignty, arbitrarily deal with persons lawfully within the peace of its dominion. But the act before us is not an act to abrogate or repeal treaties or laws in respect of Chinese laborers entitled to remain in the United States, or to expel them from the country, and no such intent can be imputed to Congress. As to them, registration for the purpose of identification is required, and the deportation denounced for failure to do so is by way of punishment to coerce compliance with that requisition. No euphemism can disguise the character of the act in this regard. It directs the performance of a judicial function in a particular way, and inflicts punishment without a judicial trial. It is, in effect, a legislative sentence of banishment, and, as such, absolutely void. Moreover, it contains within it the germs of the assertion of an unlimited and arbitrary power, in general, incompatible with the immutable principles of justice, inconsistent with the nature of our government, and in conflict with the written Constitution by which that government was created, and those principles secured.

Notes and Questions

1. Congress has an elaborate institutional machinery devoted to foreign relations. The principal committee in the Senate is the Senate Foreign Relations Committee, which has jurisdiction over an enormous array of foreign relations and related issues.* Another important committee in the Senate is the Appropriations Committee (for obvious reasons). This committee's most important foreign relations subcommittee is the Subcommittee on Foreign Operations, which handles the dispersion of funds for foreign operations (including various State Department programs) and oversees the Immigration and Naturalization Service. Another important subcommittee is the Judiciary Committee's Subcommittee on Immigration (which maintains jurisdiction over legislation on refugees, immigration, and naturalization). There is also the Armed Services Committee, which has jurisdiction over the U.S. armed forces and a variety of other military and defense matters. Finally, half a dozen committees and subcommittees in the Senate affect U.S. participation in international trade. In the House, the International Relations Committee mirrors the Senate Foreign Relations Committee as the principal committee devoted to foreign relations.** As in the Senate, there are also House committees or subcommittees on appropriations, immigration, the armed services, and international trade.

These committees and subcommittees have institutional experience and expertise that facilitate congressional influence in foreign relations. The decentralization of power in Congress may suggest a weakness, however, in Congress's

* The Senate Rules describe that jurisdiction as including: (1) the acquisition of property for embassies; (2) U.S. boundaries; (3) diplomatic service; (4) foreign economic, military, technical, and humanitarian assistance; (5) foreign loans; (6) international activities of the American National Red Cross and the International Committee of the Red Cross; (7) international aspects of nuclear energy; (8) international conferences and congresses; (9) international law as it relates to foreign policy; (10) the International Monetary Fund and other international monetary organizations (shared with the Committee on Banking, Housing, and Urban Affairs); (11) intervention abroad and declarations of war; (12) the fostering of commercial intercourse with foreign nations and the safeguarding of American business interests abroad; (13) national security and international aspects of trusteeships of the United States; (14) oceans and international environmental and scientific affairs as they relate to foreign policy; (15) protection of U.S. citizens abroad and expatriation; (16) U.S. relations with foreign nations generally; (17) treaties and executive agreements, except reciprocal trade agreements; (18) the United Nations and its affiliate organizations; (19) the World Bank group and other international development assistance organizations. See Senate Rule XXV.1(j).
** Like its counterpart, the International Relations Committee maintains a broad jurisdiction, which includes the following areas: (1) U.S. relations with foreign nations generally; (2) the acquisition of property for embassies; (3) U.S. boundaries; (4) export controls; (5) foreign loans; (6) international commodity agreements; (7) international conferences and congresses; (8) international education; (9) intervention abroad and declarations of war; (10) diplomatic service; (11) the fostering of commercial intercourse with foreign nations and the safeguarding of American business interests abroad; (12) international economic policy; (13) neutrality; (14) the protection of American citizens abroad and expatriation; (15) the American National Red Cross; (16) trading with the enemy; and (17) United Nations Organizations.

ability to conduct U.S. foreign relations. Recall that one reason for the foreign relations difficulties in the pre-constitutional period was that these relations were run by a committee (and later a Department) in the Continental Congress. A decentralized, deliberative body like Congress has difficulty acting with dispatch. It also has difficulty speaking with the unified and coherent voice that may be needed in international communication and negotiation. Because its hallmark is public deliberation, Congress also has difficulty maintaining secrecy that is often crucial to the successful conduct of foreign relations. In addition, foreign relations problems arise on a daily basis, but Congress is not always in session. These are some of the reasons why, despite its broad powers and institutional expertise, Congress generally does not *conduct* U.S. foreign relations. But Congress nonetheless exercises significant influence on U.S. foreign policy. It controls the power of the purse, its concurrence is needed in many foreign relations endeavors, and it can impose obstacles to Executive action even in areas where its affirmative participation is not required.

2. One of the most significant sources of congressional authority over foreign relations stems from its control over appropriations and spending. The Constitution provides that "no Money shall be drawn from the Treasury, but in Consequence of Appropriations made by Law" (Art. I, §9, cl. 7), and gives Congress the power to "provide for the common Defence and general Welfare of the United States" (Art. I, 8, cl. 1). In addition, the Constitution prohibits any appropriation of funds for the army "for a longer Term than two Years" (Art. I, §8, cl. 12). These provisions give Congress enormous discretion over when and how to spend money on the foreign relations activities of the United States, and thus enormous power over U.S. foreign relations. As Professor Henkin has noted, "Congress decides the degree and detail of its support [for presidential foreign relations initiatives]: it determines ultimately the State Department's budget, how much money the President shall have to spend on the armed forces under his command, how much he can contribute to United Nations programs." Louis Henkin, Foreign Affairs and the United States Constitution 74 (2d ed. 1996). In addition, "Congress and Congressional committees can use appropriations and the appropriations process to bargain also about other elements of Presidential policy in foreign affairs. Because the President usually cannot afford to veto appropriations acts, they are favorite vehicles for conditions and other 'riders' imposed on unwilling Presidents." *Id.* at 74-75. To take one recent example, in the 1990s Congress successfully conditioned payment of United Nations dues on various United Nations reforms. *See* Sean D. Murphy, *Contemporary Practice of the United States Relating to International Law: Payment of U.S. Arrears to the United Nations*, 94 Am. J. Int'l L. 348, 348 (2000). Congress's appropriations power also gives it significant control over billions of dollars in U.S. foreign aid. Thus, for example, Congress often conditions foreign aid on the satisfaction of certain human rights practices in the donee country. In addition, the appropriations power can give Congress the final say in implementing the President's international initiatives. A famous early example was the dispute over whether Congress was required to issue appropriations needed to fund bilateral commissions contemplated by the Jay Treaty, which President Washington ratified in 1795. Although the House eventually authorized the needed appropriations, it did so after expressing the view that it retained the discretion not to do so. *See* David P. Currie, The Constitution in Congress: The Federalist Period, 1789-1801, at 214 (1997). Presidents have generally recognized the constraints imposed by Congress through its appropriations authority. *See, e.g.*, Expense of Presents to

Foreign Governments How Defrayed, 4 Op. Att'y Gen. 358, 359 (1845) (stating that in "the conduct of our foreign relations," the executive "cannot exceed the amount . . . appropriated"). Nonetheless, "Congress ordinarily feels legally, politically, or morally obligated to appropriate funds to maintain the President's foreign affairs establishment and to implement his treaties and other undertakings." Henkin, *supra*, at 74. Below in Section C we consider possible constitutional limits on the conditions that Congress can impose on its appropriations. In Chapter 4, we consider the significance of Congress's control over appropriations and spending in the context of war.

3. In Article I, Section 8, Clause 3, Congress is given the power to regulate both domestic and foreign commerce. What does *Buttfield* suggest about the relationship between Congress's domestic and foreign commerce powers? Consider the following statement from a 1903 Supreme Court decision upholding a federal statute regulating interstate sale of lottery tickets:

> It is argued that the power to regulate commerce among the several states is the same as the power to regulate commerce with foreign nations, and with the Indian tribes. But is its scope the same? As in effect before observed, the power to regulate commerce with foreign nations and the power to regulate interstate commerce, are to be taken *diverso intuitu*, for the latter was intended to secure equality and freedom in commercial intercourse as between the states, not to permit the creation of impediments to such intercourse; while the former clothed Congress with that power over international commerce, pertaining to a sovereign nation in its intercourse with foreign nations, and subject, generally speaking, to no implied or reserved power in the states. The laws which would be necessary and proper in the one case would not be necessary or proper in the other.

Champion v. Ames (The "Lottery Case"), 188 U.S. 321, 373 (1903). According to *Ames*, why is the Foreign Commerce Clause not subject to implied or reserved powers? Because the states never had the power to regulate foreign commerce prior to the Constitution? Is this true? *Cf.* Japan Line, Ltd. v. County of Los Angeles, 441 U.S. 434, 448 (1979) ("Although the Constitution, Art. I, §8, cl. 3, grants Congress power to regulate commerce 'with foreign Nations' and 'among the several States' in parallel phrases, there is evidence that the Founders intended the scope of the foreign commerce power to be the greater."). In ascertaining the scope of the foreign commerce power, what is the relevance of the fact that states are prohibited under the Constitution from imposing duties on imports and exports without Congress's consent? *See* U.S. Const. art. I, §10, cl. 2.

In recent years, the Supreme Court has imposed limitations on Congress's exercise of its domestic commerce power. In United States v. Lopez, 514 U.S. 549 (1995), for example, the Court held that a federal statute prohibiting the possession of firearms near schools exceeded Congress's domestic commerce power. The Court explained that Congress has the authority under its domestic commerce power to regulate only "the use of the channels of interstate commerce"; "the instrumentalities of interstate commerce, or persons or things in interstate commerce"; and intrastate activities "having a substantial relation to interstate commerce . . . , *i.e.*, those activities that substantially affect interstate commerce." *Id.* at 558-59. *See also* United States v. Morrison, 529 U.S. 598 (2000) (holding that civil remedy provision in the Violence Against Women Act exceeded Congress's domestic commerce power and its powers under the Fourteenth Amendment). The Court also has prohibited Congress, in the exercise of its domestic powers, from "commandeering" state legislative and executive officials. *See* New York v. United States, 505 U.S. 144 (1992); Printz v. United States, 521 U.S. 898 (1997). Do these limitations apply to Congress's exercise of its foreign commerce power? For example, in order for Congress to use its foreign commerce power to regulate conduct outside the United States, must the conduct have a "substantial effect" on the United States?

We return to potential federalism restrictions on the federal government's power in foreign affairs in the discussion of the treaty power in Chapter 6.

4. Another important congressional power is reflected in the Necessary and Proper Clause, also sometimes referred to as the "Sweeping Clause," which confers on Congress the authority "[t]o make all Laws which shall be necessary and proper for carrying into Execution the foregoing Powers, and all other Powers vested by this Constitution in the Government of the United States, or in any Department or Officer thereof." *See* U.S. Const. art. I, §8, cl. 18. By its terms, the Necessary and Proper Clause gives Congress not only the ability to enact laws to implement its own powers, but also the ability to enact laws to implement the powers of the other federal branches. Thus, for example, Congress can enact laws that are "necessary and proper" to implement the President's Article II foreign affairs powers.

In McCulloch v. Maryland, 17 U.S. (4 Wheat.) 316 (1819), the Supreme Court famously adopted an expansive construction of the Necessary and Proper Clause. In upholding the constitutionality of Congress's creation of a national bank, the Court stated: "Let the end be legitimate, let it be within the scope of the constitution; and all means which are appropriate, which are plainly adapted to that end, which are not prohibited, but consistent with the letter and spirit of the constitution, are constitutional." *Id.* at 421. Despite the breadth of this power, it presumably is not unlimited. How are courts to determine whether a law falls within the scope of the Necessary and Proper Clause? Consider the following statement in *McCulloch*: "[W]here the law is not prohibited, and is really calculated to effect any of the objects intrusted to the government, to undertake here to inquire into the decree of its necessity, would be to pass the line which circumscribes the judicial department, and to tread on legislative ground. This court disclaims all pretensions to such a power." *Id.* at 423. At first glance, this passage might suggest that the scope of Congress's necessary and proper authority is largely immune from judicial scrutiny. On the other hand, the passage could be read to require a judicial determination of whether a statute "is *really* calculated to effect . . . the objects intrusted to the government." If courts are to make that determination, what test should they use? *McCulloch* suggested two possibilities. First, the Court emphasized that a necessary and proper law was one whose means were "appropriate" and "plainly adapted" toward a legitimate end. Second, it suggested that courts should examine whether Congress acted with a proper purpose or merely under the "pretext" of exercising enumerated powers. Are courts competent to perform either this means-ends test or this purpose test? Is judicial competence in applying these tests a greater concern in the foreign affairs area?

For general discussion of the scope and meaning of the Necessary and Proper Clause, see, for example, Randy E. Barnett, *Necessary and Proper*, 44 UCLA L. Rev. 745 (1997); David E. Engdhal, *The Necessary and Proper Clause as an Intrinsic Restraint on Federal Lawmaking Power*, 22 Harv. J.L. & Pub. Pol'y 107 (1998); Stephen Gardbaum, *Rethinking Constitutional Federalism*, 74 Tex. L. Rev. 795 (1996); Gary Lawson & Patricia B. Granger, *The "Proper" Scope of Federal Power: A Jurisdictional Interpretation of the* Sweeping Clause, 43 Duke L.J. 267, 297 (1993); and William Van Alstyne,

The Role of Congress in Determining Incidental Powers of the President and of the Federal Courts: A Comment on the Horizontal Effect of "The Sweeping Clause," 36 Ohio St. L.J. 788 (1975).

5. Admiralty matters raise many important foreign policy issues. Yet the Constitution provides no explicit source of authority for Congress's regulation of admiralty. During the nineteenth century, the Supreme Court located Congress's power to regulate admiralty in the Commerce Clause. *See, e.g.,* The Daniel Ball, 77 U.S. 557, 564 (1870). But during this period, the Court adhered to a narrow construction of the Commerce Clause, especially the interstate Commerce Clause, and in some circumstances congressional power over admiralty was construed accordingly. *See, e.g.,* Moore v. American Transp. Co., 65 U.S. 1, 39 (1860) ("The act can apply to vessels only which are engaged in foreign commerce, and commerce between the States."). Eventually the Court reasoned that Congress's power to regulate admiralty was "necessary and proper" to carry into execution the federal courts' Article III jurisdiction over admiralty matters. *See, e.g.,* Romero v. International Terminal Operating Co., 358 U.S. 354, 360-61 (1959); Southern Pacific Co. v. Jensen, 244 U.S. 205, 214-15 (1917). The Court has suggested only two limits on this power: First, "there are boundaries to the maritime law and admiralty jurisdiction which inhere in those subjects and cannot be altered by legislation, as by excluding a thing falling clearly within them or including a thing falling clearly without." Panama R.R. Co. v. Johnson, 264 U.S. 375, 386 (1924). Second, the enactments, "when not relating to matters whose existence or influence is confined to a more restricted field . . . shall be coextensive with and operate uniformly in the whole of the United States." *Id.* at 387. *See also* United States v. Flores, 289 U.S. 137, 148 (1933) (referring to these "well recognized limitations"). For a discussion of the Court's changing interpretations of the source of congressional power over admiralty, see Note, *From Judicial Grant to Legislative Power: The Admiralty Clause in the Nineteenth Century,* 67 Harv. L. Rev. 1214, 1230-37 (1954).

6. Congress's power to define and punish offenses against the law of nations, discussed in *Arjona,* grew out of the Founders' concern that the states might not adequately punish infractions of the law of nations (such as attacks on ambassadors), and might thereby implicate the international responsibility of the entire United States. This concern led the Continental Congress to pass a resolution in 1781 recommending that the states "provide expeditious, exemplary and adequate punishment . . . for the infractions of the immunities of ambassadors and other public ministers authorized and received as such by the United States in Congress assembled." 21 Journals of the Continental Congress 1136 (1781); *see also* 29 Journals of the Continental Congress 654-66 (1785) (similar resolution). At the Constitutional Convention in 1787, Edmund Randolph stated that one of the defects of the Articles of Confederation was that Congress "could not cause infractions of treaties or of the law of nations, to be punished: that particular states might by their conduct provoke war without controul. . . ." 1 Records of the Federal Convention of 1787, at 19 (Max Farrand ed., 1911); *see also id.* at 25 (Randolph reported to have said, "If the rights of an ambassador be invaded by any citizen it is only in a few States that any laws exist to punish the offender.").

When the Define and Punish Clause was being drafted, James Wilson expressed concern about the implications of Congress's power to "define" the law of nations: "To pretend to *define* the law of nations which depended on the authority of all the Civilized Nations of the World, would have the look of arrogance, that would make us look ridiculous." Gouverneur Morris responded: "The word *define* is proper when applied to *offenses* in this case; the law of (nations) being often too vague and deficient to be a rule." 2 Records of the Federal Convention of 1787, at 614-15 (Max Farrand ed., 1911). *Cf.* United States v. Smith, 18 U.S. (5 Wheat.) 153, 159 (1820) ("Offences, too, against the law of nations, cannot, with any accuracy, be said to be completely ascertained and defined in any public code recognised by the common consent of nations."). For more on the origins of the Define and Punish Clause, see Charles D. Siegal, *Deference and Its Dangers: Congress' Power to "Define . . . Offenses Against the Law of Nations,"* 21 Vand. J. Transnat'l L. 865, 874-79 (1988).

Are there any limits on Congress's power to incorporate international law into federal law under the Define and Punish Clause? One limit is the Bill of Rights. *See* Boos v. Barry, 485 U.S. 312 (1988) (holding that a statute enacted pursuant to the Define and Punish Clause that prohibited the display of certain signs within 500 feet of an embassy violated the First Amendment). In addition, one might think that the Define and *Punish* Clause gives Congress only criminal enforcement authority, not the authority to regulate civil suits. However, Congress has invoked the Define and Punish Clause as a basis for enacting important civil legislation relating to foreign relations, including the Foreign Sovereign Immunities Act and the Torture Victim Protection Act. For a recent argument that the clause authorizes civil as well as criminal enactments, see Beth Stephens, *Federalism and Foreign Affairs: Congress's Power to "Define and Punish . . . Offenses Against the Law of Nations,"* 42 Wm. & Mary L. Rev. 447 (2000). *But cf.* Siegal, *supra,* at 866-67 (stating that the clause permits "Congress to define violations of customary international law as domestic crimes"). For an argument that the Framers did not expect the "law of nations" to evolve over time and that the Define and Punish Clause therefore "allows for the enactment of legislation touching upon only that fixed, discrete set of areas involving intercourse with foreign nations and their citizens — including navigation, trade, war, and diplomacy — that comprise what the Framers believed to be the immutable law of nations," see Michael T. Morley, Note, *The Law of Nations and the Offenses Clause of the Constitution: A Defense of Federalism,* 112 Yale L.J. 109, 112 (2002).

Are there any other limits on Congress's define and punish power? The Torture Victim Protection Act mentioned above provides a cause of action in U.S. courts for torture by foreign citizens in foreign countries. *See* 28 U.S.C. §1350 note. Is this a valid exercise of the Define and Punish Clause? Should there be a requirement that the defendant have either a territorial or citizenship nexus with the United States? These and other questions concerning the Act are considered in Chapter 7. Finally, what if Congress attempts to define and punish something that is not in fact an offense against the law of nations? Should courts engage in an independent review of whether the punished offense is really prohibited by the law of nations, or does Congress have substantial, or perhaps plenary, authority to decide for itself what the law of nations prohibits? For a discussion of this issue, see Note, *The Offences Clause After Sosa v. Alvarez-Machain,* 118 Harv. L. Rev. 2378 (2005).

The Court in *Arjona* stated that "if the thing made punishable is one which the United States are required by their international obligations to use due diligence to prevent, it is an offense against the law of nations." Is this interpretation consistent with the text of the Define and Punish Clause? Or is the clause narrower, authorizing punishment only of acts which are themselves violations of the law of nations? *Cf.* Ex parte Quirin, 317 U.S. 1, 28 (1942) (upholding Congress's "authority to define and punish offenses against the law of nations by sanctioning, within constitutional limitations, the jurisdiction of military commissions to try persons for offenses which, according to the rules and precepts of the law of nations, and more particularly the law of war, are cognizable by such tribunals").

7. Congress also has the power in Article I, Section 8 to define and punish felonies and piracies committed on the high seas. There has been a federal piracy statute since 1790. The current statute provides that, "Whoever, on the high seas, commits the crime of piracy as defined by the law of nations, and is afterwards brought into or found in the United States, shall be imprisoned for life." 18 U.S.C. §1651. In an early decision involving a predecessor to this statute, the Supreme Court held that Congress's definition of piracy by reference to the law of nations was sufficiently precise. *See* United States v. Smith, 18 U.S. (5 Wheat.) 153, 162 (1820). The Court reasoned that the crime of piracy had a definite meaning in international law and that "Congress may as well define by using a term of a known and determinate meaning, as by an express enumeration of all the particulars included in that term." *Id*. at 159. As we discuss in Chapter 7, the Alien Tort Statute, first enacted in 1789, provides: "The district courts shall have original jurisdiction of any civil action by an alien for a tort only, committed in violation of the law of nations or a treaty of the United States." 28 U.S.C. §1350. Like the piracy statute, the Alien Tort Statute does not attempt to define the content of the law of nations. It is not clear that the Alien Tort Statute, however, was enacted pursuant to the Define and Punish Clause. Rather, it may have been based simply on Congress's power to regulate the jurisdiction of the lower federal courts (which has been implied from Congress's power to "ordain and establish" lower federal courts, see U.S. Const. art. III, §1).

8. The justifications for Congress's power to regulate various aspects of immigration have, as in the admiralty context, changed over the years. A possible basis for congressional regulation of immigration is the enumerated power to "establish an uniform Rule of Naturalization," U.S. Const. art. I, §8, cl. 4. The problem with this theory is that a power to regulate naturalization (the process by which a person becomes a U.S. citizen) is substantially narrower than a power to regulate immigration (a process that includes the admission, exclusion, and deportation of aliens, as well as the naturalization of aliens to become U.S. citizens). As a result, the Supreme Court has located the power to regulate immigration elsewhere. During most of the nineteenth century, the Court addressed Congress's power over immigration only indirectly, in the context of striking down state regulations relating to immigration under the dormant Commerce Clause. *See, e.g.,* The Passenger Cases, 48 U.S. 283 (1849).* The Court finally addressed the question directly in The Head Money Cases, 112 U.S. 580, 600 (1884), where the Court rejected a challenge to a congressional tax on ships for immigrants brought to U.S. ports, reasoning: "congress having the power to pass a law regulating immigration as a part of the commerce of this country with foreign nations, we see nothing in the statute by which it has here exercised that power forbidden by any other part of the constitution."

Toward the end of the nineteenth century, the Court moved away from a Commerce Clause justification for congressional power over immigration, and began to embrace a more extensive source of power—inherent constitutional

---

* The first federal immigration statute was not enacted until 1875; prior to that time, the several states played a major role in regulating immigration, primarily through the police power. *See* Gerald L. Neuman, *The Lost Century of American Immigration Law* (1776-1875), 93 Colum. L. Rev. 1833 (1993).

power based on national sovereignty. One of the first instances of this shift was the *Chinese Exclusion Case*, excerpted in Chapter 1. *Fong Yue Ting* extended this sovereignty rationale to cover the power to deport aliens living in the United States. Throughout the twentieth century, the Court continued to invoke the sovereignty rationale as a basis for Congress's power over immigration. *See, e.g.*, Miller v. Albright, 523 U.S. 420, 455-56 (1998); Landon v. Plasencia, 459 U.S. 21, 34 (1982); Galvan v. Press, 347 U.S. 522, 530 (1954). For articles analyzing the sources of congressional power over immigration, see Louis Henkin, *The Constitution and United States Sovereignty: A Century of* Chinese Exclusion *and Its Progeny*, 100 Harv. L. Rev. 853 (1987); Siegfried Hesse, *The Constitutional Status of the Lawfully Admitted Permanent Resident Alien: The Pre-1917 Cases*, 68 Yale L.J. 1578 (1959); Siegfried Hesse, *The Constitutional Status of the Lawfully Admitted Permanent Resident Alien: The Inherent Limits of the Power to Expel*, 69 Yale L.J. 262 (1959); Stephen Legomsky, *Immigration Law and the Principle of Plenary Congressional Power*, 1984 Sup. Ct. Rev. 255; Hiroshi Motomura, *Immigration Law After a Century of Plenary Power: Phantom Constitutional Norms and Statutory Interpretation*, 100 Yale L.J. 545 (1990); Gerald L. Neuman, *The Lost Century of American Immigration Law (1776-1875)*, 93 Colum. L. Rev. 1833 (1993).

9. The *Chinese Exclusion Case* and *Fong Yue Ting* are the founts of the "plenary power doctrine" in immigration law. This doctrine has two components. First is the idea, sketched above, that the source of congressional power over immigration is inherent constitutional power based on national sovereignty. Second, and distinct, is the notion suggested in *Fong Yue Ting* that the validity of congressional regulations of immigration involve political questions committed to the political branches rather than the courts to resolve. (In accord with modern changes in the political question doctrine, more recent cases articulate this component of the plenary power doctrine in terms of "special judicial deference" to Congress, see Fiallo v. Bell, 430 U.S. 787, 793 (1977).) *Fong Yue Ting* and subsequent cases invoked the plenary power doctrine to reject aliens' due process claims. *See, e.g.*, United States ex rel. Knauff v. Shaughnessy, 338 U.S. 537, 544 (1950) ("Whatever the procedure authorized by Congress is, it is due process as far as an alien is concerned").

The "deference" component of the plenary power doctrine has eroded in recent years. Beginning with Landon v. Plasencia, 459 U.S. 21 (1982), the Court began "to use mainstream procedural due process analysis in immigration law and made procedural due process claims potentially available to a wider circle of aliens." Hiroshi Motomura, *The Curious Evolution of Immigration Law: Procedural Surrogates for Substantive Constitutional Rights*, 92 Colum. L. Rev. 1625, 1656 (1992). More recent decisions have continued and expanded this trend. *See* Immigration and Naturalization Service v. St. Cyr, 121 S. Ct. 2271 (2001) (upholding judicial review of deportation proceedings even though expulsion statute appeared to bar it); Zadvydas v. Davis, 121 S. Ct. 2491 (2001) (holding that due process protects liberty of "all 'persons' in the United States, including aliens, whether their presence here is lawful, unlawful, temporary, or permanent"). *See also* Gabriel J. Chin, *Is There a Plenary Power Doctrine? A Tentative Apology and Prediction for Our Strange but Unexceptional Constitutional Immigration Law*, 14 Geo. Immigr. L.J. 257 (2000); Peter J. Spiro, *Explaining the End of Plenary Power*, 16 Geo. Immigr. L.J. 339 (2002).

10. To the extent that the plenary power doctrine survives, do you agree with the *Fong Yue Ting* dissents that the doctrine is (in Justice Brewer's words) "indefinite and dangerous" or (in Justice Field's words) "unlimited and despotic"? Why did

Justice Field—the author of the majority opinion in the *Chinese Exclusion Case*—dissent in *Fong Yue Ting*? Was it because of the distinction between exclusion and deportation? Is this a difference that the Constitution recognizes? Why? Is Justice Brewer right to suggest, in dissent, that deportation is more problematic than exclusion because "[t]he constitution has no extraterritorial effect"? On the extra-territorial scope of constitutional rights, see Chapter 8.

11. Does Congress have a general foreign relations power? Recall from Chapter 2 that, in the Second Hickenlooper Amendment, Congress modified the act of state doctrine articulated in *Sabbatino* to permit courts greater leeway in judging the validity of certain acts of state. What was the constitutional basis for this statute? What is the constitutional basis for congressional assertions of U.S. sovereignty over U.S. airspace, see 49 U.S.C. §40103? For federal statutes authorizing extradition in the absence of a treaty, see 18 U.S.C. §3186? Professor Henkin, unable to find a clear basis in Article I for these and other enactments, grounds them in a general "Foreign Affairs Power" akin to powers inherent in sovereignty articulated in the *Chinese Exclusion Case* and *Fong Yue Ting*. *See* Henkin, *supra*, at 70-72; *cf.* Perez v. Brownell, 356 U.S. 44, 59 (1958) (referring to the "power of Congress to deal with foreign relations"). Do you agree? Is there some other constitutional basis for these statutes? If Congress does have a general foreign relations power, what are its limits? *Cf.* Louis Henkin, *The Treaty Makers and the Law Makers: The Law of the Land and Foreign Relations*, 107 U. Pa. L. Rev. 903, 920-30 (1959) (arguing that the Foreign Affairs Power supports legislation on any matter so related to foreign affairs that the United States might deal with it by treaty).

12. In the midst of the 1798-1800 undeclared war between France and the United States, George Logan, a Pennsylvania Quaker, traveled to France and attempted to work out a peace settlement. This effort indirectly led President Adams to dispatch negotiators to France and, eventually, to obtain peace. But the Federalists in Congress were furious, and responded in 1799 by enacting the Logan Act, which prohibited private correspondence with foreign governments. The modern version of the Act provides:

> Any citizen of the United States, wherever he may be, who, without authority of the United States, directly or indirectly commences or carries on any correspondence or intercourse with any foreign government or any officer or agent thereof, with intent to influence the measures or conduct of any foreign government or of any officer or agent thereof, in relation to any disputes or controversies with the United States, or to defeat the measures of the United States, shall be fined under this title or imprisoned not more than three years, or both.
>
> This section shall not abridge the right of a citizen to apply, himself or his agent, to any foreign government or the agents thereof for redress of any injury which he may have sustained from such government or any of its agents or subjects.

18 U.S.C. §953. What is the basis of congressional authority to enact this statute? The statute's supporters argued that it was necessary and proper to implement the President's authority to negotiate with foreign nations. *See* David P. Currie, The Constitution in Congress: The Federalist Period, 1789-1801, at 262 n.208 (1997). Is this persuasive? Is there some other basis for congressional power to enact the Logan Act? The Foreign Affairs Power, perhaps? Does the Act violate the First Amendment? For discussions of the Act, see Detlev Vagts, *The Logan Act: Paper Tiger or Sleeping Giant?*, 60 Am. J. Int'l L. 268, 269-80 (1966); Kevin M. Kearney, Comment, *Private Citizens in Foreign Affairs: A Constitutional Analysis*, 36 Emory L.J.

285, 287-306 (1987); Curtis S. Simpson III, Comment, *The Logan Act of 1799: May It Rest in Peace*, 10 Cal. W. Int'l L.J. 365 (1980). For similar legislation, see The Johnson Act, 18 U.S.C. §955 (prohibiting private citizens from lending money to foreign nations in default on loans from the United States).

13. We explore other aspects of congressional power throughout this casebook, including Congress's power to preempt state law, see Chapter 5, its power to override treaty obligations as a matter of U.S. domestic law, see Chapter 6, and its power to violate customary international law, see Chapter 7. *See also* Cecil V. Crabb, Jr., Glenn J. Antizzo & Leila E. Sarieddine, Congress and the Foreign Policy Process (2000); James M. Lindsay, Congress and the Politics of U.S. Foreign Policy (1994); Thomas M. Franck & Edward Weisband, Foreign Policy by Congress (1979).

B. SOURCES OF EXECUTIVE POWER

This section explores the basic sources of Executive power in foreign affairs.* Unlike Article I's lengthy and detailed list of congressional foreign affairs powers, Article II grants relatively few enumerated foreign affairs powers to the President. Nevertheless, the President has always exercised enormous foreign relations power. Indeed, the President is often described as having the dominant role in the conduct of U.S. foreign relations. As we saw in Chapter 1, for example, the Supreme Court in *Curtiss-Wright* referred to "the very delicate, plenary and exclusive power of the President as the sole organ of the federal government in the field of international relations." The paradox of the relatively spare textual grants of power to the President and the reality of the President's broad foreign relations power is a recurring issue in this casebook. Before reading the materials that follow, carefully read Article II of the Constitution, in Appendix A, and review the Pacificus-Helvidius debate concerning the nature and scope of Executive power, in Chapter 1. *president has dominant role in foreign relations*

President Monroe's Annual Message to Congress, December 2, 1823

in 2 A Compilation of the Messages and Papers of the Presidents, 1789-1897, at 209, 218 (James D. Richardson ed., 1896)

[In the early 1820s, rumors circulated in the United States that Spain, supported by other continental European powers, was preparing to deploy a military force to restore to Spain colonies that it had lost in revolutions in South and Central America during the previous decade. At the same time, Russia was threatening to extend its empire into northwestern North America. In August 1823, George Canning, the British foreign secretary, proposed that Great Britain and the United States form an alliance to oppose any such action by the continental powers. Secretary of War John Calhoun, along with former presidents Jefferson and Madison, supported the alliance with Britain. Secretary of State John Quincy Adams strenuously opposed it.

---

* One of the Executive Branch's most important powers — the "Commander in Chief" power — is discussed in Chapter 4. Another important set of presidential powers — treaty-making and executive-agreement-making — is addressed in Chapter 6.

President opposed alliance with G.B.

He argued instead that the United States should issue a unilateral statement of policy about the inappropriateness of European meddling in the American hemisphere. President Monroe followed Adams' advice in his seventh annual message to Congress, excerpted below.]

[T]he American continents, by the free and independent condition which they have assumed and maintain, are henceforth not to be considered as subjects for future colonization by any European powers....

We owe it...to candor and to the amicable relations existing between the United States and those powers to declare that we should consider any attempt on their part to extend their system to any portion of this hemisphere as dangerous to our peace and safety. With the existing colonies or dependencies of any European power we have not interfered and shall not interfere. But with the Governments who have declared their independence and maintain it, and whose independence we have, on great consideration and on just principles, acknowledged, we could not view any interposition for the purpose of oppressing them, or controlling in any other manner their destiny, by any European power in any other light than as the manifestation of an unfriendly disposition toward the United States.

Theodore Roosevelt, An Autobiography

388-89 (1914)

The most important factor in getting the right spirit in my Administration, next to insistence upon courage, honesty, and a genuine democracy of desire to serve the plain people, was my insistence upon the theory that the executive power was limited only by specific restrictions and prohibitions appearing in the Constitution or imposed by Congress under its Constitutional powers. My view was that every executive officer and above all every executive officer in high position was a steward of the people, bound actively and affirmatively to do all he could for the people and not to content himself with the negative merit of keeping his talents undamaged in a napkin. I declined to adopt this view that what was imperatively necessary for the Nation could not be done by the President unless he could find some specific authorization to do it. My belief was that it was not only his right but his duty to do anything that the needs of the Nation demanded unless such action was forbidden by the Constitution or by the laws. Under this interpretation of executive power I did and caused to be done many things not previously done by the President and the heads of the departments. I did not usurp power, but I did greatly broaden the use of executive power. In other words, I acted for the public welfare, I acted for the common well-being of all our people, whenever and in whatever measure was necessary, unless prevented by direct constitutional or legislative prohibition.

can do anything unless expressly forbidden

William Howard Taft, Our Chief Magistrate and His Powers

139-40, 144-45 (1916)

The true view of the Executive functions is, as I conceive it, that the President can exercise no power which cannot be fairly and reasonably traced to some specific grant of power or justly implied and included within such express grant as proper

can't excercise anything unless it can be traced or implied to some grant of power

and necessary to its exercise. Such specific grant must be either in the Federal Constitution or in an act of Congress passed in pursuance thereof. There is no undefined residuum of power which he can exercise because it seems to him to be in the public interest.... The grants of Executive power are necessarily in general terms in order not to embarrass the Executive within the field of action plainly marked for him, but his jurisdiction must be justified and vindicated by affirmative constitutional or statutory provision, or it does not exist. There have not been wanting, however, eminent men in high public office holding a different view and who have insisted upon the necessity for an undefined residuum of Executive power in the public interest....

My judgment is that the view of Mr. Garfield and Mr. Roosevelt, ascribing an undefined residuum of power to the President is an unsafe doctrine and that it might lead under emergencies to results of an arbitrary character, doing irremediable injustice to private right. The mainspring of such a view is that the Executive is charged with responsibility for the welfare of all the people in a general way, that he is to play the part of a Universal Providence and set all things right, and that anything that in his judgement will help the people he ought to do, unless he is expressly forbidden not to do it. The wide field of action that this would give to the Executive one can hardly limit.

Robert Kagan, A Twilight Struggle: American Power and Nicaragua, 1977-1990

345-53 (1996)

The landslide re-election of Ronald Reagan guaranteed another battle with Congress over aid to the [Nicaraguan] contras in 1985....

The nation's overwhelming support for Reagan did not translate directly into support for the contra war in Nicaragua....

Reagan...began his campaign for contra aid after his landslide victory, taking advantage of his own popularity and Democratic unease. In each phase of the battle, he pushed the congressional consensus as far as he believed it could go and then settled, always a bit short of his goals, but always further along than before....

President Reagan himself was eager to do battle on the issue of Nicaragua. He intended to wield his restored political power to make the members of Congress "feel the heat" if they refused to "see the light." Less constrained after his landslide re-election, Reagan gave fuller voice to his moral convictions about communism and America's role in fighting it. As a means of selling his unpopular covert war in Nicaragua, President Reagan elaborated more fully on themes he had adumbrated at Westminster in 1982. Linking together the popular Afghan and unpopular Nicaraguan rebellions and putting both in a broader historical and ideological context that stretched from the American Revolution to the French Resistance, Reagan elaborated an international strategy that was revolutionary abroad and politically potent at home.

The "Reagan Doctrine," as it was dubbed by columnist Charles Krauthammer in 1985, was a sweeping application of American political philosophy and morality to the conduct of international affairs. It denied the fundamental legitimacy of all communist governments, and by implication all non-democratic governments, declared them to be essentially transient, affirmed the right of democratic movements to challenge them, and proclaimed the right, even the responsibility, of the United States to provide assistance to those movements. "There are those who say America's attempt to encourage freedom in Nicaragua interferes with the right of self-determination," Reagan said in April. "[But] when a small clique seizes a country there is no self-determination, and no chance of it." Reagan was thinking primarily about communist governments, but Secretary Shultz took the doctrine to its logical conclusion and declared that "as a matter of fundamental principle, the United States supports human rights and peaceful democratic change throughout the world, including in non-Communist, pro-Western countries." Pushed by the difficult task of selling its policy in Nicaragua, and emboldened by the continued success of democratic reform in El Salvador, Reagan and Shultz thus called for an unprecedented ideological consistency in American foreign policy.

The departure from traditional Republican policies was striking. For most of the twentieth century, Republicans had been isolationists, anti-Communists, or practitioners of realpolitik. Even Democratic presidents, from Kennedy to Carter, had hesitated to question the legitimacy of non-communist dictatorships. The Reagan Doctrine was the unique product of a unique combination of circumstances in the United States. At the height of the cold war, with the most fervently anti-communist President in American history, a Congress half-controlled by Democrats, and an American public moved by conflicting desires for national assertiveness and withdrawal, by belligerent anti-communism and post-Vietnam moralism, the Reagan doctrine came as close as any other international political strategy to answering the contradictory demands of the country.

George W. Bush, The National Security Strategy of the United States of America (Sept. 2002)

at http://www.whitehouse.gov/nsc/nss.html

.... V. Prevent Our Enemies from Threatening Us, Our Allies, and Our Friends with Weapons of Mass Destruction ....

The nature of the Cold War threat required the United States — with our allies and friends — to emphasize deterrence of the enemy's use of force, producing a grim strategy of mutual assured destruction. With the collapse of the Soviet Union and the end of the Cold War, our security environment has undergone profound transformation.

Having moved from confrontation to cooperation as the hallmark of our relationship with Russia, the dividends are evident: an end to the balance of terror that divided us; an historic reduction in the nuclear arsenals on both sides; and cooperation in areas such as counterterrorism and missile defense that until recently were inconceivable.

But new deadly challenges have emerged from rogue states and terrorists. None of these contemporary threats rival the sheer destructive power that was arrayed against us by the Soviet Union. However, the nature and motivations of these new adversaries, their determination to obtain destructive powers hitherto available only to the world's strongest states, and the greater likelihood that they will use weapons of mass destruction against us, make today's security environment more complex and dangerous ....

We must be prepared to stop rogue states and their terrorist clients before they are able to threaten or use weapons of mass destruction against the United States and our allies and friends. Our response must take full advantage of strengthened alliances, the establishment of new partnerships with former adversaries, innovation in the use of military forces, modern technologies, including the development of an effective missile defense system, and increased emphasis on intelligence collection and analysis....

It has taken almost a decade for us to comprehend the true nature of this new threat. Given the goals of rogue states and terrorists, the United States can no longer solely rely on a reactive posture as we have in the past. The inability to deter a potential attacker, the immediacy of today's threats, and the magnitude of potential harm that could be caused by our adversaries' choice of weapons, do not permit that option. We cannot let our enemies strike first....

For centuries, international law recognized that nations need not suffer an attack before they can lawfully take action to defend themselves against forces that present an imminent danger of attack. Legal scholars and international jurists often conditioned the legitimacy of preemption on the existence of an imminent threat — most often a visible mobilization of armies, navies, and air forces preparing to attack.

We must adapt the concept of imminent threat to the capabilities and objectives of today's adversaries. Rogue states and terrorists do not seek to attack us using conventional means. They know such attacks would fail. Instead, they rely on acts of terror and, potentially, the use of weapons of mass destruction — weapons that can be easily concealed, delivered covertly, and used without warning....

The United States has long maintained the option of preemptive actions to counter a sufficient threat to our national security. The greater the threat, the greater is the risk of inaction — and the more compelling the case for taking anticipatory action to defend ourselves, even if uncertainty remains as to the time and place of the enemy's attack. To forestall or prevent such hostile acts by our adversaries, the United States will, if necessary, act preemptively. Giving U.S power to act preemptively w/ terrorism

Youngstown Sheet & Tube Co. v. Sawyer

343 U.S. 579 (1952)

[During the Korean War, a labor dispute arose in the U.S. steel industry, and the United Steelworkers threatened to go on strike. In an effort to avoid a disruption in steel production, President Truman issued an executive order directing the Secretary of Commerce to take possession of and operate some of the nation's steel mills. The executive order noted that the United States and other nations were engaged "in deadly combat with the forces of aggression in Korea" and that "the weapons and other materials needed by our armed forces and by those joined with us in the defense of the free world are produced to a great extent in this country, and steel is an indispensable component of substantially all of such weapons and materials." As support for the order, President Truman invoked "the authority vested in me by the Constitution and laws of the United States, and as President of the United States and Commander in Chief of the armed forces of the United States." The mill owners challenged the constitutionality of the President's order.]

MR. JUSTICE BLACK delivered the opinion of the Court....

The President's power, if any, to issue the order must stem either from an act of Congress or from the Constitution itself. There is no statute that expressly

Nowhere is pres. given this power.

authorizes the President to take possession of property as he did here. Nor is there any act of Congress to which our attention has been directed from which such a power can fairly be implied. Indeed, we do not understand the Government to rely on statutory authorization for this seizure. There are two statutes which do authorize the President to take both personal and real property under certain conditions.

Doesn't meet req. for proper seizure under statute

However, the Government admits that these conditions were not met and that the President's order was not rooted in either of the statutes. The Government refers to the seizure provisions of one of these statutes (§201(b) of the Defense Production Act) as "much too cumbersome, involved, and time-consuming for the crisis which was at hand."

Moreover, the use of the seizure technique to solve labor disputes in order to prevent work stoppages was not only unauthorized by any congressional enactment; prior to this controversy, Congress had refused to adopt that method of settling labor disputes. When the Taft-Hartley Act was under consideration in 1947, Congress rejected an amendment which would have authorized such governmental seizures in cases of emergency. Apparently it was thought that the technique of seizure, like that of compulsory arbitration, would interfere with the process of collective bargaining. Consequently, the plan Congress adopted in that Act did not provide for seizure under any circumstances. Instead, the plan sought to bring about settlements by use of the customary devices of mediation, conciliation, investigation by boards of inquiry, and public reports. In some instances temporary injunctions were authorized to provide cooling-off periods. All this failing, unions were left free to strike after a secret vote by employees as to whether they wished to accept their employers' final settlement offer.

It is clear that if the President had authority to issue the order he did, it must be found in some provision of the Constitution. And it is not claimed that express constitutional language grants this power to the President. The contention is that presidential power should be implied from the aggregate of his powers under the Constitution. Particular reliance is placed on provisions in Article II which say that "The executive Power shall be vested in a President..."; that "he shall take Care that the Laws be faithfully executed"; and that he "shall be Commander in Chief of the Army and Navy of the United States."

The order cannot properly be sustained as an exercise of the President's military power as Commander in Chief of the Armed Forces. The Government attempts to do so by citing a number of cases upholding broad powers in military commanders engaged in day-to-day fighting in a theater of war. Such cases need not concern us here. Even though "theater of war" be an expanding concept, we cannot with faithfulness to our constitutional system hold that the Commander in Chief of the Armed Forces has the ultimate power as such to take possession of private property in order to keep labor disputes from stopping production. This is a job for the Nation's lawmakers, not for its military authorities.

can't fall under comm. in chief power

Nor can the seizure order be sustained because of the several constitutional provisions that grant executive power to the President. In the framework of our Constitution, the President's power to see that the laws are faithfully executed refutes the idea that he is to be a lawmaker. The Constitution limits his functions in the lawmaking process to the recommending of laws he thinks wise and the vetoing of laws he thinks bad. And the Constitution is neither silent nor equivocal about who shall make laws which the President is to execute. The first section of the first article says that "All legislative Powers herein granted shall be vested in a Congress of the United States...." After granting many powers to the Congress,

congress has law making power

Article I goes on to provide that Congress may "make all Laws which shall be necessary and proper for carrying into Execution the foregoing Powers, and all other Powers vested by this Constitution in the Government of the United States, or in any Department or Officer thereof." . . .

It is said that other Presidents without congressional authority have taken possession of private business enterprises in order to settle labor disputes. But even if this be true, Congress has not thereby lost its exclusive constitutional authority to make laws necessary and proper to carry out the powers vested by the Constitution "in the Government of the United States, or any Department or Officer thereof."

The Founders of this Nation entrusted the lawmaking power to the Congress alone in both good and bad times. It would do no good to recall the historical events, the fears of power and the hopes for freedom that lay behind their choice. Such a review would but confirm our holding that this seizure order cannot stand . . . . *unconstitutional*.

MR. JUSTICE FRANKFURTER, concurring . . . .

Congress has frequently — at least 16 times since 1916 — specifically provided for executive seizure of production, transportation, communications, or storage facilities. In every case it has qualified this grant of power with limitations and safeguards. This body of enactments . . . demonstrates that Congress deemed seizure so drastic a power as to require that it be carefully circumscribed whenever the President was vested with this extraordinary authority . . . .

Congress in 1947 was again called upon to consider whether governmental seizure should be used to avoid serious industrial shutdowns. Congress decided against conferring such power generally and in advance, without special Congressional enactment to meet each particular need . . . .

[N]othing can be plainer than that Congress made a conscious choice of policy in a field full of perplexity and peculiarly within legislative responsibility for choice. In formulating legislation for dealing with industrial conflicts, Congress could not more clearly and emphatically have withheld authority than it did in 1947. Perhaps as much so as is true of any piece of modern legislation, Congress acted with full consciousness of what it was doing and in the light of much recent history . . . .

It cannot be contended that the President would have had power to issue this order had Congress explicitly negated such authority in formal legislation. Congress has expressed its will to withhold this power from the President as though it had said so in so many words . . . .

Apart from his vast share of responsibility for the conduct of our foreign relations, the embracing function of the President is that "he shall take Care that the Laws be faithfully executed . . . ." Art. II, §3. The nature of that authority has for me been comprehensively indicated by Mr. Justice Holmes. "The duty of the President to see that the laws be executed is a duty that does not go beyond the laws or require him to achieve more than Congress sees fit to leave within his power." Myers v. United States, 272 U.S. 52, 177. The powers of the President are not as particularized as are those of Congress. But unenumerated powers do not mean undefined powers. The separation of powers built into our Constitution gives essential content to undefined provisions in the frame of our government.

To be sure, the content of the three authorities of government is not to be derived from an abstract analysis. The areas are partly interacting, not wholly disjointed. The Constitution is a framework for government. Therefore the way the framework has consistently operated fairly establishes that it has operated according to its true nature. Deeply embedded traditional ways of conducting government cannot supplant the Constitution or legislation, but they give meaning to the words of a text or supply them. It is an inadmissibly narrow conception of American constitutional law to confine it to the words of the Constitution and to disregard the gloss which life has written upon them. In short, a systematic, unbroken, executive practice, long pursued to the knowledge of the Congress and never before questioned, engaged in by Presidents who have also sworn to uphold the Constitution, making as it were such exercise of power part of the structure of our government, may be treated as a gloss on "executive Power" vested in the President by §1 of Art. II . . . .

MR. JUSTICE JACKSON, concurring in the judgment and opinion of the Court . . . .

A judge, like an executive adviser, may be surprised at the poverty of really useful and unambiguous authority applicable to concrete problems of executive power as they actually present themselves. Just what our forefathers did envision, or would have envisioned had they foreseen modern conditions, must be divined from materials almost as enigmatic as the dreams Joseph was called upon to interpret for Pharaoh. A century and a half of partisan debate and scholarly speculation yields no net result but only supplies more or less apt quotations from respected sources on each side of any question. They largely cancel each other.[1] And court decisions are indecisive because of the judicial practice of dealing with the largest questions in the most narrow way.

The actual art of governing under our Constitution does not and cannot conform to judicial definitions of the power of any of its branches based on isolated clauses or even single Articles torn from context. While the Constitution diffuses power the better to secure liberty, it also contemplates that practice will integrate the dispersed powers into a workable government. It enjoins upon its branches separateness but interdependence, autonomy but reciprocity. Presidential powers are not fixed but fluctuate, depending upon their disjunction or conjunction with those of Congress. We may well begin by a somewhat over-simplified grouping of practical situations in which a President may doubt, or others may challenge, his powers, and by distinguishing roughly the legal consequences of this factor of relativity.

1. When the President acts pursuant to an express or implied authorization of Congress, his authority is at its maximum, for it includes all that he possesses in his own right plus all that Congress can delegate.[2] In these circumstances, and in these only, may he be said (for what it may be worth) to personify the federal sovereignty. If his act is held unconstitutional under these circumstances, it

1. A Hamilton may be matched against a Madison. Professor Taft is counterbalanced by Theodore Roosevelt. It even seems that President Taft cancels out Professor Taft. Compare his "Temporary Petroleum Withdrawal No. 5" of September 27, 1909, United States v. Midwest Oil Co., 236 U.S. 459, 467, 468, with his appraisal of executive power in "Our Chief Magistrate and His Powers" 139-140.

2. It is in this class of cases that we find the broadest recent statements of presidential power, including those relied on here. United States v. Curtiss-Wright Corp., 299 U.S. 304, involved, not the question of the President's power to act without congressional authority, but the question of his right to act under and in accord with an Act of Congress . . . .

That case does not solve the present controversy. It recognized internal and external affairs as being in separate categories, and held that the strict limitation upon congressional delegations of power to the President over internal affairs does not apply with respect to delegations of power in external affairs. It was intimated that the President might act in external affairs without congressional authority, but not that he might act contrary to an Act of Congress . . . .

usually means that the Federal Government as an undivided whole lacks power. A seizure executed by the President pursuant to an Act of Congress would be supported by the strongest of presumptions and the widest latitude of judicial interpretation, and the burden of persuasion would rest heavily upon any who might attack it.

2. When the President acts in absence of either a congressional grant or denial of authority, he can only rely upon his own independent powers, but there is a zone of twilight in which he and Congress may have concurrent authority, or in which its distribution is uncertain. Therefore, congressional inertia, indifference or quiescence may sometimes, at least as a practical matter, enable, if not invite, measures on independent presidential responsibility. In this area, any actual test of power is likely to depend on the imperatives of events and contemporary imponderables rather than on abstract theories of law.

congress is indifferent

3. When the President takes measures incompatible with the expressed or implied will of Congress, his power is at its lowest ebb, for then he can rely only upon his own constitutional powers minus any constitutional powers of Congress over the matter. Courts can sustain exclusive presidential control in such a case only by disabling the Congress from acting upon the subject. Presidential claim to a power at once so conclusive and preclusive must be scrutinized with caution, for what is at stake is the equilibrium established by our constitutional system.

This case falls under

Into which of these classifications does this executive seizure of the steel industry fit? It is eliminated from the first by admission, for it is conceded that no congressional authorization exists for this seizure . . . .

Can it then be defended under flexible tests available to the second category? It seems clearly eliminated from that class because Congress has not left seizure of private property an open field but has covered it by three statutory policies inconsistent with this seizure . . . .

This leaves the current seizure to be justified only by the severe tests under the third grouping, where it can be supported only by any remainder of executive power after subtraction of such powers as Congress may have over the subject. In short, we can sustain the President only by holding that seizure of such strike-bound industries is within his domain and beyond control by Congress . . . .

I did not suppose, and I am not persuaded, that history leaves it open to question, at least in the courts, that the executive branch, like the Federal Government as a whole, possesses only delegated powers. The purpose of the Constitution was not only to grant power, but to keep it from getting out of hand. However, because the President does not enjoy unmentioned powers does not mean that the mentioned ones should be narrowed by a niggardly construction. Some clauses could be made almost unworkable, as well as immutable, by refusal to indulge some latitude of interpretation for changing times. I have heretofore, and do now, give to the enumerated powers the scope and elasticity afforded by what seem to be reasonable, practical implications instead of the rigidity dictated by a doctrinaire textualism.

The Solicitor General seeks the power of seizure in three clauses of the Executive Article, the first reading, "The executive Power shall be vested in a President of the United States of America." Lest I be thought to exaggerate, I quote the interpretation which his brief puts upon it: "In our view, this clause constitutes a grant of all the executive powers of which the Government is capable." If that be true, it is difficult to see why the forefathers bothered to add several specific items, including some trifling ones.[9]

The example of such unlimited executive power that must have most impressed the forefathers was the prerogative exercised by George III, and the description of its evils in the Declaration of Independence leads me to doubt that they were creating their new Executive in his image. Continental European examples were no more appealing. And if we seek instruction from our own times, we can match it only from the executive powers in those governments we disparagingly describe as totalitarian. I cannot accept the view that this clause is a grant in bulk of all conceivable executive power but regard it as an allocation to the presidential office of the generic powers thereafter stated.

The clause on which the Government next relies is that "The President shall be Commander in Chief of the Army and Navy of the United States . . . ." These cryptic words . . . , undoubtedly put[] the Nation's armed forces under presidential command. Hence, this loose appellation is sometimes advanced as support for any presidential action, internal or external, involving use of force, the idea being that it vests power to do anything, anywhere, that can be done with an army or navy.

That seems to be the logic of an argument tendered at our bar — that the President having, on his own responsibility, sent American troops abroad derives from that act "affirmative power" to seize the means of producing a supply of steel for them. To quote, "Perhaps the most forceful illustration of the scope of Presidential power in this connection is the fact that American troops in Korea, whose safety and effectiveness are so directly involved here, were sent to the field by an exercise of the President's constitutional powers." Thus, it is said, he has invested himself with "war powers."

I cannot foresee all that it might entail if the Court should indorse this argument. Nothing in our Constitution is plainer than that declaration of a war is entrusted only to Congress. Of course, a state of war may in fact exist without a formal declaration. But no doctrine that the Court could promulgate would seem to me more sinister and alarming than that a President whose conduct of foreign affairs is so largely uncontrolled, and often even is unknown, can vastly enlarge his mastery over the internal affairs of the country by his own commitment of the Nation's armed forces to some foreign venture. I do not, however, find it necessary or appropriate to consider the legal status of the Korean enterprise to discountenance argument based on it . . . .

There are indications that the Constitution did not contemplate that the title Commander in Chief *of the Army and Navy* will constitute him also Commander in Chief of the country, its industries and its inhabitants. He has no monopoly of "war powers," whatever they are. While Congress cannot deprive the President of the command of the army and navy, only Congress can provide him an army or navy to command. It is also empowered to make rules for the "Government and Regulation of land and naval Forces," by which it may to some unknown extent impinge upon even command functions.

That military powers of the Commander in Chief were not to supersede representative government of internal affairs seems obvious from the Constitution and from elementary American history . . . .

9. "[H]e may require the Opinion, in writing, of the principal Officer in each of the executive Departments, upon any Subject relating to the Duties of their respective Offices . . . ." U.S. Const., Art. II, §2. He "shall Commission all the Officers of the United States." U.S. Const., Art. II, §3. Matters such as those would seem to be inherent in the Executive if anything is.

We should not use this occasion to circumscribe, much less to contract, the lawful role of the President as Commander in Chief. I should indulge the widest latitude of interpretation to sustain his exclusive function to command the instruments of national force, at least when turned against the outside world for the security of our society. But, when it is turned inward, not because of rebellion but because of a lawful economic struggle between industry and labor, it should have no such indulgence. His command power is not such an absolute as might be implied from that office in a militaristic system but is subject to limitations consistent with a constitutional Republic whose law and policy-making branch is a representative Congress. The purpose of lodging dual titles in one man was to insure that the civilian would control the military, not to enable the military to subordinate the presidential office. No penance would ever expiate the sin against free government of holding that a President can escape control of executive powers by law through assuming his military role. What the power of command may include I do not try to envision, but I think it is not a military prerogative, without support of law, to seize persons or property because they are important or even essential for the military and naval establishment.

The third clause in which the Solicitor General finds seizure powers is that "he shall take Care that the Laws be faithfully executed...." That authority must be matched against words of the Fifth Amendment that "No person shall be...deprived of life, liberty or property, without due process of law...." One gives a governmental authority that reaches so far as there is law, the other gives a private right that authority shall go no farther. These signify about all there is of the principle that ours is a government of laws, not of men, and that we submit ourselves to rulers only if under rules.

The Solicitor General lastly grounds support of the seizure upon nebulous, inherent powers never expressly granted but said to have accrued to the office from the customs and claims of preceding administrations. The plea is for a resulting power to deal with a crisis or an emergency according to the necessities of the case, the unarticulated assumption being that necessity knows no law.

Loose and irresponsible use of adjectives colors all nonlegal and much legal discussion of presidential powers. "Inherent" powers, "implied" powers, "incidental" powers, "plenary" powers, "war" powers and "emergency" powers are used, often interchangeably and without fixed or ascertainable meanings....

In the practical working of our Government we already have evolved a technique within the framework of the Constitution by which normal executive powers may be considerably expanded to meet an emergency. Congress may and has granted extraordinary authorities which lie dormant in normal times but may be called into play by the Executive in war or upon proclamation of a national emergency.... Under this procedure we retain Government by law — special, temporary law, perhaps, but law nonetheless. The public may know the extent and limitations of the powers that can be asserted, and persons affected may be informed from the statute of their rights and duties.

In view of the ease, expedition and safety with which Congress can grant and has granted large emergency powers, certainly ample to embrace this crisis, I am quite unimpressed with the argument that we should affirm possession of them without statute. Such power either has no beginning or it has no end. If it exists, it need submit to no legal restraint. I am not alarmed that it would plunge us straightway into dictatorship, but it is at least a step in that wrong direction.

As to whether there is imperative necessity for such powers, it is relevant to note the gap that exists between the President's paper powers and his real powers. The Constitution does not disclose the measure of the actual controls wielded by the modern presidential office. That instrument must be understood as an Eighteenth-Century sketch of a government hoped for, not as a blueprint of the Government that is. Vast accretions of federal power, eroded from that reserved by the States, have magnified the scope of presidential activity. Subtle shifts take place in the centers of real power that do not show on the face of the Constitution.

Executive power has the advantage of concentration in a single head in whose choice the whole Nation has a part, making him the focus of public hopes and expectations. In drama, magnitude and finality his decisions so far overshadow any others that almost alone he fills the public eye and ear. No other personality in public life can begin to compete with him in access to the public mind through modern methods of communications. By his prestige as head of state and his influence upon public opinion he exerts a leverage upon those who are supposed to check and balance his power which often cancels their effectiveness.

...I have no illusion that any decision by this Court can keep power in the hands of Congress if it is not wise and timely in meeting its problems. A crisis that challenges the President equally, or perhaps primarily, challenges Congress. If not good law, there was worldly wisdom in the maxim attributed to Napoleon that "The tools belong to the man who can use them." We may say that power to legislate for emergencies belongs in the hands of Congress, but only Congress itself can prevent power from slipping through its fingers.... With all its defects, delays and inconveniences, men have discovered no technique for long preserving free government except that the Executive be under the law, and that the law be made by parliamentary deliberations.

Such institutions may be destined to pass away. But it is the duty of the Court to be last, not first, to give them up.

[Justice Vinson, joined by Justices Reed and Minton, filed a 48-page dissent. The thrust of the dissent's argument was that Truman's action was consistent with his Article II duty to "take Care that the Laws be faithfully executed."

The dissent first tried to put the steel seizure in historical perspective. It began by characterizing the Korean War, and more generally the Cold War, as a "more terrifying threat" than World War II. It noted that Truman's actions in the Korean War were supported by the United Nations Security Council, and by congressional enactments that (a) dramatically increased defense spending (the bulk of which went to "military equipment and supplies — guns, tanks, ships, planes and ammunition — all of which require steel"), (b) established a new military draft, and (c) created organizations and programs (such as the Marshall plan and NATO) designed to achieve victory in the Cold War. The dissent next reiterated the facts leading up to Truman's seizure of the steel mills, noting that the morning following the seizure, the President informed Congress of his actions and invited it to act otherwise if it "deem[s] some other course to be wiser," and that twelve days later, in the face of no congressional action, the President again sent a letter to Congress restating his position that "Congress can, if it wishes, reject the course of action I have followed in this matter." The dissent further noted the evidence in the record showing the importance of continued steel production to the war effort in Korea. It concluded: "Even ignoring for the moment whatever confidential information the President may possess as 'the Nation's organ for foreign affairs,' the uncontroverted affidavits in this record amply support the finding that 'a work stoppage would immediately jeopardize and imperil our national defense.'"

Second, the dissent set forth its theory of Executive power. It argued that the constitutional Framers intended to establish "an office of power and independence" characterized by "initiative," "vigor," and "energy." It then cited a long list of Executive actions throughout U.S. history showing that "[w]ith or without explicit statutory authorization, Presidents have . . . dealt with national emergencies by acting promptly and resolutely to enforce legislative programs, at least to save those programs until Congress could act." It added that "Congress and the courts have responded to such executive initiative with consistent approval."

Third, the dissent turned to Truman's seizure of the steel mills, and argued "that the President was performing his duty under the Constitution to 'take Care that the Laws be faithfully executed . . . .'" The dissent reasoned:

> Much of the argument in this case has been directed at straw men. We do not now have before us the case of a President acting solely on the basis of his own notions of the public welfare. Nor is there any question of unlimited executive power in this case. The President himself closed the door to any such claim when he sent his Message to Congress stating his purpose to abide by any action of Congress, whether approving or disapproving his seizure action. Here, the President immediately made sure that Congress was fully informed of the temporary action he had taken only to preserve the legislative programs from destruction until Congress could act . . . . The absence of a specific statute authorizing seizure of the steel mills as a mode of executing the laws — both the military procurement program and the anti-inflation program — has not until today been thought to prevent the President from executing the laws. Unlike an administrative commission confined to the enforcement of the statute under which it was created, or the head of a department when administering a particular statute, the President is a constitutional officer charged with taking care that a "mass of legislation" be executed. Flexibility as to mode of execution to meet critical situations is a matter of practical necessity. This practical construction of the "Take Care" clause . . . was adopted by this Court in *In re Neagle*, . . . and other cases . . . . There is no statute prohibiting seizure as a method of enforcing legislative programs. Congress has in no wise indicated that its legislation is not to be executed by the taking of private property (subject of course to the payment of just compensation) if its legislation cannot otherwise be executed . . . . Whatever the extent of Presidential power on more tranquil occasions, and whatever the right of the President to execute legislative programs as he sees fit without reporting the mode of execution to Congress, the single Presidential purpose disclosed on this record is to faithfully execute the laws by acting in an emergency to maintain the status quo, thereby preventing collapse of the legislative programs until Congress could act. The President's action served the same purposes as a judicial stay entered to maintain the status quo in order to preserve the jurisdiction of a court.]

Notes and Questions

1. In contrast to Congress, the Executive Branch is hierarchically ordered. The President sits atop, and exercises plenary power over, a massive bureaucracy devoted to foreign affairs. Within the White House, the National Security Council is charged with advising the President concerning foreign and military policies relating to national security. Outside the White House, the Department of State is the principal agent of the Executive Branch in the conduct of foreign relations. The State Department operates over 250 diplomatic and consular posts around the globe. It also negotiates treaties and other international agreements, represents the United States at international conferences and other non-treaty international negotiations, monitors activities of foreign nations, makes policy recommendations, and implements Executive foreign policy in many contexts. The Department of Defense is responsible for military and security affairs, the Department of Treasury is responsible for international monetary affairs, and the Department of Commerce has jurisdiction over the expansion and protection of American business activities abroad. Other departments — especially Justice, Labor, and Agriculture — also have important foreign affairs responsibilities. Overseas intelligence operations are the responsibility of the newly established Director of National Intelligence, a cabinet-level official who is the President's principal intelligence advisor and the coordinator of the entire intelligence community, including the Central Intelligence Agency. The Office of the United States Trade Representative manages U.S. trade policy. Dozens of additional agencies assist the President in conducting other aspects of U.S. foreign relations.

Institutionally, the Executive Branch has a number of advantages over Congress with respect to the conduct of foreign relations. As Edward Corwin explained, these advantages include: "the *unity* of the office, its capacity for *secrecy* and *dispatch*, and its superior sources of *information,* to which should be added the fact that it is always on hand and ready for action, whereas the houses of Congress are in adjournment much of the time." Edward S. Corwin, The President: Office and Powers 1787-1984, at 201 (Randall Bland et al. eds., 5th ed. 1984). Does the President have any other advantages over Congress in conducting foreign relations? Are there any drawbacks to the Executive Branch's organization? Given the size of the modern Executive Branch, and the differing institutional perspectives of its agencies, how unified is it in practice?

2. As noted at the outset of this section, the list of presidential foreign affairs powers in Article II is much less extensive than the list of congressional foreign affairs powers in Article I. Some of these powers, such as the President's role as Commander in Chief of the army and navy, and his power to make treaties, provided that he obtains the advice and consent of two-thirds of the senators present, are explored in detail in subsequent chapters. In this section, we consider the President's "executive" power, his power to "take Care that the Laws be faithfully executed," his power to appoint U.S. ambassadors (subject to majority approval in the Senate) and to receive foreign ambassadors, and various possible inherent and implied powers.

3. Article II, Section 1 states that "[t]he executive Power shall be vested in a President of the United States of America." What is entailed by the phrase "executive Power"? Does this "vesting clause" convey authority to the President beyond the authority conveyed by the specific powers listed in Article II? Three important influences on the Founders — Blackstone, Locke, and Montesquieu — believed that foreign relations powers should be lodged in the Executive Branch of government, as was the case with the King of England. *See* 1 William Blackstone, Commentaries on the Laws of England 245-57 (1765); John Locke, Two Treatises of Government 383-84 (Peter Laslett ed., 1963) (1690); Baron de Montesquieu, The Spirit of Laws 185 (Thomas Nugent trans., 1994) (1751); *see generally* Saikrishna B. Prakash & Michael D. Ramsey, *The Executive Power over Foreign Affairs*, 111 Yale L.J. 231, 266-69 (2001) (summarizing these views). Recall from Chapter 1 that Hamilton, relying on the differences in the "vesting" clauses of Articles I and II, argued that the Founders incorporated these views of Executive power except to the extent that foreign relations powers were specifically allocated to another branch.

Professors Prakash and Ramsey ~~have recently reinvigorated the Hamiltonian view of Executive power in foreign affairs.~~ They argue that Hamilton's view is consistent with both the original understanding of the Founders and the text of Article II. Their central contention is:

> [I]n 1787, when the Constitution provided that the President would have "the executive Power," that would have been understood to mean not only that the President would have the power to execute the laws (the primary and essential meaning of "executive power") but also that the President would have foreign affairs powers. As a result, the starting point is that foreign affairs powers are presidential, not from some shadowy implication of national sovereignty, per *Curtiss-Wright*, but from the ordinary eighteenth-century meaning of executive power.

[handwritten margin note: Hamiltonian view of executive power in foreign affairs]

> ~~[T]he President's executive foreign affairs power is residual, encompassing only those executive foreign affairs powers not allocated elsewhere by the Constitution's text.~~ The Constitution's allocation of specific foreign affairs powers or roles to Congress or the Senate are properly read as assignments away from the President. Absent these specific allocations, by Article II, Section 1, all traditionally executive foreign affairs powers would be presidential.... The Constitution's drafters believed that the English system afforded too much foreign affairs power to the monarch through the undivided possession of the executive power, and that some aspects of the traditional executive power over foreign affairs had legislative overtones (including the war and treaty-making powers). Accordingly, they divided the traditional executive power over foreign affairs by creating specific (but very substantial) exceptions to the general grant of executive power to the President. In the document they created, many key foreign affairs powers were either shared — such as the power to appoint ambassadors or make treaties — or allocated elsewhere — such as the power to declare war and issue letters of marque. As a result, once the drafting was complete, the President had a greatly diminished foreign affairs power as compared to the English monarchy. But the President retained a residual power — that is, the President, as the possessor of "the executive Power," had those executive foreign affairs powers not allocated elsewhere by the text. In short, far from suffering from huge gaps, the Constitution has a simple default rule that we call the "residual principle": Foreign affairs powers not assigned elsewhere belong to the President, by virtue of the President's executive power; while foreign affairs powers specifically allocated elsewhere are not presidential powers, in spite of the President's executive power.

Prakash & Ramsey, *supra*, at 253-54; *see also* Phillip R. Trimble, International Law: United States Foreign Relations Law ch. 1 (2002) (making similar argument). Does this "Vesting Clause Thesis" make sense of the text of Article II? What is Justice Jackson's response in *Youngstown* to the Vesting Clause Thesis? If the Vesting Clause Thesis is right, why does Article II mention some foreign affairs powers but not others? Why, for example, does it provide for a power to receive ambassadors? Wouldn't this power already be included within the "executive Power," as it is not assigned to another branch? Similarly, why, under the Vesting Clause Thesis, does Article II specifically allocate the Commander-in-Chief power to the President? Wouldn't this power also be included within the "executive Power"? Prakash and Ramsey maintain that, because the Founders had given some military powers to Congress, they wanted to be clear that the President retained the Commander-in-Chief power. But on their view, wouldn't this result already follow from the default assumption of the meaning of "executive Power"? Also, this argument raises the question: Under the Vesting Clause Thesis, is the only military-related presidential power the Commander-in-Chief power? Otherwise, wouldn't the Founders have specified the other powers (such as the power to declare peace)? We discuss war powers in more detail in Chapter 4.

For a recent critique of the Vesting Clause Thesis, see Curtis A. Bradley & Martin S. Flaherty, *Executive Power Essentialism and Foreign Affairs*, 102 Mich. L. Rev. 545 (2004). The Bradley/Flaherty article challenges the thesis on both textual and historical grounds. As stated in the introduction to their article:

> As for text, the difference in wording between the Article I and Article II Vesting Clauses can be explained in other plausible ways and need not be read as distinguishing between a limited grant of legislative powers and a plenary grant of executive power. Familiar canons of construction, such as expressio unius, and other interpretive principles further cut against the Vesting Clause Thesis. That thesis, moreover, cannot explain some of Article II's specific grants of foreign affairs authority, and it sits uneasily with the Constitution's enumerated powers structure.
>
> Given that the textual case for the Vesting Clause Thesis is at best uncertain, the persuasiveness of the thesis ultimately depends on history. Here there is a particular irony. Proponents of the Vesting Clause Thesis are often also advocates of a classically originalist approach to constitutional interpretation, pursuant to which the understanding of the Constitution's framers and ratifiers controls constitutional meaning. Yet, as we will show, the historical sources that are most relevant to the Founding, such as the records of the Federal Convention, the Federalist Papers, and the state ratification debates, contain almost nothing that supports the Vesting Clause Thesis, and much that contradicts it.
>
> Supporters of the Vesting Clause Thesis attempt to compensate for the lack of direct Founding support by focusing on political theory and practice both before and after the ratification of the Constitution. Their historical narrative thus has two central features. First, it is a story of continuity, whereby European political theory is carried forward, relatively unblemished, into American constitutional design and practice. Second, the narrative relies on what could be called "executive power essentialism" — the proposition that the Founders had in mind, and intended the Constitution to reflect, a conception of what is "naturally" or "essentially" within executive power. We argue that this historical narrative is wrong on both counts. Among other things, the narrative fails to take account of complexity within eighteenth-century political theory, the experience of state constitutionalism before 1787, and the Founders' self-conscious rejection of the British model of government. The narrative also understates the degree to which the constitutional Founders were functionalists, willing to deviate from pure political theory and essentialist categories in order to design an effective government.
>
> Moreover, as usually presented, the post-constitutional practice of the Washington Administration provides only half the story. Washington and his cabinet, perhaps unsurprisingly, tended to stake out pro-executive positions with respect to the management of U.S. diplomacy. To the extent that there was a consensus concerning these positions, that consensus was based on functional considerations related to specific constitutional grants, not the Vesting Clause. When other, more substantive issues arose — such as the power to remove executive officials (including the Secretary of State) and the power to declare neutrality — the consensus broke down and there was substantial disagreement about the sources and scope of executive power. Moreover, with the partial exception of Alexander Hamilton, neither Washington nor his cabinet actually articulated the Vesting Clause Thesis, preferring instead to make more specific and modest textual claims.

Bradley and Flaherty therefore argue that the Article II vesting clause should not be viewed as an independent source of foreign affairs authority, and that the

President's foreign affairs powers are consequently limited to the powers expressly granted in Article II. They also note, however, that it might be appropriate to interpret those express grants broadly, and that their meaning might be informed by longstanding historical practice since the Founding. Which view of presidential power is more persuasive? For Prakash and Ramsey's reply to the Bradley/Flaherty article, see Saikrishna B. Prakash and Michael D. Ramsey, *Foreign Affairs and the Jeffersonian Executive: A Defence*, 89 Minn. L. Rev. 1591 (2005).

4. Article II, Section 3 of the Constitution provides that the President "shall take Care that the Laws be faithfully executed." The term "Laws" unquestionably includes the Constitution and federal statutes. In Chapter 7, we address whether the term also includes international laws, both treaty-based and customary. For now, the question is the meaning of the President's duty to "faithfully execute[]" the laws. Professor Monaghan notes that the text of Article II "seemingly contemplates only a 'law enforcement' Executive; that is, the President simply 'executes' the will of Congress." Henry P. Monaghan, *The Protective Power of the Presidency*, 93 Colum. L. Rev. 1, 11 (1993). Is this all that the "take care" clause entails? Recall from Chapter 1 that Hamilton argued that the Take Care Clause supported the President's issuance of the Neutrality Proclamation. Does this argument move beyond the "law enforcement" conception of the Take Care Clause?

The majority opinion in *Youngstown* provides what Professor Monaghan calls the "classic illustration" of the law enforcement conception of the "take care" power when it states that "[i]n the framework of our constitution, the President's power to see that the laws are faithfully executed refutes the idea that he is to be a lawmaker." Justice Jackson similarly states that the "take care" power only "gives a governmental authority that reaches so far as there is law," and concludes that this idea is central to the notion that "ours is a government of laws, not of men, and that we submit ourselves to rulers only if under rules." Justice Vinson's dissent, on the other hand, argues that Truman's action was consistent with, and indeed compelled by, his Article II duty to execute the laws. For this broader reading of the Take Care Clause, Vinson relied in part on In re Neagle, 135 U.S. 1 (1890). The question in that case was whether the U.S. Attorney General had lawfully assigned a federal marshal to guard Justice Field, whose life had been threatened. The Court held that he had, even though the government acknowledged that no "single specific statute" authorized him to do so. It reasoned that the President's duty to execute the laws was not "limited to the enforcement of acts of Congress or of treaties of the United States according to their express terms," but rather included "the rights, duties and obligations growing out of the Constitution itself, our international relations, and all the protection implied by the nature of the government under the Constitution." Does *Neagle* support Vinson's broader reading of the "take care" power? In any event, won't the President always exercise discretion in deciding what steps are needed to faithfully execute the laws? How do courts police that discretion? Is the problem akin to the problem of judicial scrutiny of the Necessary and Proper Clause, discussed above in Section A? Should courts engage in means-ends scrutiny or purpose scrutiny in this context as well? Does Truman's action survive that scrutiny? How much incidental authority does the President possess in executing statutes and treaties?

Whatever the proper conception of the Take Care Clause, the majority in *Youngstown* seems to say that the President has no lawmaking powers. As we shall see throughout this casebook, however, the President appears to make law related to foreign relations in a number of instances — for example, when he makes "sole" executive agreements with the force of domestic law, and when he determines whether foreign heads of state are immune from suit in the United States. For analysis of the President's foreign affairs "lawmaking" powers, see Louis Henkin, Foreign Affairs and the United States Constitution 54-61 (2d ed. 1996); Monaghan, *supra*, at 47-56.

5. How does President Roosevelt's "stewardship" theory of Executive power compare with the Vesting Clause Thesis and with the Vinson/*Neagle* conception of the Take Care Clause? Note that, although President Taft disagreed with Roosevelt's broad conception of presidential power, he

> did not think the president should construe his or her powers by a wooden, clause-by-clause exegesis of the constitutional text. In the area of foreign affairs, the president's diplomatic duties, powers as commander in chief, and duty under the take care clause to carry out the obligations of the United States to its citizens and to other nations come together to create broad authority to act independently of legislative authorization.

Editor's Introduction, in William Howard Taft, Our Chief Magistrate and His Powers xlii (H. Jefferson Powell ed., 2002). What difference is there between arguing that the President has broad residual foreign affairs authority and arguing that the President's express grants of authority in Article II should be interpreted broadly?

6. The steel seizure at issue in *Youngstown* took place in the midst of, and in alleged furtherance of, the Korean War. How does the origin and presence of the war influence the different opinions in *Youngstown*? Note in particular the differences between Justice Jackson's concurrence (which views the manner in which the war was started as a reason to read Executive power narrowly) and Justice Vinson's dissent (which views the Cold War background of the war as a reason to read Executive power broadly). Which view is right?

7. Under the analysis in *Curtiss-Wright*, isn't the Korean War an "external affair" regarding which the President has plenary power? How should a court determine which tasks concern external affairs? Why does the Court take such a different approach to constitutional limits in *Youngstown*, where the majority opinion does not even cite *Curtiss-Wright*? How would you characterize the interpretive methodologies in the different opinions in *Youngstown*? Are the holdings in *Curtiss-Wright* and *Youngstown* reconcilable, as Justice Jackson suggests in footnote 2 of his concurrence? For an effort to synthesize *Curtiss-Wright* and *Youngstown*, see Roy E. Brownell II, *The Coexistence of United States v. Curtiss-Wright Export Corp. and Youngstown Sheet & Tube v. Sawyer in National Security Jurisprudence*, 16 J.L. & Pol. 1 (2000). For a symposium on *Youngstown*, which focuses on, among other things, the relevance of *Youngstown* to the post-September 11 war on terrorism, see *Youngstown at Fifty: A Symposium*, 19 Const. Commentary 3-289 (2002). *See also* Christopher Bryant & Carl Tobias, *Youngstown Revisited*, 29 Hastings Const. L.Q. 373 (2002).

8. How does Justice Frankfurter's concurrence in *Youngstown* differ from the majority opinion? Is Frankfurter's conception of presidential power broader than the majority's conception? If so, how? Does Frankfurter's analysis allow the Constitution to be informally amended by the practices of the political branches? *See also* United States v. Midwest Oil Co., 236 U.S. 459, 473 (1915) ("[I]n determining ... the existence of a power, weight should be given to the usage itself—even when the validity of the practice is the subject of investigation.").

9. Justice Jackson's concurrence in *Youngstown*, especially its articulation of three categories of presidential power, has been very influential. Indeed, courts and commentators often give more weight to Jackson's concurrence than to the majority opinion. Why do you think this is so? How much guidance does Jackson's framework provide in ascertaining the scope of presidential power? Is it clear that President Truman's actions in *Youngstown* fell within the third category, as Jackson argues? We consider Jackson's three categories in more detail in the next section.

10. The ambassadorial receipt clause in Article II has been interpreted to mean more than the ceremonial power to acknowledge representatives from foreign nations. It has long been settled, for example, that the President also has the power to recognize (or not recognize) foreign governments. *See* Banco Nacional de Cuba v. Sabbatino, 376 U.S. 398, 410 (1964) ("Political recognition is exclusively a function of the Executive."); *see also* Goldwater v. Carter, 444 U.S. 996, 1007 (1979) (Brennan, J., dissenting) ("Our cases firmly establish that the Constitution commits to the President alone the power to recognize, and withdraw recognition from, foreign regimes."). This is an important power, for non-recognized nations do not enjoy many benefits in the United States, including the right to sue in U.S. courts. *See* Pfizer Inc. v. Government of India, 434 U.S. 308, 319-20 (1978). Recall also that, in *Goldwater v. Carter*, Justice Brennan would have upheld President Carter's termination of the Taiwan defense treaty because the termination was part of Carter's recognition of mainland China.

What else might the ambassadorial receipt clause entail? As Professor Henkin notes:

> It does not fetch too far to infer also the power to do all that is involved in relations with other nations: establishing and maintaining channels for intercourse and communication; instructing and informing our ambassadors and receiving their reports, inquiries and recommendations; exchanging information and views with foreign governments. For some, it is only another step to conclude that the President must be able to decide also the contents of his communications to ambassadors and to foreign governments, including the attitudes and intentions of the United States that constitute U.S. foreign policy.

Louis Henkin, Foreign Affairs and the United States Constitution 38 (2d ed. 1996). Can the power to receive ambassadors be read as broadly as Professor Henkin conjectures?

11. Recall John Marshall's famous statement, quoted in *Curtiss-Wright*, that the President is the "sole organ of the nation in its external relations, and its sole representative with foreign nations." Marshall made this statement in 1800 as a member of the House of Representatives in defense of President John Adams. Adams had ordered the extradition to Great Britain of Thomas Nash, alias Jonathan Robbins, who was accused of murder while aboard a British ship. Although Adams acted pursuant to a treaty with Great Britain, he was criticized on the ground that the extradition request from Great Britain should have been processed by judicial action, not Executive action. It was in this context that Marshall, defending Adams, proclaimed:

> The case was in its nature a national demand made upon the nation. The parties were the two nations. They cannot come into court to litigate their claims, nor can a court decide on them. Of consequence, the demand is not a case for judicial cognizance. *The president is the sole organ of the nation in its external relations, and its sole representative with foreign nations.* Of consequence, the demand of a foreign nation can only be made on him. He possesses the whole executive power. He holds and directs the force of the nation. Of consequence, any act to be performed by the force of the nation is to be performed through him. He is charged to execute the laws. A treaty is declared to be a law. He must then execute a treaty, where he, and he alone, possesses the means of executing it.

10 Annals of Congress 596, 613 (1800) (emphasis added). In context, what did Marshall mean in describing the President as the "sole organ"? If nothing else, Marshall appears to be arguing that the President is the official head of communication for the U.S. government in foreign affairs. Where does the President obtain that authority? Is such a role implied in the President's express powers, such as his power to receive and appoint ambassadors, his power to make treaties, and his power to execute the laws? Is it implied from the fact that the presidency is a unitary institution, whereas Congress is a plural institution? For additional discussion of the Jonathan Robbins case and Marshall's defense of Adams, see Ruth Wedgwood, *The Revolutionary Martyrdom of Jonathan Robbins*, 100 Yale L.J. 229 (1990).

    12. In practice, the Executive Branch exercises a virtual monopoly over formal communications with foreign nations and also plays a lead role in announcing U.S. foreign policy. The Monroe, Reagan, and Bush Doctrines, excerpted and described above, are important examples of the exercise of this authority. Each of these doctrines announced a fundamental proposition of U.S. foreign policy without any prior consultation with Congress. What are the legal effects of these doctrines? The political effects? Is each doctrine anything more than (as Lord Clarendon said of the Monroe Doctrine) "merely the dictum of its distinguished author"? Thomas A. Bailey, A Diplomatic History of the American People 189 (6th ed. 1958). If so, why? Where did the presidents obtain the authority to announce these doctrines? In terms of presidential authority, how do these doctrines compare with Washington's Neutrality Proclamation, which we discussed in Chapter 1? Do these doctrines bind Congress or future presidents? If the answer is no, is the President's power to announce important foreign policy initiatives such as these nonetheless important? Why or why not? What does the Bush doctrine on preemption suggest about the President's role in interpreting international law for the United States?

    13. For additional commentary on the issues in this section, see Raoul Berger, *The Presidential Monopoly of Foreign Relations*, 71 Mich. L. Rev. 1 (1972); Michael J. Glennon, *Two Views of Presidential Foreign Affairs Power*: Little v. Barreme or Curtiss-Wright?, 13 Yale J. Int'l L. 5 (1988); H. Jefferson Powell, *The Founders and the President's Authority over Foreign Affairs*, 40 Wm. & Mary L. Rev. 1471 (1999); H. Jefferson Powell, *The President's Authority over Foreign Affairs: An Executive Branch Perspective*, 67 Geo. Wash. L. Rev. 527 (1999); Phillip R. Trimble, *The President's Foreign Affairs Power*, 83 Am. J. Int'l L. 750 (1989).

C. RELATIONSHIP BETWEEN CONGRESS AND THE PRESIDENT

Congress and the Executive Branch frequently interact in their regulation of foreign relations. Often they interact in harmony. At other times, each branch acquiesces in the other's actions, albeit sometimes grudgingly. And at still other times the branches act in opposition to one another. Are there limits on the ways in which the two branches can work together? Is inaction by a branch the same as acquiescence? How should conflicts between the political branches be resolved? What role should courts play in resolving such conflicts? Consider these questions as you read the materials below.

Dames & Moore v. Regan

453 U.S. 654 (1981)

[On November 4, 1979, Iranian militants seized the U.S. embassy in Tehran and began holding the U.S. diplomatic personnel there as hostages. The revolutionary Iranian government made no effort to stop the militants and soon sided with them in negotiations. The government also repudiated its predecessor government's contracts with U.S. companies. Acting pursuant to the International Emergency Economic Powers Act (IEEPA), President Carter quickly blocked the removal or transfer of Iranian assets held within the jurisdiction of the United States. Carter subsequently issued orders authorizing the initiation of judicial proceedings in U.S. courts against Iran. These orders allowed for the entry of a pre-judgment attachment in such proceedings, but not a final judgment. After the issuance of these orders, Dames & Moore filed suit against Iran and various Iranian entities seeking the recovery of money owed to its subsidiary under a service contract, and it obtained a pre-judgment attachment of the property of certain Iranian banks. On January 20, 1981, the U.S. hostages were released by Iran pursuant to the Algiers Accords, an executive agreement. Under the Accords, the United States agreed to "terminate all legal proceedings in United States courts involving claims of United States persons and institutions against Iran and its state enterprises, to nullify all attachments and judgments obtained therein, to prohibit all further litigation based on such claims, and to bring about the termination of such claims through binding arbitration [before a special tribunal to be established in the Hague]." Immediately before leaving office, President Carter issued executive orders implementing the terms of the Accords. President Reagan subsequently issued an executive order in which he reaffirmed Carter's orders and "suspended" all "claims which may be presented to the...Tribunal" and provided that such claims "shall have no legal effect in any action now pending in any court of the United States." Dames & Moore challenged the validity of the Carter and Reagan executive orders.]

JUSTICE REHNQUIST delivered the opinion of the Court....

The parties and the lower courts, confronted with the instant questions, have all agreed that much relevant analysis is contained in Youngstown Sheet & Tube Co. v. Sawyer, 343 U.S. 579 (1952)....

Although we have in the past found and do today find Justice Jackson's classification of executive actions into three general categories analytically useful, we should be mindful of Justice Holmes' admonition, quoted by Justice Frankfurter in *Youngstown, supra,* at 597 (concurring opinion), that "[the] great ordinances of the Constitution do not establish and divide fields of black and white." Springer v. Philippine Islands, 277 U.S. 189, 209 (1928) (dissenting opinion). Justice Jackson himself recognized that his three categories represented "a somewhat over-simplified grouping," 343 U.S. at 635, and it is doubtless the case that executive action in any particular instance falls, not neatly in one of three pigeonholes, but rather at some point along a spectrum running from explicit congressional authorization to explicit congressional prohibition. This is particularly true as respects cases such as the one before us, involving responses to international crises the nature of which Congress can hardly have been expected to anticipate in any detail.

... The Government ... has principally relied on §203 of the IEEPA, 50 U.S.C. §1702(a)(1), as authorization for these actions. Section 1702(a)(1) provides in part:

> *At the times and to the extent specified in section 1701 of this title, the President may, under such regulations as he may prescribe, by means of instructions, licenses, or otherwise —*

> (A) investigate, regulate, or prohibit —
> (i) any transactions in foreign exchange,
> (ii) transfers of credit or payments between, by, through, or to any banking institution, to the extent that such transfers or payments involve any interest of any foreign country or a national thereof,
> (iii) the importing or exporting of currency or securities, and
> (B) investigate, regulate, direct and compel, nullify, void, prevent or prohibit, any acquisition, holding, withholding, use, transfer, withdrawal, transportation, importation or exportation of, or dealing in, or exercising any right, power, or privilege with respect to, or transactions involving, any property in which any foreign country or a national thereof has any interest;
> by any person, or with respect to any property, subject to the jurisdiction of the United States.

The Government contends that the acts of "nullifying" the attachments and ordering the "transfer" of the frozen assets are specifically authorized by the plain language of the above statute....

Petitioner contends that we should ignore the plain language of this statute because an examination of its legislative history as well as the history of §5(b) of the Trading With the Enemy Act (hereinafter TWEA), 40 Stat. 411, as amended, 50 U.S.C. App. §5(b) (1976 ed. and Supp. III), from which the pertinent language of §1702 is directly drawn, reveals that the statute was not intended to give the President such extensive power over the assets of a foreign state during times of national emergency. According to petitioner, once the President instituted the November 14, 1979, blocking order, §1702 authorized him "only to continue the freeze or to discontinue controls."

We do not agree and refuse to read out of §1702 all meaning to the words "transfer," "compel," or "nullify." Nothing in the legislative history of either §1702 or §5(b) of the TWEA requires such a result. To the contrary, we think both the legislative history and cases interpreting the TWEA fully sustain the broad authority of the Executive when acting under this congressional grant of power. Although Congress intended to limit the President's emergency power in peacetime, we do not think the changes brought about by the enactment of the IEEPA in any way affected the authority of the President to take the specific actions taken here. We likewise note that by the time petitioner instituted this action, the President had already entered the freeze order. Petitioner proceeded against the blocked assets only after the Treasury Department had issued revocable licenses authorizing such proceedings and attachments. The Treasury Regulations provided that "unless licensed" any attachment is null and void, 31 CFR §535.203(e) (1980), and all licenses "may be amended, modified, or revoked at any time." §535.805. As such, the attachments obtained by petitioner were specifically made subordinate to further actions which the President might take under the IEEPA. Petitioner was on notice of the contingent nature of its interest in the frozen assets....

Because the President's action in nullifying the attachments and ordering the transfer of the assets was taken pursuant to specific congressional authorization, it is "supported by the strongest of presumptions and the widest latitude of judicial interpretation, and the burden of persuasion would rest heavily upon any who might attack it." *Youngstown*, 343 U.S. at 637 (Jackson, J., concurring). Under the circumstances of this case, we cannot say that petitioner has sustained that heavy burden. A contrary ruling would mean that the Federal Government as a whole lacked the power exercised by the President, see *id.*, at 636-637, and that we are not prepared to say.

...Although we have concluded that the IEEPA constitutes specific congressional authorization to the President to nullify the attachments and order the transfer of Iranian assets, there remains the question of the President's authority to suspend claims pending in American courts. Such claims have, of course, an existence apart from the attachments which accompanied them. In terminating these claims through Executive Order No. 12294, the President purported to act under authority of both the IEEPA and 22 U.S.C. §1732, the so-called "Hostage Act."

We conclude that although the IEEPA authorized the nullification of the attachments, it cannot be read to authorize the suspension of the claims. The claims of American citizens against Iran are not in themselves transactions involving Iranian property or efforts to exercise any rights with respect to such property.... The terms of the IEEPA therefore do not authorize the President to suspend claims in American courts. This is the view of all the courts which have considered the question.

The Hostage Act, passed in 1868, provides:

> Whenever it is made known to the President that any citizen of the United States has been unjustly deprived of his liberty by or under the authority of any foreign government, it shall be the duty of the President forthwith to demand of that government the reasons of such imprisonment; and if it appears to be wrongful and in violation of the rights of American citizenship, the President shall forthwith demand the release of such citizen, and if the release so demanded is unreasonably delayed or refused, the President shall use such means, not amounting to acts of war, as he may think necessary and proper to obtain or effectuate the release; and all the facts and proceedings relative thereto shall as soon as practicable be communicated by the President to Congress. Rev. Stat. §2001, 22 U.S.C. §1732.

We are reluctant to conclude that this provision constitutes specific authorization to the President to suspend claims in American courts. Although the broad language of the Hostage Act suggests it may cover this case, there are several difficulties with such a view. The legislative history indicates that the Act was passed in response to a situation unlike the recent Iranian crisis. Congress in 1868 was concerned with the activity of certain countries refusing to recognize the citizenship of naturalized Americans traveling abroad, and repatriating such citizens against their will. These countries were not interested in returning the citizens in exchange for any sort of ransom. This also explains the reference in the Act to imprisonment "in violation of the rights of American citizenship." Although the Iranian hostage-taking violated international law and common decency, the hostages were not seized out of any refusal to recognize their American citizenship — they were seized precisely *because of* their American citizenship. The legislative history is also somewhat ambiguous on the question whether Congress contemplated Presidential action such as that involved here or rather simply reprisals directed against the offending foreign country and *its* citizens.

Concluding that neither the IEEPA nor the Hostage Act constitutes specific authorization of the President's action suspending claims, however, is not to say that these statutory provisions are entirely irrelevant to the question of the validity of the President's action. We think both statutes highly relevant in the looser sense of indicating congressional acceptance of a broad scope for executive action in circumstances such as those presented in this case. As noted in Part III, *supra*, the IEEPA delegates broad authority to the President to act in times of national emergency with respect to property of a foreign country. The Hostage Act similarly indicates congressional willingness that the President have broad discretion when responding to the hostile acts of foreign sovereigns....

Although we have declined to conclude that the IEEPA or the Hostage Act directly authorizes the President's suspension of claims for the reasons noted, we cannot ignore the general tenor of Congress' legislation in this area in trying to determine whether the President is acting alone or at least with the acceptance of Congress. As we have noted, Congress cannot anticipate and legislate with regard to every possible action the President may find it necessary to take or every possible situation in which he might act. Such failure of Congress specifically to delegate authority does not, "especially . . . in the areas of foreign policy and national security," imply "congressional disapproval" of action taken by the Executive. Haig v. Agee, [453 U.S. 280, 291 (1981)]. On the contrary, the enactment of legislation closely related to the question of the President's authority in a particular case which evinces legislative intent to accord the President broad discretion may be considered to "invite" "measures on independent presidential responsibility." *Youngstown*, 343 U.S. at 637 (Jackson, J., concurring). At least this is so where there is no contrary indication of legislative intent and when, as here, there is a history of congressional acquiescence in conduct of the sort engaged in by the President. It is to that history which we now turn.

Not infrequently in affairs between nations, outstanding claims by nationals of one country against the government of another country are "sources of friction" between the two sovereigns. United States v. Pink, 315 U.S. 203, 225 (1942). To resolve these difficulties, nations have often entered into agreements settling the claims of their respective nationals.... Consistent with that principle, the United States has repeatedly exercised its sovereign authority to settle the claims of its nationals against foreign countries. Though those settlements have sometimes been made by treaty, there has also been a longstanding practice of settling such claims by executive agreement without the advice and consent of the Senate.[8] Under such agreements, the President has agreed to renounce or extinguish claims of United States nationals against foreign governments in return for lump-sum payments or the establishment of arbitration procedures. To be sure, many of these settlements were encouraged by the United States claimants themselves, since a claimant's only hope of obtaining any payment at all might lie in having his Government negotiate a diplomatic settlement on his behalf. But it is also undisputed that the "United States has sometimes disposed of the claims of its citizens without their consent, or even without consultation with them, usually without exclusive regard for their interests, as distinguished from those of the nation as a whole." Henkin, [Foreign Affairs and the Constitution 262-63 (1972)].... It is clear that the practice of settling claims continues today. Since 1952, the President

---

8. At least since the case of the "Wilmington Packet" in 1799, Presidents have exercised the power to settle claims of United States nationals by executive agreement. In fact, during the period of 1817-1917, "no fewer than eighty executive agreements were entered into by the United States looking toward the liquidation of claims of its citizens." W. McClure, International Executive Agreements 53 (1941). *See also* 14 M. Whiteman, Digest of International Law 247 (1970).

has entered into at least 10 binding settlements with foreign nations, including an $80 million settlement with the People's Republic of China.

Crucial to our decision today is the conclusion that Congress has implicitly approved the practice of claim settlement by executive agreement. This is best demonstrated by Congress' enactment of the International Claims Settlement Act of 1949, as amended, 22 U.S.C. §1621 et seq. The Act had two purposes: (1) to allocate to United States nationals funds received in the course of an executive claims settlement with Yugoslavia, and (2) to provide a procedure whereby funds resulting from future settlements could be distributed. To achieve these ends Congress created the International Claims Commission, now the Foreign Claims Settlement Commission, and gave it jurisdiction to make final and binding decisions with respect to claims by United States nationals against settlement funds. 22 U.S.C. §1623(a). By creating a procedure to implement future settlement agreements, Congress placed its stamp of approval on such agreements. Indeed, the legislative history of the Act observed that the United States was seeking settlements with countries other than Yugoslavia and that the bill contemplated settlements of a similar nature in the future.

Over the years Congress has frequently amended the International Claims Settlement Act to provide for particular problems arising out of settlement agreements, thus demonstrating Congress' continuing acceptance of the President's claim settlement authority....[10]

In addition to congressional acquiescence in the President's power to settle claims, prior cases of this Court have also recognized that the President does have some measure of power to enter into executive agreements without obtaining the advice and consent of the Senate. In United States v. Pink, 315 U.S. 203 (1942), for example, the Court upheld the validity of the Litvinov Assignment, which was part of an Executive Agreement whereby the Soviet Union assigned to the United States amounts owed to it by American nationals so that outstanding claims of other American nationals could be paid....

In light of all of the foregoing...we conclude that the President was authorized to suspend pending claims pursuant to Executive Order No. 12294. As Justice Frankfurter pointed out in *Youngstown*, 343 U.S. at 610-611, "a systematic, unbroken, executive practice, long pursued to the knowledge of the Congress and never before questioned...may be treated as a gloss on 'Executive Power' vested in the President by §1 of Art. II." Past practice does not, by itself, create power, but "long-continued practice, known to and acquiesced in by Congress, would raise a presumption that the [action] had been [taken] in pursuance of its consent...." United States v. Midwest Oil Co., 236 U.S. 459, 474 (1915). Such practice is present here and such a presumption is also appropriate. In light of the fact that Congress may be considered to have consented to the President's action in suspending claims, we cannot say that action exceeded the President's powers.

Our conclusion is buttressed by the fact that the means chosen by the President to settle the claims of American nationals provided an alternative forum, the Claims Tribunal, which is capable of providing meaningful relief.... The fact that the President has provided such a forum here means that the claimants are receiving something in return for the suspension of their claims, namely, access to an international tribunal before which they may well recover something on their claims.

---

10. Indeed, Congress has consistently failed to object to this longstanding practice of claim settlement by executive agreement, even when it has had an opportunity to do so....

Because there does appear to be a real "settlement" here, this case is more easily analogized to the more traditional claim settlement cases of the past.

Just as importantly, Congress has not disapproved of the action taken here. Though Congress has held hearings on the Iranian Agreement itself, Congress has not enacted legislation, or even passed a resolution, indicating its displeasure with the Agreement. Quite the contrary, the relevant Senate Committee has stated that the establishment of the Tribunal is "of vital importance to the United States." We are thus clearly not confronted with a situation in which Congress has in some way resisted the exercise of Presidential authority.

Finally, we re-emphasize the narrowness of our decision. We do not decide that the President possesses plenary power to settle claims, even as against foreign governmental entities. As the Court of Appeals for the First Circuit stressed, "[the] sheer magnitude of such a power, considered against the background of the diversity and complexity of modern international trade, cautions against any broader construction of authority than is necessary." But where, as here, the settlement of claims has been determined to be a necessary incident to the resolution of a major foreign policy dispute between our country and another, and where, as here, we can conclude that Congress acquiesced in the President's action, we are not prepared to say that the President lacks the power to settle such claims.

...We do not think it appropriate at the present time to address petitioner's contention that the suspension of claims, if authorized, would constitute a taking of property in violation of the Fifth Amendment to the United States Constitution in the absence of just compensation.[14] ...

Immigration and Naturalization Service v. Chadha

462 U.S. 919 (1983)

[This case involved a challenge to the constitutionality of a provision in the Immigration and Nationality Act. Section 244(a)(1) of the Act authorized the Attorney General to suspend deportation of an otherwise deportable alien if the alien met specified conditions and if his deportation would "result in extreme hardship to the alien" or his family. The Act also required the Attorney General to report such suspensions to Congress. Section 244(c)(2), the provision of the Act challenged in this case, allowed one house of Congress to veto the Attorney General's determination that suspension of deportation was appropriate. Chadha was an East Indian whose deportation was suspended by the Attorney General. Over a year later, the House of Representatives, acting without the participation of either the Senate or the President, passed a resolution under Section 244(c)(2) stating that Chadha and others did not satisfy the statutory criteria and thus would not have their deportations suspended. Chadha challenged his deportation, arguing that Section 244(c)(2) was unconstitutional.]

MR. CHIEF JUSTICE BURGER delivered the opinion of the Court ....

We turn now to the question whether action of one House of Congress under §244(c)(2) violates strictures of the Constitution. We begin, of course, with the presumption that the challenged statute is valid ....

---

14. Though we conclude that the President has settled petitioner's claims against Iran, we do not suggest that the settlement has terminated petitioner's possible taking claim against the United States. We express no views on petitioner's claims that it has suffered a taking.

By the same token, the fact that a given law or procedure is efficient, convenient, and useful in facilitating functions of government, standing alone, will not save it if it is contrary to the Constitution. Convenience and efficiency are not the primary objectives—or the hallmarks—of democratic government and our inquiry is sharpened rather than blunted by the fact that Congressional veto provisions are appearing with increasing frequency in statutes which delegate authority to executive and independent agencies....

Justice White undertakes to make a case for the proposition that the one-House veto is a useful "political invention," and we need not challenge that assertion. We can even concede this utilitarian argument although the long-range political wisdom of this "invention" is arguable. It has been vigorously debated, and it is instructive to compare the views of the protagonists. But policy arguments supporting even useful "political inventions" are subject to the demands of the Constitution which defines powers and, with respect to this subject, sets out just how those powers are to be exercised.

Explicit and unambiguous provisions of the Constitution prescribe and define the respective functions of the Congress and of the Executive in the legislative process....

THE PRESENTMENT CLAUSES

The records of the Constitutional Convention reveal that the requirement that all legislation be presented to the President before becoming law was uniformly accepted by the Framers. Presentment to the President and the Presidential veto were considered so imperative that the draftsmen took special pains to assure that these requirements could not be circumvented. During the final debate on Art. I, §7, cl. 2, James Madison expressed concern that it might easily be evaded by the simple expedient of calling a proposed law a "resolution" or "vote" rather than a "bill." 2 M. Farrand, The Records of the Federal Convention of 1787 301-302. As a consequence, Art. I, §7, cl. 3, was added.

The decision to provide the President with a limited and qualified power to nullify proposed legislation by veto was based on the profound conviction of the Framers that the powers conferred on Congress were the powers to be most carefully circumscribed. It is beyond doubt that lawmaking was a power to be shared by both Houses and the President....

The President's role in the lawmaking process also reflects the Framers' careful efforts to check whatever propensity a particular Congress might have to enact oppressive, improvident, or ill-considered measures....

The Court also has observed that the Presentment Clauses serve the important purpose of assuring that a "national" perspective is grafted on the legislative process....

BICAMERALISM

The bicameral requirement of Art. I, §§1, 7 was of scarcely less concern to the Framers than was the Presidential veto and indeed the two concepts are interdependent. By providing that no law could take effect without the concurrence of the prescribed majority of the Members of both Houses, the Framers reemphasized their belief, already remarked upon in connection with the Presentment Clauses, that legislation should not be enacted unless it has been carefully and fully considered by the Nation's elected officials....

[T]he Framers were acutely conscious that the bicameral requirement and the Presentment Clauses would serve essential constitutional functions. The President's participation in the legislative process was to protect the Executive Branch from Congress and to protect the whole people from improvident laws. The division of the Congress into two distinctive bodies assures that the legislative power would be exercised only after opportunity for full study and debate in separate settings. The President's unilateral veto power, in turn, was limited by the power of two thirds of both Houses of Congress to overrule a veto thereby precluding final arbitrary action of one person. It emerges clearly that the prescription for legislative action in Art. I, §§1, 7 represents the Framers' decision that the legislative power of the Federal government be exercised in accord with a single, finely wrought and exhaustively considered, procedure.

The Constitution sought to divide the delegated powers of the new Federal Government into three defined categories, Legislative, Executive and Judicial, to assure, as nearly as possible, that each branch of government would confine itself to its assigned responsibility. The hydraulic pressure inherent within each of the separate Branches to exceed the outer limits of its power, even to accomplish desirable objectives, must be resisted.

Although not "hermetically" sealed from one another, Buckley v. Valeo, 424 U.S., at 121, the powers delegated to the three Branches are functionally identifiable. When any Branch acts, it is presumptively exercising the power the Constitution has delegated to it. When the Executive acts, he presumptively acts in an executive or administrative capacity as defined in Art. II. And when, as here, one House of Congress purports to act, it is presumptively acting within its assigned sphere.

Beginning with this presumption, we must nevertheless establish that the challenged action under §244(c)(2) is of the kind to which the procedural requirements of Art. I, §7, apply. Not every action taken by either House is subject to the bicameralism and presentment requirements of Art. I. Whether actions taken by either House are, in law and fact, an exercise of legislative power depends not on their form but upon "whether they contain matter which is properly to be regarded as legislative in its character and effect." S. Rep. No. 1335, 54th Cong., 2d Sess., 8 (1897).

Examination of the action taken here by one House pursuant to §244(c)(2) reveals that it was essentially legislative in purpose and effect. In purporting to exercise power defined in Art. I, §8, cl. 4, to "establish an uniform Rule of Naturalization," the House took action that had the purpose and effect of altering the legal rights, duties, and relations of persons, including the Attorney General, Executive Branch officials and Chadha, all outside the Legislative Branch. Section 244(c)(2) purports to authorize one House of Congress to require the Attorney General to deport an individual alien whose deportation otherwise would be cancelled under §244. The one-House veto operated in this case to overrule the Attorney General and mandate Chadha's deportation; absent the House action, Chadha would remain in the United States. Congress has *acted* and its action has altered Chadha's status.

The legislative character of the one-House veto in this case is confirmed by the character of the Congressional action it supplants. Neither the House of Representatives nor the Senate contends that, absent the veto provision in §244(c)(2), either of them, or both of them acting together, could effectively require the Attorney General to deport an alien once the Attorney General, in the exercise of legislatively delegated authority, had determined the alien should remain in the United States. Without the challenged provision in §244(c)(2), this could have been achieved, if at all, only by legislation requiring deportation. Similarly, a veto by one House of Congress under §244(c)(2) cannot be justified as an attempt at amending the standards set out in §244(a)(1), or as a repeal of §244 as applied to Chadha. Amendment and repeal of statutes, no less than enactment, must conform with Art. I.

The nature of the decision implemented by the one-House veto in these cases further manifests its legislative character. After long experience with the clumsy, time-consuming private bill procedure, Congress made a deliberate choice to delegate to the Executive Branch, and specifically to the Attorney General, the authority to allow deportable aliens to remain in this country in certain specified circumstances. It is not disputed that this choice to delegate authority is precisely the kind of decision that can be implemented only in accordance with the procedures set out in Art. I. Disagreement with the Attorney General's decision on Chadha's deportation — that is, Congress' decision to deport Chadha — no less than Congress' original choice to delegate to the Attorney General the authority to make that decision, involves determinations of policy that Congress can implement in only one way; bicameral passage followed by presentment to the President. Congress must abide by its delegation of authority until that delegation is legislatively altered or revoked.

Finally, we see that when the Framers intended to authorize either House of Congress to act alone and outside of its prescribed bicameral legislative role, they narrowly and precisely defined the procedure for such action. There are but four provisions in the Constitution, explicit and unambiguous, by which one House may act alone with the unreviewable force of law, not subject to the President's veto: (a) The House of Representatives alone was given the power to initiate impeachments. Art. I, §2, cl. 5; (b) The Senate alone was given the power to conduct trials following impeachment on charges initiated by the House and to convict following trial. Art. I, §3, cl. 6; (c) The Senate alone was given final unreviewable power to approve or to disapprove presidential appointments. Art. II, §2, cl. 2; (d) The Senate alone was given unreviewable power to ratify treaties negotiated by the President. Art. II, §2, cl. 2.

Clearly, when the Draftsmen sought to confer special powers on one House, independent of the other House, or of the President, they did so in explicit, unambiguous terms. These carefully defined exceptions from presentment and bicameralism underscore the difference between the legislative functions of Congress and other unilateral but important and binding one-House acts provided for in the Constitution. These exceptions are narrow, explicit, and separately justified; none of them authorize the action challenged here. On the contrary, they provide further support for the conclusion that Congressional authority is not to be implied and for the conclusion that the veto provided for in §244(c)(2) is not authorized by the constitutional design of the powers of the Legislative Branch.

Since it is clear that the action by the House under §244(c)(2) was not within any of the express constitutional exceptions authorizing one House to act alone, and equally clear that it was an exercise of legislative power, that action was subject to the standards prescribed in Article I. The bicameral requirement, the Presentment Clauses, the President's veto, and Congress' power to override a veto were intended to erect enduring checks on each Branch and to protect the people from the improvident exercise of power by mandating certain prescribed steps. To preserve those checks, and maintain the separation of powers, the carefully defined limits on the power of each Branch must not be eroded. To accomplish what has been attempted by one House of Congress in this case requires action in conformity with the express procedures of the Constitution's prescription for legislative action: passage by a majority of both Houses and presentment to the President.

The veto authorized by §244(c)(2) doubtless has been in many respects a convenient shortcut; the "sharing" with the Executive by Congress of its authority over aliens in this manner is, on its face, an appealing compromise. In purely practical terms, it is obviously easier for action to be taken by one House without submission to the President; but it is crystal clear from the records of the Convention, contemporaneous writings and debates, that the Framers ranked other values higher than efficiency. The records of the Convention and debates in the States preceding ratification underscore the common desire to define and limit the exercise of the newly created federal powers affecting the states and the people. There is unmistakable expression of a determination that legislation by the national Congress be a step-by-step, deliberate and deliberative process.

The choices we discern as having been made in the Constitutional Convention impose burdens on governmental processes that often seem clumsy, inefficient, even unworkable, but those hard choices were consciously made by men who had lived under a form of government that permitted arbitrary governmental acts to go unchecked. There is no support in the Constitution or decisions of this Court for the proposition that the cumbersomeness and delays often encountered in complying with explicit Constitutional standards may be avoided, either by the Congress or by the President. *See* Youngstown Sheet & Tube Co. v. Sawyer, 343 U.S. 579 (1952). With all the obvious flaws of delay, untidiness, and potential for abuse, we have not yet found a better way to preserve freedom than by making the exercise of power subject to the carefully crafted restraints spelled out in the Constitution....

MR. JUSTICE WHITE, dissenting.

Today the Court not only invalidates §244(c)(2) of the Immigration and Nationality Act, but also sounds the death knell for nearly 200 other statutory provisions in which Congress has reserved a "legislative veto." For this reason, the Court's decision is of surpassing importance. And it is for this reason that the Court would have been well-advised to decide the case, if possible, on the narrower grounds of separation of powers, leaving for full consideration the constitutionality of other congressional review statutes operating on such varied matters as war powers and agency rulemaking, some of which concern the independent regulatory agencies.

The prominence of the legislative veto mechanism in our contemporary political system and its importance to Congress can hardly be overstated. It has become a central means by which Congress secures the accountability of executive and independent agencies. Without the legislative veto, Congress is faced with a Hobson's choice: either to refrain from delegating the necessary authority, leaving itself with a hopeless task of writing laws with the requisite specificity to cover endless special circumstances across the entire policy landscape, or in the alternative, to abdicate its law-making function to the Executive Branch and independent agencies. To choose the former leaves major national problems unresolved; to opt for the latter risks unaccountable policymaking by those not elected to fill that role. Accordingly, over the past five decades, the legislative veto has been placed in nearly 200 statutes. The device is known in every field of governmental concern: reorganization, budgets, foreign affairs, war powers, and regulation of trade, safety, energy, the environment and the economy.

[Justice White traces the history and uses of the legislative veto since the New Deal.]

Even this brief review suffices to demonstrate that the legislative veto is more than "efficient, convenient, and useful." It is an important if not indispensable political invention that allows the President and Congress to resolve major constitutional and policy differences, assures the accountability of independent regulatory agencies, and preserves Congress' control over lawmaking. Perhaps there are other means of accommodation and accountability, but the increasing reliance of Congress upon the legislative veto suggests that the alternatives to which Congress must now turn are not entirely satisfactory....

... If the legislative veto were as plainly unconstitutional as the Court strives to suggest, its broad ruling today would be more comprehensible. But, the constitutionality of the legislative veto is anything but clear-cut. The issue divides scholars, courts, attorneys general, and the two other branches of the National Government. If the veto devices so flagrantly disregarded the requirements of Article I as the Court today suggests, I find it incomprehensible that Congress, whose members are bound by oath to uphold the Constitution, would have placed these mechanisms in nearly 200 separate laws over a period of 50 years.

The reality of the situation is that the constitutional question posed today is one of immense difficulty over which the Executive and Legislative branches — as well as scholars and judges — have understandably disagreed. That disagreement stems from the silence of the Constitution on the precise question: The Constitution does not directly authorize or prohibit the legislative veto. Thus, our task should be to determine whether the legislative veto is consistent with the purposes of Art. I and the principles of Separation of Powers which are reflected in that Article and throughout the Constitution. We should not find the lack of a specific constitutional authorization for the legislative veto surprising, and I would not infer disapproval of the mechanism from its absence. From the summer of 1787 to the present the Government of the United States has become an endeavor far beyond the contemplation of the Framers. Only within the last half century has the complexity and size of the Federal Government's responsibilities grown so greatly that the Congress must rely on the legislative veto as the most effective if not the only means to insure their role as the nation's lawmakers. But the wisdom of the Framers was to anticipate that the nation would grow and new problems of governance would require different solutions. Accordingly, our Federal Government was intentionally chartered with the flexibility to respond to contemporary needs without losing sight of fundamental democratic principles.

Notes and Questions

1. Why are the foreign relations powers divided between the President and Congress? Wouldn't it have been more efficient to let the President make all foreign relations decisions and all foreign relations law? Why did the Founders give different powers to different branches? The generic response is that separation of federal powers secures liberty by diffusing authority, and increases the quality of political outcomes through an institutional division of labor. Do these justifications apply in the foreign affairs context? Why were the Founders so unclear about the allocation of authority for so many foreign relations tasks? Is there virtue in ambiguity and silence? Did the Founders expect the branches to work out the optimal allocation of foreign relations power? Is this realistic?

2. Uncertainty about the constitutional allocation of authority between the President and Congress has been resolved by two distinct, and somewhat incompatible, interpretive strategies. The first strategy, known as "formalism," emphasizes constitutional text, rule-bound-adjudication, and clearly delineated lines of demarcation between the branches. For separation-of-powers formalists, the critical threshold question is whether a particular exercise of authority is essentially legislative, executive, or judicial; once the characterization is made, the action is scrutinized for conformity to constitutional allocation. The majority opinions in *Chadha* and *Youngstown* are classic formalist opinions. The second interpretive strategy is known as "functionalism." Functionalists believe that the exigencies of modern government demand a more flexible interpretation of separation of powers. Functionalists tend to employ balancing approaches to separation-of-powers disputes, to ask whether particular institutional practices further the purposes of separation of powers, and to countenance the participation of each branch in the decision-making processes of the other. Famous functionalist opinions include Justice Jackson's concurrence in *Youngstown* and Justice White's dissent in *Chadha*. For general discussions of the distinction, see William N. Eskridge, Jr., *Relationships Between Formalism and Functionalism in Separation of Powers Cases*, 22 Harv. J.L. & Pub. Pol'y 21 (1998); Martin S. Flaherty, *The Most Dangerous Branch*, 105 Yale L.J. 1725 (1996); Thomas Merrill, *The Constitutional Principle of Separation of Powers*, 1991 Sup. Ct. Rev. 225; and Peter L. Strauss, *Formal and Functional Approaches to Separation of Powers Questions: A Foolish Inconsistency?*, 72 Cornell L. Rev. 488 (1987). For a critique of both the formalist and functionalist perspectives, and an attempt to sketch out a different approach to separation of powers, see M. Elizabeth Magill, *The Real Separation in Separation of Powers Law*, 86 Va. L. Rev. 1127 (2000), and M. Elizabeth Magill, *Beyond Powers and Branches in Separation of Powers Law*, 150 U. Pa. L. Rev. 603 (2001).

3. Which approach — formalist or functionalist — better promotes the constitutional separation of powers? Which approach is most appropriate for a case such as *Youngstown*? Is it helpful, or simplistic, for the majority in *Youngstown* to ask simply whether the steel seizure was a legislative or executive action? Couldn't it have been something of both? Isn't it a question of degree?

But is Justice Jackson's more celebrated functionalist opinion any more helpful? Consider his first category — presidential action pursuant to an express or implied congressional authorization. How does a Court discern an implied authorization? (We return to this issue below.) And, assuming that there is such an authorization, is Jackson correct to assert that if an act is held unconstitutional in this context, "it usually means that the Federal government as an undivided whole lacks power"? What about constitutional limitations on excessive delegation?

Jackson's second category is presidential action in the face of legislative silence. Again, as we shall explore below, the ascertainment of true congressional silence is a difficult interpretive question. But assuming Congress has been silent, is it helpful to assert that "there is a zone of twilight in which [the President] and Congress may have concurrent authority, or in which its distribution is uncertain"? What does Jackson mean by concurrent authority? Can the President act until Congress says otherwise? What is the source of Executive authority here? When Jackson says that such assertions of presidential power depend on "imperatives of events and contemporary imponderables," is he talking about politics? Is the validity of presidential action within the second category a political question? In the face of congressional silence, are there any limits on presidential power except *ex post* congressional disapproval?

Jackson's third category is presidential action incompatible with the express or implied will of Congress. Again the problem arises of ascertaining the implied will of Congress. Can this will be ascertained through measures other than legislation? Jackson himself viewed *Youngstown* as a case of presidential action inconsistent with the implied will of Congress. What was this conclusion based on? Had Congress explicitly prohibited this action? Was Jackson interpreting congressional silence, in the context of Congress's other actions, to mean disapproval? If he implied congressional will from silence, would this be consistent with *Chadha*'s insistence that Congress can only legislate through bicameralism and presentment?

4. Although the Supreme Court in *Dames & Moore* could point to no statute that conferred on the President the authority to suspend the private claims against Iran pending in U.S. courts, it nonetheless concluded that the presidential action "was authorized" to suspend the claims. On what basis did the Court reach this conclusion? Was it appropriate for the Court to look at the "general tenor of Congress's legislation in this area in trying to determine whether the President is acting alone or at least with the acceptance of Congress"? Do the majority opinions in *Youngstown* and *Chadha* permit this inquiry? What was the Court's basis for its "crucial" conclusion that Congress had implicitly approved the practice of claims settlement by executive agreement? And why did the Court find it "important[]" that "Congress has not disapproved of the action taken here [by the President]"? Do you agree with Professor Koh that the approach in *Dames & Moore* "elevat[es] the president's power from the twilight zone-Jackson's category two-to its height in Jackson's category one" and "effectively follow[s] the dissenting view in *Youngstown*, which had converted legislative silence into consent, thereby delegating to the President authority that Congress itself had arguably withheld"? Harold Hongju Koh, The National Security Constitution: Sharing Power after the Iran-Contra Affair 139 (1990). Professor Koh continues:

> [B]y finding legislative "approval" when Congress had given none, [*Dames & Moore*] not only inverted the Steel Seizure holding which had construed statutory non-approval of the president's act to mean legislative disapprovalbut also condoned legislative inactivity at a time that demanded interbranch dialogue and bipartisan consensus. . . . *Dames & Moore* championed unguided executive activism and congressional acquiescence in foreign affairs over the constitutional principle of balanced institutional participation.

Id. at 140. Do you agree? If so, why do you think the Court departed so drastically from the *Youngstown* approach? In stating in the passive voice that the President "was authorized" to suspend the claims, was the Court saying that it was Congress, Article II, or both, that authorized the President to suspend the claims in question? In other parts of the opinion, the Court described Congress as having "accepted" or "acquiesced in" the President's action. What difference might it make whether Congress authorized the suspension of claims or merely supported the suspension in a way that was less than authorization but more than silence?

5. As the statutory delegations described in *Dames & Moore* make clear, Congress has delegated a substantial amount of its foreign policy decisionmaking power to the President. An early such delegation was the Trading with the

Enemy Act of 1917, codified as amended, 50 U.S.C. app. §§1-6, 41-44. The TWEA essentially gave the President authority to freeze and seize assets and regulate all international transactions, simply by declaring a national emergency or war, and Presidents from Wilson to Nixon invoked it in a variety of ways as a basis for domestic and international emergency acts. *See* Harold Hongju Koh & John Choon Yoo, *Dollar Diplomacy/Dollar Defense: The Fabric of Economics and National Security Law*, 26 Int'l Law. 715, 725-34, 743 (1992). Following perceived abuses in Watergate and Vietnam, Congress enacted the International Emergency Economic Powers Act (IEEPA), one of the statutes at issue in *Dames & Moore*. IEEPA was actually designed to narrow the President's powers under TWEA by limiting them to wartime. But IEEPA also delegated very broad emergency powers in peacetime upon a presidential finding of "any unusual and extraordinary threat, which has its source in whole or substantial part outside the United States, to the national security, foreign policy, or economy of the United States, if the President declares a national emergency with respect to such threat." 50 U.S.C. §1701. The procedural requirement of a declaration of national emergency has proven to be no obstacle to the president's invocation of IEEPA, and presidents have accordingly invoked IEEPA in a variety of circumstances, including some at issue in the cases described below in Note 6. Another important source of foreign affairs authority delegated from Congress to the President is the Export Administration Act, 50 U.S.C. app. §§2401-2420, which gives the President near-plenary authority over U.S. exports. Congress has also historically delegated significant amounts of its power to regulate foreign trade to the President.

Why has Congress delegated so much of its foreign affairs power to the President? One reason that Congress historically had been so sanguine about delegations of power to the President was that it retained relatively tight control over presidential action through the use of the legislative veto. But *Chadha* calls scores of legislative veto provisions relating to foreign affairs into question. *See Chadha*, 462 U.S. at 1003-05 (White, J., dissenting). Are there any limits on such delegations? Recall that *Curtiss-Wright* rejected a challenge to an allegedly excessive delegation in the foreign affairs context even in an era in which the Supreme Court was taking delegation claims more seriously than it does today with respect to domestic affairs. We revisit the issue of delegation in Chapter 6 when we examine the somewhat different issue of whether there are any limits on the U.S. government's ability to delegate power to international organizations.

6. In addition to authority delegated to him by Congress, the President has substantial independent foreign relations authority. How should courts construe statutes that delegate authority to the Executive Branch in areas in which the Executive has independent constitutional authority to act? Because these statutes are thought to raise fewer concerns about excessive delegation of congressional authority, courts have tended to construe them broadly. A good illustration is Loving v. United States, 517 U.S. 748 (1996). The issue there was whether the general authority conferred on the President by the Uniform Code of Military Justice (UCMJ) to prescribe court martial punishments entailed authority to prescribe aggravating factors in the death penalty sentencing phase of court martial proceedings. Loving argued that reading the UCMJ to provide such authority would violate the "nondelegation doctrine" because the UCMJ did not provide "an intelligible principle to guide the President's discretion." In rejecting this argument, the Court noted that the delegation of authority "was to the President in his role as Commander in Chief." While it is arguable, said the Court, that "more explicit guidance as to how to select aggravating factors would be necessary if delegation were made to a newly created entity without independent authority in the area," in this case "the delegated duty . . . is interlinked with duties already assigned to the President by express terms of the Constitution, and the same limitations on delegation do not apply where the entity exercising the delegated authority itself possesses independent authority over the subject matter." For other decisions with similar reasoning, see, for example, Regan v. Wald, 468 U.S. 222 (1984) (finding statutory authority for restrictions on travel to Cuba), and Haig v. Agee, 453 U.S. 280 (1981) (finding statutory authority for revocation of passport).

How, if at all, is this delegation analysis relevant to the Court's decision in *Dames & Moore*? Is this what the Court has in mind in stating that "Congress cannot anticipate and legislate with regard to every possible action the President may find it necessary to take or every possible situation in which he might act"? In light of the Court's tendency to construe delegations broadly when they relate to independent presidential authority, will the President almost always be able to claim congressional authorization in the area of foreign affairs? If so, what is left of the framework established by the majority and concurring opinions in *Youngstown*?

7. What happens when Congress enacts a statute that restricts the President's exercise of his exclusive constitutional authority? As a general matter, such a statute is unconstitutional and thus not binding on the President. *See, e.g.*, Myers v. United States, 272 U.S. 52 (1926) (holding that a statute that prevented the President from removing postmasters without Senate approval was an unconstitutional limitation on the President's removal power under Article II); Youngstown Sheet & Tube Co. v. Sawyer, 343 U.S. 579, 635-38 (1952) (Jackson, J., concurring) (recognizing the existence of presidential authority that Congress cannot regulate). Beyond this general truism, however, several difficult issues are raised when there is a potential conflict between a federal statute and an exclusive presidential power.

First, what are the exclusive presidential powers that Congress cannot restrict? The Supreme Court has provided very little guidance. It has only rarely invalidated federal statutes for intruding on an exclusive presidential power, *see, e.g., Myers, supra*; Buckley v. Valeo, 424 US 1 (1976) (invalidating statute that purported to give Congress the authority to appoint commissioners to the Federal Election Commission), and it has never done so in the foreign affairs field. How can one tell which presidential powers in Article II are exclusive, and which are concurrent (i.e., legitimately subject to congressional regulation)? Could Congress recognize a different government from the one recognized by the President? Could Congress by statute revise the Monroe, Reagan, or Bush doctrines? Could it communicate directly with a foreign government on behalf of the United States? Would it matter whether it was communicating on a position that the President had already addressed? (We consider related questions concerning Congress's regulation of war in Chapter 4.)

The second issue is whether the President can disregard a statute that he deems to be unconstitutional, even though no court has declared it to be so. Since the President has a duty to take care to faithfully execute the "Laws," including the Constitution, and since statutes must conform to the Constitution, the President would seem to have the authority to disregard a statute that he believes violates Article II. This has long been the position of the Executive Branch, *see, e.g.*, Memorial of Captain Meigs, 9 Op. Att'y Gen. 462, 469-70 (1860) (asserting that the President need not enforce a statute purporting to appoint an officer); The

Attorney General's Duty to Defend and Enforce Constitutionally Objectionable Legislation, 4A Op. O.L.C. 55 (1980) (noting that *Myers, supra,* "holds that the President's constitutional duty does not require him to execute unconstitutional statutes"), and the Supreme Court appears to agree, *see Myers, supra;* Freytag v. Commissioner, 501 U.S. 868 (1991) (Scalia, J., concurring) (stating that the President has "the power to veto encroaching laws . . . or even to disregard them when they are unconstitutional"). What criteria should the President and his legal advisors employ in determining whether to disregard a statute that is believed to violate Article II? Should the President give deference to the fact that Congress passed the statute and that Congress believed it was upholding its obligation to enact constitutional legislation? Should the President, where possible, construe provisions to avoid constitutional problems? How, if at all, should the answers to the questions be affected by the likelihood of judicial review?

The third issue is what courts should do when the scope of the federal statute or the exclusivity of the presidential power is unclear. This issue came up in Department of Navy v. Egan, 484 U.S. 518 (1988). In that case, the question was whether the Merit Systems Protection Board's statutory authority to review the removal of Executive employees included the authority to review the related decision to deny the employee in question a security clearance. The Supreme Court held that the Board had no such authority, reasoning in part:

> [The President's] authority to classify and control access to information bearing on national security and to determine whether an individual is sufficiently trustworthy to occupy a position in the Executive Branch that will give that person access to such information flows primarily from this constitutional investment of power in the President and exists quite apart from any explicit congressional grant . . . . [U]nless Congress specifically has provided otherwise, courts traditionally have been reluctant to intrude upon the authority of the Executive in military . . . affairs.

Id. at 527, 530. In effect, the Court required a clear statement by Congress before it would construe the statute as intruding on Executive authority. In what circumstances should this clear statement requirement apply? When the alternate statutory construction would be unconstitutional? When it would raise important constitutional questions? Does the clear statement requirement apply only when the presidential authority in question is an exclusive one, or also when the presidential authority is merely an independent one (i.e., derived from Article II but subject to the concurrent regulation of the Congress)?

8. The Court in *Dames & Moore* relied heavily on the historical practice of Executive Branch claims settlement in support of its conclusion that Congress authorized the President to suspend claims. Especially in the foreign affairs field, historical practice plays a critical role in informing the allocation of power between the President and Congress. *See, e.g.,* American Insurance Ass'n v. Garamendi, 539 U.S. 396, 415 (2003) ("Given the fact that the practice goes back over 200 years to the first Presidential administration, and has received congressional acquiescence throughout its history, the conclusion that the President's control of foreign relations includes the settlement of claims is indisputable.") (internal quotations and citations omitted); Youngstown Sheet & Tube Co. v. Sawyer, 343 U.S. 579, 610-11 (1952) (Frankfurter, J., concurring) ("[A] systematic, unbroken executive practice, long pursued to the knowledge of Congress and never before questioned, . . . making as it were such exercise of power part of the structure of our government, may be treated as a gloss on 'executive Power' vested in the President by §1 of Art. II."). Why is this so? Because constitutional text and structure in the foreign relations context are unclear? Because the President has significant concurrent constitutional authority in the foreign affairs field? Because original understanding matters less, and practical considerations more, in this context? Some other reason? For discussion of these issues, see Michael J. Glennon, *The Use of Custom in Resolving Separation of Powers Disputes*, 64 B.U. L. Rev. 109 (1984); Peter J. Spiro, *Treaties, Executive Agreements, and Constitutional Method*, 79 Tex. L. Rev. 961 (2001).

Historical practice also is relevant in the interpretation of statutes that authorize Executive Branch action. Congress is generally presumed to be aware of relevant Executive Branch practice when it legislates, and especially when this practice is longstanding, courts will often conclude that Congress has approved the practice when it enacts a related statute. A good example is United States v. Midwest Oil Co., 236 U.S. 459 (1915), a case relied on in *Dames & Moore*. There, the President suspended a statutory land grant program in a way that did not appear to be authorized by the statute. The Supreme Court nevertheless upheld the suspension, reasoning that the President had for many years prior to the enactment of the statute exercised the power to suspend similar land grant programs. The Court explained that, "in determining the meaning of a statute or the existence of a power, weight shall be given to the usage itself–even when the validity of the practice is the subject of investigation," and added that the past Executive Branch practice created a "presumption that unauthorized acts would not have been allowed to be so often repeated as to crystallize into a regular practice."

Is it proper for courts to construe statutes to conform to past Executive Branch practice? As one commentator has noted, although courts do not always infer congressional intent to ratify prior Executive Branch practice in this way, the inference is normally "stronger in the foreign affairs arena" than in other contexts. William N. Eskridge, Jr., *Interpreting Legislative Inaction*, 87 Mich. L. Rev. 67, 74 (1988). Why might Executive Branch practice be more important in the interpretation of foreign relations statutes? One reason might be that Congress faces "practical limitations on [its] capacity to forge ex ante standards for executive national security action." Peter Raven-Hansen & William C. Banks, *Pulling the Purse Strings of the Commander in Chief*, 80 Va. L. Rev. 833, 848 (1994). Another might be that the Executive Branch has special fact-gathering and interpretive expertise in this context. *See, e.g.*, Chicago & S. Air Lines, Inc. v. Waterman S.S. Corp., 333 U.S. 103, 111 (1948). Still another reason might be one that matters in the constitutional context, namely, that the President has significant concurrent constitutional authority in the foreign affairs field. Does it make sense to extend this constitutional reasoning to the interpretation of foreign affairs statutes? Is this what the Supreme Court meant in *Dames & Moore* when it stated that "the enactment of legislation closely related to the question of the President's authority in a particular case which evinces legislative intent to accord the President broad discretion may be considered to 'invite measures on independent presidential responsibility'"?

9. As a general matter, Congress has discretion not to spend or appropriate money for whatever reason it likes, and the President cannot expend unappropriated government monies, even if the result is that he cannot carry out foreign relations activities. Matters are more complicated when Congress conditions a spending authorization or appropriation on some restriction on presidential foreign relations action, or on the achievement of a particular foreign relations goal that affects a presidential foreign relations power. It is generally accepted that

Congress has the authority to spend and appropriate monies to accomplish results that it could not mandate directly through its enumerated powers, as long as it does so for the "general Welfare of the United States." *See* U.S. Const. Art. I, §8, cl. 1; South Dakota v. Dole, 483 U.S. 203, 207 (1987); United States v. Butler, 297 U.S. 1, 65-66 (1936). However, "other constitutional provisions [outside of Article I] may provide an independent bar to the conditional grant of federal funds." *Dole*, 483 U.S. at 208. The difficult question in the foreign relations context is determining when the President's powers under Article II amount to an independent bar to congressional conditions. As Professor Powell has noted, "[i]t is often unclear whether to interpret a conditional spending provision as a legislative assumption of authority the Constitution grants to the President, or as the legitimate use of a congressional power to express congressional views on foreign policy, or even to accomplish other proper legislative goals, in a manner that affects, without usurping, presidential authority." H. Jefferson Powell, *The President's Authority over Foreign Affairs: An Executive Branch Perspective*, 67 Geo. Wash. L. Rev. 527, 552 (1999).

Consider, in this light, the Jerusalem Embassy Act of 1995, 104 Pub. L. No. 45, 109 Stat. 398 (1995), which declared it to be the policy of the United States that "Jerusalem should be recognized as the capital of Israel," and "that the United States embassy in Israel should be established in Jerusalem no later than May 31, 1999," and which conditioned half of the State Department's appropriations for the acquisition and maintenance of buildings abroad on the construction and opening in Jerusalem of the United States Embassy. The Department of Justice advised the President that such conditional appropriations "invade exclusive presidential authorities in the field of foreign affairs and are unconstitutional." Memorandum from Walter Dellinger to the Counsel to the President, Bill to Relocate United States Embassy from Tel Aviv to Jerusalem, 19 Op. O.L.C. 123 (1995). Beginning from the premise that the President has the exclusive authority to recognize governments and conduct diplomatic relations, the memorandum reasoned that "Congress cannot trammel the President's constitutional authority to conduct the Nation's foreign affairs and to recognize foreign governments by directing the relocation of an embassy," especially "where, as here, the location of the embassy is not only of great significance in establishing the United States' relationship with a single country, but may well also determine our relations with an entire region of the world." Do you agree? Does the President have the exclusive authority to determine the location of a U.S. embassy? Could Congress decline to appropriate any money for the building and maintenance of a U.S. embassy in a particular country? Could it limit appropriations to ensure that the embassy was small and had a small staff? If so, why can't it condition appropriations to ensure a particular location? For an analysis that disagrees with the Justice Department view, see Malvina Halberstam, *The Jerusalem Embassy Act*, 19 Fordham Int'l L.J. 1379 (1996).

For additional discussion of Congress's ability to affect foreign relations through its appropriations and spending powers, see William C. Banks & Peter Raven-Hansen, National Security Law and the Power of the Purse (1994); Powell, *supra*; Louis Fisher, *Presidential Independence and the Power of the Purse*, 3 U.C. Davis J. Int'l L. & Pol'y. 107 (1997); J. Gregory Sidak, *The President's Power of the Purse*, 1989 Duke L.J. 1162. We return to the issue of conditional appropriations in the discussion of war powers in Chapter 4.

10. To what extent should courts adjudicate the respective powers of Congress and the President in foreign affairs? Is there much practical difference between significant deference to presidential action (such as in *Dames & Moore*) and nonreview under the political question doctrine? What do you think now of Justice Powell's insistence in *Goldwater v. Carter* on a true conflict between the branches as a prerequisite to adjudication?

11. Professor Koh reflects conventional wisdom in maintaining that the President almost always wins in foreign affairs disputes with Congress. *See* Harold Hongju Koh, *Why the President (Almost) Always Wins in Foreign Affairs: Lessons of the Iran-Contra Affair*, 97 Yale L.J. 1255 (1988). In support of this view, Koh notes that the President usually takes the initiative in foreign policy and rarely suffers high stakes losses at the hand of Congress or the courts; and the President conducts day-to-day relations, negotiates international agreements, articulates U.S. policies toward other nations, sends troops abroad, and the like. The House and Senate, by contrast, seem reactive, acquiescent, and relatively weak. They approve Executive appointments (and rarely reject them), they consent to international agreements (and rarely reject them), and although they sometimes initiate and enact foreign relations statutes, they almost always do so via Executive delegation or with an exception allowing for Executive discretion.

Professor Martin, a political scientist, questions whether a tally of initiatives and defeats tells us much about how much influence the U.S. legislature wields. It is a fallacy, she argues, to infer the absence of influence from the absence of action. This is because of the logic of indirect influence through anticipated reaction. For example, legislators trying to maximize their preferences anticipate the effect of a presidential veto and adjust the content of proposed legislation accordingly. The veto has a potent influence on the content of legislation even though it is rarely exercised. Martin argues that Congress exercises considerable analogous influence over the President that does not manifest itself in "victories." Thus, for example, she contends that the President's decision whether to use an executive agreement in place of an Article II treaty (a phenomenon discussed in Chapter 6) is constrained by the President's need for congressional cooperation in implementing international commitments. *See* Lisa L. Martin, Democratic Commitments: Legislatures and International Cooperation (2000).

Which view is right? Does the outcome of this debate have any implications for constitutional doctrine? For the role of the courts?

4

War Powers

This chapter considers the constitutional authority of the United States to engage in war. It begins in Sections A and B with an analysis of the respective war powers of Congress and the President. Section C then examines Congress's ability to regulate the President's use of force. Section D assesses the role of civil liberties during wartime. The chapter closes with an analysis in Section E of some of the legal issues raised by the war on terrorism.

A. CONGRESS'S ROLE IN AUTHORIZING WAR

Article I, Section 8 of the Constitution confers on Congress many war-related powers, including: the power to "declare War, grant Letters of Marque and Reprisal, and make Rules concerning Captures on Land and Water" (cl. 11); the power to appropriate money for the military, which, in the case of the army, is limited to two-year periods (cls. 12-13); the power to "make Rules for the Government and Regulation of the land and naval Forces" (cl. 14); the power to "provide for calling forth the Militia to execute the Laws of the Union, suppress Insurrections and repel Invasions" (cl. 15); and the power to "provide for organizing, arming, and disciplining, the Militia, and for governing such Part of them as may be employed in the Service of the United States" (cl. 16). This section examines the meaning and scope of these powers, and considers their implications for Congress's role in authorizing the United States to engage in war.

1. Historical Background

In late eighteenth-century England, the power to wage war, like other foreign relations powers, rested exclusively with the king. As Blackstone explained in his Commentaries on the Laws of England, the king had "the sole prerogative of making war and peace," such that "in order to make a war completely effectual, it is necessary with use in England that it be publicly declared and duly proclaimed by the king's authority." 1 William Blackstone, Commentaries on the Laws of England 249-50 (1765).

Upon separating from England, the foreign affairs of the United States, including its management of the revolutionary war, were handled by the Continental Congress. The First Continental Congress, which convened in September 1774, issued the

Articles of Association, imposed an economic boycott of British goods, and threatened a ban on American exports to Britain. The Second Continental Congress, which convened in May 1775, appointed George Washington as commander in chief of the "United Colonies," as well as a dozen other generals. In November of that year, the Continental Congress established a Committee of Secret Correspondence that, primarily through Benjamin Franklin and John Adams, would later negotiate loans and gifts from France, Holland, and Spain. Following the Declaration of Independence in July 1776, the foreign affairs details of which we described in Chapter 1, the Continental Congress managed the war, continued to seek foreign assistance, and called up the state militia. The Continental Congress was a weak institution, however, with no legal authority to enact or enforce laws or to raise or finance an army, and thus was often dependent on the states for money, troops, and supplies. As a result, the Continental Army was chronically depleted, and the United States often relied for its defense on state militias that tended to be unreliable, undisciplined, and inefficient. As Washington once described the state militia during this period, "they come in you cannot tell how, go, you cannot tell when; and act, you Cannot tell where, consume your Provisions, exhaust your Stores, and leave you at last in a critical moment." Letter from George Washington to the President of the Continental Congress, December 20, 1776, in 6 The Writings of George Washington 403 (John C. Fitzpatrick ed., 1931-1944).

Under the Articles of Confederation, which took effect in 1781, the Continental Congress was given the "sole and exclusive right and power of determining on peace and war." In addition, states were prohibited from "engag[ing] in any war without the consent of the United States in Congress assembled" unless they were invaded, or threatened with imminent invasion by an Indian tribe. The Articles also provided that expenses incurred for defense would be paid out of a common treasury, financed by the states in proportion to the value of their land. These provisions worked better on paper than in practice. Congress still lacked the effective power to raise a standing national army or navy. It also lacked the power to draft individuals for military service. And states did not contribute their share to the public treasury. Thus, as Edmund Randolph explained at the Federal Convention in 1787, one of the principal defects of the Confederation had been that it did not provide "security agai[nst] foreign invasion; congress not being permitted to prevent a war nor to support it by th[eir] own authority." 1 The Records of the Federal Convention of 1787, at 19 (Max Farrand ed., 1911).

Not surprisingly, therefore, the text of the Constitution contains a number of provisions relating to the use of military force. Article I gives Congress the powers described above. Article II provides that the President "shall be Commander in Chief of the Army and Navy of the United States, and of the Militia of the several States, when called into the actual Service of the United States." Finally, Article I, Section 10 prohibits the states from engaging in war unless they are invaded or in imminent danger, and it prohibits them from keeping troops or ships of war during a time of peace without the consent of Congress.

At the Constitutional Convention, a draft of the Constitution would have given Congress the power to "make" war. The word "make" was changed during the Convention, however, to "declare." The following oft-discussed excerpt from James Madison's notes of the Convention debates reflects this change:

> Mr. Pinkney opposed the vesting this power [to make war] in the Legislature. Its proceedings were too slow. It wd. meet but once a year. The Hs. of Rps. would be

too numerous for such deliberations. The Senate would be the best depositary, being more acquainted with foreign affairs, and most capable of proper resolutions. If the States are equally represented in Senate, so as to give no advantage to large States, the power will notwithstanding be safe, as the small have their all at stake in such cases as well as the large States. It would be singular for one authority to make war, and another peace.

Mr. Butler. The Objections agst the Legislature lie in a great degree agst the Senate. He was for vesting the power in the President, who will have all the requisite qualities, and will not make war but when the Nation will support it.

Mr. Madison and Mr Gerry moved to insert "*declare*," striking out "*make*" war; leaving to the Executive the power to repel sudden attacks.

Mr. Sharman thought it stood very well. The Executive shd. be able to repel and not to commence war. "Make" better than "declare" the latter narrowing the power too much.

Mr. Gerry never expected to hear in a republic a motion to empower the Executive alone to declare war.

Mr. Elseworth. there is a material difference between the cases of making *war*, and making *peace*. It shd. be more easy to get out of war, than into it. War also is a simple and overt declaration. peace attended with intricate & secret negociations.

Mr. Mason was agst giving the power of war to the Executive, because not safely to be trusted with it; or to the Senate, because not so constructed as to be entitled to it. He was for clogging rather than facilitating war; but for facilitating peace. He preferred "*declare*" to "*make*."

On the Motion to insert *declare* — in place of *Make*, it was agreed to.

[Connecticut originally voted against this motion, but] On the remark by Mr. King that "*make*" war might be understood to "conduct" it which was an Executive function, Mr. Elseworth gave up his objection and the vote of Con[necticut] was changed to — ay.

2 The Records of the Federal Convention of 1787, at 318-19 (Max Farrand ed., 1911).

The Constitution's assignment of war powers is discussed in *The Federalist Papers*, excerpted below:

Federalist No. 24 (Hamilton)

A stranger to our politics, who was to read our newspapers at the present juncture, without having previously inspected the plan reported by the convention, would be naturally led to one of two conclusions: either that it contained a positive injunction, that standing armies should be kept up in time of peace; or that it vested in the EXECUTIVE the whole power of levying troops, without subjecting his discretion, in any shape, to the control of the legislature.

If he came afterwards to peruse the plan itself, he would be surprised to discover, that neither the one nor the other was the case; that the whole power of raising armies was lodged in the LEGISLATURE, not in the EXECUTIVE; that this legislature was to be a popular body, consisting of the representatives of the people periodically elected; and that instead of the provision he had supposed in favor of standing armies, there was to be found, in respect to this object, an important qualification even of the legislative discretion, in that clause which forbids the appropriation of money for the support of an army for any longer period than two years a precaution which, upon a nearer view of it, will appear to be a great and real security against the keeping up of troops without evident necessity.

Federalist No. 25 (Hamilton)

[If, as some suggest, the Constitution were to prohibit] the RAISING of armies in time of peace, the United States would then exhibit the most extraordinary spectacle which the world has yet seen, that of a nation incapacitated by its Constitution to prepare for defense, before it was actually invaded. As the ceremony of a formal denunciation of war has of late fallen into disuse, the presence of an enemy within our territories must be waited for, as the legal warrant to the government to begin its levies of men for the protection of the State. We must receive the blow, before we could even prepare to return it. All that kind of policy by which nations anticipate distant danger, and meet the gathering storm, must be abstained from, as contrary to the genuine maxims of a free government. We must expose our property and liberty to the mercy of foreign invaders, and invite them by our weakness to seize the naked and defenseless prey, because we are afraid that rulers, created by our choice, dependent on our will, might endanger that liberty, by an abuse of the means necessary to its preservation.

Here I expect we shall be told that the militia of the country is its natural bulwark, and would be at all times equal to the national defense. This doctrine, in substance, had like to have lost us our independence. It cost millions to the United States that might have been saved. The facts which, from our own experience, forbid a reliance of this kind, are too recent to permit us to be the dupes of such a suggestion. The steady operations of war against a regular and disciplined army can only be successfully conducted by a force of the same kind. Considerations of economy, not less than of stability and vigor, confirm this position. The American militia, in the course of the late war, have, by their valor on numerous occasions, erected eternal monuments to their fame; but the bravest of them feel and know that the liberty of their country could not have been established by their efforts alone, however great and valuable they were. War, like most other things, is a science to be acquired and perfected by diligence, by perserverance, by time, and by practice.

Federalist No. 69 (Hamilton)

The President is to be the "commander-in-chief of the army and navy of the United States, and of the militia of the several States, when called into the actual service of the United States." . . . In most of these particulars, the power of the President will resemble equally that of the king of Great Britain and of the governor of New York. The most material points of difference are these: First. The President will have only the occasional command of such part of the militia of the nation as by legislative provision may be called into the actual service of the Union. The king of Great Britain and the governor of New York have at all times the entire command of all the militia within their several jurisdictions. In this article, therefore, the power of the President would be inferior to that of either the monarch or the governor. Secondly. The President is to be commander-in-chief of the army and navy of the United States. In this respect his authority would be nominally the same with that of the king of Great Britain, but in substance much inferior to it. It would amount to nothing more than the supreme command and direction of the military and naval forces, as first General and admiral of the Confederacy; while that of the British king extends to the declaring of war and to the raising and regulating of fleets and armies, all which, by the Constitution under consideration, would appertain to the legislature.

There was also discussion of the Constitution's assignment of war powers in the state debates over ratification of the U.S. Constitution. Perhaps the most frequently quoted statement from these debates is the following excerpt of a speech by James Wilson in the Pennsylvania convention:

> This [constitutional] system will not hurry us into war; it is calculated to guard against it. It will not be in the power of a single man, or a single body of men, to involve us in such distress, for the important power of declaring war is vested in the legislature at large; this declaration must be made with the concurrence of the House of Representatives. From this circumstance we may draw a certain conclusion, that nothing but our national interest can draw us into a war.

2 The Documentary History of the Ratification of the Constitution 583 (Merrill Jensen ed., 1976). Also frequently quoted is the following statement by James Iredell at the North Carolina ratifying convention:

> I believe most of the governors of the different states have powers similar to those of the President. In almost every country, the executive has command of the military forces. From the nature of the thing, the command of armies ought to be delegated to one person only. The secrecy, dispatch, and decision, which are necessary in military operations, can only be expected from one person. The President, therefore, is to command the military forces of the United States, and this power I think a proper one; at the same time it will be found to be sufficiently guarded. A very material difference may be observed between this power, and the authority of the king of Great Britain under similar circumstances. The king of Great Britain is not only the commander-in-chief of the land and naval forces, but has power, in time of war, to raise fleets and armies. He also has authority to declare war. The President has not the power of declaring war by his own authority, nor that of raising fleets and armies. These powers are vested in other hands. The power of declaring war is expressly given to Congress, that is, to the two branches of the legislature.... They have also expressly delegated to them the powers of raising and supporting armies, and of providing and maintaining a navy.

4 Jonathan Elliot, The Debates in the Several State Conventions on the Adoption of the Federal Constitution 107-08 (1888).

2. The Quasi-War with France

The United States engaged in an "undeclared war" early in its history. Recall from Chapter 1 that in 1793, following France's declaration of war on Great Britain and other countries, President Washington issued a proclamation of neutrality. Despite this proclamation, both England and France attacked U.S. commercial shipping. John Jay negotiated a treaty with Great Britain, ratified in 1795, that reduced the British attacks. The French, perceiving the Jay Treaty to be evidence of U.S. favoritism toward the British, increased their attacks on U.S. shipping. In 1797,

Washington's successor, John Adams, sent three commissioners (including future Chief Justice John Marshall) to France to resolve the crisis. When it was later revealed that the French treated the U.S. commissioners rudely and asked them for a large bribe (an episode known as the "XYZ Affair"), public opinion in the United States turned against the French, and Congress enacted numerous statutes relating to war with France. These statutes enlarged the army and navy, empowered the President to raise troops, authorized the construction of forts and the purchase of weapons, barred commercial relations with France, declared treaties with France to be legally void, and, most important, gave the President the power to capture French warships and commission privateers. *See* David P. Currie, The Constitution in Congress: The Federalist Period, 1789-1801, at 243-44 (1997). Congress never declared war, however. This undeclared war with France is the subject of the Bas v. Tingy decision below, as well as the Little v. Barreme decision excerpted in Section C.

Bas v. Tingy

4 U.S. 37 (1800)

[During the undeclared war with France, Congress enacted two statutes concerning the recapture of American vessels. The first statute, enacted on June 28, 1798, provided:

> That whenever any vessel the property of, or employed by, any citizen of the United States, or person resident therein, or any goods or effects belonging to any such citizen, or resident, shall be re-captured by any public armed vessel of the United States, the same shall be restored to the former owner, or owners, upon due proof, he or they paying and allowing, as and for salvage to the re-captors, one-eighth part of the value of such vessel, goods and effects, free from all deduction and expenses.

The second statute, enacted the following year on March 2, 1799, differed slightly in wording:

> That for the ships or goods belonging to the citizens of the United States, or to the citizens, or subjects, of any nation in amity with the United States, or to the citizens, or subjects, of any nation in amity with the United States, if re-taken from the enemy within twenty-four hours, the owners are to allow one-eighth part of the whole value for salvage, &c. and if above ninety-six hours one-half, all of which is to be paid without any deduction whatsoever . . . that all the money accruing, of which has already accrued from the sale of prizes, shall be and remain forever a fund for the payment of the half-pay to the officers and seamen, who may be entitled to receive the same.

In this case, the commander of an American public vessel claimed that, based on the 1799 statute, he was entitled to an award of one-half of the value of an American merchant ship he had recaptured from the French. The owner of the merchant ship responded that, because Congress had not declared war on France, France was not an "enemy" and therefore the 1799 statute did not apply.]

The [Justices] delivered their opinions *seriatim* in the following manner:

JUSTICE MOORE.

This case depends on the construction of the [1799] act, for the regulation of the navy. It is objected, indeed, that the act applies only to future wars; but its provisions are obviously applicable to the present situation of things, and there is nothing to prevent an immediate commencement of its operation.

It is, however, more particularly urged, that the word "enemy" cannot be applied to the French; because the section in which it is used, is confined to such a state of war, as would authorise a re-capture of property belonging to a nation in amity with the United States, and such a state of war, it is said, does not exist between America and France. A number of books have been cited to furnish a glossary on the word enemy; yet, our situation is so extraordinary, that I doubt whether a parallel case can be traced in the history of nations. But, if words are the representatives of ideas, let me ask, by what other word the idea of the relative situation of America and France could be communicated, than by that of hostility, or war? And how can the characters of the parties engaged in hostility or war, be otherwise described than by the denomination of enemies? It is for the honour and dignity of both nations, therefore, that they should be called enemies; for, it is by that description alone, that either could justify or excuse, the scene of bloodshed, depredation and confiscation, which has unhappily occurred; and, surely, congress could only employ the language of the act of June 13, 1798, towards a nation whom she considered as an enemy....

JUSTICE WASHINGTON....
    It may, I believe, be safely laid down, that every contention by force between two nations, in external matters, under the authority of their respective governments, is not only war, but public war. If it be declared in form, it is called solemn, and is of the perfect kind; because one whole nation is at war with another whole nation; and all the members of the nation declaring war, are authorised to commit hostilities against all the members of the other, in every place, and under every circumstance. In such a war all the members act under a general authority, and all the rights and consequences of war attach to their condition.

    But hostilities may subsist between two nations more confined in its nature and extent; being limited as to places, persons, and things; and this is more properly termed imperfect war; because not solemn, and because those who are authorised to commit hostilities, act under special authority, and can go no farther than to the extent of their commission. Still, however, it is public war, because it is an external contention by force, between some of the members of the two nations, authorised by the legitimate powers. It is a war between the two nations, though all the members are not authorised to commit hostilities such as in a solemn war, where the government restrain the general power.

    Now, if this be the true definition of war, let us see what was the situation of the United States in relation to France. In March 1799, congress had raised an army; stopped all intercourse with France; dissolved our treaty; built and equip ships of war; and commissioned private armed ships; enjoining the former, and authorising the latter, to defend themselves against the armed ships of France, to attack them on the high seas, to subdue and take them as prize, and to re-capture armed vessels found in their possession. Here, then, let me ask, what were the technical characters of an American and French armed vessel, combating on the high seas, with a view the one to subdue the other, and to make prize of his property? They certainly were not friends, because there was a contention by force; nor were they private enemies, because the contention was external, and authorised by the legitimate authority of the two governments. If they were not our enemies, I know not what constitutes an enemy.

    But, secondly, it is said, that a war of the imperfect kind, is more properly called acts of hostility, or reprizal, and that congress did not mean to consider the hostility subsisting between France and the United States, as constituting a state of war.

In support of this position, it has been observed, that in no law prior to March 1799, is France styled our enemy, nor are we said to be at war. This is true; but neither of these things were necessary to be done: because as to France, she was sufficiently described by the title of the French republic; and as to America, the degree of hostility meant to be carried on, was sufficiently described without declaring war, or declaring that we were at war. Such a declaration by congress, might have constituted a perfect state of war, which was not intended by the government....

JUSTICE CHASE....

What, then, is the nature of the contest subsisting between America and France? In my judgment, it is a limited, partial, war. Congress has not declared war in general terms; but congress has authorised hostilities on the high seas by certain persons in certain cases. There is no authority given to commit hostilities on land; to capture unarmed French vessels, nor even to capture French armed vessels lying in a French port; and the authority is not given, indiscriminately, to every citizen of America, against every citizen of France; but only to citizens appointed by commissions, or exposed to immediate outrage and violence. So far it is, unquestionably, a partial war; but, nevertheless, it is a public war, on account of the public authority from which it emanates.

There are four acts, authorised by our government, that are demonstrative of a state of war. A belligerent power has a right, by the law of nations, to search a neutral vessel; and, upon suspicion of a violation of her neutral obligations, to seize and carry her into port for further examination. But by the acts of congress, an American vessel it authorised: 1st. To resist the search of a French public vessel: 2d. To capture any vessel that should attempt, by force, to compel submission to a search: 3d. To re-capture any American vessel seized by a French vessel; and 4th. To capture any French armed vessel wherever found on the high seas. This suspension of the law of nations, this right of capture and re-capture, can only be authorised by an act of the government, which is, in itself, an act of hostility. But still it is a restrained, or limited, hostility; and there are, undoubtedly, many rights attached to a general war, which do not attach to this modification of the powers of defence and aggression....As there may be a public general war, and a public qualified war; so there may, upon correspondent principles, be a general enemy, and a partial enemy. The designation of "enemy" extends to a case of perfect war; but as a general designation, it surely includes the less, as well as the greater, species of warfare. If congress had chosen to declare a general war, France would have been a general enemy; having chosen to wage a partial war, France was, at the time of the capture, only a partial enemy; but still she was an enemy.

3. The War of 1812

When war broke out between Great Britain and France in 1803, American commercial shipping got caught in the crossfire. Great Britain enacted and enforced harsh neutrality laws, and on that basis seized U.S. merchant vessels for allegedly violating the British blockade of Europe. The British also impressed thousands of U.S. sailors into service for the Royal Navy. By 1811, so-called "War Hawks" in the U.S. House of Representatives (most notably Henry Clay of Kentucky and John Calhoun of South Carolina) began to clamor for war with Great Britain, in part because of continued British interference in American shipping, but also to redress alleged British instigation of Indians on the western frontier of the United States. On June 1, 1812, President James Madison asked Congress to declare war against Great Britain. Three days later, the House of Representatives voted (79 to 49) to declare war, and after much debate, on June 17, 1812, the U.S. Senate also voted for war, 19 to 13. On June 18, 1812, President Madison signed the following measure into law:

> An Act Declaring War Between the United Kingdom of Great Britain and Ireland and the Dependencies Thereof and the United States of America and Their Territories.
>
> Be it enacted by the Senate and House of Representatives of the United States of America in Congress assembled, That war be and the same is hereby declared to exist between the United Kingdom of Great Britain and Ireland and the dependencies thereof, and the United States of America and their territories; and that the President of the United States is hereby authorized to use the whole land and naval force of the United States to carry the same into effect, and to issue to private armed vessels of the United States commissions or letters of marque and general reprisal, in such form as he shall think proper, and under the seal of the United States, against the vessels, goods, and effects of the government of the said United Kingdom of Great Britain and Ireland, and the subjects thereof.

Brown v. United States

12 U.S. 110 (1814)

[The issue in this case was whether Congress, in its act of June 18, 1812, had implicitly authorized the Executive Branch to confiscate enemy property (pine timber owned by a British citizen) located within the United States.]

MARSHALL, C.J. delivered the opinion of the Court, as follows....

Respecting the power of government no doubt is entertained. That war gives to the sovereign full right to take the persons and confiscate the property of the enemy wherever found, is conceded. The mitigations of this rigid rule, which the humane and wise policy of modern times has introduced into practice, will more or less affect the exercise of this right, but cannot impair the right itself. That remains undiminished, and when the sovereign authority shall chuse to bring it into operation, the judicial department must give effect to its will. But until that will shall be expressed, no power of condemnation can exist in the Court....

Since, in this country, from the structure of our government, proceedings to condemn the property of an enemy found within our territory at the declaration of war, can be sustained only upon the principle that they are instituted in execution of some existing law, we are led to ask, Is the declaration of war such a law? Does that declaration, by its own operation, so vest the property of the enemy in the government, as to support proceedings for its seizure and confiscation, or does it vest only a right, the assertion of which depends on the will of the sovereign power?...

The modern rule [under international law] would seem to be, that tangible property belonging to an enemy and found in the country at the commencement of war, ought not to be immediately confiscated; and in almost every commercial treaty an article is inserted stipulating for the right to withdraw such property....

The constitution of the United States was framed at a time when this rule, introduced by commerce in favor of moderation and humanity, was received throughout the civilized world. In expounding that constitution, a construction ought not lightly to be admitted which would give to a declaration of war an effect in this country it does not possess elsewhere, and which would fetter that exercise of entire discretion respecting enemy property, which may enable the government to apply to the enemy the rule that he applies to us.

If we look to the constitution itself, we find this general reasoning much strengthened by the words of that instrument.

That the declaration of war has only the effect of placing the two nations in a state of hostility, of producing a state of war, of giving those rights which war confers; but not of operating, by its own force, any of those results, such as a transfer of property, which are usually produced by ulterior measures of government, is fairly deducible from the enumeration of powers which accompanies that of declaring war. "Congress shall have power" — "to declare war, grant letters of marque and reprisal, and make rules concerning captures on land and water."

It would be restraining this clause within narrower limits than the words themselves import, to say that the power to make rules concerning captures on land and water, is to be confined to captures which are exterritorial. If it extends to rules respecting enemy property found within the territory, then we perceive an express grant to congress of the power in question as an independent substantive power, not included in that of declaring war.

The acts of congress furnish many instances of an opinion that the declaration of war does not, of itself, authorize proceedings against the persons or property of the enemy found, at the time, within the territory.

War gives an equal right over persons and property: and if its declaration is not considered as prescribing a law respecting the person of an enemy found in our country, neither does it prescribe a law for his property. The act concerning alien enemies, which confers on the president very great discretionary powers respecting their persons, affords a strong implication that he did not possess those powers by virtue of the declaration of war.

The "act for the safe keeping and accommodation of prisoners of war," is of the same character.

The act prohibiting trade with the enemy, contains this clause:

> And be it further enacted, That the president of the United States be, and he is hereby authorized to give, at any time within six months after the passage of this act, passports for the safe transportation of any ship or other property belonging to British subjects, and which is now within the limits of the United States.

The phraseology of this law shows that the property of a British subject was not considered by the legislature as being vested in the United States by the declaration of war; and the authority which the act confers on the president, is manifestly considered as one which he did not previously possess.

The proposition that a declaration of war does not, in itself, enact a confiscation of the property of the enemy within the territory of the belligerent, is believed to be entirely free from doubt. Is there in the act of congress, by which war is declared against Great Britain, any expression which would indicate such an intention?

That act, after placing the two nations in a state of war, authorizes the president of the United States to use the whole land and naval force of the United States to carry the war into effect, and "to issue to private armed vessels of the United States, commissions or letters of marque and general reprisal against the vessels, goods and effects of the government of the united kingdom of Great Britain and Ireland, and the subjects thereof."

Kennedy and Johnson expanded American involvement in Vietnam, and by July 1964 there were 21,000 U.S. forces there. All of these activities took place without specific congressional authorization. On July 31, 1964, the American destroyer *U.S.S. Maddox* was attacked by North Vietnamese forces in the Gulf of Tonkin. There is evidence, still contested, suggesting that some of the attacks in the Gulf of Tonkin may have been exaggerated or invented by the Johnson Administration in order to prompt Congress to support the war. In any event, on August 7, 1964, Congress passed the following resolution:

> ...Resolved by the Senate and House of Representatives of the United States of America in Congress assembled, That the Congress approves and supports the determination of the President, as Commander in Chief, to take all necessary measures to repel any armed attack against the forces of the United States and to prevent further aggression.
>
> Sec. 2. The United States regards as vital to its national interest and to world peace the maintenance of international peace and security in southeast Asia. Consonant with the Constitution of the United States and the Charter of the United Nations and in accordance with its obligations under the Southeast Asia Collective Defense Treaty, the United States is, therefore, prepared, as the President determines, to take all necessary steps, including the use of armed force, to assist any member or protocol state of the Southeast Asia Collective Defense Treaty requesting assistance in defense of its freedom.
>
> Sec. 3. This resolution shall expire when the President shall determine that the peace and security of the area is reasonably assured by international conditions created by action of the United Nations or otherwise, except that it may be terminated earlier by concurrent resolution of the Congress.

Joint Resolution of Congress, Pub. L. No. 88-408, 78 Stat. 384 (1964). After the Tonkin Gulf Resolution, U.S. military involvement in Vietnam increased dramatically. In February 1965, the United States began a sustained bombing campaign in North Vietnam. In March 1965, it began to send combat troops to Vietnam; by early 1968, U.S. combat troops there numbered more than half a million. In addition to the Tonkin Gulf Resolution, Congress repeatedly authorized the appropriation of money to finance the war and repeatedly renewed selective service provisions allowing for a military draft.

Orlando v. Laird

443 F.2d 1039 (2d Cir. 1971)

[In 1970, two enlistees in the U.S. Army sued to enjoin the Secretary of Defense, the Secretary of the Army, and certain commanding officers from enforcing orders directing the enlistees to report for transfer to Vietnam. Their principal claim was that these Executive Branch officials exceeded their constitutional authority by ordering the enlistees to participate in a war not properly authorized by Congress.]

ANDERSON, CIRCUIT JUDGE....

We [have previously held] that the constitutional delegation of the war-declaring power to the Congress contains a discoverable and manageable standard imposing on the Congress a duty of mutual participation in the prosecution of war. Judicial scrutiny of that duty, therefore, is not foreclosed by the political question doctrine. As we see it, the test is whether there is any action by the Congress sufficient to authorize or ratify the military activity in question. The evidentiary materials produced at the hearings in the district court clearly disclose that this test is satisfied.

The Congress and the Executive have taken mutual and joint action in the prosecution and support of military operations in Southeast Asia from the beginning of those operations. The Tonkin Gulf Resolution, enacted August 10, 1964 (repealed December 31, 1970) was passed at the request of President Johnson and, though occasioned by specific naval incidents in the Gulf of Tonkin, was expressed in broad language which clearly showed the state of mind of the Congress and its intention fully to implement and support the military and naval actions taken by and planned to be taken by the President at that time in Southeast Asia, and as might be required in the future "to prevent further aggression." Congress has ratified the executive's initiatives by appropriating billions of dollars to carry out military operations in Southeast Asia and by extending the Military Selective Service Act with full knowledge that persons conscripted under that Act had been, and would continue to be, sent to Vietnam. Moreover, it specifically conscripted manpower to fill "the substantial induction calls necessitated by the current Vietnam buildup."

There is, therefore, no lack of clear evidence to support a conclusion that there was an abundance of continuing mutual participation in the prosecution of the war. Both branches collaborated in the endeavor, and neither could long maintain such a war without the concurrence and cooperation of the other.

Although appellants do not contend that Congress can exercise its war declaring power only through a formal declaration, they argue that congressional authorization cannot, as a matter of law, be inferred from military appropriations or other war-implementing legislation that does not contain an express and explicit authorization for the making of war by the President. Putting aside for a moment the explicit authorization of the Tonkin Gulf Resolution, we disagree with appellants' interpretation of the declaration clause for neither the language nor the purpose underlying that provision prohibits an inference of the fact of authorization from such legislative action as we have in this instance. The framers' intent to vest the war power in Congress is in no way defeated by permitting an inference of authorization from legislative action furnishing the manpower and materials of war for the protracted military operation in Southeast Asia.

The choice, for example, between an explicit declaration on the one hand and a resolution and war-implementing legislation, on the other, as the medium for expression of congressional consent involves "the exercise of a discretion demonstrably committed to the . . . legislature," Baker v. Carr, [369 U.S. 186, 211 (1962)], and therefore, invokes the political question doctrine.

Such a choice involves an important area of decision making in which, through mutual influence and reciprocal action between the President and the Congress, policies governing the relationship between this country and other parts of the world are formulated in the best interests of the United States. If there can be nothing more than minor military operations conducted under any circumstances, short of an express and explicit declaration of war by Congress, then extended military operations could not be conducted even though both the Congress and the President were agreed that they were necessary and were also agreed that a formal declaration of war would place the nation in a posture in its international relations which would be against its best interests. For the judicial branch to enunciate and enforce such a standard would be not only extremely unwise but also would constitute a deep invasion of the political question domain. As the Government says, "...decisions regarding the form and substance of congressional enactments authorizing hostilities are determined by highly complex considerations of diplomacy, foreign policy and military strategy inappropriate to judicial inquiry." It would, indeed, destroy the flexibility of action which the executive and legislative branches must have in dealing with other sovereigns. What has been said and done by both the President and the Congress in their collaborative conduct of the military operations in Vietnam implies a consensus on the advisability of not making a formal declaration of war because it would be contrary to the interests of the United States to do so. The making of a policy decision of that kind is clearly within the constitutional domain of those two branches and is just as clearly not within the competency or power of the judiciary.

Notes and Questions

1. How did the allocation of war powers under the Constitution differ from the allocation of war powers under the Articles of Confederation? What accounts for the differences? What were the inadequacies under the Articles of Confederation relating to war, and how were they dealt with in the Constitution? Why did the Founders substitute the word "declare" for the word "make"? Is it relevant that Article I, Section 10 of the Constitution provides that the states may not "engage" in war? Is engaging in a war different from declaring a war?

2. The Constitution gives Congress the power to "declare War." What does that power entail? When, if ever, is a declaration of war constitutionally necessary in order for the United States to engage in war? As *Federalist No. 25* suggests, numerous wars in the eighteenth century began without a declaration, and a declaration often came, if at all, years after the initiation of direct armed conflict between two nations. *See, e.g.,* Louis Henkin, Foreign Affairs and the United States Constitution 76, 370 n.65 (2d ed. 1996); J.F. Maurice, Hostilities Without Declaration of War (1883); Clyde Eagleton, *The Form and Function of the Declaration of War,* 32 Am. J. Int'l L. 19 (1938). Throughout U.S. history, Congress has declared war in connection with only five conflicts: the War of 1812; the Mexican-American War of 1846-48; the Spanish-American War of 1898; World War I; and World War II. By contrast, the United States has utilized military force in hundreds of situations not involving declarations of war. *See* Ellen C. Collier, Instances of Use of United States Forces Abroad, 1798-1993 (C.R.S. 1993) (listing "234 instances in which the United States has used its armed forces abroad in situations of conflict or potential conflict or for other than normal peacetime purposes"). In many but not all of these undeclared wars, Congress expressly approved the use of force even though it did not declare war. *See generally* Curtis A. Bradley & Jack L. Goldsmith, *Congressional Authorization and the War on Terrorism,* 118 Harv. L. Rev. 2047, 2072-74 (2005). Taken together, these historical facts raise the question: if Congress need not issue a formal declaration of war in order for the United States to engage in hostilities with foreign nations, what is the significance of Congress's power to "declare" war?

3. One historic function of a declaration of war was to give other nations legal notice under international law. At the time of the Founding, war was a "fundamental concept in public international law," sharply distinguishable from "peace," to which particular legal consequences attached. Henkin, *supra*, at 98. During war, elaborate rules of belligerency governed relations between warring states, and equally elaborate rules of neutrality governed relations between belligerents and neutral states. "War," so understood, was different from other uses of military force, which did not by themselves necessarily trigger all of the rules of belligerency and neutrality. As the opinions in Bas v. Tingy suggest, sometimes this distinction was framed in terms of the differences between "perfect" and "imperfect" war, or between "general" and "limited" war. On this understanding, a declaration of war was a method by which states could trigger the full array of international law rules governing neutral and belligerent states on issues such as rights to seizure of vessels, shipment of contraband, and institution of blockades, as well as domestic laws related to war and emergency powers. *See, e.g.,* 1 William Blackstone, Commentaries 250; 3 E. de Vattel, The Law of Nations or the Principles of Natural Law 255 (photo. reprint 1995) (James Brown Scott ed., Charles G. Fenwick trans., Carnegie Institute of Washington 1916) (1758).

Many commentators maintain that modern international law has largely eliminated this historic function for declarations of war. As Professor Kahn explains:

> Since the advent of the United Nations (UN) Charter, war has been abolished as a category of international law. A declaration of war serves no purpose under international law; it can have no bearing on the underlying legal situation. No longer a performative utterance, it is only a meaningless utterance—not even descriptive— from the perspective of international law. . . . War has disappeared from international law because force is no longer a legitimate means of changing state entitlements. The fundamental rule of postwar international law was the prohibition on the use or threat of force. This was enshrined in Article 2(4) of the UN Charter: "All members shall refrain in their international relations from the threat or use of force against the territorial integrity or political independence of any state."

Paul W. Kahn, *War Powers and the Millennium,* 34 Loy. L.A. L. Rev. 11, 16-17 (2000). Do these changes in international law explain why the United States has not issued a formal declaration of war since World War II? How do these changes in the international law effect of war declarations affect Congress's role in U.S. warmaking? Can changes in international law alter the scope or meaning of the U.S. Constitution?

4. Even if declarations of war have lost their function under international law, and even if a declaration of war is not a constitutional prerequisite for U.S. warmaking, the Declare War Clause may still be relevant to the constitutional distribution of war powers authority between Congress and the President. Many scholars believe that Congress has the exclusive power to authorize significant offensive military operations, and they often rely on the Declare War Clause as textual support for this position. *See, e.g.,* John Hart Ely, War and Responsibility: Constitutional Lessons of Vietnam and Its Aftermath 3-10 (1993); Louis Fisher, Presidential War Power 1-16 (2d ed. 2004); Henkin, *supra,* at 76, 97-101; Harold Hongju Koh, The National Security Constitution: Sharing Power after the Iran-Contra Affair 74-77 (1990); Charles A. Lofgren, *War-making Under the Constitution: The Original Understanding,* 81 Yale L.J. 672, 695 (1972).

Does the text of the Declare War Clause support this view? The clause refers to a particular congressional action—declaring war—and does not state that Congress has the more general authority to "authorize" or "initiate" war. Do either the Founding materials excerpted above, or Bas v. Tingy, support the view that only

Congress can authorize war? Or do they merely show that Congress has the exclusive authority to declare war, and that it can authorize war without issuing a declaration, without addressing whether Congress's power to authorize war is exclusive? Would it be consistent with these materials for the President to possess the power to make war in all circumstances in which Congress has not authorized or declared it? Of what relevance is it that some statutes refer to declarations of war? For example, the Alien Enemy Act, first enacted in 1798, gives the President the power to detain and expel enemy aliens within the United States "[w]henever there is a declared war between the United States and any foreign nation or government, or any invasion or predatory incursion is perpetrated, attempted, or threatened against the territory of the United States by any foreign nation or government." 50 U.S.C. §21.

5. Post-Founding statements and practices provide clearer evidence than the constitutional text to support the view that congressional authorization is constitutionally required for some uses of force by the United States. When the United States faced attacks from Indians along the western frontier, George Washington consistently denied that he had the power to engage in offensive military actions in the absence of congressional authorization: "The Constitution vests the power of declaring war with Congress; therefore no offensive expedition of importance can be undertaken until after they have deliberated on the subject, and authorized such a measure." Letter of George Washington to Governor William Moultrie, August 28, 1793, in 33 The Writings of George Washington 73 (John C. Fitzpatrick ed., 1939). John Adams evinced a similar attitude toward presidential war power with respect to the undeclared war with France in 1798. *See* Dean Alfange Jr., The Quasi-War and Presidential Warmaking, in David Gray Adler & Larry N. George eds., The Constitution and the Conduct of Foreign Policy 274-90 (1996). Jefferson took a similar view — at least in public — with respect to attacks by the Barbary Pirates in 1801-1802. *See* Currie, Federalist Period, *supra*, at 88; *but see id.* at 127-29 (describing how Jefferson took more aggressive offensive action than his public pronouncements deemed appropriate).

For other early statements in support of Congress's authority over the initiation of war, see Letter from Thomas Jefferson to James Madison, Sept. 6, 1789, in 15 The Papers of Thomas Jefferson 397 (Julian P. Boyd ed., 1958) ("We have already given in example one effectual check to the Dog of war by transferring the power of letting him loose from the Executive to the Legislative body...."); Letter from James Madison to Thomas Jefferson, April 2, 1798, in 6 The Writings of James Madison 312 (Gaillard Hunt ed., 1906) ("The constitution supposes, what The History of all Gov[ernments] demonstrates, that the Ex[ecutive] is the branch of power most interested in war, & most prone to it. It has accordingly with studied care, vested the question of war in the Legisl[ature]."); *cf.* Talbot v. Seeman, 5 U.S. 1, 28 (1801) ("The whole powers of war being, by the constitution of the United States, vested in congress, the acts of that body can alone be resorted to as our guides in this enquiry. It is not denied, nor in the course of the argument has it been denied, that congress may authorize general hostilities, in which case the general laws of war apply to our situation; or partial hostilities, in which case the laws of war, so far as they actually apply to our situation, must be noticed.").

6. Several scholars have challenged the view that the Declare War Clause gives Congress the exclusive power to authorize war. *See, e.g.,* Robert F. Turner, Repealing the War Powers Resolution: Restoring the Rule of Law in U.S. Foreign Policy 80-81 (1991); Henry P. Monaghan, *Presidential War-making*, 50 B.U. L. Rev. 19

(special issue 1970); Eugene V. Rostow, *Great Cases Make Bad Law: The War Powers Act*, 50 Tex. L. Rev. 833, 864-66 (1972); John C. Yoo, *The Continuation of Politics by Other Means: The Original Understanding of War Powers*, 84 Cal. L. Rev. 167 (1996). Professor Yoo has presented the most developed version of this position. He argues that constitutional text should be read in its eighteenth-century context to mean that Congress's war declaration power is limited to the notification and international law functions mentioned above. In his view, "interpreting 'declare war' to mean 'authorize' or 'commence' is a twentieth-century construct inconsistent with the eighteenth century understanding of the phrase." Yoo, *supra*, at 204. He concludes that the Constitution "demanded no constitutionally correct method of waging war," *id.* at 296, that the President has broad residual power to engage in offensive military action even in the absence of congressional authorization, and that Congress retains an ultimate check on presidential war power through its appropriations power. *Id.* at 295-305. This theory makes sense of the term "declare," and comports with modern war powers practice. But does it hold up in light of evidence that the Founders were trying to limit presidential war power, and were rejecting the English model? If Professor Yoo is right, why did Washington, Adams, and Jefferson believe, when each was President, that they lacked the power to initiate offensive military actions in the absence of congressional authorization?

Professor Ramsey has attempted to reconcile Professor Yoo's textual arguments with the evidence that the Founders thought that Congress must authorize offensive hostilities. *See* Michael D. Ramsey, *Textualism and War Powers*, 69 U. Chi. L. Rev. 1543 (2002). He argues that in the eighteenth century, war could, in the words of John Locke, be "declared by word or action." Thus Congress could "declare" war either by a formal declaration, or by authorizing the commencement of hostilities even in the absence of a declaration. If Professor Ramsey's premise about the meaning of "declare" is correct, does his theory successfully vindicate the "authorization" theory of congressional war powers? Does it matter that the "word or action" theory is nowhere mentioned in the Founding debates? For a response to Professor Ramsey's arguments, see John C. Yoo, *War and the Constitutional Text*, 69 Chi. L. Rev. 1639 (2002). For Professor Ramsey's rejoinder, see Michael D. Ramsey, *Text and History in the War Powers Debate: A Reply to Professor Yoo*, 69 U. Chi. L. Rev. 1685 (2002).

7. Congress's power to "grant Letters of Marque and Reprisal" might provide further support for the congressional authorization view. A letter of marque and reprisal is a governmental authorization to a private party to engage in retaliatory action against citizens or vessels of another nation. Some scholars have argued that the marque and reprisal clause supplements the Declare War Clause, with the Declare War Clause covering perfect and large-scale wars, and the marque and reprisal clause covering imperfect and smaller wars. *See, e.g.*, Lofgren, *supra*. *But see* C. Kevin Marshall, *Putting Privateers in Their Place: The Applicability of the Marque and Reprisal Clause to Undeclared Wars*, 64 U. Chi. L. Rev. 953 (1997) (criticizing this argument). Why would a power to authorize private citizens to engage in hostilities give Congress the exclusive ability to authorize the U.S. military to engage in hostilities? Of what relevance is it that Congress no longer grants letters of marque and reprisal (and has not done so since the nineteenth century)? Note, however, that about a month after the September 11, 2001 terrorist attacks, a bill was introduced in the House of Representatives (but never voted on) that would have authorized the President to issue letters of marque and reprisal allowing for the private

capture of Osama bin Laden and others responsible for the attacks. *See* H.R. 3076 (Oct. 10, 2001).

8. What is the significance of Congress's power to appropriate money for the military, which, in the case of the army, the Constitution limits to two-year periods? In general, the two-year limit was a compromise procedural mechanism to allay American concerns about a peacetime standing army. As Professor Kohn has noted, "[n]o principle of government was more widely understood or more completely accepted by the generation of Americans that established the United States than the danger of a standing army in peacetime." Richard H. Kohn, Eagle and Sword: The Beginnings of the Military Establishment in America, 1783-1802, at 2 (1975). American concerns about standing armies were reflected in the Declaration of Independence, which castigates King George for keeping a peacetime standing army "without the consent of our legislatures." This danger to liberty was not an abstraction — few forgot the Boston Massacre of 1770, where British troops killed five civilians and created "a cause celebre up and down the seacoast . . . [that] permanently embedded the prejudice against standing armies into the American political tradition." Lois G. Schwoerer, "No Standing Armies!": The Anti-Army Ideology in Seventeenth Century England 5-6 (1974).

In the Founding debates, the main arguments against a standing army were that they were a threat to liberty, they were unnecessary because America was isolated from its main threats, and state militias sufficed for defensive purposes. Largely for reasons articulated by Hamilton in the excerpt from *Federalist No. 25* — the inadequacy of the state militia system during the revolutionary war (and during the Articles of Confederation period), and the need to deter and meet foreign attacks — most of the Founders assumed that the new Constitution would provide for a standing army, and the main issue was how to set limits on it. *See* Kohn, *supra*, at 77-78. Some suggested capping the standing army at one or two thousand troops, and others suggested a refunding requirement every year, but ultimately the two-year appropriations requirement was agreed upon. As Hamilton explained the rationale for the provision in *Federalist No. 26*, "The Legislature of the United States will be obliged by this provision, once at least in every two years, to deliberate upon the propriety of keeping a military force on foot; to come to a new resolution on the point; and to declare their sense of the matter, by a formal vote in the face of their constituents. They are not at liberty to vest in the executive department permanent funds for the support of an army."

Does the two-year appropriations limit for the army help explain the widespread early belief that Congress needed to authorize all offensive uses of U.S. military force? At the Founding, the United States had a tiny standing army (718 persons) and no standing navy, and many Founders believed that a larger standing military force was unnecessary or pernicious. In this context congressional participation — in the form of authorizing the raising of troops, and the financing of them — was literally necessary for the President to exercise military power abroad. As a result, the appropriations authority, along with Congress's authority to regulate the use of the militia, would have required — and in fact, did require — early presidents to seek and secure statutory authority to use military force for any extended period, regardless of whether war had been declared. Was this appropriation requirement the real check on presidential use of force without congressional authorization? *See* Phillip Bobbitt, *War Powers: An Essay on John Hart Ely's War and Responsibility: Constitutional Lessons of Vietnam and Its Aftermath*, 92 Mich. L. Rev. 1364, 1385, 1392, 1396 (1994); Yoo, *Continuation of Politics, supra.*

If control over appropriations is an important check on the President's ability to use force abroad, what is the significance of the fact that over the course of U.S. history, the size of the standing army has dramatically increased — from 12,000 during the War of 1812, to 50,000 during the Spanish-American War, to 250,000 following World War I, to 12 million during World War II? Today this number is about 1.5 million, with approximately one million more in the reserves. As one commentator noted in the 1960s, "America possesses a standing army, sufficiently large, sufficiently well-equipped, and sufficiently mobile to make possible, through presidential action alone and on very short notice, conflicts of unforeseeable dimensions anywhere in the world." Note, *Congress, the President, and the Power to Commit Forces to Combat*, 81 Harv. L. Rev. 1771, 1791 (1968).

9. Every time that Congress has declared war, it has additionally authorized the President to use force against the enemy. The statute commencing the War of 1812, excerpted above, is one example. Another example is the World War II joint resolution concerning the war with Germany. The title of the joint resolution made clear that the resolution did two things: it both "declar[ed] that a state of war exists between the Government of Germany and the Government and the people of the United States" and "made provision to prosecute the same." The body of the resolution did precisely these two things:

> Therefore, be it Resolved by the Senate and House of Representatives of the United States of America in Congress assembled, That the state of war between the United States and the Government of Germany which has thus been thrust upon the United States is hereby formally declared; and the President is hereby authorized and directed to employ the entire naval and military forces of the United States and the resources of the Government to carry on war against the Government of Germany; and, to bring the conflict to a successful termination, all of the resources of the country are hereby pledged by the Congress of the United States.

The identical pattern of expressly distinguishing between Congress's war declaration and its authorization for the President to use force is evident in every other statute declaring war in U.S. history — the other World War II joint resolutions, the World War I joint resolutions, and the statutes declaring war in the Spanish-American War, and the Mexican-American War. *See* Bradley & Goldsmith, *Congressional Authorization, supra*, at 2062-64.

What is the significance of this practice? Does it support the view that war declarations and war authorizations serve different aims? Does it show that congressional war authorizations, as opposed to war declarations, are what empower the President to use force abroad? Does this pattern suggest that Congress could declare war but not authorize the President to use force? What does Brown v. United States suggest about this issue?

10. Recall Justice Washington's distinction in Bas v. Tingy between an "imperfect" war that is "more confined in its nature and extent; being limited as to places, persons, and things," and a "perfect" one, in which "one whole nation is at war with another whole nation; and all the members of the nation declaring war, are authorised to commit hostilities against all the members of the other, in every place, and under every circumstance." One can group most conflicts in U.S. history into one or the other of these two categories. In addition to the Quasi-War with France, examples of limited wars include Congress's authorization of the President to use various specified military resources and methods related to the repulsion, suppression, or protection of Indians, its authorization of the President to use limited force to occupy and control Florida, and its authorization of the President to use limited force against slave traders and pirates and against the Barbary states that had been preying on U.S. shipping. *See* Bradley & Goldsmith, *Congressional Authorization, supra,* at 2073-74 & nn.112-16. By contrast, the authorizations of force in declared wars have tended not to have any limits other than to indicate who the enemy is. So, for example, the authorization against Germany in World War I simply "authorized and directed" the President "to employ the entire naval and military forces of the United States and the resources of the Government," without restriction on the method of force or targets, "to carry on war against the Imperial German Government."

What is the significance of the distinction between imperfect wars with limited authorizations to use force, and perfect wars with broad and generally unlimited authorizations to use force? Do the limited authorizations in imperfect wars implicitly restrict presidential power? Are there any limits on presidential power in perfect wars with broad authorizations? Did the Gulf of Tonkin Resolution trigger a perfect or an imperfect war?

11. What does Brown v. United States suggest about the role of war declarations? Does it support or detract from the theory that war declarations serve notice and related functions under international law? What does it suggest about how authorizations to use force should be interpreted? Is its holding based on, and thus limited to, the Constitution's assignment to Congress of the power to make rules concerning captures on land and on the particular array of statutes associated with the War of 1812? Or does it more broadly require Congress to specifically authorize the President to engage in each element of war? Is *Brown* limited to presidential seizures within the United States, or does it apply to seizure of enemy property everywhere, including the high seas? Is *Brown* consistent with the Constitution's assignment of the Commander-in-Chief power to the President? Why didn't the Court conclude that the 1812 authorization "to use the whole land and naval force of the United States to carry the [war with Great Britain] into effect" entailed the power to confiscate enemy property? Why did the Court reject Justice Story's position that in a declared war with an unqualified authorization to use force, Congress should be deemed to have conferred all of the authorities on the President permitted by the international laws of war?

12. Assuming congressional authorization is sometimes required for U.S. war-making, must this authorization take a particular form? Are there situations in which it must take the form of a declaration of war? Is the choice of the form of authorization a political question, as the court concludes in Orlando v. Laird? Assuming that the authorization need not take a particular form, what counts as authorization? Do military appropriations count? Selective service authorizations? General statutes regulating the armed services? Consider the Vietnam War. In addition to the Tonkin Gulf Resolution, Congress repeatedly authorized the appropriation of money to finance the war and repeatedly renewed selective service provisions allowing for a military draft. Is the court correct in Orlando v. Laird that these provisions, taken together, constitute congressional authorization for the war in Vietnam? *Compare* Ely, *supra,* at 12-46 (analyzing question in detail and concluding that there was authorization), *with* William Van Alstyne, *Congress, the President, and the Power to Declare War: A Requiem for Vietnam,* 121 U. Pa. L. Rev. 1, 23-24 (1972) (concluding no authorization); Alexander M. Bickel, *Congress, the President and the Power to Wage War,* 48 Chi.-Kent L. Rev. 131, 136-38 (1971) (concluding no authorization or an excessive delegation of war power authority). If authorization can be inferred from appropriations and other measures, are there any limits on the President's use of the peacetime standing army? The Office of Legal Counsel in the Clinton Administration's Department of Justice argued that "in establishing and funding a military force that is capable of being projected anywhere around the globe, Congress has given the President, as Commander in Chief, considerable discretion in deciding how that force is to be deployed." Letter from Walter Dellinger, Assistant Attorney General, Office of Legal Counsel, to Senators Robert K. Dole, Alan K. Simpson, Strom Thurmond, and William S. Cohen (Sept. 27, 1994), at http://www.usdoj.gov/olc/haiti.htm. Is this correct?

13. Are there any limits on Congress's ability to authorize the President to go to war? Must Congress specify the enemy? The purpose for the use of force? The location where force may be used? The duration of the use of force?

What if Congress authorized the President to use military force against whomever he wanted, whenever and wherever he wanted? Some scholars have argued that the Gulf of Tonkin resolution was unconstitutional because it failed to identify a particular enemy and failed to sufficiently channel the President's military discretion. *See, e.g.,* Alexander M. Bickel, *Congress, the President, and the Power to Wage War*, 48 Chi.-Kent L. Rev. 131, 137-40 (1971); Francis D. Wormuth, *The Nixon Theory of the War Power: A Critique*, 60 Cal. L. Rev. 623, 692-700 (1972). John Hart Ely, by contrast, argued that to satisfy the nondelegation doctrine, a congressional authorization to use force need only specify an enemy, and the Gulf of Tonkin Resolution did so implicitly because of its preamble. Ely, *supra*, at 25-26. *Cf.* William H. Rehnquist, *The Constitutional Issues — Administration Position*, 45 N.Y.U. L. Rev. 628, 636-37 (1970) ("It has been suggested that there may be a question of unlawful delegation of powers here [with respect to the Gulf of Tonkin Resolution], and that Congress is not free to give a blank check to the President. Whatever may be the answer to that abstract question in the domestic field, I think it is plain from United States v. Curtiss-Wright Export Corp. . . . that the principle of unlawful delegation of powers does not apply to the field of external affairs." (footnotes omitted)). What if any constitutional limits are there on Congress's ability to delegate war-making authority to the President?

14. What is the proper meaning of "war" in the Declare War Clause? Justice Washington in Bas v. Tingy asserts that "every contention by force between two nations, in external matters, under the authority of their respective governments, is not only war, but public war." Does this mean (assuming that the Declare War Clause gives Congress the exclusive authority to authorize war) that "every contention by force" abroad must be authorized by Congress? Or is the analysis in Bas v. Tingy limited to the statutory term?

The meaning of the term "war" may differ in contexts outside of Article I, Section 8. For example, the United States Court of Military Appeals concluded that the Korean War, which was never authorized by Congress, was a war for purposes of the criminal provisions of the Uniform Code of Military Justice. *See* United States v. Bancroft, 3 U.S.C.M.A. 3 (1953). It stated:

> We believe a finding that this is a time of war, within the meaning of the language of the Code, is compelled by the very nature of the present conflict; the manner in which it is carried on; the movement to, and the presence of large numbers of American men and women on, the battlefields of Korea; the casualties involved; the sacrifices required; the drafting of recruits to maintain the large number of persons in the military service;

the national emergency legislation enacted and being enacted; the executive orders promulgated; and the tremendous sums being expended for the express purpose of keeping our Army, Navy and Air Force in the Korean theatre of operations. For our purpose, it matters not whether the authorization for the military activities in Korea springs from Congressional declarations, United Nations Agreements or orders by the Chief Executive. Within the limited area in which the principles of military justice are operative, we need consider only whether the conditions facing this country are such as to permit us to conclude that we are in a state of war within the meaning of the terms as used by Congress.

Id. at 5-6. Is this analysis consistent with the conclusion in *Youngstown* that the Korean War did not give the President power under the Commander-in-Chief Clause to seize the steel mills?

Contrast this decision with United States v. Averette, 19 U.S.C.M.A. 363 (1970). In that case, a civilian employee of an Army contractor working in Vietnam during the Vietnam War was tried by court-martial for conspiracy to commit larceny and attempted larceny of government-owned property. The issue was whether it was proper to exercise court-martial jurisdiction over a civilian in this situation. Article 2(10) of the Uniform Code of Military Justice allows for court-martial jurisdiction in "time of war" over "persons serving with or accompanying an armed force in the field." 18 U.S.C. §802(a)(10). The court construed the phrase "time of war" in this Article as referring only to a war formally declared by Congress. Noting that the Supreme Court "in a series of cases . . . has disapproved the trial by courts-martial of person not members of the armed forces," the court applied what it described as a "strict and literal interpretation" of the phrase "time of war." The court acknowledged that it had construed the phrase "time of war" more broadly with respect to other provisions in the Uniform Code of Military Justice, but it noted that "[n]one of these cases dealt with military jurisdiction over civilians." One judge dissented, arguing that "there is no compelling or cogent reason to construe the phrase 'time of war' as used in Article 2(10) of the Uniform Code differently from the construction we have accorded the same phrase in other Articles of the Code." The dissenting judge also argued that, "if congressional participation is required to energize the phrase in regard to court-martial jurisdiction, sufficient congressional participation is present in connection with the Vietnam conflict to fulfill the requirement."

The question of the meaning of "war" also arises in the interpretation of private contracts. For example, life insurance policies sometimes pay different amounts depending on whether the covered party died in war. Some courts have interpreted "war" in these policies narrowly to require an "act or declaration creating or recognizing its existence by that department of the government clothed with the war-making power." Bishop v. Jones & Petty, 28 Tex. 294 (Tex. Sup. Ct. 1866). Relying on this view of "war," some courts concluded that persons who were killed at Pearl Harbor and in the Korean War did not die in time of war. *See, e.g.,* West v. Palmetto State Life Insurance Co., 25 S.E.2d 475 (S.C. 1943) (Pearl Harbor); Beley v. Pennsylvania Mutual Life Insurance Co., 373 Pa. 231 (1953) (Korea). Other courts, however, have interpreted the term "war" more broadly to include "every forcible contest between two governments, de facto, or de jure," regardless of whether there is congressional declaration or authorization. *See, e.g.,* Western Reserve Life Ins. Co. v. Meadows, 261 S.W.2d 554 (Tex. 1953) (concluding that death during Korean War was "in time of war" for purposes of life insurance policy). *See generally* Arnold McNair & Arthur D. Watts, The Legal Effects of War (4th ed. 1966).

B. THE PRESIDENT'S INDEPENDENT MILITARY POWERS

Article II of the Constitution makes the President the Commander in Chief of the armed forces. The President may also have military powers as a result of other provisions in Article II, such as the Article II "vesting clause" or the Take Care Clause. This section considers the scope of the President's independent military powers, as illustrated by a variety of conflicts throughout history.

1. The Mexican-American War

One of the United States' five declared wars was the Mexican-American War of 1846-1848, which stemmed in part from a dispute over the border between Texas and Mexico. After gaining its independence from Mexico, Texas was annexed by the United States. The southern border of Texas was in dispute, with the United States claiming that it extended down to the Rio Grande river and Mexico claiming that it extended only down to the Nueces river. In June 1845, General Zachary Taylor, at the direction of President James Polk, moved his troops to the Rio Grande. This action prompted military clashes between U.S. and Mexican forces. President Polk then delivered the following message to Congress:

> The grievous wrongs perpetrated by Mexico upon our citizens throughout a long period of years, remain unredressed; and solemn treaties, pledging her public faith for this redress, have been disregarded. A Government either unable or unwilling to enforce the execution of such treaties, fails to perform one of its plainest duties.
>
> Our commerce with Mexico has been almost annihilated. It was formerly highly beneficial to both nations; but our merchants have been deterred from prosecuting it, by the system of outrage and extortion which the Mexican authorities have pursued against them;.... [N]ow, after reiterated menaces, Mexico has passed the boundary of the United States, has invaded our territory and shed American blood upon the American soil. She has proclaimed that hostilities have commenced, and that the two nations are now at war.
>
> As war exists, and, notwithstanding all our efforts to avoid it, exists by the act of Mexico herself, we are called upon, by every consideration of duty and patriotism, to vindicate, with decision the honor, the rights, and the interests of our country....
>
> In further vindication of our rights and defense of our territory, I invoke the prompt action of Congress to recognize the existence of the war, and to place at the disposition of the Executive the means of prosecuting the war with vigor, and thus hastening the restoration of peace. To this end I recommend that authority should be given to call into the public service a large body of volunteers to serve for not less than six or twelve months unless sooner discharged. A volunteer force is, beyond question, more efficient than any other description of citizen soldiers; and it is not to be doubted that a number far beyond that required would readily rush to the field upon the call of their country. I further recommend that a liberal provision be made for sustaining our entire military force, and furnishing it with supplies and munitions of war.

President's Message to Congress, May 11, 1846, *reprinted in* Cong. Globe, 29th Cong., 1st Sess. 783 (1846).

Although some members of Congress expressed concern that the President was rushing the country into war, Congress acceded to Polk's request. On May 13, 1846, it recognized that "a state of war exists" between the United States and Mexico, and authorized the President, "for the purpose of enabling the government of the United States to prosecute said war to a speedy and successful termination," to "employ the militia, naval, and military forces of the United States, and to call for and accept the services of any number of volunteers, not exceeding fifty thousand." Act of May 13, 1846, ch. 16, 9 Stat. 9. After the war was concluded two years later, however, the House of Representatives adopted a resolution stating that the Mexican-American War was "a war unnecessarily and unconstitutionally begun by the President of the United States." Cong. Globe, 30th Cong., 1st Sess. 95 (1848). One of the House members who voted in favor of this resolution was Abraham Lincoln. Subsequently, he wrote the following letter to his friend William Herndon responding to Herndon's defense of Polk's actions:

Let me first state what I understand to be your position. It is that if it shall become necessary to repel invasion, the President may, without violation of the Constitution, cross the line and invade the territory of another country, and that whether such necessity exists in any given case the President is the sole judge....

Allow the President to invade a neighboring nation whenever he shall deem it necessary to repel an invasion, and you allow him to do so whenever he may choose to say he deems it necessary for such a purpose, and you allow him to make war at his pleasure....

• The provision of the Constitution giving the war-making power to Congress was dictated, as I understand it, by the following reasons: kings had always been involving and impoverishing their people in wars, pretending generally, if not always, that the good of the people was the object. This our convention understood to be the most oppressive of all kingly oppressions, and they resolved to so frame the Constitution that no one man should hold the power of bringing oppression upon us. But your view destroys the whole matter, and places our President where kings have always stood.

Letter from Abraham Lincoln to William H. Herndon (Feb. 15, 1848), in 2 The Writings of Abraham Lincoln 52 (Arthur Brooks Lapsley ed., 1905).

2. The Bombardment of Greytown

Durand v. Hollins

8 F. Cas. 111 (C.C.S.D.N.Y. 1860)

[In 1854, Captain George Hollins, of the *U.S.S. Cyane*, ordered the bombardment of Greytown, Nicaragua, in response to the theft and destruction of American property and an attack on an American minister. Durand, an American citizen living in Greytown, sued Hollins for destruction of his property caused by the bombardment. In defense, Hollins argued that his actions had been authorized by the Secretary of the Navy.]

NELSON, CIRCUIT JUSTICE.

The principal ground of objection to the pleas, as a defence of the action, is, that neither the president nor the secretary of the navy had authority to give the orders relied on to the defendant, and, hence, that they afford no ground of justification....

As the executive head of the nation, the president is made the only legitimate organ of the general government, to open and carry on correspondence or negotiations with foreign nations, in matters concerning the interests of the country or of its citizens. It is to him, also, the citizens abroad must look for protection of person and of property, and for the faithful execution of the laws existing and intended for their protection. For this purpose, the whole executive power of the country is placed in his hands, under the constitution, and the laws passed in pursuance thereof; and different departments of government have been organized, through which this power may be most conveniently executed, whether by negotiation or by force — a department of state and a department of the navy.

Now, as it respects the interposition of the executive abroad, for the protection of the lives or property of the citizen, the duty must, of necessity, rest in the discretion of the president. Acts of lawless violence, or of threatened violence to the citizen or his property, cannot be anticipated and provided for; and the protection, to be effectual or of any avail, may, not unfrequently, require the most prompt and decided action. Under our system of government, the citizen abroad is as much entitled to protection as the citizen at home. The great object and duty of government is the protection of the lives, liberty, and property of the people composing it, whether abroad or at home; and any government failing in the accomplishment of the object, or the performance of the duty, is not worth preserving.

I have said, that the interposition of the president abroad, for the protection of the citizen, must necessarily rest in his discretion; and it is quite clear that, in all cases where a public act or order rests in executive discretion neither he nor his authorized agent is personally civilly responsible for the consequences.... The question whether it was the duty of the president to interpose for the protection of the citizens at Greytown against an irresponsible and marauding community that had established itself there, was a public political question, in which the government, as well as the citizens whose interests were involved, was concerned, and which belonged to the executive to determine; and his decision is final and conclusive, and justified the defendant in the execution of his orders given through the secretary of the navy.

3. The Civil War

Southern forces opened fire on Fort Sumter on April 12, 1861. In the following days and weeks, President Lincoln took a number of responsive actions without authorization or input from Congress, including: convening a special session of Congress; calling up 75,000 militiamen from the states; seeking volunteers for the federal army and navy; and imposing a blockade on Southern ports. In his address to a special session of Congress on July 4, Lincoln explained the legal bases for these actions:

> Recurring to the action of the Government, it may be stated that at first a call was made for 75,000 militia, and rapidly following this a proclamation was issued for closing the ports of the insurrectionary districts by proceedings in the nature of blockade. So far all was believed to be strictly legal....
>
> Other calls were made for volunteers to serve for three years, unless sooner discharged, and also for large additions to the Regular Army and Navy. These measures, whether strictly legal or not, were ventured upon under what appeared to be a popular demand and a public necessity, trusting then, as now, that Congress would readily

ratify them. It is believed that nothing has been done beyond the constitutional competency of Congress. . . .

It was with the deepest regret that the Executive found the duty of employing the war power, in defense of the Government, forced upon him. He could but perform this duty or surrender the existence of the Government. . . .

As a private citizen the Executive could not have consented that these [U.S. governmental] institutions shall perish; much less could he in betrayal of so vast and so sacred a trust as these free people had confided to him. He felt that he had no moral right to shrink, nor even to count the chances of his own life, in what might follow. In full view of his great responsibility he has, so far, done what he has deemed his duty. You will now, according to your own judgment, perform yours.

Abraham Lincoln's Special Session Message, July 4, 1861. The next month, Congress passed a statute ratifying Lincoln's military actions:

That all the acts, proclamations and orders of the President of the United States after the fourth of March, eighteen hundred and sixty-one, respecting the army and navy of the United States, and calling out or relating to the militia or volunteers from the States, are hereby approved and in all respects legalized and made valid, to the same intent and with the same effect as if they had been issued and done under the previous express authority and direction of the Congress of the United States.

12 Stat. 326 (1861).

The Prize Cases

67 U.S. 635 (1863)

MR. JUSTICE GRIER. . . .

Had the President a right to institute a blockade of ports in possession of persons in armed rebellion against the Government, on the principles of international law, as known and acknowledged among civilized States? . . .

That a blockade de facto actually existed, and was formally declared and notified by the President on the 27th and 30th of April, 1861, is an admitted fact in these cases.

That the President, as the Executive Chief of the Government and Commander-in-chief of the Army and Navy, was the proper person to make such notification, has not been, and cannot be disputed.

The right of prize and capture has its origin in the "*jus belli*," and is governed and adjudged under the law of nations. To legitimate the capture of a neutral vessel or property on the high seas, a war must exist de facto, and the neutral must have a knowledge or notice of the intention of one of the parties belligerent to use this mode of coercion against a port, city, or territory, in possession of the other.

Let us enquire whether, at the time this blockade was instituted, a state of war existed which would justify a resort to these means of subduing the hostile force. . . .

By the Constitution, Congress alone has the power to declare a national or foreign war. It cannot declare war against a State, or any number of States, by virtue of any clause in the Constitution. The Constitution confers on the President the whole Executive power. He is bound to take care that the laws be faithfully executed. He is Commander-in-chief of the Army and Navy of the United States, and of the militia of the several States when called into the actual service of the United States. He has no power to initiate or declare a war either against a foreign nation or a domestic State. But by the Acts of Congress of February 28th, 1795, and 3d of March, 1807, he is authorized to call out the militia and use the military and naval forces of the United States in case of invasion by foreign nations, and to suppress insurrection against the government of a State or of the United States.

If a war be made by invasion of a foreign nation, the President is not only authorized but bound to resist force by force. He does not initiate the war, but is bound to accept the challenge without waiting for any special legislative authority. And whether the hostile party be a foreign invader, or States organized in rebellion, it is none the less a war, although the declaration of it be "unilateral." . . .

This greatest of civil wars was not gradually developed by popular commotion, tumultuous assemblies, or local unorganized insurrections. However long may have been its previous conception, it nevertheless sprung forth suddenly from the parent brain, a Minerva in the full panoply of war. The President was bound to meet it in the shape it presented itself, without waiting for Congress to baptize it with a name; and no name given to it by him or them could change the fact. . . .

Whether the President in fulfilling his duties, as Commander in-chief, in suppressing an insurrection, has met with such armed hostile resistance, and a civil war of such alarming proportions as will compel him to accord to them the character of belligerents, is a question to be decided by him, and this Court must be governed by the decisions and acts of the political department of the Government to which this power was entrusted. "He must determine what degree of force the crisis demands." The proclamation of blockade is itself official and conclusive evidence to the Court that a state of war existed which demanded and authorized a recourse to such a measure, under the circumstances peculiar to the case. . . .

If it were necessary to the technical existence of a war, that it should have a legislative sanction, we find it in almost every act passed at the extraordinary session of the Legislature of 1861, which was wholly employed in enacting laws to enable the Government to prosecute the war with vigor and efficiency. And finally, in 1861, we find Congress "ex major cautela" and in anticipation of such astute objections, passing an act "approving, legalizing, and making valid all the acts, proclamations, and orders of the President, &c., as if they had been issued and done under the previous express authority and direction of the Congress of the United States."

Without admitting that such an act was necessary under the circumstances, it is plain that if the President had in any manner assumed powers which it was necessary should have the authority or sanction of Congress, that on the well known principle of law, "omnis ratihabitio retrotrahitur et mandato equiparatur," this ratification has operated to perfectly cure the defect. . . .

The objection made to this act of ratification, that it is *ex post facto*, and therefore unconstitutional and void, might possibly have some weight on the trial of an indictment in a criminal Court. But precedents from that source cannot be received as authoritative in a tribunal administering public and international law.

On this first question therefore we are of the opinion that the President had a right, *jure belli*, to institute a blockade of ports in possession of the States in rebellion, which neutrals are bound to regard. . . .

MR. JUSTICE NELSON, dissenting. . . .

Upon the whole, after the most careful consideration of this case which the pressure of other duties has admitted, I am compelled to the conclusion that no civil war existed between this Government and the States in insurrection till recognized by the Act of Congress 13th of July, 1861; that the President does not possess the power under the Constitution to declare war or recognize its existence within the meaning of the law of nations, which carries with it belligerent rights, and thus change the country and all its citizens from a state of peace to a state of war; that this power belongs exclusively to the Congress of the United States, and, consequently, that the President had no power to set on foot a blockade under the law of nations, and that the capture of the vessel and cargo in this case, and in all cases before us in which the capture occurred before the 13th of July, 1861, for breach of blockade, or as enemies' property, are illegal and void, and that the decrees of condemnation should be reversed and the vessel and cargo restored.

MR. CHIEF JUSTICE TANEY, MR. JUSTICE CATRON and MR. JUSTICE CLIFFORD, concurred in the dissenting opinion of MR. JUSTICE NELSON.

4. The Korean War

The Korean War was the first large-scale military conflict in U.S. history initiated and sustained without express congressional authorization. It was also the first time a President relied on the U.N. Charter as authority for sending U.S. troops into combat. We first describe the U.N. Charter and its U.S. implementing legislation, and then examine the legal aspects of the Korean War.

The United Nations Charter.   The U.N. Charter established a Security Council, which consists of five permanent members (the United States, Russia, Great Britain, France, and China) and ten rotating nonpermanent members. The Council is charged with "primary responsibility for the maintenance of international peace and security" under the Charter. U.N. Charter, Art. 24. If the Council determines "the existence of any threat to the peace, breach of the peace, or act of aggression," *id.* at Art. 39, and if it determines that nonmilitary measures "would be inadequate or have proved to be inadequate," *id.* at Art. 42, it can authorize "such action by air, sea, or land forces as may be necessary to maintain or restore international peace and security." *Id.* Such actions "may include demonstrations, blockade, and other operations by air, sea, or land forces of Members of the United Nations."

The Charter also provides for the establishment of military force agreements between the United Nations and member countries. In Article 43(1) of the Charter, all U.N. members "undertake to make available to the Security Council, on its call and in accordance with a special agreement or agreements, armed forces, assistance, and facilities, including rights of passage, necessary for the purpose of maintaining international peace and security." These agreements, which were to be "concluded between the Security Council and Members," and "subject to ratification by the signatory states in accordance with their respective constitutional processes," would govern "the numbers and types of forces, their degree of readiness and general location, and the nature of the facilities and assistance to be provided." *Id.* at Arts. 43(2)-(3).

Finally, several provisions of the Charter place obligations on member states with respect to the above provisions. Article 49 provides: "The Members of the United Nations shall join in affording mutual assistance in carrying out the measures decided upon by the Security Council." Similarly, Article 25 provides: "The Members of the United Nations agree to accept and carry out the decisions of the

Security Council in accordance with the present Charter." *See also id.* at Art. 2(5), Art. 48(1), Art. 48(2).

The Senate gave its consent to the U.N. Charter in 1945 by a vote of 89-2. The dissenting senators (Bushfield and Wheeler) objected that, in ratifying the Charter, the United States was unconstitutionally delegating its war power to the Security Council, and to the Executive Branch's representative on the Council. Soon thereafter, Congress enacted the United Nations Participation Act, 22 U.S.C. §§287-287e, which authorizes the President to negotiate an agreement with the United Nations for the use of U.S. forces (as contemplated by Article 43 of the U.N. Charter), subject to congressional approval:

> The President is authorized to negotiate a special agreement or agreements with the Security Council which shall be subject to the approval of the Congress by appropriate Act or joint resolution, providing for the numbers and types of armed forces, their degree of readiness and general location, and the nature of facilities and assistance, including rights of passage, to be made available to the Security Council on its call for the purpose of maintaining international peace and security in accordance with article 43 of said Charter. The President shall not be deemed to require the authorization of the Congress to make available to the Security Council on its call in order to take action under article 42 of said Charter and pursuant to such special agreement or agreements the armed forces, facilities, or assistance provided for therein: Provided, That, except as authorized in section 287d-1 of this title, nothing herein contained shall be construed as an authorization to the President by the Congress to make available to the Security Council for such purpose armed forces, facilities, or assistance in addition to the forces, facilities, and assistance provided for in such special agreement or agreements.

22 U.S.C. §287d. Despite this provision, the United States has never concluded an Article 43 agreement with the Security Council.

In 1949, the U.N. Participation Act was amended to provide in relevant part:

> (a) Notwithstanding the provisions of any other law, the President, upon a request by the United Nations for cooperative action, and to the extent that he finds that it is consistent with the national interest to comply with such request may authorize, in support of such activities of the United Nations as are specifically directed to the peaceful settlement of disputes and not involving the employment of armed forces contemplated by chapter VII of the United Nations Charter—
>
>> (1) the detail to the United Nations, under such terms and conditions as the President shall determine, of personnel of the armed forces of the United States to serve as observers, guards, or in any noncombatant capacity, but in no event shall more than a total of one thousand of such personnel be so detailed at any one time. . . .

The Korean War. On June 24, 1950, North Korean forces invaded South Korea. The following day, the Security Council (with the Soviet Union absent) issued a resolution denouncing the attack and calling for an immediate ceasefire and a withdrawal of North Korean forces to the 38th parallel. The resolution also called upon members of the United Nations "to render every assistance to the United Nations in the execution of this resolution." S.C. Res. 82, U.N. SCOR, 5th Sess., 473d mtg., at 4, U.N. Doc. S/INF/4/Rev.1 (1950). On June 26, President Truman, referring to the Security Council's resolution, publicly announced a commitment of U.S. air and naval forces to assist South Korean forces in repelling the North Korean attack. The next day, on June 27, the Security Council issued another resolution calling upon "[m]embers of the United Nations to furnish such assistance to the Republic of Korea as may be necessary to repel the armed attack and to restore international peace and security in the area." S.C. Res. 83, U.N. SCOR, 5th Sess., Res. & Dec., at 4, U.N. Doc. S/INF/5/Rev.1 (1950). The Council subsequently placed the forces of 15 countries under U.S. command, and Truman appointed General Douglas MacArthur to lead these forces.

There was widespread support in Congress for Truman's initial commitment of U.S. armed forces to Korea. Some members of Congress invoked the U.N. Charter in defending Truman's actions. Senator Knowland, for example, stated:

> [The President] has been authorized to do it under the terms of our obligations to the United Nations Charter. I believe he has the authority to do it under his constitutional power as Commander in Chief of the Armed Forces of the United States.
>
> Certainly the action which has been taken to date is not one which would have required, or one in which I believe it was desirable to have, a declaration of war, as such, by the Congress of the United States. What is being done is more in the nature of police action.

96 Cong. Rec. 9540 (1950).

A few senators, however, criticized Truman for failing to obtain congressional authorization. Senator Taft, for example, argued as follows:

> [President Truman's] action unquestionably has brought about a de facto war with the Government of northern Korea. He has brought that war without consulting Congress and without congressional approval. We have a situation in which in a far distant part of the world one nation has attacked another, and if the President can intervene in Korea without congressional approval, he can go to war in Malaya or Indonesia or Iran or South America. . . .
>
> It is claimed that the Korean situation is changed by the obligations into which we have entered under the Charter of the United Nations. I think this is true, but I do not think it justifies the President's present action without approval by Congress. . . .
>
> [In the U.N. Participation Act], we have enacted the circumstances under which the President may use armed forces in support of a resolution of the Security Council of the United Nations. The first requisite is that we negotiate an agreement to determine what forces shall be used, and in what quantity, and that the agreement be approved by Congress. No agreement has ever been negotiated, of course, and no agreement has ever been presented to Congress. So far as I can see, and so far as I have studied the matter, I would say that there is no authority to use armed forces in support of the United Nations in the absence of some previous action by Congress dealing with the subject and outlining the general circumstances and the amount of the forces that can be used.

96 Cong. Rec. 9322-23 (1950).

In defending against such criticism, Secretary of State Dean Acheson (like Senator Knowland) invoked the U.N. Charter:

> All actions taken by the United States to restore the peace in Korea have been under the aegis of the United Nations. . . .
>
> We are confronted with a direct challenge to the United Nations. Whether this organization, which embodies our hopes for an international order based on peace with justice and freedom, can survive this test will depend upon the vigor with which it answers the challenge and the support which it receives from free nations.
>
> . . . This action, pursuant to the Security Council resolutions, is solely for the purpose of restoring the Republic of Korea to its status prior to the invasion from the north and of reestablishing the peace broken by that aggression.

23 Dep't of State Bull. 43, 46 (July 10, 1950). And the Truman Administration later justified its dispatch of troops to Korea without congressional authorization as

follows: "The power to send troops abroad is certainly one of the powers which the President may exercise in carrying out such a treaty as . . . the United Nations Charter." Joint Comm. of the Comms. on Foreign Relations and on Armed Services, 82d Cong., 1st Sess., Powers of the President to Send the Armed Forces Outside the United States 20 (1951).

5. The Somalia Intervention

In 1992, in response to a severe famine in Somalia, the United Nations began providing food and other relief to the affected areas. Its efforts were hampered by armed bands, however, who were stealing the commodities for their own use. The U.N. Security Council then issued Resolution 794, which authorized member states to "use all necessary means to establish as soon as possible a secure environment for humanitarian relief operations in Somalia." In response to this resolution, the first President Bush sent 28,000 U.S. troops to Somalia. The following Office of Legal Counsel memorandum analyzes the constitutionality of the President's action.

Memorandum from Timothy E. Flanigan, Assistant Attorney General, Office of Legal Counsel, to the Attorney General of the United States, "Authority to Use United States Military Forces in Somalia"

(Dec. 4, 1992), at http://www.usdoj.gov/olc/presiden.8.htm

. . . From the instructions of President Jefferson's Administration to Commodore Richard Dale in 1801 to "chastise" Algiers and Tripoli if they continued to attack American shipping, to the present, Presidents have taken military initiatives abroad on the basis of their constitutional authority. Against the background of this repeated past practice under many Presidents, this Department and this Office have concluded that the President has the power to commit United States troops abroad for the purpose of protecting important national interests. *See, e.g.,* Training of British Flying Students in the United States, 40 Op. Att'y Gen. 58, 62 (1941) (Jackson, A.G.) ("the President's authority has long been recognized as extending to the dispatch of armed forces outside of the United States, either on missions of good will or rescue, or for the purpose of protecting American lives or property or American interests"). . . .

At the core of this power is the President's authority to take military action to protect American citizens, property, and interests from foreign threats. *See, e.g.,* Presidential Powers Relating to the Situation in Iran, 4A Op. O.L.C. 115, 121 (1979) ("It is well established that the President has the constitutional power as Chief Executive and Commander-in-Chief to protect the lives and property of Americans abroad."); Presidential Power to Use the Armed Forces Abroad Without Statutory Authorization, 4A Op. O.L.C. 185, 187 (1980) ("Presidents have repeatedly employed troops abroad in defense of American lives and property."). . . . [The memorandum proceeds to discuss *Durand v. Hollins,* excerpted above.]

Applying these principles to the present case, we conclude that the President can reasonably determine that the proposed mission is necessary to protect the American citizens already in Somalia. We understand that these include private United States citizens engaged in relief operations, and United States military

personnel conducting humanitarian supply flights. The United Nations has determined that existing conditions in Somalia pose a threat to the lives and safety of
these individuals and of non-Americans also engaged in efforts to deliver food,
medicine and other relief to over two million Somalians. *See* Security Council
Resolution No. 794, U.N. SCOR, 47th Sess., 3145th mtg., U.N.Doc. S RES 794
(1992).

It is also essential to consider the safety of the troops to be dispatched as
requested by Security Council Resolution No. 794. The President may provide
those troops with sufficient military protection to insure that they are able to
carry out their humanitarian tasks safely and efficiently. He may also decide to
send sufficient numbers of troops so that those who are primarily engaged in
assisting the United Nations in noncombatant roles are defended by others who
perform a protective function.

Nor is the President's power strictly limited to the protection of American
citizens in Somalia. Past military interventions that extended to the protection
of foreign nationals provide precedent for action to protect endangered Somalians
and other non-United States citizens. For example, in 1965, President Lyndon
Johnson explained that he had ordered United States military intervention in
the Dominican Republic to protect both Americans and the citizens of other
nations. During the 1900-01 Boxer Rebellion in China, President McKinley, without prior congressional authorization, sent about 5,000 United States troops as part
of a multi-national contingent to lift the siege of the foreign quarters in Peking after
the Chinese government proved unable to control rebels. The United States has an
additional important national interest arising from the involvement of the United
Nations in the Somalian situation. In a 1950 opinion supporting President Truman's decision to support the United Nations in repelling the invasion of South
Korea, the State Department concluded that "the continued existence of the United Nations as an effective international organization is a paramount United States
interest." Authority of the President to Repel the Attack in Korea, 23 Dep't St. Bull.
173, 177 (1950). We adopt that conclusion. Here, too, maintaining the credibility of
United Nations Security Council decisions, protecting the security of United
Nations and related relief efforts, and ensuring the effectiveness of United Nations
peacekeeping operations can be considered a vital national interest, and will promote the United States' conception of a "new world order."

In Security Council Resolution No. 794, which was adopted pursuant to Chapter VII of the United Nations Charter, the Security Council has authorized the
United States and other member States to use "all necessary means" to establish
a secure environment for the delivery of essential humanitarian aid in Somalia. The
President is entitled to rely on this resolution, and on its finding that the situation in
Somalia "constitutes a threat to international peace and security," in making his
determination that the interests of the United States justify providing the military
assistance that Security Council Resolution No. 794 calls for. Moreover, American
assistance in giving effect to this and other Security Council resolutions pertaining
to Somalia would in itself strengthen the prestige, credibility and effectiveness of
the United Nations — which the President can legitimately find to be a substantial
national foreign policy objective, and which will tend further to guarantee the lives
and property of Americans abroad.

This conclusion accords with our prior opinions. During the Korean War, for
example, we took the position that a Security Council resolution authorizing the

use of force by member States to protect international peace and security could furnish a new ground for a decision by the President to use troops abroad.

> In the presence of such a resolution the President is bound to consider what the interests of the United States require. He will necessarily weigh the nature of the breach of the peace which has occurred, what its consequences will be for the United Nations if it goes unchallenged, and what it foreshadows in the way of an ultimate threat to the vital interests of the United States. In the light of these and other considerations he will then make the decisions which he, as President, must make.

Franklin S. Pollak, Power of the President to Send Troops Abroad, 34-35 (Apr. 27, 1951).

Notes and Questions

1. In *Federalist No. 69*, excerpted above in Section A, Alexander Hamilton stated that the President's authority as Commander in Chief "would amount to nothing more than the Supreme command and direction of the military and naval forces." In practice, presidents have exercised a much broader array of military powers than this description might suggest. In any event, what is entailed by the "command and direction" of the armed forces? Does it include decisions about the use of particular weaponry? The choice of military targets? The detention and trial of enemy prisoners? The termination of hostilities? What is the relationship between the President's Commander-in-Chief authority and Congress's war powers, such as its power to declare war and its power to "make Rules for the Government and Regulation of the land and naval Forces"?

2. There is general agreement that, in addition to his authority to direct the armed forces during a war, the President has the power to repel attacks on the United States. As stated in *The Prize Cases*, "If a war be made by invasion of a foreign nation, the President is not only authorized but bound to resist by force." Also, recall from Section A that, according to James Madison's notes of the Federal Convention, giving Congress the power to "declare" war would "leav[e] to the Executive the power to repel sudden attacks." What is the constitutional source of this power? How is this power reconciled with Congress's war declaration and other war-related powers?

3. What is encompassed by the President's power to repel attacks? Must the President wait for the attacks to occur, or can he act preemptively? Does the existence today of missiles and weapons of mass destruction affect the answer to this question? Once the United States is attacked, are there limits on what the President can do in response? Must his response be proportional to the attack? Could he wage a full war in response to a small-scale attack? Can he carry the conflict into another country without congressional authorization? In 1801, President Jefferson instructed the naval force that it could respond to attacks by the Barbary Pirates by disarming captured ships, but that, because of the lack of congressional authorization, they were to release the crews of the ships and take no further offensive action. *See* 11 Annals of Congress 12 (1801) (Jefferson's message to Congress). Alexander Hamilton disagreed with this limitation, arguing that once the United States is attacked, the President has full power to respond with any force that he deems suitable. *See* 25 The Papers of Alexander Hamilton 453-57 (Harold C. Syrett ed., 1997). Do you agree? What do *The Prize Cases* suggest? Could Lincoln have fought the entire Civil War without congressional authorization?

4. While *The Prize Cases* are widely viewed as supporting a broad presidential authority to repel attacks, the decision also stated that the President "has no power to initiate or declare a war either against a foreign nation or a domestic State." In addition, the Court noted that Congress had by statute authorized the President to "call out the militia and use the military and naval forces of the United States in case of invasion by foreign nations, and to suppress insurrection against the government of a State or of the United States." Lincoln went beyond that statutory authorization by calling for volunteers for the U.S. Army and Navy, and by incurring debts on behalf of the United States to fund these forces. Were these acts constitutional? What was Lincoln's answer in his July 4, 1861, message to Congress? Why would it matter that, as Lincoln claimed, the actions he took were not beyond *Congress's* power? What was the legal significance of Congress's *ex post* ratification of Lincoln's acts in August 1861? Was this *ex post* ratification necessary? Did it imply a defect in the President's actions? Did it render constitutional acts that were until then unconstitutional? Or was Congress's action legally meaningless? For analysis of these issues, see Daniel Farber, Lincoln's Constitution (2003). We return to related issues about emergency power in Section D below.

5. What are the implications of *The Prize Cases* for the interpretation of congressional authorizations to the President to use military force abroad? Recall from Section A that the Supreme Court in Brown v. United States construed the 1812 declaration of war and authorization as not empowering the President to seize enemy property in the United States without specific congressional authorization. Does *Brown* survive *The Prize Cases*? Professor Henkin maintains that *Brown* was decided in an era in which the presidential war power was "still in its infancy," and he doubts that it survived the Civil War, in which both President Lincoln and the Supreme Court agreed that the President could seize both enemy property and neutral vessels operating in violation of a blockade, even in the absence of specific congressional authorization. *See* Henkin, supra, at 104; *see also* Curtis A. Bradley & Jack L. Goldsmith, *Congressional Authorization and the War on Terrorism*, 118 Harv. L. Rev. 2047, 2093-94 (2005). Do you agree? *Cf.* David Golove, *Military Tribunals, International Law, and the Constitution: A Franckian-Madisonian Approach*, 35 N.Y.U. J. Int'l L. & Pol. 363, 385 (2003) (suggesting that Lincoln's Emancipation Proclamation, in which Lincoln freed Southern slaves without any congressional authorization, and which he justified by reference to his Commander-in-Chief authority and the laws of war, is inconsistent with *Brown*).

6. Can the President exercise his acknowledged foreign relations powers — for example, his power to dismiss an ambassador, break off diplomatic relations, or announce a new U.S. foreign policy — in a way that is likely to provoke an attack and thus trigger his defensive war powers? Is this what President Polk did with Mexico? *See also* Message from President Wilson to Congress, April 2, 1917, in 55 Cong. Rec. 103 (1917) (acknowledging that his order to U.S. merchant ships to arm themselves against attack by German submarines was "practically certain" to draw the United States into the first World War). Are there any legal limitations on the President's ability to provoke a war?

7. The court in *Durand* states that the President has the discretionary authority to use force to protect the lives and property of U.S. citizens abroad. As noted by the Office of Legal Counsel in its memorandum concerning the Somalia intervention, presidents have often invoked the authority. Modern examples include the U.S. invasion of Panama in 1989, the U.S. invasion of Grenada in 1983, and the failed attempt to rescue U.S. hostages in Iran in 1980. What is the constitutional source of this authority? Does it include protecting U.S. "interests" as well as persons and property? Does it extend to protecting *foreign* nationals and property, as suggested in the Somalia memorandum?

8. As noted above, the Truman Administration was the first to rely on the U.N. Charter as a source of authority for using force abroad. Are you convinced by the Truman Administration's arguments? Do these arguments amount to the claim that the Article II Take Care Clause permits the President to use military force to enforce the United States' international obligations? Is this claim valid? Professor Stromseth argues that it is not, reasoning that the Constitution's allocation of war powers cannot be changed by treaty. *See* Jane E. Stromseth, *Collective Force and Constitutional Responsibility: War Powers in the Post-Cold War Era*, 50 U. Miami L. Rev. 145 (1995). But does this response beg the question about what the Constitution authorizes? Isn't a treaty a "law" for purposes of the Take Care Clause? Even if it is, though, is the President's treaty enforcement authority under the Take Care Clause limited to domestic enforcement, or is international enforcement permitted as well? If the latter, is Congress's war declaration power a check on the President's take care power? Or vice-versa? Which power is more fundamental? Assuming that the Take Care Clause argument has some validity in theory, does it justify Truman's actions in Korea? In this connection, recall that Truman committed U.S. troops to Korea before the U.N. Security Council issued its authorization to use force. And note that the Security Council "recommended," and did not order, nations to "repel the armed attack" on South Korea. *See* S.C. Res. 83 (1950).

9. Consider Senator Knowland's suggested constitutional justification for Truman's actions in the Korean War. Professor Turner restates the argument this way: "When the President decides to risk the use of armed force in cooperation with the United Nations or other treaty partners in an effort to restore peace and end armed aggression, he is not 'initiating' a 'war' but defending the rule of law. No 'declaration of war' is necessary or appropriate in such circumstances." Robert F. Turner, The Constitutional Roles of Congress and the President in Declaring and Waging War, Hearings Before the Senate Judiciary Comm., 102d Cong., 1st Sess. 426 (1991). For other articulations of this view, *see, e.g.,* Walter Dellinger, *After the Cold War: Presidential Power and the Use of Military Force*, 50 U. Miami L. Rev. 107, 111-17 (1995); Thomas M. Frank & Faiza Patel, *UN Police Action in Lieu of War: "The Old Order Changeth,"* 85 Am. J. Int'l L. 63, 64, 67-69 (1991); Paul Kahn, *War Powers at the Millennium*, 34 Loy. L.A. L. Rev. 11, 51 (2000).

Is there really a distinction between a "war," which Congress must authorize before the President can send U.S. troops abroad, and a U.N.-authorized "police action" designed to prevent illegal uses of force, which Congress need not authorize? Professor Stromseth thinks not. She argues that legal uses of forces under the U.N. Charter might still be a "war" for U.S. constitutional purposes (and thus require congressional approval) because of the nature and circumstances of the operation and the magnitude of the combat risks involved. And she adds that the Security Council cannot substitute for the kind of check on unilateral presidential action that the Founders sought in Congress, because the Security Council does not represent the American people and is not politically accountable to them. *See* Stromseth, *supra*, at 157-58. Do you agree with this assessment?

Professor Kahn offers a response to one of these concerns, maintaining that the "effective check on the abuse of force would come from the Security Council, not Congress." Kahn, *supra*, at 51. Is this right? Is the Security Council a democratic institution? Does the U.S. veto power in the Security Council ensure that no U.S. troops will be dispatched unless doing so is in U.S. interests? Does the Security Council provide a sufficient check on presidential action? Does the fact that "Congress . . . retains an ultimate authority to prohibit American participation in [U.N.] police actions," see Kahn, *supra*, at 51, constitute an effective check? Or does this reverse the burden of inertia that the constitutional Founders imposed on the large-scale commitment of U.S. troops abroad?

10. Consider Senator Taft's objection to Truman's commitment of troops in Korea. Is it true that the U.N. Participation Act prohibits the use of armed forces in support of a U.N-authorized police action in the absence of a congressionally approved agreement under Article 43 of the U.N. Charter specifying the circumstances in which forces can be used? The question raises two issues. The first is: Does the U.N. Charter authorize the Security Council to call on member states to use force outside of Article 43 Agreements? Consider this answer:

> Just as Congress nowadays does not grant letters of marque and reprisal (Constitution, Article I, section 8(11)) or establish post roads (Article I, section 8(7)), so the Security Council has not made use of Article 43 of the Charter, which authorizes it to negotiate agreements with consenting member states that, preemptively, would have placed designated national military contingents at the Council's disposal. That no such agreements were made, owing to the Cold War, does not signify a lapse in the Organization's general police power, set out in Article 42, any more than the abstinence by Congress in matters of post roads signifies a lapse in its power to legislate on other matters pertaining to the Postal Service. Rather, the practice of the Security Council has evolved other means for taking coercive measures, including the use of police forces raised ad hoc in response to a specific threat to the peace. . . . [T]he central idea of a globally sanctioned police action was never abandoned; . . . the failure to implement Article 43 merely led to organic growth and the alternative creation of police action through invocation of Article 42, which does not require special agreements.

Franck & Patel, *supra*, at 66. Do you agree?

Assuming this assessment is correct, does the U.N. Participation Act nonetheless prohibit the President from sending U.S. troops abroad pursuant to a Security Council authorization in the absence of congressional authorization? Does the Participation Act make Article 43 agreements a pre-condition to the presidential use of force pursuant to a Security Council request? How do you read the proviso at the end of 22 U.S.C. §287d, which provides that "nothing herein contained shall be construed as an authorization to the President by the Congress to make available to the Security Council . . . armed forces, facilities, or assistance in addition to the forces, facilities, and assistance provided for in such special agreement or agreements"? Clearly Congress did not provide a separate authorization for Security Council-authorized presidential action, but did it affirmatively forbid it? Of what relevance is the 1949 amendment to the U.N. Participation Act, excerpted above? Can the President claim an independent power under the Take Care Clause to enforce Security Council actions even in the absence of an Article 43 Special Agreement or some other congressional authorization? In this connection, can we attribute any significance to Senator Wheeler's proposed amendment to the Participation Act, later defeated, which would have provided: "Wherever a decision to use United States armed forces arises in the Security Council, such a decision must be made by Congress." *See* 91 Cong. Rec. 11,036 (1945)?

11. There were a number of instances in the 1990s when presidents relied on the U.N. Charter as support for committing troops in the absence of congressional authorization. One example is the Somalia operation discussed in the Office of Legal Counsel memorandum. Another example is President Clinton's dispatch of 16,000 U.S. troops to Haiti in 1994 under the auspices of Security Council Resolution 940, which authorized member states to "use all necessary means to facilitate the departure from Haiti of the military leadership [and] the prompt return of the legitimately elected President and the restoration of the legitimate authorities of the Government of Haiti, and to establish and maintain a secure and stable environment." S.C. Res. 940 (July 31, 1994). Is it true, as stated in the Office of Legal Counsel's Somalia memo, that even in the absence of congressional authorization the President has the authority to use military force to "maintain[] the credibility of United Nations Security Council decisions, protect[] the security of United Nations and related relief efforts, and ensur[e] the effectiveness of United Nations peace-keeping operations"?

12. As the materials in this section suggest, Presidents have often employed U.S. troops outside the United States in the absence of congressional authorization, especially in the modern era. This has been made possible in part by the dramatic increase in the size of the standing army, as already discussed. And the enormous increase in the standing army, in turn, reflects a larger two-century evolution in the nature of international affairs and the United States' role in those affairs. In particular, throughout the twentieth century, and especially following World War II, presidential foreign relations powers increased enormously in response to the possibility of nuclear war and the United States' more prominent role as a world super-power. It is no accident that during this period presidents have asserted war-making powers more aggressively. The entire Korean War was initiated and fought without express congressional authorization. The United States' commitment of military force in Vietnam long predated the Tonkin Gulf Resolution. Most uses of force abroad in the 1980s and 1990s — including the 1999 air campaign in Kosovo, the 1994 air strikes in Bosnia, the 1992-1993 operation in Somalia, the 1989 invasion of Panama, the 1986 air strikes against Libya, the 1983 invasion of Grenada, and the 1982 deployment of troops in Lebanon — took place without express congressional authorization, and many of them without any colorable U.N. authorization.

Can these practices, in effect, change the meaning of the Constitution? For an argument along these lines, see Peter J. Spiro, *War Powers and the Sirens of Formalism*, 68 N.Y.U. L. Rev. 1338, 1355 (1993) (book review): "It is . . . the 'court of history,' an accretion of interactions among the branches, that gives rise to basic norms governing the branches' behavior in the [war powers] area." By contrast, consider the following:

> In the case of executive wars, none of the conditions for the establishment of constitutional power by usage is present. The Constitution is not ambiguous. No contemporaneous congressional interpretation attributes a power of initiating war to the President. The early Presidents, and indeed everyone in the country until the year 1950, denied that the President possessed such a power. There is no sustained body of usage to support such a claim. It can only be audacity or desperation that leads the champions of recent presidential usurpations to state that "history has legitimated the practice of presidential war-making."

Francis D. Wormuth & Edwin B. Firmage, To Chain the Dog of War: The War Power of Congress in History and Law 151 (2d ed. 1989). Who is right?

13. In 1878, in response to perceived abuses by the U.S. military in the South during Reconstruction, Congress enacted the Posse Comitatus Act. The current version of the Act provides: "Whoever, except in cases and under circumstances expressly authorized by the Constitution or Act of Congress, willfully uses any part of the Army or the Air Force as a posse comitatus or otherwise to execute the laws shall be fined under this title or imprisoned not more than two years, or both." 18 U.S.C. §1385. The term "posse comitatus" is a Latin phrase meaning the "power of the county"; the term was used at common law to refer to all those individuals over the age of 15 upon whom a sheriff could call for assistance in preventing any type of civil disorder. In effect, the Act precludes the use of the U.S. military for civilian law enforcement unless otherwise permitted by federal law.

Although the Navy and Marine Corps are not included by name in the Act, Congress directed the Secretary of Defense to "prescribe such regulations as may be necessary" to prohibit "direct participation by a member of the Army, Navy, Air Force, or Marine Corps" in civilian law enforcement activities. 10 U.S.C. §375. The Department of Defense thereafter made the Act applicable to the Navy and Marine Corps as a matter of Department of Defense policy.

Congress has enacted numerous exceptions to the Act. For example, the Armed Forces may be used to suppress insurrections against state governments or the federal government. *See* 10 U.S.C. §§331-333. They are also allowed to engage in the sharing of information and equipment with civilian authorities. *See* 10 U.S.C. §371-372. The Department of Defense also has issued a directive regulating the cooperation of military personnel with civilian law enforcement officials, and the Secretaries of the Navy and Army have issued regulations implementing this directive. These regulations generally prohibit "direct" military involvement in civilian law enforcement activities but permit "indirect" assistance such as the transfer of information obtained during the normal course of military operations or other actions that "do not subject civilians to the use [of] military power that is regulatory, prescriptive, or compulsory." The regulations do permit direct involvement, however, where the military action is undertaken "for the primary purpose of furthering a military or foreign affairs function of the United States, regardless of incidental benefits to civilian authorities." Direct involvement in civilian law enforcement is also allowed in "investigations and other actions related to enforcement of the Uniform Code of Military Justice (UCMJ)" and "investigations and other actions related to the commander's inherent authority to maintain law and order on a military installation or facility."

Even where the Posse Comitatus Act has been found to be violated, courts have generally declined to dismiss criminal prosecutions or exclude evidence on the basis of the Act, at least in the absence of "widespread and repeated" violations. *See, e.g.,* United States v. Wolffs, 594 F.2d 77 (5th Cir. 1979); United States v. Walden, 490 F.2d 372 (4th Cir. 1974). *But cf.* Bissonette v. Haig, 800 F.2d 812 (8th Cir. 1986) (allowing a private cause of action under the Fourth Amendment predicated on a violation of the Act). For other decisions discussing the scope of the Act, see, for example, United States v. Hitchcock, 263 F.3d 878 (9th Cir. 2001); United States v. Kahn, 35 F.3d 426 (9th Cir. 1994). After the September 11, 2001 terrorist attacks, the Bush Administration began reviewing the Posse Comitatus Act and other statutes to determine whether the statutes unduly restricted the ability of the military to protect domestic security. *See, e.g.,* Eric Schmitt, *Wider Role in U.S. Is Urged*, N.Y. Times, July 21, 2002, p.16.

C. CONGRESS'S ABILITY TO REGULATE THE PRESIDENT'S USE OF FORCE

In this section we consider Congress's ability to regulate the President's use of force, with a particular focus on the War Powers Resolution.

Little v. Barreme

6 U.S. 170 (1804)

[In February 1799, in the midst of the undeclared war with France, Congress passed a "non-intercourse" statute prohibiting trade with France. Section 1 of the statute prohibited vessels "owned, hired or employed, wholly or in part, by any person resident within the United States, and which shall depart therefrom" from traveling to "any port or place within the territory of the French republic, or the dependencies thereof, or to any place in the West Indies, or elsewhere under the acknowledged government of France." Vessels violating this law were "liable to be seized, and may be prosecuted and condemned, in any circuit or district court of the United States, which shall be holden within or for the district where the seizure shall be made." Section 5 of the statute provided that the President had the authority to direct the commanders of public armed ships of the United States to "stop and examine any ship or vessel of the United States on the high seas, which there may be reason to suspect to be engaged in any traffic or commerce contrary to the true tenor thereof; and if, upon examination, it shall appear that such ship or vessel is bound or sailing to any port or place within the territory of the French republic, or her dependencies, contrary to the intent of this act, it shall be the duty of the commander of such public armed vessel to seize every such ship or vessel engaged in such illicit commerce. . . ."]

MARSHALL, CHIEF JUSTICE . . . delivered the opinion of the Court.

The *Flying-Fish,* a Danish vessel having on board Danish and neutral property, was captured on the 2d of December 1799, on a voyage from Jeremie to St. Thomas's, by the United States frigate *Boston,* commanded by Captain Little, and brought into the port of Boston, where she was libelled as an American vessel that had violated the nonintercourse law.

The judge before whom the cause was tried, directed a restoration of the vessel and cargo as neutral property, but refused to award damages for the capture and detention, because in his opinion, there was probable cause to suspect the vessel to be American.

On an appeal to the circuit court this sentence was reversed, because the *Flying-Fish* was on a voyage from, not to, a French port, and was therefore, had she even been an American vessel, not liable to capture on the high seas. . . .

It is by no means clear that the president of the United States whose high duty it is to "take care that the laws be faithfully executed," and who is commander in chief of the armies and navies of the United States, might not, without any special authority for that purpose, in the then existing state of things, have empowered the officers commanding the armed vessels of the United States, to seize and send into port for adjudication, American vessels which were forfeited by being engaged in this illicit commerce. But when it is observed that the general clause of the first section of the "act, which declares that such vessels may be seized, and may be prosecuted in any district or circuit court, which shall be holden within or for the district where the seizure shall be made," obviously contemplates a seizure within the United States; and that the 5th section gives a special authority to seize on the high seas, and limits that authority to the seizure of vessels bound or sailing to a French port, the legislature seem to have prescribed that the manner in which this law shall be carried into execution, was to exclude a seizure of any vessel not bound to a French port. Of consequence, however strong the circumstances might be, which induced captain Little to suspect the *Flying-Fish* to be an American vessel, they could not excuse the detention of her, since he would not have been authorised to detain her had she been really American.

It was so obvious, that if only vessels sailing to a French port could be seized on the high seas, that the law would be very often evaded, that this act of congress appears to have received a different construction from the executive of the United States; a construction much better calculated to give it effect.

A copy of this act was transmitted by the secretary of the navy, to the captains of the armed vessels, who were ordered to consider the 5th section as a part of their instructions. The same letter contained the following clause.

> A proper discharge of the important duties enjoined on you, arising out of this act, will require the exercise of a sound and an impartial judgment. You are not only to do all that in you lies, to prevent all intercourse, whether direct or circuitous, between the ports of the United States, and those of France or her dependencies, where the vessels are apparently as well as really American, and protected by American papers only, but you are to be vigilant that vessels or cargoes really American, but covered by Danish or other foreign papers, and bound to or from French ports, do not escape you.

These orders given by the executive under the construction of the act of congress made by the department to which its execution was assigned, enjoin the seizure of American vessels sailing from a French port. Is the officer who obeys them liable for damages sustained by this misconstruction of the act, or will his orders excuse him? If his instructions afford him no protection, then the law must take its course, and he must pay such damages as are legally awarded against him; if they excuse an act not otherwise excusable, it would then be necessary to inquire whether this is a case in which the probable cause which existed to induce a suspicion that the vessel was American, would excuse the captor from damages when the vessel appeared in fact to be neutral.

I confess the first bias of my mind was very strong in favour of the opinion that though the instructions of the executive could not give a right, they might yet excuse from damages. I was much inclined to think that a distinction ought to be taken between acts of civil and those of military officers; and between proceedings within the body of the country and those on the high seas. That implicit obedience which military men usually pay to the orders of their superiors, which indeed is indispensably necessary to every military system, appeared to me strongly to imply the principle that those orders, if not to perform a prohibited act, ought to justify the person whose general duty it is to obey them, and who is placed by the laws of his country in a situation which in general requires that he should obey them. I was strongly inclined to think that where, in consequence of orders from the legitimate authority, a vessel is seized with pure intention, the claim of the injured party for damages would be against that government from which the orders proceeded, and would be a proper subject for negotiation. But I have been convinced that I was mistaken, and I have receded from this first opinion. I acquiesce in that of my brethren, which is, that the instructions cannot change the nature of the transaction, or legalize an act which without those instructions would have been a plain trespass.

It becomes therefore unnecessary to inquire whether the probable cause afforded by the conduct of the *Flying-Fish* to suspect her of being an American, would excuse Captain Little from damages for having seized and sent her into port, since had she actually been an American, the seizure would have been unlawful.

Captain Little then must be answerable in damages to the owner of this neutral vessel.

War Powers Resolution

Pub. L. No. 93-148, 87 Stat. 555 (1973)
50 U.S.C. §§1541-1548

Sec. 2. (a) It is the purpose of this joint resolution to fulfill the intent of the framers of the Constitution of the United States and insure that the collective judgment of both the Congress and the President will apply to the introduction of United States Armed Forces into hostilities, or into situations where imminent involvement in hostilities is clearly indicated by the circumstances, and to the continued use of such forces in hostilities or in such situations. . . .

(c) The constitutional powers of the President as Commander-in-Chief to introduce United States Armed Forces into hostilities, or into situations where imminent involvement in hostilities is clearly indicated by the circumstances, are exercised only pursuant to (1) a declaration of war, (2) specific statutory authorization, or (3) a national emergency created by attack upon the United States, its territories or possessions, or its armed forces.

Sec. 3. The President in every possible instance shall consult with Congress before introducing United States Armed Forces into hostilities or into situations where imminent involvement in hostilities is clearly indicated by the circumstances, and after every such introduction shall consult regularly with the Congress until United States Armed Forces are no longer engaged in hostilities or have been removed from such situations.

Sec. 4. (a) In the absence of a declaration of war, in any case in which United States Armed Forces are introduced—

(1) into hostilities or into situations where imminent involvement in hostilities is clearly indicated by the circumstances;

(2) into the territory, airspace or waters of a foreign nation, while equipped for combat, except for deployments which relate solely to supply, replacement, repair, or training of such forces; or

(3) in numbers which substantially enlarge United States Armed Forces equipped for combat already located in a foreign nation; the President shall submit within 48 hours to the Speaker of the House of Representatives and to the President pro tempore of the Senate a report, in writing, setting forth—

(A) the circumstances necessitating the introduction of United States Armed Forces;

(B) the constitutional and legislative authority under which such introduction took place; and

(C) the estimated scope and duration of the hostilities or involvement. . . .

(c) Whenever United States Armed Forces are introduced into hostilities or into any situation described in subsection (a) of this section, the President shall, so long as such armed forces continue to be engaged in such hostilities or situation, report to the Congress periodically on the status of such hostilities or situation as well as on the scope and duration of such hostilities or situation, but in no event shall he report to the Congress less often than once every six months.

Sec. 5. . . . (b) Within sixty calendar days after a report is submitted or is required to be submitted pursuant to section 4(a)(1), whichever is earlier, the President shall terminate any use of United States Armed Forces with respect to which such report was submitted (or required to be submitted), unless the Congress (1) has declared war or has enacted a specific authorization for such use of United States Armed Forces, (2) has extended by law such sixty-day period, or (3) is physically unable to meet as a result of an armed attack upon the United States. Such sixty-day period shall be extended for not more than an additional thirty days if the President determines and certifies to the Congress in writing that unavoidable military necessity respecting the safety of United States Armed Forces requires the continued use of such armed forces in the course of bringing about a prompt removal of such forces.

(c) Notwithstanding subsection (b), at any time that United States Armed Forces are engaged in hostilities outside the territory of the United States, its possessions or territories without a declaration of war or specific statutory authorization, such forces shall be removed by the President if the Congress so directs by concurrent resolution. . . .

Sec. 8. (a) Authority to introduce United States Armed Forces into hostilities or into situations wherein involvement in hostilities is clearly indicated by the circumstances shall not be inferred —

(1) from any provision of law (whether or not in effect before the date of the enactment of this joint resolution), including any provision contained in any appropriation Act, unless such provision specifically authorizes the introduction of United States Armed Forces into hostilities or into such situations and states that it is intended to constitute specific statutory authorization within the meaning of this joint resolution; or

(2) from any treaty heretofore or hereafter ratified unless such treaty is implemented by legislation specifically authorizing the introduction of United States Armed Forces into hostilities or into such situations and stating that it is intended to constitute specific statutory authorization within the meaning of this joint resolution.

President Nixon's Message Vetoing the War Powers Resolution

Oct. 24, 1973

To the House of Representatives:

I hereby return without my approval House Joint Resolution 542 — the War Powers Resolution. While I am in accord with the desire of the Congress to assert its proper role in the conduct of our foreign affairs, the restrictions which this resolution would impose upon the authority of the President are both unconstitutional and dangerous to the best interests of our Nation....

House Joint Resolution 542 would attempt to take away, by a mere legislative act, authorities which the President has properly exercised under the Constitution for almost 200 years. One of its provisions would automatically cut off certain authorities after sixty days unless the Congress extended them. Another would allow the Congress to eliminate certain authorities merely by the passage of a concurrent resolution — an action which does not normally have the force of law, since it denies the President his constitutional role in approving legislation.

I believe that both these provisions are unconstitutional. The only way in which the constitutional powers of a branch of the Government can be altered is by amending the Constitution — and any attempt to make such alterations by legislation alone is clearly without force....

While I firmly believe that a veto of House Joint Resolution 542 is warranted solely on constitutional grounds, I am also deeply disturbed by the practical consequences of this resolution. For it would seriously undermine this Nation's ability to act decisively and convincingly in times of international crisis. As a result, the confidence of our allies in our ability to assist them could be diminished and the respect of our adversaries for our deterrent posture could decline. A permanent and substantial element of unpredictability would be injected into the world's assessment of American behavior, further increasing the likelihood of miscalculation and war.

If this resolution had been in operation, America's effective response to a variety of challenges in recent years would have been vastly complicated or even made impossible. We may well have been unable to respond in the way we did during the Berlin crisis of 1961, the Cuban missile crisis of 1962, the Congo rescue operation in 1964, and the Jordanian crisis of 1970 — to mention just a few examples. In addition, our recent actions to bring about a peaceful settlement of the hostilities in the Middle East would have been seriously impaired if this resolution had been in force.

While all the specific consequences of House Joint Resolution 542 cannot yet be predicted, it is clear that it would undercut the ability of the United States to act as an effective influence for peace. For example, the provision automatically cutting off certain authorities after 60 days unless they are extended by the Congress could work to prolong or intensify a crisis. Until the Congress suspended the deadline, there would be at least a chance of United States withdrawal and an adversary would be tempted therefore to postpone serious negotiations until the 60 days were up. Only after the Congress acted would there be a strong incentive for an adversary to negotiate. In addition, the very existence of a deadline could lead to an escalation of hostilities in order to achieve certain objectives before the 60 days expired.

The measure would jeopardize our role as a force for peace in other ways as well. It would, for example, strike from the President's hand a wide range of important peace-keeping tools by eliminating his ability to exercise quiet diplomacy backed by subtle shifts in our military deployments. It would also cast into doubt authorities which Presidents have used to undertake certain humanitarian relief missions in conflict areas, to protect fishing boats from seizure, to deal with ship or aircraft hijackings, and to respond to threats of attack. Not the least of the adverse consequences of this resolution would be the prohibition contained in section 8 against fulfilling our obligations under the NATO treaty as ratified by the Senate.

Finally, since the bill is somewhat vague as to when the 60 day rule would apply, it could lead to extreme confusion and dangerous disagreements concerning the prerogatives of the two branches, seriously damaging our ability to respond to international crises....

I am particularly disturbed by the fact that certain of the President's constitutional powers as Commander in Chief of the Armed Forces would terminate automatically under this resolution 60 days after they were invoked. No overt Congressional action would be required to cut off these powers—they would disappear automatically unless the Congress extended them. In effect, the Congress is here attempting to increase its policy-making role through a provision which requires it to take absolutely no action at all.

In my view, the proper way for the Congress to make known its will on such foreign policy questions is through a positive action, with full debate on the merits of the issue and with each member taking the responsibility of casting a yes or no vote after considering those merits. The authorization and appropriations process represents one of the ways in which such influence can be exercised. I do not, however, believe that the Congress can responsibly contribute its considered, collective judgment on such grave questions without full debate and without a yes or no vote. Yet this is precisely what the joint resolution would allow. It would give every future Congress the ability to handcuff every future President merely by doing nothing and sitting still. In my view, one cannot become a responsible partner unless one is prepared to take responsible action.

[Congress subsequently overrode President Nixon's veto. The Senate vote to override was 75 to 18, see 119 Cong. Rec. 36, 198 (1973), and the House vote was 284 to 135, see *id.* at 36,221.]

Memorandum from Walter Dellinger, Assistant Attorney General, Office of Legal Counsel, to Abner J. Mikva, Counsel to the President, "Presidential Authority to Decline to Execute Unconstitutional Statutes"

(Nov. 2, 1994), at http://www.usdoj.gov/olc/nonexcut.htm

....[T]here are circumstances in which the President may appropriately decline to enforce a statute that he views as unconstitutional.

First, there is significant judicial approval of this proposition. Most notable is the Court's decision in Myers v. United States, 272 U.S. 52 (1926). There the Court sustained the President's view that the statute at issue was unconstitutional without any member of the Court suggesting that the President had acted improperly in refusing to abide by the statute. More recently, in Freytag v. Commissioner, 501 U.S. 868 (1991), all four of the Justices who addressed the issue agreed that the President has "the power to veto encroaching laws...or even to disregard them when they are unconstitutional." Id. at 906 (Scalia, J., concurring); see also Youngstown Sheet & Tube Co. v. Sawyer, 343 U.S. 579, 635-38 (1952) (Jackson, J., concurring) (recognizing existence of President's authority to act contrary to a statutory command).

Second, consistent and substantial executive practice also confirms this general proposition. Opinions dating to at least 1860 assert the President's authority to decline to effectuate enactments that the President views as unconstitutional.

See, e.g., Memorial of Captain Meigs, 9 Op. Att'y Gen. 462, 469-70 (1860) (asserting that the President need not enforce a statute purporting to appoint an officer) . . . .

While the general proposition that in some situations the President may decline to enforce unconstitutional statutes is unassailable, it does not offer sufficient guidance as to the appropriate course in specific circumstances. To continue our conversation about these complex issues, I offer the following propositions for your consideration.

1. The President's office and authority are created and bounded by the Constitution; he is required to act within its terms. Put somewhat differently, in serving as the executive created by the Constitution, the President is required to act in accordance with the laws—including the Constitution, which takes precedence over other forms of law. This obligation is reflected in the Take Care Clause and in the President's oath of office.

2. When bills are under consideration by Congress, the executive branch should promptly identify unconstitutional provisions and communicate its concerns to Congress so that the provisions can be corrected. Although this may seem elementary, in practice there have been occasions in which the President has been presented with enrolled bills containing constitutional flaws that should have been corrected in the legislative process.

3. The President should presume that enactments are constitutional. There will be some occasions, however, when a statute appears to conflict with the Constitution. In such cases, the President can and should exercise his independent judgment to determine whether the statute is constitutional. In reaching a conclusion, the President should give great deference to the fact that Congress passed the statute and that Congress believed it was upholding its obligation to enact constitutional legislation. Where possible, the President should construe provisions to avoid constitutional problems.

4. The Supreme Court plays a special role in resolving disputes about the constitutionality of enactments. As a general matter, if the President believes that the Court would sustain a particular provision as constitutional, the President should execute the statute, notwithstanding his own beliefs about the constitutional issue. If, however, the President, exercising his independent judgment, determines both that a provision would violate the Constitution and that it is probable that the Court would agree with him, the President has the authority to decline to execute the statute.

5. Where the President's independent constitutional judgment and his determination of the Court's probable decision converge on a conclusion of unconstitutionality, the President must make a decision about whether or not to comply with the provision. That decision is necessarily specific to context, and it should be reached after careful weighing of the effect of compliance with the provision on the constitutional rights of affected individuals and on the executive branch's constitutional authority. Also relevant is the likelihood that compliance or noncompliance will permit judicial resolution of the issue. . . .

6. The President has enhanced responsibility to resist unconstitutional provisions that encroach upon the constitutional powers of the Presidency. Where the President believes that an enactment unconstitutionally limits his powers, he has the authority to defend his office and decline to abide by it, unless he is convinced that the Court would disagree with his assessment. If the President does not challenge such provisions (i.e., by refusing to execute them), there often will be no occasion for judicial consideration of their constitutionality; a policy of consistent

Presidential enforcement of statutes limiting his power thus would deny the Supreme Court the opportunity to review the limitations and thereby would allow for unconstitutional restrictions on the President's authority.

Some legislative encroachments on executive authority, however, will not be justiciable or are for other reasons unlikely to be resolved in court. If resolution in the courts is unlikely and the President cannot look to a judicial determination, he must shoulder the responsibility of protecting the constitutional role of the presidency. This is usually true, for example, of provisions limiting the President's authority as Commander in Chief. Where it is not possible to construe such provisions constitutionally, the President has the authority to act on his understanding of the Constitution....

7. The fact that a sitting President signed the statute in question does not change this analysis. The text of the Constitution offers no basis for distinguishing bills based on who signed them; there is no constitutional analogue to the principles of waiver and estoppel. Moreover, every President since Eisenhower has issued signing statements in which he stated that he would refuse to execute unconstitutional provisions.... (Of course, the President is not obligated to announce his reservations in a signing statement; he can convey his views in the time, manner, and form of his choosing.)...

We recognize that these issues are difficult ones. When the President's obligation to act in accord with the Constitution appears to be in tension with his duty to execute laws enacted by Congress, questions are raised that go to the heart of our constitutional structure. In these circumstances, a President should proceed with caution and with respect for the obligation that each of the branches shares for the maintenance of constitutional government.

Campbell v. Clinton

203 F.3d 19 (D.C. Cir. 2000)

SILBERMAN, CIRCUIT JUDGE:

A number of congressmen, led by Tom Campbell of California, filed suit claiming that the President violated the War Powers Resolution and the War Powers Clause of the Constitution by directing U.S. forces' participation in the recent NATO campaign in Yugoslavia. The district court dismissed for lack of standing. We agree with the district court and therefore affirm.

I.

On March 24, 1999, President Clinton announced the commencement of NATO air and cruise missile attacks on Yugoslav targets. Two days later he submitted to Congress a report, "consistent with the War Powers Resolution," detailing the circumstances necessitating the use of armed forces, the deployment's scope and expected duration, and asserting that he had "taken these actions pursuant to [his] authority . . . as Commander in Chief and Chief Executive." On April 28, Congress voted on four resolutions related to the Yugoslav conflict: It voted down a declaration of war 427 to 2 and an "authorization" of the air strikes 213 to 213, but it also voted against requiring the President to immediately end U.S. participation in the NATO operation and voted to fund that involvement. The conflict between NATO and Yugoslavia continued for 79 days, ending on June 10 with Yugoslavia's

agreement to withdraw its forces from Kosovo and allow deployment of a NATO-
led peacekeeping force. Throughout this period Pentagon, State Department, and
NATO spokesmen informed the public on a frequent basis of developments in the
fighting.

Appellants, 31 congressmen opposed to U.S. involvement in the Kosovo intervention, filed suit prior to termination of that conflict seeking a declaratory judgment
that the President's use of American forces against Yugoslavia was unlawful under
both the War Powers Clause of the Constitution and the War Powers Resolution ("the
WPR").... Appellants claim that the President [submitted] a report sufficient to trigger the WPR on March 26, or in any event was required to submit a report by that date,
but nonetheless failed to end U.S. involvement in the hostilities after 60 days....

II....

The question whether congressmen have standing in federal court to challenge the
lawfulness of actions of the executive was answered, at least in large part, in the
Supreme Court's recent decision in Raines v. Byrd, 521 U.S. 811 (1997).... *Raines*
involved a constitutional challenge to the President's authority under the short-lived
Line Item Veto Act. Individual congressmen claimed that under that Act a President
could veto (unconstitutionally) only part of a law and thereby diminish the institutional power of Congress. Observing it had never held that congressmen have standing to assert an institutional injury as against the executive, the Court held that
petitioners in the case lacked "legislative standing" to challenge the Act....

There remains, however, a soft spot in the legal barrier against congressional
legal challenges to executive action, and it is a soft spot that appellants sought to
penetrate. In 1939 the Supreme Court in *Coleman v. Miller* voted 5-4 to recognize
the standing of Kansas State legislators in the Supreme Court to challenge the
actions of the Kansas Secretary of State and the Secretary of the State Senate.
See 307 U.S. 433 (1939). That case arose out of a State Senate vote on the ratification of a constitutional amendment, the Child Labor Amendment, proposed by
Congress in 1924. The State Senate split 20 to 20, and the Lieutenant Governor,
the presiding officer of the Senate, then cast a deciding vote in favor. The State
House subsequently also passed a ratification resolution. Thereupon the twenty
State Senators who voted against ratification plus one more (who presumably had
voted for the resolution) brought a mandamus action in the State Supreme Court
challenging the Lieutenant Governor's right to vote. They sought an order compelling the Secretary of the Senate to erase the endorsement on the resolution and
restraining the Secretary of State from authenticating the resolution and passing it
on to the Governor. The Supreme Court of Kansas entertained the action but ruled
against the plaintiffs on the merits. Granting certiorari, the United States Supreme
Court determined that "at least the twenty senators whose votes, if their contention
were sustained, would have been sufficient to defeat the resolution... have an
interest... sufficient to give the Court jurisdiction," *id.* at 446, because they have
a legal interest "in maintaining the effectiveness of their votes." *Id.* at 438.

In *Raines* the plaintiff congressmen had relied on *Coleman* to argue that they had
standing because the presidential veto had undermined the "effectiveness of their
votes." The Supreme Court noted that *Coleman* might be distinguished on grounds
that the federal constitutional separation of powers concerns that underlay its decision
in *Raines* ... were not present, or that if the Court in *Coleman* had not taken the case a
question of federal law—the ratification vel non by the Kansas Legislature—would

remain as decided by the Kansas Court. But the Court thought it unnecessary to cabin *Coleman* on those grounds. Instead, the Court emphasized that the congressmen were not asserting that their votes had been "completely nullified." ...

Here the plaintiff congressmen, by specifically defeating the War Powers Resolution authorization by a tie vote and by defeating a declaration of war, sought to fit within the *Coleman* exception to the *Raines* rule. This parliamentary tactic led to an extensive argument before us as to exactly what the Supreme Court meant by a claim that a legislator's vote was completely "nullified." ...

The Court did not suggest in *Raines* that the President "nullifies" a congressional vote and thus legislators have standing whenever the government does something Congress voted against, still less that congressmen would have standing anytime a President allegedly acts in excess of statutory authority. As the government correctly observes, appellants' statutory argument, although cast in terms of the nullification of a recent vote, essentially is that the President violated the quarter-century old War Powers Resolution. Similarly, their constitutional argument is that the President has acted illegally — in excess of his authority — because he waged war in the constitutional sense without a congressional delegation. Neither claim is analogous to a *Coleman* nullification.

We think the key to understanding the Court's treatment of *Coleman* and its use of the word nullification is its implicit recognition that a ratification vote on a constitutional amendment is an unusual situation. It is not at all clear whether once the amendment was "deemed ratified," *see Raines,* 521 U.S. at 822, the Kansas Senate could have done anything to reverse that position. We think that must be what the Supreme Court implied when it said the *Raines* plaintiffs could not allege that the "[Line Item Veto Act] would nullify their votes in the future," and that, after all, a majority of senators and congressmen could always repeal the Line Item Veto Act. The *Coleman* senators, by contrast, may well have been powerless to rescind a ratification of a constitutional amendment that they claimed had been defeated. In other words, they had no legislative remedy. Under that reading — which we think explains the very narrow possible *Coleman* exception to *Raines* — appellants fail because they continued, after the votes, to enjoy ample legislative power to have stopped prosecution of the "war."

In this case, Congress certainly could have passed a law forbidding the use of U.S. forces in the Yugoslav campaign; indeed, there was a measure — albeit only a concurrent resolution — introduced to require the President to withdraw U.S. troops. Unfortunately, however, for those congressmen who, like appellants, desired an end to U.S. involvement in Yugoslavia, this measure was defeated by a 139 to 290 vote. Of course, Congress always retains appropriations authority and could have cut off funds for the American role in the conflict. Again there was an effort to do so but it failed; appropriations were authorized. And there always remains the possibility of impeachment should a President act in disregard of Congress' authority on these matters....

SILBERMAN, CIRCUIT JUDGE, concurring....*

Prior litigation under the WPR has turned on the threshold test whether U.S. forces are engaged in hostilities or are in imminent danger of hostilities. But the question posed by appellants — whether the President's refusal to discontinue

---

* [Judge Silberman concurred in his own majority opinion in order to make the additional argument that the question presented was not suitable for judicial determination. — EDS.]

American activities in Yugoslavia violates the WPR — necessarily depends on the statute having been triggered in the first place. It has been held that the statutory threshold standard is not precise enough and too obviously calls for a political judgment to be one suitable for judicial determinations. . . . I think that is correct. . . .

Judge Tatel points to numerous cases in which a court has determined that our nation was at war, but none of these cases involved the question whether the President had "declared war" in violation of the Constitution. [Judge Silberman proceeds to discuss *Bas v. Tingy*.] . . . It is similarly irrelevant that courts have determined the existence of a war in cases involving insurance policies and other contracts, the Federal Tort Claims Act, and provisions of the military criminal code applicable in "time of war." None of these cases asked whether there was a war as the Constitution uses that word, but only whether a particular statutory or contractual provision was triggered by some instance of fighting. . . .

Even assuming a court could determine what "war" is, it is important to remember that the Constitution grants Congress the power to declare war, which is not necessarily the same as the power to determine whether U.S. forces will fight in a war. This distinction was drawn in [*The Prize Cases*], 67 U.S. 635 (1862). . . .

I read the *Prize Cases* to stand for the proposition that the President has independent authority to repel aggressive acts by third parties even without specific congressional authorization, and courts may not review the level of force selected. . . . Therefore, I assume, arguendo, that appellants are correct and only Congress has authority to initiate "war." If the President may direct U.S. forces in response to third-party initiated war, then the question any plaintiff who challenges the constitutionality of a war must answer is, who started it? The question of who is responsible for a conflict is, as history reveals, rather difficult to answer, and we lack judicial standards for resolving it. Then there is the problem of actually discovering the necessary information to answer the question, when such information may be unavailable to the U.S. or its allies, or unavailable to courts due to its sensitivity. Perhaps Yugoslavia did pose a threat to a much wider region of Europe and to U.S. civilian and military interests and personnel there. . . .

RANDOLPH, CIRCUIT JUDGE, concurring in the judgment. . . .

I believe plaintiffs lack standing, at least to litigate their constitutional claim, but for reasons the majority opinion neglects. . . .

The heart of the *Raines* decision is this: "legislators whose votes would have been sufficient to defeat (or enact) a specific legislative act have standing to sue if that legislative action goes into effect (or does not go into effect), on the ground that their votes have been completely nullified." 521 U.S. at 823.

Here, plaintiffs had the votes "sufficient to defeat" "a specific legislative action" — they defeated a declaration of war (their constitutional claim) and they blocked a resolution approving the President's continuation of the war (their statutory claim). To follow precisely the formulation in *Raines*, they would have standing only if the legislative actions they defeated went "into effect." Obviously, this did not happen: war was not declared, and the President never maintained that he was prosecuting the war with the House's approval. . . .

As to [plaintiffs'] under the War Powers Resolution, the beauty of this measure, or one of its defects . . . , is in its automatic operation: unless a majority of both Houses declares war, or approves continuation of hostilities beyond 60 days, or Congress is "physically unable to meet as a result of an armed attack upon the United States," the Resolution requires the President to withdraw the troops.

The President has nothing to veto. Congress may allow the time to run without taking any vote, or it may — as the House did here — take a vote and fail to muster a majority in favor of continuing the hostilities.

To put the matter in terms of *Raines* once again, plaintiffs had the votes "sufficient to defeat" "a specific legislative action" — they blocked a resolution authorizing the President's continuation of the war with Yugoslavia — but it is not true, in the language of *Raines*, that this "legislative action" nevertheless went "into effect." Congressional authorization simply did not occur. The President may have acted as if he had Congress's approval, or he may have acted as if he did not need it. Either way, plaintiffs' real complaint is not that the President ignored their votes; it is that he ignored the War Powers Resolution, and hence the votes of an earlier Congress, which enacted the law over President Nixon's veto. It is hard for me to see that this amounts to anything more than saying: "We, the members of Congress, have standing because the President violated one of our laws." To hold that Members of Congress may litigate on such a basis strikes me as highly problematic, not only because the principle is unconfined but also because it raises very serious separation-of-powers concerns. . . .

TATEL, CIRCUIT JUDGE, concurring:

Although I agree with Judge Silberman that Raines v. Byrd, 521 U.S. 811 (1997), . . . deprives plaintiffs of standing to bring this action, I do not share his view that the case poses a nonjusticiable political question. In my view, were this case brought by plaintiffs with standing, we could determine whether the President, in undertaking the air campaign in Yugoslavia, exceeded his authority under the Constitution or the War Powers Resolution. . . .

Whether the military activity in Yugoslavia amounted to "war" within the meaning of the Declare War Clause, U.S. Const. art. I, §8, cl. 11, is no more standardless than any other question regarding the constitutionality of government action. Precisely what police conduct violates the Fourth Amendment guarantee "against unreasonable searches and seizures?" When does government action amount to "an establishment of religion" prohibited by the First Amendment? When is an election district so bizarrely shaped as to violate the Fourteenth Amendment guarantee of "equal protection of the laws"? Because such constitutional terms are not self defining, standards for answering these questions have evolved, as legal standards always do, through years of judicial decisionmaking. Courts have proven no less capable of developing standards to resolve war powers challenges.

Since the earliest years of the nation, courts have not hesitated to determine when military action constitutes "war." [Judge Tatel proceeds to discuss Bas v. Tingy and *The Prize Cases*, excerpted above in Sections A and B.] . . .

Without undue difficulty, courts have also determined whether hostilities amount to "war" in other contexts. These have included insurance policies and other contracts, . . . the Federal Tort Claims Act, and provisions of military criminal law applicable "in time of war."

Although courts have thus determined the existence of war as defined by the Constitution, statutes, and contracts, in this case plaintiffs' War Powers Resolution claim would not even require that we do so. We would need to ask only whether, and at what time, "United States Armed Forces [were] introduced into hostilities or into situations where imminent involvement in hostilities [was] clearly indicated by the circumstances." 50 U.S.C. §1543(a)(1). On this question, the record is clear. . . .

The undisputed facts of this case are equally compelling with respect to plaintiffs' constitutional claim. If in 1799 the Supreme Court could recognize that sporadic battles between American and French vessels amounted to a state of war, and if in 1862 it could examine the record of hostilities and conclude that a state of war existed with the confederacy, then surely we, looking to similar evidence, could determine whether months of daily airstrikes involving 800 U.S. aircraft flying more than 20,000 sorties and causing thousands of enemy casualties amounted to "war" within the meaning of Article I, section 8, clause 11.

Determining whether a state of war exists would certainly be more difficult in situations involving more limited military force over a shorter period of time. But just as we never shrink from deciding a First Amendment case simply because we can imagine a more difficult one, the fact that a challenge to a different military action might present a closer question would not justify abdicating our responsibility to construe the law and apply it to the facts of this case.

Nor is the question nonjusticiable because the President, as Commander in Chief, possesses emergency authority to use military force to defend the nation from attack without obtaining prior congressional approval. Judge Silberman's suggestion notwithstanding, President Clinton does not claim that the air campaign was necessary to protect the nation from imminent attack....

The government also claims that this case is nonjusticiable because it "requires a political, not a judicial, judgment." The government has it backwards. Resolving the issue in this case would require us to decide not whether the air campaign was wise — a "policy choice[ ] and value determination[ ] constitutionally committed for resolution to the halls of Congress or the confines of the Executive Branch," Japan Whaling Ass'n v. American Cetacean Soc'y, 478 U.S. 221, 230 (1986) — but whether the President possessed legal authority to conduct the military operation. Did the President exceed his constitutional authority as Commander in Chief? Did he intrude on Congress's power to declare war? Did he violate the War Powers Resolution? Presenting purely legal issues, these questions call on us to perform one of the most important functions of Article III courts: determining the proper constitutional allocation of power among the branches of government. Although our answer could well have political implications, "the presence of constitutional issues with significant political overtones does not automatically invoke the political question doctrine. Resolution of litigation challenging the constitutional authority of one of the three branches cannot be evaded by courts because the issues have political implications...." INS v. Chadha, 462 U.S. 919, 942-43 (1983). This is so even where, as here (and as in the other cases discussed above), the issue relates to foreign policy. If "we cannot shrink [our] responsibility" to decide whether an Act of Congress requires the President to impose economic sanctions on a foreign nation for diminishing the effectiveness of an international treaty, a question rife with "political overtones," Japan Whaling Ass'n, 478 U.S. at 230, then surely we cannot shrink our responsibility to decide whether the President exceeded his constitutional or statutory authority by conducting the air campaign in Yugoslavia.

War Crimes Act of 1996 (as amended)

18 U.S.C. §2441

(a) Offense. — Whoever, whether inside or outside the United States, commits a war crime, in any of the circumstances described in subsection (b), shall be fined under this title or imprisoned for life or any term of years, or both, and if death results to the victim, shall also be subject to the penalty of death.

(b) Circumstances. — The circumstances referred to in subsection (a) are that the person committing such breach or the victim of such war crime is a member of the Armed Forces of the United States or a national of the United States (as defined in section 101 of the Immigration and Nationality Act).

(c) Definition. — As used in this section the term "war crime" means any conduct —

> (1) defined as a grave breach in any of the international conventions signed at Geneva 12 August 1949, or any protocol to such convention to which the United States is a party;
>
> (2) prohibited by Article 23, 25, 27, or 28 of the Annex to the Hague Convention IV, Respecting the Laws and Customs of War on Land, signed 18 October 1907;
>
> (3) which constitutes a violation of common Article 3 of the international conventions signed at Geneva, 12 August 1949, or any protocol to such convention to which the United States is a party and which deals with noninternational armed conflict; or
>
> (4) of a person who, in relation to an armed conflict and contrary to the provisions of the Protocol on Prohibitions or Restrictions on the Use of Mines, Booby-Traps and Other Devices as amended at Geneva on 3 May 1996 (Protocol II as amended on 3 May 1996), when the United States is a party to such Protocol, willfully kills or causes serious injury to civilians.

Notes and Questions

1. The President has a constitutional duty to "take Care that the Laws are faithfully executed." When Congress enacts a statute that restricts presidential power, the Take Care Clause requires him to abide by the statute unless it conflicts with a higher law that the President also must execute, most notably the Constitution. It follows that congressional restrictions on presidential uses of force raise the following general questions: Does the Constitution give the President a core of exclusive military powers that Congress cannot limit? If so, what falls within those exclusive presidential powers? And who decides which presidential powers are exclusive?

2. As the Dellinger memorandum notes, Presidents since the 1860s have argued for asserted exclusive Commander-in-Chief authorities that are beyond Congress' power to regulate. But the content of these authorities remain contested. *See* Youngstown Sheet & Tube Co. v. Sawyer, 343 U.S. 579, 641 (1952) (Jackson, J., concurring) ("These cryptic words [of the Commander-in-Chief clause] have given rise to some of the most persistent controversies in our constitutional history. Of course, they imply something more than an empty title. But just what authority goes with the name has plagued presidential advisers who would not waive or narrow it by nonassertion yet cannot say where it begins or ends."). The least controversial element of the exclusive Commander-in-Chief authority is that Congress cannot relieve the President of his command of the armed force of the United States. *See id.* at 641 (noting that the Commander-in-Chief Clause "undoubtedly puts the Nation's armed forces under presidential command"). Beyond that, there is

general agreement that the President alone makes strategic and tactical decisions on the battlefield. *See Youngstown,* 343 U.S. at 645 (Jackson, J., concurring) ("I should indulge the widest latitude of interpretation to sustain his exclusive function to command the instruments of national force, at least when turned against the outside world for the security of our society."); *Federalist No. 69* (noting that President's Commander-in-Chief authority "would amount to nothing more than the Supreme command and direction of the military and naval forces"). What is included within battlefield control? What if the battlefield is in the United States? What about decisions about where to send troops? What if Congress authorizes the President to use force against a particular entity, but forbids him from using force against other entities? What if it forbids him from attacking certain types of targets, or from using certain types of weapons? For matters falling with the President's exclusive authority, does this mean that Congress lacks the ability, even under the Define and Punish Clause, to criminalize actions in these areas that violate the international laws of war — for example, through the War Crimes Act of 1996?

What materials should one look to in answering these questions? Is Justice Jackson's concurrence in *Youngstown* helpful? Does the President have independent interpretive authority in answering these questions? Must he defer to Supreme Court decisions that are on point? What if there are no decisions on point? Is the Dellinger memorandum correct in claiming that the President has enhanced responsibilities to resist unconstitutional encroachments on his own power?

3. What does Little v. Barreme suggest about Congress's power to control presidential military power during wartime? Would the case have come out differently if Congress had been attempting to limit the President's power vis-à-vis an enemy ship rather than vis-à-vis a U.S. citizen engaged in commerce? What if Congress had declared war against France and authorized force without qualification except to say that the President could not fire on or seize enemy French ships found on the high seas? What does Brown v. United States, excerpted in Section A, suggest about these questions? Does the holding in *Barreme* concern the war power of the President or simply the liability of presidential subordinates? Why is the captain in *Barreme* liable for damages and the captain in *Durand* is not? Can Justice Nelson's opinion in *Durand,* excerpted in Section B, be reconciled with his dissent in *The Prize Cases?* For differing views about the significance of *Barreme,* compare Michael J. Glennon, Constitutional Diplomacy 3-8 (1991) (arguing that *Barreme* supports broad congressional authority to control the President during wartime), with Gegory J. Sidak, *The Quasi-War Cases,* 28 Harv. J.L. & Pub. Pol'y 465 (2004) (disputing that proposition).

4. What if a treaty, as opposed to a statute, purports to limit the President's Commander-in-Chief power? For example, the four Geneva Conventions of 1949 place significant restrictions on what the United States can do in a war to prisoners of war, civilians, and others. Can the Geneva Conventions restrict the President on the battlefield? Is a treaty part of the "Laws" of the United States that he must faithfully execute? Does it matter whether the treaty is self-executing (i.e., directly enforceable by U.S. courts) or non-self-executing (not directly enforceable by U.S. courts)? What if Congress has incorporated portions of the treaty into domestic law, as it has for the Geneva Conventions in the War Crimes Act of 1996? Does it matter whether the President, as opposed to one of his subordinates, makes the decision to disregard the treaty? For analysis of these issues, see Derek Jinks & David Sloss, *Is the President Bound by the Geneva Conventions?,* 90 Cornell L. Rev. 97 (2004). We return to these issues in Chapter 6 in the materials on the treaty power.

5. As the Vietnam War dragged on, Congress became increasingly resistant to U.S. involvement. In 1967, for example, it issued a "Statement of Congressional Policy" expressing "its support of efforts being made by the President of the United States and other men of good will throughout the world to prevent an expansion of the war in Vietnam and to bring that conflict to an end through a negotiated settlement which will preserve the honor of the United States, protect the vital interests of this country, and allow the people of South Vietnam to determine the affairs of that nation in their own way." In December 1970, it enacted the Cooper-Church Amendment to the U.S. defense appropriations bill, forbidding the use of any U.S. ground forces in Laos or Cambodia. In January 1971, it repealed the Tonkin Gulf Resolution. The same year, it enacted the Mansfield Amendment, which provided: "It is hereby declared to be the policy of the United States to terminate at the earliest practicable date all military operations of the United States in Indochina, and to provide for the prompt and orderly withdrawal of all United States military forces at a date certain, subject to the release of all American prisoners of war held by the Government of North Vietnam and forces allied with such Government and an accounting for all Americans missing in action who have been held by or known to such Government or such forces." However, Congress also continued to appropriate funds for military activities in Southeast Asia, and to extend selective service statutes. Do these congressional actions, taken together, constitute a withdrawal of authorization for the war in Vietnam? *Compare* Francis D. Wormuth & Edwin B. Firmage, To Chain the Dog of War: The War Power of Congress in History and Law 231 (2d ed. 1989) (arguing that they did), *with* John Hart Ely, War and Responsibility: Constitutional Lessons of Vietnam and Its Aftermath 32-34 (1993) (arguing that they did not). What would it have taken for Congress to de-authorize the war? What practical hurdles might there have been to a more unambiguous de-authorization? What about the possibility of a presidential veto? Does it make sense that Congress would need a two-thirds majority in both Houses to de-authorize a war?

6. In 1996, some members of Congress proposed a bill that would have prohibited the use of Department of Defense funds for armed forces under U.N. operational or tactical command. *See* Section 3 of H.R. 3308, 104th Cong. (1996). In effect, this law would have barred the President from placing U.S. armed forces participating in U.N. peacekeeping operations under U.N. operational or tactical control. The limitation would have allowed the President to waive the limitation if he certified to Congress 15 days in advance of the delegation that it is "in the national security interests of the United States to place any element of the armed forces under United Nations operational or tactical control," and provided a detailed report setting forth specific items of information.

This bill was never enacted, but had it been, would it have been constitutional? The President's lawyers thought not, arguing that:

> [T]he Commander-in-Chief Clause commits to the President alone the power to select the particular personnel who are to exercise tactical and operational control over U.S. forces. . . .
>
> True, Congress has the power to lay down general rules creating and regulating "the framework of the Military Establishment"; but such framework rules may not unduly constrain or inhibit the President's authority to make and to implement the decisions that he deems necessary or advisable for the successful conduct of military missions in the field, including the choice of particular persons to perform specific command functions in those missions. . . .

Moreover, in seeking to impair the President's ability to deploy U.S. Armed Forces under U.N. operational and tactical command in U.N. operations in which the United States may otherwise lawfully participate, Congress is impermissibly undermining the President's constitutional authority with respect to the conduct of diplomacy.... U.N. peacekeeping missions involve multilateral arrangements that require delicate and complex accommodations of a variety of interests and concerns, including those of the nations that provide troops or resources, and those of the nation or nations in which the operation takes place. The success of the mission may depend, to a considerable extent, on the nationality of the commanding officers, or on the degree to which the operation is perceived as a U.N. activity (rather than that of a single nation or bloc of nations). Given that the United States may lawfully participate in such U.N. operations, we believe that Congress would be acting unconstitutionally if it were to tie the President's hands in negotiating agreements with respect to command structures for those operations.

Memorandum from Walter Dellinger, Assistant Attorney General, Office of Legal Counsel, to Alan Kreczko, Legal Adviser to the National Security Council, "Placing of United States Armed Forces Under United Nations Operational or Tactical Control" (May 8, 1996), at http://www.usdoj.gov/olc/1996opinions.htm.

In response to the claim that the waiver provision meant that the bill "effects only a conditional ban on the President's constitutional authority to control the tactical and operational deployment of U.S. forces," the memorandum responded that "Congress cannot, however, burden or infringe the President's exercise of a core constitutional power by attaching conditions precedent to the exercise of that power." Finally, the President's lawyers rejected the argument that the bill was a legitimate exercise of Congress's appropriations power:

We are mindful that Congress has framed its restriction on placing troops under U.N. control as a prohibition on the obligation or expenditure of appropriated funds. That Congress has chosen to invade the President's authority indirectly, through a condition on an appropriation, rather than through a direct mandate, is immaterial. Broad as Congress' spending power undoubtedly is, it is clear that Congress may not deploy it to accomplish unconstitutional ends. In particular, as our Office has insisted over the course of several Administrations, Congress may not use its power over appropriation of public funds to attach conditions to Executive Branch appropriations requiring the President to relinquish his constitutional discretion in foreign affairs.

Id. (citations and quotations omitted). Do you agree with these arguments? Is the Commander-in-Chief power superior to the appropriations power? What is the relevance for this issue, if any, of Congress's power under Article I, §8, to "raise and support armies" and to "make rules for the government and regulation of the land and naval forces"? Do you think the President would have committed troops to U.N. command if Congress had succeeded in enacting legislation, over his veto, to cut off funds?

7. Does the War Powers Resolution meet its stated goal of "fulfill[ing] the intent of the framers of the Constitution"? To what extent does the Resolution simply express what the Constitution already requires? To what extent does it exceed what the Constitution requires? To what extent, if at all, does it impinge upon the President's war powers?

8. Does the consultation requirement in Section 3 of the War Powers Resolution have any legal effect? Even if it does not, might it nonetheless have practical significance?

9. Does the Resolution's 60-day authorization period give the President carte blanche authority to conduct military operations within that period? If so, is this consistent with Congress's war declaration power? Does the Resolution delegate some of Congress's war power to the President? If so, is such a delegation constitutional?

10. When does the 60-day period mentioned in Section 5 of the Resolution begin to run? How clear is the statutory standard governing this issue? What constitutes "hostilities"? When is "imminent involvement in hostilities . . . clearly indicated by the circumstances"? Who decides these questions?

11. Does Section 5(c)'s concurrent resolution provision (which Congress has never invoked) violate *Chadha*?

12. Since the enactment of the War Powers Resolution, there have been at least 15 significant uses of U.S. force abroad: the 1975 rescue of the U.S. merchant ship *Mayaguez*; the 1980 Iran Hostage rescue mission; the dispatch of troops to Lebanon in 1982; the 1983 invasion of Grenada; the 1986 air strikes against Libya; the 1987 escort operations to protect Persian Gulf shipping; the 1989 intervention in Panama; the 1991 Gulf War; the 1992-1993 humanitarian and combat mission in Somalia; the 1993 air strikes against Iraq in response to the attempted assassination of the first President Bush; the 1993 air strikes in Bosnia; the 1998 air strikes against the Sudan and Afghanistan; the 1999 air strikes against Yugoslavia; the war begun in Afghanistan in 2001; and the war begun in Iraq in 2003. Only three of these actions — the 1991 Gulf War, the conflict in Afghanistan, and the 2003 war in Iraq — were preceded by express congressional authorization. Two others — the Lebanon and Somalia missions — received *ex post* approval from Congress. The remaining ten actions received no congressional approval. Eight of these unauthorized actions — the *Mayaguez* incident, the attempted hostage rescue, the bombing of Libya, the Gulf escort operation, the invasions of Panama and (perhaps) Grenada, the 1993 air strikes against Iraq, and the Sudan-Afghanistan bombings — can to varying degrees be justified as responses to attacks or threatened attacks on U.S. citizens or property. The Bosnia and Yugoslavia missions lacked any ties to U.S. property or citizens.

In all of these situations, presidents justified their actions — in whole or in part — under the Commander-in-Chief and related presidential powers. In none of these situations did any president acknowledge an obligation to comply with the War Powers Resolution. President Ford "took note of" the Resolution when he sent troops on the *Mayaguez* rescue operation. Presidents Carter, Reagan, Bush, and Clinton stated that they were informing Congress of their actions "consistent with" the Resolution. In a number of these instances, presidents have also sought congressional support for military operations — sometimes successfully (as in Iraq), and sometimes not (as in Kosovo) — without acknowledging any requirement that they do so.

What do these patterns suggest about the effectiveness of the War Powers Resolution? If presidents do not feel obliged to comply with the War Powers Resolution, why do they note that their actions are consistent with the Resolution, and why do they often seek Congress's support?

13. Why has Congress not been more aggressive in insisting on presidential compliance with the War Powers Resolution? Why has Congress almost never expressed direct opposition to presidential commitments of U.S. armed forces? Why doesn't Congress withdraw appropriations? What are Congress's institutional incentives in these situations? Does congressional failure to resist a president's military operation constitute congressional authorization? Consider the following assessment: "During [the post-World War II] period a tacit deal has existed between the executive and legislative branches, not just with respect to foreign policy but more generally, to the effect that the president will take the responsibility (well, most of it) so long as he can make the decisions, and Congress will forego actual policy-making authority so long as it doesn't have to be held accountable (and can scold the President when things go wrong)." Ely, *supra*, at 54. If this assessment is accurate, how, if at all, should it affect the willingness of courts to intervene in war powers disputes?

14. According to the majority in *Campbell*, what is now required in order for legislators to have standing to bring a challenge under the War Powers Resolution? How does the majority's standing analysis compare with Justice Powell's ripeness analysis in Goldwater v. Carter (excerpted in Chapter 2)? What is Judge Randolph's disagreement with the majority's standing analysis? Who is right? What, precisely, was the constitutional claim being made by the legislative plaintiffs in *Campbell*? If their claim were correct, wouldn't that mean that their votes against authorizing the Kosovo bombing were nullified? In deciding standing, isn't a court obligated to assume that the plaintiff's claim is correct?

15. In *Campbell*, who has the better of the argument between Judges Silberman and Tatel? Is deciding the meaning of "war" in the Constitution any more difficult, or political, than deciding the meaning of other contested and important constitutional provisions? To what extent should courts defer to the President's determination about whether a conflict qualifies as a "war" for purposes of the Declare War Clause?

16. So far, no court has upheld a challenge under the War Powers Resolution. Rather, these challenges have all been dismissed under limiting doctrines such as standing, ripeness, equitable discretion, and the political question doctrine. In addition to *Campbell*, see, for example Ange v. Bush, 752 F. Supp. 509 (D.D.C. 1990) (dismissing challenge to Gulf War on political question, equitable discretion, and ripeness grounds); Lowry v. Reagan, 676 F. Supp. 333 (D.D.C. 1987) (dismissing challenge to reflagging operations in the Persian Gulf on equitable discretion and political question grounds); Sanchez-Espinoza v. Reagan, 568 F. Supp. 596 (D.D.C. 1983) (dismissing challenge to covert assistance to Nicaraguan contras on political question grounds), *aff'd on other grounds*, 770 F.2d 202 (D.C. Cir. 1985); Crockett v. Reagan, 558 F. Supp. 893 (D.D.C. 1982) (dismissing challenge to military aid to El Salvador on political question grounds), *aff'd without opinion*, 720 F.2d 1355 (D.C. Cir. 1983).

Although the D.C. Circuit affirmed the district court's decision in *Crockett* without issuing a new opinion, Judge Bork wrote a short concurrence arguing that the case should be dismissed for lack of standing. *See* 720 F.2d at 1357 (Bork, J., concurring). In arguing that "an alleged diminution in congressional influence must amount to a disenfranchisement—a nullification or diminution of a congressman's vote—before a congressional plaintiff may claim the requisite injury-in-fact necessary to confer standing to sue," *id.*, Judge Bork anticipated the approach to legislative standing subsequently adopted by the Supreme Court in Raines v. Byrd.

Do courts have the expertise and access to information necessary to resolve challenges under the War Powers Resolution? Would judicial enforcement of the Resolution deprive the President of needed flexibility, as President Nixon argued in his veto message? What do Bas v. Tingy and *The Prize Cases* suggest about these questions? In enforcing the Resolution, how much deference should courts give to the President's views regarding whether a particular situation implicates the Resolution?

17. Setting aside for the moment the fact that no court may be able to rule on the question, did the Kosovo bombing violate the War Powers Resolution? What arguments might you make that it didn't? The Justice Department's Office of Legal Counsel maintained that Congress had implicitly authorized bombings beyond the 60-day period of the War Powers Resolution through its enactment of emergency appropriations. *See* Memorandum from Randolph D. Moss, Assistant Attorney General, Office of Legal Counsel, to the Attorney General, "Authorization for Continuing Hostilities in Kosovo" (Dec. 19, 2000), at http://www.usdoj. gov/olc/final.htm. They reached this conclusion despite the fact that section 8(a)(1) of the War Powers Resolution states that appropriations shall not be construed as war authorizations unless they say so explicitly. The memorandum reasoned that Congress in 1999 intended the appropriations to be authorizations, and that the earlier 1973 Congress could not control the later Congress's intent through prospective plain statement requirements. Do you agree with this analysis?

18. Many commentators have argued that the War Powers Resolution is ineffective in limiting the President's ability to use military force. Do you agree? If so, why do you think this is so? How might the War Powers Resolution have been drafted differently? If it had been drafted differently, would it have been more effective? Besides the War Powers Resolution, what mechanisms does Congress have to limit the President's ability to engage in military operations? Are these mechanisms effective restraints on the President's use of military force?

19. For commentary on the War Powers Resolution, see, for example, Robert F. Turner, The War Powers Resolution: Its Implementation in Theory and Practice (1983); Stephen L. Carter, *The Constitutionality of the War Powers Resolution,* 70 Va. L. Rev. 101 (1984); Maj. Geoffrey S. Corn, *Clinton, Kosovo, and the Final Destruction of the War Powers Resolution,* 42 Wm. & Mary L. Rev. 1149 (2001); J. Terry Emerson, *The War Powers Resolution Tested: The President's Independent Defense Power,* 51 Notre Dame L. Rev. 187 (1975); Michael J. Glennon, *Too Far Apart: Repeal the War Powers Resolution,* 50 U. Miami L. Rev. 17 (1995); John Hart Ely, *Suppose Congress Wanted a War Powers Act that Worked,* 88 Colum. L. Rev. 1379 (1988); Eugene V. Rostow, *Great Cases Make Bad Law: The War Powers Act,* 50 Tex. L. Rev. 833 (1972); Eugene V. Rostow, *"Once More Unto the Breach": The War Powers Resolution Revisited,* 21 Val. U. L. Rev. 1 (1986); Peter M. Shane, *Learning McNamara's Lessons: How the War Powers Resolution Advances the Rule of Law,* 47 Case W. Res. L. Rev. 1281 (1997); Cyrus R. Vance, *Striking the Balance: Congress and the President Under the War Powers Resolution,* 133 U. Pa. L. Rev. 79 (1984).

D. WAR AND INDIVIDUAL LIBERTIES

This section considers the issue of protecting individual liberties during wartime.

1. The Civil War

As we learned in Chapter 1, soon after the Civil War began in April 1861, President Lincoln suspended the writ of habeas corpus in various parts of the United States, and Chief Justice Taney, riding Circuit, declared this action unconstitutional in May 1861 in *Ex parte Merryman*. In his July 4, 1861 message to Congress, Lincoln defended his actions:

> [T]he legality and propriety of what has been done [pursuant to my authorization to military authorities to suspend the writ of habeas corpus] are questioned and the attention of the country has been called to the proposition that one who is sworn to "take care that the laws be faithfully executed" should not himself violate them. . . . The whole of the laws which were required to be faithfully executed were being resisted and failing of execution in nearly one-third of the States. Must they be allowed to finally fail of execution, even had it been perfectly clear that by the use of the means necessary to their execution some single law, made in such extreme tenderness of the citizen's liberty that practically it relieves more of the guilty than of the innocent, should to a very limited extent be violated? To state the question more directly, are all the laws but one to go unexecuted and the Government itself go to pieces lest that one be violated? Even in such a case would not the official oath be broken if the Government should be overthrown, when it was believed that disregarding the single law would tend to preserve it? But it was not believed that this question was presented. It was not believed that any law was violated. The provision of the Constitution that "the privilege of the writ of habeas corpus shall not be suspended unless when in cases of rebellion or invasion the public safety may require it," is equivalent to a provision — is a provision — that such privilege may be suspended when in cases of rebellion or invasion the public safety does require it. It was decided that we have a case of rebellion, and that the public safety does require the qualified suspension of the privilege of the writ which was authorized to be made. Now, it is insisted that Congress and not the Executive is vested with this power. But the Constitution itself is silent as to which, or who, is to exercise the power; and as the provision was plainly made for a dangerous emergency, it cannot be believed the framers of the instrument intended that in every case the danger should run its course until Congress could be called together, the very assembling of which might be prevented, as was intended in this case, by the rebellion.
>
> . . . Whether there shall be any legislation upon the subject, and if any, what, is submitted entirely to the better judgment of Congress.

More than a year and a half later, Congress enacted the Habeas Corpus Act of 1863. Section 1 of the Act provided that "during the present rebellion the President of the United States, whenever, in his judgment the public safety may require it, is authorized to suspend the write of *habeas corpus* in any case throughout the United States or any part thereof." Section 2 of the Act then qualified this authorization in an important way. It required the Executive branch to furnish a list of persons other than "prisoners of war" who were imprisoned without trial in states "in which the administration of the laws has continued unimpaired in the . . . Federal courts," and required federal courts to release such persons if the grand jury did not indict them for a federal crime by the time the grand jury terminated its session.

Ex parte Milligan

71 U.S. 2 (1866)

[Lambdin Milligan, a civilian U.S. citizen living in Indiana, was a vociferous critic of Abraham Lincoln and of the U.S. Civil War. In October 1864, in the midst of the war, the U.S. general commanding the military district of Indiana arrested

Milligan. Milligan was accused of conspiracy against the government, giving aid and comfort to the rebels, initiating insurrection, disloyal practices, and violating the laws of war. He was tried before a commission of U.S. military judges established by President Lincoln exercising his powers as Commander in Chief. The commission found Milligan guilty, and sentenced him to be hanged. Milligan then petitioned a lower federal court for a writ of habeas corpus. He argued that because he was a citizen of Indiana who was not a prisoner of war, and because the grand jury of the district had met and convened without indicting him, Section 2 of the Habeas Corpus Act of 1863, which qualified the President's authority to suspend the writ of habeas corpus, was satisfied and required his release. The lower federal court certified the case to the Supreme Court.]

MR. JUSTICE DAVIS delivered the opinion of the court....

The Constitution of the United States is a law for rulers and people, equally in war and in peace, and covers with the shield of its protection all classes of men, at all times, and under all circumstances. No doctrine, involving more pernicious consequences, was ever invented by the wit of man than that any of its provisions can be suspended during any of the great exigencies of government. Such a doctrine leads directly to anarchy or despotism, but the theory of necessity on which it is based is false; for the government, within the Constitution, has all the powers granted to it, which are necessary to preserve its existence; as has been happily proved by the result of the great effort to throw off its just authority.

Have any of the rights guaranteed by the Constitution been violated in the case of Milligan? and if so, what are they?

Every trial involves the exercise of judicial power; and from what source did the military commission that tried him derive their authority? Certainly no part of the judicial power of the country was conferred on them; because the Constitution expressly vests it "in one supreme court and such inferior courts as the Congress may from time to time ordain and establish," and it is not pretended that the commission was a court ordained and established by Congress. They cannot justify on the mandate of the President; because he is controlled by law, and has his appropriate sphere of duty, which is to execute, not to make, the laws; and there is "no unwritten criminal code to which resort can be had as a source of jurisdiction."

But it is said that the jurisdiction is complete under the "laws and usages of war."

It can serve no useful purpose to inquire what those laws and usages are, whence they originated, where found, and on whom they operate; they can never be applied to citizens in states which have upheld the authority of the government, and where the courts are open and their process unobstructed. This court has judicial knowledge that in Indiana the Federal authority was always unopposed, and its courts always open to hear criminal accusations and redress grievances; and no usage of war could sanction a military trial there for any offence whatever of a citizen in civil life, in nowise connected with the military service. Congress could grant no such power; and to the honor of our national legislature be it said, it has never been provoked by the state of the country even to attempt its exercise. One of the plainest constitutional provisions was, therefore, infringed when Milligan was tried by a court not ordained and established by Congress, and not composed of judges appointed during good behavior.

Why was he not delivered to the Circuit Court of Indiana to be proceeded against according to law? No reason of necessity could be urged against it; because Congress had declared penalties against the offences charged, provided for their punishment, and directed that court to hear and determine them. . . .

Another guarantee of freedom was broken when Milligan was denied a trial by jury. . . . [T]his right — one of the most valuable in a free country — is preserved to every one accused of crime who is not attached to the army, or navy, or militia in actual service. The sixth amendment affirms that "in all criminal prosecutions the accused shall enjoy the right to a speedy and public trial by an impartial jury," language broad enough to embrace all persons and cases; but the fifth, recognizing the necessity of an indictment, or presentment, before any one can be held to answer for high crimes, "excepts cases arising in the land or naval forces, or in the militia, when in actual service, in time of war or public danger"; and the framers of the Constitution, doubtless, meant to limit the right of trial by jury, in the sixth amendment, to those persons who were subject to indictment or presentment in the fifth.

The discipline necessary to the efficiency of the army and navy, required other and swifter modes of trial than are furnished by the common law courts; and, in pursuance of the power conferred by the Constitution, Congress has declared the kinds of trial, and the manner in which they shall be conducted, for offences committed while the party is in the military or naval service. Every one connected with these branches of the public service is amenable to the jurisdiction which Congress has created for their government, and, while thus serving, surrenders his right to be tried by the civil courts. All other persons, citizens of states where the courts are open, if charged with crime, are guaranteed the inestimable privilege of trial by jury. This privilege is a vital principle, underlying the whole administration of criminal justice; it is not held by sufferance, and cannot be frittered away on any plea of state or political necessity. When peace prevails, and the authority of the government is undisputed, there is no difficulty of preserving the safeguards of liberty; for the ordinary modes of trial are never neglected, and no one wishes it otherwise; but if society is disturbed by civil commotion — if the passions of men are aroused and the restraints of law weakened, if not disregarded — these safeguards need, and should receive, the watchful care of those entrusted with the guardianship of the Constitution and laws. . . .

It is claimed that martial law covers with its broad mantle the proceedings of this military commission. The proposition is this: that in a time of war the commander of an armed force (if in his opinion the exigencies of the country demand it, and of which he is to judge), has the power, within the lines of his military district, to suspend all civil rights and their remedies, and subject citizens as well as soldiers to the rule of his will; and in the exercise of his lawful authority cannot be restrained, except by his superior officer or the President of the United States.

If this position is sound to the extent claimed, then when war exists, foreign or domestic, and the country is subdivided into military departments for mere convenience, the commander of one of them can, if he chooses, within his limits, on the plea of necessity, with the approval of the Executive, substitute military force for and to the exclusion of the laws, and punish all persons, as he thinks right and proper, without fixed or certain rules.

The statement of this proposition shows its importance; for, if true, republican government is a failure, and there is an end of liberty regulated by law. Martial law, established on such a basis, destroys every guarantee of the Constitution, and effectually renders the "military independent of and superior to the civil power"—the attempt to do which by the King of Great Britain was deemed by our fathers such an offence, that they assigned it to the world as one of the causes which impelled them to declare their independence. Civil liberty and this kind of martial law cannot endure together; the antagonism is irreconcilable; and, in the conflict, one or the other must perish....

It is essential to the safety of every government that, in a great crisis, like the one we have just passed through, there should be a power somewhere of suspending the writ of habeas corpus. In every war, there are men of previously good character, wicked enough to counsel their fellow-citizens to resist the measures deemed necessary by a good government to sustain its just authority and overthrow its enemies; and their influence may lead to dangerous combinations. In the emergency of the times, an immediate public investigation according to law may not be possible; and yet, the peril to the country may be too imminent to suffer such persons to go at large. Unquestionably, there is then an exigency which demands that the government, if it should see fit in the exercise of a proper discretion to make arrests, should not be required to produce the persons arrested in answer to a writ of habeas corpus. The Constitution goes no further. It does not say after a writ of habeas corpus is denied a citizen, that he shall be tried otherwise than by the course of the common law; if it had intended this result, it was easy by the use of direct words to have accomplished it. The illustrious men who framed that instrument were guarding the foundations of civil liberty against the abuses of unlimited power; they were full of wisdom, and the lessons of history informed them that a trial by an established court, assisted by an impartial jury, was the only sure way of protecting the citizen against oppression and wrong. Knowing this, they limited the suspension to one great right, and left the rest to remain forever inviolable. But, it is insisted that the safety of the country in time of war demands that this broad claim for martial law shall be sustained. If this were true, it could be well said that a country, preserved at the sacrifice of all the cardinal principles of liberty, is not worth the cost of preservation. Happily, it is not so....

It is difficult to see how the safety of the country required martial law in Indiana. If any of her citizens were plotting treason, the power of arrest could secure them, until the government was prepared for their trial, when the courts were open and ready to try them. It was as easy to protect witnesses before a civil as a military tribunal; and as there could be no wish to convict, except on sufficient legal evidence, surely an ordained and established court was better able to judge of this than a military tribunal composed of gentlemen not trained to the profession of the law.

It follows, from what has been said on this subject, that there are occasions when martial rule can be properly applied. If, in foreign invasion or civil war, the courts are actually closed, and it is impossible to administer criminal justice according to law, then, on the theatre of active military operations, where war really prevails, there is a necessity to furnish a substitute for the civil authority, thus overthrown, to preserve the safety of the army and society; and as no power is left but the military, it is allowed to govern by martial rule until the laws can have their free course. As necessity creates the rule, so it limits its duration; for, if this government is continued after the courts are reinstated, it is a gross usurpation of power. Martial rule can never exist where the courts are open, and in the proper and unobstructed exercise of their jurisdiction. It is also confined to the locality of actual war. Because, during the late Rebellion it could have been enforced in Virginia, where the national authority was overturned and the courts driven out, it does not follow that it should obtain in Indiana, where that authority was never disputed, and justice was always administered. And so in the case of a foreign invasion, martial rule may become a necessity in one state, when, in another, it would be "mere lawless violence."...

If the military trial of Milligan was contrary to law, then he was entitled, on the facts stated in his petition, to be discharged from custody by the terms of the act of Congress of March 3d, 1863.... Milligan avers he was a citizen of Indiana, not in the military or naval service, and was detained in close confinement, by order of the President, from the 5th day of October, 1864, until the 2d day of January, 1865, when the Circuit Court for the District of Indiana, with a grand jury, convened in session at Indianapolis; and afterwards, on the 27th day of the same month, adjourned without finding an indictment or presentment against him. If these averments were true (and their truth is conceded for the purposes of this case), the court was required to liberate him on taking certain oaths prescribed by the law, and entering into recognizance for his good behavior.

But it is insisted that Milligan was a prisoner of war, and, therefore, excluded from the privileges of the statute. It is not easy to see how he can be treated as a prisoner of war, when he lived in Indiana for the past twenty years, was arrested there, and had not been, during the late troubles, a resident of any of the states in rebellion. If in Indiana he conspired with bad men to assist the enemy, he is punishable for it in the courts of Indiana; but, when tried for the offence, he cannot plead the rights of war; for he was not engaged in legal acts of hostility against the government, and only such persons, when captured, are prisoners of war. If he cannot enjoy the immunities attaching to the character of a prisoner of war, how can he be subject to their pains and penalties?...

THE CHIEF JUSTICE [Chase] delivered the following opinion.

[Chase first argued that because Milligan satisfied the criteria of Section 2 of the Habeas Corpus Act of 1863 — i.e., that he was not a prisoner of war, was imprisoned in a state where the laws had continued unimpaired in the federal courts, and was not indicted by the grand jury during its term — the Habeas Statute required his release.]

But the [majority opinion] goes further; and as we understand it, asserts not only that the military commission held in Indiana was not authorized by Congress, but that it was not in the power of Congress to authorize it....

We cannot agree to this....

We think that Congress had power, though not exercised, to authorize the military commission which was held in Indiana....

Congress has the power not only to raise and support and govern armies but to declare war. It has, therefore, the power to provide by law for carrying on war. This power necessarily extends to all legislation essential to the prosecution of war with vigor and success, except such as interferes with the command of the forces and the conduct of campaigns. That power and duty belong to the President as commander-in-chief....

[W]hen the nation is involved in war, and some portions of the country are invaded, and all are exposed to invasion, it is within the power of Congress to determine in what states or districts such great and imminent public danger exists as justifies the authorization of military tribunals for the trial of crimes and offences against the discipline or security of the army or against the public safety....

We cannot doubt that, in such a time of public danger, Congress had power, under the Constitution, to provide for the organization of a military commission, and for trial by that commission of persons engaged in this conspiracy. The fact that the Federal courts were open was regarded by Congress as a sufficient reason for not exercising the power; but that fact could not deprive Congress of the right to exercise it. Those courts might be open and undisturbed in the execution of their functions, and yet wholly incompetent to avert threatened danger, or to punish, with adequate promptitude and certainty, the guilty conspirators....

We have confined ourselves to the question of power. It was for Congress to determine the question of expediency. And Congress did determine it. That body did not see fit to authorize trials by military commission in Indiana, but by the strongest implication prohibited them....

MR. JUSTICE WAYNE, MR. JUSTICE SWAYNE, and MR. JUSTICE MILLER, concur with me in these views.

2. World War II

Korematsu v. United States

323 U.S. 214 (1944)

[Two months after the attack on Pearl Harbor in 1941, President Roosevelt issued the following Executive Order:

WHEREAS the successful prosecution of the war requires every possible protection against espionage and against sabotage to national-defense material, national-defense premises, and national-defense utilities...

NOW, THEREFORE, by virtue of the authority vested in me as President of the United States, and Commander in Chief of the Army and Navy, I hereby authorize and direct the Secretary of War, and the Military Commanders whom he may from time to time designate, whenever he or any designated Commander deems such actions necessary or desirable, to prescribe military areas in such places and of such extent as he or the appropriate Military Commanders may determine, from which any or all persons may be excluded, and with such respect to which, the right of any person to enter, remain in, or leave shall be subject to whatever restrictions the Secretary of War or the appropriate Military Commander may impose in his discretion. The Secretary of War is hereby authorized to provide for residents of any such area who are excluded therefrom, such transportation, food, shelter, and other accommodations as may be necessary, in the judgement of the Secretary of War or the said Military Commander, and until other arrangements are made, to accomplish the purpose of this order....

I hereby further authorize and direct the Secretary of War and the said Military Commanders to take such other steps as he or the appropriate Military Commander may deem advisable to enforce compliance with the restrictions applicable to each Military area hereinabove authorized to be designated, including the use of Federal troops and other Federal Agencies, with authority to accept assistance of state and local agencies.

Executive Order No. 9066, 7 Fed. Reg. 1407. Pursuant to this Order, the Commanding General of the Western Command excluded Japanese-Americans from the West Coast area and ordered them curfewed and/or detained in relocation centers. In 1942, Congress enacted a statute that provided:

> ...whoever shall enter, remain in, leave, or commit any act in any military area or military zone prescribed, under the authority of an Executive order of the President, by the Secretary of War, or by any military commander designated by the Secretary of War, contrary to the restrictions applicable to any such area or zone or contrary to the order of the Secretary of War or any such military commander, shall, if it appears that he knew or should have known of the existence and extent of the restrictions or order and that his act was in violation thereof, be guilty of a misdemeanor and upon conviction shall be liable to a fine of not to exceed $5,000 or to imprisonment for not more than one year, or both, for each offense.

Act of Congress, of March 21, 1942, 56 Stat. 173. Korematsu, an American citizen of Japanese descent, was convicted under this statute for remaining in San Leandro, California, a "Military Area," contrary to Civilian Exclusion Order No. 34 of the Commanding General of the Western Command, U.S. Army, which directed that after May 9, 1942, all persons of Japanese ancestry should be excluded from that area.]

MR. JUSTICE BLACK delivered the opinion of the Court....

One of the series of orders and proclamations, a curfew order, which like the exclusion order here was promulgated pursuant to Executive Order 9066, subjected all persons of Japanese ancestry in prescribed West Coast military areas to remain in their residences from 8 p.m. to 6 a.m. As is the case with the exclusion order here, that prior curfew order was designed as a "protection against espionage and against sabotage." In Hirabayashi v. United States, 320 U.S. 81, we sustained a conviction obtained for violation of the curfew order. The *Hirabayashi* conviction and this one thus rest on the same 1942 Congressional Act and the same basic executive and military orders, all of which orders were aimed at the twin dangers of espionage and sabotage.

The 1942 Act was attacked in the *Hirabayashi* case as an unconstitutional delegation of power; it was contended that the curfew order and other orders on which it rested were beyond the war powers of the Congress, the military authorities and of the President, as Commander in Chief of the Army; and finally that to apply the curfew order against none but citizens of Japanese ancestry amounted to a constitutionally prohibited discrimination solely on account of race. To these questions, we gave the serious consideration which their importance justified. We upheld the curfew order as an exercise of the power of the government to take steps necessary to prevent espionage and sabotage in an area threatened by Japanese attack.

In the light of the principles we announced in the *Hirabayashi* case, we are unable to conclude that it was beyond the war power of Congress and the Executive to exclude those of Japanese ancestry from the West Coast war area at the time they did. True, exclusion from the area in which one's home is located is a far greater deprivation than constant confinement to the home from 8 p.m. to 6 a.m. Nothing short of apprehension by the proper military authorities of the gravest imminent danger to the public safety can constitutionally justify either. But exclusion from a threatened area, no less than curfew, has a definite and close relationship to the prevention of espionage and sabotage. The military authorities, charged with the primary responsibility of defending our shores, concluded that curfew provided inadequate protection and ordered exclusion. They did so, as pointed out in our

Hirabayashi opinion, in accordance with Congressional authority to the military to say who should, and who should not, remain in the threatened areas.

In this case the petitioner challenges the assumptions upon which we rested our conclusions in the *Hirabayashi* case. He also urges that by May 1942, when Order No. 34 was promulgated, all danger of Japanese invasion of the West Coast had disappeared. After careful consideration of these contentions we are compelled to reject them.

Here, as in the *Hirabayashi* case, "we cannot reject as unfounded the judgment of the military authorities and of Congress that there were disloyal members of that population, whose number and strength could not be precisely and quickly ascertained. We cannot say that the war-making branches of the Government did not have ground for believing that in a critical hour such persons could not readily be isolated and separately dealt with, and constituted a menace to the national defense and safety, which demanded that prompt and adequate measures be taken to guard against it."

Like curfew, exclusion of those of Japanese origin was deemed necessary because of the presence of an unascertained number of disloyal members of the group, most of whom we have no doubt were loyal to this country. It was because we could not reject the finding of the military authorities that it was impossible to bring about an immediate segregation of the disloyal from the loyal that we sustained the validity of the curfew order as applying to the whole group. In the instant case, temporary exclusion of the entire group was rested by the military on the same ground. The judgment that exclusion of the whole group was for the same reason a military imperative answers the contention that the exclusion was in the nature of group punishment based on antagonism to those of Japanese origin. That there were members of the group who retained loyalties to Japan has been confirmed by investigations made subsequent to the exclusion. Approximately five thousand American citizens of Japanese ancestry refused to swear unqualified allegiance to the United States and to renounce allegiance to the Japanese Emperor, and several thousand evacuees requested repatriation to Japan.

We uphold the exclusion order as of the time it was made and when the petitioner violated it. In doing so, we are not unmindful of the hardships imposed by it upon a large group of American citizens. But hardships are part of war, and war is an aggregation of hardships. All citizens alike, both in and out of uniform, feel the impact of war in greater or lesser measure. Citizenship has its responsibilities as well as its privileges, and in time of war the burden is always heavier. Compulsory exclusion of large groups of citizens from their homes, except under circumstances of direst emergency and peril, is inconsistent with our basic governmental institutions. But when under conditions of modern warfare our shores are threatened by hostile forces, the power to protect must be commensurate with the threatened danger....

It is said that we are dealing here with the case of imprisonment of a citizen in a concentration camp solely because of his ancestry, without evidence or inquiry concerning his loyalty and good disposition towards the United States. Our task would be simple, our duty clear, were this a case involving the imprisonment of a loyal citizen in a concentration camp because of racial prejudice. Regardless of the true nature of the assembly and relocation centers — and we deem it unjustifiable to call them concentration camps with all the ugly connotations that term implies — we are dealing specifically with nothing but an exclusion order. To cast this case into outlines of racial prejudice, without reference to the real military dangers which were presented, merely confuses the issue. Korematsu was not excluded from the Military Area because of hostility to him or his race. He *was* excluded because we are at war with the Japanese Empire, because the properly constituted military authorities feared an invasion of our West Coast and felt constrained to take proper security measures, because they decided that the military urgency of the situation demanded that all citizens of Japanese ancestry be segregated from the West Coast temporarily, and finally, because Congress, reposing its confidence in this time of war in our military leaders — as inevitably it must — determined that they should have the power to do just this. There was evidence of disloyalty on the part of some, the military authorities considered that the need for action was great, and time was short. We cannot — by availing ourselves of the calm perspective of hindsight — now say that at that time these actions were unjustified.

MR. JUSTICE FRANKFURTER, concurring. . . .

The provisions of the Constitution which confer on the Congress and the President powers to enable this country to wage war are as much part of the Constitution as provisions looking to a nation at peace. . . . Therefore, the validity of action under the war power must be judged wholly in the context of war. That action is not to be stigmatized as lawless because like action in times of peace would be lawless. To talk about a military order that expresses an allowable judgment of war needs by those entrusted with the duty of conducting war as "an unconstitutional order" is to suffuse a part of the Constitution with an atmosphere of unconstitutionality. The respective spheres of action of military authorities and of judges are of course very different. But within their sphere, military authorities are no more outside the bounds of obedience to the Constitution than are judges within theirs. . . . To recognize that military orders are "reasonably expedient military precautions" in time of war and yet to deny them constitutional legitimacy makes of the Constitution an instrument for dialectic subtleties not reasonably to be attributed to the hard-headed Framers, of whom a majority had had actual participation in war. If a military order such as that under review does not transcend the means appropriate for conducting war, such action by the military is as constitutional as would be any authorized action by the Interstate Commerce Commission within the limits of the constitutional power to regulate commerce. And being an exercise of the war power explicitly granted by the Constitution for safeguarding the national life by prosecuting war effectively, I find nothing in the Constitution which denies to Congress the power to enforce such a valid military order by making its violation an offense triable in the civil courts. To find that the Constitution does not forbid the military measures now complained of does not carry with it approval of that which Congress and the Executive did. That is their business, not ours.

MR. JUSTICE MURPHY, dissenting.

This exclusion of "all persons of Japanese ancestry, both alien and non-alien," from the Pacific Coast area on a plea of military necessity in the absence of martial law ought not to be approved. Such exclusion goes over "the very brink of constitutional power" and falls into the ugly abyss of racism.

In dealing with matters relating to the prosecution and progress of a war, we must accord great respect and consideration to the judgments of the military authorities who are on the scene and who have full knowledge of the military facts. . . .

At the same time, however, it is essential that there be definite limits to military discretion, especially where martial law has not been declared. Individuals must not be left impoverished of their constitutional rights on a plea of military necessity that has neither substance nor support. Thus, like other claims conflicting with the asserted constitutional rights of the individual, the military claim must subject itself to the judicial process of having its reasonableness determined and its conflicts with other interests reconciled. . . .

The main reasons relied upon by those responsible for the forced evacuation . . . do not prove a reasonable relation between the group characteristics of Japanese Americans and the dangers of invasion, sabotage and espionage. The reasons appear, instead, to be largely an accumulation of much of the misinformation, half-truths and insinuations that for years have been directed against Japanese Americans by people with racial and economic prejudices — the same people who have been among the foremost advocates of the evacuation. A military judgment based upon such racial and sociological considerations is not entitled to the great weight ordinarily given the judgments based upon strictly military considerations. Especially is this so when every charge relative to race, religion, culture, geographical location, and legal and economic status has been substantially discredited by independent studies made by experts in these matters.

The military necessity which is essential to the validity of the evacuation order thus resolves itself into a few intimations that certain individuals actively aided the enemy, from which it is inferred that the entire group of Japanese Americans could not be trusted to be or remain loyal to the United States. No one denies, of course, that there were some disloyal persons of Japanese descent on the Pacific Coast who did all in their power to aid their ancestral land. Similar disloyal activities have been engaged in by many persons of German, Italian and even more pioneer stock in our country. But to infer that examples of individual disloyalty prove group disloyalty and justify discriminatory action against the entire group is to deny that under our system of law individual guilt is the sole basis for deprivation of rights. . . .

MR. JUSTICE JACKSON, dissenting.

Korematsu was born on our soil, of parents born in Japan. The Constitution makes him a citizen of the United States by nativity and a citizen of California by residence. No claim is made that he is not loyal to this country. There is no suggestion that apart from the matter involved here he is not law-abiding and well disposed. Korematsu, however, has been convicted of an act not commonly a crime. It consists merely of being present in the state whereof he is a citizen, near the place where he was born, and where all his life he has lived. . . .

It would be impracticable and dangerous idealism to expect or insist that each specific military command in an area of probable operations will conform to conventional tests of constitutionality. When an area is so beset that it must be put under military control at all, the paramount consideration is that its measures be successful, rather than legal. The armed services must protect a society, not merely its Constitution. The very essence of the military job is to marshal physical force, to remove every obstacle to its effectiveness, to give it every strategic advantage. Defense measures will not, and often should not, be held within the limits that bind civil authority in peace. No court can require such a commander in such circumstances to act as a reasonable man; he may be unreasonably cautious and exacting. Perhaps he should be. But a commander in temporarily focusing the life of a community on defense is carrying out a military program; he is not making law in the sense the courts know the term. He issues orders, and they may have a certain authority as military commands, although they may be very bad as constitutional law.

But if we cannot confine military expedients by the Constitution, neither would I distort the Constitution to approve all that the military may deem expedient. That is what the Court appears to be doing, whether consciously or not. I cannot say, from any evidence before me, that the orders of General DeWitt were not reasonably expedient military precautions, nor could I say that they were. But even if they were permissible military procedures, I deny that it follows that they are constitutional. If, as the Court holds, it does follow, then we may as well say that any military order will be constitutional and have done with it.

The limitation under which courts always will labor in examining the necessity for a military order are illustrated by this case. How does the Court know that these orders have a reasonable basis in necessity? No evidence whatever on that subject has been taken by this or any other court. There is sharp controversy as to the credibility of the DeWitt report. So the Court, having no real evidence before it, has no choice but to accept General DeWitt's own unsworn, self-serving statement, untested by any cross-examination, that what he did was reasonable. And thus it will always be when courts try to look into the reasonableness of a military order.

In the very nature of things, military decisions are not susceptible of intelligent judicial appraisal. They do not pretend to rest on evidence, but are made on information that often would not be admissible and on assumptions that could not be proved. Information in support of an order could not be disclosed to courts without danger that it would reach the enemy. Neither can courts act on communications made in confidence. Hence courts can never have any real alternative to accepting the mere declaration of the authority that issued the order that it was reasonably necessary from a military viewpoint.

Much is said of the danger to liberty from the Army program for deporting and detaining these citizens of Japanese extraction. But a judicial construction of the due process clause that will sustain this order is a far more subtle blow to liberty than the promulgation of the order itself. A military order, however unconstitutional, is not apt to last longer than the military emergency. Even during that period a succeeding commander may revoke it all. But once a judicial opinion rationalizes such an order to show that it conforms to the Constitution, or rather rationalizes the Constitution to show that the Constitution sanctions such an order, the Court for all time has validated the principle of racial discrimination in criminal procedure and of transplanting American citizens. The principle then lies about like a loaded weapon ready for the hand of any authority that can bring forward a plausible claim of an urgent need. Every repetition imbeds that principle more deeply in our law and thinking and expands it to new purposes. . . .

I should hold that a civil court cannot be made to enforce an order which violates constitutional limitations even if it is a reasonable exercise of military authority. The courts can exercise only the judicial power, can apply only law, and must abide by the Constitution, or they cease to be civil courts and become instruments of military policy.

Of course the existence of a military power resting on force, so vagrant, so centralized, so necessarily heedless of the individual, is an inherent threat to liberty. But I would not lead people to rely on this Court for a review that seems to me wholly delusive. The military reasonableness of these orders can only be determined by military superiors. If the people ever let command of the war power fall into irresponsible and unscrupulous hands, the courts wield no power equal to its restraint. The chief restraint upon those who command the physical forces of the country, in the future as in the past, must be their responsibility to the political judgments of their contemporaries and to the moral judgments of history.

My duties as a justice as I see them do not require me to make a military judgment as to whether General DeWitt's evacuation and detention program was a reasonable military necessity. I do not suggest that the courts should have attempted to interfere with the Army in carrying out its task. But I do not think they may be asked to execute a military expedient that has no place in law under the Constitution. I would reverse the judgment and discharge the prisoner.

Ex parte Endo

323 U.S. 283 (1944)

[Appellant Mitsuye Endo, an American citizen of Japanese ancestry, was evacuated from Sacramento, California, in 1942, pursuant to the same military orders at issue in Korematsu, and was removed to the Tule Lake War Relocation Center located at Newell, Modoc County, California, an interim place of residence for Japanese evacuees. At such Centers, the War Relocation Authority was supposed to segregate loyal from disloyal evacuees, detain only the disloyal ones, and relocate loyal ones in selected communities. In connection with such relocation, the War Relocation Authority established a procedure for obtaining leave from Relocation Centers that provided, so far as indefinite leave was concerned, as follows:

> Application for leave clearance is required. An investigation of the applicant is made for the purpose of ascertaining "the probable effect upon the war program and upon the public peace and security of issuing indefinite leave" to the applicant. The grant of leave clearance does not authorize departure from the Relocation Center. Application for indefinite leave must also be made. Indefinite leave may be granted under 14 specified conditions. For example, it may be granted (1) where the applicant proposes to accept an employment offer or an offer of support that has been investigated and approved by the Authority; or (2) where the applicant does not intend to work but has "adequate financial resources to take care of himself" and a Relocation Officer has investigated and approved "public sentiment at his proposed destination", or (3) where the applicant has made arrangements to live at a hotel or in a private home approved by a Relocation Officer while arranging for employment; or (4) where the applicant proposes to accept employment by a federal or local governmental agency; or (5) where the applicant is going to live with designated classes of relatives.

Even if an applicant met these requirements, no leave was granted if the proposed place of residence or employment was within a locality where "community sentiment is unfavorable" or when the applicant planned to go to an area that had been closed by the Authority to the issuance of indefinite leave. Nor did such leave issue if the area where the applicant planned to reside or work was one that had not been cleared for relocation.

In July 1942, Endo filed a petition for a writ of habeas corpus in federal district court, alleging that she was a loyal and law-abiding citizen of the United States, that no charge had been made against her, that she was being unlawfully detained, and that she was confined in the Relocation Center under armed guard and held there against her will. Executive Branch officials acknowledged that she was a loyal and law-abiding citizen, but argued that her continued detention was nonetheless warranted because she planned to live and work in an area where community sentiment was unfavorable to the presence of even loyal Japanese-Americans who had been relocated.]

MR. JUSTICE DOUGLAS delivered the opinion of the Court.

We are of the view that Mitsuye Endo should be given her liberty. In reaching that conclusion we do not come to the underlying constitutional issues which have been argued. For we conclude that, whatever power the War Relocation Authority may have to detain other classes of citizens, it has no authority to subject citizens who are concededly loyal to its leave procedure.

It should be noted at the outset that we do not have here a question such as was presented in *Ex parte Milligan*, or in *Ex parte Quirin*, where the jurisdiction of military tribunals to try persons according to the law of war was challenged in habeas corpus proceedings. Mitsuye Endo is detained by a civilian agency, the War Relocation Authority, not by the military. Moreover, the evacuation program was not left exclusively to the military; the Authority was given a large measure of responsibility for its execution and Congress made its enforcement subject to civil penalties by the Act of March 21, 1942. Accordingly, no questions of military law are involved.

Such power of detention as the Authority has stems from Executive Order No. 9066. That order is the source of the authority delegated by General De Witt in his letter of August 11, 1942. And Executive Order No. 9102 which created the War Relocation Authority purported to do no more than to implement the program authorized by Executive Order No. 9066.

We approach the construction of Executive Order No. 9066 as we would approach the construction of legislation in this field. That Executive Order must indeed be considered along with the Act of March 21, 1942, which ratified and confirmed it as the Order and the statute together laid such basis as there is for participation by civil agencies of the federal government in the evacuation program. Broad powers frequently granted to the President or other executive officers by Congress so that they may deal with the exigencies of war time problems have been sustained. And the Constitution when it committed to the Executive and to Congress the exercise of the war power necessarily gave them wide scope for the exercise of judgment and discretion so that war might be waged effectively and successfully. At the same time, however, the Constitution is as specific in its enumeration of many of the civil rights of the individual as it is in its enumeration of the powers of his government. Thus it has prescribed procedural safeguards surrounding the arrest, detention and conviction of individuals. Some of these are contained in the Sixth Amendment, compliance with which is essential if convictions are to be sustained. And the Fifth Amendment provides that no person shall be deprived of liberty (as well as life or property) without due process of law. Moreover, as a further safeguard against invasion of the basic civil rights of the individual it is provided in Art. I, Sec. 9 of the Constitution that "The Privilege of the Writ of Habeas Corpus shall not be suspended, unless when in Cases of Rebellion or Invasion the public Safety may require it."

We mention these constitutional provisions not to stir the constitutional issues which have been argued at the bar but to indicate the approach which we think should be made to an Act of Congress or an order of the Chief Executive that touches the sensitive area of rights specifically guaranteed by the Constitution.

This Court has quite consistently given a narrower scope for the operation of the presumption of constitutionality when legislation appeared on its face to violate a specific prohibition of the Constitution. We have likewise favored that interpretation of legislation which gives it the greater chance of surviving the test of constitutionality. Those analogies are suggestive here. We must assume that the Chief Executive and members of Congress, as well as the courts, are sensitive to and respectful of the liberties of the citizen. In interpreting a war-time measure we must assume that their purpose was to allow for the greatest possible accommodation between those liberties and the exigencies of war. We must assume, when asked to find implied powers in a grant of legislative or executive authority, that the law makers intended to place no greater restraint on the citizen than was clearly and unmistakably indicated by the language they used.

The Act of March 21, 1942, was a war measure. . . . The purpose and objective of the Act and of these orders are plain. Their single aim was the protection of the war effort against espionage and sabotage. It is in light of that one objective that the powers conferred by the orders must be construed.

Neither the Act nor the orders use the language of detention. . . . Moreover, unlike the case of curfew regulations the legislative history of the Act of March 21, 1942, is silent on detention. And that silence may have special significance in view of the fact that detention in Relocation Centers was no part of the original program of evacuation but developed later to meet what seemed to the officials in charge to be mounting hostility to the evacuees on the part of the communities where they sought to go.

We do not mean to imply that detention in connection with no phase of the evacuation program would be lawful. The fact that the Act and the orders are silent on detention does not of course mean that any power to detain is lacking. Some such power might indeed be necessary to the successful operation of the evacuation program. At least we may so assume. Moreover, we may assume for the purposes of this case that initial detention in Relocation Centers was authorized. But we stress the silence of the legislative history and of the Act and the Executive Orders on the power to detain to emphasize that any such authority which exists must be implied. If there is to be the greatest possible accommodation of the liberties of the citizen with this war measure, any such implied power must be narrowly confined to the precise purpose of the evacuation program.

A citizen who is concededly loyal presents no problem of espionage or sabotage. Loyalty is a matter of the heart and mind not of race, creed, or color. He who is loyal is by definition not a spy or a saboteur. When the power to detain is derived from the power to protect the war effort against espionage and sabotage, detention which has no relationship to that objective is unauthorized. . . .

Community hostility even to loyal evacuees may have been (and perhaps still is) a serious problem. But if authority for their custody and supervision is to be sought on that ground, the Act of March 21, 1942, Executive Order No. 9066, and Executive Order No. 9102, offer no support. And none other is advanced. To read them that broadly would be to assume that the Congress and the President intended that this discriminatory action should be taken against these people wholly on account of their ancestry even though the government conceded their loyalty to this country. We cannot make such an assumption. As the President has said of these loyal citizens: "Americans of Japanese ancestry, like those of many other ancestries, have shown that they can, and want to, accept our institutions and work loyally with the rest of us, making their own valuable contribution to the national wealth and well-being. In vindication of the very ideals for which we are fighting this war it is important to us to maintain a high standard of fair, considerate, and equal treatment for the people of this minority as of all other minorities."

3. Vietnam War
New York Times Co. v. United States
403 U.S. 713 (1971)

[The New York Times and the Washington Post obtained from Daniel Ellsberg, a former Defense Department official, portions of a secret Defense Department study popularly known as the "Pentagon Papers," and began to publish them on June 12 and 17, 1971. The Pentagon Papers analyzed in detail the formulation and execution of American diplomatic and military policy in Indochina. The Executive Branch sought to enjoin further publication of the Pentagon Papers on the ground that publication would jeopardize national security and diplomatic negotiations, would result in the death of Americans, and would prolong the Vietnam War. The lower courts declined to grant an injunction, but did order a stay of publication until June 25. On that date the Supreme Court granted certiorari and continued the stay; on June 26 it heard oral arguments in the cases; and on June 30 it issued the following decision.]

PER CURIAM. . . .
   "Any system of prior restraints of expression comes to this Court bearing a heavy presumption against its constitutional validity." Bantam Books, Inc. v. Sullivan, 372 U.S. 58, 70 (1963). The Government "thus carries a heavy burden of showing justification for the imposition of such a restraint." Organization for a Better Austin v. Keefe, 402 U.S. 415, 419 (1971). The District Court for the Southern District of New York in the *New York Times* case and the District Court for the District of Columbia and the Court of Appeals for the District of Columbia Circuit in the *Washington Post* case held that the Government had not met that burden. We agree. . . .

MR. JUSTICE BLACK, with whom MR. JUSTICE DOUGLAS joins, concurring. . . .
   In the First Amendment the Founding Fathers gave the free press the protection it must have to fulfill its essential role in our democracy. The press was to serve the governed, not the governors. The Government's power to censor the press was abolished so that the press would remain forever free to censure the Government. The press was protected so that it could bare the secrets of government and inform the people. Only a free and unrestrained press can effectively expose deception in government. And paramount among the responsibilities of a free press is the duty to prevent any part of the government from deceiving the people and sending them off to distant lands to die of foreign fevers and foreign shot and shell . . . .
   [W]e are asked to hold that despite the First Amendment's emphatic command, the Executive Branch, the Congress, and the Judiciary can make laws enjoining publication of current news and abridging freedom of the press in the name of "national security." The Government does not even attempt to rely on any act of Congress. Instead it makes the bold and dangerously far-reaching contention that the courts should take it upon themselves to "make" a law abridging freedom of the

press in the name of equity, presidential power and national security, even when the representatives of the people in Congress have adhered to the command of the First Amendment and refused to make such a law. To find that the President has "inherent power" to halt the publication of news by resort to the courts would wipe out the First Amendment and destroy the fundamental liberty and security of the very people the Government hopes to make "secure." . . .

MR. JUSTICE DOUGLAS, with whom MR. JUSTICE BLACK joins, concurring. . . .

[The First Amendment] leaves . . . no room for governmental restraint on the press.

There is, moreover, no statute barring the publication by the press of the material which the Times and the Post seek to use. . . .

So any power that the Government possesses must come from its "inherent power."

The power to wage war is "the power to wage war successfully." *See* Hirabayashi v. United States, 320 U.S. 81, 93. But the war power stems from a declaration of war. The Constitution by Art. I, §8, gives Congress, not the President, power "to declare War." Nowhere are presidential wars authorized. We need not decide therefore what leveling effect the war power of Congress might have.

These disclosures may have a serious impact. But that is no basis for sanctioning a previous restraint on the press. . . .

The dominant purpose of the First Amendment was to prohibit the widespread practice of governmental suppression of embarrassing information. It is common knowledge that the First Amendment was adopted against the widespread use of the common law of seditious libel to punish the dissemination of material that is embarrassing to the powers-that-be. The present cases will, I think, go down in history as the most dramatic illustration of that principle. A debate of large proportions goes on in the Nation over our posture in Vietnam. That debate antedated the disclosure of the contents of the present documents. The latter are highly relevant to the debate in progress. . . .

MR. JUSTICE BRENNAN, concurring. . . .

"The chief purpose of [the First Amendment's] guaranty [is] to prevent previous restraints upon publication." Near v. Minnesota, [283 U.S. 697, 713 (1931)]. Thus, only governmental allegation and proof that publication must inevitably, directly, and immediately cause the occurrence of an event kindred to imperiling the safety of a transport already at sea can support even the issuance of an interim restraining order. In no event may mere conclusions be sufficient: for if the Executive Branch seeks judicial aid in preventing publication, it must inevitably submit the basis upon which that aid is sought to scrutiny by the judiciary. And therefore, every restraint issued in this case, whatever its form, has violated the First Amendment — and not less so because that restraint was justified as necessary to afford the courts an opportunity to examine the claim more thoroughly. Unless and until the Government has clearly made out its case, the First Amendment commands that no injunction may issue.

MR. JUSTICE STEWART, with whom MR. JUSTICE WHITE joins, concurring. . . .

In the absence of the governmental checks and balances present in other areas of our national life, the only effective restraint upon executive policy and power in the areas of national defense and international affairs may lie in an enlightened citizenry — in an informed and critical public opinion which alone can here protect the values of democratic government. For this reason, it is perhaps here that a press that is alert, aware, and free most vitally serves the basic purpose of the First Amendment. For without an informed and free press there cannot be an enlightened people.

Yet it is elementary that the successful conduct of international diplomacy and the maintenance of an effective national defense require both confidentiality and secrecy. Other nations can hardly deal with this Nation in an atmosphere of mutual trust unless they can be assured that their confidences will be kept. And within our own executive departments, the development of considered and intelligent international policies would be impossible if those charged with their formulation could not communicate with each other freely, frankly, and in confidence. In the area of basic national defense the frequent need for absolute secrecy is, of course, self-evident.

I think there can be but one answer to this dilemma, if dilemma it be. The responsibility must be where the power is. If the Constitution gives the Executive a large degree of unshared power in the conduct of foreign affairs and the maintenance of our national defense, then under the Constitution the Executive must have the largely unshared duty to determine and preserve the degree of internal security necessary to exercise that power successfully. It is an awesome responsibility, requiring judgment and wisdom of a high order. . . .

This is not to say that Congress and the courts have no role to play. Undoubtedly Congress has the power to enact specific and appropriate criminal laws to protect government property and preserve government secrets. Congress has passed such laws, and several of them are of very colorable relevance to the apparent circumstances of these cases. . . .

But in the cases before us we are asked neither to construe specific regulations nor to apply specific laws. We are asked, instead, to perform a function that the Constitution gave to the Executive, not the Judiciary. We are asked, quite simply, to prevent the publication by two newspapers of material that the Executive Branch insists should not, in the national interest, be published. I am convinced that the Executive is correct with respect to some of the documents involved. But I cannot say that disclosure of any of them will surely result in direct, immediate, and irreparable damage to our Nation or its people. That being so, there can under the First Amendment be but one judicial resolution of the issues before us. I join the judgments of the Court.

MR. JUSTICE WHITE, with whom MR. JUSTICE STEWART joins, concurring. . . .

At least in the absence of legislation by Congress, based on its own investigations and findings, I am quite unable to agree that the inherent powers of the Executive and the courts reach so far as to authorize remedies having such sweeping potential for inhibiting publications by the press. . . .

The Criminal Code contains numerous provisions potentially relevant to these cases. . . .

It is thus clear that Congress has addressed itself to the problems of protecting the security of the country and the national defense from unauthorized disclosure of potentially damaging information. *Cf.* Youngstown Sheet & Tube Co. v. Sawyer, 343 U.S. 579, 585-586 (1952); *see also id.*, at 593-628 (Frankfurter, J., concurring). It has not, however, authorized the injunctive remedy against threatened publication. It has apparently been satisfied to rely on criminal sanctions and their deterrent effect on the responsible as well as the irresponsible press. I am not, of course, saying that either of these newspapers has yet committed a crime or that either would commit a crime if it published all the material now in its possession. That matter must await resolution in the context of a criminal proceeding if one is instituted by the United States. . . .

MR. JUSTICE MARSHALL, concurring. . . .

It would . . . be utterly inconsistent with the concept of separation of powers for this Court to use its power of contempt to prevent behavior that Congress has specifically declined to prohibit. There would be a similar damage to the basic concept of these coequal branches of Government if when the Executive Branch has adequate authority granted by Congress to protect "national security" it can choose instead to invoke the contempt power of a court to enjoin the threatened conduct. The Constitution provides that Congress shall make laws, the President execute laws, and courts interpret laws. Youngstown Sheet & Tube Co. v. Sawyer, 343 U.S. 579 (1952). It did not provide for government by injunction in which the courts and the Executive Branch can "make law" without regard to the action of Congress. It may be more convenient for the Executive Branch if it need only convince a judge to prohibit conduct rather than ask the Congress to pass a law, and it may be more convenient to enforce a contempt order than to seek a criminal conviction in a jury trial. . . .

MR. CHIEF JUSTICE BURGER, dissenting. . . .

[Chief Justice Burger stated that he "generally" agreed with Justices Harlan and Blackmun, but, because the case was "conducted in unseemly haste," he would extend the stays pending a full trial on the merits.]

MR. JUSTICE HARLAN, with whom THE CHIEF JUSTICE and MR. JUSTICE BLACKMUN join, dissenting. . . .

It is plain to me that the scope of the judicial function in passing upon the activities of the Executive Branch of the Government in the field of foreign affairs is very narrowly restricted. This view is, I think, dictated by the concept of separation of powers upon which our constitutional system rests. . . .

The power to evaluate the "pernicious influence" of premature disclosure is not, however, lodged in the Executive alone. I agree that, in performance of its duty to protect the values of the First Amendment against political pressures, the judiciary must review the initial Executive determination to the point of satisfying itself that the subject matter of the dispute does lie within the proper compass of the President's foreign relations power. Constitutional considerations forbid "a complete abandonment of judicial control." Moreover, the judiciary may properly insist that the determination that disclosure of the subject matter would irreparably impair the national security be made by the head of the Executive Department concerned — here the Secretary of State or the Secretary of Defense — after actual personal consideration by that officer. This safeguard is required in the analogous area of executive claims of privilege for secrets of state. But in my judgment the judiciary may not properly go beyond these two inquiries and redetermine for itself the probable impact of disclosure on the national security. . . .

Even if there is some room for the judiciary to override the executive determination, it is plain that the scope of review must be exceedingly narrow. I can see no indication in the opinions of either the District Court or the Court of Appeals in

the *Post* litigation that the conclusions of the Executive were given even the deference owing to an administrative agency, much less that owing to a co-equal branch
of the Government operating within the field of its constitutional prerogative.

Notes and Questions

1. As the materials in this section show, war tests a nation's commitment to
individual liberties, for during war the tradeoffs between liberty and security are
most apparent. How should the United States reconcile its constitutional commitment to civil liberties with the need to protect national security and to wage war
successfully? Cicero answered a similar question with the now-famous maxim "inter
arma silent leges" ("in times of war the law is silent"). The Court in *Ex parte Milligan*
answered the question quite differently when it stated that the Constitution operates "equally in war and in peace," protecting "all classes of men, at all times, and
under all circumstances." 71 U.S. 2, 120-21 (1866). Former Chief Justice Rehnquist
concluded a study of the question with an intermediate position: "The laws will-
. . . not be silent in time of war, but they will speak with a somewhat different voice."
William H. Rehnquist, All the Laws But One: Civil Liberties in Wartime 225
(1998). Which of these three answers best describes the decisions excerpted in
this section?

2. What do the opinions in this section suggest about the role courts should
play in the enforcement of civil liberties during wartime? Is the political question
doctrine stronger or weaker when civil liberties are at stake? How are courts supposed to judge the validity of the President's claim of military necessity? Do the
answers to these questions depend on whether Congress has declared war? On
whether the Executive Branch acts with or without congressional authorization?
On whether judicial review takes place during or after the war? How does the
analysis from the majority and concurring opinions in *Youngstown* apply to cases
involving the curtailment of civil liberties? Realistically, do courts have the ability to
curb government restrictions on individual liberties during wartime?

3. The suspension clause of Article I, section 9, clause 2 of the Constitution
provides that the "Privilege of the Writ of Habeas Corpus shall not be suspended,
unless when in Cases of Rebellion or Invasion the public Safety may require it." Did
Lincoln have the authority to suspend the writ of habeas corpus before Congress
authorized him to do so in March 1863? Or was Chief Justice Taney right in *Ex parte
Merryman*, excerpted in Chapter 1, that Congress has the exclusive power to suspend the writ? Does it matter that the suspension clause is written in the passive
voice and thus does not name the entity that has the power to suspend? What is the
significance of the fact that the suspension clause is in Article I, which regulates
the powers of Congress, and that all of the other clauses of Article I, section 9 where
the suspension clause appears contemplate qualifications on congressional power?
What about Lincoln's argument that it would be absurd to assign the suspension
power exclusively to a branch of government that might not be able to meet in an
emergency? If a bomb in the Capitol killed every member of Congress, would the
federal government lack the authority to suspend the writ until a new Congress
could be elected? On the other hand, perhaps the Constitution does not contemplate such an extreme situation? In a recent decision that we analyze in the next
section, every Justice of the Supreme Court assumed, with little analysis and in
dicta, that only Congress could suspend the writ of habeas corpus. *See* Hamdi v.

Rumsfeld, 124 S. Ct. 2633 (2004). For an argument that the President has a concurrent authority to suspend the writ of habeas corpus in the absence of contrary action by Congress, see Daniel Farber, Lincoln's Constitution 158-63 (2003).

4. Assuming that the Constitution permits only Congress to suspend the writ, can it be argued that Lincoln nonetheless acted appropriately because it was an emergency and the fate of the United States was at stake? This was the thrust of Lincoln's famous "all the laws but one" argument in his address to Congress. Are you persuaded? Can an emergency ever justify the President in disregarding the Constitution or otherwise not complying with the law?

Answers to this question divide into three groups. An "absolutist" perspective "contends that the government has no emergency power to deal with crisis other than that specifically provided by the Constitution." Jules Lobel, *Emergency Power and the Decline of Liberalism,* 98 Yale L.J. 1385, 1386-87 (1989). This approach is essentially represented by the *Milligan* majority opinion. A "relativist" perspective "argues that the Constitution is a flexible document that permits the President to take whatever measures are necessary in crisis situations." *Id.* at 1388. An example of the relativist perspective can be found in President Franklin Roosevelt's claim that the President has the constitutional power to ignore statutory provisions when "necessary to avert a disaster which would interfere with the winning of the war." *Id.* Professor Lobel notes:

> Both the relativist and absolutist views have an underlying philosophical unity, as both eviscerate the dichotomy between constitutional normalcy and extra-constitutional emergency. The first does so by denying the need for emergency power; the second does so by interpreting the Constitution to provide the Executive with the authority to use such extraordinary power.

98 Yale L.J. at 1388. By contrast, a third view, "liberal constitutionalism," preserves the distinction between normal and emergency power. On this view, "[n]ormalcy permit[s] a governmental structure based on separation of powers, respect for civil liberties and the rule of law, while emergencies require[] strong executive rule, premised not on law and respect for civil liberties, but rather on discretion to take a wide range of actions to preserve the government." *Id.* Lincoln's "all the laws but one" explanation for his suspension of the writ of habeas corpus, combined with his acknowledgment that Congress could judge his actions, is an example of liberal constitutionalism. Similarly, Jefferson wrote:

> A strict observance of the written laws is doubtless one of the high duties of a good citizen, but it is not the highest. The laws of necessity, of self-preservation, of saving our country when in danger, are of higher obligation. To lose our country by a scrupulous adherence to written law, would be to lose the law itself, with life, liberty, property and all those who are enjoying them with us; thus absurdly sacrificing the end to the means. . . . The officer who is called to act on this superior ground, does indeed risk himself on the justice of the controlling powers of the Constitution, and his station makes it his duty to incur that risk. . . . The line of discrimination between cases may be difficult; but the good officer is bound to draw it at his own peril, and throw himself on the justice of his country and the rectitude of his motives.

Letter from Thomas Jefferson to John B. Colvin, Sept. 20, 1810, in 11 The Works of Thomas Jefferson 146, 148-49 (Paul L. Ford ed., 1905).

Which of these three views is most persuasive? What are the advantages and dangers of each of these three views? Is the absolutist perspective practical? How can the relativist perspective be cabined to ensure that the President does not abuse emergency power? Under the liberal perspective, how are emergency situations distinguished from normal ones? Who decides? Which perspective gives a President the right incentives to act only in true emergencies?

In considering these questions, what is the relevance of the oath clause for the President, which requires him to "solemnly swear (or affirm) that [he] will faithfully execute the Office of President of the United States, and will to the best of [his] Ability, preserve, protect and defend the Constitution of the United States"? U.S. Const. art. II, §1, cl. 8. By contrast to the President's oath, all other federal and state officers are required merely to "support" the Constitution. U.S. Const. art. VI, cl. 3. Does the President's unique constitutional duty to "preserve, protect and defend the Constitution" entail a unique authority to disregard law, including the Constitution, when he deems an emergency threat to the Constitution to require it? For a critical analysis of this question in the context of Lincoln's actions, see Michael Stokes Paulsen, *The Constitution of Necessity*, 79 Notre Dame L. Rev. 1257 (2004).

5. *Milligan* raises the question of the constitutional validity of military commissions. A military commission is a non-Article III military court used in three situations: (a) to try enemy belligerents for violations of the laws of war; (b) to administer justice in territory occupied by the military; and (c) to replace civilian courts where martial law has been declared. (A military commission should not be confused with a court martial, which tries members of the U.S. military forces under the Uniform Code of Military Justice, 10 U.S.C. §§801 et seq.) Military commissions typically try defendants before military judges rather than a jury, and typically feature more relaxed procedural and evidentiary rules than are found in civilian trials. Why are trials with these characteristics needed in the military context? Why not have all trials during war in civilian courts?

Military commissions or entities like them have been used throughout U.S. history. During the Revolutionary War, such commissions tried and convicted scores of British spies. Some of these trials were authorized by resolutions of the Continental Congress; others were authorized by U.S. generals in the field. General Andrew Jackson used what we would today call a military commission during the War of 1812 to try a British spy, and again in 1818 to try defendants accused of inciting and assisting the Creek Indians to make war against the United States. In the Mexican-American War, what we today call military commissions were labeled "Councils of War" and were employed extensively by General Winfield Scott. During the U.S. Civil War, military commissions were used in thousands of cases. The United States also used military commissions in the Philippines after the Spanish-American War, and in World War I to try German civilians for various crimes committed in the occupied Rhineland. During and following World War II, U.S. military commissions operated in the United States and in France, Germany, Austria, Italy, Japan, and Korea. We will return to the issue of military commissions in the war on terrorism materials in Section E.

6. What is the holding of *Milligan*? What is the relationship between the majority opinion's constitutional analysis and its analysis of the Habeas Corpus Act of 1863? Why didn't the Court rely exclusively on the Habeas Act, like the dissent? What is at stake in the disagreement between the majority and dissent? Is the discussion of martial law in the last few paragraphs of the majority opinion consistent with its earlier unqualified statements about the applicability of the Constitution during wartime? (Note 14 below discusses the concept of martial law.)

7. The Supreme Court appeared to significantly qualify *Milligan* in *Ex parte Quirin*, 317 U.S. 1 (1942). *Quirin* involved the military commission trial of eight

Nazi saboteurs, including one American citizen, captured in the United States in 1942. The Court in *Quirin* held that Congress had authorized the military commission trials, and that the trials were constitutional. Congressional authorization, the Court reasoned, stemmed from, among other things, Article 15 of the Articles of War. Article 15 stated that Congress's 1916 creation of statutory jurisdiction for courts-martial of U.S. soldiers did not "deprive military commissions . . . of concurrent jurisdiction in respect of offenders or offenses that . . . by the law of war may be triable by such military commissions." Although by its terms Article 15 appeared simply to preserve the historical authority of the President to establish military commissions, the Supreme Court in *Quirin* held that this provision also constituted congressional authorization for the use of military commissions. The Court noted that "by the Articles of War, and especially Article 15, Congress has explicitly provided, so far as it may constitutionally do so, that military tribunals shall have jurisdiction to try offenders or offenses against the law of war in appropriate cases," and held that "Congress [in Article 15] has authorized trial of offenses against the law of war before such commissions."

As for the constitutionality of using military commissions, the Court distinguished *Milligan* on two grounds. First, it noted that Milligan, unlike the Nazi saboteurs, was not part of or associated with the armed forces of the enemy, and thus was not an enemy belligerent entitled to the status of a prisoner of war or subject to the penalties imposed upon unlawful belligerents. Second, the Court reasoned that the Constitution's jury trial provisions were intended only to preserve jury trial rights available at common law, and that the common law did not extend jury trial rights to properly constituted military commissions. Are these arguments persuasive? Why is status as a belligerent or prisoner of war, or the absence of that status, relevant to the constitutionality of military commissions? Did *Milligan* invoke these factors in interpreting the Constitution, or the Habeas Corpus Act of 1863? Why might this matter? Turning to the Court's jury trial argument, can it be reconciled with the fact that "cases arising in the land or naval forces," which is presumably a reference to the trials of U.S. soldiers, is expressly excepted from the Fifth Amendment jury trial right?

8. Under the analysis in *Quirin*, a properly constituted military commission need not comply with the Constitution's procedural requirements for criminal trials, such as the requirement of a jury. But where does Congress, or the President, obtain the constitutional authority to establish such commissions in the first place? Do these commissions fall within Congress's power to declare war? To regulate the armed forces? To define and punish offenses against the law of nations? Do they fall within the President's Commander-in-Chief powers? The general "executive Power"? Or are they part of what the Court suggested in *Curtiss-Wright* were the national government's "powers of external sovereignty" — derived, for example, from international law? *Cf.* Ex parte Vallandigham, 68 U.S. 243, 249 (1863) (stating that military commissions derive their authority from "the common law of war").

Relatedly, is Congress's power to establish military commissions exclusive of the President, or is it concurrent? Could the President, in the absence of congressional approval, establish military commissions under his authority as Commander in Chief? The Court in *Quirin* declined to address this question. But might one interpret Congress's recognition of a preexisting authority, in combination with the historical practice described in Note 5, and with the conceptualization of military tribunals as tools for meting out justice in times of war, to mean that the President can on his or her own establish the tribunals, at least in the absence of congressional disapproval of this practice? *See* Madsen v. Kinsella, 343 U.S. 341, 348 (1952) ("In the absence of attempts by Congress to limit the President's power, it appears that, as Commander-in-Chief of the Army and Navy of the United States, he may, in time of war, establish and prescribe the jurisdiction and procedure of military commissions, and of tribunals in the nature of such commissions, in the territory occupied by the United States by force of arms."). *See also* Military Commissions, 11 Op. Att'y Gen. 305 (1865) (making similar point).

9. The Supreme Court's decisions in *Hirabayashi, Korematsu,* and *Endo* involved the legality, respectively, of World War II curfew orders for Japanese-Americans, exclusion orders for Japanese-Americans, and detentions of Japanese-Americans. Why did the Court uphold the first two and invalidate the third? Was it really because the detention order in *Endo* was not authorized by Congress or the President? Would *Endo* have come out differently if Congress in World War II had expressly authorized the detention of an admittedly loyal Japanese-American on the ground that community sentiment was unfavorable to her release? If not, why did the Court go out of its way to say that it was not reaching the constitutional question? Compare, in this regard, the analysis of the majority opinion in *Milligan*.

10. At the time of the Japanese exclusion order at issue in *Korematsu*, the Japanese Navy was regularly sinking ships off the west coast and firing upon land facilities in California and Oregon, and there was intelligence information suggesting that a Japanese invasion of the west coast was imminent, and was being facilitated by Japanese-Americans in the United States. *See* United States Department of War, Final Report: Japanese Evacuation from the West Coast 1942 (1978). Nonetheless, the decision in *Korematsu* is widely decried. In part this is because the exclusion order overtly discriminated on the basis of race, and also because it focused only on individuals of Japanese ancestry and not on individuals of German or Italian ancestry, even though the United States was also at war with Germany and Italy. Another reason is that many analysts now believe that the order was a disproportionate response to the threat of sabotage, invasion, and espionage by Japanese agents. See, for example, Greg Robinson, By Order of the President: FDR and the Internment of Japanese Americans (2001). Is this *ex post* perspective — which Justice Black's majority opinion in *Korematsu* refers to as the "calm perspective of hindsight" — the proper perspective from which to determine the validity of military orders in response to perceived emergencies? Can judges second-guess military claims of emergency in the midst of a war in which the nation's security is threatened? In answering this question, is it relevant that most claims of emergency or necessity turn out, after the fact, to have been exaggerated? What do you make of Justice Jackson's proposed solution to this conundrum, and Justice Frankfurter's implicit response?

11. The Court in *Endo* employs a canon of statutory construction of wartime congressional authorizations that is very protective of civil liberties, and that appears to impose a clear statement requirement before civil liberties will be contracted. Is such a canon appropriate? Is it consistent with the principle, articulated in decisions like *Curtiss-Wright* and *Dames & Moore*, that congressional authorizations to the President should be construed broadly? Can these decisions be reconciled with *Endo*? Is *Endo* even consistent with *Quirin*, decided less than two years earlier, which as noted above broadly construed the Articles of War to authorize presidential use of military commissions? Might the difference be that *Quirin* involved presidential action against enemy belligerents, while *Endo* involved presidential action against an innocent non-belligerent? Why might this distinction matter? For analysis of these issues, see Curtis A. Bradley & Jack L. Goldsmith,

Congressional Authorization and the War on Terrorism, 118 Harv. L. Rev. 2047, 2102-07 (2005); Cass R. Sunstein, *Minimalism at War*, 2004 Sup. Ct. Rev. 47.

12. Can you discern a common rationale in the various opinions supporting the judgment in the *Pentagon Papers* case? Would the result have been different if Congress had prohibited publication of the information that the New York Times and Washington Post sought to publish? What is the relevance of *Youngstown Steel* to this question? What was the relevance of the fact that the Vietnam War was not a *declared* war, or that at the time of the opinion in 1971, there was widespread national debate over the course and legitimacy of the war?

The *Pentagon Papers* case pits the First Amendment's prior restraint doctrine against the Executive's broad powers in foreign affairs and national security. Although the First Amendment prevailed in the *Pentagon Papers* case, it need not always do so. As the Court stated in Near v. Minnesota, 283 U.S. 697, 716 (1931):

> [The] protection even as to previous restraint is not absolutely unlimited. But the limitation has been recognized only in exceptional cases. . . . No one would question but that a government might prevent actual obstruction to its recruiting service or the publication of the sailing dates of transports or the number and location of troops. . . . The security of the community life may be protected against incitements to acts of violence and the overthrow by force of orderly government.

Id. at 716. What do the various opinions in the *Pentagon Papers* case say about how courts should determine whether the threat to U.S. security is so overwhelming as to permit a prior restraint? What kind of showing could the government have made to demonstrate that national security would be undermined by the publication? Won't it always be necessary for courts to judge how convincing this showing is? Can courts do this with confidence?

Free speech rights have often been curtailed in wartime. An early example is the Sedition Act, enacted during the administration of John Adams on the eve of the undeclared war with France, which provided for fines and imprisonment for the publication of any "false, scandalous and malicious writing," against the government. Another example is the Espionage Act of 1917, which, among other things, provided for fines and imprisonment for speech intended to create resistance to the military draft during World War I. *See* Schenck v. United States, 249 U.S. 47 (1919) (upholding one of the many prosecutions under this statute). For an account of the treatment of free speech during wartime throughout U.S. history, see Geoffrey R. Stone, Perilous Times: Free Speech in Wartime (2004).

13. Former Chief Justice Rehnquist has described a "generally ameliorative trend" in civil liberties during wartime. *See* Rehnquist, All the Laws But One, *supra,* at 221. He notes that World Wars I and II were each, by comparison to the prior war, characterized by increased congressional and judicial involvement in the protection of civil liberties, and diminished governmental attempts to suppress criticism of the war effort. *Id.* at 219-21. Is this an accurate statement? If so, what explains this trend?

14. The Court in *Milligan* suggested that a military commission would have been proper if martial law had legitimately been in effect in Indiana. In Duncan v. Kahanamoku, 327 U.S. 304, 315 (1946), the Court stated:

> [T]he term "martial law" . . . has been employed in various ways by different people and at different times. By some it has been identified as "military law" limited to members of, and those connected with, the armed forces. Others have said that the term does not imply a system of established rules but denotes simply some kind of day to day expression of a general's will dictated by what he considers the imperious necessity of the moment.

See also William E. Birkhimer, Military Government and Martial Law 10 (3d ed. rev. 1914) (defining martial law as "the carrying on of government in domestic territory by military agencies, in whole or in part, with the consequent suspension of some or all civil agencies"). The Constitution does not specifically contemplate martial law, and some commentators believe that the federal government's powers in an emergency are limited to suspending the writ of habeas corpus, see U.S. Const. Art. I, §9, cl. 2, and calling out the militia to "suppress Insurrections and repel Invasions," see U.S. Const. Art. I, §8, cl. 15. *See* Jules Lobel, *Emergency Power and the Decline of Liberalism*, 98 Yale L.J. 1385, 1387 (1989). It is generally agreed that martial law, to the extent valid, can only be imposed out of "military necessity in the actual presence of war." United States v. Diekelman, 92 U.S. 520, 526 (1875). But what does "necessity" entail? And who decides? Does the President have the legal authority to use the armed forces to respond to emergencies within the United States? If so, to what extent is this authority derived from the Constitution? Whatever the source of the President's national emergency power, does the Constitution permit the President to use this power to override civilian rule? Even if it does not, are there situations in which compliance with the Constitution is not the paramount value? To put it differently, are there situations in which the President's duty to protect the nation overrides his or her duty to take care that the laws are faithfully executed?

For further discussion of martial law, see Birkhimer, *supra*; Charles Fairman, The Law of Martial Rule (2d ed. 1943); Robert S. Rankin, When Civil Law Fails: Martial Law and Its Legal Basis in the United States (1939); Frederick Bernays Wiener, A Practical Manual of Martial Law (1940); Major Kirk L. Davies, *The Imposition of Martial Law in the United States*, 49 A.F. L. Rev. 67 (2000); George M. Dennison, *Martial Law: The Development of a Theory of Emergency Powers*, 1776-1861, 18 Am. J. Legal Hist. 52 (1974); Charles Fairman, *The Law of Martial Rule and the National Emergency*, 55 Harv. L. Rev. 1253 (1942); Max Radin, *Martial Law and the State of Siege*, 30 Cal. L. Rev. 634 (1942).

E. THE WAR ON TERRORISM

On September 11, 2001, nineteen individuals connected to the al Qaeda terrorist network hijacked four U.S. airliners. The hijackers crashed two of the airliners into the World Trade Center in New York, and another into the Pentagon in Northern Virginia. The fourth airliner crashed in Pennsylvania, apparently after a struggle between the passengers and the hijackers. The attacks killed thousands of people and caused billions of dollars in property damage. This section analyzes legal issues arising from the subsequent "war on terrorism."

Joint Resolution of Congress Authorizing the Use of Force

Pub. L. No. 107-40 (Sept. 18, 2001)

JOINT RESOLUTION

To authorize the use of United States Armed Forces against those responsible for the recent attacks launched against the United States.

WHEREAS, on September 11, 2001, acts of treacherous violence were committed against the United States and its citizens; and

WHEREAS, such acts render it both necessary and appropriate that the United States exercise its right to self-defense and to protect United States citizens both at home and abroad; and

WHEREAS, in light of the threat to the national security and foreign policy of the United States posed by these grave acts of violence; and

WHEREAS, such acts continue to pose an unusual and extraordinary threat to the national security and foreign policy of the United States; and

WHEREAS, the President has authority under the Constitution to take action to deter and prevent acts of international terrorism against the United States: Now, therefore, be it

Resolved by the Senate and the House of Representatives of the United States of America in Congress assembled, . . .

Section 2   Authorization for Use of United States Armed Forces

(a) IN GENERAL. — That the President is authorized to use all necessary and appropriate force against those nations, organizations, or persons he determines planned, authorized, committed, or aided the terrorist attacks that occurred on September 11, 2001, or harbored such organizations or persons, in order to prevent any future acts of international terrorism against the United States by such nations, organizations or persons.

(b) War Powers Resolution Requirements —

(1) SPECIFIC STATUTORY AUTHORIZATION. — Consistent with Section 8(a)(1) of the War Powers Resolution, the Congress declares that this section is intended to constitute specific statutory authorization within the meaning of Section 5(b) of the War Powers Resolution.

(2) APPLICABILITY OF OTHER REQUIREMENTS. — Nothing in this resolution supercedes any requirement of the War Powers Resolution.

President's Letter to Congress on American Campaign Against Terrorism

(Sept. 24, 2001)

Dear Mr. Speaker: (Dear Mr. President:)

On the morning of September 11, 2001, terrorists hijacked four U.S. commercial airliners. These terrorists coldly murdered thousands of innocent people on those airliners and on the ground, and deliberately destroyed the towers of the World Trade Center and surrounding buildings and a portion of the Pentagon.

In response to these attacks on our territory, our citizens, and our way of life, I ordered the deployment of various combat-equipped and combat support forces to a number of foreign nations in the Central and Pacific Command areas of operations. In the future, as we act to prevent and deter terrorism, I may find it necessary to order additional forces into these and other areas of the world, including into foreign nations where U.S. Armed Forces are already located.

I have taken these actions pursuant to my constitutional authority to conduct U.S. foreign relations and as Commander in Chief and Chief Executive. It is not now possible to predict the scope and duration of these deployments, and the actions necessary to counter the terrorist threat to the United States. It is likely that the American campaign against terrorism will be a lengthy one.

I am providing this report as part of my efforts to keep the Congress informed, consistent with the War Powers Resolution and Senate Joint Resolution 23, which I signed on September 18, 2001. As you know, officials of my Administration and I have been regularly communicating with the leadership and other Members of Congress about the actions we are taking to respond to the threat of terrorism and we will continue to do so. I appreciate the continuing support of the Congress, including its passage of Senate Joint Resolution 23, in this action to protect the security of the United States of America and its citizens, civilian and military, here and abroad.

President's Letter to Congress on American Response to Terrorism

(Oct. 9, 2001)

Dear Mr. Speaker: (Dear Mr. President:)

At approximately 12:30 p.m. (EDT) on October 7, 2001, on my orders, U.S. Armed Forces began combat action in Afghanistan against Al Qaida terrorists and their Taliban supporters. This military action is a part of our campaign against terrorism and is designed to disrupt the use of Afghanistan as a terrorist base of operations.

We are responding to the brutal September 11 attacks on our territory, our citizens, and our way of life, and to the continuing threat of terrorist acts against the United States and our friends and allies. This follows the deployment of various combat-equipped and combat support forces to a number of locations in the Central and Pacific Command areas of operations, as I reported to the Congress on September 24, to prepare for the campaign to prevent and deter terrorism.

I have taken these actions pursuant to my constitutional authority to conduct U.S. foreign relations as Commander in Chief and Chief Executive. It is not possible to know at this time either the duration of combat operations or the scope and duration of the deployment of U.S. Armed Forces necessary to counter the terrorist threat to the United States. As I have stated previously, it is likely that the American campaign against terrorism will be lengthy. I will direct such additional measures as necessary in exercise of our right to self-defense and to protect U.S. citizens and interests.

I am providing this report as part of my efforts to keep the Congress informed, consistent with the War Powers Resolution and Public Law 107-40. Officials of my Administration and I have been communicating regularly with the leadership and other members of Congress, and we will continue to do so. I appreciate the continuing support of the Congress, including its enactment of Public Law 107-40, in these actions to protect the security of the United States of America and its citizens, civilian and military, here and abroad.

Military Order of President George W. Bush, "Detention, Treatment, and Trial of Certain Non-Citizens in the War Against Terrorism"

(Nov. 13, 2001)

By the authority vested in me as President and as Commander in Chief of the Armed Forces of the United States by the Constitution and the laws of the United States of America, including the Authorization for Use of Military Force Joint Resolution (Public Law 107-40, 115 Stat. 224) and sections 821 and 836 of title 10, United States Code, it is hereby ordered as follows....

Section 2. DEFINITION AND POLICY.

(a) The term "individual subject to this order" shall mean any individual who is not a United States citizen with respect to whom I determine from time to time in writing that:

(1) there is reason to believe that such individual, at the relevant times,

(i) is or was a member of the organization known as al Qaeda;

(ii) has engaged in, aided or abetted, or conspired to commit, acts of international terrorism, or acts in preparation therefor, that have caused, threaten to cause, or have as their aim to cause, injury to or adverse effects on the United States, its citizens, national security, foreign policy, or economy; or

(iii) has knowingly harbored one or more individuals described in subparagraphs (i) or (ii) of subsection 2(a)(1) of this order; and

(2) it is in the interest of the United States that such individual be subject to this order....

Section 4. AUTHORITY OF THE SECRETARY OF DEFENSE REGARDING TRIALS OF INDIVIDUALS SUBJECT TO THIS ORDER.

(a) Any individual subject to this order shall, when tried, be tried by military commission for any and all offenses triable by military commission that such individual is alleged to have committed, and may be punished in accordance with the penalties provided under applicable law, including life imprisonment or death.

(b) As a military function and in light of the findings [above]..., the Secretary of Defense shall issue such orders and regulations, including orders for the appointment of one or more military commissions, as may be necessary to carry out subsection (a) of this section.

(c) Orders and regulations issued under subsection (b) of this section shall include, but not be limited to, rules for the conduct of the proceedings of military commissions, including pretrial, trial, and post-trial procedures, modes of proof, issuance of process, and qualifications of attorneys, which shall at a minimum provide for—

(1) military commissions to sit at any time and any place, consistent with such guidance regarding time and place as the Secretary of Defense may provide;

(2) a full and fair trial, with the military commission sitting as the triers of both fact and

(3) admission of such evidence as would, in the opinion of the presiding officer of the military commission ... have probative value to a reasonable person;

(4) in a manner consistent with the protection of [classified information],

(A) the handling of, admission into evidence of, and access to materials and information, and

(B) the conduct, closure of, and access to proceedings;

(5) conduct of the prosecution by one or more attorneys designated by the Secretary of Defense and conduct of the defense by attorneys for the individual subject to this order;

(6) conviction only upon the concurrence of two-thirds of the members of the commission present at the time of the vote, a majority being present;

(7) sentencing only upon the concurrence of two-thirds of the members of the commission present at the time of the vote, a majority being present; and

(8) submission of the record of the trial, including any conviction or sentence, for review and final decision by me or by the secretary of defense if so designated by me for that purpose. . . .

Section 6. ADDITIONAL AUTHORITIES OF THE SECRETARY OF DEFENSE.

(a) As a military function and in light of the findings [above], the Secretary of Defense shall issue such orders and regulations as may be necessary to carry out any of the provisions of this order. . . .

Section 7. RELATIONSHIP TO OTHER LAW AND FORUMS. . . .

(b) With respect to any individual subject to this order —

(1) military tribunals shall have exclusive jurisdiction with respect to offenses by the individual; and

(2) the individual shall not be privileged to seek any remedy or maintain any proceeding, directly or indirectly, or to have any such remedy or proceeding sought on the individual's behalf, in

(i) any court of the United States, or any State thereof

(ii) any court of any foreign nation, or

(iii) any international tribunal.

Hamdi v. Rumsfeld

124 S. Ct. 2633 (2004)

[Shortly after the September 11 attacks, Congress enacted an Authorization for Use of Military Force ("AUMF"), which is excerpted above. Subsequently, U.S. armed forces were sent to Afghanistan, where they engaged in combat with the al Qaeda terrorist organization and the Taliban regime that ruled much of Afghanistan. During that conflict, the U.S. government acquired custody of Yaser Hamdi, a U.S. citizen who was seized in Afghanistan by members of the Northern Alliance (a coalition of Afghanistan groups opposed to the Taliban government) and turned over to the U.S. military. The military subsequently moved Hamdi to the U.S. naval base at Guantanamo Bay, Cuba. Upon learning that he was a U.S. citizen, the military transferred him to a naval brig in Norfolk, Virginia, and then subsequently to a brig in South Carolina. The U.S. government maintained that Hamdi was an "enemy combatant" who could be held without trial. Hamdi's father filed a petition on his behalf in a federal court in Virginia, seeking habeas corpus relief. In response to the petition, the government filed a short declaration (the "Mobbs Declaration") stating that Hamdi had traveled to Afghanistan in the summer of 2001, had affiliated himself with the Taliban military, and had surrendered to Northern Alliance forces while carrying a rifle. The district court concluded that this declaration was insufficient to support Hamdi's detention, calling it "little more than the government's 'sayso.'" The Fourth Circuit reversed, holding that, because it was "undisputed that Hamdi was captured in a zone of active combat in a foreign theater of conflict," no factual inquiry or evidentiary hearing allowing Hamdi to be heard or to rebut the Government's assertions was necessary or proper. The Fourth Circuit also rejected the argument that Hamdi's detention as an enemy combatant was precluded by 18 U.S.C. §4001(a), which provides that "no citizen shall be imprisoned or otherwise detained by the United States except pursuant to an Act of Congress."]

JUSTICE O'CONNOR announced the judgment of the Court and delivered an opinion, in which THE CHIEF JUSTICE, JUSTICE KENNEDY, and JUSTICE BREYER join....

II

The threshold question before us is whether the Executive has the authority to detain citizens who qualify as "enemy combatants." There is some debate as to the proper scope of this term, and the Government has never provided any court with the full criteria that it uses in classifying individuals as such. It has made clear, however, that, for purposes of this case, the "enemy combatant" that it is seeking to detain is an individual who, it alleges, was "'part of or supporting forces hostile to the United States or coalition partners'" in Afghanistan and who "'engaged in an armed conflict against the United States'" there. We therefore answer only the narrow question before us: whether the detention of citizens falling within that definition is authorized.

The Government maintains that no explicit congressional authorization is required, because the Executive possesses plenary authority to detain pursuant to Article II of the Constitution. We do not reach the question whether Article II provides such authority, however, because we agree with the Government's alternative position, that Congress has in fact authorized Hamdi's detention, through the AUMF.

Our analysis on that point, set forth below, substantially overlaps with our analysis of Hamdi's principal argument for the illegality of his detention. He posits that his detention is forbidden by 18 U.S.C. §4001(a). Section 4001(a) states that "no citizen shall be imprisoned or otherwise detained by the United States except pursuant to an Act of Congress." Congress passed §4001(a) in 1971 as part of a bill to repeal the Emergency Detention Act of 1950, which provided procedures for executive detention, during times of emergency, of individuals deemed likely to engage in espionage or sabotage. Congress was particularly concerned about the possibility that the Act could be used to reprise the Japanese internment camps of World War II. The Government again presses two alternative positions. First, it argues that §4001(a), in light of its legislative history and its location in Title 18, applies only to "the control of civilian prisons and related detentions," not to military detentions. Second, it maintains that §4001(a) is satisfied, because Hamdi is being detained "pursuant to an Act of Congress" — the AUMF. Again, because we conclude that the Government's second assertion is correct, we do not address the first. In other words, for the reasons that follow, we conclude that the AUMF is explicit congressional authorization for the detention of individuals in the narrow category we describe (assuming, without deciding, that such authorization is required), and that the AUMF satisfied §4001(a)'s requirement that a detention be "pursuant to an Act of Congress" (assuming, without deciding, that §4001(a) applies to military detentions).

The AUMF authorizes the President to use "all necessary and appropriate force" against "nations, organizations, or persons" associated with the September 11, 2001, terrorist attacks. There can be no doubt that individuals who fought against the United States in Afghanistan as part of the Taliban, an organization known to have supported the al Qaeda terrorist network responsible for those attacks, are individuals Congress sought to target in passing the AUMF. We conclude that detention of individuals falling into the limited category we are considering, for the duration of the particular conflict in which they were captured, is so fundamental and accepted an incident to war as to be an exercise of the "necessary and appropriate force" Congress has authorized the President to use.

The capture and detention of lawful combatants and the capture, detention, and trial of unlawful combatants, by "universal agreement and practice," are "important incidents of war." Ex parte Quirin, [317 U.S. 1, 28 (1942)]. The purpose of detention is to prevent captured individuals from returning to the field of battle and taking up arms once again. . . .

There is no bar to this Nation's holding one of its own citizens as an enemy combatant. In Quirin, one of the detainees, Haupt, alleged that he was a naturalized United States citizen. We held that "citizens who associate themselves with the military arm of the enemy government, and with its aid, guidance and direction enter this country bent on hostile acts, are enemy belligerents within the meaning of . . . the law of war." Id., at 37-38. While Haupt was tried for violations of the law of war, nothing in Quirin suggests that his citizenship would have precluded his mere detention for the duration of the relevant hostilities. Nor can we see any reason for drawing such a line here. A citizen, no less than an alien, can be "part of or supporting forces hostile to the United States or coalition partners" and "engaged in an armed conflict against the United States," Brief for Respondents 3; such a citizen, if released, would pose the same threat of returning to the front during the ongoing conflict.

In light of these principles, it is of no moment that the AUMF does not use specific language of detention. Because detention to prevent a combatant's return to the battlefield is a fundamental incident of waging war, in permitting the use of "necessary and appropriate force," Congress has clearly and unmistakably authorized detention in the narrow circumstances considered here.

Hamdi objects, nevertheless, that Congress has not authorized the indefinite detention to which he is now subject. The Government responds that "the detention of enemy combatants during World War II was just as 'indefinite' while that war was being fought." We take Hamdi's objection to be not to the lack of certainty regarding the date on which the conflict will end, but to the substantial prospect of perpetual detention. We recognize that the national security underpinnings of the "war on terror," although crucially important, are broad and malleable. As the Government concedes, "given its unconventional nature, the current conflict is unlikely to end with a formal cease-fire agreement." The prospect Hamdi raises is therefore not far-fetched. If the Government does not consider this unconventional war won for two generations, and if it maintains during that time that Hamdi might, if released, rejoin forces fighting against the United States, then the position it has taken throughout the litigation of this case suggests that Hamdi's detention could last for the rest of his life.

It is a clearly established principle of the law of war that detention may last no longer than active hostilities.... [The Court cites various treaty provisions and other materials.]

Hamdi contends that the AUMF does not authorize indefinite or perpetual detention. Certainly, we agree that indefinite detention for the purpose of interrogation is not authorized. Further, we understand Congress' grant of authority for the use of "necessary and appropriate force" to include the authority to detain for the duration of the relevant conflict, and our understanding is based on longstanding law-of-war principles. If the practical circumstances of a given conflict are entirely unlike those of the conflicts that informed the development of the law of war, that understanding may unravel. But that is not the situation we face as of this date. Active combat operations against Taliban fighters apparently are ongoing in Afghanistan.... The United States may detain, for the duration of these hostilities, individuals legitimately determined to be Taliban combatants who "engaged in an armed conflict against the United States." If the record establishes that United States troops are still involved in active combat in Afghanistan, those detentions are part of the exercise of "necessary and appropriate force," and therefore are authorized by the AUMF.

Ex parte Milligan, 71 U.S. 2 (1866), does not undermine our holding about the Government's authority to seize enemy combatants, as we define that term today. In that case, the Court made repeated reference to the fact that its inquiry into whether the military tribunal had jurisdiction to try and punish Milligan turned in large part on the fact that Milligan was not a prisoner of war, but a resident of Indiana arrested while at home there. That fact was central to its conclusion. Had Milligan been captured while he was assisting Confederate soldiers by carrying a rifle against Union troops on a Confederate battlefield, the holding of the Court might well have been different. The Court's repeated explanations that Milligan was not a prisoner of war suggest that had these different circumstances been present he could have been detained under military authority for the duration of the conflict, whether or not he was a citizen....

III

Even in cases in which the detention of enemy combatants is legally authorized, there remains the question of what process is constitutionally due to a citizen who disputes his enemy-combatant status. Hamdi argues that he is owed a meaningful and timely hearing and that "extra-judicial detention [that] begins and ends with the submission of an affidavit based on third-hand hearsay" does not comport with the Fifth and Fourteenth Amendments. The Government counters that any more process than was provided below would be both unworkable and "constitutionally intolerable." Our resolution of this dispute requires a careful examination both of the writ of habeas corpus, which Hamdi now seeks to employ as a mechanism of judicial review, and of the Due Process Clause, which informs the procedural contours of that mechanism in this instance.

A

Though they reach radically different conclusions on the process that ought to attend the present proceeding, the parties begin on common ground. All agree that, absent suspension, the writ of habeas corpus remains available to every individual detained within the United States. U.S. Const., Art. I, §9, cl. 2 ("The Privilege of the Writ of Habeas Corpus shall not be suspended, unless when in Cases of Rebellion or Invasion the public Safety may require it"). Only in the rarest of circumstances has Congress seen fit to suspend the writ. At all other times, it has remained a critical check on the Executive, ensuring that it does not detain individuals except in accordance with law. See INS v. St. Cyr, 533 U.S. 289, 301 (2001). All agree suspension of the writ has not occurred here. Thus, it is undisputed that Hamdi was properly before an Article III court to challenge his detention under 28 U.S.C. §2241. Further, all agree that §2241 and its companion provisions provide at least a skeletal outline of the procedures to be afforded a petitioner in federal habeas review. Most notably, §2243 provides that "the person detained may, under oath, deny any of the facts set forth in the return or allege any other material facts," and §2246 allows the taking of evidence in habeas proceedings by deposition, affidavit, or interrogatories.

The simple outline of §2241 makes clear both that Congress envisioned that habeas petitioners would have some opportunity to present and rebut facts and that courts in cases like this retain some ability to vary the ways in which they do so as mandated by due process. The Government recognizes the basic procedural protections required by the habeas statute, but asks us to hold that, given both the flexibility of the habeas mechanism and the circumstances presented in this case, the presentation of the Mobbs Declaration to the habeas court completed the required factual development. It suggests two separate reasons for its position that no further process is due.

B

First, the Government urges the adoption of the Fourth Circuit's holding below — that because it is "undisputed" that Hamdi's seizure took place in a combat zone, the habeas determination can be made purely as a matter of law, with no further hearing or factfinding necessary. This argument is easily rejected. As the dissenters from the denial of rehearing en banc noted, the circumstances surrounding Hamdi's seizure cannot in any way be characterized as "undisputed," as "those circumstances are neither conceded in fact, nor susceptible to concession in law, because Hamdi has not been permitted to speak for himself or even through counsel as to those circumstances." Further, the "facts" that constitute the alleged concession are insufficient to support Hamdi's detention. Under the definition of enemy combatant that we accept today as falling within the scope of Congress' authorization, Hamdi would need to be "part of or supporting forces hostile to the United States or coalition partners" and "engaged in an armed conflict against the United States" to justify his detention in the United States for the duration of the relevant conflict.

The habeas petition states only that "when seized by the United States Government, Mr. Hamdi resided in Afghanistan." An assertion that one resided in a country in which combat operations are taking place is not a concession that one was "captured in a zone of active combat operations in a foreign theater of war," and certainly is not a concession that one was "part of or supporting forces hostile to the United States or coalition partners" and "engaged in an armed conflict against the United States." Accordingly, we reject any argument that Hamdi has made concessions that eliminate any right to further process.

C

The Government's second argument requires closer consideration. This is the argument that further factual exploration is unwarranted and inappropriate in light of the extraordinary constitutional interests at stake. Under the Government's most extreme rendition of this argument, "respect for separation of powers and the limited institutional capabilities of courts in matters of military decision-making in connection with an ongoing conflict" ought to eliminate entirely any individual process, restricting the courts to investigating only whether legal authorization exists for the broader detention scheme. At most, the Government argues, courts should review its determination that a citizen is an enemy combatant under a very deferential "some evidence" standard. Under this review, a court would assume the accuracy of the Government's articulated basis for Hamdi's detention, as set forth in the Mobbs Declaration, and assess only whether that articulated basis was a legitimate one.

In response, Hamdi emphasizes that this Court consistently has recognized that an individual challenging his detention may not be held at the will of the Executive without recourse to some proceeding before a neutral tribunal to determine whether the Executive's asserted justifications for that detention have basis in fact and warrant in law. He argues that the Fourth Circuit inappropriately "ceded power to the Executive during wartime to define the conduct for which a citizen may be detained, judge whether that citizen has engaged in the proscribed conduct, and imprison that citizen indefinitely," and that due process demands that he receive a hearing in which he may challenge the Mobbs Declaration and adduce his own counter evidence. The District Court, agreeing with Hamdi, apparently believed that the appropriate process would approach the process that accompanies a criminal trial. It therefore disapproved of the hearsay nature of the Mobbs Declaration and anticipated quite extensive discovery of various military affairs. Anything less, it concluded, would not be "meaningful judicial review."

Both of these positions highlight legitimate concerns. And both emphasize the tension that often exists between the autonomy that the Government asserts is necessary in order to pursue effectively a particular goal and the process that a citizen contends he is due before he is deprived of a constitutional right. The ordinary mechanism that we use for balancing such serious competing interests, and for determining the procedures that are necessary to ensure that a citizen is not "deprived of life, liberty, or property, without due process of law," U.S. Const., Amdt. 5, is the test that we articulated in Mathews v. Eldridge, 424 U.S. 319 (1976). *Mathews* dictates that the process due in any given instance is determined by weighing "the private interest that will be affected by the official action" against the Government's asserted interest, "including the function involved" and the burdens the Government would face in providing greater process. 424 U.S., at 335. The

Mathews calculus then contemplates a judicious balancing of these concerns, through an analysis of "the risk of an erroneous deprivation" of the private interest if the process were reduced and the "probable value, if any, of additional or substitute safeguards." Ibid. We take each of these steps in turn.

1

It is beyond question that substantial interests lie on both sides of the scale in this case. Hamdi's "private interest . . . affected by the official action," is the most elemental of liberty interests — the interest in being free from physical detention by one's own government. . . .

Nor is the weight on this side of the *Mathews* scale offset by the circumstances of war or the accusation of treasonous behavior, for "it is clear that commitment for any purpose constitutes a significant deprivation of liberty that requires due process protection," Jones v. United States, 463 U.S. 354, 361 (1983) (emphasis added; internal quotation marks omitted), and at this stage in the Mathews calculus, we consider the interest of the erroneously detained individual. . . . Moreover, as critical as the Government's interest may be in detaining those who actually pose an immediate threat to the national security of the United States during ongoing international conflict, history and common sense teach us that an unchecked system of detention carries the potential to become a means for oppression and abuse of others who do not present that sort of threat. . . .

2

On the other side of the scale are the weighty and sensitive governmental interests in ensuring that those who have in fact fought with the enemy during a war do not return to battle against the United States. As discussed above, the law of war and the realities of combat may render such detentions both necessary and appropriate, and our due process analysis need not blink at those realities. Without doubt, our Constitution recognizes that core strategic matters of warmaking belong in the hands of those who are best positioned and most politically accountable for making them. Dep't of the Navy v. Egan, 484 U.S. 518, 530 (1988) (noting the reluctance of the courts "to intrude upon the authority of the Executive in military and national security affairs"); Youngstown Sheet & Tube Co. v. Sawyer, 343 U.S. 579, 587 (1952) (acknowledging "broad powers in military commanders engaged in day-to-day fighting in a theater of war").

The Government also argues at some length that its interests in reducing the process available to alleged enemy combatants are heightened by the practical difficulties that would accompany a system of trial-like process. In its view, military officers who are engaged in the serious work of waging battle would be unnecessarily and dangerously distracted by litigation half a world away, and discovery into military operations would both intrude on the sensitive secrets of national defense and result in a futile search for evidence buried under the rubble of war. To the extent that these burdens are triggered by heightened procedures, they are properly taken into account in our due process analysis.

3

Striking the proper constitutional balance here is of great importance to the Nation during this period of ongoing combat. But it is equally vital that our calculus not give short shrift to the values that this country holds dear or to the privilege that is American citizenship. It is during our most challenging and uncertain moments that our Nation's commitment to due process is most severely tested; and it is in those times that we must preserve our commitment at home to the principles for which we fight abroad....

With due recognition of these competing concerns, we believe that neither the process proposed by the Government nor the process apparently envisioned by the District Court below strikes the proper constitutional balance when a United States citizen is detained in the United States as an enemy combatant. That is, "the risk of erroneous deprivation" of a detainee's liberty interest is unacceptably high under the Government's proposed rule, while some of the "additional or substitute procedural safeguards" suggested by the District Court are unwarranted in light of their limited "probable value" and the burdens they may impose on the military in such cases.

We therefore hold that a citizen-detainee seeking to challenge his classification as an enemy combatant must receive notice of the factual basis for his classification, and a fair opportunity to rebut the Government's factual assertions before a neutral decisionmaker....

At the same time, the exigencies of the circumstances may demand that, aside from these core elements, enemy combatant proceedings may be tailored to alleviate their uncommon potential to burden the Executive at a time of ongoing military conflict. Hearsay, for example, may need to be accepted as the most reliable available evidence from the Government in such a proceeding. Likewise, the Constitution would not be offended by a presumption in favor of the Government's evidence, so long as that presumption remained a rebuttable one and fair opportunity for rebuttal were provided. Thus, once the Government puts forth credible evidence that the habeas petitioner meets the enemy-combatant criteria, the onus could shift to the petitioner to rebut that evidence with more persuasive evidence that he falls outside the criteria. A burden-shifting scheme of this sort would meet the goal of ensuring that the errant tourist, embedded journalist, or local aid worker has a chance to prove military error while giving due regard to the Executive once it has put forth meaningful support for its conclusion that the detainee is in fact an enemy combatant. In the words of *Mathews*, process of this sort would sufficiently address the "risk of erroneous deprivation" of a detainee's liberty interest while eliminating certain procedures that have questionable additional value in light of the burden on the Government.

We think it unlikely that this basic process will have the dire impact on the central functions of warmaking that the Government forecasts. The parties agree that initial captures on the battlefield need not receive the process we have discussed here; that process is due only when the determination is made to continue to hold those who have been seized. The Government has made clear in its briefing that documentation regarding battlefield detainees already is kept in the ordinary course of military affairs. Any factfinding imposition created by requiring a knowledgeable affiant to summarize these records to an independent tribunal is a minimal one. Likewise, arguments that military officers ought not have to wage war under the threat of litigation lose much of their steam when factual disputes at enemy-combatant hearings are limited to the alleged combatant's acts. This focus meddles little, if at all, in the strategy or conduct of war, inquiring only into the appropriateness of continuing to detain an individual claimed to have taken up arms against the United States. While we accord the greatest respect and consideration to the judgments of military authorities in matters relating to the actual prosecution of a war, and recognize that the scope of that discretion necessarily is wide, it does not infringe on the core role of the military for the courts to exercise their own time-honored and constitutionally mandated roles of reviewing and resolving claims like those presented here....

D

In so holding, we necessarily reject the Government's assertion that separation of powers principles mandate a heavily circumscribed role for the courts in such circumstances. Indeed, the position that the courts must forgo any examination of the individual case and focus exclusively on the legality of the broader detention scheme cannot be mandated by any reasonable view of separation of powers, as this approach serves only to condense power into a single branch of government. We have long since made clear that a state of war is not a blank check for the President when it comes to the rights of the Nation's citizens. Youngstown Sheet & Tube, 343 U.S., at 587. Whatever power the United States Constitution envisions for the Executive in its exchanges with other nations or with enemy organizations in times of conflict, it most assuredly envisions a role for all three branches when individual liberties are at stake. Likewise, we have made clear that, unless Congress acts to suspend it, the Great Writ of habeas corpus allows the Judicial Branch to play a necessary role in maintaining this delicate balance of governance, serving as an important judicial check on the Executive's discretion in the realm of detentions. Thus, while we do not question that our due process assessment must pay keen attention to the particular burdens faced by the Executive in the context of military action, it would turn our system of checks and balances on its head to suggest that a citizen could not make his way to court with a challenge to the factual basis for his detention by his government, simply because the Executive opposes making available such a challenge. Absent suspension of the writ by Congress, a citizen detained as an enemy combatant is entitled to this process.

Because we conclude that due process demands some system for a citizen detainee to refute his classification, the proposed "some evidence" standard is inadequate. Any process in which the Executive's factual assertions go wholly unchallenged or are simply presumed correct without any opportunity for the alleged combatant to demonstrate otherwise falls constitutionally short. As the Government itself has recognized, we have utilized the "some evidence" standard in the past as a standard of review, not as a standard of proof. That is, it primarily has been employed by courts in examining an administrative record developed after an adversarial proceeding — one with process at least of the sort that we today hold is constitutionally mandated in the citizen enemy-combatant setting. This standard therefore is ill suited to the situation in which a habeas petitioner has received no prior proceedings before any tribunal and had no prior opportunity to rebut the Executive's factual assertions before a neutral decisionmaker.

Today we are faced only with such a case. Aside from unspecified "screening" processes, and military interrogations in which the Government suggests Hamdi could have contested his classification, Hamdi has received no process. An interrogation by one's captor, however effective an intelligence-gathering tool, hardly constitutes a constitutionally adequate factfinding before a neutral decisionmaker.... Plainly, the "process" Hamdi has received is not that to which he is entitled under the Due Process Clause.

There remains the possibility that the standards we have articulated could be met by an appropriately authorized and properly constituted military tribunal. Indeed, it is notable that military regulations already provide for such process in related instances, dictating that tribunals be made available to determine the status of enemy detainees who assert prisoner-of-war status under the Geneva Convention. In the absence of such process, however, a court that receives a petition for a writ of habeas corpus from an alleged enemy combatant must itself ensure that the minimum requirements of due process are achieved. Both courts below recognized as much, focusing their energies on the question of whether Hamdi was due an opportunity to rebut the Government's case against him. The Government, too, proceeded on this assumption, presenting its affidavit and then seeking that it be evaluated under a deferential standard of review based on burdens that it alleged would accompany any greater process. As we have discussed, a habeas court in a case such as this may accept affidavit evidence like that contained in the Mobbs Declaration, so long as it also permits the alleged combatant to present his own factual case to rebut the Government's return. We anticipate that a District Court would proceed with the caution that we have indicated is necessary in this setting, engaging in a factfinding process that is both prudent and incremental. We have no reason to doubt that courts faced with these sensitive matters will pay proper heed both to the matters of national security that might arise in an individual case and to the constitutional limitations safeguarding essential liberties that remain vibrant even in times of security concerns.

IV

Hamdi asks us to hold that the Fourth Circuit also erred by denying him immediate access to counsel upon his detention and by disposing of the case without permitting him to meet with an attorney. Since our grant of certiorari in this case, Hamdi has been appointed counsel, with whom he has met for consultation purposes on several occasions, and with whom he is now being granted unmonitored meetings. He unquestionably has the right to access to counsel in connection with the proceedings on remand. No further consideration of this issue is necessary at this stage of the case....

JUSTICE SOUTER, with whom JUSTICE GINSBURG joins, concurring in part, dissenting in part, and concurring in the judgment....

The threshold issue is how broadly or narrowly to read the Non-Detention Act, the tone of which is severe: "No citizen shall be imprisoned or otherwise detained by the United States except pursuant to an Act of Congress." Should the severity of the Act be relieved when the Government's stated factual justification for incommunicado detention is a war on terrorism, so that the Government may be said to act "pursuant" to congressional terms that fall short of explicit authority to imprison individuals? With one possible though important qualification, the answer has to be no. For a number of reasons, the prohibition within §4001(a) has to be read broadly to accord the statute a long reach and to impose a burden of justification on the Government.

First, the circumstances in which the Act was adopted point the way to this interpretation. The provision superseded a cold-war statute, the Emergency Detention Act of 1950, which had authorized the Attorney General, in time of emergency, to detain anyone reasonably thought likely to engage in espionage or sabotage. That statute was repealed in 1971 out of fear that it could authorize a repetition of the World War II internment of citizens of Japanese ancestry; Congress meant to preclude another episode like the one described in Korematsu v. United States,

323 U.S. 214 (1944). See H. R. Rep. No. 92-116, pp. 2, 4-5 (1971). While Congress might simply have struck the 1950 statute, in considering the repealer the point was made that the existing statute provided some express procedural protection, without which the Executive would seem to be subject to no statutory limits protecting individual liberty. It was in these circumstances that a proposed limit on Executive action was expanded to the inclusive scope of §4001(a) as enacted.

The fact that Congress intended to guard against a repetition of the World War II internments when it repealed the 1950 statute and gave us §4001(a) provides a powerful reason to think that §4001(a) was meant to require clear congressional authorization before any citizen can be placed in a cell. It is not merely that the legislative history shows that §4001(a) was thought necessary in anticipation of times just like the present, in which the safety of the country is threatened. To appreciate what is most significant, one must only recall that the internments of the 1940's were accomplished by Executive action. Although an Act of Congress ratified and confirmed an Executive order authorizing the military to exclude individuals from defined areas and to accommodate those it might remove, see Ex parte Endo, 323 U.S. 283, 285-288 (1944), the statute said nothing whatever about the detention of those who might be removed; internment camps were creatures of the Executive, and confinement in them rested on assertion of Executive authority. When, therefore, Congress repealed the 1950 Act and adopted §4001(a) for the purpose of avoiding another Korematsu, it intended to preclude reliance on vague congressional authority (for example, providing "accommodations" for those subject to removal) as authority for detention or imprisonment at the discretion of the Executive (maintaining detention camps of American citizens, for example). In requiring that any Executive detention be "pursuant to an Act of Congress," then, Congress necessarily meant to require a congressional enactment that clearly authorized detention or imprisonment.

Second, when Congress passed §4001(a) it was acting in light of an interpretive regime that subjected enactments limiting liberty in wartime to the requirement of a clear statement and it presumably intended §4001(a) to be read accordingly. This need for clarity was unmistakably expressed in Ex parte Endo, decided the same day as Korematsu. Endo began with a petition for habeas corpus by an interned citizen claiming to be loyal and law-abiding and thus "unlawfully detained." 323 U.S. at 294. The petitioner was held entitled to habeas relief in an opinion that set out this principle for scrutinizing wartime statutes in derogation of customary liberty:

> "In interpreting a wartime measure we must assume that [its] purpose was to allow for the greatest possible accommodation between . . . liberties and the exigencies of war. We must assume, when asked to find implied powers in a grant of legislative or executive authority, that the law makers intended to place no greater restraint on the citizen than was clearly and unmistakably indicated by the language they used." Id. at 300.

Congress's understanding of the need for clear authority before citizens are kept detained is itself therefore clear, and §4001(a) must be read to have teeth in its demand for congressional authorization.

Finally, even if history had spared us the cautionary example of the internments in World War II, even if there had been no Korematsu, and Endo had set out no principle of statutory interpretation, there would be a compelling reason to read §4001(a) to demand manifest authority to detain before detention is authorized. The defining character of American constitutional government is its constant tension between security and liberty, serving both by partial helpings of each. In a government of separated powers, deciding finally on what is a reasonable degree of guaranteed liberty whether in peace or war (or some condition in between) is not well entrusted to the Executive Branch of Government, whose particular responsibility is to maintain security. For reasons of inescapable human nature, the branch of the Government asked to counter a serious threat is not the branch on which to rest the Nation's entire reliance in striking the balance between the will to win and the cost in liberty on the way to victory; the responsibility for security will naturally amplify the claim that security legitimately raises. A reasonable balance is more likely to be reached on the judgment of a different branch, just as Madison said in remarking that "the constant aim is to divide and arrange the several offices in such a manner as that each may be a check on the other — that the private interest of every individual may be a sentinel over the public rights." The Federalist No. 51, p. 349 (J. Cooke ed. 1961). Hence the need for an assessment by Congress before citizens are subject to lockup, and likewise the need for a clearly expressed congressional resolution of the competing claims.

Under this principle of reading §4001(a) robustly to require a clear statement of authorization to detain, none of the Government's arguments suffices to justify Hamdi's detention.

First, there is the argument that §4001(a) does not even apply to wartime military detentions, a position resting on the placement of §4001(a) in Title 18 of the United States Code, the gathering of federal criminal law. The text of the statute does not, however, so limit its reach, and the legislative history of the provision shows its placement in Title 18 was not meant to render the statute more restricted than its terms. The draft of what is now §4001(a) as contained in the original bill prohibited only imprisonment unauthorized by Title 18. See H. R. Rep. No. 92- 116, at 4. In response to the Department of Justice's objection that the original draft seemed to assume wrongly that all provisions for the detention of convicted persons would be contained in Title 18, the provision was amended by replacing a reference to that title with the reference to an "Act of Congress." Id., at 3. The Committee on the Judiciary, discussing this change, stated that "[limiting] detention of citizens . . . to situations in which . . . an Act of Congres[s] exists" would "assure that no detention camps can be established without at least the acquiescence of the Congress." Id., at 5. This understanding, that the amended bill would sweep beyond imprisonment for crime and apply to Executive detention in furtherance of wartime security, was emphasized in an extended debate. . . . This legislative history indicates that Congress was aware that §4001(a) would limit the Executive's power to detain citizens in wartime to protect national security, and it is fair to say that the prohibition was thus intended to extend not only to the exercise of power to vindicate the interests underlying domestic criminal law, but to statutorily unauthorized detention by the Executive for reasons of security in wartime, just as Hamdi claims.

Next, there is the Government's claim, accepted by the Court, that the terms of the Force Resolution are adequate to authorize detention of an enemy combatant under the circumstances described, a claim the Government fails to support sufficiently to satisfy §4001(a) as read to require a clear statement of authority to detain. Since the Force Resolution was adopted one week after the attacks of September 11, 2001, it naturally speaks with some generality, but its focus is clear, and that is on the use of military power. It is fairly read to authorize the use of armies and weapons, whether against other armies or individual terrorists. But, like the statute discussed in *Endo*, it never so much as uses the word detention, and there is no reason to think Congress might have perceived any need to augment Executive power to deal with dangerous citizens within the United States, given the well-stocked statutory arsenal of defined criminal offenses covering the gamut of actions that a citizen sympathetic to terrorists might commit....

Even so, there is one argument for treating the Force Resolution as sufficiently clear to authorize detention of a citizen consistently with §4001(a). Assuming the argument to be sound, however, the Government is in no position to claim its advantage.

Because the Force Resolution authorizes the use of military force in acts of war by the United States, the argument goes, it is reasonably clear that the military and its Commander in Chief are authorized to deal with enemy belligerents according to the treaties and customs known collectively as the laws of war. Accordingly, the United States may detain captured enemies, and Ex parte Quirin, 317 U.S. 1 (1942), may perhaps be claimed for the proposition that the American citizenship of such a captive does not as such limit the Government's power to deal with him under the usages of war. Thus, the Government here repeatedly argues that Hamdi's detention amounts to nothing more than customary detention of a captive taken on the field of battle: if the usages of war are fairly authorized by the Force Resolution, Hamdi's detention is authorized for purposes of §4001(a).

There is no need, however, to address the merits of such an argument in all possible circumstances. For now it is enough to recognize that the Government's stated legal position in its campaign against the Taliban (among whom Hamdi was allegedly captured) is apparently at odds with its claim here to be acting in accordance with customary law of war and hence to be within the terms of the Force Resolution in its detention of Hamdi. In a statement of its legal position cited in its brief, the Government says that "the Geneva Convention applies to the Taliban detainees." Office of the White House Press Secretary, Fact Sheet, Status of Detainees at Guantanamo (Feb. 7, 2002). Hamdi presumably is such a detainee, since according to the Government's own account, he was taken bearing arms on the Taliban side of a field of battle in Afghanistan. He would therefore seem to qualify for treatment as a prisoner of war under the Third Geneva Convention, to which the United States is a party. Article 4 of the Geneva Convention (III) Relative to the Treatment of Prisoners of War, Aug. 12, 1949, [1955] 6 U.S. T. 3316, 3320, T. I. A. S. No. 3364.

By holding him incommunicado, however, the Government obviously has not been treating him as a prisoner of war, and in fact the Government claims that no Taliban detainee is entitled to prisoner of war status. This treatment appears to be a violation of the Geneva Convention provision that even in cases of doubt, captives are entitled to be treated as prisoners of war "until such time as their status has been determined by a competent tribunal." Art. 5, 6 U.S. T., at 3324. The Government answers that the President's determination that Taliban detainees do not qualify as prisoners of war is conclusive as to Hamdi's status and removes any doubt that would trigger application of the Convention's tribunal requirement. But reliance on this categorical pronouncement to settle doubt is apparently at odds with the military regulation, Enemy Prisoners of War, Retained Personnel, Civilian Internees and Other Detainees, Army Reg. 190-8, §§1-5, 1-6 (1997), adopted to implement the Geneva Convention, and setting out a detailed procedure for a military tribunal to determine an individual's status. See, e.g., id., §1-6 ("A competent tribunal shall be composed of three commissioned officers"; a "written record shall be made of proceedings"; "[p]roceedings shall be open" with certain exceptions;

"[p]ersons whose status is to be determined shall be advised of their rights at the beginning of their hearings," "allowed to attend all open sessions," "allowed to call witnesses if reasonably available, and to question those witnesses called by the Tribunal," and to "have a right to testify"; and a tribunal shall determine status by a "[p]reponderance of evidence"). One of the types of doubt these tribunals are meant to settle is whether a given individual may be, as Hamdi says he is, an "[i]nnocent civilian who should be immediately returned to his home or released." *Id.*, 1-6e(10)(*c*). The regulation, jointly promulgated by the Headquarters of the Departments of the Army, Navy, Air Force, and Marine Corps, provides that "[p]ersons who have been determined by a competent tribunal not to be entitled to prisoner of war status may not be executed, imprisoned, or otherwise penalized without further proceedings to determine what acts they have committed and what penalty should be imposed." *Id.*, §1-6*g*. The regulation also incorporates the Geneva Convention's presumption that in cases of doubt, "persons shall enjoy the protection of the . . . Convention until such time as their status has been determined by a competent tribunal." *Id.*, §1-6*a*. Thus, there is reason to question whether the United States is acting in accordance with the laws of war it claims as authority.

Whether, or to what degree, the Government is in fact violating the Geneva Convention and is thus acting outside the customary usages of war are not matters I can resolve at this point. What I can say, though, is that the Government has not made out its claim that in detaining Hamdi in the manner described, it is acting in accord with the laws of war authorized to be applied against citizens by the Force Resolution. I conclude accordingly that the Government has failed to support the position that the Force Resolution authorizes the described detention of Hamdi for purposes of §4001(a).

[Despite their reading of §4001(a), Justices Souter and Ginsburg joined the plurality's call for a hearing at which Hamdi could present evidence to contest his status as an enemy combatant, in order "to give practical effect to the conclusions of eight members of the Court rejecting the Government's position."]

[Justice Scalia filed a dissent, joined by Justice Stevens. Relying on Ex parte Milligan, they argued that a U.S. citizen could not be held by the government in the United States without trial absent a suspension of the writ of habeas corpus. They also criticized the plurality for its "Mr. Fix-it Mentality" and for "view[ing] it as its mission to Make Everything Come Out Right, rather than merely to decree the consequences, as far as individual rights are concerned, of the other two branches' actions and omissions." "The problem with this approach," they said, "is not only that it steps out of the courts' modest and limited role in a democratic society; but that by repeatedly doing what it thinks the political branches ought to do it encourages their lassitude and saps the vitality of government by the people."]

[Justice Thomas filed a dissent. He agreed with the plurality that the AUMF constituted a congressional authorization of the detention. He disagreed, however, with the plurality's due process analysis. Citing decisions such as *The Prize Cases*, *Curtiss-Wright*, and *Dames & Moore*, he argued that, "[b]y detaining Hamdi, the President, in the prosecution of a war and authorized by Congress, has acted well within his authority. Hamdi thereby received all the process to which he was due under the circumstances. I therefore believe that this is no occasion to balance the competing interests, as the plurality unconvincingly attempts to do."]

Notes and Questions

1. *Background.* After the September 11 terrorist attacks, the U.S. military detained hundreds of al Qaeda and Taliban prisoners in both Afghanistan and at the U.S. naval base at Guantanamo Bay, Cuba. The U.S. military also detained some individuals within the United States, including at least two U.S. citizens — Yaser Hamdi and Jose Padilla. The Bush Administration maintained that both the foreign detainees and the U.S. citizen detainees qualified as "enemy combatants" who could be held without trial until the end of hostilities.

A number of World War II-era decisions are potentially relevant to these detentions. In Ex parte Quirin, 317 U.S. 1 (1942), which is discussed in the Notes in Section D, the Supreme Court upheld the constitutional authority of the President to try eight German agents, including an alleged U.S. citizen, by means of a military commission. The agents had been apprehended after sneaking into the United States with the intent of carrying out acts of sabotage. The Court construed the Articles of War (the predecessor to the current Uniform Code of Military Justice) as authorizing the President to use military commissions to try offenses against the laws of war. The Court therefore concluded that it was "unnecessary for present purposes to determine to what extent the President as Commander in Chief has constitutional power to create military commissions without the support of Congressional legislation." *Id.* at 29. The President's delegated power to use a military commission, the court reasoned, applied even with respect to the alleged U.S. citizen:

> Citizenship in the United States of an enemy belligerent does not relieve him from the consequences of a belligerency which is unlawful because in violation of the law of war. Citizens who associate themselves with the military arm of the enemy government, and with its aid, guidance and direction enter this country bent on hostile acts, are enemy belligerents [under international law].

Id. at 37-38. The Court further explained that international law allows the use of military commissions for unlawful combatants, and in doing so noted that lawful combatants are subject to detention:

> By universal agreement and practice, the law of war draws a distinction between the armed forces and the peaceful populations of belligerent nations and also between those who are lawful and unlawful combatants. Lawful combatants are subject to capture and detention as prisoners of war by opposing military forces. Unlawful combatants are likewise subject to capture and detention, but in addition they are subject to trial and punishment by military tribunals for acts which render their belligerency unlawful.

Id. at 30-31. *See also* Colepaugh v. Looney, 235 F.2d 429 (10th Cir. 1956) (denying habeas corpus relief to U.S. citizen tried by military commission for violating the laws of war during World War II).

Another potentially relevant decision is Johnson v. Eisentrager, 339 U.S. 763 (1950). That case involved a habeas corpus petition filed by 21 German nationals who were being held at a U.S. military prison in post-World War II occupied Germany. The petitioners had been tried by a U.S. military commission in China and had been found guilty of violating the laws of war by engaging in continued military activity against the United States after Germany's surrender. In a 6-3 decision, the Court held that U.S. courts lacked jurisdiction to hear the petition. The Court noted:

> We are here confronted with a decision whose basic premise is that these prisoners are entitled, as a constitutional right, to sue in some court of the United States for a writ of

habeas corpus. To support that assumption we must hold that a prisoner of our military authorities is constitutionally entitled to the writ, even though he (a) is an enemy alien; (b) has never been or resided in the United States; (c) was captured outside of our territory and there held in military custody as a prisoner of war; (d) was tried and convicted by a Military Commission sitting outside the United States; (e) for offenses against laws of war committed outside the United States; (f) and is at all times imprisoned outside the United States.

The Court also explained that "the privilege of litigation has been extended to aliens, whether friendly or enemy, only because permitting their presence in the country implied protection," whereas "[n]o such basis can be invoked here, for these prisoners at no relevant time were within any territory over which the United States is sovereign, and the scenes of their offense, their capture, their trial and their punishment were all beyond the territorial jurisdiction of any court of the United States."

Also potentially relevant is In re Territo, 156 F.2d 142 (9th Cir. 1946), in which the U.S. Court of Appeals for the Ninth Circuit held that the U.S. military could hold even a U.S. citizen as a prisoner of war until the end of hostilities. In that case, a U.S. citizen was captured in Italy while serving in the Italian Army during World War II and was held in the United States as a prisoner of war. Citing Quirin, the court concluded that "all persons who are active in opposing an army in war may be captured and except for spies and other non-uniformed plotters and actors for the enemy are prisoners of war." Id. at 145. The court further explained that, "The object of capture is to prevent the captured individual from serving the enemy. He is disarmed and from then on he must be removed as completely as practicable from the front, treated humanely and in time exchanged, repatriated or otherwise released." Id.

In addition to these decisions, there is at least one treaty that may be relevant — the 1949 Geneva Convention Relative to the Treatment of Prisoners of War, also known as the Third Geneva Convention. The Convention applies "to all cases of declared war or of any other armed conflict which may arise between two or more of the High Contracting Parties." Both the United States and Afghanistan are parties to the Convention. Article 4 of the Convention defines prisoners of war (POWs) as follows:

Prisoners of war, in the sense of the present Convention, are persons belonging to one of the following categories, who have fallen into the power of the enemy:

1. Members of the armed forces of a Party to the conflict as well as members of militias or volunteer corps forming part of such armed forces.

2. Members of other militias and members of other volunteer corps, including those of organized resistance movements, belonging to a Party to the conflict and operating in or outside their own territory, even if this territory is occupied, provided that such militias or volunteer corps, including such organized resistance movements, fulfil the following conditions:

(a) That of being commanded by a person responsible for his subordinates;
(b) That of having a fixed distinctive sign recognizable at a distance;
(c) That of carrying arms openly;
(d) That of conducting their operations in accordance with the laws and customs of war.

3. Members of regular armed forces who profess allegiance to a government or an authority not recognized by the Detaining Power.

Article 5 of the Convention further provides that, "Should any doubt arise as to whether persons, having committed a belligerent act and having fallen into the hands of the enemy, belong to any of the categories enumerated in Article 4, such persons shall enjoy the protection of the present Convention until such time as their status has been determined by a competent tribunal."

The Convention proceeds to set forth a variety of rights for POWs. For example: Article 17 provides that POWs, when interrogated, are required to give only their name, rank, and a few other pieces of information. Article 25 states that POWs "shall be quartered under conditions as favorable as those for the forces of the Detaining Power who are billeted in the same area." Article 71 gives POWs the right to send and receive letters and cards. Article 87 states that, "Prisoners of war may not be sentenced by the military authorities and courts of the Detaining Power to any penalties except those provided for in respect of members of the armed forces of the said Power who have committed the same acts." Article 102 states that a POW can be validly sentenced "only if the sentence has been pronounced by the same courts according to the same procedure as in the case of members of the armed forces of the Detaining Power." And Article 118 provides that POWs "shall be released and repatriated without delay after the cessation of active hostilities."

In a Fact Sheet issued on February 7, 2002, the White House stated that neither the al Qaeda detainees nor the Taliban detainees at Guantanamo were entitled to POW status under the Convention. *See* Fact Sheet: White House on Status of Detainees at Guantanamo (Feb. 7, 2002), at http://usinfo.state.gov/topical/pol/terror/02020700.htm. The Fact Sheet reasons that the Convention does not apply to al Qaeda detainees because al Qaeda is not a state and is not a party to the Convention. It also reasons that, although the Convention does apply to the Taliban detainees (because the Taliban had been in control of much of Afghanistan), these detainees also are not entitled to POW status. The White House Press Secretary explained this point as follows:

> Under Article 4 of the Geneva Convention, . . . Taliban detainees are not entitled to POW status. To qualify as POWs under Article 4, al Qaeda and Taliban detainees would have to have satisfied four conditions: They would have to be part of a military hierarchy; they would have to have worn uniforms or other distinctive signs visible at a distance; they would have to have carried arms openly; and they would have to have conducted their military operations in accordance with the laws and customs of war.
>
> The Taliban have not effectively distinguished themselves from the civilian population of Afghanistan. Moreover, they have not conducted their operations in accordance with the laws and customs of war. Instead, they have knowingly adopted and provided support to the unlawful terrorist objectives of al Qaeda.

But the Fact Sheet also states that the United States "is treating and will continue to treat all of the individuals detained at Guantanamo humanely and, to the extent appropriate and consistent with military necessity, in a manner consistent with the principles of the Third Geneva Convention of 1949." The Fact Sheet goes on to explain: "The detainees will receive much of the treatment normally afforded to POWs by the Third Geneva Convention. However, the detainees will not receive some of the specific privileges afforded to POWs, including: — access to a canteen to purchas e food, soap, and tobacco — a monthly advance of pay — the ability to have and consult personal financial accounts — the ability to receive scientific equipment, musical instruments, or sports outfits."

2. The U.S. military has often detained enemy combatants without trial during time of war. In World War II, for example, it detained more than 400,000 enemy combatants in prisoner-of-war camps within the United States. *See generally* Arnold Krammer, Nazi Prisoners of War in America (1996). A large majority of the prisoners were German, but some were Italian or Japanese, and a handful were U.S. citizens who had served with enemy forces. How relevant is this World War II-era practice, and judicial precedents like *Quirin* and *Territo*, to the post-September 11 detentions? How is the post-September 11 conflict different from World War II? In applying the World War II precedent, does it matter that Congress did not declare war after the September 11 attacks? That al Qaeda is not a nation-state? That the conflict with al Qaeda, and with international terrorism more generally, may last indefinitely? What exactly is the scope of the war on terrorism? Is it limited to the conflict between the United States and al Qaeda? Does it extend to the broader broader conflict with Islamic terrorists? To the conflict with all terrorists of global reach? *Cf.* President George W. Bush, Address to a Joint Session of Congress and the American People (Sept. 20, 2001) ("Our enemy is a radical network of terrorists, and every government that supports them. Our war on terror begins with al Qaeda, but it does not end there. It will not end until every terrorist group of global reach has been found, stopped and defeated."), at http://www.whitehouse.gov/news/releases/ 2001/09/20010920-8.html.

3. Shortly after the September 11 attacks, Congress enacted an Authorization for Use of Military Force (AUMF), which is excerpted above. Why didn't Congress declare war? How does the AUMF compare with past authorizations of force? To use the language of Bas v. Tingy, is it a limited authorization triggering an imperfect war, or a broad authorization triggering a perfect war? How does it define the enemy? What limitations does it contain? What is encompassed by the phrase "all necessary and appropriate force"? To what extent should courts defer to presidential interpretations of the AUMF?

4. What are the holdings of the Court in *Hamdi*? On what basis does the plurality find congressional authorization for Hamdi's detention? What are the arguments for and against construing the AUMF as authorizing the detention of U.S. citizens? Why does the plurality look to the "fundamental incidents of war" to give content to the AUMF? What are the "fundamental incidents of war" authorized by the AUMF? Does this "fundamental incidents" idea work for the broader conflict with al Qaeda? For the global war on terrorism?

5. For purposes of its decision, the plurality in *Hamdi* defines "enemy combatant" as an individual who is part of or supporting forces hostile to the United States or its coalition partners and who has engaged in armed conflict against the United States. Are these the only individuals who can be detained under the authority of the AUMF? What about members of al Qaeda picked up outside of Afghanistan? What does the text of the AUMF suggest?

6. Under the plurality's analysis, enemy combatants can be held until the end of hostilities. How does this "end of hostilities" test apply in the war on terrorism? If the war on terrorism lasts indefinitely, does this mean that the President has the authority to detain alleged terrorists indefinitely without trial? What is the significance of the plurality's statement that, "[i]f the practical circumstances of a given conflict are entirely unlike those of the conflicts that informed the development of the law of war, that understanding may unravel"?

7. The plurality in *Hamdi* does not address the scope of the President's independent constitutional authority in the war on terrorism but rather considers only the authority conferred by the AUMF. Based on the materials in the other sections of this chapter, what independent powers do you think the President has in the war on terrorism, beyond those conferred by the AUMF? For example, can he use force against terrorists that do not have a connection to the September 11 attacks? In considering this question, what is the significance of the "whereas" clause in the AUMF that states "the President has authority under the Constitution to take action to deter and prevent acts of international terrorism against the United States"?

In a memorandum prepared shortly after September 11, the Justice Department's Office of Legal Counsel concluded that "the President has the constitutional power not only to retaliate against any person, organization, or State suspected of involvement in terrorist attacks on the United States, but also against foreign States suspected of harboring or supporting such organizations" and that the President "may deploy military force preemptively against terrorist organizations or the States that harbor or support them, whether or not they can be linked to the specific terrorist incidents of September 11." Memorandum from John C. Yoo, Deputy Assistant Attorney General, to the Deputy Counsel to the President, "The President's Constitutional Authority to Conduct Military Operations Against Terrorists and Nations Supporting Them" (Sept. 25, 2001), at http://www.usdoj.gov/olc/warpowers925.htm. Does this conclusion follow from the previously accepted principles of independent presidential war power explored in Section B? If this conclusion is correct, did the AUMF add anything to the President's authority? If not, why did the President seek its enactment? Are the limitations that Congress included in the AUMF legally irrelevant?

8. In considering the incidents of war — either when determining what Congress has authorized or in determining the scope of the President's independent war powers — of what relevance is international law? Should a congressional authorization of force, such as the one issued after September 11, be construed as implicitly authorizing presidential actions permitted under the international laws of war? Should courts assume that Congress has not authorized presidential actions that would violate the international laws of war? Should courts assume that Congress has affirmatively prohibited violations of the international laws of war? Should the President be able to receive the benefits of the international laws of war (such as the authority to detain enemy combatants and try war criminals by military commissions), while avoiding the burdens imposed by those laws (such as the protections given to prisoners of war in the Third Geneva Convention)? Is that a fair characterization of the Bush Administration's position? For discussion of the relationship between the AUMF and international law, see Curtis A. Bradley & Jack L. Goldsmith, *Congressional Authorization and the War on Terrorism*, 118 Harv. L. Rev. 2047, 2087-2102 (2005); Ryan Goodman & Derek Jinks, *International Law, U.S. War Powers, and the Global War on Terrorism*, 118 Harv. L. Rev. 2653 (2005); and Ingrid Brunk Wuerth, *Authorizations for the Use of Force, International Law, and the Charming Betsy Canon*, 46 B.C. L. Rev. 293 (2005).

9. Is the plurality's treatment of 18 U.S.C. §4001(a) persuasive? What are the arguments for and against the clear statement requirement advocated by Justices Souter and Ginsburg? What constitutes a clear statement? Was a clear statement required for the detention of U.S.-citizen prisoners during World War II? For discussion of the possible use of a clear statement requirement in the war on terrorism, compare Cass R. Sunstein, *Administrative Law Goes to War*, 118 Harv. L. Rev. 2663 (2005) (arguing in favor of a clear statement requirement for presidential actions that restrict "constitutionally sensitive interests"), with Curtis A. Bradley &

Jack L. Goldsmith, *Rejoinder: The War on Terrorism: International Law, Clear Statement Requirements, and Constitutional Design*, 118 Harv. L. Rev. 2683 (2005) (arguing for a narrower clear statement requirement for presidential actions that restrict the liberty of noncombatants in the United States).

10. What must the government do in order to satisfy the plurality's due process analysis? Would a military process be sufficient? Are only U.S. citizen enemy combatants entitled to the due process protections outlined by the plurality?

11. Several months after the Supreme Court's decision, the government released Hamdi and allowed him to return to his family in Saudi Arabia. *See* Joel Brinkley & Eric Lichtblau, *U.S. Releases Saudi-American It Had Captured in Afghanistan*, N.Y. Times, Oct. 12, 2004, at A15. As a result, no hearing was conducted to determine his status.

12. Jose Padilla, a U.S. citizen, was suspected of having ties to al Qaeda and of planning to engage in bombings in the United States. He was arrested on a material witness warrant at Chicago's O'Hare International Airport, after arriving from Pakistan. Initially, he was transferred by the Justice Department to New York as part of a grand jury investigation. At this point, a federal public defender was appointed to represent him. Subsequently, President Bush designated Padilla an "enemy combatant," and Padilla was transferred to military custody in South Carolina. After that, he was denied any further access to his lawyer. The public defender then filed a petition for a writ of habeas corpus on his behalf in a federal district court in New York, directed against Secretary of Defense Donald Rumsfeld. The court held the government had the constitutional authority to detain Padilla as an enemy combatant, but that the government was required to give him access to a lawyer so that he could develop and present facts concerning his habeas petition. On appeal, the U.S. Court of Appeals for the Second Circuit held that 18 U.S.C. §4001(a) prohibits the U.S. government from detaining U.S. citizens on U.S. soil in the absence of specific congressional authorization, and that the AUMF did not constitute such specific authorization. As a result, it ordered the government to release Padilla.

In Rumsfeld v. Padilla, 124 S. Ct. 2711 (2004), decided the same day as *Hamdi*, the Supreme Court reversed the judgment of the Second Circuit and remanded the case for dismissal without prejudice, holding that Padilla's habeas petition had been filed in the wrong judicial district. In a 5-4 decision, the Court reasoned that the petition should have been filed in the district where Padilla's immediate custodian was located, which was South Carolina, not New York. The Court stated that "longstanding practice confirms that in habeas challenges to present physical confinement . . . the default rule is that the proper respondent is the warden of the facility where the prisoner is being held, not the Attorney General or some other remote supervisory official." As a result, the Court did not reach the merits of the habeas petition. A footnote in the four-Justice dissent in *Padilla*, however, expresses the view that "the Non-Detention Act, 18 U.S.C. §4001(a), prohibits—and the Authorization for Use of Military Force Joint Resolution, 115 Stat. 224, adopted on September 18, 2001, does not authorize—the protracted, incommunicado detention of American citizens arrested in the United States." And Justice Breyer, who was in the plurality in *Hamdi*, was one of the dissenters in *Padilla*.

What are the implications of *Hamdi* for the ultimate resolution of Padilla's case? Under *Hamdi*, does the Executive Branch even have the authority to continue holding Padilla? Is the detention of Padilla an "incident of war" implicitly authorized by the AUMF? Does the rationale for detention discussed in *Hamdi*—preventing the enemy from returning to hostilities—apply to Padilla? What relevant differences are there between the detention of Hamdi and the detention of Padilla?

In Padilla v. Hanft, 423 F.3d 386 (4th Cir. 2005), the U.S. Court of Appeals for the Fourth Circuit concluded that the President had authority under the AUMF to detain Padilla as an enemy combatant. The court noted that the government had presented evidence indicating that, before coming to the United States, Padilla, like Hamdi, had associated with forces in Afghanistan that were hostile to the United States and had taken up arms against the United States. After subsequently escaping to Pakistan, the evidence indicated that Padilla received directions from al Qaeda to travel to the United States for the purpose of continuing the war against the United States by blowing up apartment buildings. Based on these facts, the court reasoned that, "[a]s the AUMF authorized Hamdi's detention by the President, so also does it authorize Padilla's detention." The fact that Padilla was seized on U.S. soil does not eliminate the detention authority granted by the AUMF, said the court, because "Padilla poses the same threat of returning to the battlefield as Hamdi posed at the time of the Supreme Court's adjudication of Hamdi's petition." The court also noted that the plurality in *Hamdi* relied on *Quirin*, which involved the capture of a U.S. citizen on U.S. soil.

13. As noted above, the U.S. military has detained hundreds of foreign citizens at the U.S. naval base at Guantanamo Bay, Cuba. The United States occupies the base pursuant to a 1903 lease agreement with Cuba, pursuant to which the United States "recognizes the continuance of the ultimate sovereignty of the Republic of Cuba over the [leased areas]," while the Republic of Cuba "consents that during the period of occupation by the United States . . . the United States shall exercise complete jurisdiction and control over and within said areas." A 1934 treaty between Cuba and the United States further provided that the lease would remain in effect "[s]o long as the United States of America shall not abandon the . . . naval station at Guantanamo." Family members of a number of the Guantanamo detainees filed habeas corpus petitions in federal court, arguing that the detentions were unlawful. The U.S. Court of Appeals for the D.C. Circuit upheld dismissal of the petitions for lack of jurisdiction. The court reasoned that, under Johnson v. Eisentrager, "'the privilege of litigation' does not extend to aliens in military custody who have no presence in 'any territory over which the United States is sovereign.'"

In a 6-3 decision, issued the same day as the *Hamdi* and *Padilla* decisions, the Supreme Court reversed, holding that federal courts "have jurisdiction to determine the legality of the Executive's potentially indefinite detention of individuals who claim to be wholly innocent of wrongdoing." Rasul v. Bush, 124 S. Ct. 2686, 2699 (2004). The Court noted that the petitioners in this case

> differ from the *Eisentrager* detainees in critical respects: They are not nationals of countries at war with the United States, and they deny that they have engaged in or plotted acts of aggression against the United States; they have never been afforded access to any tribunal, must less charged with and convicted of wrongdoing; and for more than two years they have been imprisoned in territory over which the United States exercises exclusive jurisdiction and control.

The Court also reasoned that *Eisentrager* had addressed only the constitutional right of the detainees there to habeas corpus relief, not their right to relief under the habeas statute. The Court explained that the Court in *Eisentrager* had assumed that the habeas statute required the presence of the habeas petitioners within the judicial district where the habeas petition was filed, a proposition later disavowed by the Court with respect to individuals detained outside the territorial jurisdiction of any district court. In addition, the Court held that the presumption against extraterritoriality did not bar application of the habeas statute to the detainees at Guantanamo. "Whatever traction the presumption against extraterritoriality might have in other contexts," the Court stated, "it certainly has no application to the operation of the habeas statute with respect to persons detained with 'the territorial jurisdiction' of the United States," including, said the Court, the Guantanamo Bay Naval Base. The Court also reasoned that application of the statute to Guantanamo was consistent with the historical reach of the writ of habeas corpus, including its reach under British common law. Although the Court did not purport to address the merits of the petitioners' habeas claims, it did observe in footnote 15 of its opinion that "Petitioners' allegations — that, although they have engaged neither in combat nor in acts of terrorism against the United States, they have been held in Executive detention for more than two years in territory subject to the long-term, exclusive jurisdiction and control of the United States, without access to counsel and without being charged with any wrongdoing — unquestionably describe 'custody in violation of the Constitution or laws or treaties of the United States' [within the meaning of the habeas statute]."

Justice Kennedy concurred in the judgment. He reasoned that, although *Eisentrager* "indicates that there is a realm of political authority over military affairs where the judicial power may not enter," this case was distinguishable from *Eisentrager*. Whereas in *Eisentrager* the detainees "were proven enemy aliens found and detained outside the United States, and . . . the existence of jurisdiction would have had a clear harmful effect on the Nation's military affairs," in this case Guantanamo Bay "is in every practical respect a United States territory, and it is on far removed from any hostilities," and "the detainees at Guantanamo Bay are being held indefinitely, and without benefit of any legal proceeding to determine their status."

Justice Scalia issued a dissent, joined by Chief Justice Rehnquist and Justice Thomas. Scalia accused the majority of effectively overturning *Eisentrager* and improperly extending the reach of the habeas statute, a matter that should have been left to Congress. He also argued that "the Court springs a trap on the Executive, subjecting Guantanamo Bay to the oversight of the federal courts even though it has never before been thought to be within their jurisdiction — and thus making it a foolish place to have housed alien wartime detainees." In addition, he predicted that, by allowing aliens captured in a foreign theater of combat to bring a habeas corpus action against the Secretary of Defense, the majority's decision would have "breathtaking" consequences. "From this point forward," he stated, "federal courts will entertain petitions from these prisoners, and others like them around the world, challenging actions and events far away, and forcing the courts to oversee one aspect of the Executive's conduct of a foreign war." Scalia also disagreed with the majority's conclusion that the presumption against extraterritoriality was inapplicable to Guantanamo Bay. U.S. laws should not be presumed to apply to foreign territory, he argued, merely because the territory is subject to U.S. jurisdiction and control.

Are the detainees at Guantanamo Bay entitled to the same due process rights as Hamdi? If not, what sort of hearing are they entitled to? Should courts apply the "some evidence" standard, rejected by the Court for Hamdi? Can the Guantanamo detainees, unlike Hamdi and Padilla, file their habeas corpus petitions anywhere in the United States? *See* Gherebi v. Bush, 2004 U.S. App. LEXIS 14094 (9th Cir. July 8, 2004) (transferring case brought by Guantanamo detainees from the Ninth

Circuit to the District of Columbia Circuit); Gherebi v. Bush, 338 F. Supp. 2d 91 (D.D.C. 2004) (holding that it had jurisdiction to hear habeas petition). To what extent does the jurisdictional holding of *Rasul* apply outside the context of Guantanamo Bay?

Would the detainees at Guantanamo have any greater rights if they were moved to the continental United States and detained there? Would transferring them to other locations abroad for continued detention under U.S. control eliminate their right to seek habeas corpus review? What about transferring them to a friendly foreign country that would have ultimate control over their detention, interrogation, and trial? In Abu Ali v. Ashcroft, 350 F. Supp. 2d 28 (D.D.C. 2004), the court held that a U.S. citizen held in Saudi Arabia by Saudi authorities, allegedly at the behest of the U.S. government, could pursue jurisdictional discovery to support his claim that he was effectively in the custody of the United States. Saudi Arabia subsequently transferred him to U.S. custody, and a prosecution was initiated against him for allegedly being involved in a plot to assassinate President Bush.

14. What rights do enemy combatants have to access to a lawyer when pursuing habeas corpus relief? In *Hamdi*, which involved a U.S. citizen detained in the United States, the plurality noted at the end of its opinion that Hamdi was challenging the Fourth Circuit's refusal to allow him immediate access to counsel. The plurality observed that, since it had granted certiorari, Hamdi had been appointed counsel and was now being granted unmonitored meetings with counsel. The plurality stated that Hamdi "unquestionably has the right to access to counsel in connection with the proceedings on remand" and that "[n]o further consideration of this issue is necessary at this stage of the case." What if any implications do these statements have for Guantanamo detainees seeking to obtain the assistance of counsel? *See* Al Odah v. United States, 346 F. Supp. 2d 1 (D.D.C. 2004) (holding that Guantanamo detainees had a statutory right to be represented by counsel to pursue habeas claims, and that the government could not conduct real-time monitoring of their meetings with counsel).

15. Shortly after the Supreme Court decisions discussed above, the Department of Defense announced the creation of "Combatant Status Review Tribunals" to review challenges by detainees at Guantanamo to their designation as enemy combatants. *See* Memorandum for the Secretary of the Navy, Order Establishing Combatant Status Review Tribunal (July 7, 2004), at http://www.defenselink.mil/news/Jul2004/d20040707review.pdf. Under this process, each detainee at Guantanamo has been given notice of the factual basis for his detention and an opportunity, with the assistance of a "personal representative" (a military officer who will not act as a lawyer or advocate), to challenge his designation as an enemy combatant. The challenges are heard by panels of three commissioned officers not involved in the detainee's apprehension, detention, interrogation, or screening. The detainees have the right to call witnesses if reasonably available, question other witnesses, testify, and introduce relevant documentary evidence. Do these tribunals satisfy the due process standards outlined in *Hamdi*? Do they need to? What deference should courts give to the determinations made by these tribunals? Is the procedure legally deficient by not permitting attorney representation before the tribunals? Is the definition of "enemy combatant" that has been adopted for the tribunals ("an individual who was part of or supporting Taliban or al Qaeda forces, or associated forces that are engaged in hostilities against the United States or its coalition partners") too broad? How does it compare with the definition used by the plurality in *Hamdi*?

16. In the spring of 2004, while *Hamdi* and *Rasul* were under consideration, the Executive Branch established an Administrative Review Board that, using formal procedures, reviews whether enemy combatants should continue to be detained or should be released, with or without conditions. In making its recommendation, the Board considers whether each detainee "remains a threat to the United States and its allies in the ongoing armed conflict against al Qaida and its affiliates and supporters or if there is any other reason that it is in the interest of the United States and its allies for the enemy combatant to remain in the control of [the Department of Defense]." *See* http://www.defenselink.mil/news/May2004/d20040518gtmoreview.pdf.

17. Do the CSRT and ARB processes satisfy whatever due process rights apply to the detainees at Guantanamo? In early 2005, federal district court judges in Washington, D.C. reached conflicting conclusions about the rights of these detainees. In one decision, the court reasoned that nonresident aliens captured and detained outside the United States have no cognizable constitutional rights. *See* Khalid v. Bush, 355 F. Supp. 2d 311 (D.D.C. 2005). In the other decision, the court held that at least fundamental constitutional rights (including the right not to be deprived of liberty without due process) apply to Guantanamo Bay, emphasizing the same factors that were emphasized by the majority in *Rasul* in concluding that habeas jurisdiction extended to Guantanamo. *See* In re Guantanamo Detainee Cases, 355 F. Supp. 2d 443 (D.D.C. 2004). That court also concluded that the Guantanamo detainees were not being given due process, e.g., inability to review the classified evidence relied upon by the government, and lack of appointment of a lawyer.

18. Are there any legal restrictions on the U.S. government's ability to transfer detainees to other countries? What if the detainee alleges that he will be tortured or otherwise mistreated in the other country? What if he alleges that he will be detained indefinitely there without counsel? In any event, should the U.S. government be required to give notice to a U.S. court of its intent to transfer a detainee, since the transfer could deprive the court of habeas corpus jurisdiction with respect to that detainee? On the last question, compare Al-Joudi v. Bush, 2005 U.S. Dist. LEXIS 6265 (D.D.C. Apr. 4, 2005) (enjoining the government from transferring certain detainees at Guantanamo without first giving their counsel and the court 30-days notice); and Abdah v. Bush, 2005 U.S. Dist. LEXIS 4942 (D.D.C. May 29, 2005) (same), with Almurbati v. Bush, 366 F. Supp. 72 (D.D.C. 2005) (declining to require advance notice, but requiring the government to submit a declaration to the court stating "that any transfers or repatriations were not made for the purpose of merely continuing the petitioners' detention on behalf of the United States or for the purpose of extinguishing this Court of jurisdiction over the petitioners' actions for habeas relief or for a reason unrelated to the decision that the petitioners' detention is no longer warranted by the United States").

19. In his November 13, 2001 order, excerpted above, President Bush authorized the use of military commissions to try (a) present and former members of al Qaeda, (b) individuals who "engaged in, aided or abetted, or conspired to commit, acts of international terrorism, or acts in preparation therefore, that have caused, threatened to cause, or have as their aim to cause, injury to or adverse effects on the United States, its citizens, national security, foreign policy, or economy," and (c) those who knowingly harbored any of these individuals. Under the order, the military commissions are authorized to try these various individuals for "any and all offenses triable by military commission that such individual is alleged to have committed."

The November 13 directed the Secretary of Defense to issue whatever regulations were necessary to establish the commissions. Since then, the Department of Defense has issued numerous orders and instructions relating to the commissions. These orders and instructions, among other things, establish extensive procedures for the commissions and define the crimes that can be tried before the commissions.

President Bush subsequently determined that 15 individuals being detained at the U.S. Naval Base in Guantanamo Bay, Cuba were subject to his November 13 order and were eligible to be tried before military commissions. In 2004, it was announced that four of these individuals had been charged with war crimes and would be tried by military commissions. The commission proceedings for these individuals began in August 2004, almost three years after issuance of the November 13 order. They were suspended, however, as a result of litigation. *See* Hamdan v. Rumsfeld, 344 F. Supp. 2d 152 (D.D.C. 2004), *rev'd*, 415 F.3d 33 (D.C. Cir. 2005).

Although the November 13 order states that the individuals tried by military commissions shall have no right to seek review in any U.S. court, the counsel to the President stated shortly after issuance of the order that the order "preserves judicial review in civilian courts," and that "anyone arrested, detained or tried *in the United States* by a military commission will be able to challenge the lawfulness of the commission's jurisdiction through a habeas corpus proceeding in a federal court." He also noted that the order had been modeled on the military commission order issued by President Franklin Roosevelt in World War II that was construed by the Supreme Court in *Quirin* as permitting habeas review. In addition, as noted above, the Supreme Court held in *Rasul* that habeas jurisdiction extends to Guantanamo Bay, Cuba, where the military commission proceedings are being held.

As noted in Section D, military commissions have historically been used by the United States for three basic purposes: to try enemy belligerents for crimes triable by the laws of war, including war crimes; to administer justice in territory occupied by the United States; and to replace civilian courts where martial law has been declared. The commissions established by President Bush's November 13 order fall within the first category. Except for two offenses that Congress has specifically authorized to be tried before military commissions (spying and aiding the enemy), the historical jurisdiction of these commissions has been limited to trying offenses governed by the international laws of war. The November 13 order appears to recognize this limitation, noting in one of its "Findings" that it is appropriate that individuals subject to the order be tried "for violation of the laws of war and other applicable laws by military tribunals." Moreover, the Department of Defense stated in the Crimes and Elements that it adopted for the commissions that they "derive from the law of armed conflict, a body of law that is sometimes referred to as the law of war."

Where did President Bush obtain the legal authority to establish the military commissions? The November 13 order cites as authority the Commander-in-Chief power, the AUMF, and sections 821 and 836 of the Uniform Code of Military Justice (UCMJ). Section 821 of the UCMJ states that "[t]he provisions of this chapter conferring jurisdiction upon courts-martial do not deprive military commissions ... of concurrent jurisdiction with respect to offenders or offenses that by statute or by the law of war may be tried by military commissions." Section 836 authorizes the President to prescribe "pretrial, trial, and post-trial procedures, including modes of proof, for cases arising under this chapter triable in ... military military commissions and other military tribunals."

Consider first the Commander-in-Chief power. Does this power implicitly include the authority to establish military commissions during a war? What, if anything, does *Quirin* (discussed above and in Section D) suggest about this question? Does it matter that the war on terrorism is not a declared war? Of what relevance is *Ex parte Milligan*, excerpted above in section D? In *Quirin*, the Court distinguished *Milligan* as follows: "the Court [in *Milligan*] was at pains to point out that Milligan, a citizen twenty years resident in Indiana, who had never been a resident of any of the states in rebellion, was not an enemy belligerent either entitled to the status of a prisoner of war or subject to the penalties imposed upon unlawful belligerents." Is this a fair distinction? What are the implications of this distinction for the President's authority to use military commissions to try terrorists? How does the plurality in *Hamdi* distinguish *Milligan*?

Now consider the AUMF. Does it implicitly authorize the creation of military commissions? Are such commissions part of the "necessary and appropriate force" that the President has been authorized to use? How does this issue compare with the issue of detention addressed in *Hamdi*?

Finally, consider the UCMJ provisions. The UCMJ replaced the Articles of War, which had themselves been recodified in 1916. In the 1916 recodification of the Articles of War, Congress expanded court-martial jurisdiction (i.e., jurisdiction over members of the U.S. military) to include offenses against the laws of war. Article 15 of the recodified Articles of War, the predecessor to Section 821 of the UCMJ, stated that the creation of statutory jurisdiction for courts martial did not "deprive military commissions . . . of concurrent jurisdiction with respect to offenders or offenses that . . . by the law of war may be tried by military commission." Although by its terms this provision appears simply to recognize the historical authority of the President to establish military commissions, the Supreme Court in *Quirin* held that this provision also constituted congressional *authorization* for the creation of military commissions. The Court noted that "Congress [in Article 15] has explicitly provided, so far as it may constitutionally do so, that military tribunals shall have jurisdiction to try offenders or offenses against the law of war in appropriate cases," and held that "Congress [in Article 15] has authorized trial of offenses against the law of war before such commissions." In 1950, Congress recodified Article 15 as Section 821 of the UCMJ without changing the reference to military commissions. Moreover, the legislative history of Section 821 indicates that Congress was aware of and accepted the Court's interpretation. What does this background suggest about President Bush's authority to establish military commissions? *Compare* Neal K. Katyal & Laurence H. Tribe, *Waging War, Deciding Guilt: Trying the Military Tribunals*, 111 Yale L.J. 1259 (2002) (arguing that the President lacked authority to establish commissions), *with* Curtis A. Bradley & Jack L. Goldsmith, *The Constitutional Validity of Military Commissions*, 3 Green Bag 2d 249 (2002) (arguing that he had authority).

In Hamdan v. Rumsfeld, 415 F.3d 33 (D.C. Cir. 2005), the U.S. Court of Appeals for the D.C. Circuit held that President Bush had the authority to use military commissions to try enemy combatants in the war on terrorism. The court relied on, among other things, the AUMF, *Quirin*, and Section 821 of the Uniform Code of Military Justice. The court rejected the argument that the President's use of the commissions was barred by the Third Geneva Convention, concluding that the Convention does not confer judicially enforceable private rights, and also that the conflict with al Qaeda is not covered by the Convention.

20. Some individuals associated with al Qaeda have been subjected to criminal prosecution in federal court. Before the September 11 attacks, individuals implicated in the 1993 bombing of the World Trade Center and the 1998 bombings of the U.S. embassies in Kenya and Tanzania were tried in federal court. *See* United States v. Yousef, 327 F.3d 56 (2d Cir. 2003); United States v. Bin Laden, 91 F. Supp. 2d 600 (2000).

After September 11, Richard Reid, a U.S. citizen who attempted to detonate a shoe bomb on a U.S. airliner, was prosecuted in a federal district court in Massachusetts. He pleaded guilty and was subsequently sentenced to life imprisonment. At his sentencing hearing, Reid proclaimed his allegiance to Osama bin Laden, and said, "I am at war with your country." The "American Taliban," John Walker Lindh, also was prosecuted in federal court. He pleaded guilty in return for a 20-year prison sentence. In a decision issued prior to the plea bargain, the federal district court in Lindh's case ruled that he did not have immunity from prosecution under the Third Geneva Convention because he had not satisfied the conditions specified in Article 4(2) of the Convention. In reaching this conclusion, the court gave some deference, although not absolute deference, to the Executive Branch's construction of the Convention. *See* United States v. Lindh, 212 F. Supp. 2d 541 (E.D. Va. 2002).

In addition, the alleged "20th hijacker," Zacarias Moussaoui, was prosecuted in a federal district court in Virginia, and he eventually pleaded guilty. The Moussaoui proceedings, however, raised questions about whether national security can be sufficiently protected in such trials, as Moussaoui sought access to other suspected terrorists and to classified evidence, and sought to have his proceedings open to the public. Because of these concerns, there were suggestions at times that the U.S. government might move Moussaoui to military custody and thereby either hold him without trial or subject him to a military trial.

Should the government have complete freedom of choice in deciding whether to prosecute someone or hold them indefinitely without trial? Or are there situations in which the government should be required either to release someone or bring a criminal prosecution against them? If so, how are courts to identify these situations? Note that, in June 2003, President Bush declared a Qatari citizen who was scheduled to be tried in a civilian federal court to be an enemy combatant and, on that basis, transferred him from civilian to military custody, where he remains as of August 2005. *See* Eric Lichtblau, *Bush Declares Student an Enemy Combatant*, N.Y. Times, June 24, 2003, at A15.

21. During 2004, the press obtained a series of internal Executive Branch legal memoranda concerning the war on terrorism. These memoranda concerned, among other things, the applicability of the Geneva Conventions to the detainees at Guantanamo, the permissible interrogation methods for such detainees, and the meaning of the federal criminal torture statute. These memoranda generated substantial controversy, in part because it was perceived that their aggressive interpretations of both international and domestic law helped foster a climate that led to an abuse of prisoners by U.S. personnel in Iraq. The most controversial of these memoranda concerned the interpretation of the federal criminal torture statute and its relationship to executive power. *See* Memorandum from Jay S. Bybee, Assistant Attorney General, Office of Legal Counsel, to Alberto R. Gonzales, "Standards of Conduct for Interrogation Under 18 U.S.C. §§2340-2340A" (Aug. 1, 2002), at http://www.washingtonpost.com/wpsrv/nation/documents/dojinterrogationmemo20020801.pdf. Among other things, this memorandum argued that the President was not bound by the torture statute when exercising his Commander-in-Chief powers. It reasoned that "[a]ny effort by Congress to regulate the interrogation of battlefield combatants would violate the Constitution's sole vesting of the Commander-in-Chief authority in the President.... Congress can no more interfere with the President's conduct of the interrogation of enemy combatants than it can dictate strategic or tactical decisions on the battlefield." In light of the materials in Section C, is this reasoning persuasive? Would this reasoning render the Geneva Conventions, and the implementing War Crimes Statute, 18 U.S.C. §2441, unconstitutional? In response to the controversy surrounding this memo, it was officially withdrawn by the Department of Justice in the summer of 2004. In December 2004, the Department issued a new memorandum, adopting a broader conception of what constitutes torture, and expressly declining to address the issue of the President's authority to disregard the torture statute. *See* Memorandum from Daniel Levin, Assistant Attorney General, Office of Legal Counsel, to James B. Comey, Assistant Attorney General, "Legal Standards Applicable Under 18 U.S.C. §§2340-2340A" (Dec. 30, 2004), at http://www.usdoj.gov/olc/18usc23402340a2.htm. The December 2004 memorandum did not revisit the merits of the earlier Commander-in-Chief argument, but rather merely stated: "Because the discussion in that memorandum concerning the President's Commander-in-Chief power and the potential defenses to liability was — and remains — unnecessary, it has been eliminated from the analysis that follows. Consideration of the bounds of any such authority would be inconsistent with the President's unequivocal directive that United States personnel not engage in torture." For a discussion of the claims about executive power in the original memorandum (and in other Bush administration memoranda relating to the war on terrorism), see Michael D. Ramsay, *Torturing Executive Power*, 93 Georgetown L.J. 1213(2005).

22. Numerous books and articles have been written about the legal aspects of the war on terrorism. The books include David Cole, Enemy Aliens (2003); Philip B. Heymann, Terrorism, Freedom, and Security: Winning Without War (2003); and Derek Jinks, The Rules of War: The Geneva Conventions in the Age of Terror (2005). The articles include Bruce Ackerman, *The Emergency Constitution*, 113 Yale L.J. 1029 (2004); Diane Marie Amann, *Guantanamo*, 42 Colum. J. Transnat'l L. 263 (2004); Bradley & Goldsmith, *Congressional Authorization, supra*; David Golove, *Military Tribunals, International Law, and the Constitution: A Franckian-Madisonian Approach*, 35 N.Y.U. J. Int'l L. Pol'y 363 (2003); Derek Jinks & David Sloss, *Is the President Bound by the Geneva Conventions?*, 90 Cornell L. Rev. 97 (2004); Michael Stokes Paulsen, *Youngstown Goes to War*, 19 Const. Comm. 215 (2002); and Katyal & Tribe, *Waging War, Deciding Guilt, supra*.

5

States and Foreign Relations

As discussed in Chapter 1, state interference in foreign relations was a significant problem during the Articles of Confederation period. The Constitution addressed this problem by enhancing the foreign relations powers of the national government vis-à-vis the states in a number of significant ways: Article I, Section 10 bars states from performing certain foreign relations functions, such as treaty-making; Article I, Section 8 and Article II broadly authorize the federal political branches to conduct foreign relations through the enactment of federal statutes and treaties; the Supremacy Clause in Article VI establishes that these federal enactments are supreme over state law; Article III extends the federal judicial power to cases involving these federal enactments and to other transnational controversies; and the "take care" clause in Article II authorizes the President to enforce federal enactments.

Because of the national government's broad constitutional authority over foreign relations, some commentators have suggested that the United States' system of federalism is irrelevant to an understanding of U.S. foreign relations law. There is dicta in Supreme Court opinions that might support this conclusion. In United States v. Belmont, 301 U.S. 324, 331 (1937), for example, the Court stated: "[I]n respect of our foreign relations generally, state lines disappear. As to such purposes the State . . . does not exist." In fact, as the materials in this chapter illustrate, states are far from irrelevant to U.S. foreign relations. State law regulates many aspects of a foreign national's activities in the United States, and state courts often decide cases involving foreign parties or events. In addition, although states and municipalities are precluded from entering into treaties with foreign nations, they often engage in less formal international relations, such as sending international missions to foreign countries and establishing sister-city relationships. States and municipalities also sometimes take positions on international economic and political issues — through, for example, their purchasing and investment decisions. Even when such foreign relations activities trigger complaints by foreign governments or international institutions, the federal political branches often decline to preempt them.

This chapter introduces the theme of federalism and foreign relations. It begins with cases involving statutory and treaty preemption. These cases raise interpretive questions concerning how courts should determine whether federal political branch enactments have in fact preempted state authority. Next, the chapter turns to preemption doctrines not tied to a statute or treaty, namely, "Executive

Branch preemption" (the power of the Executive Branch to take action in a way that results in preemption of state law) and "dormant foreign affairs preemption" (the power of federal courts to preempt state activities related to foreign affairs in the absence of political branch action). We then examine the idea of a jurisdictional "federal common law of foreign relations." Subsequent chapters consider other federalism issues, including possible federalism-based limitations on the treaty power, see Chapter 6, and the relationship between customary international law and state law, see Chapter 7.

Although the focus of this chapter is on federalism, the reader should pay close attention to the separation of powers issues implicated in the materials that follow. One of the underlying questions in these materials is whether federal *courts* should, in the absence of clear guidance from the federal *political branches*, limit state authority in the name of a federal foreign relations interest. In light of this question, consider whether the doctrines developed in this chapter are consistent with what you learned in Chapter 2 concerning the relative competence and authority of federal courts and the federal political branches in the foreign relations field. Consider also how the separation of powers issues in Chapter 3 concerning presidential-congressional relations in foreign relations differ from the separation of powers issues in this chapter.

A. STATUTORY PREEMPTION

Hines v. Davidowitz

312 U.S. 52 (1941)

[This case concerned the validity of Pennsylvania's 1939 Alien Registration Act. The Act required certain aliens 18 years or older, in order to avoid fine or imprisonment, to register with the state, provide certain information, pay a $1 annual registration fee, and receive and carry an alien registration card. A three-judge district court enjoined enforcement of the Act, holding that it denied aliens equal protection of the laws and encroached on the legislative powers constitutionally vested in the federal government. After that decision but before Supreme Court review, Congress enacted a federal Alien Registration Act. The federal statute required registration of aliens 14 years and over, and required registered aliens to provide detailed information and finger-printing. But, unlike the state statute, the federal statute did not require aliens to carry or produce a registration card, and it made only the willful failure to register a criminal offense. The plaintiffs argued, among other things, that the Pennsylvania statute was preempted by the federal statute.]

MR. JUSTICE BLACK delivered the opinion of the Court....

First. That the supremacy of the national power in the general field of foreign affairs, including power over immigration, naturalization and deportation, is made clear by the Constitution, was pointed out by the authors of *The Federalist* in 1787, and has since been given continuous recognition by this Court. When the national government by treaty or statute has established rules and regulations touching the rights, privileges, obligations or burdens of aliens as such, the treaty or statute is the supreme law of the land.....

One of the most important and delicate of all international relationships, recognized immemorially as a responsibility of government, has to do with the protection of the just rights of a country's own nationals when those nationals are in another country. Experience has shown that international controversies of the gravest moment, sometimes even leading to war, may arise from real or imagined wrongs to another's subjects inflicted, or permitted, by a government. This country, like other nations, has entered into numerous treaties of amity and commerce since its inception — treaties entered into under express constitutional authority, and binding upon the states as well as the nation. Among those treaties have been many which not only promised and guaranteed broad rights and privileges to aliens sojourning in our own territory, but secured reciprocal promises and guarantees for our own citizens while in other lands. And apart from treaty obligations, there has grown up in the field of international relations a body of customs defining with more or less certainty the duties owing by all nations to alien residents — duties which our State Department has often successfully insisted foreign nations must recognize as to our nationals abroad. In general, both treaties and international practices have been aimed at preventing injurious discriminations against aliens....

Legal imposition of distinct, unusual and extraordinary burdens and obligations upon aliens — such as subjecting them alone, though perfectly law-abiding, to indiscriminate and repeated interception and interrogation by public officials — thus bears an inseparable relationship to the welfare and tranquillity of all the states, and not merely to the welfare and tranquillity of one. Laws imposing such burdens are not mere census requirements, and even though they may be immediately associated with the accomplishment of a local purpose, they provoke questions in the field of international affairs. And specialized regulation of the conduct of an alien before naturalization is a matter which Congress must consider in discharging its constitutional duty "To establish an Uniform Rule of Naturalization...." It cannot be doubted that both the state and the federal registration laws belong "to that class of laws which concern the exterior relation of this whole nation with other nations and governments."[16] Consequently the regulation of aliens is so intimately blended and intertwined with responsibilities of the national government that where it acts, and the state also acts on the same subject, "the act of Congress, or the treaty, is supreme; and the law of the State, though enacted in the exercise of powers not controverted, must yield to it."[17] And where the federal government, in the exercise of its superior authority in this field, has enacted a complete scheme of regulation and has therein provided a standard for the registration of aliens, states cannot, inconsistently with the purpose of Congress, conflict or interfere with, curtail or complement, the federal law, or enforce additional or auxiliary regulations. There is not — and from the very nature of the problem there cannot be — any rigid formula or rule which can be used as a universal pattern to determine the meaning and purpose of every act of Congress. This Court, in considering the validity of state laws in the light of treaties or federal laws touching the same subject, has made use of the following expressions: conflicting; contrary to; occupying the field; repugnance; difference; irreconcilability; inconsistency; violation; curtailment; and interference. But none of these expressions provides an infallible constitutional test or an exclusive constitutional yardstick. In the final

16. Henderson v. Mayor of New York, 92 U.S. 259, 273.
17. Gibbons v. Ogden, 22 U.S. 1 (1824).

analysis, there can be no one crystal clear distinctly marked formula. Our primary function is to determine whether, under the circumstances of this particular case, Pennsylvania's law stands as an obstacle to the accomplishment and execution of the full purposes and objectives of Congress. And in that determination, it is of importance that this legislation is in a field which affects international relations, the one aspect of our government that from the first has been most generally conceded imperatively to demand broad national authority. Any concurrent state power that may exist is restricted to the narrowest of limits; the state's power here is not bottomed on the same broad base as is its power to tax. And it is also of importance that this legislation deals with the rights, liberties, and personal freedoms of human beings, and is in an entirely different category from state tax statutes or state pure food laws regulating the labels on cans.

Our conclusion is that appellee is correct in his contention that the power to restrict, limit, regulate, and register aliens as a distinct group is not an equal and continuously existing concurrent power of state and nation, but that whatever power a state may have is subordinate to supreme national law. We proceed therefore to an examination of Congressional enactments to ascertain whether or not Congress has acted in such manner that its action should preclude enforcement of Pennsylvania's law.

Second. For many years Congress has provided a broad and comprehensive plan describing the terms and conditions upon which aliens may enter this country, how they may acquire citizenship, and the manner in which they may be deported. Numerous treaties, in return for reciprocal promises from other governments, have pledged the solemn obligation of this nation to the end that aliens residing in our territory shall not be singled out for the imposition of discriminatory burdens. Our Constitution and our Civil Rights Act have guaranteed to aliens "the equal protection of the laws [which] is a pledge of the protection of equal laws." With a view to limiting prospective residents from foreign lands to those possessing the qualities deemed essential to good and useful citizenship in America, carefully defined qualifications are required to be met before aliens may enter our country. These qualifications include rigid requirements as to health, education, integrity, character, and adaptability to our institutions. Nor is the alien left free from the application of federal laws after entry and before naturalization. If during the time he is residing here he should be found guilty of conduct contrary to the rules and regulations laid down by Congress, he can be deported. At the time he enters the country, at the time he applies for permission to acquire the full status of citizenship, and during the intervening years, he can be subjected to searching investigations as to conduct and suitability for citizenship. And in 1940 Congress added to this comprehensive scheme a complete system for alien registration.

The nature of the power exerted by Congress, the object sought to be attained, and the character of the obligations imposed by the law, are all important in considering the question of whether supreme federal enactments preclude enforcement of state laws on the same subject. . . .

[The purpose of the 1940 statute], as announced by the chairman of the Senate subcommittee which drafted the final bill, was to "work . . . the new provisions into the existing [immigration and naturalization] laws, so as to make a harmonious whole." That "harmonious whole" included the "Uniform Rule of Naturalization" the Constitution empowered the Congress to provide. And as a part of that "harmonious whole," under the federal Act aliens need not carry cards, and can only be punished for willful failure to register. Further, registration records and fingerprints must be kept secret and cannot be revealed except to agencies — such as a state — upon consent of the Commissioner and the Attorney General.

We have already adverted to the conditions which make the treatment of aliens, in whatever state they may be located, a matter of national moment. And whether or not registration of aliens is of such a nature that the Constitution permits only of one uniform national system, it cannot be denied that the Congress might validly conclude that such uniformity is desirable. The legislative history of the Act indicates that Congress was trying to steer a middle path, realizing that any registration requirement was a departure from our traditional policy of not treating aliens as a thing apart, but also feeling that the Nation was in need of the type of information to be secured. Having the constitutional authority so to do, it has provided a standard for alien registration in a single integrated and allembracing system in order to obtain the information deemed to be desirable in connection with aliens. When it made this addition to its uniform naturalization and immigration laws, it plainly manifested a purpose to do so in such a way as to protect the personal liberties of law-abiding aliens through one uniform national registration system, and to leave them free from the possibility of inquisitorial practices and police surveillance that might not only affect our international relations but might also generate the very disloyalty which the law has intended guarding against. Under these circumstances, the Pennsylvania Act cannot be enforced. . . .

MR. JUSTICE STONE, dissenting:

Undoubtedly Congress, in the exercise of its power to legislate in aid of powers granted by the Constitution to the national government may greatly enlarge the exercise of federal authority and to an extent which need not now be defined, it may, if such is its will, thus subtract from the powers which might otherwise be exercised by the states. Assuming, as the Court holds, that Congress could constitutionally set up an exclusive registration system for aliens, I think it has not done so and that it is not the province of the courts to do that which Congress has failed to do.

At a time when the exercise of the federal power is being rapidly expanded through Congressional action, it is difficult to overstate the importance of safeguarding against such diminution of state power by vague inferences as to what Congress might have intended if it had considered the matter or by reference to our own conceptions of a policy which Congress has not expressed and which is not plainly to be inferred from the legislation which it has enacted. The Judiciary of the United States should not assume to strike down a state law which is immediately concerned with the social order and safety of its people unless the statute plainly and palpably violates some right granted or secured to the national government by the Constitution or similarly encroaches upon the exercise of some authority delegated to the United States for the attainment of objects of national concern. . . .

It is conceded that the federal act in operation does not at any point conflict with the state statute, and it does not by its terms purport to control or restrict state authority in any particular. But the government says that Congress by passing the federal act, has "occupied the field" so as to preclude the enforcement of the state statute and that the administration of the latter might well conflict with Congressional policy to protect the civil liberty of aliens against the harassments of intrusive police surveillance. Little aid can be derived from the vague and illusory but often repeated formula that Congress "by occupying the field" has excluded from it all state legislation. Every Act of Congress occupies some field, but we must know the boundaries of that field before we can say that it has precluded a state from the exercise of any power reserved to it by the Constitution. To discover the boundaries we look to the federal statute itself, read in the light of its constitutional setting and its legislative history.

Federal statutes passed in aid of a granted power obviously supersede state statutes with which they conflict. But we are pointed to no such conflict here. In the exercise of such powers Congress also has wide scope for prohibiting state regulation of matters which Congress may, but has not undertaken to regulate itself. But no words of the statute or of any committee report, or any Congressional debate indicate that Congress intended to withdraw from the states any part of their constitutional power over aliens within their borders. We must take it that Congress was not unaware that some nineteen states have statutes or ordinances requiring some form of registration for aliens, seven of them dating from the last war. The repeal of this legislation is not to be inferred from the silence of Congress in enacting a law which at no point conflicts with the state legislation and is harmonious with it.

Here compliance with the state law does not preclude or even interfere with compliance with the act of Congress. The enforcement of both acts involves no more inconsistency, no more inconvenience to the individual, and no more embarrassment to either government than do any of the laws, state and national, such as revenue laws, licensing laws, or police regulations, where interstate commerce is involved, which are equally applied to the citizen because he is subject, as are aliens, to a dual sovereignty.

De Canas v. Bica

424 U.S. 351 (1976)

MR. JUSTICE BRENNAN delivered the opinion of the Court.

California Labor Code Ann. §2805(a) provides that "[n]o employer shall knowingly employ an alien who is not entitled to lawful residence in the United States if such employment would have an adverse effect on lawful resident workers." The question presented in this case is whether §2805(a) is unconstitutional either because it is an attempt to regulate immigration and naturalization or because it is pre-empted under the Supremacy Clause, Art. VI, cl. 2, of the Constitution, by the Immigration and Nationality Act (INA), the comprehensive federal statutory scheme for regulation of immigration and naturalization....

Power to regulate immigration is unquestionably exclusively a federal power. But the Court has never held that every state enactment which in any way deals with aliens is a regulation of immigration and thus per se pre-empted by this constitutional power, whether latent or exercised.... [T]here would have been no need, in cases such as... Hines v. Davidowitz, 312 U.S. 52 (1941), even to discuss the relevant congressional enactments in finding pre-emption of state regulation if all state regulation of aliens was ipso facto regulation of immigration, for the existence *vel non* of federal regulation is wholly irrelevant if the Constitution of its own force requires pre-emption of such state regulation. In this case, California has sought to strengthen its economy by adopting federal standards in imposing criminal sanctions against state employers who knowingly employ aliens who have no federal right to employment within the country; even if such local regulation has some purely speculative and indirect impact on immigration, it does not thereby become a constitutionally proscribed regulation of immigration that Congress itself would be powerless to authorize or approve. Thus, absent congressional action, §2805 would not be an invalid state incursion on federal power.

Even when the Constitution does not itself commit exclusive power to regulate a particular field to the Federal Government, there are situations in which state regulation, although harmonious with federal regulation, must nevertheless be invalidated under the Supremacy Clause. As we stated in Florida Lime & Avocado Growers v. Paul, 373 U.S. 132, 142 (1963): "[F]ederal regulation . . . should not be deemed pre-emptive of state regulatory power in the absence of persuasive reasons — either that the nature of the regulated subject matter permits no other conclusion, or that the Congress has unmistakably so ordained."

In this case, we cannot conclude that pre-emption is required either because "the nature of the . . . subject matter [regulation of employment of illegal aliens] permits no other conclusion," or because "Congress has unmistakably so ordained" that result.

States possess broad authority under their police powers to regulate the employment relationship to protect workers within the State. Child labor laws, minimum and other wage laws, laws affecting occupational health and safety, and workmen's compensation laws are only a few examples. California's attempt in §2805(a) to prohibit the knowing employment by California employers of persons not entitled to lawful residence in the United States, let alone to work here, is certainly within the mainstream of such police power regulation. Employment of illegal aliens in times of high unemployment deprives citizens and legally admitted aliens of jobs; acceptance by illegal aliens of jobs on substandard terms as to wages and working conditions can seriously depress wage scales and working conditions of citizens and legally admitted aliens; and employment of illegal aliens under such conditions can diminish the effectiveness of labor unions. These local problems are particularly acute in California in light of the significant influx into that State of illegal aliens from neighboring Mexico. In attempting to protect California's fiscal interests and lawfully resident labor force from the deleterious effects on its economy resulting from the employment of illegal aliens, §2805(a) focuses directly upon these essentially local problems and is tailored to combat effectively the perceived evils.

Of course, even state regulation designed to protect vital state interests must give way to paramount federal legislation. But we will not presume that Congress, in enacting the INA, intended to oust state authority to regulate the employment relationship covered by §2805(a) in a manner consistent with pertinent federal laws. Only a demonstration that complete ouster of state power — including state power to promulgate laws not in conflict with federal laws — was "'the clear and manifest purpose of Congress'" would justify that conclusion. Florida Lime & Avocado Growers v. Paul, *supra*, at 146, quoting Rice v. Santa Fe Elevator Corp., 331 U.S. 218, 230 (1947). Respondents have not made that demonstration. They fail to point out, and an independent review does not reveal, any specific indication in either the wording or the legislative history of the INA that Congress intended to preclude even harmonious state regulation touching on aliens in general, or the employment of illegal aliens in particular.

Nor can such intent be derived from the scope and detail of the INA. The central concern of the INA is with the terms and conditions of admission to the country and the subsequent treatment of aliens lawfully in the country. The comprehensiveness of the INA scheme for regulation of immigration and naturalization, without more, cannot be said to draw in the employment of illegal aliens as "plainly within...[that] central aim of federal regulation." San Diego Unions v. Garmon, 359 U.S. 236, 244 (1959). This conclusion is buttressed by the fact that comprehensiveness of legislation governing entry and stay of aliens was to be expected in light of the nature and complexity of the subject. As the Court said in another legislative context: "Given the complexity of the matter addressed by Congress..., a detailed statutory scheme was both likely and appropriate, completely apart from any questions of pre-emptive intent." New York Dept. of Social Services v. Dublino, 413 U.S. 405, 415 (1973)....

Hines v. Davidowitz, 312 U.S. 52 (1941), and Pennsylvania v. Nelson, 350 U.S. 497 (1956), upon which respondents rely, are fully consistent with this conclusion. *Hines* held that Pennsylvania's Alien Registration Act of 1939 was pre-empted by the federal Alien Registration Act. *Nelson* held that the Pennsylvania Sedition Act was pre-empted by the federal Smith Act. Although both cases relied on the comprehensiveness of the federal regulatory schemes in finding pre-emptive intent, both federal statutes were in the specific field which the States were attempting to regulate, while here there is no indication that Congress intended to preclude state law in the area of employment regulation. And *Nelson* stated that even in the face of the general immigration laws, States would have the right "to enforce their sedition laws at times when the Federal Government has not occupied the field and is not protecting the entire country from seditious conduct." Moreover, in neither *Hines* nor *Nelson* was there affirmative evidence, as here, that Congress sanctioned concurrent state legislation on the subject covered by the challenged state law. Furthermore, to the extent those cases were based on the predominance of federal interest in the fields of immigration and foreign affairs, there would not appear to be a similar federal interest in a situation in which the state law is fashioned to remedy local problems, and operates only on local employers, and only with respect to individuals whom the Federal Government has already declared cannot work in this country. Finally, the Pennsylvania statutes in *Hines* and *Nelson* imposed burdens on aliens lawfully within the country that created conflicts with various federal laws.

Crosby v. National Foreign Trade Council

530 U.S. 363 (2000)

[In June 1996, Massachusetts adopted a statute that generally barred state entities from buying goods or services from any person or organization identified on a state-compiled "restricted purchase list" as doing business with Burma (also called Myanmar). The statute contained three exceptions, for situations in which the procurement was essential and, in the absence of the restricted bid, there would be no bids or insufficient competition; the procurement was for medical supplies; or the procurement efforts elicited no bids or offers that were less than 10 percent greater than the restricted bid.

In September 1996, Congress passed a statute imposing a set of mandatory and conditional sanctions on Burma. The federal statute imposed several sanctions directly on Burma—banning most federal aid to the Burmese Government, instructing U.S. representatives in international financial institutions to vote against loans or other assistance to or for Burma, and providing that no entry visa was to be issued to any Burmese government official unless required by treaty or to staff the Burmese mission to the United Nations. These sanctions were to remain in effect "until such time as the President determines and certifies to Congress that Burma has made measurable and substantial progress in improving human rights practices and implementing democratic government." The federal statute also authorized the President to prohibit "United States persons" from "new investment" in Burma, and directed him to do so if he determined and certified to Congress that the Burmese Government had physically harmed, rearrested, or exiled Daw Aung San Suu Kyi (the opposition leader selected to receive the Nobel Peace Prize), or had committed "large-scale repression of or violence against the Democratic opposition." The statute also directed the President to work to develop "a comprehensive, multilateral strategy to bring democracy to and improve human rights practices and the quality of life in Burma." The statute further required the President to report periodically to certain committee chairmen on the progress toward democratization and better living conditions in Burma as well as on the development of the required strategy. Finally, the statute authorized the President "to waive, temporarily or permanently, any sanction [under the federal statute] . . . if he determines and certifies to Congress that the application of such sanction would be contrary to the national security interests of the United States."

In May 1997, President Clinton issued an executive order certifying that the Government of Burma had "committed large-scale repression of the democratic opposition in Burma" and finding that the Burmese Government's actions and policies constituted "an unusual and extraordinary threat to the national security and foreign policy of the United States," a threat characterized as a national emergency. The order proceeded to prohibit new investment in Burma "by United States persons," any approval or facilitation by a United States person of such new investment by foreign persons, and any transaction meant to evade or avoid the ban. The order generally incorporated the exceptions and exemptions in the statute. Finally, the order delegated to the Secretary of State the tasks of working with the Association of Southeast Asian Nations (ASEAN) and other countries to develop a strategy for democracy, human rights, and the quality of life in Burma, and of making the required congressional reports.

In this case, a trade group challenged the validity of the Massachusetts statute based on a variety of preemption arguments.]

JUSTICE SOUTER delivered the opinion of the Court. . . .

A fundamental principle of the Constitution is that Congress has the power to preempt state law. Art. VI, cl. 2. Even without an express provision for preemption, we have found that state law must yield to a congressional Act in at least two circumstances. When Congress intends federal law to "occupy the field," state law in that area is preempted. And even if Congress has not occupied the field, state law is naturally preempted to the extent of any conflict with a federal statute. . . . Hines v. Davidowitz. . . . We will find preemption where it is impossible for a private party to comply with both state and federal law, . . . and where "under the circumstances of [a] particular case, [the challenged state law] stands as an obstacle to the accomplishment and execution of the full purposes and objectives of Congress." *Hines*. What is a sufficient obstacle is a matter of judgment, to be informed by examining the federal statute as a whole and identifying its purpose and intended effects:

> For when the question is whether a Federal act overrides a state law, the entire
> scheme of the statute must of course be considered and that which needs must be

implied is of no less force than that which is expressed. If the purpose of the act cannot otherwise be accomplished — if its operation within its chosen field else must be frustrated and its provisions be refused their natural effect — the state law must yield to the regulation of Congress within the sphere of its delegated power. Savage v. Jones, 225 U.S. 501, 533 (1912), quoted in *Hines, supra,* at 67, n.20.

Applying this standard, we see the state Burma law as an obstacle to the accomplishment of Congress's full objectives under the federal Act. We find that the state law undermines the intended purpose and "natural effect" of at least three provisions of the federal Act, that is, its delegation of effective discretion to the President to control economic sanctions against Burma, its limitation of sanctions solely to United States persons and new investment, and its directive to the President to proceed diplomatically in developing a comprehensive, multilateral strategy towards Burma.[8]

First, Congress clearly intended the federal act to provide the President with flexible and effective authority over economic sanctions against Burma. Although Congress immediately put in place a set of initial sanctions (prohibiting bilateral aid, support for international financial assistance, and entry by Burmese officials into the United States), it authorized the President to terminate any and all of those measures upon determining and certifying that there had been progress in human rights and democracy in Burma. It invested the President with the further power to ban new investment by United States persons, dependent only on specific Presidential findings of repression in Burma. And, most significantly, Congress empowered the President "to waive, temporarily or permanently, any sanction [under the federal act]...if he determines and certifies to Congress that the application of such sanction would be contrary to the national security interests of the United States."

This express investiture of the President with statutory authority to act for the United States in imposing sanctions with respect to the government of Burma, augmented by the flexibility to respond to change by suspending sanctions in the interest of national security, recalls Justice Jackson's observation in Youngstown Sheet & Tube Co. v. Sawyer, 343 U.S. 579, 635 (1952): "When the President acts pursuant to an express or implied authorization of Congress, his authority is at its maximum, for it includes all that he possesses in his own right plus all that Congress can delegate." *See also id.* at 635-636, n.2 (noting that the President's power in the area of foreign relations is least restricted by Congress and citing United States v. Curtiss-Wright Export Corp., 299 U.S. 304 (1936)). Within the sphere defined by Congress, then, the statute has placed the President in a position with as much discretion to exercise economic leverage against Burma, with an eye toward national security, as our law will admit. And it is just this plenitude of Executive authority that we think controls the issue of preemption here. The President has been given this authority not merely to make a political statement but to achieve a political result, and the fullness of his authority shows the importance in the

8. We leave for another day a consideration in this context of a presumption against preemption. Assuming, *arguendo,* that some presumption against preemption is appropriate, we conclude, based on our analysis below, that the state Act presents a sufficient obstacle to the full accomplishment of Congress's objectives under the federal Act to find it preempted. *See* Hines v. Davidowitz, 312 U.S. 52, 67 (1941).

Because our conclusion that the state Act conflicts with federal law is sufficient to affirm the judgment below, we decline to speak to field preemption as a separate issue,...or to pass on the First Circuit's rulings addressing the foreign affairs power or the dormant Foreign Commerce Clause. *See* Ashwander v. TVA, 297 U.S. 288, 346-347 (1936) (concurring opinion).

congressional mind of reaching that result. It is simply implausible that Congress would have gone to such lengths to empower the President if it had been willing to compromise his effectiveness by deference to every provision of state statute or local ordinance that might, if enforced, blunt the consequences of discretionary Presidential action.

And that is just what the Massachusetts Burma law would do in imposing a different, state system of economic pressure against the Burmese political regime. As will be seen, the state statute penalizes some private action that the federal Act (as administered by the President) may allow, and pulls levers of influence that the federal Act does not reach. But the point here is that the state sanctions are immediate, and perpetual, there being no termination provision. This unyielding application undermines the President's intended statutory authority by making it impossible for him to restrain fully the coercive power of the national economy when he may choose to take the discretionary action open to him, whether he believes that the national interest requires sanctions to be lifted, or believes that the promise of lifting sanctions would move the Burmese regime in the democratic direction. Quite simply, if the Massachusetts law is enforceable the President has less to offer and less economic and diplomatic leverage as a consequence. In Dames & Moore v. Regan, 453 U.S. 654 (1981), we used the metaphor of the bargaining chip to describe the President's control of funds valuable to a hostile country; here, the state Act reduces the value of the chips created by the federal statute. It thus "stands as an obstacle to the accomplishment and execution of the full purposes and objectives of Congress." *Hines,* 312 U.S. at 67.

Congress manifestly intended to limit economic pressure against the Burmese Government to a specific range. The federal Act confines its reach to United States persons, imposes limited immediate sanctions, places only a conditional ban on a carefully defined area of "new investment," and pointedly exempts contracts to sell or purchase goods, services, or technology. These detailed provisions show that Congress's calibrated Burma policy is a deliberate effort "to steer a middle path," *Hines, supra.*[13]

The State has set a different course, and its statute conflicts with federal law at a number of points by penalizing individuals and conduct that Congress has explicitly exempted or excluded from sanctions. While the state Act differs from the federal in relying entirely on indirect economic leverage through third parties with Burmese connections, it otherwise stands in clear contrast to the congressional scheme in the scope of subject matter addressed. It restricts all contracts between the State and companies doing business in Burma, except when purchasing medical supplies and other essentials (or when short of comparable bids). It is specific in targeting contracts to provide financial services, and general goods and services, to the Government of Burma, and thus prohibits contracts between the State and United States persons for goods, services, or technology, even though those transactions are explicitly exempted from the ambit of new investment prohibition when

13. The fact that Congress repeatedly considered and rejected targeting a broader range of conduct lends additional support to our view. Most importantly, the federal Act, as passed, replaced the original proposed [statute], which barred "any investment in Burma" by a United States national without exception or limitation. Congress also rejected a competing amendment, which similarly provided that "United States nationals shall not make any investment in Burma," and would have permitted the President to impose conditional sanctions on the importation of "articles which are produced, manufactured, grown, or extracted in Burma," and would have barred all travel by United States nationals to Burma. Congress had rejected an earlier amendment that would have prohibited all United States investment in Burma, subject to the President's power to lift sanctions.

the President exercises his discretionary authority to impose sanctions under the federal Act.

As with the subject of business meant to be affected, so with the class of companies doing it: the state Act's generality stands at odds with the federal discreteness. The Massachusetts law directly and indirectly imposes costs on all companies that do any business in Burma, save for those reporting news or providing international telecommunications goods or services, or medical supplies. It sanctions companies promoting the importation of natural resources controlled by the government of Burma, or having any operations or affiliates in Burma. The state Act thus penalizes companies with pre-existing affiliates or investments, all of which lie beyond the reach of the federal act's restrictions on "new investment" in Burmese economic development. The state Act, moreover, imposes restrictions on foreign companies as well as domestic, whereas the federal Act limits its reach to United States persons.

The conflicts are not rendered irrelevant by the State's argument that there is no real conflict between the statutes because they share the same goals and because some companies may comply with both sets of restrictions. The fact of a common end hardly neutralizes conflicting means, and the fact that some companies may be able to comply with both sets of sanctions does not mean that the state Act is not at odds with achievement of the federal decision about the right degree of pressure to employ. *See Hines*, 312 U.S. at 61 ("The basic subject of the state and federal laws is identical"); *id.* at 67 (finding conflict preemption). " 'Conflict is imminent' " when " 'two separate remedies are brought to bear on the same activity.' " Wisconsin Dept. of Industry v. Gould Inc., 475 U.S. 282 (1986) (quoting Garner v. Teamsters, 346 U.S. 485, 498-499 (1953)). Sanctions are drawn not only to bar what they prohibit but to allow what they permit, and the inconsistency of sanctions here undermines the congressional calibration of force.

Finally, the state Act is at odds with the President's intended authority to speak for the United States among the world's nations in developing a "comprehensive, multilateral strategy to bring democracy to and improve human rights practices and the quality of life in Burma." Congress called for Presidential cooperation with members of ASEAN and other countries in developing such a strategy, directed the President to encourage a dialogue between the government of Burma and the democratic opposition, and required him to report to the Congress on the progress of his diplomatic efforts. As with Congress's explicit delegation to the President of power over economic sanctions, Congress's express command to the President to take the initiative for the United States among the international community invested him with the maximum authority of the National Government, *cf. Youngstown Sheet & Tube Co.*, 343 U.S. at 635, in harmony with the President's own constitutional powers, U.S. Const., Art. II, §2, cl. 2 ("[The President] shall have Power, by and with the Advice and Consent of the Senate, to make Treaties" and "shall appoint Ambassadors, other public Ministers and Consuls"); §3 ("[The President] shall receive Ambassadors and other public Ministers"). This clear mandate and invocation of exclusively national power belies any suggestion that Congress intended the President's effective voice to be obscured by state or local action.

Again, the state Act undermines the President's capacity, in this instance for effective diplomacy. It is not merely that the differences between the state and federal Acts in scope and type of sanctions threaten to complicate discussions; they compromise the very capacity of the President to speak for the Nation with one voice in dealing with other governments. We need not get into any general consideration of limits of state action affecting foreign affairs to realize that the President's maximum power to persuade rests on his capacity to bargain for the benefits of access to the entire national economy without exception for enclaves fenced off willy-nilly by inconsistent political tactics. When such exceptions do qualify his capacity to present a coherent position on behalf of the national economy, he is weakened, of course, not only in dealing with the Burmese regime, but in working together with other nations in hopes of reaching common policy and "comprehensive" strategy.

While the threat to the President's power to speak and bargain effectively with other nations seems clear enough, the record is replete with evidence to answer any skeptics. First, in response to the passage of the state Act, a number of this country's allies and trading partners filed formal protests with the National Government.... Second, the EU and Japan have gone a step further in lodging formal complaints against the United States in the World Trade Organization (WTO), claiming that the state Act violates certain provisions of the Agreement on Government Procurement, and the consequence has been to embroil the National Government for some time now in international dispute proceedings under the auspices of the WTO. In their brief before this Court, EU officials point to the WTO dispute as threatening relations with the United States, and note that the state Act has become the topic of "intensive discussions" with officials of the United States at the highest levels, those discussions including exchanges at the twice yearly EU-U.S. Summit. Third, the Executive has consistently represented that the state Act has complicated its dealings with foreign sovereigns and proven an impediment to accomplishing objectives assigned it by Congress....[22] This evidence in combination is more than sufficient to show that the state Act stands as an obstacle in addressing the congressional obligation to devise a comprehensive, multilateral strategy....

The State's remaining argument is unavailing. It contends that the failure of Congress to preempt the state Act demonstrates implicit permission. The State points out that Congress has repeatedly declined to enact express preemption provisions aimed at state and local sanctions, and it calls our attention to the large number of such measures passed against South Africa in the 1980s, which various authorities cited have thought were not preempted. The State stresses that Congress was aware of the state Act in 1996, but did not preempt it explicitly when it adopted its own Burma statute. The State would have us conclude that Congress's continuing failure to enact express preemption implies approval, particularly in light of occasional instances of express preemption of state sanctions in the past.

The argument is unconvincing on more than one level. A failure to provide for preemption expressly may reflect nothing more than the settled character of implied preemption doctrine that courts will dependably apply, and in any event, the existence of conflict cognizable under the Supremacy Clause does not depend on express congressional recognition that federal and state law may conflict, *Hines*. The State's inference of congressional intent is unwarranted here, therefore, simply because the silence of Congress is ambiguous. Since we never ruled on whether state and local sanctions against South Africa in the 1980s were preempted or otherwise invalid, arguable parallels between the two sets of federal and state Acts do not tell us much about the validity of the latter.

22. The United States, in its brief as *amicus curiae*, continues to advance this position before us. This conclusion has been consistently presented by senior United States officials.

Notes and Questions

1. The Supremacy Clause makes clear that federal statutes can preempt state law. Sometimes Congress expressly states its intent to preempt. For example, the Employee Retirement Income Security Act (ERISA) provides that it "shall supersede any and all State laws insofar as they . . . relate to any employee benefit plan" covered by the Act. 29 U.S.C. §1144(a). Similarly, the federal copyright statute expressly preempts "legal or equitable rights [under state law] that are equivalent to any of the exclusive rights within the general scope of copyright as specified by [the federal statute]." 17 U.S.C. §301(a). Most federal statutes, however, do not contain express preemption provisions. In these situations, preemption can still be found in the following circumstances: *Conflict preemption* occurs when it is impossible to comply with a federal statute (which is otherwise silent about preemption) and a state law. In this context, preemption follows by necessary implication from the fact of conflict. *Obstacle preemption* first identifies the "purposes and objectives" of a federal statute that is silent about preemptive scope; preemption follows if the state statute "stands as an obstacle to the accomplishment" of these purposes and objectives. *Field preemption* can occur in one of two ways. First, a federal regulatory scheme can be "so pervasive" as to imply that "Congress left no room for the States to supplement it." *See* English v. General Electric Co., 496 U.S. 72, 79 (1990). Second, a "federal interest" in the field addressed by a federal statute may be "so dominant" that federal law "will be assumed to preclude enforcement of state laws on the same subject." *See* Rice v. Santa Fe Elevator Corp., 331 U.S. 218, 230 (1947). Which type of preemption was at issue in each of the three cases above?

2. As Justice Stone suggests in his dissent in *Hines*, obstacle and field preemption may require courts to speculate about a statute's purposes and objectives. *See also* Karen A. Jordan, *The Shifting Preemption Paradigm: Conceptual and Interpretive Issues,* 51 Vand. L. Rev. 1149 (1998); Caleb Nelson, *Preemption,* 86 Va. L. Rev. 225 (2000). What were the purported statutory purposes and objectives in *Hines* and *Crosby*? How did the Supreme Court discern those purposes and objectives? Do courts have the competence, or the authority, to speculate about Congress's goals in this way? In the context of foreign relations statutes, does this speculation entail the exercise of foreign policy judgment?

3. Under obstacle preemption, even if a court has correctly identified a statute's objectives, it must also determine whether the state law in question interferes with those objectives. What evidence should a court look at in resolving this issue? What weight did the Court in *Crosby* give to Congress's failure to preempt the Massachusetts statute? To the views of the Executive Branch? To the views and complaints of foreign governments? What weight, if any, should be given to these sources?

4. Courts sometimes invoke presumptions to assist them in deciding whether a statute, silent on its face about preemption, nonetheless preempts state law. In the domestic context, courts often presume that Congress does not intend to preempt state law, especially the historic police powers of the states, unless Congress makes its preemptive intent clear. *See, e.g.,* Gregory v. Ashcroft, 501 U.S. 452, 464 (1991). This presumption is grounded in structural constitutional principles of federalism. It is designed to ensure that Congress considers the federal-state balance when enacting legislation and that any preemption of state law is attributable to the policy judgments of Congress, where the states are represented. *See, e.g.,* Kenneth Starr et al., The Law of Preemption 40-55 (1991); Laurence H. Tribe, 1 American Constitutional Law 1174-75 (3d ed. 2000); Paul Wolfson, *Preemption and Federalism: The Missing Link,* 16 Hastings Const. L.Q. 69, 111-14 (1988). The Court in *Hines,* however, appeared to embrace a presumption in favor of preemption for foreign relations statutes. The Court reasoned that, unlike its treatment of domestic matters, the Constitution evinces a preference for federal control of foreign relations. Although *De Canas,* like *Hines,* involved a federal immigration statute, the Court in *De Canas* did not apply a presumption in favor of preemption, but instead appeared to apply a presumption against preemption. What explains this difference between these decisions?

In answering this question, consider United States v. Locke, 529 U.S. 89 (2000), decided a few months before *Crosby*. In *Locke*, the Court held that Washington state regulations concerning remedies for oil spills were preempted by the federal Port and Waterways Safety Act of 1972 (PWSA). In the course of its analysis, the Court stated:

> The state laws now in question bear upon national and international maritime commerce, and in this area there is no beginning assumption that concurrent regulation by the State is a valid exercise of its police powers. Rather, we must ask whether the local laws in question are consistent with the federal statutory structure, which has as one of its objectives a uniformity of regulation for maritime commerce. No artificial presumption aids us in determining the scope of appropriate local regulation under the PWSA.

Id. at 108-09. What does this passage suggest about the proper presumption? Does it reject a presumption against preemption? If so, to what extent? Does the Court's reasoning here apply to all foreign relations cases? Or only to ones involving "national and maritime commerce" when the "federal statutory structure" suggests federal uniformity as an objective? Even if the Court rejects a presumption against preemption, does it embrace a presumption in favor of preemption? Is the Court in *Locke* avoiding presumptions, as in *Crosby*, or doing something else?

5. Which of the two presumptive canons should courts embrace when a federal foreign relations statute implicates a traditional state prerogative? This was the situation in *Crosby*, because states traditionally have exercised significant control over how they spend state funds on state projects. In footnote 8, the Court in *Crosby* avoided the question of what presumption, if any, is appropriate. But does *Crosby* implicitly embrace the *Hines* canon? What presumptive canon, if any, should it have embraced? Which is more important — the protection of state prerogatives, or a uniform federal foreign relations policy? How do courts decide? Should the canons cancel one another out? In answering this question, what is the significance, if any, of the waning of the distinction between domestic and foreign affairs? For purposes of deciding which presumption applies, how do courts even tell which federal statutes are "foreign relations statutes"?

6. The Court in *Hines* states: "Our system of government is such that the interest of the cities, counties and states, no less than the interest of the people of the whole nation, imperatively requires that federal power in the field affecting foreign relations be left entirely free from local interference." What does this statement mean? Does it mean that states can never act in a way that affects relations with other nations? Does it mean that federal power to preempt state foreign relations activity is unlimited?

7. In support of its conclusion that the Massachusetts statute stood as an obstacle to Congress's desire for the President to establish a "comprehensive, multilateral strategy" for dealing with Myanmar, the Court in *Crosby* cited the formal complaints lodged by the European Union and Japan against the United States in the World Trade Organization (WTO). The Court also noted that "EU officials point to the WTO dispute as threatening relations with the United States." The petitioners in *Crosby*, however, argued that the WTO proceedings, taken in context, demonstrated that the political branches did *not* wish to preempt the state law. First, when the case before the WTO was first brought, the Executive Branch criticized the action and pledged to "defend the [state] measure." Second, when Congress enacted implementing legislation for the WTO, it specified that U.S. courts could only declare state laws inconsistent with the WTO "in an action brought by the United States for the purpose of declaring such law or application invalid," 19 U.S.C. §3512(b)(2)(A), something that never occurred with respect to the Massachusetts statute. Should the Court have given more weight to these actions by the Executive Branch and Congress?

8. *Crosby* has provoked substantial academic commentary that is noteworthy for its widely differing interpretations of the opinion. *See, e.g.*, Sarah H. Cleveland, Crosby *and the "One-Voice" Myth in U.S. Foreign Relations*, 46 Vill. L. Rev. 975, 1013 (2001) ("The Court's willingness to invalidate a state measure that was perceived as digressing from federal policy, however incidentally, is more akin to dormant constitutional preemption . . . than to the simple statutory preemption the Court purported to apply."); Jack L. Goldsmith, *Statutory Foreign Affairs Preemption*, 2001 Sup. Ct. Rev. 175 (arguing that *Crosby* rejects judicial foreign relations effects test and reaffirms trend towards formalism in U.S. foreign relations law); Daniel Halberstam, *The Foreign Affairs of Federal Systems: A National Perspective on the Benefits of State Participation*, 46 Vill. L. Rev. 1015, 1066 (2001) ("The Supreme Court's decision in *Crosby* is thus susceptible to two readings, one suggesting strong federal exclusivity, and another signaling openness to state participation in foreign affairs."); Edward Swaine, Crosby *as Foreign Relations Law*, 41 Va. J. Int'l L. 481 (2001) (describing *Crosby* as an effort to engage in constitutional avoidance and judicial minimalism, and criticizing this effort); Mark Tushnet, *Globalization and Federalism in a Post-*Printz *World*, 36 Tulsa L.J. 11 (2000) (arguing that *Crosby* reflects "the Court's limited willingness to develop a robust law of federalism"); Carlos Manuel Vazquez, *W[h]ither* Zschernig?, 46 Vill. L. Rev. 1259, 1323 (2001) ("[I]t is only a slight exaggeration to say that *Crosby* is a dormant foreign affairs case in disguise."); Ernest A. Young, *Dual Federalism, Concurrent Jurisdiction, and the Foreign Affairs Exception*, 69 Geo. Wash. L. Rev. 139 (2001) (arguing that *Crosby* embraces a presumption in favor of preemption for foreign relations statutes). *See also* Sanford Levinson, *Compelling Collaboration with Evil? A Comment on Crosby v. National Foreign Trade Council*, 69 Fordham L. Rev. 2189, 2200 (2001) (criticizing the Court in *Crosby* for "mouthing Cold War platitudes at a time when they make increasingly little sense").

B. TREATY PREEMPTION

This section focuses on issues relating to treaty preemption. As we learned in Chapter 1, the failure of states to comply with treaty obligations, and the inability of the federal government to compel state compliance, was a significant problem under the Articles of Confederation. The constitutional Framers attempted to address this problem by, among other things, creating a Supremacy Clause that made treaties, in addition to federal statutes and the Constitution, supreme over state law.

Clark v. Allen

331 U.S. 503 (1947)

MR. JUSTICE DOUGLAS delivered the opinion of the Court.

Alvina Wagner, a resident of California, died in 1942, leaving real and personal property situate there. By a will dated December 23, 1941, and admitted to probate in a California court in 1942, she bequeathed her entire estate to four relatives who are nationals and residents of Germany. Six heirs-at-law, residents of California, filed a petition for determination of heirship in the probate proceedings claiming that the German nationals were ineligible as legatees under California law.[1]

There has never been a hearing on that petition. For in 1943 the Alien Property Custodian, to whose functions the Attorney General has recently succeeded, vested in himself all right, title and interest of the German nationals in the estate of this decedent. He thereupon instituted this action in the District Court against the executor under the will and the California heirs-at-law for a determination that they had no interest in the estate and that he was entitled to the entire net estate, after payment of administration and other expenses. The District Court granted judgment for the Custodian on the pleadings. The Circuit Court of Appeals . . . held for respondents. The case is here again on a petition for a writ of certiorari which we granted because the issues raised are of national importance.

First. Our problem starts with the Treaty of Friendship, Commerce and Consular Rights with Germany, signed December 8, 1923, and proclaimed October 14, 1925. It has different provisions governing the testamentary disposition of realty and personalty, which we will treat separately. The one pertaining to realty, contained in Article IV, reads as follows:

> Where, on the death of any person holding real or other immovable property or interests therein within the territories of one High Contracting Party, such property or interests therein would, by the laws of the country or by a testamentary disposition, descend or pass to a national of the other High Contracting Party, whether resident or non-resident, were he not disqualified by the laws of the country where such property or interests therein is or are situated, such national shall be allowed a term of three years in which to sell the same, this term to be reasonably prolonged if circumstances render it necessary, and withdraw the proceeds thereof, without restraint or

---

1. Section 259, California Probate Code, in 1942 provided:

> The rights of aliens not residing within the United States or its territories to take either real or personal property or the proceeds thereof in this State by succession or testamentary disposition, upon the same terms and conditions as residents and citizens of the United States is dependent in each case upon the existence of a reciprocal right upon the part of citizens of the United States to take real and personal property and the proceeds thereof upon the same terms and conditions as residents and citizens of the respective countries of which such aliens are inhabitants and citizens and upon the rights of citizens of the United States to receive by payment to them within the United States or its territories money originating from the estates of persons dying within such foreign countries.

Section 259.2 provided:

> If such reciprocal rights are not found to exist and if no heirs other than such aliens are found eligible to take such property, the property shall be disposed of as escheated property.

interference, and exempt from any succession, probate or administrative duties or
charges other than those which may be imposed in like cases upon the nationals of the
country from which such proceeds may be drawn.

The rights secured are in terms a right to sell within a specified time plus a right to
withdraw the proceeds and an exemption from discriminatory taxation. It is plain
that those rights extend to the German heirs of "any person" holding realty in the
United States. And though they are not expressed in terms of ownership or the
right to inherit, that is their import and meaning.

If, therefore, the provisions of the treaty have not been superseded or abrogated, they prevail over any requirements of California law which conflict with
them....

[The Court concludes that the treaty has not been superseded or abrogated,
either by statute, treaty, or the outbreak of war, and that it therefore preempts
inconsistent state law.]

...So far as the right of inheritance of realty under Article IV of the present
treaty is concerned, we find no incompatibility with national policy, for reasons
already given....

Third. The problem of the personalty raises distinct questions. Article IV of the
treaty contains the following provision pertaining to it:

Nationals of either High Contracting Party may have full power to dispose of their
personal property of every kind within the territories of the other, by testament,
donation, or otherwise, and their heirs, legatees and donees, of whatsoever nationality,
whether resident or non-resident, shall succeed to such personal property, and may
take possession thereof, either by themselves or by others acting for them, and retain
or dispose of the same at their pleasure subject to the payment of such duties or
charges only as the nationals of the High Contracting Party within whose territories
such property may be or belong shall be liable to pay in like cases.

A practically identical provision of the Treaty of 1844 with Wurttemburg, Art. III, 8
Stat. 588, was before the Court in Frederickson v. Louisiana, 23 How. 445. In that
case the testator was a citizen of the United States, his legatees being citizens and
residents of Wurttemberg. Louisiana, where the testator was domiciled, levied a
succession tax of 10 per cent on legatees not domiciled in the United States. The
Court held that the treaty did not cover the "case of a citizen or subject of the
respective countries residing at home, and disposing of property there in favor
of a citizen or subject of the other..." pp. 447-448. That decision was made in 1860.
In 1917 the Court followed it in cases involving three other treaties. Petersen v.
Iowa, 245 U.S. 170; Duus v. Brown, 245 U.S. 176; Skarderud v. Tax Commission,
245 U.S. 633.

The construction adopted by those cases is, to say the least, permissible when
the syntax of the sentences dealing with realty and personalty is considered. So far
as realty is concerned, the testator includes "any person"; and the property covered
is that within the territory of either of the high contracting parties. In case of
personalty, the provision governs the right of "nationals" of either contracting
party to dispose of their property within the territory of the "other" contracting
party; and it is "such personal property" that the "heirs, legatees and donees" are
entitled to take.

Petitioner, however, presents a detailed account of the history of the clause
which was not before the Court in Frederickson v. Louisiana, and which bears
out the construction that it grants the foreign heir the right to succeed to his

inheritance or the proceeds thereof. But we do not stop to review that history. For the consistent judicial construction of the language since 1860 has given it a character which the treaty-making agencies have not seen fit to alter. And that construction is entirely consistent with the plain language of the treaty. We therefore do not deem it appropriate to change that construction at this late date, even though as an original matter the other view might have much to commend it.

We accordingly hold that Article IV of the treaty does not cover personalty located in this country and which an American citizen undertakes to leave to German nationals. We do not know from the present record the nationality of Alvina Wagner. But since the issue arises on the Government's motion for judgment on the pleadings, we proceed on the assumption less favorable to it, viz., that she was an American citizen.

Fourth. It is argued, however, that even though the provision of the treaty is inapplicable, the personalty may not be disposed of pursuant to the California statute because that statute is unconstitutional. . . . The challenge to the statute is that it is an extension of state power into the field of foreign affairs, which is exclusively reserved by the Constitution to the Federal Government. That argument is based on the fact that under the statute the right of nonresident aliens to take by succession or testamentary disposition is dependent upon the existence of a reciprocal right on the part of citizens of the United States to take personalty on the same terms and conditions as residents and citizens of the other nation. The argument is that by this method California seeks to promote the right of American citizens to inherit abroad by offering to aliens reciprocal rights of inheritance in California. Such an offer of reciprocal arrangements is said to be a matter for settlement by the Federal Government on a nation-wide basis.

In *Blythe* v. *Hinckley*, 180 U.S. 333, California had granted aliens an unqualified right to inherit property within its borders. The alien claimant was a citizen of Great Britain with whom the United States had no treaty providing for inheritance by aliens in this country. The argument was that a grant of rights to aliens by a State was, in absence of a treaty, a forbidden entry into foreign affairs. The Court rejected the argument as being an extraordinary one. The objection to the present statute is equally farfetched.

Rights of succession to property are determined by local law. Those rights may be affected by an overriding federal policy, as where a treaty makes different or conflicting arrangements. Then the state policy must give way. *Cf.* Hines v. Davidowitz, 312 U.S. 52. But here there is no treaty governing the rights of succession to the personal property. Nor has California entered the forbidden domain of negotiating with a foreign country, United States v. Curtiss-Wright Corp., 299 U.S. 304, 316-17, or making a compact with it contrary to the prohibition of Article I, Section 10 of the Constitution. What California has done will have some incidental or indirect effect in foreign countries. But that is true of many state laws which none would claim cross the forbidden line.

In re World War II Era Japanese Forced Labor Litigation
114 F. Supp. 2d 939 (N.D. Cal. 2000)

VAUGHN R. WALKER, UNITED STATES DISTRICT JUDGE.
On December 23, 1941, after mounting a brave resistance against an overwhelming foe, the small American garrison on Wake Island in the South Pacific

surrendered to Imperial Japanese forces. James King, a former United States Marine, was among the troops and civilians taken prisoner by the invaders. He was ultimately shipped to Kyushu, Japan, where he spent the remainder of the war toiling by day as a slave laborer in a steel factory and enduring maltreatment in a prison camp by night. When captured, King was 20 years old, 5 feet 11 inches tall and weighed 167 pounds. At the conclusion of the war, he weighed 98 pounds.

James King is one of the plaintiffs in these actions against Japanese corporations for forced labor in World War II; his experience, and the undisputed injustice he suffered, are representative. King and the other plaintiffs seek judicial redress for this injustice. . . .

In addressing the motions to dismiss, the court refers again to a complaint that is representative of the actions by United States and Allied POWs, King v. Nippon Steel Corp., No. 99-504.

As noted at the outset of this order, plaintiff King seeks redress for wrongs inflicted by his captors half a century ago. In count one of the complaint, [King] asserts a claim under California Code of Civil Procedure §354.6, a new law that permits an action by a "prisoner-of-war of the Nazi regime, its allies or sympathizers" to "recover compensation for labor performed as a Second World War slave labor victim . . . from any entity or successor in interest thereof, for whom that labor was performed." Cal Code Civ. Pro. §354.6. Count two is an unjust enrichment claim in which plaintiff seeks disgorgement and restitution of economic benefits derived from his labor. In count three, plaintiff seeks damages in tort for battery, intentional infliction of emotional distress and unlawful imprisonment. Count four alleges that defendant's failure to reveal its prior exploitation of prisoner labor to present-day customers in California and elsewhere constitutes an unfair business practice under California Business and Professions Code §17204. . . .

The Treaty of Peace with Japan was signed at San Francisco on September 8, 1951, by the representatives of the United States and 47 other Allied powers and Japan. Treaty of Peace with Japan, [1952] 3 UST 3169, TIAS No. 2490 (1951). President Truman, with the advice and consent of the Senate, ratified the treaty and it became effective April 28, 1952.

Article 14 provides the terms of Japanese payment "for the damage and suffering caused by it during the war." *Id.* at Art. 14(a). For present purposes, the salient features of the agreement are: (1) a grant of authority of Allied powers to seize Japanese property within their jurisdiction at the time of the treaty's effective date; (2) an obligation of Japan to assist in the rebuilding of territory occupied by Japanese forces during the war and (3) *waiver* of all "other claims of the Allied Powers and their nationals arising out of any actions taken by Japan and its nationals in the course of the prosecution of the war." *Id.* at Art. 14(a)-(b) (emphasis added).

It is the waiver provision that defendants argue bars plaintiffs' present claims. In its entirety, the provision reads:

(b) Except as otherwise provided in the present Treaty, the Allied Powers waive all reparations claims of the Allied Powers, other claims of the Allied Powers and their nationals arising out of any actions taken by Japan and its nationals in the course of the prosecution of the war, and claims of the Allied Powers for direct military costs of occupation.

Id. at Art. 14(b).

On its face, the treaty waives "all" reparations and "other claims" of the "nationals" of Allied powers "arising out of any actions taken by Japan and its nationals during the course of the prosecution of the war." The language of this waiver is strikingly broad, and contains no conditional language or limitations, save for the opening clause referring to the provisions of the treaty. The interests of Allied prisoners of war are addressed in Article 16, which provides for transfer of Japanese assets in neutral or enemy jurisdictions to the International Committee of the Red Cross for distribution to former prisoners and their families. *Id.* at Art. 16. The treaty specifically exempts from reparations, furthermore, those Japanese assets resulting from "the resumption of trade and financial relations subsequent to September 2, 1945." *Id.* at Art. 14(a)(2)(II)(iv).

To avoid the preclusive effect of the treaty, plaintiffs advance an interpretation of Article 14(b) that is strained and, ultimately, unconvincing. Although the argument has several shades, it comes down to this: the signatories of the treaty did not understand the Allied waiver to apply to prisoner of war claims because the provision did not expressly identify such claims, in contrast to the corresponding Japanese waiver provision of Article 19. Article 19(b) states that the Japanese waiver includes "any claims and debts arising in respect to Japanese prisoners of war and civilian internees in the hands of the Allied Powers."

That the treaty is more specific in Article 19 does not change the plain meaning of the language of Article 14. If the language of Article 14 were ambiguous, plaintiffs' expressio unius argument would have more force. But plaintiffs cannot identify any ambiguity in the language of Article 14. To do so would be to inject hidden meaning into straightforward text. . . .

The court does not find the treaty language ambiguous, and therefore its analysis need go no further. To the extent that Articles 19(b) raises any uncertainty, however, the court "may look beyond the written words to the history of the treaty, the negotiations, and the practical construction adopted by the parties." Air France v. Saks, 470 U.S. 392, 396 (1985). These authorities are voluminous and therefore of doubtful utility due to the potential for misleading selective citation. Counsel for both sides have proved themselves skilled in scouring these documents for support of their positions, and that both sides have succeeded to a certain degree underscores the questionable value of such resort to drafting history. Nevertheless, the court has conducted its own review of the historical materials, and concludes that they reinforce the conclusion that the Treaty of Peace with Japan was intended to bar claims such as those advanced by plaintiffs in this litigation.

The official record of treaty negotiations establishes that a fundamental goal of the agreement was to settle the reparations issue once and for all. . . .

The policy of the United States that Japanese liability for reparations should be sharply limited was informed by the experience of six years of United States-led occupation of Japan. During the occupation the Supreme Commander of the Allied Powers (SCAP) for the region, General Douglas MacArthur, confiscated Japanese assets in conjunction with the task of managing the economic affairs of the vanquished nation and with a view to reparations payments. It soon became clear that Japan's financial condition would render any aggressive reparations plan an exercise in futility. Meanwhile, the importance of a stable, democratic Japan as a bulwark to communism in the region increased. At the end of 1948, MacArthur expressed the view that "the use of reparations as a weapon to retard the reconstruction of a viable economy in Japan should be combated with all possible means" and "recommended that the reparations issue be settled finally and without delay." Memorandum from General Headquarters of SCAP to Department of the Army (Dec. 14, 1948).

That this policy was embodied in the treaty is clear not only from the negotiations history but also from the Senate Foreign Relations Committee report recommending approval of the treaty by the Senate. The committee noted, for example:

> Obviously insistence upon the payment of reparations in any proportion commensurate with the claims of the injured countries and their nationals would wreck Japan's economy, dissipate any credit that it may possess at present, destroy the initiative of its people, and create misery and chaos in which the seeds of discontent and communism would flourish. In short, [it] would be contrary to the basic purposes and policy of . . . the United States.

Japanese Peace Treaty and Other Treaties Relating to Security in the Pacific, S. Rep. No. 82-2, 82d Cong, 2d Sess. 12 (1952). The committee recognized that the treaty provisions "do not give a direct right of return to individual claimants except in the case of those having property in Japan," *id.* at 13, and endorsed the position of the State Department that "United States nationals, whose claims are not covered by the treaty provisions . . . must look for relief to the Congress of the United States," *id.* at 14.

Indeed, the treaty went into effect against the backdrop of congressional response to the need for compensation for former prisoners of war, in which many, if not all, of the plaintiffs in the present cases participated. *See* War Claims Act of 1948, 50 USC §§2001-2017p (establishing War Claims Commission and assigning top priority to claims of former prisoners of war).

Were the text of the treaty to leave any doubt that it waived claims such as those advanced by plaintiffs in these cases, the history of the Allied experience in post-war Japan, the drafting history of the treaty and the ratification debate would resolve it in favor of a finding of waiver.

As one might expect, considering the acknowledged inadequacy of compensation for victims of the Japanese regime provided under the treaty, the issue of additional reparations has arisen repeatedly since the adoption of that agreement some 50 years ago. This is all the more understandable in light of the vigor with which the Japanese economy has rebounded from the abyss.

The court finds it significant, as further support for the conclusion that the treaty bars plaintiffs' claims, that the United States, through State Department officials, has stood firmly by the principle of finality embodied in the treaty. This position was expressed in recent congressional testimony by Ronald J. Bettauer, deputy legal advisor, as follows:

> The 1951 Treaty of Peace with Japan settles all war-related claims of the U.S. and its nationals, and precludes the possibility of taking legal action in United States domestic courts to obtain additional compensation for war victims from Japan or its nationals — including Japanese commercial enterprises.

POW Survivors of the Bataan Death March, Hearing before the Senate Committee on the Judiciary (June 28, 2000) (statement of Ronald J. Bettauer, United States Department of State).

In another recent example, in response to a letter from Senator Orrin Hatch expressing "disappointment" with the "fifty-five year old injustice imposed on our military forces held as prisoners of war in Japan" and urging the Secretary of State to take action, a State Department representative wrote:

> The Treaty of Peace with Japan has, over the past five decades, served to sustain U.S. security interests in Asia and to support peace and stability in the region. We strongly

believe that the U.S. must honor its international agreements, including the [treaty]. There is, in our view, no justification for the U.S. to attempt to reopen the question of international commitments and obligations under the 1951 Treaty in order now to seek a more favorable settlement of the issue of Japanese compensation.

This explanation obviously offers no consolation to the victims of Japanese wartime aggression. Regrettably, however, it was impossible when the Treaty was negotiated — and it remains impossible today, 50 years later — to compensate fully for the suffering visited upon the victims of the war.

Letter of Jan. 18, 2000, from US Dept. of State to The Hon. Orrin Hatch at 2.

The conclusion that the 1951 treaty constitutes a waiver of the instant claims, as stated above and argued in the brief of the United States as amicus curiae in this case, carries significant weight. *See* Kolovrat v. Oregon, 366 U.S. 187, 194 (1961) ("While courts interpret treaties for themselves, the meaning given them by the departments of government particularly charged with their negotiation and enforcement is given great weight."); Sullivan v. Kidd, 254 U.S. 433, 442 (1921) ("The construction placed upon the treaty before us and consistently adhered to by the Executive Department of the Government, charged with the supervision of our foreign relations, should be given much weight."). The government's position also comports entirely with the court's own analysis of the treaty and its history.

Notes and Questions

1. Treaties differ from statutes in important respects. To become law, statutes require the agreement of a majority of both Houses of Congress and the President, or two-thirds of both Houses in situations in which the President vetoes the statute. Treaties, by contrast, are made by the President with the advice and consent of two-thirds of the Senate. Unlike statutes, which might or might not be classified as implicating foreign relations, all treaties by definition implicate relations with other nations. Also unlike statutes, treaties have a dual domestic law/international law nature. Furthermore, as discussed below in Chapter 6, only "self-executing" treaties preempt inconsistent state law. Thus with treaties, unlike with statutes, courts must answer the prior interpretive question of whether the treaty is self-executing before addressing the preemption question. Finally, as also discussed in Chapter 6, the Supreme Court has held that the treaty power is not limited to the scope of Congress's legislative powers. How, if at all, should these differences be reflected in different doctrines of preemption under the Supremacy Clause?

2. The first decision to strike down a state statute as inconsistent with a federal treaty was Ware v. Hylton, 3 U.S. 199 (1796). The Supreme Court held that the 1783 Treaty of Peace with Great Britain, which provided that British "creditors... shall meet with no lawful impediment to recovery... of all bona fide debts," preempted a 1780 Virginia statute that precluded such a recovery if the debt had already been paid to the state. *Ware* is also important for another reason: it, and not Marbury v. Madison, 5 U.S. 137 (1803), was the first Supreme Court decision to exercise judicial review. As David Currie has noted:

The most important constitutional holding of Ware v. Hylton was that the federal courts had the power to determine the constitutionality of state laws. This crucial point, so painstakingly established with respect to federal laws a few years later in Marbury v. Madison, passed almost unnoticed.

David P. Currie, The Constitution in the Supreme Court: The First Hundred Years, 1789-1888, at 39 (1985).

3. Which presumptive canon—in favor of preemption, against preemption, or no presumption at all—is appropriate in the treaty context? The Supreme Court has not provided clear answers to these questions. Sometimes the Court has suggested that the general presumption against preemption should apply to treaties. *See, e.g.,* Guaranty Trust Co. v. United States, 304 U.S. 126, 143 (1938) ("Even the language of a treaty wherever reasonably possible will be construed so as not to override state laws or to impair rights arising under them."); United States v. Pink, 315 U.S. 203, 230 (1942) ("Even treaties . . . will be carefully construed so as not to derogate from the authority and jurisdiction of the States of this Nation unless clearly necessary to effectuate the national policy"). At other times, the Court has suggested that the presumption against preemption may not apply with respect to treaties. *See* El Al Israel Airlines v. Tseng, 525 U.S. 155, 175 (1999) (asserting that because "the nation-state, not subdivisions within one nation, is the focus of the [Warsaw] Convention and the perspective of our treaty partners, . . . [o]ur home-centered preemption analysis [with its presumption against preemption] . . . should not be applied, mechanically, in construing our international obligations"). What is the right approach?

4. What presumption, if any, was applied in *Clark v. Allen*? In *Japanese Forced Labor Litigation*? To what extent was the preemption analysis in these decisions affected by the nature of the state activity in question? Why did the Court in *Clark* conclude that the treaty did not apply to personal property?

5. The court in *Japanese Forced Labor Litigation* gave special deference to the views of the Executive Branch in interpreting the meaning of the treaty. Is this deference appropriate? Recall the discussion in Chapter 2 of deference to the Executive Branch in the treaty context.

6. What deference, if any, should courts give to the views of foreign governments on questions of treaty interpretation? More or less deference than on matters of statutory interpretation?

7. The court in *Japanese Forced Labor Litigation* quotes Air France v. Saks, 470 U.S. 392, 396 (1985), for the proposition that, if treaty terms raise any uncertainty, courts "may look beyond the written words to the history of the treaty, the negotiations, and the practical construction adopted by the parties." When should courts rely on the text of treaties alone? When should they look to their context and negotiation history? How do the views of the Executive Branch intersect with these considerations? Should courts use international law rules of treaty interpretation, such as those reflected in the Vienna Convention on the Law of Treaties (which disfavor reliance on drafting history)? For a discussion of these and other issues of treaty interpretation, see David J. Bederman, *Revivalist Canons and Treaty Interpretation*, 41 U.C.L.A. L. Rev. 953 (1994); and Michael P. Van Alstine, *Dynamic Treaty Interpretation*, 146 U. Pa. L. Rev. 687 (1998).

8. A federal statute can preempt state law only if the statute is constitutionally valid. Is this also true of treaties? If so, to what extent are treaties subject to procedural or substantive constitutional limitations? These questions are considered in Chapter 6.

9. The materials above are focused on Article II treaties—that is, treaties concluded by the United States through the process specified in Article II of the Constitution, which requires the advice and consent of two-thirds of the Senate. Many international agreements concluded by the United States, however, do not go through this process. We consider the effect of these "executive agreements" below in Section C and also in Chapter 6.

C. DORMANT AND EXECUTIVE BRANCH PREEMPTION

Zschernig v. Miller

389 U.S. 429 (1968)

MR. JUSTICE DOUGLAS delivered the opinion of the Court.

This case concerns the disposition of the estate of a resident of Oregon who died there intestate in 1962. Appellants are decedent's sole heirs and they are residents of East Germany. Appellees include members of the State Land Board that petitioned the Oregon probate court for the escheat of the net proceeds of the estate under the provisions of Ore. Rev. Stat. §111.070 (1957), which provides for escheat in cases where a nonresident alien claims real or personal property unless three requirements are satisfied:

> (1) the existence of a reciprocal right of a United States citizen to take property on the same terms as a citizen or inhabitant of the foreign country;
> (2) the right of United States citizens to receive payment here of funds from estates in the foreign country; and
> (3) the right of the foreign heirs to receive the proceeds of Oregon estates "without confiscation."

The Oregon Supreme Court held that the appellants could take the Oregon realty involved in the present case by reason of Article IV of the 1923 Treaty of Friendship, Commerce and Consular Rights with Germany but that by reason of the same Article, as construed in Clark v. Allen, 331 U.S. 503, they could not take the personalty. We noted probable jurisdiction.

The Department of Justice, appearing as amicus curiae, submits that, although the 1923 Treaty is still in force, Clark v. Allen should be overruled insofar as it construed the personalty provision of Article IV. That portion of Article IV speaks of the rights of "nationals of either High Contracting Party" to dispose of "their personal property of every kind within the territories of the other." That literal language and its long consistent construction, we held in Clark v. Allen, "does not cover personalty located in this country and which an American citizen undertakes to leave to German nationals."

We do not accept the invitation to re-examine our ruling in Clark v. Allen. For we conclude that the history and operation of this Oregon statute make clear that §111.070 is an intrusion by the State into the field of foreign affairs which the Constitution entrusts to the President and the Congress. *See* Hines v. Davidowitz.

[O]ne of the conditions of inheritance under the Oregon statute requires "proof that such foreign heirs, distributees, devisees or legatees may receive the benefit, use or control of money or property from estates of persons dying in this state without confiscation, in whole or in part, by the governments of such foreign countries," the burden being on the nonresident alien to establish that fact.

This provision came into Oregon's law in 1951. Prior to that time the rights of aliens under the Oregon statute were defined in general terms of reciprocity, similar to the California Act which we had before us in Clark v. Allen. We held in Clark v. Allen that a general reciprocity clause did not on its face intrude on the federal domain. We noted that the California statute, then a recent enactment, would have only "some incidental or indirect effect in foreign countries."

Had that case appeared in the posture of the present one, a different result would have obtained. We were there concerned with the words of a statute on its face, not the manner of its application. State courts, of course, must frequently read, construe, and apply laws of foreign nations. It has never been seriously suggested that state courts are precluded from performing that function, albeit there is a remote possibility that any holding may disturb a foreign nation — whether the matter involves commercial cases, tort cases, or some other type of controversy. At the time Clark v. Allen was decided, the case seemed to involve no more than a routine reading of foreign laws. It now appears that in this reciprocity area under inheritance statutes, the probate courts of various States have launched inquiries into the type of governments that obtain in particular foreign nations — whether aliens under their law have enforceable rights, whether the so-called "rights" are merely dispensations turning upon the whim or caprice of government officials, whether the representation of consuls, ambassadors, and other representatives of foreign nations is credible or made in good faith, whether there is in the actual administration in the particular foreign system of law any element of confiscation....

In its brief amicus curiae, the Department of Justice states that: "The government does not . . . contend that the application of the Oregon escheat statute in the circumstances of this case unduly interferes with the United States' conduct of foreign relations."

The Government's acquiescence in the ruling of Clark v. Allen certainly does not justify extending the principle of that case, as we would be required to do here to uphold the Oregon statute as applied; for it has more than "some incidental or indirect effect in foreign countries," and its great potential for disruption or embarrassment makes us hesitate to place it in the category of a diplomatic bagatelle.

As we read the decisions that followed in the wake of Clark v. Allen, we find that they radiate some of the attitudes of the "cold war," where the search is for the "democracy quotient" of a foreign regime as opposed to the Marxist theory. The Oregon statute introduces the concept of "confiscation," which is of course opposed to the Just Compensation Clause of the Fifth Amendment. And this has led into minute inquiries concerning the actual administration of foreign law, into the credibility of foreign diplomatic statements, and into speculation whether the fact that some received delivery of funds should "not preclude wonderment as to how many may have been denied 'the right to receive.'" *See* State Land Board v. Kolovrat, 220 Ore. 448, 461-462, 349 P.2d 255, 262, *rev'd sub nom.* Kolovrat v. Oregon, 366 U.S. 187, on other grounds....

That kind of state involvement in foreign affairs and international relations — matters which the Constitution entrusts solely to the Federal Government — is not sanctioned by Clark v. Allen. Yet such forbidden state activity has infected each of the three provisions of §111.070, as applied by Oregon.... As one reads the Oregon decisions, it seems that foreign policy attitudes, the freezing or thawing of the "cold war," and the like are the real desiderata. Yet they of course are matters for the Federal Government, not for local probate courts. In short, it would seem that Oregon judges in construing §111.070 seek to ascertain whether "rights" protected by foreign law are the same "rights" that citizens of Oregon enjoy.... The statute as construed seems to make unavoidable judicial criticism of nations established on a more authoritarian basis than our own.

It seems inescapable that the type of probate law that Oregon enforces affects international relations in a persistent and subtle way. The practice of state courts in withholding remittances to legatees residing in Communist countries or in preventing them from assigning them is notorious. The several States, of course, have traditionally regulated the descent and distribution of estates. But those regulations must give way if they impair the effective exercise of the Nation's foreign policy. Where those laws conflict with a treaty, they must bow to the superior federal policy. Yet, even in absence of a treaty, a State's policy may disturb foreign relations. As we stated in Hines v. Davidowitz: "Experience has shown that international controversies of the gravest moment, sometimes even leading to war, may arise from real or imagined wrongs to another's subjects inflicted, or permitted, by a government." Certainly a State could not deny admission to a traveler from East Germany nor bar its citizens from going there. If there are to be such restraints, they must be provided by the Federal Government. The present Oregon law is not as gross an intrusion in the federal domain as those others might be. Yet, as we have said, it has a direct impact upon foreign relations and may well adversely affect the power of the central government to deal with those problems.

The Oregon law does, indeed, illustrate the dangers which are involved if each State, speaking through its probate courts, is permitted to establish its own foreign policy.

MR. JUSTICE HARLAN, concurring in the result....

[Justice Harlan first argues that the Oregon statute is preempted by the 1923 treaty, even with respect to the inheritance of personal property.]

Upon my view of this case, it would be unnecessary to reach the issue whether Oregon's statute governing inheritance by aliens amounts to an unconstitutional infringement upon the foreign relations power of the Federal Government. However, since this is the basis upon which the Court has chosen to rest its decision, I feel that I should indicate briefly why I believe the decision to be wrong on that score, too....

Prior decisions have established that in the absence of a conflicting federal policy or violation of the express mandates of the Constitution the States may legislate in areas of their traditional competence even though their statutes may have an incidental effect on foreign relations. Application of this rule to the case before us compels the conclusion that the Oregon statute is constitutional. Oregon has so legislated in the course of regulating the descent and distribution of estates of Oregon decedents, a matter traditionally within the power of a State. Apart from the 1923 treaty, which the Court finds it unnecessary to consider, there is no specific interest of the Federal Government which might be interfered with by this statute. The appellants concede that Oregon might deny inheritance rights to all nonresident aliens. Assuming that this is so, the statutory exception permitting inheritance by aliens whose countries permit Americans to inherit would seem to be a measure wisely designed to avoid any offense to foreign governments and thus any conflict with general federal interests: a foreign government can hardly object to the denial of rights which it does not itself accord to the citizens of other countries.

The foregoing would seem to establish that the Oregon statute is not unconstitutional on its face. And in fact the Court seems to have found the statute unconstitutional only as applied. Its notion appears to be that application of the parts of the statute which require that reciprocity actually exist and that the alien heir actually be able to enjoy his inheritance will inevitably involve the state courts in evaluations of foreign laws and governmental policies, and that this is likely to result in offense to foreign governments. There are several defects in this rationale. The most glaring is that it is based almost entirely on speculation. My Brother Douglas does cite a few unfortunate remarks made by state court judges in applying statutes resembling the one before us. However, the Court does not mention, nor does the record reveal, any instance in which such an occurrence has been the occasion for a diplomatic protest, or, indeed, has had any foreign relations consequence whatsoever. The United States says in its brief as amicus curiae that it

> does not . . . contend that the application of the Oregon escheat statute in the circumstances of this case unduly interferes with the United States' conduct of foreign relations.

At an earlier stage in this case, the Solicitor General told this Court:

> The Department of State has advised us . . . that State reciprocity laws, including that of Oregon, have had little effect on the foreign relations and policy of this country. . . . Appellants' apprehension of a deterioration in international relations, unsubstantiated by experience, does not constitute the kind of "changed conditions" which might call for re-examination of Clark v. Allen.

Essentially, the Court's basis for decision appears to be that alien inheritance laws afford state court judges an opportunity to criticize in dictum the policies of foreign governments, and that these dicta may adversely affect our foreign relations. In addition to finding no evidence of adverse effect in the record, I believe this rationale to be untenable because logically it would apply to many other types of litigation which come before the state courts. It is true that, in addition to the many state court judges who have applied alien inheritance statutes with proper judicial decorum, some judges have seized the opportunity to make derogatory remarks about foreign governments. However, judges have been known to utter dicta critical of foreign governmental policies even in purely domestic cases, so that the mere possibility of offensive utterances can hardly be the test.

If the flaw in the statute is said to be that it requires state courts to inquire into the administration of foreign law, I would suggest that that characteristic is shared by other legal rules which I cannot believe the Court wishes to invalidate. For example, the Uniform Foreign Money-Judgments Recognition Act provides that a foreign-country money judgment shall not be recognized if it "was rendered under a system which does not provide impartial tribunals or procedures compatible with the requirements of due process of law." When there is a dispute as to the content of foreign law, the court is required under the common law to treat the question as one of fact and to consider any evidence presented as to the actual administration of the foreign legal system. And in the field of choice of law there is a nonstatutory rule that the tort law of a foreign country will not be applied if that country is shown to be "uncivilized." Surely, all of these rules possess the same "defect" as the statute now before us. Yet I assume that the Court would not find them unconstitutional.

American Insurance Association v. Garamendi

123 S. Ct. 2374 (2003)

[The proceeds of many life insurance policies issued to Jews in Europe before World War II were never paid to the policyholders or their heirs, either because the proceeds were confiscated by the Nazis, the insurance companies denied the existence of the policies or claimed that they had lapsed from unpaid premiums, or the German government would not provide heirs with documentation of the policy-holder's death. In 1999, California enacted the Holocaust Victim Insurance Relief Act (HVIRA). This statute required any insurer doing business in California to disclose information about all policies sold in Europe between 1920 and 1945 by the company itself or by any company related to it. After the war, the United States entered into a number of reparations agreements to resolve claims against Germany. These agreements included, most recently, the German Foundation Agreement, signed by President Clinton and German Chancellor Schröder in July 2000. In this agreement, Germany agreed to enact legislation establishing a foundation funded with 10 billion Deutschmarks contributed equally by the German Government and German companies, to be used to compensate all those "who suffered at the hands of German companies during the National Socialist era." The President entered into similar agreements with Austria and France. In the agreements, the United States promised that it would try to persuade its courts, and state and local governments, to respect the foundations as the exclusive means for resolving World War II-era claims against private companies. The agreements also provided that the foundations would work with a voluntary organization — the International Commission on Holocaust Era Insurance Claims (ICHEIC) — to determine and settle outstanding insurance claims. The petitioners in this case, American and European insurance companies, challenged the validity of HVIRA.]

JUSTICE SOUTER delivered the opinion of the Court. . . .

The principal argument for preemption made by petitioners and the United States as *amicus curiae* is that HVIRA interferes with foreign policy of the Executive Branch, as expressed principally in the executive agreements with Germany, Austria, and France. The major premises of the argument, at least, are beyond dispute. There is, of course, no question that at some point an exercise of state power that touches on foreign relations must yield to the National Government's policy, given the "concern for uniformity in this country's dealings with foreign nations" that animated the Constitution's allocation of the foreign relations power to the National Government in the first place. Banco Nacional de Cuba v. Sabbatino, 376 U.S. 398, 427, n.25 (1964). . . .

Nor is there any question generally that there is executive authority to decide what that policy should be. Although the source of the President's power to act in foreign affairs does not enjoy any textual detail, the historical gloss on the "executive Power" vested in Article II of the Constitution has recognized the President's "vast share of responsibility for the conduct of our foreign relations." Youngstown Sheet & Tube Co. v. Sawyer, 343 U.S. 579, 610-611 (1952) (Frankfurter, J., concurring). While Congress holds express authority to regulate public and private dealings with other nations in its war and foreign commerce powers, in foreign affairs the President has a degree of independent authority to act. . . .

At a more specific level, our cases have recognized that the President has authority to make "executive agreements" with other countries, requiring no ratification by the Senate or approval by Congress, this power having been exercised since the early years of the Republic. *See* Dames & Moore v. Regan, 453 U.S. 654, 679, 682-683 (1981); United States v. Pink, 315 U.S. 203, 223, 230 (1942); United States v. Belmont, 301 U.S. 324, 330-331 (1937). . . . Given the fact that the practice goes back over 200 years to the first Presidential administration, and has received congressional acquiescence throughout its history, the conclusion "that the President's control of foreign relations includes the settlement of claims is indisputable." Pink, *supra*, at 240 (Frankfurter, J., concurring). . . .

The executive agreements at issue here do differ in one respect from those just mentioned insofar as they address claims associated with formerly belligerent states, but against corporations, not the foreign governments. But the distinction does not matter. Historically, wartime claims against even nominally private entities have become issues in international diplomacy, and three of the postwar settlements dealing with reparations implicating private parties were made by the Executive alone.[8] Acceptance of this historical practice is supported by a good pragmatic reason for depending on executive agreements to settle claims against foreign corporations associated with wartime experience. As shown by the history of insurance confiscation mentioned earlier, untangling government policy from private initiative during war time is often so hard that diplomatic action settling claims against private parties may well be just as essential in the aftermath of hostilities as diplomacy to settle claims against foreign governments. While a sharp line between public and private acts works for many purposes in the domestic law, insisting on the same line in defining the legitimate scope of the Executive's international negotiations would hamstring the President in settling international controversies.

Generally, then, valid executive agreements are fit to preempt state law, just as treaties are,[9] and if the agreements here had expressly preempted laws like HVIRA, the issue would be straightforward. But petitioners and the United States as *amicus curiae* both have to acknowledge that the agreements include no preemption clause, and so leave their claim of preemption to rest on asserted interference with the foreign policy those agreements embody. Reliance is placed on our decision in Zschernig v. Miller, 389 U.S. 429 (1968). . . .

[The court describes both the majority opinion and Justice Harlan's concurrence in *Zschernig*.]

It is a fair question whether respect for the executive foreign relations power requires a categorical choice between the contrasting theories of field and conflict preemption evident in the *Zschernig* opinions,[11] but the question requires no answer here. For even on Justice Harlan's view, the likelihood that state legislation will produce something more than incidental effect in conflict with express foreign policy of the National Government would require preemption of the state law. And

---

8. The Yalta and Potsdam Agreements envisioning dismantling of Germany's industrial assets, public and private, and the follow-up Paris Agreement aspiring to settle the claims of western nationals against the German Government and private agencies were made as executive agreements.

9. Subject, that is, to the Constitution's guarantees of individual rights. See Reid v. Covert, 354 U.S. 1, 15-19 (1957); Boos v. Barry, 485 U.S. 312, 324 (1988). Even Justice Sutherland's reading of the National Government's "inherent" foreign affairs power in United States v. Curtiss-Wright Export Corp., 299 U.S. 304 (1936), contained the caveat that the power, "like every other governmental power, must be exercised in subordination to the applicable provisions of the Constitution." *Id.*, at 320.

11. The two positions can be seen as complementary. If a State were simp ly to take a position on a matter of foreign policy with no serious claim to be addressing a traditional state responsibility, field preemption might be the appropriate doctrine, whether the National Government had acted and, if it had, without reference to the degree of any conflict, the principle having been established that the Constitution entrusts foreign policy exclusively to the National Government. *See, e.g.*, Hines v. Davidowitz, 312 U.S. 52, 63 (1941). Where, however, a State has acted within what Justice Harlan called its "traditional competence," 389 U.S., at 459, but in a way that affects foreign relations, it might make good sense to require a conflict, of a clarity or substantiality that would vary with the strength or the traditional importance of the state concern asserted. Whether the strength of the federal foreign policy interest should itself be weighed is, of course, a further question. . . .

since on his view it is legislation within "areas of . . . traditional competence" that gives a State any claim to prevail, it would be reasonable to consider the strength of the state interest, judged by standards of traditional practice, when deciding how serious a conflict must be shown before declaring the state law preempted. . . . Judged by these standards, we think petitioners and the Government have demonstrated a sufficiently clear conflict to require finding preemption here.

IV

A

To begin with, resolving Holocaust-era insurance claims that may be held by residents of this country is a matter well within the Executive's responsibility for foreign affairs. Since claims remaining in the aftermath of hostilities may be "sources of friction" acting as an "impediment to resumption of friendly relations" between the countries involved, *Pink, supra*, at 225, there is a "longstanding practice" of the national Executive to settle them in discharging its responsibility to maintain the Nation's relationships with other countries, *Dames & Moore*, 453 U.S., at 679. The issue of restitution for Nazi crimes has in fact been addressed in Executive Branch diplomacy and formalized in treaties and executive agreements over the last half century, and although resolution of private claims was postponed by the Cold War, securing private interests is an express object of diplomacy today, just as it was addressed in agreements soon after the Second World War. Vindicating victims injured by acts and omissions of enemy corporations in wartime is thus within the traditional subject matter of foreign policy in which national, not state, interests are overriding, and which the National Government has addressed.

The exercise of the federal executive authority means that state law must give way where, as here, there is evidence of clear conflict between the policies adopted by the two. The foregoing account of negotiations toward the three settlement agreements is enough to illustrate that the consistent Presidential foreign policy has been to encourage European governments and companies to volunteer settlement funds in preference to litigation or coercive sanctions. . . . As for insurance claims in particular, the national position, expressed unmistakably in the executive agreements signed by the President with Germany and Austria, has been to encourage European insurers to work with the ICHEIC to develop acceptable claim procedures, including procedures governing disclosure of policy information. . . . . This position, of which the agreements are exemplars, has also been consistently supported in the high levels of the Executive Branch, as mentioned already. . . . [12] The approach taken serves to resolve the several competing matters of national concern apparent in the German Foundation Agreement: the national interest in maintaining amicable relationships with current European allies; survivors' interests in a "fair and prompt" but nonadversarial resolution of their claims so as to "bring some measure of justice . . . in their lifetimes"; and the companies' interest in securing "legal peace" when they settle claims in this fashion. 39 Int'l

12. In Barclays Bank PLC v. Franchise Tax Bd. of Cal., 512 U.S. 298, 328-330 (1994), we declined to give policy statements by Executive Branch officials conclusive weight as against an opposing congressional policy in determining whether California's "worldwide combined reporting" tax method violated the Foreign Commerce Clause. The reason, we said, is that "the Constitution expressly grants Congress, not the President, the power to 'regulate Commerce with foreign Nations.'" *Id.*, at 329 (quoting Art. I, §8, cl. 3). As we have discussed, however, in the field of foreign policy the President has the "lead role." First Nat. City Bank v. Banco Nacional de Cuba, 406 U.S. 759, 767 (1972).

Legal Materials, at 1304. As a way for dealing with insurance claims, moreover, the voluntary scheme protects the companies' ability to abide by their own countries' domestic privacy laws limiting disclosure of policy information.

California has taken a different tack of providing regulatory sanctions to compel disclosure and payment, supplemented by a new cause of action for Holocaust survivors if the other sanctions should fail. The situation created by the California legislation calls to mind the impact of the Massachusetts Burma law on the effective exercise of the President's power, as recounted in the statutory preemption case, Crosby v. National Foreign Trade Council, 530 U.S. 363 (2000). HVIRA's economic compulsion to make public disclosure, of far more information about far more policies than ICHEIC rules require, employs "a different, state system of economic pressure," and in doing so undercuts the President's diplomatic discretion and the choice he has made exercising it. *Id.*, at 376. Whereas the President's authority to provide for settling claims in winding up international hostilities requires flexibility in wielding "the coercive power of the national economy" as a tool of diplomacy, *id.*, at 377, HVIRA denies this, by making exclusion from a large sector of the American insurance market the automatic sanction for noncompliance with the State's own policies on disclosure. "Quite simply, if the [California] law is enforceable the President has less to offer and less economic and diplomatic leverage as a consequence." Ibid. (citing Dames & Moore, 453 U.S., at 673). The law thus "compromises the very capacity of the President to speak for the Nation with one voice in dealing with other governments" to resolve claims against European companies arising out of World War II. 530 U.S., at 381.[14]

Crosby's facts are replicated again in the way HVIRA threatens to frustrate the operation of the particular mechanism the President has chosen. The letters from Deputy Secretary Eizenstat to California officials show well enough how the portent of further litigation and sanctions has in fact placed the Government at a disadvantage in obtaining practical results from persuading "foreign governments and foreign companies to participate voluntarily in organizations such as ICHEIC." Brief for United States as Amicus Curiae 15.... In addition to thwarting the Government's policy of repose for companies that pay through the ICHEIC, California's indiscriminate disclosure provisions place a handicap on the ICHEIC's effectiveness (and raise a further irritant to the European allies) by undercutting European privacy protections. It is true, of course, as it is probably true of all elements of HVIRA, that the disclosure requirement's object of obtaining compensation for Holocaust victims is a goal espoused by the National Government as well. But "the fact of a common end hardly neutralizes conflicting means," *Crosby, supra*, at 379, and here HVIRA is an obstacle to the success of the National Government's chosen "calibration of force" in dealing with the Europeans using a voluntary approach, 530 U.S., at 380.

B

The express federal policy and the clear conflict raised by the state statute are alone enough to require state law to yield. If any doubt about the clarity of the conflict

---

14. It is true that the President in this case is acting without express congressional authority, and thus does not have the "plenitude of Executive authority" that "controlled the issue of preemption" in Crosby v. National Foreign Trade Council, 530 U.S. 363, 376 (2000). But in *Crosby* we were careful to note that the President possesses considerable independent constitutional authority to act on behalf of the United States on international issues, *id.*, at 381, and conflict with the exercise of that authority is a comparably good reason to find preemption of state law.

remained, however, it would have to be resolved in the National Government's favor, given the weakness of the State's interest, against the backdrop of traditional state legislative subject matter, in regulating disclosure of European Holocaust-era insurance policies in the manner of HVIRA.

The commissioner would justify HVIRA's ambitious disclosure requirement as protecting "legitimate consumer protection interests" in knowing which insurers have failed to pay insurance claims. But, quite unlike a generally applicable "blue sky" law, HVIRA effectively singles out only policies issued by European companies, in Europe, to European residents, at least 55 years ago. Cal. Ins. Code Ann. §13804(a); *see also* §790.15(a) (mandating license suspension only for "failure to pay any valid claim from Holocaust survivors"). Limiting the public disclosure requirement to these policies raises great doubt that the purpose of the California law is an evaluation of corporate reliability in contemporary insuring in the State.

Indeed, there is no serious doubt that the state interest actually underlying HVIRA is concern for the several thousand Holocaust survivors said to be living in the State. §13801(d) (legislative finding that roughly 5,600 documented Holocaust survivors reside in California). But this fact does not displace general standards for evaluating a State's claim to apply its forum law to a particular controversy or transaction, under which the State's claim is not a strong one. "Even if a plaintiff evidences his desire for forum law by moving to the forum, we have generally accorded such a move little or no significance." Phillips Petroleum Co. v. Shutts, 472 U.S. 797, 820 (1985); *see* Allstate Ins. Co. v. Hague, 449 U.S. 302, 311 (1981) ("[A] postoccurrence change of residence to the forum State — standing alone — is insufficient to justify application of forum law").

But should the general standard not be displaced, and the State's interest recognized as a powerful one, by virtue of the fact that California seeks to vindicate the claims of Holocaust survivors? The answer lies in recalling that the very same objective dignifies the interest of the National Government in devising its chosen mechanism for voluntary settlements, there being about 100,000 survivors in the country, only a small fraction of them in California. As against the responsibility of the United States of America, the humanity underlying the state statute could not give the State the benefit of any doubt in resolving the conflict with national policy.

C

The basic fact is that California seeks to use an iron fist where the President has consistently chosen kid gloves. We have heard powerful arguments that the iron fist would work better, and it may be that if the matter of compensation were considered in isolation from all other issues involving the European allies, the iron fist would be the preferable policy. But our thoughts on the efficacy of the one approach versus the other are beside the point, since our business is not to judge the wisdom of the National Government's policy; dissatisfaction should be addressed to the President or, perhaps, Congress. The question relevant to preemption in this case is conflict, and the evidence here is "more than sufficient to demonstrate that the state Act stands in the way of [the President's] diplomatic objectives." Crosby, *supra*, at 386....

V

[The Court concludes in this Part that Congress has not affirmatively authorized the California statute.]

JUSTICE GINSBURG, with whom JUSTICE STEVENS, JUSTICE SCALIA, and JUSTICE THOMAS join, dissenting. . . .

The President's primacy in foreign affairs, I agree with the Court, empowers him to conclude executive agreements with other countries. Our cases do not catalog the subject matter meet for executive agreement, but we have repeatedly acknowledged the President's authority to make such agreements to settle international claims. And in settling such claims, we have recognized, an executive agreement may preempt otherwise permissible state laws or litigation. The executive agreements to which we have accorded preemptive effect, however, warrant closer inspection than the Court today endeavors. . . .

[Justice Ginsburg discusses the facts of *Belmont* and *Pink*, which are covered in Chapter 6 of the casebook, and *Dames & Moore*, which is excerpted in Chapter 3. In those decisions, the Court enforced executive agreements that resolved U.S. claims against foreign governments and treated the agreements as preemptive federal law.]

Together, *Belmont*, *Pink*, and *Dames & Moore* confirm that executive agreements directed at claims settlement may sometimes preempt state law. The Court states that if the executive "agreements here had expressly preempted laws like HVIRA, the issue would be straightforward." One can safely demur to that statement, for, as the Court acknowledges, no executive agreement before us expressly preempts the HVIRA. Indeed, no agreement so much as mentions the HVIRA's sole concern: public disclosure.

B

Despite the absence of express preemption, the Court holds that the HVIRA interferes with foreign policy objectives implicit in the executive agreements. I would not venture down that path. . . .

We have not relied on *Zschernig* since it was decided, and I would not resurrect that decision here. The notion of "dormant foreign affairs preemption" with which *Zschernig* is associated resonates most audibly when a state action "reflects a state policy critical of foreign governments and involves 'sitting in judgment' on them." L. Henkin, Foreign Affairs and the United States Constitution 164 (2d ed. 1996). The HVIRA entails no such state action or policy. It takes no position on any contemporary foreign government and requires no assessment of any existing foreign regime. It is directed solely at private insurers doing business in California, and it requires them solely to disclose information in their or their affiliates' possession or control. I would not extend *Zschernig* into this dissimilar domain.[4]

Neither would I stretch *Belmont*, *Pink*, or *Dames & Moore* to support implied preemption by executive agreement. In each of those cases, the Court gave effect to the express terms of an executive agreement. In *Dames & Moore*, for example, the Court addressed an agreement explicitly extinguishing certain suits in domestic courts. Here, however, none of the executive agreements extinguish any underlying claim for relief. The United States has agreed to file precatory statements

4. The Court also places considerable weight on Crosby v. National Foreign Trade Council, 530 U.S. 363 (2000). As the Court acknowledges, however, *Crosby* was a statutory preemption case. The state law there at issue posed "an obstacle to the accomplishment of Congress's full objectives under the [relevant] federal Act." 530 U.S., at 373. That statutory decision provides little support for preempting a state law by inferring preclusive foreign policy objectives from precatory language in executive agreements.

advising courts that dismissing Holocaust-era claims accords with American foreign policy, but the German Foundation Agreement confirms that such statements have no legally binding effect. It remains uncertain, therefore, whether even *litigation* on Holocaust-era insurance claims must be abated in deference to the German Foundation Agreement or the parallel agreements with Austria and France. Indeed, ambiguity on this point appears to have been the studied aim of the American negotiating team.

If it is uncertain whether insurance *litigation* may continue given the executive agreements on which the Court relies, it should be abundantly clear that those agreements leave *disclosure* laws like the HVIRA untouched. The contrast with the Litvinov Assignment at issue in *Belmont* and *Pink* is marked. That agreement spoke directly to claim assignment in no uncertain terms; *Belmont* and *Pink* confirmed that state law could not invalidate the very assignments accomplished by the agreement. Here, the Court invalidates a state disclosure law on grounds of conflict with foreign policy "embodied" in certain executive agreements, although those agreements do not refer to state disclosure laws specifically, or even to information disclosure generally. It therefore is surely an exaggeration to assert that the "HVIRA threatens to frustrate the operation of the particular mechanism the President has chosen" to resolve Holocaust-era claims. If that were so, one might expect to find some reference to laws like the HVIRA in the later-in-time executive agreements. There is none.

To fill the agreements' silences, the Court points to statements by individual members of the Executive Branch. . . . But we have never premised foreign affairs preemption on statements of that order. *Cf.* Barclays Bank PLC v. Franchise Tax Bd. of Cal., 512 U.S. 298, 329-330 (1994) ("Executive Branch actions — press releases, letters, and *amicus* briefs" that "express federal policy but lack the force of law" cannot render a state law unconstitutional under the Foreign Commerce Clause.). We should not do so here lest we place the considerable power of foreign affairs preemption in the hands of individual sub-Cabinet members of the Executive Branch. Executive officials of any rank may of course be expected "faithfully [to] represent the President's policy," but no authoritative text accords such officials the power to invalidate state law simply by conveying the Executive's views on matters of federal policy. The displacement of state law by preemption properly requires a considerably more formal and binding federal instrument.

Sustaining the HVIRA would not compromise the President's ability to speak with one voice for the Nation. To the contrary, by declining to invalidate the HVIRA in this case, we would reserve foreign affairs preemption for circumstances where the President, acting under statutory or constitutional authority, has spoken clearly to the issue at hand. . . . And judges should not be the expositors of the Nation's foreign policy, which is the role they play by acting when the President himself has not taken a clear stand. As I see it, courts step out of their proper role when they rely on no legislative or even executive text, but only on inference and implication, to preempt state laws on foreign affairs grounds.

Notes and Questions

1. Is *Zschernig* consistent with Clark v. Allen, excerpted above in Section B? What did *Clark* suggest about the validity of state inheritance laws that are not preempted by a federal statute or treaty?

2. Prior to *Zschernig*, courts did not preempt state foreign relations activities in the absence of controlling enacted federal law, even though states frequently caused foreign relations controversies. *See* Louis Henkin, Foreign Affairs and the United States Constitution 162 (2d ed. 1996) (describing *Zschernig* as "new" constitutional doctrine); Jack L. Goldsmith, *Federal Courts, Foreign Affairs, and Federalism*, 83 Va. L. Rev. 1617, 1643-58 (1997). In addition, at least two pre-*Zschernig* Supreme Court decisions were dismissive of the idea of dormant foreign affairs preemption. *See* Clark v. Allen, 331 U.S. 503, 516-17 (1947) (rejecting dormant foreign relations challenge to a state anti-alien inheritance statute as "farfetched"); Blythe v. Hinckley, 180 U.S. 333, 340 (1901) (rejecting as "extraordinary" the argument that a California statute permitting aliens to inherit real property invaded the unexercised treaty power).

Nonetheless, *Zschernig* did have precursors. Prior to 1968, the closest the Court came to a dormant foreign affairs preemption doctrine was in Holmes v. Jennison, 39 U.S. 540 (1840), a case involving Vermont's attempted extradition of an alleged criminal to Canada. Writing for a plurality of four Justices, Chief Justice Taney maintained that federal power in "foreign intercourse" was exclusive, and that a concurrent state power to extradite was "incompatible and inconsistent with the powers conferred on the federal government." The four other participating Justices, by contrast, all rejected a dormant preemption argument. On remand from the Supreme Court's 4-4 decision, the Vermont Supreme Court held that the extradition constituted "an agreement between the governor of this state, in behalf of the state, and the governor of Canada" in violation of Article I, Section 10 of the U.S. Constitution. *See* Ex parte Holmes, 12 Vt. 631, 640 (1840). Although most commentators today believe that the extradition power is an exclusive federal power, and the Court has suggested this in dicta, see Valentine v. United States, 299 U.S. 5, 8 (1936) (stating that "it cannot be doubted that the power to provide for extradition is a national power; it pertains to the national government and not to the States"), the Court has never expressly held this.

Another area in which the Court has hinted at dormant foreign affairs preemption is immigration. In the nineteenth century, states exercised control over many immigration matters. *See* Gerald L. Neuman, *The Lost Century of American Immigration Law (1776-1875)*, 93 Colum. L. Rev. 1833 (1993). This practice abated in the last half of the nineteenth century after the Supreme Court invoked the dormant Commerce Clause to invalidate certain state laws regulating the migration of aliens, and the federal political branches began to enact immigration statutes and enter into treaties that regulated the issue. One prominent early dormant Commerce Clause decision concerning immigration was Chy Lung v. Freeman, 92 U.S. 275 (1875). There, the Court invalidated a California state commissioner's power to demand indemnification bonds for certain vaguely described classes of immigrants disembarking at California ports. The Court reasoned that because the Constitution "has forbidden the States to hold negotiations with any foreign nations . . . and has taken the whole subject of these relations [as reserved for the federal government]," the Framers could not be held to have "done so foolish a thing as to leave it in the power of the States to pass laws whose enforcement renders the general government liable to just recriminations that it must answer, while it does not prohibit to the States the acts for which it is held responsible." And in a passage quoted favorably in Hines v. Davidowitz, the Court added: "If [the United States] should get into a difficulty which would lead to war, or to suspension of intercourse, would California alone suffer, or all the Union?"

Although the reasoning in *Chy Lung* is similar to the reasoning in *Zschernig*, *Chy Lung* did not establish a stand-alone doctrine of dormant foreign affairs preemption. After *Chy Lung*, states enacted numerous anti-alien statutes that produced stormy diplomatic controversy, but no court or commentator hinted that the statutes could be preempted in the absence of a controlling federal treaty, statute, or textual constitutional prohibition. *See* Goldsmith, *supra*, at 1653-54; Dennis James Palumbo, The States and American Foreign Relations 147-92 (1960) (unpublished Ph.D. dissertation, University of Chicago). And, even as late as *Hines*, the Court stated that it was still an open question whether "federal power in [immigration], whether exercised or unexercised, is exclusive." Many post-*Hines* decisions, including *De Canas*, refer to an exclusive federal immigration power, but no Supreme Court decision has clearly rested on this ground.

3. What is the constitutional source for dormant foreign affairs preemption? Read Article I, Section 10 of the Constitution. Among other things, this Section excludes state authority in a defined set of "high" foreign relations functions, such as treaty-making and warmaking. Now read the foreign relations powers conferred on the federal government in Articles I, Section 8 and in Article II, Sections 2-3. Are these powers *exclusive* (which means that they can be exercised only by the federal government)? Or are they, like most other powers conferred on the federal government, *concurrent* (which means that they can be exercised by both state and federal governments until the federal government affirmatively acts to preempt state authority)? Now consider the Tenth Amendment, which provides that the "powers not delegated to the United States by the Constitution, nor prohibited by it to the States, are reserved to the States respectively, or to the people." What implications, if any, can one draw from these textual provisions? *Compare* Goldsmith, *supra*, at 1642 (arguing that the "most natural inference . . . is that all foreign relations matters not excluded by Article I, Section 10 fall within the concurrent power of the state and federal governments until preempted by federal statute or treaty"), *with* Brannon P. Denning & Jack H. McCall, Jr., *The Constitutionality of State and Local "Sanctions" Against Foreign Countries: Affairs of State, States' Affairs, or a Sorry State of Affairs?*, 26 Hastings Const. L.Q. 307, 337 (1999) ("[T]he various provisions related to foreign affairs can be read to contain a structural or 'penumbral' restriction on state actions affecting foreign affairs, even in the absence of a congressional enactment.").

4. As noted earlier in this chapter, the Constitution assigns the treaty power to the federal government and provides that treaties are the supreme law of the land and thereby preempt inconsistent state law. Does the federal government's treaty power also have *dormant* preemptive effect? In other words, are state activities that might interfere with the treaty power preempted even in the absence of a treaty? For an argument to this effect, see Edward T. Swaine, *Negotiating Federalism: State Bargaining and the Dormant Treaty Power*, 49 Duke L.J. 1127 (2000). If the treaty power does have a dormant preemptive effect, what is the scope of the preemption? Is every state law or activity that might be the subject of a future treaty preempted? Professor Swaine suggests that the dormant treaty power "does not preclude all state activities affecting foreign relations," but rather precludes states from "direct or indirect negotiating . . . with foreign powers on matters of national concern." *Id.* at 1138. What constitutes "indirect negotiating"? What are "matters of national concern"? How does the dormant treaty power as articulated by Professor Swaine compare with the dormant preemption doctrine announced in *Zschernig*?

5. Another justification for dormant foreign affairs preemption is a functional one. Even if federal courts are not as well suited as the federal political branches to perform the foreign relations inquiries in support of dormant preemption, the federal political branches cannot redress every state foreign relations activity. Moreover, the federal courts are at least in a better position than states to identify and police U.S. foreign relations interests. And any errors the courts might make in inappropriately preempting state law can always be corrected by subsequent federal legislation. Is this argument persuasive? Do the federal political branches need the assistance of federal courts in policing states for harmful foreign relations activity? Are courts well suited to assist in this task? What effect does dormant foreign affairs preemption have on the political branches that are primarily responsible for conducting U.S. foreign relations? Are there any other costs to dormant foreign affairs preemption?

6. What is the scope of the prohibition on state activity announced in *Zschernig*? What matters in answering this question: Foreign relations effects? The state's purpose in engaging in the activity? Both? Neither?

7. What is the relationship between statutory preemption and dormant foreign affairs preemption? At first glance, it might appear that the presence of a congressional statute makes the judicial decision whether to preempt more straightforward, or at least easier from a policy perspective. But is this true? As the federal Burma statute in *Crosby* illustrates, Congress often provides no concrete guidance about the preemptive scope of its statutes. Does this mean that courts deciding whether a statute preempts state law are effectively in the same position as they are in dormant preemption cases? Or does the presence of the federal statute provide courts with guidance about preemption, even though the statute is silent regarding preemptive scope? Is one method of preemption more legitimate than the other? Why?

8. Should courts always consider statutory before dormant preemption? In explaining why it addressed statutory preemption and not dormant preemption, footnote 8 in *Crosby* cited Justice Brandeis's celebrated concurring opinion in Ashwander v. Valley Authority, 297 U.S. 288, 341 (1936), which provides in pertinent part:

> The Court will not pass upon a constitutional question although properly presented by the record, if there is also present some other ground upon which the case may be disposed of. . . . Thus, if a case can be decided on either of two grounds, one involving a constitutional question, the other a question of statutory construction or general law, the Court will decide only the latter.

If a court considers and rejects a statutory preemption argument (i.e., if it concludes that there is no conflict between the federal and state enactments and that Congress did not intend to preempt), is it appropriate to strike down the state law nonetheless on the basis of a judicially developed preemption doctrine?

9. After *Zschernig*, the Supreme Court began to invoke a doctrine akin to dormant foreign affairs preemption in the context of applying the dormant Foreign Commerce Clause. Article I, Section 8, Clause 3 of the Constitution gives Congress the power to regulate commerce "among the several States" and "with foreign Nations." Even in the absence of affirmative congressional regulation, the Supreme Court has long invoked the "dormant" Commerce Clause as a basis for judicial preemption of state laws that unduly burden interstate or foreign commerce. The Court has devised a number of tests for such preemption.

With respect to the regulation of *interstate* commerce, the Court performs essentially a two-step inquiry. First, state laws that facially discriminate against interstate commerce are subject to strict scrutiny, and are "virtually per se invalid."

Oregon Waste Systems, Inc. v. Department of Environmental Quality, 511 U.S. 93, 99 (1994). Second, even a nondiscriminatory state law can be invalidated under the dormant Commerce Clause if "the burden imposed on [foreign] commerce is clearly excessive in relation to the putative local benefits." Pike v. Bruce Church, Inc., 397 U.S. 137, 142 (1970).

With respect to the regulation of *foreign* commerce, courts apply similar discrimination and balancing tests, with two differences. First, they apply the discrimination and balancing tests in a more searching manner with respect to foreign commerce. *See, e.g.,* Kraft General Foods v. Iowa Dep't of Revenue & Finance, 505 U.S. 71, 79 (1992) ("The constitutional prohibition against state taxation of foreign commerce is broader than the protection afforded to interstate commerce . . . in part because matters of concern to the entire Nation are implicated."). Second, beginning in Japan Line Ltd. v. County of Los Angeles, 441 U.S. 434 (1979), the Supreme Court imposed a new, and independent, prohibition under the dormant Foreign Commerce Clause: The state law must not prevent the federal government from speaking with "one voice" in foreign relations. The one-voice test under the dormant Foreign Commerce Clause requires courts to analyze the extent to which state law will "offend" a foreign nation, and to distinguish a state law that "merely has foreign resonances" from one that "implicates foreign affairs." Container Corp. of America v. Franchise Tax Board, 463 U.S. 159, 194 (1983).

In Barclays Bank v. Franchise Tax Board of California, 512 U.S. 298 (1994), the Supreme Court appeared to back away from the "one-voice test" for dormant Foreign Commerce Clause preemption. *Barclays Bank* involved a challenge to California's method of taxing foreign multinational corporations. The taxation method was different from the federal government's method and had drawn extensive international protest, and numerous countries filed amicus curiae briefs urging the Supreme Court to invalidate it. The Court nevertheless rejected the challenge because it could "discern no 'specific indications of congressional intent' to bar the state action." Emphasizing that "the Constitution does 'not make the judiciary the overseer of our government,'" the Court decided to "leave it to Congress — whose voice, in this area, is the Nation's — to evaluate whether the national interest is best served by tax uniformity, or state autonomy." Is the reasoning in *Barclays Bank* consistent with *Zschernig*? Is the Court's conception of the judicial role in *Barclays Bank* consistent with *Zschernig*? What does *Garamendi* suggest about *Barclays Bank* 's effect on *Zschernig*? Does *Barclays Bank* survive *Garamendi*?

10. The Court's preemption analysis in *Garamendi* was influenced by the presence of a "sole" executive agreement — i.e., an agreement between the United States and another country that the President entered into on his own constitutional authority, without recourse to the Senate or Congress. As discussed in detail in Chapter 6, the Supreme Court, beginning in United States v. Belmont, 301 U.S. 324 (1937), determined that such sole executive agreements could, at least in some circumstances, preempt state law. Did the Court in *Garamendi* hold that the California statute was preempted by the executive agreement? If not, how did the executive agreement influence the Court's decision? How does the Court's analysis in *Garamendi* differ from its analysis in *Crosby* (also authored by Justice Souter), where a statute was in issue? What is the relevance, in this connection, of footnote 11 of the Court's opinion? Under the analysis in *Garamendi*, does the Executive Branch even need an executive agreement to preempt state law under *Garamendi*? Could the mere unilateral announcement of a foreign policy by the President be enough to preempt state law?

11. Professors Ku and Yoo sharply distinguish *Garamendi* from *Zschernig*:

Although *Garamendi* might be understood as a defeat for "foreign relations federalism" and state participation in matters relating to foreign affairs, it is hardly an unqualified endorsement of *Zschernig*'s reliance on federal courts to police state activities. Rather, *Garamendi*'s reliance on the statements and actions of executive branch officials to discern a "consistent Presidential foreign policy" in conflict with the state law affirms that the federal executive, rather than the federal courts, holds the primary responsibility for determining which state laws and policies unduly interfere with national policies.

Julian Ku & John Yoo, *Beyond Formalism in Foreign Affairs: A Functional Approach to the Alien Tort Statute*, 2004 Sup. Ct. Rev. 153, 210. Do you agree with this analysis? Since the courts and not the Executive will have the final say on the content of the relevant policy and whether it is sufficiently weighty for preemption, and since courts decide when and whether to rely on Executive Branch policy statements, could one argue instead that the real effect of *Garamendi* is to enhance judicial (as opposed to Executive) power over foreign relations?

Some commentators agree that *Garamendi* enhances Executive power, but they argue that it does so in a constitutionally problematic way. Consider this analysis:

The Constitution's Article VI places the power of preemption in the legislative branch by making laws and treaties, but not executive decrees, the supreme law of the land. In unusual cases, state laws might be displaced by the judiciary, or by the President pursuant to executive agreements with foreign nations. Giving mere executive policy preemptive effect, as the Court did in *Garamendi*, bypasses these constitutional processes and concentrates power in the executive branch. That is particularly problematic in foreign affairs, where the President's substantial authority over the military and the organs of diplomacy already gives rise to broad independent power. The President's lack of lawmaking authority balances these other great executive powers, because without lawmaking authority, the President needs the support of other branches to fully effectuate foreign policy. This highlights an often overlooked way that federalism reinforces checks and balances at the national level. A robust foreign affairs federalism promotes a cooperative approach to foreign affairs, because the President will need the support of Congress to oust disruptive state laws; as a result, more foreign affairs decision making will be done by Congress (or the Senate). In contrast, allowing the President unilaterally to oust states from foreign affairs, as the Court did in *Garamendi*, means that more foreign affairs disputes may be decided only by the President, through a concentration of executive and lawmaking power that is contrary to the first principles of separation of powers.

Michael D. Ramsey & Brannon P. Denning, *American Association v. Garamendi and Executive Preemption in Foreign Affairs*, 46 Wm. & Mary L. Rev. 825, 829-30 (2004). Do you agree with this analysis?

12. Does the Supreme Court have a coherent view of the proper role of the views of the Executive Branch in its various preemption doctrines? In *Zschernig* the Court appeared to ignore Department of Justice statements denying that the Oregon escheat statute interfered with the conduct of U.S. foreign relations. In *Barclays Bank* the Court similarly discounted Executive Branch statements. In *Garamendi*, by contrast, the Court relied on Executive Branch statements. Similarly, in the context of statutory preemption in *Crosby* (excerpted in the last section), the Court appeared to give great weight to Executive Branch representations about the foreign relations difficulties caused by the Massachusetts statute. Is there any way to reconcile these decisions?

13. Should the war on terrorism following the September 11, 2001, attacks on the United States affect the dormant and Executive Branch preemption doctrines? Is having one voice in foreign affairs now more important than it was before September 11? Is the war on terrorism analogous to the Cold War situation that existed at the time of *Zschernig*?

14. Several states have enacted "Buy American" statutes that require private contractors with state agencies to provide goods made in the United States. Should these statutes be subject to dormant foreign affairs preemption? Lower courts have reached different conclusions. Most have upheld state Buy-American laws. For example, in upholding Pennsylvania's Buy-American law, the Third Circuit Court of Appeals reasoned as follows:

> The Pennsylvania statute exhibits none of the dangers attendant on the statute reviewed in *Zschernig*, for Pennsylvania's statute provides no opportunity for state administrative officials or judges to comment on, let alone key their decisions to, the nature of foreign regimes. On its face the statute applies to steel from any foreign source, without respect to whether the source country might be considered friend or foe. Nor is there any indication from the record that the statute has been selectively applied according to the foreign policy attitudes of Commonwealth courts or the Commonwealth's Attorney General. And while it is possible that sub-national government procurement restrictions may become a topic of intense international scrutiny, and a target in international trade negotiations, that possibility alone cannot justify this court's invalidation of the Commonwealth's statute. This is especially true when Congress has recently directed its attention to such restrictions and has taken no steps to preempt them through federal legislation.

Trojan Technologies, Inc. v. Pennsylvania, 916 F.2d 903 (3d Cir. 1990). *See also* North American Salt Co. v. Ohio Dep't of Transportation, 701 N.E.2d 454, 462-63 (Ohio Ct. App. 1997) (upholding Ohio statute); K.S.B. Technical Sales Corp. v. North Jersey District Water Supply Commission, 381 A.2d 774 (N.J. 1977) (upholding New Jersey statute).

By contrast, a California appellate court invalidated a California Buy American Act. It reasoned as follows:

> The California Buy American Act, in effectively placing an embargo on foreign products, amounts to a usurpation by this state of the power of the federal government to conduct foreign trade policy. That there are countervailing state policies which are served by the retention of such an act is "wholly irrelevant to judicial inquiry" (United States v. Pink, 315 U.S. 203, 233) since "[it] is inconceivable that any of them can be interposed as an obstacle to the effective operation of a federal constitutional power." (United States v. Belmont, 301 U.S. 324, 332). Foreign trade is properly a subject of national concern, not state regulation. State regulation can only impede, not foster, national trade policies. The problems of trade expansion or non-expansion are national in scope, and properly should be national in scope in their resolution.

Bethlehem Steel Corp. v. Board of Commissioners, 276 Cal. App. 2d 221, 80 Cal. Rptr. 800 (Ct. App. 2d Dist. 1969). How should this issue be resolved after *Crosby* and *Garamendi*?

15. A precursor to the debate over the validity of the Massachusetts Burma statute in *Crosby* was a similar debate in the 1980s over the validity of various state sanctions against South Africa. The Supreme Court never addressed the issue, and, once again, the lower courts are divided. In New York Times Co. v. City of New York Commission on Human Rights, 361 N.E.2d 963 (N.Y. 1977), the New York

Court of Appeals held that New York's requirement that the *New York Times* not carry an advertisement for employment opportunities in South Africa was inconsistent with *Zschernig*. Similarly, the Illinois Supreme Court invalidated an Illinois statute that excluded South African coins from state tax exemptions that applied to coins and currency issued by other nations. The court reasoned that the "sole motivation [for the law] was disapproval of a nation's policies" and that the legislation effectively "imposed, or at least encouraged, an economic boycott of the South African Krugerrand," and thus was "outside the realm of permissible state activity." Springfield Rare Coin Galleries, Inc. v. Johnson, 503 N.E.2d 300, 307 (Ill. 1986). *See also* Tayyari v. New Mexico State University, 495 F. Supp. 1365, 1376-80 (D.N.M. 1980) (finding that a state university's decision to bar admission or readmission of Iranian students could affect international relations and thus was impermissible).

In contrast, the Maryland Court of Appeals upheld a Baltimore ordinance that required city pension funds to divest their holdings in companies engaged in business in South Africa. It reasoned that the ordinance survived scrutiny under *Zschernig* because the divestiture "requires no continuing investigation, assessment or commentary by local government officials or employees into the laws or operations of the South African government," and because Baltimore's purpose in enacting the ordinance was simply "to ensure that the City's pension funds would not be invested in a manner that was morally offensive to many Baltimore residents and many beneficiaries of the pension funds." Board of Trustees of the Employees' Retirement System of Baltimore v. Mayor and City Council of Baltimore, 562 A.2d 720, 746 (Md. App. 1989).

Another similarity between the South Africa sanctions debate and the Burma sanctions debate is that, as in the Burma situation, the federal government imposed its own sanctions on South Africa. *See* Comprehensive Anti-Apartheid Act of 1986, 22 U.S.C. §§2151, 2346(d), 5001-5116 (Supp. IV 1986). This statute, like the federal Burma statute, said nothing on its face about preemption. The only court to consider whether the federal statute preempted state sanctions was *Board of Trustees of the Employees' Retirement System, supra*. The court applied a presumption against preemption after concluding that state regulation of employee pension investments "is clearly a matter of traditional local regulation." It then considered the legislative history in detail and concluded that the "evidence with respect to congressional intent is wholly inadequate to overcome this presumption." 562 A.2d at 741-44.

16. There is a substantial literature on dormant foreign affairs preemption. In addition to the books and articles cited in the notes above, see Louis Henkin, Foreign Affairs and the United States Constitution ch. VI (2d ed. 1996); Richard B. Bilder, *The Role of Cities and States in Foreign Relations*, 83 Am. J. Int'l L. 821 (1989); Sarah H. Cleveland, Crosby *and the "One-Voice" Myth in U.S. Foreign Relations*, 46 Vill. L. Rev. 975 (2001); Howard N. Fenton, III, *The Fallacy of Federalism in Foreign Affairs: State and Local Foreign Policy Trade Restrictions*, 13 Nw. J. Int'l L. & Bus. 563 (1993); Harold G. Maier, *Preemption of State Law: A Recommended Analysis*, 83 Am. J. Int'l L. 832 (1989); Michael D. Ramsey, *The Power of the States in Foreign Affairs: The Original Understanding of Foreign Policy Federalism*, 75 Notre Dame L. Rev. 341 (1999); Michael H. Shuman, *Dateline Main Street: Courts v. Local Foreign Policies*, 86 Foreign Policy (1992); Peter J. Spiro, *Foreign Relations Federalism*, 70 U. Colo. L. Rev. 1223, 1233-34 (1999); Arthur Weisburd, *State Courts, Federal Courts, and International Cases*, Yale J. Int'l L. 1 (1995). In the political science and international relations fields, see Earl H. Fry, The Expanding Role of State and Local Governments in U.S. Foreign Affairs (1998); Brian Hocking, Localizing Foreign Policy: Governments and Multilayered Diplomacy (1993); Foreign Relations and Federal States (Brian Hocking ed., 1993); John M. Kline, State Government Influence in U.S. International Economic Policy (1983); John M. Kline, *Continuing Controversies over State and Local Foreign Policy Sanctions in the United States*, 29 Publius 111 (Spring 1999).

D. FEDERAL COMMON LAW OF FOREIGN RELATIONS

[Reread Section V of Banco Nacional de Cuba v. Sabbatino, 376 U.S. 398 (1964), excerpted in Chapter 2.]

Republic of the Philippines v. Marcos

806 F.2d 344 (2d Cir. 1986)

[In this case, the Republic of the Philippines ("The Republic") sued its former President, Ferdinand Marcos, his wife Imelda, and several of their acquaintances, alleging a conspiracy in which five properties in New York had been purchased for the benefit of the Marcoses from the proceeds of moneys and assets stolen from the Philippine government. The complaint further alleged that the defendants were seeking to liquidate or transfer these New York properties, and it sought injunctive relief to prevent such actions pending a determination of the true ownership of the properties. The case was originally filed in state court, and then removed by the defendants to a federal district court. The district court granted the injunction, reasoning that the Republic had satisfied the standard for injunctive relief by "amply show[ing] 'sufficiently serious questions going to the merits to make them a fair ground for litigation' together with irreparable harm and a balance of hardships tipping in [the Republic's] favor."]

OAKES, CIRCUIT JUDGE. . . .
    [The district court judge] thought the issue of jurisdiction not to be "open to serious doubt" because this is a case "arising under the Constitution, laws or treaties of the United States" and is therefore within federal question jurisdiction under 28 U.S.C. §1331. We agree.
    We recognize that the likelihood or inevitability that federal law matters will be raised in the answer or some subsequent pleading does not bring a case within federal question jurisdiction. Rather, we are to examine the "well-pleaded complaint" to determine whether it relies on any doctrine of federal law. . . . Thus, we must analyze the plaintiff's complaint separate and apart from any defenses that the defendants have asserted or might assert in the future, to see if this action arises under federal law.
    Such an examination shows that the plaintiff's claims necessarily require determinations that will directly and significantly affect American foreign relations. In Banco Nacional de Cuba v. Sabbatino, 376 U.S. 398, 425 (1964), the Supreme Court stated that issues involving "our relationships with other members of the

international community must be treated exclusively as an aspect of federal law."
While the issue in *Sabbatino* involved application of the act of state doctrine, in
holding that the doctrine was to be applied as a matter of federal law the Court
reasoned that foreign policy matters, entrusted by the Constitution primarily to the
executive branch, have "'constitutional' underpinnings," and that the problems
that arise when foreign policy matters come before the courts "are uniquely federal
in nature." As Judge Leval pointed out, two months after the *Sabbatino* decision the
late Henry Friendly wrote that in the *Sabbatino* case "the Supreme Court has found
in the Constitution a mandate to fashion a federal law of foreign relations."
Friendly, *In Praise of Erie and of the New Federal Common Law*, 39 N.Y.U. L. Rev.
383, 408 n.119 (1964). The same judge wrote for this court in Republic of Iraq v.
First National City Bank, 353 F.2d 47, 50 (2d Cir. 1965), *cert. denied*, 382 U.S. 1027
(1966), that:

> The Supreme Court has declared that a question concerning the effect of an act of state
> "must be treated exclusively as an aspect of federal law." . . . We deem that ruling to be
> applicable here even though, as we conclude below, this is not a case in which the courts
> of the forum are bound to respect the act of the foreign state.

The opinion in *Republic of Iraq* went on to say that the decision whether to enforce
the act of a foreign sovereign affecting property in the United States "is closely tied
to our foreign affairs, with consequent need for nationwide uniformity," and that
"when property confiscated is within the United States at the time of the attempted
confiscation, our courts will give effect to acts of state 'only if they are consistent with
the policy and law of the United States.'" The principles stated in *Sabbatino* and
Republic of Iraq extend beyond the act of state doctrine context in which both cases
arose and support the existence of federal jurisdiction where the allegations in the
complaint, as in this case, concern efforts by a foreign government to reach or
obtain property located here. . . .

Weighing in favor of the application of federal common law here is the fact that
prior to the filing of the complaint in the New York State Supreme Court, The
Republic of the Philippines had already promulgated Executive Order No. 1
appointing the President's Commission on Good Government and charging it
with the recovery of all ill-gotten wealth accumulated "by the former President."
And, prior to the removal to federal court, Executive Order No. 2 had been promulgated freezing the assets of the Marcoses in the Philippines and appealing to
foreign governments to freeze assets in their countries. Whether any confiscatory
action by the Philippines will be entitled to credit in the United States courts is a
question for another day, but it is surely a question that will be governed by federal
law within the original jurisdiction of the court under section 1331 of the Judicial
Code.

On the face of the complaint, to be sure, the plaintiff brought this case under a
theory more nearly akin to a state cause of action for conversion, requiring the
imposition of a constructive trust or equitable lien upon the "ill-gotten" gains,
rather than under stated federal common law. But a "well-pleaded" complaint
can be read in one of two ways to implicate federal law. As was held in Avco
Corp. v. Aero Lodge No. 735 376 F.2d 337, 340 (6th Cir. 1967), *aff'd*, 390 U.S.
557 (1968), federal court jurisdiction may not be defeated simply by pleading a
state cause of action when that cause of action had been preempted by federal
law. . . . Discussing *Avco* in [Franchise Tax Board of California v. Construction
Laborers Vacation Trust, 463 U.S. 1 (1983)], the Supreme Court said that *Avco*

had held that federal jurisdiction exists even though the plaintiff pleads a state cause of action if federal law "is so powerful as to displace entirely any state cause of action." Our question then would be whether the federal common law in the area of foreign affairs is so "powerful," or important, as to displace a purely state cause of action of constructive trust. We think it probably is: an action brought by a foreign government against its former head of state arises under federal common law because of the necessary implications of such an action for United States foreign relations. But even if we were wrong on this point, at the least this case presents "the presence of a federal issue in a state-created cause of action." This is true because the action is brought by a foreign government against its former head of state to regain property allegedly obtained as the result of acts while he was head of state.

We hold that federal jurisdiction is present in any event because the claim raises, as a necessary element, the question whether to honor the request of a foreign government that the American courts enforce the foreign government's directives to freeze property in the United States subject to future process in the foreign state. The question whether to honor such a request by a foreign government is itself a federal question to be decided with uniformity as a matter of federal law, and not separately in each state, regardless of whether the overall claim is viewed as one of federal or state common law.

Torres v. Southern Peru Copper

113 F.3d 540 (5th Cir. 1997)

POLITZ, CHIEF JUDGE. . . .

Plaintiffs are approximately 700 Peruvian citizens who allege that they have been harmed by sulfur dioxide emissions from Southern Peru Copper Corporation's copper smelting and refining operations in Ilo, Peru. Plaintiffs originally sued SPCC and other defendants in Texas state court alleging state law causes of action such as negligence, intentional tort, and nuisance. Defendants removed the case to federal court; the plaintiffs filed a motion to remand. The district court denied the motion, holding that although diversity jurisdiction was lacking, federal question jurisdiction existed. The district court then dismissed the case on the basis of forum non conveniens and comity among nations. Plaintiffs timely appealed. . . .

We analyze a removal action on the basis of federal question jurisdiction under the well-pleaded complaint rule, which requires disclosure of the federal question on the face of the complaint. The complaint must state a cause of action created by federal law or it must assert a state-law cause of action requiring the "resolution of a substantial question of federal law." In making our jurisdictional determination, we examine the entire record for a proper understanding of the true nature of the complaint. . . .

Plaintiffs maintain that because they have asserted only state-law tort claims, the well-pleaded complaint rule precludes us from finding federal question jurisdiction. The state of Peru has protested the lawsuit by filing a letter with the State Department and by submitting an amicus brief to this court. Peru maintains that the litigation implicates some of its most vital interests and, hence, will affect its relations with the United States. SPCC therefore contends that plaintiffs' complaint raises substantial questions of federal law by implicating the federal common law of foreign relations.

That Peru has injected itself into this lawsuit does not, standing alone, create a question of federal law. Its vigorousness in opposing the action, however, has alerted us to the foreign policy issues implicated by this case, which we have confirmed by a close review of the record. The mining industry in Peru, of which SPCC is the largest company, is critical to that country's economy, contributing up to 50% of its export income and 11% of its gross domestic product. Furthermore, the Peruvian government has participated substantially in the activities for which SPCC is being sued. By way of example, the government: (1) owns the land on which SPCC operates; (2) owns the minerals which SPCC extracts; (3) owned the Ilo refinery from 1975 until 1994, during which time pollution from the refinery may have contributed to the injuries complained of by plaintiffs; and (4) grants concessions that allow SPCC to operate in return for an annual fee. Moreover, the government extensively regulates the mining industry. This action therefore strikes not only at vital economic interests but also at Peru's sovereign interests by seeking damages for activities and policies in which the government actively has been engaged. On the record before us we must conclude that plaintiffs' complaint raises substantial questions of federal common law by implicating important foreign policy concerns.[8] We accordingly affirm the district court's conclusion that it had federal question jurisdiction.

Pacheco de Perez v. AT&T Co.

139 F.3d 1368 (11th Cir. 1998)

BARKETT, CIRCUIT JUDGE:

In these two consolidated cases, plaintiffs-appellants, individuals injured in a 1993 gas pipeline explosion in Venezuela, appeal from the district court's order denying their motion to remand the case to the Georgia state courts and dismissing the action under the doctrine of forum non conveniens.

The explosion, which killed fifty people and injured many others, occurred during the laying of fiber-optic cable in the town of Tejerias, Venezuela, when a machine used to dig a trench for the cable struck a gas pipeline. Plaintiffs allege that defendants-appellees AT&T Company ("AT&T"), a New York corporation, and several citizens of Georgia who worked for AT&T, participated in the acts or omissions that caused the explosion.

Before filing the present actions, many of the plaintiffs in this case filed and dismissed actions based on the same claims against the same or similar defendants in other federal district courts. Specifically, most of the plaintiffs brought two diversity tort actions in the United States District Court for the Eastern District of California, which they voluntarily dismissed, and later filed two similar suits in the United States District Court for the District of New Jersey, which they also voluntarily dismissed. The several suits named AT&T, AT&T International, and AT&T Andinos, among others, as potentially liable defendants.

Thereafter, plaintiffs filed two separate actions in Georgia state court, asserting various state law claims against AT&T and the individual employees of AT&T. Defendants removed the cases to the United States District Court for the Northern

---

8. *See* Republic of Philippines v. Marcos, 806 F.2d 344, 352 (2d Cir. 1986) (concluding that although plaintiff brought action on state-law theory, "an examination shows that the plaintiff's claims necessarily require determinations that will directly and significantly affect American foreign relations").

District of Georgia. The district court consolidated the two actions, denied the plaintiffs' motion to remand, and dismissed the consolidated actions under the doctrine of forum non conveniens.

The threshold question on appeal is whether, as the plaintiffs argue, the district court should have remanded the case back to the Georgia state court for lack of federal jurisdiction. Although there is complete diversity among the parties, removal of a case on diversity grounds is not permitted if one or more of the defendants is a citizen of the state in which the suit was originally filed. 28 U.S.C. §1441(b). Accordingly, because the individual defendants in this case are Georgia citizens, removal would not ordinarily be permitted on diversity grounds....

As their third alternative theory of federal jurisdiction, defendants assert that the plaintiffs' claims implicate the federal common law of foreign relations. The Supreme Court has held that the area of international relations is governed exclusively by federal law....Where a state law action has as a substantial element an issue involving foreign relations or foreign policy matters, federal jurisdiction is present. The cases addressing this area of federal common law generally involve disputes in which a foreign government, or its instrumentality, is a named party to the lawsuit, or where the actions of a foreign government are a direct focus of the litigation.

The Fifth Circuit has extended the area of federal jurisdiction based on the federal common law of foreign relations to disputes between private parties that implicate the "vital economic and sovereign interests" of the nation where the parties' dispute arose. Torres [v. Southern Peru Copper Corp., 113 F.3d 540 (5th Cir. 1997)]....

Citing *Torres*, defendants argue that the plaintiffs' action implicates the economic and sovereign interests of Venezuela to such a significant extent that federal jurisdiction based upon the federal common law of foreign relations exists in this case. Defendants note that the factors considered by the Fifth Circuit in this jurisdictional inquiry include whether the injuries occurred on foreign soil, whether the foreign government's policy decisions or actions are brought into question by the suit, whether the foreign government was involved in the alleged wrongdoing, and whether the action strikes at the heart of the economic and sovereign interests of the foreign nation. Defendants assert that the record shows that the plaintiffs' injuries occurred only in Venezuela; that the gas pipeline that exploded was owned and operated by a government-owned Venezuelan corporation; that the cable-laying project was initiated by the national telephone company, 49% of which is owned by the Venezuelan government, and that a ministry of the government was responsible for the issuing of permits for the fiber-optic cable project; that the plaintiffs' action calls into question the laying of the gas pipeline, an act done by the government-owned corporation; that the Venezuelan National Congress has conducted hearings into the accident; and that the fiber-optic cable project is "vital" to the Venezuelan economy. All of these factors, the defendants argue, support a finding that the substantial interests of Venezuela are implicated by this litigation and that, therefore, federal jurisdiction is proper.

We conclude that the federal common law of foreign relations will not support federal jurisdiction in this case. First, although the court in *Torres* stated "that Peru has injected itself into this lawsuit does not, standing alone, create a question of federal law," we think it significant, for purposes of this case, that the Venezuelan government has taken no position on whether this lawsuit proceeds in the United

States or in Venezuela. Without such an indication from the foreign nation, we are reluctant to find that the plaintiffs' private cause of action sounding in Georgia tort law implicates important foreign policy on the face of the plaintiffs' pleadings. It seems more likely to us that any issues involving the participation of the Venezuelan government, or its corporate entities, will arise in the form of a defense by AT&T. Federal question jurisdiction, however, cannot be based upon a federal defense.

Second, we find that the evidence regarding Venezuela's interests in the plaintiffs' action is too speculative and tenuous to confer federal jurisdiction over this case.... In this case,... while the record shows that Venezuelan governmental entities or corporations partially owned by the government participated in activities that may have had an effect on the events giving rise to the explosion, the evidence of Venezuela's direct participation in any tortious actions is weaker than the evidence of the Peruvian government's involvement in *Torres*, and there is no evidence regarding the relative importance of the fiber-optic cable project, or the telecommunications industry in general, to the Venezuelan national economy. Although this litigation might significantly affect AT&T's business operations in Venezuela, it is not clear that the lawsuit threatens the economic vitality of Venezuela itself. While we do not doubt that the gas pipeline explosion was a significant event in Venezuela, we conclude that the defendants have failed to show that the plaintiffs' complaints are so intertwined with the sovereign interests of Venezuela as to place this case within the purview of the federal courts.

Patrickson v. Dole Food Co.

251 F.3d 795 (9th Cir. 2001)

KOZINSKI, CIRCUIT JUDGE:

We consider whether the federal courts have jurisdiction over a class action brought by Latin American banana workers against multinational fruit and chemical companies alleged to have exposed the workers to a toxic pesticide.

I

Dibromochloropropane (DBCP) is a powerful pesticide. Tough on pests, it's no friend to humans either. Absorbed by the skin or inhaled, it's alleged to cause sterility, testicular atrophy, miscarriages, liver damage, cancer and other ailments that you wouldn't wish on anyone. Originally manufactured by Dow Chemical and Shell Oil, the pesticide was banned from general use in the United States by the Environmental Protection Agency in 1979. But the chemical companies continued to distribute it to fruit companies in developing nations.

In our case, banana workers from Costa Rica, Ecuador, Guatemala and Panama brought a class action against Dole Food Company, other major fruit companies and chemical companies (hereinafter "Dole") for injuries allegedly sustained from exposure to DBCP in their home countries. This case represents one front in a broad litigation war between these plaintiffs' lawyers and these defendants. In some of the cases, plaintiffs have reportedly won multimillion dollar settlements. In others, defendants have managed to have the cases dismissed for forum non conveniens.

The merits are not before us. Instead, we must decide whether the case is properly in federal court. The workers brought suit in Hawaii state court.

Dole...removed [the case] based on federal-question jurisdiction, 28 U.S.C. §1331. The district court denied plaintiffs' remand motion and then dismissed the case for forum non conveniens.

II

Dole was entitled to remove the case to federal court if plaintiffs could have brought it there to begin with. *See* 28 U.S.C. §1441(a). We must therefore consider whether plaintiffs could have brought the case in district court under federal-question jurisdiction.... [1]

A.   Federal-Question Jurisdiction

We are courts of limited jurisdiction. This means we hear only those cases that Congress directs and the Constitution permits us to hear. Under Article III, federal courts may assert jurisdiction over federal questions, extending to all cases "arising under this Constitution, the Laws of the United States, and Treaties made, or which shall be made, under their Authority." U.S. Const. art. III, §2. Although any federal ingredient may be sufficient to satisfy Article III, the statutory grant of jurisdiction under 28 U.S.C. §1331 requires more. *See* Verlinden B.V. v. Central Bank of Nigeria, 461 U.S. 480, 495 (1983) ("Article III 'arising under' jurisdiction is broader than federal-question jurisdiction under §1331....").

Even if the case turns entirely on the validity of a federal defense, federal courts may not assert jurisdiction unless a federal right or immunity is "an element, and an essential one, of the plaintiff's cause of action." This venerable "well-pleaded complaint" rule keeps us from becoming entangled in state law controversies on the conjecture that federal law may come into play at some point during the litigation; it also ensures that Congress retains control over the size of federal court dockets.

Under conventional principles, the class action here unquestionably arises under state law. Plaintiffs seek relief under the common law of Hawaii for negligence, conspiracy, strict liability, intentional torts and breach of implied warranty. None of the claims has an element premised on a right created by Congress or the Constitution. Dole nonetheless argues that we have federal-question jurisdiction because the case calls for an application of the federal common law of foreign relations.

Although there is no general federal common law, "there are enclaves of federal judge-made law which bind the States." Banco Nacional de Cuba v. Sabbatino, 376 U.S. 398, 426 (1964). In *Sabbatino*, the Court held that one of those enclaves concerns the legal principles governing the nation's relationship with other members of the international community. The case considered whether the "act of state doctrine" requires U.S. courts to recognize the validity of the Cuban government's expropriation of private property. A long-standing common law principle, the act of state doctrine precludes courts from questioning the legality of actions that a foreign government has taken within its own borders. *Sabbatino* considered whether the doctrine was a matter of state or federal law.

Because the Constitution gives the federal government exclusive authority to manage the nation's foreign affairs, the Court concluded that "rules of international law should not be left to divergent and perhaps parochial state

---

1. Because Dole Food Company is a citizen of the forum state, defendants could not remove based on diversity of citizenship. *See* 28 U.S.C. §1441(b).

interpretations." *Sabbatino.* Whether a foreign state's act is given legal force in the courts of the United States is a "uniquely federal" question directly implicating our nation's foreign affairs. Therefore, it was appropriate to fashion a single federal standard to govern such cases, rather than rely on a patchwork of separate state standards. Equally important, the Supreme Court in *Sabbatino* reserved to itself ultimate review of all cases raising the act of state doctrine, rather than leaving them to the various state supreme courts.

Federal-question jurisdiction was not an issue in *Sabbatino*; the district court already had jurisdiction because of diversity of citizenship. The question presented was what substantive law would apply — state law pursuant to Erie R.R. Co. v. Tompkins, 304 U.S. 64 (1938), or federal law. *Sabbatino* held that the common law of foreign relations falls outside *Erie*'s general rule and so federal law applies. Federal common law is, of course, federal law; so if a plaintiff's claim arises under the federal common law recognized by *Sabbatino*, the federal courts will have jurisdiction under 28 U.S.C. §1331.[2]

This is as far as *Sabbatino* goes, and it's not far enough, because nothing in plaintiffs' complaint turns on the validity or invalidity of any act of a foreign state. Plaintiffs seek compensation for injuries sustained from the defendants' manufacture, sale and use of DBCP. Plaintiffs don't claim that any foreign government participated in such activities or that the defendants acted under the color of foreign law. The case — at least as framed by plaintiffs — does not require us to evaluate any act of state or apply any principle of international law. The common law of foreign relations will become an issue only when — and if — it is raised as a defense.

Dole nonetheless argues that we must assert federal-question jurisdiction because the case concerns a vital sector of the economies of foreign countries and so has implications for our nation's relations with those countries. Plaintiffs represent a class of perhaps thousands of foreign nationals who allege that large multinational corporations harmed them in their home countries. Dole argues that, by granting relief, American courts would damage the banana industry — one of the most important sectors of those countries' economies — and cast doubt on the balance those governments have struck between agricultural development and labor safety. Although plaintiffs allege only state law claims, Dole argues, this case implicates the "uniquely federal" interest in foreign relations, and so must be heard in a federal forum. In essence, Dole interprets *Sabbatino* as creating an exception not only to *Erie*, but to the well-pleaded complaint rule as well. Dole's position is not without support. [The Court describes Torres v. Southern Peru Copper Corp., excerpted above.] While reaching the opposite result on the facts before it, the Eleventh Circuit seems to have adopted the Fifth Circuit's theory in *Torres*. [The court describes Pacheco de Perez v. AT&T Co., excerpted above.]

Torres and *Pacheco de Perez* relied principally on Republic of Philippines v. Marcos [excerpted above], which seems to have been the first case to conclude that "there is federal question jurisdiction over actions having important foreign policy implications." . . . *Marcos* . . . broadly suggest[ed] that federal-question jurisdiction could "probably" be premised on the fact that a case may affect our nation's foreign relations, whether or not federal law is raised by the plaintiff's complaint:

---

2. Although the act of state doctrine generally serves as a defense, it can also be used affirmatively as the basis of a claim. *See* Restatement (Third) of Foreign Relations Law §443 cmt. i (1986) (noting that an act of state may be "necessary to a litigant's claim or defense").

"An action brought by a foreign government against its former head of state arises under federal common law because of the necessary implications of such an action for United States foreign relations." This reads far too much into *Sabbatino*. As noted, *Sabbatino* was about choice of law, not jurisdiction. The Court left no doubt that the substantive law of foreign relations must be federal, and it stressed the need for national uniformity. But *Sabbatino* does not say that federal courts alone are competent to develop this body of law. To the contrary, *Sabbatino* notes that the law of foreign relations is like other "enclaves of federal judge-made law which bind the States," such as the rules filling the interstices of federal statutes and the laws regulating interstate boundary issues. The Court's reference to binding the states makes sense only if one assumes that state courts will be called upon to apply the law of foreign relations. *Sabbatino* says as much: "The act of state doctrine is a principle of decision binding on federal and state courts alike...."

State courts apply federal law in a wide variety of cases and, by doing so, they necessarily develop it. This does not undermine the nationwide uniformity of federal law much more than having somewhat different applications of federal law in the various federal circuits. Ultimately, the Supreme Court has the final say on any question of federal law, whether it arises in federal or state court, and this is thought sufficient to ensure nationwide uniformity in areas as diverse as criminal procedure, patent law and labor law.

We see no reason to treat the federal common law of foreign relations any differently than other areas of federal law. Certainly, federal courts have preeminence in developing all areas of federal law by virtue of the fact that almost all cases premised on federal law may be brought in or removed to federal court. In addition, Congress has provided federal jurisdiction in certain cases implicating our foreign relations, regardless of the nature of the claim. *See, e.g.,* 28 U.S.C. §1251(b)(1) (suits where ambassadors or other foreign government officials are parties); *id.* §1351 (suits against foreign consuls or other diplomatic personnel); *id.* §1330 (suits against a foreign state); *see also id.* §1350 (suits brought by an alien for a tort committed in violation of international law). What Congress has not done is to extend federal-question jurisdiction to all suits where the federal common law of foreign relations might arise as an issue. We interpret congressional silence outside these specific grants of jurisdiction as an endorsement of the well-pleaded complaint rule.

We therefore decline to follow *Marcos*, *Torres* and *Pacheco de Perez* insofar as they stand for the proposition that the federal courts may assert jurisdiction over a case simply because a foreign government has expressed a special interest in its outcome. It may well be that our foreign relations will be implicated by the pendency of a lawsuit on a subject that affects that government's sovereign interests; the courts in *Marcos* and *Torres* certainly believed this to be the case. But we see no logical connection between such an effect and the assertion of federal-question jurisdiction. That the case is litigated in federal court, rather than state court, will not reduce the impact of the case on the foreign government. Federal judges cannot dismiss a case because a foreign government finds it irksome, nor can they tailor their rulings to accommodate a non-party. Federal judges, like state judges, are bound to decide cases before them according to the rule of law. If a foreign government finds the litigation offensive, it may lodge a protest with our government; our political branches can then respond in whatever way they deem appropriate—up to and including passing legislation. Our government may, of course, communicate its own views as to the conduct of the litigation, and the court—whether state or federal — can take those views into account. But it is quite a different matter to suggest that courts — state or federal — will tailor their rulings to accommodate the expressed interests of a foreign nation that is not even a party.

Nor do we understand how a court can go about evaluating the foreign policy implications of another government's expression of interest. Assuming that foreign relations are an appropriate consideration at all, the relevant question is not whether the foreign government is pleased or displeased by the litigation, but how the case affects the interests of the United States. That is an inherently political judgment, one that courts — whether state or federal — are not competent to make. *See* Container Corp. of Am. v. Franchise Tax Bd., 463 U.S. 159 (1983) ("This Court has little competence in determining precisely when foreign nations will be offended by particular acts. . . ."); Chicago & S. Air Lines, Inc. v. Waterman S.S. Corp., 333 U.S. 103, 111 (1948) ("The very nature of executive decisions as to foreign policy is political, not judicial."). If courts were to take the interests of the foreign government into account, they would be conducting foreign policy by deciding whether it serves our national interests to continue with the litigation, dismiss it on some ground such as forum non conveniens, or deal with it in some other way.[8] *See* Jack L. Goldsmith, *Federal Courts, Foreign Affairs, and Federalism*, 83 Va. L. Rev. 1617, 1667 (1997). Because such political judgments are not within the competence of either state or federal courts, we can see no support for the proposition that federal courts are better equipped than state courts to deal with cases raising such concerns.[9]

As Justice Frankfurter noted in Romero v. International Terminal Operating Co., 358 U.S. 354 (1959), federal courts must be hesitant "to expand the jurisdiction of the federal courts through a broad reading of jurisdictional statutes." If federal courts are so much better suited than state courts for handling cases that might raise foreign policy concerns, Congress will surely pass a statute giving us that jurisdiction. Because we see no evidence that Congress meant for the federal courts to assert jurisdiction over cases simply because foreign governments have an interest in them, we must part company with our sister circuits.

Notes and Questions

1. Is *Sabbatino* properly read as authorizing a broad "federal common law of foreign relations"? If so, what is the scope of this federal common law? The court in *Marcos* holds that the Philippines' action for conversion of property — normally a

---

8. We note, for example, that the Fifth Circuit in *Torres* had before it an amicus brief from the government of Peru, but none from our own government. Based on Peru's representations, the court concluded that Peru had a vital interest in the case and the litigation might adversely affect Peru's relations with the United States. Apparently, the Fifth Circuit believed that it served the interests of the United States to avoid this consequence, so it asserted jurisdiction and affirmed the dismissal on grounds of forum non conveniens. But it is just as plausible that our government did not express its views because it was indifferent to Peru's discomfort or even reveled in it. Courts should not put themselves in the position of having to make such judgments.

9. We are particularly troubled by the suggestion in *Pacheco de Perez* (echoed by Dole in our case) that federal jurisdiction will hinge on whether a foreign government has taken a position in support or in opposition to the litigation. The Eleventh Circuit noted that the Peruvian government in *Torres* had opposed the litigation, both in a communication to our State Department and an amicus brief filed in the Fifth Circuit. The Eleventh Circuit found it significant that, by contrast, "the Venezuelan government has taken no position on whether the Pacheco de Perez lawsuit proceeds in the United States or in Venezuela."

state law issue — implicates the federal common law of foreign relations "because of the necessary implications of such an action for our foreign relations." What, precisely, are these implications? Are all issues that implicate U.S. foreign relations governed by the federal common law of foreign relations? If not, how do courts determine whether implications for foreign relations are sufficiently serious as to implicate the federal common law of foreign relations? And how do courts tell what federal rule will best serve U.S. foreign relations interests?

2. What is the relationship between the federal common law holding of *Sabbatino* and *Zschernig's* dormant foreign affairs preemption doctrine (which is discussed in Section C)? One could argue that the federal common law created in *Sabbatino* is the exercise of a "legislative" power in the federal judiciary, while dormant foreign affairs preemption is a species of structural constitutional preemption. *See* Louis Henkin, Foreign Affairs and the United States Constitution 139-40, 162-65 (2d ed. 1996). Or one could argue that the two decisions involve functionally identical judicial lawmaking powers because both decisions (a) assert that the Constitution's assignment of foreign relations powers to the federal government entails a self-executing exclusion of state authority; (b) justify preemption as needed to protect political branch prerogatives in foreign relations; and (c) are ultimately subject to congressional revision. *See* Jack L. Goldsmith, *Federal Courts, Foreign Affairs, and Federalism*, 83 Va. L. Rev. 1617, 1630 (1997). Which view is right? Does it matter?

3. As discussed in Chapter 2, the lower federal courts can hear only those cases that (a) fall with the bounds of their Article III judicial power and (b) are authorized by a statutory grant of subject matter jurisdiction. For federal question jurisdiction under 28 U.S.C. §1331, a federal law issue must appear on the face of the well-pleaded complaint. This is true regardless of whether the case is originally filed in federal court or removed to federal court from state court. What were the federal law issues in *Marcos* and *Torres*? Did they appear on the face of the plaintiffs' well-pleaded complaints? One gloss on the well-pleaded complaint rule is that, in situations in which federal law completely preempts a cause of action, any claim that comes within the scope of the preemption necessarily arises under federal law. *See, e.g.,* Franchise Tax Board of California v. Construction Laborers Vacation Trust, 463 U.S. 1 (1983); Avco Corp. v. Aero Lodge No. 735, 390 U.S. 557 (1968). Did *Marcos* and *Torres* involve situations of complete preemption? (In Beneficial National Bank v. Anderson, 123 S. Ct. 2058 (2003), the Supreme Court, citing *Avco* and *Franchise Tax Board*, reaffirmed the complete preemption doctrine. Applying that doctrine, the Court held that an action filed in state court to recover damages from a national bank for allegedly charging excessive interest in violation of both state common law and a state statute could be removed to federal court because a federal statute (the National Bank Act) was intended to provide the exclusive cause of action for usury claims against national banks. Justice Scalia filed a dissent, joined by Justice Thomas, in which he questioned the validity of the complete preemption doctrine.)

4. The court in *Dole* characterizes *Marcos* and *Torres* as arguing for a federal common law of foreign relations exception to the well-pleaded complaint rule. Is this an accurate characterization? Could one argue that the tort claims in *Marcos* and *Torres* were themselves governed by a federal common law of foreign relations and thus "arose under" federal law? Does *Sabbatino* support such an argument?

5. Some commentators have suggested that, in order to protect federal interests, Congress has the power in some instances to create "protective jurisdiction"—that is, federal jurisdiction over cases that do not fall within any of the categories of jurisdiction listed in Article III of the Constitution but that nonetheless implicate important federal interests. *See, e.g.*, Paul J. Mishkin, *The Federal "Question" in the District Courts*, 53 Colum. L. Rev. 57 (1953); Herbert Wechsler, *Federal Jurisdiction and the Revision of the Judicial Code*, 13 Law & Contemp. Probs. 216 (1948). This theory is controversial, and the Supreme Court has never endorsed it. Can *Marcos* and *Torres* properly be viewed as exercising "protective jurisdiction"? Does *Dole* implicitly reject this jurisdictional theory? For an argument that a jurisdictional federal common law of foreign relations cannot be justified as a form of protective jurisdiction, see Andrew C. Baak, Comment, *The Illegitimacy of Protective Jurisdiction over Foreign Affairs*, 70 U. Chi. L. Rev. 1487 (2003).

6. What explains the different outcomes in *Torres* and *Perez*? Do these decisions provide sufficient predictability concerning the circumstances under which federal courts can exercise subject matter jurisdiction? Are courts competent to make the assessments called for by these decisions?

7. Compare the treatment of foreign government protests in *Torres* with their treatment in *Dole*. What if any weight should federal courts give to such protests in determining whether they have jurisdiction to hear a case? Are such protests less or more relevant here than they are in connection with dormant foreign affairs preemption, discussed in the last section?

8. Numerous other lower court decisions in recent years have considered whether to base federal jurisdiction on a federal common law of foreign relations. Consider two interesting examples. In In re Tobacco/Governmental Health Care Costs Litigation, 100 F. Supp. 2d 31 (D.D.C. 2000), *appeals dismissed*, 287 F. 3d 192 (D.C. Cir. 2002), Bolivia and Venezuela brought separate state lawsuits against scores of tobacco companies, alleging state common law torts. The lawsuits were removed to federal court on the basis of the federal common law of foreign relations and transferred by the Judicial Panel on Multi-District Litigation to the federal district court in the District of Columbia. That court granted the plaintiffs' motion to remand, rejecting the federal common law of foreign relations removal for reasons similar to those articulated in *Dole*. In In re World War II Era Japanese Forced Labor Litigation, 114 F. Supp. 2d 939 (N.D. Cal. 2000), excerpted above in Section B, U.S. servicemen sued various Japanese corporations for forced labor during World War II. Here again, the plaintiffs sued in state court on state law claims, and the defendants removed on the ground that the case implicated the federal common law of foreign relations. The court in that case rejected remand motions, however, reasoning that "plaintiffs' claims arise out of world war and are enmeshed with the momentous policy choices that arose in the war's aftermath." *Id.* at 943.

For additional decisions basing jurisdiction on a federal common law of foreign relations, see Sequihua v. Texaco Inc., 847 F. Supp. 61 (S.D. Tex. 1994), and Grynberg Production Corp. v. British Gas, plc, 817 F. Supp. 1338 (E.D. Tex. 1993). For additional decisions declining to base jurisdiction on a federal common law of foreign relations, see Marathon Oil Co. v. Ruhrgas, A.G., 115 F.3d 315 (5th Cir. 1997); Aquafaith Shipping, Ltd. v. Jarillas, 963 F.2d 806 (5th Cir. 1992); Sao Paulo v. American Tobacco Co., 2000 U.S. Dist. LEXIS 9617 (E.D. La. 2000); Rio de Janeiro v. Philip Morris Cos., 1999 U.S. Dist. LEXIS 21958 (E.D. Tex. 1999);

Potabe v. Robichaux, 1999 U.S. Dist. LEXIS 9798 (E.D. La. 1999); and Republic of Panama v. American Tobacco Co., 1999 U.S. Dist. LEXIS 8135 (E.D. La. 1999). For a recent decision holding that state law claims relating to the expropriation of property during the Nazi regime in Germany should be treated as governed by federal common law, see Ungaro-Banages v. Dresdner Bank AG, 379 F.3d 1227, 1332-33 (11th Cir. 2004), a different portion of which is excerpted in Chapter 2 in the materials on comity.

6

Treaties and Other International Agreements

Article II of the Constitution grants the President the power "by and with the Advice and Consent of the Senate, to make Treaties, provided two thirds of the Senators present concur." The U.S. treaty-making process operates essentially as follows:* Representatives of the President negotiate the terms of the treaty with foreign nations, and the President or his representative signs the completed draft. The President then transmits the treaty to the Senate for its advice and consent. If the treaty receives the required two-thirds vote, the Senate sends a resolution to the President approving the treaty. The President has the discretion at this point to ratify or not ratify the treaty. Ratification is the act by which a nation formally declares its intent to be bound by a treaty. When the President signs the instrument of ratification and the Secretary of State affixes the Seal of the United States, the U.S. ratification process is complete. Even at this point, however, the United States is not bound by the terms of the treaty. The treaty becomes binding on the United States when the instrument of ratification is either exchanged (as is usually the process with respect to bilateral treaties) or deposited at a specified place (as is usually the process with respect to multilateral treaties).

[handwritten margin note: Process of making treaties]

The materials that follow explore the domestic status and scope of treaties and other international agreements.** A number of the issues discussed below surfaced early in U.S. history, in connection with the 1794 Jay Treaty with Great Britain. As background reading for this chapter, here is a brief description of the Jay Treaty and the controversies surrounding it.

David P. Currie, The Constitution in Congress: The Federalist Period, 1789-1801

at 209-15 (1997)

The United States were close to war with Great Britain in 1794, and in April President Washington sent John Jay to London to try to forestall it. The Senate

---

* *See* Congressional Research Service, Treaties and Other International Agreements: The Role of the United States Senate, S. Prt. 106-71, 106th Cong., 2d Sess. 6-12 (2001) ("CRS Study").

** Although not explored in this chapter, it should be kept in mind that the United States also often makes *non-binding* international commitments. These commitments, which are not "treaties" under either U.S. law or international law, can nevertheless be an important component of U.S. foreign policy. Such commitments are typically made by the Executive Branch without formal senatorial or congressional involvement.

approved Jay's appointment, but not without protest. For at the time of his nomination John Jay was Chief Justice of the United States, and some senators had the temerity to suggest that he belonged on the Bench. . . .

Jay went to England, and he did not resign until the following year, after he was elected Governor of New York. . . .

Meanwhile Jay's labors had borne fruit; Washington submitted the treaty he had negotiated to a special session of the Senate in June 1795. Like its author, the treaty encountered heavy weather in the Senate.

The first hurdle was a two-pronged Republican challenge to its constitutionality. Article IX of the treaty, which guaranteed the right of British subjects to own land, was attacked as beyond federal authority; various commercial provisions — including Article XV, which promised that neither country would impose higher duties on the other's ships or goods than upon those of other nations — were alleged to imply "a power in the President and Senate, to control, and even annihilate the constitutional right of the Congress of the United States over their commercial intercourse with foreign nations." . . . [T]he Senate rejected the constitutional challenge by a bare 20-10 vote on what has been described as strict party lines.

The second difficulty came from the Federalists, who had provided the votes to sustain the treaty's validity. Article XII purported to reopen trade between the United States and the British West Indies, but on onerous terms: It permitted U.S. citizens to transport West Indian goods only in small vessels and only to the United States and could be read (contrary to its probable intention) to forbid American ships to carry American cotton. The upper House disapproved this article and gave only conditional consent to the treaty. . . .

Serious pressure was brought to bear on the President not to sign the treaty even after the Senate approved it, confirming the understanding (which had prevailed since the First Congress) that ratification was a separate and discretionary act. Overcoming doubts as to the desirability of the treaty, Washington gave his final approval, and the battle shifted to the House of Representatives.

For, in addition to renouncing U.S. claims of freedom to trade with France in exchange for a promise by the British to evacuate forts in the Northwest Territory that they continued to occupy in violation of the peace treaty of 1783, Jay's agreement provided for the establishment of bilateral commissions to resolve a New England border dispute, the rights of British creditors, and claims for depredations against U.S. shipping. The President sent the fully ratified treaty to both Houses of Congress, in the evident expectation that they would appropriate money to cover the attendant expenses.

Before anyone moved to do so, however, Representative Edward Livingston of New York fired the first shot by offering a resolution requesting the President to provide the House with the instructions that Jay had been given when he undertook his mission in England, as well as other documents and correspondence relevant to the treaty. The debate on this resolution lasted an entire month and was one of the most impressive and fundamental ever conducted in Congress. . . .

At length the House approved Livingston's resolution by the lopsided vote of sixty-two to thirty-seven, suggesting that a substantial majority agreed that the House had discretion in implementing the treaty. But the President refused to turn over the requested information. . . .

Representative Thomas Blount responded by proposing another resolution, which the House promptly adopted by a similarly decisive vote, affirming its discretion to refuse to implement any treaty affecting a subject within congressional power and its right to request information without giving reasons.

Deprived of the materials it professed to find crucial to its deliberations, the House proceeded to debate the merits of the treaty. As it did so petitions began to pour in, most significantly from the Republican West, urging that Congress appropriate the necessary funds. For control of the northwestern forts was critical to the prevention of Indian raids and thus to settlement of the Northwest Territory. With their constituents vociferously against them, a number of House opponents gave up the fight; having asserted its right not to appropriate money, the House voted to do so after all.

A. SELF-EXECUTION

Article VI of the Constitution provides that "all Treaties made, or which shall be made, under the Authority of the United States, shall be the supreme Law of the Land; and the Judges in every State shall be bound thereby, any Thing in the Constitution or Laws of any State to the Contrary notwithstanding." This language could be read to suggest that every treaty ratified by the United States has the status of judicially enforceable federal law. Since early in U.S. history, however, the Supreme Court has recognized a distinction between "self-executing" and "non-self-executing" treaties, and it has held that, in the absence of implementing legislation, only self-executing treaties are judicially enforceable. The Court first relied on this distinction in Foster v. Neilson, 27 U.S. (2 Pet.) 253 (1829), a case involving a treaty with Spain in which Spain ceded Florida to the United States. In an opinion by Chief Justice Marshall, the Court concluded that a provision in the treaty preserving grants of land that had been made by Spain in the ceded territory was not self-executing. Marshall explained that the treaty provision, the English version of which provided that the grants of land "shall be ratified and confirmed to the persons in possession of the lands," was in "the language of contract," and thus would not take effect as domestic law until implemented by the legislature. *Id.* at 315. The Court further stated:

> A treaty is in its nature a contract between two nations, not a legislative act. It does not generally effect, of itself, the object to be accomplished, especially so far as its operation is infra-territorial; but is carried into execution by the sovereign power of the respective parties to the instrument.
>
> In the United States a different principle is established. Our constitution declares a treaty to be the law of the land. It is, consequently, to be regarded in courts of justice as equivalent to an act of the legislature, whenever it operates of itself without the aid of any legislative provision. But when the terms of the stipulation import a contract, when either of the parties engages to perform a particular act, the treaty addresses itself to the political, not the judicial department; and the legislature must execute the contract before it can become a rule for the Court.

Id. at 314. Interestingly, several years later the Court changed its mind about this particular treaty provision. After examining the Spanish version of the provision, the English translation of which provided that the grants of land "shall remain ratified and confirmed," the Court concluded that the provision was in fact self-executing. *See* United States v. Percheman, 32 U.S. (7 Pet.) 51, 88-89 (1833).

The decisions below address various implications of this distinction between self-executing and non-self-executing treaties, as well as the factors that courts consider in making this distinction.

Asakura v. City of Seattle

265 U.S. 332 (1924)

claiming treaty violation

[A Seattle ordinance required pawnbrokers to obtain licenses, but prohibited the granting of such licenses to noncitizens. Asakura, a pawnbroker who was a citizen of Japan, sued in state court to enjoin enforcement of the ordinance on the ground that it violated a treaty between the United States and Japan that granted "national treatment" (i.e., equal treatment with U.S. citizens) to Japanese citizens who engaged in trade in the United States.]

MR. JUSTICE BUTLER delivered the opinion of the Court. . . .

Does the ordinance violate the treaty? Plaintiff in error invokes and relies upon the following provisions: "The citizens or subjects of each of the High Contracting Parties shall have liberty to enter, travel and reside in the territories of the other to carry on trade, wholesale and retail, to own or lease and occupy houses, manufactories, warehouses and shops, to employ agents of their choice, to lease land for residential and commercial purposes, and generally to do anything incident to or necessary for trade upon the same terms as native citizens or subjects, submitting themselves to the laws and regulations there established. . . . The citizens or subjects of each . . . shall receive, in the territories of the other, the most constant protection and security for their persons and property, . . ."

A treaty made under the authority of the United States "shall be the supreme law of the land; and the judges in every State shall be bound thereby, any thing in the constitution or laws of any State to the contrary notwithstanding." Constitution, Art. VI, §2.

The treaty-making power of the United States is not limited by any express provision of the Constitution, and, though it does not extend "so far as to authorize what the Constitution forbids," it does extend to all proper subjects of negotiation between our government and other nations. Geofroy v. Riggs, 133 U.S. 258, 266, 267. . . . The treaty is binding within the State of Washington. The rule of equality established by it cannot be rendered nugatory in any part of the United States by municipal ordinances or state laws. It stands on the same footing of supremacy as do the provisions of the Constitution and laws of the United States. It operates of itself without the aid of any legislation, state or national; and it will be applied and given authoritative effect by the courts. . . .

prefer interpret. favorable to rights

It remains to be considered whether the business of pawnbroker is "trade" within the meaning of the treaty. Treaties are to be construed in a broad and liberal spirit, and, when two constructions are possible, one restrictive of rights that may be claimed under it and the other favorable to them, the latter is to be preferred. . . . The ordinance defines "pawnbroker" to "mean and include every person whose business or occupation [it] is to take and receive by way of pledge, pawn or exchange, goods, wares or merchandise, or any kind of personal property whatever, for the repayment or security of any money loaned thereon, or to loan money on deposit of personal property"; and defines "pawnshop" to "mean and include every place at which the business of pawnbroker is carried on." The language of the treaty is comprehensive. The phrase "to carry on trade" is broad. That it is not to be given a restricted meaning is plain. The clauses "to own or lease... shops,... to lease land for... commercial purposes, and generally to do anything incident to or necessary for trade," and "shall receive... the most constant protection and security for their... property..." all go to show the intention of the parties that the citizens or subjects to either shall have liberty in the territory of the other to engage in all kinds and classes of business that are or reasonably may be embraced within the meaning of the word "trade" as used in the treaty.... The ordinance violates the treaty.

United States v. Postal

589 F.2d 862 (5th Cir. 1979)

[The defendants were sailing near the Florida Keys in a vessel registered in the Grand Cayman Islands, a territory of the United Kingdom. Because their vessel displayed no flag and did not exhibit a name or home port on its stern, a U.S. Coast Guard ship approached the vessel approximately 8.75 miles from the U.S. coast to inquire about its origin, destination, and nationality. After receiving conflicting information from the defendants, the Coast Guard boarded the vessel when it was approximately 10.5 miles from the coast. Later, the Coast Guard re-boarded the vessel when it was approximately 16.3 miles from the U.S. coast. During this inspection, the Coast Guard found a substantial quantity of marijuana. The defendants were later convicted of the federal crimes of conspiracy to import marijuana and possession of marijuana with intent to distribute. On appeal they argued that the United States lacked jurisdiction to prosecute them. They relied on various treaty provisions, including Article 6 of the Convention on the High Seas, which provides that "Ships shall sail under the flag of one State only and, save in exceptional cases expressly provided for in international treaties or in these articles, shall be subject to its exclusive jurisdiction on the high seas." The Convention does not define the "high seas," but the court of appeals assumed that this phrase covered anything beyond three miles from the coast. In the first part of its opinion, the court concluded that the first boarding was justified under the international law right of approach (in order to check the ship's nationality), but that the second boarding violated the Convention.]

TJOFLAT, CIRCUIT JUDGE....

Article 6 of the United States Constitution declares treaties made "under the Authority of the United States (to) be the supreme Law of the Land," but it was early decided that treaties affect the municipal law of the United States only when those treaties are given effect by congressional legislation or are, by their nature, self-executing. Whitney v. Robertson, 124 U.S. 190, 194 (1888); Foster v. Neilson, 27 U.S. (2 Pet.) 253, 311 (1829)....

[S]elf-executing treaties may act to deprive the United States, and hence its courts, of jurisdiction over property and individuals that would otherwise be subject to that jurisdiction. The law of treaties teaches, however, that treaties may have this effect only when self-executing. Therefore, the determinative issue in the case before us is whether article 6 of the Convention on the High Seas is self-executing. We hold that it is not.

The question whether a treaty is self-executing is a matter of interpretation for the courts when the issue presents itself in litigation, Restatement (Second) of Foreign Relations Law of the United States §154(1) (1965), and, as in the case of all matters of interpretation, the courts attempt to discern the intent of the parties to the agreement so as to carry out their manifest purpose. The parties' intent may be apparent from the language of the treaty, or, if the language is ambiguous, it may be divined from the circumstances surrounding the treaty's promulgation.

The self-execution question is perhaps one of the most confounding in treaty law....A treaty may expressly provide for legislative execution. An example is found in articles 27 through 29 of the Convention on the High Seas, each of which begins with the preamble "Every State shall take the necessary legislative measures to...." Such provisions are uniformly declared executory. *See* Foster v. Neilson, 27 U.S. (2 Pet.) 253, 311-12 (1829). And it appears that treaties cannot affect certain subject matters without implementing legislation. "A treaty cannot be self-executing...to the extent that it involves governmental action that under the Constitution can be taken only by the Congress." Restatement (Second) of Foreign Relations Law of the United States §141(3) (1965). Thus, since article 1, section 9 of the Constitution prohibits the drawing of money from the treasury without congressional enactment, it is doubtful that a treaty could appropriate moneys. The same appears to be the case with respect to criminal sanctions.

Apart from those few instances in which the language of the provision expressly calls for legislative implementation or the subject matter is within the exclusive jurisdiction of Congress, the question is purely a matter of interpretation. In carrying out our interpretive task, "we may look beyond the written words to the history of the treaty, the negotiations, and the practical construction adopted by the parties." Choctaw Nation of Indians v. United States, 318 U.S. 423, 431-32 (1943) (citations omitted). In the specific context of determining whether a treaty provision is self-executing, we may refer to several factors:

> the purposes of the treaty and the objectives of its creators, the existence of domestic procedures and institutions appropriate for direct implementation, the availability and feasibility of alternative enforcement methods, and the immediate and long-range consequences of self- or non-self-execution.

People of Saipan v. United States Department of Interior, 502 F.2d 90, 97 (9th Cir. 1974), *cert. denied*, 420 U.S. 1003 (1975). With these principles in mind, we proceed to examine the treaty provision in issue here, article 6 of the Convention on the High Seas.

Article 6 declares the exclusivity of a nation's jurisdiction over the vessels entitled to fly its flag: "Ships shall sail under the flag of one State only and, save in exceptional cases expressly provided for in international treaties or in these articles, shall be subject to its exclusive jurisdiction on the high seas." On its face, this language would bear a self-executing construction because it purports to preclude the exercise of jurisdiction by foreign states in the absence of an exception embodied in treaty. We are admonished, however, to interpret treaties in the context of their promulgation, and we think the context of article 6 compels the conclusion that it is not self-executing....

The Convention on the High Seas is a multilateral treaty which has been ratified by over fifty nations, some of which do not recognize treaties as self-executing. It is difficult therefore to ascribe to the language of the treaty any common intent that the treaty should of its own force operate as the domestic law of the ratifying nations. This is not to say that by entering into such a multilateral treaty the United States cannot without legislation execute provisions of it, but one would expect that in these circumstances the United States would make that intention clear. The lack of mutuality between the United States and countries that do not recognize treaties as self-executing would seem to call for as much. Here there was no such manifestation....

A literal reading of article 6 would prohibit the exercise of jurisdiction in all cases that do not come within exceptions embodied in treaty. Therefore, if the article were self-executing, the United States would lack jurisdiction... over vessels and their crews seized in the enforcement of interests not expressly recognized by treaty.[25]

Since its inception, the United States has asserted limited jurisdiction over vessels on the high seas, generally but not always within the twelve-mile limit, to enforce a variety of interests not expressly authorized in treaties. As early as 1790, the United States professed authority to board vessels beyond the three-mile territorial sea. In An Act to Provide More Effectually for the Collection of Duties, ch. 35, 1 Stat. 145 (1790), the United States first specified a twelve-mile limit in which foreign vessels bound for the United States could be boarded to examine their manifests and inspect their cargoes. The Act also prohibited the unloading of foreign goods within twelve miles. Severe sanctions, including fines and forfeitures, were imposed for violation of its provisions....

The 1790 Act is the progenitor of successive enactments authorizing the boarding and searching of foreign vessels within twelve miles of the coast of the United States and imposing penalties for violations of customs provisions operating within that limit. Through the years the courts have had numerous occasions to address the issue of the propriety of the exercise of United States jurisdiction over foreign vessels within twelve miles but beyond three miles under these statutes and in the absence of treaty....

It is clear, therefore, that the consistent attitude of the United States has been that it may assert limited jurisdiction over foreign vessels within twelve miles of its coast. Although the conventions we construe today do provide for some control within this zone, the ambit of this control is much narrower than that which the United States has customarily asserted. A self-executing interpretation, which would eviscerate many of these provisions, would, therefore, be wholly inconsonant with the historical policy of the United States.

Frolova v. Union of Soviet Socialist Republics

761 F.2d 370 (7th Cir. 1985)

[Lois Becker, an American citizen, traveled to the Soviet Union in 1981, where she met and married Andrei Frolov, a Soviet citizen. She returned to the United States as Lois Frolova when her visa expired in June 1981, but her husband stayed behind because he did not have permission needed to leave the Soviet Union. In September 1981 and March 1982, Mr. Frolov's request to leave the U.S.S.R. was

---

25. This statement is subject to the qualification that the United States would not lack jurisdiction to adjudicate seizures made pursuant to federal legislation enacted after the date of ratification (April 12, 1961) since subsequent federal legislation overrides prior self-executing treaty provisions, Whitney v. Robertson, 124 U.S. 190, 194 (1888); Edye v. Robertson (The Head Money Cases), 112 U.S. 580, 599 (1884)....

denied. In May 1982, Lois Frolova filed this suit, seeking injunctive and monetary relief from the Soviet Union on the ground that its refusal to permit her husband to emigrate caused her mental anguish, physical distress, and loss of her rights of consortium. When Mr. Frolova was allowed to emigrate in June 1982, Mrs. Frolova abandoned her request for injunctive relief but not her claim for damages. The district court discussed, but did not decide, whether the Soviet Union was immune from suit under the Foreign Sovereign Immunities Act of 1976 ("FSIA"), 28 U.S.C. §§1601 et seq. Instead, the court dismissed the case on the ground that Mr. Frolov's emigration request was an act of state that was not the proper subject of litigation in U.S. courts.]

BAUER, WOOD, and COFFEY, CIRCUIT JUDGES.
PER CURIAM. . . .
    We need not discuss the applicability of the act of state doctrine because we conclude that under the FSIA the Soviet Union was entitled to sovereign immunity and that the district court, as a result, lacked jurisdiction. Accordingly, we affirm the district court's dismissal of this action. . . .
    [Frolova argues] that the U.S.S.R. is not entitled to sovereign immunity because of the international agreement exception found in 28 U.S.C. §1604 ("Subject to existing international agreements..."). She contends that the provisions of the United Nations Charter, 59 Stat. 1033 (1945), and the Helsinki Accords (officially entitled Conference on Security and Cooperation in Europe: Final Act), 73 Dept. of State Bull. 323 (1975), may be enforced by private litigants.
    Treaties made by the United States are the law of the land, U.S. Const. art. VI, but if not implemented by appropriate legislation they do not provide the basis for a private lawsuit unless they are intended to be self-executing. Whether a treaty is self-executing is an issue for judicial interpretation, Restatement (Second) of Foreign Relations Law of the United States, §154(1) (1965), and courts consider several factors in discerning the intent of the parties to the agreement: (1) the language and purposes of the agreement as a whole; (2) the circumstances surrounding its execution; (3) the nature of the obligations imposed by the agreement; (4) the availability and feasibility of alternative enforcement mechanisms; (5) the implications of permitting a private right of action; and (6) the capability of the judiciary to resolve the dispute. Of course, if the parties' intent is clear from the treaty's language courts will not inquire into the remaining factors.
    The provisions of the United Nations Charter on which plaintiff relies are Articles 55 and 56.[4] We have found no case holding that the U.N. Charter is self-executing nor has plaintiff provided us with one. There are, however, quite a few decisions stating that the Charter is not self-executing. Indeed, a significant number of decisions have rejected the precise argument made here with respect to

    4. Article 55 provides:

With a view to the creation of conditions of stability and wellbeing which are necessary for peaceful and friendly relations among nations based on respect for the principle of equal rights and self-determination of peoples, the United Nations shall promote...
        c. universal respect for, and observance of, human rights and fundamental freedoms for all without distinction as to race, sex, language, or religion.

    Article 56 provides:

All Members pledge themselves to take joint and separate action in cooperation with the Organization for the achievement of the purposes set forth in Article 55.

Articles 55 and 56. We agree with those rulings: Articles 55 and 56 do not create rights enforceable by private litigants in American courts.

To begin with, the articles are phrased in broad generalities, suggesting that they are declarations of principles, not a code of legal rights. In Article 56, for example, the member nations pledge to assist in achieving the principles of Article 55. This is not the kind of promissory language that will create a judicially-enforceable right.... Articles 55 and 56 create obligations on the member nations (and the United Nations itself); they do not confer rights on individual citizens....

Moreover, judicial resolution of cases bearing significantly on sensitive foreign policy matters, like the case before us, might have serious foreign policy implications which courts are ill-equipped to anticipate or handle. Soviet emigration policies have been the subject of a long-running battle between American policymakers and the Kremlin, often generating conflict between the White House and Congress. Judicial intervention into such a delicate political issue would be ill-advised and could have unforeseen consequences for American-Soviet relations.

There is no basis for concluding that Articles 55 and 56 are privately enforceable. Unless the United Nations alters its fundamental nature and amends its Charter, individuals having grievances based on Articles 55 and 56 will have to be satisfied with diplomatic channels and the court of world opinion to resolve their disputes; they may not bring suit in American courts.

> A treaty is primarily a compact between independent nations. It depends for the enforcement of its provisions on the interest and the honor of the governments which are parties to it. If these fail, its infraction becomes the subject of international negotiations and reclamations, so far as the injured party chooses to seek redress, which may in the end be enforced by actual war. It is obvious that with all this the judicial courts have nothing to do and can give no redress.

Head Money Cases, 112 U.S. 580, 598 (1884).

Notes and Questions

1. The Court in *Asakura* did not use the term "self-executing," but it found the treaty provision there to be judicially enforceable. Why? Why did the courts in *Postal* and *Frolova* find the treaty provisions in those cases to be non-self-executing? The courts in *Postal* and *Frolova* recite a variety of factors to be considered in determining whether a treaty is self-executing. *See also* People of Saipan v. United States Department of Interior, 502 F.2d 90, 97 (9th Cir. 1974), quoted in *Postal*. What is the source of these factors? How much guidance do they give courts and litigants?

2. Is the distinction between self-executing and non-self-executing treaties consistent with the language of the Supremacy Clause, which provides that "all" treaties "shall" be supreme federal law? Is it consistent with the Founders' concern about state treaty violations during the pre-constitutional period, discussed in Chapter 1? Does the Constitution require self-execution even when the U.S. treaty-makers do not intend such a result? What purpose is served by the distinction between self-executing and non-self-executing treaties? What problems, if any, would be created if courts treated all treaties as self-executing?

3. What, precisely, is a self-executing treaty? At the most general level, it is a treaty that can be enforced by courts without domestic implementing legislation. Is a self-executing treaty the same thing as a treaty that gives private parties a right to sue in U.S. courts? Can a non-self-executing treaty ever be enforced by a court—for example, as a defense to a state criminal charge, or when the federal government is suing to enforce the treaty? Is there a single non-self-execution "doctrine" that answers these and related questions? Consider the following analysis by Professor Vazquez:

> Bringing coherence and analytical clarity to this area of the law requires recognition that the self-execution "doctrine" addresses at least four distinct types of reasons why a treaty might be judicially unenforceable. First, a treaty might be judicially unenforceable because the parties (or perhaps the U.S. treaty makers unilaterally) made it judicially unenforceable. This is primarily a matter of intent. Second, a treaty might be judicially unenforceable because the obligation it imposes is of a type that, under our system of separated powers, cannot be enforced directly by the courts. This branch of the doctrine calls for a judgment concerning the allocation of treaty-enforcement power as between the courts and the legislature. Third, a treaty might be judicially unenforceable because the treaty makers lack the constitutional power to accomplish by treaty what they purported to accomplish. This branch of the doctrine calls for a judgment about the allocation of legislative power between the treaty makers and the lawmakers. Finally, a treaty provision might be judicially unenforceable because it does not establish a private right of action and there is no other legal basis for the remedy being sought by the party relying on the treaty. Unlike the first three categories of non-self-executing treaties, a treaty that is non-self-executing in the fourth sense will be judicially unenforceable only in certain contexts. These four issues are sufficiently distinct and require sufficiently differing analyses that they should be thought of as four distinct doctrines.

Carlos Manuel Vazquez, *The Four Doctrines of Self-Executing Treaties,* 89 Am. J. Int'l L. 695, 722-23 (1995). Is this helpful?

4. In determining whether a treaty was intended to be self-executing, should courts look at the intent of all the parties to the treaty, or just the intent of the U.S. treaty-makers? What does *Foster v. Neilson* suggest? What do the three decisions excerpted above suggest? In deciding whose intent to consider, does it matter whether the treaty is bilateral or multilateral? Of what significance is the fact that in many countries, such as the United Kingdom, all treaties are considered non-self-executing? Is it likely that treaties with numerous parties will have a single intent concerning self-execution?

5. The Restatement (Third) of Foreign Relations Law states:

> In the absence of special agreement, it is ordinarily for the United States to decide how it will carry out its international obligations. Accordingly, the intention of the United States determines whether an agreement is to be self-executing in the United States or should await implementation by legislation or appropriate executive or administrative action.

Restatement (Third) of the Foreign Relations Law of the United States §111, cmt. h (1987). On this point, the Restatement appears to be at odds with what a number of courts have said about self-execution. *See, e.g.,* Diggs v. Richardson, 555 F.2d 848, 851 (D.C. Cir. 1976) ("In determining whether a treaty is self-executing courts look to the *intent of the signatory parties* as manifested by the language of the instrument, and, if the instrument is uncertain, recourse must be had to the circumstances surrounding its execution.") (emphasis added). On the other hand, it is arguable that, despite what courts have said, they end up looking primarily to the actual or likely intent of the U.S. treaty-makers rather than to the intent of all the ratifying parties.

Assuming the Restatement approach is correct, whose intent constitutes the intent of the United States? The intent of the approving senators? The intent of the ratifying president? The intent of *subsequent* senators or presidents? What do *Postal* and *Frolova* suggest? Whose intent counts when a court determines whether a *statute* is judicially enforceable? Are there relevant differences on this issue between a statute and a treaty? Recall from Chapter 2 that courts often give deference to the views of the Executive Branch concerning the meaning of treaties. Should courts similarly defer to Executive Branch views concerning whether a treaty is self-executing? *See, e.g.,* More v. Intelcom Support Services, Inc., 960 F.2d 466 (5th Cir. 1992) (deferring to the Executive Branch on this issue and analogizing to the *Chevron* deference doctrine).

6. After deciding whose intent counts, the next question is what must have been intended. If the relevant actors make their intent (of self-execution or non-self-execution) plain in the treaty, then there is no interpretive difficulty. But what if (as is usually the case) the treaty is silent or ambiguous about self-execution? Should there be a presumption in favor of self-execution or against self-execution? There appears to be some division in the courts on this issue. Compare, for example, Goldstar (Panama) S.A. v. United States, 967 F.2d 965, 968 (4th Cir. 1992) ("International treaties are not presumed to create rights that are privately enforceable."), with Beharry v. Reno, 183 F. Supp. 2d 584, 593 (E.D.N.Y. 2002) ("Treaties are generally treated as self-executing, that is, they are enforceable in courts once signed and ratified."), *rev'd on other grounds*, 329 F.3d 51 (2d Cir. 2003).

Which default rule is more consistent with the Supremacy Clause? With separation of powers principles? With federalism principles? What are the institutional consequences of each of the two default rules? Which default rule is more likely to spur the treaty-makers to address the question of non-self-execution? Of what significance is the fact that non-self-executing treaties are still binding on the United States on the international plane?

7. The Senate and President sometimes attach declarations to their ratification of treaties, especially human rights treaties, stating that the treaties are not self-executing. Although these declarations are not part of the negotiated text of the treaties, they are typically included with the U.S. instrument of ratification. Although these declarations have generated academic controversy, courts have generally given effect to them. We consider these declarations in more detail in Section E.

8. As illustrated by *Postal* and *Frolova*, courts in recent years have often been reluctant to find multilateral treaties to be self-executing. *But see* Trans World Airlines, Inc. v. Franklin Mint Corp., 466 U.S. 243, 281 (1984) (concluding that the Warsaw Convention, a multilateral treaty governing international air carriage liability, was self-executing). Courts have been especially disinclined to find provisions in the U.N. Charter to be self-executing. In addition to *Frolova*, see, for example, Hitai v. INS, 343 F.2d 466 (2d Cir. 1965); Sei Fujii v. State, 242 P.2d 617 (1952). Note that, by contrast, courts commonly assume that certain types of bilateral treaties, such as extradition treaties and Friendship, Commerce, and Navigation (FCN) treaties, are self-executing. *See, e.g.,* Cheung v. United States, 213 F.3d 82, 94 (2d Cir. 2000) (extradition treaty); Spiess v. C. Itoh & Co. (America), 643 F.2d 353 (5th Cir. 1981) (FCN treaty); *see also Asakura.* Why do you think there is this difference in treatment between bilateral and multilateral treaties? Is the court's argument in *Postal* about reciprocity convincing?

9. To what extent should the identity of the breaching party affect the determination of whether a treaty is judicially enforceable? In particular, should courts be more willing to enforce treaties against states and localities (as in *Asakura*) than against either the federal government (as in *Postal*) or foreign nations (as in *Frolova*)? If so, why?

10. Professor Yoo has argued that as an original matter, treaties that touched on subjects within Congress's Article I powers could not be self-executing, but rather needed domestic implementing legislation before having domestic force. Treaties that regulated areas that would be beyond Congress's legislative powers, by contrast, did not impinge upon the legislative power and could apply as self-executing federal law even in the absence of implementing legislation. Professor Yoo concludes that, at the very least, the Constitution requires treaties to be non-self-executing unless the treaty-makers clearly specify the contrary. *See* John C. Yoo, *Globalism and the Constitution: Treaties, Non-Self-Execution, and the Original Understanding*, 99 Colum. L. Rev. 1955 (1999). For a challenge to Professor Yoo's views based on historical materials, see Martin S. Flaherty, *History Right? Historical Scholarship, Original Understanding, and "Supreme Law of the Land,"* 99 Colum. L. Rev. 2095 (1999). For a challenge to his views based on structural constitutional arguments, and in particular the implications of the Supremacy Clause, see Carlos M. Vazquez, *Laughing at Treaties*, 99 Colum. L. Rev. 2154 (1999). For Professor Yoo's reply, see John C. Yoo, *Treaties and Public Lawmaking: A Textual and Structural Defense of Non-Self-Execution*, 99 Colum. L. Rev. 2218 (1999).

How does Professor Yoo's theory fit with the text of the Supremacy Clause? With the reasons the Founders included treaties in that Clause? With the excerpt at the beginning of this section from Foster v. Neilson? With decisions such as *Asakura*?

11. For other scholarship on self-execution, see Edwin Dickinson, *Are the Liquor Treaties Self-Executing?*, 20 Am. J. Int'l L. 444 (1926); Yuji Iwasawa, *The Doctrine of Self-Executing Treaties in the United States: A Critical Analysis*, 26 Va. J. Int'l L. 627 (1986); Jordan J. Paust, *Self-Executing Treaties*, 82 Am. J. Int'l L. 760 (1988); Stefan A. Riesenfeld, *The Doctrine of Self-Executing Treaties and U.S. v. Postal: Win at Any Price?*, 74 Am. J. Int'l L. 892 (1980); and Carlos Manuel Vazquez, *The Four Doctrines of Self-Executing Treaties*, 89 Am. J. Int'l L. 695 (1995).

B. LAST-IN-TIME RULE

The Constitution provides that both treaties and federal statutes are part of the supreme law of the land and thus preempt inconsistent state law. The Constitution does not specify, however, the relationship between treaties and statutes. What should a court do if confronted with a conflict between a self-executing treaty and a federal statute? The decisions below consider this question.

Whitney v. Robertson

124 U.S. 190 (1888)

MR. JUSTICE FIELD delivered the opinion of the court.

The plaintiffs are merchants, doing business in the city of New York, and in August, 1882, they imported a large quantity of "centrifugal and molasses sugars," the produce and manufacture of the island of San Domingo. These goods were similar in kind to sugars produced in the Hawaiian Islands, which are admitted free of duty under the treaty with the king of those islands, and the act of Congress, passed to carry the treaty into effect. They were duly entered at the custom house at the port of New York, the plaintiffs claiming that by the treaty with the Republic of San Domingo [the Dominican Republic] the goods should be admitted on the same terms, that is, free of duty, as similar articles, the produce and manufacture of the Hawaiian Islands. The defendant, who was at the time collector of the port, refused to allow this claim, treated the goods as dutiable articles under the acts of Congress, and exacted duties on them to the amount of $21,936. The plaintiffs appealed from the collector's decision to the Secretary of the Treasury, by whom the appeal was denied. They then paid under protest the duties exacted, and brought the present action to recover the amount.

[The Court first holds that the "most favored nation" provision in the treaty with the Dominican Republic precluded discrimination but did not require the United States to extend to the Republic special concessions given to other countries for valuable consideration.]

But, independently of considerations of this nature, there is another and complete answer to the pretensions of the plaintiffs. The act of Congress under which the duties were collected authorized their exaction. It is of general application, making no exception in favor of goods of any country. It was passed after the treaty with the Dominican Republic, and, if there be any conflict between the stipulations of the treaty and the requirements of the law, the latter must control. A treaty is primarily a contract between two or more independent nations, and is so regarded by writers on public law. For the infraction of its provisions a remedy must be sought by the injured party through reclamations upon the other. When the stipulations are not self-executing they can only be enforced pursuant to legislation to carry them into effect, and such legislation is as much subject to modification and repeal by Congress as legislation upon any other subject. If the treaty contains stipulations which are self-executing, that is, require no legislation to make them operative, to that extent they have the force and effect of a legislative enactment. Congress may modify such provisions, so far as they bind the United States, or supersede them altogether. By the Constitution a treaty is placed on the same footing, and made of like obligation, with an act of legislation. Both are declared by that instrument to be the supreme law of the land, and no superior efficacy is given to either over the other. When the two relate to the same subject, the courts will always endeavor to construe them so as to give effect to both, if that can be done without violating the language of either; but if the two are inconsistent, the one last in date will control the other, provided always the stipulation of the treaty on the subject is self-executing. If the country with which the treaty is made is dissatisfied with the action of the legislative department, it may present its complaint to the executive head of the government, and take such other measures as it may deem essential for the protection of its interests. The courts can afford no redress....

It follows, therefore, that when a law is clear in its provisions, its validity cannot be assailed before the courts for want of conformity to stipulations of a previous treaty not already executed. Considerations of that character belong to another department of the government. The duty of the courts is to construe and give effect to the latest expression of the sovereign will.

Cook v. United States

288 U.S. 102 (1933)

[The Eighteenth Amendment, which took effect in 1920, outlawed (among other things) the importation of intoxicating liquor into the United States. This Prohibition Amendment was repealed by the Twenty First Amendment in 1933. In 1922, Congress enacted a statute, §581 of the Tariff Act, authorizing the Coast Guard to stop and inspect vessels within 12 miles of the U.S. coast to determine if any violation of law had been committed. This statute was reenacted in 1930. Pursuant to the statute, the Coast Guard stopped a British ship that was about 11-1/2 miles from the coast and found liquor on board. The Customs Service subsequently imposed a fine on the master of the ship for failing to disclose the liquor on the ship's manifest. The master of the ship, Cook, argued that a 1924 treaty between the United States and Great Britain modified the earlier statute and precluded the United States from exercising jurisdiction over the ship. The treaty gave the United States jurisdiction only over British vessels that could reach the U.S. coast within one hour. The vessel in this case could not go over 10 miles an hour and was more than 10 miles from the coast. The Government responded that the Treaty did not modify §581 of the 1922 statute, and that if it did, the reenactment of §581 without change in 1930 removed the alleged modification.]

MR. JUSTICE BRANDEIS delivered the opinion of the Court....

Second. The Treaty, being later in date than the Act of 1922, superseded, so far as inconsistent with the terms of the Act, the authority which had been conferred by §581 upon officers of the Coast Guard to board, search and seize beyond our territorial waters. Whitney v. Robertson, 124 U.S. 190, 194. For in a strict sense the Treaty was self-executing, in that no legislation was necessary to authorize executive action pursuant to its provisions.

The purpose of the provisions for seizure in §581, and their practical operation, as an aid in the enforcement of the laws prohibiting alcoholic liquors, leave no doubt that the territorial limitations there established were modified by the Treaty. This conclusion is supported by the course of administrative practice. Shortly after the Treaty took effect, the Treasury Department issued amended instructions for the Coast Guard which pointed out, after reciting the provisions of §581, that "in cases of special treaties, the provisions of those treaties shall be complied with"; and called attention particularly to the recent treaties dealing with the smuggling of intoxicating liquors. The Commandant of the Coast Guard, moreover, was informed in 1927, as the Solicitor General states, that all seizures of British vessels captured in the rum-smuggling trade should be within the terms of the Treaty and that seizing officers should be instructed to produce evidence, not that the vessel was found within the four-league limit, but that she was apprehended within one hour's sailing distance from the coast.

Third. The Treaty was not abrogated by re-enacting §581 in the Tariff Act of 1930 in the identical terms of the Act of 1922. A treaty will not be deemed to have been abrogated or modified by a later statute unless such purpose on the part of Congress has been clearly expressed. Here, the contrary appears. The committee reports and the debates upon the Act of 1930, like the re-enacted section itself, make no reference to the Treaty of 1924. Any doubt as to the construction of the section should be deemed resolved by the consistent departmental practice existing before its reenactment....

Searches and seizures in the enforcement of the laws prohibiting alcoholic liquors are governed, since the 1930 Act, as they were before, by the provisions of the Treaty. Section 581, with its scope narrowed by the Treaty, remained in force after its reenactment in the Act of 1930. The section continued to apply to the boarding, search and seizure of all vessels of all countries with which we had no relevant treaties. It continued also, in the enforcement of our customs laws not related to the prohibition of alcoholic liquors, to govern the boarding of vessels of those countries with which we had entered into treaties like that with Great Britain.

Breard v. Greene

523 U.S. 371 (1998)

PER CURIAM.

Angel Francisco Breard is scheduled to be executed by the Commonwealth of Virginia this evening at 9:00 p.m. Breard, a citizen of Paraguay, came to the United States in 1986, at the age of 20. In 1992, Breard was charged with the attempted rape and capital murder of Ruth Dickie. At his trial in 1993, the State presented overwhelming evidence of guilt, including semen found on Dickie's body matching Breard's DNA profile and hairs on Dickie's body identical in all microscopic characteristics to hair samples taken from Breard. Breard chose to take the witness stand in his defense. During his testimony, Breard confessed to killing Dickie, but explained that he had only done so because of a Satanic curse placed on him by his father-in-law. Following a jury trial in the Circuit Court of Arlington County, Virginia, Breard was convicted of both charges and sentenced to death. On appeal, the Virginia Supreme Court affirmed Breard's convictions and sentences, and we denied certiorari. State collateral relief was subsequently denied as well.

Breard then filed a motion for habeas relief under 28 U.S.C. §2254 in Federal District Court on August 20, 1996. In that motion, Breard argued for the first time that his conviction and sentence should be overturned because of alleged violations of the Vienna Convention on Consular Relations (Vienna Convention), April 24, 1963, [1970] 21 U.S.T. 77, T.I.A.S. No. 6820, at the time of his arrest. Specifically, Breard alleged that the Vienna Convention was violated when the arresting authorities failed to inform him that, as a foreign national, he had the right to contact the Paraguayan Consulate. The District Court rejected this claim, concluding that Breard procedurally defaulted the claim when he failed to raise it in state court and that Breard could not demonstrate cause and prejudice for this default. The Fourth Circuit affirmed. Breard has petitioned this Court for a writ of certiorari.

In September 1996, the Republic of Paraguay, the Ambassador of Paraguay to the United States, and the Consul General of Paraguay to the United States (collectively Paraguay) brought suit in Federal District Court against certain Virginia officials, alleging that their separate rights under the Vienna Convention had been violated by the Commonwealth's failure to inform Breard of his rights under the treaty and to inform the Paraguayan consulate of Breard's arrest, conviction, and sentence. In addition, the Consul General asserted a parallel claim under 42 U.S.C. §1983, alleging a denial of his rights under the Vienna Convention. The District Court concluded that it lacked subject-matter jurisdiction over these suits because Paraguay was not alleging a "continuing violation of federal law" and therefore could not bring its claims within the exception to Eleventh Amendment immunity established in Ex parte Young, 209 U.S. 123 (1908). The Fourth Circuit affirmed on Eleventh Amendment grounds. Paraguay has also petitioned this Court for a writ of certiorari.

On April 3, 1998, nearly five years after Breard's conviction became final, the Republic of Paraguay instituted proceedings against the United States in the International Court of Justice (ICJ), alleging that the United States violated the Vienna Convention at the time of Breard's arrest. On April 9, the ICJ noted jurisdiction and issued an order requesting that the United States "take all measures at its disposal to ensure that Angel Francisco Breard is not executed pending the final decision in these proceedings. . . ." The ICJ set a briefing schedule for this matter, with oral argument likely to be held this November. Breard then filed a petition for an original writ of habeas corpus and a stay application in this Court in order to "enforce" the ICJ's order. Paraguay filed a motion for leave to file a bill of complaint in this Court, citing this Court's original jurisdiction over cases "affecting Ambassadors . . . and Consuls." U.S. Const., Art. III, §2.

It is clear that Breard procedurally defaulted his claim, if any, under the Vienna Convention by failing to raise that claim in the state courts. Nevertheless, in their petitions for certiorari, both Breard and Paraguay contend that Breard's Vienna Convention claim may be heard in federal court because the Convention is the "supreme law of the land" and thus trumps the procedural default doctrine. This argument is plainly incorrect for two reasons.

First, while we should give respectful consideration to the interpretation of an international treaty rendered by an international court with jurisdiction to interpret such, it has been recognized in international law that, absent a clear and express statement to the contrary, the procedural rules of the forum State govern the implementation of the treaty in that State. This proposition is embodied in the Vienna Convention itself, which provides that the rights expressed in the Convention "shall be exercised in conformity with the laws and regulations of the receiving State," provided that "said laws and regulations must enable full effect to be given to the purposes for which the rights accorded under this Article are intended." Article 36(2), [1970] 21 U.S. T., at 101. It is the rule in this country that assertions of error in criminal proceedings must first be raised in state court in order to form the basis for relief in habeas. Claims not so raised are considered defaulted. By not asserting his Vienna Convention claim in state court, Breard failed to exercise his rights under the Vienna Convention in conformity with the laws of the United States and the Commonwealth of Virginia. Having failed to do so, he cannot raise a claim of violation of those rights now on federal habeas review.

Second, although treaties are recognized by our Constitution as the supreme law of the land, that status is no less true of provisions of the Constitution itself, to which rules of procedural default apply. We have held "that an Act of Congress . . . is on a full parity with a treaty, and that when a statute which is subsequent in time is inconsistent with a treaty, the statute to the extent of conflict renders the treaty null." Reid v. Covert, 354 U.S. 1, 18 (1957) (plurality opinion); *see also* Whitney v. Robertson, 124 U.S. 190, 194 (1888) (holding that if a treaty and a federal statute conflict, "the one last in date will control the other"). The Vienna Convention — which arguably confers on an individual the right to consular assistance following arrest — has continuously been in effect since 1969. But in 1996, before Breard filed his habeas petition raising claims under the Vienna Convention, Congress enacted the Antiterrorism and Effective Death Penalty Act (AEDPA), which provides that a habeas petitioner alleging that he is held in violation of "treaties of the United States" will, as a general rule, not be afforded an evidentiary hearing if he "has failed to develop the factual basis of [the] claim in State court proceedings." 28 U.S.C.A. §§2254(a), (e)(2) (Supp. 1998). Breard's ability to obtain relief based on violations of the Vienna Convention is subject to this subsequently-enacted rule, just as any claim arising under the United States Constitution would be. This rule prevents Breard from establishing that the violation of his Vienna Convention rights prejudiced him. Without a hearing, Breard cannot establish how the Consul would have advised him, how the advice of his attorneys differed from the advice the Consul could have provided, and what factors he considered in electing to reject the plea bargain that the State offered him.

Notes and Questions

1. As illustrated by *Whitney* and *Breard*, Congress's ability to override treaties, for purposes of U.S. domestic law, is well settled. *See also, e.g.,* Reid v. Covert, 354 U.S. 1, 18 (1957) (plurality); Chae Chan Ping v. United States (*Chinese Exclusion Case*), 130 U.S. 581, 600-01 (1889); Edye v. Robertson (*Head Money Cases*), 112 U.S. 580, 597-98 (1884). In one of the earliest articulations of this proposition, a court explained the basis for it as follows:

> To refuse to execute a treaty, for reasons which approve themselves to the conscientious judgment of the nation, is a matter of the utmost gravity and delicacy; but the power to do so, is prerogative, of which no nation can be deprived, without deeply affecting its independence. That the people of the United States have deprived their government of this power in any case, I do not believe. That it must reside somewhere, and be applicable to all cases, I am convinced. I feel no doubt that it belongs to congress. That, inasmuch as treaties must continue to operate as part of our municipal law, and be obeyed by the people, applied by the judiciary and executed by the president, while they continue unrepealed, and inasmuch as the power of repealing these municipal laws must reside somewhere, and no body other than congress possesses it, then legislative power is applicable to such laws whenever they relate to subjects, which the constitution has placed under that legislative power.

Taylor v. Morton, 23 F. Cas. 784, 786 (C.C.D. Mass. 1855). How does this explanation for why statutes can override treaties compare with the explanation given in *Whitney*?

2. Today, the proposition that Congress can override treaties for purposes of U.S. domestic law is referred to as a component of the "last-in-time rule," pursuant to which treaties and statutes are given equal weight in the U.S. legal system. What is the basis for giving statutes and treaties equal weight? Treaties and statutes are both mentioned in the Supremacy Clause, but is every form of law mentioned in the Clause equal in status? Given that two-thirds of the Senate must consent in order for the United States to enter into a treaty, why should a simple majority of Congress have the ability to override a treaty? Given that the President is granted the power to make treaties (with the advice and consent of the Senate), why should Congress (if it passes a veto-proof statute) have the ability to override a treaty against the wishes of the President? What, if anything, does *Chadha*, excerpted in Chapter 3, suggest about these questions? Would U.S. treaty practice change if statutes could not override treaties? Would it change if treaties could not override statutes? In considering these questions, keep in mind that when Congress overrides a treaty as a matter of U.S. domestic law, the treaty still binds the United States under international law until validly terminated.

3. In *Whitney*, the last-in-time rule was applied to override an earlier treaty. As illustrated by *Cook*, the last-in-time rule can work the other way as well. That is, later-in-time treaties can, at least in theory, override earlier federal statutes. *See also* Opinion of Caleb Cushing, Copyright Convention with Great Britain (Feb. 16, 1854), 6 Op. Atty. Gen. 291 (1854) (expressing the view that a treaty could override an earlier federal statute). This is relatively rare, however, and *Cook* is the only Supreme Court decision recognizing such an override. Courts have allowed treaties to supersede the requirements of federal statutes in the area of income taxation, but that is in part because the Internal Revenue Code specifically provides that the income tax laws are to be applied "with due regard to any treaty obligation of the United States which applies to such taxpayer." 26 U.S.C. §894(a)(1); *cf.* 26 U.S.C. §7852(d)(1) ("For purposes of determining the relationship between a provision of a treaty and any law of the United States affecting revenue, neither the treaty nor the law shall have preferential status by reason of its being a treaty or law."). Why are there not more decisions allowing treaties to override statutes? Are the justifications the same for allowing later treaties to supersede earlier statutes as they are for allowing later statutes to supersede earlier treaties? What is the relationship between the self-execution doctrine and the ability of treaties to override statutes?

Courts. will not apply the last-in-time rule to override a treaty or statute absent a clear conflict with a subsequent treaty or statute. *See, e.g.,* Trans World Airlines, Inc. v. Franklin Mint Corp., 466 U.S. 243, 252 (1984); Johnson v. Browne, 205 U.S. 309, 321 (1907); United States v. Lee Yen Tai, 185 U.S. 213, 222 (1902); *see also Cook*. This clear conflict rule can be viewed as an application of the general presumption against the repeal of law by implication. In addition, the requirement of a clear conflict for overriding a treaty can be viewed as a component of the "*Charming Betsy*" canon of construction that we will consider in Chapter 7, whereby courts will construe federal statutes, where reasonably possible, so that they do not violate international law.

Did the Court in *Breard* overlook these principles? Was there a clear conflict between the 1996 habeas amendments and the consular notice provision in the Vienna Convention? *Cf.* Roeder v. Islamic Republic of Iran, 333 F.3d 228, 236 (D.C. Cir. 2003) (declining to construe statutory amendments as overriding Algiers Accords between Iran and the United States because "[t]he amendments do not, on their face, say anything about the Accords"). Even if there was a clear conflict, why wasn't the order from the International Court of Justice the operative last-in-time rule? Because it was not itself a new treaty? For discussion of these and other aspects of the *Breard* case, see *Agora: Breard*, 92 Am. J. Int'l L. 666-712 (1998); Curtis A. Bradley, *Breard, Our Dualist Constitution, and the Internationalist Conception*, 51 Stan. L. Rev. 529 (1999); Sanja Djajic, *The Effect of International Court of Justice Decisions on Municipal Courts in the United States: Breard v. Greene*, 23 Hastings Int'l & Comp. L. Rev. 27 (1999); Erik G. Luna & Douglas J. Sylvester, *Beyond* Breard, 17 Berkeley J. Int'l L. 147 (1999).

4. Following the *Breard* litigation, foreign citizen defendants brought numerous challenges to their convictions and sentences based on violations of the consular notice provision in the Vienna Convention on Consular Relations. Many of these challenges were brought on direct appeal and thus were not subject to the habeas corpus limitations applied in *Breard*. Nevertheless, most courts rejected the challenges. In some cases, courts found that the treaty violation was harmless error.

In other cases, courts held that the treaty did not give the criminal defendants a right to the relief they were seeking, such as dismissal of the indictment or suppression of evidence. *See, e.g.,* United States v. Page, 232 F.3d 526 (6th Cir. 2000); United States v. Lawal, 231 F.3d 1045 (7th Cir. 2000); United States v. Li, 206 F.3d 56 (1st Cir. 2000); United States v. Lombera-Camorlinga, 206 F.3d 882 (9th Cir. 2000); United States v. Cordoba-Mosquera, 212 F.3d 1194 (11th Cir. 2000). If the consular notice provision of the Vienna Convention is self-executing, as most courts have assumed, why did it not provide a right to relief in these cases? On this question, consider these excerpts from the dissent and concurrence in one of these decisions. From the dissent:

> By its unambiguous text the Supremacy Clause declares treaties to be "the supreme Law of the Land," and thus automatically incorporates these international agreements into the domestic law of the United States, without the need for further action once the treaty is ratified by the Senate. The effect is to render treaty provisions enforceable in the courts at the behest of affected individuals, in applicable cases. . . .
>
> Unfortunately, we are no longer in the same playing field that existed when the Court decided *Foster* and *Percheman*, whose holding has since been distorted beyond recognition with the tail end of the quoted language often wagging the principal rule established by those cases. . . . The bottom line to [the more recent] cases seems to be that we should look to the "intent" of the treaty to determine whether it is self-executing, or more in point, whether it creates rights that individuals can enforce in the courts. As the majority purports to recognize, however, we begin this inquiry with the terms of the treaty. . . . If we look to this guideline as the starting point to our inquest in the present appeal, I fail to see why further analysis is required or is *appropriate*.

United States v. Li, 206 F.3d at 70-71 (Torruella, C.J., dissenting). From the concurrence:

> Our dissenting brother's emphasis on the self-executing character of the treaties in question does not sway our thinking. The label "self-executing" usually is applied to any treaty that according to its terms takes effect upon ratification and requires no separate implementing statute. Whether the terms of such a treaty provide for private rights, enforceable in domestic courts, is a wholly separate question. That courts sometimes discuss both concepts together . . . does not detract from their distinctiveness. At bottom, the questions remain separate. It follows inexorably that the self-executing character of a treaty does not by itself establish that the treaty creates private rights.

Id. at 67-68 (Selya, J., concurring). Is the distinction in the concurrence between self-execution and private rights persuasive? Note that the Executive Branch had expressed the view in a number of these cases that the Convention did not confer the rights being sought, and the courts gave deference to this view.

5. After deciding the *Breard* case, the International Court of Justice (ICJ) was presented with a similar dispute involving German nationals on death row. Two brothers of German nationality, Walter and Karl LaGrand, were arrested in Arizona in 1982 for committing murder during an attempted armed robbery. They were convicted and sentenced to death, but they were not informed of their rights under the Vienna Convention on Consular Relations. After exhausting appellate and state post-conviction proceedings, the LaGrands filed petitions for writs of habeas corpus in the 1990s, raising for the first time the Vienna Convention violation. After these petitions were denied, and after Karl LaGrand was executed, Germany filed a suit against the United States in the ICJ, seeking, among other things, a stay of Walter LaGrand's execution. As in the *Breard* case, the ICJ issued a provisional order stating that the United States should "take all measures at its disposal" to ensure that the execution was not carried out while the ICJ heard the case. Despite this order, neither Arizona's governor nor the U.S. Supreme Court granted a stay of execution, and Walter LaGrand was executed. Unlike Paraguay in the *Breard* case, however, Germany did not abandon its case before the ICJ at this point, and the ICJ subsequently issued a final decision in the case. In its decision, the ICJ held that the United States had violated the Vienna Convention; that the United States had also violated the ICJ's provisional order, which the Court held was legally binding; and that in future situations in which German nationals "have been subjected to prolonged detention or convicted and sentenced to severe penalties," the United States would be required "to allow the review and reconsideration of the conviction and sentence by taking account of the violation of the rights set forth in the Convention." LaGrand Case (Germany v. United States of America), ICJ, No. 104 (June 27, 2001), 40 I.L.M. 1069, 1100. The ICJ also stated, however, that "[t]his obligation can be carried out in various ways" and that "[t]he choice of means must be left to the United States." *Id.* The U.S. Executive Branch subsequently maintained that the United States could comply with this decision through consideration of Vienna Convention violations in state clemency proceedings, and it therefore continued to maintain that U.S. courts should not grant relief based on the Convention.

6. In January 2003, Mexico brought suit against the United States in the ICJ. Mexico alleged that the United States had violated the consular notice rights of 54 Mexican nationals who were awaiting execution in ten U.S. states. (Mexico subsequently amended its claims to cover only 52 individuals in nine U.S. states.) The ICJ issued a preliminary order in early February 2003 stating that the United States "shall take all measures necessary to ensure" that three of the individuals in question — whom the court determined to be "at risk of execution in the coming months, or possibly even weeks" — were not executed during the court's consideration of the case.

The ICJ issued its final judgment in the case in March 2004. *See* Case Concerning Avena and Other Mexican Nationals (Mexico v. United States of America) (31 March 2004), at http://www.icj-cij.org. The ICJ concluded that the United States had violated the Vienna Convention on Consular Relations with respect to 51 of the Mexican nationals. Consistent with its decision in *LaGrand*, the ICJ held that Article 36 of the Vienna Convention confers individual rights on arrested foreign nationals. It also held that, when there has been a violation of the Convention and severe penalties have been imposed, the United States is obligated to provide "review and reconsideration" of the defendant's conviction and sentence. Such review and reconsideration, said the ICJ, should "guarantee that the violation and the possible prejudice caused by that violation will be fully examined and taken into account in the review and reconsideration process." The ICJ also said that this review and reconsideration "should occur within the overall judicial proceedings relating to the individual defendant concerned." In addition, the ICJ suggested that U.S. procedural default rules should not be applied to bar review and reconsideration, at least in certain circumstances. The ICJ rejected Mexico's argument, however, that there is an automatic right to a new trial, new sentencing, or suppression of evidence when there has been a violation of the Convention.

7. What is the status of the *Avena* decision in U.S. courts? Is the ICJ's interpretation of the Vienna Convention on Consular Relations binding on U.S. courts? If not binding, should its interpretation of the Vienna Convention nevertheless be given deference? Even if the Executive Branch disagrees with the interpretation?

In Medellin v. Dretke, 371 F.3d 270 (5th Cir. 2004), the U.S. Court of Appeals for the Fifth Circuit considered a habeas corpus challenge by one of the 51 Mexican citizens covered by the *Avena* decision. Notwithstanding *Avena*, the Fifth Circuit held that the petitioner could not seek federal habeas relief based on the Vienna Convention violation because (a) the petitioner was barred under the federal habeas statute from raising the violation due to the fact that he had not raised it in his state trial, and (b) Article 36 of the Vienna Convention does not confer judicially enforceable individual rights. For the first proposition, the court relied on the Supreme Court's decision in *Breard*. For the second proposition, the court relied on its prior precedent, which it said it was bound to apply absent a contrary *en banc* decision from its Circuit or contrary decision from the Supreme Court.

The Supreme Court granted certiorari in *Medellin* to decide two questions:

> 1. In a case brought by a Mexican national whose rights were adjudicated in the *Avena* Judgment, must a court in the United States apply as the rule of decision, notwithstanding any inconsistent United States precedent, the *Avena* holding that the United States courts must review and reconsider the national's conviction and sentence, without resort to procedural default doctrines?
>
> 2. In a case brought by a foreign national of a State party of the Vienna Convention, should a court in the United States give effect to the *LaGrand* and *Avena* Judgments as a matter of international judicial comity and in the interest of uniform treaty interpretation?

In an *amicus* brief to the Court, the Executive Branch argued that provisions in the federal habeas statute barred federal court consideration of Medellin's claims. *See* Brief of the United States as Amicus Curiae Supporting Respondent in Medellin v. Dretke (Feb. 2005), at http://www.usdoj.gov/osg/briefs/2004/3mer/1ami/2004-5928.mer.ami.html. To the extent that there was a conflict between those provisions and rights derived from the Vienna Convention, the Executive further argued, the statutory provisions would be controlling since they were later in time. In addition, the Executive argued that Article 36 of the Vienna Convention did not confer judicially enforceable private rights, and that the *Avena* decision was not privately enforceable in U.S. courts. At the same time that it filed this brief, however, President Bush sent a memorandum to the Attorney General stating that the United States would discharge its international obligations under the *Avena* judgment by "having State courts give effect to the [ICJ] decision in accordance with general principles of comity in cases filed by the 51 Mexican nationals addressed in that decision." Based in part on this memorandum, Medellin filed an application for a writ of habeas corpus with a Texas state court.

Subsequently, in Medellin v. Dretke, 125 S. Ct. 2088 (2005), the Court issued a *per curiam* decision declining to resolve the questions upon which it had granted certiorari. The Court noted that the state court proceedings might provide Medellin with the relief that he was seeking. The Court also noted that there were a number of hurdles Medellin would have to overcome in order to qualify for federal habeas corpus relief, including the requirement in the federal habeas statute that, in order to appeal the denial of habeas corpus relief, the petitioner must make a "a substantial showing of the denial of a *constitutional* right." 28 U.S.C. §2253(c)(2) (emphasis added). Justice O'Connor filed a dissent, joined by three other Justices, arguing that the case should have been remanded to the Fifth Circuit so that it could decide "(1) whether the International Court of Justice's judgment in Medellin's favor, *Case Concerning Avena and Other Mexican Nationals (Mex. v. U.S.)*, 2004 I. C. J. No. 128

(Judgment of Mar. 31), is binding on American courts; (2) whether Article 36(1)(b) of the Convention creates a judicially enforceable individual right; and (3) whether Article 36(2) of the Convention sometimes requires state procedural default rules to be set aside so that the treaty can be given 'full effect.'" The dissenters argued that the requirement in the habeas statute of a showing of a denial of a constitutional right should not preclude consideration of these issues because Texas had not relied on that requirement until it filed its merits brief with the Supreme Court, and the dissenters argued that the requirement was waivable. They acknowledged, however, that "wherever the [Vienna] Convention, which has been in continuous force since 1969, conflicts with [the later-in-time habeas statute], the statute must govern."

The Supreme Court did not decide the legal effect of President Bush's memorandum. In its *amicus* brief, the Executive Branch had argued that the memorandum was binding on state courts and preempted any contrary state law, such as state procedural default rules. The Executive relied on, among other things, the President's authority to take care that the laws, including treaty obligations, are faithfully executed. These treaty obligations, the Executive explained, include Article 94 of the United Nations Charter, which states that "[e]ach Member of the United Nations undertakes to comply with the decision of the International Court of Justice in any case to which it is a party." The Executive also relied on the *Garamendi* decision, excerpted in Chapter 5.

If a treaty does not itself confer judicially enforceable rights, does the Take Care Clause nevertheless give the President the authority to create such rights? Does *Garamendi* support a presidential power to create preemptive federal law to implement treaty obligations?

8. For academic discussion of the last-in-time rule, see, for example, Louis Henkin, *The Constitution and United States Sovereignty: A Century of* Chinese Exclusion *and Its Progeny*, 100 Harv. L. Rev. 853 (1987); Julian Ku, *Treaties as Laws: A Defense of the Last-in-Time Rule for Treaties and Federal Statutes*, 80 Ind. L.J. 319 (2005); Jules Lobel, *The Limits of Constitutional Power: Conflicts Between Foreign Policy and International Law*, 71 Va. L. Rev. 1071 (1985); Detlev Vagts, *The United States and Its Treaties: Observance and Breach*, 95 Am. J. Int'l L. 313 (2001); and Peter Westen, *The Place of Foreign Treaties in the Courts of the United States: A Reply to Louis Henkin*, 101 Harv. L. Rev. 511 (1987).

C. SEPARATION OF POWERS AND DELEGATION LIMITATIONS

In this section we consider separation of powers and related limitations on the treaty power. We begin by considering the relationship between the treaty power and the powers of Congress. We then consider possible limits on the treaty-makers' ability to delegate authority to international institutions.

1. Relationship of the Treaty Power with Congress's Powers

Edwards v. Carter

580 F.2d 1055 (D.C. Cir. 1978)

FAHY, SENIOR CIRCUIT JUDGE, and MCGOWAN and MACKINNON, CIRCUIT JUDGES. PER CURIAM.

This is an appeal from the District Court's dismissal of a challenge to appellee's use of the treaty power to convey to the Republic of Panama United States properties, including the Panama Canal, located in the Panama Canal Zone. Appellants, sixty members of the House of Representatives, sought a declaratory judgment that the exclusive means provided in the Constitution for disposal of United States property requires approval of both Houses of Congress, see Art. IV, §3, cl. 2, and that therefore the Panama Canal Zone may not be returned to Panama through the Treaty process, which invests the treaty-making power in the President by and with the advice and consent of two-thirds of the Senators present, see Art. II, §2, cl. 2. Appellee contends that the Constitution permits United States territory to be disposed of either through congressional legislation or through the treaty process, and that therefore the President's decision to proceed under the treaty power is constitutionally permissible. . . .

II

Article IV, §3, cl. 2 of the Constitution states in its entirety:

The Congress shall have Power to dispose of and make all needful Rules and Regulations respecting the Territory or other Property belonging to the United States; and nothing in this Constitution shall be so construed as to Prejudice any Claims of the United States, or of any particular State.

Appellants contend that this clause gives Congress exclusive power to convey to foreign nations any property, such as the Panama Canal, owned by the United States. We find such a construction to be at odds with the wording of this and similar grants of power to the Congress, and, most significantly, with the history of the constitutional debates.

The grant of authority to Congress under the property clause states that "The Congress shall have Power . . . ," not that only the Congress shall have power, or that the Congress shall have exclusive power. In this respect the property clause is parallel to Article I, §8, which also states that "The Congress shall have Power. . . ." Many of the powers thereafter enumerated in §8 involve matters that were at the time the Constitution was adopted, and that are at the present time, also commonly the subject of treaties. The most prominent example of this is the regulation of commerce with foreign nations, Art. I, §8, cl. 3, and appellants do not go so far as to contend that the treaty process is not a constitutionally allowable means for regulating foreign commerce. It thus seems to us that, on its face, the property clause is intended not to restrict the scope of the treaty clause, but, rather, is intended to permit Congress to accomplish through legislation what may concurrently be accomplished through other means provided in the Constitution.

The American Law Institute's Restatement of Foreign Relations, directly addressing this issue, comes to the same conclusion we reach:

The mere fact, however, that a congressional power exists does not mean that the power is exclusive so as to preclude the making of a self-executing treaty within the area of that power.

ALI Restatement of Foreign Relations Law (2d), §141, at 435 (1965). The section of the Restatement relied on by the dissent merely states that the treaty power, like all powers granted to the United States, is limited by other restraints found in the Constitution on the exercise of governmental power. Of course the correctness of this proposition as a matter of constitutional law is clear. *See* Reid v. Covert, 354 U.S. 1 (1957); Geoffroy v. Riggs, 133 U.S. 258 (1890); Asakura v. Seattle, 265 U.S. 332 (1924), also relied on by the dissent. To urge, as does the dissent, that the transfer of the Canal Zone property by treaty offends this well-settled principle — that the treaty power can only be exercised in a manner which conforms to the Constitution — begs the very question to be decided, namely, whether Art. IV, §3, cl. 2 places in the Congress the *exclusive* authority to dispose of United States property.

There are certain grants of authority to Congress which are, by their very terms, exclusive. In these areas, the treaty-making power and the power of Congress are not concurrent; rather, the only department of the federal government authorized to take action is the Congress. For instance, the Constitution expressly provides only one method — congressional enactment — for the appropriation of money:

> No Money shall be drawn from the Treasury, but in Consequence of Appropriations made by Law.

Art. I, §9, cl. 7. Thus, the expenditure of funds by the United States cannot be accomplished by self-executing treaty; implementing legislation appropriating such funds is indispensable. Similarly, the constitutional mandate that "all Bills for raising Revenue shall originate in the House of Representatives," Art. I, §7, cl. 1, appears, by reason of the restrictive language used, to prohibit the use of the treaty power to impose taxes.[7]

These particular grants of power to Congress operate to limit the treaty power because the language of these provisions clearly precludes any method of appropriating money or raising taxes other than through the enactment of laws by the full Congress. This is to be contrasted with the power-granting language in Art. I, §8, and in Art. IV, §3, cl. 2. Rather than stating the particular matter of concern and providing that the enactment of a law is the only way for the federal government to take action regarding that matter, these provisions state simply that Congress shall have power to take action on the matters enumerated.

Thus it appears from the very language used in the property clause that this provision was not intended to preclude the availability of self-executing treaties as a means for disposing of United States property. The history of the drafting and ratification of that clause confirms this conclusion. The other clause in Art. IV, §3, concerns the procedures for admission of new states into the Union, and the debates at the Constitutional Convention clearly demonstrate that the property clause was intended to delineate the role to be played by the central government in the disposition of Western lands which were potential new states. Several individual states had made territorial claims to portions of these lands; and as finally enacted

---

7. The dissent argues that because the power to declare war is exclusively reserved to Congress by Art. I, §8, so also must be the power to dispose of United States property, which power is granted to Congress in the same language as the war-making power. The sui generis nature of a declaration of war and the unique history indicating the Framers' desire to have both Houses of Congress concur in such a declaration, may place it apart from the other congressional powers enumerated in Art. I, §8 and in Art. IV, §3, cl. 2. The history, discussed *infra*, of the constitutional convention and ratifying conventions with respect to the property clause and the treaty clause, on the other hand, clearly demonstrates the Framers' intention to allow disposition of the United States property through self-executing treaty. Moreover, while there are numerous instances in past treaty practice of the latter, we know of no instance in which the United States has been in a state of formally declared war without a congressional declaration thereof.

the property clause, introduced in the midst of the Convention's consideration of the admission of new states, sought to preserve both federal claims and conflicting state claims to certain portions of the Western lands.

The proceedings of the Virginia state ratifying convention provide further evidence of the limited scope of the property clause. During a debate in which the meaning of the clause was questioned, Mr. Grayson noted that the sole purpose for including this provision was to preserve the property rights of the states and the federal government to the Western territory as these rights existed during the Confederation.

This history demonstrates the limited concerns giving rise to the inclusion of Article IV, §3, cl. 2 in the Constitution. Whether or not this historical perspective might serve as a basis for restricting the scope of congressional power under the property clause, we view it as persuasive evidence for rejecting the claim that Article IV is an express limitation on the treaty power, foreclosing the availability of that process as a constitutionally permissible means of disposing of American interests in the Panama Canal Zone.

III

The debates over the treaty clause at the Constitutional Convention and state ratifying conventions even more directly demonstrate the Framers' intent to permit the disposition of United States property by treaty without House approval. As originally reported to the Convention, authority to make treaties would have been entrusted to a majority of the Senate, without even Presidential participation. However, this structure was thought to entrust too much power to the Senate, and the provision was subsequently amended to include an active Presidential role. Nonetheless, concern over the extensive scope of the power remained; particularly worrisome was the potential use of treaties as a means of effecting territorial cessions. Elbridge Gerry expressed this fear when he noted that "in Treaties of peace the dearest interests will be at stake, as the fisheries, territory, etc. In treaties of peace also there is more danger to the extremities of the Continent, of being sacrificed than on any other occasion."

Concern about the sweeping character of the treaty clause led to several proposed amendments aimed at limiting its exercise. One amendment would have restricted this power by requiring that "no Treaty of Peace affecting Territorial rights should be made without the concurrence of two thirds of the (members of the Senate present.)." For some delegates, however, merely increasing the level of Senate approval did not go far enough towards ensuring the proper exercise of the treaty power. Thus Connecticut's Roger Sherman proposed an amendment providing that "no such [territorial] rights should be ceded without the sanction of the Legislature."

The Committee of Eleven, in whose hands this issue finally rested, rejected the proposed amendment for House participation. Instead, a provision requiring a two-thirds Senate vote for the passage of all treaties was adopted. This choice clearly indicates the Framers' satisfaction was a supermajoritarian requirement in the Senate, rather than House approval, to serve as a check upon the improvident cession of United States territory.

That the two-thirds voting requirement did not affect the scope of the treaty power, but only made ratification of treaties more difficult, was clearly understood at the state ratifying conventions. An amendment proposed at the Virginia Convention provided that

> no treaty ceding, contracting, restraining, or suspending the territorial rights or claims of the United States . . . shall be made, but in case of the most urgent and extreme necessity; nor shall any such treaty be ratified without the concurrence of three fourths of the whole number of the members of both houses respectively.

This, and a similar amendment offered at the North Carolina Convention, evidence the broad interpretation given Article II, §2 at the time of its inception. As was true of the effort at the Constitutional Convention to introduce House participation in ratification of treaties, these state attempts to limit the treaty power as now contained in the Constitution also failed.

That those who framed and ratified the Constitution rejected several express attempts to limit the treaty power in the manner now urged by appellants greatly undermines the interpretation of that power they press upon us. From this evidence we conclude that the disposition of property pursuant to the treaty power and without the express approval of the House of Representatives was both contemplated and authorized by the makers of the Constitution.

IV

In view of the lack of ambiguity as to the intended effects of the treaty and property clauses, it may be surprising that judicial pronouncements over the past two centuries relating to these constitutional provisions are somewhat vague and conflicting. However, none of the actual holdings in these cases addressed the precise issue before us—whether the property clause prohibits the transfer of United States property to foreign nations through self-executing treaties. While, therefore, neither the holdings nor the dicta of these previous cases are dispositive of the case before us, we believe that in the main they support the conclusions we have stated heretofore. . . .

V

While certain earlier judicial interpretations of the interplay between the property clause and the treaty clause may be somewhat confused and less than dispositive of the precise issue before us, past treaty practice is thoroughly consistent with the revealed intention of the Framers of these clauses. In addition to the treaties with Indian tribes upheld in the cases discussed above, there are many other instances of self-executing treaties with foreign nations, including Panama, which cede land or other property assertedly owned by the United States. That some transfers have been effected through a congressional enactment instead of, or in addition to, a treaty signed by the President and ratified by two-thirds of the Senate present lends no support to appellants' position in this case, because, as stated previously, self-executing treaties and congressional enactments are alternative, concurrent means provided in the Constitution for disposal of United States property. . . .

It is important to the correct resolution of the legal issue now before us not to confuse what the Constitution permits with what it prohibits. In deciding that Article IV, §3, cl. 2 is not the exclusive method contemplated by the Constitution for disposing of federal property, we hold that the United States is not prohibited from employing an alternative means constitutionally authorized. Our judicial function in deciding this lawsuit is confined to assessing the merits of the claim of appellants that in the conduct of foreign relations in this matter, involving, inter alia, the transfer of property of the United States, the treaty power as contained in Article II, §2, cl. 2, was not legally available. We hold, contrarily, that this choice of procedure was clearly consonant with the Constitution. . . .

MacKINNON, CIRCUIT JUDGE, dissenting:

The United States Constitution in Article IV, §3, cl. 2 provides that "The *Congress* shall have power *to dispose of . . . property* belonging to the United States . . ." (emphasis added). Because of this specific constitutional provision, it is my opinion that the treaty clause does not authorize the President to dispose of the large property interests of the United States in the Panama Canal treaty without the approval of *Congress* to the transfer of the *property* involved. Yet the pending treaty with the Republic of Panama would violate the Constitution and disenfranchise the 435 members of the House of Representatives from voting as members of "the Congress" upon the proposal to "dispose of" eight billion dollars worth of Canal "property belonging to the United States." Since we are supposedly a participatory democracy, where the right and duty of the entire Congress to participate in that decision is clearly stated in the Constitution, and has been recognized by prior Presidents, it is almost impossible to understand the motivation for excluding the House of Representatives from exercising its constitutional authority.

Notes and Questions

1. As a general matter, it does not violate separation of powers for the President and Senate to enter into a treaty that regulates a subject falling within Congress's powers. Thus, for example, the United States has throughout its history entered into treaties regulating international trade, even though Congress has the power to regulate international trade through its foreign commerce power. Separation of powers problems can arise, however, if a treaty regulates a matter *exclusively* assigned to Congress. Unfortunately, it is often unclear whether a particular matter is exclusively assigned to Congress.

2. Are you convinced by the majority's reading in *Edwards* of Article IV, §3, cl. 2? Does the text of that clause show that Congress's property power is nonexclusive? Besides constitutional text, what does the majority look to? How, if at all, does the majority respond to the dissent's argument about participatory democracy?

3. The court in *Edwards* claims (and it has long been assumed) that Congress's power under Article I, §9, cl. 7 — "No Money shall be drawn from the Treasury, but in Consequence of Appropriations made by Law" — is exclusive. *See also* Turner v. American Baptist Missionary Union, 24 F. Cas. 344, 345-46 (C.C.D. Mich. 1852). But why is that so? Doesn't the Supremacy Clause suggest that treaties, like statutes, are "Law"? Or does it suggest the opposite, by distinguishing between treaties and "Laws of the United States"? In this regard, recall Hamilton's argument in Pacificus that the word "Laws" in the Article II Take Care Clause includes treaties and other international law.

4. The court in *Edwards* also states that Congress's power to declare war is exclusive. Again, why is this so? Is this exclusivity based on constitutional text or on something else? Based on the materials in Chapter 4, is the war power in fact exclusive?

5. It is generally accepted that treaties may not by themselves create domestic criminal liability in the United States. *See also, e.g.,* Restatement (Third) of the Foreign Relations Law of the United States §111, cmt. i and reporters' note 6 (1987); Hopson v. Kreps, 622 F.2d 1375, 1380 (9th Cir. 1980); The Over the Top, 5 F.2d 838, 845 (D. Conn. 1925). *But see* Edwin D. Dickinson, *Are the Liquor Treaties Self Executing?*, 20 Am. J. Int'l L. 444, 449-50 (1926) (questioning this proposition). What is the basis for this restriction? Does Article I explicitly confer power on Congress to make federal criminal law? Where do you think the power comes from? Why would this congressional power be exclusive of the treaty power? Is it relevant that the Supreme Court, as mentioned in Chapter 1, has long disallowed a federal common law of crimes?

6. The court in *Edwards* reiterates the conventional wisdom that taxes may not be imposed by treaty because Article I, Section 7 provides that "All Bills for raising Revenue shall originate in the House of Representatives." Are you convinced? Could one argue that this limitation applies only to "Bills" and not to treaties? How could an agreement with another nation be used as a vehicle to impose domestic taxes?

7. It is generally understood that the exercise of jurisdiction by the lower federal courts requires authorization from both Article III of the Constitution and a federal statute. Can a treaty create federal court jurisdiction in the absence of a statute authorizing the jurisdiction? Consider, for example, Article 3(b) of the Supplementary U.S.-U.K Extradition Treaty, which provides that "[a] finding [by a federal magistrate] under paragraph (a) [of the Treaty] shall be immediately appealable by either party to the United States district court, or court of appeals, as appropriate." Under the current U.S. extradition statute, federal magistrates are directed to make determinations of extraditability, and there is no provision for appeal of those determinations within the federal court system. (The topic of extradition is covered in Chapter 8 of the casebook.) Does Article 3(b) confer federal court jurisdiction? For a discussion of this issue, see John T. Parry, *No Appeal: The U.S.-U.K. Supplementary Extradition Treaty's Effort to Create Federal Jurisdiction*, 25 Loy. L.A. Int'l & Comp. L. Rev. 543 (2003).

8. When treaties do regulate in areas within the exclusive control of Congress, what is the proper remedy? Should a U.S. court deem the treaty constitutionally invalid? Should it decline to review the validity of the treaty, pursuant to the political question doctrine? Or should it simply construe the treaty to be non-self-executing? Would non-self-execution adequately address the separation of powers issue?

9. Given the exclusivity of the appropriations clause in Article I, §9, cl. 7, does Congress have a *duty* to appropriate funds pursuant to a treaty? This issue came up in connection with the Jay Treaty discussed at the beginning of this chapter. This treaty, concluded by the President and Senate, required the appropriation of funds to cover expenditures for bilateral commissions set up under the treaty to resolve several outstanding disputes between the United States and Great Britain. Some congressmen argued that the House of Representatives was obliged to appropriate funds for the treaty because the treaty was the law of the land binding on the House. Others countered that the appropriations power was independent of the treaty power and was intended as a check on the other two branches of government. *See generally* David P. Currie, The Constitution in Congress: The Federalist Period, 1789-1801, at 211-17 (1997). Which is the better view?

2. Delegation of Authority to International Institutions

The *Edwards* decision focuses on the ability of the U.S. treaty-makers to bypass domestic lawmaking procedures, particularly procedures that would normally require the involvement of the House of Representatives.* A different set of separation of powers issues is implicated by delegations of authority from the U.S. treaty-makers to international institutions. Since World War II, there has been a vast growth in the number and importance of international institutions, many of which possess lawmaking or adjudicative authority. In committing itself to these institutions (usually by treaty or congressional-executive agreement), the United States has consented to have these institutions make certain decisions that can affect the United States' rights and duties under international law and, in some instances, the enforceability of U.S. domestic law.

Without prejudging their constitutionality, one could describe the relationships between the United States and these institutions as raising "delegation concerns." *See generally* Curtis A. Bradley, *International Delegations, the Structural Constitution, and Non-Self-Execution*, 55 Stan. L. Rev. 1557 (2003). There are a variety of U.S. legal doctrines and constitutional provisions relating to separation of powers and federalism that limit delegations or divisions of authority, at least some of which may be implicated by delegations of authority to international institutions. The doctrines and provisions most likely to be relevant are:

Nondelegation Doctrine. The Supreme Court has stated that "Congress generally cannot delegate its legislative power to another Branch." Mistretta v. United States, 488 U.S. 361, 372 (1989). At least in theory, this doctrine "forces a politically accountable Congress to make the policy choices, rather than leave this to unelected administrative officials." Erwin Chemerinsky, Constitutional Law: Principles and Policies 235 (1997). Under this doctrine, when Congress delegates power, it must "lay down by legislative act an intelligible principle to which the person or body authorized to [act] is directed to conform." J.W. Hampton, Jr. & Co. v. United States, 276 U.S. 394, 409 (1928). This "intelligible principle" requirement "seeks to enforce the understanding that Congress may not delegate the power to make laws and so may delegate no more than the authority to make policies and rules that implement its statutes." Loving v. United States, 517 U.S. 748, 758 (1996).

The Supreme Court has nevertheless allowed Congress to delegate substantial interpretive and regulatory authority to the Executive Branch and the Judiciary, and it has not found a violation of the "intelligible principle" requirement since the mid-1930s. The Court has explained that its nondelegation doctrine "has been driven by a practical understanding that in our increasingly complex society, replete with ever changing and more technical problems, Congress simply cannot do its job absent an ability to delegate power under broad general directives." *Mistretta*, 488 U.S. at 372. Although some Supreme Court Justices and academic commentators have called for reinvigorating the nondelegation doctrine, the Court has not yet shown an inclination to do so. *See, e.g.*, Whitman v. American Trucking Associations, 531 U.S. 457 (2001) (finding that broad delegation of authority to the

---

* The reverse scenario — the ability of Congress to bypass the Article II treaty-making process — is addressed below in Section H in the discussion of congressional-executive agreements.

EPA satisfied the "intelligible principle" requirement).** Furthermore, as we saw in Chapter 1, the Court has applied the nondelegation doctrine even less strictly in the foreign affairs area, explaining that "congressional legislation which is to be made effective through negotiation and inquiry within the international field must often accord to the President a degree of discretion and freedom from statutory restriction which would not be admissible were domestic affairs alone involved." United States v. Curtiss-Wright Export Corp., 299 U.S. 304, 320 (1936).

The Appointments Clause. The Appointments Clause in Article II of the Constitution gives the President the power to appoint, with the advice and consent of the Senate, ambassadors, other public ministers and consuls, Supreme Court Justices, and all other "Officers of the United States" whose appointment is not otherwise provided for in the Constitution. It also states that Congress may vest the appointment of "inferior Officers" in either the President, the courts, or in the heads of departments. The Supreme Court has made clear that "[u]nless their selection is elsewhere provided for [in the Constitution], all officers of the United States are to be appointed in accordance with the Clause." Buckley v. Valeo, 424 U.S. 1, 132 (1976). The Court also has stated that "any appointee exercising significant authority pursuant to the laws of the United States is an 'Officer of the United States,' and must, therefore, be appointed in the manner prescribed" by the Clause. Id. at 126. The Clause does not apply, however, to "lesser functionaries subordinate to officers of the United States." Id. at 126 n.162. These requirements, the Court has explained, are designed both to prevent aggrandizement of power by one branch at the expense of another and to ensure public accountability in the appointments process.

Limits on Non-Article III Courts. Article III of the Constitution provides that "[t]he judicial Power of the United States, shall be vested in one supreme Court, and in such inferior Courts as the Congress may from time to time ordain and establish," and it also specifies that the federal judicial power is to be exercised by judges who "shall hold their Offices during good Behaviour, and [who] shall, at stated Times, receive for their Services a Compensation, which shall not be diminished during their Continuance in Office." This language has been interpreted as at least sometimes precluding the vesting of the judicial power of the United States in tribunals that are not ordained and established by Congress and that do not have the Article III tenure and salary protections.

Although the Supreme Court invalidated an important piece of bankruptcy reform legislation on the ground that it unconstitutionally delegated judicial power to non-Article III courts, see Northern Pipeline Construction Co. v. Marathon Pipe Line Co., 458 U.S. 50 (1982), the Court has not provided clear guidance about when such courts are allowed or disallowed. There was no majority opinion in the bankruptcy case, and the Court's *holding* was limited to the narrow proposition that "Congress may not vest in a non-Article III court the power to adjudicate, render final judgment, and issue binding orders in a traditional contract action arising under state law, without consent of the litigants, and subject only to ordinary

** The court has sometimes construed statutory delegations narrowly, however, in order to avoid constitutional concerns. *See generally* John F. Manning, *The Nondelegation Doctrine as a Canon of Avoidance*, 2000 Sup. Ct. Rev. 223; Cass R. Sunstein, *Nondelegation Canons*, 67 U. Chi. L. Rev. 315 (2000). In addition, the Court has invalidated statutory delegations on *other* separation of powers grounds, such as (in *Chada*, for example) a failure to satisfy the Constitution's bicameralism and presentment requirements.

appellate review." Thomas v. Union Carbide Agricultural Products Co., 473 U.S. 568, 584 (1985). In subsequent decisions, the Court has applied a case-by-case balancing approach, whereby it weighs the need for the non-Article III court against the danger to separation of powers. In assessing this balance, the Court considers a variety of factors, and it has indicated that non-Article III courts are more likely to be permitted if the parties consent, if appellate review is available in an Article III court, and if the dispute involves "public rights" created by the government. *See* Commodity Futures Trading Commission v. Schor, 478 U.S. 833 (1986); Thomas v. Union Carbide, *supra*.

In a more recent decision, Nguyen v. United States, 123 S. Ct. 2130 (2003), the Supreme Court held that a federal appeals court lacked jurisdiction to review a narcotics conviction from the District Court of Guam, because one of the judges on the appellate panel was a territorial-court judge (from the District Court for the Northern Mariana Islands) appointed for a ten-year term, rather than an Article III judge appointed with life tenure. Although a federal statute allows "one or more district judges within the circuit" to sit on a court of appeals "whenever the business of that court so requires," the Supreme Court concluded that Congress's reference to "district judges" was intended to encompass only Article III judges. In rejecting the government's argument that the defendants had waived this statutory argument by failing to raise it before the appellate court, the Court observed that the statute "embodies weighty congressional policy concerning the proper organization of the federal courts." Citing *Northern Pipeline*, the Court also noted that "Congress' decision to preserve the Article III character of the courts of appeals is more than a trivial concern."

Hayburn's Case. An early Supreme Court case, Hayburn's Case, 2 U.S. (2 Dall.) 409 (1792), has come to stand for the proposition that Congress may not vest review of the decisions of Article III courts in officials of the Executive Branch. That case involved a 1792 statute that authorized pensions for disabled veterans of the Revolutionary War. The statute provided that the federal circuit courts were to determine the appropriate disability payments, but that the Secretary of War had the discretion either to adopt or reject the courts' findings. The Supreme Court did not address the constitutionality of this arrangement, but the views of several circuit courts (reflecting the views of five Supreme Court Justices) were reported with the case, and these courts reasoned that the statute was unconstitutional because it asked the federal courts to do something that was not "judicial." *See also* Miller v. French, 530 U.S. 327, 343 (2000) (Hayburn's Case "'stands for the principle that Congress cannot vest review of the decisions of Article III courts in officials of the Executive Branch'") (quoting Plaut v. Spendthrift Farm, Inc., 514 U.S. 211, 218 (1995)). Hayburn's Case is also frequently cited for the broader proposition that the federal courts may not issue advisory opinions.

Interference with Judicial Power. In Plaut v. Spendthrift Farm, Inc., 514 U.S. 211 (1995), the Court held that Congress does not have the power to reopen, retroactively, a federal court's final judgment in a civil case. In that case, Congress had authorized the reinstitution of certain lawsuits that had been dismissed on statute-of-limitations grounds. Analogizing to *Hayburn's Case*, the Court held that Congress's reopening of a final judgment unconstitutionally interferes with the power of the federal courts to decide cases, in violation of Article III of the Constitution and principles of separation of powers. The Constitution, reasoned the Court, "gives the Federal Judiciary the power, not merely to rule on cases, but to *decide* them, subject to review only by superior courts in the Article III hierarchy — with an understanding, in short, that 'a judgment conclusively resolves the case' because 'a "judicial Power" is one to render dispositive judgments.'" *Id.* at 218-19 (quoting Frank Easterbrook, *Presidential Review*, 40 Case W. Res. L Rev. 905, 926 (1999)).

Anti-Commandeering. The Court has held that Congress may not "commandeer" state legislatures or executive branch officials to implement federal regulatory programs. *See* Printz v. United States, 521 U.S. 898 (1997); New York v. United States, 505 U.S. 144 (1992). In addition to finding that such commandeering violates the "dual sovereignty" implicit in the Constitution, the Court has explained that commandeering undermines political accountability, because "it may be state officials who will bear the brunt of public disapproval, while the federal officials who devised the regulatory program may remain insulated from the electoral ramifications of their decision." *New York*, 505 U.S. at 168-69. The Court also has expressed concern that such commandeering could allow Congress to implement federal law without the assistance of the President, thereby enhancing its power vis-à-vis the Executive Branch. *See id.* at 922-23. Among other things, these anti-commandeering decisions suggest (as do some of the Court's separation of powers decisions) that the Court's concerns about accountability and aggrandizement of power extend beyond horizontal delegations of authority.

Consider the relevance of these constitutional doctrines and provisions to the U.S. relationship with the following international institutions (as well as to two scenarios listed at the end that do not involve international institutions). In doing so, think about how constitutional principles, which were formulated primarily with domestic issues in mind, should be applied to the international arena. Should these principles be applied in a formal way, with an emphasis on constitutional text, structure, and history, or in a functional way, with an emphasis on the practical needs of the United States and the changing nature of the international community? *Compare* Julian G. Ku, *The Delegation of Federal Power to International Organizations: New Problems with Old Solutions*, 85 Minn. L. Rev. 71, 121 (2000) (arguing for a formal approach in this area because international institutions lack the accountability and political legitimacy of domestic institutions), *with* Louis Henkin, Foreign Affairs and the United States Constitution 272 (2d ed. 1996) ("It is difficult to accept that United States participation in contemporary forms of multinational cooperation should depend on 'technicalities' about 'delegation,' 'judicial power,' and 'case or controversy,' and on forms and devices to satisfy them.").

U.N. Security Council. The U.N. Security Council, established by the U.N. Charter, consists of five permanent members (the United States, Russia, Great Britain, France, and China) and ten rotating non-permanent members. Under the Charter, the Council is charged with "primary responsibility for the maintenance of international peace and security." If the Security Council determines "the existence of any threat to the peace, breach of the peace, or act of aggression," it may call upon member states to take measures "not involving the use of armed force," such as "complete or partial interruption of economic relations and of rail, sea, air, postal, telegraphic, radio, and other means of communication, and the severance of diplomatic relations." If it determines that nonmilitary measures "would be inadequate or have proved to be inadequate," the Council can authorize "such action by air, sea, or land forces as may be necessary to maintain or restore international peace and security." Such actions "may include demonstrations, blockade, and other operations by air, sea, or land forces of Members of the United Nations."

The United States has promised in the Charter to "accept and carry out the decisions of the Security Council." Does this commitment raise delegation concerns? Does the U.S. veto power on the Security Council remove such concerns? The D.C. Circuit was faced with these issues in Diggs v. Richardson, 555 F.2d 848 (D.C. Cir. 1976). In that case, the Security Council had issued a resolution calling upon all nations to cease certain relationships with South Africa, because of its occupation of the former U.N. territory of Namibia. Relying on this resolution, a group of plaintiffs sought declaratory and injunctive relief prohibiting the U.S. government from continuing to deal with South Africa concerning the importation of seal furs from Namibia. The D.C. Circuit upheld dismissal of the lawsuit, concluding that the UN resolution was not self-executing. The court noted, among other things, that the resolution was not addressed to the judicial branch, did not by its terms confer individual rights, addressed foreign relations issues within the discretion of the Executive Branch, and did not provide specific standards. Does treating Security Council resolutions as non-self-executing eliminate delegation concerns? For additional discussion of the status of Security Council resolutions in the United States, see James A.R. Nafziger & Edward M. Wise, *The Status in United States Law of Security Council Resolutions Under Chapter VII of the United Nations Charter*, 46 Am. J. Comp. L. 421 (1998).

Another way in which the U.S. relationship with the Security Council might raise delegation concerns is with respect to the use of military force. Can the U.S. treatymakers delegate to the Security Council the decision of when to use military force? Can they delegate command authority over U.S. forces to the Council and its agents? These and related questions are explored in Chapter 4. *See also* Michael J. Glennon & Allison R. Hayward, *Collective Security and the Constitution: Can the Commander in Chief Power Be Delegated to the United Nations?*, 82 Geo. L.J. 1573 (1994).

International Court of Justice. The U.N. Charter also established the International Court of Justice (ICJ), which has jurisdiction to resolve international law disputes between nations. A member of the United Nations, such as the United States, is bound to "comply with the decision of the International Court of Justice in any case to which it is a party." The Court can only hear cases, however, in which both parties have consented in some fashion to the Court's jurisdiction. For many years, the United States consented generally to the Court's jurisdiction. But in 1985, after the Court exercised jurisdiction over a suit brought against the United States by Nicaragua, the United States withdrew its general consent. As a result, it can now be sued in the Court only if it has consented to the Court's jurisdiction in a particular treaty with the complaining party or if it gives its specific consent to jurisdiction at the time the suit is filed. The United States continues to be a party, however, to a number of treaties that contain clauses authorizing the Court to resolve disputes arising under the treaties.

Does the United States' consent to the ICJ's jurisdiction, along with its commitment to comply with the ICJ's decisions, raise delegation concerns — for example, by interfering with the federal courts' exercise of their judicial power? Does your answer depend on whether the ICJ's orders are self-executing? What, if anything, does the Supreme Court's *Breard* decision (excerpted in Section B) suggest about these issues? Consider also Committee of United States Citizens Living in Nicaragua v. Reagan, 859 F.2d 929 (D.C. Cir. 1988). In that case, various plaintiffs challenged the United States' failure to abide by an ICJ decision holding that the United States was "under a duty immediately to cease and to refrain" from assisting the contra rebel forces in Nicaragua. The court rejected this challenge, for two reasons. First, it concluded that, under the last-in-time rule, Congress had effectively overridden the United States' obligation to comply with the ICJ's decision, because Congress had continued to authorize assistance to the contras after the ICJ's decision. Second, citing its earlier decision in *Diggs*, the court concluded that the U.N. Charter obligation to comply with ICJ decisions was not self-executing. Do the last-in-time rule and the non-self-execution doctrine remove delegation concerns associated with ICJ decisions? (Recall from Section B that the Supreme Court granted certiorari in Medellin v. Dretke to consider the legal effect of an ICJ decision, but ultimately dismissed the case without addressing the merits. In that case, the petitioner was arguing that an ICJ decision that directed the United States to provide review and reconsideration of the convictions and sentences of 51 Mexican nationals (including the petitioner) had direct effect in the U.S. legal system and preempted state rules of criminal procedure. The Executive Branch disputed that argument, but it defended the President's authority to direct the state courts to provide review and reconsideration in the covered cases.)

World Trade Organization. The United States is a party to the World Trade Organization, which was established in 1995 to administer the General Agreement on Tariffs and Trade (GATT) and related treaties. This organization includes a Dispute Settlement Body (DSB), which adjudicates trade disputes between the member countries. The DSB's decisions are binding, and, if the losing party does not comply with a decision, the DSB may authorize the prevailing party to impose trade sanctions on the losing party. The United States has already participated in a number of cases before the DSB, both as a plaintiff and as a defendant. As defendant, the United States has lost a number of significant cases, including a case challenging clean air regulations issued by the Environmental Protection Agency, a case challenging U.S. limits on shrimp imports designed to protect sea turtles, and a case challenging U.S. tax treatment of foreign sales corporations. Does U.S. participation in the World Trade Organization raise delegation concerns? Note that the legislation implementing the U.S. commitment to the WTO provides that (a) "No provision of [the GATT], nor the application of any such provision to any person or circumstance, that is inconsistent with any law of the United States shall have effect"; and (b) the GATT may not be enforced in a U.S. court *against a state* "except in an action brought by the United States for the purpose of declaring such law or application invalid." Do these limitations remove delegation concerns?

In addition to its dispute settlement powers, the WTO has the power to adopt binding interpretations of the GATT and related treaties. These interpretations require the vote of only a three-fourths' majority of the WTO members. Thus, at least in theory, the WTO has the power to adopt interpretations of the treaties that are contrary to the views of the United States. In agreeing to give this interpretive authority to the WTO, has the United States effectively delegated away some of its treaty-making, or treaty-interpreting, power? If so, is such a delegation constitutional? Note that the United States has the right to withdraw from the WTO upon giving six months' notice. Does that right eliminate the delegation concerns?

For a statute raising delegation concerns relating to both the World Trade Organization and the Security Council, consider the Clean Diamond Trading Act. This Act, which was enacted in 2003, authorizes the President to restrict trade in "conflict diamonds" used by rebel groups in Africa to finance their activities. Section 15 of the Act provides:

> This Act shall take effect on the date on which the President certifies to the Congress that —
>> (1) an applicable waiver that has been granted by the World Trade Organization is in effect; or
>> (2) an applicable decision in a resolution adopted by the United Nations Security Council pursuant to Chapter VII of the Charter of the United Nations is in effect.
> The Act shall remain in effect during those periods in which, as certified by the President to the Congress, an applicable waiver or decision referred to in paragraph (1) or (2) is in effect.

In his signing statement, President Bush stated that if section 15 "imposed a mandatory duty on the President to certify to the Congress whether either of the two specified events has occurred and whether either remains in effect, a serious question would exist as to whether section 15 unconstitutionally delegated legislative power to international bodies." To avoid this constitutional question, President Bush stated that he would construe the provision "as giving the President broad discretion whether to certify to Congress that an applicable waiver or decision is in effect" and "as imposing no obligation on the President to withdraw an existing certification in response to any particular event." *See* Statement by the President (April 25, 2003), at http://www.whitehouse.gov/news/releases/2003/04/20030425-9 .html. Was there in fact a constitutional problem here?

NAFTA. In 1993, the United States became a party, along with Canada and Mexico, to the North American Free Trade Agreement (NAFTA). At least two aspects of NAFTA raise potential delegation concerns. First, Chapter 19 of NAFTA allows certain import decisions of the member countries to be reviewed by binational arbitral panels. These panels apply the substantive law of the importing country, and their decisions are binding and final. Thus, in the case of the United States, the panels can exercise final review over the application of U.S. trade law by the International Trade Commission (a federal administrative agency). In situations in which a matter is referred by a panel back to the Commission, the Commission is bound by statute to "take action not inconsistent with the decision" of the panel. The panel members, however, will not necessarily be Article III judges. Nor is their selection subject to the Article II appointments process. Does this scheme raise delegation concerns? In particular, does it violate the limits on non-Article III courts? The scheme was challenged in the D.C. Circuit on various delegation grounds, but the plaintiff (a trade association) was found to lack standing, so the D.C. Circuit did not address the delegation issues. *See* American Coalition for Competitive Trade v. Clinton, 128 F.3d 761 (D.C. Cir. 1997). For a discussion of delegation issues associated with the binational review system established under the predecessor to NAFTA (the United States-Canada Free Trade Agreement), see Jim C. Chen, *Appointments with Disaster: The Unconstitutionality of Binational Arbitral Review Under the United States-Canada Free Trade Agreement,* 49 Wash. & Lee L. Rev. 1455 (1992).

A second feature of NAFTA that may raise delegation concerns is its provision for challenges by investors to the practices of the member countries. Chapter 11 of

NAFTA requires each country to accord investors of the other two countries certain minimum standards of treatment, including protection against uncompensated expropriation. Investors who allege a violation of Chapter 11 may submit claims to a panel of three private arbitrators who can award monetary damages but not injunctive relief. (Under U.S. law, however, an award against the U.S. government by a foreign court or tribunal is paid only after the Attorney General certifies that it is in the interest of the United States to make the payment. *See* 28 U.S.C. §2414.)

The potential intersection between Chapter 11 of NAFTA and U.S. domestic institutions is illustrated by a Chapter 11 arbitration filed against the United States in 1998 by a Canadian funeral home operator, The Loewen Group. The Chapter 11 arbitration concerned the treatment that Loewen received in a civil lawsuit in a Mississippi state court. In that lawsuit, the owner of a funeral home in Mississippi charged Loewen with unfair and deceptive trading practices and breach of contract. The plaintiff sought approximately $26 million in damages, but the jury awarded a total of $500 million, which included $400 million in punitive damages. Under Mississippi state law, Loewen was required to post a bond in the amount of 125 percent of the judgment (i.e., $625 million) in order to appeal, and the Mississippi Supreme Court refused to waive that requirement. Loewen settled the case for $175 million.

In its Chapter 11 proceeding, Loewen alleged that the plaintiffs' attorneys in the Mississippi case had been allowed to appeal to anti-Canadian, racial, and class biases (e.g., by suggesting that Loewen was prejudiced against African-Americans), and that these biases had affected the verdict. It argued that the unfairness of the Mississippi proceedings and the bond requirement violated Chapter 11 because they constituted an expropriation of property, unequal treatment of a foreign company, and a denial of justice. Loewen sought damages in the amount of $725 million, which included not only what it paid out in the settlement but also compensation for business losses allegedly sustained as a result of the verdict.

The U.S. government contested Loewen's claims. In a preliminary ruling, the arbitration panel held that a nation's judicial proceedings may be challenged under Chapter 11 (which refers to "measures adopted or maintained by a party"). In its final decision, however, the arbitration tribunal ruled in favor of the United States. *See* Award, The Loewen Group, Inc. and United States of America, Case No. ARB(AF)/98/3 (June 26, 2003), at http://www.state.gov/documents/ organization/22094.pdf. The tribunal held that Loewen's assignment of its NAFTA claims to a Canadian corporation owned and controlled by a United States corporation destroyed the diversity of nationality required for NAFTA arbitration. The tribunal also held that the claims should be dismissed on the merits because the claimants had failed to show that they had no reasonably available and adequate remedy under United States law. While concluding that the trial and verdict in the Mississippi case "were clearly improper and discreditable and cannot be squared with minimum standards of international law and fair and equitable treatment," the tribunal noted that Loewen had failed to appeal the Mississippi trial court's decision either to the Mississippi Supreme Court or the U.S. Supreme Court, and it reasoned that "a court decision which can be challenged through the judicial process does not amount to a denial of justice at the international level." The tribunal concluded its opinion as follows: "In the last resort, a failure by [a] nation to provide adequate means of remedy may amount to an international wrong but only in the last resort. The line may be hard to draw, but it is real. Too great a readiness to step from outside into the domestic arena, attributing the shape of an international wrong to what is really a local error (however serious), will damage both the integrity of the domestic judicial system and the viability of NAFTA itself."

In another NAFTA case, a Canadian company filed an action against the United States for alleged expropriation after the Massachusetts Supreme Judicial Court dismissed the company's suit against the Boston Redevelopment Authority (a municipal entity) for interference with contractual relations. Like *Loewen*, this case was resolved in favor of the United States. The panel concluded that the decision of the Massachusetts court was consistent with international standards of justice and that Massachusetts did not violate international law by making the Boston Redevelopment Authority immune from suit for interference with contractual relations. *See* Award, Mondev Int'l Ltd. v. United States, Case No. ARB(AF)/99/2 (Oct. 11, 2002), at http://www.state.gov/documents/organization/14442.pdf.

When applied to review the fairness of U.S. judicial proceedings, does Chapter 11 constitute a delegation of Article III judicial power to an international body? When applied to review *state* court proceedings, does it violate principles of federalism? For additional discussion of the *Loewen* and *Mondev* decisions, see William S. Dodge, *ICSID Arbitral Awards Addressing the Protection of Foreign Investment Under NAFTA Chapter 11*, 98 Am. J. Int'l L. 155 (2004). For a description of other Chapter 11 cases filed against the United States, see U.S. State Department, Office of the Legal Adviser, NAFTA Investor-State Arbitrations, at http://www.state.gov/s/l/c3439.htm.

Chemical Weapons Convention. In 1997, the United States ratified the Chemical Weapons Convention, which bans the development, retention, and use of chemical weapons. The Convention further establishes a new international organization, the Organization for the Prohibition of Chemical Weapons, which has the power to verify Convention compliance by ordering inspections of public and private facilities in the United States. Inspections are conducted by the organization's Technical Secretariat, members of which are not appointed by or removable by U.S. officials. Is the authority exercised by these officials consistent with the Appointments Clause? Do these officials exercise "significant federal authority"? Does the delegation of authority to the PCW undermine the principles of accountability served by the Appointments Clause? Should Appointments Clause limitations even apply in the context of U.S. participation in international institutions? Is it possible to argue, using *Curtiss-Wright* by analogy, that the treaty power is not subject to the same Appointments Clause restrictions as domestic legislation? For a consideration of these and related questions, see John C. Yoo, *The New Sovereignty and the Old Constitution: The Chemical Weapons Convention and the Appointments Clause*, 15 Const. Commentary 87 (1998).

International Criminal Court. In 1998, approximately 120 nations agreed on the text of a treaty that establishes a permanent International Criminal Court. The treaty, entitled the "Rome Statute of the International Criminal Court," recently took effect after it had been ratified by 60 nations. Under the treaty, an international court, based in The Hague, has jurisdiction to try the offenses of genocide, crimes against humanity, war crimes, and the crime of aggression. Despite expressing a number of concerns about the treaty, President Clinton signed it shortly before leaving office. In 2002, however, the Bush Administration informed the United Nations that the United States had no intention of ratifying the treaty.

If the United States *did* become a party to the treaty, the court would have jurisdiction to try U.S. citizens for the covered offenses, even if committed in the United States.* In trying these offenses, the court would apply the terms of the treaty, other applicable treaties, "rules of international law, including the established principles of the international law of armed conflict," and, as a last resort, "general principles of law derived by the Court from national laws of legal systems of the world including, as appropriate, the national laws of States that would normally exercise jurisdiction over the crime." As a party to the treaty, the United States would be required to "cooperate fully with the Court in its investigation and prosecution of crimes within the jurisdiction of the Court," and to "comply with requests for arrest and surrender." Some commentators have argued that the extent of the court's jurisdiction is such that U.S. participation in the court would violate the constitutional limits on non-Article III courts. *See, e.g.,* Lee A. Casey, *The Case Against the International Criminal Court,* 25 Fordham Int'l L.J. 840 (2002). *But see* Audrey Benison, *International Criminal Tribunals: Is There a Substantive Limitation on the Treaty Power?,* 37 Stan. J. Int'l L. 75 (2001) (arguing that U.S. participation in the court would be constitutional); Paul D. Marquardt, *Law Without Borders: The Constitutionality of an International Criminal Court,* 33 Colum. J. Transnat'l L. 73 (1995) (same). Note that the United States has already statutorily committed itself to extradite suspects to the ad hoc international criminal tribunals established for former Yugoslavia and Rwanda. *See* National Defense Authorization Act for Fiscal Year 1996, Pub. L. No. 104-106, §1342, 110 Stat. 186, 486; *see also* Ntakirutimana v. Reno, 184 F.3d 419 (5th Cir. 1999) (upholding extradition to the Rwandan tribunal).

Congress has enacted a controversial statute concerning the U.S. relationship with the International Criminal Court. This statute, entitled the American Servicemembers' Protection Act, broadly precludes federal, state, and local government assistance to the International Criminal Court. *See* Pub. L. No. 107-206, 116 Stat. 820, tit. II (Aug. 2, 2002). The Act also prohibits U.S. military assistance to countries that are parties to the Court, subject to waiver by the President on the basis of national interest or if the country in question enters into an agreement with the United States "preventing the International Criminal court from proceeding against United States personnel present in such country." (The Bush Administration has entered into a number of such agreements, and has suspended military assistance to countries that have not entered into such agreements.) The Act further authorizes the President to use "all means necessary and appropriate" to obtain the release of U.S. and allied soldiers and government employees detained or imprisoned by the court.

International Labour Organization. The United States is a member of the International Labour Organization (ILO). The ILO was founded in 1919, and it became the first specialized agency of the United Nations in 1946. It promulgates conventions and recommendations for labor rights such as freedom of association, the right to organize, collective bargaining, abolition of forced labor, and equality

---

* Even if the United States does not become a party to the treaty, the court will purportedly have jurisdiction to try U.S. citizens for offenses committed in the territory of nations that are parties to the treaty.

of opportunity and treatment. Although member states are not required to adopt the proposed conventions and recommendations, they are required under the ILO Constitution to bring the conventions and recommendations "before the authority or authorities within whose competence the matter lies, for the enactment of legislation or other action." The ILO also has claimed that members have an obligation to respect certain conventions regardless of whether they have ratified them. In addition, the ILO Constitution can itself be amended by a two-thirds' vote.

Judicial Application of Foreign Law.   U.S. courts routinely apply foreign law in civil cases when called for by choice of law principles. They also regularly enforce foreign civil judgments and foreign arbitral awards that are based on foreign law. Do these applications of foreign law raise delegation concerns? What about the Lacey Act, a federal statute that makes it a crime to "import, export, transport, sell, receive, acquire, or purchase in interstate or foreign commerce . . . any fish or wildlife taken, possessed, transported, or sold . . . in violation of any foreign law," 16 U.S.C. §3372(a)(2)(a)? *See, e.g.,* United States v. McNab, 324 F.3d 1266 (11th Cir. 2003) (upholding prosecutions under the Lacey Act premised on violations of Honduran law). *Cf.* United States v. Pasquantino, 125 S. Ct. 1766 (2005) (upholding prosecution under federal wire fraud statute for liquor smuggling operation designed to evade Canadian tax laws); Small v. United States, 125 S. Ct. 1752 (2005) (construing the phrase "convicted in any court" in statute prohibiting gun ownership to mean only U.S. courts).

Judicial Application of Customary International Law.   When you study the materials in Chapter 7 concerning judicial application of customary international law, consider whether such application can raise delegation concerns. In addition, pay attention to the connections between modern customary international law and the resolutions and decisions of international institutions, including the international institutions discussed above.

Notes and Questions

1. Of the above examples, which, if any, seem constitutionally problematic? What types of arrangements with international institutions are most likely to raise delegation concerns? What types of arrangements are least likely to raise these concerns? For example, is a delegation of adjudicative authority more or less constitutionally problematic than a delegation of legislative or executive authority?

2. To what extent can the constitutional concerns posed by international delegations be reduced or eliminated by treating the output of international institutions (such as their decisions or resolutions) as non-self-executing within the U.S. legal system? If Congress is required to implement the output of international institutions before they have domestic effect, does that eliminate the constitutional concerns? In which of the above examples, if any, would such a congressional role not eliminate constitutional concerns?

3. To what extent does a U.S. veto power — such as on the U.N. Security Council — reduce delegation concerns? Who decides for the United States whether to exercise the veto?

4. The United States has the legal right to withdraw from most international institutions. To what extent does the ability by the United States to withdraw from an international institution reduce delegation concerns? How easy is it to withdraw in practice?

5. Are there parallels between the growth of international regulatory bodies and the rise of the administrative state during and after the New Deal in the United States? If so, what do these parallels suggest about either the policy wisdom of U.S. delegations of authority to international institutions, or the constitutionality of such delegations?

6. There has been much writing in recent years about a "democratic deficit" in international institutions (especially in the European Union) — for example, that they are not sufficiently accountable, and that their decisionmaking is not sufficiently transparent. *See, e.g.*, Peter L. Lindseth, *Democratic Legitimacy and the Administrative Character of Supranationalism: The Example of the European Community*, 99 Colum. L. Rev. 628 (1999); Eric Stein, *International Integration and Democracy: No Love at First Sight*, 95 Am. J. Int'l L. 489 (2001); Paul B. Stephan, *Accountability and International Lawmaking: Rules, Rents and Legitimacy*, 17 Nw. J. Int'l L. & Bus. 681 (1996-1997). What implications, if any, might such a democratic deficit have for the constitutionality of international delegations by the United States?

7. In a qualified defense of U.S. delegations of authority to international institutions, Professor Swaine argues as follows:

> While the judiciary may be ill equipped to strike down international delegations on constitutional grounds, the conceptual relevance of nondelegation and federalism to international delegations is not so easily dismissed. International delegations are demonstrably different from domestic delegations of legislative authority — primarily because the United States is just one of many principals directing its international agents. And for this reason, among others, the role of international delegations in reassigning authority from the states is more problematic than when that authority is assumed (and retained) by the national government.
>
> It does not follow, however, that international delegations are an affront to the Constitution. Such measures are constitutional in two important and reinforcing senses. International delegations are troubling precisely because they are constitutional in character: That is, legislative authority conferred on international institutions is difficult to reclaim. By the same token, however, this kind of commitment indirectly promotes a more specific constitutional value: the diffusion of political authority prized by federalism. While delegating national power to international institutions redistributes national legislative authority (including that which might otherwise fall to the states), it provides a bulwark against the concentration of political power in the national government that is consistent with the ambitions of federalism.
>
> Viewed this way, international delegations are constitutional in an important — and neglected — regard: They advance a constitutional value that deserves to be measured against any harm to constitutional values that they may risk. This does not, of course, amount to a concrete finding that international delegations should always withstand constitutional scrutiny, even in terms of the nondelegation and federalism doctrines. It does, however, warrant resisting a preemptive, undifferentiated constitutional objection to such activities, particularly any that would condemn them outright. It is also a small step toward a more sophisticated analysis, one particularly relevant to Congress and the President, for distinguishing types of delegations that are most problematic.

Edward T. Swaine, *The Constitutionality of International Delegations*, 104 Colum. L. Rev. 1492, 1501 (2004). Do you agree that international delegations can promote the values of U.S. federalism by diluting the power of the national government? Or do they simply move power even further away from U.S. states and localities?

8. For additional discussion of the constitutionality of U.S. delegations of authority to international institutions, see Bradley, *supra*; David M. Golove, *The New Confederalism: Treaty Delegations of Legislative, Executive, and Judicial Authority*, 55 Stan. L. Rev. 1697 (2003); Jenny S. Martinez, *Towards an International Judicial System*, 56 Stan. L. Rev. 429 (2003); Ernest A. Young, *The Trouble with Global Constitutionalism*, 38 Tex. Int'l L.J. 527 (2003); and A. Mark Weisburd, *International Courts and American Courts*, 21 Mich. J. Int'l L. 877 (2000).

D. RELATIONSHIP BETWEEN TREATY POWER AND AMERICAN FEDERALISM

The Constitution makes clear that treaties are the supreme law of the land and therefore preempt inconsistent state law. The Supreme Court confirmed this proposition in an early decision, Ware v. Hylton, 3 U.S. (3 Dall.) 199 (1796), which held that the treaty between the United States and Great Britain ending the Revolutionary War preempted a Virginia statute providing for the discharge of debts owed to British creditors. Despite the settled supremacy of treaties over state law, questions remain about the relationship between the treaty power and U.S. federalism. Can treaties create domestic law that is beyond the scope of Congress's legislative powers? Does Congress have the authority under the Necessary and Proper Clause to enact legislation to implement treaties if the legislation would otherwise fall outside the scope of its legislative powers? Is the treaty power subject to any Tenth Amendment limitations? Can treaties "commandeer" state legislatures or executive branches? Can treaties override the sovereign immunity of the states? Are there any limits to the subject matters that can be regulated by treaty? These and other federalism issues are considered below.

Missouri v. Holland

252 U.S. 416 (1920)

MR. JUSTICE HOLMES delivered the opinion of the Court.

This is a bill in equity brought by the State of Missouri to prevent a game warden of the United States from attempting to enforce the Migratory Bird Treaty Act of July 3, 1918, c. 128, 40 Stat. 755, and the regulations made by the Secretary of Agriculture in pursuance of the same. The ground of the bill is that the statute is an unconstitutional interference with the rights reserved to the States by the Tenth Amendment, and that the acts of the defendant done and threatened under that authority invade the sovereign right of the State and contravene its will manifested in statutes. . . . A motion to dismiss was sustained by the District Court on the ground that the act of Congress is constitutional. . . . The State appeals.

On December 8, 1916, a treaty between the United States and Great Britain was proclaimed by the President. It recited that many species of birds in their annual migrations traversed certain parts of the United States and of Canada, that they were of great value as a source of food and in destroying insects injurious to vegetation, but were in danger of extermination through lack of adequate protection. It therefore provided for specified close seasons and protection in other forms, and agreed that the two powers would take or propose to their law-making bodies the necessary measures for carrying the treaty out. 39 Stat. 1702. The above mentioned Act of July 3, 1918, entitled an act to give effect to the convention, prohibited the killing, capturing or selling any of the migratory birds included in the terms of the treaty except as permitted by regulations compatible with those terms, to be made by the Secretary of Agriculture. Regulations were proclaimed on July 31, and October 25, 1918. 40 Stat. 1812; 1863. It is unnecessary to go into any details, because, as we have said, the question raised is the general one whether the treaty and statute are void as an interference with the rights reserved to the States.

To answer this question it is not enough to refer to the Tenth Amendment, reserving the powers not delegated to the United States, because by Article II, §2, the power to make treaties is delegated expressly, and by Article VI treaties made under the authority of the United States, along with the Constitution and laws of the United States made in pursuance thereof, are declared the supreme law of the land. If the treaty is valid there can be no dispute about the validity of the statute under Article I, §8, as a necessary and proper means to execute the powers of the Government. The language of the Constitution as to the supremacy of treaties being general, the question before us is narrowed to an inquiry into the ground upon which the present supposed exception is placed.

It is said that a treaty cannot be valid if it infringes the Constitution, that there are limits, therefore, to the treaty-making power, and that one such limit is that what an act of Congress could not do unaided, in derogation of the powers reserved to the States, a treaty cannot do. An earlier act of Congress that attempted by itself and not in pursuance of a treaty to regulate the killing of migratory birds within the States had been held bad in the District Court. United States v. Shauver, 214 Fed. Rep. 154. United States v. McCullagh, 221 Fed. Rep. 288. Those decisions were supported by arguments that migratory birds were owned by the States in their sovereign capacity for the benefit of their people, and that under cases like Geer v. Connecticut, 161 U.S. 519, this control was one that Congress had no power to displace. The same argument is supposed to apply now with equal force.

Whether the two cases cited were decided rightly or not they cannot be accepted as a test of the treaty power. Acts of Congress are the supreme law of the land only when made in pursuance of the Constitution, while treaties are declared to be so when made under the authority of the United States. It is open to question whether the authority of the United States means more than the formal acts prescribed to make the convention. We do not mean to imply that there are no qualifications to the treaty-making power; but they must be ascertained in a different way. It is obvious that there may be matters of the sharpest exigency for the national well being that an act of Congress could not deal with but that a treaty followed by such an act could, and it is not lightly to be assumed that, in matters requiring national action, "a power which must belong to and somewhere reside in every civilized government" is not to be found. Andrews v. Andrews, 188 U.S. 14, 33. What was said in that case with regard to the powers of the States applies with equal force to the powers of the nation in cases where the States individually are incompetent to act. We are not yet discussing the particular case before us but only are considering the validity of the test proposed. With regard to that we may add that when we are dealing with words that also are a constituent act, like the Constitution of the United States, we must realize that they have called into life a being the development of which could not have been foreseen completely by the most gifted of its begetters. It was enough for them to realize or to hope that they had created an organism; it has taken a century and has cost their successors much sweat and blood to prove that they created a nation. The case before us must be considered in the light of our whole experience and not merely in that of what was said a hundred years ago. The treaty in question does not contravene any prohibitory words to be found in the Constitution. The only question is whether it is forbidden by some invisible radiation from the general terms of the Tenth Amendment. We must consider what this country has become in deciding what that Amendment has reserved.

The State as we have intimated founds its claim of exclusive authority upon an assertion of title to migratory birds, an assertion that is embodied in statute. No doubt it is true that as between a State and its inhabitants the State may regulate the killing and sale of such birds, but it does not follow that its authority is exclusive of paramount powers. To put the claim of the State upon title is to lean upon a slender reed. Wild birds are not in the possession of anyone; and possession is the beginning of ownership. The whole foundation of the State's rights is the presence within their jurisdiction of birds that yesterday had not arrived, tomorrow may be in another State and in a week a thousand miles away. If we are to be accurate we cannot put the case of the State upon higher ground than that the treaty deals with creatures that for the moment are within the state borders, that it must be carried out by officers of the United States within the same territory, and that but for the treaty the State would be free to regulate this subject itself.

As most of the laws of the United States are carried out within the States and as many of them deal with matters which in the silence of such laws the State might regulate, such general grounds are not enough to support Missouri's claim. Valid treaties of course "are as binding within the territorial limits of the States as they are elsewhere throughout the dominion of the United States." Baldwin v. Franks, 120 U.S. 678, 683. No doubt the great body of private relations usually fall within the control of the State, but a treaty may override its power. We do not have to invoke the later developments of constitution law for this proposition; it was recognized as early as Hopkirk v. Bell, 3 Cranch, 454, with regard to statutes of limitation, and even earlier, as to confiscation, in Ware v. Hylton, 3 Dall. 199. It was assumed by Chief Justice Marshall with regard to the escheat of land to the State in Chirac v. Chirac, 2 Wheat. 259, 275. . . . So as to a limited jurisdiction of foreign consuls within a State. Wildenhus's Case, 120 U.S. 1. . . . Further illustration seems unnecessary, and it only remains to consider the application of established rules to the present case.

Here a national interest of very nearly the first magnitude is involved. It can be protected only by national action in concert with that of another power. The subject-matter is only transitorily within the State and has no permanent habitat therein. But for the treaty and the statute there soon might be no birds for any powers to deal with. We see nothing in the Constitution that compels the Government to sit by while a food supply is cut off and the protectors of our forests and our crops are destroyed. It is not sufficient to rely upon the States. The reliance is vain, and were it otherwise, the question is whether the United States is forbidden to act. We are of opinion that the treaty and statute must be upheld.

United States v. Lue

134 F.3d 79 (2d Cir. 1998)

[Defendant and his co-conspirators met in New York City in May 1991 to plan the kidnapping of Chan Fung Chung. In April 1992, they attempted to kidnap Chung in Manhattan, but were thwarted by a firefighter and an off-duty police officer. Defendant was arrested by New York City police officers with a handgun in his possession. Following the arrest, defendant pleaded guilty to (1) violating 18 U.S.C. §1203, the Act for the Prevention and Punishment of the Crime of Hostage-Taking ("Hostage Taking Act"), and (2) carrying a firearm in relation to the hostage taking in violation of 18 U.S.C. §924(c). Pursuant to the plea agreement, defendant sought review of the district court's denial of his motion to dismiss the hostage taking charge, arguing that the Hostage Taking Act exceeded Congress's Article I authority and violated the principles of federalism embodied in the Tenth Amendment.]

WALKER, CIRCUIT JUDGE. . . .

DISCUSSION

A. The Hostage Taking Act . . .

[T]he International Convention Against the Taking of Hostages, Dec. 18, 1979, T.I.A.S. No. 11,081 ("Hostage Taking Convention" or "Convention") . . . binds the signatories to take specific steps to adopt "effective measures for the prevention, prosecution and punishment of all acts of taking of hostages as manifestations of international terrorism." Hostage Taking Convention, preamble, T.I.A.S. No. 11,081. In particular, the signatories agreed that

> any person who seizes or detains and threatens to kill, to injure or to continue to detain another person (hereinafter referred to as the "hostage") in order to compel a third party, namely, a State, an international intergovernmental organization, a natural or juridical person, or a group of persons, to do or abstain from doing any act as an explicit or implicit condition for the release of the hostage commits the offense of taking of hostages . . . within the meaning of this Convention.

Id. art. 1. The signatories also agreed to make hostage taking punishable in accordance with the deep gravity of the offense. *See id.* art. 2. Presumably to accommodate jurisdictional concerns, the terms of the Convention are inapplicable if a covered offense was committed within a single nation, the hostage and the alleged offender are nationals of that nation, and the alleged offender is found within the territory of that nation. *Id.* art. 13.

Pursuant to its obligation under the Convention, in late 1984, Congress passed, and the President signed, the Hostage Taking Act, which provides in pertinent part:

> (a) Except as provided in subsection (b) of this section, whoever, whether inside or outside the United States, seizes or detains and threatens to kill, to injure, or to continue to detain another person in order to compel a third person or a governmental organization to do or abstain from doing any act as an explicit or implicit condition for the release of the person detained, or attempts or conspires to do so, shall be punished by imprisonment for any term of years or for life and, if the death of any person results, shall be punished by death or life imprisonment. . . .
>
> (b)(2) It is not an offense under this section if the conduct required for the offense occurred inside the United States, each alleged offender and each person seized or detained are nationals of the United States, and each alleged offender is found in the United States, unless the governmental organization sought to be compelled is the Government of the United States. 18 U.S.C. §1203. This statute is the focus of defendant's constitutional challenge.

B.   Necessary and Proper Clause...

At the outset we note that Congress's authority under the Necessary and Proper Clause extends beyond those powers specifically enumerated in Article I, section 8. As the clause specifically states, "Congress shall have Power...to make all Laws which shall be necessary and proper for carrying into Execution the foregoing powers, and all other Powers vested by this Constitution in the Government of the United States, or in any Department or Officer thereof." U.S. Const. art. I, §8, cl. 18. Accordingly, Congress may enact laws necessary to effectuate the treaty power, enumerated in Article II of the Constitution. *See* Missouri v. Holland, 252 U.S. 416, 432 (1920).

1.   The Treaty Power

[D]efendant's contention that entry into the Hostage Taking Convention was beyond the Executive's authority under Article II to sign (and Congress to assent to) treaties...rests on the fundamental, but somewhat ambiguous, proposition in Asakura v. City of Seattle that the Executive's treaty power "extends to all proper subjects of negotiation between our government and other nations." 265 U.S. 332, 341 (1924) (citing Missouri v. Holland, 252 U.S. 416 (1920); In re Ross, 140 U.S. 453, 463 (1891); Geofroy v. Riggs, 133 U.S. 258, 266, 267 (1890)). But, defendant argues that the Hostage Taking Convention regulates matters of purely domestic concern not touching on relations with other nations. Accordingly, he concludes that entry into the Convention was beyond the constitutional authority of the executive....

[D]efendant fails to acknowledge the breadth of the *Asakura* Court's statement of the extent of that power. In *Asakura*, the Court held that the executive's treaty power "extends to all *proper subjects* of negotiation between our government and other nations." *Asakura*, 265 U.S. at 341 (citing *Geofroy*, 133 U.S. at 266) (emphasis added). Invoking this standard simply begs the question: What is a "proper subject" of negotiation between governments? Admittedly, there must be certain outer limits, as yet undefined, beyond which the executive's treaty power is constitutionally invalid. *See, e.g.,* Laurence H. Tribe, *Taking Text and Structure Seriously: Reflections on Free-Form Method in Constitutional Interpretation*, 108 Harv. L. Rev. 1221, 1261 n.133 (1995) (noting that the Treaty Power is subject to certain structural limitations and offering as an example of such limitations: "The President and the Senate could not...create a fully operating national health care system in the United States by treaty with Canada...."). But within such generous limits, it is not the province of the judiciary to impinge upon the Executive's prerogative in matters pertaining to foreign affairs.

The defendant relies far too heavily on a dichotomy between matters of purely domestic concern and those of international concern, a dichotomy appropriately criticized by commentators in the field.

> Contrary to what was once suggested, the Constitution does not require that an international agreement deal only with "matters of international concern." The references in the Constitution presumably incorporate the concept of treaty and of other agreements in international law. International law knows no limitations on the purpose or subject matter of international agreements, other than that they may not conflict with a peremptory norm of international law. States may enter into an agreement on any matter of concern to them, and international law does not look behind their motives or purposes in doing so. Thus, the United States may make an agreement on any subject suggested by its national interests in relations with other nations.

Restatement (Third) of the Foreign Relations Law of the United States §302, cmt. c (1986) (citation omitted). The circumstances of *Asakura* exemplify the breadth of the treaty power. The treaty in that case embodied a reciprocal-privileges agreement whereby the then-subjects of Japan would enjoy certain enumerated privileges in the United States which the citizens of the United States would also enjoy in Japan. The privileges entailed such "purely domestic" matters as the ability to "carry on trade, wholesale and retail, to own or lease and occupy houses, manufactories, warehouses and shops" as well as other matters. 265 U.S. at 340. *See also Holland*, 252 U.S. at 431-32 (treaty regulating the killing, capture, or selling of migratory birds); *Geofroy*, 133 U.S. at 266 (treaty addressing rights of inheritance).

Whatever the potential outer limit on the treaty power of the Executive, the Hostage Taking Convention does not transgress it. At the most general level, the Convention addresses — at least in part — the treatment of foreign nationals while they are on local soil, a matter of central concern among nations. More specifically, the Convention addresses a matter of grave concern to the international community: hostage taking as a vehicle for terrorism. In fact, the preamble of the Convention explicitly so states:

> the taking of hostages is an offence of grave concern to the international community and . . . in accordance with the provisions of this Convention, any person committing an act of hostage taking shall either be prosecuted or extradited. . . . [I]t is urgently necessary to develop international cooperation between States in devising and adopting effective measures for the prevention, prosecution and punishment of all acts of taking of hostages as manifestations of international terrorism.

Hostage Taking Convention, preamble, T.I.A.S. No. 11,081. In short, the Hostage Taking Convention is well within the boundaries of the Constitution's treaty power.

2. *The Hostage Taking Act* . . .

If the Hostage Taking Convention is a valid exercise of the Executive's treaty power, there is little room to dispute that the legislation passed to effectuate the treaty is valid under the Necessary and Proper Clause. *See Holland*, 252 U.S. at 432 (noting that, under normal circumstances, "if the treaty is valid there can be no dispute about the validity of [a] statute [passed] under Article I, Section 8, as a necessary and proper means to execute the powers of the Government").

Defendant makes much of language in McCulloch v. Maryland, 17 U.S. (4 Wheat.) 316 (1819), noting that for a statute to pass muster under the Necessary and Proper Clause it must be "plainly adapted" to satisfying a constitutionally permissible end. *Id.* at 421 ("Let the end be legitimate, let it be within the scope of the constitution, and all means which are appropriate, which are plainly adapted to that end, which are not prohibited, but consist with the letter and spirit of the constitution, are constitutional."). In effect, however, the "plainly adapted" standard requires that the effectuating legislation bear a rational relationship to a permissible constitutional end. Were this not the case, any congressional enactment not passed pursuant to an expressly enumerated power would be subject to challenge on some more rigorous means-ends analysis. Such thoroughgoing judicial involvement in the day-to-day enactments of Congress would undercut the foundation on which *McCulloch* rests: the need to preserve a realm of flexibility in which Congress can carry out its delegated responsibilities. *See id.* (reasoning that the "constitution must allow to the national legislature . . . discretion[] with respect to the means by which the powers it confers are to be carried into execution"). The Act here plainly bears a rational relationship to the Convention; indeed, it tracks the language of the Convention in all material respects.

C. Federalism Challenge

[D]efendant [next] contends that because the Hostage Taking Act potentially criminalizes "domestic, non-political abductions," Brief of Defendant-Appellant at 22, and because such abductions "are not in any meaningful way a uniquely international (or national) problem," *id.*, the Act violates the principles of federalism embodied in the Tenth Amendment. We reject this argument.

The Tenth Amendment provides, in full: "The powers not delegated to the United States by the Constitution, nor prohibited by it to the States, are reserved to the States respectively, or to the people." U.S. Const. amend. X. The Constitution expressly vests the power to enter into treaties in the Executive, U.S. Const. art II, §2, cl. 2; accordingly, the power wielded by the Executive (with the advice and consent of the Senate) is "delegated" to the federal government and not "reserved" to the states. As one distinguished commentator has noted:

> Since the Treaty Power was delegated to the federal government, whatever is within its scope is not reserved to the states: the Tenth Amendment is not material. Many matters, then, may appear to be "reserved to the States" as regards domestic legislation if Congress does not have power to regulate them; but they are not reserved to the states so as to exclude their regulation by international agreement.

Louis Henkin, Foreign Affairs and the United States Constitution 191 (2d ed. 1996). Thus, the treaty power is not subject to meaningful limitation under the terms of the Tenth Amendment.

Missouri v. Holland, 252 U.S. 416 (1920), on which defendant relies heavily, is not to the contrary. In *Holland*, the State of Missouri argued that the Migratory Bird Treaty Act of 1918, regulating the killing, capturing, or selling of certain migratory birds, pursuant to a treaty entered into between the United States and Great Britain (on behalf of Canada), was an unconstitutional interference with the rights reserved to the states by the Tenth Amendment. *See* 252 U.S. at 430-32. In that case, prior to the United States' entry into the treaty with Great Britain (and, thus, prior to the passage of the Migratory Bird Treaty Act), Congress—acting on its own—had attempted in an earlier act to regulate similar conduct and two federal courts had ruled that the act was beyond Congress's authority under the Tenth Amendment. *See id.* at 432. On this basis, Missouri argued, as summarized by Justice Holmes in his opinion for the Court, "what an act of Congress could not do unaided, in derogation of the powers reserved to the States, a treaty cannot do." *Id.* The Court rejected this argument:

> It is obvious that there may be matters of the sharpest exigency for the national well being that an act of Congress could not deal with but that a treaty followed by such an act could, and it is not lightly to be assumed that, in matters requiring national action, "a power which must belong to and somewhere reside in every civilized government" is not to be found.

Id. at 433 (quoting Andrews v. Andrews, 188 U.S. 14, 33 (1903)). The Court, finding an important national interest at stake, held that no "invisible radiation from the general terms of the Tenth Amendment" would require invalidation of the Act. The same is true in this case.

Defendant's primary Tenth Amendment challenge to the Hostage Taking Act rests on his contention that hostage taking is a local concern and that, under *Holland*, a legislative enactment effectuating a treaty will not pass muster under the Tenth Amendment unless such an enactment addresses a uniquely national or international matter. Such a reading finds some support in the language of the Court's opinion. *See, e.g., id.* at 434. However, we need not decide the question, because in this case there is a sufficient national (indeed, international) interest supporting Congress's passage of the Hostage Taking Act.

Notes and Questions

1. One important difference between treaties and federal statutes is that treaties bind the United States to international obligations. In that sense, treaties (and executive agreements, see Section G) can accomplish something that cannot be accomplished by legislation. Nevertheless, prior to *Holland*, the Supreme Court had never expressly held that the federal government has broader power to make changes to U.S. laws and entitlements through the use of treaties than it has through the enactment of federal statutes. There were a number of treaties before *Holland*, however, that arguably did exceed the scope of Congress's legislative powers. One notable example is the 1803 treaty between the United States and France for the Louisiana Purchase. In addition to providing for the acquisition by the United States of a vast amount of new territory, the treaty provided that the territory would be "incorporated into the Union of the United States." President Jefferson had doubts that the treaty was constitutional, explaining to a senator that, "The Constitution has made no provision for our holding foreign territory, still less for incorporating foreign nations into our Union." Although Jefferson initially suggested that a constitutional amendment be passed to give the federal government this power, he changed his mind and urged ratification and implementation of the treaty in the absence of such an amendment. *See* David P. Currie, The Constitution in Congress: The Jeffersonians, 1801-1829, at 95-107 (2001). Despite Jefferson's constitutional doubts, is a power to acquire territory implied from Congress's power in Article IV, §3, cl. 2, to "dispose of and make all needful Rules and Regulations respecting the Territory or other Property belonging to the United States," which we looked at in Edwards v. Carter (excerpted in Section C)? And is a power to admit such acquired territory into the Union implied from the statement in Article IV, §3, cl. 1, that "New States may be admitted by the Congress into this Union"? For an argument that Jefferson's constitutional concerns about the Louisiana Purchase were valid, and that the incorporation of the Louisiana Territory into the federal union exceeded the federal government's treaty power, see Robert Knowles, *The Balance of Forces and the Empire of Liberty: States' Rights and the Louisiana Purchase*, 88 Iowa L. Rev. 343 (2003).

2. Even before *Holland*, the Supreme Court had never invalidated a treaty on federalism grounds. Moreover, the Court often referred to the treaty power in broad and general terms. The Court nevertheless suggested at times that the treaty power was limited by the United States' federal structure. *See, e.g.,* Holmes v. Jennison, 39 U.S. (14 Pet.) 540, 569 (1840) (stating that the exercise of the treaty power must be "consistent with . . . the distribution of powers between the general and state governments"); New Orleans v. United States, 35 U.S. (10 Pet.) 662, 736

(1836) (noting that the federal government is "one of limited powers" and that its authority cannot be "enlarged under the treaty-making power"). U.S. officials also sometimes expressed this view. An 1831 Attorney General opinion, for example, stated that the federal government was "under a constitutional obligation to respect [the reserved powers of the states] in the formation of treaties." 2 Op. Att'y Gen. 437 (1831). In addition, in a number of instances in the late nineteenth and early twentieth centuries, U.S. officials declined to enter into negotiations concerning private international law treaties because of a purported concern that the treaties would infringe on the reserved powers of the states. *See* Kurt H. Nadelmann, *Ignored State Interests: The Federal Government and International Efforts to Unify Rules of Private Law,* 102 U. Pa. L. 323 (1923). Similarly, U.S. representatives insisted a few years before *Holland* that they could not agree to a treaty regulating certain labor conditions because those matters were within the reserved powers of the states. *See* James T. Shotwell, Historical Significance of the International Labour Conference, in Labour as an International Problem 41 (E. John Salano ed., 1920). These states' rights concerns continued to inhibit U.S. participation in private international law, labor, and other treaty regimes even after *Holland*. *See* Pittman B. Potter, *Inhibitions on the Treaty-Making Power of the United States,* 29 Am. J. Int'l L. 456 (1934).

3. In recent years, the Supreme Court has imposed a number of federalism restraints on Congress's domestic lawmaking powers. In particular, it has imposed limits on the scope of Congress's powers under the Commerce Clause and Fourteenth Amendment, *see, e.g.,* United States v. Morrison, 529 U.S. 598 (2000); City of Boerne v. Flores, 521 U.S. 507 (1997); United States v. Lopez, 514 U.S. 549 (1995); prohibited Congress from "commandeering" state legislatures and executive officials, *see, e.g.,* Printz v. United States, 521 U.S. 898 (1997); New York v. United States, 505 U.S. 144 (1992); and limited the ability of Congress to override the immunity of states from private lawsuits, *see, e.g.,* Alden v. Maine, 527 U.S. 706 (1999); Seminole Tribe of Florida v. Florida, 517 U.S. 44 (1996). To what extent should these limitations apply to the treaty power? For example, in *City of Boerne,* the Supreme Court held that the Religious Freedom Restoration Act exceeded Congress's powers under the Fourteenth Amendment. Could Congress validly enact this statute as an implementation of the religious freedom provision in the International Covenant on Civil and Political Rights, a treaty ratified by the United States in 1992? For an argument that it could, see Gerald L. Neuman, *The Global Dimension of RFRA,* 14 Const. Commentary 33 (1997).

4. The Tenth Amendment provides that "[t]he powers not delegated to the United States by the Constitution, nor prohibited to it by the States, are reserved to the States respectively, or to the people." Article II of the Constitution clearly delegates the power to enter into treaties to the national government, and in Article I, Section 10 it expressly prohibits states from entering into treaties. Does this make the Tenth Amendment irrelevant to the treaty power? Consider this argument from Professor Louis Henkin: "Since the Treaty Power was delegated to the federal government, whatever is within its scope is not reserved to the states: the Tenth Amendment is not material." Louis Henkin, Foreign Affairs and the United States Constitution 191 (2d ed. 1996). By contrast, consider the following argument in an article published in 1909:

> This argument indeed proves that the states did not reserve the power to make treaties and hence have no such power even in the exercise of their reserved powers. But it fails

to prove that the federal government in the exercise of its undoubted treaty-making power is not limited by those restrictions which the first ten amendments have placed on the power of the federal government. It proves that the federal power to make treaties is exclusive, but it does not prove that it is unlimited, or that [it] is not limited by the tenth amendment.

William E. Mikell, *The Extent of the Treaty-Making Power of the President and Senate of the United States* (pt. 2), 57 U. Pa. L. Rev. 528, 539-40 (1909). Which view is more persuasive?

5. The Supreme Court sometimes uses the "Tenth Amendment" as a shorthand phrase for "any implied constitutional limitations on [the national government's] authority to regulate state activities, whether grounded in the Tenth Amendment itself or in principles of federalism derived generally from the Constitution." South Carolina v. Baker, 485 U.S. 505, 511 n.5 (1988). Does *Holland* address the relationship between that broader "Tenth Amendment" and the treaty power? For example, does *Holland* immunize the treaty power from anti-commandeering restrictions? State sovereign immunity limitations? Compare, for example, Martin Flaherty, *Are We to Be a Nation? Federal Power vs. "States' Rights" in Foreign Affairs*, 70 U. Colo. L. Rev. 1277, 1279 (1999) (arguing that the anti-commandeering restrictions do not limit the treaty power), with Louis Henkin, Foreign Affairs and the United States Constitution 467 (2d ed. 1996) (assuming that the restrictions do limit the treaty power). Note that the Supreme Court has indicated, albeit in a brief per curiam decision, that the treaty power is subject to state sovereign immunity limitations. *See* Breard v. Greene, 523 U.S. 371, 376-77 (1998), which we discussed above in connection with the last-in-time rule. *See also* Carlos Manuel Vazquez, *Treaties and the Eleventh Amendment*, 42 Va. J. Int'l L. 713 (2002) (concluding that the treaty power is subject to state sovereign immunity limitations).

6. The central holding of *Holland* is that the treaty power can be used to regulate matters beyond the scope of Congress's legislative powers. As a textual matter, this conclusion might seem obvious: Congress's legislative powers are referred to in Article I, whereas the treaty power is referred to in Article II. This structure might suggest that the limitations in Article I apply only to Congress's enactments, not treaties. On the other hand, as we saw above in the separation of powers materials, some provisions of Article I are thought to limit the treaty power — for example, the requirement in Article I, Section 9 that an appropriations statute be passed in order to draw money from the treasury, and the requirement in Article I, Section 7 that all revenue bills originate in the House of Representatives. Furthermore, it is now settled that the treaty power is limited by the First Amendment, yet that Amendment refers only to Congress, not the treaty-makers ("Congress shall make no law..."). Although the First Amendment has been held to apply to the *states* by virtue of the Fourteenth Amendment Due Process Clause, there is no equivalent textual basis for applying the First Amendment to the federal treaty-makers. Nevertheless, as discussed below in Note 10, the Supreme Court has made clear that the federal government may not use the treaty power to subvert the First Amendment and other individual rights protections. Can it similarly be argued that the federal treaty-makers should be disallowed from subverting the general federalism structure of the Constitution? By way of comparison, the Supreme Court held in Erie Railroad Co. v. Tompkins, 304 U.S. 64, 78 (1938), that the federal courts (which are governed by Article III, not Article I) could not have more lawmaking power than Congress because this would be inconsistent with the United States' federal structure. Is this structural argument persuasive?

7. One common argument for not imposing judicially enforced federalism limitations in the domestic arena is that there are sufficient political safeguards to protect federalism. This argument was first developed by Professor Herbert Wechsler in the 1950s and then further developed by Professor Jesse Choper in the 1970s. *See* Herbert Wechsler, *The Political Safeguards of Federalism: The Role of the States in the Composition and Selection of the National Government,* 54 Colum. L. Rev. 543 (1954); Jesse H. Choper, *The Scope of the National Power vis-à-vis the States: The Dispensability of Judicial Review,* 86 Yale L.J. 1552 (1977). The Supreme Court relied heavily on this political safeguards theory in its 1985 *Garcia* decision, in which a 5-4 majority of the Court largely abandoned judicial enforcement of the Tenth Amendment. *See* Garcia v. San Antonio Metro. Transit Auth., 469 U.S. 528 (1985). In recent years, the Supreme Court has arguably backed away from *Garcia,* although the decision has not yet been overruled. *See* John C. Yoo, *The Judicial Safeguards of Federalism,* 70 S. Cal. L. Rev. 1311 (1997).

The political safeguards theory was developed with domestic legislation in mind. How well does the theory apply in the context of the treaty power? On the one hand, it would seem that there are more federalism safeguards in the treaty process than in the domestic legislative process, because a treaty requires the approval of two-thirds of the Senate. Moreover, the Senate often has acted to protect state interests in the treaty process — for example, by attaching "federalism understandings" to its consent to human rights treaties. On the other hand, the treaty negotiation process is dominated by the President, who may not be particularly sensitive to state (as opposed to majoritarian) interests. The treaty process is also more opaque than the domestic legislative process, which might make it less open to state influence and input. Perhaps more important, most international agreements concluded by the United States in recent years have been in the form of congressional-executive agreements rather than Article II treaties and thus have not been subject to the two-thirds senatorial consent requirement. Many commentators (and the Restatement (Third) of Foreign Relations Law) have asserted that congressional-executive agreements are *completely interchangeable* with Article II treaties. We discuss these agreements below in Section G.

8. The Second Optional Protocol to the International Covenant on Civil and Political Rights, which has been ratified by over 40 countries but not by the United States, prohibits the use of the death penalty. Could the President and Senate validly ratify this treaty and thereby preempt U.S. states from utilizing the death penalty? In answering this question, does it matter whether Congress has the constitutional power to abolish the death penalty in the absence of a treaty?

9. The least controversial holding of *Holland* has been the proposition that, if a treaty is constitutionally valid, Congress can use its authority under the Necessary and Proper Clause to enact legislation to implement the treaty, even if Congress would lack the authority to enact such legislation in the absence of the treaty. The court in *Lue* treated this proposition as settled. Professor Rosenkranz, however, has recently challenged this proposition. *See* Nicholas Quinn Rosenkranz, *Executing the Treaty Power,* 118 Harv. L. Rev. 1867 (2005), He points out that the Necessary and Proper Clause gives Congress the authority to make laws necessary and proper for carrying into execution "Powers" vested in other parts of the government, and he argues that, when applied to the "Power . . . to make Treaties" in Article II, it gives Congress only the authority to enact legislation to facilitate the *making* of treaties, not legislation to implement particular treaties. Consequently, he contends that, when a treaty is not self-executing, Congress can enact legislation to implement the treaty only if the legislation falls within its independent legislative powers. However, Professor Rosenkranz accepts the principal holding of *Holland* — i.e., that the treaty power is not itself limited to the scope of Congress's legislative powers — and thus under his analysis a self-executing treaty could create domestic law that exceeded Congress's legislative powers. Are you persuaded by his construction of the Necessary and Proper Clause? Does his distinction between self-executing and non-self-executing treaties make sense? If the U.S. treatymakers have the authority to change domestic law directly through a self-executing treaty, why is it constitutionally problematic for them to make the treaty non-self-executing and leave the details of implementation to Congress?

10. Are there constitutional limits on the subject matters that can be regulated by treaties? Article II of the Constitution states that the President and Senate have the power to make treaties, but it does not define the word "treaty." Can a treaty regulate "internal" or "domestic" matters? In order to be valid under U.S. law, must a treaty obligation be reciprocal? Must it be of mutual concern to the parties to the treaty?

When discussing treaties, the Founders appeared to have had in mind particular treaty subjects such as "war, peace, and commerce." Federalist No. 64 (Jay). This does not necessarily mean, however, that the Founders intended to preclude treaty-making on other subjects. Indeed, their decision not to specify subject matter limitations on the treaty power might have reflected a desire to preserve flexibility for the treaty-makers. Given the lack of any express constitutional limitations on the treaty power, how should a court go about determining the scope of that power?

In a number of nineteenth and early twentieth century decisions, the Supreme Court described the treaty power in broad, but not unlimited, terms. Probably its most widely quoted description of the scope of the treaty power is the following:

> The treaty power, as expressed in the Constitution, is in terms unlimited except by those restraints which are found in that instrument against the action of the government or of its departments, and those arising from the nature of the government itself and of that of the States. It would not be contended that it extends so far as to authorize what the Constitution forbids, or a change in the character of the government or in that of one of the States, or a cession of any portion of the territory of the latter, without its consent.... But with these exceptions, it is not perceived that there is any limit to the questions which can be adjusted touching any matter which is properly the subject of negotiation with a foreign country.

Geofroy v. Riggs, 133 U.S. 258, 267 (1890). For similarly broad descriptions, see, for example, Santovincenzo v. Egan, 284 U.S. 30, 40 (1931) ("The treaty-making power is broad enough to cover all subjects that properly pertain to our foreign relations...."); Asakura v. City of Seattle, 265 U.S. 332, 341 (1924) ("The treaty-making power ... extends to all proper subjects of negotiation with foreign governments."). Interestingly, *Santovincenzo* was authored by Chief Justice Hughes, who two years earlier had suggested in a speech to the American Society of International Law that the treaty power might be limited to "matters of international concern." *See* 1929 Proc. Am. Soc. Int'l L. 194. What treaties, if any, would be precluded by the language in *Geofroy* or *Santovincenzo*? By Hughes' suggested "matters of international concern" test?

The Restatement (Second) of Foreign Relations Law, published in 1965, states that the United States has the constitutional power to enter into international agreements as long as "the matter is of international concern." Restatement

(Second) of the Foreign Relations Law of the United States §117(1)(a) (1965). The comments to this provision explain that an international agreement of the United States "must relate to the external concerns of the nation as distinguished from matters of a purely internal nature." *Id.*, cmt. b. The Restatement (Third), published in 1987, rejects the Restatement (Second)'s subject matter limitation. The Restatement (Third) states that, "[c]ontrary to what was once suggested, the Constitution does not require that an international agreement deal only with 'matters of international concern.' . . . The United States may make an agreement on any subject suggested by its national interests in relations with other nations." Restatement (Third) of the Foreign Relations Law of the United States §302, cmt. c (1987). Why do you think the Restatement changed its position?

11. In *Lue*, note the interrelationship between (a) the subject matter scope of the treaty power, (b) the Necessary and Proper Clause, and (c) potential federalism limits on the treaty power. Does the court articulate a clear test for subject matter limits on the treaty power? With respect to the Necessary and Proper Clause, do you agree with the court that the Act "plainly bears a rational relationship to the Convention" and "tracks the language of the Convention in all material respects"? Does the court's federalism analysis depart at all from *Holland*? For a decision similar to *Lue*, see United States v. Ferreira, 275 F.3d 1020 (11th Cir. 2001).

12. In the 1950s, there were a number of proposals to amend the Constitution to limit the treaty power. One of the key supporters of these proposed amendments was Senator John Bricker of Ohio, and the proposals are often referred to collectively as the "Bricker Amendment." In general, the proposed amendments were intended to preclude treaties from being self-executing and to make clear that treaties could not override the reserved powers of the states. Some versions also would have restricted the use of executive agreements. One of the proposed amendments fell only one vote short of obtaining the necessary two-thirds vote in the Senate. As part of its efforts to defeat the Bricker Amendment, the Eisenhower Administration promised the Senate that it would not enter into any of the human rights treaties being developed at that time and would not attempt to use the treaty power to regulate domestic matters. For additional discussion of the Bricker Amendment controversy, see Duane Tananbaum, The Bricker Amendment Controversy: A Test of Eisenhower's Political Leadership (1988). What, if anything, does the Bricker Amendment controversy suggest about the scope of the treaty power?

13. Starting in the 1980s, the United States began ratifying some of the human rights treaties. As discussed in the next section, the United States has consistently attached a series of reservations, understandings, and declarations ("RUDs") limiting or clarifying the U.S. obligations under the treaties. These RUDs typically include a declaration that the substantive terms of the treaty will not be considered self-executing (and thus will not preempt inconsistent state law) and an understanding that the treaty "shall be implemented by the Federal Government to the extent that it exercises legislative and judicial jurisdiction over the matters covered therein, and otherwise by the state and local governments." In reading the materials in the next section, consider what, if anything, these RUDs suggest about the scope of the treaty power.

14. The United States and other federal nations such as Canada have sometimes negotiated to have "federal" clauses included in treaties. These clauses typically limit the obligations of the federal nation to matters within its national legislative jurisdiction, and call upon it merely to recommend adoption of these obligations by its constituent states. Article 11 of the U.N. Convention on the

Recognition and Enforcement of Foreign Arbitral Awards, for example, provides in relevant part:

> In the case of a federal or non-unitary State, the following provisions shall apply:
>
>> (a) With respect to those articles of this Convention that come within the legislative jurisdiction of the federal authority, the obligations of the federal Government shall to this extent be the same as those of Contracting States which are not federal States;
>> (b) With respect to those articles of this Convention that come within the legislative jurisdiction of constituent states or provinces which are not, under the constitutional system of the federation, bound to take legislative action, the federal Government shall bring such articles with a favourable recommendation to the notice of the appropriate authorities of constituent states or provinces at the earliest possible moment....

Similarly, Article 28 of the American Convention on Human Rights (which the United States has signed but not ratified), provides in relevant part:

> 1. Where a State Party is constituted as a federal state, the national government of such State Party shall implement all the provisions of the Convention over whose subject matter it exercises legislative and judicial jurisdiction.
> 2. With respect to the provisions over whose subject matter the constituent units of the federal state have jurisdiction, the national government shall immediately take suitable measures, in accordance with its constitution and its laws, to the end that the competent authorities of the constituent units may adopt appropriate provisions for the fulfillment of this Convention.

What, if anything, do these clauses suggest about the relationship between the treaty power and American federalism?

15. A proposed optional protocol to the Convention Against Torture and Other Cruel, Inhuman and Degrading Treatment or Punishment would create an international inspection system for places of detention. If approved by the United States, the protocol would, among other things, allow international monitors to inspect state prisons. In explaining a decision by the United States to abstain from voting on the protocol, a U.S. representative stated that the "overall approach and certain specific provisions [of the draft protocol] are contrary to our Constitution, particularly with respect to matters of search and seizure," and that, "in view of our Federal system of government, the regime established by the draft would be overly intrusive." John Davison, Deputy U.S. Representative on the United Nations Economic and Social Council, Explanation of Vote (July 24, 2002), available at http://www.state.gov/p/io/rls/rm/2002/12200.htm. What weight should be given to statements like this one when interpreting the treaty power?

16. Consider the federalism argument that the U.S. government made before the International Court of Justice in the *LaGrand Case* discussed above in the notes in Section B (involving a violation by the state of Arizona of the Vienna Convention on Consular Relations). The government explained that, under the U.S. constitutional system, states "remain sovereign and the masters of their affairs within the areas of their responsibility reserved to them by the U.S. Constitution," and that "[o]ne of the most important functions reserved to the states is criminal law enforcement." As a result of the U.S. federal system, the government contended, "Federal Government officials do not have legal power to stop peremptorily the enforcement of a criminal sentence by the state of Arizona." Is this contention constitutionally correct? In any event, why would the federal government, which normally favors national control over foreign relations, make these statements? *See also* Note, *Too Sovereign But Not Sovereign Enough: Are U.S. States Beyond the Reach of the Law of Nations?*, 116 Harv. L. Rev. 2654, 2677 (2003) (arguing that the federal government has "ample means" to ensure state compliance with the Vienna Convention).

17. What does *Holland* suggest about the relationship between the treaty power and individual rights? Some commentators feared that the analysis in *Holland* would allow the treaty-makers the power to override the individual rights protections in the Bill of Rights. *See, e.g.,* Thomas Reed Powell, *Constitutional Law in 1919-20,* 19 Mich. L. Rev. 1, 13 (1920) (noting that the Court's "hint that there may be no other test to be applied than whether the treaty has been duly concluded indicates that the Court might hold that specific constitutional limitations in favor of individual liberty and property are not applicable to deprivations wrought by treaties"). Was that a fair concern? The Supreme Court largely dispelled this concern in Reid v. Covert, 354 U.S. 1 (1957), in which it held that Fifth Amendment guarantees to a grand jury indictment and trial by jury applied to trials conducted overseas pursuant to an executive agreement. A plurality of the Court distinguished *Holland* as follows:

> There is nothing in Missouri v. Holland, 252 U.S. 416, which is contrary to the position taken here. There the Court carefully noted that the treaty involved was not inconsistent with any specific provision of the Constitution. The Court was concerned with the Tenth Amendment which reserves to the States or the people all power not delegated to the National Government. To the extent that the United States can validly make treaties, the people and the States have delegated their power to the National Government and the Tenth Amendment is no barrier.

Id. at 18. Is that a valid distinction? In Boos v. Barry, 485 U.S. 312 (1988), the Court confirmed that the treaty power is subject to individual rights limitations. There, the Court held that legislation prohibiting the display of any sign within 500 feet of a foreign embassy if that sign tends to bring that foreign government into "public odium" or "public disrepute" violated the First Amendment, notwithstanding the fact that the legislation implemented a treaty.

18. In a recent Indian law decision, *United States v. Lara,* 541 U.S. 193 (2004), the Supreme Court referred favorably to *Missouri v. Holland,* stating:

> The treaty power does not literally authorize Congress to act legislatively, for it is an Article II power authorizing the President, not Congress, "to make Treaties." U.S. Const., Art. II, §2, cl. 2. But, as Justice Holmes pointed out, treaties made pursuant to that power can authorize Congress to deal with "matters" with which "otherwise Congress could not deal." Missouri v. Holland, 252 U.S. 416, 433 (1920); *see also* L. Henkin, Foreign Affairs and the U.S. Constitution 72 (2d ed. 1996).

19. For additional discussion of whether the treaty power should be subject to federalism limitations, compare Curtis A. Bradley, *The Treaty Power and American Federalism,* 97 Mich. L. Rev. 390 (1998) (arguing that it should), and Curtis A. Bradley, *The Treaty Power and American Federalism, Part II,* 99 Mich. L. Rev. 98 (2000) (same), with David M. Golove, *Treaty-Making and the Nation: The Historical Foundations of the Nationalist Conception of the Treaty Power,* 98 Mich. L. Rev. 1075 (2000) (arguing against federalism limitations). *See also* Robert Anderson IV, *"Ascertained in a Different Way": The Treaty Power at the Crossroads of Contract, Compact, and Constitution,* 69 Geo. Wash. L. Rev. 189 (2001); Audrey I. Benison, *International Criminal Tribunals: Is There a Substantive Limitation on the Treaty Power?,* 37 Stan. J. Int'l L. 75 (2001); Edward T. Swaine, *Does Federalism Constrain the Treaty Power?,*

103 Colum. L. Rev. 403 (2003); Janet R. Carter, Note, *Commandeering Under the Treaty Power*, 76 N.Y.U. L. Rev. 598 (2001); Note, *Restructuring the Modern Treaty Power*, 114 Harv. L. Rev. 2478 (2001). For additional discussion of the historical background and context of *Holland*, see Charles A. Lofgren, *Missouri v. Holland in Historical Perspective*, 1975 Sup. Ct. Rev. 77.

E. CONDITIONAL CONSENT

The U.S. treaty-makers sometimes condition their consent to a treaty by attaching reservations, understandings, and declarations — collectively known as "RUDs" — to the U.S. ratification of the treaty. The precise meaning of these terms is often elusive, but subject to the qualifications in the materials below, the following definitions are generally accurate: Reservations are acts of non-consent to particular treaty terms; they are "specific qualifications or stipulations that modify U.S. obligations without necessarily changing treaty language." Congressional Research Service, Treaties and Other International Agreements: The Role of the United States Senate, S. Prt. 106-71, 106th Cong., 2d Sess. 39, at 125 (2001) ("CRS Study"). Understandings are "interpretive statements that clarify or elaborate, rather than change, the provisions of an agreement and that are deemed to be consistent with the obligations imposed by the agreement." *Id.* Declarations are "statements of purpose, policy, or position related to matters raised by the treaty in question but not altering or limiting any of its provisions." *Id.* at 126. Sometimes the President proposes RUDs to a treaty when he submits the treaty to the Senate for its advice and consent. At other times the Senate unilaterally imposes RUDs, "granting its advice and consent only subject to certain stipulations that the President must accept before proceeding to ratification." *Id.* at 124.

Power Authority of New York v. Federal Power Commission

247 F.2d 538 (D.C. Cir. 1957)

[Petitioner, an agency of the State of New York, applied to the Federal Power Commission for a license to construct a power project utilizing all of the Niagara River water which, under a 1950 treaty between the United States and Canada, was available for American exploitation. In consenting to the treaty, the Senate had attached the following, which it called a "reservation":

> The United States on its part expressly reserves the right to provide by Act of Congress for redevelopment, for the public use and benefit, of the United States' share of the waters of the Niagara River made available by the provisions of the Treaty, and no project for redevelopment of the United States' share of such waters shall be undertaken until it be specifically authorized by Act of Congress.

The Commission dismissed petitioner's application on the ground that it lacked authority to issue the license. It reasoned that "[s]ince the reservation here was intended by the Senate as part of the treaty and was intended to prevent our jurisdiction attaching to the water made available by the treaty, it is entirely authoritative with us as the Supreme Law of the Land under Article VI of the Constitution." Petitioner then brought this review proceeding.]

BAZELON, CIRCUIT JUDGE....

The parties agree that, if the reservation to the 1950 treaty is not "Law of the Land," the order should be set aside. Since the reservation did not have the concurrence of the House of Representatives, it is not "Law of the Land" by way of legislation. The question is whether it became "Law of the Land" as part of the treaty.

The Commission argues that the reservation is an effective part of the treaty because: (1) it was a condition of the Senate's consent to the ratification of the Treaty; (2) the condition was sanctioned by the President, was "accepted" by Canada, and was included in the exchange of ratifications; and (3) it "thus became a part of the Treaty." Simple as this argument seems, we cannot agree with it.

The treaty was signed on behalf of the United States and Canada on February 27, 1950. It defined the quantity of Niagara River water which was to be available for power purposes and provided that it "shall be divided equally between the United States of America and Canada." How each party was to exploit its share of the water was left for that party to decide. In transmitting the treaty to the Senate on May 2, 1950, the President pointed out that the treaty did not determine how the United States was to exploit its share of the water....

The Foreign Relations Committee of the Senate agreed that the question was "domestic in nature" and "concerns the United States constitutional process alone." It recommended the reservation because, without it, "the redevelopment for power purposes would be governed by the Federal Power Act. The Committee intends by the reservation to retain that power in the hands of Congress." The Senate accepted the Committee's recommendation and consented to the ratification of the treaty with the reservation on August 9, 1950.

Meanwhile, the Canadian Parliament had approved the treaty as signed, without the reservation.... [W]ithout waiting for Canadian reaction to the reservation, the President ratified the treaty subject to the reservation. On September 21, 1951, the Canadian Ambassador...advised that his government accepted the reservation and would indicate its acceptance "by a statement to be included in the Protocol of exchange of ratifications." Two weeks later, without resubmitting the treaty to Parliament for approval of the reservation, the Canadian Government ratified the treaty. In the Protocol, on October 10, 1950, Canada inserted the following statement: "Canada accepts the above-mentioned reservation because its provisions relate only to the internal application of the Treaty within the United States and do not affect Canada's rights or obligations under the Treaty." ...

Unquestionably the Senate may condition its consent to a treaty upon a variation of its terms. The effect of such a "consent," by analogy to contract law, is to reject the offered treaty and to propose the variation as a counter-offer which will become a binding agreement only if accepted by the other party. But, if what the Senate seeks to add was implicit in the original offer, the purported "conditional acceptance" is an acceptance and the contract arises without a further acceptance by the other party being required. The disposition of the United States share of the water covered by this treaty was, even apart from the reservation, something "which we in the United States must settle under our own procedures and laws." The reservation, therefore, made no change in the treaty. It was merely an expression of domestic policy which the Senate attached to its consent. It was not a counter-offer requiring Canadian acceptance before the treaty could become effective. That Canada did "accept" the reservation does not change its character. The Canadian acceptance, moreover, was not so much an acceptance as a disclaimer of interest. It is of some significance in this regard that the Canadian Government, although it had submitted the original treaty to the Parliament for its approval, found it unnecessary to resubmit the treaty to Parliament after the reservation was inserted. Also significant is the fact that the President ratified the treaty with the reservation without even waiting for Canada to "accept."

A true reservation which becomes a part of a treaty is one which alters "the effect of the treaty in so far as it may apply in the relations of (the) State with the other State or States which may be parties to the treaty." Report of the Harvard Research in International Law 29 Am. J. Int'l L. Supp. 843, 857 (1935). It creates "a different relationship between" the parties and varies "the obligations of the party proposing it...." 2 Hyde, International Law, Chiefly As Interpreted and Applied by the United States (2d revised ed. 1945) 1435. The purported reservation to the 1950 treaty makes no change in the relationship between the United States and Canada under the treaty and has nothing at all to do with the rights or obligations of either party.... The Senate could, of course, have attached to its consent a reservation to the effect that the rights and obligations of the signatory parties should not arise until the passage of an act of Congress. Such a reservation, if accepted by Canada, would have made the treaty executory. But the Senate did not seek to make the treaty executory. By the terms of its consent, the rights and obligations of both countries arose at once on the effective date of the treaty. All that the Senate sought to make executory was the purely municipal matter of how the American share of the water was to be exploited.

A party to a treaty may presumably attach to it a matter of purely municipal application, neither affecting nor intended to affect the other party. But such matter does not become part of the treaty....

The constitutionality of the reservation as a treaty provision was extensively argued by the parties. The respondent merely suggests that "there is no apparent limit" to what may be done under the treaty power, citing State of Missouri v. Holland, 1920, 252 U.S. 416....

In State of Missouri v. Holland, 252 U.S. at page 433, Mr. Justice Holmes questioned, but did not decide, whether there was any constitutional limitation on the treaty-making power other than the formal requirements prescribed for the making of treaties. The treaty he sustained related to a "national interest of very nearly the first magnitude" which "can be protected only by national action in concert with that of another power." And it conferred rights and imposed obligations upon both signatories. The treaty power's relative freedom from constitutional restraint, so far as it attaches to "any matter which is properly the subject of negotiation with a foreign country," Ware v. Hylton, 1796, 3 Dall. 199, is a long-established fact. No court has ever said, however, that the treaty power can be exercised without limit to affect matters which are of purely domestic concern and do not pertain to our relations with other nations.

Our present Secretary of State [Dulles] has said that the treaty power may be exercised with respect to a matter which "reasonably and directly affects other nations in such a way that it is properly a subject for treaties which become contracts between nations as to how they should act"; and not with respect to matters "which do not essentially affect the actions of nations in relation to international affairs, but are purely internal." He had earlier said:

> I do not believe that treaties should, or lawfully can, be used as a device to circumvent the constitutional procedures established in relation to what are essentially matters of domestic concern.

Charles Evans Hughes, just before he became Chief Justice and after he had been Secretary of State, addressing himself to the question whether there is any constitutional limitation of the treaty power, said:

> ...The power is to deal with foreign nations with regard to matters of international concern. It is not a power intended to be exercised, it may be assumed, with respect to matters that have no relation to international concerns.... The nation has the power to make any agreement whatever in a constitutional manner that relates to the conduct of our international relations, unless there can be found some express prohibition in the Constitution, and I am not aware of any which would in any way detract from the power as I have defined it in connection with our relations with other governments. But if we attempted to use the treaty-making power to deal with matters which did not pertain to our external relations but to control matters which normally and appropriately were within the local jurisdiction of the States, then I again say there might be ground for implying a limitation upon the treaty-making power that it is intended for the purpose of having treaties made relating to foreign affairs and not to make laws for the people of the United States in their internal concerns through the exercise of the asserted treaty-making power.

In the Dulles view this reservation, if part of the treaty, would be an invalid exercise of the treaty power. In the Hughes view, its constitutionality would be a matter of grave doubt. "The path of constitutional concern in this situation is clear." United States v. Witkovich, 1957, 353 U.S. 194. We construe the reservation as an expression of the Senate's desires and not a part of the treaty. We do not decide the constitutional question....

BASTIAN, CIRCUIT JUDGE (dissenting)....

I must disagree with the implication in the majority opinion that this reservation, if a part of the treaty, would be invalid.... We are told that the reservation is void because it is regarded as of "purely domestic concern" and therefore not a valid subject matter for a treaty reservation. It is elementary law that treaties may and frequently do affect domestic concerns. Indeed, treaties may repeal previous municipal law passed by the Congress or by state legislatures. Therefore, if this reservation is void, it is not because it affects domestic law to the extent that it requires that the Federal Power Act not apply to the additional water power made available by the treaty.

If void, it must be because the reservation is not only of domestic concern, but is also remote from the valid subject matter of the treaty, and is not inspired by consideration of or pertinent to international relations or policy. While it is true that the President and officials of the Department of State have referred to the question of how the water power made available by the treaty was to be exploited as a matter of domestic concern, certainly that question is not remote from but is germane to the subject matter of the treaty. At the time the treaty was submitted to the Senate for ratification, the question of how and by whom water-power resources of the Niagara River would be exploited was a controversial issue in the Congress. With this controversy in mind, the Senate Foreign Relations Committee, in its report on the treaty, pointed out that extensive public hearings on implementing legislation would probably be necessary. The Committee recognized that it would take considerable time to complete such hearings and to obtain final Congressional action on the pending legislation. Yet the Committee and the Senate as a whole were reluctant to jeopardize the rights which this country would receive under the proposed treaty by delaying its ratification until after Congress had acted upon the pending legislation concerning Niagara River power development....

Because of the possibility that the Canadians might in the absence of the treaty be compelled to take some unilateral action in harnessing the Niagara power, because undue delay might prejudice our good relations with Canada, and in view of an asserted acute power shortage in Canada requiring speedy ratification, this reservation was intimately and inseparably bound up in international questions. In this context it is not purely a domestic concern. If the subject matter of the reservation is domestic in nature, it was nonetheless inspired by, an outgrowth of, and inextricably connected with, an admittedly valid subject matter of a treaty. It is not required as a condition to validity that the reservation be in and of itself, treated in artificial isolation or detachment, a domestic matter properly a subject of contract between sovereigns. It is sufficient if it is directly related to a general subject which is properly a matter for contract between sovereigns, and if international policies and considerations are the raison d'etre of the reservation. As no properly negotiated and ratified treaty of the United States has ever been held invalid there can be no binding judicial authority in support of petitioner's argument for unconstitutionality....

My colleagues recognize that the Senate could have made the treaty executory by providing in its consent that the rights and obligations of both signatory parties take effect only after passage of an act of Congress. They say, however, that the Senate did not do so. While I agree with this, I cannot agree that the Senate has no power to make the treaty executory as to this country alone.

There are many instances where the Senate has extended to the House of Representatives a voice in determining how treaties will be implemented. The Senate has on many occasions done this by insisting that a treaty not be effective until approved or implemented by an act of Congress. This is particularly so as regards treaties affecting revenues. It is also worthy of note that denial of House participation in domestic legislation effectuated by treaty has been one of the most common causes of controversy over the treaty power.

It is my view that recognition of the Senate's power to condition its consent to a treaty upon its remaining executory on both sides until Congress passes legislation to give the treaty operative effect carries with it recognition that the Senate may condition its consent upon the treaty not having an operative effect in this country alone until Congress acts. In either event the treaty rights and duties are the same. In one instance both parties are bound to await an act of Congress before exercising their rights under the treaty, whereas in the second instance, which is the case here, only this country is bound to await an act of Congress before availing itself of the rights allotted by the treaty. Why cannot the Senate make the reduction to use of the treaty rights by the United States await an act of Congress?

International Covenant on Civil and Political Rights

999 U.N.T.S. 171, 6 I.L.M. 368
Opened for Signature, December 19, 1966
Ratified by the United States on June 5, 1992

ARTICLE 4

1. In time of public emergency which threatens the life of the nation and the existence of which is officially proclaimed, the States Parties to the present

Covenant may take measures derogating from their obligations under the present Covenant to the extent strictly required by the exigencies of the situation, provided that such measures are not inconsistent with their other obligations under international law and do not involve discrimination solely on the ground of race, colour, sex, language, religion or social origin.

2. No derogation from articles 6, 7, 8 (paragraphs 1 and 2), 11, 15, 16 and 18 may be made under this provision.

3. Any State Party to the present Covenant availing itself of the right of derogation shall immediately inform the other States Parties to the present Covenant, through the intermediary of the Secretary-General of the United Nations, of the provisions from which it has derogated and of the reasons by which it was actuated. A further communication shall be made, through the same intermediary, on the date on which it terminates such derogation....

ARTICLE 6

1. Every human being has the inherent right to life. This right shall be protected by law. No one shall be arbitrarily deprived of his life....

4. Anyone sentenced to death shall have the right to seek pardon or commutation of the sentence. Amnesty, pardon or commutation of the sentence of death may be granted in all cases.

5. Sentence of death shall not be imposed for crimes committed by persons below eighteen years of age and shall not be carried out on pregnant women.

6. Nothing in this article shall be invoked to delay or to prevent the abolition of capital punishment by any State Party to the present Covenant.

ARTICLE 7

No one shall be subjected to torture or to cruel, inhuman or degrading treatment or punishment. In particular, no one shall be subjected without his free consent to medical or scientific experimentation....

ARTICLE 9

1. Everyone has the right to liberty and security of person. No one shall be subjected to arbitrary arrest or detention. No one shall be deprived of his liberty except on such grounds and in accordance with such procedures as are established by law.

2. Anyone who is arrested shall be informed, at the time of arrest, of the reasons for his arrest and shall be promptly informed of any charges against him.

3. Anyone arrested or detained on a criminal charge shall be brought promptly before a judge or other officer authorized by law to exercise judicial power and shall be entitled to trial within a reasonable time or to release. It shall not be the general rule that persons awaiting trial shall be detained in custody, but release may be subject to guarantees to appear for trial, at any other stage of the judicial proceedings, and, should occasion arise, for execution of the judgement.

4. Anyone who is deprived of his liberty by arrest or detention shall be entitled to take proceedings before a court, in order that court may decide without delay on the lawfulness of his detention and order his release if the detention is not lawful.

5. Anyone who has been the victim of unlawful arrest or detention shall have an enforceable right to compensation....

ARTICLE 17

1. No one shall be subjected to arbitrary or unlawful interference with his privacy, family, home or correspondence, nor to unlawful attacks on his honour and reputation.

2. Everyone has the right to the protection of the law against such interference or attacks.

ARTICLE 18

1. Everyone shall have the right to freedom of thought, conscience and religion. This right shall include freedom to have or to adopt a religion or belief of his choice, and freedom, either individually or in community with others and in public or private, to manifest his religion or belief in worship, observance, practice and teaching.

2. No one shall be subject to coercion which would impair his freedom to have or to adopt a religion or belief of his choice.

3. Freedom to manifest one's religion or beliefs may be subject only to such limitations as are prescribed by law and are necessary to protect public safety, order, health, or morals or the fundamental rights and freedoms of others.

4. The States Parties to the present Covenant undertake to have respect for the liberty of parents and, when applicable, legal guardians to ensure the religious and moral education of their children in conformity with their own convictions....

ARTICLE 20

1. Any propaganda for war shall be prohibited by law.

2. Any advocacy of national, racial or religious hatred that constitutes incitement to discrimination, hostility or violence shall be prohibited by law....

ARTICLE 26

All persons are equal before the law and are entitled without any discrimination to the equal protection of the law. In this respect, the law shall prohibit any discrimination and guarantee to all persons equal and effective protection against discrimination on any ground such as race, colour, sex, language, religion, political or other opinion, national or social origin, property, birth or other status.

U.S. Reservations, Declarations, and Understandings, International Covenant on Civil and Political Rights

138 CONG. REC. S4781-01 (DAILY ED., APR. 2, 1992)

I. The Senate's advice and consent is subject to the following reservations:

(1) That Article 20 does not authorize or require legislation or other action by the United States that would restrict the right of free speech and association protected by the Constitution and laws of the United States.

(2) That the United States reserves the right, subject to its Constitutional constraints, to impose capital punishment on any person (other than a pregnant woman) duly convicted under existing or future laws permitting the imposition of capital punishment, including such punishment for crimes committed by persons below eighteen years of age.

(3) That the United States considers itself bound by Article 7 to the extent that "cruel, inhuman or degrading treatment or punishment" means the cruel and unusual treatment or punishment prohibited by the Fifth, Eighth and/or Fourteenth Amendments to the Constitution of the United States....

II. The Senate's advice and consent is subject to the following understandings, which shall apply to the obligations of the United States under this Covenant:

(1) That the Constitution and laws of the United States guarantee all persons equal protection of the law and provide extensive protections against discrimination. The United States understands distinctions based upon race, color, sex, language, religion, political or other opinion, national or social origin, property, birth or any other status—as those terms are used in Article 2, paragraph 1 and Article 26—to be permitted when such distinctions are, at minimum, rationally related to a legitimate governmental objective. The United States further understands the prohibition in paragraph 1 of Article 4 upon discrimination, in time of public emergency, based "solely" on the status of race, color, sex, language, religion or social origin not to bar distinctions that may have a disproportionate effect upon persons of a particular status....

(5) That the United States understands that this Covenant shall be implemented by the Federal Government to the extent that it exercises legislative and judicial jurisdiction over the matters covered therein, and otherwise by the state and local governments; to the extent that state and local governments exercise jurisdiction over such matters, the Federal Government shall take measures appropriate to the Federal system to the end that the competent authorities of the state or local governments may take appropriate measures for the fulfillment of the Covenant.

III. The Senate's advice and consent is subject to the following declarations:

(1) That the United States declares that the provisions of Articles 1 through 27 of the Covenant are not self-executing....

IV. The Senate's advice and consent is subject to the following proviso, which shall not be included in the instrument of ratification to be deposited by the President:

Nothing in this Covenant requires or authorizes legislation, or other action, by the United States of America prohibited by the Constitution of the United States as interpreted by the United States.

Louis Henkin, U.S. Ratification of Human Rights Conventions: The Ghost of Senator Bricker

89 Am. J. Int'l L. 341 (1995)

....The package of reservations, understandings and declarations [RUDs] the United States has been attaching to its ratifications of human rights conventions appears to be guided by several "principles." . . . I address each of these "principles" in turn.

CONSTITUTIONAL LIMITATIONS ON TREATIES

Under accepted United States constitutional jurisprudence, treaties are subject to constitutional limitations: none of the three branches — the Executive, the Congress, or the courts — can give effect to a treaty provision that is inconsistent with the Constitution. Therefore, a reservation to avoid an obligation that the United States could not carry out because of constitutional limitations is appropriate, indeed necessary.

Such a reservation may have been required when the United States ratified the International Covenant on Civil and Political Rights, in respect of the obligation in Article 20 to prohibit war propaganda and "racial hate speech." In that case, however, had the executive branch been disposed to avoid entering a reservation, it might have contented itself with an "understanding" that would construe Article 20 as requiring only that a state party prohibit speech that incites to unlawful action. That, indeed, is the plausible interpretation of Article 20(2), and as so understood could be implemented by the United States under the Constitution. . . . Instead, the United States entered a reservation that seems designed not to avoid constitutional difficulties but to resist change in United States law.

REJECTING HIGHER INTERNATIONAL STANDARDS

By its reservations, the United States apparently seeks to assure that its adherence to a convention will not change, or require change, in U.S. laws, policies or practices, even where they fall below international standards. For example, in ratifying the International Covenant on Civil and Political Rights, the United States refused to accept a provision prohibiting capital punishment for crimes committed by persons under eighteen years of age. . . .

Reservations designed to reject any obligation to rise above existing law and practice are of dubious propriety: if states generally entered such reservations, the convention would be futile. The object and purpose of the human rights conventions, it would seem, are to promote respect for human rights by having countries — mutually — assume legal obligations to respect and ensure recognized rights in accordance with international standards. Even friends of the United States have objected that its reservations are incompatible with that object and purpose and are therefore invalid.

By adhering to human rights conventions subject to these reservations, the United States, it is charged, is pretending to assume international obligations but in fact is undertaking nothing. It is seen as seeking the benefits of participation in the convention (e.g., having a U.S. national sit on the Human Rights Committee established pursuant to the Covenant) without assuming any obligations or burdens. The United States, it is said, seeks to sit in judgment on others but will not submit its human rights behavior to international judgment. To many, the attitude reflected in such reservations is offensive: the conventions are only for other states, not for the United States. . . .

THE "FEDERALISM" CLAUSE

The "federalism" clause attached to U.S. ratifications of human rights conventions has been denominated an "understanding," a designation ordinarily used for an interpretation or clarification of a possibly ambiguous provision in the treaty. The federalism clause in the instruments of ratification of the human rights conventions is not an understanding in that sense, but may be intended to alert other parties to United States intent in the matter of implementation....

The United States has proposed "federalism" clauses in the past, presumably to assuage "states' rights" sensibilities. At one time, the United States sought to limit its obligations under particular treaties to those matters that were "within the jurisdiction" of the federal Government, and to exclude any international obligation as to matters subject to the jurisdiction of the states. Some early versions of the federal-state clause reflected a misapprehension about "the jurisdiction" of the federal Government, as regards the reach of both its treaty power and congressional legislative power. There are no significant "states' rights" limitations on the treaty power. There is little that is not "within the jurisdiction of the United States," i.e., within the treaty power, or within the legislative power of Congress under the Commerce Power, under its authority to implement the Fourteenth Amendment, or under its power to do what is necessary and proper to carry out its treaty obligations. In time, recognizing that virtually any matter governed by treaty was "within the jurisdiction" of the United States, the executive branch took to declaring that the convention shall be implemented by the federal Government to the extent that it "exercises jurisdiction" over matters covered by the treaty, leaving to the states implementation of matters over which the states exercise jurisdiction.

Such a statement is deeply ambiguous. The federal Government exercises jurisdiction over all matters covered in a human rights convention, if only by making the treaty. It exercises jurisdiction over such matters because Congress has the power to legislate, and has legislated, in respect of them. In any event, as a matter of international treaty law, such a statement is not an "understanding" or a reservation, and raises no international difficulties. International law requires the United States to carry out its treaty obligations but, in the absence of special provision, does not prescribe how, or through which agencies, they shall be carried out. As a matter of international law, then, the United States could leave the implementation of any treaty provision to the states. Of course, the United States remains internationally responsible for any failure of implementation.

The "federalism" declarations that have been attached to human rights conventions thus serve no legal purpose. But some see such declarations as another sign that the United States is resistant to international human rights agreements, setting up obstacles to their implementation and refusing to treat human rights conventions as treaties dealing with a subject of national interest and international concern.

THE NON-SELF-EXECUTING DECLARATION

The United States has been declaring the human rights agreements it has ratified to be non-self-executing.

The U.S. practice of declaring human rights conventions non-self-executing is commonly seen as of a piece with the other RUDs. As the reservations designed to deny international obligations serve to immunize the United States from external judgment, the declaration that a convention shall be non-self-executing is designed to keep its own judges from judging the human rights conditions in the United States by international standards. To critics, keeping a convention from having any effect as United States law confirms that United States adherence remains essentially empty.

The non-self-executing declaration has been explained — and justified — as designed to assure that changes in U.S. law will be effected only by "democratic processes" — therefore, by legislation, not by treaty. That argument, of course, impugns the democratic character of every treaty made or that will be made by the President with the consent of the Senate.

Whatever may be appropriate in a special case, as a general practice such a declaration is against the spirit of the Constitution; it may be unconstitutional. Article VI of the Constitution provides expressly for lawmaking by treaty: treaties are declared to be the supreme law of the land. The Framers intended that a treaty should become law *ipso facto*, when the treaty is made; it should not require legislative implementation to convert it into United States law. In effect, lawmaking by treaty was to be an alternative to legislation by Congress.

Nothing in the Constitution or in the history of its adoption suggests that the Framers contemplated that some treaties might not be law of the land. That was a later suggestion by John Marshall, because he found that some promises *by their character* could not be "self-executing": when the United States undertook to do something in the future that could be done only by legislative or other political act, the treaty did not — could not — carry out the undertaking. Marshall did not contemplate that treaty undertakings that could be given effect as law by the Executive and the courts, or by the states, should not be carried out by them, but might be converted into promises that Congress would legislate. Surely, there is no evidence of any intent, by the Framers (or by John Marshall), to allow the President or the Senate, by their *ipse dixit*, to prevent a treaty that by its character *could* be law of the land from becoming law of the land. . . .

The pattern of non-self-executing declarations threatens to subvert the constitutional treaty system. That, for the present at least, the non-self-executing declaration is almost exclusively a concomitant of U.S. adherence to human rights conventions will appear to critics as an additional indication that the United States does not take such conventions seriously as international obligations.

THE GHOST OF SENATOR BRICKER

There is more at issue in the United States RUDs than their effect on a particular treaty; at stake in United States human rights reservation policy is the integrity of the constitutional system for concluding treaties. I recall some background.

Between 1950 and 1955 Senator Bricker of Ohio led a movement to amend the Constitution in ways designed to make it impossible for the United States to adhere to human rights treaties. The campaign for the Bricker Amendment apparently represented a move by anti-civil-rights and "states' rights" forces to seek to prevent — in particular — bringing an end to racial discrimination and segregation by international treaty.

In its principal version, the Bricker Amendment included the following provision: "A treaty shall become effective in the United States only through legislation which would be valid in the absence of treaty." The clause would have rendered all treaties non-self-executing. It would also have prevented congressional implementation of a treaty by legislation that was not within congressional power apart from the treaty, overruling *Missouri v. Holland.*

In the end, leaders of the legal profession mobilized and, by persuading President Eisenhower and Secretary Dulles to oppose the amendment, succeeded in defeating it. But the human rights movement paid a high price for that victory.

To help defeat the amendment, the Eisenhower administration promised that the United States would not accede to international human rights covenants or conventions.

In retrospect, the Bricker Amendment, if adopted, would have damaged the treaty power by making all treaties not self-executing, but it would not have prevented adherence to human rights treaties or their implementation by Congress. Limiting the power of Congress to implement treaties would not have proved to be serious for human rights: In 1954 the Constitution itself was interpreted as forbidding segregation, and the courts enforced desegregation without any human rights treaty or act of Congress. Within a few years it became clear that the powers of Congress apart from its power to implement treaties—notably the Commerce Power and the power to implement the Fourteenth Amendment—were broad enough to support civil rights legislation. The civil rights campaign in the United States became entirely domestic, and any thought of effecting change in United States law by treaty was abandoned. The Bricker Amendment campaign became ancient history.

It soon appeared, however, that—apart from the condition of human rights in the United States—United States foreign policy required U.S. support for, if not leadership in, the international human rights movement, and required U.S. adherence to international human rights conventions. Successive administrations slowly abandoned President Eisenhower's commitment. But Senator Bricker's ghost has proved to be alive in the Senate, and successive administrations have become infected with his ideology.

Senator Bricker lost his battle, but his ghost is now enjoying victory in war. For the package of reservations, understandings and declarations achieves virtually what the Bricker Amendment sought, and more.

Notes and Questions

1. Approximately 15 percent of all Article II treaties since the Founding have been ratified subject to conditions. *See* Kevin C. Kennedy, *Conditional Approval of Treaties by the U.S. Senate,* 19 Loy. L.A. Int'l & Comp. L.J. 89, 91, 97 (1996). As mentioned in the introduction to this chapter, the Senate usually proposes these conditions, but sometimes the President does as well. The Senate's power to give its conditional consent has two justifications. First, conditional consent is viewed as a component of the Senate's larger power to withhold consent altogether. Second, conditional consent is viewed as a substitute for the Senate's envisioned *ex ante* advice role that was effectively repudiated by the Washington administration in the early 1790s. In order to preserve its ability to "advise" (as well as consent) regarding treaty terms, the Senate has since the 1790s asserted the power to condition its consent on amendments to the negotiated treaty. *See* CRS Study, *supra*; Samuel B. Crandall, Treaties, Their Making and Enforcement 70 (1904); Ralston Hayden, The Senate and Treaties, 1789-1817, at 110-11 (1920).

2. The first example of conditional consent by the Senate was a reservation made in connection with the Jay Treaty, discussed at the beginning of this chapter. A bare two-thirds of the Senate gave their advice and consent to the treaty in 1795, but only on the condition that an article of the treaty relating to trade between the United States and the British West Indies be suspended. Britain accepted this condition without complaint, and the treaty was eventually ratified. *See* Hayden, *supra*, at 87; George H. Haynes, The Senate of the United States 607-08 (1938). A few years later, the Senate gave its advice and consent to a treaty with Tunisia on the condition that an article in the treaty be suspended and renegotiated, and the article was in fact renegotiated prior to ratification. Treaty of Amity, Commerce, and Navigation, Aug. 28, 1797, U.S.-Tunis., T.S. No. 360, at 1088 n.1. The Senate again exercised its conditional consent power in connection with an 1800 treaty between the United States and France. Hayden, *supra*, at 121.

The United States' treaty partners did not always respond favorably to the Senate's conditions. In negotiating an 1803 boundary treaty with the United States, Great Britain would not accept the amendment proposed by the Senate, and the treaty was never ratified. The head of the British Foreign Office at that time criticized the United States's conditional consent practice, calling it "new, unauthorized and not to be sanctioned." *Id.* at 150. Great Britain similarly complained about conditions proposed by the Senate in connection with an 1824 treaty concerning the African slave trade. *See* 5 John Bassett Moore, A Digest of International Law 748, at 200 (1906). Over time, however, this practice became generally accepted by the international community. The United States engaged in this practice in connection with numerous treaties during the nineteenth and early twentieth centuries, generally without controversy, as did many of its treaty partners. *See generally* David Hunter Miller, Reservations to Treaties: Their Effect and the Procedure in Regard Thereto (1919).

3. Was what the Senate called a "reservation" in the U.S.-Canada Treaty at issue in *Power Authority* really a reservation? Did it, like the reservations to the ICCPR, in any way qualify the United States' international obligations? Should courts defer to the Senate's characterization of its conditional consent, or should it, as the *Power Authority* court did, look behind the labels to determine how the condition operates in practice? Whatever the condition is called, isn't it clear that the President and the Senate intended to qualify U.S. ratification of the treaty on the condition having binding domestic effect? Should courts second-guess such clear political branch wishes in the treaty context?

4. Why did the court in *Power Authority* view the "reservation" as precatory and not part of the treaty? Because it did not impose reciprocal obligations on Canada? Because the President ratified the treaty without waiting for Canada to accept the reservation? Because the reservation concerned a matter of purely domestic concern?

5. If valid, the "reservation" in *Power Authority* would have abrogated the preexisting domestic statute that, by its terms, governed the development of the Niagara River waters. The court in *Power Authority* thus might have believed that the Senate was attempting, through its conditional consent power, to change existing law without the involvement of the House of Representatives. *See* Opinion of Phillip C. Jessup & Oliver J. Lissitzyn for the Power Authority of the State of New York (Dec. 1955), quoted in William W. Bishop, Jr., Reservations to Treaties, II Receuil des Cours at 319-20 (1961). What would have been wrong with the Senate doing this? We know from the last-in-time rule that treaties can supersede prior statutes, so why wouldn't the Senate and President have had that authority here? Does *Power Authority* apply an interpretive presumption against overriding federal legislation by means of treaty conditions? Would such a presumption be any different than the general presumption against repealing federal statutes, which applies even in the last-in-time rule context? Professor Henkin contested the Jessup/Lissitzyn characterization of the Niagara reservation, arguing that "[t]he President and Senate have merely refused to throw new and valuable resources into an old established system of development which Congress may not have intended and may not now desire." Louis Henkin, *The Treaty Makers and the Law Makers: The Niagara Reservation*, 56 Colum. L. Rev. 1151, 1174 (1956). How would Henkin's characterization affect the validity of the reservation?

6. The majority in *Power Authority* acknowledges that the Senate could have conditioned its consent in a way that precluded he international obligation with Canada from coming into effect until passage of an Act of Congress. In a number of instances in the nineteenth and early twentieth centuries, the Senate consented to treaties on the condition that the treaties, or particular articles in the treaties, would take effect only after Congress passed legislation implementing them. For example, a provision in an 1875 trade treaty with Hawaii stated that the treaty would not take effect "until a law to carry it into operation shall have been passed by the Congress of the United States of America." Convention between the United States of America and His Majesty the King of the Hawaiian Islands, Jan. 30, 1875, U.S.-Hawaii, art. V, 19 Stat. 625, 627. Relatedly, the Senate has often reserved certain implementation duties for Congress. For example, in an 1899 treaty with Spain concerning the acquisition of Puerto Rico and the Philippines, the U.S. treaty-makers included a provision stating that "the civil rights and political status of the native inhabitants of the territories hereby ceded to the United States shall be determined by the Congress." Treaty of Peace Between the United States of America and the Kingdom of Spain, Dec. 10, 1898, U.S.-Spain, art. IX, 30 Stat. 1754, 1759. *See also* Fourteen Diamond Rings v. United States, 183 U.S. 176, 182, 184-85 (1901) (Brown, J., concurring) (stating that there was "no doubt" that the U.S. treaty-makers could provide that customs relations between territories ceded by treaty and the United States "should remain unchanged until legislation had been had upon the subject").

How did the reservation in *Power Authority* differ from these well-settled practices? Why did the majority believe these differences had constitutional significance?

7. The ICCPR RUDs, excerpted above, are typical of the RUDs that the United States has attached to most of the human rights treaties that it has ratified. Such RUDs were first proposed by President Carter in 1979 as a way of overcoming decades-long opposition in the Senate — including, most famously, the Bricker Amendment debate — to ratification of human rights treaties. There were many reasons for this opposition, including concerns that (a) provisions in the human rights treaties might conflict with U.S. constitutional guarantees; (b) the vaguely worded terms in the treaties would, if self-executing, sow confusion in the law by superseding inconsistent state law and prior inconsistent federal legislation; (c) even if courts ultimately decided that each of the differently worded provisions in the ICCPR did not require a change in domestic law, litigation of these issues would be costly and would generate substantial legal uncertainty; and (d) the human rights treaties would affect the balance of power between state and federal governments. *See* Four Treaties Relating to Human Rights, Hearings before the Comm. on Foreign Relations, 96th Cong. 21 (1979) (testimony of Deputy Secretary of State Warren Christopher concerning ICCPR). RUDs were a response to these concerns that made it possible for the Senate to ratify not only the ICCPR, but also the Genocide Convention, the Torture Convention, and the Convention on the Elimination of All Forms of Racial Discrimination.

8. Unlike the "reservation" in *Power Authority*, the reservations to the ICCPR were included in the original treaty ratification instruments and clearly constitute non-consent to particular treaty terms in the ICCPR. Are such reservations constitutional? The examples of conditional consent outlined in Note 2 were all reservations, and thus the practice of reservations goes back to the beginning of the Nation. Some commentators, however, have argued that reservations are in tension with separation of powers principles, either because they violate the President's constitutional prerogatives in making treaties, or because they constitute an improper "line-item veto" whereby the Senate is in effect trying to change the terms of the treaty. Do these arguments apply to RUDs to human rights treaties, which have largely been proposed by presidents? Assuming they do, is it relevant that the Senate must attach a RUD before, and not after, ratification, see Fourteen Diamond Rings v. United States, 183 U.S. 176, 180 (1901) ("The meaning of the treaty cannot be controlled by subsequent explanations of some of those who may have voted to ratify it"); and that the President always retains the discretion to refuse to ratify a treaty that the Senate has consented to conditionally? As for the line-tem veto argument, the Supreme Court struck down a line-item veto statute in Clinton v. New York, 524 U.S. 417 (1998), because the Court found that it gave "the President the unilateral power to change the text of duly enacted statutes." *Id.* at 447. Do RUDs give the Senate unilateral power to change the text of duly ratified treaties? Or are they analogous to a bill passed by both Houses of Congress in the sense that the President retains the discretion to decline to make them binding U.S. law?

9. The ICCPR established a Human Rights Committee ("HRC") that is charged with receiving reports submitted by nations under the ICCPR's self-reporting provisions and issuing "such general comments as it may consider appropriate." The HRC technically has no official power to issue binding legal interpretations of the ICCPR. Nonetheless, the HRC has declared itself to be the definitive interpreter of whether a reservation to the ICCPR is consistent with the international law rule that a reservation cannot violate the treaty's "object and purpose." See ICCPR Human Rights Comm., General Comment 24(52), 52d Sess., 1382d mtg. P 10, U.N. Doc. CCPR/C/21/Rev.1/ Add. 6 (1994), at 18. The HRC also has stated that the execution of juvenile offenders violates the object and purpose test, and that the remedy for this violation is that the entire treaty, including the provision to which the United States reserved, remains binding on the United States. *See id.;* Human Rights Committee, Comments on United States of America, U.N. Doc. CCPR/C/79/Add. 50 (1995). In short, the HRC appears to have maintained that the U.S. reservation with respect to the juvenile death penalty is invalid under international law and that the United States is bound by the ICCPR's prohibition on the juvenile death penalty even though it specifically declined to consent to it.

In "Observations" responding to the HRC, the United States government contested these conclusions. It disagreed with the legal analysis supporting the view that the reservation to the death penalty provision violates the ICCPR's object and purpose, and it maintained that it is inconsistent with the principle of state consent to bind a nation to a term to which it had attached a reservation. *See* Observations by the United States on General Comment 24, 3 Int'l Hum. Rts. Rep. 265 (1996). France and Great Britain also objected to the HRC's conclusion that a nation could be bound to a treaty provision to which it had attempted to reserve out of. *See* Observations by France on General Comment 24 on

Reservations to the ICCPR, 4 Int'l Hum. Rts. Rep. 6, 6-8 (1997); Observations by the United Kingdom on General Comment 24, 3 Int'l Hum. Rts. Rep. 261, 261-69 (1996); *cf.* Report of the International Law Commission on the Work of Its Forty-Ninth Session, U.N. GAOR, 52d Sess., Supp. No. 10, U.N. Doc. A/52/10 (1997) (similar conclusions). The United States reservation with respect to the juvenile death penalty no longer has practical significance in light of the Supreme Court's decision in Roper v. Simmons, 125 S. Ct. 1183 (2005), which declared the juvenile death penalty unconstitutional. But the HRC position nonetheless raises the more general question about the implications for domestic U.S. law of the possible invalidity of reservations under international law. If a reservation were invalid under international law, would it nonetheless bind U.S. courts?

This issue arises in connection with the United States' ratification of the Chemical Weapons Convention (CWC) in 1994. Article 22 of the CWC prohibits State Parties from attaching reservations to its Articles. Nonetheless, the United States ratified the CWC subject to twenty-eight "conditions." Some of these conditions — such as the one providing the president with the power to refuse a contemplated CWC inspection on the grounds of protecting national security, and the one asserting a congressional right to make reservations to the Convention despite the no reservation clause — appear to amount to non-consent to particular treaty terms, and thus to be "reservations" as that term is typically understood. Assuming that the "conditions" violate the treaty, are they nevertheless legal under domestic law? When the President "takes care" to faithfully execute the treaty, does his constitutional duty require him, or prohibit him, from giving effect to the "conditions"?

10. Why does the United States attach non-self-execution declarations to human rights treaties? The State Department's Legal Adviser offered this answer: "[T]he decision to make the treaty 'non-self-executing' reflects a strong preference, both within the Administration and in the Senate, not to use the unicameral treaty power of the U.S. Constitution to effect direct changes in the domestic law of the United States." Statement by Conrad K. Harper, USUN Press Release #49-(95), at 3 (Mar. 29, 1995). Professor Henkin offers different reasons in his article excerpted above. Who is right?

11. Are declarations of non-self-execution constitutional? They do not have the same historical pedigree as reservations, but they are analogous to the long-standing practice, recounted in Note 6, of conditioning consent on subsequent congressional action. Is Professor Henkin right that non-self-execution conditions are inconsistent with the Supremacy Clause? Does the term "shall" in the Supremacy Clause suggest an irrebuttable presumption that otherwise self-executing treaties be treated as self-executing? In answering this question, is it relevant that Congress frequently specifies that federal *statutes* do not preempt state law, do not invalidate prior federal law, or do not create a private cause of action? Does it matter that it is widely believed that Congress can declare congressional-executive agreements — which are equivalent to treaties on the international plane (we study these in Section G below) — to be non-self-executing? Does it matter that it has long been settled that, notwithstanding the Supremacy Clause, some treaties are non-self-executing? Does it matter that the non-self-execution declaration for the ICCPR was included within the U.S. instrument of ratification that defines the nature of the U.S. obligations to other countries?

12. Does *Power Authority* suggest that the domestic enforcement of treaties is a domestic rather than an international matter? If so, would this support the view that non-self-execution declarations exceed the scope of the treaty power? For arguments to this effect, see Malvina Halberstam, *United States Ratification of the Convention on the Elimination of All Forms of Discrimination Against Women*, 31 Geo. Wash. J. Int'l L. & Econ. 49, 69 (1997); John Quigley, *The International Covenant on Civil and Political Rights and the Supremacy Clause*, 42 DePaul L. Rev. 1287, 1303-05 (1993); Stefan A. Riesenfeld & Frederick M. Abbott, *The Scope of U.S. Senate Control Over the Conclusion and Operation of Treaties*, 67 Chi.-Kent L. Rev. 571, 590-600 (1991). *But see* Curtis A. Bradley & Jack L. Goldsmith, *Treaties, Human Rights, and Conditional Consent*, 149 U. Pa. L. Rev. 399, 452-53 (2000) (arguing that *Power Authority* and the treaty power do not affect the validity of non-self-execution declarations).

13. One commentator has argued that the non-self-execution declarations merely preclude the implication of a private cause of action under the treaties and do not preclude courts from applying the treaties in situations not requiring the implication of a private cause of action — for example, as a defense to a criminal prosecution, or in a civil suit in which some other law provides a right to sue. *See* David Sloss, *The Domestication of International Human Rights: Non-Self-Executing Declarations and Human Rights Treaties*, 24 Yale J. Int'l L. 129 (1999). *But see* Bradley & Goldsmith, *supra*, at 421-22 (contesting that construction of the declarations). To date, courts have treated the non-self-execution declarations as precluding all judicial enforcement of the treaties, not just the implication of a private cause of action.

14. Do you agree with Professor Henkin's criticisms of the RUDs packages that the United States attaches to human rights treaties? Supporters of RUDs emphasize that RUDs have had wide bipartisan support and were crucial in breaking the logjam in domestic politics that had prevented U.S. ratification of any of the major human rights treaties. They also note that the RUDs do not make U.S. ratification of human rights treaties empty promises. The United States has in fact enacted domestic criminal, civil, and immigration laws to implement the Genocide and Torture Conventions. *See* 18 U.S.C. §1091 (1994) (genocide); 18 U.S.C. §2340A (1994) (torture). Furthermore, even with the RUDs, the United States has bound itself to almost all of the obligations in each of the four major human rights treaties it has ratified, and thus has promised not to retreat from those protections. In addition, the United States has opened its domestic human rights practices to official international scrutiny by filing with international bodies associated with the treaties reports that describe and defend U.S. human rights practices. Finally, supporters of RUDs note that there is no evidence linking U.S. RUDs practice with a diminution of human rights protections around the world, and indeed that international human rights law has flourished during the period that U.S. RUDs were introduced. *See generally* Bradley & Goldsmith, *supra*, at 456-68. Which view is right?

15. Another complaint about RUDs is that they are "anti-majoritarian" because they allow a minority of senators to force limitations on treaties through their power to block the two-thirds advice and consent needed for ratification. *See, e.g.*, Stefan A. Riesenfeld & Frederick M. Abbott, *The Scope of U.S. Senate Control Over the Conclusion and Operation of Treaties*, 67 Chi.-Kent L. Rev. 571, 600-01 (1991). It is true that a minority of senators can insist on a package of RUDs as a precondition of senatorial consent to the treaty. Is this minority power of conditional consent any more problematic than Article II's super-majoritarian treaty-making procedure? Does this anti-majoritarian feature of the treaty process distinguish it from other constitutional provisions designed to protect minority interests, including Article I's bicameralism and presentment process, Article II's impeachment process, Article V's constitutional amendment process, and the Bill of Rights?

16. To date, every court to have considered the issue has given effect to the U.S. RUDs to human rights treaties. Many of these cases have involved the legality under the ICCPR of the juvenile death penalty, an issue, as noted above, now mooted by the *Roper* decision. *See, e.g.*, Beazley v. Johnson, 242 F.3d 248 (5th Cir. 2001); Domingues v. Nevada, 114 Nev. 783, 961 P.2d 1279 (1998). For similar conclusions in other contexts, see, for example, Flores v. S. Peru Copper Corp., 343 F.3d 140, 164 (2d Cir. 2003) (enforcing ICCPR non-self-execution declaration in context of environmental tort suit under the Alien Tort Statute); Bannerman v. Snyder, 325 F.3d 722, 724 (6th Cir. 2003) (enforcing ICCPR non-self-execution declaration in criminal context).

17. Can a non-self-executing treaty be enforced by the Executive Branch — for example, by an Executive Order? Consider the following Executive Order, promulgated by President Clinton, which purported to implement human rights treaties that had been declared by the U.S. treaty-makers to be non-self-executing:

By the authority vested in me as President by the Constitution and the laws of the United States of America, and bearing in mind the obligations of the United States pursuant to the [ICCPR], the Convention Against Torture and Other Cruel, Inhuman or Degrading Treatment or Punishment (CAT), the Convention on the Elimination of All Forms of Racial Discrimination (CERD), and other relevant treaties concerned with the protection and promotion of human rights to which the United States is now or may become a party in the future, it is hereby ordered as follows:

SEC. 1. IMPLEMENTATION OF HUMAN RIGHTS OBLIGATIONS.

(a) It shall be the policy and practice of the Government of the United States, being committed to the protection and promotion of human rights and fundamental freedoms, fully to respect and implement its obligations under the international human rights treaties to which it is a party, including the ICCPR, the CAT, and the CERD.

(b) It shall also be the policy and practice of the Government of the United States to promote respect for international human rights, both in our relationships with all other countries and by working with and strengthening the various international mechanisms for the promotion of human rights, including, inter alia, those of the United Nations, the International Labor Organization, and the Organization of American States.

SEC. 2. RESPONSIBILITY OF EXECUTIVE DEPARTMENTS AND AGENCIES.

(a) All executive departments and agencies . . . shall maintain a current awareness of United States international human rights obligations that are relevant to their functions and shall perform such functions so as to respect and implement those obligations fully. The head of each agency shall designate a single contact officer who will be responsible for overall coordination of the implementation of this order. Under this order, all such agencies shall retain their established institutional roles in the implementation, interpretation, and enforcement of Federal law and policy.

(b) The heads of agencies shall have lead responsibility, in coordination with other appropriate agencies, for questions concerning implementation of human rights obligations that fall within their respective operating and program responsibilities and authorities or, to the extent that matters do not fall within the operating and program responsibilities and authorities of any agency, that most closely relate to their general areas of concern.

SEC. 3. HUMAN RIGHTS INQUIRIES AND COMPLAINTS.

Each agency shall take lead responsibility, in coordination with other appropriate agencies, for responding to inquiries, requests for information, and complaints about violations of human rights obligations that fall within its areas of responsibility or, if the matter does not fall within its areas of responsibility, referring it to the appropriate agency for response. . . .

SEC. 6. JUDICIAL REVIEW, SCOPE, AND ADMINISTRATION.

(a) Nothing in this order shall create any right or benefit, substantive or procedural, enforceable by any party against the United States, its agencies or instrumentalities, its officers or employees, or any other person.

(b) This order does not supersede Federal statutes and does not impose any justiciable obligations on the executive branch. . . .

Implementation of Human Rights Treaties, Exec. Order No. 13107, 63 Fed. Reg. 68,991 (1998).

The Order refers to "the authority vested in me as President by the Constitution." What authority is it referring to? The President's power to make treaties with the advice and consent of the Senate? The President's duty to take care that the laws are faithfully executed? The "executive Power" vested by Article II? The Order appears to be directed only at the Executive Branch, and it expressly does not create a right to sue. Could President Clinton have constitutionally ordered state compliance with non-self-executing treaties? Could he constitutionally have provided for judicial enforcement of such treaties?

F. INTERPRETATION AND TERMINATION OF TREATIES

In this section, we consider the allocation of authority between the three branches of government to interpret (and reinterpret) treaties, and the scope of the President's domestic authority to terminate treaties.

1. Treaty Interpretation by U.S. Courts

El Al Israel Airlines v. Tseng

525 U.S. 155 (1999)

[The Convention for the Unification of Certain Rules Relating to International Transportation by Air, popularly known as the Warsaw Convention, governs air carrier liability for "all international transportation of persons, baggage, or goods performed by aircraft for hire," Ch. I, Art. 1(1). The Warsaw Convention imposes liability for, among other things, bodily injuries suffered as a result of an "accident . . . on board the aircraft or in the course of any of the operations of embarking or disembarking," Ch. III, Art. 17. In a prior decision, the Supreme Court had held that liability could not be imposed under this provision for mental or psychic injuries unaccompanied by physical injuries. In this case Tsui Yuan Tseng sued El Al Israel Airlines under New York state law for psychic tort damages that allegedly resulted from an intrusive security search at John F. Kennedy International Airport. The Second Circuit Court of Appeals held that the Warsaw Convention did not preempt such state-law tort claims. The Supreme Court granted certiorari to address the question whether the Convention precludes a passenger from maintaining an action for damages under state law when the Convention itself allows no recovery.]

JUSTICE GINSBURG delivered the Opinion of the Court....

Our inquiry begins with the text of Article 24, which prescribes the exclusivity of the Convention's provisions for air carrier liability. "It is our responsibility to give the specific words of the treaty a meaning consistent with the shared expectations of the contracting parties." Air France v. Saks, 470 U.S. 392, 399 (1985). "Because a treaty ratified by the United States is not only the law of this land, see U.S. Const., Art. II, §2, but also an agreement among sovereign powers, we have traditionally considered as aids to its interpretation the negotiating and drafting history (*travaux preparatoires*) and the postratification understanding of the contracting parties." Zicherman v. Korean Air Lines Co., 516 U.S. 217, 226 (1996).

Article 24 provides that "cases covered by article 17" — or in the governing French text, "les cas prevus a l'article 17" — may "only be brought subject to the conditions and limits set out in the Convention." ... In Tseng's view, and in the view of the Court of Appeals, "les cas prevus a l'article 17" means those cases in which a passenger could actually maintain a claim for relief under Article 17. So read, Article 24 would permit any passenger whose personal injury suit did not satisfy the liability conditions of Article 17 to pursue the claim under local law.

In El Al's view, on the other hand, and in the view of the United States as *amicus curiae*, "les cas prevus a l'article 17" refers generically to all personal injury cases stemming from occurrences on board an aircraft or in embarking or disembarking, and simply distinguishes that class of cases (Article 17 cases) from cases involving damaged luggage or goods, or delay (which Articles 18 and 19 address). So read, Article 24 would preclude a passenger from asserting any air transit personal injury claims under local law, including claims that failed to satisfy Article 17's liability conditions, notably, because the injury did not result from an "accident," see *Saks*, 470 U.S. at 405, or because the "accident" did not result in physical injury or physical manifestation of injury, see Eastern Airlines v. Floyd, 499 U.S. 530, 552 (1991).

Respect is ordinarily due the reasonable views of the Executive Branch concerning the meaning of an international treaty. *See* Sumitomo Shoji America, Inc. v. Avagliano, 457 U.S. 176, 184-185 (1982) ("Although not conclusive, the meaning attributed to treaty provisions by the Government agencies charged with their negotiation and enforcement is entitled to great weight."). We conclude that the Government's construction of Article 24 is most faithful to the Convention's text, purpose, and overall structure.

The cardinal purpose of the Warsaw Convention, we have observed, is to "achieve uniformity of rules governing claims arising from international air transportation." *Floyd*, 499 U.S. at 552. The Convention signatories, in the treaty's preamble, specifically "recognized the advantage of regulating in a uniform manner the conditions of...the liability of the carrier." To provide the desired uniformity, Chapter III of the Convention sets out an array of liability rules which, the treaty declares, "apply to all international transportation of persons, baggage, or goods performed by aircraft." *Ibid.* In that Chapter, the Convention describes and defines the three areas of air carrier liability (personal injuries in Article 17, baggage or goods loss, destruction, or damage in Article 18, and damage occasioned by delay in Article 19), the conditions exempting air carriers from liability (Article 20), the monetary limits of liability (Article 22), and the circumstances in which air carriers may not limit liability (Articles 23 and 25). Given the Convention's comprehensive scheme of liability rules and its textual emphasis on uniformity, we would be hard put to conclude that the delegates at Warsaw meant to subject air carriers to the distinct, nonuniform liability rules of the individual signatory nations....

A complementary purpose of the Convention is to accommodate or balance the interests of passengers seeking recovery for personal injuries, and the interests of air carriers seeking to limit potential liability. Before the Warsaw accord, injured passengers could file suits for damages, subject only to the limitations of the forum's laws, including the forum's choice of law regime. This exposure inhibited the growth of the then-fledgling international airline industry. Many international air carriers at that time endeavored to require passengers, as a condition of air travel, to relieve or reduce the carrier's liability in case of injury. The Convention drafters designed Articles 17, 22, and 24 of the Convention as a compromise between the interests of air carriers and their customers worldwide. In Article 17 of the Convention, carriers are denied the contractual prerogative to exclude or limit their liability for personal injury. In Articles 22 and 24, passengers are limited in the amount of damages they may recover, and are restricted in the claims they may pursue by the conditions and limits set out in the Convention.

Construing the Convention, as did the Court of Appeals, to allow passengers to pursue claims under local law when the Convention does not permit recovery could produce several anomalies. Carriers might be exposed to unlimited liability under diverse legal regimes, but would be prevented, under the treaty, from contracting out of such liability. Passengers injured physically in an emergency landing might be subject to the liability caps of the Convention, while those merely traumatized in the same mishap would be free to sue outside of the Convention for potentially unlimited damages. The Court of Appeals' construction of the Convention would encourage artful pleading by plaintiffs seeking to opt out of the Convention's liability scheme when local law promised recovery in excess of that prescribed by the treaty. Such a reading would scarcely advance the predictability that adherence to the treaty has achieved worldwide....

The drafting history of Article 17 is consistent with our understanding of the preemptive effect of the Convention. The preliminary draft of the Convention submitted to the conference at Warsaw made air carriers liable "in the case of death, wounding, or any other bodily injury suffered by a traveler." In the later draft that prescribed what is now Article 17, airline liability was narrowed to encompass only bodily injury caused by an "accident." It is improbable that, at the same time the drafters narrowed the conditions of air carrier liability in Article 17, they intended, in Article 24, to permit passengers to skirt those conditions by pursuing claims under local law.

Inspecting the drafting history, the Court of Appeals stressed a proposal made by the Czechoslovak delegation to state in the treaty that, in the absence of a stipulation in the Convention itself, "'the provisions of laws and national rules relative to carriage in each [signatory] State shall apply.'" That proposal was withdrawn upon amendment of the Convention's title to read: "CONVENTION FOR THE UNIFICATION OF *CERTAIN* RULES RELATING TO INTERNATIONAL TRANSPORTATION BY AIR." The Second Circuit saw in this history an indication "that national law was intended to provide the passenger's remedy where the Convention did not expressly apply."

The British House of Lords, in Sidhu v. British Airways plc, [1997] 1 All E.R. 193, considered the same history, but found it inconclusive. Inclusion of the word "certain" in the Convention's title, the Lords reasoned, accurately indicated that "the Convention is concerned with certain rules only, not with all the rules relating to international carriage by air." *Id.*, at 204. For example, the Convention does not say "anything...about the carrier's obligations of insurance, and in particular about compulsory insurance against third party risks." *Ibid.* The Convention, in other words, is "a partial harmonization, directed to the particular issues with which it deals," *ibid.*, among them, a carrier's liability to passengers for personal injury. As to those issues, the Lords concluded, "the aim of the Convention is to unify." *Ibid.* Pointing to the overall understanding that the Convention's objective was to "ensure uniformity," *id.*, at 209, the Lords suggested that the Czechoslovak delegation may have meant only to underscore that national law controlled "chapters of law relating to international carriage by air with which the Convention was not attempting to deal." *Ibid.* In light of the Lords' exposition, we are satisfied that the withdrawn Czechoslovak proposal will not bear the weight the Court of Appeals placed on it. . . .

Tseng urges that federal preemption of state law is disfavored generally, and particularly when matters of health and safety are at stake. Tseng overlooks in this regard that the nation-state, not subdivisions within one nation, is the focus of the Convention and the perspective of our treaty partners. Our home-centered preemption analysis, therefore, should not be applied, mechanically, in construing our international obligations.

Decisions of the courts of other Convention signatories corroborate our understanding of the Convention's preemptive effect. In *Sidhu*, the British House of Lords considered and decided the very question we now face concerning the Convention's exclusivity when a passenger alleges psychological damages, but no physical injury, resulting from an occurrence that is not an "accident" under Article 17. *See* 1 All E.R. at 201, 207. Reviewing the text, structure, and drafting history of the Convention, the Lords concluded that the Convention was designed to "ensure that, in all questions relating to the carrier's liability, it is the provisions of the Convention which apply and that the passenger does not have access to any other remedies, whether under the common law or otherwise, which may be available within the particular country where he chooses to raise his action." *Ibid.* Courts of other nations bound by the Convention have also recognized the treaty's encompassing preemptive effect. The "opinions of our sister signatories," we have observed, are "entitled to considerable weight." *Saks*, 470 U.S. at 404. The text, drafting history, and underlying purpose of the Convention, in sum, counsel us to adhere to a view of the treaty's exclusivity shared by our treaty partners.

JUSTICE STEVENS, dissenting. . . .

Everyone agrees that the literal text of the treaty does not preempt claims of personal injury that do not arise out of an accident. It is equally clear that nothing in the drafting history requires that result. On the contrary, the amendment to the title of the Convention made in response to the proposal advanced by the Czechoslovak delegation, suggests that the parties assumed that local law would apply to all nonaccident cases. I agree with the Court that that inference is not strong enough, in itself, to require that the ambiguity be resolved in the plaintiff's favor. It suffices for me, however, that the history is just as ambiguous as the text. I firmly believe that a treaty, like an Act of Congress, should not be construed to preempt state law unless its intent to do so is clear. For this reason, I respectfully dissent.

2. The Role of the President and Senate in Treaty Interpretation

In the 1972 Treaty on the Limitation of Anti-Ballistic Missile Systems ("ABM Treaty") between the United States and the Soviet Union, each party agreed "not to develop, test, or deploy ABM systems or components," and to restrict land-based ABM systems to two sites. In March 1983, President Reagan initiated the Strategic Defense Initiative (SDI) that sought to establish a space-based method to render incoming ballistic missile warheads "impotent and obsolete." Two years later, the Reagan Administration announced a new interpretation of the ABM treaty that permitted research and development of ABM systems that, like the SDI system, used technologies not in existence in 1972. This new interpretation departed from prior Executive Branch interpretations of the ABM treaty that were presented to the Senate during the ratification process, and some argued that the Executive was bound by the earlier interpretations. In response to this claim, Abraham Sofaer, then-Legal Adviser to the State Department, argued that Executive Branch representations to the Senate were binding on the Executive after ratification only if they were "generally understood," "clearly intended," and "relied upon" by the Senate during the ratification process. *See* David A. Koplow, *Constitutional Bait and Switch: Executive Reinterpretation of Arms Control Treaties*, 137 Penn. L. Rev. 153, 1374 (1989) (deriving this position from various sources, including Sofaer's testimony before the Senate). Below is an Executive Branch legal analysis in support of Sofaer's view.

Memorandum from Charles J. Cooper, Assistant Attorney General, Office of Legal Counsel, to Abraham D. Sofaer, Legal Adviser, Department of State, "Relevance of Senate Ratification History to Treaty Interpretation"

11 Op. Atty. Gen. 28 (Apr. 9, 1987)

This memorandum responds to your request for the views of this Office concerning the relevance of the Senate's deliberations on ratification of a treaty to subsequent interpretations of ambiguous treaty language by the Executive Branch. We use the term "deliberations" or "ratification record" to encompass sources such as hearings, committee reports, and floor debates, which are generally analogous to the "legislative history" of domestic statutes. Our focus is on the relevance of those sources to interpretation of a treaty as domestic law, i.e., their relevance to the President's constitutional responsibility to "take Care that the Laws be faithfully executed." U.S. Const. art. II, §3. We understand that you are reviewing separately the relevance that would be ascribed under international law to the Senate's ratification record.

The question you raise does not lend itself to any clear or easy answer....

Under [the] separation of powers, the President has a dual role with respect to treaties. First, the President is responsible for "making" treaties, i.e., entering into negotiations with foreign governments and reaching agreement on specific provisions. U.S. Const. art. II, §2, cl. 2. Second, as part of his responsibility to "take Care that the Laws be faithfully executed," and as the "sole organ of the federal government in the field of international relations," the President is responsible for enforcing and executing international agreements, a responsibility that necessarily "involves also the obligation and authority to interpret what the treaty requires." L. Henkin, Foreign Affairs and the Constitution 167 (1972).[4]

The President's authority to make treaties is shared with the Senate, which must consent by a two-thirds vote. This "JOINT AGENCY of the Chief Magistrate of the Union, and of two-thirds of the members of [the Senate]"[6] reflects the Framers' recognition that the negotiation and acceptance of treaties incorporates both legislative and executive responsibilities. . . . Rather than vest either Congress or the President with the sole power to make treaties, the Framers sought to combine the judgment of both, providing that the President shall make the treaties, but subject to the "advice and consent" of the Senate. Thus, the Framers included the Senate in the treaty-making process because the result of that process, just as the result of the legislative process, is essentially a law that has "the effect of altering the legal rights, duties and relations of persons . . . outside the Legislative Branch." INS v. Chadha, 462 U.S. at 952. [H]owever, conceptually the constitutional division of treaty-making responsibility between the Senate and the President is essentially the reverse of the division of law-making authority, with the President being the draftsman of the treaty and the Senate holding the authority to grant or deny approval.

In practice, the Senate's formal participation in the treaty-making process begins after negotiation of the treaty. At that time, the President transmits the treaty to the Senate, with a detailed description and analysis of the treaty, and any protocols, annexes, or other documents that the President considers to be integral parts of the proposed treaty. Under the Senate's rules, treaties are referred to the Senate Foreign Relations Committee, which may hold hearings to develop a record explaining the purposes, provisions, and significance of the agreement. Typically, the principal witnesses at such hearings are representatives of the Executive Branch. The Foreign Relations Committee then issues a report to the full Senate, with its recommendation on approval of the treaty.

The Senate's practice has been to approve, to disapprove, or to approve with conditions, treaties negotiated by the Executive Branch. Express conditions imposed by the Senate may include "understandings," which interpret or clarify the obligations undertaken by the parties to the treaty but do not change those obligations, or "reservations" and "amendments," which condition the Senate's consent on amendment or limitation of the substantive obligations of the parties under the agreement. On occasion, the Senate has accompanied its consent by "declarations," which state the Senate's position, opinion, or intention on issues raised by the treaty, although not on the provisions of the specific treaty itself.

A. Express Conditions

When the Senate includes express conditions as part of its resolution of consent to ratification, the President may, if he objects, either refuse to ratify the treaty or resubmit it to the Senate with the hope that it will be approved unconditionally the

4. The President's interpretation of a treaty is, of course, subject to review by the courts in a case or controversy that meets Article III requirements. See U.S. Const. art. III, §2 ("The judicial Power shall extend to all Cases, . . . arising under this Constitution, the Laws of the United States, and Treaties made, or which shall be made, under their Authority").

6. The Federalist No. 66, at 406 (A. Hamilton) (C. Rossiter ed. 1961).

second time. If the President proceeds with ratification, however, such understandings or other conditions expressly imposed by the Senate are generally included by the President with the treaty documents deposited for ratification or communicated to the other parties at the same time the treaty is deposited for ratification. Because such conditions are considered to be part of the United States' position in ratifying the treaty, they are generally binding on the President, both internationally and domestically, in his subsequent interpretation of the treaty.

B. Statements in the Ratification Record

The more difficult question is what relevance, if any, the President must give to less formal, contemporaneous indications of the Senate's understanding of the treaty, i.e., statements in committee reports, hearings, and debates which may reflect an understanding of certain treaty provisions by some Senators, but which were not embodied in any formal understanding or condition approved by the entire Senate.[14] With the not insubstantial exception of representations made or confirmed by the Executive Branch (discussed below), we believe such statements have only limited probative value and therefore are entitled to little weight in subsequent interpretations of the treaty.

First, it must be observed that a treaty is fundamentally a "contract between or among sovereign nations," and the primary responsibility — whether of the executive or the courts — is "to give the specific words of the treaty a meaning consistent with the shared expectations of the contracting parties." Air France v. Saks, 470 U.S. 392, 399 (1985). International agreements, like "other contracts . . . are to be read in the light of the conditions and circumstances existing at the time they were entered into, with a view to effecting the objects and purposes of the States thereby contracting." Rocca v. Thompson, 223 U.S. 317, 331-332 (1912). Necessarily, the best evidence of the intent of the parties is the language and structure of the treaty and, secondarily, direct evidence of the understanding reached by the parties, as reflected in the negotiating record and subsequent administrative construction, rather than unilateral, post-negotiation statements made during the Senate ratification debates.

Moreover, the constitutional role of the Senate is limited to approval or disapproval of the treaty, much as the President's constitutional role in enacting domestic legislation is limited to his veto power. The Senate may, if it chooses, amend or interpret the treaty by attaching explicit conditions to its consent, which are then transmitted to, and either accepted or rejected by, the other parties. Absent such conditions, the Senate does not participate in setting the terms of the agreement between the parties, and therefore statements made by Senators, whether individually in hearings and debates or collectively in committee reports, should be accorded little weight unless confirmed by the Executive. . . .

Indeed, profound foreign policy implications would be raised if the United States were to supplement or alter treaty obligations to foreign governments based on statements made by members of the Senate during its consideration of the treaty that were not communicated to those governments in the form of express

---

14. It is clear that post hoc expressions of legislative intent, after the treaty has been duly ratified, cannot change the legal effect of an international agreement to which the Senate has given its approval. *See* Fourteen Diamond Rings v. United States, 183 U.S. 176, 179-180 (1901) (resolution adopted by Congress after the Senate had consented to ratification of a treaty is "absolutely without legal significance"). Congress may, of course, in effect validate an Executive Branch interpretation of a treaty by passing legislation consistent with that view.

conditions. "Foreign governments dealing with us must rely upon the official instruments of ratification as an expression of the full intent of the government of the United States, precisely as we expect from foreign governments." Coplin v. United States, 6 Ct. Cl. at 145....

On the other hand, statements made to the Senate by representatives of the Executive Branch as to the meaning of a treaty should have considerably more weight in subsequent interpretations of ambiguous terms of the treaty. Such statements do not present as substantial a threat to the reliance interests of foreign governments, because the Executive Branch negotiated the treaty and is therefore in a position to represent authoritatively the meaning of the agreement that emerged from the negotiating process. Moreover, given that the Senate's constitutional role is limited to approving a treaty already negotiated by the Executive Branch and that much of the extra-textual evidence of a treaty's meaning remains in the control of the Executive Branch, we believe the Senate itself has a substantial reliance interest in statements made by the Executive Branch officials seeking that approval.

Accordingly, consistent with the President's role as the nation's exclusive negotiator of treaties with foreign governments, we believe that statements made to the Senate by the Executive Branch during the ratification debates are relevant in much the same way that contemporaneous statements by congressional draftsmen or sponsors of domestic legislation are relevant to any subsequent interpretation of the statute. We note that because of the primary role played by the Executive Branch in the negotiation of treaties and the implementation of foreign policy, courts generally accord substantial deference — albeit not conclusive effect — to interpretations advanced by the Executive Branch. Although the courts often rely on interpretative statements made by the Executive Branch prepared well after negotiation and ratification of the treaty,[21] they find particularly persuasive a consistent pattern of Executive Branch interpretation, reflected in the application of the treaty by the Executive and the course of conduct of the parties in implementing the agreement. Much as contemporaneous administrative construction of domestic statutes by agencies charged with their implementation is generally accorded considerable deference by the courts, particularly when those agencies have made explicit representations to Congress during consideration of the legislation, statements made to the Senate by members of the Executive Branch about the scope and meaning of a treaty would be relevant evidence of the Executive Branch's view, and therefore would be accorded deference by a court in assessing the domestic effect of the treaty.

The weight to be given to an interpretative statement made by an Executive Branch official to the Senate during the ratification process will likely depend upon such factors as the formality of the statement, the identity and position of the Executive Branch official making the statement, the level of attention and interest focused on the meaning of the relevant treaty provision, and the consistency with which members of the Executive Branch adhered at the time to the view of the treaty provision reflected in the statement. All of these factors affect the degree to which the Senate could reasonably have relied upon the statement and, in turn, the weight that courts will attach to it. At one extreme, a single statement made by a middle-level Executive Branch official in response to a question at a hearing would

---

21. On occasion, the State Department makes specific suggestions to the court about the interpretation of an agreement.... The courts in fact often invite the United States to file amicus briefs giving the views of the Executive Branch in cases to which the United States is not a party.

not be regarded as definitive. Rather, in interpreting the domestic effect of a treaty, the courts would likely accord such a statement in the ratification record a degree of significance subordinate to more direct evidence of the mutual intent of the parties, such as the language and context of the treaty, diplomatic exchanges between the President and the other treaty parties, the negotiating record, and the practical construction of the provision reflected in the parties' course of dealings under the treaty. Moreover, courts often give substantial weight to the Executive Branch's current interpretation of the treaty, in recognition of the President's unique role in shaping foreign policy and communicating with foreign governments, and, accordingly, would be unlikely to bind future chief executives on the basis of an isolated remark of an Executive Branch official in a previous administration. In general, therefore, less formal statements made by the Executive Branch before the Senate (such as the one described in the preceding hypothetical) will be but one source of relevant evidence to be considered in interpreting an ambiguous treaty provision.

In contrast, in a case in which the statements by the Executive Branch amount to a formal representation by the President concerning the meaning of a particular treaty provision, the ratification record may be conclusive. If, for example, the ratification record unequivocally shows that the President presented the treaty to the Senate based on specific, official representations regarding the meaning of an ambiguous provision, that the Senate regarded that understanding as important to its consent, and that the Senate relied on the representations made by the Executive Branch in approving the treaty (and thus in refraining from attaching a formal reservation setting forth the understanding), we believe the President would, in effect, be estopped from taking a contrary position in his subsequent interpretation of the treaty, just as he would be bound by a formal reservation or understanding passed by the Senate to the same effect. Obviously, a President could not negotiate a treaty with other nations on the basis of one understanding of its import, submit the treaty to the Senate on a wholly different understanding, and then, in implementing the treaty, rely solely on the understanding he had reached with the other parties. Similarly, he could not reach a secret agreement with the other party that substantially modifies the obligations and authorities created by the text of the treaty submitted to the Senate, and then seek to use the secret agreement as a basis for actions inconsistent with the text of the treaty. Such results would essentially eviscerate the Senate's constitutional advice and consent role, because it would deprive the Senate of a fair opportunity to determine whether, or with what conditions, the treaty should become the "supreme Law of the Land." Accordingly, in such extreme cases, we have little doubt that, as a matter of domestic law, the courts would construe the treaty as presented to and accepted by the Senate, even if as a matter of international law the treaty might have a different meaning.[25]

---

25. Although courts generally seek to construe treaties consistent with their international import, on occasion courts have adopted constructions of particular treaties that conflict with the President's view of the international obligations created by the treaty. Moreover, Congress can enact domestic legislation that is inconsistent with existing treaty obligations, and thus has the effect of tying the President's hands domestically, while leaving the international obligations intact. It would not be unprecedented, therefore, for a court to construe a treaty more narrowly — or more broadly — as a matter of domestic law than the President construes the treaty as a matter of international law.

The "Sofaer doctrine" generated substantial criticism and debate — in Congress, among academic commentators, and in the international community. Congress subsequently imposed conditions on Defense Department appropriations forbidding the testing of new technologies that would violate the original, narrower construction of the Treaty. The Reagan administration subsequently announced that, while it considered its broad interpretation of the Treaty "fully justified," it would follow a narrower interpretation in practice.

Several years later, the Senate gave its consent to the Treaty on the Elimination of Their Intermediate-Range and Shorter-Range Missiles ("I.N.F. Treaty"), a treaty with the Soviet Union that called for the elimination of ground-based missiles capable of reaching distances between 300 and 3500 miles. The Senate attached the following condition — the so-called "Biden Condition" — to its advice and consent:

> The Senate's advice and consent to ratification of the I.N.F. Treaty is subject to the condition, based on the treaty clauses of the Constitution, that:
> 1. The United States shall interpret the treaty in accordance with the common understanding of the treaty shared by the President and the Senate at the time the Senate gave its advice and consent to ratification;
> 2. Such common understanding is based on: a) first, the text of the treaty and the provisions of this resolution of ratification; and b) second, the authoritative representations which were provided by the President and his representatives to the Senate and its committees, in seeking Senate consent to ratification, insofar as such representations were directed to the meaning and legal effect of the text of the treaty; and
> 3. The United States shall not agree to or adopt an interpretation different from that common understanding except pursuant to Senate advice and consent to a subsequent treaty or protocol, or the enactment of a statute; and
> 4. If, subsequent to ratification of the treaty, a question arises as to the interpretation of a provision of the treaty on which no common understanding was reached in accordance with paragraph 2, that provision shall be interpreted in accordance with applicable United States law.

134 Cong. Rec.. S6724 (daily ed. May 26, 1988). The condition was adopted by the Senate by a vote of 72 to 27.

3. The President's Authority to Terminate Treaties

Goldwater v. Carter

617 F.2d 697 (D.C. Cir. 1979)

[This case concerned the constitutional validity of President Carter's termination of a defense treaty with Taiwan, which he announced in conjunction with his decision to recognize mainland China. In Chapter 2, we looked at the Supreme Court's decision in this case, in which the Court dismissed the case based on justiciability considerations and did not reach the merits. The lower courts had reached the merits, however, with the district court holding that the termination would not be effective unless approved by either two-thirds of the Senate or a majority of both houses of Congress, and the court of appeals holding that the termination was effective without further senatorial or congressional action. The court of appeals decision is excerpted below.]

Opinion for the court PER CURIAM. . . .

[W]e think it important at the outset to stress that the Treaty, as it was presented to the Senate in 1954 and consented to by it, contained an explicit provision for termination by either party on one year's notice. The Senate, in the course of giving its consent, exhibited no purpose and took no action to reserve a role for itself by amendment, reservation, or condition in the effectuation of this provision. Neither has the Senate, since the giving of the notice of termination, purported to take any final or decisive action with respect to it, either by way of approval or disapproval. The constitutional issue we face, therefore, is solely and simply the one of whether the President in these precise circumstances is, on behalf of the United States, empowered to terminate the Treaty in accordance with its terms. It is our view that he is, and that the limitations which the District Court purported to place on his action in this regard have no foundation in the Constitution. . . .

Various considerations enter into our determination that the President's notice of termination will be effective on January 1, 1980. The result we reach draws upon their totality, but in listing them hereinafter we neither assign them hierarchical values nor imply that any one factor or combination of factors is determinative.

1. We turn first to the argument, embraced by the District Court, drawn from the language of Article II, §2, of the Constitution. It is that, since the President clearly cannot enter into a treaty without the consent of the Senate, the inference is inescapable that he must in all circumstances seek the same senatorial consent to terminate that treaty. As a matter of language alone, however, the same inference would appear automatically to obtain with respect to the termination by the President of officers appointed by him under the same clause of the Constitution and subject to Senate confirmation. But the Supreme Court has read that clause as not having such an inevitable effect in any and all circumstances. Compare Myers v. United States, 272 U.S. 52 (1926) with In re Humphrey's Executor v. United States, 295 U.S. 602 (1935). In the area of foreign relations in particular, where the constitutional commitment of powers to the President is notably comprehensive, it has never been suggested that the services of Ambassadors appointed by the President, confirmed by the Senate, and of critical importance as they are to the successful conduct of our foreign relations may not be terminated by the President without the prior authorization of that body.

Expansion of the language of the Constitution by sequential linguistic projection is a tricky business at best. Virtually all constitutional principles have unique elements and can be distinguished from one another. As the Supreme Court has recognized with respect to the clause in question, it is not abstract logic or sterile symmetry that controls, but a sensible and realistic ascertainment of the meaning of the Constitution in the context of the specific action taken.

2. The District Court's declaration, in the alternative, that the necessary authority in this instance may be granted by a majority of each house of Congress presumably has its source in the Supremacy Clause of Article VI. The argument is that a treaty, being a part of the "supreme Law of the Land," can only be terminated at the least by a subsequent federal statute.

The central purpose of the Supremacy Clause has been accepted to be that of causing each of the designated supreme laws Constitution, statute, and treaty to prevail, for purposes of domestic law, over state law in any form. Article VI speaks explicitly to the judges to assure that this is so. But these three types of supreme law are not necessarily the same in their other characteristics, any more than are the circumstances and terms of their creation the same. Certainly the Constitution is silent on the matter of treaty termination. And the fact that it speaks to the common characteristic of supremacy over state law does not provide any basis for concluding that a treaty must be unmade either by (1) the same process by which it was made, or (2) the alternative means by which a statute is made or terminated.

3. The constitutional institution of advice and consent of the Senate, provided two-thirds of the Senators concur, is a special and extraordinary condition of the exercise by the President of certain specified powers under Article II. It is not lightly to be extended in instances not set forth in the Constitution. Such an extension by implication is not proper unless that implication is unmistakably clear.

The District Court's absolutist extension of this limitation to termination of treaties, irrespective of the particular circumstances involved, is not sound. The making of a treaty has the consequences of an entangling alliance for the nation. Similarly, the amending of a treaty merely continues such entangling alliances, changing only their character, and therefore also requires the advice and consent of the Senate. It does not follow, however, that a constitutional provi sion for a special concurrence (two-thirds of the Senators) prior to entry into an entangling alliance necessarily applies to its termination in accordance with its terms.

4. The Constitution specifically confers no power of treaty termination on either the Congress or the Executive. We note, however, that the powers conferred upon Congress in Article I of the Constitution are specific, detailed, and limited, while the powers conferred upon the President by Article II are generalized in a manner that bespeaks no such limitation upon foreign affairs powers. "Section 1. The executive Power shall be vested in a President. . . ." Although specific powers are listed in Section 2 and Section 3, these are in many instances not powers necessary to an Executive, while "The executive Power" referred to in Section 1 is nowhere defined. There is no required twothirds vote of the Senate conditioning the exercise of any power in Section 1.

In some instances this difference is reflective of the origin of the particular power in question. In general, the powers of the federal government arise out of specific grants of authority delegated by the states hence the enumerated powers of Congress in Article I, Section 8. The foreign affairs powers, however, proceed directly from the sovereignty of the Union. "(I)f they had never been mentioned in the Constitution, (they) would have vested in the federal government as necessary concomitants of nationality." United States v. Curtiss-Wright Export Corp., 299 U.S. 304, 318 (1936).

The President is the constitutional representative of the United States with respect to external affairs. It is significant that the treaty power appears in Article II of the Constitution, relating to the executive branch, and not in Article I, setting forth the powers of the legislative branch. It is the President as Chief Executive who is given the constitutional authority to enter into a treaty; and even after he has obtained the consent of the Senate it is for him to decide whether to ratify a treaty and put it into effect. Senatorial confirmation of a treaty concededly does not obligate the President to go forward with a treaty if he concludes that it is not in the public interest to do so.

Thus, in contrast to the lawmaking power, the constitutional initiative in the treaty-making field is in the President, not Congress. It would take an unprecedented feat of judicial construction to read into the Constitution an absolute condition precedent of congressional or Senate approval for termination of all treaties, similar to the specific one relating to initial approval. And it would unalterably affect the balance of power between the two Branches laid down in Articles I and II.

5. Ultimately, what must be recognized is that a treaty is sui generis. It is not just another law. It is an international compact, a solemn obligation of the United States and a "supreme Law" that supersedes state policies and prior federal laws. For clarity of analysis, it is thus well to distinguish between treaty-making as an international act and the consequences which flow domestically from such act. In one realm the Constitution has conferred the primary role upon the President; in the other, Congress retains its primary role as lawmaker. The fact that the Constitution, statutes, and treaties are all listed in the Supremacy Clause as being superior to any form of state law does not mean that the making and unmaking of treaties can be analogized to the making and unmaking of domestic statutes any more than it can be analogized to the making or unmaking of a constitutional amendment.

The recognized powers of Congress to implement (or fail to implement) a treaty by an appropriation or other law essential to its effectuation, or to supersede for all practical purposes the effect of a treaty on domestic law, are legislative powers, not treaty-making or treaty termination powers. The issue here, however, is not Congress' legislative powers to supersede or affect the domestic impact of a treaty; the issue is whether the Senate (or Congress) must in this case give its prior consent to discontinue a treaty which the President thinks it desirable to terminate in the national interest and pursuant to a provision in the treaty itself. The existence, in practical terms, of one power does not imply the existence, in constitutional terms, of the other.

6. If we were to hold that under the Constitution a treaty could only be terminated by exactly the same process by which it was made, we would be locking the United States into all of its international obligations, even if the President and two-thirds of the Senate minus one firmly believed that the proper course for the United States was to terminate a treaty. Many of our treaties in force, such as mutual defense treaties, carry potentially dangerous obligations. These obligations are terminable under international law upon breach by the other party or change in circumstances that frustrates the purpose of the treaty. In many of these situations the President must take immediate action. The creation of a constitutionally obligatory role in all cases for a two-thirds consent by the Senate would give to one-third plus one of the Senate the power to deny the President the authority necessary to conduct our foreign policy in a rational and effective manner.

7. Even as to the formal termination of treaties, as the District Court pointed out, "a variety of means have been used to terminate treaties." There is much debate among the historians and scholars as to whether in some instances the legislature has been involved at all; they are agreed that, when involved, that involvement with the President has taken many different forms. . . .

The District Court concluded that the diversity of historical precedents left an inconclusive basis on which to decide the issue of whether the President's power to terminate a treaty must always be "shared" in some way by the Senate or Congress. We agree. Yet we think it is not without significance that out of all the historical precedents brought to our attention, in no situation has a treaty been continued in force over the opposition of the President.

There is on the other hand widespread agreement that the President has the power as Chief Executive under many circumstances to exercise functions regarding treaties which have the effect of either terminating or continuing their vitality. Prominent among these is the authority of the President as Chief Executive (1) to determine whether a treaty has terminated because of a breach, Charlton v. Kelly,

229 U.S. 447, 473-476, (1913); and (2) to determine whether a treaty is at an end due to changed circumstances.

In short, the determination of the conduct of the United States in regard to treaties is an instance of what has broadly been called the "foreign affairs power" of the President. We have no occasion to define that term, but we do take account of its vitality. The *Curtiss-Wright* opinion, written by a Justice who had served in the United States Senate, declares in oft-repeated language that the President is "the sole organ of the federal government in the field of international relations." That status is not confined to the service of the President as a channel of communication, as the District Court suggested, but embraces an active policy determination as to the conduct of the United States in regard to a treaty in response to numerous problems and circumstances as they arise.

8. How the vital functions of the President in implementing treaties and in deciding on their viability in response to changing events can or should interact with Congress' legitimate concerns and powers in relating to foreign affairs is an area into which we should not and do not prematurely intrude. History shows us that there are too many variables to lay down any hard and fast constitutional rules.

We cannot find an implied role in the Constitution for the Senate in treaty termination for some but not all treaties in terms of their relative importance. There is no judicially ascertainable and manageable method of making any distinction among treaties on the basis of their substance, the magnitude of the risk involved, the degree of controversy which their termination would engender, or by any other standards. We know of no standards to apply in making such distinctions. The facts on which such distinctions might be drawn may be difficult of ascertainment; and the resolution of such inevitable disputes between the two Branches would be an improper and unnecessary role for the courts. To decide whether there was a breach or changed circumstances, for example, would involve a court in making fundamental decisions of foreign policy and would create insuperable problems of evidentiary proof. This is beyond the acceptable judicial role. All we decide today is that two-thirds Senate consent or majority consent in both houses is not necessary to terminate this treaty in the circumstances before us now.

9. The circumstances involved in the termination of the Mutual Defense Treaty with the Republic of China include a number of material and unique elements. Prominent is assertion by the officials of both the Republic of China and the People's Republic of China that each of them is the government of China, intending the term China to comprehend both the mainland of China and the island of Taiwan. In the 1972 Shanghai Communique, the United States acknowledged that position and did not challenge it. It is in this context that the recent Joint Communique set forth as of January 1, 1979 that the United States recognizes the People's Republic of China as "the sole legal government of China." This action made reference to "the people of Taiwan," stating that the peoples of the United States and Taiwan "will maintain cultural, commercial and other unofficial relations." This formulation was confirmed by the Taiwan Relations Act.

It is undisputed that the Constitution gave the President full constitutional authority to recognize the PRC and to derecognize the ROC. What the United States has evolved for Taiwan is a novel and somewhat indefinite relationship, namely, of unofficial relations with the people of Taiwan. The subtleties involved in maintaining amorphous relationships are often the very stuff of diplomacy a field in which the President, not Congress, has responsibility under our Constitution.

The President makes a responsible claim that he has authority as Chief Executive to determine that there is no meaningful vitality to a mutual defense treaty when there is no recognized state. That is not to say that the recognition power automatically gives the President authority to take any action that is required or requested by the state being recognized. We do not need to reach this question. Nevertheless, it remains an important ingredient in the case at bar that the President has determined that circumstances have changed so as to preclude continuation of the Mutual Defense Treaty with the ROC; diplomatic recognition of the ROC came to an end on January 1, 1979, and now there exists only "cultural, commercial and other unofficial relations" with the "people on Taiwan."

10. Finally, and of central significance, the treaty here at issue contains a termination clause. The existence of Article X of the ROC treaty, permitting termination by either party on one year's notice, is an overarching factor in this case, which in effect enables all of the other considerations to be knit together.

Without derogating from the executive power of the President to decide to act contrary to the wording of a treaty for example, because of a breach by the other party (Charlton v. Kelly, supra), or because of a doctrine of fundamental change of circumstances (rebus sic stantibus) the President's authority as Chief Executive is at its zenith when the Senate has consented to a treaty that expressly provides for termination on one year's notice, and the President's action is the giving of notice of termination.

As already noted, we have no occasion to decide whether this factor would be determinative in a case lacking other factors identified above, e. g., under a notice of withdrawal from the NATO treaty unaccompanied by derecognition of the other signatories. No specific restriction or condition on the President's action is found within the Constitution or this treaty itself. The termination clause is without conditions and without designation as to who shall act to terminate it. No specific role is spelled out in either the Constitution or this treaty for the Senate or the Congress as a whole. That power consequently devolves upon the President, and there is no basis for a court to imply a restriction on the President's power to terminate not contained in the Constitution, in this treaty, or in any other authoritative source.

In December 2001, President Bush determined that the United States would terminate its obligations under the ABM treaty that was the subject of the reinterpretation debate, recounted above. Here is the text of the December 13, 2001 Diplomatic Notes sent to Russia, Belarus, Kazakhstan, and the Ukraine (the notes were sent to these countries because the Soviet Union had disintegrated in the interim, and these were the resulting countries that had nuclear weapons):

> The Embassy of the United States of America has the honor to refer to the Treaty between the United States of America and the Union of Soviet Socialist Republics (USSR) on the Limitation of Anti-Ballistic Missile Systems signed at Moscow May 26, 1972.
>
> Article XV, paragraph 2, gives each Party the right to withdraw from the Treaty if it decides that extraordinary events related to the subject matter of the treaty have jeopardized its supreme interests.
>
> The United States recognizes that the Treaty was entered into with the USSR, which ceased to exist in 1991. Since then, we have entered into a new strategic

relationship with Russia that is cooperative rather than adversarial, and are building strong relationships with most states of the former USSR.

Since the Treaty entered into force in 1972, a number of state and non-state entities have acquired or are actively seeking to acquire weapons of mass destruction. It is clear, and has recently been demonstrated, that some of these entities are prepared to employ these weapons against the United States. Moreover, a number of states are developing ballistic missiles, including long-range ballistic missiles, as a means of delivering weapons of mass destruction. These events pose a direct threat to the territory and security of the United States and jeopardize its supreme interests. As a result, the United States has concluded that it must develop, test, and deploy anti-ballistic missile systems for the defense of its national territory, of its forces outside the United States, and of its friends and allies.

Pursuant to Article XV, paragraph 2, the United States has decided that extraordinary events related to the subject matter of the Treaty have jeopardized its supreme interests. Therefore, in the exercise of the right to withdraw from the Treaty provided in Article XV, paragraph 2, the United States hereby gives notice of its withdrawal from the Treaty. In accordance with the terms of the Treaty, withdrawal will be effective six months from the date of this notice.

The White House also issued the following Fact Sheet related to the ABM treaty withdrawal:

The circumstances affecting U.S. national security have changed fundamentally since the signing of the ABM Treaty in 1972. The attacks against the U.S. homeland on September 11 vividly demonstrate that the threats we face today are far different from those of the Cold War. During that era, now fortunately in the past, the United States and the Soviet Union were locked in an implacably hostile relationship. Each side deployed thousands of nuclear weapons pointed at the other. Our ultimate security rested largely on the grim premise that neither side would launch a nuclear attack because doing so would result in a counter-attack ensuring the total destruction of both nations.

Today, our security environment is profoundly different. The Cold War is over. The Soviet Union no longer exists. Russia is not an enemy, but in fact is increasingly allied with us on a growing number of critically important issues. The depth of United States-Russian cooperation in counterterrorism is both a model of the new strategic relationship we seek to establish and a foundation on which to build further cooperation across the broad spectrum of political, economic and security issues of mutual interest.

Today, the United States and Russia face new threats to their security. Principal among these threats are weapons of mass destruction and their delivery means wielded by terrorists and rogue states. A number of such states are acquiring increasingly longer-range ballistic missiles as instruments of blackmail and coercion against the United States and its friends and allies. The United States must defend its homeland, its forces and its friends and allies against these threats. We must develop and deploy the means to deter and protect against them, including through limited missile defense of our territory.

Under the terms of the ABM Treaty, the United States is prohibited from defending its homeland against ballistic missile attack. We are also prohibited from cooperating in developing missile defenses against long-range threats with our friends and allies. Given the emergence of these new threats to our national security and the imperative of defending against them, the United States is today providing formal notification of its withdrawal from the ABM Treaty. As provided in Article XV of that Treaty, the effective date of withdrawal will be six months from today.

At the same time, the United States looks forward to moving ahead with Russia in developing elements of a new strategic relationship. . . .

4. Presidential "Unsigning" of Treaties

Under contemporary treaty practice, a nation's signature of a treaty, especially a multilateral treaty, does not make the nation a party to the treaty. Rather, nations typically become parties to treaties by an act of ratification—either by depositing an instrument of ratification with a depository (for multilateral treaties) or exchanging instruments of ratification (for bilateral treaties). According to Article 18 of the Vienna Convention on the Law of Treaties, however, a nation that signs a treaty is "obliged to refrain from acts which would defeat the object and purpose" of the treaty "until it shall have made its intention clear not to become a party to the treaty." Although the United States has not ratified the Vienna Convention, Executive Branch officials have stated on a number of occasions that they view at least much of the Convention as reflecting binding customary international law.

On December 31, 2000, shortly before leaving office, President Clinton signed the treaty establishing the International Criminal Court. Under that treaty, an international court, based in The Hague, Netherlands, has jurisdiction to try the offenses of genocide, crimes against humanity, war crimes, and the crime of aggression. In signing the treaty, President Clinton stated that:

In signing..., we are not abandoning our concerns about significant flaws in the treaty.

In particular, we are concerned that when the court comes into existence, it will not only exercise authority over personnel of states that have ratified the treaty, but also claim jurisdiction over personnel of states that have not.

With signature, however, we will be in a position to influence the evolution of the court. Without signature, we will not.

In May 2002, at President Bush's direction, the Under Secretary of State for Arms Control, John Bolton, sent the following letter to the Secretary-General of the United Nations:

Dear Mr. Secretary-General:

This is to inform you, in connection with the Rome Statute of the International Criminal Court adopted on July 17, 1998, that the United States does not intend to become a party to the treaty. Accordingly, the United States has no legal obligations arising from its signature on December 31, 2000. The United States requests that its intention not to become a party, as expressed in this letter, be reflected in the depositary's status lists relating to this treaty.

Press Statement, International Criminal Court: Letter from John Bolton to UN Secretary General Kofi Annan (May 6, 2002), at www.state.gov/r/pa/prs/ps/2002/9968.htm. The sending of this letter was described by some commentators as "unsigning" the International Criminal Court treaty, although the Administration did not attempt to physically remove the U.S. signature.

In explaining the Administration's action, Marc Grossman, the Under Secretary for Political Affairs, stated:

Here's what America believes in:

• We believe in justice and the promotion of the rule of law.
• We believe those who commit the most serious crimes of concern to the international community should be punished.

- We believe that states, not international institutions are primarily responsible for ensuring justice in the international system.
- We believe that the best way to combat these serious offenses is to build domestic judicial systems, strengthen political will and promote human freedom.

We have concluded that the International Criminal Court does not advance these principles. Here is why:

- We believe the ICC undermines the role of the United Nations Security Council in maintaining international peace and security.
- We believe in checks and balances. The Rome Statute creates a prosecutorial system that is an unchecked power.
- We believe that in order to be bound by a treaty, a state must be party to that treaty. The ICC asserts jurisdiction over citizens of states that have not ratified the treaty. This threatens US sovereignty.
- We believe that the ICC is built on a flawed foundation. These flaws leave it open for exploitation and politically motivated prosecutions.

President Bush has come to the conclusion that the United States can no longer be a party to this process. In order to make our objections clear, both in principle and philosophy, and so as not to create unwarranted expectations of U.S. involvement in the Court, the President believes that he has no choice but to inform the United Nations, as depository of the treaty, of our intention not to become a party to the Rome Statute of the International Criminal Court. This morning, at the instruction of the President, our mission to the United Nations notified the UN Secretary General in his capacity as the depository for the Rome Statute of the President's decision. These actions are consistent with the Vienna Convention on the Law of Treaties.

Marc Grossman, Under Secretary for Political Affairs, Remarks to the Center for Strategic and International Studies, Washington, D.C. (May 6, 2002), at *http:// www.state. gov/p/ 9949.htm*,

Notes and Questions

1. As *El Al* illustrates, when interpreting a treaty, the Supreme Court sometimes looks beyond the treaty's text to its purpose and drafting history and to the post-ratification practices of the treaty parties. In other cases, however, the Court relies on the treaty's text to the exclusion of these other factors. An example of the latter approach can be found in Chan v. Korean Airlines, 490 U.S. 122 (1989). The issue in *Chan* was whether an airline forfeited the Warsaw Convention's liability limitation by failing to provide notice of the limitation to passengers in the 10-point type required by a private accord among air carriers. The Court determined that the text of the Convention clearly limited liability in this context, and that in the absence of textual ambiguity recourse to drafting history or other evidence of what the drafters intended was inappropriate. When should courts look beyond the treaty's text to other materials? Is the drafting history of a treaty like the legislative history of a statute? Is it more or less relevant to the treaty's meaning than legislative history is to a statute's meaning? Is intent easier to discern with treaties than it is with statutes? Does it matter whether the treaty is bilateral or multilateral?

In answering these questions, consider the Vienna Convention on the Law of Treaties, 1155 U.N.T.S. 331, adopted 22 May 1969, entry into force 27 January 1980. Article 31(1) of the Vienna Convention provides that "[a] treaty shall be interpreted in good faith in accordance with the ordinary meaning to be given to the terms of the treaty in their context and in the light of its object and purpose." Article 32 provides that "[r]ecourse may be had to supplementary means of interpretation, including the preparatory work of the treaty and the circumstances of its conclusion, in order to confirm the meaning resulting from the application of article 31, or to determine the meaning when the interpretation according to article 31: (a) leaves the meaning ambiguous or obscure; or (b) leads to a result which is manifestly absurd or unreasonable." The United States has not ratified the Vienna Convention, but the State Department has stated that many of its provisions reflect customary international law, and lower courts have applied its terms in a number of cases. Is the Supreme Court's approach to treaty interpretation in *El Al* and *Chan* consistent with these Articles? For discussion of the tension between the requirements of the Vienna Convention and U.S. interpretation practice, see Evan Criddle, *The Vienna Convention on the Law of Treaties in U.S. Treaty Interpretation*, 44 Va. J. Int'l L. 431 (2004).

2. The majority in *El Al* relies on the decisions of courts in other countries, which it says are entitled to "considerable weight." Why is this so? Is the deference in this context stronger or weaker than the deference courts pay to Executive Branch interpretation of treaties, which we analyzed in Chapter 2? What happens if foreign court interpretations conflict with the Executive's interpretation?

In Olympic Airways v. Husain, 541 U.S. 644 (2004), there was disagreement among the Supreme Court Justices over the degree of deference owed to foreign court decisions in the interpretation of treaties. *Husain* involved the question whether an airline's failure to move a passenger away from a smoking area, resulting in the passenger's death, could be an "accident" under Article 17 of the Warsaw Convention. Relying largely on earlier Supreme Court decisions and dictionary definitions, the majority concluded that it could. The majority rejected reliance on two contrary intermediate appellate courts from the United Kingdom and Australia on the ground that "there are substantial factual distinctions between these cases," and "the respective courts of last resort — the House of Lords and High Court of Australia — have yet to speak." *Id.* at 655 n. 9. In dissent, Justice Scalia disagreed, reasoning:

> We can, and should, look to decisions of other signatories when we interpret treaty provisions. Foreign constructions are evidence of the original shared understanding of the contracting parties. Moreover, it is reasonable to impute to the parties an intent that their respective courts strive to interpret the treaty consistently.... Finally, even if we disagree, we surely owe the conclusions reached by appellate courts of other signatories the courtesy of respectful consideration.... To the extent the Court implies that [the foreign court decisions] merit only slight consideration because they were not decided by courts of last resort, I note that our prior Warsaw Convention cases have looked to decisions of intermediate appellate foreign courts as well as supreme courts.

Id. at 661-62 & n.2. Are you convinced by Justice Scalia's reasons for deferring to foreign judicial treaty interpretations? What if the Supreme Court relied on the lower court decisions and they were overturned on appeal? If there are just a few foreign decisions on point, does deference to those decisions run the risk on entrenching a possibly wrong initial decision?

3. As *El Al* shows, one difference between a U.S. statute and a treaty is that the latter can be written in more than one authoritative language. Recall from Section A that Chief Justice Marshall changed his mind about the meaning of the treaty at issue in *Foster v. Neilson* after consulting the Spanish language version of the treaty in *United States v. Percheman*. Which version — English, or some other language — is dispositive for U.S. courts? Article 33 of the Vienna Convention on the Law of Treaties states that in the event of a discrepancy between two or more authoritative languages that is not clarified by the normal rules of interpretation, "the meaning which best reconciles the texts, having regard to the object and purpose of the treaty, shall be adopted." To the extent that the Vienna Convention binds the United States, must a U.S. court take into account and reconcile non-English versions of the treaty when they conflict on a particular point with the English version? Does *Percheman* support this view? Are federal judges generally equipped to do this? Does it matter that the Senate considered and consented to only the English-language version?

4. The majority and dissent in *El Al* disagree over whether the presumption against preemption of state law that applies to statutes also applies to treaties. In light of the analysis of these issues in Chapter 5, which side has the better of the argument here? When Justice Ginsburg says that "our home-centered preemption analysis . . . should not be applied, mechanically, in construing our international obligations," does she mean that it has no relevance in the treaty context, or that it has less relevance?

5. Of what relevance to the interpretation of a treaty are statements made, either by the Senate or the Executive Branch, during the Senate advice and consent process? Why should a statement by a Senator, or even a Senate Foreign Relations Committee report, matter to the interpretation of a treaty? Do such statements and reports have more weight, or less, than they would for the interpretation of statutes? What about presidential statements to the Senate? If these statements can form part of the meaning of a treaty, then isn't it possible that the President could make a representation to the Senate on an interpretation of the treaty that does not accord with the understanding of the country or countries with which he negotiated? As the Cooper memorandum notes, foreign governments do not monitor hearings before the Senate Foreign Relations Committee, and must rely on the official instruments of ratification, including any express formal conditions on consent, as an expression of the United States' intent. Is this why the Cooper memorandum suggests that certain representations by the President can form part of the meaning of the treaty under *domestic* law but not under *international* law? Does it make sense to conclude that a treaty might have different meanings under domestic and international law? Is the Cooper memorandum's conclusion on this point consistent with the aim of the constitutional Founders to ensure that the United States had adequate domestic mechanisms to ensure compliance with treaties?

6. In connection with the ABM reinterpretation controversy, where does the President obtain the authority to reinterpret treaties? Does it flow from his Article II power to "take Care that the Laws be faithfully executed"? From his role as the "sole organ" of the United States with respect to foreign affairs? From his role in making treaties? From the Article II Vesting Clause, since the power to reinterpret is not expressly placed anywhere else? Note that Executive Branch agencies are permitted to change their interpretations of statutes that they are charged with administering, and that such changed interpretations, if reasonable, receive deference from courts. *See, e.g.,* FDA v. Brown & Williamson Tobacco Corp., 529 U.S. 120, 156-57 (2000); Chevron, U.S.A., Inc. v. NRDC, Inc., 467 U.S. 837, 863 (1984). Are treaties comparable to statutes administered by agencies? How does this issue of treaty reinterpretation relate to the deference that courts often give to the Executive Branch with respect to treaty interpretation issues, which we considered in Chapter 2?

   7. Under what circumstances will Executive representations to the Senate preclude the President from reinterpreting a treaty? Does the formality of the representation matter? Whether the Executive Branch representative is a Cabinet Secretary as opposed to a mid-level official? Whether the Executive Branch has been consistent in its view? The Cooper memorandum says that these factors inform the degree to which the Senate reasonably relies on the representation in consenting to the treaty. Why does that matter to the President's authority to reinterpret a treaty? Should it be the words of the treaty, and any formal conditions on consent, that matter? Why should the representations of one administration limit the reasonable interpretations of a treaty's text by another administration?

   8. As the materials above make clear, the Reagan Administration's attempt to reinterpret the ABM treaty failed because of substantial political opposition. What does this say about the tools that the Senate and, more broadly, the Congress have for dealing with Executive Branch reinterpretation of treaties? How does this effectiveness inform your view of the legitimacy of Executive reinterpretation?

   9. Is the Biden condition constitutional? Is it like a conditional consent to the treaty that alters the treaty's terms, or does it purport to affect how other constitutional interpreters must construe the treaty's language? Professor Glennon takes the former view:

> The Senate well might have insisted that the INF Treaty actually be changed. Instead, the Senate chose a more restrained course; one that did not endanger the Treaty's ratification. It conditioned its consent upon adherence to a canon of construction tailored to this specific agreement. Rather than inject the Senate into the process of interpretation that occurs after the Senate's consent, therefore, the Condition simply shaped the meaning of the document to which the Senate consented. The President remains free, as he is with all other treaties, to interpret the INF Treaty to which the Senate consented. But he cannot interpret a treaty other than the one to which the Senate consented — subject to the Biden Condition — for to do so would be to make a new treaty.

Michael J. Glennon, *The Constitutional Power of the United States Senate to Condition its Consent to Treaties,* 67 Chi.-Kent. L. Rev. 533, 552 (1991). President Reagan, by contrast, took the latter view, and had this response: "I cannot accept the proposition that a condition in a resolution to ratification can alter the allocation of rights and duties under the Constitution; nor could I . . . accept any diminution claimed to be effected by such a condition in the constitutional powers and responsibilities of the Presidency." 24 Weekly Comp./Pres. Doc. 779, 780 (June 13, 1988). Which characterization of the Biden condition is right? If Reagan was correct in his construction of what the Biden condition purports to do, is it an unconstitutional intrusion on presidential or judicial power? If Glennon is correct, does this make it constitutional?

   10. What is the source of the President's power to terminate a treaty? Article II of the Constitution requires that, in order to make a treaty, presidents must obtain the advice and consent of two-thirds of the Senate. Does this requirement imply that presidents must also obtain two-thirds Senate consent before they can terminate a treaty? Or does the Constitution's silence about treaty termination mean that the President possesses the authority to terminate, on a Hamiltonian vesting clause rationale? Is the analogy in *Goldwater* to the President's power to remove appointed officials persuasive? *Cf.* Morrison v. Olson, 487 U.S. 654 (1988) (allowing Congress to impose a "good cause" limitation on President's ability to remove independent counsel).

If the President lacks the authority to terminate a treaty, who has it? We know from the prior Section that Congress can, with presidential consent or by over-riding a veto, effectively abrogate a U.S. treaty commitment with a subsequent federal statute. Even that action, however, will not necessarily terminate the treaty under international law. In any event, does it make sense to make this the only mechanism to terminate treaties? What about a requirement that the President and two-thirds of the Senate must agree before a treaty is terminated? Does it make sense to give 34 Senators a veto power to prevent treaty termination? To enact a federal statute, Congress must either obtain presidential consent or override a presidential veto, and it is well settled that the same limitation applies to congressional repeal of a federal statute. Is the termination of a treaty analogous to the repeal of a statute for these purposes? Does the answer to this question depend on whether the treaty is self-executing?

In answering these questions, what is the significance of the fact that many constitutional Founders believed that it should be difficult for the United States to enter into treaties? Gouverneur Morris remarked at the Federal Convention, for example, that "[t]he more difficulty in making treaties, the more value will be set on them," and James Madison observed that it had been too easy to make treaties in the pre-constitutional period. As a practical matter, does the United States need more flexibility in the termination of its treaty commitments than in the making of such commitments?

11. Might the President have the authority to terminate treaties under some circumstances but not others? For example, both the Taiwan treaty and the ABM treaty contained termination clauses. Would it matter to the President's power to terminate if a treaty lacked such a clause? Would the reason for the termination matter? Would it matter, for example, if the President's termination was (a) consistent with international law and was based on a material breach of the treaty by the other party, (b) consistent with international law, but based merely on policy reasons, or (c) contrary to international law?

12. The historical practice concerning U.S. treaty termination is contested, in part because each treaty termination is in some respects unique. In many instances, presidents have sought and obtained congressional consent for treaty terminations. The earliest example of this was Congress's termination of treaties with France in 1798, at the request of President Adams. Another example was a joint resolution passed by Congress in 1846 authorizing President Polk to terminate a treaty with Great Britain relating to the Oregon territory. In other instances, presidents have sought and obtained the consent of the Senate. President Buchanan terminated a commercial treaty with Denmark in 1858, for example, after receiving Senate authorization. In still other instances, presidents have acted unilaterally, as President Carter did in terminating the Taiwan treaty. In the *Goldwater* case, the Executive Branch cited thirteen other such instances in which the President had unilaterally terminated a treaty. In a dissent in *Goldwater* that is not excerpted above, Judge MacKinnon challenged the Executive Branch's assertion after canvassing the historical record in detail. After concluding that "Congressional participation in termination has been the overwhelming historical practice," he had this to say about the 13 examples of unilateral Executive termination:

> In five instances Congress by direct authorization, or inconsistent legislation supplied the basis for the President's action; in two instances the putative abrogation was withdrawn and no termination resulted; one treaty was already terminated by the demise of the country; one treaty had become void by a change in the basic facts upon which the treaty was grounded; four treaties had already been abrogated by the other party; and [one] was not terminated.

What is at stake over the historical record of treaty terminations? If the President had terminated many treaties unilaterally in the past, why would that support his authority to do so with respect to the Taiwan treaty? Premised on the belief that history did not provide significant support for unilateral presidential termination of treaties, Judge MacKinnon expressed this view about the role of historical practice in constitutional interpretation: "Practice may not make perfect a constitutional power. Yet a prevailing practice, especially when begun in the light provided by the dawn of the Constitution, emanates a precedential aura of constitutional significance." Do you agree? Does the truth of this statement depend on how obviously "prevailing" the practice is? On whether the practice has or has not been controversial?

13. In June 2002, 32 members of the House of Representatives brought suit in federal district court against President Bush and other Executive Branch officials, challenging the Bush Administration's authority to withdraw from the ABM Treaty. The House members argued that because the Constitution classifies treaties, like federal statutes, as the "supreme law of the land," the President does not have the authority to terminate a treaty without congressional consent, just as he cannot terminate a statute without congressional consent. In December 2002, the district court dismissed the suit. Relying on Raines v. Byrd (excerpted in Chapter 2), the court concluded that the House members lacked standing. The court also held that the case raised a nonjusticiable political question, for reasons similar to those articulated by then-Justice Rehnquist in his plurality opinion in Goldwater v. Carter (also excerpted in Chapter 2). *See* Kucinich v. Bush, 236 F. Supp. 2d 1 (D.D.C. 2002).

14. Recall the controversy, discussed in Section B, over the International Court of Justice's holdings that the United States had violated the Vienna Convention on Consular Relations, and its instructions for various forms of relief within the U.S. legal system. The ICJ had jurisdiction in these cases pursuant to the Optional Protocol to the Vienna Convention, which the United States ratified in 1969. In March 2005, in the same month in which the President announced that the United States would comply with the ICJ's *Avena* decision through state court proceedings, Secretary of State Condoleezza Rice sent a letter to the Secretary-General of the United Nations informing him that the United States "hereby withdraws" from the Optional Protocol. Unlike the Taiwan defense treaty and the ABM treaty, the Protocol does not specifically provide for withdrawal, and some have argued that under international law the United States either lacks the right to withdraw from the Protocol, or at least has an obligation to provide a year's notice prior to its withdrawal, which it apparently did not do. Does the absence of a termination provision in the Optional Protocol, or possible international law problems with the termination, affect the President's domestic authority to terminate the treaty?

15. Are the issues of treaty reinterpretation and treaty termination analytically or constitutionally distinguishable? Might the President have one power but not the other? Or do the two go hand in hand? In answering these questions, compare President Reagan's attempted reinterpretation of the ABM treaty in the 1980s, which was controversial, and President's Bush's termination of the ABM treaty in 2001, which was relatively uncontroversial.

16. Throughout its history, the United States has signed numerous treaties that it has not subsequently ratified. This phenomenon has been especially evident in the last several decades. During this period, the United States has signed, but has not yet ratified, a variety of important multilateral treaties. These treaties include significant human rights agreements such as the International Covenant on Economic, Social, and Cultural Rights (signed in 1977); the American Convention on Human Rights (signed in 1977); the Convention on the Elimination of All Forms of Discrimination Against Women (signed in 1980); and the Convention on the Rights of the Child (signed in 1995). They also include important environmental treaties such as the Kyoto Protocol on Global Warming (signed in 1998); the Rio Convention on Biological Diversity (signed in 1993); and an agreement revising the seabed mining provisions of the Law of the Sea Convention (signed in 1994). Another example of a signed but unratified treaty, much discussed in connection with the war on terrorism, is the First Additional Protocol to the Geneva Conventions (signed in 1977).

A long delay in ratification does not necessarily mean that the United States will not become a party to a treaty. At least since World War I, it has not been uncommon for a significant period of time to elapse between U.S. signature and ratification of a treaty. Two particularly dramatic examples are the Geneva Protocol for the Prohibition of the Use in War of Asphyxiating, Poisonous or Other Gases, and of Bacteriological Methods of Warfare, which the United States signed in 1925 but did not ratify until 1975, fifty years later, and the Convention on the Prevention and Punishment of the Crime of Genocide, which the United States signed in 1948 but did not ratify until 1989, forty-one years later. Another example is the Convention on the Elimination of All Forms of Discrimination Against Women (CEDAW). The United States signed CEDAW in 1980. In 2002, despite objections from the Bush Administration, the Democratic-controlled Senate Foreign Relations Committee voted to send the Convention to the full Senate for advice and consent. Although no vote was held at that time in the Senate, many supporters of the Convention continue to be hopeful of U.S. ratification.

What do you think explains the phenomenon of signed but unratified treaties? Why might a President sign a treaty knowing that there is little prospect that the Senate will give its consent to the treaty? Why might a President sign a treaty even though he has no present plan to move forward with ratification? Why did President Clinton sign the treaty establishing the International Criminal Court knowing that the incoming Bush Administration was likely to oppose the treaty?

17. According to Article 18 of the Vienna Convention on the Law of Treaties, a nation that signs a treaty is obligated not to take actions that would defeat the object and purpose of the treaty. Assuming Article 18 reflects customary international law, does the President have the constitutional authority to impose this sort of obligation on the United States based merely on his signature of a treaty? If so, what is the source of this authority? Are there any constitutional limits on this authority? If these signing obligations are treated as non-self-executing, does that eliminate any potential constitutional problems? Did President Clinton's signature of the International Criminal Court treaty impose obligations on the United States?

18. Does the President have the constitutional authority to terminate the effects of a prior presidential signature of a treaty, as President Bush did with respect to the treaty establishing the International Criminal Court? If so, what is the source of that authority? Is it implied from the President's authority to sign the treaty in the first place? From the fact that the United States cannot ratify a treaty without presidential agreement? From the President's role as chief spokesperson for the United States in foreign affairs? How does this issue compare with the issue of the President's authority to terminate treaties?

Although the Bush Administration's announcement concerning the International Criminal Court treaty was described by some commentators as unprecedented, there have been other instances in which an Administration has announced an intention not to ratify a treaty signed by its precedessor, although not through a formal letter to the United Nations. For example, President Carter signed the SALT II nuclear reduction treaty in 1979, but the Reagan Administration announced in 1982 that the United States had no intention of ratifying that treaty. Secretary of State Alexander Haig explained to the Senate Foreign Relations Committee that "[t]his proposal has been abandoned by this administration," and that "we consider SALT II dead and have so informed the Soviets." Similarly, the Reagan Administration announced in 1987 that it would not ratify the First Additional Protocol to the Geneva Conventions on the laws of war, which President Carter had signed in 1977. President Reagan explained in a message to the Senate that the Protocol was "fundamentally and irreconcilably flawed," that the problems with the Protocol were "so fundamental in character that they cannot be remedied through reservations," and that he therefore had "decided not to submit the Protocol to the Senate in any form."

19. For additional discussion of the issue of treaty interpretation, see Michael P. Van Alstine, *Dynamic Treaty Interpretation*, 146 U. Pa. L. Rev. 687 (1998); Michael P. Van Alstine, *Federal Common Law in an Age of Treaties*, 89 Cornell L. Rev. 892 (2004); David J. Bederman, *Revivalist Canons and Treaty Interpretation*, 41 UCLA L. Rev. 953 (1994); Alex Glashausser, *Difference and Deference in Treaty Interpretation*, 50 Vill. L. Rev. 25 (2005); John Norton Moore, *Treaty Interpretation, the Constitution and the Rule of Law*, 42 Va. J. Int'l L. 163 (2001).

For additional discussion of the issue of treaty reinterpretation, see Raymond L. Garthoff, Policy versus Law: The Reinterpretation of the ABM Treaty (1987); Joseph R. Biden, Jr. & John B. Ritch III, *The Treaty Power: Upholding a Constitutional Partnership*, 137 U. Pa. L. Rev. 1529 (1989); Abram Chayes & Antonia Handler Chayes, *Testing and Development of "Exotic" Systems Under the ABM Treaty: The Great Reinterpretation Caper*, 99 Harv. L. Rev. 1956 (1986); Kevin C. Kennedy, *Treaty Interpretation by the Executive Branch: The ABM Treaty and "Star Wars" Testing and Development*, 80 Am. J. Int'l L. 854 (1986); David A. Koplow, *Constitutional Bait and Switch: Executive Reinterpretation of Arms Control Treaties*, 137 U. Pa. L. Rev. 1353 (1989); Eugene V. Rostow, *The Reinterpretation Debate and Constitutional Law*, 137 U. Pa. L. Rev. 1451 (1989); Abraham D. Sofaer, *The ABM Treaty and the Strategic Defense Initiative*, 99 Harv. L. Rev. 1972 (1986); Phillip R. Trimble, *The Constitutional Common Law of Treaty Interpretation: A Reply to the Formalists*, 137 U. Pa. L. Rev. 1461 (1989); John Yoo, *Politics as Law?: The Anti-Ballistic Missile Treaty, the Separation of Powers, and Treaty Interpretation*, 89 Cal. L. Rev. 851 (2001). For a response to Professor Yoo's article, and Professor Yoo's reply, see Michael P. Van Alstine, *The Judicial Power and Treaty Delegation*, 90 Cal. L. Rev. 1263 (2002), and John C. Yoo, *Treaty Interpretation and the False Sirens of Delegation*, 90 Cal. L. Rev. 1305 (2002).

For additional discussion of the issue of treaty termination, see David Gray Adler, The Constitution and the Termination of Treaties (1986); Victoria Maria Kraft, The U.S. Constitution and Foreign Policy: Terminating the Taiwan Treaty (1991); Treaty Termination: Hearings on S. Res. 15 Before the Senate Comm. on Foreign Relations, 96th Cong. (Apr. 9-11, 1979); Restatement (Third) of the Foreign Relations Law of the United States §339 (1987); Restatement (Second) of the Foreign Relations Law of the United States §163 (1965); Raoul Berger, *The President's Unilateral Termination of the Taiwan Treaty*, 75 Nw. U. L. Rev. 577 (1980); Louis Henkin, *Litigating the President's Power to Terminate Treaties*, 73 Am. J. Int'l L. 647 (1979); James J. Moriarty, *Congressional Claims for Treaty Termination Powers in the Age of the Diminished Presidency*, 14 Conn. J. Int'l L. 123 (1999); Randall H. Nelson, *The Termination of Treaties and Executive Agreements by the United States: Theory and Practice*, 42 Minn. L. Rev. 879 (1958); Anna Mamalakis Pappas, *The Constitutional Allocation of Competence in the Termination of Treaties*, 13 N.Y.U. J. Int'l L. & Pol. 473 (1981); David J. Scheffer, Comment, *The Law of Treaty Termination as Applied to the United States De-Recognition of the Republic of China*, 19 Harv. Int'l L.J. 931 (1978); Jonathan York Thomas, *The Abuse of History: A Refutation of the State Department Analysis of Alleged Instances of Independent Presidential Treaty Termination*, 6 Yale Studies in World Pub. Ord. 27 (1979).

For additional discussion of issues associated with the signing and unsigning of treaties, see Michael J. Glennon, Constitutional Diplomacy 169-75 (1990); Edward T. Swaine, *Unsigning*, 55 Stan. L. Rev. 2061, 2064-65 (2003); David C. Scott, Note, *Presidential Power to "Un-Sign" Treaties*, 69 U. Chi. L. Rev. 1447 (2002); *see also* Curtis A. Bradley, *ASIL Insight: U.S. Announces Intent Not to Ratify International Criminal Court Treaty* (May 2002), at http://www.asil.org/insights/insigh87.htm.

G. EXECUTIVE AGREEMENTS

Executive agreements are international agreements concluded by the United States without resort to the two-thirds senatorial advice and consent process specified in Article II. There are three types of executive agreements: executive agreements authorized by an existing Article II treaty; congressional-executive agreements (those concluded by the President with the advance authorization or subsequent approval of a majority of both houses of Congress); and sole executive agreements (those concluded solely by the President). As the chart below indicates, the vast majority of international agreements entered into by the United States in the modern era have been executive agreements rather than Article II treaties.

Period	Treaties	Executive Agreements
1789-1839	60	27
1839-1889	215	238
1889-1939	524	917
1939-1989	702	11,698
Total	1,501	12,880

Source: Congressional Research Service, Treaties and Other International Agreements: The Role of the United States Senate, S. Prt. 106-71, 106th Cong., 2d Sess. 39 (2001) ("CRS Study").

The materials below consider the scope and constitutionality of congressional-executive agreements and sole executive agreements.

1. Congressional-Executive Agreements

Congressional-executive agreements are international agreements authorized in advance, or approved after the fact, by a majority of both Houses of Congress. Although the United States has entered into many such agreements, they are not free from controversy. The materials below discuss constitutional concerns that were raised with respect to two important trade agreements concluded pursuant to the congressional-executive agreement process — the 1992 North American Free Trade Agreement (NAFTA) and the 1994 General Agreement on Tariffs and Trade (GATT). These materials are followed by a letter from two leading members of the Senate Foreign Relations Committee arguing that significant arms control agreements must be concluded pursuant to the Article II treaty process.

Made in the USA Foundation v. United States

56 F. Supp. 2d 1226 (N.D. Ala. 1999), *aff'd on other grounds*,
242 F.3d 1300 (11th Cir. 2001)

ROBERT B. PROPST, DISTRICT JUDGE. . . .

In 1990 the United States, Mexico and Canada initiated negotiations with the intention of creating a "free trade zone" through the elimination or reduction of tariffs and other barriers to trade. After two years of negotiations, the leaders of the three countries signed the North American Free Trade Agreement ("NAFTA" or the "Agreement") on December 17, 1992. Congress approved and implemented NAFTA on December 8, 1993 with the passage of NAFTA Implementation Act ("Implementation Act"), which was passed by a vote of 234 to 200 in the House and 61 to 38 in the Senate. The Implementation Act served two purposes, to "approve" NAFTA and to provide a series of laws to "locally" enforce NAFTA's provisions. The enactment of the Implementation Act brought to a close a lengthy period of rancorous debate over NAFTA. The instant suit seeks to reopen that debate by pulling back NAFTA's coat and demonstrating that the Agreement and Implementation Act stand on sand rather than on firm Constitutional ground. Brought to bear in this case is an almost century-long bout of Constitutional theorizing about whether the Treaty Clause, contained in Article II, Section 2 of the United States Constitution (the "Treaty Clause"), creates the exclusive means of making certain types of international agreements.

Neither NAFTA nor the Implementation Act were subjected to the procedures outlined in the Treaty Clause. The President purportedly negotiated and concluded NAFTA pursuant to his constitutional responsibility for conducting the foreign affairs of the United States and in accordance with the Omnibus Trade and Competitiveness Act of 1988, 19 U.S.C. §2901, et seq. ("Trade Act of 1988"), and the Trade Act of 1974, 19 U.S.C. §2101, et seq. ("Trade Act of 1974"), under the so-called fast track procedure. Congress then approved and implemented NAFTA by enacting the Implementation Act, allegedly pursuant to its power to legislate in the areas of tariffs and domestic and foreign commerce.

The plaintiffs contend that this failure to go through the Article II, Section 2, prerequisites renders the Agreement and, apparently, the Implementation Act, unconstitutional. The Government denies this....

The Government argues that the Treaty Clause of Article II is not the exclusive means for entering into an international agreement such as NAFTA or for adopting legislation implementing such an agreement. To begin with, the Government notes that the plaintiffs concede the existence of some kinds of valid and binding international agreements that do not constitute Article II treaties. This concession, comments the Government, is unsurprising in light of the fact that there exist several types of non-Article II treaty international agreements that have been well-established as valid under United States law. Such agreements include: (1) congressional-executive agreements — agreements negotiated by the President that are either pre- or post-approved by a simple majority of Congress; (2) executive agreements authorized expressly or implicitly by an existing treaty; and (3) presidential or sole executive agreements — agreements concluded unilaterally by the President pursuant to his constitutional authority. The Government notes that nothing in the Constitutional text elevates the Article II treaty ratification process over Article I's law making powers. Plaintiffs' claims represent, according to the Government, nothing more than an attempt to engraft an artificial and illegitimate hierarchy onto the Constitution.

The plaintiffs argue that the Government's argument as to exclusivity is persuasive only to the extent that it promotes the position that some international agreements do not rise to the level of treaties and do not require approval of two-thirds of the Senate. They argue that acceptance of the executive agreement and/or the congressional-executive agreement as all-purpose alternatives to the Treaty Clause represents an acceptance of the principle that the Constitution may be amended without reference to Article V of the Constitution. They note that in the 1930's and 1940's when advocates of the congressional-executive agreement first garnered significant support for their use, there was a widespread recognition of the fact that in order to make the practice constitutional an amendment would be necessary. A movement in favor of such an amendment took place in 1943-45, but was abandoned when advocates decided that it was "ridiculous to suppose that two-thirds of the Senate would voluntarily surrender its treaty-making prerogatives by supporting a formal constitutional amendment." Thus, according to [Laurence H. Tribe, *Taking Text and Structure Seriously: Reflections on the Free-Form Method in Constitutional Interpretation,* 108 Harv. L. Rev. 1221 (1995)], rather than properly amending the Constitution, politicians and academics chose to ignore the intent of the Framers and historical precedent in favor of political prudence and "strategic compromise." Tribe at 1280-86.

The plaintiffs reject the Government's characterization of the broad powers of the President and Congress with respect to international agreement-making. They claim that the Government's description of the powers of the President is so broad as to leave nothing beyond the scope of unilateral executive agreements as long as such agreements deal with "foreign affairs." Similarly, the Government's characterization of Congress's power lacks any defined boundaries, and, in effect, amounts to a total interchangeability argument....

According to the Government, the text of the Constitution, as interpreted by the Supreme Court, allows for the utilization of executive agreements whenever there exists constitutional authority outside of the Treaty Clause allowing the

President to negotiate and conclude an international agreement and allowing Congress to enact the legislation required for a given agreement's implementation. The Government, citing the Constitutional authority granted to both the President and Congress, and noting that the Supreme Court has characterized Congress's power to regulate "Commerce with foreign Nations" as "broad," "comprehensive," "plenary," and "complete," argues that NAFTA and the Implementation Act fall squarely within the combined enumerated powers of the two political branches. Further, it argues that the Agreement and the Act stand at the intersection of Congress's and the President's power over foreign commerce and foreign affairs, respectively, and that each provision of the Implementation Act could, therefore, have been enacted in the absence of any agreement with Mexico and Canada.

While acknowledging that NAFTA could have been ratified as a treaty, the Government contends that the congressional-executive agreement process was certainly acceptable, that the Treaty Clause does not expressly prohibit the employment of an alternative procedure, and that the congressional-executive agreement method may have been the Constitutionally preferable method by which to approve of and implement NAFTA. Thus, the Supreme Court, in holding that a later act of Congress may override a treaty, stated that the House's action with respect to such legislation "does not render it less entitled to respect in the matter of its repeal or modification than a treaty.... If there be any difference in this regard, it would seem to be in favor of an act in which all three of the bodies [the President, House and Senate] participate."[269]

The plaintiffs argue that the text of the Constitution supports their contention that international agreements that have the substance of a treaty cannot be adopted without the approval of two-thirds of the Senate. In doing so, they begin by contending that the most "natural" reading of the Treaty Clause is one that reads the clause as creating the exclusive method by which to conclude that certain class of international agreements called "treaties." They, like Tribe, argue that basic provisions of the Constitution that define the locus of power for certain governmental actions are properly construed as creating the exclusive means by which to exercise those powers. Both the plaintiffs and Tribe assert that the Treaty Clause represents such a provision. They therefore argue that any other reading of the Treaty Clause renders it a "dead letter," and allows the corruption of one of the Constitution's fundamental provisions.

The plaintiffs argue that the language of the Compacts Clause, U.S. Const., Art. I, §10, clauses 1 and 3, is perfectly consistent with the contention that the Treaty Clause represents the exclusive method by which to conclude certain international agreements. The Compacts Clause was, as noted above, meant to represent an absolute bar with respect to the States' ability to enter into treaties with foreign powers. However, the Clause permits the States to enter into other international agreements with the consent of Congress. The plaintiffs argue that to the extent the Compact Clause evidences the Framers' recognition of a distinction between treaties and other international agreements, the Treaty Clause indicates that they intended to limit the federal government's method of concluding those things called treaties, while leaving open the question of how the federal government is to make other international agreements. Thus, the plaintiffs argue that in addressing "treaties" and not those other international agreements termed "agreements"

---

269. Head Money Cases, 112 U.S. 580, 599 (1884).

and "compacts," the Treaty Clause clearly establishes that those agreements that do constitute treaties must be subjected to its more rigorous procedural requirements in order to be considered valid. . . .

The most significant issue before the court is whether the Treaty Clause is an exclusive means of making an international agreement under the circumstances of this case. It is clear that there is no explicit language in the Constitution which makes the Treaty Clause exclusive as to all international agreements. On the other hand, the broad breadth of the Commerce Clause, particularly the Foreign Commerce Clause, has been repeatedly emphasized. The inability of the Congress under the Articles of Confederation to regulate commerce was one of the main weaknesses which led to the call of the Constitutional Convention. The Annapolis Convention of 1786 was called to discuss problems which had resulted from this weakness. This meeting, in turn, led to the Constitutional Convention. The Commerce Clause was clearly intended to address this concern. The "Power" to regulate commerce, foreign and interstate and with Indian Tribes, was specifically given to Congress. The Treaty Clause makes no specific reference to commerce of any type. . . .

In the absence of specific limiting language in or relating to the Treaty Clause, I am led to conclude that the Foreign Commerce power of Congress is at least concurrent with the Treaty Clause power when an agreement, as is the case here, is dominated by provisions specifically related to foreign commerce and has other provisions which are reasonably "necessary and proper" for "carrying all others into execution." . . . Further, I note that the President, in negotiating the Agreement in connection with the fast track legislation, was acting pursuant to his constitutional responsibility for conducting the Nation's foreign affairs and pursuant to a grant of authority from Congress.[352] The foregoing, considered in light of at least some degree of presumption of constitutionality to which the Agreement is entitled, leads me to ultimately conclude that NAFTA and the Implementation Act were made and approved in a constitutional manner.[354] One thing is clear. This court does not have jurisdiction to review the wisdom of NAFTA or to determine whether it is in the best interest of the Nation. . . .

In 1994, after years of negotiation, the "Uruguay Round" of the General Agreement on Tariffs and Trade (GATT) was concluded and over 100 nations, including the United States, signed a "Final Act" that encompassed a variety of agreements. These agreements included detailed provisions concerning free trade

352. Again, according to *Youngstown*, the President's power is at its pinnacle when he acts in concert with Congress. . . .

354. In reaching my conclusion, I do not accept a theory of total interchangeability. As the Supreme Court has stated, "it is obvious that there may be matters of the sharpest exigency for the national well being that an act of Congress could not deal with but that a treaty followed by such an act could." Missouri v. Holland, 252 U.S. 416, 433 (1920). Further, the Justice Department has stated that it does not disagree with the premise that some agreements with foreign nations "may have to be ratified as treaties." Memorandum, Walter Dellinger, Asst. Atty. Gen. to Ambassador Michael Kantor, November 22, 1994. Similarly, while purportedly speaking on behalf of the Senate Judiciary Committee, Senator Dirksen, in 1956, rejected the "doctrine that treaties and executive agreements are wholly interchangeable." Senate Rep. No. 1716, 84th Congress, 2nd Session 9 (1956). Thus, there may exist circumstances where the procedures outlined in the Treaty Clause must be adhered to in order to adopt an international agreement. However, it is not entirely clear what those circumstances are. In any case, in light of Congress's enumerated powers in the areas dealt with by NAFTA, I conclude that such circumstances are not present in this case. My opinion is limited to the area of foreign commerce and related enumerated powers coupled with Presidential power(s) and the powers under the Necessary and Proper Clause.

of goods and services and the protection of intellectual property, as well as an agreement calling for the establishment of a World Trade Organization that would adjudicate international trade disputes and formulate trade policy. The Clinton Administration's decision to ratify this treaty through the congressional-executive agreement process rather than through the Article II senatorial consent process prompted a written debate between Professor Laurence Tribe of the Harvard Law School and Assistant Attorney General Walter Dellinger. Here is an excerpt from a memorandum in which Dellinger responds to some of Professor Tribe's arguments:

Memorandum from Walter Dellinger, Assistant Attorney General, to Michael Kantor, U.S. Trade Representative

July 29, 1994

In a recent letter to Senator Robert Byrd, Professor Laurence H. Tribe took the position that "if there is any category of international agreement or accord that must surely be submitted to the Senate for approval under the usually rigorous two-thirds rule of the Treaty Clause, that category must include agreements like the Uruguay Round, which represents not merely a traditional trade agreement but a significant restructuring of the power alignment between the National Government and the States." Professor Tribe contends that the legal regime that would ensue from the enactment of the GATT implementing legislation "would entail a significant shift of sovereignty from state and local governments to the proposed World Trade Organization (WTO), in which the interests of these entities would be represented exclusively by the U.S. Trade Representative." Professor Tribe concludes that "the legal regime put in place by the Uruguay Round represents a structural rearrangement of state-federal relations of the sort that requires ratification by two-thirds of the Senate."

We disagree....Congress has frequently enacted major international trade agreements that apply to the States, including agreements that raise the possibility that State law might be challenged as inconsistent with our international obligations....

The Constitution itself recognizes the possibility of international agreements other than "treaties" in the sense of Art. II, §2, cl. 2....[W]hile a state may not enter into a "Treaty" with a foreign power, it may (with Congress's approval) enter into an "Agreement or Compact" with one....Accordingly, from the beginning of the Republic to the present, Presidents and Congresses have elected to enter into international agreements in preference to formal treaties....

We do not understand Professor Tribe to be arguing that trade agreements in all cases must be approved by two-thirds of the Senate. Rather, he appears to be claiming that the GATT Uruguay Round has some specific feature that requires that *it* — unlike other trade agreements — be ratified in the manner prescribed by the Treaty Clause....We are hard pressed, however, to identify with any certainty what this assertedly distinguishing feature of the GATT Uruguay Round is, or why it should entail the constitutional consequences that Professor Tribe seeks to draw from it.

Conceivably, Professor Tribe might mean only that the GATT Uruguay Round will change the relative balance of control over various trade-related matters between federal and state governments. But such a shift would in itself raise no substantive constitutional issues: it has long been settled that if federal legislation is within the substantive scope of a delegated power, it is constitutional, even though its purpose is to reconfigure state-federal relations. To deny that GATT Uruguay Round falls within the substantive scope of Congress's combined powers under the Interstate and Foreign Commerce Clause would be a radical attack upon the modern understanding of federal power: it would be an attempt to carve out of the scope of the Commerce Clause matters that are part of or are closely related to that Clause's core meaning, which is that Congress can control the conditions of all trade and commerce that affect more states than one. We doubt that Professor Tribe is taking so extreme a stance.

While Professor Tribe says little about the specific nature of "restructuring of the power alignment as between the National Government and the States" that, in his view, triggers the application of the Treaty Clause, he does claim that enactment of the GATT implementing legislation "would entail a significant shift of sovereignty from state and local governments to the proposed World Trade Organization (WTO), in which the interests of those entities would be represented exclusively by" [the U.S. Trade Representative]. We assume, therefore, that it is this particular feature of the GATT Uruguay Round that, in Professor Tribe's opinion, implicates the requirement for Senate approval under the Treaty Clause. Professor Tribe thus appears to be arguing that because the GATT Uruguay Round would diminish state sovereignty while augmenting the authority of the WTO — a foreign forum in which the states would be unable to represent themselves — that agreement can only be adopted in accordance with a procedure that provides maximum protection to the states. That procedure is found in the treaty ratification process, in which the states, by virtue of their equal representation in the Senate, are peculiarly well positioned to defend their own interests.

We do not dispute that the "the Constitution's federal structure imposes limitations on the Commerce Clause." Garcia v. San Antonio Metro. Transit Auth., 469 U.S. 528, 547 (1985). We also agree that state sovereignty within the federal system is "protected by procedural safeguards inherent in the structure of the federal system." Id. at 552. Finally, we agree that among the procedural devices in the Constitution for protecting the rights and interests of the states, the equal representation of the states in the Senate is particularly important.

We do not understand, however, why the asserted transfer of state authority to the WTO (even were this the case) should require the approval of two-thirds of the Senate, rather than a majority of both Houses of Congress. . . . Congress's powers vis-à-vis the States are no less "broad" under the Foreign Commerce Clause than they are under the Interstate Commerce Clause. If the Constitution permits Congress, when acting under the Interstate Commerce Clause, to affect the scope of state authority by majority votes of both Houses (together, of course, with Presidential approval), we see no reason why the states should be entitled to a different and more protective procedure when Congress affects them by acting under the Foreign Commerce Clause. In both contexts, the states may rely on their influence on the legislative process.

Letter from Senators Biden and Helms to Secretary of State Powell

March 15, 2002

[In November 2001, President Bush suggested that he and Russian President Vladimir Putin could achieve large cuts in nuclear weapons through an informal "handshake," but added that "if we need to write it down on a piece of paper, I'll be glad to do that." Presidential News Conference, November 19, 2001, in 37 Public Papers of the President No. 46 (2001). Some commentators interpreted this statement to be a proposal to achieve arms control through some kind of an executive agreement rather than through the Article II treaty process. During testimony before the Senate Foreign Relations Committee in February 2002, Secretary of State Colin Powell announced that the President did in fact intend to negotiate a legally binding agreement with Russia. One month later, the senior Democratic and Republican members of the Senate Foreign Relations Committee sent Secretary of State Powell the following letter.]

Dear Mr. Secretary:

Your February 5 testimony before the Committee on Foreign Relations indicates that the Administration has decided to negotiate a legally-binding agreement with the Russian Federation on further strategic arms reductions. Various subsequent reports left the same impression.

Clearly, any such agreement would most likely include significant obligations by the United States regarding deployed U.S. strategic nuclear warheads. We are therefore convinced that such an agreement would constitute a treaty subject to the advice and consent of the Senate.

With the exception of the SALT I agreement,* every significant arms control agreement during the past three decades has been transmitted to the Senate pursuant to the Treaty Clause of the Constitution. Mr. Secretary, we see no reason whatsoever to alter this practice, especially since it clearly appears that a legally binding bilateral agreement with Russia would in all likelihood incorporate (or continue) certain aspects of the START I Treaty.

Indeed, the question of Senate prerogative regarding international arms control agreements has been previously addressed by the Senate. In Declaration (5) of the START I Treaty resolution of ratification, the Senate stated its intent to consider for approval all international agreements obligating the United States to reduce or limit its military power in a significant manner, pursuant to the treaty power set forth in Article II, Section 2, Clause 2 of the Constitution.

Mr. Secretary, it is therefore clear that no Constitutional alternative exists to transmittal of the concluded agreement to the Senate for its advice and consent. . . .

Joseph R. Biden, Jr. (Chairman)
Jesse Helms (Ranking Member)

[President Bush subsequently made clear that he would submit the referenced arms reduction treaty with Russia to the Senate for its advice and consent. He and President Putin signed this treaty in May 2002, the Senate unanimously gave its advice and consent to the treaty in March 2003, and the treaty was formally ratified in June 2003.]

Notes and Questions

1. There have been congressional-executive agreements since early in U.S. history. In 1792, for example, Congress authorized the Postmaster General to

---

* [The 1972 SALT I arms control agreement was approved as a congressional-executive agreement rather than as an Article II treaty. *See* Strategic Arms Limitation I Agreement, Pub. L. No. 79-448, 86 Stat. 746. — EDS.]

conclude international agreements concerning the exchange of mail. *See* Act of Feb. 20, 1792, ch. 7, §26, 1 Stat. 232, 239. Most of the congressional-executive agreements before World War II, like the postal agreements, involved *ex ante* delegations of authority by Congress rather than *ex post* approval by Congress of agreements already negotiated. Since the War, however, many congressional-executive agreements have involved *ex post* approvals. Some of these agreements have been quite significant. Famous examples of congressional-executive agreements include the Bretton Woods Agreement (which established the International Monetary Fund and the World Bank), the GATT and NAFTA trade agreements, the SALT I arms control agreement, and the U.N. Headquarters Agreement. Is there constitutional significance in the distinction between *ex ante* and *ex post* congressional-executive agreements? Is one more legitimate than the other?

2. During the period 1789-1839, the United States entered into 60 treaties and 27 non-treaty international agreements (a category that includes congressional executive agreements and sole executive agreements). As noted in the introduction to this section, from 1939-1989, the United States entered into 702 treaties and 11,698 non-treaty agreements. *See* CRS Study, *supra*, at 39. Most of these non-treaty agreements were congressional-executive agreements; one study found that 88.3 percent of the non-treaty agreements between 1946 and 1972 were congressional-executive agreements. *See id.* at 41. Why was there such a substantial increase in the relative use of congressional-executive agreements? Is this related to the mid-century rise in Executive Branch power in foreign affairs? Might it reflect the increasing number and complexity of U.S. government activities abroad? What, if anything, does the frequent use of congressional-executive agreements suggest about their constitutionality? Is it relevant that congressional-executive agreements have not generated significant inter-branch conflict?

3. Although the Supreme Court has never directly addressed the constitutionality of congressional-executive agreements, it has appeared to assume their validity in several decisions. In Weinberger v. Rossi, 456 U.S. 25 (1982), for example, the Court interpreted the word "treaty" in an employment discrimination statute as referring not only to Article II treaties but also congressional-executive agreements. The Court noted that the United States has entered into numerous such agreements, that they are binding on the United States, and that Congress sometimes uses the word treaty to refer to them. *See also* B. Altman & Co. v. United States, 224 U.S. 583 (1912) (construing the word "treaty" in a jurisdictional statute as including congressional-executive agreements); Field v. Clark, 143 U.S. 649 (1892) (upholding congressional delegation of tariff authority to the Executive Branch and citing, among other things, the history of congressional authorizations of executive trade agreements).

4. What does the text of the Constitution suggest about the validity of congressional-executive agreements? Does the Article II treaty clause indicate that all international agreements entered into by the United States must go through the two-thirds senatorial advice and consent process? Does it indicate that at least *some* international agreements must go through this process? Do Congress's Article I powers provide a basis for congressional-executive agreements? Is Congress's power to make legislation on certain subjects tantamount to a power to approve international agreements on those subjects? Of what relevance to this issue is Congress's Necessary and Proper power? What does INS v. Chadha, which we considered in Chapter 3, suggest about this issue? Are congressional-executive agreements more "democratic" than Article II treaties? If so, does this matter?

5. Congress can override presidential vetoes and enact legislation by two-thirds approval of both Houses. Does it follow that both houses of Congress could, through a two-thirds vote, enter into a congressional-executive agreement without the President's approval? If not, what does this tell us about the validity of congressional-executive agreements?

6. How are congressional-executive agreements terminated? The President does not normally have the power to unilaterally abrogate statutes. But, as we learned from Goldwater v. Carter, the President might have the power to terminate a treaty. Can the President also terminate a congressional-executive agreement? If so, would this termination preclude domestic enforcement of the congressional-executive agreement?

7. Assuming congressional-executive agreements are valid, are they completely interchangeable with treaties? In other words, could any U.S. international agreement be entered into by either method? The Restatement (Third) of Foreign Relations Law maintains that "the prevailing view is that the Congressional-Executive agreement can be used as an alternative to the treaty method in every instance," and adds that "which procedure should be used is a political judgment, made in the first instance by the President." Restatement (Third) of the Foreign Relations Law of the United States §303 cmt. e (1987); *see also* Louis Henkin, Foreign Affairs and the United States Constitution 218 (2d ed. 1996); Bruce Ackerman & David Golove, *Is NAFTA Constitutional?*, 108 Harv. L. Rev. 799 (1995). Several scholars have recently questioned this conventional wisdom, arguing in various (and not always consistent) ways that treaties and congressional-executive agreements are not, and should not be, perfectly interchangeable. See, for example, John C. Yoo, *Laws as Treaties?: The Constitutionality of Congressional-Executive Agreements*, 99 Mich. L. Rev. 757 (2001); Peter J. Spiro, *Constitutional Method and the Great Treaty Debate*, 79 Tex. L. Rev. 961 (2001); and Joel R. Paul, *The Geopolitical Constitution: Executive Expediency and Executive Agreements*, 86 Cal. L. Rev. 671 (1998).

In considering the substitutability of treaties and congressional-executive agreements, what is the relevance, if any, of the fact that the following types of international agreements are almost always concluded by the treaty process: political treaties (such as the agreements in which the United States joined NATO and the United Nations); arms control agreements (with the exception of SALT I); human rights agreements; and extradition agreements? *See* Yoo, *supra*, at 803-13; Spiro, *supra*, at 996-1002. Why have presidents consistently submitted these types of international agreements to the Senate? Does this practice have constitutional significance?

8. Does interchangeability mean that if an international agreement fails to obtain the required two-thirds senatorial consent in the Article II process, the President can simply resubmit it to Congress for a majority vote? Or must the President choose one method and stick to it? Consider the fate of the Comprehensive Nuclear Test Ban Treaty. In October 1999, the Senate declined to give the requisite two-thirds consent to the Treaty. Fifty-one Senators voted against the Treaty, forty-eight in its favor. If President Clinton could have persuaded two "no" votes to switch (thereby giving him a majority of support in the Senate), could he have resubmitted the Treaty to the House and Senate as a congressional-executive agreement?

9. How, if at all, do the separation of powers issues discussed above in Section C relate to the issue of interchangeability? How about the federalism issues discussed in Section D? Are Professor Tribe's federalism arguments (discussed in the above excerpt of the Dellinger memo) persuasive? Is Dellinger's reliance on the Commerce Clause a sufficient response?

10. Assuming that every type of international agreement that could be done by treaty could also be done by congressional-executive agreement, are the two forms of international agreement treated alike for other purposes? For example, does the analysis of Missouri v. Holland, excerpted above in Section D, apply to congressional-executive agreements? Do congressional-executive agreements warrant the same degree of judicial deference to Executive Branch interpretation as treaties? Do the same rules of self-execution that apply to treaties also apply to congressional-executive agreements? How about the last-in-time rule? Do the same separation of powers limitations that apply to treaties (such as the bar on creating domestic criminal law by treaty) apply to congressional-executive agreements?

11. Article I, Section 10 shows that the Founders knew of international agreements other than what they called "treaties." But does this cut for or against the validity of congressional-executive agreements? On the one hand, it suggests that "treaties" are not the exclusive way to make international agreements. On the other hand, the fact that Article II of the constitution refers only to a federal government power "treaties" might cut against the validity of congressional-executive agreements. Or is it absurd to attribute to the Founders the view that there were certain international agreements that the federal government could not enter into? Even assuming that Congress has the power to enter into compacts, cf. B. Altman & Co. v. United States, 224 U.S. 583, 601 (1912) (describing a congressional-executive agreement as a compact), does this support the interchangeability thesis, or undermine it?

12. In 1997, President Clinton agreed to submit the Flank Agreement, an update of the Treaty on Armed Conventional Forces in Europe ("CFE Treaty"), to the Senate for its Article II consent. This action marked an abandonment of an earlier decision to seek only a congressional majority approval for the Flank Agreement. See Phillip R. Trimble & Alexander W. Koff, *All Fall Down: The Treaty Power in the Clinton Administration,* 16 Berkeley J. Int'l L. 55 (1998). In connection with the original CFE Treaty, the Senate had attached, as a condition of its consent, a declaration stating that international agreements that "reduce or limit the armed forces or armaments of the United States in a militarily significant manner" can be approved only pursuant to the Article II treaty process. See 137 Cong. Rec. S17846 (daily ed. Nov. 23, 1991). In a letter to the Senate, a presidential advisor noted that submission of the Flank agreement for Senate approval was "without prejudice to its legal position vis-à-vis the approval options we believe are available to us." Letter from Samuel R. Berger, Assistant to the President for National Security Affairs, to Trent Lott, Majority Leader of the Senate, dated March 25, 1997, quoted in The Arms Control Reporter 1997 at 603.D.45. What does this episode suggest about the validity of congressional-executive agreements? About the limits on those agreements? About how the Senate's treaty prerogatives can be enforced? About the role of courts in policing these issues?

13. What is the significance of the Biden-Helms letter to President Bush, excerpted above? Do you think this letter influenced the President to submit the arms control agreement with Russia to the Senate? Is the letter a signal of political difficulties with the Senate should the President decide not to submit the agreement there? Does the letter have *legal* significance?

14. The *Made in the USA Foundation* decision, excerpted above, was affirmed by the Eleventh Circuit in an opinion referred to in Chapter 2, Section C. As explained there, the Eleventh Circuit noted that "certain international agreements may well require Senate ratification as treaties through the constitutionally-mandated procedures of Art. II, §2," but it declined to adjudicate the challenge to NAFTA, concluding that, at least in the context of that case, "the issue of what kinds of agreements require Senate ratification pursuant to the Art. II, §2 procedures presents a nonjusticiable political question." Made in the USA Foundation v. United States, 242 F.3d 1300, 1302, 1319 (11th Cir. 2001). Was this a proper application of the political question doctrine? Was this case more like Goldwater v. Carter, where the Supreme Court declined to exercise judicial review, or INS v. Chadha, where the Court exercised judicial review?

15. Consider 22 U.S.C. §7401 (enacted in November 1999), which prohibits the United States from becoming a party to the International Criminal Court by any means other than an Article II treaty. What weight, if any, should a U.S. court give to such a prohibition in considering the scope of the President's executive agreement power? Does Congress have the constitutional authority to limit the use of executive agreements? What does the three-tiered framework for presidential power set forth by Justice Jackson in his concurrence in *Youngstown* suggest?

16. When concluding an international agreement, what factors do you think influence the President's choice between using a sole executive agreement, a congressional-executive agreement, and an Article II treaty? Professor Setear argues that Presidents will sometimes use congressional-executive agreements or treaties rather than sole executive agreements in order to send a "costly, credible signal" to the other treaty parties that the United States is committed to the treaty. *See* John K. Setear, *The President's Rational Choice of a Treaty's Preratification Pathway: Article II, Congressional-Executive Agreement, or Executive Agreement?*, 31 J. Leg. Stud. S5 (2002). Do you agree? Can you think of examples? Can you think of other international or domestic factors that might influence the President's decision?

17. In recent years scholars have engaged in a lively debate about the legitimacy of congressional-executive agreements. *See, e.g.*, Ackerman & Golove, *supra*; David M. Golove, *Against Free-Form Formalism*, 73 N.Y.U. L. Rev. 1791 (1998); Paul, *supra*; Spiro, *supra*; Tribe, *supra*; Yoo, *supra; see also* Detlev F. Vagts, *International Agreements, the Senate, and the Constitution*, 36 Colum. J. Transnat'l L. 143 (1997). For an earlier debate, see Edwin Borchard, *Shall the Executive Agreement Replace the Treaty?*, 53 Yale L.J. 664 (1944); Edwin Borchard, *Treaties and Executive Agreements — A Reply*, 54 Yale L.J. 616 (1945); Myres McDougal & Asher Lans, *Treaties and Congressional-Executive or Presidential Agreements: Interchangeable Instruments of National Policy* (pt. 1), 54 Yale L.J. 184 (1945); and Myres McDougal & Asher Lans, *Treaties and Congressional-Executive or Presidential Agreements: Interchangeable Instruments of National Policy* (pt. 2), 54 Yale L.J. 534 (1945).

2. Sole Executive Agreements

"Sole executive agreements" are executive agreements concluded by the President without specific congressional approval. The Supreme Court has upheld the validity of sole executive agreements in several decisions. In addition to the materials excerpted below, review Dames & Moore v. Regan, which is excerpted in Chapter 3.

United States v. Belmont

301 U.S. 324 (1937)

MR. JUSTICE SUTHERLAND delivered the opinion of the Court.

This is an action at law brought by petitioner against respondents in a federal district court to recover a sum of money deposited by a Russian corporation (Petrograd Metal Works) with August Belmont, a private banker doing business in New York City under the name of August Belmont & Co. August Belmont died in 1924; and respondents are the duly-appointed executors of his will....

The corporation had deposited with Belmont, prior to 1918, the sum of money which petitioner seeks to recover. In 1918, the Soviet Government duly enacted a decree by which it dissolved, terminated and liquidated the corporation (together with others), and nationalized and appropriated all of its property and assets of every kind and wherever situated, including the deposit account with Belmont. As a result, the deposit became the property of the Soviet Government, and so remained until November 16, 1933, at which time the Soviet Government released and assigned to petitioner all amounts due to that government from American nationals, including the deposit account of the corporation with Belmont. Respondents failed and refused to pay the amount upon demand duly made by petitioner.

The assignment was effected by an exchange of diplomatic correspondence between the Soviet Government and the United States. The purpose was to bring about a final settlement of the claims and counterclaims between the Soviet Government and the United States; and it was agreed that the Soviet Government would take no steps to enforce claims against American nationals; but all such claims were released and assigned to the United States, with the understanding that the Soviet Government was to be duly notified of all amounts realized by the United States from such release and assignment. The assignment and requirement for notice are parts of the larger plan to bring about a settlement of the rival claims of the high contracting parties. The continuing and definite interest of the Soviet Government in the collection of assigned claims is evident; and the case, therefore, presents a question of public concern, the determination of which well might involve the good faith of the United States in the eyes of a foreign government. The court below held that the assignment thus effected embraced the claim here in question; and with that we agree.

That court, however, took the view that the situs of the bank deposit was within the State of New York; that in no sense could it be regarded as an intangible property right within Soviet territory; and that the nationalization decree, if enforced, would put into effect an act of confiscation. And it held that a judgment for the United States could not be had, because, in view of that result, it would be contrary to the controlling public policy of the State of New York. The further contention is made by respondents that the public policy of the United States would likewise be infringed by such a judgment. The two questions thus presented are the only ones necessary to be considered.

First. We do not pause to inquire whether in fact there was any policy of the State of New York to be infringed, since we are of opinion that no state policy can prevail against the international compact here involved....

We take judicial notice of the fact that coincident with the assignment set forth in the complaint, the President recognized the Soviet Government, and normal diplomatic relations were established between that government and the

Government of the United States, followed by an exchange of ambassadors. The effect of this was to validate, so far as this country is concerned, all acts of the Soviet Government here involved from the commencement of its existence. The recognition, establishment of diplomatic relations, the assignment, and agreements with respect thereto, were all parts of one transaction, resulting in an international compact between the two governments. That the negotiations, acceptance of the assignment and agreements and understandings in respect thereof were within the competence of the President may not be doubted. Governmental power over internal affairs is distributed between the national government and the several states. Governmental power over external affairs is not distributed, but is vested exclusively in the national government. And in respect of what was done here, the Executive had authority to speak as the sole organ of that government. The assignment and the agreements in connection therewith did not, as in the case of treaties, as that term is used in the treaty making clause of the Constitution (Art. II, §2), require the advice and consent of the Senate.

A treaty signifies "a compact made between two or more independent nations with a view to the public welfare." Altman & Co. v. United States, 224 U.S. 583, 600. But an international compact, as this was, is not always a treaty which requires the participation of the Senate. There are many such compacts, of which a protocol, a modus vivendi, a postal convention, and agreements like that now under consideration are illustrations. The distinction was pointed out by this court in the *Altman* case, *supra*, which arose under §3 of the Tariff Act of 1897, authorizing the President to conclude commercial agreements with foreign countries in certain specified matters. We held that although this might not be a treaty requiring ratification by the Senate, it was a compact negotiated and proclaimed under the authority of the President, and as such was a "treaty" within the meaning of the Circuit Court of Appeals Act, the construction of which might be reviewed upon direct appeal to this court.

Plainly, the external powers of the United States are to be exercised without regard to state laws or policies. The supremacy of a treaty in this respect has been recognized from the beginning. Mr. Madison, in the Virginia Convention, said that if a treaty does not supersede existing state laws, as far as they contravene its operation, the treaty would be ineffective. "To counteract it by the supremacy of the state laws, would bring on the Union the just charge of national perfidy, and involve us in war." 3 Elliot's Debates 515. And see Ware v. Hylton, 3 Dall. 199, 236-237. And while this rule in respect of treaties is established by the express language of cl. 2, Art. VI, of the Constitution, the same rule would result in the case of all international compacts and agreements from the very fact that complete power over international affairs is in the national government and is not and cannot be subject to any curtailment or interference on the part of the several states. Compare United States v. Curtiss-Wright Export Corp., 299 U.S. 304, 316, et seq. In respect of all international negotiations and compacts, and in respect of our foreign relations generally, state lines disappear. As to such purposes the State of New York does not exist. Within the field of its powers, whatever the United States rightfully undertakes, it necessarily has warrant to consummate. And when judicial authority is invoked in aid of such consummation, state constitutions, state laws, and state policies are irrelevant to the inquiry and decision. It is inconceivable that any of them can be interposed as an obstacle to the effective operation of a federal constitutional power. *Cf.* Missouri v. Holland, 252 U.S. 416; Asakura v. Seattle, 265 U.S. 332, 341.

U.S. State Department, Foreign Affairs Manual

11 FAM 721.3: Considerations for Selecting among
Constitutionally Authorized Procedures

In determining a question as to the procedure which should be followed for any particular international agreement, due consideration is given to the following factors. . . .

a. The extent to which the agreement involves commitments or risks affecting the nation as a whole;
b. Whether the agreement is intended to affect State laws;
c. Whether the agreement can be given effect without the enactment of subsequent legislation by the Congress;
d. Past U.S. practice as to similar agreements;
e. The preference of the Congress as to a particular type of agreement;
f. The degree of formality desired for an agreement;
g. The proposed duration of the agreement, the need for prompt conclusion of the agreement, and the desirability of conducting a routine or short-term agreement; and
h. The general international practice as to similar agreements.

In determining whether any international agreement should be brought into force as a treaty or as an international agreement other than a treaty, the utmost care is to be exercised to avoid any invasion or compromise of the constitutional powers of the Senate, the Congress as a whole, or the President.

Case-Zablocki Act

1 U.S.C. §112b (first enacted in 1972)

(a) The Secretary of State shall transmit to the Congress the text of any international agreement (including the text of any oral international agreement, which agreement shall be reduced to writing), other than a treaty, to which the United States is a party as soon as practicable after such agreement has entered into force with respect to the United States but in no event later than sixty days thereafter. However, any such agreement the immediate public disclosure of which would, in the opinion of the President, be prejudicial to the national security of the United States shall not be so transmitted to the Congress but shall be transmitted to the Committee on Foreign Relations of the Senate and the Committee on [International Relations] of the House of Representatives under an appropriate injunction of secrecy to be removed only upon due notice from the President. Any department or agency of the United States Government which enters into any international agreement on behalf of the United States shall transmit to the Department of State the text of such agreement not later than twenty days after such agreement has been signed.

Notes and Questions

1. Presidents have entered into "sole" executive agreements since the beginning of the nation. *See* Wilfred McClure, International Executive Agreements 53

(1941); Michael D. Ramsey, *Executive Agreements and the (Non)Treaty Power*, 77 N.C. L. Rev. 133 (1998). These agreements bind the United States on the international plane just as would a treaty with Senate participation. Most sole executive agreements have concerned relatively insignificant matters such as protocols, modus vivendi, and postal agreements. But they also have included very important matters, such as the World War II agreements at Yalta and Potsdam, the Litvinov agreement at issue in *Belmont*, and the Algiers Accords at issue in Dames & Moore v. Regan (excerpted in Chapter 3). What is the constitutional authority for sole executive agreements? Are there any limits on sole executive agreements? How would limits be discerned? How would they be enforced?

2. The asserted basis for the Litvinov agreement was the President's power to recognize foreign governments. This power, in turn, purportedly stems from the President's power in Article II to "receive Ambassadors and other public Ministers." Does the recognition power flow from this Article II provision? In any event, does the power to recognize include the power to make international agreements relating to recognition? If so, how related must the agreements be to the recognition?

3. As both Dames & Moore v. Regan and American Insurance Association v. Garamendi (excerpted in Chapter 5) suggest, a prominent subject of sole executive agreements concerns the settlement of claims of American nationals against foreign governments. This practice dates back to the founding of the Nation. *See* Evan T. Bloom, Note, *The Executive Claims Settlement Power: Constitutional Authority and Foreign Affairs Applications*, 85 Colum. L. Rev. 155 (1985) (recounting this history). As the Court noted in *Garamendi*, the first example was "as early as 1789, when the Washington administration settled demands against the Dutch Government by American citizens who lost their cargo when Dutch privateers overtook the schooner *Wilmington Packet*." Traditionally these Executive agreements resolved claims against foreign sovereigns, and were practically the only recourse that U.S. citizens had to recovering property and related losses from foreign governments. But as the litigation in *Garamendi* shows, beginning in the 1990s, President Clinton extended such agreements to include claims by U.S. citizens against private parties where there may have been alternate mechanisms of redress. *See generally* Ingrid Brunk Wuerth, *The Dangers of Deference: International Claim Settlement by the President*, 44 Harv. Int'l L.J. 1 (2003) (describing and criticizing this trend).

Why exactly does the President have the power to enter into international agreements that settle claims between U.S. citizens and foreign governments? Some settlements occur when the U.S. victims have little alternate recourse, and thus might be said to be consensual. Others occur in the context of recognition (such as in *Belmont*) or in emergency or war situations where the President is arguably exercising Commander-in-Chief authority (such as in *Dames & Moore*). But where does the President obtain the authority settle claims outside these contexts? From his role as the "sole organ" of communication in foreign relations? From the Article II Vesting Clause?

4. Consider Article I, Section 10 of the Constitution, which prohibits states from entering into "any Treaty," and requires that they obtain congressional consent before entering into "any Agreement or Compact . . . with a foreign Power." What is the difference between a "Treaty" and an "Agreement or Compact"? Is this distinction relevant to the validity of sole executive agreements? The Supreme Court discussed this distinction in Holmes v. Jennison, 39 U.S. (14 Pet.) 540 (1840). In that case, the issue was whether Vermont was precluded by Article I,

Section 10 from extraditing an individual to Canada. A plurality of the Court concluded that, although Vermont's agreement with Canada to extradite the individual was not a "treaty," it was an "agreement" and thus required congressional authorization. The Court stated:

> But it may be said, that here is no treaty; and, undoubtedly, in the sense in which that word is generally understood, there is no treaty between Vermont and Canada. For when we speak of "a treaty," we mean an instrument written and executed with the formalities customary among nations; and as no clause in the Constitution ought to be interpreted differently from the usual and fair import of the words used, if the decision of this case depended upon the word above mentioned, we should not be prepared to say that there was any express prohibition of the power exercised by the state of Vermont.
>
> But the question does not rest upon the prohibition to enter into a treaty. In the very next clause of the Constitution, the states are forbidden to enter into any "agreement" or "compact" with a foreign nation; and as these words could not have been idly or superfluously used by the framers of the Constitution, they cannot be construed to mean the same thing with the word treaty. They evidently mean something more, and were designed to make the prohibition more comprehensive.
>
> A few extracts from an eminent writer on the laws of nations, showing the manner in which these different words have been used, and the different meanings sometimes attached to them, will, perhaps, contribute to explain the reason for using them all in the Constitution; and will prove that the most comprehensive terms were employed in prohibiting to the states all intercourse with foreign nations[:]
>
>> Vattel, page 192, sec. 152, says: "A treaty, in Latin faedus, is a compact made with a view to the public welfare, by the superior power, either for perpetuity, or for a considerable time."
>>
>> Section 153. "The compacts which have temporary matters for their object, are called agreements, conventions, and pactions. They are acomplished by one single act, and not by repeated acts. These compacts are perfected in their execution once for all; treaties receive a successive execution, whose duration equals that of the treaty."
>>
>> Section 154. Public treaties can only be made by the "supreme power, by sovereigns who contract in the name of the state. Thus conventions made between sovereigns respecting their own private affairs, and those between a sovereign and a private person, are not public treaties."
>>
>> Section 206, page 218. "The public compacts called conventions, articles of agreement, &c., when they are made between sovereigns, differ from treaties only in their object."

Id. at 571-72. Does this distinction between treaties and agreements and compacts suggest possible limits on the sole executive agreement power? Does it help explain the historical practice of presidential settlement of claims?

5. Even assuming that presidents have the power to make executive agreements that bind the United States on the international plane, does it follow that these agreements preempt state law? The *Belmont* decision was the first decision to hold that a sole executive agreement preempts state law. *See also* United States v. Pink, 315 U.S. 203 (1942) (reaffirming *Belmont*). What does the language of the Supremacy Clause suggest about the preemptive power of executive agreements? Assuming, as stated in *Belmont*, that "in respect of our foreign relations generally, ... the State of New York does not exist," does it follow that there are no limits on the power of the President to make executive agreements that preempt state law?

What about separation of powers concerns, such as a concern with undermining the Senate's constitutional role in treaty-making or Congress's constitutional role in creating federal legislation?

6. Take another look at Dames & Moore v. Regan. Most of that decision focuses on the domestic sources of authority for President Carter's and President Reagan's Executive Orders nullifying and transferring attached Iranian funds, and suspending claims in U.S. courts. Why didn't the Court rely more heavily on the Algiers Accords, the executive agreement that ended the hostage crisis? After all, this agreement obligated the United States to "terminate all legal proceedings" in U.S. courts, to "nullify all attachments...obtained therein," and to "prohibit all further litigation based on such claims." Does the Court's failure to rely more heavily on the Algiers Accords as the source of presidential power suggest a retrenchment from *Belmont*? Or does it reflect the fact that the Executive Orders at issue in *Dames & Moore* arguably limited the effect of a federal statute (the Foreign Sovereign Immunities Act)?

7. How much guidance do the factors listed in the State Department's manual, excerpted above, provide in deciding whether an international agreement should go through the Article II treaty process? Do these factors adequately protect the constitutional powers of the Senate? Of the full Congress? Assuming it were proper for a court to evaluate the validity of an executive agreement, how much weight, if any, should it give to these factors?

8. What is the significance of Congress's enactment of the Case-Zablocki Act, excerpted above, for the validity of executive agreements? Is the Act constitutional? Judicially enforceable? A Senate study concludes that the Act "has been helpful in apprising Congress of executive agreements as defined by the Act," and that the Act "has contributed to improved relations between Congress and the executive branch in the area of executive agreements." CRS Study, *supra*, at 225. Between 1978 and 1999, more than 7,000 agreements were transmitted to Congress pursuant to the Act. *See id.* at 226-27.

9. For an overview of the sole executive agreement power, see Louis Henkin, Foreign Affairs and the United States Constitution 219-26 (2d ed. 1996). For articles critical of this power, see Joel R. Paul, *The Geopolitical Constitution: Executive Expediency and Executive Agreements*, 86 Cal. L. Rev. 671 (1998); Ramsey, *supra*. For a good historical account of the context and significance of *Belmont*, see G. Edward White, *The Transformation of the Constitutional Regime of Foreign Relations*, 85 Va. L. Rev. 1, 111-34 (1999).

7

Customary International Law and International Human Rights Litigation

Customary international law is the law of the international community that "results from a general and consistent practice of states followed by them from a sense of legal obligation." Restatement (Third) of the Foreign Relations Law of the United States §102(2) (1987). Like treaties, customary international law binds the United States on the international plane. At the time of the Founding, customary international law was referred to as the "law of nations," a term that in its broadest sense included not only what we today call customary international law, but also the law merchant, maritime law, and the law of conflict of laws.

As we learned in Chapter 1, the Founders hoped to establish a federal government that would be able to ensure that the United States (and its constituent parts, the States) carried out international obligations under both treaties and customary international law. Nonetheless, the Constitution emphasizes treaties much more than customary international law. Article I, Section 10 denies states the ability to enter into treaties. Article II grants the President the power to make treaties, with the advice and consent of two-thirds of the Senate. Article III grants the federal courts the power to hear cases arising under treaties. And Article VI states that treaties are part of the supreme law of the land. By contrast, the only reference to customary international law is in Article I, §8, cl. 10, which authorizes Congress to "define and punish...Offences against the Law of Nations."

Congress has significant authority, under the Define and Punish Clause and other clauses of Article I, to incorporate customary international law into U.S. federal law. This authority raises two types of issues that we explore in this chapter: first, the status of customary international law in the U.S. legal system in the absence of such congressional incorporation; second, the degree to which Congress has in fact incorporated customary international law into the domestic legal system, an issue that arises frequently in the context of international human rights litigation. Section A examines the status of customary international law in the U.S. legal system and assesses the possible consequences of treating customary international law as federal law. Section B discusses the Alien Tort Statute, the principal statutory basis for human rights litigation — litigation that typically involves alleged violations of customary international law. It also examines the Torture Victim Protection Act, in which Congress expressly incorporated certain human rights norms into federal statutory law. Section C analyzes various sovereign immunity defenses that can arise in human rights litigation in U.S. courts. Section D considers human rights litigation against private parties, particularly corporations. Section E examines human rights-related civil lawsuits against terrorists and supporters of terrorism. Section F discusses: the relevance of international law, including customary international law, to the interpretation of Federal Statutes. Section G explores an issue related to customary international law but that also builds on other issues explored in this book — judicial reliance on foreign and international materials in constitutional interpretation.

A. "PART OF OUR LAW"

The Paquete Habana

175 U.S. 677 (1900)

[During the Spanish–American War, a U.S. naval squadron was enforcing a blockade around Cuba. In doing so, it seized two Cuban vessels while they were engaged in catching and transporting fish off the coast of Cuba. A federal district court condemned the fishing vessels as prizes of war. The masters and owners of the vessels appealed to the Supreme Court.]

MR. JUSTICE GRAY delivered the opinion of the court. . . .

By an ancient usage among civilized nations, beginning centuries ago, and gradually ripening into a rule of international law, coast fishing vessels, pursuing their vocation of catching and bringing in fresh fish, have been recognized as exempt, with their cargoes and crews, from capture as prize of war.

This doctrine, however, has been earnestly contested at the bar; and no complete collection of the instances illustrating it is to be found, so far as we are aware, in a single published work, although many are referred to and discussed by the writers on international law. . . . It is therefore worth the while to trace the history of the rule, from the earliest accessible sources, through the increasing recognition of it, with occasional setbacks, to what we may now justly consider as its final establishment in our own country and generally throughout the civilized world. . . .

[The Court proceeds to look at statements and practices by England and France starting in the 1400s. This evidence included instructions by these governments to their admirals as well as various treaty provisions. This evidence was not uniform — in the late 1700s, for example, France stopped following the practice because of its perception that French fishing vessels were not receiving the same treatment.]

The doctrine which exempts coast fishermen with their vessels and cargoes from capture as prize of war has been familiar to the United States from the time of the War of Independence. . . .

[The Court notes, among other things, that England and France had abstained from interfering with coastal fishing during the Revolutionary War. The Court admitted, however, that those two countries had failed to exempt fishing vessels from capture during the period of the French Revolution. The Court also notes that the United States had recognized the exemption of coastal fishing boats from capture in its war with Mexico.]

International law is part of our law, and must be ascertained and administered by the courts of justice of appropriate jurisdiction, as often as questions of right depending upon it are duly presented for their determination. For this purpose, where there is no treaty, and no controlling executive or legislative act or juricial decision, resort must be had to the customs and usages of civilized nations; and, as evidence of these, to the works of jurists and commentators, who by years of labor, research and experience, have made themselves peculiarly well acquainted with the subjects of which they treat. Such works are resorted to by judicial tribunals, not for the speculations of their authors concerning what the law ought to be, but for trustworthy evidence of what the law really is. Hilton v. Guyot, 159 U.S. 113, 163, 164, 214, 215. . . .

[The Court then refers to the views of leading European commentators on international law. This evidence also was not uniform. Two English commentators, for example, although noting that the exemption was common practice, did not believe that it had become a settled rule of customary international law.]

This review of the precedents and authorities on the subject appears to us abundantly to demonstrate that at the present day, by the general consent of the civilized nations of the world, and independently of any express treaty or other public act, it is an established rule of international law, founded on considerations of humanity to a poor and industrious order of men, and of the mutual convenience of belligerent States, that coast fishing vessels, with their implements and supplies, cargoes and crews, unarmed, and honestly pursuing their peaceful calling of catching and bringing in fresh fish, are exempt from capture as prize of war.

The exemption, of course, does not apply to coast fishermen or their vessels, if employed for a warlike purpose, or in such a way as to give aid or information to the enemy; nor when military or naval operations create a necessity to which all private interests must give way.

Nor has the exemption been extended to ships or vessels employed on the high sea in taking whales or seals, or cod or other fish which are not brought fresh to market, but are salted or otherwise cured and made a regular article of commerce.

This rule of international law is one which prize courts, administering the law of nations, are bound to take judicial notice of, and to give effect to, in the absence of any treaty or other public act of their own government in relation to the matter. . . .

The position taken by the United States during the recent war with Spain was quite in accord with the rule of international law, now generally recognized by civilized nations, in regard to coast fishing vessels.

On April 21, 1898, the Secretary of the Navy gave instructions to Admiral Sampson, commanding the North Atlantic Squadron, to "immediately institute a blockade of the north coast of Cuba, extending from Cardenas on the east to Bahia Honda on the west." The blockade was immediately instituted accordingly. On April 22, the President issued a proclamation, declaring that the United States had instituted and would maintain that blockade, "in pursuance of the laws of the United States, and the law of nations applicable to such cases." And by the act of Congress of April 25, 1898, c. 189, it was declared that the war between the United States and Spain existed on that day, and had existed since and including April 21.

On April 26, 1898, the President issued another proclamation, which, after reciting the existence of the war, as declared by Congress, contained this further recital: "It being desirable that such war should be conducted upon principles in harmony with the present views of nations and sanctioned by their recent practice." This recital was followed by specific declarations of certain rules for the conduct of the war by sea, making no mention of fishing vessels. But the proclamation clearly manifests the general policy of the Government to conduct the war in accordance with the principles of international law sanctioned by the recent practice of nations.

On April 28, 1898, (after the capture of the two fishing vessels now in question,) Admiral Sampson telegraphed to the Secretary of the Navy as follows: "I find that a large number of fishing schooners are attempting to get into Havana from their fishing grounds near the Florida reefs and coasts. They are generally manned by excellent seamen, belonging to the maritime inscription of Spain, who have already served in the Spanish navy, and who are liable to further service. As these trained men are naval reserves, have a semi-military character, and would be most valuable to the Spaniards as artillerymen, either afloat or ashore, I recommend that they should be detained prisoners of war, and that I should be authorized to deliver them to the commanding officer of the army at Key West." To that communication the Secretary of the Navy, on April 30, 1898, guardedly answered: "Spanish fishing vessels attempting to violate blockade are subject, with crew, to capture, and any such vessel or crew considered likely to aid enemy may be detained." The Admiral's despatch assumed that he was not authorized, without express order, to arrest coast fishermen peaceably pursuing their calling; and the necessary implication and evident intent of the response of the Navy Department were that Spanish coast fishing vessels and their crews should not be interfered with, so long as they neither attempted to violate the blockade, nor were considered likely to aid the enemy....

Upon the facts proved in either case, it is the duty of this court, sitting as the highest prize court of the United States, and administering the law of nations, to declare and adjudge that the capture was unlawful, and without probable cause.

Filartiga v. Pena-Irala

630 F.2d 876 (2d Cir. 1980)

[Joel Filartiga and his daughter Dolly, citizens of Paraguay, sued Pena-Irala, also a citizen of Paraguay, for torturing and wrongfully killing Joelito Filartiga, Joel's son and Dolly's brother, in Paraguay. The complaint alleged that the torture and killing took place while Pena-Irala was Inspector General of Police in Asuncion, Paraguay. The Filartigas served Pena-Irala with process while he was living in the United States beyond the terms of his visa. Following this service but before trial, the INS deported Pena-Irala back to Paraguay. The district court dismissed the Filartigas' complaint for lack of subject matter jurisdiction.]

KAUFMAN, CIRCUIT JUDGE....

[Appellants'] cause of action is stated as arising under "wrongful death statutes; the U.N. Charter; the Universal Declaration on Human Rights; the U.N. Declaration Against Torture; the American Declaration of the Rights and Duties of Man; and other pertinent declarations, documents and practices constituting the customary international law of human rights and the law of nations," as well as 28 U.S.C. §1350, Article II, §2 and the Supremacy Clause of the U.S. Constitution. Jurisdiction is claimed under the general federal question provision, 28 U.S.C. §1331 and, principally on this appeal, under the Alien Tort Statute, 28 U.S.C. §1350....

II

Appellants rest their principal argument in support of federal jurisdiction upon the Alien Tort Statute, 28 U.S.C. §1350, which provides: 'The district courts shall have original jurisdiction of any civil action by an alien for a tort only, committed in violation of the law of nations or a treaty of the United States." Since appellants do not contend that their action arises directly under a treaty of the United States,[7] a threshold question on the jurisdictional issue is whether the conduct alleged violates the law of nations. In light of the universal condemnation of torture in numerous international agreements, and the renunciation of torture as an instrument of official policy by virtually all of the nations of the world (in principle if not in practice), we find that an act of torture committed by a state official against one held in detention violates established norms of the international law of human rights, and hence the law of nations.

The Supreme Court has enumerated the appropriate sources of international law. The law of nations "may be ascertained by consulting the works of jurists, writing professedly on public law; or by the general usage and practice of nations; or by judicial decisions recognizing and enforcing that law." United States v. Smith, 18 U.S. (5 Wheat.) 153, 160-61 (1820). In *Smith*, a statute proscribing "the crime of piracy (on the high seas) as defined by the law of nations," 3 Stat. 510(a) (1819), was held sufficiently determinate in meaning to afford the basis for a death sentence. The *Smith*, Court discovered among the works of Lord Bacon, Grotius, Bochard and other commentators a genuine consensus that rendered the crime "sufficiently and constitutionally defined." *Smith, supra*, 18 U.S. (5 Wheat.) at 162....

[*The Paquete] Habana* is particularly instructive for present purposes, for it held that the traditional prohibition against seizure of an enemy's coastal fishing vessels during wartime, a standard that began as one of comity only, had ripened over the preceding century into "a settled rule of international law" by "the general assent of civilized nations." *Id.* at 694; *accord, id.* at 686. Thus it is clear that courts must interpret international law not as it was in 1789, but as it has evolved and exists among the nations of the world today. *See* Ware v. Hylton, 3 U.S. (3 Dall.) 199 (1796) (distinguishing between "ancient" and "modern" law of nations).

The requirement that a rule command the "general assent of civilized nations" to become binding upon them all is a stringent one. Were this not so, the courts of one nation might feel free to impose idiosyncratic legal rules upon others, in the name of applying international law. Thus, in Banco Nacional de Cuba v. Sabbatino, 376 U.S. 398 (1964), the Court declined to pass on the validity of the Cuban government's expropriation of a foreign-owned corporation's assets, noting the sharply conflicting views on the issue propounded by the capital-exporting, capital-importing, socialist and capitalist nations.

The case at bar presents us with a situation diametrically opposed to the conflicted state of law that confronted the *Sabbatino* Court. Indeed, to paraphrase that Court's statement, *id.* at 428, there are few, if any, issues in international law today on which opinion seems to be so united as the limitations on a state's power to torture persons held in its custody.

The United Nations Charter (a treaty of the United States, see 59 Stat. 1033 (1945)) makes it clear that in this modern age a state's treatment of its own citizens is a matter of international concern. It provides:

---

7. Appellants "associate themselves with" the argument of some of the amici curiae that their claim arises directly under a treaty of the United States, but nonetheless primarily rely upon treaties and other international instruments as evidence of an emerging norm of customary international law, rather than independent sources of law.

> With a view to the creation of conditions of stability and well-being which are necessary for peaceful and friendly relations among nations...the United Nations shall promote...universal respect for, and observance of, human rights and fundamental freedoms for all without distinctions as to race, sex, language or religion.

Id. Art. 55. And further:

> All members pledge themselves to take joint and separate action in cooperation with the Organization for the achievement of the purposes set forth in Article 55.

Id. Art. 56.

While this broad mandate has been held not to be wholly self-executing, ... this observation alone does not end our inquiry. For although there is no universal agreement as to the precise extent of the "human rights and fundamental freedoms" guaranteed to all by the Charter, there is at present no dissent from the view that the guaranties include, at a bare minimum, the right to be free from torture. This prohibition has become part of customary international law, as evidenced and defined by the Universal Declaration of Human Rights, General Assembly Resolution 217 (III)(A) (Dec. 10, 1948) which states, in the plainest of terms, "no one shall be subjected to torture." The General Assembly has declared that the Charter precepts embodied in this Universal Declaration "constitute basic principles of international law."

Particularly relevant is the Declaration on the Protection of All Persons from Being Subjected to Torture, General Assembly Resolution 3452, 30 U.N. GAOR Supp. (No. 34) 91, U.N. Doc. A/1034 (1975)... The Declaration expressly prohibits any state from permitting the dastardly and totally inhuman act of torture. Torture, in turn, is defined as "any act by which severe pain and suffering, whether physical or mental, is intentionally inflicted by or at the instigation of a public official on a person for such purposes as...intimidating him or other persons." The Declaration goes on to provide that "(w)here it is proved that an act of torture or other cruel, inhuman or degrading treatment or punishment has been committed by or at the instigation of a public official, the victim shall be afforded redress and compensation, in accordance with national law." This Declaration, like the Declaration of Human Rights before it, was adopted without dissent by the General Assembly....

These U.N. declarations are significant because they specify with great precision the obligations of member nations under the Charter. Since their adoption, "(m)embers can no longer contend that they do not know what human rights they promised in the Charter to promote." Sohn, "A Short History of United Nations Documents on Human Rights," in The United Nations and Human Rights, 18th Report of the Commission (Commission to Study the Organization of Peace ed. 1968). Moreover, a U.N. Declaration is, according to one authoritative definition, "a formal and solemn instrument, suitable for rare occasions when principles of great and lasting importance are being enunciated." 34 U.N. ESCOR, Supp. (No. 8) 15, U.N. Doc. E/cn.4/1/610 (1962) (memorandum of Office of Legal Affairs, U.N. Secretariat). Accordingly, it has been observed that the Universal Declaration of Human Rights "no longer fits into the dichotomy of 'binding treaty' against 'nonbinding pronouncement,' but is rather an authoritative statement of the international community." E. Schwelb, Human Rights and the International Community 70 (1964). Thus, a Declaration creates an expectation of adherence, and "insofar as the expectation is gradually justified by State practice, a declaration may by custom become recognized as laying down rules binding upon the States." 34 U.N.

ESCOR, *supra*. Indeed, several commentators have concluded that the Universal Declaration has become, in toto, a part of binding, customary international law.

Turning to the act of torture, we have little difficulty discerning its universal renunciation in the modern usage and practice of nations. *Smith, supra*, 18 U.S. (5 Wheat.) at 160-61. The international consensus surrounding torture has found expression in numerous international treaties and accords. . . . The substance of these international agreements is reflected in modern municipal i.e. national law as well. Although torture was once a routine concomitant of criminal interrogations in many nations, during the modern and hopefully more enlightened era it has been universally renounced. According to one survey, torture is prohibited, expressly or implicitly, by the constitutions of over fifty-five nations, including both the United States and Paraguay. . . . We have been directed to no assertion by any contemporary state of a right to torture its own or another nation's citizens. Indeed, United States diplomatic contacts confirm the universal abhorrence with which torture is viewed:

> In exchanges between United States embassies and all foreign states with which the United States maintains relations, it has been the Department of State's general experience that no government has asserted a right to torture its own nationals. Where reports of torture elicit some credence, a state usually responds by denial or, less frequently, by asserting that the conduct was unauthorized or constituted rough treatment short of torture.[15]

Memorandum of the United States as Amicus Curiae at 16 n.34.

Having examined the sources from which customary international law is derived—the usage of nations, judicial opinions and the works of jurists—we conclude that official torture is now prohibited by the law of nations. . . . The treaties and accords cited above, as well as the express foreign policy of our own government, all make it clear that international law confers fundamental rights upon all people vis-à-vis their own governments. While the ultimate scope of those rights will be a subject for continuing refinement and elaboration, we hold that the right to be free from torture is now among them. We therefore turn to the question whether the other requirements for jurisdiction are met.

III

Appellee submits that even if the tort alleged is a violation of modern international law, federal jurisdiction may not be exercised consistent with the dictates of Article III of the Constitution. The claim is without merit. Common law courts of general jurisdiction regularly adjudicate transitory tort claims between individuals over whom they exercise personal jurisdiction, wherever the tort occurred. Moreover, as part of an articulated scheme of federal control over external affairs, Congress provided, in the first Judiciary Act, §9(b), 1 Stat. 73, 77 (1789), for federal jurisdiction over suits by aliens where principles of international law are in issue. The constitutional basis for the Alien Tort Statute is the law of nations, which has always been part of the federal common law.

---

15. The fact that the prohibition of torture is often honored in the breach does not diminish its binding effect as a norm of international law. As one commentator has put it, "The best evidence for the existence of international law is that every actual State recognizes that it does exist and that it is itself under an obligation to observe it. States often violate international law, just as individuals often violate municipal law; but no more than individuals do States defend their violations by claiming that they are above the law." J. Brierly, The Outlook for International Law 4-5 (Oxford 1944)

It is not extraordinary for a court to adjudicate a tort claim arising outside of its territorial jurisdiction. A state or nation has a legitimate interest in the orderly resolution of disputes among those within its borders, and where the lex loci delicti commissi is applied, it is an expression of comity to give effect to the laws of the state where the wrong occurred. . . .

During the eighteenth century, it was taken for granted on both sides of the Atlantic that the law of nations forms a part of the common law. 1 Blackstone, Commentaries 263-64 (1st Ed. 1765-69); 4 *id.* at 67. Under the Articles of Confederation, the Pennsylvania Court of Oyer and Terminer at Philadelphia, per McKean, Chief Justice, applied the law of nations to the criminal prosecution of the Chevalier de Longchamps for his assault upon the person of the French Consul-General to the United States, noting that "(t)his law, in its full extent, is a part of the law of this state. . . ." Respublica v. DeLongchamps, 1 U.S. (1 Dall.) 113, 119 (1784). . . .

[O]ne of the principal defects of the Confederation that our Constitution was intended to remedy was the central government's inability to "cause infractions of treaties or of the law of nations, to be punished." 1 Farrand, Records of the Federal Convention 19 (Rev. ed. 1937) (Notes of James Madison). . . .

As ratified, the judiciary article contained no express reference to cases arising under the law of nations. Indeed, the only express reference to that body of law is contained in Article I, §8, cl. 10, which grants to the Congress the power to "define and punish . . . offenses against the law of nations." Appellees seize upon this circumstance and advance the proposition that the law of nations forms a part of the laws of the United States only to the extent that Congress has acted to define it. This extravagant claim is amply refuted by the numerous decisions applying rules of international law uncodified in any act of Congress. *E.g.,* Ware v. Hylton, 3 U.S. (3 Dall.) 199, (1796); *The Paquete Habana, supra,* 175 U.S. 677; *Sabbatino, supra,* 376 U.S. 398 (1964). A similar argument was offered to and rejected by the Supreme Court in United States v. Smith, *supra,* 18 U.S. (5 Wheat.) 153, 158-60, and we reject it today. As John Jay wrote in The Federalist No. 3, at 22 (1 Bourne ed. 1901), "Under the national government, treaties and articles of treaties, as well as the laws of nations, will always be expounded in one sense and executed in the same manner, whereas adjudications on the same points and questions in the thirteen states will not always accord or be consistent." Federal jurisdiction over cases involving international law is clear.

Thus, it was hardly a radical initiative for Chief Justice Marshall to state in The Nereide, 13 U.S. (9 Cranch) 388, 422 (1815), that in the absence of a congressional enactment,[20] United States courts are "bound by the law of nations, which is a part of the law of the land." These words were echoed in *The Paquete Habana, supra,* 175 U.S. at 700: "international law is part of our law, and must be ascertained and administered by the courts of justice of appropriate jurisdiction, as often as questions of right depending upon it are duly presented for their determination."

The Filartigas urge that 28 U.S.C. §1350 be treated as an exercise of Congress's power to define offenses against the law of nations. While such a reading is possible, see Lincoln Mills v. Textile Workers, 353 U.S. 448 (1957) (jurisdictional statute

---

20. The plainest evidence that international law has an existence in the federal courts independent of acts of Congress is the long-standing rule of construction first enunciated by Chief Justice Marshall: "an act of congress ought never to be construed to violate the law of nations, if any other possible construction remains. . . ." The Charming Betsy, 6 U.S. (2 Cranch), 64, 67 (1804), quoted in Lauritzen v. Larsen, 345 U.S. 571, 578 (1953).

authorizes judicial explication of federal common law), we believe it is sufficient here to construe the Alien Tort Statute, not as granting new rights to aliens, but simply as opening the federal courts for adjudication of the rights already recognized by international law. The statute nonetheless does inform our analysis of Article III, for we recognize that questions of jurisdiction "must be considered part of an organic growth—part of the evolutionary process," and that the history of the judiciary article gives meaning to its pithy phrases. Romero v. International Terminal Operating Co., 358 U.S. 354, 360 (1959). The Framers' overarching concern that control over international affairs be vested in the new national government to safeguard the standing of the United States among the nations of the world therefore reinforces the result we reach today.

Although the Alien Tort Statute has rarely been the basis for jurisdiction during its long history, in light of the foregoing discussion, there can be little doubt that this action is properly brought in federal court.[22] This is undeniably an action by an alien, for a tort only, committed in violation of the law of nations. The paucity of suits successfully maintained under the section is readily attributable to the statute's requirement of alleging a "*violation* of the law of nations" (emphasis supplied) at the jurisdictional threshold. Courts have, accordingly, engaged in a more searching preliminary review of the merits than is required, for example, under the more flexible "arising under" formulation. Compare O'Reilly de Camara v. Brooke, 209 U.S. 45, 52 (1907) (question of Alien Tort Statute jurisdiction disposed of "on the merits") (Holmes, J.), with Bell v. Hood, 327 U.S. 678 (1946) (general federal question jurisdiction not defeated by the possibility that the averments in the complaint may fail to state a cause of action). Thus, the narrowing construction that the Alien Tort Statute has previously received reflects the fact that earlier cases did not involve such well-established, universally recognized norms of international law that are here at issue. . . .

In the twentieth century the international community has come to recognize the common danger posed by the flagrant disregard of basic human rights and particularly the right to be free of torture. Spurred first by the Great War, and then the Second, civilized nations have banded together to prescribe acceptable norms of international behavior. From the ashes of the Second World War arose the United Nations Organization, amid hopes that an era of peace and cooperation had at last begun. Though many of these aspirations have remained elusive goals, that circumstance cannot diminish the true progress that has been made. In the modern age, humanitarian and practical considerations have combined to lead the nations of the world to recognize that respect for fundamental human rights is in their individual and collective interest. Among the rights universally proclaimed by all nations, as we have noted, is the right to be free of physical torture. Indeed, for purposes of civil liability, the torturer has become like the pirate and slave trader before him hostis humani generis, an enemy of all mankind. Our holding today, giving effect to a jurisdictional provision enacted by our First Congress, is a small but important step in the fulfillment of the ageless dream to free all people from brutal violence.

---

22. We recognize that our reasoning might also sustain jurisdiction under the general federal question provision, 28 U.S.C. §1331. We prefer, however, to rest our decision upon the Alien Tort Statute, in light of that provision's close coincidence with the jurisdictional facts presented in this case.

Notes and Questions

1. What differences are there between the sources and content of the customary international law at issue in *The Paquete Habana* and the sources and content of the customary international law at issue in *Filartiga*? Do both decisions satisfy the Restatement definition of customary international law set forth at the beginning of this chapter?

The Paquete Habana and *Filartiga* arguably represent different conceptions of customary international law. Under this view, *The Paquete Habana* reflects a traditional conception of customary international law that emphasized the importance of state consent as embodied in state practice that developed slowly over a substantial period of time. By contrast, *Filartiga* represents a modern conception of customary international law that focuses less on state practice and state consent and instead emphasizes General Assembly Resolutions (which in themselves are technically not a source of international law, but which nonetheless may have normative force as representing the views of the nations of the world); positions taken at multilateral treaty conferences, regardless of whether the treaties have been ratified; and the pronouncements of international bodies, such as human rights committees and the International Law Commission. For more elaborate descriptions of the differences outlined in this paragraph, see Restatement (Third) of the Foreign Relations Law of the United States §102, reporters' note 2 (1987); Jeffrey M. Blum & Ralph G. Steinhardt, *Federal Jurisdiction over International Human Rights Claims: The Alien Tort Claims Act After Filartiga v. Pena-Irala*, 22 Harv. Int'l L.J. 53, 98-102 (1981); and Curtis A. Bradley & Jack L. Goldsmith, *Customary International Law as Federal Common Law: A Critique of the Modern Position*, 110 Harv. L. Rev. 815, 838-42 (1997).

To the extent there are differences between these conceptions of customary international law, these differences raise at least two sets of questions. The first concerns the significance of these differences for the legitimacy of international law *per se*. Is one conception of customary international law more legitimate than the other? For various perspectives, see Jack L. Goldsmith & Eric A. Posner, The Limits of International Law 132-33 (2005); Blum & Steinhardt, *supra*, at 98-102; and J. Patrick Kelly, *The Twilight of Customary International Law*, 40 Va. J. Int'l L. 449 (2000).

The second set of questions concerns the relevance of the distinction between traditional and modern customary international law for purposes of the *domestic* status of this law in the U.S. legal system. Consider the distinction as you work through the questions below.

2. The domestic legal status of customary international law has been the subject of significant debate. As mentioned above, the text of the Constitution contains little reference to customary international law. Yet, as Chapter 1 made clear, the Founders wanted to ensure that the United States abided by its obligations under customary international law. Why, in this light, would the Founders say so much about treaties and so little about customary international law? Why would they refer to the law of nations only in the Define and Punish Clause?

3. Although the Constitution does not mention customary international law in either Article III or Article VI, those Articles do refer to the "Laws of the United States," and some scholars have argued that the Founders intended that phrase to encompass customary international law. Isn't that argument undermined by the express reference to the law of nations in Article I? Is it likely that the Founders would have wanted *all* of the law of nations to be included within Articles III and VI, including the law merchant? Would the Founders have considered customary international law to be "made in Pursuance [of the Constitution]," as required by the Supremacy Clause? If not, is it likely that they intended the phrase "Laws of the United States" in Article III to be broader than the similar phrase in Article VI? For a discussion of these and related issues, compare Curtis A. Bradley, *The Alien Tort Statute and Article III*, 42 Va. J. Int'l L. 587 (2002) (arguing that the phrase "Laws of the United States" was not intended to encompass the law of nations in either Article III or Article VI), with William S. Dodge, *The Constitutionality of the Alien Tort Statute: Some Observations on Text and Context*, 42 Va. J. Int'l L. 687 (2002) (arguing that the phrase "Laws of the United States" in Article III was intended to encompass the law of nations). *See also* Michael D. Ramsey, *International Law as Part of Our Law: A Constitutional Perspective*, 29 Pepp. L. Rev. 187 (2001) (suggesting that "Laws of the United States" in Article III may be broader than "Laws of the United States . . . made in Pursuance [of the Constitution]" in Article VI).

4. The drafting history of Article III might have implications for the domestic status of customary international law. Some of the proposed drafts would have included cases arising under the law of nations within the federal courts' jurisdiction. The Pinckney Plan proposed giving the Supreme Court appellate jurisdiction over state court decisions "in all Causes wherein Questions shall arise . . . on the Law of Nations." 2 The Records of the Federal Convention of 1787, at 136 (Max Farrand ed., 1911). Similarly, there is evidence suggesting that the New Jersey Plan would have given the federal judiciary the authority to hear, on appeal, all cases "which may arise . . . on the Law of Nations, or general commercial or marine Laws." *Id.* at 157. But these proposals were never adopted. Instead, the draft that emerged from the Convention's Committee of Detail listed specific cases and controversies, some of which, such as admiralty cases and controversies involving ambassadors, would be likely to involve the law of nations. *See id.* at 186. What, if anything, does this drafting history suggest?

5. In England, as noted by Blackstone, "the law of nations . . . is here adopted in its full extent by the common law, and is held to be a part of the law of the land." 4 William Blackstone, Commentaries on The Laws of England 67 (1769); *see also* Triquet v. Bath, 3 Burr. 1478, 1481, 97 Eng. Rep. 936, 938 (K.B. 1764) (Mansfield, J.) (stating that "[t]he law of nations, in its full extent was part of the law of England"). Prior to the Constitution, state courts in the United States applied customary international law as part of state common law. A prominent example was the Pennsylvania Supreme Court's decision in Respublica v. DeLongchamps, 1 U.S. (1 Dall.) 113 (1784), a case discussed in *Filartiga*. *DeLongchamps* involved the prosecution of a French citizen for his assault upon the French Consul-General to the United States, an offense considered at that time to be a violation of the law of nations. The Pennsylvania court explained that the law of nations, "in its full extent, is part of the law of this State, and is to be collected from the practice of different Nations, and the authority of writers." *Id.* at 119.

It is unclear to what extent this understanding changed after the adoption of the Constitution. As noted in Chapter 1, several Founders, in connection with neutrality prosecutions in the 1790s, stated that the law of nations was part of this country's laws. *See, e.g.,* Henfield's Case, 11 F. Cas. 1099, 1100-01 (C.C.D. Pa. 1793) (No. 6360) (Grand Jury charge of Jay, C.J.); *id.* at 1117 (Grand Jury charge of Wilson, J.); *see also* Charge to the Grand Jury for the District of New York (Apr. 4, 1790), in New Hampshire Gazette (Portsmouth 1790) (Chief Justice

Jay instructs that law of nations was "part of the laws of this, and of every other civilized nation."). In another Grand Jury Charge, Justice Iredell explained:

> The Common Law of England, from which our own is derived, fully recognizes the principles of the Law of Nations, and applies them in all cases falling under its jurisdiction, where the nature of the subject requires it. . . . In whatever manner the Law of Nations is violated, it is a subject of national, not personal complaint.

Charge to the Grand Jury for the District of South Carolina (May 12, 1794), in Gazette of the United States (Philadelphia 1794). Attorneys General Edmund Randolph and Charles Lee made similar statements in official legal opinions in the 1790s. Randolph specifically noted that this conclusion was unaffected by the fact that the law of nations was "not specially adopted by the Constitution or any municipal act." 1 Op. Att'y Gen. 26, 27 (1792) (Attorney General Randolph); *see also id.* at 68 (1797) (Attorney General Lee).

What did these statements mean? For the view that these statements show that customary international law was viewed as federal law, see Jordan J. Paust, International Law as Law of the United States 5-8 (1996); Edwin Dickinson, *The Law of Nations as Part of the National Law of the United States*, 101 U. Pa. L. Rev. 26 (1952); Douglas J. Sylvester, *International Law as Sword or Shield? Early American Foreign Policy and the Law of Nations*, 32 N.Y.U. J. Int'l L. & Pol. 1 (1999). For the view that these statements meant simply that customary international law provided a non-federal rule of decision in cases otherwise within the federal courts' jurisdiction, see Bradley, *The Alien Tort Statute and Article III, supra*; Stewart Jay, *The Status of the Law of Nations in Early American Law*, 42 Vand. L. Rev. 819, 832 (1989); Arthur Weisburd, The *Executive Branch and International Law*, 41 Vand. L. Rev. 1205, 1222-23 (1988); *cf.* Robert C. Palmer, *The Federal Common Law of Crime,*, 4 L. & Hist. Rev. 267, 294-96 (1986) (arguing that these statements meant that customary international law was state law).

6. Whatever its status at the Founding, it appears that by the late 1790s and early 1800s, customary international law was not viewed as federal law within the meaning of Articles III and VI. In Ware v. Hylton, 3 U.S. 199, 281 (1796), the Court considered whether Virginia's confiscation of debts owed to British creditors was consistent with the Treaty of Peace with Great Britain and the law of nations. As to the latter point, Justices Chase and Iredell concluded (without disagreement from the other Justices) that customary international law did not preempt inconsistent state law. *See id.* at 229 (Chase, J.); *id.* at 265-66 (Iredell, J.); *see generally* David P. Currie, The Constitution in the Supreme Court: The First Hundred Years, 1789-1888, at 38 & n.46 (1985). In the early nineteenth century, the Supreme Court held that nonwritten common law (including, presumably, customary international law) could not serve as the basis for a criminal prosecution in the federal courts. *See* United States v. Hudson & Goodwin, 11 U.S. (7 Cranch) 32, 34 (1812); United States v. Coolidge, 14 U.S. (1 Wheat.) 415, 416-17 (1816). In a legal opinion in 1802, Jefferson's Attorney General, Levi Lincoln, wrote that "an aggravated violation against the law of nations" did not contravene any "provision in the Constitution [or] any law of the United States," and that the "law of nations is considered as a part of the municipal law of each State." 5 Op. Att'y Gen. 691, 692 (1802).

7. In the nineteenth and early twentieth centuries, the law of nations was treated as an element of "general common law," a body of law most famously identified with Swift v. Tyson, 41 U.S. 1 (1842). General common law was a type of customary law that U.S. courts applied as "rules of decision in particular cases without insisting that the law be attached to any particular sovereign." William A. Fletcher, *The General Common Law and Section 34 of the Judiciary Act of 1798: The Example of Marine Insurance*, 97 Harv. L. Rev. 1513, 1517 (1984). General common law was not considered part of the "Laws of the United States" within the meaning of Articles III and VI of the Constitution; federal court interpretations of general common law were not binding on the states; and a case "arising under" general common law did not by that fact alone establish federal question jurisdiction. *See* Bradford R. Clark, *Federal Common Law: A Structural Reinterpretation*, 144 U. Pa. L. Rev. 1245, 1276-92 (1996); Fletcher, *supra*, at 1521-27. The Supreme Court expressly referred to customary international law as "general law" or "common law" during this period, and in several cases it declined to review state court determinations of customary international law because of the lack of a federal question. *See, e.g.,* Oliver Am. Trading Co. v. Mexico, 264 U.S. 440, 442-43 (1924) (foreign sovereign immunity); New York Life Ins. Co. v. Hendren, 92 U.S. 286, 286-87 (1875) ("laws of war"). Was customary international law's status as non-federal general common law consistent with the Founders' commitment to federal control over U.S. foreign relations? If so, how? If not, why did courts treat customary international law in this fashion?

8. In light of this historical background, what is the meaning of the statement in *The Paquete Habana* that "international law is part of our law"? Does the Court view customary international law as federal law or general common law? In answering this question, what is the significance of the Court's statements that customary international law applies "where there is no treaty, and no controlling executive or legislative act," and that courts must "give effect to" customary international law "in the absence of any treaty or other public act of [the] government in relation to the matter"?

9. The Supreme Court overruled *Swift v. Tyson* in Erie Railroad Co. v. Tompkins, 304 U.S. 64 (1938), stating that "there is no general federal common law," and holding that "[e]xcept in matters governed by the Federal Constitution or by Act of Congress, the law to be applied in any case is the law of the State." One reason the Court in *Erie* rejected the notion of a general common law in the federal courts was the Court's belief that "law in the sense in which courts speak of it today does not exist without some definite authority behind it." *Id.* at 79. *Erie* did not, however, eliminate the lawmaking powers of federal courts. *Erie* ruled that federal court development of general common law was illegitimate not because it was a form of judicial lawmaking per se, but rather because it was *unauthorized* lawmaking not grounded in a sovereign source. Federal courts thus retain some power to make federal common law when authorized to do so in some fashion by the Constitution or a federal statute or treaty. *See, e.g.,* Larry Kramer, *The Lawmaking Power of the Federal Courts*, 12 Pace L. Rev. 263, 268-88 (1992); Thomas Merrill, *The Common Law Powers of Federal Courts*, 52 U. Chi. L. Rev. 1, 17 (1985). This grounding of federal common lawmaking in a federal sovereign source makes the new federal common law, unlike the pre-*Erie* general common law, federal law within the meaning of Article II ("take care" clause), Article III (arising under jurisdiction), and Article VI (the Supremacy Clause). What are the implications of *Erie* and post-*Erie* federal common law for the domestic status of customary international law? In the absence of congressional incorporation, should its applicability now be treated a matter of state law? Or did it become federal common law in the post-*Erie* sense? Alternatively, is it possible that customary international law survived as general common law?

10. Professor Philip Jessup (who later served as a judge on the International Court of Justice) was the first commentator to recognize the need for an examination of *Erie*'s implications for the domestic status of customary international law. One year after *Erie*, Jessup acknowledged in a brief essay that, if *Erie* were "applied broadly, it would follow that hereafter a state court's determination of a rule of international law would be a finding regarding the law of the state and would not be reviewed by the Supreme Court of the United States." Philip C. Jessup, *The Doctrine of Erie Railroad v. Tompkins Applied to International Law*, 33 Am. J. Int'l L. 740, 742 (1939). However, Jessup argued against this construction of *Erie*. He reasoned that the Court in *Erie* was not thinking about international law, and that it "would be as unsound as it would be unwise" to bind federal courts to state court interpretations of customary international law. *Id* at 743.

The first judicial decision to consider the domestic legal status of customary international law after *Erie*, Bergman v. De Sieyes, 170 F.2d 360 (2d Cir. 1948), appeared to conclude, contrary to Jessup, that the applicability of customary international law was to be determined by state law. In *Bergman* a diversity case removed to New York federal court, the issue was whether an ambassador in transit to another country was entitled under customary international law to immunity from service of process. The court, in an opinion by Judge Learned Hand, explained that "[the New York state courts'] interpretation of international law is controlling upon us, and we are to follow them so far as they have declared themselves."*Id.* at 361. After analyzing three New York decisions and a variety of international sources, Hand concluded that "the courts of New York would today hold"that an ambassador in transit is immune under customary international law from service of process in New York. *Id.* Judge Hand added the following caveat: "Whether an avowed refusal to accept a well-established doctrine of international law, or a plain misapprehension of it, would present a federal question we need not consider, for neither is present here." *Id.* Does Hand's approach make sense? What is the significance of his caveat? What are the consequences of the view that customary international law is state law? Is this what the Founders would have wanted? Does Hand's opinion survive the Supreme Court's subsequent decision in *Sabbatino*, which we considered in Chapter 2? More specifically, does the logic of *Sabbatino*'s federal common law analysis entail the conclusion that customary international law is post-*Erie* federal common law? Does the holding of *Sabbatino* — barring judicial review of the validity of certain acts of state under customary international law — support or weaken the view that customary international law is federal common law? What is the significance of the Court's favorable reference in *Sabbatino* to Jessup's article and the Court's statement that Jessup's "basic rationale is equally applicable to the act of state doctrine"?

11. *Filartiga* was the first decision in the post-*Erie* period to squarely hold that customary international law has the status of federal common law. *Filartiga* itself makes clear one implication of this holding: a case arising under customary international law "arises under" federal law for purposes of Article III federal jurisdiction. Is this a proper construction of Article III? Is the court in *Filartiga* correct in stating that customary international law has "always been part of the federal common law"? Does a case under customary international law also "arise under"federal law for purposes of statutory federal question jurisdiction, 28 U.S.C. §1331? We return to this statutory jurisdiction issue in the next section.

12. A second possible consequence of *Filartiga*'s holding is that customary international law binds the President under Article II, which provides that the

President "shall take Care that the Laws be faithfully executed." *See* U.S. Const., Art. II, §3. Is customary international law included within the "Laws" that the President must faithfully execute? Recall from Chapter 1 that Hamilton, writing as Pacificus, argued that customary international law was included within the "Laws." But he made this argument as support for an *enhancement* of presidential power, contending that President Washington's power to execute the laws included an ability to issue the Neutrality Proclamation and thereby execute customary international law rules relating to neutrality. But does the President have the domestic authority to *violate* customary international law? Most courts that have considered this question have held that he does. *See, e.g.,* Barrera-Echavarria v. Rison, 44 F.3d 1441, 1451 (9th Cir. 1995); Gisbert v. United States Attorney General, 988 F.2d 1437, 1448 (5th Cir. 1993); Garcia-Mir v. Meese, 788 F.2d 1446, 1454-55 (11th Cir. 1986). These decisions rely heavily on the statement from The *Paquete Habana* that customary international law is to be applied by U.S. courts "only 'where there is no treaty and no controlling executive or legislative act or judicial decision....'" *Garcia-Mir, supra,* 788 F. 2d at 1454 (quoting The *Paquete Habana,* 175 U.S. at 700). The President normally cannot violate a federal statute; so why can the President violate federal law in the form of customary international law? If the President can violate customary international law, does this suggest that perhaps it is not federal law after all? Is it possible that customary international law is part of the "Laws of the United States" within the meaning of Article VI but not part of "the Laws" in the Article II take care clause? In answering these questions, what is the significance of the observation in *Sabbatino* that "[w]hen articulating principles of international law in its relations with other states, the Executive Branch speaks not only as an interpreter of generally accepted and traditional rules, as would the courts, but also as an advocate of standards it believes desirable for the community of nations and protective of national concerns"?

At least one court has relied on customary international law to override Executive Branch action. In Fernandez v. Wilkinson, 505 F. Supp. 787, 195, 198 (D. Kan. 1980), the district court ordered the Immigration and Naturalization Service to release from a federal penitentiary a Cuban citizen awaiting deportation because the court found that, although the detention was consistent with "the United States Constitution [and] our statutory laws," it nevertheless violated customary international law. Note, however, that the Tenth Circuit affirmed this decision on different grounds, looking to international law in ascertaining the constitutional requirements of due process, and then interpreting the relevant immigration statutes to avoid a conflict with these requirements. *See* Fernandez v. Wilkinson, 654 F.2d 1382, 1388-90 (10th Cir. 1981).

Assuming the President has the authority to violate customary international law, do lower level Executive Branch officials also have this authority? The court in *Garcia-Mirir, supra,* addressed this issue. In that case, Cuban refugees who were being detained as unadmitted and excludable aliens sued the Attorney General, arguing that, among other things, the detention was prolonged and arbitrary in violation of customary international law. The plaintiffs and their *amici* tried to distinguish *The Paquete Habana* by arguing that the "controlling executive action" could come only from an act by the President and not, as in this case, by the Attorney General. In rejecting this argument, the court reasoned as follows:

> [The Paquete Habana] involved the capture and sale as war prize of several fishing boats during the Spanish-American War. The Supreme Court found this contrary to

the dictates of international law. The amicus characterizes the facts of the case such that the Secretary of the Navy authorized the capture and that the Supreme Court held that this did not constitute a controlling executive act because it was not ordered by the President himself. This is a mischaracterization. After the capture of the two vessels at issue, an admiral telegraphed the Secretary for permission to seize fishing ships, to which the Secretary responded that only those vessels "'likely to aid enemy may be detained'" 175 U.S. at 713. Seizing fishing boats aiding the enemy would be in obvious accord with international law. But the facts of The Paquete Habana showed the boats in question to be innocent of aiding the Spanish. The Court held that the ships were seized in violation of international law because they were used solely for fishing. It was the admiral who acted in excess of the clearly delimited authority granted by the Secretary, who instructed him to act only consistent with international law. Thus The Paquete Habana does not support the proposition that the acts of cabinet officers cannot constitute controlling executive acts. At best it suggests that lower level officials cannot by their acts render international law inapplicable. That is not an issue in this case, where the challenge is to the acts of the Attorney General.

788 F.2d at 1454. Does this passage suggest that the President and his cabinet officers can violate customary international law, but lower level officials cannot? Does that make sense? Could the President expressly delegate his power to violate customary international law to lower level officials?

For discussion of these and other issues concerning the relationship between customary international law and the Executive Branch, see Essays, *Agora: May the President Violate Customary International Law?*, 80 Am. J. Int'l L. 913 (1986); Essays, *Agora: May the President Violate Customary International Law? (Cont'd)*, 81 Am. J. Int'l L. 371 (1987); *The Authority of the United States Executive to Interpret, Articulate or Violate the Norms of International Law*, 80 Am. Soc'y Int'l L. Proc. 297 (1986); Michael J. Glennon, *Raising* The Paquete Habana: *Is Violation of Customary International Law by the Executive Unconstitutional?*, 80 Nw. U. L. Rev. 321 (1985); Arthur M. Weisburd, *The Executive Branch and International Law*, 41 Vand. L. Rev. 1205 (1988).

13. A third possible consequence of the view that customary international law is federal common law is that it preempts inconsistent state law pursuant to the Supremacy Clause. This is the view of the Restatement and of a number of international law scholars. *See, e.g.*, Restatement (Third), *supra*, §111(1); Jordan J. Paust, International Law as Law of the United States 6-7 (1996); Lea Brilmayer, *Federalism, State Authority, and the Preemptive Power of International Law*, 1994 Sup. Ct. Rev. 295, 295, 302-04; Louis Henkin, *International Law as Law in the United States*, 82 Mich. L. Rev. 1555, 1560-62 (1984); Harold Hongju Koh, *Is International Law Really State Law?*, 111 Harv. L. Rev. 1824 (1998).

Is the view that customary international law is preemptive federal law consistent with the text of the Supremacy Clause? The Supremacy Clause states that the Constitution, treaties, and "Laws of the United States which shall be made in Pursuance [*of the Constitution*]" are supreme over state law. As Professor Henkin notes:

Customary international law, it will be argued, is the law of the international community of which the United States is a member, not a law of the United States directly. Strictly, customary international law is not 'made' it results from the practice of states. If it is 'made,' not all of it was made 'pursuant' to the Constitution, since much of it antedated the Constitution. If it is made, it is not made by the United States and through its governmental institutions alone but by them together with many foreign governments in a process to which the United States contributes only in an uncertain way and to an indeterminate degree.

Louis Henkin, Foreign Affairs and the United States Constitution 508 n.16 (2d ed. 1996). Is this argument persuasive? How might customary international law be made to fit within the text of the Supremacy Clause?

There is little precedent for the proposition that customary international law can preempt an inconsistent state law. One state court decision, however, might be read to support this proposition: In Republic of Argentina v. City of New York, 250 N.E.2d 698 (Ct. App. N.Y. 1969), the New York Court of Appeals held that the City of New York could not assess taxes against Argentina's consulate property because the assessment would violate customary international law. The court did not explain its views about the precise status of customary international law, but the court might have implicitly been accepting Argentina's argument that customary international law had the status of preemptive federal law.

14. A final possibility is that customary international law, as federal common law, binds Congress. Lower courts have consistently held that Congress can violate customary international law. *See, e.g.*, United States v. Yousef, 327 F.3d 56, 93 (2d Cir. 2003); United States v. Yunis, 924 F.2d 1086, 1091 (D.C. Cir. 1991); *Garcia-Mir, supra*. However, as discussed in Chapter 6, the Supreme Court has held that self-executing treaties and federal statutes are essentially equal in status, such that the later in time prevails as a matter of U.S. domestic law. This invites the argument that a newly developed norm of customary international law, like a new treaty, could supersede a prior inconsistent federal statute. As the Restatement (Third) explains: "Since international customary law and an international agreement have equal authority in international law, and both are law of the United States, arguably later customary law should be given effect as law of the United States, even in the face of an earlier law or agreement, just as a later international agreement of the United States is given effect in the face of an earlier law or agreement." Restatement (Third), §115 reporters' note 4. Is this argument persuasive? Can courts exercise other federal common law powers to invalidate a federal statute? For a rare decision suggesting that customary international law can supersede a federal statute if it develops after the enactment of the statute, see Beharry v. Reno, 183 F. Supp. 2d 584 (E.D.N.Y. 2002), *rev'd on other grounds*, 329 F.3d 51 (2d Cir. 2003). *But see* Guaylupo-Moya v. Gonzales, 423 F.3d 121 (2d Cir. 2005) ("[T]o the extent that *Beharry* purports to declare that international law should override the plain language and effect of the relevant statutes, that reasoning was in error; clear congressional action trumps customary international law and previously enacted treaties.").

15. There has been substantial commentary in recent years concerning the domestic status of customary international law in the absence of political branch incorporation of such law. The leading academic view following *Filartiga* was that all of customary international law has the status of self-executing federal common law that courts were bound to apply even in the absence of congressional authorization. See, for example, Restatement (Third) of Foreign Relations Law, §111; Lea Brilmayer, *Federalism, State Authority, and the Preemptive Power of International Law*, 1994 Sup. Ct. Rev. 295; Louis Henkin, *International Law as Law in the United States*, 82 Mich. L. Rev. 1555 (1984).

This conventional wisdom that customary international law has the status of federal common law became the subject of significant academic debate beginning in the mid-1990s. Articles challenging this conventional wisdom include Curtis A. Bradley & Jack L. Goldsmith, *Customary International Law as Federal Common Law: A Critique of the Modern Position*, 110 Harv. L. Rev. 815 (1997); Curtis A. Bradley & Jack

L. Goldsmith, *Federal Courts and the Incorporation of International Law*, 111 Harv. L. Rev. 2260 (1998); and A.M. Weisburd, *State Courts, Federal Courts, and International Cases*, 20 Yale J. Int'l L. 1 (1995); *see also* Phillip R. Trimble, *A Revisionist View of Customary International Law*, 33 UCLA L. Rev. 665 (1986). Articles defending the conventional wisdom include Ryan Goodman & Derek P. Jinks, *Filartiga's Firm Footing: International Human Rights and Federal Common Law*, 66 Fordham L. Rev. 463 (1997); Harold Hongju Koh, *Is International Law Really State Law?*, 111 Harv. L. Rev. 1824 (1998); Gerald L. Neuman, *Sense and Nonsense About Customary International Law: A Response to Professors Bradley and Goldsmith*, 66 Fordham L. Rev. 371 (1997); and Beth Stephens, *The Law of Our Land: Customary International Law as Federal Law After Erie*, 66 Fordham L. Rev. 393 (1997). In the course of this debate, some scholars staked out an interesting middle-ground position whereby customary international law would be applied by U.S. courts as non-federal common law of the sort that was applied prior to *Erie*. *See* Ernest A. Young, *Sorting Out the Debate over Customary International Law*, 42 Va. J. Int'l L. 365 (2002); T. Alexander Aleinikoff, *International Law, Sovereignty, and American Constitutionalism: Reflections on the Customary International Law Debate*, 98 Am. J. Int'l L. 91 (2004); *cf.* Weisburd, *supra*. For an insightful discussion of the intellectual history of the Restatement (Third)'s claim that customary international law has the status of federal common law, see Paul B. Stephan, *Courts, the Constitution, and Customary International Law: The Intellectual Origins of the Restatement (Third) of the Foreign Relations Law of the United States*, 44 Va. J. Int'l L. 33 (2003).

B. THE ALIEN TORT STATUTE AND TORTURE VICTIM PROTECTION ACT

The Alien Tort Statute ("ATS") at issue in *Filartiga* provides that "[t]he district courts shall have original jurisdiction of any civil action by an alien for a tort only, committed in violation of the law of nations or a treaty of the United States." 28 U.S.C. §1350. The ATS was, in a slightly different form, part of the Judiciary Act of 1789 that first created and organized the U.S. federal court system. There is little mention of the ATS in the legislative history of the Judiciary Act, and its original purposes are uncertain. As Judge Friendly once stated, "This old but little used section is a kind of legal Lohengrin; although it has been with us since the first Judiciary Act . . . no one seems to know whence it came." IIT v. Vencap, Ltd., 519 F.2d 1001, 1015 (2d Cir. 1975).

Filartiga breathed new life into the ATS with its holding that federal courts had jurisdiction under the statute and Article III to adjudicate lawsuits between aliens concerning violations of international human rights standards committed in other countries. The *Filartiga* holding was purely jurisdictional, however, and did not identify the source of the plaintiffs' cause of action. An important court of appeals decision four years after *Filartiga* focused on this question. In Tel-Oren v. Libyan Arab Republic, 726 F.2d 774 (D.C. Cir. 1984), aliens who were victims of a terrorist attack in Israel sued the Palestine Liberation Organization and others under the ATS, alleging violations of customary international law prohibitions on torture and summary execution. The court dismissed the suit, but the judges could not agree on the reason for dismissal. Judge Robb reasoned that the case raised nojusticiable political questions. Judge Edwards reasoned that, although the ATS implicitly created a cause of action for violations of customary international law, such a cause of action was limited to suits against state actors. Judge Bork argued that neither the ATS nor customary international law created a cause of action. He also argued that judicial implication of a cause of action would impermissibly interfere with political branch control of U.S. foreign relations, and that courts should wait for "affirmative action by Congress" before allowing the ATS to be used as the vehicle for international human rights litigation.

In 1992, Congress provided "affirmative action" with regard to the international human rights violations of torture and extra-judicial killing by enacting the Torture Victim Protection Act, excerpted below.

Torture Victim Protection Act

Pub. L. No. 102-256, §2, 106 Stat. 73 (Mar. 12, 1992)

(a) Liability. An individual who, under actual or apparent authority, or color of law, of any foreign nation—

(1) subjects an individual to torture shall, in a civil action, be liable for damages to that individual; or

(2) subjects an individual to extrajudicial killing shall, in a civil action, be liable for damages to the individual's legal representative, or to any person who may be a claimant in an action for wrongful death.

(b) Exhaustion of remedies. A court shall decline to hear a claim under this section if the claimant has not exhausted adequate and available remedies in the place in which the conduct giving rise to the claim occurred.

(c) Statute of limitations. No action shall be maintained under this section unless it is commenced within 10 years after the cause of action arose.

SEC. 3. DEFINITIONS

(a) Extrajudicial killing. For the purposes of this Act, the term "extrajudicial killing" means a deliberated killing not authorized by a previous judgment pronounced by a regularly constituted court affording all the judicial guarantees which are recognized as indispensable by civilized peoples. Such term, however, does not include any such killing that, under international law, is lawfully carried out under the authority of a foreign nation.

(b) Torture. For the purposes of this Act—

(1) the term "torture" means any act, directed against an individual in the offender's custody or physical control, by which severe pain or suffering (other than pain or suffering arising only from or inherent in, or incidental to, lawful sanctions), whether physical or mental, is intentionally inflicted on that individual for such purposes as obtaining from that individual or a third person information or a confession, punishing that individual for an act that individual or a third person has committed or is suspected of having committed, intimidating or coercing that individual or a third person, or for any reason based on discrimination of any kind; and

(2) mental pain or suffering refers to prolonged mental harm caused by or resulting from—

(A) the intentional infliction or threatened infliction of severe physical pain or suffering;

(B) the administration or application, or threatened administration or application, of mind altering substances or other procedures calculated to disrupt profoundly the senses or the personality;

(C) the threat of imminent death; or

(D) the threat that another individual will imminently be subjected to death, severe physical pain or suffering, or the administration or application of mind altering substances or other procedures calculated to disrupt profoundly the senses or personality.

Sosa v. Alvarez-Machain

124 S. Ct. 2739 (2004)

[The United States Drug Enforcement Administration (DEA) recruited petitioner Sosa and other Mexican nationals to abduct respondent Alvarez-Machain (Alvarez), also a Mexican national, from Mexico to stand trial in the United States for allegedly assisting in the murder and torture of a DEA agent. Following his acquittal, Alvarez sued Sosa and others under the ATS for violating customary international law prohibitions on arbitrary arrest and detention.]

JUSTICE SOUTER delivered the opinion of the Court....

The parties and *amici* here advance radically different historical interpretations of [the ATS]. Alvarez says that the ATS was intended not simply as a jurisdictional grant, but as authority for the creation of a new cause of action for torts in violation of international law. We think that reading is implausible. As enacted in 1789, the ATS gave the district courts "cognizance" of certain causes of action, and the term bespoke a grant of jurisdiction, not power to mold substantive law. The fact that the ATS was placed in §9 of the Judiciary Act, a statute otherwise exclusively concerned with federal-court jurisdiction, is itself support for its strictly jurisdictional nature. Nor would the distinction between jurisdiction and cause of action have been elided by the drafters of the Act or those who voted on it.... In sum, we think the statute was intended as jurisdictional in the sense of addressing the power of the courts to entertain cases concerned with a certain subject.

But holding the ATS jurisdictional raises a new question, this one about the interaction between the ATS at the time of its enactment and the ambient law of the era. Sosa would have it that the ATS was stillborn because there could be no claim for relief without a further statute expressly authorizing adoption of causes of action. *Amici* professors of federal jurisdiction and legal history take a different tack, that federal courts could entertain claims once the jurisdictional grant was on the books, because torts in violation of the law of nations would have been recognized within the common law of the time. We think history and practice give the edge to this latter position.

"When the United States declared their independence, they were bound to receive the law of nations, in its modern state of purity and refinement." Ware v. Hylton, 3 Dall. 199, 281 (1796) (Wilson, J.). In the years of the early Republic, this law of nations comprised two principal elements, the first covering the general norms governing the behavior of national states with each other: "the science which teaches the rights subsisting between nations or states, and the obligations correspondent to those rights," E. de Vattel, The Law of Nations, Preliminaries §3 (J. Chitty et al. transl. and ed. 1883) (hereinafter Vattel) (footnote omitted), or "that code of public instruction which defines the rights and prescribes the duties of nations, in their intercourse with each other," 1 James Kent Commentaries *1. This aspect of the law of nations thus occupied the executive and legislative domains, not the judicial. *See* 4 W. Blackstone, Commentaries on the Laws of England 68 (1769) (hereinafter Commentaries) ("Offenses against" the law of nations are "principally incident to whole states or nations").

The law of nations included a second, more pedestrian element, however, that did fall within the judicial sphere, as a body of judge-made law regulating the conduct of individuals situated outside domestic boundaries and consequently carrying an international savor. To Blackstone, the law of nations in this sense was implicated "in mercantile questions, such as bills of exchange and the like; in all marine causes, relating to freight, average, demurrage, insurances, bottomry...; [and] in all disputes relating to prizes, to shipwrecks, to hostages, and ransom bills." *Id*., at 67. The law merchant emerged from the customary practices of international traders and admiralty required its own transnational regulation. And it was the law of nations in this sense that our precursors spoke about when the Court explained the status of coast fishing vessels in wartime grew from "ancient usage among civilized nations, beginning centuries ago, and gradually ripening into a rule of international law...." The Paquete Habana, 175 U.S. 677, 686 (1900).

There was, finally, a sphere in which these rules binding individuals for the benefit of other individuals overlapped with the norms of state relationships. Blackstone referred to it when he mentioned three specific offenses against the law of nations addressed by the criminal law of England: violation of safe conducts, infringement of the rights of ambassadors, and piracy. 4 Commentaries 68. An assault against an ambassador, for example, impinged upon the sovereignty of the foreign nation and if not adequately redressed could rise to an issue of war. *See* Vattel 463-464. It was this narrow set of violations of the law of nations, admitting of a judicial remedy and at the same time threatening serious consequences in international affairs, that was probably on minds of the men who drafted the ATS with its reference to tort.

Before there was any ATS, a distinctly American preoccupation with these hybrid international norms had taken shape owing to the distribution of political power from independence through the period of confederation. The Continental Congress was hamstrung by its inability to "cause infractions of treaties, or of the law of nations to be punished," J. Madison, Journal of the Constitutional Convention 60 (E. Scott ed. 1893), and in 1781 the Congress implored the States to vindicate rights under the law of nations. In words that echo Blackstone, the congressional resolution called upon state legislatures to "provide expeditious, exemplary, and adequate punishment" for "the violation of safe conducts or passports,... of hostility against such as are in amity,...with the United States,... infractions of the immunities of ambassadors and other public ministers ... [and] "infractions of treaties and conventions to which the United States are a party." 21 Journals of the Continental Congress 1136-1137 (G. Hunt ed. 1912) (hereinafter Journals of the Continental Congress). The resolution recommended that the States "authorise suits... for damages by the party injured, and for compensation to the United States for damage sustained by them from an injury done to a foreign power by a citizen." *Id.*, at 1137.... Apparently only one State acted upon the recommendation, ... but Congress had done what it could to signal a commitment to enforce the law of nations.

Appreciation of the Continental Congress's incapacity to deal with this class of cases was intensified by the so-called Marbois incident of May 1784, in which a French adventurer, Longchamps, verbally and physically assaulted the Secretary of the French Legion in Philadelphia. Congress called again for state legislation addressing such matters, and concern over the inadequate vindication of the law of nations persisted through the time of the constitutional convention. During the Convention itself, in fact, a New York City constable produced a reprise of the Marbois affair and Secretary Jay reported to Congress on the Dutch Ambassador's protest, with the explanation that "the federal government does not appear ... to be vested with any judicial Powers competent to the Cognizance and Judgment of such Cases." Casto, [The Federal Courts' Protective Jurisdiction Over Torts Committed in Violation of the Law of Nations, 18 Conn. L. Rev. 467, 494 & n. 152 (1986)].

The Framers responded by vesting the Supreme Court with original jurisdiction over "all Cases affecting Ambassadors, other public ministers and Consuls," U.S. Const., Art. III, §2, and the First Congress followed through. The Judiciary Act reinforced this Court's original jurisdiction over suits brought by diplomats, see 1 Stat. 80, ch. 20, §13, created alienage jurisdiction, §11 and, of course, included the ATS, §9....

[D]espite considerable scholarly attention, it is fair to say that a consensus understanding of what Congress intended has proven elusive.

Still, the history does tend to support two propositions. First, there is every reason to suppose that the First Congress did not pass the ATS as a jurisdictional convenience to be placed on the shelf for use by a future Congress or state legislature that might, some day, authorize the creation of causes of action or itself decide to make some element of the law of nations actionable for the benefit of foreigners. The anxieties of the preconstitutional period cannot be ignored easily enough to think that the statute was not meant to have a practical effect. Consider that the principal draftsman of the ATS was apparently Oliver Ellsworth, previously a member of the Continental Congress that had passed the 1781 resolution and a member of the Connecticut Legislature that made good on that congressional request. Consider, too, that the First Congress was attentive enough to the law of nations to recognize certain offenses expressly as criminal, including the three mentioned by Blackstone. *See* An Act for the Punishment of Certain Crimes Against the United States, §8, 1 Stat. 113-114 (murder or robbery, or other capital crimes, punishable as piracy if committed on the high seas), and §28, *id.* at 118 (violation of safe conducts and assaults against ambassadors punished by imprisonment and fines described as "infract[ions of] the law of nations"). It would have been passing strange for Ellsworth and this very Congress to vest federal courts expressly with jurisdiction to entertain civil causes brought by aliens alleging violations of the law of nations, but to no effect whatever until the Congress should take further action. There is too much in the historical record to believe that Congress would have enacted the ATS only to leave it lying fallow indefinitely.

The second inference to be drawn from the history is that Congress intended the ATS to furnish jurisdiction for a relatively modest set of actions alleging violations of the law of nations. Uppermost in the legislative mind appears to have been offenses against ambassadors; violations of safe conduct were probably understood to be actionable; and individual actions arising out of prize captures and piracy may well have also been contemplated. But the common law appears to have understood only those three of the hybrid variety as definite and actionable, or at any rate, to have assumed only a very limited set of claims. . . .

We think it is correct, then, to assume that the First Congress understood that the district courts would recognize private causes of action for certain torts in violation of the law of nations, though we have found no basis to suspect Congress had any examples in mind beyond those torts corresponding to Blackstone's three primary offenses: violation of safe conducts, infringement of the rights of ambassadors, and piracy. We assume, too, that no development in the two centuries from the enactment of §1350 to the birth of the modern line of cases beginning with Filartiga v. Pena-Irala, 630 F.2d 876 (CA2 1980), has categorically precluded federal courts from recognizing a claim under the law of nations as an element of common law; Congress has not in any relevant way amended §1350 or limited civil common law power by another statute. Still, there are good reasons for a restrained conception of the discretion a federal court should exercise in considering a new cause of action of this kind. Accordingly, we think courts should require any claim based on the present-day law of nations to rest on a norm of international character accepted by the civilized world and defined with a specificity comparable to the features of the 18th-century paradigms we have recognized. This requirement is fatal to Alvarez's claim.

A series of reasons argue for judicial caution when considering the kinds of individual claims that might implement the jurisdiction conferred by the early statute. First, the prevailing conception of the common law has changed since 1789 in a way that counsels restraint in judicially applying internationally generated norms. When §1350 was enacted, the accepted conception was of the common law as "a transcendental body of law outside of any particular State but obligatory within it unless and until changed by statute." Black and White Taxicab & Transfer Co. v. Brown and Yellow Taxicab & Transfer Co., 276 U.S. 518, 533 (1928) (Holmes, J., dissenting). Now, however, in most cases where a court is asked to state or formulate a common law principle in a new context, there is a general understanding that the law is not so much found or discovered as it is either made or created. Holmes explained famously in 1881 that

> in substance the growth of the law is legislative . . . [because t]he very considerations which judges most rarely mention, and always with an apology, are the secret root from which the law draws all the juices of life. I mean, of course, considerations of what is expedient for the community concerned. The Common Law 31-32 (Howe ed. 1963).

One need not accept the Holmesian view as far as its ultimate implications to acknowledge that a judge deciding in reliance on an international norm will find a substantial element of discretionary judgment in the decision.

Second, along with, and in part driven by, that conceptual development in understanding common law has come an equally significant rethinking of the role of the federal courts in making it. Erie R. Co. v. Tompkins, 304 U.S. 64 (1938), was the watershed in which we denied the existence of any federal "general" common law, which largely withdrew to havens of specialty, some of them defined by express congressional authorization to devise a body of law directly. Elsewhere, this Court has thought it was in order to create federal common law rules in interstitial areas of particular federal interest. And although we have even assumed competence to make judicial rules of decision of particular importance to foreign relations, such as the act of state doctrine, see Banco Nacional de Cuba v. Sabbatino, 376 U.S. 398, 427 (1964), the general practice has been to look for legislative guidance before exercising innovative authority over substantive law. It would be remarkable to take a more aggressive role in exercising a jurisdiction that remained largely in shadow for much of the prior two centuries.

Third, this Court has recently and repeatedly said that a decision to create a private right of action is one better left to legislative judgment in the great majority of cases. The creation of a private right of action raises issues beyond the mere consideration whether underlying primary conduct should be allowed or not, entailing, for example, a decision to permit enforcement without the check imposed by prosecutorial discretion. Accordingly, even when Congress has made it clear by statute that a rule applies to purely domestic conduct, we are reluctant to infer intent to provide a private cause of action where the statute does not supply one expressly. While the absence of congressional action address- ing private rights of action under an international norm is more equivocal than its failure to provide such a right when it creates a statute, the possible collateral consequences of making international rules privately actionable argue for judicial caution.

Fourth, the subject of those collateral consequences is itself a reason for a high bar to new private causes of action for violating international law, for the potential implications for the foreign relations of the United States of recognizing such causes should make courts particularly wary of impinging on the discretion of the Legislative and Executive Branches in managing foreign affairs. It is one thing for American courts to enforce constitutional limits on our own State and Federal Governments' power, but quite another to consider suits under rules that would go so far as to claim a limit on the power of foreign governments over their own citizens, and to hold that a foreign government or its agent has transgressed those limits. Yet modern international law is very much concerned with just such questions, and apt to stimulate calls for vindicating private interests in §1350 cases. Since many attempts by federal courts to craft remedies for the violation of new norms of international law would raise risks of adverse foreign policy consequences, they should be undertaken, if at all, with great caution. *Cf.* Tel-Oren v. Libyan Arab Republic, 726 F.2d 774, 813 (CADC 1984) (Bork, J., concurring) (expressing doubt that §1350 should be read to require "our courts [to] sit in judgment of the conduct of foreign officials in their own countries with respect to their own citizens").

The fifth reason is particularly important in light of the first four. We have no congressional mandate to seek out and define new and debatable violations of the law of nations, and modern indications of congressional understanding of the judi- cial role in the field have not affirmatively encouraged greater judicial creativity. It is true that a clear mandate appears in the Torture Victim Protection Act of 1991, 106 Stat. 73, providing authority that "establishes an unambiguous and modern basis for" federal claims of torture and extrajudicial killing, H.R. Rep. No. 102-367, pt. 1, p.3 (1991). But that affirmative authority is confined to specific subject matter, and although the legislative history includes the remark that §1350 should "remain intact to permit suits based on other norms that already exist or may ripen in the future into rules of customary international law," Congress as a body has done nothing to promote such suits. Several times, indeed, the Senate has expressly declined to give the federal courts the task of interpreting and applying international human rights law, as when its ratification of the International Covenant on Civil and Political Rights declared that the substantive provisions of the document were not self-executing.

These reasons argue for great caution in adapting the law of nations to private rights. Justice Scalia concludes that caution is too hospitable, and a word is in order to summarize where we have come so far and to focus our difference with him on whether some norms of today's law of nations may ever be recognized legitimately by federal courts in the absence of congressional action beyond §1350. All Members of the Court agree that §1350 is only jurisdictional. We also agree, or at least Justice Scalia does not dispute, that the jurisdiction was originally understood to be available to enforce a small number of international norms that a federal court could properly recognize as within the common law enforceable without further statutory authority. Justice Scalia concludes, however, that two subsequent developments should be understood to preclude federal courts from recognizing any further international norms as judicially enforceable today, absent further congressional action. As described before, we now tend to understand common law not as a discoverable reflection of universal reason but, in a positivistic way, as a product of human choice. And we now adhere to a conception of limited judicial power first expressed in reorienting federal diversity jurisdiction, see Erie R. Co. v. Tompkins, 304 U.S. 64 (1938), that federal courts have no authority to derive "general" common law.

Whereas Justice Scalia sees these developments as sufficient to close the door to further independent judicial recognition of actionable international norms, other considerations persuade us that the judicial power should be exercised on the understanding that the door is still ajar subject to vigilant doorkeeping, and thus open to a narrow class of international norms today. *Erie* did not in terms bar any judicial recognition of new substantive rules, no matter what the circumstances, and post-*Erie* understanding has identified limited enclaves in which federal courts may derive some substantive law in a common law way. For two centuries we have affirmed that the domestic law of the United States recognizes the law of nations. It would take some explaining to say now that federal courts must avert their gaze entirely from any international norm intended to protect individuals.

We think an attempt to justify such a position would be particularly unconvincing in light of what we know about congressional understanding bearing on this issue lying at the intersection of the judicial and legislative powers. The First Congress, which reflected the understanding of the framing generation and included some of the Framers, assumed that federal courts could properly identify some international norms as enforceable in the exercise of §1350 jurisdiction. We think it would be unreasonable to assume that the First Congress would have expected federal courts to lose all capacity to recognize enforceable international norms simply because the common law might lose some metaphysical cachet on the road to modern realism. Later Congresses seem to have shared our view. The position we take today has been assumed by some federal courts for 24 years, ever since the Second Circuit decided Filartiga v. Pena-Irala, 630 F.2d 876 (CA2 1980), and for practical purposes the point of today's disagreement has been focused since the exchange between Judge Edwards and Judge Bork in Tel-Oren v. Libyan Arab Republic, 726 F.2d 774 (CADC 1984), Congress, however, has not only expressed no disagreement with our view of the proper exercise of the judicial power, but has responded to its most notable instance by enacting legislation supplementing the judicial determination in some detail. *See supra* (discussing the Torture Victim Protection Act).

While we agree with Justice Scalia to the point that we would welcome any congressional guidance in exercising jurisdiction with such obvious potential to affect foreign relations, nothing Congress has done is a reason for us to shut the door to the law of nations entirely. It is enough to say that Congress may do that at any time (explicitly, or implicitly by treaties or statutes that occupy the field) just as it may modify or cancel any judicial decision so far as it rests on recognizing an international norm as such.[19]

We must still, however, derive a standard or set of standards for assessing the particular claim Alvarez raises, and for this case it suffices to look to the historical antecedents. Whatever the ultimate criteria for accepting a cause of action subject to jurisdiction under §1350, we are persuaded that federal courts should not recognize private claims under federal common law for violations of any international law norm with less definite content and acceptance among civilized nations than the historical paradigms familiar when §1350 was enacted. *See, e.g.,* United States v. Smith, 18 U.S. 153, 5 Wheat. 153, 163-180 (1820) (illustrating the specificity with which the law of nations defined piracy). This limit upon judicial recognition is generally consistent with the reasoning of many of the courts and judges who faced the issue before it reached this Court. And the determination whether a norm is sufficiently definite to support a cause of action[20] should (and, indeed, inevitably must) involve an element of judgment about the practical consequences of making that cause available to litigants in the federal courts.[21]

---

19. Our position does not . . . imply that every grant of jurisdiction to a federal court carries with it an opportunity to develop common law (so that the grant of federal-question jurisdiction would be equally as good for our purposes as §1350). Section 1350 was enacted on the congressional understanding that courts would exercise jurisdiction by entertaining some common law claims derived from the law of nations; and we know of no reason to think that federal-question jurisdiction was extended subject to any comparable congressional assumption. Further, our holding today is consistent with the division of responsibilities between federal and state courts after *Erie*, as a more expansive common law power related to 28 U.S.C. §1331 might not be.

20. A related consideration is whether international law extends the scope of liability for a violation of a given norm to the perpetrator being sued, if the defendant is a private actor such as a corporation or individual. . . .

21. This requirement of clear definition is not meant to be the only principle limiting the availability of relief in the federal courts for violations of customary international law, though it disposes of this case. For example, the European Commission argues as *amicus curiae* that basic principles of international law require that before asserting a claim in a foreign forum, the claimant must have exhausted any remedies available in the domestic legal system, and perhaps in other fora such as international claims tribunals. *Cf.* Torture Victim Protection Act of 1991, §2(b), 106 Stat. 73 (exhaustion requirement). We would certainly consider this requirement in an appropriate case.

Another possible limitation that we need not apply here is a policy of case-specific deference to the political branches. For example, there are now pending in federal district court several class actions seeking damages from various corporations alleged to have participated in, or abetted, the regime of apartheid that formerly controlled South Africa. *See* In re South African Apartheid Litigation, 238 F. Supp. 2d 1379 (JPML 2002) (granting a motion to transfer the cases to the Southern District of New York). The Government of South Africa has said that these cases interfere with the policy embodied by its Truth and Reconciliation Commission, which "deliberately avoided a 'victors' justice' approach to the crimes of apartheid and chose instead one based on confession and absolution, informed by the principles of reconciliation, reconstruction, reparation and goodwill." The United States has agreed. In such cases, there is a strong argument that federal courts should give serious weight to the Executive Branch's view of the case's impact on foreign policy. *Cf.* Republic of Aus. v. Altmann, 124 S. Ct. 2240 (2004) (discussing the State Department's use of statements of interest in cases involving the Foreign Sovereign Immunities Act of 1976, 28 U.S.C. §1602 *et seq.*)

Thus, Alvarez's detention claim must be gauged against the current state of international law, looking to those sources we have long, albeit cautiously, recognized.

> Where there is no treaty, and no controlling executive or legislative act or judicial decision, resort must be had to the customs and usages of civilized nations; and, as evidence of these, to the works of jurists and commentators, who by years of labor, research and experience, have made themselves peculiarly well acquainted with the subjects of which they treat. Such works are resorted to by judicial tribunals, not for the speculations of their authors concerning what the law ought to be, but for trustworthy evidence of what the law really is.

The Paquete Habana, 175 U.S., at 700.

To begin with, Alvarez cites two well-known international agreements that, despite their moral authority, have little utility under the standard set out in this opinion. He says that his abduction by Sosa was an "arbitrary arrest" within the meaning of the Universal Declaration of Human Rights (Declaration). And he traces the rule against arbitrary arrest not only to the Declaration, but also to article nine of the International Covenant on Civil and Political Rights (Covenant), to which the United States is a party, and to various other conventions to which it is not. But the Declaration does not of its own force impose obligations as a matter of international law. And, although the Covenant does bind the United States as a matter of international law, the United States ratified the Covenant on the express understanding that it was not self-executing and so did not itself create obligations enforceable in the federal courts. Accordingly, Alvarez cannot say that the Declaration and Covenant themselves establish the relevant and applicable rule of international law. He instead attempts to show that prohibition of arbitrary arrest has attained the status of binding customary international law.

Here, it is useful to examine Alvarez's complaint in greater detail. As he presently argues it, the claim does not rest on the cross-border feature of his abduction. Although the District Court granted relief in part on finding a violation of international law in taking Alvarez across the border from Mexico to the United States, the Court of Appeals rejected that ground of liability for failure to identify a norm of requisite force prohibiting a forcible abduction across a border. Instead, it relied on the conclusion that the law of the United States did not authorize Alvarez's arrest, because the DEA lacked extraterritorial authority under 21 U.S.C. §878, and because Federal Rule of Criminal Procedure 4(d)(2) limited the warrant for Alvarez's arrest to "the jurisdiction of the United States." It is this position that Alvarez takes now: that his arrest was arbitrary and as such forbidden by international law not because it infringed the prerogatives of Mexico, but because no applicable law authorized it.

Alvarez thus invokes a general prohibition of "arbitrary" detention defined as officially sanctioned action exceeding positive authorization to detain under the domestic law of some government, regardless of the circumstances. Whether or not this is an accurate reading of the Covenant, Alvarez cites little authority that a rule so broad has the status of a binding customary norm today.[27] He certainly cites

27. Specifically, he relies on a survey of national constitutions; a case from the International Court of Justice; and some authority drawn from the federal courts. None of these suffice. The [national constitution survey] does show that many nations recognize a norm against arbitrary detention, but that consensus is at a high level of generality. The [ICJ] case . . . involved a different set of international norms and mentioned the problem of arbitrary detention only in passing; the detention in that case was, moreover, far longer and harsher than Alvarez's. And the authority from the federal courts, to the extent

nothing to justify the federal courts in taking his broad rule as the predicate for a federal lawsuit, for its implications would be breathtaking. His rule would support a cause of action in federal court for any arrest, anywhere in the world, unauthorized by the law of the jurisdiction in which it took place, and would create a cause of action for any seizure of an alien in violation of the Fourth Amendment, supplanting the actions under Rev. Stat. §1979, 42 U.S.C. §1983 and Bivens v. Six Unknown Fed. Narcotics Agents, 403 U.S. 388 (1971), that now provide damages remedies for such violations. It would create an action in federal court for arrests by state officers who simply exceed their authority; and for the violation of any limit that the law of any country might place on the authority of its own officers to arrest. And all of this assumes that Alvarez could establish that Sosa was acting on behalf of a government when he made the arrest, for otherwise he would need a rule broader still.

Alvarez's failure to marshal support for his proposed rule is underscored by the Restatement (Third) of Foreign Relations Law of the United States (1987), which says in its discussion of customary international human rights law that a "state violates international law if, as a matter of state policy, it practices, encourages, or condones . . . prolonged arbitrary detention." Id., §702. Although the Restatement does not explain its requirements of a "state policy" and of "prolonged" detention, the implication is clear. Any credible invocation of a principle against arbitrary detention that the civilized world accepts as binding customary international law requires a factual basis beyond relatively brief detention in excess of positive authority. Even the Restatement's limits are only the beginning of the enquiry, because although it is easy to say that some policies of prolonged arbitrary detentions are so bad that those who enforce them become enemies of the human race, it may be harder to say which policies cross that line with the certainty afforded by Blackstone's three common law offenses. In any event, the label would never fit the reckless policeman who botches his warrant, even though that same officer might pay damages under municipal law.

Whatever may be said for the broad principle Alvarez advances, in the present, imperfect world, it expresses an aspiration that exceeds any binding customary rule having the specificity we require. Creating a private cause of action to further that aspiration would go beyond any residual common law discretion we think it appropriate to exercise. It is enough to hold that a single illegal detention of less than a day, followed by the transfer of custody to lawful authorities and a prompt arraignment, violates no norm of customary international law so well defined as to support the creation of a federal remedy. . . .

[Justice Breyer joined the portion of the Court's opinion concerning the Alien Tort Statute, but wrote separately to note another consideration that he believed courts should take into account in deciding whether to exercise jurisdiction under the Statute: "I would ask whether the exercise of jurisdiction under the ATS is consistent with those notions of comity that lead each nation to respect the sovereign rights of other nations by limiting the reach of its laws and their enforcement." Specifically, he suggested looking to whether there was consensus that the claim in question was subject to "universal jurisdiction." (The concept of universal jurisdiction is discussed in Chapter 8 of the casebook.)]

---

it supports Alvarez's position, reflects a more assertive view of federal judicial discretion over claims based on customary international law than the position we take today.

JUSTICE SCALIA, with whom THE CHIEF JUSTICE and JUSTICE THOMAS join, concurring in part and concurring in the judgment. . . .

The analysis in the Court's opinion departs from my own in this respect: After concluding . . . that "the ATS is a jurisdictional statute creating no new causes of action," the Court addresses at length . . . the "good reasons for a restrained conception of the *discretion* a federal court should exercise in considering a new cause of action" under the ATS. (Emphasis added.) By framing the issue as one of "discretion," the Court skips over the antecedent question of authority. This neglects the "lesson of *Erie*," that "grants of jurisdiction alone" (which the Court has acknowledged the ATS to be) "are not themselves grants of law-making authority." Meltzer, [Customary International Law, Foreign Affairs, and Federal Common Law, 42 Va. J. Int'l L. 513, 541 (2002)]. On this point, the Court observes only that no development between the enactment of the ATS (in 1789) and the birth of modern international human rights litigation under that statute (in 1980) "has categorically *precluded* federal courts from recognizing a claim under the law of nations as an element of common law." (Emphasis added). This turns our jurisprudence regarding federal common law on its head. The question is not what case or congressional action prevents federal courts from applying the law of nations as part of the general common law; it is what *authorizes* that peculiar exception from *Erie*'s fundamental holding that a general common law *does not exist*.

The Court would apparently find authorization in the understanding of the Congress that enacted the ATS, that "district courts would recognize private causes of action for certain torts in violation of the law of nations." But as discussed above, that understanding rested upon a notion of general common law that has been repudiated by *Erie*.

The Court recognizes that *Erie* was a "watershed" decision heralding an avulsive change, wrought by "conceptual development in understanding common law . . . [and accompanied by an] equally significant rethinking of the role of the federal courts in making it." The Court's analysis, however, does not follow through on this insight, interchangeably using the unadorned phrase "common law" . . . to refer to pre-*Erie* general common law and post-*Erie* federal common law. This lapse is crucial, because the creation of post-*Erie* federal common law is rooted in a positivist mindset utterly foreign to the American common-law tradition of the late 18th century. Post-*Erie* federal common lawmaking (all that is left to the federal courts) is so far removed from that general-common-law adjudication which applied the "law of nations" that it would be anachronistic to find authorization to do the former in a statutory grant of jurisdiction that was thought to enable the latter.* Yet that is precisely what the discretion-only analysis . . . suggests.

---

* The Court conjures the illusion of common-law-making continuity between 1789 and the present by ignoring fundamental differences. The Court's approach places the law of nations on a federal-law footing unknown to the First Congress. At the time of the ATS's enactment, the law of nations, being part of general common law, was *not* supreme federal law that could displace state law. By contrast, a judicially created federal rule based on international norms *would be* supreme federal law. Moreover, a federal-common-law cause of action of the sort the Court reserves discretion to create would "arise under" the laws of the United States, not only for purposes of Article III but also for purposes of *statutory* federal-question jurisdiction.

The lack of genuine continuity is thus demonstrated by the fact that today's opinion renders the ATS unnecessary for federal jurisdiction over (so-called) law-of-nations claims. If the law of nations can be transformed into federal law on the basis of (1) a provision that merely grants jurisdiction, combined with (2) some residual judicial power (from whence nobody knows) to create federal causes of action in cases implicating foreign relations, then a grant of federal-question jurisdiction would give rise to a power to create international-law-based federal common law just as effectively as would the

Because today's federal common law is not our Framers' general common law, the question presented by the suggestion of discretionary authority to enforce the law of nations is not whether to extend old-school general-common-law adjudication. Rather, it is whether to create new federal common law. The Court masks the novelty of its approach when it suggests that the difference between us is that we would "close the door to further independent judicial recognition of actionable international norms," whereas the Court would permit the exercise of judicial power "on the understanding that the door is still ajar subject to vigilant door-keeping." The general common law was the old door. We do not close that door today, for the deed was done in *Erie*. Federal common law is a *new* door. The question is not whether that door will be left ajar, but whether this Court will open it. . . .

To be sure, today's opinion does not itself precipitate a direct confrontation with Congress by creating a cause of action that Congress has not. But it invites precisely that action by the lower courts, even while recognizing (1) that Congress understood the difference between granting jurisdiction and creating a federal cause of action in 1789, (2) that Congress understands that difference today, and (3) that the ATS itself supplies only jurisdiction. In holding open the possibility that judges may create rights where Congress has not authorized them to do so, the Court countenances judicial occupation of a domain that belongs to the people's representatives. One does not need a crystal ball to predict that this occupation will not be long in coming, since the Court endorses the reasoning of "many of the courts and judges who faced the issue before it reached this Court," including the Second and Ninth Circuits.

The Ninth Circuit brought us the judgment that the Court reverses today. Perhaps its decision in this particular case, like the decisions of other lower federal courts that receive passing attention in the Court's opinion, "reflects a more assertive view of federal judicial discretion over claims based on customary international law than the position we take today." But the verbal formula it applied is the same verbal formula that the Court explicitly endorses. Endorsing the very formula that led the Ninth Circuit to its result in this case hardly seems to be a recipe for restraint in the future. . . .

Though it is not necessary to resolution of the present case, one further consideration deserves mention: Despite the avulsive change of *Erie*, the Framers who included reference to "the Law of Nations" in Article I, §8, cl. 10, of the Constitution would be entirely content with the post-*Erie* system I have described, and quite terrified by the "discretion" endorsed by the Court. That portion of the general common law known as the law of nations was understood to refer to the accepted practices of nations in their dealings with one another (treatment of ambassadors, immunity of foreign sovereigns from suit, etc.) and with actors on the high seas hostile to all nations and beyond all their territorial jurisdictions (pirates). Those accepted practices have for the most part, if not in their entirety, been enacted into United States statutory law, so that insofar as they are concerned the demise of the general common law is inconsequential. The notion that a law of nations, redefined to mean the consensus of states on *any* subject, can be used by a private citizen to control a sovereign's treatment of *its own citizens* within *its own territory* is a

---

ATS. This would mean that the ATS became largely superfluous as of 1875, when Congress granted general federal-question jurisdiction subject to a $500 amount-in-controversy requirement, Act of Mar. 3, 1875, §1, 18 Stat. 470, and entirely superfluous as of 1980, when Congress eliminated the amount-in-controversy requirement, Pub. L. 96-486, 94 Stat. 2369.

20th-century invention of internationalist law professors and human-rights advocates. The Framers would, I am confident, be appalled by the proposition that, for example, the American peoples' democratic adoption of the death penalty, see, e.g., Tex. Penal Code Ann. §12.31 (2003), could be judicially nullified because of the disapproving views of foreigners.

We Americans have a method for making the laws that are over us. We elect representatives to two Houses of Congress, each of which must enact the new law and present it for the approval of a President, whom we also elect. For over two decades now, unelected federal judges have been usurping this lawmaking power by converting what they regard as norms of international law into American law. Today's opinion approves that process in principle, though urging the lower courts to be more restrained.

Notes and Questions

1. As the Court in *Sosa* suggests, the original purposes of the ATS are uncertain. Is it plausible to think that the ATS was a response to the pre-constitutional events that the Court recounts? Are you convinced by the Court's suggestion that the Framers who drafted the phrase "torts only committed in violation of the law of nations" in the ATS probably had in mind the three international law violations—violation of safe conducts, infringement of the rights of ambassadors, and piracy—that, according to Blackstone, applied to individuals? Do you think the ATS was, as the Court speculates, a response to the Articles of Confederation's inability to ensure compliance with U.S. international obligations? Does the Marbois affair recounted by the Court support this conclusion? Is the Court correct that, whatever the ATS's precise purposes might have been, the First Congress that drafted the ATS did not view it "as a jurisdictional convenience to be placed on the shelf for use by a future Congress or state legislature that might, some day, authorize the creation of causes of action or itself decide to make some element of the law of nations actionable for the benefit of foreigners"? To the extent that the pre-constitutional events cited by the Court suggest a desire to comply with international law obligations, and to avoid conflicts with foreign nations, is the use of the ATS today consistent with these purposes?

For various perspectives on the original meaning and scope of the ATS, see Anne-Marie Burley, *The Alien Tort Statute and the Judiciary Act of 1789: A Badge of Honor*, 83 Am. J. Int'l L. 461 (1989); Curtis A. Bradley, *The Alien Tort Statute and Article III*, 42 Va. J. Int'l L. 587 (2002); William R. Casto, *The Federal Courts' Protective Jurisdiction over Torts Committed in Violation of the Law of Nations*, 18 Conn. L. Rev. 467 (1986); William S. Dodge, *The Historical Origins of the Alien Tort Statute: A Response to the "Originalists,"* 19 Hastings Int'l & Comp. L. Rev. 221 (1996); John M. Rogers, *The Alien Tort Statute and How Individuals "Violate" International Law*, 21 Vand. J. Transnat'l L. 47 (1988); Joseph Modeste Sweeney, *A Tort Only in Violation of the Law of Nations*, 18 Hastings Int'l & Comp. L. Rev. 445 (1995); Arthur Weisburd, *The Executive Branch and International Law*, 41 Vand. L. Rev. 1205 (1988).

2. The ATS requires that the plaintiff be an alien, and today the ATS is often used by aliens to sue other aliens. Would the First Congress have envisioned that the ATS would be a vehicle for alien-versus-alien suits concerning violations of the law of nations? If so, which category of Article III jurisdiction would they have thought these cases would fall into? What, if anything, does the Court in *Sosa* suggest about the relationship between the ATS and Article III? *Cf.* Mossman v. Higginson, 4 U.S. (4 Dall.) 12 (1800) (holding that the alien diversity provision in Article III does not extend to suits between aliens and therefore construing Article 11 of the Judiciary Act, which gave the circuit courts jurisdiction over suits "where an alien is a party," as "confined to suits between citizens and foreigners"). *See also* Bradley, *The Alien Tort Statute and Article III*, *supra*.

3. Prior to *Filartiga*, only two courts had upheld jurisdiction under the ATS since the statute had been enacted in 1789. *See* Adra v. Clift, 195 F. Supp. 857 (D. Md. 1961) (holding that a mother's concealment of her half-Lebanese child's name and nationality, resulting in the child being given a falsified Iraqi passport, was a tort in violation of the law of nations for purposes of the ATS); Bolchos v. Darrell, 3 F. Cas. 810 (D.S.C. 1795) (No. 1607) (finding jurisdiction under both an admiralty statute and the ATS in a case involving dispute about ownership of slaves on board a captured Spanish vessel). Why did the ATS not serve as a basis for jurisdiction in more cases?

Part of the answer is that, before *Filartiga*, courts generally held that the law of nations did not regulate the ways in which nations treated their own citizens. *See, e.g.*, Dreyfus v. Von Finck, 534 F.2d 24, 31 (2d Cir. 1976) ("[V]iolations of international law do not occur when the aggrieved parties are nationals of the acting state."). This view reflected a pre-World War II conception of customary international law, in which "it was thought to be antithetical for there to be international legal rights that individuals could assert against states, especially against their own governments." Mark W. Janis, An Introduction to International Law 257 (4th ed. 2003). But after World War II, several developments — most notably the Nuremberg trials, the United Nations General Assembly's 1948 Universal Declaration of Human Rights, and a series of international human rights agreements — led to the view that "how a state treats individual human beings . . . is a matter of international concern and a proper subject for regulation by international law." Restatement (Third) of Foreign Relations Law of the United States, pt. VII introductory note at 144-45. As we noted in the previous section, beginning with *Filartiga*, courts began to view a customary international human rights law based on these and related sources as cognizable in cases brought under the ATS.

4. With the exception of Judge Bork's concurrence in *Tel-Oren*, most courts after *Filartiga* and before the Supreme Court's decision in *Sosa* concluded that the ATS itself provided a cause of action. *See, e.g.*, In re Estate of Ferdinand Marcos, Human Rights Litigation, 25 F.3d 1467, 1474-75 (9th Cir. 1994); *cf.* Abebe-Jira v. Negewo, 72 F.3d 844, 848 (11th Cir. 1996) (interpreting ATS as delegating to the federal courts the task of fashioning remedies, including causes of action, to give effect to the federal policies underlying the ATS).

In *Sosa*, the Court unanimously rejected this view, holding that the ATS is merely a jurisdictional statute that does not itself confer any causes of action. Nevertheless, a majority of the Court left open some room for judicial creation of causes of action in ATS cases. What justifications does the majority give for doing so? Does the fact that Congress in 1789 would have expected some causes of action for violations of international law to be available as a matter of general common law compel the conclusion that, after the abolition of general common law and the adoption of much stricter standards for finding causes of action, courts may create federal common law causes of action when applying the ATS? In applying a statute, is a court obligated not only to apply what Congress enacted but also to attempt to recreate the jurisprudential landscape that Congress legislated against? Does such an approach contradict *Erie*, which rejected on constitutional grounds the notion, going back to the beginning of the Nation, that federal courts sitting in diversity would apply a general common law? Both the diversity jurisdiction statute and the ATS originated in the Judiciary Act of 1789. Why did the Court in *Erie* reject, rather than recreate, the jurisprudential landscape of 1789? Why did the Court in *Erie* update the law that applies under the diversity statute by holding that *state* common law governed, while *Sosa* updated the law that applies under the ATS by holding that *federal* common law governed? Because *Erie* involved a domestic tort and *Sosa* involved customary international law? Because there will be substantially fewer causes of action available under the ATS than under the diversity statute?

5. After *Sosa*, when is it appropriate for courts to recognize a cause of action in a case brought under the ATS? How specific must the international consensus be in order to support a cause of action? What evidence would show that a norm of international law has been "accepted by the civilized world and defined with a specificity comparable to the features of the 18th-century paradigms [discussed by the Court]"? For example, what weight should be given to non-binding UN resolutions or treaties that have not been ratified by the United States, or that have been ratified subject to a reservation stating that the treaty is not self-executing? Are these materials irrelevant sources of law, or merely insufficient by themselves to support a cause of action? Why, precisely, did the Court decline to find a cause of action for Alvarez's claim of arbitrary arrest?

6. What are the implications of *Sosa* for the domestic status of customary international law outside the context of the ATS? Is it possible to maintain, after *Sosa*, that *all* of customary international law is self-executing federal common law? That *none* of it is? Do courts have the authority to create a federal common law cause of action for violations of customary international law in cases not brought under the Alien Tort Statute — for example, in cases brought by U.S. citizens, where jurisdiction is premised either on the general federal question statute or the diversity statute, or the case is brought in state court? What, if anything, does *Sosa* suggest about whether customary international law applies automatically to preempt state law under the Supremacy Clause? How does *Garamendi*, the decision excerpted in Chapter 5 concerning Executive Branch preemption of state law, affect the answer to this question?

7. After *Sosa*, can customary international law serve as a basis for federal question jurisdiction under 28 U.S.C. §1331? What does footnote 19 of *Sosa* suggest? Of what relevance is footnote 19 to the questions in the previous note? Prior to *Sosa*, several lower courts rejected the claim that customary international law could be a basis for federal jurisdiction under §1331. *See, e.g.*, Princz v. Federal Republic of Germany, 26 F.3d 1166, 1176 (D.C. Cir. 1994); Xuncax v. Gramajo, 886 F. Supp. 162, 193-94 (D. Mass. 1995); Handel v. Artukovic, 601 F. Supp. 1421, 1426 (C.D. Cal. 1985).

8. Are there circumstances short of wholesale incorporation of customary international law, but outside the ATS context, in which courts can nonetheless apply customary international law as federal common law? In First National City Bank v. Banco Para El Comercio Exterior De Cuba, 462 U.S. 611 (1983), for example, the Supreme Court looked to federal common law, which it viewed to be informed both by "international law principles and by articulated congressional policies," to determine when to pierce the corporate veil of separate juridical entities in suits under the Foreign Sovereign Immunities Act. Customary international law might be similarly relevant to filling in gaps in the Foreign Sovereign

Immunities Act with regard to head-of-state immunity issues. *See* Curtis A. Bradley & Jack L. Goldsmith, *Pinochet and International Human Rights Litigation*, 97 Mich. L. Rev. 2129, 2166-67 (1999). One might also think that to the extent that federal courts apply principles of treaty interpretation from the Vienna Convention on the Law of Treaties, which binds the United States at most as customary international law, such principles would also apply as federal common law to bind state courts in their interpretation of treaties. *Cf.* Chubb & Son, Inc. v. Asiana Airlines, 214 F.3d 301 (2d Cir. 2000) (looking to principles of customary international law as embodied in the Vienna Convention on the Law of Treaties to ascertain whether a treaty existed between United States and Korea).

9. In footnote 21, the Court in *Sosa* refers to the possibility of "case-specific deference to the political branches," and, after describing the State Department's involvement in an ATS case involving South Africa, states that "[i]n such cases, there is a strong argument that federal courts should give serious weight to the Executive Branch's view of the case's impact on foreign policy." Should the Executive Branch's views of the foreign policy implications of a case affect the decision whether to recognize a cause of action? What deference should courts give to the Executive about whether to recognize a cause of action, or whether to allow a particular case to go forward? The Executive has recently opposed aiding and abetting liability, for example, on the ground that it could hurt U.S. trade and foreign relations. Should courts defer to that view?

Sosa marks the third decision in recent years (the other two are *Garamendi* (excerpted in Chapter 5) and *Altmann* (excerpted in Chapter 2)) in which the Supreme Court has emphasized the possibility of case-specific deference to the Executive's views in deciding foreign relations cases. Will the Court's contemplated role for case-by-case Executive suggestions thrust the Executive Branch into the same politicized situation that it was in during the days prior to the enactment of the Foreign Sovereign Immunities Act when (as discussed in Chapter 2) the Executive Branch essentially adjudicated foreign sovereign immunity determinations? Prior to the September 11 attacks, the Court had in a series of foreign relations decisions rejected case-by-case reliance on the Executive's views. *See* Jack L. Goldsmith, *The New Formalism in United States Foreign Relations Law*, 66 Colo. L. Rev. 1395 (1999). Might the September 11 attacks and the ensuing war on terrorism have something to do with the Court's change of course in this context?

10. In addition to the cause of action and Executive suggestion issues addressed in *Sosa*, the Court suggests in footnote 21 that another possible limitation in ATS cases is that the plaintiff may need to exhaust remedies. What would be the source of this limitation? Would a plaintiff have to exhaust remedies in foreign forums, international forums, or both?

Justice Breyer suggests an additional limitation grounded in international comity. Are courts competent to decide whether comity would be promoted or undermined by adjudicating a human rights lawsuit?

Lower courts have considered two other possible limitations in ATS cases. One is the act of state doctrine, analyzed in Chapter 2. Most courts that have considered the act of state doctrine in the ATS context have found it not to apply. *See, e.g.,* Kadic v. Karadzic, 70 F.3d 232, 249-50 (2d Cir. 1995); Doe v. Unocal Corp., 395 F.3d 932, 959-60 (9th Cir. 2002). These courts note that the Supreme Court stated in *Sabbatino* that the act of state doctrine applies only "in the absence of a treaty or other unambiguous agreement regarding controlling legal principles," *Sabbatino,* 376 U.S. at 430, and they reason that there is "unambiguous agreement" concerning the norm in question. Did the Court's reference to "unambiguous agreement" include customary international law? *Compare* Ryan Goodman & Derek P. Jinks, Filartiga's *Firm Footing: International Human Rights and Federal Common Law*, 66 Fordham L. Rev. 463, 481-97 (1997) (arguing that it did), *with* Gary B. Born, International Civil Litigation in United States Courts 743 (3d ed. 1996) (stating that "*Sabbatino* appears to have rejected any such possibility" of a customary international law exception to the act of state doctrine). Which is the better view? Does *Sosa* have any implications for the availability of the act of state doctrine in ATS cases?

Another possible limitation on ATS suits is the doctrine of *forum non conveniens*, also analyzed in Chapter 2. Should courts apply this doctrine in ATS cases? For relevant decisions, see, for example, Abdullahi v. Pfizer, 2003 U.S. App. LEXIS 20704 (2d Cir. Oct. 8, 2003) (remanding for further consideration of whether Nigeria would be an adequate alternative forum in case concerning allegedly improper medical treatment administered by U.S. company in Nigeria); Aguinda v. Texaco, 303 F.3d 470 (2d Cir. 2002) (dismissing ATS suit by citizens of Peru and Ecuador alleging that defendant oil company polluted rain forests and rivers in their countries); Delgado v. Shell Oil Co., 231 F.3d 165 (2d Cir. 2000) (dismissing ATS suit against U.S. and foreign companies for injuries allegedly caused by exposure to a nematocide in several foreign countries); Wiwa v. Royal Dutch Petroleum Co., 226 F.3d 88 (2d Cir. 2000) (declining to dismiss suit against foreign companies for alleged human rights abuses committed in Nigeria); Aguinda v. Texaco, Inc., 142 F. Supp. 2d 534 (S.D.N.Y. 2001) (dismissing ATS suit against U.S. company for injuries caused by waste disposal practices in Ecuador). *See also* Kathryn Lee Boyd, *The Inconvenience of Victims: Abolishing Forum Non Conveniens in U.S. Human Rights Litigation*, 39 Va. J. Int'l L. 41 (1998); Paul B. Stephan, *A Becoming Modesty — U.S. Litigation in the Mirror of International Law*, 52 DePaul L. Rev. 627 (2002); Aric K. Short, *Is the Alien Tort Statute Sacrosanct? Retaining Forum Non Conveniens in Human Rights Litigation*, 33 N.Y.U. J. Int'l L. & Pol. 1001 (2001).

11. The ATS refers to both the "law of nations" and "a treaty of the United States." Most suits under the ATS have involved only alleged violations of the law of nations, in part because the treaties that might be relevant to the plaintiffs' claims have either not been ratified by the United States or have been declared by the U.S. treatymakers to be non-self-executing. A recent ATS case involving an alleged treaty violation is Jogi v. Voges, 425 F.3d 367 (7th Cir. 2005). There, the U.S. Court of Appeals for the Seventh Circuit held that a claim could be brought under the ATS for a violation of the requirement in Article 36 of the Vienna Convention on Consular Relations that foreign nationals arrested in the United States be advised that they have the right to have their consulate notified of the arrest and to communicate with the consulate. (This requirement is discussed in more detail in connection with the *Breard* decision excerpted in Chapter 6.) The court concluded that Article 36 of the Convention is self-executing, and that it may be enforced through a private right of action for damages. The court reasoned that its prior decisions had precluded other remedies to enforce the Convention and that, "In the absence of any administrative remedy or other alternative to measures we have already rejected (such as suppression of evidence), a damages action is the only avenue left."

Is the violation of Article 36 a "tort"? Do you think that those who drafted and ratified Article 36 intended for it to confer a private right of action for damages?

12. As the Court notes in *Sosa*, the legislative history of the Torture Victim Protection Act (TVPA) expresses support for the *Filartiga* approach to human rights litigation under the ATS. Despite this legislative history, is the text of the TVPA in fact consistent with the *Filartiga* approach to human rights litigation? Note that the TVPA, unlike the ATS, is limited to two specifically defined violations of international law and contains a statute of limitations and an exhaustion requirement. In this light, does the TVPA narrow ATS-style human rights litigation with respect to torture and extrajudicial killing? Or could a plaintiff avoid the limitations of the TVPA by bringing their torture or extrajudicial claim under the ATS? These questions were addressed in Enahoro v. Abubakar, 408 F.3d 877 (7th Cir. 2005), which held that a suit for torture and extrajudicial killing could not be brought under the ATS because the TVPA "occupied the field" of civil human rights lawsuits for these causes of action. The court reasoned that it would make no sense for Congress to codify a cause of action for torture and extrajudicial killing with the procedural restrictions in the TVPA if plaintiffs could simply plead these causes of action under the ATS alone and avoid the TVPA's procedural requirements. The court reasoned that this conclusion was consistent with the Supreme Court's insistence in *Sosa* on "vigilant doorkeeping" in developing private rights of action in human rights cases. Do you agree with this analysis?

Should the TVPA's exhaustion requirement apply in ATS suits not involving torture and extrajudicial killing? Most courts prior to *Sosa* held that the TVPA's exhaustion requirement did not apply in ATS cases. *See, e.g.*, Doe v. Saravia, 348 F. Supp. 2d 1112, 1157-58 (E.D. Cal. 2004); Sarei v. Rio Tinto Plc, 221 F. Supp. 2d 1116, 1133 (C.D. Cal. 2002). Why would Congress want an exhaustion requirement for torture and extrajudicial killing suits, but not, say, for suits involving prolonged and arbitrary detention?

A related issue is whether the ten-year statute of limitations in the TVPA applies to ATS claims. Most courts have held that it does, reasoning that the ATS doesn't specify a statute of limitations and the TVPA is the closest analogy. *See, e.g.*, Arce v. Garcia, 400 F.3d 1340, 1345-46 (11th Cir. 2005); Papa v. United States, 281 F.3d 1004, 1012-13 (9th Cir. 2002). Are these decisions correct? Does it make sense to apply the TVPA's statute of limitations but not its exhaustion requirement in ATS cases?

13. The first President Bush expressed the following concerns upon signing the TVPA:

> With rare exceptions, the victims of [acts covered by the TVPA] will be foreign citizens. There is thus a danger that U.S. courts may become embroiled in difficult and sensitive disputes in other countries, and possibly ill-founded or politically motivated suits, which have nothing to do with the United States and which offer little prospect of successful recovery. Such potential abuse of this statute undoubtedly would give rise to serious frictions in international relations and would also be a waste of our own limited and already overburdened judicial resources.

Statement by President George Bush Upon Signing H.R. 2092, 28 Weekly Comp. Pres. Doc. 465, March 16, 1992, reprinted in 1992 U.S.C.C.A.N. 91. Are these concerns justified? Do you think the cases covered in this section were politically motivated? Assuming they were, what's wrong with politically motivated lawsuits to redress gross human rights abuses? If President Bush was worried about problematic cases brought under the TVPA, why did he sign the legislation?

14. What is the constitutional authority for Congress to enact the TVPA? The Majority Senate Report explained congressional authority as follows:

> Congress clearly has authority to create a private right of action for torture and extrajudicial killings committed abroad. Under article III of the Constitution, the Federal judiciary has the power to adjudicate cases "arising under" the "law of the United States." The Supreme Court has held that the law of the United States includes international law. In Verlinden B.V. v. Central Bank of Nigeria, 461 U.S. 480, 481 (1983),

the Supreme Court held that the "arising under" clause allows Congress to confer jurisdiction on U.S. courts to recognize claims brought by a foreign plaintiff against a foreign defendant. Congress' ability to enact this legislation also derives from article I, section 8 of the Constitution, which authorizes Congress "to define and punish... Offenses against the Laws of Nations."... The law of nations is "part of our law, and must be ascertained and administered by the courts of justice of appropriate jurisdiction, as often as questions of right depending upon it are duly presented for their determination." The Paquete Habana, 175 U.S. 677, 700 (1900).

S. Rep. No. 249, 102d Cong., 1st Sess. (1991). The Minority Senate Report disagreed:

> [The TVPA] appears to over-extend Congress' constitutional authority. Congress has the power to "define and punish Piracies and Felonies committed on the high Seas, and Offenses against the Law of Nations." But as the Department of Justice has noted, (t)he reference in the constitutional text to "punish(ing) Piracies and Felonies... and Offenses" suggests that the Founders intended that Congress use this power to define crimes. It is a difficult and unresolved question, therefore, whether that power extends to creating a civil cause of action in this country for disputes that have no factual nexus with the United States or its citizens. In short, we simply do not agree with the contention in the majority views that Congress "clearly has authority to create a private right of action for torture and extrajudicial killings committed abroad." [*Verlinden*] involved a contract between a Dutch corporation and the Government of Nigeria (which wished to purchase 240,000 metric tons of cement). When Central Bank of Nigeria issued an unconfirmed letter of credit through Morgan Guaranty Trust Company of New York, the Dutch corporation filed suit, claiming an anticipatory breach of contract. The connection to the United States in this case is clear: while the plaintiff and defendant in the breach of contract suit were foreign entities, an instrumentality of that breach however unintended was a United States corporation, Morgan Guaranty Trust Company, of New York, which acted as a correspondent bank to the Central Bank of Nigeria. Thus, the *Verlinden* case does consider some actions occurring within the United States, while [the TVPA] would address actions which occurred wholly outside the United States, with no connection to the United States.

Id. Who has the better of this argument? Does Congress's power here depend, as the Majority Report suggests, on whether the law of nations is automatically part of the laws of the United States? Does the Define and Punish Clause in fact have a penal law limitation and a nexus requirement, as the Minority Report suggests?

15. Can the TVPA be justified on some basis in Article I other than the Define and Punish Clause? How about the Commerce Clause? Can the TVPA be justified as an implementation of the Convention Against Torture and Other Cruel, Inhuman or Degrading Treatment or Punishment, ratified by the United States in 1994, which requires that nations "prosecute or extradite" torturers found in their territory? With regard to this latter question, the Majority Report states that the TVPA

> will carry out the intent of the Convention Against Torture and Other Cruel, Inhuman or Degrading Treatment or Punishment, ... The convention obligates state parties to adopt measures to ensure that torturers within their territories are held legally accountable for their acts. This legislation will do precisely that — by making sure that torturers and death squads will no longer have a safe haven in the United States.

S. Rep. No. 249, 102d Cong., 1st Sess. 4 (1991). The Minority Report took a somewhat different view:

> The Department of Justice noted, and we agree, that "(s)uch a unilateral assertion of extraterritorial jurisdiction would be in tension with the framework of the (U.N. Convention Against Torture and other Cruel, Inhuman or Degrading Treatment or

Punishment)." According to the administration, the convention requires countries to provide remedies for acts of torture which took place only within their own territory. In fact the convention specifically declined to extend coverage to acts committed outside the country in which the lawsuit is brought. We do not wish to second-guess the experts who drafted this treaty, and believe it is unwise to do explicitly what its drafters chose not to do — extend the coverage to extraterritorial actions.

Id. Does the Convention Against Torture authorize the TVPA, or is the TVPA in tension with the Convention? Who decides this legal question — a majority of Congress, or courts?

16. The TVPA applies to any foreign official who "subjects an individual" to torture or extrajudicial killing. According to the TVPA's legislative history, the statute also applies to "anyone with higher authority who authorized, tolerated or knowingly ignored those acts," S. Rep. No. 102-249, at 9 (1991), and courts have construed the statute as applying to those individuals as well. *See, e.g.*, Hilao v. Marcos, 103 F.3d 767, 778-79 (9th Cir. 1996); Xuncax v. Gramajo, 886 F. Supp. 162, 172 (D. Mass. 1995). Why aren't those individuals mentioned in the statute itself? Should liability be based on mere legislative history, which is not voted on by Congress and not signed by the President? On the other hand, can command responsibility be reasonably inferred from the statutory term "subjects"?

In any event, what if the person in charge was unable to control the actions of his or her subordinates? The U.S. Court of Appeals for the Eleventh Circuit addressed this issue in Ford v. Garcia, 289 F.3d 1283 (11th Cir. 2002). That case concerned the torture and murder, in 1980, of three American nuns and a layperson in El Salvador by members of the Salvadoran National Guard. The Guardsmen who committed these acts were eventually convicted and sentenced to prison terms. Some years later, representatives of the victims' estates brought suit under the TVPA against two former Salvadoran officials residing in Florida: the Director of the Salvadoran National Guard at the time of the killings, and El Salvador's Minister of Defense at the time of the killings. At trial, the defendants argued that they did not have the ability to control their troops during the relevant time period, and the jury returned a verdict in their favor. The Eleventh Circuit affirmed. Relying on the TVPA's legislative history, the appeals court concluded that the statute implicitly adopts the international law doctrine of command responsibility. Under this doctrine, said the court, "effective control of a commander over his troops is required before liability will be imposed." *Id.* at 1290. In support of this conclusion, the court relied on decisions from the international criminal tribunals for former Yugoslavia and Rwanda, as well as the treaty establishing the permanent international criminal court. The court further concluded from these materials that the trial court had not committed reversible error in instructing the jury that the plaintiffs had the ultimate burden of persuasion to show that the defendants had effective control over their troops. Was it proper for the court to look to international law in construing the statute's scope and burden of proof?

17. For discussions of *Sosa* and its implications, see William S. Dodge, *Bridging Erie: Customary International Law in the U.S. Legal System After Sosa v. Alvarez-Machain*, 12 Tulsa J. Comp. & Int'l L. 87 (2004); Eugene Kontorovich, *Implementing Sosa v. Alvarez-Machain: What Piracy Teaches About the Limits of the Alien Tort Statute*, 80 Notre Dame L. Rev. 111 (2004); Julian Ku & John C. Yoo, *Beyond Formalism in Foreign Affairs: A Functional Approach to the Alien Tort Statute*, 2004 Sup. Ct. Rev. 153; Ralph G. Steinhardt, *Laying One Bankrupt Critique to Rest: Sosa v. Alvarez-Machain and the Future of International Human Rights Litigation in U.S. Courts*, 57 Vand. L. Rev. 2241 (2004).

C. SOVEREIGN IMMUNITY DEFENSES

Chuidian v. Philippine National Bank

912 F.2d 1095 (9th Cir. 1990)

WALLACE, CIRCUIT JUDGE.

Chuidian, a Philippine citizen, sued Daza, a Philippine citizen and an official of the Philippine government, after Daza instructed the Philippine National Bank (Bank) to dishonor a letter of credit issued by the Republic of the Philippines to Chuidian. The district court dismissed for lack of subject matter jurisdiction, and Chuidian timely appeals....

The central issue in this appeal is whether Daza is entitled to sovereign immunity for acts committed in his official capacity as a member of the [Commission on Good Government, a Philippine Agency charged with recovering the "ill-gotten wealth" accumulated by former President Ferdinand Marcos and his associates]. Daza argues that he qualifies as an "agency or instrumentality of a foreign state," 28 U.S.C. §1603(b), and hence is entitled to immunity pursuant to the [Foreign Sovereign Immunities] Act, 28 U.S.C. §1604. Chuidian contends either that Daza is not covered by the Act, or, in the alternative, that this case falls within the exceptions to immunity expressly provided by the Act. See 28 U.S.C. §§1605-07. The government, in a "Statement of Interest of the United States," takes a third position. Under the government's view, Daza is not covered by the Act because he is an individual rather than a corporation or an association, but he is nevertheless entitled to immunity under the general principles of sovereign immunity expressed in the Restatement (Second) of Foreign Relations Law §66(b).

We initially consider whether the Act applies to an individual such as Daza acting in his official capacity as an employee of a foreign sovereign....

The government and Chuidian argue that the definition of "agency or instrumentality of a foreign state" in §1603(b) includes only agencies, ministries, corporations, and other associations, and is not meant to encompass individuals. Such a reading draws some significant support from the legislative history of §1603(b), which reads in part:

The first criterion [§1603(b)(1)]... is intended to include a corporation, association, foundation or any other entity which, under the law of the foreign state where it was created, can sue or be sued in its own name....

The second criterion [§1603(b)(2)] requires that the entity be either an organ of a foreign state... or that a majority of the entity's shares or other ownership interest be owned by a foreign state....

As a general matter, entities which meet the definition of an "agency or instrumentality of a foreign state" could assume a variety of forms, including a state trading corporation, a mining enterprise, a transport organization such as a shipping line or airline, a steel company, a central bank, an export association, a governmental procurement agency or a department or ministry....

House Report at 6614.

This language from the House Report indicates that Congress was primarily concerned with *organizations* acting for the foreign state, and may not have expressly contemplated the case of *individuals* acting as sovereign instrumentalities. At least one court has so concluded.

Chuidian and the United States thus argue that Daza's immunity cannot be evaluated under the provisions of the Act. Chuidian argues that Daza therefore cannot be granted immunity: the Act provides the sole source of sovereign immunity, and Daza does not qualify under its definition of a foreign state. The government, on the other hand, urges us to apply the pre-Act common law of immunity. In its view, the Act replaces common law only in the context of "foreign states" as defined by section 1603(b); elsewhere — i.e., for entities covered by the common law but not covered by the Act — common law principles remain valid. The government further argues that Daza is immune under the common law principles of the Second Restatement; Chuidian contends that even if the old common law applies, an exception to immunity is applicable.

We are persuaded by neither of these arguments. While section 1603(b) may not explicitly include individuals within its definition of foreign instrumentalities, neither does it expressly exclude them. The terms "agency," "instrumentality," "organ," "entity," and "legal person," while perhaps more readily connoting an organization or collective, do not in their typical legal usage necessarily exclude individuals. Nowhere in the text or legislative history does Congress state that individuals are *not* encompassed within the section 1603(b) definition; indeed, aside from some language which is more commonly associated with the collective, the legislative history does not even hint of an intent to exclude individual officials from the scope of the Act. Such an omission is particularly significant in light of numerous statements that Congress intended the Act to codify the existing common law principles of sovereign immunity. As pointed out above, pre-1976 common law expressly extended immunity to individual officials acting in their official capacity. If in fact the Act does not include such officials, the Act contains a substantial unannounced departure from prior common law.

The most that can be concluded from the preceding discussion is that the Act is ambiguous as to its extension to individual foreign officials. Under such circumstances, we decline to limit its application as urged by Chuidian and the government. We conclude that the consequences of such a limitation, whether they be the loss of immunity urged by Chuidian or the reversion to pre-Act common law as urged by the government, would be entirely inconsistent with the purposes of the Act.

It is generally recognized that a suit against an individual acting in his official capacity is the practical equivalent of a suit against the sovereign directly. Thus, to take Chuidian's argument first, we cannot infer that Congress, in passing the Act, intended to allow unrestricted suits against individual foreign officials acting in their official capacities. Such a result would amount to a blanket abrogation of foreign sovereign immunity by allowing litigants to accomplish indirectly what the Act barred them from doing directly. It would be illogical to conclude that Congress would have enacted such a sweeping alteration of existing law implicitly and without comment. Moreover, such an interpretation would defeat the purposes of the Act: the statute was intended as a comprehensive codification of immunity and its exceptions. The rule that foreign states can be sued only pursuant to the specific provisions of sections 1605-07 would be vitiated if litigants could avoid immunity simply by recasting the form of their pleadings.

Similarly, we disagree with the government that the Act can reasonably be interpreted to leave intact the pre-1976 common law with respect to foreign officials. Admittedly, such a result would not effect the sweeping changes which would accompany the rule suggested by Chuidian: the government merely proposes that immunity of foreign states be evaluated under the Act and immunity of individuals be evaluated under the (substantially similar) provisions of the Second Restatement. Nevertheless, such a rule would also work to undermine the Act.

The principal distinction between pre-1976 common law practice and post-1976 statutory practice is the role of the State Department. If individual immunity is to be determined in accordance with the Second Restatement, presumably we would once again be required to give conclusive weight to the State Department's determination of whether an individual's activities fall within the traditional exceptions to sovereign immunity. As observed previously, there is little practical difference between a suit against a state and a suit against an individual acting in his official capacity. Adopting the rule urged by the government would promote a peculiar variant of forum shopping, especially when the immunity question is unclear. Litigants who doubted the influence and diplomatic ability of their sovereign adversary would choose to proceed against the official, hoping to secure State Department support, while litigants less favorably positioned would be inclined to proceed against the foreign state directly, confronting the Act as interpreted by the courts without the influence of the State Department.

Absent an explicit direction from the statute, we conclude that such a bifurcated approach to sovereign immunity was not intended by the Act. First, every indication shows that Congress intended the Act to be comprehensive, and courts have consistently so interpreted its provisions. Yet the rule urged by the government would in effect make the statute optional: by artful pleading, litigants would be able to take advantage of the Act's provisions or, alternatively, choose to proceed under the old common law.

Second, a bifurcated interpretation of the Act would be counter to Congress's stated intent [in the legislative history] of removing the discretionary role of the State Department. Under the government's interpretation, the pre-1966 common law would apply, in which the State Department had a discretionary role at the option of the litigant. But the Act is clearly intended as a mandatory rather than an optional procedure. To convert it to the latter by allowing suits against individual officials to proceed under the old common law would substantially undermine the force of the statute. There is no showing that Congress intended such a limited effect in passing a supposedly comprehensive codification of foreign sovereign immunity.

Furthermore, no authority supports the continued validity of the pre-1976 common law in light of the Act. Indeed, the American Law Institute recently issued the Restatement (Third) of Foreign Relations Law, superseding the Second Restatement relied upon by the government in this action. The new Restatement deletes in its entirety the discussion of the United States common law of sovereign immunity, and substitutes a section analyzing such issues exclusively under the Act.

For these reasons, we conclude that Chuidian's suit against Daza for acts committed in his official capacity . . . must be analyzed under the framework of the Act. We thus join the majority of courts which have similarly concluded that section 1603(b) can fairly be read to include individuals sued in their official capacity. . . .

Chuidian argues in the alternative that Daza did not commit the acts complained of while acting in his official capacity. According to Chuidian, Daza acted out of malice against Chuidian, and also acted at the direction of Garcia, an enemy of Chuidian's to whom Daza owed personal favors. Thus, Chuidian contends, we should treat Daza's obstruction of the payment as a private rather than a governmental act.

Plainly Daza would not be entitled to sovereign immunity for acts not committed in his official capacity. We have recognized several circumstances in which a suit against a sovereign's employee is distinct from a suit against the sovereign. Obviously, "if the officer purports to act as an individual and not as an official, a suit directed against that action is not a suit against the sovereign." Larson v. Domestic and Foreign Commerce Corp., 337 U.S. 682, 689 (1949). As we stated in United States v. Yakima Tribal Court, 806 F.2d 853, 859 (9th Cir. 1986), *cert. denied*, 481 U.S. 1069 (1987), "if an employee of the United States acts completely outside his governmental authority, he has no immunity. An obvious example would be if a dispute occurs pertaining to the sale of an employee's personal house, his government employment provides him with no shield to liability."

Here, however, while Daza may or may not have acted with an individual *motive*, it is clear that in ordering the payment not be made he purported to act as an official, not as an individual. Indeed, only his authority as a member of the Commission enabled him to prevent the payment. Thus, his actions, far from being "completely outside his governmental authority," *id.*, were entirely dependent upon it.

Sovereign immunity similarly will not shield an official who acts beyond the scope of his authority. "Where the officer's powers are limited by statute, his actions beyond those limitations are considered individual and not sovereign actions. The officer is not doing the business which the sovereign has empowered him to do. . . ." *Larson*, 337 U.S. at 689.

Chuidian argues that Daza was not authorized to use his office for personal purposes, and hence his actions against Chuidian are ultra vires and not subject to immunity. But Chuidian once more confuses the motive with the actions arising from the motive. Chuidian has not alleged any respect in which Daza's *actions* departed from his statutory mandate. As a member of the Commission, Daza was entitled to investigate possible fraudulent transfers to Marcos associates. Daza clearly had the power to prevent the payment in aid of his investigation; indeed, he had the power to seek an injunction if the Bank refused to comply.

Chuidian does not argue otherwise. Rather, he contends that Daza's personal motive renders his actions ultra vires even though the actions themselves were fully authorized. Under Chuidian's view, every otherwise proper sovereign action would be subject to judicial examination to ensure that the acting officer did not derive some personal satisfaction from the commission of his official duty. There is no authority to support such a radical expansion of the exceptions to sovereign immunity.

The most Chuidian can allege is that Daza experienced a convergence between his personal interest and his official duty and authority. Such a circumstance does not serve to make his action any less an action of his sovereign. Therefore, we hold that the district court did not err in dismissing the claims against Daza in his individual capacity.

Ye v. Zemin

383 F.3d 620 (7th Cir. 2004)

[Practitioners of Falun Gong, a spiritual movement of Chinese origin, sued the President of China, Ziang Zemin, alleging that he was responsible for various abuses against the Falun Gong in China, including torture, genocide, arbitrary arrest, and imprisonment. The Executive Branch filed a suggestion of immunity on behalf of Zemin, and the district court dismissed the case based on the doctrine of "head-of-state immunity."]

MANION, CIRCUIT JUDGE. . . .

The appellants' first argument relates to the assertion by the United States, which the district court took as dispositive, that President Jiang was immune from the appellants' suit. The appellants argue that the actions President Jiang is accused of amount to violations of *"jus cogens"* norms of international law and that immunity may not be conferred upon a person accused of violating these norms....

The FSIA does not...address the immunity of foreign heads of states. The FSIA refers to foreign states, not their leaders. The FSIA defines a foreign state to include a political subdivision, agency or instrumentality of a foreign state but makes no mention of heads of state. 28 U.S.C. §603(a). Because the FSIA does not apply to heads of states, the decision concerning the immunity of foreign heads of states remains vested where it was prior to 1976—with the Executive Branch....

In this case the Executive Branch entered a suggestion of immunity. The appellants argue, however, that the Executive Branch has no power to immunize a head of state (or any person for that matter) for acts that violate *jus cogens* norms of international law....

The appellants' position, therefore, is that, in at least a particular class of cases (those involving *jus cogens* norms), a court cannot defer to the position of the Executive Branch with respect to immunity for heads of states. The Supreme Court has held, however, that the Executive Branch's suggestion of immunity is conclusive and not subject to judicial inquiry. [The court here cites and quotes from pre-FSIA sovereign immunity decisions.]

The appellants present their argument as one of international law—under customary international law, a state cannot provide immunity to a defendant accused of violating *jus cogens* norms. Our first concern, however, is to ascertain the proper relationship between the Executive and Judicial Branches insofar as the immunity of foreign leaders is concerned. The obligation of the Judicial Branch is clear—a determination by the Executive Branch that a foreign head of state is immune from suit is conclusive and a court must accept such a determination without reference to the underlying claims of a plaintiff....

Our deference to the Executive Branch is motivated by the caution we believe appropriate of the Judicial Branch when the conduct of foreign affairs is involved.... The determination to grant (or not grant) immunity can have significant implications for this country's relationship with other nations. A court is ill-prepared to assess these implications and resolve the competing concerns the Executive Branch is faced with in determining whether to immunize a head of state....

Although our decision in [Sampson v. Federal Republic of Germany, 250 F.3d 1145, 1149-50 (7th Cir. 2001)] was one of statutory interpretation, we believe it is also instructive here. In *Sampson* we held that the FSIA did not include an implied exception to its general grant of sovereign immunity to foreign states where a foreign state was accused of violating *jus cogens* norms. Because the FSIA contained no such exception, Germany was immune from suit brought by a survivor of Auschwitz in the Northern District of Illinois.

Our interpretation of the FSIA confirmed that Congress could grant immunity to a foreign state for acts that amounted to violations of *jus cogens* norms. Just as the FSIA is the Legislative Branch's determination that a nation should be immune from suit in the courts of this country, the immunity of foreign leaders remains the province of the Executive Branch. The Executive Branch's determination that a foreign leader should be immune from suit even when the leader is accused of acts that violate *jus cogens* norms is established by a suggestion of immunity. We are no more free to ignore the Executive Branch's determination than we are free to ignore a legislative determination concerning a foreign state....Pursuant to their respective authorities, Congress or the Executive Branch can create exceptions to blanket immunity. In such cases the courts would be obliged to respect such exceptions. In the present case the Executive Branch has recognized the immunity of President Jiang from the appellants' suit. The district court was correct to accept this recognition as conclusive.

Enahoro v. Abubakar

408 F.3d 877 (7th Cir. 2005)

[Seven Nigerian citizens sued a Nigerian general, Abdulsalami Abubakar, who had been part of a military council that had ruled Nigeria from 1993-99, and had himself operated as Nigeria's head of state for one of those years. The plaintiffs alleged that Abubakar was responsible for various acts of torture and killing. The district court held that he was entitled to common law "head-of-state immunity" for the year during which he was head of state, but that he was not entitled to immunity under the FSIA. Abubakar appealed the denial of FSIA immunity. The plaintiffs did not appeal the ruling concerning head-of-state immunity. The Executive Branch did not express a view in either the district court or court of appeals concerning these issues.]

EVANS, CIRCUIT JUDGE.

A courtroom in Chicago, one would think, is an unlikely place for considering a case involving seven Nigerian citizens suing an eighth Nigerian for acts committed in Nigeria. It sounds like the sort of fare that would be heard in a courtroom on the African continent. But this case ended up in Chicago, and that leads us to consider the claims of seven Nigerian citizens against a Nigerian general over alleged torture and murder in Nigeria. The path the plaintiffs are pursuing is, as we shall see, quite thorny. . . .

General Abubakar contends that he has immunity for official conduct taken while he was a Nigerian public official and a member of the ruling council. Underlying his argument is his contention that the FSIA applies to individuals in government, not just foreign governments and agencies. . . .

Under the FSIA, a foreign state is "presumptively immune from the jurisdiction of United States courts. . . ." Saudi Arabia v. Nelson, 507 U.S. 349, 355 (1993). That immunity exists unless one of the statutory exceptions to immunity applies. See 28 U.S.C. §§1605 & 1607. Ironically, however, the FSIA is also the sole basis for jurisdiction over a foreign state. Title 28 U.S.C. §§1604 and 1330(a) work together. Section 1330 confers jurisdiction when the state is not entitled to immunity under one of the exceptions in the FSIA. Argentine Republic v. Amerada Hess Shipping Corp., 488 U.S. 428, 434 (1989).

In this case, no one contends that an exception to immunity applies. If Abubakar is covered by the FSIA, he is immune; no exception is relevant; and the suit would have to be dismissed. Therefore, the only issue is whether the statute applies to individuals, who are connected with the government, as opposed to the state itself and its agencies. We have recently looked at a similar question. Ye v. Zemin, 383 F.3d 620 (7th Cir. 2004), involved a head of state, and we concluded that the FSIA did not apply to heads of state: "The FSIA defines a foreign state to include a political subdivision, agency or instrumentality of a foreign state but makes no mention of heads of state." Ye, 383 F.3d at 625. We noted that the FSIA did not seem to subscribe to Louis XIV's not-so-modest view that "L'etat, c'est moi." How much less, then, could the statute apply to persons, like General Abubakar, when he was simply a member of a committee, even if, as seems likely, a committee that ran the country?

The language of the Act supports our conclusion. The over-riding concern of the Act, as set out in 28 U.S.C. §1602, is allowing judgments against foreign sovereigns "in connection with their commercial activities." The statute was passed so immunity determinations in such contexts would be made "by courts of the United States and of the States . . .", not by the executive branch of the government. Section 1604 provides that a "foreign state" is immune unless certain exceptions apply. Under §1603(a), a foreign state includes "a political subdivision of a foreign state or an agency or instrumentality of a foreign state. . . ." In turn,

> (b) an "agency or instrumentality of a foreign state" means any entity — (1) which is a separate legal person, corporate or otherwise, and (2) which is an organ of a foreign state or political subdivision thereof, or a majority of whose shares or other ownership interest is owned by a foreign state or political subdivision thereof, and (3) which is neither a citizen of a State of the United States as defined in section 1332(c) and (d) of this title nor created under the laws of any third country.

The definition does not explicitly include individuals who either head the government or participate in it at some high level.

Abubakar argues, however, that "separate legal person" must mean an individual. We suppose it could. But if it was a natural person Congress intended to refer to, it is hard to see why the phrase "separate legal person" would be used, having as it does the ring of the familiar legal concept that corporations are persons, which are subject to suit. Given that the phrase "corporate or otherwise" follows on the heels of "separate legal person," we are convinced that the latter phrase refers to a legal fiction — a business entity which is a legal person. If Congress meant to include individuals acting in the official capacity in the scope of the FSIA, it would have done so in clear and unmistakable terms.

It is true, however, that this issue is a long way from being settled. The FSIA has been applied to individuals, but in those cases one thing is clear: the individual must have been acting in his official capacity. If he is not, there is no immunity. . . .

In our case, we conclude, based on the language of the statute, that the FSIA does not apply to General Abubakar; it is therefore also clear that the Act does not provide jurisdiction over the case.

Notes and Questions

1. As discussed in Chapter 2, foreign states cannot be sued in U.S. courts unless one of the exceptions set forth in the Foreign Sovereign Immunities Act (FSIA) is satisfied. In addition, the exception in the FSIA for non-commercial tort claims has a strict territorial limitation: it applies only when the damage or injury occurs in the United States. See 28 U.S.C. §1605(a)(5). As a result, foreign governments generally cannot be sued in U.S. courts for torts committed abroad. (An important exception is the provision in the FSIA for suits against state sponsors of terrorism, discussed below in Section E.)

2. The FSIA does not contain a general exception for violations of international law, and the Supreme Court has held that "immunity is granted in those cases

involving alleged violations of international law that do not come within one of the
FSIA's exceptions." Argentine Republic v. Amerada Hess Shipping Corp., 488 U.S.
428, 436 (1989). The FSIA does, however, contain an exception for situations in
which a foreign state has "waived its immunity...by implication," 28 U.S.C.
§1605(a)(1), and some litigants and commentators have argued that a foreign
state's violation of *jus cogens* norms of international law (fundamental norms that
nations cannot opt out of, such as the prohibitions on genocide and torture) constitutes such an implicit waiver of immunity. *See, e.g.,* Adam C. Belsky et al., *Implied
Waiver Under the FSIA: A Proposed Exception to Immunity for Violations of Peremptory
Norms of International Law,* 71 Cal. L. Rev. 365 (1989). To date, courts have uniformly rejected this argument, holding that even the most egregious conduct does
not constitute a waiver of immunity under the FSIA. *See, e.g.,* Sampson v. Federal
Republic of Germany, 250 F.3d 1145 (7th Cir. 2001); Smith v. Socialist People's
Libyan Arab Jamahiriya, 101 F.3d 239, 344-45 (2d Cir. 1996); Princz v. Federal
Republic of Germany, 26 F.3d 1166 (D.C. Cir. 1994); Siderman de Blake v. Republic of Argentina, 965 F.2d 699, 718-19 (9th Cir. 1992). In rejecting a *jus cogens*
limitation on head-of-state immunity (the contours of which are discussed below),
the court in *Zemin* analogized to its earlier FSIA decision in *Sampson.*

   3. The FSIA confers immunity on "foreign states," which are defined to
include agencies and instrumentalities of foreign states. An agency or instrumentality is in turn defined as "a separate legal person, corporate or otherwise," that is
either an organ or political subdivision of a foreign state or has a majority of its
shares or other ownership interests owned by a foreign state or political subdivision. Is the court's extension of FSIA immunity in *Chuidian* to individuals acting in
an official capacity consistent with the text of the FSIA? Its legislative history? Its
purposes? To date, most courts to have considered the issue have agreed with
Chuidian. See, e.g., Byrd v. Corporacion Forestal y Indus. de Olancho S.A., 182
F.3d 380, 388-89 (5th Cir. 1999); Junquist v. Nahyan, 115 F.3d 1020, 1027
(D.C. Cir. 1997). In *Abubakar,* however, the court expresses the view that the
FSIA does not apply to individuals. Which is the better view? If individual officials
are not covered by the FSIA, does this mean that they lack any immunity from suit?
That plaintiffs can circumvent the limitations of the FSIA by simply suing officials
rather than governments?

   4. Under the analysis in *Chuidian,* the FSIA applies to suits against foreign
officials acting in their official capacity, but not to suits against foreign officials
acting in their personal capacity. What should a court look at in order to determine
whether someone was acting in an official capacity? Should a court attempt to
discern the defendant's motive in engaging in the actions? What body of law governs the official capacity determination? The court in *Chuidian* looked to foreign
law; was this appropriate? If the defendant's actions are illegal under foreign law,
does this prevent them from being official? What if they are illegal under U.S. law?
International law? *Cf.* Saudi Arabia v. Nelson, 507 U.S. 349, 361 (1993) (describing
alleged police abuse in Saudi Arabia as "peculiarly sovereign in nature" and thus as
not falling within the FSIA's commercial activity exception).

   5. The extension of the FSIA to foreign officials acting in an official capacity is
a potential obstacle to human rights cases brought under the Alien Tort Statute and
Torture Victim Protection Act. Do you see why? To date, however, the FSIA has
not in fact been a significant obstacle to these cases: in many of these cases
(such as *Filartiga*) the FSIA has not been invoked, and in cases where it has been
invoked courts have tended to conclude that the foreign official was not acting

in an official capacity when he or she committed the human rights abuses, *see, e.g.*, Hilao v. Marcos, 25 F.3d 1467, 1470 (9th Cir. 1994); Cabiri v. Assasie-Gyimah, 921 F. Supp. 1189, 1198 (S.D.N.Y. 1996); Xuncax v. Gramajo, 886 F. Supp. 162, 174-76 (D. Mass. 1995). Most violations of international human rights law require "state action." Does it make sense to conclude that there is state action for purposes of the international law violation while also finding a lack of official capacity for purposes of immunity? Note that there is a similar tension in U.S. civil rights law: An abuse of authority by an individual state official is considered state action for purposes of the Fourteenth Amendment, see Home Telephone & Telegraph Co. v. Los Angeles, 227 U.S. 278 (1913), and for purposes of the civil rights statute, 42 U.S.C. §1983, see Monroe v. Pape, 365 U.S. 167 (1961), but it is not considered state action for purposes of state sovereign immunity in either injunctive actions or damage actions filed against the official personally. *See* Ex parte Young, 209 U.S. 123 (1908); Hafer v. Melo, 502 U.S. 21 (1992). Should foreign sovereign immunity be subject to the same limitations as the sovereign immunity of U.S. states?

6. Most courts have concluded that, even if the FSIA applies to lower-level foreign officials acting in an official capacity, it does not apply to heads of state. Nevertheless, almost every court to address the issue, including the court in *Zemin*, has recognized a doctrine of "head-of-state immunity." In addition, courts have almost always granted head-of-state immunity when the Executive Branch has suggested it. *See, e.g.* Tachiona v. Mugabe, 169 F. Supp. 2d 259 (S.D.N.Y. 2001) (granting immunity to Zimbabwe's president and foreign minister); Lafontant v. Aristide, 844 F. Supp. 128 (E.D.N.Y. 1994) (granting immunity to exiled president of Haiti); Alicog v. Kingdom of Saudi Arabia, 860 F. Supp. 369, 382 (S.D. Tex. 1994) (granting immunity to King of Saudi Arabia); Saltany v. Reagan, 702 F. Supp. 319, 320 (D.D.C. 1988) (granting immunity to prime minister of Great Britain).

The court in *Zemin* reasons that head-of-state immunity is governed by the same Executive suggestion regime that applied to foreign state immunity prior to the enactment of the FSIA. As discussed in Chapter 2, from approximately the late 1930s through the enactment of the FSIA in 1976, Executive suggestions of immunity were treated as binding by the courts. One of the reasons for the enactment of the FSIA, however, was to transfer immunity determinations from the Executive Branch to the courts. Is it correct to conclude that an Executive suggestion regime survived the enactment of the FSIA? If so, what precisely is the source of the Executive's authority to make binding suggestions of immunity? Could Congress validly amend the FSIA to transfer this issue to the courts, as it did for foreign state immunity?

If the Executive suggests that a court *deny* immunity to a head of state, is that suggestion also binding? There have not been many cases raising this question. Consider, however, United States v. Noriega, 117 F.3d 1206 (11th Cir. 1997). That case involved the criminal trial and prosecution of Manuel Noriega, a Panamanian general who had become the de facto leader of Panama after its democratically elected leader was ousted from power. In December 1989, the United States sent troops to Panama, seized Noriega, and brought him to the United States. He was subsequently tried on various charges relating to cocaine trafficking. One of his defenses was that he had head-of-state immunity from prosecution. The U.S. Court of Appeals for the Eleventh Circuit rejected this argument, reasoning that "[t]he Executive Branch has not merely refrained from taking a position on this matter; to the contrary, by pursuing Noriega's capture and this prosecution, the Executive

Branch has manifested its clear sentiment that Noriega should be denied head-of-state immunity." *Id.* at 1212.

What should a court do when the Executive declines to express a view about head-of-state immunity? Some courts have indicated that an Executive suggestion is a prerequisite for immunity. *See, e.g.,* Jungquist v. Nahyan, 940 F. Supp. 312, 321 (D.D.C. 1996). Other courts have relied on the lack of an Executive suggestion simply as a factor weighing against immunity. *See, e.g.,* First American Corp. v. Al-Nahyan, 948 F. Supp. 1107, 1121 (D.D.C. 1996). Other courts (including the district court in *Abubakar*) have reasoned that, when lacking guidance from the Executive, a court should decide for itself whether the head of state is entitled to immunity. *See* In re Doe, 860 F.2d 40, 45 (2d Cir. 1988); Abiola v. Abubakar, 267 F. Supp. 2d 907, 915 (N.D. Ill. 2003). Which of these approaches is preferable? What, if anything, should be inferred from the Executive Branch's failure to file a suggestion of immunity?

7. Should head-of-state immunity extend to high-level officials other than the head of state? To the head-of-state's family members? In cases in which the Executive Branch has suggested extending head-of-state immunity to these additional individuals, courts have generally done so. *See, e.g.,* Kline v. Keneko, 535 N.Y.S.2d 303 (Sup. Ct. 1988) (granting immunity to president's wife), *aff'd mem. sub nom.* Kline v. Cordero de la Madrid, 546 N.Y.S. 2d 506 (App. Div. 1989); Kilroy v. Windsor, No. C-78-291, slip op. (N.D. Ohio, Dec. 7, 1978) (unpublished) (granting immunity to Prince Charles of England); Chong Boon Kim v. Kim Yong Shik, 58 Am. J. Int'l L. 186 (Haw. Cir. Ct., Sept. 9, 1963) (granting immunity to foreign minister). *But see* El-Hadad v. Embassy of the U.A.E., 60 F. Supp. 2d 69, 82 n.10 (D.D.C. 1999) (reasoning that head-of-state immunity is limited to heads of state); Republic of Philippines v. Marcos, 665 F. Supp. 793, 797 (N.D. Cal. 1987) (refusing to grant immunity to Philippine Solicitor General, despite suggestion of immunity from the State Department).

8. Courts have held that a foreign state may waive a head-of-state's immunity. *See, e.g.,* In re Doe, 860 F.2d 40, 44-45 (2d Cir. 1988); In re Grand Jury Proceedings, 817 F.2d 1108, 1111 (4th Cir. 1987); Paul v. Avril, 812 F. Supp. 207, 210 (S.D. Fla. 1992). These courts have reasoned that "[b]ecause it is the state that gives the power to lead and the ensuing trappings of power—including immunity—the state may therefore take back that which it bestowed upon its erstwhile leaders." *Doe,* 860 F.2d at 45. Is this persuasive? How explicit should courts require the waiver to be? What if the Executive Branch suggests that a court disregard a waiver? *Cf. Lafontant,* 844 F. Supp. at 134 (declining to recognize waiver by ostensible new government of Haiti because the Executive Branch had not recognized the new government as legitimate).

9. What if a *former* head of state seeks immunity in U.S. courts? To date, most former-head-of-state immunity claims have been resolved on the basis of a waiver by the ex-head-of-state's new government. Some courts have suggested in dicta that former-head-of-state immunity does not extend to private (as opposed to official) acts. *See, e.g.,* In re Doe, 860 F.2d at 44; Republic of the Philippines v. Marcos, 806 F.2d 344, 360 (2d Cir. 1986); United States v. Noriega, 746 F. Supp. 1506, 1519 n.11 (S.D. Fla. 1990). At least one court has questioned the availability of any immunity for former heads of state. *See* Roxas v. Marcos, 969 P.2d 1209, 1252 (Haw. 1998). By contrast, the district court in *Abubakar* held that a former head of state is entitled to immunity "in the absence of any doctrine restricting a head of state's immunity for the type of conduct alleged in the complaint or a denial of immunity from the State Department." Abiola v. Abubakar, 267 F. Supp. 2d 907, 916 (N.D. Ill. 2003). The court reasoned that "the rationale for head-of-state-immunity is no less implicated when a former head of state is sued in a United States court for acts committed while head of state than it is when a sitting head of state is sued." *Id.* Do you agree?

10. In *Zemin*, although it is not very clear from the court of appeals' opinion, the defendant had resigned his presidency while the litigation was pending in the district court. Why was the Executive Branch's suggestion of immunity still binding on the courts after the resignation? Does the suggestion of immunity relate to subject matter jurisdiction, personal jurisdiction, or the merits of the lawsuit? If the defendant had resigned the presidency before the lawsuit was initiated, would an Executive suggestion of immunity still have been binding? That is, does the Executive Branch have the authority to issue binding suggestions of immunity for former heads of state? If so, are there any limits on this authority?

11. Head-of-state immunity is governed on the international plane by customary international law. As discussed in Section A, some commentators have argued that customary international law has the status of federal common law that applies in U.S. courts even in the absence of political branch authorization. What do the head-of-state immunity decisions suggest about the status of customary international law in U.S. courts? By looking for Executive Branch authorization for head-of-state immunity, are courts implying that they lack independent authority to convert customary international law into federal law?

12. In a case that received worldwide attention, the British House of Lords held in 1999 that the former president of Chile, Augusto Pinochet, was not entitled to immunity from criminal extradition proceedings relating to charges of torture. The House of Lords decision is difficult to summarize, since, as is typical, each of the Law Lords issued their own opinion. A majority of the Law Lords, however, appeared to conclude that whatever customary international law immunity Pinochet possessed with respect to acts of torture had impliedly been abrogated in 1988 by a treaty outlawing torture. *See* Regina v. Bow Street Magistrate, Ex parte Pinochet, [1999] 2 W.L.R. 827 (H.L.). Note that most of these Law Lords indicated that they would have granted Pinochet immunity even on the post-1988 charges of torture if he had still been a sitting head of state. Should sitting heads of state be entitled to absolute immunity? Even with respect to the most serious human rights violations? Conversely, should heads of state lose their absolute immunity once they are out of office? What incentives might such an immunity regime create? Does the reasoning of the *Pinochet* decision support or undermine international human rights litigation in U.S. courts?

13. In 2002, the International Court of Justice issued an important decision concerning official immunity. *See* Case Concerning the Arrest Warrant of 11 April 2000 (Democratic Republic of the Congo v. Belgium), 41 I.L.M. 536 (2002). In that case, an investigating judge in Belgium had issued an arrest warrant directed at Congo's Minister for Foreign Affairs, charging him with war crimes and crimes against humanity. The warrant was based on a controversial Belgian statute allowing for "universal jurisdiction" over certain egregious violations of international law committed anywhere in the world. (The universal jurisdiction basis for prescriptive jurisdiction is discussed in Chapter 8.) The International Court of Justice held that Belgium had violated Congo's rights under customary international law by issuing the arrest warrant.

The Court began by noting that "in international law it is firmly established that, as also diplomatic and consular agents, certain holders of high-ranking office in a State, such as the Head of a State, Head of Government and Minister for Foreign Affairs, enjoy immunities from jurisdiction in other States, both civil and criminal." *Id*. at 549. The Court next examined the functions of a Minister of Foreign Affairs and concluded that these functions were such that "throughout the duration of his or her office, [a Minister of Foreign Affairs] when abroad enjoys full immunity from criminal jurisdiction and inviolability." *Id*. at 550. The Court rejected any distinction for these purposes between acts performed in an official capacity and acts performed in a personal capacity, reasoning that "[t]he consequences of such impediment to the exercise of [the Minister's] official functions are equally serious" regardless of whether the official is charged in his or her official or personal capacity. *Id*.

The Court further held that the Minister's immunity extended even to charges of war crimes and crimes against humanity. The Court considered state practice and the decisions of national courts, including the *Pinochet* decision, as well as treaties establishing international criminal tribunals, and said that it was "unable to deduce from this practice that there exists under customary international law any form of exception to the rule according immunity from criminal jurisdiction and inviolability to incumbent Ministers for Foreign Affairs, where they are suspected of having committed war crimes or crimes against humanity." *Id*. at 551. In reasoning at odds with some of the reasoning in the *Pinochet* decision, the Court also noted that the existence of treaties calling for the extension of national jurisdiction over international crimes "in no way affects immunities under customary international law." *Id*. The Court's decision may be distinguishable from the *Pinochet* decision, however, in that it involved the immunity of a *sitting* Minister, whereas *Pinochet* involved the immunity of a *former* head of state. Indeed, the Court specifically observed that a foreign state could prosecute a former Minister for acts "committed . . . in a private capacity" without violating the former Minister's immunity. *Id*. at 552.

What implications, if any, does the International Court's decision have for U.S. law concerning head-of-state immunity? For suits brought under the FSIA against individual officials?

14. In recent years, an increasing number of international human rights claims have been directed against the U.S. government and its officials. The U.S. government is immune from suit in U.S. courts, however, except to the extent that it has waived its immunity. Moreover, courts have held that any waiver of immunity must be explicit. The U.S. government's waiver of immunity for tort claims is set forth in the Federal Tort Claims Act (FTCA), 28 U.S.C. §1346(b)(1), §§2671-2680. This waiver is subject to procedural requirements (such as exhaustion of administrative remedies) and various exceptions. The exceptions include the retention of immunity for "[a]ny claim arising in a foreign country." 28 U.S.C. §2680(k). In Sosa v. Alvarez-Machain, the Supreme Court (in a portion of the decision not excerpted above in Section B) rejected a "headquarters doctrine" limitation on this provision that had been adopted by some lower courts, whereby the U.S. government would have been subject to suit for acts or omissions in the United States that caused harm abroad. The FTCA also retains sovereign immunity for (a) "any claim . . . based upon the exercise or performance or the failure to exercise or perform a discretionary function or duty on the part of a federal agency or an employee of the Government, whether or not the discretion be abused," and

(b) "any claim arising out of combatant activities of the military or naval forces, or the Coast Guard, during time of war." 28 U.S.C. §2680(a), (j).

The Federal Employers Liability Reform and Tort Compensation Act of 1988 (also known as the "Westfall Act") further provides that, for civil actions arising out of the wrongful acts of an employee acting within the scope of his or her official duties, the U.S. government is to be substituted as the defendant and the action is to proceed only under the FTCA. *See* 28 U.S.C. §2679(b)(1), (d)(1). Although this provision does not apply to an action "which is brought for a violation of a statute of the United States under which such action against an individual is otherwise authorized," 28 U.S.C. §2679(b)(2)(B), courts have held that the ATS does not constitute such a statute, a holding that appears to be further supported by the Supreme Court's conclusion in *Sosa* that the ATS does not create a cause of action. The TVPA could arguably constitute such a statute, but it applies only to actions taken under color of foreign law and thus is normally inapplicable to actions by the U.S. government and its officials. Suits against the U.S. government and its officials concerning their foreign affairs activities are also particularly likely to implicate the political question doctrine. *See, e.g.*, Schneider v. Kissinger, 310 F. Supp. 2d 251 (D.D.C. 2004) (holding that political question doctrine barred judicial consideration of claims against former National Security Advisor for allegedly having assisted in a failed coup attempt in Chile in 1970); Bancoult v. McNamara, 370 F. Supp. 2d 1 (D.D.C. 2004) (holding that political question doctrine barred judicial consideration of claims against the U.S. government for alleged forcible removal of indigenous population on islands in the Indian Ocean in the 1960s and 1970s).

15. For discussion of the FSIA and head-of-state immunity issues in this section, see David J. Bederman, *Dead Man's Hand: Reshuffling Foreign Sovereign Immunities in U.S. Human Rights Litigation*, 25 Ga. J. Int'l & Comp. L. 255 (1995-1996); Curtis A. Bradley & Jack L. Goldsmith, Pinochet *and International Human Rights Litigation*, 97 Mich. L. Rev. 2129 (1999); Joseph W. Dellapenna, *Head of State Immunity — Foreign Sovereign Immunities Act — Suggestion by the State Department*, 88 Am. J. Int'l L. 528 (1994); Amber Fitzgerald, *The Pinochet Case: Head of State Immunity Within the United States*, 22 Whittier L. Rev. 987 (2001); Jerrold L. Mallory, Note, *Resolving the Confusion Over Head of State Immunity: The Defined Right of Kings*, 86 Colum. L. Rev. 169 (1986); Shobha Varughese George, Note, *Head-of-State Immunity in the United States Courts: Still Confused After All These Years*, 64 Fordham L. Rev. 1051 (1995).

D. HUMAN RIGHTS LITIGATION AGAINST NON-STATE ACTORS

Kadic v. Karadzic

70 F.3d 232 (2d Cir. 1995)

[Croat and Muslim citizens of Bosnia-Herzegovina, formerly a republic of Yugoslavia, sued Radovan Karadzic, the president of a self-proclaimed Bosnian-Serb republic within Bosnia-Herzegovina. Invoking the ATS and the TVPA, the plaintiffs alleged that Karadzic was responsible for acts of genocide, rape, forced prostitution and impregnation, torture and other cruel, inhuman, and degrading treatment, assault and battery, sex and ethnic inequality, summary execution, and wrongful death. They served Karadzic with process when he was in New York as an invitee of the United Nations.]

JON O. NEWMAN, CHIEF JUDGE:

Most Americans would probably be surprised to learn that victims of atrocities committed in Bosnia are suing the leader of the insurgent Bosnian-Serb forces in a United States District Court in Manhattan. Their claims seek to build upon the foundation of this Court's decision in Filartiga v. Pena-Irala, 630 F.2d 876 (2d Cir. 1980), which recognized the important principle that the venerable Alien Tort Act, 28 U.S.C. §1350 (1988), enacted in 1789 but rarely invoked since then, validly creates federal court jurisdiction for suits alleging torts committed anywhere in the world against aliens in violation of the law of nations. The pending appeals pose additional significant issues as to the scope of the Alien Tort Act: whether some violations of the law of nations may be remedied when committed by those not acting under the authority of a state; if so, whether genocide, war crimes, and crimes against humanity are among the violations that do not require state action; and whether a person, otherwise liable for a violation of the law of nations, is immune from service of process because he is present in the United States as an invitee of the United Nations....

Our decision in *Filartiga* established that [the Alien Tort Statute] confers federal subject-matter jurisdiction when the following three conditions are satisfied: (1) an alien sues (2) for a tort (3) committed in violation of the law of nations (i.e., international law). The first two requirements are plainly satisfied here, and the only disputed issue is whether plaintiffs have pleaded violations of international law.

Because the Alien Tort Act requires that plaintiffs plead a "violation of the law of nations" at the jurisdictional threshold, this statute requires a more searching review of the merits to establish jurisdiction than is required under the more flexible "arising under" formula of section 1331. Thus, it is not a sufficient basis for jurisdiction to plead merely a colorable violation of the law of nations. There is no federal subject-matter jurisdiction under the Alien Tort Act unless the complaint adequately pleads a violation of the law of nations (or treaty of the United States)....

Karadzic contends that appellants have not alleged violations of the norms of international law because such norms bind only states and persons acting under color of a state's law, not private individuals. In making this contention, Karadzic advances the contradictory positions that he is not a state actor, see Brief for Appellee at 19, even as he asserts that he is the President of the self-proclaimed Republic of Srpska, see statement of Radovan Karadzic, May 3, 1993, submitted with Defendant's Motion to Dismiss. For their part, the *Kadic* appellants also take somewhat inconsistent positions in pleading defendant's role as President of Srpska, and also contending that "Karadzic is not an official of any government."...

We do not agree [with the district court] that the law of nations, as understood in the modern era, confines its reach to state action. Instead, we hold that certain forms of conduct violate the law of nations whether undertaken by those acting under the auspices of a state or only as private individuals. An early example of the application of the law of nations to the acts of private individuals is the prohibition against piracy.... Later examples are prohibitions against the slave trade and certain war crimes....

Karadzic disputes the application of the law of nations to any violations committed by private individuals, relying on *Filartiga* and the concurring opinion of Judge Edwards in *Tel-Oren*. *Filartiga* involved an allegation of torture committed by a state official. Relying on the United Nations' Declaration on the Protection of All Persons from Being Subjected to Torture, G.A. Res. 3452, U.N. GAOR, U.N. Doc. A/1034 (1975) (hereinafter "Declaration on Torture"), as a definitive statement of norms of customary international law prohibiting states from permitting torture, we ruled that "*official* torture is now prohibited by the law of nations." *Filartiga*, 630 F.2d at 884 (emphasis added). We had no occasion to consider whether international law violations other than torture are actionable against private individuals, and nothing in *Filartiga* purports to preclude such a result.

Nor did Judge Edwards in his scholarly opinion in *Tel-Oren* reject the application of international law to any private action. On the contrary, citing piracy and slave-trading as early examples, he observed that there exists a "handful of crimes to which the law of nations attributes individual responsibility," 726 F.2d at 795. Reviewing authorities similar to those consulted in *Filartiga*, he merely concluded that torture — the specific violation alleged in *Tel-Oren* — was not within the limited category of violations that do not require state action.

Karadzic also contends that Congress intended the state-action requirement of the Torture Victim Act to apply to actions under the Alien Tort Act. We disagree. Congress enacted the Torture Victim Act to codify the cause of action recognized by this Circuit in *Filartiga*, and to further extend that cause of action to plaintiffs who are U.S. citizens. *See* H.R. Rep. No. 367, 102d Cong., 2d Sess., at 4 (1991), *reprinted in* 1992 U.S.C.C.A.N. 84, 86 (explaining that codification of *Filartiga* was necessary in light of skepticism expressed by Judge Bork's concurring opinion in *Tel-Oren*). At the same time, Congress indicated that the Alien Tort Act "has other important uses and should not be replaced," because

> claims based on torture [or] summary executions do not exhaust the list of actions that may appropriately be covered [by the Alien Tort Act]. That statute should remain intact to permit suits based on other norms that already exist or may ripen in the future into rules of customary international law.

Id. The scope of the Alien Tort Act remains undiminished by enactment of the Torture Victim Act....

[I]t will be helpful to group the appellants' claims into three categories: (a) genocide, (b) war crimes, and (c) other instances of inflicting death, torture, and degrading treatment.

(a) Genocide. In the aftermath of the atrocities committed during the Second World War, the condemnation of genocide as contrary to international law quickly achieved broad acceptance by the community of nations. In 1946, the General Assembly of the United Nations declared that genocide is a crime under international law that is condemned by the civilized world, whether the perpetrators are "private individuals, public officials or statesmen." G.A. Res. 96(I), 1 U.N. GAOR, U.N. Doc. A/64/Add.1, at 188-89 (1946). The General Assembly also affirmed the principles of Article 6 of the Agreement and Charter Establishing the Nuremberg War Crimes Tribunal for punishing " 'persecutions on political, racial, or religious grounds,'" regardless of whether the offenders acted "'as individuals or as members of organizations,'" In re Extradition of Demjanjuk, 612 F. Supp. 544, 555 n.11 (N.D. Ohio 1985) (quoting Article 6).

The Convention on the Prevention and Punishment of the Crime of Genocide, 78 U.N.T.S. 277, entered into force Jan. 12, 1951, for the United States Feb. 23, 1989 (hereinafter "Convention on Genocide"), provides a more specific articulation of the prohibition of genocide in international law. The Convention, which has been ratified by more than 120 nations, including the United States, see U.S. Dept. of State, Treaties in Force 345 (1994), defines "genocide" to mean

> any of the following acts committed with intent to destroy, in whole or in part, a national, ethnical, racial or religious group, as such:
>
> (a) Killing members of the group;
>
> (b) Causing serious bodily or mental harm to members of the group;
>
> (c) Deliberately inflicting on the group conditions of life calculated to bring about its physical destruction in whole or in part;
>
> (d) Imposing measures intended to prevent births with the group;
>
> (e) Forcibly transferring children of the group to another group.

Convention on Genocide art. II. Especially pertinent to the pending appeal, the Convention makes clear that "persons committing genocide . . . shall be punished, *whether they are constitutionally responsible rulers, public officials or private individuals.*" *Id*. art. IV (emphasis added). These authorities unambiguously reflect that, from its incorporation into international law, the proscription of genocide has applied equally to state and non-state actors.

The applicability of this norm to private individuals is also confirmed by the Genocide Convention Implementation Act of 1987, 18 U.S.C. §1091 (1988), which criminalizes acts of genocide without regard to whether the offender is acting under color of law, see *id*. §1091(a) ("whoever" commits genocide shall be punished), if the crime is committed within the United States or by a U.S. national, *id*. §1091(d). Though Congress provided that the Genocide Convention Implementation Act shall not "be construed as creating any substantive or procedural right enforceable by law by any party in any proceeding," *id*. §1092, the legislative decision not to create a new private remedy does not imply that a private remedy is not already available under the Alien Tort Act. Nothing in the Genocide Convention Implementation Act or its legislative history reveals an intent by Congress to repeal the Alien Tort Act insofar as it applies to genocide, and the two statutes are surely not repugnant to each other. Under these circumstances, it would be improper to construe the Genocide Convention Implementation Act as repealing the Alien Tort Act by implication.

Appellants' allegations that Karadzic personally planned and ordered a campaign of murder, rape, forced impregnation, and other forms of torture designed to destroy the religious and ethnic groups of Bosnian Muslims and Bosnian Croats clearly state a violation of the international law norm proscribing genocide, regardless of whether Karadzic acted under color of law or as a private individual. The District Court has subject-matter jurisdiction over these claims pursuant to the Alien Tort Act.

(b) War crimes. Plaintiffs also contend that the acts of murder, rape, torture, and arbitrary detention of civilians, committed in the course of hostilities, violate the law of war. Atrocities of the types alleged here have long been recognized in international law as violations of the law of war. Moreover, international law imposes an affirmative duty on military commanders to take appropriate measures within their power to control troops under their command for the prevention of such atrocities.

After the Second World War, the law of war was codified in the four Geneva Conventions, which have been ratified by more than 180 nations, including the United States. Common article 3, which is substantially identical in each of the four Conventions, applies to "armed conflicts not of an international character" and binds "each Party to the conflict...to apply, as a minimum, the following provisions":

> Persons taking no active part in the hostilities...shall in all circumstances be treated humanely, without any adverse distinction founded on race, colour, religion or faith, sex, birth or wealth, or any other similar criteria.
>
> To this end, the following acts are and shall remain prohibited at any time and in any place whatsoever with respect to the above-mentioned persons:
>
> > (a) violence to life and person, in particular murder of all kinds, mutilation, cruel treatment and torture;
>
> > (b) taking of hostages;
>
> > (c) outrages upon personal dignity, in particular humiliating and degrading treatment;
>
> > (d) the passing of sentences and carrying out of executions without previous judgment pronounced by a regularly constituted court....

Geneva Convention I art. 3(1). Thus, under the law of war as codified in the Geneva Conventions, all "parties" to a conflict—which includes insurgent military groups—are obliged to adhere to these most fundamental requirements of the law of war.

The offenses alleged by the appellants, if proved, would violate the most fundamental norms of the law of war embodied in common article 3, which binds parties to internal conflicts regardless of whether they are recognized nations or roving hordes of insurgents. The liability of private individuals for committing war crimes has been recognized since World War I and was confirmed at Nuremberg after World War II, and remains today an important aspect of international law. The District Court has jurisdiction pursuant to the Alien Tort Act over appellants' claims of war crimes and other violations of international humanitarian law.

(c) Torture and summary execution. In *Filartiga*, we held that official torture is prohibited by universally accepted norms of international law, and the Torture Victim Act confirms this holding and extends it to cover summary execution. Torture Victim Act §§2(a), 3(a). However, torture and summary execution—when not perpetrated in the course of genocide or war crimes—are proscribed by international law only when committed by state officials or under color of law.

In the present case, appellants allege that acts of rape, torture, and summary execution were committed during hostilities by troops under Karadzic's command and with the specific intent of destroying appellants' ethnic-religious groups. Thus, many of the alleged atrocities are already encompassed within the appellants' claims of genocide and war crimes. Of course, at this threshold stage in the proceedings it cannot be known whether appellants will be able to prove the specific intent that is an element of genocide, or prove that each of the alleged torts were committed in the course of an armed conflict, as required to establish war crimes. It suffices to hold at this stage that the alleged atrocities are actionable under the Alien Tort Act, without regard to state action, to the extent that they were committed in pursuit of genocide or war crimes, and otherwise may be pursued against Karadzic to the extent that he is shown to be a state actor. Since the meaning of the state action requirement for purposes of international law violations will likely arise on remand and has already been considered by the District Court, we turn next to that requirement....

In dismissing plaintiffs' complaints for lack of subject-matter jurisdiction, the District Court concluded that the alleged violations required state action and that the "Bosnian-Serb entity" headed by Karadzic does not meet the definition of a state. Appellants contend that they are entitled to prove that Srpska satisfies the definition of a state for purposes of international law violations and, alternatively, that Karadzic acted in concert with the recognized state of the former Yugoslavia and its constituent republic, Serbia.

(a) Definition of a state in international law. The definition of a state is well established in international law:

> Under international law, a state is an entity that has a defined territory and a permanent population, under the control of its own government, and that engages in, or has the capacity to engage in, formal relations with other such entities.

Restatement (Third) §201.

Although the Restatement's definition of statehood requires the capacity to engage in formal relations with other states, it does not require recognition by other states. Recognized states enjoy certain privileges and immunities relevant to judicial proceedings, see, e.g., Pfizer Inc. v. India, 434 U.S. 308, 318-20 (1978) (diversity jurisdiction); Banco Nacional de Cuba v. Sabbatino, 376 U.S. 398, 408-12 (1964) (access to U.S. courts); Lafontant, 844 F. Supp. at 131 (head-of-state immunity), but an unrecognized state is not a juridical nullity. Our courts have regularly given effect to the "state" action of unrecognized states....

The customary international law of human rights, such as the proscription of official torture, applies to states without distinction between recognized and unrecognized states. It would be anomalous indeed if non-recognition by the United States, which typically reflects disfavor with a foreign regime—sometimes due to human rights abuses—had the perverse effect of shielding officials of the unrecognized regime from liability for those violations of international law norms that apply only to state actors.

Appellants' allegations entitle them to prove that Karadzic's regime satisfies the criteria for a state, for purposes of those international law violations requiring state action. Srpska is alleged to control defined territory, control populations within its power, and to have entered into agreements with other governments. It has a president, a legislature, and its own currency. These circumstances readily appear to satisfy the criteria for a state in all aspects of international law. Moreover, it is likely that the state action concept, where applicable for some violations like "official" torture, requires merely the semblance of official authority. The inquiry, after all, is whether a person purporting to wield official power has exceeded internationally recognized standards of civilized conduct, not whether statehood in all its formal aspects exists.

(b) Acting in concert with a foreign state. Appellants also sufficiently alleged that Karadzic acted under color of law insofar as they claimed that he acted in concert with the former Yugoslavia, the statehood of which is not disputed. The "color of law" jurisprudence of 42 U.S.C. §1983 is a relevant guide to whether a defendant has engaged in official action for purposes of jurisdiction under the Alien Tort Act. A private individual acts under color of law within the meaning of section 1983 when he acts together with state officials or with significant state aid. *See* Lugar v. Edmondson Oil Co., 457 U.S. 922, 937 (1982). The appellants are entitled to prove their allegations that Karadzic acted under color of law of Yugoslavia by acting in concert with Yugoslav officials or with significant Yugoslavian aid.

In re South African Apartheid Litigation

346 F. Supp. 2d 538 (S.D.N.Y. 2004)

[This case involved class action lawsuits brought against multinational corporations that did business in South Africa during that country's racially discriminatory and repressive apartheid regime.]

SPRIZZO, DISTRICT JUDGE....

Plaintiffs have alleged a veritable cornucopia of international law violations, including forced labor, genocide, torture, sexual assault, unlawful detention, extra-judicial killings, war crimes, and racial discrimination. Plaintiffs link defendants to these alleged international law violations in three ways. Plaintiffs contend that defendants engaged in state action by acting under color of law in perpetrating these international law violations, that defendants aided and abetted the apartheid regime in the commission of these violations, and that defendants' business activities alone are sufficient to make out an international law violation.

Although it is clear that the actions of the apartheid regime were repugnant, and that the decisions of the defendants to do business with that regime may have been morally suspect or "embarrassing," it is this Court's job to apply the law and not some normative or moral ideal... Given the [Supreme] Court's ruling in *Sosa*, as well as the Second Circuit's decision in [Flores v. Southern Peru Copper, 343 F.3d 140 (2d Cir. 2003)], it is clear that none of the theories pleaded by plaintiffs support jurisdiction under the ATCA.

First, it is plain from relevant Second Circuit authority that plaintiffs have not pleaded facts that would allow this Court to find that defendants engaged in state action by acting under color of law in perpetrating the complained-of acts. In Bigio v. Coca-Cola Co., 239 F.3d 440 (2d Cir. 2001), the Court explained that state action under the ATCA, which is derived from the color of law requirement of 42 U.S.C. §1983, required that a private individual "'act[] together with state officials or with significant state aid.'" *Bigio*, 239 F.3d at 448 (quoting Kadic v. Karadzic, 70 F.3d 232, 245 (2d Cir. 1995)).

The *Bigio* Court found that Coca-Cola did not act under color of law when it purchased property that it knew the Egyptian government had seized from Jewish landowners. The Court concluded that "an indirect economic benefit from unlawful state action is not sufficient" to establish state action.

Here, plaintiffs do not allege actions by the defendants that elevate them to the status of state actors in the commission of torture, genocide, killings, and other serious crimes. At most, by engaging in business with the South African regime, defendants benefited from the unlawful state action of the apartheid government....

Because this Court does not find state action, it need not consider whether the actions of the apartheid regime violated the law of nations so as to support jurisdiction under the ATCA.

Because defendants did not engage in state action, plaintiffs will need to show that either aiding and abetting international law violations or doing business in apartheid South Africa are violations of the law of nations that are "accepted by the civilized world and defined with a specificity comparable to the features of the 18th-century paradigms" such as piracy and crimes against ambassadors. *Sosa*, 124 S. Ct. at 2761-62.

The Second Circuit has described the standard as a violation of "those rules that States universally abide by, or accede to, out of a sense of legal obligation and mutual concern." *Flores*, 343 F.3d at 154. The *Flores* Court stressed the requirement that the norm be a legal obligation, and not acceded to merely for moral or political reasons. *Id.* at 154. Also, the norm must be sufficiently definite and not so general as to be simply "aspirational." *Id.*

Plaintiffs here point to little that would lead this Court to conclude that aiding and abetting international law violations is itself an international law violation that is universally accepted as a legal obligation. Plaintiffs point to the International Criminal Tribunals for the former Yugoslavia, ICTY STAT. art. 7(1), and Rwanda, ICTR STAT. art 6(1), respectively, the Nuremberg trials, the International Convention on the Suppression and Punishment of the Crime of Apartheid ("Apartheid Convention"), November 30, 1973, art. I, 1015 U.N.T.S. 243, 245, and this Court's ruling in Presbyterian Church of Sudan v. Talisman Energy, Inc., 244 F. Supp. 2d 289 (S.D.N.Y. 2003). None of these sources establishes a clearly-defined norm for ATCA purposes.

The International Criminal Tribunals and rulings pursuant thereto, besides dealing with criminal and not civil matters, are not binding sources of international law. *See* Flores, 343 F.3d at 169-70. The same applies for the Nuremberg trials. The Apartheid Convention, which similarly dealt with the criminal repercussions for aiding apartheid, was not ratified by a number of major world powers, including the United States, Great Britain, Germany, France, Canada, and Japan. Without the backing of so many major world powers, the Apartheid Convention is not binding international law. *See Flores*, 343 F.3d at 163 n.33.

Finally, this Court declines the invitation to follow the lead of *Presbyterian Church* in finding that aider and abettor liability is recognized under the ATCA. This is especially true since the applicability of that concept in a civil context is dubious at best.

In Central Bank of Denver v. First Interstate Bank of Denver, 511 U.S. 164 (1994), the Supreme Court, in dealing with the issue of aiding and abetting in the civil context, stated that the concept was "at best uncertain in application." Therefore, the Court held that where Congress has not explicitly provided for aider and abettor liability in civil causes of action, it should not be inferred. The Court reasoned that in the context of Rule 10b-5 actions, allowing aider and abettor liability would only serve to compound the problems that already existed with the cause of action, including vexatious litigation and strike suits. . . .

Central Bank applies with special force here. Although the ATCA points to international law for the causes of action over which it grants jurisdiction, the ATCA presently does not provide for aider and abettor liability, and this Court will not write it into the statute. In refusing to do so, this Court finds this approach to be heedful of the admonition in Sosa that Congress should be deferred to with respect to innovative interpretations of that statute.

This conclusion is strengthened by the policies behind *Central Bank* and is in accord with the framework announced by *Sosa*. To allow for expanded liability, without congressional mandate, in an area that is so ripe for non-meritorious and blunderbuss suits would be an abdication of this Court's duty to engage in "vigilant doorkeeping." *Sosa*, 124 S. Ct. at 2764...

This Court is also mindful of the collateral consequences and possible foreign relations repercussions that would result from allowing courts in this country to hear civil suits for the aiding and abetting of violations of international norms across the globe. To do so would not be consistent with the "restrained conception" of new international law violations that the Supreme Court has mandated for the lower federal courts.

The final possible basis upon which to ground ATCA jurisdiction here is the theory that defendants violated the law of nations by doing business in apartheid South Africa. Although plaintiffs repeatedly indicated that "this lawsuit is not about whether a company can do business with a repressive regime," plaintiffs' complaints are almost solely composed of allegations of defendants' business activities within South Africa and the consequences that flowed therefrom.

Plaintiffs have pointed to a multitude of sources that they claim establishes that doing business with the apartheid regime was a violation of the law of nations. Plaintiffs rely on several treaties — the U.N. Charter, the Convention on the Prevention and Punishment of the Crime of Genocide ("Genocide Convention"), the Convention Against Torture and Other Cruel, Inhuman or Degrading Treatment or Punishment ("Convention Against Torture"), the International Covenant on Civil and Political Rights ("ICCPR"), and the Apartheid Convention — as well as a number of General Assembly and Security Council declarations and resolutions and the Restatement (Third) of Foreign Relations Law.

Although treaties that set forth definite rules and enjoy overwhelming acceptance and adherence are valid sources of international norms for ATCA purposes, the treaties relied on by plaintiffs suffer from a number of defects that preclude findings that any of them provide applicable customary international law.

Although the Genocide Convention and the Convention Against Torture, which prohibit "acts committed with intent to destroy, in whole or in part, a national, ethnical, racial or religious group," Genocide Convention, art. 2, and "any act by which severe pain or suffering, whether physical or mental, is intentionally inflicted on a person...for any reason based on discrimination of any kind," Convention Against Torture, art. 1, respectively, may apply to the acts undertaken by the apartheid regime itself, they nonetheless do not describe the actions undertaken by defendants here. While both punish complicity in engaging in such acts, both conventions are criminal in nature, and neither is self-executing. *See* Genocide Convention, art. 5; Convention Against Torture, (declaring that United States deems articles one through sixteen not to be self-executing). Therefore, there is no private liability under the treaties in United States courts. It follows that no liability based upon any alleged violation of these norms can form an adequate predicate for jurisdiction under the ATCA.

The ICCPR, which the United States also deemed not to be self-executing, see *Sosa*, 124 S. Ct. at 2767, deals primarily with ensuring that state actors do not violate the rights of their citizens. For example, the ICCPR proclaims that "each State

Party to the present Covenant undertakes to respect and to ensure to all individuals within its territory and subject to its jurisdiction the rights recognized in the present Covenant," ICCPR, art. 2, which include the right not to be enslaved, art. 8, the right to be free from arbitrary detention, art. 9, and the right to be equal before the law, art. 26. Again, although these provisions may apply to the apartheid regime, they do not apply to the actions of defendants.

The other authorities relied on by plaintiffs simply do not create binding international law. As stated earlier, the Apartheid Convention, not having been adopted by most world powers, did not create binding international law actionable under the ATCA. The UN Charter, General Assembly resolutions, and the Declaration of Human Rights ("Declaration") are also insufficient for that purpose.

The UN Charter and the Declaration speak in broad aspirational language that does not meet the specificity required under the ATCA. For example, the Declaration advances a number of the ideals later set forth in the treaties that plaintiffs rely upon, see arts. 4, 5, 7, 9 (prohibiting slavery, torture, discrimination, and arbitrary arrest), as well as the goal of "equal pay for equal work," see art. 23. The Declaration, however, creates no legal obligations, and the language cited above, which could arguably be applied to defendants here, is simply not specific enough to create binding legal rules....

General Assembly resolutions are similarly not valid sources of international law. *See Flores*, 343 F.3d at 165. Although the UN repeatedly condemned apartheid, it simply does not have the power to legally bind member states. The only binding sanction passed by the UN was an embargo that prohibited all states from exporting arms to the apartheid regime. Moreover, like the treaties discussed above, this Security Council resolution simply does not apply to defendants.

The only materials that plaintiffs cite that even apply to defendants are a series of General Assembly resolutions that "condemn []...transnational corporations and financial institutions that have increased political, economic and military collaboration with the racist minority regime of South Africa." ... Despite the strong rhetoric, these resolutions simply recommend that nations pass legislation that will cut off the apartheid regime from the rest of the world. They do not impose binding legal obligations.

Even if this Court were swayed by the non-binding General Assembly resolutions calling for an end to defendants' business activities in South Africa, it is clear from history and from the factors announced by the Court in *Sosa*, and discussed above, that the opinions expressed by these resolutions never matured into customary international law actionable under the ATCA.

Moreover, as *Sosa* points out, this Court must be aware of the collateral consequences that would result from finding a new international law violation that would support ATCA jurisdiction. In this case, those consequences are not only far-reaching but would raise the prospect of serious impediments to the flow of international commerce. Indeed, the South African government has indicated that it does not support this litigation and that it believes that allowing this action to proceed would preempt the ability of the government to handle domestic matters and would discourage needed investment in the South African economy. Similarly, the United States government has expressed its belief that the adjudication of this suit would cause tension between the United States and South Africa and would serve to hamper the policy of encouraging positive change in developing countries via economic investment. As the *Sosa* Court made clear, these opinions as to the foreign relations consequences of this action certainly deserve great weight. *See*

Sosa, 124 S. Ct. at 2766 n.21 (mentioning this case specifically and stating that "in such cases, there is a strong argument that federal courts should give serious weight to the Executive Branch's view of the case's impact on foreign policy").

In a world where many countries may fall considerably short of ideal economic, political, and social conditions, this Court must be extremely cautious in permitting suits here based upon a corporation's doing business in countries with less than stellar human rights records, especially since the consequences of such an approach could have significant, if not disastrous, effects on international commerce. Moreover, to infer such causes of action under the ATCA would expand precipitously the jurisdiction of the federal courts and would not be consistent with the "extraordinary care and restraint" that this Court must exercise in recognizing new violations of customary international law.

Finally, far from there being a congressional mandate to recognize a cause of action here, history indicates that Congress, consistent with most other world powers, supported and encouraged business investment in apartheid South Africa. The Comprehensive Anti-Apartheid Act of 1986, 100 Stat. 1086, placed a minimal amount of restrictions on business activities with South Africa. This policy of constructive engagement was similar to the policies of many of the world powers at the time. . . . As the government makes clear in this case, the United States still relies on the tool of economic investment as a means to achieve greater respect for human rights and a reduction in poverty in developing countries. Therefore, under the framework set forth by the Court in *Sosa*, this Court finds that doing business in apartheid South Africa is not a violation of international law that would support jurisdiction in federal court under the ATCA. . . .

The Torture Victim Protection Act of 1991 ("TVPA"), 28 U.S.C. §1350 note, establishes a civil action against an "individual who, under actual or apparent authority, or color of law, of any foreign nation"subjects another to "torture" or "extrajudicial killing." In order to hear an action under this provision, the Court must be satisfied that plaintiff has exhausted all remedies in the place where the conduct occurred.

Here, defendants did not engage in torture or extrajudicial killings. Because this is abundantly clear, Digwamaje plaintiffs rely on the concept of aider and abettor liability to make the necessary connection between defendants and the prohibited conduct. Plaintiffs . . . look to [Wiwa v. Royal Dutch Petroleum Co., 2002 U.S. Dist. LEXIS 3293, No. 96 Civ. 8386, 2002 WL 319887, at *15-16 (S.D.N.Y. Feb. 28, 2002)] for support. . . .

This Court believes that *Wiwa* is distinguishable. In *Wiwa*, defendants were found to be acting under color of law in the perpetration of torture and extrajudicial killings. Here, defendants were not acting under color of law. Since a prerequisite to TVPA liability is that the individual be acting under color of law, this Court finds that creating aider and abettor liability for private actors not acting under color of law would be inconsistent with the statute and precluded by *Central Bank*.

Notes and Questions

1. Unlike governments and officials, non-state actors typically are not entitled to sovereign immunity defenses. (Under some circumstances, however, private U.S. government contractors may be able to benefit from the U.S. government's immunity. *See* Boyle v. United Technologies Corp., 487 U.S. 500 (1988).) It is also likely to be easier to collect a monetary judgment against a non-state actor than against a state actor, especially if the non-state actor is a corporation that has assets in the United States. Before *Karadzic*, however, there were few lawsuits brought against corporations based on international human rights law, in part because it was thought that most human rights norms could be violated only by state actors.

The *Karadzic* decision opened up the possibility of bringing human rights suits against non-state actors, either on the theory that they can themselves violate international human rights law or on the theory that their involvement with foreign government actors renders their conduct state action. Is this a legitimate extension of *Filartiga*? Is it justified on the basis of the ATS? On the basis of customary international law? Why did international law traditionally focus on state actors? Why were there exceptions to this state action requirement for pirates and slave traders? What criteria does the court in *Karadzic* use for identifying international law rules that regulate private behavior? For identifying when a non-state actor is engaged in state action?

2. The Convention on the Prevention and Punishment of the Crime of Genocide, which the United States ratified in 1989, defines the crime of genocide, extends the prohibition on genocide to non-state actors, and requires signatories to prosecute or extradite certain offenders found within their territories. The Genocide Convention Implementation Act ("GCIA"), 18 U.S.C. §1091 (1988), implements these obligations in the United States, but makes clear that the Act shall not "be construed as creating any substantive or procedural right enforceable by law by any party in any proceeding."*Id.* at §1092. What does the court in *Karadzic* mean when it says that the GCIA does not repeal the ATS by implication? What is the court assuming about the cause of action in ATS cases? Even if the GCIA does not implicitly repeal the ATS, isn't it relevant in determining whether Congress authorized the implication of a private civil cause of action for genocide under the ATS?

3. On September 25, 2000, a jury awarded the plaintiffs in the *Karadzic* case $4.5 billion in damages. As in many international human rights cases in U.S. courts, the plaintiffs have little prospect of recovering this award. Does this mean the case was a waste of time? After the verdict, one of the plaintiffs said that the case "was not about monetary damages, but about gaining recognition of the acts committed by Bosnian Serb ultra-nationalists." The jury foreman added: "I hope the world gets the message.... What happened was reprehensible." David Rohde, *Jury in New York Orders Bosnian Serb to Pay Billions*, N.Y. Times, Sept. 26, 2000, at A10. Will unenforceable jury verdicts awarded in U.S. courts in fact achieve these ends? Are these appropriate ends to pursue in federal courts?

4. Since *Karadzic*, numerous lawsuits have been brought under the ATS against private corporations, from the United States and abroad, with respect to alleged human rights and environmental abuses committed in foreign countries. In addition to the South Africa apartheid decision excerpted above, see, for example, Doe I v. Unocal, 395 F.3d 932 (9th Cir. 2002) (suit by Burmese villagers against oil companies for alleged use of slave labor); Flores v. Southern Peru Copper Corp., 343 F.3d 140 (2d Cir. 2003) (suit by residents of Peru concerning environmental pollution from mining and refinery operations in Peru by a company that was incorporated in the United States but had its principal place of business in Peru); and Wiwa v. Royal Dutch Petroleum Co., 226 F.3d 88 (2d Cir. 2000) (suit by Nigerians against non-U.S. corporation for alleged human rights abuses in Nigeria).

5. The court in *Karadzic* acknowledged that, except for a few offenses such as genocide and war crimes, customary international law is violated only by governmental conduct. *See also, e.g.*, Bigio v. Coca-Cola Co., 239 F.3d 440, 448 (2d Cir. 2000). When should conduct by private individuals or corporations be treated as governmental conduct for purposes of international law? In attempting to answer this question, courts have relied on decisions considering whether private parties are acting under "color of law" for purposes of the U.S. civil rights statute, 42 U.S.C. §1983. Although these Section 1983 decisions use a variety of tests and are not entirely consistent, in general they hold that "[a] private individual acts under 'color of law' within the meaning of section 1983 when he acts together with state officials or with significant state aid." Doe v. Unocal Corp., 110 F. Supp. 2d 1294, 1305 (C.D. Cal. 2000). Are these decisions a proper source of guidance on this issue?

6. Because corporations generally do not participate directly in human rights abuses, a central question is whether and to what extent corporations can be held liable in human rights lawsuits for aiding and abetting governmental abuses. What does *Sosa* suggest about whether aiding and abetting claims can be brought under the ATS? What are the implications of footnote 20 of the Court's opinion, in which the Court states that one consideration in deciding whether to find a cause of action in an ATS case "is whether international law extends the scope of liability for a violation of a given norm to the perpetrator being sued, if the defendant is a private actor such as a corporation or individual"?

Before *Sosa*, the Ninth Circuit had addressed the issue of corporate aiding and abetting liability in Doe I v. Unocal Corp., 395 F.3d 932 (9th Cir. 2002). In that case, various plaintiffs from Myanmar (formerly Burma) sued Unocal Corporation and others under the ATS, alleging violations of international law stemming from forced labor, rape, and torture perpetrated by the Myanmar military in connection with the construction of a gas pipeline in Myanmar. The Ninth Circuit concluded that the standard for whether Unocal aided and abetted the Myanmar military's human rights abuses was whether Unocal provided "knowing practical assistance or encouragement that has a substantial effect on the perpetration of the crime." The court went on to hold that a reasonable factfinder could conclude that Unocal's conduct met this standard. The Ninth Circuit subsequently decided to rehear this case *en banc*. After holding oral argument, the Ninth Circuit stayed the issuance of its decision in order to wait for the Supreme Court's decision in *Sosa*. After *Sosa*, the parties filed supplemental briefs, and the U.S. government filed an *amicus curiae* brief arguing that the Ninth Circuit should not recognize an aiding and abetting cause of action under the ATS. The parties subsequently entered into a settlement agreement resolving the case, so no decision was issued by the Ninth Circuit. For another pre-*Sosa* decision endorsing the idea of corporate aiding and abetting liability under the ATS, see Presbyterian Church of Sudan v. Talisman Energy, Inc., 244 F. Supp. 2d 289 (S.D.N.Y. 2004).

7. In opposing ATS aiding and abetting liability in *Unocal*, the Justice Department argued that "the creation of civil aiding and abetting liability is a legislative act that the courts should not undertake without a conclusion that Congress so intended, and there is no indication in either the language or history of the ATS that Congress intended such a vast expansion of suits in this sensitive foreign policy area." Is this persuasive? Given that the ATS is merely a jurisdictional statute that does not itself create causes of action, aren't *all* causes of action under the ATS, in a sense, "legislative"? And could Congress have intended *any* of the modern international human rights lawsuits? If not, can congressional intent be the test in determining which modern claims can be brought in ATS cases? On the other hand, would allowing aiding and abetting liability be consistent with the cautious approach to ATS litigation suggested by the Court in *Sosa*?

8. Even before *Unocal*, the Executive Branch had expressed concern about particular corporate ATS cases. For example, in an ATS suit against Exxon Mobil Corporation for alleged human rights abuses in Indonesia, the court invited the State Department to express a non-binding opinion about whether the suit would adversely affect U.S. interests. In response to this invitation, the State Department submitted a letter to the court (which was conveyed by the Justice Department) stating that it believed that adjudicating the lawsuit at this time would "risk a potentially serious adverse impact on significant interests of the United States, including interests relating directly to the on-going struggle against terrorism" and could "diminish [the United States'] ability to work with the Government of Indonesia (GOI) on a variety of important programs, including efforts to promote human rights in Indonesia." Letter from William H. Taft, IV, Legal Adviser to the Department of State, to Judge Louis F. Oberdorfer, July 29, 2002. What weight should a court give to such a letter? What does *Sosa* suggest?

As the Supreme Court noted in *Sosa*, the State Department also had the Justice Department convey a letter to the court in the South African apartheid case. That letter stated, among other things, that the litigation "risks potentially serious adverse consequences for significant interests of the United States." Letter from William H. Taft, IV to Shannen W. Coffin, Deputy Attorney General, Oct. 27, 2003. *See also* Letter from William H. Taft, IV to Honorable Robert D. McCallum, Assistant Attorney General, Oct. 31, 2001 (expressing concern about suit against corporations for allegedly acting in concert with government of Papua New Guinea in causing environmental harm and human rights abuses).

9. In the South Africa apartheid decision, excerpted above, the court rejects a cause of action in ATS cases for corporate aiding and abetting. Does the court properly apply *Sosa*? Does it properly apply the *Central Bank* decision that it discusses concerning aiding and abetting liability for securities fraud? Does the court persuasively distinguish the international criminal law materials that recognize aiding and abetting liability? Is there a stronger case for aiding and abetting liability under the TVPA than under the ATS? Did the court need to completely reject aiding and abetting liability in order to find for the defendants? Should corporations ever be liable for knowingly facilitating governmental human rights abuses? What if a corporation specifically asked a foreign government to commit the abuses — for example, in order to stop protesters from disrupting a construction project? At that point, would the corporation be so directly involved that aiding and abetting liability would be unnecessary? *See also* Doe v. Exxon Mobil Corp., 2005 U.S. Dist. LEXIS 23557 D.D.C. Oct. 14, 2005 (rejecting aiding and abetting liability).

10. Another important decision involving the issue of corporate liability under the ATS is Flores v. Southern Peru Copper, 343 F.3d 140 (2d Cir. 2003), which is referred to in the South Africa apartheid decision. In that case, a group of Peruvian citizens brought personal injury claims under the ATS against a U.S. company, Southern Peru Copper, arguing that the company's copper mining, refining, and smelting operations in Peru had caused the plaintiffs or their decedents severe lung disease. Southern Peru's conduct, argued the plaintiffs, violated customary international law by infringing upon their "right to life," "right to health," and right to "sustainable development."

In upholding the dismissal of the plaintiffs' claims, the Second Circuit began by reviewing the case law since *Filartiga*, and the controversy and uncertainties associated with that decision, and stated: "[N]either Congress nor the Supreme Court has definitively resolved the complex and controversial decisions regarding the meaning of the ATCA. Whatever the differing perspectives among jurists and scholars — differences that ultimately can be resolved only by Congress or the Supreme Court — *Filartiga* remains the law of this Circuit, and we analyze plaintiffs' claims under the framework set forth in that case and its progeny." The court then explained that, in order for a principle to become a rule of customary international law, states must universally abide by it; it must be followed out of a sense of legal obligation; and it must be of mutual concern between states and not merely a matter "in which States are separately and independently interested." The purported international law rule must also, said the court, be "clear and unambiguous."

Applying this framework, the court reasoned that the purported rights to life and health were too indefinite to constitute rules of customary international law. The court also concluded, after considering a variety of treaties, nonbinding resolutions and declarations, and decisions of international tribunals, that there was no international law right against intranational pollution. In doing so, the court emphasized, among other things, that the United Nations General Assembly does not have the authority to create enforceable legal obligations. The court also declined to give weight to affidavits submitted by several international law scholars that asserted that there was a right against intranational pollution, noting that "although scholars may provide accurate descriptions of the *actual* customs and practices and legal obligations of States, only the courts may determine whether these customs and practices give rise to a rule of customary international law."

This decision predated *Sosa*. How does it compare with the Supreme Court's approach to the cause of action asserted in *Sosa*? Is it, as the court in the South Africa apartheid decision implies, complementary to the approach outlined in *Sosa*?

11. Detainees at the Guantanamo Bay naval base have sued various U.S. military and civilian officials under the ATS for alleged torture and other mistreatment. In Rasul v. Bush, 542 U.S. 466 (2004), which as discussed in Chapter 4 held that U.S. courts could hear habeas corpus challenges filed on behalf of the Guantanamo detainees, the Supreme Court observed near the end of its opinion that aliens detained in military custody are not categorically excluded from the "privilege of litigation" in U.S. courts, and it noted that the ATS "explicitly confers the privilege of suing for an actionable 'tort . . . committed in violation of the law of nations or a treaty of the United States' on aliens alone." What obstacles are the detainees likely to face in their ATS suits?

12. For additional discussion of human rights litigation against corporations and other non-state actors, see, for example, Kathryn L. Boyd, *Collective Rights Adjudication in U.S. Courts: Enforcing Human Rights at the Corporate Level*, 1999 B.Y.U.L. Rev. 1139; Armin Rosencranz & Richard Campbell, *Foreign Environmental and Human Rights Suits Against U.S. Corporations in U.S. Courts*, 18 Stan. Envtl. L.J. 145 (1999); Beth Stephens, *The Amorality of Profit: Transnational Corporations and Human Rights*, 20 Berkeley J. Int'l L. 45 (2002); *Developments in the Law: Corporate Liability for Violations of International Human Rights Law*, 114 Harv. L. Rev. 2025 (2001).

E. CIVIL SUITS RELATING TO TERRORISM

Boim v. Quranic Literacy Institute

291 F.3d 1000 (7th Cir. 2002)

[Mr. and Mrs. Boim sued the Quranic Literacy Institute ("QLI") and the Holy Land Foundation for Relief and Development ("HLF"), alleging that these nonprofit organizations raised and funneled money to the Hamas terrorist organization, which murdered their son David in Israel. The Boims sought to recover damages under 18 U.S.C. §2333, which provides, in relevant part:

> Any national of the United States injured in his or her person, property, or business by reason of an act of international terrorism, or his or her estate, survivors, or heirs, may sue therefor in any appropriate district court of the United States and shall recover threefold the damages he or she sustains and the cost of the suit, including attorney's fees.

"International terrorism" is in turn defined as activities that:

> (A) involve violent acts or acts dangerous to human life that are a violation of the criminal laws of the United States or of any State, or that would be a criminal violation if committed within the jurisdiction of the United States or of any State;
> (B) appear to be intended —
>
>> (i) to intimidate or coerce a civilian population;
>>
>> (ii) to influence the policy of a government by intimidation or coercion; or
>>
>> (iii) to affect the conduct of a government by assassination or kidnapping;
> and
>
>> (C) occur primarily outside the territorial jurisdiction of the United States, or transcend national boundaries in terms of the means by which they are accomplished, the persons they appear intended to intimidate or coerce, or the locale in which their perpetrators operate or seek asylum.

18 U.S.C. §2331(1).]

ROVNER, CIRCUIT JUDGE. . . .

The plaintiffs' first theory is that the simple provision of funds to Hamas by QLI and HLF constitutes an act of international terrorism because it "involves violent acts or acts dangerous to human life." The Boims liken payments to Hamas to murder for hire: the person who pays for the murder does not himself commit a violent act, but the payment "involves" violent acts in the sense that it brings about the violent act and provides an incentive for someone else to commit it. The Boims urge us to adopt a very broad definition of "involves" that would include any activity that touches on and supports a violent act. They argue that David's murder was indisputably a violent act, and we have no quarrel with that premise. But they further argue that the provision of money or in-kind services to persons outside the country who set up the infrastructure used to recruit and train David's murderers, buy their weapons, and compensate their families also "involves" violent acts. The defendants, in turn, urge us to read the statute to hold liable only those who actually commit a violent act.

No court has yet considered the meaning or scope of sections 2331 and 2333, and so we write upon a tabula rasa. The starting point in all statutory analysis is the plain language of the statute itself. We look to the language in order to determine what Congress intended, and we also look to the statute's structure, subject matter, context and history for this same purpose. The controversy here centers on the definition of international terrorism, and in particular on the definition of the word "involve," which is susceptible to many meanings. The statutory definition of international terrorism in section 2331(1) is drawn *verbatim* from the Foreign Intelligence Surveillance Act, 50 U.S.C. §1801(c) ("FISA"). No court has yet expounded on the meaning or scope of "international terrorism" as it is used in FISA either, so we are not aided by that origin. A dictionary definition of "involve" demonstrates the many levels of participation that could constitute involvement. To involve is: to enfold or envelop so as to encumber; to engage as a participant; to oblige to take part; to occupy (as oneself) absorbingly; to commit emotionally; to relate closely; to have within or as part of itself; to require as a necessary accompaniment; to have an effect on. Webster's Ninth New Collegiate Dictionary (1983). Because of these many possibilities, we agree with the district court that we must look to the structure, context and legislative history of the statute to determine what Congress intended.

The government, in its very helpful *amicus curiae* brief, delineates some of the legislative history of sections 2331 and 2333. That history, in combination with the language of the statute itself, evidences an intent by Congress to codify general common law tort principles and to extend civil liability for acts of international terrorism to the full reaches of traditional tort law. . . . Although the statute defines the class of plaintiffs who may sue, it does not limit the class of defendants, and we must therefore look to tort law and the legislative history to determine who may be held liable for injuries covered by the statute.

The legislative record is replete with references to the then-recent decision in Klinghoffer v. S.N.C. Achille Lauro Ed Altri-Gestione Motonave Achille Lauto In Amministrazione, 739 F. Supp. 854 (S.D.N.Y. 1990), vacated, 937 F.2d 44 (2d Cir. 1991). . . . Leon Klinghoffer was a U.S. citizen who was murdered in a terrorist attack on a cruise ship in the Mediterranean Sea. The district court found that his survivors' claims were cognizable in federal court under federal admiralty jurisdiction and the Death on the High Seas Act because the tort occurred in navigable waters. The repeated favorable references to *Klinghoffer* indicate a desire on the part of Congress to extend this liability to land-based terrorism that occurred in a foreign country. . . .

The statute clearly is meant to reach beyond those persons who themselves commit the violent act that directly causes the injury. The Senate report on the bill notes that "the substance of [an action under section 2333] is not defined by the statute, because the fact patterns giving rise to such suits will be as varied and numerous as those found in the law of torts. This bill opens the courthouse door to victims of international terrorism." S. Rep. 102-342, at 45 (1992). This same report also remarks that the legislation, with "its provisions for compensatory damages, treble damages, and the imposition of liability *at any point along the causal chain of terrorism*," would "*interrupt, or at least imperil, the flow of money.*" *Id*. at 22 (emphasis added). . . . All of this history indicates an intent by Congress to allow a plaintiff to recover from anyone along the causal chain of terrorism.

But to the extent that the Boims urge a reading of the statute that would lead to liability for merely giving money to Hamas, a group which then sponsored a terrorist act in the manner the Boims have alleged, we agree with the district court, the defendants and the government that those allegations would be inadequate. To say that funding *simpliciter* constitutes an act of terrorism is to give the statute an almost unlimited reach. Any act which turns out to facilitate terrorism, however remote that act may be from actual violence and regardless of the actor's intent, could be construed to "involve" terrorism. Without also requiring the plaintiffs to show knowledge of and intent to further the payee's violent criminal acts, such a broad definition might also lead to constitutional infirmities by punishing mere association with groups that engage in terrorism, as we shall discuss later in addressing the First Amendment concerns raised here.

Additionally, the statute itself requires that in order to recover, a plaintiff must be injured "by reason of" an act of international terrorism. The Supreme Court has interpreted identical language to require a showing of proximate cause. *See* Holmes v. Securities Investor Protection Corp., 503 U.S. 258, 265-68 (1992) (interpreting "by reason of" language in civil RICO provision to require a showing that the defendant's conduct proximately caused the plaintiff's injury). Foreseeability is the cornerstone of proximate cause, and in tort law, a defendant will be held liable only for those injuries that might have reasonably been anticipated as a natural consequence of the defendant's actions. In the circumstances of this case, the Boims cannot show that David Boim was injured "by reason of" the defendants' payments to Hamas in the traditional tort sense of causation unless they can also show that murder was the reasonably foreseeable result of making the donation. To hold the defendants liable for donating money without knowledge of the donee's intended criminal use of the funds would impose strict liability. Nothing in the language of the statute or its structure or history supports that formulation. The government, in its *amicus* brief, maintains that funding may be enough to establish liability if the plaintiff can show that the provider of funds was generally aware of the donee's terrorist activity, and if the provision of funds substantially assisted the terrorist act in question. We will consider the government's proposed standard separately in our discussion of aiding and abetting liability. For now we note only that the complaint cannot be sustained on the theory that the defendants themselves committed an act of international terrorism when they donated unspecified amounts of money to Hamas, neither knowing nor suspecting that Hamas would in turn financially support the persons who murdered David Boim. In the very least, the plaintiffs must be able to show that murder was a reasonably foreseeable result of making a donation. Thus, the Boims' first theory of liability under section 2333, funding *simpliciter* of a terrorist organization, is insufficient because it sets too vague a standard, and because it does not require a showing of proximate cause.

The Boims' second theory of liability is that the defendants' violation of sections 2339A and 2339B, the criminal counterparts to section 2333, gives rise to civil liability under section 2333. The Boims further contend that sections 2339A and 2339B demonstrate Congress' intent to include the provision of material support to terrorist organizations in the definition of international terrorism for the purposes of section 2333. The district court concluded that Congress viewed violations of sections 2339A and 2339B as "activities involving violent acts or acts dangerous to human life," and therefore found that violations of sections 2339A and 2339B gave rise to civil liability under section 2333. Because much of the conduct the Boims alleged occurred before the passage of sections 2339A and 2339B, however, the district court ruled that the Boims would have to rely primarily on their aiding and abetting theory.

In 1994, Congress passed 18 U.S.C. §2339A, which criminalizes the provision of material support to terrorists:

> Whoever, within the United States, provides material support or resources or conceals or disguises the nature, location, source, or ownership of material support or resources, knowing or intending that they are to be used in preparation for, or in carrying out, a violation of section 32, 37, 81, 175, 351, 831, 842(m) or (n), 844(f) or (i), 930(c), 956, 1114, 1116, 1203, 1361, 1362, 1363, 1366, 1751, 1992, 2155, 2156, 2280, 2281, 2332, 2332a, 2332b, 2332c, or 2340A of this title or section 46502 of title 49, or in preparation for, or in carrying out, the concealment or an escape from the commission of any such violation, shall be fined under this title, imprisoned not more than 10 years, or both.

18 U.S.C. §2339A(a). "Material support or resources" is a defined term:

> In this section, the term 'material support or resources' means currency or other financial securities, financial services, lodging, training, safehouses, false documentation or identification, communications equipment, facilities, weapons, lethal substances, explosives, personnel, transportation, and other physical assets, except medicine or religious materials.

18 U.S.C. §2339A(b). Two years later, Congress extended criminal liability to those providing material support to foreign terrorist organizations:

> Whoever, within the United States or subject to the jurisdiction of the United States, knowingly provides material support or resources to a foreign terrorist organization, or attempts or conspires to do so, shall be fined under this title or imprisoned not more than 10 years, or both.

18 U.S.C. §2339B(a)(1). Section 2339B adopts the definition of "material support or resources" provided in section 2339A, and looks to 8 U.S.C. §1189 for the definition of "terrorist organization."

Most of these arguments are tautologous. For example, sections 2339A and 2339B certainly do proscribe different conduct than sections 2332, 2332a, 2332b and 2332d. These latter provisions address the primary perpetrators of violent acts of terrorism, while sections 2339A and 2339B apply to those persons who provide material support to the primary perpetrators of violent acts of terrorism. When it passed sections 2339A and 2339B, Congress undoubtedly intended that the persons providing financial support to terrorists should also be held criminally liable for those violent acts. Indeed, as we have already noted, the Congressional record for section 2333 indicates an intention to cut off the flow of money in support of terrorism generally. Sections 2339A and 2339B further this goal by imposing criminal liability for financial support of terrorist activities and organizations. The fact that Congress imposed lesser criminal penalties for the financial supporters indicates perhaps that they found the financiers less dangerous or less culpable than the terrorists they finance, but it does not in any way indicate that Congress meant to limit civil liability to those who personally committed acts of terrorism. On the contrary, it would be counterintuitive to conclude that Congress imposed criminal liability in sections 2339A and 2339B on those who financed terrorism, but did not intend to impose civil liability on those same persons through section 2333.

Section 2339A prohibits the provision of material support for an extensive list of violent crimes associated with terrorism — assassination, kidnapping, arson, destruction of aircraft — that make clear what types of conduct Congress had in mind when it defined "international terrorism" in section 2331(1) as not just the violent acts themselves, but also "activities that *involve* violent acts or acts dangerous to human life." There is no textual, structural or logical justification for construing the civil liability imposed by section 2333 more narrowly than the corresponding criminal provisions. Because Congress intended to impose criminal liability for funding violent terrorism, we find that it also intended through sections 2333 and 2331(1) to impose civil liability for funding at least as broad a class of violent terrorist acts. If the plaintiffs could show that HLF and QLI violated either section 2339A or section 2339B, that conduct would certainly be sufficient to meet the definition of "international terrorism" under sections 2333 and 2331. Such acts would give rise to civil liability under section 2333 so long as knowledge and intent are also shown, as we shall discuss shortly in the context of aiding and abetting.

We hasten to add that, although proof of a criminal violation under sections 2339A or 2339B might satisfy the definition of international terrorism under section 2333, such proof is not necessary to sustain a section 2333 claim. As we discuss in the context of aiding and abetting, we believe Congress intended for civil liability for financing terrorism to sweep more broadly than the conduct described in sections 2339A and 2339B. We also note that the district court seems to have inadvertently redefined the term "material" in the context of sections 2339A and 2339B as meaning substantial or considerable. The statute itself defines "material support or resources" as "currency or other financial securities, financial services, lodging, training, safehouses, false documentation or identification, communications equipment, facilities, weapons, lethal substances, explosives, personnel, transportation, and other physical assets, except medicine or religious materials." 18 U.S.C. §2339A(b). Thus, the term relates to the type of aid provided rather than whether it is substantial or considerable. For civil liability, section 2333 requires that the plaintiff be injured "by reason of" the act of international terrorism. Because we believe Congress intended to import standard tort law into section 2333, causation may be demonstrated as it would be in traditional tort law. Congress has made clear, though, through the criminal liability imposed in sections 2339A and 2339B, that even small donations made knowingly and intentionally in support of terrorism may meet the standard for civil liability in section 2333. Congress' goal of cutting off funding for terrorism would be seriously compromised if terrorist organizations could avoid liability by simply pooling together small donations to fund a terrorist act.

We turn finally to 28 U.S.C. §1605(a)(7). In relevant part, the statute provides:

> A foreign state shall not be immune from the jurisdiction of courts of the United States or of the States in any case . . . in which money damages are sought against a foreign state for personal injury or death that was caused by an act of torture, extrajudicial killing, aircraft sabotage, hostage taking, or the provision of material support or resources (as defined in section 2339A of title 18) for such an act if such act or provision of material support is engaged in by an official, employee, or agent of such foreign state while acting within the scope of his or her office, employment, agency[.]

Contrary to the defendants' characterization, the district court did not rely solely on the passage of section 1605(a)(7) in finding that Congress viewed the provision of material support and resources as an act of international terrorism. After finding support in both the text and the structure of sections 2333 and 2331 for this proposition, the court found further reasons in section 1605(a)(7). As the district court noted, "Considering that Congress has permitted foreign states that have been designated state sponsors of terrorism to be sued in United States courts for violating §2339A, it is hard to argue that Congress did not intend to include such violations in its definition of 'terrorism' under the statutory scheme." We take the district court to mean that section 1605(a)(7) implies a foreign state may be sued in the United States for acts that would give rise to criminal liability under section 2339A, not that section 2339A itself has a civil provision. The mechanism for suing a foreign state for these acts that would give rise to criminal liability under section 2339A is section 2333. The defendants complain that Congress did not specifically mention section 2333 as the device by which plaintiffs might sue foreign governments for violations of section 2339A, but they fail to point to any other source of civil liability. We agree that Congress made clear in section 1605(a)(7) its intent to characterize violations of section 2339A as acts of international terrorism under section 2333.

The district court believed there was a timing problem for the Boims in making their case under these criminal provisions because much of the funding conduct allegedly committed by HLF and QLI occurred prior to the passage of sections 2339A and 2339B. Indeed, Hamas was not designated a terrorist organization under section 1189 until 1997, after David's murder. Certainly HLF and QLI could not be held criminally liable for conduct that occurred before the statutes were enacted, but that argument misses the point. We are using sections 2339A and 2339B not as independent sources of liability under section 2333, but to amplify what Congress meant by "international terrorism." Sections 2339A and 2339B merely lend further support to our finding that Congress considered the provision of material support to terrorists an act of international terrorism. This reading simply amplifies the conclusion we have already reached by examining the language and legislative history of section 2333. Sections 2339A and 2339B provide criminal liability for the provision of material support, and section 2333 provides civil liability. The Boims may thus show that QLI and HLF committed an act of international terrorism subject to civil liability under section 2333 by proving that QLI and HLF provided material support to terrorist organizations. No timing problem arises because sections 2339A and 2339B merely elucidate conduct that was already prohibited by section 2333.

We turn next to the Boims' theory that HLF and QLI may be held civilly liable under section 2333 for aiding and abetting an act of international terrorism. Under this theory, the Boims urge us to find that aiding and abetting a violent act is conduct that "involves" a violent act as that word is used in section 2331(1). HLF and QLI contend that section 2333 does not provide for aiding and abetting liability, and that the Supreme Court in *Central Bank* held that aiding and abetting liability is available only when a statute expressly provides for it. *See* Central Bank of Denver N.A. v. First Interstate Bank of Denver, N.A., 511 U.S. 164 (1994); Alexander v. Sandoval, 532 U.S. 275 (2001). . . .

The *Central Bank* analysis [which rejected aiding and abetting liability under section 10(b) of the Securities Exchange Act of 1934] provides guidance but is not determinative here for a number of reasons. First, *Central Bank* addressed extending aiding and abetting liability to an implied right of action, not an express right of action as we have here in section 2333. Second, Congress expressed an intent in the terms and history of section 2333 to import general tort law principles, and those principles include aiding and abetting liability. Third, Congress expressed an intent in section 2333 to render civil liability at least as extensive as criminal liability in the context of the terrorism cases, and criminal liability attaches to aiders and abettors of terrorism. Fourth, failing to extend section 2333 liability to aiders and abettors is contrary to Congress' stated purpose of cutting off the flow of money to terrorists at every point along the chain of causation. . . .

Finally, if we failed to impose liability on aiders and abettors who knowingly and intentionally funded acts of terrorism, we would be thwarting Congress' clearly expressed intent to cut off the flow of money to terrorists at every point along the causal chain of violence. Unlike section 10(b) where Congress' intent could be met without imposing liability on aiders and abettors, Congress' purpose here could not be met unless liability attached beyond the persons directly involved in acts of violence. The statute would have little effect if liability were limited to the persons who pull the trigger or plant the bomb because such persons are unlikely to have assets, much less assets in the United States, and would not be deterred by the statute. Also, and perhaps more importantly, there would not be a trigger to pull or a bomb to blow up without the resources to acquire such tools of terrorism and to bankroll the persons who actually commit the violence. Moreover, the organizations, businesses and nations that support and encourage terrorist acts are likely to have reachable assets that they wish to protect. The only way to imperil the flow of money and discourage the financing of terrorist acts is to impose liability on those who knowingly and intentionally supply the funds to the persons who commit the violent acts. For all of these distinguishing reasons, we do not think *Central Bank* controls the result here, but that aiding and abetting liability is both appropriate and called for by the language, structure and legislative history of section 2333.

[The court proceeds to hold that it would not offend the First Amendment to impose liability on the defendants as long as the Boims prove that the defendants knew of Hamas' illegal activities and contributed money to Hamas with the desire to help those activities succeed.]

Cicippio-Puleo v. Islamic Republic of Iran

353 F.3d 1024 (D.C. Cir. 2004)

[The Hizbollah terrorist organization, which was supported by Iran, kidnapped Joseph Cicippio in Lebanon and held him hostage from 1986-1991. Mr. Cicippio and his wife later sued Iran for damages under the "state sponsor of terrorism" exception to the Foreign Sovereign Immunities Act, 28 U.S.C. §1605(a)(7), and the "Flatow Amendment," 28 U.S.C. §1605 note. The state sponsor of terrorism exception provides:

> A foreign state shall not be immune from the jurisdiction of courts of the United States or of the States in any case —
>
> > (7) not otherwise covered by paragraph (2), in which money damages are sought against a foreign state for personal injury or death that was caused by an act of torture, extrajudicial killing, aircraft sabotage, hostage taking, or the provision of material support or resources (as defined in section 2339A of title 18) for such an act if such act or provision of material support is engaged in by an official, employee, or agent of such foreign state while acting within the scope of his or her

office, employment, or agency, except that the court shall decline to hear a claim under this paragraph —

> (A) if the foreign state was not designated as a state sponsor of terrorism under section 6(j) of the Export Administration Act of 1979 or section 620A of the Foreign Assistance Act of 1961 at the time the act occurred, unless later so designated as a result of such act or the act is related to Case Number 1:00CV03110(EGS) in the United States District Court for the District of Columbia; and

> (B) even if the foreign state is or was so designated, if —

> (i) the act occurred in the foreign state against which the claim has been brought and the claimant has not afforded the foreign state a reasonable opportunity to arbitrate the claim in accordance with accepted international rules of arbitration; or
> (ii) neither the claimant nor the victim was a national of the United States (as that term is defined in section 101(a)(22) of the Immigration and Nationality Act when the act upon which the claim is based occurred.

The Flatow Amendment provides in relevant part:

> An official, employee, or agent of a foreign state designated as a state sponsor of terrorism designated under section 6(j) of the Export Administration Act of 1979 while acting within the scope of his or her office, employment, or agency shall be liable to a United States national or the national's legal representative for personal injury or death caused by acts of that official, employee, or agent for which the courts of the United States may maintain jurisdiction under section 1605(a)(7) of title 28, United States Code, for money damages which may include economic damages, solatium, pain, and suffering, and punitive damages if the acts were among those described in section 1605(a)(7).

The district court awarded Mr. Cicippio $20 million in damages and awarded Mrs. Cicippio $10 million in damages. Iran never entered an appearance in the case and no appeal was taken from the judgment. Mr. Cicippio's children and siblings subsequently sued Iran under the state sponsor of terrorism exception and the Flatow Amendment for the emotional distress and loss of solatium they suffered as a result of Mr. Cicippio's ordeal. The district court dismissed their claims, holding that the plaintiffs had not met the common law requirements for recovery for emotional distress or loss of solatium.]

EDWARDS, CIRCUIT JUDGE. . . .

Section 1605(a)(7) waives the sovereign immunity of a designated "foreign state" in actions in which money damages are sought for personal injury or death caused by one of the specified acts of terrorism, if the act of terrorism or provision of material support is engaged in by "an official, employee, or agent of such foreign state while acting within the scope of his or her office, employment, or agency." 28 U.S.C. §1605(a)(7). Section 1605(a)(7) is merely a jurisdiction-conferring provision that does not otherwise provide a cause of action against either a foreign state or its agents. However, the Flatow Amendment, 28 U.S.C. §1605 note, undoubtedly does provide a cause of action against "an official, employee, or agent of a foreign state designated as a state sponsor of terrorism" "for personal injury or death caused by acts of that official, employee, or agent for which the courts of the

United States may maintain jurisdiction under section 1605(a)(7)." The question here is whether the Flatow Amendment, which does not refer to "foreign state," may be construed, either alone or in conjunction with section 1605(a)(7), to provide a cause of action against a foreign state. . . .

This court . . . has never affirmed a judgment that the Flatow Amendment, either alone or in conjunction with section 1605(a)(7), provides a cause of action against a foreign state. . . .

We now hold that neither 28 U.S.C. §1605(a)(7) nor the Flatow Amendment, nor the two considered in tandem, creates a private right of action against a foreign government. Section 1605(a)(7) merely waives the immunity of a foreign state without creating a cause of action against it, and the Flatow Amendment only provides a private right of action against officials, employees, and agents of a foreign state, not against the foreign state itself. Because we hold that there is no statutory cause of action against Iran under these provisions, we affirm the District Court's judgment without deciding whether the evidence presented by the plaintiffs is sufficient to recover for intentional infliction of emotional distress or loss of solatium.

There is a clearly settled distinction in federal law between statutory provisions that waive sovereign immunity and those that create a cause of action. It cannot be assumed that a claimant has a cause of action for damages against a government agency merely because there has been a waiver of sovereign immunity. *See* FDIC v. Meyer, 510 U.S. 471, 483-84 (1994). As the Supreme Court has noted:

> The first inquiry is whether there has been a waiver of sovereign immunity. If there has been such a waiver, as in this case, the second inquiry comes into play — that is, whether the source of substantive law upon which the claimant relies provides an avenue for relief.

Id. at 484.

The Supreme Court has also made it clear that the federal courts should be loathe to "imply" a cause of action from a jurisdictional provision that "creates no cause of action of its own force and effect . . . [and] imposes no liabilities." *See* Touche Ross & Co. v. Redington, 442 U.S. 560, 577 (1979). "The ultimate question is one of congressional intent, not one of whether this Court thinks that it can improve upon the statutory scheme that Congress enacted into law." *Id.* at 578. In adhering to this view, the Supreme Court has declined to construe statutes to imply a cause of action where Congress has not expressly provided one.

Unsurprisingly, the Supreme Court has applied the distinction between immunity and liability in interpreting the FSIA itself, explaining that "the language and history of the FSIA clearly establish that the Act was not intended to affect the substantive law determining the liability of a foreign state or instrumentality." First Nat'l City Bank v. Banco Para El Comercio Exterior de Cuba, 462 U.S. 611, 620 (1983). With this case law to guide us, there can be little doubt of the outcome in this case.

The language of section 1605(a)(7) and the Flatow Amendment — the only provisions upon which plaintiffs rely — is clear. In declaring that "[a] foreign state shall not be immune from the jurisdiction of courts of the United States or of the States . . . ," 28 U.S.C. §1605(a)(7) merely abrogates the immunity of foreign states from the jurisdiction of the courts in lawsuits for damages for certain enumerated acts of terrorism. It does not impose liability or mention a cause of action. The statute thus confers subject matter jurisdiction on federal courts over such lawsuits, but does not create a private right of action.

As noted above, the Flatow Amendment imposes liability and creates a cause of action. But the liability imposed by the provision is precisely limited to "an official, employee, or agent of a foreign state designated as a state sponsor of terrorism." "Foreign states" are not within the compass of the cause of action created by the Flatow Amendment. In short, there is absolutely nothing in section 1605(a)(7) or the Flatow Amendment that creates a cause of action against foreign states for the enumerated acts of terrorism.

We also agree with the United States that, insofar as the Flatow Amendment creates a private right of action against officials, employees, and agents of foreign states, the cause of action is limited to claims against those officials in their *individual*, as opposed to their official, capacities:

> As the Supreme Court repeatedly has explained, an *official*-capacity claim against a government official is in substance a claim against the government itself. . . . By definition, a damages judgment in an official-capacity suit is enforceable against the state itself (and only against the state). Thus, to construe the Flatow Amendment as permitting official-capacity claims would eviscerate the recognized distinction between suits against governments and suits against individual government officials. . . . The text of the Flatow Amendment and Section 1605(a)(7), as well as all relevant background interpretive principles . . . foreclose any such construction.

Br. for the United States as *Amicus Curiae* at 17.

The plaintiffs and *amicus curiae* dispute both the meaning and relevance of the legislative history of the FSIA or the Flatow Amendment in support of their competing arguments to the court. The legislative history is largely irrelevant, however, because the statutory language is clear — nothing in section 1605(a)(7) or the Flatow Amendment establishes a cause of action against *foreign states*. And, as we explain below, there is nothing in the legislative history that raises any serious doubts about the meaning of the statute.

In 1976, the House Judiciary Committee Report explained that the FSIA was "not intended to affect the substantive law of liability." H.R. Rep. No. 94-1487, at 12 (1976). It stated that the statute was intended to preempt other federal or state law that accorded sovereign immunity, and to discontinue the practice of judicial deference to suggestions of immunity from the executive branch. But the statute was not intended to affect "the attribution of responsibility between or among entities of a foreign state; for example, whether the proper entity of a foreign state has been sued; or whether an entity sued is liable in whole or in part for the claimed wrong."

When Congress passed section 1605(a)(7), the Conference Committee report explained:

> This subtitle provides that nations designated as state sponsors of terrorism under section 6(j) of the Export Administration Act of 1979 will be amenable to suit in U.S. courts for terrorist acts. It permits U.S. federal courts to hear claims seeking money damages for personal injury or death against such nations and arising from terrorist acts they commit, or direct to be committed, against American citizens or nationals outside of the foreign state's territory, and for such acts within the state's territory if the state involved has refused to arbitrate the claim.

H.R. Conf. Rep. No. 104-518, at 112 (1996). It is noteworthy that the legislative history does not say that section 1605(a)(7) imposes liability against foreign states or creates a cause of action against them.

When Congress later passed the appropriations bill that included the Flatow Amendment, there was very little legislative history purporting to explain the enactment. The Conference Report said: "The conference agreement inserts language expanding the scope of monetary damage awards available to American victims of international terrorism. The conferees intend that this section shall apply to cases pending upon enactment of this Act." H.R. Conf. Rep. No. 104-863, at 987 (1996). As the United States notes in its brief, "on its face, that statement addresses only issues of damages and retroactivity, not the question whether foreign states are proper defendants in the first place." Br. for the United States as *Amicus Curiae* at 12. We agree. Thus, the legislative history of the Flatow Amendment is not inconsistent with the clear terms of the statute.

Subsequent enactments by Congress providing for the payment or enforcement of judgments entered against foreign states in cases brought under §1605(a)(7) fail to establish that Congress created a cause of action against foreign states. *See* Victims of Trafficking and Violence Protection Act of 2000, Pub. L. No. 106-386, §2002, 114 Stat. 1464, 1541-43; Terrorism Risk Insurance Act of 2002, Pub. L. No. 107-297, §201, 116 Stat. 2322, 2337-39. As we explained in *Roeder*, these statutes merely provide for payment "*if* an individual has a judgment against Iran," but they do not address or resolve the anterior question "whether plaintiffs are legally entitled to such a judgment." It is entirely plausible for Congress to direct the United States to compensate victims of terrorism without purporting to establish or support a cause of action against foreign state sponsors of terrorism.

There is nothing anomalous in Congress's approach in enacting the Flatow Amendment. As we noted [Price v. Socialist People's Libyan Arab Jamhiriya, 294 F.3d 82 (D.C. Cir. 2002)], the passage of §1605(a)(7) involved a delicate legislative compromise. While Congress sought to create a judicial forum for the compensation of victims and the punishment of terrorist states, it proceeded with caution, in part due to executive branch officials' concern that other nations would respond by subjecting the American government to suits in foreign countries.

The plaintiffs suggest that our construction of the Flatow Amendment "will mean that what Congress gave with one hand in section 1605(a)(7) it immediately took away with the other in the Flatow Amendment." We disagree. Section 1605(a)(7) does not purport to grant victims of terrorism a *cause of action* against foreign states, or against officials, employees, or agents of those states acting in either their official or personal capacities. Therefore, the Flatow Amendment's authorization of a limited cause of action against officials, employees, and agents acting in their personal capacities takes nothing away from §1605(a)(7). What §1605(a)(7) does is to make it clear that designated foreign state sponsors of terrorism will be amenable to suits in United States courts for acts of terrorism in cases in which there is a viable cause of action.

Clearly, Congress's authorization of a cause of action against officials, employees, and agents of a foreign state was a significant step toward providing a judicial forum for the compensation of terrorism victims. Recognizing a federal cause of action against foreign states undoubtedly would be an even greater step toward that end, but it is a step that Congress has yet to take. And it is for Congress, not the courts, to decide whether a cause of action should lie against foreign states. Therefore, we decline to imply a cause of action against foreign states when Congress has not expressly recognized one in the language of section 1605(a)(7) or the Flatow Amendment.

Although we affirm the District Court's dismissal of plaintiffs' complaint for failure to state a claim under section 1605(a)(7) and the Flatow Amendment, we will nonetheless remand the case. The Cicippios' suit was filed in the wake of judgments in favor of Mr. and Mrs. Cicippio and other hostage victims, so they may have been misled in assuming that the Flatow Amendment afforded a cause of action against foreign state sponsors of terrorism. We will therefore remand the case to allow plaintiffs an opportunity to amend their complaint to state a cause of action under some other source of law, including state law. . . .

In remanding, we do not mean to suggest, one way or the other, whether plaintiffs have a viable cause of action. The possibility that an alternative source of law might support such a claim was addressed only by *amici*, and we do not ordinarily decide issues not raised by parties. Accordingly, we will leave it to the District Court in the first instance to address any amended complaint that is offered by plaintiffs.

Notes and Questions

1. The principal statute at issue in *Boim*, 18 U.S.C. §2333, was enacted in 1992 and was a recodification of a statute that had been enacted in 1990 and then repealed because of a technical deficiency in 1991. This statute was not invoked as a basis for suit until approximately 2000. For other cases considering this statute, see Ungar v. Palestine Liberation Organization, 402 F.3d 274 (1st Cir. 2005) (affirming judgment against the Palestinian Authority and the Palestine Liberation Organization and rejecting defendants' political question and sovereign immunity arguments); and Knox v. Palestine Liberation Organization, 306 F. Supp. 2d 424 (S.D.N.Y. 2004) (declining to dismiss and holding that the PLO was not entitled to sovereign immunity).

2. Was the court in *Boim* correct in concluding that the mere provision of funds to a terrorist organization is not an act of international terrorism covered by 18 U.S.C. §2333? Is the court's reasoning on this issue inconsistent with its subsequent reasoning concerning liability for the provision of material support to terrorist organizations and the existence of aiding and abetting liability? Under the court's analysis, what is the relationship between 18 U.S.C. §2333, and the criminal provisions, 18 U.S.C. §§2339A and 2339B? How does the issue of aiding and abetting liability under 18 U.S.C. §2333 compare with the issue of aiding and abetting liability under the ATS and TVPA, discussed in the last section?

3. The "state sponsor of terrorism" exception to foreign sovereign immunity, 28 U.S.C. §1605(a)(7), was enacted in 1996 as an amendment to the Foreign Sovereign Immunities Act. By its terms, this exception applies only to countries included on the State Department's official list of terrorist states. Until recently, seven states were on the list: Cuba, Iran, Iraq, Libya, North Korea, Sudan, and Syria. In late 2004, Iraq was removed from the list because of the regime change that had taken place in that country. Recent improvements in U.S.-Libya relations may lead it to be removed from the list as well, although it was still on the list as of October 2005. States not on the list have the immunity from suit provided for in the FSIA, even if they are alleged to be connected to terrorism. Thus, for example, in a suit relating to the September 11 terrorist attacks, claims against Saudi Arabia were dismissed on the basis of sovereign immunity. See Burnett v. Al Baraka Investment and Development Corp., 349 F. Supp. 2d 765 (S.D.N.Y. 2005). (However, if a state is on the list and is then removed from the list, it will continue to lack immunity for suits relating to conduct that took place while it was on the list.)

4. Before *Cicippio*, there were numerous judgments, some of them involving hundreds of millions of dollars, entered against foreign states based on 28 U.S.C.

§1605(a)(7) and the Flatow Amendment. In many of these cases, the defendant state did not make an appearance, and did not appeal the judgment. To the extent they focused on the issue, the district judges in these cases concluded that, even though the Flatow Amendment did not expressly refer to suits against foreign states that were sponsors of terrorism, Congress had implicitly authorized such suits. As one judge explained:

> First, the text of the Flatow Amendment suggests, although admittedly does not explicitly state, that a cause of action exists against foreign states proper. Before addressing the text of the Flatow Amendment, however, it is important to recognize that the provision must be read in conjunction with 28 U.S.C. §1605(a)(7).... "The operative language of 28 U.S.C. §1605(a)(7) parallels the definition of respondeat superior: an employer is liable is some cases for damages 'proximately resulting from acts of [an] employee done within [the] scope of his employment in the employer's service.'" Flatow [v. The Islamic Reublic of Iran], 999 F. Supp. [1, 26 (D.D.C. 1998)] (footnote omitted). Thus, under 28 U.S.C. §1605(a)(7), the sovereign immunity of a foreign state will be abrogated if its "official, employee, or agent" provides material resources to the entity that commits the terrorist act. The Flatow Amendment likewise provides that an "official, employee, or agent" of a foreign state shall be liable if their actions were taken "while acting within the scope of his or her office, employment, or agency[.]" 28 U.S.C. §1605(a)(7) note. In light of the identical language used in both statutory provisions, the Court finds that the respondeat superior implications of section 1605(a)(7) are equally applicable to the Flatow Amendment. Thus, in *Flatow*, the Court opined that "the state sponsored terrorism exception to immunity and the Flatow Amendment similarly employ the principles of *respondeat superior* and command responsibility to create both subject matter jurisdiction and a federal cause of action." *Flatow*, 999 F. Supp. at 26. Moreover, by referring to officials, employees, and agents of foreign states, the Flatow Amendment makes clear that they can, in addition to the foreign state itself, be held liable for providing material support to groups that perform terrorist acts. When viewed in this light, it becomes clear that the omission of "foreign state" from the Flatow Amendment is the beginning, rather than the end, of the inquiry. It also shows that to interpret the text of the Flatow Amendment as denying a cause of action against the foreign state itself would turn the scheme of §1605(a)(7) on its head. Instead of using the acts of officials, employees, and agents to support liability against the foreign state, the same language would be used in the Flatow Amendment to deny victims of state-sponsored terrorism a cause of action against the responsible foreign state.

Cronin v. Islamic Republic of Iran, 238 F. Supp. 2d 222, 232 (D.D.C. 2002). Which is more persuasive — this analysis, or the analysis in *Cicippio*?

5. If the court is correct in *Cicippio*, why did Congress enact the state sponsor of terrorism exception? Why did it enact the Flatow Amendment? Why would Congress strip foreign states of immunity, and then enact a cause of action statute that did not apply to them? Do the subsequent enactments by Congress concerning the payment of judgments against state sponsors of terrorism (referred to in *Cicippio*) show that Congress thought there was a cause of action against those states?

6. After *Cicippio*, can plaintiffs rely on sources of law other than the Flatow Amendment for their cause of action? What about federal common law? State law? Foreign law? *See* Acree v. Republic of Iraq, 370 F.3d 41, 59 (D.C. Cir. 2004) (stating that, "as in any case, a plaintiff proceeding under the FSIA must identify a particular cause of action arising out of a specific source of law," and holding that reliance on "generic common law" is not sufficient); Price v. Socialist People's Libyan Arab Jamahiriya, 384 F. Supp. 2d 120 (D.D.C. July 26, 2005) (entering judgment against Libya based on state tort law for torture and other abuse); Damarell v. Islamic Republic of Iran, 2005 U.S. Dist. LEXIS 5343 (D.D.C. Mar. 29, 2005) (holding that plaintiffs could state a claim under state law for bombing of U.S. embassy, but not under federal common law). How does this issue compare with the cause of action issue in ATS and TVPA litigation, discussed above in Section B?

7. The *Cicippio* decision may have substantially limited the effect of the FSIA's state sponsor of terrorism exception. Consider, for example, Acree v. Republic of Iraq, 370 F.3d 41 (D.C. Cir. 2004). In that case, 17 U.S. service members who had been held as prisoners of war during the 1991 Gulf War brought suit against Iraq, alleging that they had been tortured. The district court awarded the plaintiffs over $900 million. While the case was pending, the U.S. invaded Iraq and removed its president, Saddam Hussein, from power. In an appropriations bill enacted after Hussein's removal, the Emergency Wartime Supplemental Appropriations Act, Congress authorized the President to exempt Iraq from laws otherwise applicable to countries that have supported terrorism. The President exercised this authority in a Presidential Determination, making "inapplicable with respect to Iraq . . . any other provision of law that applies to countries that have supported terrorism." The plaintiffs nevertheless sought to satisfy their judgment by attaching frozen Iraqi bank accounts. The Executive Branch opposed the attachment, arguing that the Presidential Determination had exempted Iraqi funds from a statute (discussed below in Note 8) that made frozen assets of state sponsors of terrorism available for attachment. The district court agreed with the Executive Branch and therefore declined to allow recovery against the Iraqi accounts. The U.S. Court of Appeals for the D.C. Circuit affirmed, albeit on different grounds. Although noting that it was a close question, the appeals court concluded that the exemption provision in the Appropriations Act was "aimed at legal provisions that prevent obstacles to assistance and funding for the new Iraqi Government and was not intended to alter the jurisdiction of the federal courts under the FSIA." However, the court also concluded that, in light of its earlier decision in *Cicippio*, the plaintiffs had failed to state a claim, since they were relying only on Section 1605(a)(7) and the Flatow Amendment, neither of which creates a cause of action against foreign states.

8. Receiving a damages award from a court does not guarantee recovery of money from the defendant. If the defendant does not voluntarily pay the judgment, the plaintiff must find assets of the defendant that he or she can enforce the judgment against. When it enacted 28 U.S.C. §1605(a)(7), Congress attempted to facilitate execution by making clear that in cases brought under this exception, the property executed against need not be "involved in the act upon which the claim is based." 28 U.S.C. §1610(b)(2). Nevertheless, the only property owned by state sponsors of terrorism within the United States tends to be either frozen assets or diplomatic property, neither of which is ordinarily subject to execution.

In 1998, Congress (in Section 117 of an appropriations statute) amended the execution provisions to allow plaintiffs in cases brought under section 1605(a)(7) to attach and execute on frozen assets, including frozen diplomatic property. The amendment also directed the Executive Branch to assist prevailing plaintiffs in "identifying, locating, and executing against the property of that foreign state or any agency or instrumentality of such state." *See* 28 U.S.C. §1610(f). But a provision in the amendment also gave the President the authority to waive the implementation of at least part of the amendment "in the interest of national security," and

President Clinton immediately invoked this authority upon signing the legislation. He explained his action as follows:

> I am concerned about section 117 of the Treasury/General Government appropriations section of the Act, which amends the Foreign Sovereign Immunities Act. If this section were to result in attachment and execution against foreign embassy properties, it would encroach on my authority under the Constitution to "receive Ambassadors and other public Ministers." Moreover, if applied to foreign diplomatic or consular property, section 117 would place the United States in breach of its international treaty obligations. It would put at risk the protection we enjoy at every embassy and consulate throughout the world by eroding the principle that diplomatic property must be protected regardless of bilateral relations. Absent my authority to waive section 117's attachment provision, it would also effectively eliminate use of blocked assets of terrorist states in the national security interests of the United States, including denying an important source of leverage. In addition, section 117 could seriously affect our ability to enter into global claims settlements that are fair to all U.S. claimants, and could result in U.S. taxpayer liability in the event of a contrary claims tribunal judgment. To the extent possible, I shall construe section 117 in a manner consistent with my constitutional authority and with U.S. international legal obligations, and for the above reasons, I have exercised the waiver authority in the national security interest of the United States.

Statement by President William J. Clinton Upon Signing H.R. 4328, 34 Weekly Comp. Pres. Doc. 2108 (Nov. 2, 1998).

Despite this presidential waiver, plaintiffs who had obtained a judgment against Cuba relating to its shooting down of civilian planes over international waters attempted to enforce their judgment against monies owed by AT&T and other U.S. telecommunications companies to the Cuban state telecommunications company. A 1992 statute and implementing regulations authorized payments to Cuba on a case-by-case basis for telecommunications services, notwithstanding the general freeze on Cuban assets. The district court allowed the plaintiffs to enforce the judgment against such payments, despite the Executive Branch's claim that the President had effectively waived the 1998 execution provisions. *See* Alejandre v. Republic of Cuba, 42 F. Supp. 2d 1317 (S.D. Fla. 1999). That decision was vacated on appeal, however, on the ground that the Cuban telecommunications company was a separate entity from the defendants involved in the case and thus could not be held liable for the defendants' wrongdoing. *See* Alejandre v. Republic of Cuba, 183 F.3d 1277 (11th Cir. 1999). Another district court, in a case against Iran, subsequently held that the President had effectively waived the enforcement of the execution provisions. *See* Flatow v. Islamic Republic of Iran, 76 F. Supp. 2d 16 (D.D.C. 1999).

In response to these decisions, Congress, in a section of the Victims of Trafficking and Violence Protection Act of 2000 (VTVPA), amended the execution provisions again. This time Congress provided for payment by the U.S. government of the compensatory damage judgments already awarded in the cases against Iran and Cuba. Under this scheme, plaintiffs were given a choice of taking 110 percent of their compensatory damages and waiving all other damage claims or taking 100 percent of their compensatory damages and preserving their right to seek recovery of punitive damages. The statute substitutes the U.S. government as the claimant in these actions, so that it can seek recovery of this money in the future if it so chooses. In early 2001, the federal government liquidated $96.7 million in frozen Cuban assets and paid that amount to the plaintiffs in the *Alejandre* case.

Is Congress's approach in the VTVPA a good solution to the execution problem? Should this scheme be limited to suits against Iran and Cuba? To judgments already awarded? What happens when the frozen assets are exhausted?

9. In Flatow v. Islamic Republic of Iran, 308 F.3d 1065 (9th Cir. 2002), the U.S. Court of Appeals for the Ninth Circuit held that the plaintiff could not enforce his multimillion dollar punitive damages judgment against Iran by levying on real estate in California held by an Iranian government-owned bank. The court concluded that the bank was juridically separate from the government of Iran and thus was not liable for the judgment against the Iranian government. The court concluded its opinion by stating:

> This panel joins other courts in expressing regret that its holding forestalls the Flatow family's efforts to execute their judgment against Iran.... There has, however, been substantial payment of damages through the legislation passed by the United States Congress.... The government of Iran should pay its debt to the Flatow family, but [the bank] cannot be held liable for the debt. We follow the clear path set out by the applicable case law.

Id. at 1075. The legislation referred to by the court was the VTVPA, discussed above. The plaintiff in this case exercised his right to receive compensation under the Act and was paid $26 million by the Department of the Treasury in January 2001.

10. In a 2002 statute, the Terrorism Risk Insurance Act (TRIA), Congress attempted to make it easier for prevailing plaintiffs to enforce their compensatory damage judgments against state sponsors of terrorism. TRIA provides that

> in every case in which a person has obtained a judgment against a terrorist party on a claim based upon an act of terrorism, or for which a terrorist party is not immune under section 1605(a)(7) of title 28, United States Code, the blocked assets of that terrorist party (including the blocked assets of any agency or instrumentality of that terrorist party) shall be subject to execution or attachment in aid of execution in order to satisfy such judgment to the extent of any compensatory damages for which such terrorist party has been adjudged liable.

This statute included only a limited president waiver provision:

> (b) Presidential Waiver. —
>
> (1) In general. — Subject to paragraph (2), upon determining on an asset-by-asset basis that a waiver is necessary in the national security interest, the President may waive the requirements of subsection (a) in connection with (and prior to the enforcement of) any judicial order directing attachment in aid of execution or execution against any property subject to the Vienna Convention on Diplomatic Relations or the Vienna Convention on Consular Relations.
>
> (2) Exception. — A waiver under this subsection shall not apply to —
>
> (A) property subject to the Vienna Convention on Diplomatic Relations or the Vienna Convention on Consular Relations that has been used by the United States for any nondiplomatic purpose (including use as rental property), or the proceeds of such use; or
>
> (B) the proceeds of any sale or transfer for value to a third party of any asset subject to the Vienna Convention on Diplomatic Relations or the Vienna Convention on Consular Relations.

The Executive Branch opposed this section, but it supported the insurance provisions in the remainder of the statute, and President Bush decided to sign the statute into law. What does this suggest about the political process for foreign relations lawmaking? For a decision holding that an acceptance of a compensatory payment under the VTVPA constitutes a relinquishment of the ability to enforce a judgment under TRIA, see Hegna v. Islamic Republic of Iran, 376 F.3d 226 (4th Cir. 2004); *see also* Hegna v. Islamic Republic of Iran, 380 F.3d 1000 (7th Cir. 2004) (holding that properties in Chicago were not subject to attachment because they were within the scope of the relinquishments in the VTVPA).

11. What should a court do if faced with a conflict between 28 U.S.C. §1605(a)(7) and a treaty or executive agreement? This issue has arisen in connection with lawsuits brought against Iran relating to the 1979-1981 hostage crisis. The Algiers Accords (which were concluded by the United States as a presidential executive agreement) are a potential obstacle to these suits because they purport to settle claims against Iran relating to the hostage crisis. In November 2001, Congress enacted an appropriations bill, section 626(c) of which purported to exempt cases relating to the Iran hostage crisis from the requirement in section 1605(a)(7) that the foreign state defendant have been designated a sponsor of terrorism at the time of the act complained of or have been subsequently designated a sponsor of terrorism based on that act. The legislative history of this provision (and of a technical correction of the amendment enacted a month later) suggests that Congress intended to allow claims against Iran based on the hostage crisis and that it disapproved of efforts by the Executive Branch to have these cases dismissed. In signing this legislation, however, President Bush stated that the Executive Branch would act, and encourage courts to act, "in a manner consistent with the obligations of the United States under the Algiers Accords that achieved the release of U.S. hostages in 1981."

Despite section 626(c), the D.C. Circuit upheld the dismissal of a suit against Iran relating to the hostage crisis, noting that "[t]here is . . . no clear expression in anything Congress enacted abrogating the Algiers Accords." The court explained that, "Executive agreements are essentially contracts between nations, and like contracts between individuals, executive agreements are expected to be honored by the parties. Congress (or the President acting alone) may abrogate an executive agreement, but legislation must be clear to ensure that Congress — and the President — have considered the consequences." Roeder v. Islamic Republic of Iran, 333 F.3d 228 (D.C. Cir. 2003). Why did the President sign section 626(c) if he did not want suits against Iran relating to the hostage crisis to proceed? Why did Congress not state its intent more clearly?

12. 28 U.S.C. §1605(a)(7) does not itself determine which nations lose their immunity by virtue of their involvement in terrorism. Instead, as noted above, that determination is delegated to the Executive Branch. Is this delegation of authority consistent with the separation of powers structure of the Constitution, which assigns the power to regulate the jurisdiction of the federal courts to Congress rather than to the Executive? In Rein v. Socialist People's Libyan Arab Jamahiriya, 162 F.3d 748 (2d Cir. 1998), the court held that there was no violation of separation of powers in a suit against Libya, because Libya was listed as a state sponsor of terrorism in 1996, when section 1605(a)(7) was enacted. The court expressed no opinion about whether it would be constitutional to apply section 1605(a)(7) to a nation that was not listed as a state sponsor of terrorism in 1996. For decisions reaching a similar conclusion, see Price v. Socialist People's Libyan Arab Jamahiriya, 110 F. Supp. 2d 10 (D.D.C. 2000); and Daliberti v. Republic of Iraq, 97 F. Supp. 2d 38 (D.D.C. 2000). If the Executive Branch changes the list of state sponsors of terrorism, is it improperly determining federal court jurisdiction? Does it matter whether the Executive is adding or deleting states from the list? How, if at all, is this Executive role different from the pre-FSIA regime, under which the Executive Branch could control the grant of immunity on a case-by-case basis?

13. The State Department opposed the enactment of an exception to immunity for state sponsors of terrorism. In testimony before a Senate subcommittee in 1994, a representative from the State Department explained:

> Consistency of the FSIA with established international practice is important. If we deviate from that practice and assert jurisdiction over foreign states for acts that are generally perceived by the international community as falling within the scope of immunity, this would tend to erode the credibility of the FSIA. We have made substantial efforts over the years to persuade foreign states to participate in our judicial system — to appear and defend in actions against them under the FSIA. That kind of broad participation serves the interests of all. If we expand our jurisdiction in ways that causes other states to question our statute, this could undermine the broad participation we seek. It could also undermine our ability to influence other states to abandon the theory of absolute immunity and adopt the restrictive view of sovereign immunity, which the United States has followed for over forty years....
>
> This bill could also lead to other undesirable consequences for our foreign relations. Current U.S. law allows the U.S. Government to fine-tune the application of sanctions against state-sponsors of terrorism, increasing or decreasing them when in the national interest. In addition, the U.S. Government frequently coordinates closely with other nations at the UN and elsewhere on the imposition of sanctions and the development of joint positions vis-à-vis acts of terrorism. The possibility of civil suits and potential judgments against state-sponsors of terrorism would inject a new unpredictable element in these very delicate relationships. Such proceedings could in some instances interfere with U.S. counter-terrorism objectives. They could also raise difficult issues involving sensitive intelligence and national security information....
>
> Restrictions on immunity have a reciprocal dimension. If the United States extends the jurisdiction of its courts to embrace cases involving alleged wrongdoing by a foreign state outside the United States, we would have to expect that some other states could do likewise. However, there is of course no guarantee that any action taken by other states would precisely mirror our own. If other states were to expand the jurisdiction of their own courts, they might not limit such action to terrorism, for example, but could seek to include as well other kinds of alleged wrongdoing that could be of concern to us.

The Foreign Sovereign Immunities Act, Hearings on S. 825 before the Subcommittee on Courts and Administrative Practice of the Senate Committee on the Judiciary, 103d Cong., 2d Sess. 14-15 (June 21, 1994) (Statement of Jamison S. Borek). Are these concerns valid? Have subsequent events supported or undermined these concerns? Are there ways that 28 U.S.C. §1605(a)(7) could be amended to address these concerns?

14. What effect might 28 U.S.C. §1605(a)(7) have on future relations between the United States and the nations that are subject to suit? Does it create a risk of retaliation by these nations? Consider two examples: (a) In November 2000, Iran's

Parliament enacted a law that allows Iranian "victims of US interference since the 1953 coup d'etat" to sue the United States in Iranian courts. This law was reportedly enacted as a "measure of reciprocity" in response to the recent suits allowed in U.S. courts against Iran. (b) In 2003, Libya enacted a law that gave Libyan courts jurisdiction over foreign nationals and their government if that government allows lawsuits in its courts against Libya. It was reported in early 2004 that a suit had been brought under this law in Libya seeking billions of dollars in damages from the United States and the United Kingdom for air strikes that took place in 1986. Should the United States be concerned about such retaliatory measures?

15. For additional discussion of civil remedies relating to terrorism, see Jack Goldsmith & Ryan Goodman, *U.S. Civil Litigation and International Terrorism*, in Civil Litigation and Terrorism (John Norton Moore ed., 2003); Joseph W. Dellapenna, *Civil Remedies for International Terrorism*, 12 DePaul Bus. L.J. 169 (1999); Joseph W. Glannon & Jeffrey Atik, *Politics and Personal Jurisdiction: Suing State Sponsors of Terrorism Under the 1996 Amendments to the Foreign Sovereign Immunities Act*, 87 Georgetown L.J. 675 (1999); Walter W. Heiser, *Civil Litigation as a Means of Compensating Victims of International Terrorism*, 3 San Diego Int'l L.J. 1 (2002); William P. Hoye, *Fighting Fire With . . . Mire? Civil Remedies and the New War on State-Sponsored Terrorism*, 12 Duke J. Comp. & Int'l L. 105 (2002); W. Michael Reisman & Monica Hakimi, *Illusion and Reality in the Compensation of Victims of International Terrorism*, 54 Ala. L. Rev. 561 (2001); and Seth N. Stratton, *Taking Terrorists to Court: A Practice Evaluation of Civil Suits Against Terrorists Under the Anti-Terrorism Act*, 9 Suffolk J. Trial & App. Adv. 27 (2004).

F. THE *CHARMING BETSY* CANON

The materials below consider the influence that international law—both customary and treaty-based—can have on the interpretation of federal statutes. As you will see, this interpretive role is where customary international law may have its most significant effect in the U.S. legal system.

United States v. Palestine Liberation Organization

695 F. Supp. 1456 (S.D.N.Y. 1988)

EDMUND L. PALMIERI, UNITED STATES DISTRICT JUDGE. . . .

The United Nations' Headquarters in New York were established as an international enclave by the Agreement Between the United States and the United Nations Regarding the Headquarters of the United Nations (the "Headquarters Agreement"). This agreement followed an invitation extended to the United Nations by the United States, one of its principal founders, to establish its seat within the United States.

As a meeting place and forum for all nations, the United Nations, according to its charter, was formed to:

> maintain international peace and security . . . ; to develop friendly relations among nations, based on [respect for] the principle of equal rights and self-determination of peoples . . . ; to achieve international cooperation in solving international problems

of an economic, social, cultural or humanitarian character...; and be a centre for harmonizing the actions of nations in the attainment of these common ends.

U.N. Charter art. 1. Today, 159 of the United Nations' members maintain missions to the U.N. in New York. In addition, the United Nations has, from its incipiency, welcomed various non-member observers to participate in its proceedings. Of these, several non-member nations, intergovernmental organizations, and other organizations currently maintain "Permanent Observer Missions" in New York.

The PLO falls into the last of these categories and is present at the United Nations as its invitee. *See* Headquarters Agreement, §11. The PLO has none of the usual attributes of sovereignty. It is not accredited to the United States and does not have the benefits of diplomatic immunity. There is no recognized state it claims to govern. It purports to serve as the sole political representative of the Palestinian people. The PLO nevertheless considers itself to be the representative of a state, entitled to recognition in its relations with other governments, and is said to have diplomatic relations with approximately one hundred countries throughout the world.

In 1974, the United Nations invited the PLO to become an observer at the U.N., to "participate in the sessions and the work of the General Assembly in the capacity of observer."...

Since 1974, the PLO has continued to function without interruption as a permanent observer and has maintained its Mission to the United Nations without trammel, largely because of the Headquarters Agreement, which we discuss below.

In October 1986, members of Congress requested the United States Department of State to close the PLO offices located in the United States. That request proved unsuccessful, and proponents of the request introduced legislation with the explicit purpose of doing so.

The result was the ATA, 22 U.S.C. §§5201-5203. It is of a unique nature. We have been unable to find any comparable statute in the long history of Congressional enactments. The PLO is stated to be "a terrorist organization and a threat to the interests of the United States, its allies, and to international law and should not benefit from operating in the United States." 22 U.S.C. §5201(b)....

The ATA, which became effective on March 21, 1988, forbids the establishment or maintenance of "an office, headquarters, premises, or other facilities or establishments within the jurisdiction of the United States at the behest or direction of, or with funds provided by" the PLO, if the purpose is to further the PLO's interests. 22 U.S.C. §5202(3). The ATA also forbids spending the PLO's funds or receiving anything of value except informational material from the PLO, with the same *mens rea* requirement. *Id.* §§5202(1) and (2).

Ten days before the effective date, the Attorney General wrote the Chief of the PLO Observer Mission to the United Nations that "maintaining a PLO Observer Mission to the United Nations will be unlawful," and advised him that upon failure of compliance, the Department of Justice would take action in federal court....

The United States commenced this lawsuit the day the ATA took effect, seeking injunctive relief to accomplish the closure of the Mission. The United States Attorney for this District has personally represented that no action would be taken to enforce the ATA pending resolution of the litigation in this court....

If the ATA were construed as the government suggests, it would be tantamount to a direction to the PLO Observer Mission at the United Nations that it close its doors and cease its operations *instanter*. Such an interpretation would fly in the face of the Headquarters Agreement, a prior treaty between the United Nations and the United States, and would abruptly terminate the functions the Mission has performed for many years. This conflict requires the court to seek out a reconciliation between the two.

Under our constitutional system, statutes and treaties are both the supreme law of the land, and the Constitution sets forth no order of precedence to differentiate between them. U.S. Const. art. VI, cl. 2. Wherever possible, both are to be given effect.... Only where a treaty is irreconcilable with a later enacted statute and Congress has clearly evinced an intent to supersede a treaty by enacting a statute does the later enacted statute take precedence....

The long standing and well-established position of the Mission at the United Nations, sustained by international agreement, when considered along with the text of the ATA and its legislative history, fails to disclose any clear legislative intent that Congress was directing the Attorney General, the State Department or this Court to act in contravention of the Headquarters Agreement. This court acknowledges the validity of the government's position that Congress *has the power* to enact statutes abrogating prior treaties or international obligations entered into by the United States. However, unless this power is clearly and unequivocally exercised, this court is under a duty to interpret statutes in a manner consonant with existing treaty obligations. This is a rule of statutory construction sustained by an unbroken line of authority for over a century and a half. Recently, the Supreme Court articulated it in Weinberger v. Rossi, [456 U.S. 25, 32 (1982)]:

> It has been maxim of statutory construction since the decision in Murray v. The Charming Betsy, 6 U.S. (2 Cranch) 64 (1804), that "an act of Congress ought never to be construed to violate the law of nations, if any other possible construction remains."

The American Law Institute's recently revised Restatement (Third) Foreign Relations Law of the United States (1988) reflects this unbroken line of authority:

§115. INCONSISTENCY BETWEEN INTERNATIONAL LAW OR AGREEMENT AND DOMESTIC LAW: LAW OF THE UNITED STATES

> (1)(a) An Act of Congress supersedes an earlier rule of international law or a provision of an international agreement as law of the United States *if the purpose of the act to supersede the earlier rule or provision is clear* [or] if the act and the earlier rule or provision cannot be fairly reconciled. (emphasis supplied).

We believe the ATA and the Headquarters Agreement cannot be reconciled except by finding the ATA inapplicable to the PLO Observer Mission.

The obligation of the United States to allow transit, entry and access stems not only from the language of the Headquarters Agreement but also from forty years of practice under it. Section 11 of the Headquarters Agreement reads, in part,

> The federal, state or local authorities of the United States shall not impose any impediments to transit to or from the headquarters district of: (1) representatives of Members..., (5) other persons invited to the headquarters district by the United Nations...on official business.

These rights could not be effectively exercised without the use of offices. The ability to effectively organize and carry out one's work, especially as a liaison to an international organization, would not be possible otherwise....

In addition, there can be no dispute that over the forty years since the United States entered into the Headquarters Agreement it has taken a number of actions consistent with its recognition of a duty to refrain from impeding the functions of observer missions to the United Nations.... After the United Nations invited the PLO to participate as a permanent observer, the Department of State took the position that it was required to provide access to the U.N. for the PLO. The State Department at no time disputed the notion that the rights of entry, access and residence guaranteed to invitees include the right to maintain offices.... The United States has, for fourteen years, acted in a manner consistent with a recognition of the PLO's rights in the Headquarters Agreement. This course of conduct under the Headquarters Agreement is important evidence of its meaning....

It seemed clear to those in the executive branch that closing the PLO mission would be a departure from the United States' practice in regard to observer missions, and they made their views known to members of Congress who were instrumental in the passage of the ATA. In addition, United States representatives to the United Nations made repeated efforts to allay the concerns of the U.N. Secretariat by reiterating and reaffirming the obligations of the United States under the Headquarters Agreement.

"Although not conclusive, the meaning attributed to treaty provisions by the Government agencies charged with their negotiation and enforcement is entitled to great weight." Sumitomo Shoji America, Inc. v. Avagliano, 457 U.S. 176, 184-85 (1982). The interpretive statements of the United Nations also carry some weight, especially because they are in harmony with the interpretation given to the Headquarters Agreement by the Department of State.

The lengths to which our courts have sometimes gone in construing domestic statutes so as to avoid conflict with international agreements are suggested by a passage from Justice Field's dissent in [Chew Heong v. United States, 112 U.S. 536, 560-61 (1884)]:

> I am unable to agree with my associates in their construction of the act... restricting the immigration into this country of Chinese laborers. That construction appears to me to be in conflict with the language of that act, and to require the elimination of entire clauses and the interpolation of new ones. It renders nugatory whole provisions which were inserted with sedulous care. The change thus produced in the operation of the act is justified on the theory that to give it any other construction would bring it into conflict with the treaty; and that we are not at liberty to suppose that Congress intended by its legislation to disregard any treaty stipulations.

Chew Heong concerned the interplay of legislation regarding Chinese laborers with treaties on the same subject. During the passage of the statute at issue in *Chew Heong*, "it was objected to the legislation sought that the treaty of 1868 stood in the way, and that while it remained unmodified, such legislation would be a breach of faith to China...." *Id.* at 569. In spite of that, and over Justice Field's dissent, the Court, in Justice Field's words, "narrow[ed] the meaning of the act so as measurably to frustrate its intended operation." Four years after the decision in *Chew Heong*, Congress amended the act in question to nullify that decision. With the amended statute, there could be no question as to Congress' intent to supersede the treaties, and it was the later enacted statute which took precedence. *The Chinese Exclusion Case, supra,* 130 U.S. at 598-99 (1889).

The principles enunciated and applied in *Chew Heong* and its progeny require the clearest of expressions on the part of Congress. We are constrained by these decisions to stress the lack of clarity in Congress' action in this instance. Congress' failure to speak with one clear voice on this subject requires us to interpret the ATA as inapplicable to the Headquarters Agreement. This is so, in short, for the reasons which follow.

First, neither the Mission nor the Headquarters Agreement is mentioned in the ATA itself. Such an inclusion would have left no doubt as to Congress' intent on a matter which had been raised repeatedly with respect to this act, and its absence here reflects equivocation and avoidance, leaving the court without clear interpretive guidance in the language of the act. Second, while the section of the ATA prohibiting the maintenance of an office applies "notwithstanding any provision of law to the contrary," 22 U.S.C. §5202(3), it does not purport to apply notwithstanding any *treaty*. The absence of that interpretive instruction is especially relevant because elsewhere in the same legislation Congress expressly referred to "United States law (including any treaty)." 101 Stat. at 1343. Thus Congress failed, in the text of the ATA, to provide guidance for the interpretation of the act, where it became repeatedly apparent before its passage that the prospect of an interpretive problem was inevitable. Third, no member of Congress expressed a clear and unequivocal intent to supersede the Headquarters Agreement by passage of the ATA. In contrast, most who addressed the subject of conflict denied that there would be a conflict: in their view, the Headquarters Agreement did not provide the PLO with any right to maintain an office. . . .

A more complete explanation begins, of course, with the statute's language. The ATA reads, in part:

> It shall be unlawful, if the purpose be to further the interests of the PLO . . .
>
> > (3) notwithstanding any provision of law to the contrary, to establish or maintain an office, headquarters, premises, or other facilities or establishments within the jurisdiction of the United States at the behest or direction of, or with funds provided by the PLO . . .

22 U.S.C. §5202(3).

The Permanent Observer Mission to the United Nations is nowhere mentioned *in haec verba* in this act, as we have already observed. It is nevertheless contended by the United States that the foregoing provision requires the closing of the Mission, and this in spite of possibly inconsistent international obligations. According to the government, the act is so clear that this possibility is nonexistent. The government argues that its position is supported by the provision that the ATA would take effect "notwithstanding any provision of law to the contrary," 22 U.S.C. §5202(3), suggesting that Congress thereby swept away any inconsistent international obligations of the United States. In effect, the government urges literal application of the maxim that in the event of conflict between two laws, the one of later date will prevail: *leges posteriores priores contrarias abrogant*.

We cannot agree. The proponents of the ATA were, at an early stage and throughout its consideration, forewarned that the ATA would present a potential conflict with the Headquarters Agreement. It was especially important in those circumstances for Congress to give clear, indeed unequivocal guidance, as to how an interpreter of the ATA was to resolve the conflict. Yet there was no reference to the Mission in the text of the ATA, despite extensive discussion of the Mission in the floor debates. Nor was there reference to the Headquarters Agreement, or to any treaty, in the ATA or in its "notwithstanding" clause, despite the textual expression of intent to supersede treaty obligations in other sections of the Foreign Relations Authorization Act, of which the ATA formed a part. Thus Congress failed to provide unequivocal interpretive guidance in the text of the ATA, leaving open the possibility that the ATA could be viewed as a law of general application and enforced as such, without encroaching on the position of the Mission at the United Nations.

That interpretation would present no inconsistency with what little legislative history exists. There were conflicting voices both in Congress and in the executive branch before the enactment of the ATA. Indeed, there is only one matter with respect to which there was unanimity—the condemnation of terrorism. This, however, is extraneous to the legal issues involved here. At oral argument, the United States Attorney conceded that there was no evidence before the court that the Mission had misused its position at the United Nations or engaged in any covert actions in furtherance of terrorism. If the PLO is benefiting from operating in the United States, as the ATA implies, the enforcement of its provisions outside the context of the United Nations can effectively curtail that benefit.

Ma v. Reno

208 F.3d 815 (9th Cir. 2000), *reaffirmed and amended after remand*, 257 F.3d 1095 (9th Cir. 2001)

REINHARDT, CIRCUIT JUDGE. . . .

Petitioner Kim Ho Ma's family fled Cambodia in 1979 and took Ma, who was then two years old, with them. After spending over five years in refugee camps, Ma's family lawfully entered the United States in 1985 as refugees. Ma's status was adjusted to that of a lawful permanent resident in 1987. In 1996, he was convicted, by a jury, of first degree manslaughter following a gang-related shooting. He was sentenced to 38 months in prison, but eventually served only 26 after receiving credit for good behavior. He was tried as an adult, although he was only seventeen years of age at the time of the crime. Although the INS repeatedly refers to Ma's criminal record, this was his only criminal conviction.

Ma's conviction made him removable as an alien convicted of certain crimes under 8 U.S.C. §1227(a)(2). Because he was released by the state authorities after April 1, 1997, the INS's authority to take him into custody was governed by the permanent custody rules of the Illegal Immigration Reform and Immigrant Responsibility Act of 1996 (IIRIRA) (codified at 8 U.S.C. §1231). The INS took Ma into custody following his release from prison and initiated removal proceedings against him. An immigration judge found Ma removable, and furthermore found him ineligible for asylum or withholding of deportation because of his conviction. Ma appealed this ruling to the Board of Immigration Appeals (BIA). The BIA affirmed the immigration judge's decision. Although Ma's order of removal became final on October 26, 1998, the INS could not remove him within the ninety day period during which it is authorized to do so because the United States had, and still has, no repatriation agreement with Cambodia. As a result, Ma remained in detention until he filed this petition for a writ of habeas corpus, which was granted by the district court on September 29, 1999. He is now twenty-two and has been in custody (and, but for the district court's decision, would have been incarcerated) for nearly five years, although his sentence accounts for only a little over two years of that period. . . .

Although the bulk of the parties' arguments, as well as the district court's ruling, address the constitutionality of the INS's detention policy, we must first determine whether Congress provided the INS with the authority to detain Ma indefinitely, as the Attorney General contends.

In general, after an alien is found removable, the Attorney General is required to remove that alien within ninety days after the removal order becomes administratively final. Many aliens, however, cannot be removed within the ninety day period for various reasons. First, some individual cases may simply require more time for processing. Second, there are cases involving aliens who have been ordered removed to countries with whom the United States does not have a repatriation agreement, such as Cambodia, Laos, and Vietnam. Finally, there may be those aliens whose countries refuse to take them for other reasons, and yet others who may be effectively "stateless" because of their race and/or place of birth. Ma falls in the second category.

Under the statute, aliens who cannot be removed at the end of ninety days fall into two groups. Those in the first group must be released subject to supervisory regulations that require them, among other things, to appear regularly before an immigration officer, provide information to that official, notify INS of any change in their employment or residence within 48 hours, submit to medical and psychiatric testing, and comply with substantial restrictions on their travel. 8 U.S.C. §1231(a)(3). Those in the second group "may be detained beyond the removal period" and, if released, shall be subject to the same supervisory provisions applicable to aliens in the first group. 8 U.S.C. §1231(a)(6). Aliens in the second group include, among others, persons removable because of criminal convictions (such as drug offenses, certain crimes of moral turpitude, "aggravated felonies," firearms offenses, and various other crimes). 8 U.S.C. §1227(a)(2). Ma's criminal conviction places him in the second group.

INS argues that its authority to "detain beyond the removal period" gives it the authority to detain indefinitely aliens who fall in the second group and who cannot be removed in the reasonably foreseeable future.[13] Ma argues the opposite — that the INS's authority to detain aliens beyond the removal period does not extend to cases in which removal is not likely in the reasonably foreseeable future. On its face, the statute's text compels neither interpretation: while §1231(a)(6) allows for the detention of group two aliens "beyond" ninety days, it is silent about how long beyond the ninety day period such detention is authorized. Thus, any construction of the statute must read in some provision concerning the length of time beyond the removal period detention may continue, whether it be "indefinitely," "for a reasonable time," or some other temporal measure.

We hold that Congress did not grant the INS authority to detain indefinitely aliens who, like Ma, have entered the United States and cannot be removed to their native land pursuant to a repatriation agreement. To the contrary, we construe the statute as providing the INS with authority to detain aliens only for a reasonable time beyond the statutory removal period. In cases in which an alien has already entered the United States and there is no reasonable likelihood that a foreign

---

13. Although we recognize that, in general, the Attorney General's interpretation of the immigration laws is entitled to substantial deference, INS v. Aguirre-Aguirre, 526 U.S. 415, 425 (1999), we have held that *Chevron* principles (Chevron U.S.A. v. Natural Resources Defense Council, 467 U.S. 837 (1984)) are not applicable where a substantial constitutional question is raised by an agency's interpretation of a statute it is authorized to construe. . . . As we explain *infra*, the agency's interpretation raises just such a substantial question.

government will accept the alien's return in the reasonably foreseeable future, we conclude that the statute does not permit the Attorney General to hold the alien beyond the statutory removal period. Rather, the alien must be released subject to the supervisory authority provided in the statute.

We adopt our construction of the statute for several reasons. First, and most important, the result we reach allows us to avoid deciding whether or not INS's indefinite detention policy violates the due process guarantees of the Fifth Amendment. Second, our reading is the most reasonable one — it better comports with the language of the statute and permits us to avoid assuming that Congress intended a result as harsh as indefinite detention in the absence of any clear statement to that effect. Third, reading an implicit "reasonable time" limitation into the statute is consistent with our case law interpreting a similar provision in a prior immigration statute. Finally, the interpretation we adopt is more consonant with international law. . . .

In interpreting the statute to include a reasonable time limitation, we are also influenced by amicus curiae Human Rights Watch's argument that we should apply the well-established *Charming Betsy* rule of statutory construction which requires that we generally construe Congressional legislation to avoid violating international law. Weinberger v. Rossi, 456 U.S. 25, 32 (1982) (citing Murray v. The Schooner Charming Betsy, 6 U.S. (2 Cranch) 64, 117-118 (1804)). We have reaffirmed this rule on several occasions. . . .

We recently recognized that "a clear international prohibition" exists against prolonged and arbitrary detention. Martinez v. City of Los Angeles, 141 F.3d 1373, 1384 (9th Cir. 1998).[28] Furthermore, Article 9 of the International Covenant on Civil and Political Rights (ICCPR), which the United States has ratified, see 138 Cong. Rec. S4781-84 (Apr. 2, 1992), provides that "no one shall be subjected to arbitrary arrest and detention." . . . ; *see also* Trans World Airlines, Inc. v. Franklin Mint Corp., 466 U.S. 243, 252 (1984) (holding that ambiguous Congressional action should not be construed to abrogate a treaty).

In the present case, construing the statute to authorize the indefinite detention of removable aliens might violate international law. . . . Given the strength of the rule of international law, our construction of the statute renders it consistent with the *Charming Betsy* rule.

Notes and Questions

1. The Supreme Court has long sought to construe federal statutes so that they do not violate international law. In Talbot v. Seeman, 5 U.S. (1 Cranch) 1 (1801), the Court considered the amount of salvage that should be awarded to a U.S. navy

---

28. This court has held that within the domestic legal structure, international law is displaced by "a properly enacted statute, provided it be constitutional, even if that statute violates international law." Alvarez-Mendez v. Stock, 941 F.2d 956, 963 (9th Cir. 1991) (involving prolonged detention of excludable aliens); *see also* Barrera-Echavarria v. Rison, 44 F.3d 1441, 1451 (9th Cir. 1995). Those rulings, however, do not suggest that courts should refrain from applying the *Charming Betsy* principle. Rather, they stand for the proposition that when Congress has clearly abrogated international law through legislation, that legislation nonetheless has the full force of law. *See* Restatement (Third) of [Foreign Relations] Law §115(1)(a) ("An Act of Congress supercedes an earlier rule of international law or a provision of an international agreement as law of the United States if the purpose of the act to supercede the earlier rule or provision is clear and if the act and the earlier rule or provision cannot be fairly reconciled"). Although Congress may override international law in enacting a statute, we do not presume that Congress had such an intent when the statute can reasonably be reconciled with the law of nations.

captain for seizing, during the undeclared war between the United States and France, a neutral ship that had been captured by the French. The captain cited a 1799 federal statute that allowed salvage in the amount of one-half the value of the ship and its cargo in the case of ships seized "belonging to . . . subjects of any nation in amity with the United States, if re-taken from the enemy . . . after ninety-six hours." The Court was concerned, however, that allowing such a large salvage for a neutral vessel would violate customary international law, given that neutral vessels were ordinarily not subject to *any* salvage under such law. In an opinion by Chief Justice Marshall, the Court acknowledged that the language of the statute could be read as supporting the captain's claim. Nevertheless, the Court said that "the laws of the United States ought not, if it be avoidable, so to be construed as to infract the common principles and usages of nations." *Id.* at 43. The Court proceeded to construe the statute as applying only in the case of vessels from countries at war with the capturing country and thus as inapplicable in this case. The Court explained that, "[b]y this construction the act of Congress will never violate those principles which we believe, and which it is our duty to believe, the legislature of the United States will always hold sacred." *Id.* at 44.

The Court reaffirmed this canon of construction in Murray v. The Schooner Charming Betsy, 6 U.S. (2 Cranch) 64 (1804), albeit without citing back to the *Talbot* decision. Like *Talbot*, the *Charming Betsy* case concerned events relating to the undeclared war with France. During that war, the United States passed the Non-intercourse Act of 1800, which prohibited trade "between any person or persons resident within the United States or under their protection, and any person or persons resident within the territories of the French Republic, or any of the dependencies thereof." To enforce the statute, the U.S. Navy was under orders from President Adams to seize any vessel suspected of trading with the French. A Navy frigate subsequently seized the schooner *Charming Betsy* on the high seas, suspecting her of engaging in trade with Guadaloupe, a French dependency, in violation of the statute. The owner of the ship had been born in the United States but had moved as a child to St. Thomas, a Danish island, and had become a Danish citizen. He argued that, because he was a citizen of a neutral country, the seizure of his vessel violated international law rules of neutrality. The Court, again in an opinion by Chief Justice Marshall, recited among the "principles . . . believed to be correct" and "which ought to be kept in view in construing the act now under consideration," the following proposition: "an act of Congress ought never to be construed to violate the law of nations if any other possible construction remains. . . ." 6 U.S. at 118. The Court proceeded to construe the Nonintercourse Act as not applying to the owner of the vessel, because he was not at the time of the seizure a resident of the United States or "under [its] protection." *Id.* at 120. The canon of construction invoked by the Court is today commonly referred to as the "*Charming Betsy* canon."

2. What, if anything, does the *Charming Betsy* canon tell us about the status of international law in U.S. courts? What is the relationship between the canon and the last-in-time rule between treaties and statutes, discussed in Chapter 6? Should the canon apply equally to potential conflicts with treaties and customary international law? In *Filartiga v. Pena-Irala*, which we considered above in Section A, the court cited the *Charming Betsy* canon as "[t]he plainest evidence that international law has an existence in the federal courts independent of acts of Congress." *See* 630 F.2d 876, 887 n.20. What does this statement mean? Is it correct?

3. The Restatement (Third) of Foreign Relations Law describes the *Charming Betsy* canon in somewhat softer terms than the language used by Chief Justice Marshall. The Restatement (Third) states that "[w]here fairly possible, a United States statute is to be construed so as not to conflict with international law or with an international agreement of the United States." Restatement (Third) of the Foreign Relations Law of the United States §114 (1987). Under either formulation of the canon, what evidence will be sufficient to show that Congress intended a result contrary to international law?

4. What international law was implicated in the *PLO* decision excerpted above? How was the statute there ambiguous? What did the legislative history suggest about Congress's intent? What would Congress need to have done to show a clear intent to override the UN Headquarters Agreement? In Ma v. Reno, why didn't the court defer to the INS's construction of the statute?

5. The Supreme Court has long held that statutes should be construed, where reasonably possible, so that they do not violate the Constitution. *See* Edward J. DeBartolo Corp. v. Florida Gulf Coast Bldg. & Constr. Trades Council, 485 U.S. 568, 575 (1988); Ashwander v. TVA, 297 U.S. 288, 346 (1936) (Brandeis J., concurring). What relationship, if any, is there between this constitutional avoidance canon and the *Charming Betsy* canon? Why do you think the Court attempts to avoid finding statutes unconstitutional? Are there similar reasons for attempting to avoid finding statutes in violation of international law? What, if anything, does Ma v. Reno suggest about this issue?

6. What is the relationship between the *Charming Betsy* canon and deference to the Executive Branch, either pursuant to the *Chevron* doctrine or, more generally, as a matter of "foreign affairs deference"? Should the canon override such deference? Does the answer depend on whether the international law violation involves a treaty or customary international law? What deference, if any, did the courts in the above decisions give to the Executive Branch? For discussion of the relationship between the *Charming Betsy* canon and *Chevron* deference, see Curtis A. Bradley, Chevron *Deference and Foreign Affairs*, 86 Va. L. Rev. 649, 685-90 (2000). Note that, as we have previously discussed, the Executive Branch may receive deference in its interpretation of international law. As a result, it may be in a position to influence a court's determination of whether there is a potential conflict with international law, and thus whether to apply the *Charming Betsy* canon at all. Note also that courts normally accept the interpretation by administrative agencies of their own regulations. For a decision holding that an interpretation by the Office of Foreign Assets Control (OFAC) of one of its sanctions regulations relating to Cuba should receive deference even if the interpretation entailed a violation of treaty commitments, see Havana Club Holding, S.A. v. Galleon, S.A., 203 F.3d 116 (2d Cir. 2000). The court there explained that, "[w]hether or not deference to an administrative agency's interpretation of its own provisions would override treaty provisions in other contexts, we have no doubt that Congress, whose purpose we are ultimately obliged to follow on this issue, expects that OFAC's restrictive interpretation of [the sanctions provision in question] will override any conflicting treaty protection."

7. The Supreme Court appears to have inadvertently confused matters concerning the relationship between the *Charming Betsy* canon and both the constitutional avoidance canon and *Chevron* deference. In NLRB v. Catholic Bishop of Chicago, the Court, in invoking the constitutional avoidance canon, stated as follows: "In a number of cases the Court has heeded the essence of Mr. Chief Justice

Marshall's admonition in Murray v. The Charming Betsy, 2 Cranch 64, 118 (1804), by holding that an Act of Congress ought not be construed to violate the Constitution if any other possible construction remains available." 440 U.S. 490, 500 (1979). But there is no such admonition in the *Charming Betsy* decision, only the admonition about not violating international law. The phrasing of the *Charming Betsy* canon is similar to the constitutional avoidance canon, so it is possible that this caused the Court in *Catholic Bishop* to include the mistaken reference. Whatever the reason, the Court repeated the mistaken citation in DeBartolo Corp. v. Florida Gulf Coast Trades Council, a decision that holds that the constitutional avoidance canon trumps *Chevron* deference. 485 U.S. 569, 575-78 (1988); *see also, e.g.*, INS v. St. Cyr, 121 S. Ct. 2271, 2279 n.12 (2001). This reference has in turn led at least one commentator, as well as the Court of International Trade in several decisions, to conclude that the Supreme Court has already held that the *Charming Betsy* canon trumps *Chevron* deference. *See* Ronald A. Brand, *Direct Effect of International Economic Law in the United States and European Union*, 17 Nw. J. Int'l L. & Bus. 557, 571 n.76 (1996/97); Hyundai Elecs. Co. v. United States, 53 F. Supp. 2d 1334, 1344 (Ct. Int'l Trade 1999). Consistent with its prior decisions, the Court of International Trade held in Usinor v. United States, 2002 Ct. Int'l Trade LEXIS 98 (C.I.T. July 19, 2002), that "the reasonability of an agency's interpretation [under *Chevron*] must be gauged against such [international] obligations."

8. Courts frequently invoke the *Charming Betsy* canon to limit the extraterritorial application of U.S. laws in ways that would arguably violate international law norms of prescriptive jurisdiction. *See, e.g.*, F. Hoffman-La Roche Ltd. v. Empagran S.A., 124 S. Ct. 2359, 2366 (2004); Hartford Fire Insurance Co. v. California, 509 U.S. 764, 814-16 (Scalia, J., dissenting); McCulloch v. Sociedad Nacional de Marineros de Honduras, 372 U.S. 10, 21 (1962). (We consider the extraterritorial application of U.S. law in the next chapter.) In this and other contexts where the canon if most frequently applied, the statute in question regulates primary conduct.

Does the canon also apply in the different context of a grant of discretionary enforcement authority to the President? Consider the 2001 Authorization for the Use of Military Force (AUMF), analyzed in Chapter 4, which authorized the President to use "all necessary and appropriate force" against (among others) the terrorists responsible for the September 11 attacks. Does the *Charming Betsy* canon apply to the interpretation of this statute? Does the answer depend on the purpose of the canon? One purpose of the canon is to avoid having judges, who are politically unaccountable and inexpert in foreign affairs, erroneously place the United States in violation of international law through their construction of a statute. Is this purpose served by applying it to authorizing statutes like the AUMF? *Cf.* United States v. Corey, 232 F.3d 1166, 1179 n.9 (9th Cir. 2000) ("These concerns [underlying the *Charming Betsy* canon] are obviously much less serious where the interpretation arguably violating international law is urged upon us by the Executive Branch of our government. When construing a statute with potential foreign policy implications, we must presume that the President has evaluated the foreign policy consequences of such an exercise of U.S. law and determined that it serves the interests of the United States."); Authority of the Federal Bureau of Investigation to Override International Law in Extraterritorial Law Enforcement Activities, 13 Op. Off. Legal Counsel 163, 171 (1989) (concluding that the *Charming Betsy* canon was not applicable to "broad authorizing statutes 'carrying into execution'" core Executive powers). For discussion of these issues, compare Ingrid Brunk

Wuerth, *Authorizations for the Use of Force, International Law, and the Charming Betsy Canon*, 46 B.C. L. Rev. 293, 324-28 (2005) (arguing that canon does apply to authorizing statutes), with Curtis A. Bradley & Jack L. Goldsmith, *Congressional Authorization and the War on Terrorism*, 118 Harv. L. Rev. 2047, 2097-98 (2005) (suggesting that it may not apply to such statutes).

9. Sometimes the issue is not whether a statute violates international law, but rather whether the statute extends as far as international law would allow. This issue has come up in connection with suits brought under the Foreign Sovereign Immunities Act (FSIA), which provides that foreign states are immune from suit in U.S. courts unless the suit falls within one of the Act's specified exceptions to immunity. Although the FSIA does not contain an express exception to immunity for violations of *jus cogens* norms of international law, some litigants and scholars have agued that the FSIA's exception for situations in which a foreign state has "waived its immunity . . . by implication" should be construed to include situations in which a foreign state has acted contrary to *jus cogens* norms. Supporters of this construction sometimes invoke the *Charming Betsy* canon. They reason that foreign states are not entitled under international law to immunity from suit for violations of *jus cogens* norms, and that, pursuant to the *Charming Betsy* canon, the FSIA should be construed similarly to deny immunity in this situation.

As mentioned above in the notes in Section C, courts have rejected this construction of the FSIA. *See, e.g.*, Sampson v. Federal Republic of Germany, 250 F.3d 1145 (7th Cir. 2001); Smith v. Socialist People's Libyan Arab Jamahiriya, 101 F.3d 239, 344-45 (2d Cir. 1996); Princz v. Federal Republic of Germany, 26 F.3d 1166 (D.C. Cir. 1994); Siderman de Blake v. Republic of Argentina, 965 F.2d 699, 718-19 (9th Cir. 1992). Consider one court's explanation of why this construction does not follow from the *Charming Betsy* canon:

> While the *Charming Betsy* canon directs courts to construe ambiguous statutes to avoid conflicts with international law, international law itself does not mandate Article III jurisdiction over foreign sovereigns. In other words, although jus cogens norms may address sovereign immunity in contexts where the question is whether international law itself provides immunity, e.g., the Nuremberg proceedings, jus cogens norms do not require Congress (or any government) to create jurisdiction. Because international law is silent on the grant of federal court jurisdiction at issue, we interpret the FSIA without reference to the Charming Betsy canon. . . .
>
> [A]lthough international law is "part of our law," it does not follow that federal statutes must be read to reflect the norms of international law. . . . Since customary international law in the modern era is often based on the contents of multi-lateral treaties to which the United States attaches reservations (or refuses to join at all), there is little reason to indulge in a presumption that Congress intends courts to mold ambiguous statutes into consistency with international law. Use of the canon so as to effectively incorporate customary international law into federal statutes when the political branches of our government may have rejected the international law at issue seems dubious at best.

Sampson, 250 F.3d at 1151-53. Is the court's analysis persuasive? For a more expansive view of the role of the *Charming Betsy* canon, in the context of federal immigration law, see Beharry v. Reno, 183 F. Supp. 2d 584, 591 (S.D.N.Y. 2002) (relying on *Charming Betsy* for the proposition that "[i]mmigration statutes must be woven into the seamless web of our national and international law"), *rev'd on other grounds*, 329 F.3d 51 (2d Cir. 2003).

10. For general discussions of the *Charming Betsy* canon, see Curtis A. Bradley, *The Charming Betsy Canon and Separation of Powers: Rethinking the Interpretive Role of International Law*, 86 Geo. L.J. 479 (1998); Ralph G. Steinhardt, *The Role of International Law as a Canon of Domestic Statutory Construction*, 43 Vand. L. Rev. 1103 (1990); Jonathan Turley, *Dualistic Values in an Age of International Legisprudence*, 44 Hastings L.J. 185 (1993). *See also* Jane A. Restani & Ira Bloom, *Interpreting International Trade Statutes: Is the Charming Betsy Sinking?*, 24 Fordham Int'l L.J. 1533 (2001); Michael F. Williams, Note, *Charming Betsy, Chevron, and the World Trade Organization: Thoughts on the Interpretive Effect of International Trade Law*, 32 Law & Pol'y Int'l Bus. 677 (2001). For a historical description of the *Charming Betsy* case, see Frederick C. Leiner, *The Charming Betsy and the Marshall Court*, 14 Am. J. Leg. Hist. 1 (2001).

G. RELIANCE ON FOREIGN AND INTERNATIONAL MATERIALS IN CONSTITUTIONAL INTERPRETATION

Roper v. Simmons

125 S. Ct. 1183 (2005)

[Simmons committed a gruesome murder at age 17 and was later convicted of capital murder and sentenced to death. He argued that the Eighth Amendment's ban on cruel and unusual punishments prohibits the execution of individuals who commit their capital offenses before the age of 18.]

JUSTICE KENNEDY delivered the opinion of the Court.

This case requires us to address, for the second time in a decade and a half, whether it is permissible under the Eighth and Fourteenth Amendments to the Constitution of the United States to execute a juvenile offender who was older than 15 but younger than 18 when he committed a capital crime. In Stanford v. Kentucky, 492 U.S. 361 (1989), a divided Court rejected the proposition that the Constitution bars capital punishment for juvenile offenders in this age group. We reconsider the question.

The Eighth Amendment provides: "Excessive bail shall not be required, nor excessive fines imposed, nor cruel and unusual punishments inflicted." The provision is applicable to the States through the Fourteenth Amendment....

The prohibition against "cruel and unusual punishments," like other expansive language in the Constitution, must be interpreted according to its text, by considering history, tradition, and precedent, and with due regard for its purpose and function in the constitutional design. To implement this framework we have established the propriety and affirmed the necessity of referring to "the evolving standards of decency that mark the progress of a maturing society" to determine which punishments are so disproportionate as to be cruel and unusual. Trop v. Dulles, 356 U.S. 86, 100-101 (1958) (plurality opinion).

[After determining that there was a national consensus against the death penalty for juveniles, and that the death penalty is disproportionate punishment for offenders under 18, the Court turned to consider foreign and international law.]

Our determination that the death penalty is disproportionate punishment for offenders under 18 finds confirmation in the stark reality that the United States is the only country in the world that continues to give official sanction to the juvenile death penalty. This reality does not become controlling, for the task of interpreting the Eighth Amendment remains our responsibility. Yet at least from the time of the Court's decision in *Trop*, the Court has referred to the laws of other countries and to international authorities as instructive for its interpretation of the Eighth Amendment's prohibition of "cruel and unusual punishments." 356 U.S., at 102-103 (plurality opinion) ("The civilized nations of the world are in virtual unanimity that statelessness is not to be imposed as punishment for crime"); *see also* Atkins v. Virginia, 536 U.S. 304, 317, n. 21 (2002) (recognizing that "within the world community, the imposition of the death penalty for crimes committed by mentally retarded offenders is overwhelmingly disapproved"); Thompson v. Oklahoma, 487 U.S. 815, 830-831 & n. 31 (1988) (plurality opinion) (noting the abolition of the juvenile death penalty "by other nations that share our Anglo-American heritage, and by the leading members of the Western European community," and observing that "we have previously recognized the relevance of the views of the international community in determining whether a punishment is cruel and unusual"); Enmund v. Florida, 458 U.S. 782, 796-797, n. 22 (1982) (observing that "the doctrine of felony murder has been abolished in England and India, severely restricted in Canada and a number of other Commonwealth countries, and is unknown in continental Europe"); Coker v. Georgia, 433 U.S. 584, 596, n. 10 (1977) (plurality opinion) ("It is . . . not irrelevant here that out of 60 major nations in the world surveyed in 1965, only 3 retained the death penalty for rape where death did not ensue").

As respondent and a number of amici emphasize, Article 37 of the United Nations Convention on the Rights of the Child, which every country in the world has ratified save for the United States and Somalia, contains an express prohibition on capital punishment for crimes committed by juveniles under 18. United Nations Convention on the Rights of the Child, Art. 37, Nov. 20, 1989, 1577 U.N.T.S. 3 (entered into force Sept. 2, 1990). No ratifying country has entered a reservation to the provision prohibiting the execution of juvenile offenders. Parallel prohibitions are contained in other significant international covenants. *See* International Covenant for Civil and Political Rights, Art. 6(5), 999 U.N.T.S., at 175 (prohibiting capital punishment for anyone under 18 at the time of offense) (signed and ratified by the United States subject to a reservation regarding Article 6(5); American Convention on Human Rights: Pact of San Jose, Costa Rica, Art. 4(5), Nov. 22, 1969, 1144 U.N.T.S. 146 (entered into force July 19, 1978) (same); African Charter on the Rights and Welfare of the Child, Art. 5(3), OAU Doc. CAB/ LEG/24.9/49 (1990) (entered into force Nov. 29, 1999) (same).

Respondent and his amici have submitted, and petitioner does not contest, that only seven countries other than the United States have executed juvenile offenders since 1990: Iran, Pakistan, Saudi Arabia, Yemen, Nigeria, the Democratic Republic of Congo, and China. Since then each of these countries has either abolished capital punishment for juveniles or made public disavowal of the practice. In sum, it is fair to say that the United States now stands alone in a world that has turned its face against the juvenile death penalty.

Though the international covenants prohibiting the juvenile death penalty are of more recent date, it is instructive to note that the United Kingdom abolished the juvenile death penalty before these covenants came into being. The United Kingdom's experience bears particular relevance here in light of the historic ties between our countries and in light of the Eighth Amendment's own origins. . . .

As of now, the United Kingdom has abolished the death penalty in its entirety; but, decades before it took this step, it recognized the disproportionate nature of the juvenile death penalty; and it abolished that penalty as a separate matter.... In the 56 years that have passed since the United Kingdom abolished the juvenile death penalty, the weight of authority against it there, and in the international community, has become well established.

It is proper that we acknowledge the overwhelming weight of international opinion against the juvenile death penalty, resting in large part on the understanding that the instability and emotional imbalance of young people may often be a factor in the crime. The opinion of the world community, while not controlling our outcome, does provide respected and significant confirmation for our own conclusions.

Over time, from one generation to the next, the Constitution has come to earn the high respect and even, as Madison dared to hope, the veneration of the American people. The document sets forth, and rests upon, innovative principles original to the American experience, such as federalism; a proven balance in political mechanisms through separation of powers; specific guarantees for the accused in criminal cases; and broad provisions to secure individual freedom and preserve human dignity. These doctrines and guarantees are central to the American experience and remain essential to our present-day self-definition and national identity. Not the least of the reasons we honor the Constitution, then, is because we know it to be our own. It does not lessen our fidelity to the Constitution or our pride in its origins to acknowledge that the express affirmation of certain fundamental rights by other nations and peoples simply underscores the centrality of those same rights within our own heritage of freedom....

JUSTICE O'CONNOR, dissenting....

[Justice O'Connor disagreed with the majority's conclusion that the execution of juvenile offenders violates the Eighth Amendment, reasoning that neither the objective evidence of contemporary societal values, nor the Court's moral proportionality analysis, sufficed to justify the conclusion. She then had this to say about the Court's discussion of foreign and international law.]

Without question, there has been a global trend in recent years towards abolishing capital punishment for under-18 offenders. Very few, if any, countries other than the United States now permit this practice in law or in fact. While acknowledging that the actions and views of other countries do not dictate the outcome of our Eighth Amendment inquiry, the Court asserts that "the overwhelming weight of international opinion against the juvenile death penalty...does provide respected and significant confirmation for [its] own conclusions." Because I do not believe that a genuine national consensus against the juvenile death penalty has yet developed, and because I do not believe the Court's moral proportionality argument justifies a categorical, age-based constitutional rule, I can assign no such confirmatory role to the international consensus described by the Court. In short, the evidence of an international consensus does not alter my determination that the Eighth Amendment does not, at this time, forbid capital punishment of 17-year-old murderers in all cases.

Nevertheless, I disagree with Justice Scalia's contention that foreign and international law have no place in our Eighth Amendment jurisprudence. Over the course of nearly half a century, the Court has consistently referred to foreign and international law as relevant to its assessment of evolving standards of decency. This inquiry reflects the special character of the Eighth Amendment, which, as the

Court has long held, draws its meaning directly from the maturing values of civilized society. Obviously, American law is distinctive in many respects, not least where the specific provisions of our Constitution and the history of its exposition so dictate. But this Nation's evolving understanding of human dignity certainly is neither wholly isolated from, nor inherently at odds with, the values prevailing in other countries. On the contrary, we should not be surprised to find congruence between domestic and international values, especially where the international community has reached clear agreement — expressed in international law or in the domestic laws of individual countries — that a particular form of punishment is inconsistent with fundamental human rights. At least, the existence of an international consensus of this nature can serve to confirm the reasonableness of a consonant and genuine American consensus. The instant case presents no such domestic consensus, however, and the recent emergence of an otherwise global consensus does not alter that basic fact. . . .

JUSTICE SCALIA, with whom THE CHIEF JUSTICE and JUSTICE THOMAS join, dissenting. . . .

Though the views of our own citizens are essentially irrelevant to the Court's decision today, the views of other countries and the so-called international community take center stage.

The Court begins by noting that "Article 37 of the United Nations Convention on the Rights of the Child, which every country in the world has ratified save for the United States and Somalia, contains an express prohibition on capital punishment for crimes committed by juveniles under 18." The Court also discusses the International Covenant on Civil and Political Rights (ICCPR), which the Senate ratified only subject to a reservation that reads:

> The United States reserves the right, subject to its Constitutional restraints, to impose capital punishment on any person (other than a pregnant woman) duly convicted under existing or future laws permitting the imposition of capital punishment, including such punishment for crime committed by persons below eighteen years of age.

Senate Committee on Foreign Relations, International Covenant on Civil and Political Rights, S. Exec. Rep. No. 102-23, (1992).

Unless the Court has added to its arsenal the power to join and ratify treaties on behalf of the United States, I cannot see how this evidence favors, rather than refutes, its position. That the Senate and the President — those actors our Constitution empowers to enter into treaties, see Art. II, §2 — have declined to join and ratify treaties prohibiting execution of under-18 offenders can only suggest that our country has either not reached a national consensus on the question, or has reached a consensus contrary to what the Court announces. That the reservation to the ICCPR was made in 1992 does not suggest otherwise, since the reservation still remains in place today. It is also worth noting that, in addition to barring the execution of under-18 offenders, the United Nations Convention on the Rights of the Child prohibits punishing them with life in prison without the possibility of release. If we are truly going to get in line with the international community, then the Court's reassurance that the death penalty is really not needed, since "the punishment of life imprisonment without the possibility of parole is itself a severe sanction," gives little comfort. . . .

[The] basic premise of the Court's argument — that American law should conform to the laws of the rest of the world — ought to be rejected out of hand. In fact the Court itself does not believe it. In many significant respects the laws of most other countries differ from our law — including not only such explicit provisions of our Constitution as the right to jury trial and grand jury indictment, but even many interpretations of the Constitution prescribed by this Court itself. The Court-pronounced exclusionary rule, for example, is distinctively American. When we adopted that rule in Mapp v. Ohio, 367 U.S. 643, 655 (1965), it was "unique to American Jurisprudence." Bivens v. Six Unknown Fed. Narcotics Agents, 403 U.S. 388, 415 (1971) (Burger, C.J., dissenting). Since then a categorical exclusionary rule has been "universally rejected" by other countries, including those with rules prohibiting illegal searches and police misconduct, despite the fact that none of these countries "appears to have any alternative form of discipline for police that is effective in preventing search violations." Bradley, Mapp Goes Abroad, 52 Case W. Res. L. Rev. 375, 399-400 (2001). England, for example, rarely excludes evidence found during an illegal search or seizure and has only recently begun excluding evidence from illegally obtained confessions. Canada rarely excludes evidence and will only do so if admission will "bring the administration of justice into disrepute." The European Court of Human Rights has held that introduction of illegally seized evidence does not violate the "fair trial" requirement in Article 6, §1, of the European Convention on Human Rights.

The Court has been oblivious to the views of other countries when deciding how to interpret our Constitution's requirement that "Congress shall make no law respecting an establishment of religion..." Amdt. 1. Most other countries — including those committed to religious neutrality — do not insist on the degree of separation between church and state that this Court requires. For example, whereas "we have recognized special Establishment Clause dangers where the government makes direct money payments to sectarian institutions," Rosenberger v. Rector and Visitors of Univ. of Va., 515 U.S. 819, 842 (1995) (citing cases), countries such as the Netherlands, Germany, and Australia allow direct government funding of religious schools on the ground that "the state can only be truly neutral between secular and religious perspectives if it does not dominate the provision of so key a service as education, and makes it possible for people to exercise their right of religious expression within the context of public funding." S. Monsma & J. Soper, The Challenge of Pluralism: Church and State in Five Democracies 207 (1997). England permits the teaching of religion in state schools. Even in France, which is considered "America's only rival in strictness of church-state separation," "the practice of contracting for educational services provided by Catholic schools is very widespread." C. Glenn, The Ambiguous Embrace: Government and Faith-Based Schools and Social Agencies 110 (2000).

And let us not forget the Court's abortion jurisprudence, which makes us one of only six countries that allow abortion on demand until the point of viability. Though the Government and amici in cases following Roe v. Wade, 410 U.S. 113 (1973), urged the Court to follow the international community's lead, these arguments fell on deaf ears.

The Court's special reliance on the laws of the United Kingdom is perhaps the most indefensible part of its opinion. It is of course true that we share a common history with the United Kingdom, and that we often consult English sources when asked to discern the meaning of a constitutional text written against the backdrop of 18th-century English law and legal thought. If we applied that approach today, our task would be an easy one. As we explained in Harmelin v. Michigan, 501 U.S. 957, 973-974 (1991), the "Cruell and Unusuall Punishments" provision of the English Declaration of Rights was originally meant to describe those punishments "'out of [the Judges'] Power'" — that is, those punishments that were not authorized by common law or statute, but that were nonetheless administered by the Crown or the Crown's judges. Under that reasoning, the death penalty for under-18 offenders would easily survive this challenge. The Court has, however — I think wrongly — long rejected a purely originalist approach to our Eighth Amendment, and that is certainly not the approach the Court takes today. Instead, the Court undertakes the majestic task of determining (and thereby prescribing) our Nation's current standards of decency. It is beyond comprehension why we should look, for that purpose, to a country that has developed, in the centuries since the Revolutionary War — and with increasing speed since the United Kingdom's recent submission to the jurisprudence of European courts dominated by continental jurists — a legal, political, and social culture quite different from our own. If we took the Court's directive seriously, we would also consider relaxing our double jeopardy prohibition, since the British Law Commission recently published a report that would significantly extend the rights of the prosecution to appeal cases where an acquittal was the result of a judge's ruling that was legally incorrect. We would also curtail our right to jury trial in criminal cases since, despite the jury system's deep roots in our shared common law, England now permits all but the most serious offenders to be tried by magistrates without a jury.

The Court should either profess its willingness to reconsider all these matters in light of the views of foreigners, or else it should cease putting forth foreigners' views as part of the reasoned basis of its decisions. To invoke alien law when it agrees with one's own thinking, and ignore it otherwise, is not reasoned decision-making, but sophistry.[9]

The Court responds that "it does not lessen our fidelity to the Constitution or our pride in its origins to acknowledge that the express affirmation of certain fundamental rights by other nations and peoples simply underscores the centrality of those same rights within our own heritage of freedom." To begin with, I do not believe that approval by "other nations and peoples" should buttress our commitment to American principles any more than (what should logically follow) disapproval by "other nations and peoples" should weaken that commitment. More importantly, however, the Court's statement flatly misdescribes what is going on here. Foreign sources are cited today, not to underscore our "fidelity" to the Constitution, our "pride in its origins," and "our own [American] heritage." To the contrary, they are cited to set aside the centuries-old American practice — a practice still engaged in by a large majority of the relevant States — of letting a jury of 12 citizens decide whether, in the particular case, youth should be the basis for withholding the death penalty. What these foreign sources "affirm," rather than repudiate, is the Justices' own notion of how the world ought to be, and their diktat that it shall be so henceforth in America. The Court's parting attempt to downplay the significance of its extensive discussion of foreign law is unconvincing. "Acknowledgment" of foreign approval has no place in the legal opinion of this

9. .... Justice O'Connor asserts that an international consensus can at least "serve to confirm the reasonableness of a consonant and genuine American consensus." Surely not unless it can also demonstrate the unreasonableness of such a consensus. Either America's principles are its own, or they follow the world; one cannot have it both ways.... Justice O'Connor finds it unnecessary to consult foreign law in the present case because there is "no ... domestic consensus" to be confirmed. But since she believes that the Justices can announce their own requirements of "moral proportionality" despite the absence of consensus, why would foreign law not be relevant to that judgment? If foreign law is powerful enough to supplant the judgment of the American people, surely it is powerful enough to change a personal assessment of moral proportionality.

Court unless it is part of the basis for the Court's judgment — which is surely what it parades as today.

Notes and Questions

1. In addition to the majority opinion in *Roper*, the Supreme Court has in a number of recent constitutional decisions referred to foreign or international law materials. In Lawrence v. Texas, 123 S. Ct. 2472 (2003), in striking down a Texas anti-sodomy law and overturning Bowers v. Hardwick, 478 U.S. 186 (1986), the Court cited to British law and to a decision by the European Court of Human Rights:

> The sweeping references by Chief Justice Burger [in his concurrence in *Bowers*] to the history of Western civilization and to Judeo-Christian moral and ethical standards did not take account of other authorities pointing in an opposite direction. A committee advising the British Parliament recommended in 1957 repeal of laws punishing homosexual conduct. Parliament enacted the substance of those recommendations 10 years later.
>
> Of even more importance, almost five years before *Bowers* was decided the European Court of Human Rights considered a case with parallels to *Bowers* and to today's case. An adult male resident in Northern Ireland alleged he was a practicing homosexual who desired to engage in consensual homosexual conduct. The laws of Northern Ireland forbade him that right. He alleged that he had been questioned, his home had been searched, and he feared criminal prosecution. The court held that the laws proscribing the conduct were invalid under the European Convention on Human Rights. Authoritative in all countries that are members of the Council of Europe (21 nations then, 45 nations now), the decision is at odds with the premise in *Bowers* that the claim put forward was insubstantial in our Western civilization.

In his dissent in that case (joined by two other Justices), Justice Scalia objected that these foreign law materials were not relevant to the constitutional analysis and were not responsive to the majority opinion in *Bowers*:

> Constitutional entitlements do not spring into existence because some States choose to lessen or eliminate criminal sanctions on certain behavior. Much less do they spring into existence, as the Court seems to believe, because *foreign nations* decriminalize conduct. The *Bowers* majority opinion *never* relied on "values we share with a wider civilization," but rather rejected the claimed right to sodomy on the ground that such a right was not "'deeply rooted in *this Nation's* history and tradition,'" 478 U.S., at 193-194 (emphasis added). *Bowers'* rational-basis holding is likewise devoid of any reliance on the views of a 'wider civilization,' see *id.*, at 196. The Court's discussion of these foreign views (ignoring, of course, the many countries that have retained criminal prohibitions on sodomy) is therefore meaningless dicta. Dangerous dicta, however, since "this Court...should not impose foreign moods, fads, or fashions on Americans." Foster v. Florida, 537 U.S. 990 n. (2002) (Thomas, J., concurring in denial of certiorari).

In Grutter v. Bollinger, 539 U.S. 306 (2003), which upheld the University of Michigan law school's use of affirmative action in admissions, Justice Ginsburg began her concurrence by noting that "[t]he Court's observation that race-conscious programs 'must have a logical end point' accords with the international understanding of the office of affirmative action." She then proceeded to cite and quote from the Convention on the Elimination of All Forms of Racial

Discrimination, and the Convention on the Elimination of All Forms of Discrimination Against Women.

In Atkins v. Virginia, 536 U.S. 304 (2002), the Court held that the execution of persons with mental retardation violated the Eighth Amendment, and it observed in a footnote that "within the world community, the imposition of the death penalty for crimes committed by mentally retarded offenders is overwhelmingly disapproved." In dissent, Justice Scalia argued that the practices of the world community are "irrelevant" and noted that the world community's "notions of justice are (thankfully) not always those of our people."

Finally, in Printz v. United States, 521 U.S. 898 (1997), Justice Breyer dissented from the majority's conclusion that the Brady Handgun Violence Prevention Act's provisions requiring the Attorney General to command the chief law enforcement officer of each local jurisdiction to conduct background checks for handgun purchasers exceeded Congress's power. Justice Breyer reasoned:

> [T]he United States is not the only nation that seeks to reconcile the practical need for a central authority with the democratic virtues of more local control. At least some other countries, facing the same basic problem, have found that local control is better maintained through application of a principle that is the direct opposite of the principle the majority derives from the silence of our Constitution. The federal systems of Switzerland, Germany, and the European Union, for example, all provide that constituent states, not federal bureaucracies, will themselves implement many of the laws, rules, regulations, or decrees enacted by the central "federal" body. They do so in part because they believe that such a system interferes less, not more, with the independent authority of the "state," member nation, or other subsidiary government, and helps to safeguard individual liberty as well.
>
> Of course, we are interpreting our own Constitution, not those of other nations, and there may be relevant political and structural differences between their systems and our own. Cf. The Federalist No. 20, pp. 134-138 (C. Rossiter ed. 196 1) (J. Madison and A. Hamilton) (rejecting certain aspects of European federalism). But their experience may nonetheless cast an empirical light on the consequences of different solutions to a common legal problem—in this case the problem of reconciling central authority with the need to preserve the liberty-enhancing autonomy of a smaller constituent governmental entity. Cf. id., No. 42, p. 268 (J. Madison) (looking to experiences of European countries); id., No. 43, pp. 275, 276 (J. Madison) (same).

The majority, in an opinion by Justice Scalia, responded to this argument as follows:

> Justice Breyer's dissent would have us consider the benefits that other countries, and the European Union, believe they have derived from federal systems that are different from ours. We think such comparative analysis inappropriate to the task of interpreting a constitution, though it was of course quite relevant to the task of writing one. The Framers were familiar with many federal systems, from classical antiquity down to their own time; they are discussed in Nos. 18-20 of The Federalist. Some were (for the purpose here under discussion) quite similar to the modern "federal" systems that Justice Breyer favors. Madison's and Hamilton's opinion of such systems could not be clearer. Federalist No. 20, after an extended critique of the system of government established by the Union of Utrecht for the United Netherlands, concludes:
>
> > I make no apology for having dwelt so long on the contemplation of these federal precedents. Experience is the oracle of truth; and where its responses are unequivocal, they ought to be conclusive and sacred. The important truth, which it unequivocally pronounces in the present case, is that a sovereignty over

sovereigns, a government over governments, a legislation for communities, as contra distinguished from individuals, as it is a solecism in theory, so in practice it is subversive of the order and ends of civil polity...." Id., at 138.

Antifederalists, on the other hand, pointed specifically to Switzerland—and its then 400 years of success as a "confederate republic"—as proof that the proposed Constitution and its federal structure was unnecessary. The fact is that our federalism is not Europe's. It is "the unique contribution of the Framers to political science and political theory." United States v. Lopez, 514 U.S. 549, 575 (1995) (Kennedy, J., concurring) (citing Friendly, Federalism: A Forward, 86 Yale L. J. 1019 (1977)).

2. What legal force is the Court in *Roper* giving to foreign and international materials? Is it treating those materials like precedents? Persuasive authority? As a common law court in one U.S. state might treat a common law decision in another? Do these materials merely confirm the Court's judgment reached through independent means? Are they used as *factual* evidence of a consensus against the juvenile death penalty rather than as legal authority? How, if at all, do the majority opinion and Justice O'Connor's dissenting opinion differ regarding the use of these materials?

3. Under any of the theories in Note 2 of how the international and foreign materials might be used, why are they relevant to an analysis of the Eighth Amendment? Is it because of the term "unusual" in the Eighth Amendment? Did the Framers of the U.S. Constitution intend for the meaning of the prohibitions in the Eighth Amendment to change in accordance with changing global opinions as reflected in international and foreign law? Is that the relevant question? If we uncovered clear evidence that the Framers intended "unusual" to mean "unusual within the U.S. legal culture," or "unusual in 1791," would that rebut the analysis in *Roper*? Note, in this connection, that Justice Scalia, the leading critic of the Court's use of foreign and international materials, often relies on English precedents to help elucidate the original understanding of the Constitution. How does that differ from the *Roper* majority's use of foreign precedents?

4. The Court in *Roper* refers to both foreign court materials and international law materials. Do these two sets of materials have the same relevance to U.S. constitutional interpretation? Are foreign court interpretations of analogous constitutional provisions more relevant to U.S. constitutional law than what international instruments say? Or are international instruments more relevant to the extent that they reflect a broader consensus?

✱ 5. Under the Court's analysis in *Roper*, would it be appropriate to rely on foreign and international materials in the interpretation of every constitutional provision? Does the relevance of such materials depend on the constitutional clause in question? Consider, in this regard, some historical uses of foreign and international materials in Supreme Court adjudication:

Examples quickly illustrate that international law cannot be and has not been irrelevant to constitutional interpretation. First of all, several clauses in the U.S. Constitution make open reference to institutions of international law. For example, the Constitution authorizes Congress to "declare war," to "grant letters of marque and reprisal," and to "define offenses against the law of nations"; it authorizes the president to "receive ambassadors" and to "make treaties"; it extends the judicial power to cases involving "ambassadors" and "consuls," and to certain cases involving "foreign states" or their "citizens or subjects." All of these references assume an international law background, which does not provide an exclusive source for the meaning of the constitutional text but does provide an essential resource for construing it.

Textual references to international law do not incorporate and make constitutionally binding as such the entire bodies of international norms to which they relate. Thus, the Treaty Clause has neither frozen the eighteenth-century law of treaties as permanently obligatory for the United States nor given constitutional status to the evolving international law of treaties as it exists from time to time. Rather, sound constitutional interpretation combines other constitutional principles and structures with conceptions derived from contemporary international practice in order to determine the scope and effect of the treaty power and the place of treaties within the U.S. constitutional system. In the twentieth century, the treaty power enabled the United States to create and join international organizations, and to enter into agreements *with* international organizations, facilitating forms of international cooperation that were unimagined in the eighteenth century.

In the late nineteenth and early twentieth centuries, after the Civil War had vindicated the Union's claim to nationhood, the Supreme Court repeatedly invoked international law doctrines and writers in support of its elaboration of powers inherent in national sovereignty. The Court rationalized some of these inherent powers as interpretations of enumerated powers but implied others structurally as freestanding powers. The latter included the power to acquire new territory by discovery and occupation, the power to control the entry and residence of aliens, and the power to require citizens residing abroad to return. To the extent that these arguments relied on older publicists such as Vattel, they may be construed as imputing earlier international law doctrines to the framers; to the extent that they relied on current authors and later instances of state practice, their claims of necessary sovereign powers addressed the international regime of their own period.

Inherent sovereign powers construed as ancillary to enumerated powers included the power to govern overseas territories acquired by treaty as colonies, the power to conscript soldiers, the federal power of eminent domain, and even the federal power to make paper money legal tender. In some of these cases, no international obligation or relationship was implicated, and the publicists served less as guides to genuinely international law than as theorists of sovereignty and compilers of general principles of public law common to "civilized nations." Such usage blurs the distinction between employing international law as an interpretive aid and employing foreign law, but those two categories can be difficult to separate, given that patterns of state practice provide evidence of international law.

Foreign law played a well-known role in the debates over the relationship between the Bill of Rights and the Fourteenth Amendment. . . .

Even if it were true, as Justice Antonin Scalia has argued,* that the role of foreign law in interpreting due process should be exclusively negative — to rebut an appearance of fundamentality — that would still confirm the propriety of external influence on constitutional interpretation.

The Supreme Court has also invoked international and foreign sources in construing other constitutional amendments, including the Thirteenth Amendment, the Eighteenth Amendment, and . . . the Eighth Amendment.

---

* [The reference here is to Justice Scalia's dissent in Thompson v. Oklahoma, 487 U.S. 815 (1988), where he said, in the context of denying the relevance of foreign and international materials to an analysis of the constitutionality if the juvenile death penalty: "We must never forget that it is a Constitution for the United States of America that we are expounding. The practices of other nations, particularly other democracies, can be relevant to determining whether a practice uniform among our people is not merely a historical accident, but rather so 'implicit in the concept of ordered liberty' that it occupies a place not merely in our mores but, text permitting, in our Constitution as well." *See* Palko v. Connecticut, 302 U.S. 319, 325 (1937) (Cardozo, J.). But where there is not first a settled consensus among our own people, the views of other nations, however enlightened the Justices of this Court may think them to be, cannot be imposed upon Americans through the Constitution." — EDS.]

Gerald L. Neuman, *The Uses of International Law in Constitutional Interpretation*, 98 Am. J. Int'l. L. 82 (2004).

6. Professor Alford is less sanguine about the trend of using foreign and international materials to inform constitutional interpretation:

> [The canon of authoritative materials from which constitutional common law reasoning might go forward] has traditionally been viewed as encompassing text, structure, history, and national experience. Including a new source fundamentally destabilizes the equilibrium of constitutional decision making. Using international law as an interpretive aid also ignores the Supremacy Clause, which renders all of our laws subject to, and not source material for, our Constitution.
>
> But even assuming that using international sources to interpret the Constitution were appropriate, I am doubtful that it would be advisable....
>
> The first misuse of international sources — particularly evident in death penalty litigation — occurs when the "global opinions of humankind" are ascribed constitutional value to thwart the domestic opinions of Americans. To the extent that value judgments are a source of constitutional understandings of community standards, in the hierarchical ranking of relative values domestic majoritarian judgments should hold sway over international majoritarian values. Using global opinions as a means of constitutional interpretation dramatically undermines sovereignty by utilizing the one vehicle — constitutional supremacy — that can trump the democratic will reflected in state and federal legislative and executive pronouncements....
>
> The second misuse of international sources occurs when treaties are elevated to a status they do not enjoy under our federal system. The entire edifice of constitutional law rests on the foundation that the acts of the political branches are subject to and limited by the Constitution. Proposing that international law be part of the canon of constitutional material improperly empowers the political branches to create source materials — treaties and executive agreements — that serve as interpretive inputs to the process of constitutional decision making....
>
> The third misuse of international sources occurs when the Court references them haphazardly, relying on only those materials that are readily at its fingertips. In the international legal arena, where the Court has little or no expertise, the Court is unduly susceptible to selective and incomplete presentations of the true state of international and foreign affairs. If the suggestion is that international sources may "cast an empirical light on the consequences of different solutions to a common legal problem," it is incumbent upon the Court to engage in empirical rather than haphazard comparativism. It is far from evident that this is what the Court is doing....
>
> A final misuse occurs when international and foreign materials are used selectively. In a country that "considers itself the world's foremost protector of civil liberties," what is perhaps most surprising about the enthusiasm for comparativism is the assumption that it will enhance rather than diminish basic human rights in this country. This assumption is either blind to our visionary leadership, deaf to the discord in the international instruments, or selectively mute in giving voice to only certain topics for comparison.

Roger P. Alford, *Misusing International Sources to Interpret the Constitution*, 98 Am. J. Int'l L. 57 (2004). Which if any of these "misuses" occurred in *Roper*? How can Professor Alford's concerns be reconciled with Professor Neuman's historical summary?

7. As Justice Scalia points out in his dissent in *Roper*, the Court has not yet invoked foreign and international materials as a basis for moving U.S. constitutional law in a less progressive direction. For example, the U.S. Constitution protects abortion, free speech, and criminal procedure rights more vigorously than international or foreign law typically require. Should the Court rethink its doctrines in these areas? Or are international and foreign materials only potentially relevant when they are more rights-protecting, perhaps akin to the notion that state constitutional law can be more rights-protecting, but not less so, than U.S. Constitutional rights? Relatedly, is the practice of relying on foreign and international materials to inform the meaning of the U.S. Constitution sufficiently respectful of the values of diversity? Are there unique practices in the United States, grounded in the United States particular history and culture, that are worth preserving? For example, the United States has one of the most speech-protective constitutional doctrines in the world. How should courts determine which unique practices are and are not worth preserving?

8. Was it problematic for the Court in *Roper* to rely on a treaty that the United States has not ratified (the Convention on the Rights of the Child) and a treaty that the United States had made non-self-executing and to which the United States attached a reservation on the issue of the juvenile death penalty (the International Covenant on Civil and Political Rights) as a basis for interpreting the Eighth Amendment? Why wasn't the political branches' self-conscious effort not to eliminate the juvenile death penalty by treaty more relevant to the cruelty and unusualness of the juvenile death penalty than the views in other nations? What does the answer to this question suggest about answers to the questions in Note 2? Is the Court's use of treaties in *Roper* consistent with the respect that courts generally pay to U.S. reservations, understandings, and declarations when claims based on treaties are brought before them (see Chapter 6, Section E)? Is it consistent with the Court's restrictive conception of customary international law sources in *Sosa*?

9. What is the relationship between the Court's reliance in *Roper* on foreign and international materials and the *Charming Betsy* canon discussed in the previous Section? Does the *Charming Betsy* canon apply to constitutional interpretation? How would it work in that context? For example, would it require interpreting the Eighth Amendment to prohibit criminal punishments that violate international law? If the Eighth Amendment did not prohibit such criminal punishments, would that mean that the Eighth Amendment was in violation of international law? Or is it the federal or state enactment of the criminal punishments that would violate international law? And, if those enactments were clear, would there be any role for the *Charming Betsy* canon? In any event, does the Court in *Roper* conclude that the execution of juvenile offenders in the United States violates international law?

10. In 2005, a bill was pending before both the House and Senate that provided:

> In interpreting and applying the Constitution of the United States, a court of the United States may not rely upon any constitution, law, administrative rule, Executive order, directive, policy, judicial decision, or any other action of any foreign state or international organization or agency, other than English constitutional and common law up to the time of the adoption of the Constitution of the United States.

If this bill were enacted, would it be constitutional?

11. An enormous literature has sprung up in recent years analyzing and debating the use of foreign and international materials in constitutional interpretation. Representative examples include *Agora: The United States Constitution and International Law*, 98 Am. J. Int'l L. 42 (2004); Roger Alford, *In Search of a Theory for Constitutional Comparativism*, 52 UCLA L. Rev. 639 (2005); Daniel Bodansky, *The Use of International Sources in Constitutional Opinion*, 32 Ga. J. Int'l & Comp. L. 421

(2004); David Fontana, *Refined Comparativism in Constitutional Law*, 49 UCLA L. Rev. 539 (2001); Ruth Bader Ginsburg, *Looking Beyond Our Borders: The Value of a Comparative Perspective in Constitutional Adjudication*, 22 Yale L. & Pol'y Rev. 329 (2004); Vicki C. Jackson, *Transnational Discourse, Relational Authority, and the U.S. Court: Gender Equality*, 37 Loy. L.A. L. Rev. 271 (2003); Vicki C. Jackson, *Narratives of Federalism: Of Continuities and Comparative Constitutional Experience*, 51 Duke L.J. 223 (2001); Vicki C. Jackson, *Ambivalent Resistance and Comparative Constitutionalism: Opening Up the Conversation on "Proportionality," Rights and Federalism*, 1 U. Pa. J. Const. L. 583 (1999); Richard Posner, *No Thanks, We Already Have Our Own Laws*, Legal Aff., July-Aug. 2004; Anne-Marie Slaughter, *A Global Community of Courts*, 44 Harv. Int'l L.J. 191, 193 (2003); Mark Tushnet, *Transnational/Domestic Constitutional Law*, 37 Loy. L.A. L. Rev. 239, 245 (2003); Mark Tushnet, *The Possibilities of Comparative Constitutional Law*, 108 Yale L.J. 1225 (1999); Patricia M. Wald, *The Use of International Law in the American Adjudicative Process*, 27 Harv. J.L. & Pub. Pol'y 431 (2004); Michael Wells, *International Norms in Constitutional Law*, 32 Ga. J. Int'l & Comp. L. 429 (2004); J. Harvie Wilkinson III, *The Use of International Law in Judicial Decisions*, 27 Harv. J.L. & Pub. Pol'y 423 (2004).

8

Extraterritoriality

This chapter considers the application of U.S. laws and enforcement authority beyond the nation's borders. Section A examines the extraterritorial application of the U.S. Constitution's individual rights protections. Section B then explores the extraterritorial application of U.S. federal statutes. Section C describes various aspects of U.S. extradition law. Finally, Section D considers the legal consequences of the United States' extraterritorial abduction of criminal suspects.

A. THE CONSTITUTION ABROAD

Reid v. Covert

354 U.S. 1 (1957)

[Clarice Covert, a civilian, killed her husband, a sergeant in the United States Air Force, at an airbase in England. Dorothy Smith, also a civilian, killed her husband, an Army officer, at a post in Japan. Both women were tried by a court-martial for murder—in England and Japan, respectively—under the Uniform Code of Military Justice (UCMJ), Article 2(11) of which provides:

The following persons are subject to this code:....

> Subject to the provisions of any treaty or agreement to which the United States is or may be a party or to any accepted rule of international law, all persons serving with, employed by, or accompanying the armed forces without the continental limits of the United States....

Both women claimed that they were insane at the time of the murder; both were found guilty and sentenced to life in prison; and both filed petitions for a writ of habeas corpus, arguing that the Constitution prohibited their trial by military authorities. One court granted the writ; another denied it. The Supreme Court consolidated the cases and initially held that the military trials were constitutional. The Court subsequently granted rehearing and issued the following decision.]

Mr. Justice Black announced the judgment of the Court and delivered an opinion, in which The Chief Justice, Mr. Justice Douglas, and Mr. Justice Brennan join....

I

At the beginning we reject the idea that when the United States acts against citizens abroad it can do so free of the Bill of Rights. The United States is entirely a creature of the Constitution. Its power and authority have no other source. It can only act in accordance with all the limitations imposed by the Constitution. When the Government reaches out to punish a citizen who is abroad, the shield which the Bill of Rights and other parts of the Constitution provide to protect his life and liberty should not be stripped away just because he happens to be in another land. This is not a novel concept. To the contrary, it is as old as government....

The rights and liberties which citizens of our country enjoy are not protected by custom and tradition alone, they have been jealously preserved from the encroachments of Government by express provisions of our written Constitution.

Among those provisions, Art. III, §2 and the Fifth and Sixth Amendments are directly relevant to these cases. Article III, §2 lays down the rule that:

> The Trial of all Crimes, except in Cases of Impeachment, shall be by Jury; and such Trial shall be held in the State where the said Crimes shall have been committed; but when not committed within any State, the Trial shall be at such Place or Places as the Congress may by Law have directed.

The Fifth Amendment declares:

> No person shall be held to answer for a capital, or otherwise infamous crime, unless on a presentment or indictment of a Grand Jury, except in cases arising in the land or naval forces, or in the Militia, when in actual service in time of War or public danger;

And the Sixth Amendment provides:

> In all criminal prosecutions, the accused shall enjoy the right to a speedy and public trial, by an impartial jury of the State and district wherein the crime shall have been committed.

The language of Art. III, §2 manifests that constitutional protections for the individual were designed to restrict the United States Government when it acts outside of this country, as well as here at home. After declaring that *all* criminal trials must be by jury, the section states that when a crime is "not committed within any State, the Trial shall be at such Place or Places as the Congress may by Law have directed." If this language is permitted to have its obvious meaning, §2 is applicable to criminal trials outside of the States as a group without regard to where the offense is committed or the trial held. From the very first Congress, federal statutes have implemented the provisions of §2 by providing for trial of murder and other crimes committed outside the jurisdiction of any State "in the district where the offender is apprehended, or into which he may first be brought." The Fifth and Sixth Amendments, like Art. III, §2, are also all inclusive with their sweeping references to "no person" and to "all criminal prosecutions."

This Court and other federal courts have held or asserted that various constitutional limitations apply to the Government when it acts outside the continental United States. While it has been suggested that only those constitutional rights which are "fundamental" protect Americans abroad, we can find no warrant, in logic or otherwise, for picking and choosing among the remarkable collection of "Thou shalt nots" which were explicitly fastened on all departments and agencies of the Federal Government by the Constitution and its Amendments. Moreover, in view of our heritage and the history of the adoption of the Constitution and the Bill of Rights, it seems peculiarly anomalous to say that trial before a civilian judge and by an independent jury picked from the common citizenry is not a fundamental right....

The keystone of supporting authorities mustered by the Court's opinion last June to justify its holding that Art. III, §2, and the Fifth and Sixth Amendments did not apply abroad was In re Ross, 140 U.S. 453. The *Ross* case is one of those cases that cannot be understood except in its peculiar setting; even then, it seems highly unlikely that a similar result would be reached today. Ross was serving as a seaman on an American ship in Japanese waters. He killed a ship's officer, was seized and tried before a consular "court" in Japan. At that time, statutes authorized American consuls to try American citizens charged with committing crimes in Japan and certain other "non-Christian" countries. These statutes provided that the laws of the United States were to govern the trial except:

> where such laws are not adapted to the object, or are deficient in the provisions necessary to furnish suitable remedies, the common law and the law of equity and admiralty shall be extended in like manner over such citizens and others in those countries; and if neither the common law, nor the law of equity or admiralty, nor the statutes of the United States, furnish appropriate and sufficient remedies, the ministers in those countries, respectively, shall, by decrees and regulations which shall have the force of law, supply such defects and deficiencies.

The consular power approved in the *Ross* case was about as extreme and absolute as that of the potentates of the "non-Christian" countries to which the statutes applied. Under these statutes consuls could and did make the criminal laws, initiate charges, arrest alleged offenders, try them, and after conviction take away their liberty or their life—sometimes at the American consulate. Such a blending of executive, legislative, and judicial powers in one person or even in one branch of the Government is ordinarily regarded as the very acme of absolutism. Nevertheless, the Court sustained Ross' conviction by the consul. It stated that constitutional protections applied "only to citizens and others within the United States, or who are brought there for trial for alleged offences committed elsewhere, and not to residents or temporary sojourners abroad." Despite the fact that it upheld Ross' conviction under United States laws passed pursuant to asserted constitutional authority, the Court went on to make a sweeping declaration that "[t]he Constitution can have no operation in another country."

The *Ross* approach that the Constitution has no applicability abroad has long since been directly repudiated by numerous cases. That approach is obviously erroneous if the United States Government, which has no power except that granted by the Constitution, can and does try citizens for crimes committed abroad. Thus the *Ross* case rested, at least in substantial part, on a fundamental misconception and the most that can be said in support of the result reached there is that the consular court jurisdiction had a long history antedating the adoption of the Constitution. The Congress has recently buried the consular system of trying Americans. We are not willing to jeopardize the lives and liberties of Americans by disinterring it. At best, the *Ross* case should be left as a relic from a different era.

The Court's opinion last Term also relied on the "Insular Cases" to support its conclusion that Article III and the Fifth and Sixth Amendments were not applicable to the trial of Mrs. Smith and Mrs. Covert. We believe that reliance was misplaced. The "Insular Cases," which arose at the turn of the century, involved territories which had only recently been conquered or acquired by the United States. These territories, governed and regulated by Congress under Art. IV, §3, had entirely different cultures and customs from those of this country. This Court, although closely divided, ruled that certain constitutional safeguards were not applicable to these territories since they had not been "expressly or impliedly incorporated" into the Union by Congress. While conceding that "fundamental" constitutional rights applied everywhere, the majority found that it would disrupt long-established practices and would be inexpedient to require a jury trial after an indictment by a grand jury in the insular possessions.

The "Insular Cases" can be distinguished from the present cases in that they involved the power of Congress to provide rules and regulations to govern temporarily territories with wholly dissimilar traditions and institutions whereas here the basis for governmental power is American citizenship. None of these cases had anything to do with military trials and they cannot properly be used as vehicles to support an extension of military jurisdiction to civilians. Moreover, it is our judgment that neither the cases nor their reasoning should be given any further expansion. The concept that the Bill of Rights and other constitutional protections against arbitrary government are inoperative when they become inconvenient or when expediency dictates otherwise is a very dangerous doctrine and if allowed to flourish would destroy the benefit of a written Constitution and undermine the basis of our Government. If our foreign commitments become of such nature that the Government can no longer satisfactorily operate within the bounds laid down by the Constitution, that instrument can be amended by the method which it prescribes. But we have no authority, or inclination, to read exceptions into it which are not there.

II

At the time of Mrs. Covert's alleged offense, an executive agreement was in effect between the United States and Great Britain which permitted United States' military courts to exercise exclusive jurisdiction over offenses committed in Great Britain by American servicemen or their dependents. For its part, the United States agreed that these military courts would be willing and able to try and to punish all offenses against the laws of Great Britain by such persons. In all material respects, the same situation existed in Japan when Mrs. Smith killed her husband. Even though a court-martial does not give an accused trial by jury and other Bill of Rights protections, the Government contends that Art. 2(11) of the UCMJ, insofar as it provides for the military trial of dependents accompanying the armed forces in Great Britain and Japan, can be sustained as legislation which is necessary and proper to carry out the United States' obligations under the international agreements made with those countries. The obvious and decisive answer to this, of course, is that no agreement with a foreign nation can confer power on the Congress, or on any other branch of Government, which is free from the restraints of the Constitution.

Article VI, the Supremacy Clause of the Constitution, declares:

> This Constitution, and the Laws of the United States which shall be made in Pursuance thereof; and all Treaties made, or which shall be made, under the Authority of the United States, shall be the supreme Law of the Land;

There is nothing in this language which intimates that treaties and laws enacted pursuant to them do not have to comply with the provisions of the Constitution. Nor is there anything in the debates which accompanied the drafting and ratification of the Constitution which even suggests such a result. These debates as well as the history that surrounds the adoption of the treaty provision in Article VI make it clear that the reason treaties were not limited to those made in "pursuance" of the Constitution was so that agreements made by the United States under the Articles of Confederation, including the important peace treaties which concluded the Revolutionary War, would remain in effect. It would be manifestly contrary to the objectives of those who created the Constitution, as well as those who were responsible for the Bill of Rights—let alone alien to our entire constitutional history and tradition—to construe Article VI as permitting the United States to exercise power under an international agreement without observing constitutional prohibitions. In effect, such construction would permit amendment of that document in a manner not sanctioned by Article V. The prohibitions of the Constitution were designed to apply to all branches of the National Government and they cannot be nullified by the Executive or by the Executive and the Senate combined.

There is nothing new or unique about what we say here. This Court has regularly and uniformly recognized the supremacy of the Constitution over a treaty. . . .

This Court has also repeatedly taken the position that an Act of Congress, which must comply with the Constitution, is on a full parity with a treaty, and that when a statute which is subsequent in time is inconsistent with a treaty, the statute to the extent of conflict renders the treaty null. It would be completely anomalous to say that a treaty need not comply with the Constitution when such an agreement can be overridden by a statute that must conform to that instrument. . . .

MR. JUSTICE HARLAN, concurring in the result.

I concur in the result, on the narrow ground that where the offense is capital, Article 2(11) cannot constitutionally be applied to the trial of civilian dependents of members of the armed forces overseas in times of peace.

Since I am the only one among today's majority who joined in the Court's opinions of June 11, 1956, which sustained the court-martial jurisdiction in these cases, I think it appropriate to state the reasons which led to my voting, first, to rehear these cases, and, now, to strike down that jurisdiction.

. . . The powers of Congress, unlike those of the English Parliament, are constitutionally circumscribed. Under the Constitution Congress has only such powers as are expressly granted or those that are implied as reasonably necessary and proper to carry out the granted powers. Hence the constitutionality of the statute here in question must be tested, not by abstract notions of what is reasonable "in the large," so to speak, but by whether the statute, as applied in these instances, is a reasonably necessary and proper means of implementing a power granted to Congress by the Constitution. To say that the validity of the statute may be rested upon the inherent "sovereign powers" of this country in its dealings with foreign nations seems to me to be no more than begging the question. As I now see it, the validity of this court-martial jurisdiction must depend upon whether the statute, as applied to these women, can be justified as an exercise of the power, granted to Congress by Art. I, §8, cl. 14 of the Constitution, "To make Rules for the Government and Regulation of the land and naval Forces." I can find no other constitutional power to which this statute can properly be related.

...We return, therefore, to the *Ross* question: to what extent do these provisions of the Constitution apply outside the United States?

As I have already stated, I do not think that it can be said that these safeguards of the Constitution are never operative without the United States, regardless of the particular circumstances. On the other hand, I cannot agree with the suggestion that every provision of the Constitution must always be deemed automatically applicable to American citizens in every part of the world. For *Ross* and the *Insular Cases* do stand for an important proposition, one which seems to me a wise and necessary gloss on our Constitution. The proposition is, of course, not that the Constitution "does not apply" overseas, but that there are provisions in the Constitution which do not *necessarily* apply in all circumstances in every foreign place.... In other words, what *Ross* and the *Insular Cases* hold is that the particular local setting, the practical necessities, and the possible alternatives are relevant to a question of judgment, namely, whether jury trial *should* be deemed a necessary condition of the exercise of Congress' power to provide for the trial of Americans overseas.

I think the above thought is crucial in approaching the cases before us. Decision is easy if one adopts the constricting view that these constitutional guarantees as a totality do or do not "apply" overseas. But, for me, the question is *which* guarantees of the Constitution *should* apply in view of the particular circumstances, the practical necessities, and the possible alternatives which Congress had before it. The question is one of judgment, not of compulsion. And so I agree with my brother Frankfurter that, in view of *Ross* and the *Insular Cases*, we have before us a question analogous, ultimately, to issues of due process; one can say, in fact, that the question of which specific safeguards of the Constitution are appropriately to be applied in a particular context overseas can be reduced to the issue of what process is "due" a defendant in the particular circumstances of a particular case.

On this basis, I cannot agree with the sweeping proposition that a full Article III trial, with indictment and trial by jury, is required in every case for the trial of a civilian dependent of a serviceman overseas. The Government, it seems to me, has made an impressive showing that at least for the run-of-the-mill offenses committed by dependents overseas, such a requirement would be...impractical and...anomalous....

Again, I need not go into details, beyond stating that except for capital offenses, such as we have here, to which, in my opinion, special considerations apply, I am by no means ready to say that Congress' power to provide for trial by court-martial of civilian dependents overseas is limited by Article III and the Fifth and Sixth Amendments. Where, if at all, the dividing line should be drawn among cases not capital, need not now be decided. We are confronted here with capital offenses alone; and it seems to me particularly unwise now to decide more than we have to. Our far-flung foreign military establishments are a new phenomenon in our national life, and I think it would be unfortunate were we unnecessarily to foreclose, as my four brothers would do, our future consideration of the broad questions involved in maintaining the effectiveness of these national outposts, in the light of continuing experience with these problems.

So far as capital cases are concerned, I think they stand on quite a different footing than other offenses. In such cases the law is especially sensitive to demands for that procedural fairness which inheres in a civilian trial where the judge and trier of fact are not responsive to the command of the convening authority. I do not concede that whatever process is "due" an offender faced with a fine or a prison sentence necessarily satisfies the requirements of the Constitution in a capital case.

The distinction is by no means novel; nor is it negligible, being literally that between life and death. And, under what I deem to be the correct view of *Ross* and the *Insular Cases*, it is precisely the kind of distinction which plays a large role in the process of weighing the competing considerations which lead to sound judgment upon the question whether certain safeguards of the Constitution should be given effect in the trial of an American citizen abroad. In fact, the Government itself has conceded that one grave offense, treason, presents a special case: "The gravity of this offense is such that we can well assume that, whatever difficulties may be involved in trial far from the scene of the offense . . . the trial should be in our courts." I see no reason for not applying the same principle to any case where a civilian dependent stands trial on pain of life itself. The number of such cases would appear to be so negligible that the practical problems of affording the defendant a civilian trial would not present insuperable problems.

United States v. Verdugo-Urquidez

494 U.S. 259 (1990)

[Verdugo-Urquidez, a citizen and resident of Mexico, was believed by the United States Drug Enforcement Agency (DEA) to be a leader of an organization in Mexico that smuggled narcotics into the United States. In cooperation with U.S. officials, Mexican police officials apprehended Verdugo-Urquidez and brought him to the U.S. Border Patrol station in Calexico, California, where U.S. officials arrested him pursuant to a U.S. arrest warrant. U.S. officials subsequently searched Verdugo-Urquidez's home in Mexico without a U.S. search warrant but with the authorization of Mexican officials. A U.S. district court suppressed the evidence of criminality discovered during this search, reasoning that the Fourth Amendment applied to the searches and that the DEA agents had failed to justify searching Verdugo-Urquidez's premises without a warrant. A divided panel of the Court of Appeals for the Ninth Circuit affirmed.]

CHIEF JUSTICE REHNQUIST delivered the opinion of the Court. . . .
    Before analyzing the scope of the Fourth Amendment, we think it significant to note that it operates in a different manner than the Fifth Amendment, which is not at issue in this case. The privilege against self-incrimination guaranteed by the Fifth Amendment is a fundamental trial right of criminal defendants. Although conduct by law enforcement officials prior to trial may ultimately impair that right, a constitutional violation occurs only at trial. The Fourth Amendment functions differently. It prohibits "unreasonable searches and seizures" whether or not the evidence is sought to be used in a criminal trial, and a violation of the Amendment is "fully accomplished" at the time of an unreasonable governmental intrusion. United States v. Calandra, 414 U.S. 338, 354 (1974); United States v. Leon, 468 U.S. 897, 906 (1984). For purposes of this case, therefore, if there were a constitutional violation, it occurred solely in Mexico. Whether evidence obtained from respondent's Mexican residences should be excluded at trial in the United States is a remedial question separate from the existence vel non of the constitutional violation.
    The Fourth Amendment provides:

The right of the people to be secure in their persons, houses, papers, and effects, against unreasonable searches and seizures, shall not be violated, and no Warrants shall issue, but upon probable cause, supported by Oath or affirmation, and particularly describing the place to be searched, and the persons or things to be seized.

That text, by contrast with the Fifth and Sixth Amendments, extends its reach only to "the people." . . . "[T]he people" seems to have been a term of art employed in select parts of the Constitution. The Preamble declares that the Constitution is ordained and established by "the People of the United States." The Second Amendment protects "the right of the people to keep and bear Arms," and the Ninth and Tenth Amendments provide that certain rights and powers are retained by and reserved to "the people." *See also* U.S. Const., Amdt. 1 ("Congress shall make no law . . . abridging . . . the right of *the people* peaceably to assemble") (emphasis added); Art. I, §2, cl. 1 ("The House of Representatives shall be composed of Members chosen every second Year by *the People* of the several States") (emphasis added). While this textual exegesis is by no means conclusive, it suggests that "the people" protected by the Fourth Amendment, and by the First and Second Amendments, and to whom rights and powers are reserved in the Ninth and Tenth Amendments, refers to a class of persons who are part of a national community or who have otherwise developed sufficient connection with this country to be considered part of that community. The language of these Amendments contrasts with the words "person" and "accused" used in the Fifth and Sixth Amendments regulating procedure in criminal cases.

What we know of the history of the drafting of the Fourth Amendment also suggests that its purpose was to restrict searches and seizures which might be conducted by the United States in domestic matters. The Framers originally decided not to include a provision like the Fourth Amendment, because they believed the National Government lacked power to conduct searches and seizures. Many disputed the original view that the Federal Government possessed only narrow delegated powers over domestic affairs, however, and ultimately felt an Amendment prohibiting unreasonable searches and seizures was necessary. . . . The driving force behind the adoption of the Amendment . . . was widespread hostility among the former colonists to the issuance of writs of assistance empowering revenue officers to search suspected places for smuggled goods, and general search warrants permitting the search of private houses, often to uncover papers that might be used to convict persons of libel. The available historical data show, therefore, that the purpose of the Fourth Amendment was to protect the people of the United States against arbitrary action by their own Government; it was never suggested that the provision was intended to restrain the actions of the Federal Government against aliens outside of the United States territory.

There is likewise no indication that the Fourth Amendment was understood by contemporaries of the Framers to apply to activities of the United States directed against aliens in foreign territory or in international waters. Only seven years after the ratification of the Amendment, French interference with American commercial vessels engaged in neutral trade triggered what came to be known as the "undeclared war" with France. In an Act to "protect the Commerce of the United States" in 1798, Congress authorized President Adams to "instruct the commanders of the public armed vessels which are, or which shall be employed in the service of the United States, to subdue, seize and take any armed French vessel, which shall be found within the jurisdictional limits of the United States, or elsewhere, on the high seas." §1 of An Act Further to Protect the Commerce of the United States, ch. 68, 1 Stat. 578. This public naval force consisted of only 45 vessels, so Congress also gave the President power to grant to the owners of private armed ships and vessels of the United States "special commissions," which would allow them "the same license and authority for the subduing, seizing and capturing any armed French vessel, and for the recapture of the vessels, goods and effects of the people of the United States, as the public armed vessels of the United States may by law have." §2, 1 Stat. 579; *see* U.S. Const., Art. I, §8, cl. 11 (Congress has power to grant letters of marque and reprisal). Under the latter provision, 365 private armed vessels were commissioned before March 1, 1799; together, these enactments resulted in scores of seizures of foreign vessels under congressional authority. Some commanders were held liable by this Court for unlawful seizures because their actions were beyond the scope of the congressional grant of authority, *see, e.g.*, Little v. Barreme, 2 Cranch 170, 177-178 (1804); *cf.* Talbot v. Seeman, 1 Cranch 1, 31 (1801) (seizure of neutral ship lawful where American captain had probable cause to believe vessel was French), but it was never suggested that the Fourth Amendment restrained the authority of Congress or of United States agents to conduct operations such as this.

The global view taken by the Court of Appeals of the application of the Constitution is also contrary to this Court's decisions in the *Insular Cases*, which held that not every constitutional provision applies to governmental activity even where the United States has sovereign power. *See, e.g.*, Balzac v. Porto Rico, 258 U.S. 298 (1922) (Sixth Amendment right to jury trial inapplicable in Puerto Rico); Ocampo v. United States, 234 U.S. 91 (1914) (Fifth Amendment grand jury provision inapplicable in Philippines); Dorr v. United States, 195 U.S. 138 (1904) (jury trial provision inapplicable in Philippines); Hawaii v. Mankichi, 190 U.S. 197 (1903) (provisions on indictment by grand jury and jury trial inapplicable in Hawaii); Downes v. Bidwell, 182 U.S. 244 (1901) (Revenue Clauses of Constitution inapplicable to Puerto Rico). In *Dorr*, we declared the general rule that in an unincorporated territory—one not clearly destined for statehood—Congress was not required to adopt "a system of laws which shall include the right of trial by jury, and that *the Constitution does not, without legislation and of its own force, carry such right to territory so situated.*" 195 U.S., at 149 (emphasis added). Only "fundamental" constitutional rights are guaranteed to inhabitants of those territories. *Id.*, at 148; *Balzac, supra*, at 312-313. If that is true with respect to territories ultimately governed by Congress, respondent's claim that the protections of the Fourth Amendment extend to aliens in foreign nations is even weaker. And certainly, it is not open to us in light of the *Insular Cases* to endorse the view that every constitutional provision applies wherever the United States Government exercises its power.

Indeed, we have rejected the claim that aliens are entitled to Fifth Amendment rights outside the sovereign territory of the United States. In Johnson v. Eisentrager, 339 U.S. 763 (1950), the Court held that enemy aliens arrested in China and imprisoned in Germany after World War II could not obtain writs of habeas corpus in our federal courts on the ground that their convictions for war crimes had violated the Fifth Amendment and other constitutional provisions. The *Eisentrager* opinion acknowledged that in some cases constitutional provisions extend beyond the citizenry; "the alien . . . has been accorded a generous and ascending scale of rights as he increases his identity with our society." *Id.*, at 770. But our rejection of extraterritorial application of the Fifth Amendment was emphatic:

> Such extraterritorial application of organic law would have been so significant an innovation in the practice of governments that, if intended or apprehended, it could scarcely have failed to excite contemporary comment. Not one word can be

cited. No decision of this Court supports such a view. Cf. Downes v. Bidwell, 182 U.S. 244 [(1901)]. None of the learned commentators on our Constitution has even hinted at it. The practice of every modern government is opposed to it.

Id., at 784. If such is true of the Fifth Amendment, which speaks in the relatively universal term of "person," it would seem even more true with respect to the Fourth Amendment, which applies only to "the people."

To support his all-encompassing view of the Fourth Amendment, respondent points to language from the plurality opinion in Reid v. Covert, 354 U.S. 1 (1957). . . . The plurality [in *Reid* stated]:

> The United States is entirely a creature of the Constitution. Its power and authority have no other source. It can only act in accordance with all the limitations imposed by the Constitution. When the Government reaches out to punish *a citizen* who is abroad, the shield which the Bill of Rights and other parts of the Constitution provide to protect his life and liberty should not be stripped away just because he happens to be in another land.

Id., at 5-6 (emphasis added; footnote omitted).

Respondent urges that we interpret this discussion to mean that federal officials are constrained by the Fourth Amendment wherever and against whomever they act. But the holding of *Reid* stands for no such sweeping proposition: it decided that United States citizens stationed abroad could invoke the protection of the Fifth and Sixth Amendments. The concurring opinions by Justices Frankfurter and Harlan in *Reid* resolved the case on much narrower grounds than the plurality and declined even to hold that United States citizens were entitled to the full range of constitutional protections in all overseas criminal prosecutions. Since respondent is not a United States citizen, he can derive no comfort from the *Reid* holding.

Verdugo-Urquidez also relies on a series of cases in which we have held that aliens enjoy certain constitutional rights. These cases, however, establish only that aliens receive constitutional protections when they have come within the territory of the United States and developed substantial connections with the country. Respondent is an alien who has had no previous significant voluntary connection with the United States, so these cases avail him not.

Justice Stevens' concurrence in the judgment takes the view that even though the search took place in Mexico, it is nonetheless governed by the requirements of the Fourth Amendment because respondent was "lawfully present in the United States . . . even though he was brought and held here against his will." But this sort of presence — lawful but involuntary — is not of the sort to indicate any substantial connection with our country. The extent to which respondent might claim the protection of the Fourth Amendment if the duration of his stay in the United States were to be prolonged — by a prison sentence, for example — we need not decide. When the search of his house in Mexico took place, he had been present in the United States for only a matter of days. We do not think the applicability of the Fourth Amendment to the search of premises in Mexico should turn on the fortuitous circumstance of whether the custodian of its nonresident alien owner had or had not transported him to the United States at the time the search was made. . . .

Not only are history and case law against respondent, but as pointed out in Johnson v. Eisentrager, 393 U.S. 763 (1950), the result of accepting his claim would have significant and deleterious consequences for the United States in conducting activities beyond its boundaries. The rule adopted by the Court of Appeals would apply not only to law enforcement operations abroad, but also to other foreign policy operations which might result in "searches or seizures." The United States frequently employs armed forces outside this country — over 200 times in our history — for the protection of American citizens or national security. Application of the Fourth Amendment to those circumstances could significantly disrupt the ability of the political branches to respond to foreign situations involving our national interest. Were respondent to prevail, aliens with no attachment to this country might well bring actions for damages to remedy claimed violations of the Fourth Amendment in foreign countries or in international waters....

We think that the text of the Fourth Amendment, its history, and our cases discussing the application of the Constitution to aliens and extraterritorially require rejection of respondent's claim. At the time of the search, he was a citizen and resident of Mexico with no voluntary attachment to the United States, and the place searched was located in Mexico. Under these circumstances, the Fourth Amendment has no application.

For better or for worse, we live in a world of nation-states in which our Government must be able to "functio[n] effectively in the company of sovereign nations." Perez v. Brownell, 356 U.S. 44, 57 (1958). Some who violate our laws may live outside our borders under a regime quite different from that which obtains in this country. Situations threatening to important American interests may arise halfway around the globe, situations which in the view of the political branches of our Government require an American response with armed force. If there are to be restrictions on searches and seizures which occur incident to such American action, they must be imposed by the political branches through diplomatic understanding, treaty, or legislation....

JUSTICE KENNEDY, concurring....

The conditions and considerations of this case would make adherence to the Fourth Amendment's warrant requirement impracticable and anomalous. Just as the Constitution in the *Insular Cases* did not require Congress to implement all constitutional guarantees in its territories because of their "wholly dissimilar traditions and institutions," the Constitution does not require United States agents to obtain a warrant when searching the foreign home of a nonresident alien. If the search had occurred in a residence within the United States, I have little doubt that the full protections of the Fourth Amendment would apply. But that is not this case. The absence of local judges or magistrates available to issue warrants, the differing and perhaps unascertainable conceptions of reasonableness and privacy that prevail abroad, and the need to cooperate with foreign officials all indicate that the Fourth Amendment's warrant requirement should not apply in Mexico as it does in this country. For this reason, in addition to the other persuasive justifications stated by the Court, I agree that no violation of the Fourth Amendment has occurred in the case before us. The rights of a citizen, as to whom the United States has continuing obligations, are not presented by this case.

I do not mean to imply, and the Court has not decided, that persons in the position of the respondent have no constitutional protection. The United States is prosecuting a foreign national in a court established under Article III, and all of the trial proceedings are governed by the Constitution. All would agree, for instance, that the dictates of the Due Process Clause of the Fifth Amendment protect the defendant. Indeed, as Justice Harlan put it, "the question of which specific safeguards... are appropriately to be applied in a particular context... can be reduced to the issue of what process is 'due' a defendant in the particular circumstances of a particular case." *Reid, supra*, at 75. Nothing approaching a violation of due process has occurred in this case....

JUSTICE BRENNAN, with whom JUSTICE MARSHALL joins, dissenting....

I

Particularly in the past decade, our Government has sought, successfully, to hold foreign nationals criminally liable under federal laws for conduct committed entirely beyond the territorial limits of the United States that nevertheless has effects in this country. Foreign nationals must now take care not to violate our drug laws, our antitrust laws, our securities laws, and a host of other federal criminal statutes....

The Constitution is the source of Congress' authority to criminalize conduct, whether here or abroad, and of the Executive's authority to investigate and prosecute such conduct. But the same Constitution also prescribes limits on our Government's authority to investigate, prosecute, and punish criminal conduct, whether foreign or domestic....

The Court today creates an antilogy: the Constitution authorizes our Government to enforce our criminal laws abroad, but when Government agents exercise this authority, the Fourth Amendment does not travel with them. This cannot be. At the very least, the Fourth Amendment is an unavoidable correlative of the Government's power to enforce the criminal law.

A...

What the majority ignores...is the most obvious connection between Verdugo-Urquidez and the United States: he was investigated and is being prosecuted for violations of United States law and may well spend the rest of his life in a United States prison. The "sufficient connection" is supplied not by Verdugo-Urquidez, but by the Government. Respondent is entitled to the protections of the Fourth Amendment because our Government, by investigating him and attempting to hold him accountable under United States criminal laws, has treated him as a member of our community for purposes of enforcing our laws. He has become, quite literally, one of the governed. Fundamental fairness and the ideals underlying our Bill of Rights compel the conclusion that when we impose "societal obligations," such as the obligation to comply with our criminal laws, on foreign nationals, we in turn are obliged to respect certain correlative rights, among them the Fourth Amendment.

By concluding that respondent is not one of "the people" protected by the Fourth Amendment, the majority disregards basic notions of mutuality. If we expect aliens to obey our laws, aliens should be able to expect that we will obey our Constitution when we investigate, prosecute, and punish them....

Mutuality is essential to ensure the fundamental fairness that underlies our Bill of Rights. Foreign nationals investigated and prosecuted for alleged violations of United States criminal laws are just as vulnerable to oppressive Government behavior as are United States citizens investigated and prosecuted for the same alleged violations. Indeed, in a case such as this where the Government claims the existence of an international criminal conspiracy, citizens and foreign nationals may be codefendants, charged under the same statutes for the same conduct and facing the same penalties if convicted. They may have been investigated by the same agents pursuant to the same enforcement authority. When our Government holds these codefendants to the same standards of conduct, the Fourth Amendment, which protects the citizen from unreasonable searches and seizures, should protect the foreign national as well.

Mutuality also serves to inculcate the values of law and order. By respecting the rights of foreign nationals, we encourage other nations to respect the rights of our citizens. Moreover, as our Nation becomes increasingly concerned about the domestic effects of international crime, we cannot forget that the behavior of our law enforcement agents abroad sends a powerful message about the rule of law to individuals everywhere. . . . This principle is no different when the United States applies its rules of conduct to foreign nationals. If we seek respect for law and order, we must observe these principles ourselves. Lawlessness breeds lawlessness.

Finally, when United States agents conduct unreasonable searches, whether at home or abroad, they disregard our Nation's values. For over 200 years, our country has considered itself the world's foremost protector of liberties. The privacy and sanctity of the home have been primary tenets of our moral, philosophical, and judicial beliefs. Our national interest is defined by those values and by the need to preserve our own just institutions. We take pride in our commitment to a Government that cannot, on mere whim, break down doors and invade the most personal of places. We exhort other nations to follow our example. How can we explain to others — and to ourselves — that these long cherished ideals are suddenly of no consequence when the door being broken belongs to a foreigner?

The majority today brushes aside the principles of mutuality and fundamental fairness that are central to our Nation's constitutional conscience. The Court articulates a "sufficient connection" test but then refuses to discuss the underlying principles upon which any interpretation of that test must rest. I believe that by placing respondent among those governed by federal criminal laws and investigation him for violations of those laws, the Government has made him a part of our community for purposes of the Fourth Amendment.

B

In its effort to establish that respondent does not have sufficient connection to the United States to be considered one of "the people" protected by the Fourth Amendment, the Court relies on the text of the Amendment, historical evidence, and cases refusing to apply certain constitutional provisions outside the United States. None of these, however, justifies the majority's cramped interpretation of the Fourth Amendment's applicability. . . .

[T]he Framers of the Bill of Rights did not purport to "create" rights. Rather, they designed the Bill of Rights to prohibit our Government from infringing rights and liberties presumed to be pre-existing. *See, e.g.*, U.S. Const., Amdt. 9 ("The enumeration in the Constitution of certain rights, shall not be construed to deny or disparage others retained by the people"). The Fourth Amendment, for example, does not create a new right of security against unreasonable searches and seizures. It states that "[t]he right of the people to be secure in their persons, houses, papers, and effects, against unreasonable searches and seizures, shall not be violated. . . ." The focus of the Fourth Amendment is on what the Government can and cannot do, and how it may act, not on against whom these actions may be taken. Bestowing rights and delineating protected groups would have been inconsistent with the drafters' fundamental conception of a Bill of Rights as a limitation on the Government's conduct with respect to all whom it seeks to govern. It is thus extremely unlikely that the Framers intended the narrow construction of the term "the people" presented today by the majority....

C

The majority's rejection of respondent's claim to Fourth Amendment protection is apparently motivated by its fear that application of the Amendment to law enforcement searches against foreign nationals overseas "could significantly disrupt the ability of the political branches to respond to foreign situations involving our national interest." The majority's doomsday scenario—that American Armed Forces conducting a mission to protect our national security with no law enforcement objective "would have to articulate specific facts giving them probable cause to undertake a search or seizure,"—is fanciful. Verdugo-Urquidez is protected by the Fourth Amendment because our Government, by investigating and prosecuting him, has made him one of "the governed." Accepting respondent as one of "the governed," however, hardly requires the Court to accept enemy aliens in wartime as among "the governed" entitled to invoke the protection of the Fourth Amendment.

Moreover, with respect to non-law-enforcement activities not directed against enemy aliens in wartime but nevertheless implicating national security, doctrinal exceptions to the general requirements of a warrant and probable cause likely would be applicable more frequently abroad, thus lessening the purported tension between the Fourth Amendment's strictures and the Executive's foreign affairs power. Many situations involving sensitive operations abroad likely would involve exigent circumstances such that the warrant requirement would be excused. Therefore, the Government's conduct would be assessed only under the reasonableness standard, the application of which depends on context.

In addition, where the precise contours of a "reasonable" search and seizure are unclear, the Executive Branch will not be "plunge[d] ... into a sea of uncertainty," that will impair materially its ability to conduct foreign affairs. Doctrines such as official immunity have long protected Government agents from any undue chill on the exercise of lawful discretion. Similarly, the Court has recognized that there may be certain situations in which the offensive use of constitutional rights should be limited. In most cases implicating foreign policy concerns in which the reasonableness of an overseas search or seizure is unclear, application of the Fourth Amendment will not interfere with the Executive's traditional prerogative in foreign affairs because a court will have occasion to decide the constitutionality of such a search only if the Executive decides to bring a criminal prosecution and introduce evidence seized abroad. When the Executive decides to conduct a search as part of an ongoing criminal investigation, fails to get a warrant, and then seeks to introduce the fruits of that search at trial, however, the courts must enforce the Constitution.

Notes and Questions

1. The preamble to the Constitution provides: "We the People of the United States, in Order to ... secure the Blessings of Liberty to ourselves and our Posterity, do ordain and establish this Constitution for the United States of America." The Supremacy Clause states that "[t]his Constitution . . . shall be the supreme Law of the Land." And Article III authorizes federal court jurisdiction over, among other things, suits involving foreign citizens, subjects, and ambassadors. What, if anything, do these provisions suggest about the geographical scope of the U.S. Constitution?

2. *Reid* and *Verdugo-Urquidez* were decided against a complex background of Supreme Court decisions concerning the geographical scope of U.S. constitutional rights. Such rights obviously apply with full force to U.S. citizens within the United States. Aliens within the United States are also considered persons entitled to constitutional protection. *See, e.g.,* Zadvydus v. Davis, 533 U.S. 678, 693 (2001); Yick Wo v. Hopkins, 118 U.S. 356 (1886). Even aliens not within the United States are entitled to some constitutional protection, at least with respect to governmental actions taken within the United States that affect their interests. *See, e.g.,* Asahi Metal Indus. Co. v. Superior Court, 480 U.S. 102 (1987) (extending due process limits on personal jurisdiction to claim against Japanese corporation). With respect to governmental actions taken wholly outside the United States, constitutional protection has been less certain. In the nineteenth century, the Supreme Court expressed skepticism about the extent to which the Constitution applied in this situation. *See, e.g.,* In re Ross, 140 U.S. 453, 464 (1891) (reasoning that the Constitution did not apply to the trial of an American seaman by an American consular tribunal in Japan because "[t]he Constitution can have no operation in another country"). In the *Insular Cases,* the Court held that the United States need only confer "fundamental" constitutional rights on citizens and aliens alike in "unincorporated" possessions abroad over which the United States exercised sovereignty. *See, e.g.,* DeLima v. Bidwell, 182 U.S. 1 (1901). For a comprehensive discussion of this line of cases, see Gerald L. Neuman, *Whose Constitution?,* 100 Yale L.J. 909 (1991). Do *Ross* and the *Insular Cases* survive *Reid?*

3. There are at least four possible approaches to the application of constitutional rights. First, a "universalist" approach "require[s] that constitutional provisions that create rights with no express limitations as to the persons or places covered should be interpreted as applicable to every person and at every place." Second, a "membership" approach "legitimates government through the idea of an actual or hypothetical agreement embodying the consent of the governed who have established the state and empowered it to govern." On this view, "beneficiaries have rights based in the contract; nonbeneficiaries are relegated to whatever rights they may have independent of the contract." The only difficult issue is the identity of the parties to the contract. Third, under a "territorial" model, "the Constitution constrains the United States government only when it acts within the borders of the United States." Fourth, and finally, a "balancing" approach holds that "the government's reduced right to obedience [abroad] and reduced means of enforcement [abroad] may call for a reciprocal reduction in individual rights [abroad]." *See* Neuman, *supra,* at 916-21. Which of these four approaches is normatively most attractive? Which does our Constitution embrace? Which approach is embraced by the opinions in *Reid* and *Verdugo-Urquidez?*

4. Are you convinced by the reasoning of the *Reid* plurality? Doesn't the plurality's claim that the United States "can only act in accordance with all the limitations imposed by the Constitution" beg the question whether the Constitution limits federal action abroad? Are you convinced by the inferences of extraterritorial reach that the plurality draws from Article III, §2? Do you think the drafters of

Article III had extraterritoriality in mind? Even if we accept the inference of extra-territoriality from Article III, should we draw the same conclusion from the Fifth and Sixth Amendments' "sweeping references to 'no person' and to 'all criminal prosecutions'"? In answering these questions, what is the relevance, if any, of Congress's Article I power to "make Rules for the Government and Regulation of the land and naval forces"?

   5. What are the differences in reasoning between the *Reid* plurality and Justice Harlan's concurrence? Harlan disagrees with "the suggestion that every provision of the Constitution must always be deemed automatically applicable to American citizens in every part of the world." And yet he concludes that the United States must respect the right to trial by jury and indictment by grand jury when prosecuting civilians abroad for capital crimes. How does Harlan know the extent to which the Constitution applies abroad? What guidance does he provide for future cases? Because of Harlan's concurrence, the *Reid* holding was technically limited to capital cases. The Supreme Court extended *Reid*'s holding to noncapital cases in Kinsella v. United States ex rel. Singleton, 361 U.S. 234 (1960).

   6. Is *Verdugo-Urquidez* consistent with *Reid*? Do you agree with the *Verdugo-Urquidez* majority that the Fourth Amendment violation, if any, took place in Mexico rather than in the United States? In a trial within the United States, should the scope of constitutional protection turn on the characterization of where a violation occurs? What are the criteria for determining where a violation occurs? What about Justice Brennan's claim that, by making Verdugo-Urquidez the subject of a U.S. investigation, and by holding him accountable under U.S. law, the United States made him one of the "governed" for purposes of the Bill of Rights?

   7. The Fourth Amendment protects the "right of *the people*." Does this mean U.S. citizens? Aren't aliens "people" too? If aliens are covered by this reference, does this mean that the Fourth Amendment should protect against unreasonable searches in foreign countries by foreign officials?

   8. Does the Fifth Amendment Due Process Clause limit Congress's power to apply its criminal laws to aliens abroad? Consider United States v. Davis, 905 F.2d 245 (9th Cir. 1990), which involved a prosecution of an alien under the Maritime Drug Law Enforcement Act, 46 U.S.C. app. §§1903(a), 1903(j) ("MDLEA"), for possession with intent to distribute marijuana found on a boat on the high seas. The court held that "in order to apply extraterritorially a federal criminal statute to a defendant consistently with due process, there must be a sufficient nexus between the defendant and the United States . . . so that such application would not be arbitrary or fundamentally unfair." *Id.* at 248-49. The court concluded that a sufficient nexus existed because the transaction was aimed at the United States. *Id.* at 249. In the same opinion, the court applied *Verdugo* and held that "the protections of the fourth amendment do not extend to the search of the [defendant's boat] on the high seas." *Id.* at 251.

   In United States v. Klimavicius-Viloria, 144 F.3d 1249 (9th Cir. 1998), the Ninth Circuit followed *Davis* in imposing a due process "nexus" limitation on the application of the MDLEA. The court explained the requirement as follows:

> The MDLEA contains no nexus requirement. The nexus requirement is a judicial gloss applied to ensure that a defendant is not improperly haled before a court for trial. We have explained the need for the requirement this way: "A defendant [on a foreign flag ship] would have a legitimate expectation that because he has submitted himself to the laws of one nation [the foreign flag nation], other nations will not be entitled to exercise jurisdiction without some nexus." United States v. Caicedo, 47 F.3d 370, 372 (9th Cir. 1995).

The nexus requirement serves the same purpose as the "minimum contacts" test in personal jurisdiction. It ensures that a United States court will assert jurisdiction only over a defendant who "should reasonably anticipate being haled into court" in this country. World-Wide Volkswagen v. Woodsen, 444 U.S. 286 (1980).

Id. at 1257.

Why should the Fifth Amendment apply abroad to protect aliens when the Fourth Amendment does not? Are there any other relevant differences between *Davis* and *Klimavicius-Viloria*, on the one hand, and *Verdugo-Urquidez*, on the other? A number of courts disagree with *Davis* and *Klimavicius-Viloria*, concluding that the Due Process Clause does not impose a nexus requirement with respect to enforcement of the MDLEA. *See, e.g.*, United States v. Rendon, 354 F.3d 1320, 1325 (11th Cir. 2003); United States v. Suerte, 291 F.3d 366 (5th Cir. 2002); United States v. Perez-Oviedo, 281 F.3d 400 (3d Cir. 2002); United States v. Cardales, 168 F.3d 548 (1st Cir. 1999). Which view is right? Should the due process analysis that applies to personal jurisdiction extend to the extraterritorial application of U.S. law? Compare Lea Brilmayer & Charles Norchi, *Federal Extraterritoriality and Fifth Amendment Due Process*, 105 Harv. L. Rev. 1217 (1992) (arguing that it should), with Friedrich Juenger, *Constitutional Control of Extraterritoriality?: A Comment on Professor Brilmayer's Appraisal*, 50 Law & Contemp. Probs. 39 (1987) (arguing that it should not).

9. The Fifth Amendment states that no "person" "shall be compelled in any criminal case to be a witness against himself." In United States v. Balsys, 524 U.S. 666 (1998), the Supreme Court held that this protection did not apply to a federal government request for testimony when the only danger of prosecution was in a foreign country. The Court construed the self-incrimination clause as "providing a witness with the right against compelled self-incrimination when reasonably fearing prosecution *by the government whose power the Clause limits*, but not otherwise." *Id.* at 674 (emphasis added). What, if anything, does this decison suggest about the scope of the Fifth Amendment's other protections?

10. The Court in *Verdugo-Urquidez* discusses Johnson v. Eisentrager, 339 U.S. 763 (1950), which we considered in Chapter 4. In *Eisentrager*, German nationals were captured by the U.S. Army in China, tried and convicted in China by a U.S. military commission for violations of the laws of war, and imprisoned in Germany. Claiming that their trial, conviction, and imprisonment violated the Fifth Amendment and other constitutional provisions, the aliens filed a petition for a writ of habeas corpus with the federal district court in Washington, D.C. Ordering a dismissal of the petition, the Supreme Court held that nonresident enemy aliens, captured and imprisoned abroad, do not have the right to seek habeas corpus relief from a U.S. court. One reason the Court gave for its conclusion was that the Fifth Amendment did not apply extraterritorially to enemy aliens.

The viability of this proposition is uncertain as a result of Rasul v. Bush, 124 S. Ct. 2686 (2004), a decision also discussed in Chapter 4. The Court in *Rasul* held that the federal habeas corpus statute extended to the U.S. naval base at Guantanamo Bay, Cuba, where the U.S. military has detained hundreds of "enemy combatants" in the war on terrorism. Although the Court in *Rasul* did not address the applicability of the Constitution to Guantanamo Bay, it did state in footnote 15 that:

> Petitioners' allegations — that, although they have engaged neither in combat nor in acts of terrorism against the United States, they have been held in Executive detention for more than two years in territory subject to the long-term, exclusive jurisdiction and control of the United States, without access to counsel and without being charged with

any wrongdoing—unquestionably describe "custody in violation of the Constitution or laws or treaties of the United States" [within the meaning of the habeas statute]. *Cf.* United States v. Verdugo-Urquidez, 494 U.S. 259, 277-278 (1990) (Kennedy, J., concurring), and cases cited therein.

Moreover, Justice Kennedy's concurrence in *Rasul* distinguished *Eisentrager*, reasoning that, whereas in *Eisentrager* the detainees "were proven enemy aliens found and detained outside the United States, and . . . the existence of jurisdiction would have had a clear harmful effect on the Nation's military affairs," in this case Guantanamo Bay "is in every practical respect a United States territory, and it is one far removed from any hostilities," and "the detainees at Guantanamo Bay are being held indefinitely, and without benefit of any legal proceeding to determine their status."

Two district court decisions after *Rasul* reached conflicting conclusions about the applicability of the Fifth Amendment to Guantanamo Bay. The court in In re Guantanamo Cases, 355 F. Supp. 2d 443 (D.D.C. 2005), relied on *Verdugo-Urquidez*'s reaffirmation of the *Insular Cases*, footnote 15 of the *Rasul* majority, and Justice Kennedy's concurrence in *Rasul* in concluding that fundamental constitutional protections under the Due Process Clause apply to Guantanamo Bay. By contrast, the court in Khalid v. Bush, 355 F. Supp. 2d 311 (D.D.C. 2005), reasoned that Guantanamo Bay was outside the sovereign territory of the United States, and that nothing in *Rasul* affected *Eisentrager*'s holding about the lack of extraterritorial application of the Fifth Amendment. Which of these decisions is correct? Does the answer turn on the legal status of Guantanamo Bay? What does it mean for a place to be under U.S. jurisdiction and control but outside its sovereignty? Why would the Constitution extend to places where the United States exercises sovereignty but not to where it exercises non-sovereign control? If the Constitution applies to Guantanamo Bay, does it also extend to other places where the United States has exercised territorial control—for example, in Afghanistan or Iraq? See generally Gerald Neuman, Closing the Guantanamo Loophole, 50 Loy. L. Rev. 1 (2004); Kal Raustiala, The Geography of Justice, 73 Fordham L. Rev. 2501 (2005); Kermit Roosevelt III, Guantanamo and the Conflict of Laws: Rasul and Beyond, 153 U. Pa. L. Rev. 2017 (2005).

B. FEDERAL STATUTES ABROAD

1. Presumption Against Extraterritoriality

Equal Employment Opportunity Commission v. Arabian American Oil Co.

499 U.S. 244 (1991)

[In 1979, petitioner Boureslan, a naturalized U.S. citizen of Lebanese descent, was hired by a subsidiary of respondent Arabian American Oil Co. (Aramco), a Delaware company that had its principal place of business in Saudi Arabia, to work as a cost engineer in Houston. A year later he was transferred, at his request, to Saudi Arabia. After being fired in 1984, he brought suit against Aramco under Title VII of the Civil Rights Act of 1964, claiming that he had been discriminated against on the basis of race, religion, and national origin. The Equal Employment Opportunity Commission (EEOC) intervened in support of his suit. The courts below held that Title VII did not apply to U.S. citizens employed abroad by U.S. employers.]

REHNQUIST, C.J., delivered the opinion of the Court, in which WHITE, O'CONNOR, KENNEDY, and SOUTER, JJ., joined. . . .

Both parties concede, as they must, that Congress has the authority to enforce its laws beyond the territorial boundaries of the United States. *Cf.* Foley Bros., Inc. v. Filardo, 336 U.S. 281, 284-285 (1949); Benz v. Compania Naviera Hidalgo, S.A., 353 U.S. 138, 147 (1957). Whether Congress has in fact exercised that authority in this case is a matter of statutory construction. It is our task to determine whether Congress intended the protections of Title VII to apply to United States citizens employed by American employers outside of the United States.

It is a longstanding principle of American law "that legislation of Congress, unless a contrary intent appears, is meant to apply only within the territorial jurisdiction of the United States." *Foley Bros.*, 336 U.S., at 285. This "canon of construction . . . is a valid approach whereby unexpressed congressional intent may be ascertained." *Ibid.* It serves to protect against unintended clashes between our laws and those of other nations which could result in international discord. . . .

In applying this rule of construction, we look to see whether "language in the [relevant Act] gives any indication of a congressional purpose to extend its coverage beyond places over which the United States has sovereignty or has some measure of legislative control." *Foley Bros., supra*, at 285. We assume that Congress legislates against the backdrop of the presumption against extraterritoriality. Therefore, unless there is "the affirmative intention of the Congress clearly expressed," *Benz, supra*, at 147, we must presume it "is primarily concerned with domestic conditions." *Foley Bros., supra*, at 285.

Boureslan and the EEOC contend that the language of Title VII evinces a clearly expressed intent on behalf of Congress to legislate extraterritorially. . . . Title VII prohibits various discriminatory employment practices based on an individual's race, color, religion, sex, or national origin. *See* §§2000e-2, 2000e-3. An employer is subject to Title VII if it has employed 15 or more employees for a specified period and is "engaged in an industry affecting commerce." An industry affecting commerce is "any activity, business, or industry in commerce or in which a labor dispute would hinder or obstruct commerce or the free flow of commerce and includes any activity or industry 'affecting commerce' within the meaning of the Labor-Management Reporting and Disclosure Act of 1959 [(LMRDA)] [29 U.S.C. §§401 et seq.]." §2000e(h). "Commerce," in turn, is defined as "trade, traffic, commerce, transportation, transmission, or communication among the several States; or between a State and any place outside thereof; or within the District of Columbia, or a possession of the United States; or between points in the same State but through a point outside thereof." §2000e(g).

Petitioners argue that by its plain language, Title VII's "broad jurisdictional language" reveals Congress's intent to extend the statute's protections to employment discrimination anywhere in the world by a United States employer who affects trade "between a State and any place outside thereof." More precisely, they assert that since Title VII defines "States" to include States, the District of Columbia, and specified territories, the clause "between a State and any place outside thereof" must be referring to areas beyond the territorial limit of the United States. Reply Brief for Petitioner EEOC 3.

Respondents offer several alternative explanations for the statute's expansive language. They contend that the "or between a State and any place outside thereof" clause "provides the jurisdictional nexus required to regulate commerce that is not wholly within a single state, presumably as it affects both interstate and foreign commerce" but not to "regulate conduct exclusively *within* a foreign country." Brief for Respondents 21, n.14. They also argue that since the definitions of the terms "employer," "commerce," and "industry affecting commerce" make no mention of "commerce with foreign nations," Congress cannot be said to have intended that the statute apply overseas. In support of this argument, petitioners point to Title II of the Civil Rights Act of 1964, governing public accommodation, which specifically defines commerce as it applies to foreign nations. Finally, respondents argue that while language present in the first bill considered by the House of Representatives contained the terms "foreign commerce" and "foreign nations," those terms were deleted by the Senate before the Civil Rights Act of 1964 was passed. They conclude that these deletions "[are] inconsistent with the notion of a clearly expressed congressional intent to apply Title VII extraterritorially." *Id.*, at 7.

We need not choose between these competing interpretations as we would be required to do in the absence of the presumption against extraterritorial application discussed above. Each is plausible, but no more persuasive than that. The language relied upon by petitioners — and it is they who must make the affirmative showing — is ambiguous, and does not speak directly to the question presented here. The intent of Congress as to the extraterritorial application of this statute must be deduced by inference from boilerplate language which can be found in any number of congressional Acts, none of which have ever been held to apply overseas. . . .

Petitioners' reliance on Title VII's jurisdictional provisions also finds no support in our case law; we have repeatedly held that even statutes that contain broad language in their definitions of "commerce" that expressly refer to "*foreign* commerce" do not apply abroad. . . .

[I]n McCulloch v. Sociedad Nacional de Marineros de Honduras, 372 U.S. 10 (1963), we addressed whether Congress intended the National Labor Relations Act (NLRA), 29 U.S.C. §§151-168, to apply overseas. Even though the NLRA contained broad language that referred by its terms to foreign commerce, §152(6), this Court refused to find a congressional intent to apply the statute abroad because there was not "any specific language" in the Act reflecting congressional intent to do so. *McCulloch, supra*, at 19.

The EEOC places great weight on an assertedly similar "broad jurisdictional grant in the Lanham Act" that this Court held applied extraterritorially in Steele v. Bulova Watch Co., 344 U.S. 280, 286 (1952). In *Steele*, we addressed whether the Lanham Act, designed to prevent deceptive and misleading use of trademarks, applied to acts of a United States citizen consummated in Mexico. The Act defined commerce as "all commerce which may lawfully be regulated by Congress." 15 U.S.C. §1127. The stated intent of the statute was "to regulate commerce within the control of Congress by making actionable the deceptive and misleading use of marks in such commerce." *Ibid.* While recognizing that "the legislation of Congress will not extend beyond the boundaries of the United States unless a contrary legislative intent appears," the Court concluded that in light of the fact that the allegedly unlawful conduct had some effects within the United States, coupled with the Act's "broad jurisdictional grant" and its "sweeping reach into 'all commerce which may lawfully be regulated by Congress,' " the statute was properly interpreted as applying abroad. *Steele, supra*, at 285, 287.

The EEOC's attempt to analogize these cases to *Steele* is unpersuasive. The Lanham Act by its terms applies to "all commerce which may lawfully be regulated by Congress." The Constitution gives Congress the power "to regulate Commerce with foreign Nations, and among the several States, and with the Indian Tribes." U.S. Const., Art. I, §8, cl. 3. Since the Act expressly stated that it applied to the extent of Congress' power over commerce, the Court in *Steele* concluded that Congress intended that the statute apply abroad. By contrast, Title VII's more limited, boilerplate "commerce" language does not support such an expansive construction of congressional intent. Moreover, unlike the language in the Lanham Act, Title VII's definition of "commerce" was derived expressly from the LMRDA, a statute that this Court had held, prior to the enactment of Title VII, did not apply abroad.

Thus petitioner's argument based on the jurisdictional language of Title VII fails both as a matter of statutory language and of our previous case law. Many Acts of Congress are based on the authority of that body to regulate commerce among the several States, and the parts of these Acts setting forth the basis for legislative jurisdiction will obviously refer to such commerce in one way or another. If we were to permit possible, or even plausible, interpretations of language such as that involved here to override the presumption against extraterritorial application, there would be little left of the presumption.

Petitioners argue that Title VII's "alien exemption provision," 42 U.S.C. §2000e-1, "clearly manifests an intention" by Congress to protect United States citizens with respect to their employment outside of the United States. The alien-exemption provision says that the statute "shall not apply to an employer with respect to the employment of aliens outside any State." Petitioners contend that from this language a negative inference should be drawn that Congress intended Title VII to cover United States *citizens* working abroad for United States employers. There is "[n]o other plausible explanation [that] the alien exemption exists," they argue, because "[i]f Congress believed that the statute did not apply extraterritorially, it would have had no reason to include an exemption for a certain category of individuals employed outside the United States." Since "[t]he statute's jurisdictional provisions cannot possibly be read to confer coverage only upon aliens employed outside the United States," petitioners conclude that "Congress could not rationally have enacted an exemption for the employment of aliens abroad if it intended to foreclose *all* potential extraterritorial applications of the statute."

Respondents resist petitioners' interpretation of the alien-exemption provision and assert two alternative raisons d'etre for that language. First, they contend that since aliens are included in the statute's definition of employee,* and the definition of commerce includes possessions as well as "States," the purpose of the exemption is to provide that employers of aliens in the possessions of the United States are not covered by the statute. Thus, the "outside any State" clause means outside any State, but within the control of the United States. Respondents argue that "[t]his reading of the alien exemption provision is consistent with and supported by the historical development of the provision." . . .

Second, respondents assert that by negative implication, the exemption "confirms the coverage of aliens in the United States." . . .

---

* Title VII defines "employee" as:

an individual employed by an employer, except that the term "employee" shall not include any person elected to public office in any State or political subdivision of any State by the qualified voters thereof, or any person chosen by such officer to be on such officer's personal staff, or an appointee on the policy making level or an immediate adviser with respect to the exercise of the constitutional or legal powers of the office. The exemption set forth in the preceding sentence shall not include employees subject to the civil service laws of a State government, governmental agency or political subdivision.

42 U.S.C. §2000e(f).

If petitioners are correct that the alien-exemption clause means that the statute applies to employers overseas, we see no way of distinguishing in its application between United States employers and foreign employers. Thus, a French employer of a United States citizen in France would be subject to Title VII — a result at which even petitioners balk. The EEOC assures us that in its view the term "employer" means only "American employer," but there is no such distinction in this statute and no indication that the EEOC in the normal course of its administration had produced a reasoned basis for such a distinction. Without clearer evidence of congressional intent to do so than is contained in the alien-exemption clause, we are unwilling to ascribe to that body a policy which would raise difficult issues of international law by imposing this country's employment-discrimination regime upon foreign corporations operating in foreign commerce.

This conclusion is fortified by the other elements in the statute suggesting a purely domestic focus. The statute as a whole indicates a concern that it not unduly interfere with the sovereignty and laws of the States. *See, e.g.*, 42 U.S.C. §2000h-4 (stating that the Act should not be construed to exclude the operation of state law or invalidate any state law unless inconsistent with the purposes of the Act); §2000e-5 (requiring the EEOC to accord substantial weight to findings of state or local authorities in proceedings under state or local law); §2000e-7 (providing that nothing in Title VII shall affect the application of state or local law unless such law requires or permits practices that would be unlawful under Title VII); §§2000e-5(c), (d), and (e) (provisions addressing deferral to state discrimination proceedings). While Title VII consistently speaks in terms of "States" and state proceedings, it fails even to mention foreign nations or foreign proceedings.

Similarly, Congress failed to provide any mechanisms for overseas enforcement of Title VII. . . .

It is also reasonable to conclude that had Congress intended Title VII to apply overseas, it would have addressed the subject of conflicts with foreign laws and procedures. In amending the Age Discrimination in Employment Act of 1967 (ADEA), 29 U.S.C. §621 et seq., to apply abroad, Congress specifically addressed potential conflicts with foreign law by providing that it is not unlawful for an employer to take any action prohibited by the ADEA "where such practices involve an employee in a workplace in a foreign country, and compliance with [the ADEA] would cause such employer . . . to violate the laws of the country in which such workplace is located." §623(f)(1). Title VII, by contrast, fails to address conflicts with the laws of other nations. . . .

Our conclusion today is buttressed by the fact that "when it desires to do so, Congress knows how to place the high seas within the jurisdictional reach of a statute." Argentine Republic v. Amerada Hess Shipping Corp., 488 U.S. 428, 440 (1989). Congress' awareness of the need to make a clear statement that a statute applies overseas is amply demonstrated by the numerous occasions on which it has expressly legislated the extraterritorial application of a statute. . . . Indeed, after several courts had held that the ADEA did not apply overseas, Congress amended §11(f) to provide: "The term 'employee' includes any individual who is a citizen of the United States employed by an employer in a workplace in a foreign country." 29 U.S.C. §630(f). Congress also amended §4(g)(1), which states: "If an employer controls a corporation whose place of incorporation is in a foreign country, any practice by such corporation prohibited under this section shall be presumed to be such practice by such employer." §623(h)(1). The expressed purpose of these changes was to "make provisions of the Act apply to citizens of the United States employed in foreign countries by U.S. corporations or their subsidiaries." S. Rep. No. 98-467, p. 2 (1984). Congress, should it wish to do so, may similarly amend Title VII and in doing so will be able to calibrate its provisions in a way that we cannot....

JUSTICE MARSHALL, with whom JUSTICE BLACKMUN and JUSTICE STEVENS join, dissenting....

I

Because it supplies the driving force of the majority's analysis, I start with "[t]he canon ... that legislation of Congress, unless a contrary intent appears, is meant to apply only within the territorial jurisdiction of the United States." *Ibid.* The majority recasts this principle as "the need to make *a clear statement* that a statute applies overseas." So conceived, the presumption against extraterritoriality allows the majority to derive meaning from various instances of statutory silence — from Congress' failure, for instance, "to mention foreign nations or foreign proceedings," "to provide any mechanisms for overseas enforcement," or to "addres[s] the subject of conflicts with foreign laws and procedures." At other points, the majority relies on its reformulation of the presumption to avoid the "need [to] choose between ... competing interpretations" of affirmative statutory language that the majority concludes "does not speak *directly* to the question" of extraterritoriality. In my view, the majority grossly distorts the effect of this rule of construction upon conventional techniques of statutory interpretation....

[T]he presumption against extraterritoriality is *not* a "clear statement" rule. Clear-statement rules operate less to reveal *actual* congressional intent than to shield important values from an *insufficiently strong* legislative intent to displace them. When they apply, such rules foreclose inquiry into extrinsic guides to interpretation, and even compel courts to select less plausible candidates from within the range of permissible constructions. The Court's analysis in *Foley Brothers* was by no means so narrowly constrained. Indeed, the Court considered the entire range of conventional sources "whereby *unexpressed* congressional intent may be ascertained," 336 U.S., at 285 (emphasis added), including legislative history, statutory structure, and administrative interpretations. Subsequent applications of the presumption against extraterritoriality confirm that we have not imposed the drastic clear-statement burden upon Congress before giving effect to its intention that a particular enactment apply beyond the national boundaries. *See, e.g.,* Steele v. Bulova Watch Co., 344 U.S. 280, 286-287 (1952) (relying on "broad jurisdictional grant" to find intention that Lanham Act applies abroad)....

II

A...

Confirmation that Congress did *in fact* expect Title VII's central prohibition to have an extraterritorial reach is supplied by the so-called "alien exemption" provision. The alien-exemption provision states that Title VII "shall not apply to an employer with respect to the employment of aliens *outside any State.*" 42 U.S.C. §2000e-1 (emphasis added). Absent an intention that Title VII *apply* "outside any State," Congress would have had no reason to craft this extraterritorial exemption. And because only discrimination against aliens is exempted, employers remain accountable for discrimination against United States citizens abroad.

The inference arising from the alien-exemption provision is more than sufficient to rebut the presumption against extraterritoriality....

Notwithstanding the basic rule of construction requiring courts to give effect to all of the statutory language, the majority never advances an alternative explanation of the alien-exemption provision that is consistent with the majority's own conclusion that Congress intended Title VII to have a purely domestic focus. The closest that the majority comes to attempting to give meaning to the alien-exemption provision is to identify without endorsement "two alternative raisons d'etre for that language" offered by respondents. Neither of these explanations is even minimally persuasive....

IV

In the hands of the majority, the presumption against extraterritoriality is transformed from a "valid approach whereby unexpressed congressional intent may be ascertained," *Foley Bros.*, 336 U.S., at 285, into a barrier to any genuine inquiry into the sources that reveal Congress' actual intentions. Because the language, history, and administrative interpretations of the statute all support application of Title VII to United States companies employing United States citizens abroad, I dissent.

Hartford Fire Insurance Co. v. California

509 U.S. 764 (1993)

[The Sherman Act makes every contract, combination, or conspiracy in unreasonable restraint of interstate or foreign commerce illegal. Respondents in this case alleged that reinsurers in London violated the Sherman Act by conspiring to (a) coerce primary insurers in the United States to offer comprehensive general liability (CGL) insurance on a "claims-made" rather than "occurrence" basis, and (b) limit coverage of pollution risks in North America, thereby rendering pollution liability coverage almost entirely unavailable.]

JUSTICE SOUTER announced the judgment of the Court and delivered the opinion of the Court with respect to Parts I, II-A, III, and IV, and an opinion concurring in the judgment with respect to Part II-B.* ...

III ...

At the outset, we note that the District Court undoubtedly had jurisdiction of these Sherman Act claims, as the London reinsurers apparently concede. Although the proposition was perhaps not always free from doubt, see American Banana Co. v. United Fruit Co., 213 U.S. 347 (1909), it is well established by now that the Sherman Act applies to foreign conduct that was meant to produce and did in fact produce some substantial effect in the United States. *See* Matsushita Elec. Industrial Co. v. Zenith Radio Corp., 475 U.S. 574, 582, n. 6 (1986); United States v. Aluminum Co. of America, 148 F.2d 416, 444 (CA2 1945) (L. Hand, J.); Restatement (Third) of Foreign Relations Law of the United States §415, and Reporters' Note 3 (1987) (hereinafter Restatement (Third) Foreign Relations Law); 1 P. Areeda & D. Turner, Antitrust Law P236 (1978); *cf.* Continental Ore Co. v. Union Carbide & Carbon Corp., 370 U.S. 690, 704 (1962); Steele v. Bulova Watch Co.,

---

* JUSTICE WHITE, JUSTICE BLACKMUN, and JUSTICE STEVENS join this opinion in its entirety, and THE CHIEF JUSTICE joins Parts I, II-A, III, and IV.

344 U.S. 280, 288 (1952); United States v. Sisal Sales Corp., 274 U.S. 268, 275-276 (1927).[22] Such is the conduct alleged here: that the London reinsurers engaged in unlawful conspiracies to affect the market for insurance in the United States and that their conduct in fact produced substantial effect.[23]

According to the London reinsurers, the District Court should have declined to exercise such jurisdiction under the principle of international comity.[24] The Court of Appeals agreed that courts should look to that principle in deciding whether to exercise jurisdiction under the Sherman Act. This availed the London reinsurers nothing, however. To be sure, the Court of Appeals believed that "application of [American] antitrust laws to the London reinsurance market 'would lead to significant conflict with English law and policy,'" and that "[s]uch a conflict, unless outweighed by other factors, would by itself be reason to decline exercise of jurisdiction." But other factors, in the court's view, including the London reinsurers' express purpose to affect United States commerce and the substantial nature of the effect produced, out-weighed the supposed conflict and required the exercise of jurisdiction in this litigation.

When it enacted the FTAIA, Congress expressed no view on the question whether a court with Sherman Act jurisdiction should ever decline to exercise such jurisdiction on grounds of international comity. We need not decide that question here, however, for even assuming that in a proper case a court may decline to exercise Sherman Act jurisdiction over foreign conduct (or, as Justice Scalia would put it, may conclude by the employment of comity analysis in the first instance that there is no jurisdiction), international comity would not counsel against exercising jurisdiction in the circumstances alleged here.

The only substantial question in this litigation is whether "there is in fact a true conflict between domestic and foreign law." Societe Nationale Industrielle Aerospatiale v. United States Dist. Court for Southern Dist. of Iowa, 482 U.S. 522, 555 (1987) (Blackmun, J., concurring in part and dissenting in part). The London reinsurers contend that applying the Act to their conduct would conflict significantly with British law, and the British Government, appearing before us as amicus curiae, concurs. They assert that Parliament has established a comprehensive regulatory regime over the London reinsurance market and that the conduct alleged here was perfectly consistent with British law and policy. But this is not to state a conflict. "[T]he fact that conduct is lawful in the state in which it took place will not,

---

22. Justice Scalia believes that what is at issue in this litigation is prescriptive, as opposed to subject-matter, jurisdiction. The parties do not question prescriptive jurisdiction, however, and for good reason: it is well established that Congress has exercised such jurisdiction under the Sherman Act.

23. Under §402 of the Foreign Trade Antitrust Improvements Act of 1982 (FTAIA), 96 Stat. 1246, 15 U.S.C. §6a, the Sherman Act does not apply to conduct involving foreign trade or commerce, other than import trade or import commerce, unless "such conduct has a direct, substantial, and reasonably foreseeable effect" on domestic or import commerce. §6a(1)(A). The FTAIA was intended to exempt from the Sherman Act export transactions that did not injure the United States economy, see H.R. Rep. No. 97-686, pp. 2-3, 9-10 (1982), and it is unclear how it might apply to the conduct alleged here. Also unclear is whether the Act's "direct, substantial, and reasonably foreseeable effect" standard amends existing law or merely codifies it. We need not address these questions here. Assuming that the FTAIA's standard affects this litigation, and assuming further that that standard differs from the prior law, the conduct alleged plainly meets its requirements.

24. Justice Scalia contends that comity concerns figure into the prior analysis whether jurisdiction exists under the Sherman Act. This contention is inconsistent with the general understanding that the Sherman Act covers foreign conduct producing a substantial intended effect in the United States, and that concerns of comity come into play, if at all, only after a court has determined that the acts complained of are subject to Sherman Act jurisdiction. In any event, the parties conceded jurisdiction at oral argument, and we see no need to address this contention here.

of itself, bar application of the United States antitrust laws," even where the foreign state has a strong policy to permit or encourage such conduct. Restatement (Third) Foreign Relations Law §415, Comment j. No conflict exists, for these purposes, "where a person subject to regulation by two states can comply with the laws of both." Restatement (Third) Foreign Relations Law §403, Comment e.[25] Since the London reinsurers do not argue that British law requires them to act in some fashion prohibited by the law of the United States, or claim that their compliance with the laws of both countries is otherwise impossible, we see no conflict with British law. *See* Restatement (Third) Foreign Relations Law §403, Comment e, §415, Comment j. We have no need in this litigation to address other considerations that might inform a decision to refrain from the exercise of jurisdiction on grounds of international comity. . . .

SCALIA, J., delivered . . . a dissenting opinion . . . [in which O'CONNOR, KENNEDY, and THOMAS, J.J., joined]. . . .

It is important to distinguish two distinct questions raised by this petition: whether the District Court had jurisdiction, and whether the Sherman Act reaches the extraterritorial conduct alleged here. On the first question, I believe that the District Court had subject-matter jurisdiction over the Sherman Act claims against all the defendants (personal jurisdiction is not contested). Respondents asserted nonfrivolous claims under the Sherman Act, and 28 U.S.C. §1331 vests district courts with subject-matter jurisdiction over cases "arising under" federal statutes. . . . [T]hat is sufficient to establish the District Court's jurisdiction over these claims. . . .

The second question — the extraterritorial reach of the Sherman Act — has nothing to do with the jurisdiction of the courts. It is a question of substantive law turning on whether, in enacting the Sherman Act, Congress asserted regulatory power over the challenged conduct. *See* EEOC v. Arabian American Oil Co., 499 U.S. 244, 248 (1991) (*Aramco*) ("It is our task to determine whether Congress intended the protections of Title VII to apply to United States citizens employed by American employers outside of the United States"). If a plaintiff fails to prevail on this issue, the court does not dismiss the claim for want of subject-matter jurisdiction — want of power to adjudicate; rather, it decides the claim, ruling on the merits that the plaintiff has failed to state a cause of action under the relevant statute.

There is, however, a type of "jurisdiction" relevant to determining the extraterritorial reach of a statute; it is known as "legislative jurisdiction," *Aramco, supra*, at 253; Restatement (First) Conflict of Laws §60 (1934), or "jurisdiction to prescribe," 1 Restatement (Third) of Foreign Relations Law of the United States 235 (1987) (hereinafter Restatement (Third)). This refers to "the authority of a state to make its law applicable to persons or activities," and is quite a separate matter from "jurisdiction to adjudicate," *see id.*, at 231. There is no doubt, of course, that Congress possesses legislative jurisdiction over the acts alleged in this complaint: Congress has broad power under Article I, §8, cl. 3, "to regulate Commerce with foreign Nations," and this Court has repeatedly upheld its power to make laws applicable to persons or activities beyond our territorial boundaries where

---

25. Justice Scalia says that we put the cart before the horse in citing this authority, for he argues it may be apposite only after a determination that jurisdiction over the foreign acts is reasonable. But whatever the order of cart and horse, conflict in this sense is the only substantial issue before the Court.

United States interests are affected. But the question in this litigation is whether, and to what extent, Congress *has* exercised that undoubted legislative jurisdiction in enacting the Sherman Act.

Two canons of statutory construction are relevant in this inquiry. The first is the "longstanding principle of American law 'that legislation of Congress, unless a contrary intent appears, is meant to apply only within the territorial jurisdiction of the United States.' " *Aramco, supra*, at 248 (quoting Foley Bros., Inc. v. Filardo, 336 U.S. 281, 285 (1949)). Applying that canon in *Aramco*, we held that the version of Title VII of the Civil Rights Act of 1964 then in force, 42 U.S.C. §§2000e to 2000e-17 (1988 ed.), did not extend outside the territory of the United States even though the statute contained broad provisions extending its prohibitions to, for example, " 'any activity, business, or industry in commerce.' " *Id.*, at 249 (quoting 42 U.S.C. §2000e(h)). We held such "boilerplate language" to be an insufficient indication to override the presumption against extraterritoriality. *Id.*, at 251; *see also id.*, at 251-253. The Sherman Act contains similar "boilerplate language," and if the question were not governed by precedent, it would be worth considering whether that presumption controls the outcome here. We have, however, found the presumption to be overcome with respect to our antitrust laws; it is now well established that the Sherman Act applies extraterritorially. *See* Matsushita Elec. Industrial Co. v. Zenith Radio Corp., 475 U.S. 574, 582, n. 6 (1986); Continental Ore Co. v. Union Carbide & Carbon Corp., 370 U.S. 690, 704 (1962); *see also* United States v. Aluminum Co. of America, 148 F.2d 416 (CA2 1945).

But if the presumption against extraterritoriality has been overcome or is otherwise inapplicable, a second canon of statutory construction becomes relevant: "[A]n act of congress ought never to be construed to violate the law of nations if any other possible construction remains." Murray v. Schooner Charming Betsy, 6 U.S. 64 (1804) (Marshall, C.J.). This canon is "wholly independent" of the presumption against extraterritoriality. *Aramco, supra*, at 264 (Marshall, J., dissenting). It is relevant to determining the substantive reach of a statute because "the law of nations," or customary international law, includes limitations on a nation's exercise of its jurisdiction to prescribe. *See* Restatement (Third) §§401-416. Though it clearly has constitutional authority to do so, Congress is generally presumed not to have exceeded those customary international-law limits on jurisdiction to prescribe.

Consistent with that presumption, this and other courts have frequently recognized that, even where the presumption against extraterritoriality does not apply, statutes should not be interpreted to regulate foreign persons or conduct if that regulation would conflict with principles of international law....

More recent lower court precedent has also tempered the extraterritorial application of the Sherman Act with considerations of "international comity." The "comity" they refer to is not the comity of courts, whereby judges decline to exercise jurisdiction over matters more appropriately adjudged elsewhere, but rather what might be termed "prescriptive comity": the respect sovereign nations afford each other by limiting the reach of their laws. That comity is exercised by legislatures when they enact laws, and courts assume it has been exercised when they come to interpreting the scope of laws their legislatures have enacted. It is a traditional component of choice-of-law theory.... Considering comity in this way is just part of determining whether the Sherman Act prohibits the conduct at issue.

In sum, the practice of using international law to limit the extraterritorial reach of statutes is firmly established in our jurisprudence. In proceeding to apply that practice to the present cases, I shall rely on the Restatement (Third) for the relevant principles of international law. Its standards appear fairly supported in the decisions of this Court construing international choice-of-law principles and in the decisions of other federal courts .... Whether the Restatement precisely reflects international law in every detail matters little here, as I believe this litigation would be resolved the same way under virtually any conceivable test that takes account of foreign regulatory interests.

Under the Restatement, a nation having some "basis" for jurisdiction to prescribe law should nonetheless refrain from exercising that jurisdiction "with respect to a person or activity having connections with another state when the exercise of such jurisdiction is unreasonable." Restatement (Third) §403(1). The "reasonableness" inquiry turns on a number of factors including, but not limited to: "the extent to which the activity takes place within the territory [of the regulating state]," *id.*, §403(2)(a); "the connections, such as nationality, residence, or economic activity, between the regulating state and the person principally responsible for the activity to be regulated," *id.*, §403(2)(b); "the character of the activity to be regulated, the importance of regulation to the regulating state, the extent to which other states regulate such activities, and the degree to which the desirability of such regulation is generally accepted," *id.*, §403(2)(c); "the extent to which another state may have an interest in regulating the activity," *id.*, §403(2)(g); and "the likelihood of conflict with regulation by another state," *id.*, §403(2)(h). Rarely would these factors point more clearly against application of United States law. The activity relevant to the counts at issue here took place primarily in the United Kingdom, and the defendants in these counts are British corporations and British subjects having their principal place of business or residence outside the United States. Great Britain has established a comprehensive regulatory scheme governing the London reinsurance markets, and clearly has a heavy "interest in regulating the activity," *id.*, §403(2)(g). Finally, §2(b) of the McCarran-Ferguson Act allows state regulatory statutes to override the Sherman Act in the insurance field, subject only to the narrow "boycott" exception set forth in §3(b) — suggesting that "the importance of regulation to the [United States]," Restatement (Third) §403(2)(c), is slight. Considering these factors, I think it unimaginable that an assertion of legislative jurisdiction by the United States would be considered reasonable, and therefore it is inappropriate to assume, in the absence of statutory indication to the contrary, that Congress has made such an assertion.

It is evident from what I have said that the Court's comity analysis, which proceeds as though the issue is whether the courts should "decline to exercise ...jurisdiction," rather than whether the Sherman Act covers this conduct, is simply misdirected. I do not at all agree, moreover, with the Court's conclusion that the issue of the substantive scope of the Sherman Act is not in the cases. To be sure, the parties did not make a clear distinction between adjudicative jurisdiction and the scope of the statute. Parties often do not, as we have observed (and have declined to punish with procedural default) before. It is not realistic, and also not helpful, to pretend that the only really relevant issue in this litigation is not before us. In any event, if one erroneously chooses, as the Court does, to make adjudicative jurisdiction (or, more precisely, abstention) the vehicle for taking account of the needs of prescriptive comity, the Court still gets it wrong. It concludes that no "true conflict" counseling nonapplication of United States law (or rather, as it thinks, United States judicial jurisdiction) exists unless compliance with United States law would constitute a *violation* of another country's law. That breathtakingly broad proposition ... will bring the Sherman Act and other laws into sharp and unnecessary conflict with the legitimate interests of other countries — particularly our closest trading partners.

In the sense in which the term "conflict" ... is generally understood in the field of conflicts of laws, there is clearly a conflict in this litigation. The petitioners here ... were not compelled by any foreign law to take their allegedly wrongful actions, but that no more precludes a conflict-of-laws analysis here than it did there. Where applicable foreign and domestic law provide different substantive rules of decision to govern the parties' dispute, a conflict-of-laws analysis is necessary.

Literally the *only* support that the Court adduces for its position is §403 of the Restatement (Third) — or more precisely Comment e to that provision, which states:

> Subsection (3) [which says that a State should defer to another state if that State's interest is clearly greater] applies only when one state requires what another prohibits, or where compliance with the regulations of two states exercising jurisdiction consistently with this section is otherwise impossible. It does not apply where a person subject to regulation by two states can comply with the laws of both.

The Court has completely misinterpreted this provision. Subsection (3) of §403 (requiring one State to defer to another in the limited circumstances just described) comes into play only after subsection (1) of §403 has been complied with — i.e., after it has been determined that the exercise of jurisdiction by *both* of the two States is not "unreasonable." That prior question is answered by applying the factors (inter alia) set forth in subsection (2) of §403, that is, precisely the factors that I have discussed in text and that the Court rejects.[11]

Hoffman-La Roche Ltd. v. Empagran S.A.

124 S. Ct. 2359 (2004)

[Purchasers of vitamins filed a class action suit alleging that various vitamin manufacturers and distributors had engaged in a conspiracy to raise vitamin prices in the United States and foreign countries, in violation of U.S. antitrust law. The issue in this appeal was whether foreign purchasers of the vitamins could maintain an action under the Sherman Act for their foreign harm, in light of the Foreign Trade Antitrust Improvements Act of 1982 (FTAIA). The FTAIA provides that the Sherman Act "shall not apply to conduct involving trade or commerce ... with foreign nations (other than import trade or import commerce)" unless the conduct has "a direct, substantial and reasonably foreseeable effect" on domestic commerce, U.S. imports, or U.S. exports, and "such effect gives rise to a claim" under the Sherman Act.]

JUSTICE BREYER delivered the opinion of the Court....

The price-fixing conduct significantly and adversely affects both customers outside the United States and customers within the United States, but the adverse foreign effect is independent of any adverse domestic effect. In these

---

11. The Court skips directly to subsection (3) of §403, apparently on the authority of Comment j to §415 of the Restatement (Third). But the preceding commentary to §415 makes clear that "any exercise of [legislative] jurisdiction under this section is subject to the requirement of reasonableness" set forth in §403(2). Restatement (Third) §415, Comment a. Comment j refers back to the conflict analysis set forth in §403(3), which, as noted above, comes after the reasonableness analysis of §403(2).

circumstances, we find that the FTAIA exception does not apply (and thus the Sherman Act does not apply) for two main reasons.

First, this Court ordinarily construes ambiguous statutes to avoid unreasonable interference with the sovereign authority of other nations.... This rule of construction reflects principles of customary international law — law that (we must assume) Congress ordinarily seeks to follow. *See* Restatement (Third) of Foreign Relations Law of the United States §§403(1), 403(2) (1986) (hereinafter Restatement) (limiting the unreasonable exercise of prescriptive jurisdiction with respect to a person or activity having connections with another State); Murray v. Schooner Charming Betsy, 6 U.S. 64 (1804) ("[A]n act of Congress ought never to be construed to violate the law of nations if any other possible construction remains"); Hartford Fire Insurance Co. v. California, 509 U.S. 764 (1993) (Scalia, J., dissenting) (identifying rule of construction as derived from the principle of "prescriptive comity").

This rule of statutory construction cautions courts to assume that legislators take account of the legitimate sovereign interests of other nations when they write American laws. It thereby helps the potentially conflicting laws of different nations work together in harmony — a harmony particularly needed in today's highly interdependent commercial world.

No one denies that America's antitrust laws, when applied to foreign conduct, can interfere with a foreign nation's ability independently to regulate its own commercial affairs. But our courts have long held that application of our antitrust laws to foreign anticompetitive conduct is nonetheless reasonable, and hence consistent with principles of prescriptive comity, insofar as they reflect a legislative effort to redress domestic antitrust injury that foreign anticompetitive conduct has caused. *See* United States v. Aluminum Co. of America, 148 F.2d 416, 443-444 (CA2 1945) (L. Hand, J.)

But why is it reasonable to apply those laws to foreign conduct insofar as that conduct causes independent foreign harm and that foreign harm alone gives rise to the plaintiff's claim? Like the former case, application of those laws creates a serious risk of interference with a foreign nation's ability independently to regulate its own commercial affairs. But, unlike the former case, the justification for that interference seems insubstantial. Why should American law supplant, for example, Canada's or Great Britain's or Japan's own determination about how best to protect Canadian or British or Japanese customers from anticompetitive conduct engaged in significant part by Canadian or British or Japanese or other foreign companies?

We recognize that principles of comity provide Congress greater leeway when it seeks to control through legislation the actions of American companies; and some of the anticompetitive price-fixing conduct alleged here took place in America. But the higher foreign prices of which the foreign plaintiffs here complain are not the consequence of any domestic anticompetitive conduct that Congress sought to forbid, for Congress did not seek to forbid any such conduct insofar as it is here relevant, i.e., insofar as it is intertwined with foreign conduct that causes independent foreign harm. Rather Congress sought to release domestic (and foreign) anticompetitive conduct from Sherman Act constraints when that conduct causes foreign harm. Congress, of course, did make an exception where that conduct also causes domestic harm.

We thus repeat the basic question: Why is it reasonable to apply this law to conduct that is significantly foreign insofar as that conduct causes independent foreign harm and that foreign harm alone gives rise to the plaintiff's claim? We can find no good answer to the question....

[E]ven where nations agree about primary conduct, say price fixing, they disagree dramatically about appropriate remedies. The application, for example, of American private treble-damages remedies to anticompetitive conduct taking place abroad has generated considerable controversy. And several foreign nations have filed briefs here arguing that to apply our remedies would unjustifiably permit their citizens to bypass their own less generous remedial schemes, thereby upsetting a balance of competing considerations that their own domestic antitrust laws embody. . . .

Respondents alternatively argue that comity does not demand an interpretation of the FTAIA that would exclude independent foreign injury cases across the board. Rather, courts can take (and sometimes have taken) account of comity considerations case by case, abstaining where comity considerations so dictate.

In our view, however, this approach is too complex to prove workable. The Sherman Act covers many different kinds of anticompetitive agreements. Courts would have to examine how foreign law, compared with American law, treats not only price fixing but also, say, information-sharing agreements, patent-licensing price conditions, territorial product resale limitations, and various forms of joint venture, in respect to both primary conduct and remedy. The legally and economically technical nature of that enterprise means lengthier proceedings, appeals, and more proceedings — to the point where procedural costs and delays could themselves threaten interference with a foreign nation's ability to maintain the integrity of its own antitrust enforcement system. Even in this relatively simple price-fixing case, for example, competing briefs tell us (1) that potential treble-damage liability would help enforce widespread anti-price-fixing norms (through added deterrence) and (2) the opposite, namely that such liability would hinder antitrust enforcement (by reducing incentives to enter amnesty programs). How could a court seriously interested in resolving so empirical a matter — a matter potentially related to impact on foreign interests — do so simply and expeditiously? . . .

Where foreign anticompetitive conduct plays a significant role and where foreign injury is independent of domestic effects, Congress might have hoped that America's antitrust laws, so fundamental a component of our own economic system, would commend themselves to other nations as well. But, if America's antitrust policies could not win their own way in the international marketplace for such ideas, Congress, we must assume, would not have tried to impose them, in an act of legal imperialism, through legislative fiat.

Second, the FTAIA's language and history suggest that Congress designed the FTAIA to clarify, perhaps to limit, but not to expand in any significant way, the Sherman Act's scope as applied to foreign commerce. And we have found no significant indication that at the time Congress wrote this statute courts would have thought the Sherman Act applicable in these circumstances. . . .

Taken together, these two sets of considerations, the one derived from comity and the other reflecting history, convince us that Congress would not have intended the FTAIA's exception to bring independently caused foreign injury within the Sherman Act's reach.

Respondents point to several considerations that point the other way. For one thing, the FTAIA's language speaks in terms of the Sherman Act's applicability to certain kinds of conduct. The FTAIA says that the Sherman Act applies to foreign "conduct" with a certain kind of harmful domestic effect. Why isn't that the end of the matter? How can the Sherman Act both apply to the conduct when one person sues but not apply to the same conduct when another person sues? . . .

Moreover, the exception says that it applies if the conduct's domestic effect gives rise to "*a* claim," not to "*the plaintiff's* claim" or "*the claim at issue*" 15 U.S.C. §6a(2) [15 USCS §6a(2)] (emphasis added). The alleged conduct here did have domestic effects, and those effects were harmful enough to give rise to "a" claim. Respondents concede that this claim is not their own claim; it is someone else's claim. But, linguistically speaking, they say, that is beside the point. Nor did Congress place the relevant words "gives rise to a claim" in the FTAIA to suggest any geographical limitation; rather it did so for a here neutral reason, namely, in order to make clear that the domestic effect must be an adverse (as opposed to a beneficial) effect.

Despite their linguistic logic, these arguments are not convincing. Linguistically speaking, a statute can apply and not apply to the same conduct, depending upon other circumstances; and those other circumstances may include the nature of the lawsuit (or of the related underlying harm). It also makes linguistic sense to read the words "a claim" as if they refer to the "plaintiff's claim" or "the claim at issue."

At most, respondents' linguistic arguments might show that respondents' reading is the more natural reading of the statutory language. But those arguments do not show that we must accept that reading. And that is the critical point. The considerations previously mentioned — those of comity and history — make clear that the respondents' reading is not consistent with the FTAIA's basic intent. If the statute's language reasonably permits an interpretation consistent with that intent, we should adopt it. And, for the reasons stated, we believe that the statute's language permits the reading that we give it.

Finally, respondents point to policy considerations that we have previously discussed, namely, that application of the Sherman Act in present circumstances will (through increased deterrence) help protect Americans against foreign-caused anticompetitive injury. As we have explained, however, the plaintiffs and supporting enforcement-agency amici have made important experience-backed arguments (based upon amnesty-seeking incentives) to the contrary. We cannot say whether, on balance, respondents' side of this empirically based argument or the enforcement agencies' side is correct. But we can say that the answer to the dispute is neither clear enough, nor of such likely empirical significance, that it could overcome the considerations we have previously discussed and change our conclusion.

For these reasons, we conclude that petitioners' reading of the statute's language is correct. That reading furthers the statute's basic purposes, it properly reflects considerations of comity, and it is consistent with Sherman Act history....

JUSTICE SCALIA, with whom JUSTICE THOMAS joins, concurring in the judgment.

I concur in the judgment of the Court because the language of the statute is readily susceptible of the interpretation the Court provides and because only that interpretation is consistent with the principle that statutes should be read in accord with the customary deference to the application of foreign countries' laws within their own territories.

Notes and Questions

1. The Supreme Court has applied a presumption against extraterritoriality since early in the nation's history. For example, in United States v. Palmer, 16 U.S.

610 (1818), the Court held that a federal piracy statute did not extend to a robbery committed on the high seas by foreign citizens on board a foreign ship. Although the Court acknowledged that the words of the statute, which purported to cover "any person or persons," were "broad enough to comprehend every human being," the Court reasoned that mere "general words" should not be construed to cover the conduct of foreign citizens outside U.S. territory. In *Palmer* the presumption was formulated as one against the application of federal laws to *foreigners* outside the United States, but over time it came to apply to U.S. citizens as well. The Supreme Court continued to apply the presumption during the twentieth century, especially with respect to labor-related statutes. *See, e.g.*, McCulloch v. Sociedad Nacional de Marineros de Honduras, 372 U.S. 10, 19-22 (1963) (National Labor Relations Act); Benz v. Compania Naviera Hidalgo, S.A., 353 U.S. 138, 143-46 (1957) (Labor Management Relations Act); Foley Bros., Inc. v. Filardo, 336 U.S. 281, 285 (1949) (Eight Hour Law).

2. What are the justifications for the judge-made presumption against extraterritoriality? To comply with congressional wishes? To avoid foreign relations controversy? To defer to the Executive? To comply with international law? To keep courts out of foreign affairs? Some combination? Something else?

Should the presumption be applied in a case, such as *Aramco*, where the defendant is a U.S. citizen or corporation? Should the Court abandon the presumption and simply attempt to discern legislative intent? How does the presumption differ from the *Charming Betsy* canon? (Note that the dissents in both *Aramco* and *Hartford Fire* make much of the distinction, and note also the use of the canon in *Empagran*.) What is the relationship between the two doctrines? Is the *Charming Betsy* canon sufficient to address concerns associated with extraterritoriality? Why not apply a presumption *in favor* of extraterritoriality? Or a presumption that statutes extend to the limits of Congress's powers?

3. What evidence of intent must Congress provide in order to overcome the presumption? What materials is a court allowed to look at in making this determination? Can it, for example, look at the legislative history of the statute?

4. Congress quickly overturned the specific holding of *Aramco* concerning the scope of Title VII. In the Civil Rights Act of 1991, Congress amended the definition of "employee" in Title VII to provide that, "[w]ith respect to employment in a foreign country, [the term "employee"] includes an individual who is a citizen of the United States." 42 U.S.C. §2000e(f). Congress also added the following provisions, in 42 U.S.C. §2000e-1:

> (b) It shall not be unlawful under [this statute] . . . for an employer (or a corporation controlled by an employer), labor organization, employment agency, or joint labor-management committee controlling apprenticeship or other training or retraining (including on-the-job training programs) to take any action otherwise prohibited by such section, with respect to an employee in a workplace in a foreign country if compliance with such section would cause such employer (or such corporation), such organization, such agency, or such committee to violate the law of the foreign country in which such workplace is located.
>
> (c) (1) If an employer controls a corporation whose place of incorporation is a foreign country, any practice prohibited by [this statute] engaged in by such corporation shall be presumed to be engaged in by such employer.
>
> (2) [This statute] shall not apply with respect to the foreign operations of an employer that is a foreign person not controlled by an American employer.

Does this statute show that the Court in *Aramco* erred in its original interpretation of Title VII? Or does it show the system of separation of powers working well? Consider this assessment:

> One can understand the Court's fears that, if it entered this thicket of international complications, it might well get major elements wrong, and would thus strongly benefit from the explicit legislative guidance that a preference-eliciting default rule would provide. Which is precisely what happened. Congress promptly overrode *Aramco* less than nine months later. But it did not simply codify a general conflicts of interests balancing approach. Rather, it limited extraterritorial application to discrimination in foreign workplaces by American employers against American citizens, excluding discrimination in foreign workplaces by foreign employers against American citizens as well as by American employers against foreign nationals. Congress also provided that the statute did not apply to extraterritorial conduct that was required by foreign law, and added provisions specifying how to treat foreign firms controlled by American firms. In short, the preference-eliciting default rule provoked Congress into providing just the sort of nuanced specificity and limitations that the Court would have had difficulty divining.

Einer Elhauge, *Preference-Eliciting Statutory Default Rules*, 102 Colum. L. Rev. 2162, 2240-41 (2002). Do you agree?

5. The Supreme Court has reaffirmed the presumption in two decisions after *Aramco*. *See* Sale v. Haitian Centers Council, 509 U.S. 155 (1993); Smith v. United States, 507 U.S. 197 (1993). In both of those decisions, the Court noted that the presumption applies even when there is no serious risk of conflict with the laws of another nation. In the absence of such a risk of conflict, what purpose does the presumption serve?

6. A number of academic commentators have criticized the presumption, arguing that it is inconsistent with modern international law, which allows for some extraterritorial regulation; with modern state choice-of-law rules, which generally employ a multifactored balancing analysis rather than a strict territorial presumption; and with the modern legislative focus of Congress, which they contend is often international in scope. *See, e.g.*, Gary B. Born, *A Reappraisal of the Extraterritorial Reach of U.S. Law*, 24 Law & Pol'y Int'l Bus. 1 (1992); Larry Kramer, *Vestiges of Beale: Extraterritorial Application of American Law*, 1991 Sup. Ct. Rev. 179; Jonathan Turley, *"When in Rome": Multinational Misconduct and the Presumption Against Extraterritoriality*, 84 Nw. U. L. Rev. 598 (1990). One commentator summed up the criticism by stating that "the world in which a presumption against extraterritoriality made sense is gone." Kramer, *supra*, at 184. For a defense of the presumption grounded in separation of powers principles, see Curtis A. Bradley, *Territorial Intellectual Property Rights in an Age of Globalism*, 37 Va. J. Int'l L. 505, 550-61 (1997). For a defense of the presumption grounded in principles of formalism, see Jack L. Goldsmith, *The New Formalism in United States Foreign Relations Law*, 70 U. Colo. L. Rev. 1395 (1999). For an argument that the presumption should be applied only to situations in which the extraterritorial conduct does not have effects within the United States, see William S. Dodge, *Understanding the Presumption Against Extraterritoriality*, 16 Berkeley J. Int'l L. 85 (1998).

7. *Hartford Fire* was decided against the historical backdrop of a long and varied history of the extraterritorial application of U.S. antitrust laws. The Supreme Court originally construed the Sherman Act law to be strictly territorial. *See* American Banana Co. v. United Fruit Co., 213 U.S. 347 (1909). In 1927, the Court said that the Sherman Act applied to "deliberate acts, here and elsewhere,

[that] brought about forbidden results within the United States." United States v. Sisal Sales Corp., 274 U.S. 268, 276 (1927). Eighteen years later, the Second Circuit, in a case referred to it because the Supreme Court did not have a quorum of disinterested Justices, held that U.S. antitrust law applies to agreements made abroad "if they were intended to affect imports and did affect them." United States v. Aluminum Co. of Am., 148 F.2d 416, 444 (2d Cir. 1945) (en banc). The Supreme Court appeared to endorse this "effects test" in later cases. *See* Matsushita Elec. Indus. Co. v. Zenith Radio Corp., 475 U.S. 574, 582 n.6 (1985); Continental Ore Co. v. Union Carbide & Carbon Corp., 370 U.S. 690, 704 (1962). In the 1970s and 1980s, lower courts applied the effects test aggressively to regulate extraterritorial conduct, spawning controversy with some of the United States' closest trading partners. Some lower courts modified the extraterritorial scope of the Sherman Act by engaging in comity analysis that balanced the interests of foreign nations and sometimes resulted in nonapplication of the Sherman Act even when the effects test was satisfied. *See, e.g.*, Mannington Mills v. Congoleum, 595 F.2d 1287 (3d Cir. 1979); Timberlane Lumber Co. v. Bank of America, 549 F.2d 597 (9th Cir. 1976). *But see* Laker Airways v. Sabena, 731 F.2d 909 (D.C. Cir. 1984) (granting virtually no deference to other states' interests). For discussions of this history, see Roger P. Alford, *The Extraterritorial Application of Antitrust Laws: A Postscript on Hartford Fire Insurance Co. v. California*, 34 Va. J. Int'l L. 213 (1993); Kenneth W. Dam, *Extraterritoriality in an Age of Globalization: The* Hartford Fire *Case*, 1993 Sup. Ct. Rev. 289 (1994); Robert C. Reuland, Hartford Fire Insurance Co., *Comity, and the Extraterritorial Reach of United States Antitrust Laws*, 29 Tex. Int'l L.J. 159 (1994).

8. Although *Hartford Fire* was decided after *Aramco*, the majority in *Hartford Fire* does not apply (or even consider) the presumption against extraterritoriality. Why not? Because of *stare decisis*? Because the allegedly illegal conduct produced substantial effects in the United States? Some other reason?

9. Subject matter jurisdiction is usually thought of as the court's power to hear a case; prescriptive jurisdiction is usually thought of as a nation's authority to regulate conduct. In *Hartford Fire*, the majority and dissent disagree over whether the extraterritoriality issue is one of subject matter jurisdiction or prescriptive jurisdiction. Who is right? Does it matter? The majority in *Hartford Fire* suggests that there is no issue of prescriptive jurisdiction in the case because it is settled that U.S. antitrust laws have extraterritorial effect. Is that right?

10. What position does the majority take in *Hartford Fire* concerning the role of comity analysis in limiting the application of U.S. antitrust analysis? What position does it take concerning the first comity factor — conflict with foreign law or policy? Note that some commentators construed *Hartford Fire* as precluding the use of comity analysis in antitrust cases absent what the Court calls a "true conflict" between U.S. law and foreign law. Is that a correct reading of the decision? Compare, for example, Alford, *supra*, at 220 (reading the decision that way), and Reuland, *supra*, at 161 (same), with Bradley, *supra*, at 557-60 (arguing against that reading of the decision). Is the *Hartford Fire* decision consistent with the *Charming Betsy* canon?

For additional discussion of these and other aspects of *Hartford Fire*, see, in addition to the articles cited above, Andreas F. Lowenfeld, *Conflict, Balancing of Interests, and the Exercise of Jurisdiction to Prescribe: Reflections on the Insurance Antitrust Case*, 89 Am. J. Int'l L. 42 (1995); Phillip R. Trimble, *The Supreme Court and International Law: The Demise of Restatement Section 403*, 89 Am. J. Int'l L. 53 (1995); and

Larry Kramer, *Extraterritorial Application of American Law After the Insurance Antitrust Case: A Reply to Professors Lowenfeld and Trimble*, 89 Am. J. Int'l L. 750 (1995).

11. Congress enacted the Foreign Trade Antitrust Improvements Act (FTAIA) in 1982 to clarify the application of U.S. antitrust laws to foreign conduct. In pertinent part, the FTAIA states that the antitrust laws will not apply to non-import commerce with foreign nations unless the conduct at issue has a "direct, substantial, and reasonably foreseeable effect" on domestic commerce and "such effect gives rise to a claim under" the antitrust laws. 15 U.S.C. §6a. In *Empagran*, the Court holds that U.S. antitrust law, as modified by the FTAIA, does not apply to the foreign effects of foreign anticompetitive conduct, where the foreign effects are independent of any domestic effects.

What rule of statutory construction does the Court apply in *Empagran*? What is the relationship between that rule and the presumption against extraterritoriality? What is its relationship with the *Charming Betsy* canon? How does the Court's discussion of comity in *Empagran* compare with the majority's discussion of comity in *Hartford Fire*? Did the Court in *Empagran* in effect adopt Justice Scalia's dissent from *Hartford Fire*? Why does the Court in *Empagran* reject the case-by-case approach to comity suggested by the respondents?

For various perspectives on the relationship between *Hartford Fire* and *Empagran*, see Susan E. Burnett, *US Judicial Imperialism Post-Empagran*, 18 Emory Int'l L. Rev. 555, 607-09 (2004); John K. Setear, *A Forest With No Trees: The Supreme Court and International Law in the 2003 Term*, 91 Va. L. Rev. 579, 610-11 (2005); Christopher Sprigman, *Fix Prices Globally, Get Sued Locally? U.S. Jurisdiction over International Cartels*, 72 U. Chi. L. Rev. 265, 280-81 (2005); Jaafar A. Riazi, *Finding Subject Matter Jurisdiction Over Antitrust Claims Of Extraterritorial Origin*, 54 DePaul L. Rev. 1277, 1279 (2005).

12. Like the Supreme Court's approach to the Sherman Act in *Hartford Fire*, lower courts have declined to apply a strict presumption against extraterritoriality to securities laws, the Racketeer Influenced and Corrupt Organizations (RICO) Act, and bankruptcy law. Courts also decline to apply the presumption to criminal laws that are "by their nature" concerned with extraterritorial conduct. The genesis of this exception (which is framed somewhat differently by different circuits) is the Supreme Court's decision in United States v. Bowman, 260 U.S. 94 (1922), in which the Court stated that the presumption against extraterritoriality "should not be applied to criminal statutes which are, as a class, not logically dependent on their locality for the Government's jurisdiction, but are enacted because of the right of the Government to defend itself against obstruction, or fraud wherever perpetrated, especially if committed by its own citizens, officers or agents." *Id*. at 98. For decisions applying this exception, see, for example, United States v. Delgado-Garcia, 374 F.3d 1337 (D.C. Cir. 2004) (attempted smuggling of aliens into the United States); United States v. Plummer, 221 F.3d 1298 (11th Cir. 2000) (attempted cigar smuggling); United States v. Harvey, 2 F.3d 1318 (3d Cir. 1993) (sexual exploitation of children); United States v. Larsen, 952 F.2d 1099 (9th Cir. 1991) (drug possession and attempted distribution). For a decision applying criminal antitrust laws to foreign conduct, see United States v. Nippon Paper Industries Co., 109 F.3d 1 (1st Cir. 1997). Should courts be more or less reluctant to apply U.S. criminal laws extraterritorially than they are to apply U.S. civil laws extraterritorially?

13. Maritime law is another context in which the Court does not apply the presumption. A good example is Lauritzen v. Larsen, 345 U.S. 571 (1953), which held that a Danish seaman on a Danish ship in Havana harbor could not recover under the Jones Act. The Court did not reach this conclusion through application of the presumption against extraterritoriality, but rather by balancing seven factors that might affect the extraterritorial application of the Jones Act, namely: the place of the wrongful act, the law of the flag, allegiance or domicile of the injured, allegiance of the defendant shipowner, place of contract, inaccessibility of the foreign forum, and the law of the forum. *Id*. at 583-90. It is unclear why *Lauritzen* used this balancing approach rather than a flat presumption against extraterritoriality, but the decision has been followed in subsequent maritime cases. *See* Hellenic Line Ltd. v. Rhoditis, 398 U.S. 306 (1970); Romero v. International Terminal Operating Co., 358 U.S. 354 (1959). Is there something about maritime law that requires a different test for extraterritoriality?

14. In Spector v. Norwegian Cruise Line Ltd., 125 S. Ct. 2169 (2005), the Supreme Court held that Title III of the Americans with Disabilities Act generally applied to foreign-flag cruise ships sailing in U.S. waters. Title III provides that: "no individual shall be discriminated against on the basis of disability in the full and equal enjoyment of goods, services, facilities, privileges, advantages, or accommodations of any place of public accommodation." It also prohibits discrimination against disabled individuals on "specified public transportation services provided by a private entity that is primarily engaged in the business of transporting people and whose operations affect commerce." *Spector* was not an extraterritoriality case *per se*, since it concerned the application of a federal statute within U.S. territorial waters. Nevertheless, applying Title III to foreign cruise ships will have extraterritorial effects, since these ships sail outside the United States.

The Court in *Spector* stated that "a clear statement of congressional intent is necessary before a general statutory requirement can interfere with matters that concern a foreign-flag vessel's internal affairs and operations, as contrasted with statutory requirements that concern the security and well-being of United States citizens or territory." It also reasoned that, "[w]hile the clear statement rule could limit Title III's application to foreign-flag cruise ships in some instances, when it requires removal of physical barriers, it would appear the rule is inapplicable to many other duties Title III might impose." Beyond those statements, however, there was no majority rationale for the Court's decision. The disagreement among the Justices about how to apply the "interference with internal affairs" clear statement rule parallels to some extent debates over the proper application of the presumption against extraterritoriality.

In a plurality opinion, Justice Kennedy and three other Justices proposed an "application-by-application" approach to the clear statement rule, such that a federal statute such as Title III would be deemed to apply to foreign-flag ships sailing in U.S. waters to the extent that its application did not interfere with the ship's internal affairs. In a concurrence, Justice Ginsburg and Justice Breyer proposed an even more limited approach to the clear statement rule, whereby it would be applied only to the extent that a particular application of a federal statute would conflict with international obligations or pose a potential for international discord. By contrast, Justice Scalia and three other Justices argued in dissent that Title III should be deemed not to apply to foreign-flag cruise ships at all because some aspects of this statute relate to the internal affairs of the ships, and Congress had not clearly expressed an intent to apply Title III to foreign ships. Which is the best approach? Is it better to apply a clear statement rule such as this one, or the presumption against extraterritoriality, in an application-by-application way or in a categorical way? Which approach is more likely to reflect congressional intent? Which approach is more likely to prompt legislative action?

15. So when *should* courts invoke the presumption against extraterritoriality? Lower courts appear confused. For example, in the course of interpreting the National Environmental Policy Act, one court stated that the presumption does not apply when conduct or effects occur partially in the United States. *See* Environmental Defense Fund v. Massey, 986 F. 2d 528, 531 (D.C. Cir. 1993). Another court, by contrast, applied the presumption in construing the Copyright Act even though acts abroad caused harmful local effects. *See* Subafilms Ltd. v. MGM-Pathe Communications Co., 24 F.3d 1088, 1097 (9th Cir. 1994) (en banc). For other decisions applying the presumption after *Aramco*, see, for example, Asplundh Tree Expert Co. v. National Labor Relations Board, 365 F.3d 168 (3d Cir. 2004) (holding that the National Labor Relations Act did not apply to foreign conduct of U.S. employer); and ARC Ecology v. U.S. Department of the Air Force, 411 F.3d 1092 (9th Cir. 2005) (holding that the Comprehensive Environmental Response, Compensation, and Liability Act (CERCLA) does not apply extraterritorially).

16. Two Supreme Court decisions, decided the same Term as *Empagran*, touched on the presumption against extraterritoriality. In Small v. United States, 125 S. Ct. 1752 (2005), the Court held that a federal statute that makes it a crime for anyone to possess a firearm if they have "been convicted in any court, of a crime punishable by imprisonment for a term exceeding one year" is implicitly referring only to convictions in U.S. courts. The Court therefore held that the statute did not apply to a U.S. citizen who was convicted in Japan of attempting to smuggle firearms and ammunition into that country, served a five-year prison sentence there, and subsequently purchased a firearm in the United States. In reaching this conclusion, the Court referred favorably to the presumption against extraterritoriality and noted that, "although the presumption against extraterritorial application does not apply directly to this case, we believe a similar assumption is appropriate when we consider the scope of the phrase 'convicted in any court' here."

In Pasquantino v. United States, 125 S. Ct. 1766 (2005), the Court held that the federal wire fraud statute could be applied to prosecute a conspiracy in the United States to defraud Canada of liquor taxes. The majority denied that it was giving extraterritorial effect to the wire fraud statute:

> Petitioners used U.S. interstate wires to execute a scheme to defraud a foreign sovereign of tax revenue. Their offense was complete the moment they executed the scheme inside the United States. . . . This domestic element of petitioners' conduct is what the Government is punishing in this prosecution, no less than when it prosecutes a scheme to defraud a foreign individual or corporation, or a foreign government acting as a market participant. In any event, the wire fraud statute punishes frauds executed "in interstate or foreign commerce" . . . , so this is surely not a statute in which Congress had only "domestic concerns in mind." Small v. United States, [125 S. Ct. 1752, 1755 (2005)].

The four dissenters, by contrast, argued that the *Aramco* presumption against extraterritoriality provided a reason for construing the wire fraud statute not to reach the conduct in question.

What do these decisions suggest about the Court's current commitment to the presumption against extraterritorialty?

17. States sometimes apply their laws extraterritorially in ways that implicate U.S. foreign relations. For example, California in 1999 enacted the Holocaust

Victim Insurance Relief Act, which required any insurer doing business in California that sold insurance policies to persons in Europe that were in effect between 1920 and 1945 to file certain information about those policies with the California Insurance Commissioner. A Florida Holocaust insurance act had similar reporting requirements. Both statutes imposed disclosure obligations that in some sense regulated corporate activity outside the United States. Both statutes were challenged on dormant foreign affairs preemption and related grounds, and as we studied in Chapter 5, the Supreme Court in American Insurance Ass'n v. Garamendi held that the California statute was preempted because it was inconsistent with Executive Branch policy as embodied in certain sole executive agreements. But in the courts of appeals, both statutes were also challenged on different grounds relevant to this chapter, namely, that they violated the Fourteenth Amendment Due Process Clause.

In the interstate context, when one state applies its laws in a way that regulates activity in another state, the Due Process Clause and the Full Faith and Credit Clause, taken together, have been interpreted to provide modest restrictions on the application of state and local law to activities in another state. In general, the state need only have "a significant contact or significant aggregation of contacts, creating state interests, such that choice of its law is neither arbitrary nor fundamentally unfair." Allstate Insurance Co. v. Hague, 449 U.S. 302, 312-13 (1981) (plurality opinion). The Court in *Hague* applied this standard to conclude that Minnesota could apply its insurance law of "stacking" to an accident in Wisconsin, involving a Wisconsin domiciliary who took out insurance in Wisconsin, primarily because the decedent worked in Minnesota and his wife (who was seeking recovery in the case) moved there after the litigation began. In Phillips Petroleum v. Shutts, 472 U.S. 797 (1985), by contrast, the Court applied the same standard to conclude that Kansas could not apply its law for determining interest on royalties for land leased entirely outside of Kansas and that had no other connection to Kansas.

The application of the "significant aggregation of contacts" test to state laws that apply outside the United States (as opposed to applying in another state) is somewhat uncertain because the test purports to flow from both the Due Process and Full Faith and Credit Clauses, but the latter Clause concerns only sister-state relations and does not govern the application of state law abroad. However, the Supreme Court in an older case, which was reaffirmed in *Hague* and *Shutts*, held that the Due Process Clause considered alone does regulate the extraterritorial application of state law abroad, and it emphasized the fairness of applying the law to the defendant (as opposed to concerns about offending the foreign sovereign). *See* Home Insurance Co. v. Dick, 281 U.S. 397 (1930).

What implications do these precedents have for the state Holocaust insurance statutes? In Gerling Global Reinsurance Corp. of Am. v. Gallagher, 267 F.3d 1228 (11th Cir. 2001), the Eleventh Circuit concluded that the Florida statute ran afoul of the *Hague* test to the extent that it required production of information regarding Holocaust-era policies issued outside Florida by German entities having only some corporate affiliation with the plaintiffs and no other contacts to Florida. By contrast, in Gerling Global Reinsurance Corp. of Am. v. Low, 296 F.3d 832 (9th Cir. 2002), *reversed on other grounds*, American Insurance Ass'n v. Garamendi, 539 U.S. 396 (2003), the Ninth Circuit concluded that *Hague*, *Shutts*, and *Dick* were inapposite because the California laws did not affect the substance of the contractual relationship between the plaintiffs and the insurance companies, but rather merely required information disclosure.

How does the *Hague/Shutts* analysis differ from the presumption against extra-territoriality and the comity analysis that apply to federal statutes? Why are the analyses different? Which analysis is more restrictive?

2. International Law of Prescriptive Jurisdiction

United States v. Noriega

746 F. Supp. 1506 (S.D. Fla. 1990)

[In February 1988, a federal grand jury in Miami indicted General Manuel Noriega for participating in an international conspiracy to import cocaine into and out of the United States, in violation of various federal laws, including RICO. Noriega was at the time the Commander in Chief of the Panamanian Defense Forces and the de facto leader of Panama. In December 1989, Noriega declared that a "state of war" existed between Panama and the United States, and a few days later U.S. troops in Panama were fired upon and one was killed. President H.W. Bush subsequently ordered U.S. troops into combat in Panama, where they eventually captured Noriega and brought him to the United States.]

WILLIAM H. HOEVELER, UNITED STATES DISTRICT JUDGE. . . .

The first issue confronting the Court is whether the United States may exercise jurisdiction over Noriega's alleged criminal activities. Noriega maintains that "the extraterritorial application of the criminal law is unreasonable under the unique facts of this case, and cannot be relied upon to secure jurisdiction over a leader of a sovereign nation who has personally performed no illegal acts within the borders of the United States." Although the defendant attempts to weave his asserted status as a foreign leader into his challenge to the extraterritorial application of this coun-try's criminal laws, the question of whether the United States may proscribe con-duct which occurs beyond its borders is separate from the question of whether Noriega is immune from prosecution as a head of state. This distinction is made clear in the defendant's own discussion of the applicable international law on extra-territorial jurisdiction, which does not look to a foreign defendant's official status but rather to the nature and effect of the conduct at issue. The Court therefore reserves analysis of Noriega's claim to head of state immunity and confines its discussion here to the ability of the United States to reach and prosecute acts committed by aliens outside its territorial borders.[4] While the indictment cites specific instances of conduct occurring within the United States, including the shipment of cocaine from Panama to Miami and several flights to and from Miami by Noriega's alleged co-conspirators, the activity ascribed to Noriega occurred solely in Panama with the exception of the one trip to Cuba. Noriega is charged with providing safe haven to international narcotic traffickers by allow-ing Panama to be used as a location for the manufacture and shipment of cocaine destined for this country's shores.

Where a court is faced with the issue of extraterritorial jurisdiction, the analysis to be applied is 1) whether the United States has the power to reach the conduct in question under traditional principles of international law; and 2) whether the stat-utes under which the defendant is charged are intended to have extraterritorial

---

4. No jurisdictional obstacle would be present were the defendant a United States citizen, since a country may regulate the acts of its citizens wherever they occur. . . .

effect. As Noriega concedes, the United States has long possessed the ability to attach criminal consequences to acts occurring outside this country which produce effects within the United States. Strassheim v. Daily, 221 U.S. 280, 285 (1911); Restatement (Third) of the Foreign Relations Law of the United States §402(1)(c). For example, the United States would unquestionably have authority to prosecute a person standing in Canada who fires a bullet across the border which strikes a second person standing in the United States. *See* Restatement (Third), §402, Comment d. "All the nations of the world recognize 'the principle that a man who outside of a country willfully puts in motion a force to take effect in it is answerable at the place where the evil is done. . . .' " Rivard v. United States, 375 F.2d 882, 887 (5th Cir.) (citations omitted). The objective territorial theory of jurisdiction, which focuses on the effects or intended effects of conduct, can be traced to Justice Holmes' statement that "acts done outside a jurisdiction, but intended to produce or producing effects within it, justify a State in punishing the cause of the harm as if he had been present at the effect, if the State should succeed in getting him within its power." Strassheim v. Daily, 221 U.S. at 285. Even if the extraterritorial conduct produces no effect within the United States, a defendant may still be reached if he was part of a conspiracy in which some co-conspirator's activities took place within United States territory. . . .

More recently, international law principles have expanded to permit jurisdiction upon a mere showing of intent to produce effects in this country, without requiring proof of an overt act or effect within the United States. According to the Restatement (Third):

> Cases involving intended but unrealized effect are rare, but international law does not preclude jurisdiction in such instances, subject to the principle of reasonableness. When the intent to commit the proscribed act is clear and demonstrated by some activity, and the effect to be produced by the activity is substantial and foreseeable, the fact that a plan or conspiracy was thwarted does not deprive the target state of jurisdiction to make its law applicable.

§402, Comment d.

In the drug smuggling context, the "intent doctrine" has resulted in jurisdiction over persons who attempted to import narcotics into the United States but never actually succeeded in entering the United States or delivering drugs within its borders. The fact that no act was committed and no repercussions were felt within the United States did not preclude jurisdiction over conduct that was clearly directed at the United States.

These principles unequivocally support jurisdiction in this case. The indictment charges Noriega with conspiracy to import cocaine into the United States and alleges several overt acts performed within the United States in furtherance of the conspiracy. Specifically, the indictment alleges that co-conspirators of Noriega purchased a Lear jet in Miami, which was then used to transport drug proceeds from Miami to Panama. Moreover, Noriega's activities in Panama, if true, undoubtedly produced effects within this country as deleterious as the hypothetical bullet fired across the border. The indictment alleges that, as a result of Noriega's facilitation of narcotics activity in Panama, 2,141 pounds of cocaine were illegally brought into Miami from Panama. While the ability of the United States to reach and proscribe extraterritorial conduct having effects in this country does not depend on the amount of narcotics imported into the United States or the magnitude of the consequences, the importation of over 2,000 pounds of cocaine clearly has a harmful impact and merits jurisdiction. Finally, even if no overt acts or effects occurred within the territorial borders, the object of the alleged conspiracy was to import cocaine into the United States and therefore an intent to produce effects is present.

The defendant's argument that the exercise of jurisdiction over his alleged activities in Panama is unreasonable is simply unsupportable in light of established principles of international law and the overwhelming case law in this Circuit upholding jurisdiction under similar circumstances. Other than asserting his status as a foreign leader, which presents a different question from the one posed here, Noriega does not distinguish this case from those cited above. He cites the principle of reasonableness recently articulated in the Restatement (Third) §403, but fails to say how extending jurisdiction over his conduct would be unreasonable. In fact, the defendant's invocation of a reasonableness requirement supports rather than undermines the application of jurisdiction in the present case. Thus, for example, Noriega quotes the following language from the Restatement:

> In applying the principle of reasonableness, the exercise of criminal (as distinguished from civil) jurisdiction in relation to acts committed in another state may be perceived as particularly intrusive. . . .
> It is generally accepted by enforcement agencies of the United States government that criminal jurisdiction over activity with substantial foreign elements should be exercised more sparingly than civil jurisdiction over the same activity, and only upon strong justification.

Restatement (Third) §403, Reporters' Note 8. However, the same section of the Restatement establishes that narcotics offenses provide the strong justification meriting criminal jurisdiction: "Prosecution for activities committed in a foreign state have generally been limited to serious and universally condemned offenses, such as treason or traffic in narcotics, and to offenses by and against military forces. In such cases the state in whose territory the act occurs is not likely to object to regulation by the state concerned." *Id.* (citations omitted). The Restatement therefore explicitly recognizes the reasonableness of extending jurisdiction to narcotics activity such as that alleged here. Even if another state were likely to object to jurisdiction here, the United States has a strong interest in halting the flow of illicit drugs across its borders. In assessing the reasonableness of extraterritorial jurisdiction, one of the factors to be considered is the character of the activity to be regulated, including the importance of regulation to the regulating state and the degree to which the desire to regulate is generally accepted. Restatement (Third) §403(1)(c). The consensus of the American public on the need to stem the flow of drugs into this country is well publicized and need not be elaborated upon in detail. Further, the Court notes that the United States has an affirmative duty to enact and enforce legislation to curb illicit drug trafficking under the Single Convention on Narcotics Drugs, 18 U.S.T. 1409, T.I.A.S. No. 6298, New York, March 30, 1961, ratified by the United States, 1967, amended 26 U.S.T. 1441, T.I.A.S. No. 8118. Given the serious nature of the drug epidemic in this country, certainly the efforts of the United States to combat the problem by prosecuting conduct directed against itself cannot be subject to the protests of a foreign government profiting at its expense. In any case, the Court is not made aware of any instance in which the Republic of Panama objected to the regulation of drug trafficking by the United States. In sum, because Noriega's conduct in Panama is alleged to have resulted in a direct effect within the United States, the Court concludes that extraterritorial jurisdiction is appropriate as a matter of international law.

United States v. Yunis

924 F.2d 1086 (D.C. Cir. 1991)

[Fawaz Yunis was one of several men who hijacked a Royal Jordanian Airlines flight from Beirut, Lebanon. The plane took off and eventually landed back in Beirut, where the hijackers, including Yunis, released the hostages (including two Americans), blew up the plane, and fled. The FBI subsequently arrested Yunis on a yacht in international waters in the eastern Mediterranean. Yunis was brought to the United States, where he was convicted of conspiracy, 18 U.S.C. §371, hostage taking, 18 U.S.C. §1203, and air piracy, 49 U.S.C. App. §1472(n). Yunis appealed.]

MIKVA, CHIEF JUDGE...
   Yunis appeals first of all from the district court's denial of his motion to dismiss for lack of subject matter and personal jurisdiction. Appellant's principal claim is that, as a matter of domestic law, the federal hostage taking and air piracy statutes do not authorize assertion of federal jurisdiction over him. Yunis also suggests that a contrary construction of these statutes would conflict with established principles of international law, and so should be avoided by this court. Finally, appellant claims that the district court lacked personal jurisdiction because he was seized in violation of American law.

1. HOSTAGE TAKING ACT

The Hostage Taking Act provides, in relevant part:

> (a) Whoever, whether inside or outside the United States, seizes or detains and threatens to kill, to injure, or to continue to detain another person in order to compel a third person or a governmental organization to do or to abstain from any act... shall be punished by imprisonment by any term of years or for life.
>
>   (b)(1) It is not an offense under this section if the conduct required for the offense occurred outside the United States unless—
>
>   (A) the offender or the person seized or detained is a national of the United States;
>
>   (B) the offender is found in the United States; or
>
>   (C) the governmental organization sought to be compelled is the Government of the United States.

18 U.S.C. §1203. Yunis claims that this statute cannot apply to an individual who is brought to the United States by force, since those convicted under it must be "found in the United States." But this ignores the law's plain language. Subsections (A), (B), and (C) of section 1203(b)(1) offer independent bases for jurisdiction where "the offense occurred outside the United States." Since two of the passengers on Flight 402 were U.S. citizens, section 1203(b)(1)(A), authorizing assertion of U.S. jurisdiction where "the offender or the person seized or detained is a national of the United States," is satisfied. The statute's jurisdictional requirement has been

met regardless of whether or not Yunis was "found" within the United States under section 1203(b)(1)(B).

Appellant's argument that we should read the Hostage Taking Act differently to avoid tension with international law falls flat. Yunis points to no treaty obligations of the United States that give us pause. Indeed, Congress intended through the Hostage Taking Act to execute the International Convention Against the Taking of Hostages, which authorizes any signatory state to exercise jurisdiction over persons who take its nationals hostage "if that State considers it appropriate." International Convention Against the Taking of Hostages, opened for signature Dec. 18, 1979, art. 5, para. 1, 34 U.N. GAOR Supp. (No. 39), 18 I.L.M. 1456, 1458.

Nor is jurisdiction precluded by norms of customary international law. The district court concluded that two jurisdictional theories of international law, the "universal principle" and the "passive personal principle," supported assertion of U.S. jurisdiction to prosecute Yunis on hijacking and hostage-taking charges. Under the universal principle, states may prescribe and prosecute "certain offenses recognized by the community of nations as of universal concern, such as piracy, slave trade, attacks on or hijacking of aircraft, genocide, war crimes, and perhaps certain acts of terrorism," even absent any special connection between the state and the offense. *See* Restatement (Third) of the Foreign Relations Law of the United States §§404, 423 (1987). Under the passive personal principle, a state may punish non-nationals for crimes committed against its nationals outside of its territory, at least where the state has a particularly strong interest in the crime. *See id.* at §402 comment g.

Relying primarily on the Restatement, Yunis argues that hostage taking has not been recognized as a universal crime and that the passive personal principle authorizes assertion of jurisdiction over alleged hostage takers only where the victims were seized because they were nationals of the prosecuting state. Whatever merit appellant's claims may have as a matter of international law, they cannot prevail before this court. Yunis seeks to portray international law as a self-executing code that trumps domestic law whenever the two conflict. That effort misconceives the role of judges as appliers of international law and as participants in the federal system. Our duty is to enforce the Constitution, laws, and treaties of the United States, not to conform the law of the land to norms of customary international law. *See* U.S. Const. art. VI. As we said in Committee of U.S. Citizens Living in Nicaragua v. Reagan, 859 F.2d 929 (D.C. Cir. 1988): "Statutes inconsistent with principles of customary international law may well lead to international law violations. But within the domestic legal realm, that inconsistent statute simply modifies or supersedes customary international law to the extent of the inconsistency." *Id.* at 938.

To be sure, courts should hesitate to give penal statutes extraterritorial effect absent a clear congressional directive. Similarly, courts will not blind themselves to potential violations of international law where legislative intent is ambiguous. *See* Murray v. The Schooner Charming Betsy, 6 U.S. (2 Cranch) 64, 118 (1804) ("[A]n act of congress ought never to be construed to violate the law of nations, if any other possible construction remains. . . ."). But the statute in question reflects an unmistakable congressional intent, consistent with treaty obligations of the United States, to authorize prosecution of those who take Americans hostage abroad no matter where the offense occurs or where the offender is found. Our inquiry can go no further.

2. ANTIHIJACKING ACT

The Antihijacking Act provides for criminal punishment of persons who hijack aircraft operating wholly outside the "special aircraft jurisdiction" of the United States, provided that the hijacker is later "found in the United States." 49 U.S.C. App. §1472(n). Flight 402, a Jordanian aircraft operating outside of the United States, was not within this nation's special aircraft jurisdiction. Yunis urges this court to interpret the statutory requirement that persons prosecuted for air piracy must be "found" in the United States as precluding prosecution of alleged hijackers who are brought here to stand trial. But the issue before us is more fact-specific, since Yunis was indicted for air piracy while awaiting trial on hostage-taking and other charges; we must determine whether, once arrested and brought to this country on those other charges, Yunis was subject to prosecution under the Antihijacking Act as well.

The Antihijacking Act of 1974 was enacted to fulfill this nation's responsibilities under the Convention for the Suppression of Unlawful Seizure of Aircraft (the "Hague Convention"), which requires signatory nations to extradite or punish hijackers "present in" their territory. Convention for the Suppression of Unlawful Seizure of Aircraft, Dec. 16, 1970, art. 4, para. 2, Dec. 16, 1970, 22 U.S.T. 1643, 1645, T.I.A.S. No. 7192. This suggests that Congress intended the statutory term "found in the United States" to parallel the Hague Convention's "present in [a contracting state's] territory," a phrase which does not indicate the voluntariness limitation urged by Yunis. Moreover, Congress interpreted the Hague Convention as requiring the United States to extradite or prosecute "offenders in its custody," evidencing no concern as to how alleged hijackers came within U.S. territory. S. Rep. No. 13, 93d Cong., 1st Sess. at 3. From this legislative history we conclude that Yunis was properly indicted under section 1472(n) once in the United States and under arrest on other charges.

The district court correctly found that international law does not restrict this statutory jurisdiction to try Yunis on charges of air piracy. Aircraft hijacking may well be one of the few crimes so clearly condemned under the law of nations that states may assert universal jurisdiction to bring offenders to justice, even when the state has no territorial connection to the hijacking and its citizens are not involved. But in any event we are satisfied that the Antihijacking Act authorizes assertion of federal jurisdiction to try Yunis regardless of hijacking's status vel non as a universal crime. Thus, we affirm the district court on this issue.

Notes and Questions

1. It is generally agreed that customary international law imposes limits on a nation's prescriptive jurisdiction. Under this view, a nation's exercise of prescriptive jurisdiction, in order to be lawful, must fall within one of five categories: territoriality; nationality; the protective principle; passive personality; or universality. Under the territoriality category, nations may regulate conduct that takes place within their territory or has substantial effects within their territory. Under the nationality category, nations may regulate the conduct of their citizens both inside and outside their territory. Under the protective principle, nations may regulate certain conduct outside their territory that threatens their national security or government operations. Under the passive personality category, nations may

regulate certain conduct that harms their nationals abroad. Finally, under the
universality category, nations may regulate certain egregious conduct committed
anywhere in the world. *See* Restatement (Third) of the Foreign Relations Law of the
United States §§402, 404 (1987); United States v. Pizzarusso, 388 F.2d 8 (2d Cir.
1968). Another "category" in which the exercise of prescriptive jurisdiction is
permissible is when one nation specifically agrees with another nation (for example, in a treaty) to allow the other nation to regulate within the first nation's territory. If nothing else, this category follows from the proposition that nations can
override customary international law between themselves by agreement.

2. Prescriptive jurisdiction over conduct or persons within a country's territorial boundaries has long been uncontroversial. This concept of territorial jurisdiction also includes conduct that occurs outside a country but has effects within that
country. An early endorsement of this proposition came in the decision of the
Permanent Court of International Justice in The Case of the S.S. Lotus, 1927
PCIJ, Ser. A, No. 10. In that case, a French steamship and a Turkish steamship
collided on the high seas, causing eight Turkish nationals to die. The court held
that Turkey could apply its criminal laws to a French officer on the French ship, on
the theory that his negligence had caused the collision. For conduct that occurs
outside a nation's territory, what effects are sufficient to allow the nation to regulate
the conduct? How, if at all, is the defendant's intent relevant to this analysis?
Should this territorial category of jurisdiction also apply to situations in which a
defendant engages in lawful conduct within the territory that has harmful effects
outside the territory? What does the *Noriega* decision suggest with respect to these
questions?

3. Under customary international law, nations have broad authority to regulate the conduct of their own nationals around the world. *See, e.g.*, Blackmer v.
United States, 284 U.S. 421 (1932) (upholding application of federal subpoena
statute to U.S. citizen living in France). What is the rationale for this nationality
category of jurisdiction? What limits, if any, should there be for this category of
prescriptive jurisdiction?

Consider 18 U.S.C. §2423(c), which provides that "[a]ny United States citizen
or alien admitted for permanent residence who travels in foreign commerce, and
engages in any illicit sexual conduct with another person shall be fined under this
title or imprisoned not more than 30 years, or both." The phrase "illicit sexual
contact" is defined to include commercial and other sexual acts with persons under
18 years of age. This statute was enacted as part of the Prosecutorial Remedies and
Other Tools to End the Exploitation of Children Today Act (the PROTECT Act).
See Pub. L. No. 108-21, 117 Stat. 650 (2003). Is it consistent with international law?
See United States v. Clark, 315 F. Supp. 2d 1127 (W.D. Wash. 2004) (concluding
that the statute is supported by both the nationality principle and the universality
principle).

4. Somewhat less settled is the passive personality category, which would allow
nations to assert jurisdiction, especially criminal jurisdiction, over aliens who injure
their nationals abroad. Historically, the United States disputed the validity of this
category of jurisdiction. For example, in the *Cutting Case* in 1887, the Secretary of
State protested when Mexico arrested a U.S. citizen for libeling a Mexican citizen in
the United States. *See* 2 John Bassett Moore, International Law Digest 232-40
(1906). In recent years, however, the United States and other countries have
increasingly relied upon this category of jurisdiction as a basis for regulating terrorist attacks on their citizens. In addition to the *Yunis* decision excerpted above,

see, for example, United States v. Yousef, 327 F.3d 56 (2003). What conduct should be covered by this category of prescriptive jurisdiction?

Consider United States v. Neil, 312 F.3d 419 (9th Cir. 2002). In that case, the court affirmed the conviction of a foreign citizen who, while working as an employee aboard a foreign cruise ship, engaged in sexual contact with a 12-year-old passenger, who was an American citizen, while the ship was in Mexican territorial waters. The cruise ship departed from and returned to one of California's harbors. Upon her return, the young female victim missed several days of school and underwent psychological counseling. The defendant had argued that the United States did not have extraterritorial jurisdiction over the crime. The applicable U.S. statute (18 U.S.C. §2344(a)) makes it a criminal offense to "knowingly engage in a sexual act with another person who has attained the age of 12 years but has not attained the age of 16 years." This statute applies in the "special maritime and territorial jurisdiction of the United States," which is defined elsewhere as including, "[t]o the extent permitted by international law, any foreign vessel during a voyage having a scheduled departure from or arrival in the United States with respect to an offense committed by or against a national of the United States." 18 U.S.C. §7(8). The court of appeals found that international law supported extraterritorial jurisdiction in this case under the territorial principle and the passive personality principle. Do you agree?

5. The Restatement (Third) of Foreign Relations Law contends that, in addition to falling within one of the above categories, the exercise of prescriptive jurisdiction must also be reasonable (except, apparently, for exercises of universal jurisdiction). *See* Restatement (Third), §403(1). The Restatement (Third) also sets forth a variety of factors to be considered in assessing reasonableness. These factors include the connection between the regulating state's territory and the regulated activity, the connection between the regulating state and the person being regulated, the importance of the regulation to the regulating state, the importance of the regulation to the international political, legal, or economic system, the extent to which the regulation is consistent with the traditions of the international legal system, the extent to which another state may have an interest in regulating, and the likelihood of conflict with the regulations of another nation. *See id.* §403(2). Commentators have debated whether this reasonableness requirement is in fact reflected in customary international law. *Compare* Philip R. Trimble, *The Supreme Court and International Law: The Demise of Restatement Section 403*, 89 Am. J. Int'l L. 53 (1995) (arguing that international law does not contain reasonableness limitation), *with* Andreas F. Lowenfeld, International Litigation and the Quest for Reasonableness (1996) (defending reasonableness limitation on jurisdiction to prescribe). *See also* David B. Massey, Note, *How the American Law Institute Influences Customary Law: The Reasonableness Requirement of the Restatement of Foreign Relations Law*, 22 Yale J. Int'l L. 419 (1997). How would one determine if the reasonableness requirement is really reflected in customary international law? Do U.S. courts have the necessary information and expertise to apply the reasonableness factors? Assuming they are part of customary international law, what effect do these factors have on the predictability of prescriptive jurisdiction law?

6. All but one of the five categories of prescriptive jurisdiction require a territorial or nationality connection between the regulating nation and the conduct, offender, or victim. The exception is the category of universal jurisdiction. What conduct is subject to universal jurisdiction? If a treaty confers universal jurisdiction over particular conduct, does it allow a nation to exercise such jurisdiction over citizens of countries that have not ratified the treaty?

In United States v. Yousef, 327 F.3d 56 (2d Cir. 2003), the Court disagreed with the suggestion in *Yunis* (and in the Restatement (Third)) that certain acts of terrorism may fall within the category of universal jurisdiction. The court reasoned as follows:

> The class of crimes subject to universal jurisdiction traditionally included only piracy.... In modern times, the class of crimes over which States can exercise universal jurisdiction has been extended to include war crimes and acts identified after the Second World War as "crimes against humanity." ...
>
> The concept of universal jurisdiction has its origins in prosecutions of piracy, which States and legal scholars have acknowledged for at least 500 years as a crime against all nations both because of the threat that piracy poses to orderly transport and commerce between nations and because the crime occurs statelessly on the high seas. ...
>
> Universal jurisdiction over violations of the laws of war was not suggested until the Second World War.... Following the Second World War, the United States and other nations recognized "war crimes" and "crimes against humanity," including "genocide," as crimes for which international law permits the exercise of universal jurisdiction. ...
>
> A commentator of the time explained that war crimes are "similar to piratical acts" because "in both situations there is... a lack of any adequate judicial system operating on the spot where the crime takes place — in the case of piracy it is because the acts are on the high seas and in the case of war crimes because of a chaotic condition or irresponsible leadership in time of war." Willard B. Cowles, Universality of Jurisdiction Over War Crimes, 33 Cal. L. Rev. 177, 194 (1945).
>
> The historical restriction of universal jurisdiction to piracy, war crimes, and crimes against humanity demonstrates that universal jurisdiction arises under customary international law only where crimes (1) are universally condemned by the community of nations, and (2) by their nature occur either outside of a State or where there is no State capable of punishing, or competent to punish, the crime (as in a time of war).
>
> Unlike those offenses supporting universal jurisdiction under customary international law — that is, piracy, war crimes, and crimes against humanity — that now have fairly precise definitions and that have achieved universal condemnation, "terrorism" is a term as loosely deployed as it is powerfully charged. ... [T]he mere existence of the phrase "state-sponsored terrorism" proves the absence of agreement on basic terms among a large number of States that terrorism violates public international law. Moreover, there continues to be strenuous disagreement among States about what actions do or do not constitute terrorism, nor have we shaken ourselves free of the cliche that "one man's terrorist is another man's freedom fighter."

Is this persuasive? Note that the court there proceeded to hold that the prosecution in question (for a conspiracy to bomb U.S. airliners abroad) was supported by a treaty, the Montreal Convention for the Suppression of Unlawful Acts Against the Safety of Civil Aviation, and also by the protective principle. The court also noted that, even if the prosecution did not comport with international law restrictions on prescriptive jurisdiction, Congress had the power to override those restrictions for purposes of U.S. law.

For a general discussion of universal jurisdiction, see Kenneth C. Randall, *Universal Jurisdiction Under International Law*, 66 Tex. L. Rev. 785 (1988). *See also* Symposium, *Universal Jurisdiction: Myths, Realities, and Prospects*, 35 New Eng. L. Rev. 227-469 (2001). For discussion of the costs and benefits of universal jurisdiction, compare Henry A. Kissinger, *The Pitfalls of Universal Jurisdiction*, 80 Foreign

Aff. 86 (July/Aug. 2001), with Kenneth Roth, *The Case for Universal Jurisdiction*, 80 Foreign Aff. 150 (Sept./Oct. 2001).

7. Most U.S. criminal statutes expressly or implicitly require a connection to the United States or a U.S. national and thus do not assert universal jurisdiction. Even the federal genocide statute, enacted in 1988, requires that the offense occur in the United States or that the offender be a U.S. national. *See* 18 U.S.C. §1091(d). A federal torture statute, enacted in 1994, does assert universal jurisdiction, in that it criminalizes acts of official torture committed in foreign nations by foreign citizens. *See* 18 U.S.C. §2340A. But there are no reported cases applying that statute. Why are there not more examples of universal jurisdiction in U.S. criminal law? By contrast, as we discussed in Chapter 7, a number of U.S. courts have asserted a form of universal jurisdiction in *civil* cases, in the context of international human rights litigation. What explains this difference between U.S. criminal and civil litigation? For a discussion of these and other issues, see Curtis A. Bradley, *Universal Jurisdiction and U.S. Law*, 2001 Chi. Leg. Forum 323.

8. Some European countries have laws allowing for universal criminal jurisdiction. In the late 1990s, British courts famously had to decide whether to allow the extradition of Augusto Pinochet, former President of Chile, to Spain. In that case, Spain was seeking to try Pinochet, under a universal jurisdiction statute, for human rights abuses committed in Chile. The British House of Lords upheld Spain's extradition request with respect to some of the charges, but the British government decided not to extradite Pinochet due to his ill health, and he was allowed to return to Chile. The House of Lords' decision is discussed in more detail in Chapter 7, in connection with head-of-state immunity. *See also* Curtis A. Bradley, *The "Pinochet Method" and Political Accountability*, 3 Green Bag 2d 5 (1999).

In 1993, Belgium enacted a law allowing for jurisdiction over certain egregious violations of international law committed anywhere in the world. In June 2001, four Rwandan Hutus were convicted, in a Belgian court, of committing genocide in Rwanda, in violation of the statute. A group of Palestinians subsequently initiated an investigation in Belgium seeking to have Israeli Prime Minister Ariel Sharon tried for his alleged involvement in the massacre of Palestinian refugees in Lebanon in 1982. In February 2002, the International Court of Justice held that Belgium could not apply its universal jurisdiction statute to Congo's Minister for Foreign Affairs because he was immune from arrest and prosecution under customary international law. The Court did not decide, however, whether the Belgian statute was otherwise consistent with international law. (This decision, like the *Pinochet* decision, is discussed in Chapter 7.)

In February 2003, Belgium's highest court ruled that Sharon could be tried under the universal jurisdiction statute once he left office, a decision that triggered substantial protest from the Israeli government. Subsequently, a criminal complaint was filed under the law against former President George H.W. Bush and others in connection with the bombing of a civilian shelter in Baghdad that killed hundreds of people in the 1991 Persian Gulf War. Later, a criminal complaint was brought against U.S. General Tommy Franks for alleged war crimes committed in the 2003 war in Iraq. (Criminal complaints in Belgium, as in many European countries, can be filed by private citizens and groups.) In response to these developments, the United States threatened to withhold financing for a new NATO headquarters in Belgium if the country did not change the law. Belgium subsequently amended the statute to require that the accused or victim be a national or resident of Belgium. For a discussion of the history of the Belgian statute and the controversy that it generated, see Steven R. Ratner, *Belgium's War Crimes Statute: A Postmortem*, 97 Am. J. Int'l L. 888 (2003).

9. What effect, if any, should the customary international law of prescriptive jurisdiction have on the application of U.S. law? What should a court do if faced with a clear conflict between this customary international law and an extraterritorial federal statute? What should a court do if a statute overcomes the presumption against extraterritoriality but nonetheless conflicts with customary international law? Does the evidence needed to overcome the presumption against extraterritoriality automatically overcome the *Charming Betsy* canon? If not, what counts as evidence needed to overcome the *Charming Betsy* canon when the international law at issue is customary international law?

C. EXTRADITION

It is not uncommon for someone to commit a crime in one country and then flee to another. The normal process for obtaining custody of a criminal suspect located in another country is extradition. Extradition is "the surrender by one nation to another of an individual accused or convicted of an offense outside of its own territory, and within the territorial jurisdiction of the other, which, being competent to try and to punish him, demands his surrender." Terlinden v. Ames, 184 U.S. 270, 289 (1902).

Extradition from the United States to other countries is governed by the federal extradition statute, 18 U.S.C. §§3181-3196. The extradition process is ordinarily initiated by a request from a foreign nation to the Department of State. If the Department of State determines that the request is within the relevant extradition treaty, it will forward the request to the Department of Justice. If the Department of Justice similarly concludes that the extradition request is proper, it forwards the request to the U.S. Attorney for the judicial district where the person sought is located. The U.S. Attorney then files a complaint with an appropriate judicial officer, seeking an arrest warrant. The judicial officer will then hold a hearing to determine whether (a) the crime charged is an extraditable crime under the treaty, and (b) there is probable cause to believe that the person committed the crime. If these requirements are met, the judicial officer will certify to the Secretary of State that the person is extraditable. Upon receiving such certification, the Secretary of State has the discretion to extradite but is not obligated to do so. The certification is not subject to direct appeal, but it is subject to collateral challenge through a habeas corpus action. If the judicial officer determines that the individual is *not* extraditable, the government may not appeal. It may, however, bring another extradition proceeding against the individual before a different judicial officer.

The United States not only extradites suspects to other countries, it also seeks extradition of suspects located abroad. Under international law, nations are not obligated to extradite a suspect to another country in the absence of an extradition treaty with that country, although some nations will do so as a matter of comity. *See* Factor v. Laubenheimer, 290 U.S. 276, 287 (1933). The United States currently has bilateral extradition treaties with over 100 nations.

Here is an excerpt of a fairly standard U.S. extradition treaty:

Treaty on Extradition Between the United States of America and Canada, 27 U.S.T. 983

Entered into force March 22, 1976
Amended by Protocol that entered into force November 26, 1991

ARTICLE 1

Each Contracting Party agrees to extradite to the other, in the circumstances and subject to the conditions described in this Treaty, persons found in its territory who have been charged with, or convicted of, any of the offenses covered by Article 2 of this Treaty committed within the territory of the other. . . .

ARTICLE 2

(1) Extradition shall be granted for conduct which constitutes an offense punishable by the laws of both Contracting Parties by imprisonment or other form of detention for a term exceeding one year or any greater punishment. . . .

ARTICLE 4

(1) Extradition shall not be granted in any of the following circumstances:

(i) When the person whose surrender is sought is being proceeded against, or has been tried and discharged or punished in the territory of the requested State for the offense for which his extradition is requested.

(ii) When the prosecution for the offense has become barred by lapse of time according to the laws of the requesting State.

(iii) When the offense in respect of which extradition is requested is of a political character, or the person whose extradition is requested proves that the extradition request has been made for the purpose of trying or punishing him for an offense of the above-mentioned character. If any question arises as to whether a case comes within the provisions of this subparagraph, the authorities of the Government on which the requisition is made shall decide.

(2) For the purpose of this Treaty, the following offenses shall be deemed not to be offenses within subparagraph (iii) of paragraph 1 of this Article: . . .

(ii) Murder, manslaughter or other culpable homicide, malicious wounding or inflicting grievous bodily harm;

(iii) An offense involving kidnapping, abduction, or any form of unlawful detention, including taking a hostage;

(iv) An offense involving the placing or use of explosives, incendiaries or destructive devices or substances capable of endangering life or of causing grievous bodily harm or substantial property damage. . . .

ARTICLE 6

When the offense for which extradition is requested is punishable by death under the laws of the requesting State and the laws of the requested State do not permit such punishment for that offense, extradition may be refused unless the requesting State provides such assurances as the requested State considers sufficient that the death penalty shall not be imposed, or, if imposed, shall not be executed. . . .

ARTICLE 9

(1) The request for extradition shall be made through the diplomatic channel.

(2) The request shall be accompanied by a description of the person sought, a statement of the facts of the case, the text of the laws of the requesting State describing the offense and prescribing the punishment for the offense, and a statement of the law relating to the limitation of the legal proceedings.

(3) When the request relates to a person who has not yet been convicted, it must also be accompanied by a warrant of arrest issued by a judge or other judicial officer of the requesting State and by such evidence as, according to the laws of the requested State, would justify his arrest and committal for trial if the offense had been committed there, including evidence proving the person requested is the person to whom the warrant of arrest refers.

(4) When the request relates to a person already convicted, it must be accompanied by the judgment of conviction and sentence passed against him in the territory of the requesting State, by a statement showing how much of the sentence has not been served, and by evidence proving that the person requested is the person to whom the sentence refers.

ARTICLE 10

(1) Extradition shall be granted only if the evidence be found sufficient, according to the laws of the place where the person sought shall be found, either to justify his committal for trial if the offense of which he is accused had been committed in its territory or to prove that he is the identical person convicted by the courts of the requesting State.

(2) The documentary evidence in support of a request for extradition or copies of these documents shall be admitted in evidence in the examination of the request for extradition when, in the case of a request emanating from Canada, they are authenticated by an officer of the Department of Justice of Canada and are certified by the principal diplomatic or consular officer of the United States in Canada, or when, in the case of a request emanating from the United States, they are authenticated by an officer of the Department of State of the United States and are certified by the principal diplomatic or consular officer of Canada in the United States. . . .

ARTICLE 12

(1) A person extradited under the present Treaty shall not be detained, tried or punished in the territory of the requesting State for an offense other than that for which extradition has been granted nor be extradited by that State to a third State unless:

> (i) He has left the territory of the requesting State after his extradition and has voluntarily returned to it;
> (ii) He has not left the territory of the requesting State within thirty days after being free to do so; or
> (iii) The requested State has consented to his detention, trial, punishment for an offense other than that for which extradition was granted or to his extradition to a third State, provided such other offense is covered by Article 2.

(2) The foregoing shall not apply to offenses committed after the extradition.

The above treaty contains a number of standard features, including:

Dual Criminality Requirement. As illustrated by Article 2(1) of the treaty, extradition treaties typically require "dual criminality" — that is, the conduct in question must be a crime in both the requesting state and the sending state. These treaties also typically require that the crime be a serious offense in both jurisdictions — for example, a crime punishable by at least one year in prison. Why do you think extradition treaties contain these requirements?

It is well settled that the two nations' laws need not be exactly the same in order to satisfy the dual criminality requirement. Rather, "[i]t is enough if the particular act charged is criminal in both jurisdictions." Collins v. Loisel, 259 U.S. 309, 312 (1922); *see also* Brauch v. Raiche, 618 F.2d 843 (1st Cir. 1980). What law should U.S. courts look to in determining whether the conduct in question would be a crime in the United States? Federal law? State law? If state law, which state's law? *See, e.g.*, DeSilva v. DiLeonardi, 125 F.3d 1110, 1113 (7th Cir. 1997) ("Acts are considered criminal 'in this country' if they would be unlawful under federal statutes, the law of the state where the accused is found, or the law of the preponderance of the states."); Yau-Leung v. Soscia, 649 F.2d 914, 918 (2d Cir. 1981) ("The phrase 'under the law of the United States of America' in an extradition treaty referring to American criminal law must be taken as including both state and federal law absent evidence that it was intended to the contrary."). What if the requesting state is seeking to try someone for conduct occurring outside the requesting state's borders, but the requested state would not apply its own laws extraterritorially to such conduct? *Compare* Demjanjuk v. Petrovsky, 776 F.2d 571 (6th Cir. 1985) (concluding that it was sufficient that the United States would prosecute the conduct if it had occurred within the United States), *with* Regina v. Bow Street Metropolitan Stipendiary Magistrate, Ex parte Pinochet Ugarte, 2 W.L.R. 827 (H.L. 1999) (requiring that the conduct have been an extraterritorial crime in Great Britain when committed).

Political Offense Exception. Another common provision in extradition treaties is a "political offense" exception, such as the one in Article 4(1)(iii) of the above treaty with Canada. What are the justifications for this exception? What factors should a court look at in evaluating the political offense exception? How much deference, if any, should it give to the views of the Executive Branch? For decisions considering these questions, see, for example, Quinn v. Robinson, 783 F.2d 776 (9th Cir. 1986); Eain v. Wilkes, 641 F.2d 504 (7th Cir. 1981); and In re Mackin, 668 F.2d 122 (2d Cir. 1981).

Some extradition treaties refer to a political offense exception without defining the term. Before 1985, this was the case with respect to the U.S. extradition treaty with Great Britain, which provided simply that "extradition shall not be granted if . . . the offense for which extradition is requested is regarded by the requested party as one of a political character." In this situation, courts have distinguished between "pure" and "relative" political offenses. Pure political offenses are acts, such as treason, sedition, and espionage, which are aimed directly at a government and do not violate the private rights of individuals. Courts typically have treated these offenses as non-extraditable. Relative political offenses are common crimes committed in connection with a political act. For those offenses, courts (applying a variety of tests) have examined whether the nexus between the crime and the political act is sufficiently close to warrant treating the crime as non-extraditable.

The political offense exception in the U.S.-British extradition treaty was successfully invoked in a number of cases in the 1970s and 1980s by alleged members of the Irish Republican Army. *See, e.g.,* In re McMullen, No. 3-78-1899 M.G. (N.D. Cal. 1979), *reprinted in* 132 Cong. Rec. 16,585 (1986); In re Mackin, No. 86 Cr. Misl., *app. denied,* 668 F.2d 122 (2d Cir. 1981); In re Doherty, 599 F. Supp. 270 (S.D.N.Y. 1984). These decisions drew protests from the British government, and the United States and Great Britain eventually negotiated a supplemental extradition treaty, which provides:

> For the purposes of the Extradition Treaty, none of the following offenses shall be regarded as an offense of a political character:
>
> > (a) an offense within the scope of the Convention for the Suppression of Unlawful Seizure of Aircraft, opened for signature at The Hague on 16 December 1970;
> >
> > (b) an offense within the scope of the Convention for the Suppression of Unlawful Acts Against the Safety of Civil Aviation, opened for signature at Montreal on 23 September 1971;
> >
> > (c) an offense within the scope of the Convention on the Prevention and Punishment of Crimes against Internationally Protected Persons, including Diplomatic Agents, opened for signature at New York on 14 December 1973;
> >
> > (d) an offense within the scope of the International Convention Against the Taking of Hostages, opened for signature at New York on 18 December 1979;
> >
> > (e) murder;
> >
> > (f) manslaughter;
> >
> > (g) maliciously wounding or inflicting grievous bodily harm;
> >
> > (h) kidnapping, abduction, false imprisonment or unlawful detention, including the taking of a hostage;
> >
> > (i) the following offenses relating to explosives:
> >
> > > (1) the causing of an explosion likely to endanger life or cause serious damage to property; or
> > >
> > > (2) conspiracy to cause such an explosion; or
> > >
> > > (3) the making or possession of an explosive substance by a person who intends either himself or through another person to endanger life or cause serious damage to property;
> >
> > (j) the following offenses relating to firearms or ammunition:
> >
> > > (1) the possession of a firearm or ammunition by a person who intends either himself or through another person to endanger life; or
> > >
> > > (2) the use of a firearm by a person with intent to resist or prevent the arrest or detention of himself or another person;
> >
> > (k) damaging property with intent to endanger life or with reckless disregard as to whether the life of another would thereby be endangered;
> >
> > (l) an attempt to commit any of the foregoing offenses.

Supplementary Treaty Concerning the Extradition Treaty Between the Government of the United States of America and the Government of the United Kingdom of Great Britain and Northern Ireland, June 25, 1985. Does this supplemental treaty improperly interfere with the role of the courts? *See* In re Extradition of

McMullen, 989 F.2d 603 (2d Cir. 1993) (concluding that it does not). Note that Article 4(2) of the above treaty with Canada similarly excludes certain offenses from the political offense exception.

Statute of Limitations. Another common restriction in extradition treaties is a statute of limitations. Many treaties allow the extraditee to invoke both the statute of limitations of the requested state as well as that of the requesting state. Some treaties, however (such as the above treaty with Canada), refer only to the statute of limitations of the requesting state. *See* Murphy v. United States, 199 F.3d 599 (2d Cir. 1999) (discussing treaty with Canada). Note that statutes of limitation are often tolled during the time a person is a fugitive or fighting extradition. *See, e.g.,* 18 U.S.C. §3290 ("No statute of limitations shall extend to any person fleeing from justice."). In determining the appropriate U.S. statute of limitations, should a court look to federal or state law? *See, e.g.,* Garcia-Guillern v. United States, 450 F.2d 1189, 1193 n.1 (5th Cir. 1971) ("A treaty is an agreement between two nations and the statutes of limitations of the various states of the United States should not be used to interfere with obligations under a treaty if the crime has not prescribed according to the federal statute of limitations.").

Specialty Doctrine. U.S. courts have long enforced the "specialty doctrine," which limits the charges that can be filed against suspects extradited to the United States. The Supreme Court first recognized this limitation in United States v. Rauscher, 119 U.S. 407 (1886). There, William Rauscher, the second mate on a ship, killed one of the crew members of the ship while on the high seas. A U.S. grand jury indicted Rauscher, but he fled to Great Britain before the United States could take him into custody. The United States requested extradition in order to try Rauscher for committing murder on the high seas, and Great Britain granted the request. The United States then attempted to try him for "inflicting cruel and unusual punishment." The Supreme Court held that this was improper. The Court explained that, "according to the doctrine of publicists and writers on international law, the country receiving the offender against its laws from another country had no right to proceed against him for any other offence than that for which he had been delivered up." *Id.* at 419. The Court further concluded that the extradition treaty between the United States and Great Britain "did not intend to depart in this respect from the recognized public law which had prevailed in the absence of treaties." *Id.* at 420. Finally, the Court noted that two U.S. extradition statutes implicitly assumed the specialty doctrine. *Id.* at 423-24. Under the specialty doctrine, the Court stated, an individual extradited to the United States "shall be tried only for the offence with which he is charged in the extradition proceedings and for which he was delivered up, and that if not tried for that, or after trial and acquittal, he shall have a reasonable time to leave the country before he is arrested upon the charge of any other crime committed previous to his extradition." *Id.* at 424. Chief Justice Waite dissented, arguing that any immunity that Rauscher might have from prosecution must stem from the extradition treaty, and that there was nothing in the extradition treaty with Great Britain requiring the specialty doctrine.

In the absence of a treaty provision incorporating the specialty doctrine, what is the legal source of this doctrine? Customary international law? Federal (or general) common law? International comity? What status does this doctrine have in U.S. courts? Should it supersede prosecutorial decisions made by the Executive

Branch? Why have a specialty doctrine? What would happen to cooperative extradition among nations if one country started prosecuting extradited criminals for offenses other than the ones for which they were extradited? For a consideration of these and other questions, see Jacques Semmelman, *The Doctrine of Specialty in the Federal Courts: Making Sense of United States v. Rauscher*, 34 Va. J. Int'l L. 71 (1993).

Should a court apply the specialty doctrine when the sending state does not object to the prosecution? Most courts have held that the specialty doctrine does not apply if the sending state specifically consents to the prosecution. *See, e.g.*, United States v. Tse, 135 F.3d 200 (1st Cir. 1998); United States v. Puentes, 50 F.3d 1567 (11th Cir. 1995). Courts are divided over whether the extraditee can raise the specialty doctrine when the sending state is silent. Some courts have concluded that the extraditee cannot raise the doctrine unless the sending state affirmatively objects to the new prosecution. *See, e.g.*, United States v. Kaufman, 874 F.2d 242, 243 (5th Cir. 1989). Other courts have held that, in the face of silence, the court must guess whether the sending state would object to the new prosecution. *See, e.g.*, United States v. Andonian, 29 F.3d 1432 (9th Cir. 1995). Still other courts have held that the extraditee may raise the specialty doctrine unless the sending state expressly waives this limitation. *See, e.g.*, *Puentes, supra*. What is the right approach? Note that many extradition treaties today expressly refer to the specialty doctrine. See, for example, Article 12 in the above treaty with Canada.

When the United States requests extradition of a suspect from another country, the extradition process is governed not only by the relevant treaty, but also by the laws of the other country. Such laws may impose barriers to U.S. extradition requests. For example, some nations will not extradite their own citizens. This became an issue in the case of Samuel Sheinbein, who fled to Israel after committing a grisly murder in Maryland in 1997. Israel controversially refused to extradite Sheinbein to the United States, after determining that he qualified for Israeli citizenship (even though Sheinbein had never lived in Israel and his father had lived there only briefly). *See* Melinda Henneberger, *Israel Refuses to Extradite a Murder Suspect*, N.Y. Times, Oct. 1, 1997, at A12. Instead, Sheinbein was tried in Israel, where he was found guilty and sentenced to 24 years in prison. (Israel has since changed its law to allow extradition of Israeli citizens. If the citizen is also a resident of Israel at the time of the offense, the law requires that the requesting state agree that it will allow the person to serve their term of imprisonment, if any, in Israel.) Note that the United States will extradite its own nationals, as long as the extradition treaty with the requesting nation allows for such extradition. *See* Charlton v. Kelly, 229 U.S. 447, 467 (1913).

In addition, some nations will not extradite to the United States if the suspect is likely to face the death penalty. In most cases, extradition is allowed once the relevant state or federal authorities provide an assurance that they will not seek the death penalty. In one case from Italy, however, extradition was denied notwithstanding such assurances from state authorities (in Florida). *See* John Tagliabue, *Italian Court Blocks Extradition, Citing Death Penalty in Florida*, N.Y. Times, June 28, 1996, at A7. Interestingly, Italy subsequently allowed some of the trial to take place in Florida, albeit under Italian law and with Italian judges. In a case from Mexico, state authorities (in California) refused to provide an assurance that they would not seek the death penalty, so Mexico decided to try the suspect itself. *See* Nicholas Riccardi, *Mexico Will Try Fugitive Wanted in Slayings of 4*, L.A. Times, Oct. 2, 1997, at B1. More recently, concerns about the U.S. death penalty surfaced in connection with U.S. efforts to obtain custody of and try individuals suspected of involvement in the September 11, 2001, terrorist attacks. *See* T.R. Reid, *Europeans Reluctant to Send Terror Suspects to U.S.; Allies Oppose Death Penalty and Bush's Plan for Secret Military Tribunals*, Wash. Post, Nov. 29, 2001, at A23. Some extradition treaties expressly refer to a death penalty limitation. See, for example, Article 6 in the above treaty with Canada.

Even when extradition to the United States is approved, the extradition proceedings in the foreign country may take substantial time. This was the case, for example, with respect to Ira Einhorn, who was charged with killing his girlfriend in 1977 in Philadelphia. The United States requested his extradition from France in 1997, and, although French courts ultimately approved the extradition, Einhorn was able to delay extradition through court challenges and appeals to political officials. *See* Linda Lloyd, *Einhorn Will Appeal Extradition from France on 1977 Murder Charges*, Philadelphia Inquirer, Sept. 20, 2000. Einhorn was finally extradited to the United States in July 2001. *See* Francis X. Clines, *France Sending Fugitive Home to U.S. for New Trial*, N.Y. Times, July 20, 2001.

Extradition from the United States implicates a variety of constitutional issues, some of which are explored in the materials below.

Lo Duca v. United States

93 F.3d 1100 (2d Cir. 1996) (as amended)

[In 1993, Paolo Lo Duca, an Italian citizen living in New York, was convicted in Italy on drug charges. Italy subsequently submitted an application to the United States, pursuant to an extradition treaty between the two countries, asking for Lo Duca's extradition. Lo Duca was arrested and a magistrate judge found that he was subject to extradition. Lo Duca then brought a habeas corpus action arguing that the federal extradition statute is unconstitutional.]

JON O. NEWMAN, CHIEF JUDGE ....

Lo Duca presents two alternative contentions, consideration of which depends upon our resolution of an initial question: do judicial officers acting pursuant to section 3184 exercise the "judicial power" of the United States under Article III of the Constitution? If an extradition officer does exercise Article III power, then Lo Duca contends that the statutory scheme is unconstitutional since it subjects Article III judgments to revision by the Executive Branch. On the other hand, if an extradition officer does not exercise Article III power, then Lo Duca contends that Congress has unconstitutionally authorized federal judges and magistrate judges to engage in extrajudicial activities.

This is not the first time that our Circuit has considered the question of whether extradition officers exercise Article III power. In *Austin*, we recently held that the function performed by an extradition officer is not an exercise of the judicial power of the United States. Austin [v. Healey, 5 F.3d 598, 603 (2d. Cir. 1993)]. This holding accords with the decisions of the First, Eleventh, and District of Columbia Circuits....

This conclusion is bolstered by the fact that, although direct judicial review of an extradition proceeding is not available, there is the possibility for what has been called "executive revision," pursuant to the discretionary authority of the Executive Branch to refuse extradition. The first case involving executive revision arose in a different context in Hayburn's Case, 2 U.S. (2 Dall.) 409 (1792) (1855). Congress had provided that the circuit courts should decide in the first instance whether individual veterans were eligible for disability pensions. These determinations, however, were subject to revision by the Secretary of War. Chief Justice Jay and Justice Cushing, sitting as members of the Circuit Court of the District of New York, held that "the [pension adjusting] duties assigned to the Circuit Courts... are not of [judicial] description...; inasmuch as [the statute] subjects the decisions of these courts... to the consideration and suspension of the Secretary at War...." *Id.* at 410 n.1. Similar statements regarding the non-judicial nature of the power granted by Congress were made by Justices Wilson, Blair, and Iredell in their capacities as circuit judges. *Id.* Thus, the various Justices held that the statute failed to accomplish a grant of judicial power under Article III, and in that regard, the fact that the statute contemplated executive revision was dispositive.

Chief Justice Jay and Justice Cushing additionally explained that the statute could be considered, not as a grant of Article III power, but "as appointing commissioners for the purposes mentioned in it...." *Id.* "[T]he Judges of this Court regard themselves as being the commissioners designated by the act, and therefore as being at liberty to accept or decline that office." *Id.* The Justices concluded that "the Judges of this Court will... adjourn the court from day to day... and... proceed as commissioners to execute the business of this act in the same court room, or chamber." *Id.* Notably, the Justices found no constitutional impediment to their rendering adjudicatory decisions under the statute, as long as those decisions were distinct from their judicial functions regarding cases and controversies under Article III.

In United States v. Ferreira, 54 U.S. (13 How.) 40 (1852) (1870), the Supreme Court considered a similar statute authorizing federal district judges in Florida to adjust certain claims made by the Spanish inhabitants of that state against the United States. *Id.* at 45. Those determinations were subject to approval by the Secretary of the Treasury. *Id.* The Supreme Court held that "such a tribunal is not a judicial one.... The authority conferred on the respective judges was nothing more than that of a commissioner...." *Id.* at 47. As the Supreme Court elaborated:

> The powers conferred by these acts of Congress upon the judge... are, it is true, judicial in their nature. For judgment and discretion must be exercised by both of them. But it is nothing more than the power ordinarily given by law to a commissioner appointed to adjust claims to lands or money under a treaty.... [It] is not judicial..., in the sense in which judicial power is granted by the constitution to the courts of the United States.

Id. at 48. Thus, the Supreme Court found it unexceptional that the judges, as commissioners, acted in an "adjudicatory" capacity.[5]

___

5. The Constitution itself provides numerous situations where some form of adjudication is required outside the context of Article III. For example, the executive decision to grant a Presidential pardon may be based on a review of the law and facts that would normally be reserved to the province of

Instead of focusing on the misleading distinction between adjudicatory and non-adjudicatory functions, *Ferreira* relied on the fact that the decisions of the district judges were subject to executive revision. The Supreme Court found it "too evident for argument" that the statute did not confer Article III power since

> neither the evidence, nor [the judge's] award, are to be filed in the court in which he presides, nor recorded there; but he is required to transmit, both the decision and the evidence upon which he decided, to the Secretary of the Treasury; and the claim is to be paid if the Secretary thinks it just and equitable, but not otherwise.

Id. at 46-47. Thus, the fact of executive revision led the Supreme Court in *Ferreira* to hold that those judges, acting as commissioners, did not exercise Article III power. Similarly, in this case, it is dispositive that, since the decisions of extradition officers are subject to revision by the Secretary of State, those officers do not exercise judicial power within the meaning of Article III.[6]

Lastly, we point out that, as a matter of statutory language, section 3184 closely tracks the holdings of . . . *Hayburn's Case* and *Ferreira* by granting jurisdiction over extradition complaints not to "courts" but to individual enumerated "justices," "judges," and "magistrates," including judges of state courts of general jurisdiction. *See* 18 U.S.C. §3184. . . . This distinction between "courts" and "judges" in the context of extradition proceedings has been long recognized. . . . We note that, traditionally, it is "courts" and not "judges" that exercise Article III power. *See* U.S. Const. art. III, §1 ("The judicial power of the United States shall be vested in one supreme Court, and in such inferior Courts as the Congress may from time to time ordain and establish."). The use of the word "judges" in section 3184 is more consistent with a statute appointing commissioners "by official, instead of personal descriptions." *Hayburn's Case*, 2 U.S. (2 Dall.) at 410 n.1.

Having examined the text of the statute, its structural correlation with Article III, and the relevant historical precedents, we conclude that our holding in *Austin* was correct—extradition officers do not exercise judicial power under Article III of the Constitution. *Austin*, 5 F.3d at 603. We therefore turn to Lo Duca's following arguments, which contend that section 3184 is unconstitutional precisely because it does not confer Article III power.

A. *TIDEWATER* CLAIM

Lo Duca first argues that section 3184 violates the doctrine of separation of powers insofar as it seeks to require Article III courts to conduct non-Article III extradition proceedings. *See* National Mutual Insurance Co. v. Tidewater Transfer Co., 337 U.S. 582 (1949). In *Tidewater*, the Supreme Court confronted the question whether Congress could expand the jurisdiction of federal courts beyond the class of cases and controversies enumerated in Article III. In three separate opinions, six Justices reaffirmed the traditional view that federal courts are courts of limited jurisdiction

---

courts. Similarly, the executive decision to veto legislation may be based on an opinion that such legislation is unconstitutional.

6. Lo Duca notes that, as a practical matter, extradition officers certainly appear to exercise judicial power—they issue arrest warrants, preside in courtrooms, and use other judicial resources. These actions, however, are not incompatible with their designation as commissioners acting in a non-Article III capacity. Their authority to issue arrest warrants derives not from any inherent judicial power, but rather from the text of section 3184 itself. *See* 18 U.S.C. §3184. Lo Duca does not contend that this task is such an "essential attribute of judicial power" that it can be exercised only within the confines of Article III.

whose judicial powers are bounded by Article III. *See id.* at 607 (Rutledge, J., joined by Murphy, J., concurring in the judgment); *id.* at 635 (Vinson, C.J., joined by Douglas, J., dissenting); *id.* at 647 (Frankfurter, J., joined by Reed, J., dissenting). Justice Jackson expressed a contrary view in his plurality opinion announcing the judgment of the Court. *Id.* at 583 (Jackson, J., joined by Black and Burton, JJ.). He wrote that, under Article I, Congress could grant jurisdiction for federal courts to hear non-Article III cases. *See Tidewater*, 337 U.S. at 592-93. Justices Rutledge and Murphy, who "strongly dissented" from that reasoning, nonetheless concurred in the result on other grounds. *See id.* at 604, 626 (Rutledge, J., concurring in the judgment) (calling the opinion of Justice Jackson a "dangerous doctrine").

In cases reaching as far back as Marbury v. Madison, 5 U.S. (1 Cranch) 137 (1803), the Supreme Court has held that Congress may not expand the jurisdiction of federal courts beyond the limits established by Article III. . . . Lo Duca relies on these cases to contend that the Constitution prevents Congress from vesting federal courts with jurisdiction over non-Article III extradition complaints.

Without questioning these cases, the Government responds that federal courts are not the subject of section 3184. Rather, "§3184 vests individual judges with jurisdiction over extradition requests." [In re Mackin, 668 F.2d 122, 130 n.11 (2d Cir. 1981)]. This distinction between "courts" and "judges" is dispositive. . . . Only individual justices, judges, and magistrate judges are authorized to act under the statute. Since they function, as in *Hayburn's Case* and in *Ferreira*, as commissioners, they are not bound by the limits of Article III.

B. *MISTRETTA* CLAIM

Lo Duca next argues that, insofar as section 3184 requires judges to act in an extrajudicial capacity, the statute runs afoul of Mistretta v. United States, 488 U.S. 361 (1989). In *Mistretta*, the Supreme Court was concerned with the possibility that Congress might compromise the independence of Article III judges by requiring them to participate in extrajudicial activities. This concern, however, does not apply with equal force to those who are not Article III judges. Thus, Lo Duca's claim founders at the outset since his extradition proceedings were conducted solely by federal magistrate judges. Then-Magistrate Judge Ross issued the warrant under which Lo Duca was arrested. Magistrate Judge Gold conducted the subsequent extradition hearing and granted the certificate of extraditability. Since federal magistrate judges are not Article III judges, the Constitution does not accord them the same protections against Congressional expansion of their duties. . . . Nothing in *Mistretta* suggests that federal magistrate judges would be precluded from conducting extradition proceedings.

Lo Duca argues nonetheless that, if Article III judges cannot act as extradition officers, then they lack the power to delegate those duties to a magistrate judge under the Federal Magistrates Act, 28 U.S.C. §636(b) (1994). This argument presupposes that magistrate judges serve as extradition officers in their capacity as "adjuncts" to Article III courts under section 636(b). Yet, as this Court has pointed out, magistrate judges acting under section 3184 do not rely on the Federal Magistrates Act for their authority. Rather, section 3184 contains its own independent grant of authority to allow magistrate judges to hear extradition complaints. 18 U.S.C. §3184. Once a magistrate judge is authorized to act under section 3184, that officer does not need subsequent permission from a supervising court on a case-by-case basis. A magistrate judge serving as an extradition officer pursuant to section 3184 acts as a commissioner, in the same capacity as any other enumerated justice or judge under section 3184.

In any event, even if Lo Duca's extradition proceedings had been conducted by a federal judge, there would be no violation of *Mistretta*. On the contrary, *Mistretta* expressly states that federal judges may participate in extrajudicial activities as long as two requirements are met. First, the judge must be acting "in an individual, not judicial, capacity." *Mistretta*, 488 U.S. at 404. Second, "a particular extrajudicial assignment [must not] undermine[] the integrity of the Judicial Branch." *Id*. We have already held that judges acting pursuant to section 3184 do so as commissioners in an individual capacity. We now consider whether the particular task of adjudicating extradition complaints might undermine the integrity of the Judicial Branch.

Mistretta was concerned with two possible subversions of judicial integrity. The first was the possibility that Congress might force federal judges to perform extrajudicial tasks. *See id.* at 405-06; *but see id.* at 406 n.29 (Congress may require Chief Judges of Courts of Appeals to participate in Judicial Conference of United States). In this case, however, we have no reason to believe that any federal judge has been forced to conduct an extradition proceeding. Moreover, since we are instructed to construe federal statutes to avoid constitutional infirmity, we read section 3184 as merely authorizing federal judges to act as extradition officers.... Section 3184 states that an extradition officer "*may* . . . issue his warrant for the apprehension of the person so charged, that he *may* be brought before such justice, judge, or magistrate, to the end that the evidence of criminality *may* be heard and considered." 18 U.S.C. §3184 (emphasis added).

Mistretta was also concerned with the possibility that certain extrajudicial activities might undermine the integrity of the Judicial Branch by weakening public confidence. *See Mistretta*, 488 U.S. at 407-08. We believe that, in this particular context, history sufficiently allays this concern. For nearly 150 years, federal judges have adjudicated extradition complaints under section 3184 with no indication of any adverse consequences. Of course, this is hardly surprising since an extradition proceeding is "an essentially neutral endeavor and one in which judicial participation is peculiarly appropriate." *Id.* at 407. We conclude that the extrajudicial duties authorized by section 3184 do not undermine the integrity of the Judicial Branch, and *Mistretta* does not prohibit federal judges from hearing extradition complaints.

C. APPOINTMENTS CLAUSE CLAIM

Lo Duca's final argument invokes the Appointments Clause of the Constitution. U.S. Const. art. II, §2, cl. 2. He contends that, insofar as judicial officers acting under section 3184 do not serve in their traditional capacity as "justice," "judge," or "magistrate," they must receive a second appointment to carry out their duties as "extradition officer." This argument might carry some weight if the description of extradition officers in section 3184 included persons who held no prior office, but extradition officers have already been appointed to one position — either justice, judge, or magistrate judge. Where Congress provides additional duties that are "germane" to an already existing position, the Appointments Clause does not require a second appointment.... The duties performed by an extradition officer are virtually identical to those performed every day by judges and magistrate judges in the course of preliminary criminal proceedings. This case is a far cry from *Mistretta*, where participation on the Sentencing Commission entailed duties that were substantially different from a judge's normal tasks. Since extradition proceedings are sufficiently germane to the traditional duties of judges and magistrate judges, under the Appointments Clause, these judicial officers do not require a second appointment to hear extradition complaints.[11]

Ntakirutimana v. Reno

184 F.3d 419 (5th Cir. 1999)

[In 1994, the UN Security Council created an international criminal tribunal to try individuals responsible for genocide in Rwanda. In 1995, President Clinton entered into an executive agreement committing the United States to extradite suspects to the tribunal, and Congress enacted legislation in 1996 to implement this agreement. The Rwandan tribunal subsequently indicted Elizaphan Ntakirutimana, a Rwandan citizen living in Texas, on charges of genocide and other crimes. A magistrate judge refused to extradite Ntakirutimana, concluding that suspects could not be extradited from the United States except pursuant to an extradition treaty approved by two-thirds of the Senate. A federal district court judge overturned this decision, holding that extradition was proper. Ntakirutimana then filed a petition for a writ of habeas corpus, which the district court denied.]

EMILIO M. GARZA, CIRCUIT JUDGE....

To determine whether a treaty is required to extradite Ntakirutimana, we turn to the text of the Constitution. Ntakirutimana contends that Article II, Section 2, Clause 2 of the Constitution requires a treaty to extradite. This Clause, which enumerates the President's foreign relations power, provides in part that "[the President] shall have Power, by and with the Advice and Consent of the Senate, to make Treaties, provided two thirds of the Senators present concur; and he shall nominate, and by and with the Advice and Consent of the Senate, shall appoint Ambassadors, other public Ministers and Consuls...." U.S. Const. art. II, §2, cl. 2. This provision does not refer either to extradition or to the necessity of a treaty to extradite. The Supreme Court has explained, however, that "the power to surrender is clearly included within the treaty-making power and the corresponding power of appointing and receiving ambassadors and other public ministers." Terlinden v. Ames, 184 U.S. 270, 289 (1902) (citation omitted).

Yet, the Court has found that the Executive's power to surrender fugitives is not unlimited. In Valentine v. United States, 299 U.S. 5 (1936), the Supreme Court considered whether an exception clause in the United States's extradition treaty with France implicitly granted to the Executive the discretionary power to surrender citizens. The Court first stated that the power to provide for extradition is a national power that "is not confided to the Executive in the absence of treaty or legislative provision." Id. at 8. The Court explained:

---

11. Some might question whether the task of hearing extradition complaints, which is a non-judicial task for purposes of Article III, is nevertheless "germane" to the traditionally judicial task of determining probable cause. We think that this situation falls within a narrow (perhaps unique) set of circumstances where the function is technically non-judicial in nature, but sufficiently similar to judicial functions so as to satisfy the "germaneness" requirement.

[The power to extradite] rests upon the fundamental consideration that the Constitution creates no executive prerogative to dispose of the liberty of the individual. Proceedings against him must be authorized by law. There is no executive discretion to surrender him to a foreign government, unless that discretion is granted by law. It necessarily follows that as the legal authority does not exist save as it is given by act of Congress or by the terms of a treaty, it is not enough that the statute or treaty does not deny the power to surrender. It must be found that statute or treaty confers the power.

Id. at 9.

The Court then considered whether any statute authorized the Executive's discretion to extradite. The Court commented that:

Whatever may be the power of the Congress to provide for extradition independent of treaty, that power has not been exercised save in relation to a foreign country or territory "occupied by or under the control of the United States." Aside from that limited provision, the Act of Congress relating to extradition simply defines the procedure to carry out an existing extradition treaty or convention.

Id. at 9 (citations omitted). The Court concluded that no statutory basis conferred the power on the Executive to surrender a citizen to the foreign government. *See id.* at 10. The Court subsequently addressed whether the treaty conferred the power to surrender, and found that it did not. *See id.* at 18. The Court concluded that, "we are constrained to hold that [the President's] power, in the absence of statute conferring an independent power, must be found in the terms of the treaty and that, as the treaty with France fails to grant the necessary authority, the President is without the power to surrender the respondents." *Id.* The Court added that the remedy for this lack of power "lies with the Congress, or with the treaty-making power wherever the parties are willing to provide for the surrender of citizens." *Id.*

Valentine indicates that a court should look to whether a treaty *or statute* grants executive discretion to extradite. Hence, *Valentine* supports the constitutionality of using the Congressional-Executive Agreement to extradite Ntakirutimana. Ntakirutimana attempts to distinguish *Valentine* on the ground that the case dealt with a *treaty* between France and the United States. Yet, *Valentine* indicates that a statute suffices to confer authority on the President to surrender a fugitive. Ntakirutimana suggests also that *Valentine* expressly challenged the power of Congress, independent of treaty, to provide for extradition. *Valentine*, however, did not place a limit on Congress's power to provide for extradition. *See id.* at 9 ("Whatever may be the power of the Congress to provide for extradition independent of treaty . . ."). Thus, although some authorization by law is necessary for the Executive to extradite, neither the Constitution's text nor *Valentine* require that the authorization come in the form of a treaty.

Notwithstanding the Constitution's text or *Valentine*, Ntakirutimana argues that the intent of the drafters of the Constitution supports his interpretation. He alleges that the delegates to the Constitutional Convention intentionally placed the Treaty power exclusively in the President and the Senate. The delegates designed this arrangement because they wanted a single executive agent to negotiate agreements with foreign powers, and they wanted the senior House of Congress — the Senate — to review the agreements to serve as a check on the executive branch. Ntakirutimana also claims that the rejection of alternative proposals suggests that the framers believed that a treaty is the only means by which the United States can enter into a binding agreement with a foreign nation.

We are unpersuaded by Ntakirutimana's extended discussion of the Constitution's history. Ntakirutimana does not cite to any provision in the Constitution or any aspect of its history that requires a treaty to extradite. Ntakirutimana's argument, which is not specific to extradition, is premised on the assumption that a treaty is required for an international agreement. To the contrary, "the Constitution, while expounding procedural requirements for treaties alone, apparently contemplates alternate modes of international agreements." Laurence H. Tribe, American Constitutional Law §4-5, at 228-29 (2d ed. 1988). "The Supreme Court has recognized that of necessity the President may enter into certain binding agreements with foreign nations not strictly congruent with the formalities required by the Constitution's Treaty Clause." United States v. Walczak, 783 F.2d 852, 855 (9th Cir. 1986) (citations omitted) (executive agreement). More specifically, the Supreme Court has repeatedly stated that a treaty or statute may confer the power to extradite. . . .

Ntakirutimana next argues that historical practice establishes that a treaty is required to extradite. According to Ntakirutimana, the United States has never surrendered a person except pursuant to an Article II treaty, and the only involuntary transfers without an extradition treaty have been to "a foreign country or territory 'occupied by or under the control of the United States.'" Valentine, 299 U.S. at 9. This argument fails for numerous reasons. First, Valentine did not suggest that this "historical practice" limited Congress's power. Second, the Supreme Court's statements that a statute may confer the power to extradite also reflect a historical understanding of the Constitution. Even if Congress has rarely exercised the power to extradite by statute, a historical understanding exists nonetheless that it may do so. Third, in some instances in which a fugitive would not have been extraditable under a treaty, a fugitive has been extradited pursuant to a statute that "filled the gap" in the treaty. Thus, we are unconvinced that the President's practice of usually submitting a negotiated treaty to the Senate reflects a historical understanding that a treaty is required to extradite.

We are unpersuaded by Ntakirutimana's other arguments. First, he asserts that the failure to require a treaty violates the Constitution's separation of powers. He contends that if a treaty is not required, then "the President alone could make dangerous agreements with foreign governments" or "Congress could legislate foreign affairs." This argument is not relevant to an Executive-Congressional agreement, which involves neither the President acting unilaterally nor Congress negotiating with foreign countries. Second, Ntakirutimana argues that "statutes cannot usurp the Treaty making power of Article II." The Supreme Court, however, has held that statutes can usurp a treaty. This is confirmed by the "last in time" rule that, if a statute and treaty are inconsistent, then the last in time will prevail. This rule explicitly contemplates that a statute and a treaty may at times cover the same subject matter. Third, Ntakirutimana contends that not requiring a treaty reads the treaty-making power out of the Constitution. Yet, the treaty-making power remains unaffected, because the President may still elect to submit a negotiated treaty to the Senate, instead of submitting legislation to Congress. . . .

HAROLD R. DEMOSS, CIRCUIT JUDGE, dissenting. . . .

II

The "Congressional-Executive Agreement" method of ratifying the Surrender Agreement with the Tribunal runs afoul of the Constitution's Treaty Clause, and

§1342 alone is constitutionally insufficient to ratify the Surrender Agreement which has been invoked to support the extradition.

A...

The Constitution's treaty procedure must be followed in order to ratify an extradition agreement which contractually binds our nation to respect obligations to another nation. The intent of the framers could not be clearer on this point. Our Founding Fathers were very concerned about the new nation becoming entangled in foreign alliances. The possibility of giving the President full authority for foreign affairs was considered and rejected. In *The Federalist No. 75*, Alexander Hamilton argued that it would be "utterly unsafe and improper" to completely entrust foreign affairs to a President, who is elected for only four years at a time. The Founders were especially concerned with the possibility that, in the conduct of foreign policy, American officials might become seduced by their foreign counterparts or a President might actually betray the country. Thus, while primary responsibility for foreign affairs was given to the President, a significant restraint and "check" on the use of the treaty power was created by requiring for treaties the advice and consent of two-thirds of the Senate. *See* The Federalist No. 69 (Alexander Hamilton) (noting that this "check" is a major distinction between the presidency and England's monarchy, in which the king was "the sole and absolute representative of the nation in all foreign transactions"). The decision to require approval of two-thirds of Senators was controversial and hotly debated, but it was ultimately decided that sheer importance of the treaty power merited such a treatment. Treaties cannot be accomplished by any means other than the Article II treaty ratification procedure.

Of course, not all agreements with foreign countries require the full Article II "treaty" treatment in order to be effective. The Constitution implicitly recognizes a hierarchy of arrangements with foreign countries, of which treaties are the most sacrosanct. Compare U.S. Const. art. I, §10, cl. 1 ("No State shall enter into any Treaty, Alliance, or Confederation..."), with U.S. Const. art. I, §10, cl. 3 ("No State shall, without the Consent of Congress... enter into any Agreement or Compact with another State, or with a foreign Power...."). The Attorney General's primary argument in defense of the enforceability of the extradition agreement with the Tribunal follows this line of thought. She has argued, and the majority echoes, that the Constitution contains no explicit reference to extradition.

But the fact of the matter is that while the Constitution has no provisions explicitly relating to extradition, it likewise has no provisions explicitly relating to executive agreements. It only mentions treaties. Our national government is one of limited, enumerated powers. All agree that the Surrender Agreement is not a treaty. We are therefore left to read between the lines to ascertain whether the President and Congress have wrongfully attempted by ordinary legislative procedures, to exercise a power governed by the Treaty Clause or whether some source of power other than the Treaty Clause enables the President and Congress to bind the country to the Surrender Agreement.

Our inquiry is significantly informed by a demonstration of what specific powers are encompassed by the Treaty Clause. "A treaty is in its nature a contract between two nations, not a legislative act." Foster v. Neilson, 27 U.S. (2 Pet.) 253, 314 (1829).... It is precisely the position of the Attorney General that the Surrender Agreement is a valid contract with a foreign authority and that it has the force of law. In Alexander's day, an agreement with those characteristics was called a treaty.

If the Treaty Clause is to have any meaning there is some variety of agreements which *must* be accomplished through the formal Article II process. Otherwise, the heightened consideration dictated by Article II could be avoided by the President and a majority of Congress simply by substituting the label of "executive agreement" for that of "treaty." The Supreme Court has recognized this principle:

> Express power is given to the President, by and with the advice and consent of the Senate, to make treaties, provided two-thirds of the senators present concur, and inasmuch as the power is given, in general terms, without any description of the objects intended to be embraced within its scope, *it must be assumed that the framers of the Constitution intended that it should extend to all those objects which in the intercourse of nations had usually been regarded as the proper subjects of negotiation and treaty,* if not inconsistent with the nature of our government and the relation between the States and the United States.

Holden v. Joy, 84 U.S. (17 Wall.) 211, 242-43 (1872) (emphasis supplied).

Plainly, an extradition agreement is a type of agreement historically found in a treaty and therefore governed by the Treaty Clause. Extradition, which is defined as "the surrender by one nation to another of an individual accused or convicted of an offense outside of its own territory, and within the territorial jurisdiction of the other, which, being competent to try and to punish him, demands the surrender," Terlinden v. Ames, 184 U.S. 270, 289 (1902), has usually been regarded as the proper subject of negotiation and treaty. Historically, the United States has not surrendered a person to a foreign authority (excluding countries or territories controlled by the United States) in the absence of a valid extradition treaty. Every extradition agreement ever entered into by the United States (before the advent of the new Tribunals) has been accomplished by treaty, including the Jay Treaty (1795) and the Webster Ashburton Treaty (1842). The original extradition statutes, enacted in 1848, required the existence of an extradition treaty, and there was no exception until §1342 was passed to accommodate the Tribunals for Rwanda and the former Yugoslavia. Furthermore, "the principles of international law recognize no *right* to extradition apart from treaty." Factor v. Laubenheimer, 290 U.S. 276, 287 (1933).

The insistence on the use of the treaty power for certain types of international agreements comports with the Founding Fathers' intention that the President not have unfettered discretion to enter agreements with foreign nations. *See* The Federalist No. 75 (Alexander Hamilton). Unless the Article II procedure is insisted upon, the President can exercise such plenary power simply by denominating his agreements as something other than "treaties."

Notably, the United States has publicly declared to the entire world that it can only enter into an extradition agreement through a treaty. In its fifth reservation to the Convention on the Prevention and Punishment of the Crime of Genocide, Dec. 9, 1948, 78 U.N.T.S. 277, the United States proclaimed to the international diplomatic community that it "reserves the right to effect its participation in any such tribunal only by a treaty entered into specifically for that purpose with the advice and consent of the Senate." There is no treaty which has been entered into "with the advice and consent of the Senate" which authorizes the participation in the Tribunal by the United States. This reservation clearly evidences the intent and expectation of the United States that the only way its participation in the Tribunal could take place was by a duly negotiated and ratified treaty on that subject. A reading of the Treaty Clause of the Constitution which permits the semantic shenanigans suggested by the Attorney General is an insult to the intricate structure of the Constitution, which seeks to avoid tyranny and ensure democracy through a deliberate separation of power and a delicate system of checks and balances. . . .

B

The Attorney General and my colleagues in the majority place great reliance on Valentine v. United States ex rel. Neidecker, 299 U.S. 5 (1936), in which the Court stated: "It cannot be doubted that the power to provide for extradition is a national power; it pertains to the national government and not to the states. But, albeit a national power, it is not confided to the Executive in the absence of treaty or legislative provision." 299 U.S. at 8 (internal citation omitted). *Valentine* was a case that did involve a treaty — its stray reference to "legislative provision" is pure dicta, and certainly not a plain holding that extradition may be accomplished by the President simply on the basis of congressional approval. Likewise, in Terlinden v. Ames, 184 U.S. 270 (1902), in which the Court noted that "in the United States, the general opinion and practice have been that extradition should be declined in the absence of a conventional or legislative provision," 184 U.S. at 289, there was also a valid extradition treaty, and the reference to a "legislative provision" is again dicta

The Attorney General insists that the President has the power to unilaterally enter an extradition agreement with foreign nations, the only distinction between that variety of agreement and an Article II treaty being that only a treaty will impose upon the President a duty to extradite. In defense of this principle, the Attorney General points to Factor v. Laubenheimer, 290 U.S. 276 (1933), which states:

> While a government may, if agreeable to its own constitution and laws, voluntarily exercise the power to surrender a fugitive from justice to the country from which he had fled, and it has been said that it is under a moral duty to do so, the legal right to demand his extradition and the correlative duty to surrender him to the demanding country exist only when created by treaty.

290 U.S. at 286 (internal citation omitted); *see also* United States v. Rauscher, 119 U.S. 407 (1886).

But these cases do not support the Attorney General's position. The quoted passage stands for the unremarkable propositions that a sovereign nation can (and perhaps should), if consistent with its own laws, surrender to another sovereign nation one of the surrendering nation's own citizens who is accused of crimes by that other sovereign nation, but that no such duty or legal obligation arises absent a treaty. Those propositions do not mean that the President, acting unilaterally, can enter non-binding executive agreements to extradite, or that Congress may ratify such an agreement. The Attorney General does not purport to act pursuant to some sort of sovereign power to surrender Ntakirutimana; she has consciously premised her argument on the validity and enforceability of the Surrender Agreement. This is plain from the briefs filed in this Court. Given that the Surrender Agreement is the authority invoked by the Attorney General, it is the authority which we must consider.

III

The executive and legislative branches of government erroneously disregarded their obligation to respect the structure provided by the Constitution when they purported to enter this extradition agreement.[14] We should issue a writ of habeas corpus, and Ntakirutimana should not be surrendered. The extradition agreement in place between the United States and the Tribunal is unenforceable, as it has not been properly ratified. The agreement's implementing legislation is unconstitutional insofar as it purports to ratify the Surrender Agreement by a means other than that prescribed by the Treaty Clause. The two acts seek impermissibly to evade the mandatory constitutional route for implementing such an agreement.[15] I therefore respectfully dissent.[16]

Notes and Questions

1. The first reported U.S. extradition case was United States v. Rob[b]ins, 27 F. Cas. 825 (D.S.C. 1799). In that case, Jonathan Robbins was extradited to Great Britain, pursuant to the Jay Treaty, and hanged for participating in a violent mutiny aboard a British vessel. The extradition took place notwithstanding Robbins' claim that he was a U.S. citizen who had been impressed into service by the British. The case was very controversial and generated a number of debates relating to the scope of the treaty power, the foreign affairs powers of the Executive Branch, and the role of an independent judiciary. *See generally* Ruth Wedgwood, *The Revolutionary Martyrdom of Jonathan Robbins*, 100 Yale L.J. 229 (1990). It was in defending President John Adams's authority to extradite Jonathan Robbins pursuant to an extradition treaty that John Marshall (while in the House of Representatives) described the President as the "sole organ of the nation in its external relations." *See* John Marshall, Address Before the House of Representatives (Mar. 7, 1800), in 10 Annals of Cong. 596, 613 (Washington, Gales & Seaton 1851).

2. A version of the current extradition statute has been in place since 1848. In 1995, the U.S. District Court for the District of Columbia nevertheless held that this statutory scheme was unconstitutional. The court reasoned that the scheme violated Article III of the Constitution because it allowed the Executive Branch the power, in effect, to exercise appellate review over federal judicial decisions. *See* LoBue v. Christopher, 893 F. Supp. 65 (D.D.C. 1995). This decision was

---

14. It is not true, as has been suggested in the media, that "[i]f Mr. Ntakirutimana's constitutional argument prevails, it will diminish the ability of the United States to cooperate in international war crimes prosecutions." *War Crimes and Extradition*, Wash. Post, Apr. 10, 1999, at A20, *available in* 1999 WL 2210242. All that is required for participation is conformance with the Constitution. If the President wishes to bind the United States to an agreement such as the Surrender Agreement, he must obtain the advice and consent of two-thirds of the Senate as provided in Article II.

15. Whether executive and legislative actions such as those giving rise to this case reflect, as political commentator George Will has suggested, a disturbing trend of "dilution of American democracy," I leave for others to judge. George Will, *See You in Congress . . .*, Wash. Post, May 20, 1999, at A29, *available in* 1999 WL 17003981 *and* Sacramento Post, *Sacbee Voices — George Will* (visited July 27, 1999) *http://www.sacbee.com/voices/national/will/wil_19990520.htm.*

16. Ntakirutimana challenges the Tribunal itself as an ultra vires creation of the United Nations Security Council. His is not a novel argument — the authority of the ad hoc Tribunals for Rwanda and the former Yugoslavia has been hotly debated in academia . . . , rejected by Rwanda's neighbors who refuse to accept the ICTR's process, and fully litigated in the Tribunal for the former Yugoslavia. To the extent that the viability of the Tribunal is a legitimate subject of foreign policy within the realm of the Executive, separation-of-powers concerns justify our Court in abstaining from the political question of the Tribunal's authority.

subsequently vacated by the D.C. Circuit for lack of jurisdiction. *See* 82 F.3d 1081 (D.C. Cir. 1996). (The D.C. Circuit concluded that the petitioners should have brought their challenge in a habeas corpus action in the federal district in which they were being held, which was the Northern District of Illinois.) Needless to say, the district court's decision generated significant attention and controversy. At least for now, however, the *Lo Duca* decision excerpted above appears to have put the issue to rest. *See also* Lopez-Smith v. Hood, 121 F.3d 1322, 1327 (9th Cir. 1997) (agreeing with *Lo Duca*). Should the fact that the U.S. extradition process has operated without apparent constitutional deficiency for 150 years count in favor of the modern constitutionality of the practice? What is the relevance, if any, of the fact that, before 1848, extradition was committed to the discretion of the Executive Branch?

3. What is the strongest constitutional argument against the extradition statute? That the magistrate performs an extrajudicial function in issuing a certificate of extraditability? That it exercises a judicial function that is non-final in light of the Secretary of State's discretion? That the Secretary of State exercises a judicial function? Are you convinced by the court's conclusion in *Lo Duca* that extradition magistrates act in an individual rather than judicial capacity? Would the analysis in *Lo Duca* have been different if the extradition statute had allowed the Secretary of State to overturn findings of *non*-extraditability? Is there a connection between the constitutional issues in *Lo Duca* and the constitutional issues in *Ntakirutimana*?

4. Should the "congressional-executive agreement" power, which we considered in Chapter 6, extend to extradition? In resolving this question, what weight, if any, should be given to the fact that extradition has generally been conducted pursuant to Article II treaties? Are there special policy reasons in the extradition context for insisting on adherence to the Article II process? In answering this question, what is the relevance, if any, of the fact that extradition treaties are generally considered to be self-executing in U.S. courts? *See* Terlinden v. Ames, 184 U.S. 270, 288 (1902); United States v. Balsys, 119 F.3d 122, 138 n.14 (2d Cir. 1997), *rev'd on other grounds*, 524 U.S. 666 (1998). Assuming that a treaty is not the exclusive basis for extradition, what clause in Article I authorizes the congressional-executive agreement at issue in *Ntakirutimana*? Or is the agreement justified under an inherent congressional foreign affairs power? Could Congress have authorized the extradition by a statute that was not an international agreement? On the issues in this note, see generally Evan J. Wallach, *Extradition to the Rwandan War Crimes Tribunal: Is Another Treaty Required?*, 3 UCLA J. Int'l L. & For. Aff. 59 (1998).

5. In considering whether to extradite a suspect, U.S. courts apply a rule of "non-inquiry," a doctrine that counsels against judicial inquiry into the procedures or treatment that the suspect will face in the requesting state. As one court explained, "[c]ourts have chosen to defer these questions to the executive branch because of its exclusive power to conduct foreign affairs." United States v. Manzi, 888 F.2d 204, 206 (1st Cir. 1989); *see also* United States v. Smyth, 61 F.3d 711, 714 (9th Cir. 1995) ("Undergirding this principle is the notion that courts are ill-equipped as institutions and ill-advised as a matter of separation of powers and foreign relations policy to make inquiries into and pronouncements about the workings of foreign countries' justice systems."). Is it proper for courts to defer in this way?

Some courts have suggested in dicta that there may be a "humanitarian" exception to the rule of non-inquiry, pursuant to which courts could bar extradition if the suspect would likely face procedures or punishment "so antipathetic to a federal court's sense of decency" to compel relaxation of the rule. *See* Gallina v. Fraser, 278 F.2d 77, 79 (2d Cir. 1960); *see also, e.g.*, Emami v. U.S. District Court, 834 F.2d 1444, 1453 (9th Cir. 1987). By contrast, some courts have stated that humanitarian considerations relating to the likely treatment of the suspect are proper considerations only for the Secretary of State, not the courts. *See, e.g.*, Martin v. Warden, 993 F.2d 824, 830 (11th Cir. 1993); *see also* Ahmad v. Wigen, 910 F.2d 1063, 1067 (2d Cir. 1990) (stating that "it is the function of the Secretary of State to determine whether extradition should be denied on humanitarian grounds"). What is the right approach?

Note that Article 3 of the United Nations Convention Against Torture and Other Cruel, Inhuman, or Degrading Treatment or Punishment, which the United States has ratified, prohibits extradition of persons likely to face torture in the requesting nation. In 1998, Congress enacted legislation implementing this provision, as part of the Foreign Affairs Reform and Restructuring Act of 1998 ("FARR Act"). This legislation states that it is "the policy of the United States not to expel, extradite, or otherwise effect the involuntary return of any person to a country in which there are substantial grounds for believing the person would be in danger of being subjected to torture." FARR Act, §2242(a). The legislation also directs "the appropriate agencies" to "prescribe regulations to implement the obligations of the United States under Article 3" of the Torture Convention. *Id.*, §2242(b). The Department of State subsequently adopted regulations setting out a procedure for the Secretary of State to identify individuals who qualify for relief under the Torture Convention. *See* 22 C.F.R. §§95.2-95.3. Both §2242 and the regulations provided, however, that they did not provide courts with jurisdiction to review claims for breach of these provisions. In a subsequently vacated decision, the U.S. Court of Appeals for the Ninth Circuit suggested that the legislation and regulations superseded the common law rule of non-inquiry, and thereby allowed judicial review of the Secretary of State's extradition decision on the ground that the Secretary is not complying with Article 3 of the Torture Convention. The court invoked, among other things, the *Charming Betsy* canon. *See* Cornejo-Barreto v. Seifert, 218 F.3d 1004, 1014 (9th Cir. 2000). In a later decision in that case, the Ninth Circuit disapproved the reasoning in its earlier decision and held that the rule of non-inquiry barred judicial review. *See* Cornejo-Barreto v. Siefert, 379 F.3d 1075 (9th Cir. 2004). That decision was also vacated, however, by a grant of rehearing en banc, and then by a determination of mootness when Mexico dropped its extradition request.

6. Can one of the U.S. states extradite a criminal to a foreign country or tribunal, or is international extradition exclusively a federal function? If it is exclusively a federal function, is this so by virtue of the Constitution, the extradition statute, or particular extradition treaties?

Strange as it may now seem, during the first half of the nineteenth century, "extradition was practiced by some of the states, which made and granted demands for the surrender of fugitive criminals in international cases." 1 John Basset Moore, A Treatise on Extradition and Interstate Rendition 54 (1891); *see generally id*. at 53-71 (collecting state extradition statutes and extradition cases). In Holmes v. Jennison, 39 U.S. 540 (1840), the Supreme Court split 4-4 concerning the constitutionality of this practice. Chief Justice Taney authored an opinion for four Justices reasoning that Vermont's attempted extradition to Canada was a foreign compact prohibited by Article I, Section 10 of the Constitution. *Id*. at 570-74. Taney also argued that the extradition power was exclusively federal, although he did not make clear whether this was because of dormant preemption or because the absence of federal extradition treaties constituted the affirmative "policy of the general government." *Id*. at 574; *see generally id*. at 570-75. In contrast, the four other participating Justices all rejected the dormant preemption argument. *See id*. at 579-86 (Thompson, J.); *id*. at 586-94 (Barbour, J.) (rejecting dormant preemption and foreign compacts clause arguments); *id*. at 594-98 (Catron, J.) (rejecting dormant preemption argument but stating that additional facts might reveal an agreement between Vermont and Canada that would violate the foreign compacts clause); *id*. at 614 (Baldwin, J.) (joining "fully and cordially" in opinions of Thompson, Barbour, and Catron).

By the turn of the century it appears that the extradition power was viewed as exclusive even in the absence of federal enactments, although it was never established whether this was so because of the foreign compacts clause or because of dormant preemption. Thus, for example, in United States v. Rauscher, 119 U.S. 407 (1886), the Court in dicta approved of Taney's opinion in *Holmes* that the extradition power was exclusively federal without making clear whether this was because of Article I, §10 or dormant preemption. Moore's famous 1891 treatise viewed it as "settled doctrine" that the extradition power was exclusive, but emphasized that the issue "has by no means been free from controversy, and has never been actually decided by the Supreme Court of the United States." Moore, *supra*, at 53. The issue became less important as the federal government began to regulate the issue by statute and treaty. *See Rauscher*, 119 U.S. at 414-15 (noting that the exclusivity of the extradition power "in the absence of treaties or acts of Congress on the subject, is now of very little importance, since, with nearly all the nations of the world with whom our relations are such that fugitives from justice may be found within their dominions or within ours, we have treaties which govern the rights and conduct of the parties in such cases" and [t]hese treaties are also supplemented by acts of Congress, and both are in their nature exclusive"); *cf*. Valentine v. United States, 299 U.S. 5, 8 (1936) (stating, in case interpreting federal extradition treaty, that "[i]t cannot be doubted that the power to provide for extradition is a national power; it pertains to the national government and not to the States").

What would happen today if a foreign nation with which the United States did not have an extradition treaty requested extradition of a criminal from a state governor? Would the Constitution prevent the governor from responding? What about the federal extradition statute? In considering these questions, recall the cases and doctrines discussed in Chapter 5.

7. For general discussions of U.S. extradition law, see Restatement (Third) of the Foreign Relations Law of the United States §§475-478 (1987); and M. Cherif Bassiouni, International Extradition: United States Law and Practice (3d ed. 1996).

D. EXTRATERRITORIAL ABDUCTION

United States v. Alvarez-Machain
504 U.S. 655 (1992)

[Humberto Alvarez-Machain, a Mexican citizen and a medical doctor, was indicted in a U.S. federal court for participating in the kidnap and murder of a U.S. Drug Enforcement Agency (DEA) agent in Mexico. DEA officials attempted to gain custody of Alvarez-Machain through informal negotiations with Mexico, but were unsuccessful. DEA officials then offered to pay a reward for the delivery of Alvarez-Machain to the United States. On April 2, 1990, Alvarez-Machain was kidnapped in Guadalajara, Mexico, and flown by private plane to El Paso, Texas, where DEA officials arrested him. The Mexican government officially protested the U.S. government's involvement in the abduction. Alvarez-Machain subsequently moved to dismiss the indictment against him on the ground that his abduction violated the extradition treaty between the United States and Mexico. The district court granted his motion and ordered that he be repatriated to Mexico, and the appeals court affirmed.]

CHIEF JUSTICE REHNQUIST delivered the opinion of the Court. . . .

Although we have never before addressed the precise issue raised in the present case, we have previously considered proceedings in claimed violation of an extradition treaty and proceedings against a defendant brought before a court by means of a forcible abduction. We addressed the former issue in United States v. Rauscher, 119 U.S. 407 (1886); more precisely, the issue whether the Webster-Ashburton Treaty of 1842, 8 Stat. 576, which governed extraditions between England and the United States, prohibited the prosecution of defendant Rauscher for a crime other than the crime for which he had been extradited. Whether this prohibition, known as the doctrine of specialty, was an intended part of the treaty had been disputed between the two nations for some time. Justice Miller delivered the opinion of the Court, which carefully examined the terms and history of the treaty; the practice of nations in regards to extradition treaties; the case law from the States; and the writings of commentators, and reached the following conclusion:

> [A] person who has been brought within the jurisdiction of the court *by virtue of proceedings under an extradition treaty,* can only be tried for one of the offences described in that treaty, and for the offence with which he is charged in the proceedings for his extradition, until a reasonable time and opportunity have been given him, after his release or trial upon such charge, to return to the country from whose asylum he had been forcibly taken under those proceedings.

Id., at 430 (emphasis added).

In addition, Justice Miller's opinion noted that any doubt as to this interpretation was put to rest by two federal statutes which imposed the doctrine of specialty upon extradition treaties to which the United States was a party. *Id.,* at 423. Unlike the case before us today, the defendant in *Rauscher* had been brought to the United States by way of an extradition treaty; there was no issue of a forcible abduction.

In Ker v. Illinois, 119 U.S. 436 (1886), also written by Justice Miller and decided the same day as *Rauscher*, we addressed the issue of a defendant brought before the court by way of a forcible abduction. Frederick Ker had been tried and convicted in an Illinois court for larceny; his presence before the court was procured by means of forcible abduction from Peru. A messenger was sent to Lima with the proper warrant to demand Ker by virtue of the extradition treaty between Peru and the United States. The messenger, however, disdained reliance on the treaty processes, and instead forcibly kidnapped Ker and brought him to the United States. We distinguished Ker's case from *Rauscher*, on the basis that Ker was not brought into the United States by virtue of the extradition treaty between the United States and Peru, and rejected Ker's argument that he had a right under the extradition treaty to be returned to this country only in accordance with its terms. We rejected Ker's due process argument more broadly, holding in line with "the highest authorities" that "such forcible abduction is no sufficient reason why the party should not answer when brought within the jurisdiction of the court which has the right to try him for such an offence, and presents no valid objection to his trial in such court." *Ker, supra*, at 444.

In Frisbie v. Collins, 342 U.S. 519 (1952), we applied the rule in *Ker* to a case in which the defendant had been kidnapped in Chicago by Michigan officers and brought to trial in Michigan. We upheld the conviction over objections based on the Due Process Clause and the federal Kidnapping Act and stated:

> This Court has never departed from the rule announced in [Ker] that the power of a court to try a person for crime is not impaired by the fact that he had been brought within the court's jurisdiction by reason of a "forcible abduction." No persuasive reasons are now presented to justify overruling this line of cases. They rest on the sound basis that due process of law is satisfied when one present in court is convicted of crime after having been fairly apprized of the charges against him and after a fair trial in accordance with constitutional procedural safeguards. There is nothing in the Constitution that requires a court to permit a guilty person rightfully convicted to escape justice because he was brought to trial against his will.

Frisbie, supra, at 522 (citation and footnote omitted).

The only differences between *Ker* and the present case are that *Ker* was decided on the premise that there was no governmental involvement in the abduction, 119 U.S. at 443; and Peru, from which Ker was abducted, did not object to his prosecution.[9] Respondent finds these differences to be dispositive, . . . contending that they show that respondent's prosecution, like the prosecution of Rauscher, violates the implied terms of a valid extradition treaty. The Government, on the other hand, argues that *Rauscher* stands as an "exception" to the rule in *Ker* only when an extradition treaty is invoked, and the terms of the treaty provide that its breach will limit the jurisdiction of a court. Therefore, our first inquiry must be whether the abduction of respondent from Mexico violated the Extradition Treaty between the United States and Mexico. If we conclude that the Treaty does not prohibit respondent's abduction, the rule in *Ker* applies, and the court need not inquire as to how respondent came before it.

In construing a treaty, as in construing a statute, we first look to its terms to determine its meaning. The Treaty says nothing about the obligations of the United States and Mexico to refrain from forcible abductions of people from the territory of the other nation, or the consequences under the Treaty if such an abduction occurs. Respondent submits that Article 22(1) of the Treaty, which states that it "shall apply to offenses specified in Article 2 [including murder] committed

---

9. Ker also was not a national of Peru, whereas respondent is a national of the country from which he was abducted. Respondent finds this difference to be immaterial.

before and after this Treaty enters into force," 31 U.S.T., at 5073-5074, evidences an intent to make application of the Treaty mandatory for those offenses. However, the more natural conclusion is that Article 22 was included to ensure that the Treaty was applied to extraditions requested after the Treaty went into force, regardless of when the crime of extradition occurred.

More critical to respondent's argument is Article 9 of the Treaty, which provides:

> 1. Neither Contracting Party shall be bound to deliver up its own nationals, but the executive authority of the requested Party shall, if not prevented by the laws of that Party, have the power to deliver them up if, in its discretion, it be deemed proper to do so.
> 2. If extradition is not granted pursuant to paragraph 1 of this Article, the requested Party shall submit the case to its competent authorities for the purpose of prosecution, provided that Party has jurisdiction over the offense.

Id., at 5065.

According to respondent, Article 9 embodies the terms of the bargain which the United States struck: If the United States wishes to prosecute a Mexican national, it may request that individual's extradition. Upon a request from the United States, Mexico may either extradite the individual or submit the case to the proper authorities for prosecution in Mexico. In this way, respondent reasons, each nation preserved its right to choose whether its nationals would be tried in its own courts or by the courts of the other nation. This preservation of rights would be frustrated if either nation were free to abduct nationals of the other nation for the purposes of prosecution. More broadly, respondent reasons, as did the Court of Appeals, that all the processes and restrictions on the obligation to extradite established by the Treaty would make no sense if either nation were free to resort to forcible kidnapping to gain the presence of an individual for prosecution in a manner not contemplated by the Treaty.

We do not read the Treaty in such a fashion. Article 9 does not purport to specify the only way in which one country may gain custody of a national of the other country for the purposes of prosecution. In the absence of an extradition treaty, nations are under no obligation to surrender those in their country to foreign authorities for prosecution. *Rauscher*, 119 U.S. at 411-412; Factor v. Laubenheimer, 290 U.S. 276, 287 (1933); *cf.* Valentine v. United States ex rel. Neidecker, *supra*, at 8-9 (United States may not extradite a citizen in the absence of a statute or treaty obligation). Extradition treaties exist so as to impose mutual obligations to surrender individuals in certain defined sets of circumstances, following established procedures. *See* 1 J. Moore, A Treatise on Extradition and Interstate Rendition §72 (1891). The Treaty thus provides a mechanism which would not otherwise exist, requiring, under certain circumstances, the United States and Mexico to extradite individuals to the other country, and establishing the procedures to be followed when the Treaty is invoked.

The history of negotiation and practice under the Treaty also fails to show that abductions outside of the Treaty constitute a violation of the Treaty. As the Solicitor General notes, the Mexican Government was made aware, as early as 1906, of the *Ker* doctrine, and the United States' position that it applied to forcible abductions made outside of the terms of the United States-Mexico Extradition Treaty.[11]

---

11. In correspondence between the United States and Mexico growing out of the 1905 Martinez incident, in which a Mexican national was abducted from Mexico and brought to the United States for

Nonetheless, the current version of the Treaty, signed in 1978, does not attempt to establish a rule that would in any way curtail the effect of *Ker*. Moreover, although language which would grant individuals exactly the right sought by respondent had been considered and drafted as early as 1935 by a prominent group of legal scholars sponsored by the faculty of Harvard Law School, no such clause appears in the current Treaty.

Thus, the language of the Treaty, in the context of its history, does not support the proposition that the Treaty prohibits abductions outside of its terms. The remaining question, therefore, is whether the Treaty should be interpreted so as to include an implied term prohibiting prosecution where the defendant's presence is obtained by means other than those established by the Treaty.

Respondent contends that the Treaty must be interpreted against the backdrop of customary international law, and that international abductions are "so clearly prohibited in international law" that there was no reason to include such a clause in the Treaty itself. Brief for Respondent 11. The international censure of international abductions is further evidenced, according to respondent, by the United Nations Charter and the Charter of the Organization of American States. Respondent does not argue that these sources of international law provide an independent basis for the right respondent asserts not to be tried in the United States, but rather that they should inform the interpretation of the Treaty terms.

The Court of Appeals deemed it essential, in order for the individual defendant to assert a right under the Treaty, that the affected foreign government had registered a protest. Respondent agrees that the right exercised by the individual is derivative of the nation's right under the Treaty, since nations are authorized, notwithstanding the terms of an extradition treaty, to voluntarily render an individual to the other country on terms completely outside of those provided in the treaty. The formal protest, therefore, ensures that the "offended" nation actually objects to the abduction and has not in some way voluntarily rendered the individual for prosecution. Thus the Extradition Treaty only prohibits gaining the defendant's presence by means other than those set forth in the Treaty when the nation from which the defendant was abducted objects.

This argument seems to us inconsistent with the remainder of respondent's argument. The Extradition Treaty has the force of law, and if, as respondent asserts, it is self-executing, it would appear that a court must enforce it on behalf of an individual regardless of the offensiveness of the practice of one nation to the other nation. In *Rauscher*, the Court noted that Great Britain had taken the position in other cases that the Webster-Ashburton Treaty included the doctrine of specialty, but no importance was attached to whether or not Great Britain had protested

---

trial, the Mexican Charge wrote to the Secretary of State protesting that as Martinez' arrest was made outside of the procedures established in the extradition treaty, "the action pending against the man can not rest [on] any legal foundation." Letter of Balbino Davalos to Secretary of State, *reprinted in* Papers Relating to the Foreign Relations of the United States, H.R. Doc. No. 1, 59th Cong., 2d Sess., pt. 2, p. 1121 (1906). The Secretary of State responded that the exact issue raised by the Martinez incident had been decided by *Ker*, and that the remedy open to the Mexican Government, namely, a request to the United States for extradition of Martinez' abductor, had been granted by the United States. Letter of Robert Bacon to Mexican Charge, *reprinted in* Papers Relating to the Foreign Relations of the United States, H.R. Doc. No. 1, *supra*, at 1121-1122. Respondent and the Court of Appeals stress a statement made in 1881 by Secretary of State James Blaine to the Governor of Texas to the effect that the extradition treaty in its form at that time did not authorize unconsented to abductions from Mexico. This misses the mark, however, for the Government's argument is not that the Treaty authorizes the abduction of respondent, but that the Treaty does not prohibit the abduction.

the prosecution of Rauscher for the crime of cruel and unusual punishment as opposed to murder.

More fundamentally, the difficulty with the support respondent garners from international law is that none of it relates to the practice of nations in relation to extradition treaties. In *Rauscher*, we implied a term in the Webster-Ashburton Treaty because of the practice of nations with regard to extradition treaties. In the instant case, respondent would imply terms in the Extradition Treaty from the practice of nations with regards to international law more generally. Respondent would have us find that the Treaty acts as a prohibition against a violation of the general principle of international law that one government may not "exercise its police power in the territory of another state." Brief for Respondent 16. There are many actions which could be taken by a nation that would violate this principle, including waging war, but it cannot seriously be contended that an invasion of the United States by Mexico would violate the terms of the Extradition Treaty between the two nations.[15]

In sum, to infer from this Treaty and its terms that it prohibits all means of gaining the presence of an individual outside of its terms goes beyond established precedent and practice. In *Rauscher*, the implication of a doctrine of specialty into the terms of the Webster-Ashburton Treaty, which, by its terms, required the presentation of evidence establishing probable cause of the crime of extradition before extradition was required, was a small step to take. By contrast, to imply from the terms of this Treaty that it prohibits obtaining the presence of an individual by means outside of the procedures the Treaty establishes requires a much larger inferential leap, with only the most general of international law principles to support it. The general principles cited by respondent simply fail to persuade us that we should imply in the United States-Mexico Extradition Treaty a term prohibiting international abductions.

Respondent and his amici may be correct that respondent's abduction was "shocking," and that it may be in violation of general international law principles. Mexico has protested the abduction of respondent through diplomatic notes, and the decision of whether respondent should be returned to Mexico, as a matter outside of the Treaty, is a matter for the Executive Branch. We conclude, however, that respondent's abduction was not in violation of the Extradition Treaty between the United States and Mexico, and therefore the rule of Ker v. Illinois is fully applicable to this case. The fact of respondent's forcible abduction does not therefore prohibit his trial in a court in the United States for violations of the criminal laws of the United States. . . .

JUSTICE STEVENS, with whom JUSTICE BLACKMUN and JUSTICE O'CONNOR join, dissenting. . . .

[This] case is unique for several reasons. It does not involve an ordinary abduction by a private kidnaper, or bounty hunter, as in Ker v. Illinois, 119 U.S. 436 (1886); nor does it involve the apprehension of an American fugitive who

---

15. In the same category are the examples cited by respondent in which, after a forcible international abduction, the offended nation protested the abduction and the abducting nation then returned the individual to the protesting nation. These may show the practice of nations under customary international law, but they are of little aid in construing the terms of an extradition treaty, or the authority of a court to later try an individual who has been so abducted. More to the point for our purposes are cases such as *The Richmond*, 13 U.S. 102 (1815), and *The Merino*, 22 U.S. 391 (1824), both of which hold that a seizure of a vessel in violation of international law does not affect the jurisdiction of a United States court to adjudicate rights in connection with the vessel. . . .

committed a crime in one State and sought asylum in another, as in Frisbie v. Collins, 342 U.S. 519 (1952). Rather, it involves this country's abduction of another country's citizen; it also involves a violation of the territorial integrity of that other country, with which this country has signed an extradition treaty....

The extradition treaty with Mexico is a comprehensive document containing 23 articles and an appendix listing the extraditable offenses covered by the agreement. The parties announced their purpose in the preamble: The two governments desire "to cooperate more closely in the fight against crime and, to this end, to mutually render better assistance in matters of extradition." From the preamble, through the description of the parties' obligations with respect to offenses committed within as well as beyond the territory of a requesting party, the delineation of the procedures and evidentiary requirements for extradition, the special provisions for political offenses and capital punishment, and other details, the Treaty appears to have been designed to cover the entire subject of extradition. Thus, Article 22, entitled "Scope of Application," states that the "Treaty shall apply to offenses specified in Article 2 committed before and after this Treaty enters into force," and Article 2 directs that "extradition shall take place, subject to this Treaty, for willful acts which fall within any of [the extraditable offenses listed in] the clauses of the Appendix." Moreover, as noted by the Court, Article 9 expressly provides that neither contracting party is bound to deliver up its own nationals, although it may do so in its discretion, but if it does not do so, it "shall submit the case to its competent authorities for purposes of prosecution."

The Government's claim that the Treaty is not exclusive, but permits forcible governmental kidnapping, would transform these, and other, provisions into little more than verbiage. For example, provisions requiring "sufficient" evidence to grant extradition (Art. 3), withholding extradition for political or military offenses (Art. 5), withholding extradition when the person sought has already been tried (Art. 6), withholding extradition when the statute of limitations for the crime has lapsed (Art. 7), and granting the requested country discretion to refuse to extradite an individual who would face the death penalty in the requesting country (Art. 8), would serve little purpose if the requesting country could simply kidnap the person. As the Court of Appeals for the Ninth Circuit recognized in a related case, "each of these provisions would be utterly frustrated if a kidnapping were held to be a permissible course of governmental conduct." United States v. Verdugo-Urquidez, 939 F.2d 1341, 1349 (1991). In addition, all of these provisions "only make sense if they are understood as *requiring* each treaty signatory to comply with those procedures whenever it wishes to obtain jurisdiction over an individual who is located in another treaty nation." *Id.*, at 1351.

It is true, as the Court notes, that there is no express promise by either party to refrain from forcible abductions in the territory of the other nation. Relying on that omission,[10] the Court, in effect, concludes that the Treaty merely creates an optional method of obtaining jurisdiction over alleged offenders, and that the parties silently reserved the right to resort to self-help whenever they deem

---

10. The Court resorts to the same method of analysis as did the dissent in United States v. Rauscher, 119 U.S. 407 (1886). Chief Justice Waite would only recognize an explicit provision, and in the absence of one, he concluded that the treaty did not require that a person be tried only for the offense for which he had been extradited: "The treaty requires a delivery up to justice, on demand, of those accused of certain crimes, but says nothing about what shall be done with them after the delivery has been made. It might have provided that they should not be tried for any other offences than those for which they were surrendered, but it has not." *Id.*, at 434. That approach was rejected by the Court in *Rauscher* and should also be rejected by the Court here.

force more expeditious than legal process.[11] If the United States, for example, thought it more expedient to torture or simply to execute a person rather than to attempt extradition, these options would be equally available because they, too, were not explicitly prohibited by the Treaty. That, however, is a highly improbable interpretation of a consensual agreement, which on its face appears to have been intended to set forth comprehensive and exclusive rules concerning the subject of extradition. In my opinion, "the manifest scope and object of the treaty itself," *Rauscher*, 119 U.S. at 422, plainly imply a mutual undertaking to respect the territorial integrity of the other contracting party. That opinion is confirmed by a consideration of the "legal context" in which the Treaty was negotiated. . . .

In *Rauscher*, the Court construed an extradition treaty that was far less comprehensive than the 1978 Treaty with Mexico. The 1842 treaty with Great Britain determined the boundary between the United States and Canada, provided for the suppression of the African slave trade, and also contained one paragraph authorizing the extradition of fugitives "in certain cases." 8 Stat. 576. In Article X, each nation agreed to "deliver up to justice all persons" properly charged with any one of seven specific crimes, including murder. 119 U.S. at 421. After *Rauscher* had been extradited for murder, he was charged with the lesser offense of inflicting cruel and unusual punishment on a member of the crew of a vessel on the high seas. Although the treaty did not purport to place any limit on the jurisdiction of the demanding state after acquiring custody of the fugitive, this Court held that he could not be tried for any offense other than murder. Thus, the treaty constituted the exclusive means by which the United States could obtain jurisdiction over a defendant within the territorial jurisdiction of Great Britain.

The Court noted that the treaty included several specific provisions, such as the crimes for which one could be extradited, the process by which the extradition was to be carried out, and even the evidence that was to be produced, and concluded that "the fair purpose of the treaty is, that the person shall be delivered up to be tried for that offence and for no other." *Id.*, at 423. The Court reasoned that it did not make sense for the treaty to provide such specifics only to have the person "pas[s] into the hands of the country which charges him with the offence, free from all the positive requirements and just implications of the treaty under which the transfer of his person takes place." *Id.*, at 421. To interpret the treaty in a contrary way would mean that a country could request extradition of a person for one of the seven crimes covered by the treaty, and then try the person for another crime, such as a political crime, which was clearly not covered by the treaty; this result, the Court concluded, was clearly contrary to the intent of the parties and the purpose of the treaty.

Rejecting an argument that the sole purpose of Article X was to provide a procedure for the transfer of an individual from the jurisdiction of one sovereign to another, the Court stated:

> No such view of solemn public treaties between the great nations of the earth can be sustained by a tribunal called upon to give judicial construction to them.
>
> The opposite view has been attempted to be maintained in this country upon the ground that there is no express limitation in the treaty of the right of the country in which the offence was committed to try the person for the crime alone for which he was extradited, and that once being within the jurisdiction of that country, no matter by

---

11. To make the point more starkly, the Court has, in effect, written into Article 9 a new provision, which says: "Notwithstanding paragraphs 1 and 2 of this Article, either Contracting Party can, without the consent of the other, abduct nationals from the territory of one Party to be tried in the territory of the other."

what contrivance or fraud or by what pretence of establishing a charge provided for by the extradition treaty he may have been brought within the jurisdiction, he is, when here, liable to be tried for any offence against the laws as though arrested here originally. This proposition of the absence of express restriction in the treaty of the right to try him for other offences than that for which he was extradited, is met by the manifest scope and object of the treaty itself.

Id., at 422.

Thus, the Extradition Treaty, as understood in the context of cases that have addressed similar issues, suffices to protect the defendant from prosecution despite the absence of any express language in the Treaty itself purporting to limit this Nation's power to prosecute a defendant over whom it had lawfully acquired jurisdiction.

Although the Court's conclusion in *Rauscher* was supported by a number of judicial precedents, the holdings in these cases were not nearly as uniform as the consensus of international opinion that condemns one nation's violation of the territorial integrity of a friendly neighbor. It is shocking that a party to an extradition treaty might believe that it has secretly reserved the right to make seizures of citizens in the other party's territory....

In the *Rauscher* case, the legal background that supported the decision to imply a covenant not to prosecute for an offense different from that for which extradition had been granted was far less clear than the rule against invading the territorial integrity of a treaty partner that supports Mexico's position in this case. If *Rauscher* was correctly decided — and I am convinced that it was — its rationale clearly dictates a comparable result in this case.[26]

A critical flaw pervades the Court's entire opinion. It fails to differentiate between the conduct of private citizens, which does not violate any treaty obligation, and conduct expressly authorized by the Executive Branch of the Government, which unquestionably constitutes a flagrant violation of international law,[27] and in my opinion, also constitutes a breach of our treaty obligations. Thus, at the outset of its opinion, the Court states the issue as "whether a criminal defendant, abducted to the United States from a nation with which it has an extradition treaty, thereby acquires a defense to the jurisdiction of this country's courts." That, of course, is the question decided in Ker v. Illinois, 119 U.S. 436 (1886); it is not, however, the question presented for decision today....

As the Court observes at the outset of its opinion, there is reason to believe that respondent participated in an especially brutal murder of an American law enforcement agent. That fact, if true, may explain the Executive's intense interest in punishing respondent in our courts. Such an explanation, however, provides no justification for disregarding the Rule of Law that this Court has a duty to uphold.

---

26. Just as Rauscher had standing to raise the treaty violation issue, respondent may raise a comparable issue in this case. Certainly, if an individual who is not a party to an agreement between the United States and another country is permitted to assert the rights of that country in our courts, as is true in the specialty cases, then the same rule must apply to the individual who has been a victim of this country's breach of an extradition treaty and who wishes to assert the rights of that country in our courts after that country has already registered its protest.

27. "In the international legal order, treaties are concluded by states against a background of customary international law. Norms of customary international law specify the circumstances in which the failure of one party to fulfill its treaty obligations will permit the other to rescind the treaty, retaliate, or take other steps." Vazquez, *Treaty-Based Rights and Remedies of Individuals*, 92 Colum. L. Rev. 1082, 1157 (1992).

That the Executive may wish to reinterpret[34] the Treaty to allow for an action that the Treaty in no way authorizes should not influence this Court's interpretation. Indeed, the desire for revenge exerts "a kind of hydraulic pressure . . . before which even well settled principles of law will bend," Northern Securities Co. v. United States, 193 U.S. 197, 401 (1904) (Holmes, J., dissenting), but it is precisely at such moments that we should remember and be guided by our duty "to render judgment evenly and dispassionately according to law, as each is given understanding to ascertain and apply it." United States v. Mine Workers, 330 U.S. 258, 342 (1947) (Rutledge, J., dissenting). The way that we perform that duty in a case of this kind sets an example that other tribunals in other countries are sure to emulate.

Notes and Questions

1. Did the United States have jurisdiction under international law to apply its laws to Alvarez-Machain — that is, did it have *prescriptive jurisdiction*? If Alvarez-Machain had voluntarily entered the United States, would it have been permissible under international law for the United States to try him under U.S. law? If so, why should the United States not also have the right to secure his arrest in Mexico?

2. As discussed in Section B above, the international law of prescriptive jurisdiction is not strictly territorial. By contrast, enforcement jurisdiction is still widely considered to be territorial in nature. Under this view, nations have no authority to conduct an arrest in another country without that country's consent. *See, e.g.*, Restatement (Third) of Foreign Relations Law of the United States §432(2) (1987) ("A state's law enforcement officers may exercise their functions in the territory of another state only with the consent of the other state, given by duly authorized officials of that state."). Why is enforcement jurisdiction limited by territory? Should international law ever allow cross-border arrests?

3. To understand the *Alvarez-Machain* decision, one needs to understand the "*Ker-Frisbie* doctrine." This doctrine takes its name from two Supreme Court decisions, Ker v. Illinois, 119 U.S. 436 (1886), and Frisbie v. Collins, 342 U.S. 519 (1952). In those decisions — one of which (*Ker*) involved an international abduction, and the other of which (*Frisbie*) involved an interstate abduction — the Supreme Court held that a prosecution need not be dismissed merely because the defendant's custody has been improperly obtained. In other words, there is no "exclusionary rule of the body": unlike unlawfully obtained evidence, the physical custody of the defendant is not ordinarily excluded merely because it was unlawfully obtained. The one exception to this rule, the Court suggested in *Ker*, is when the defendant's custody has been obtained in violation of a self-executing treaty. *See also* Cook v. United States, 288 U.S. 102, 121-22 (1933) (reaching this conclusion regarding seizure of property in violation of a treaty). The facts of *Ker* and *Frisbie* are described in the majority and dissenting opinions in *Alvarez-Machain*. What differences are there between the facts of those cases and the

---

34. Certainly, the Executive's view has changed over time. At one point, the Office of Legal Counsel advised the administration that such seizures were contrary to international law because they compromised the territorial integrity of the other nation and were only to be undertaken with the consent of that nation. 4B Op. Off. Legal Counsel 549, 556 (1980). More recently, that opinion was revised, and the new opinion concluded that the President did have the authority to override customary international law. Hearing before the Subcommittee on Civil and Constitutional Rights of the House Committee on the Judiciary, 101st Cong., 1st Sess., 4-5 (1989) (statement of William P. Barr, Assistant Attorney General, Office of Legal Counsel, U.S. Department of Justice).

facts of *Alvarez-Machain?* Should those differences matter? For a discussion of the *Ker-Frisbie* doctrine, see Wayne R. LaFave, Search and Seizure: A Treatise on the Fourth Amendment §1.9 (3d ed. 1996).

4. What evidence does the majority in *Alvarez-Machain* cite to show that the extradition treaty is not violated? Is this evidence persuasive? Is it, as the majority contends, too great an inferential leap to conclude that the treaty forbids abductions? How does the Court's approach to treaty interpretation in this case compare with its approach in the *Rauscher* case, which is discussed in the majority and dissenting opinions?

5. It is widely accepted that customary international law prohibits nations from carrying out abductions in other countries. *See* Michael Glennon, *State-Sponsored Abduction: A Comment on* Alvarez-Machain, 86 Am. J. Int'l L. 746 (1992). So, even assuming the Court was correct in Alvarez-Machain regarding the meaning of the extradition treaty, why was customary international law not a sufficient basis for relief? Note that, on remand, the Ninth Circuit expressed some uncertainty regarding whether the Supreme Court had addressed the customary international law argument. *See* United States v. Alvarez-Machain, 971 F.2d 310 (9th Cir. 1992), *amended*, 1992 U.S. App. LEXIS 28367 (9th Cir. Nov. 3, 1992). What do you think? Does *Alvarez-Machain* have any implications for the debate, discussed in Chapter 7, about whether customary international law is self-executing domestic federal law?

6. The *Alvarez-Machain* decision was heavily criticized by Mexico and other nations. *See* William J. Aceves, *The Legality of Transborder Abductions: A Study of United States v. Alvarez-Machain*, 3 Sw. J. of L. & Trade Am. 101 (1996). It also was generally criticized by academic commentators. *See, e.g.*, Jonathan A. Bush, *How Did We Get Here? Foreign Abductions After* Alvarez-Machain, 45 Stan. L. Rev. 939 (1993); Andrew L. Strauss, *A Global Paradigm Shattered: The Jurisdictional Nihilism of the Supreme Court's Abduction Decision in* Alvarez-Machain, 4 Temp. L. Rev. 1209 (1994); Douglas J. Sylvester, *Customary International Law, Forcible Abductions, and America's Return to the "Savage State,"* 42 Buff. L. Rev. 555 (1994). For a rare defense of the decision, see Malvina Halberstam, *In Defense of the Supreme Court Decision in* Alvarez-Machain, 86 Am. J. Int'l L. 736 (1992).

In 1994, the Clinton Administration negotiated with Mexico a modification to the bilateral extradition treaty that would expressly prohibit "trans-border abductions" like the one in *Alvarez-Machain*. For reasons that are unclear, the treaty amendment was never submitted to the Senate for its advice and consent.

7. In an ironic twist, the case against Alvarez-Machain was thrown out on remand for lack of evidence. *See* United States v. Alvarez-Machain, No. CR-87-422-(G)-ER (C.D. Cal. Dec. 14, 1992). Subsequently, Alvarez-Machain brought a civil suit against the U.S. government and the Mexican citizens involved in his abduction. After a number of decisions in the lower courts, Alvarez-Machain's claims were ordered dismissed by the Supreme Court in the Sosa v. Alvarez-Machain decision excerpted in Chapter 7. (The Court determined that Alvarez-Machain's claims against the U.S. government did not fall within an exception in the Federal Tort Claims Act and thus were barred by the government's sovereign immunity, and that Alvarez-Machain did not have a cognizable claim under the Alien Tort Statute.)

8. For post-*Alvarez-Machain* decisions allowing the prosecution of abducted defendants because of the lack of a violation of the relevant extradition treaty, see, for example, United States v. Noriega, 117 F.3d 1206 (11th Cir. 1997) (seizure of general in Panama so that he could be tried on drug charges); and Kasi v. Angelone, 300 F.3d 487 (4th Cir. 2002) (seizure of individual in Pakistan so that he could be tried for shooting CIA employees in Virginia). The United States is not the only nation that has engaged in extraterritorial abductions. In 1960, for example, Israel abducted Nazi war criminal Adolf Eichmann from Argentina. In response, the U.N. Security Council passed a resolution condemning the abduction and requesting that Israel make "appropriate reparations" to Argentina in accordance with the U.N. Charter and rules of international law. *See* Question Relating to the Case of Adolf Eichmann, S.C. Res. 138, U.N. SCOR, 15th Sess., 868th mtg. at 4, U.N. Doc. s/4349 (1960).

9. In a decision predating *Alvarez-Machain*, the U.S. Court of Appeals for the Second Circuit suggested that a court could use its supervisory powers to dismiss a prosecution when an individual is severely mistreated by the government or its agents in connection with an abduction. *See* United States v. Toscanino, 500 F.2d 267, 275 (2d Cir. 1974). The Second Circuit subsequently held that this exception applies only where the defendant can prove "the use of torture, brutality and similar outrageous conduct." United States ex rel. Lujan v. Gengler, 510 F.2d 62, 65 (2d Cir. 1975). The precise scope of this mistreatment exception, and its viability after *Alvarez-Machain*, are uncertain. *See, e.g.*, United States v. Matta-Ballesteros, 71 F.3d 754 (9th Cir. 1995) (mere kidnapping by the government does not fall within this exception); *cf.* United States v. Best, 304 F.3d 308, 312 (3d Cir. 2002) ("Subsequent decisions of the Supreme Court indicate that there is reason to doubt the soundness of the *Toscanino* exception, even as limited to its flagrant facts.").

10. There has been uncertainty at times regarding the *statutory* authority of U.S. law enforcement officials to make arrests in foreign countries without those countries' consent. A federal statute provides that "[t]he Attorney General may appoint officials to detect and prosecute crimes against the United States." 28 U.S.C. §533(1). Another statute gives FBI agents the authority to "make arrests . . . for any felony cognizable under the laws of the United States if they have reasonable grounds to believe that the person to be arrested has committed or is committing such felony." 18 U.S.C. §3052. Neither statute contains an explicit geographic limitation or an explicit directive to comply with international law. Nevertheless, in a 1980 memorandum to the Attorney General, the Office of Legal Counsel ("OLC") concluded that the FBI lacked the authority to make arrests in foreign countries without those countries' consent. *See* Extraterritorial Apprehension by the Federal Bureau of Investigation, 4B Op. Off. Legal Counsel 543 (1980). Among other things, the 1980 memorandum reasoned that such an arrest would violate international law, and it relied on the *Charming Betsy* canon of construction. Nine years later, the OLC reversed itself, concluding that the FBI did have statutory authority to make extraterritorial arrests, even if such arrests violate international law. *See* Authority of the Federal Bureau of Investigation to Override International Law in Extraterritorial Law Enforcement Activities, 13 Op. Off. Legal Counsel 164 (1989). The 1989 memorandum concluded that the *Charming Betsy* canon was "wholly inapposite" to the statutes in question, reasoning that the FBI is an agency through which the President carries out his constitutional law enforcement duties, that the President himself has the power to violate customary international law, and that "it must be presumed that Congress intended to grant the President's instrumentality the authority to act in contravention of international law when directed to do so." *Id*. at 172. Which memorandum was correct? For a discussion of the OLC memoranda, see Curtis A. Bradley, Chevron *Deference and Foreign Affairs*, 86 Va. L. Rev. 649, 697-99 (2000). (These memoranda are also mentioned in footnote 34 of the dissent in *Alvarez-Machain*.)

Appendices

Appendices

A

Constitution of the United States

We the People of the United States, in Order to form a more perfect Union, establish Justice, insure domestic Tranquility, provide for the common defense, promote the general Welfare, and secure the Blessings of Liberty to ourselves and our Posterity, do ordain and establish this Constitution for the United States of America.

Article I.

Section 1. All legislative Powers herein granted shall be vested in a Congress of the United States, which shall consist of a Senate and House of Representatives.

Section 2. The House of Representatives shall be composed of Members chosen every second Year by the People of the several States, and the Electors in each State shall have the Qualifications requisite for Electors of the most numerous Branch of the State Legislature.

No Person shall be a Representative who shall not have attained to the Age of twenty five Years, and been seven Years a Citizen of the United States, and who shall not, when elected, be an Inhabitant of that State in which he shall be chosen.

Representatives and direct Taxes shall be apportioned among the several States which may be included within this Union, according to their respective Numbers, which shall be determined by adding to the whole Number of free Persons, including those bound to Service for a Term of Years, and excluding Indians not taxed, three fifths of all other Persons. The actual Enumeration shall be made within three Years after the first Meeting of the Congress of the United States, and within every subsequent Term of ten Years, in such Manner as they shall by Law direct. The Number of Representatives shall not exceed one for every thirty Thousand, but each State shall have at Least one Representative; and until such enumeration shall be made, the State of New Hampshire shall be entitled to chuse three, Massachusetts eight, Rhode-Island and Providence Plantations one, Connecticut five, New-York six, New Jersey four, Pennsylvania eight, Delaware one, Maryland six, Virginia ten, North Carolina five, South Carolina five, and Georgia three.

When vacancies happen in the Representation from any State, the Executive Authority thereof shall issue Writs of Election to fill such Vacancies.

The House of Representatives shall chuse their Speaker and other Officers; and shall have the sole Power of Impeachment.

Section 3. The Senate of the United States shall be composed of two Senators from each State, chosen by the Legislature thereof for six Years; and each Senator shall have one Vote.

Immediately after they shall be assembled in Consequence of the first Election, they shall be divided as equally as may be into three Classes. The Seats of the Senators of the first Class shall be vacated at the Expiration of the second Year, of the second Class at the Expiration of the fourth Year, and of the third Class at the Expiration of the sixth Year, so that one third may be chosen every second Year; and if Vacancies happen by Resignation, or otherwise, during the Recess of the Legislature of any State, the Executive thereof may make temporary Appointments until the next Meeting of the Legislature, which shall then fill such Vacancies.

No Person shall be a Senator who shall not have attained to the Age of thirty Years, and been nine Years a Citizen of the United States, and who shall not, when elected, be an Inhabitant of that State for which he shall be chosen.

The Vice President of the United States shall be President of the Senate, but shall have no Vote, unless they be equally divided.

The Senate shall chuse their other Officers, and also a President pro tempore, in the Absence of the Vice President, or when he shall exercise the Office of President of the United States.

The Senate shall have the sole Power to try all Impeachments. When sitting for that Purpose, they shall be on Oath or Affirmation. When the President of the United States is tried, the Chief Justice shall preside: And no Person shall be convicted without the Concurrence of two thirds of the Members present.

Judgment in Cases of Impeachment shall not extend further than to removal from Office, and disqualification to hold and enjoy any Office of honor, Trust or Profit under the United States: but the Party convicted shall nevertheless be liable and subject to Indictment, Trial, Judgment and Punishment, according to Law.

Section 4. The Times, Places and Manner of holding Elections for Senators and Representatives, shall be prescribed in each State by the Legislature thereof; but the Congress may at any time by Law make or alter such Regulations, except as to the Places of chusing Senators.

The Congress shall assemble at least once in every Year, and such Meeting shall be on the first Monday in December, unless they shall by Law appoint a different Day.

Section 5. Each House shall be the Judge of the Elections, Returns and Qualifications of its own Members, and a Majority of each shall constitute a Quorum to do Business; but a smaller Number may adjourn from day to day, and may be authorized to compel the Attendance of absent Members, in such Manner, and under such Penalties as each House may provide.

Each House may determine the Rules of its Proceedings, punish its Members for disorderly Behaviour, and, with the Concurrence of two thirds, expel a Member.

Each House shall keep a Journal of its Proceedings, and from time to time publish the same, excepting such Parts as may in their Judgment require Secrecy; and the Yeas and Nays of the Members of either House on any question shall, at the Desire of one fifth of those Present, be entered on the Journal.

Neither House, during the Session of Congress, shall, without the Consent of the other, adjourn for more than three days, nor to any other Place than that in which the two Houses shall be sitting.

Section 6. The Senators and Representatives shall receive a Compensation for their Services, to be ascertained by Law, and paid out of the Treasury of the United States. They shall in all Cases, except Treason, Felony and Breach of the Peace, be privileged from Arrest during their Attendance at the Session of their respective Houses, and in going to and returning from the same; and for any Speech or Debate in either House, they shall not be questioned in any other Place.

No Senator or Representative shall, during the Time for which he was elected, be appointed to any civil Office under the Authority of the United States, which shall have been created, or the Emoluments whereof shall have been encreased during such time; and no Person holding any Office under the United States, shall be a Member of either House during his Continuance in Office.

Section 7. All Bills for raising Revenue shall originate in the House of Representatives; but the Senate may propose or concur with Amendments as on other Bills.

Every Bill which shall have passed the House of Representatives and the Senate, shall, before it become a Law, be presented to the President of the United States: If he approve he shall sign it, but if not he shall return it, with his Objections to that House in which it shall have originated, who shall enter the Objections at large on their Journal, and proceed to reconsider it. If after such Reconsideration two thirds of that House shall agree to pass the Bill, it shall be sent, together with the Objections, to the other House, by which it shall likewise be reconsidered, and if approved by two thirds of that House, it shall become a Law. But in all such Cases the Votes of both Houses shall be determined by yeas and Nays, and the Names of the Persons voting for and against the Bill shall be entered on the Journal of each House respectively. If any Bill shall not be returned by the President within ten Days (Sundays excepted) after it shall have been presented to him, the Same shall be a Law, in like Manner as if he had signed it, unless the Congress by their Adjournment prevent its Return, in which Case it shall not be a Law.

Every Order, Resolution, or Vote to which the Concurrence of the Senate and House of Representatives may be necessary (except on a question of Adjournment) shall be presented to the President of the United States; and before the Same shall take Effect, shall be approved by him, or being disapproved by him, shall be repassed by two thirds of the Senate and House of Representatives, according to the Rules and Limitations prescribed in the Case of a Bill.

Section 8. The Congress shall have Power To lay and collect Taxes, Duties, Imposts and Excises, to pay the Debts and provide for the common Defence and general Welfare of the United States; but all Duties, Imposts and Excises shall be uniform throughout the United States;

To borrow Money on the credit of the United States;

To regulate Commerce with foreign Nations, and among the several States, and with the Indian Tribes;

To establish an uniform Rule of Naturalization, and uniform Laws on the subject of Bankruptcies throughout the United States;

To coin Money, regulate the Value thereof, and of foreign Coin, and fix the Standard of Weights and Measures;

To provide for the Punishment of counterfeiting the Securities and current Coin of the United States;

To establish Post Offices and post Roads;

To promote the Progress of Science and useful Arts, by securing for limited Times to Authors and Inventors the exclusive Right to their respective Writings and Discoveries;

To constitute Tribunals inferior to the supreme Court;

To define and punish Piracies and Felonies committed on the high Seas, and Offences against the Law of Nations;

To declare War, grant Letters of Marque and Reprisal, and make Rules concerning Captures on Land and Water;

To raise and support Armies, but no Appropriation of Money to that Use shall be for a longer Term than two Years;

To provide and maintain a Navy;

To make Rules for the Government and Regulation of the land and naval Forces;

To provide for calling forth the Militia to execute the Laws of the Union, suppress Insurrections and repel Invasions;

To provide for organizing, arming, and disciplining, the Militia, and for governing such Part of them as may be employed in the Service of the United States, reserving to the States respectively, the Appointment of the Officers, and the Authority of training the Militia according to the discipline prescribed by Congress;

To exercise exclusive Legislation in all Cases whatsoever, over such District (not exceeding ten Miles square) as may, by Cession of particular States, and the Acceptance of Congress, become the Seat of the Government of the United States, and to exercise like Authority over all Places purchased by the Consent of the Legislature of the State in which the Same shall be, for the Erection of Forts, Magazines, Arsenals, dock-Yards, and other needful Buildings;—And

To make all Laws which shall be necessary and proper for carrying into Execution the foregoing Powers, and all other Powers vested by this Constitution in the Government of the United States, or in any Department or Officer thereof.

Section 9. The Migration or Importation of such Persons as any of the States now existing shall think proper to admit, shall not be prohibited by the Congress prior to the Year one thousand eight hundred and eight, but a Tax or duty may be imposed on such Importation, not exceeding ten dollars for each Person.

The Privilege of the Writ of Habeas Corpus shall not be suspended, unless when in Cases of Rebellion or Invasion the public Safety may require it.

No Bill of Attainder or ex post facto Law shall be passed.

No Capitation, or other direct, Tax shall be laid, unless in Proportion to the Census or enumeration herein before directed to be taken.

No Tax or Duty shall be laid on Articles exported from any State.

No Preference shall be given by any Regulation of Commerce or Revenue to the Ports of one State over those of another; nor shall Vessels bound to, or from, one State, be obliged to enter, clear, or pay Duties in another.

No Money shall be drawn from the Treasury, but in Consequence of Appropriations made by Law; and a regular Statement and Account of the Receipts and Expenditures of all public Money shall be published from time to time.

No Title of Nobility shall be granted by the United States: And no Person holding any Office of Profit or Trust under them, shall, without the Consent of the Congress, accept of any present, Emolument, Office, or Title, of any kind whatever, from any King, Prince, or foreign State.

Section 10. No State shall enter into any Treaty, Alliance, or Confederation; grant Letters of Marque and Reprisal; coin Money; emit Bills of Credit; make any Thing but gold and silver Coin a Tender in Payment of Debts; pass any Bill of

Attainder, ex post facto Law, or Law impairing the Obligation of Contracts, or grant any Title of Nobility.

No State shall, without the Consent of the Congress, lay any Imposts or Duties on Imports or Exports, except what may be absolutely necessary for executing it's inspection Laws: and the net Produce of all Duties and Imposts, laid by any State on Imports or Exports, shall be for the Use of the Treasury of the United States; and all such Laws shall be subject to the Revision and Controul of the Congress.

No State shall, without the Consent of Congress, lay any Duty of Tonnage, keep Troops, or Ships of War in time of Peace, enter into any Agreement or Compact with another State, or with a foreign Power, or engage in War, unless actually invaded, or in such imminent Danger as will not admit of delay.

Article II.

Section 1. The executive Power shall be vested in a President of the United States of America. He shall hold his Office during the Term of four Years, and, together with the Vice President, chosen for the same Term, be elected, as follows:

Each State shall appoint, in such Manner as the Legislature thereof may direct, a Number of Electors, equal to the whole Number of Senators and Representatives to which the State may be entitled in the Congress: but no Senator or Representative, or Person holding an Office of Trust or Profit under the United States, shall be appointed an Elector.

The Electors shall meet in their respective States, and vote by Ballot for two Persons, of whom one at least shall not be an Inhabitant of the same State with themselves. And they shall make a List of all the Persons voted for, and of the Number of Votes for each; which List they shall sign and certify, and transmit sealed to the Seat of the Government of the United States, directed to the President of the Senate. The President of the Senate shall, in the Presence of the Senate and House of Representatives, open all the Certificates, and the Votes shall then be counted. The Person having the greatest Number of Votes shall be the President, if such Number be a Majority of the whole Number of Electors appointed; and if there be more than one who have such Majority, and have an equal Number of Votes, then the House of Representatives shall immediately chuse by Ballot one of them for President; and if no Person have a Majority, then from the five highest on the List the said House shall in like Manner chuse the President. But in chusing the President, the Votes shall be taken by States, the Representation from each State having one Vote; A quorum for this purpose shall consist of a Member or Members from two thirds of the States, and a Majority of all the States shall be necessary to a Choice. In every Case, after the Choice of the President, the Person having the greatest Number of Votes of the Electors shall be the Vice President. But if there should remain two or more who have equal Votes, the Senate shall chuse from them by Ballot the Vice President.

The Congress may determine the Time of chusing the Electors, and the Day on which they shall give their Votes; which Day shall be the same throughout the United States.

No Person except a natural born Citizen, or a Citizen of the United States, at the time of the Adoption of this Constitution, shall be eligible to the Office of President; neither shall any Person be eligible to that Office who shall not have attained to the Age of thirty five Years, and been fourteen Years a Resident within the United States.

In Case of the Removal of the President from Office, or of his Death, Resignation, or Inability to discharge the Powers and Duties of the said Office, the Same shall devolve on the Vice President, and the Congress may by Law provide for the Case of Removal, Death, Resignation or Inability, both of the President and Vice President, declaring what Officer shall then act as President, and such Officer shall act accordingly, until the Disability be removed, or a President shall be elected.

The President shall, at stated Times, receive for his Services, a Compensation, which shall neither be increased nor diminished during the Period for which he shall have been elected, and he shall not receive within that Period any other Emolument from the United States, or any of them.

Before he enter on the Execution of his Office, he shall take the following Oath or Affirmation: — "I do solemnly swear (or affirm) that I will faithfully execute the Office of President of the United States, and will to the best of my Ability, preserve, protect and defend the Constitution of the United States."

Section 2. The President shall be Commander in Chief of the Army and Navy of the United States, and of the Militia of the several States, when called into the actual Service of the United States; he may require the Opinion, in writing, of the principal Officer in each of the executive Departments, upon any Subject relating to the Duties of their respective Offices, and he shall have Power to grant Reprieves and Pardons for Offences against the United States, except in Cases of Impeachment.

He shall have Power, by and with the Advice and Consent of the Senate, to make Treaties, provided two thirds of the Senators present concur; and he shall nominate, and by and with the Advice and Consent of the Senate, shall appoint Ambassadors, other public Ministers and Consuls, Judges of the supreme Court, and all other Officers of the United States, whose Appointments are not herein otherwise provided for, and which shall be established by Law: but the Congress may by Law vest the Appointment of such inferior Officers, as they think proper, in the President alone, in the Courts of Law, or in the Heads of Departments.

The President shall have Power to fill up all Vacancies that may happen during the Recess of the Senate, by granting Commissions which shall expire at the End of their next Session.

Section 3. He shall from time to time give to the Congress Information of the State of the Union, and recommend to their Consideration such Measures as he shall judge necessary and expedient; he may, on extraordinary Occasions, convene both Houses, or either of them, and in Case of Disagreement between them, with Respect to the Time of Adjournment, he may adjourn them to such Time as he shall think proper; he shall receive Ambassadors and other public Ministers; he shall take Care that the Laws be faithfully executed, and shall Commission all the Officers of the United States.

Section 4. The President, Vice President and all civil Officers of the United States, shall be removed from Office on Impeachment for, and Conviction of, Treason, Bribery, or other high Crimes and Misdemeanors.

Article III.

Section 1. The judicial Power of the United States shall be vested in one supreme Court, and in such inferior Courts as the Congress may from time to time ordain and establish. The Judges, both of the supreme and inferior Courts, shall hold their Offices during good Behaviour, and shall, at stated Times, receive for their Services a Compensation, which shall not be diminished during their Continuance in Office.

Section 2. The judicial Power shall extend to all Cases, in Law and Equity, arising under this Constitution, the Laws of the United States, and Treaties made, or which shall be made, under their Authority; — to all Cases affecting Ambassadors, other public Ministers and Consuls; — to all Cases of admiralty and maritime Jurisdiction; — to Controversies to which the United States shall be a Party; — to Controversies between two or more States; — between a State and Citizens of another State; — between Citizens of different States; — between Citizens of the same State claiming Lands under Grants of different States, and between a State, or the Citizens thereof, and foreign States, Citizens or Subjects.

In all Cases affecting Ambassadors, other public Ministers and Consuls, and those in which a State shall be Party, the supreme Court shall have original Jurisdiction. In all the other Cases before mentioned, the supreme Court shall have appellate Jurisdiction, both as to Law and Fact, with such Exceptions, and under such Regulations as the Congress shall make.

The Trial of all Crimes, except in Cases of Impeachment, shall be by Jury; and such Trial shall be held in the State where the said Crimes shall have been committed; but when not committed within any State, the Trial shall be at such Place or Places as the Congress may by Law have directed.

Section 3. Treason against the United States, shall consist only in levying War against them, or in adhering to their Enemies, giving them Aid and Comfort. No Person shall be convicted of Treason unless on the Testimony of two Witnesses to the same overt Act, or on Confession in open Court.

The Congress shall have Power to declare the Punishment of Treason, but no Attainder of Treason shall work Corruption of Blood, or Forfeiture except during the Life of the Person attainted.

Article IV.

Section 1. Full Faith and Credit shall be given in each State to the public Acts, Records, and judicial Proceedings of every other State. And the Congress may by general Laws prescribe the Manner in which such Acts, Records and Proceedings shall be proved, and the Effect thereof.

Section 2. The Citizens of each State shall be entitled to all Privileges and Immunities of Citizens in the several States.

A Person charged in any State with Treason, Felony, or other Crime, who shall flee from Justice, and be found in another State, shall on Demand of the executive Authority of the State from which he fled, be delivered up, to be removed to the State having Jurisdiction of the Crime.

No Person held to Service or Labour in one State, under the Laws thereof, escaping into another, shall, in Consequence of any Law or Regulation therein, be discharged from such Service or Labour, but shall be delivered up on Claim of the Party to whom such Service or Labour may be due.

Section 3. New States may be admitted by the Congress into this Union; but no new State shall be formed or erected within the Jurisdiction of any other State; nor any State be formed by the Junction of two or more States, or Parts of States, without the Consent of the Legislatures of the States concerned as well as of the Congress.

The Congress shall have Power to dispose of and make all needful Rules and Regulations respecting the Territory or other Property belonging to the United

States; and nothing in this Constitution shall be so construed as to Prejudice any Claims of the United States, or of any particular State.

Section 4. The United States shall guarantee to every State in this Union a Republican Form of Government, and shall protect each of them against Invasion; and on Application of the Legislature, or of the Executive (when the Legislature cannot be convened), against domestic Violence.

Article V.

The Congress, whenever two thirds of both Houses shall deem it necessary, shall propose Amendments to this Constitution, or, on the Application of the Legislatures of two thirds of the several States, shall call a Convention for proposing Amendments, which, in either Case, shall be valid to all Intents and Purposes, as Part of this Constitution, when ratified by the Legislatures of three fourths of the several States, or by Conventions in three fourths thereof, as the one or the other Mode of Ratification may be proposed by the Congress; Provided that no Amendment which may be made prior to the Year One thousand eight hundred and eight shall in any Manner affect the first and fourth Clauses in the Ninth Section of the first Article; and that no State, without its Consent, shall be deprived of its equal Suffrage in the Senate.

Article VI.

All Debts contracted and Engagements entered into, before the Adoption of this Constitution, shall be as valid against the United States under this Constitution, as under the Confederation.

This Constitution, and the Laws of the United States which shall be made in Pursuance thereof; and all Treaties made, or which shall be made, under the Authority of the United States, shall be the supreme Law of the Land; and the Judges in every State shall be bound thereby, any Thing in the Constitution or Laws of any State to the Contrary notwithstanding.

The Senators and Representatives before mentioned, and the Members of the several State Legislatures, and all executive and judicial Officers, both of the United States and of the several States, shall be bound by Oath or Affirmation, to support this Constitution; but no religious Test shall ever be required as a Qualification to any Office or public Trust under the United States.

Article VII.

The Ratification of the Conventions of nine States, shall be sufficient for the Establishment of this Constitution between the States so ratifying the Same.

ARTICLES IN ADDITION TO, AND AMENDMENT OF, THE CONSTITUTION OF THE UNITED STATES OF AMERICA

Amendment I

Congress shall make no law respecting an establishment of religion, or prohibiting the free exercise thereof; or abridging the freedom of speech, or of the press; or the right of the people peaceably to assemble, and to petition the Government for a redress of grievances.

Amendment II

A well regulated Militia, being necessary to the security of a free State, the right of the people to keep and bear Arms, shall not be infringed.

Amendment III

No Soldier shall, in time of peace be quartered in any house, without the consent of the Owner, nor in time of war, but in a manner to be prescribed by law.

Amendment IV

The right of the people to be secure in their persons, houses, papers, and effects, against unreasonable searches and seizures, shall not be violated, and no Warrants shall issue, but upon probable cause, supported by Oath or affirmation, and particularly describing the place to be searched, and the persons or things to be seized.

Amendment V

No person shall be held to answer for a capital, or otherwise infamous crime, unless on a presentment or indictment of a Grand Jury, except in cases arising in the land or naval forces, or in the Militia, when in actual service in time of War or public danger; nor shall any person be subject for the same offence to be twice put in jeopardy of life or limb; nor shall be compelled in any criminal case to be a witness against himself, nor be deprived of life, liberty, or property, without due process of law; nor shall private property be taken for public use, without just compensation.

Amendment VI

In all criminal prosecutions, the accused shall enjoy the right to a speedy and public trial, by an impartial jury of the State and district wherein the crime shall have been committed, which district shall have been previously ascertained by law, and to be informed of the nature and cause of the accusation; to be confronted with the witnesses against him; to have compulsory process for obtaining witnesses in his favor, and to have the Assistance of Counsel for his defence.

Amendment VII

In suits at common law, where the value in controversy shall exceed twenty dollars, the right of trial by jury shall be preserved, and no fact tried by a jury, shall be otherwise reexamined in any Court of the United States, than according to the rules of the common law.

Amendment VIII

Excessive bail shall not be required, nor excessive fines imposed, nor cruel and unusual punishments inflicted.

Amendment IX

The enumeration in the Constitution, of certain rights, shall not be construed to deny or disparage others retained by the people.

Amendment X

The powers not delegated to the United States by the Constitution, nor prohibited by it to the States, are reserved to the States respectively, or to the people.

Amendment XI

Passed by Congress March 4, 1794. Ratified February 7, 1795.

The Judicial power of the United States shall not be construed to extend to any suit in law or equity, commenced or prosecuted against one of the United States by Citizens of another State, or by Citizens or Subjects of any Foreign State.

Amendment XII

Passed by Congress December 9, 1803. Ratified June 15, 1804.

The Electors shall meet in their respective states and vote by ballot for President and Vice-President, one of whom, at least, shall not be an inhabitant of the same state with themselves; they shall name in their ballots the person voted for as President, and in distinct ballots the person voted for as Vice-President, and they shall make distinct lists of all persons voted for as President, and of all persons voted for as Vice-President, and of the number of votes for each, which lists they shall sign and certify, and transmit sealed to the seat of the government of the United States, directed to the President of the Senate; — the President of the Senate shall, in the presence of the Senate and House of Representatives, open all the certificates and the votes shall then be counted; — The person having the greatest number of votes for President, shall be the President, if such number be a majority of the whole number of Electors appointed; and if no person have such majority, then from the persons having the highest numbers not exceeding three on the list of those voted for as President, the House of Representatives shall choose immediately, by ballot, the President. But in choosing the President, the votes shall be taken by states, the representation from each state having one vote; a quorum for this purpose shall consist of a member or members from two-thirds of the states, and a majority of all the states shall be necessary to a choice. And if the House of Representatives shall not choose a President whenever the right of choice shall devolve upon them, before the fourth day of March next following, then the Vice-President shall act as President, as in case of the death or other constitutional disability of the President. The person having the greatest number of votes as Vice-President, shall be the Vice-President, if such number be a majority of the whole number of Electors appointed, and if no person have a majority, then from the two highest numbers on the list, the Senate shall choose the Vice-President; a quorum for the purpose shall consist of two-thirds of the whole number of Senators, and a majority of the whole number shall be necessary to a choice. But no person constitutionally ineligible to the office of President shall be eligible to that of Vice-President of the United States.

Amendment XIII

Passed by Congress January 31, 1865. Ratified December 6, 1865.

Section 1. Neither slavery nor involuntary servitude, except as a punishment for crime whereof the party shall have been duly convicted, shall exist within the United States, or any place subject to their jurisdiction.

Section 2. Congress shall have power to enforce this article by appropriate legislation.

Amendment XIV

Passed by Congress June 13, 1866. Ratified July 9, 1868.

Section 1. All persons born or naturalized in the United States, and subject to the jurisdiction thereof, are citizens of the United States and of the State wherein they reside. No State shall make or enforce any law which shall abridge the privileges or immunities of citizens of the United States; nor shall any State deprive any person of life, liberty, or property, without due process of law; nor deny to any person within its jurisdiction the equal protection of the laws.

Section 2. Representatives shall be apportioned among the several States according to their respective numbers, counting the whole number of persons in each State, excluding Indians not taxed. But when the right to vote at any election for the choice of electors for President and Vice-President of the United States, Representatives in Congress, the Executive and Judicial officers of a State, or the members of the Legislature thereof, is denied to any of the male inhabitants of such State, being twenty-one years of age, and citizens of the United States, or in any way abridged, except for participation in rebellion, or other crime, the basis of representation therein shall be reduced in the proportion which the number of such male citizens shall bear to the whole number of male citizens twenty-one years of age in such State.

Section 3. No person shall be a Senator or Representative in Congress, or elector of President and Vice-President, or hold any office, civil or military, under the United States, or under any State, who, having previously taken an oath, as a member of Congress, or as an officer of the United States, or as a member of any State legislature, or as an executive or judicial officer of any State, to support the Constitution of the United States, shall have engaged in insurrection or rebellion against the same, or given aid or comfort to the enemies thereof. But Congress may by a vote of two-thirds of each House, remove such disability.

Section 4. The validity of the public debt of the United States, authorized by law, including debts incurred for payment of pensions and bounties for services in suppressing insurrection or rebellion, shall not be questioned. But neither the United States nor any State shall assume or pay any debt or obligation incurred in aid of insurrection or rebellion against the United States, or any claim for the loss or emancipation of any slave; but all such debts, obligations and claims shall be held illegal and void.

Section 5. The Congress shall have the power to enforce, by appropriate legislation, the provisions of this article.

Amendment XV

Passed by Congress February 26, 1869. Ratified February 3, 1870.

Section 1. The right of citizens of the United States to vote shall not be denied or abridged by the United States or by any State on account of race, color, or previous condition of servitude.

Section 2. The Congress shall have the power to enforce this article by appropriate legislation.

Amendment XVI

Passed by Congress July 2, 1909. Ratified February 3, 1913.

The Congress shall have power to lay and collect taxes on incomes, from whatever source derived, without apportionment among the several States, and without regard to any census or enumeration.

Amendment XVII

Passed by Congress May 13, 1912. Ratified April 8, 1913.

The Senate of the United States shall be composed of two Senators from each State, elected by the people thereof, for six years; and each Senator shall have one vote. The electors in each State shall have the qualifications requisite for electors of the most numerous branch of the State legislatures.

When vacancies happen in the representation of any State in the Senate, the executive authority of such State shall issue writs of election to fill such vacancies: *Provided*, That the legislature of any State may empower the executive thereof to make temporary appointments until the people fill the vacancies by election as the legislature may direct.

This amendment shall not be so construed as to affect the election or term of any Senator chosen before it becomes valid as part of the Constitution.

Amendment XVIII

Passed by Congress December 18, 1917. Ratified January 16, 1919. Repealed by amendment 21.

Section 1. After one year from the ratification of this article the manufacture, sale, or transportation of intoxicating liquors within, the importation thereof into, or the exportation thereof from the United States and all territory subject to the jurisdiction thereof for beverage purposes is hereby prohibited.

Section 2. The Congress and the several States shall have concurrent power to enforce this article by appropriate legislation.

Section 3. This article shall be inoperative unless it shall have been ratified as an amendment to the Constitution by the legislatures of the several States, as provided in the Constitution, within seven years from the date of the submission hereof to the States by the Congress.

Amendment XIX

Passed by Congress June 4, 1919. Ratified August 18, 1920.

The right of citizens of the United States to vote shall not be denied or abridged by the United States or by any State on account of sex.

Congress shall have power to enforce this article by appropriate legislation.

Amendment XX

Passed by Congress March 2, 1932. Ratified January 23, 1933.

Section 1. The terms of the President and the Vice President shall end at noon on the 20th day of January, and the terms of Senators and Representatives at noon on the 3d day of January, of the years in which such terms would have ended if this article had not been ratified; and the terms of their successors shall then begin.

Section 2. The Congress shall assemble at least once in every year, and such meeting shall begin at noon on the 3d day of January, unless they shall by law appoint a different day.

Section 3. If, at the time fixed for the beginning of the term of the President, the President elect shall have died, the Vice President elect shall become President. If a President shall not have been chosen before the time fixed for the beginning of his term, or if the President elect shall have failed to qualify, then the Vice President elect shall act as President until a President shall have qualified; and the Congress may by law provide for the case wherein neither a President elect nor a Vice President shall have qualified, declaring who shall then act as President, or the manner in which one who is to act shall be selected, and such person shall act accordingly until a President or Vice President shall have qualified.

Section 4. The Congress may by law provide for the case of the death of any of the persons from whom the House of Representatives may choose a President whenever the right of choice shall have devolved upon them, and for the case of the death of any of the persons from whom the Senate may choose a Vice President whenever the right of choice shall have devolved upon them.

Section 5. Sections 1 and 2 shall take effect on the 15th day of October following the ratification of this article.

Section 6. This article shall be inoperative unless it shall have been ratified as an amendment to the Constitution by the legislatures of three-fourths of the several States within seven years from the date of its submission.

Amendment XXI

Passed by Congress February 20, 1933. Ratified December 5, 1933.

Section 1. The eighteenth article of amendment to the Constitution of the United States is hereby repealed.

Section 2. The transportation or importation into any State, Territory, or Possession of the United States for delivery or use therein of intoxicating liquors, in violation of the laws thereof, is hereby prohibited.

Section 3. This article shall be inoperative unless it shall have been ratified as an amendment to the Constitution by conventions in the several States, as provided in the Constitution, within seven years from the date of the submission hereof to the States by the Congress.

Amendment XXII

Passed by Congress March 21, 1947. Ratified February 27, 1951.

Section 1. No person shall be elected to the office of the President more than twice, and no person who has held the office of President, or acted as President, for more than two years of a term to which some other person was elected President shall be elected to the office of President more than once. But this Article shall not apply to any person holding the office of President when this Article was proposed by Congress, and shall not prevent any person who may be holding the office of President, or acting as President, during the term within which this Article becomes operative from holding the office of President or acting as President during the remainder of such term.

Section 2. This article shall be inoperative unless it shall have been ratified as an amendment to the Constitution by the legislatures of three-fourths of the several States within seven years from the date of its submission to the States by the Congress.

Amendment XXIII

Passed by Congress June 16, 1960. Ratified March 29, 1961.

Section 1. The District constituting the seat of Government of the United States shall appoint in such manner as Congress may direct:

A number of electors of President and Vice President equal to the whole number of Senators and Representatives in Congress to which the District would be entitled if it were a State, but in no event more than the least populous State; they shall be in addition to those appointed by the States, but they shall be considered, for the purposes of the election of President and Vice President, to be electors appointed by a State; and they shall meet in the District and perform such duties as provided by the twelfth article of amendment.

Section 2. The Congress shall have power to enforce this article by appropriate legislation.

Amendment XXIV

Passed by Congress August 27, 1962. Ratified January 23, 1964.

Section 1. The right of citizens of the United States to vote in any primary or other election for President or Vice President, for electors for President or Vice President, or for Senator or Representative in Congress, shall not be denied or abridged by the United States or any State by reason of failure to pay poll tax or other tax.

Section 2. The Congress shall have power to enforce this article by appropriate legislation.

Amendment XXV

Passed by Congress July 6, 1965. Ratified February 10, 1967.

Section 1. In case of the removal of the President from office or of his death or resignation, the Vice President shall become President.

Section 2. Whenever there is a vacancy in the office of the Vice President, the President shall nominate a Vice President who shall take office upon confirmation by a majority vote of both Houses of Congress.

Section 3. Whenever the President transmits to the President pro tempore of the Senate and the Speaker of the House of Representatives his written declaration that he is unable to discharge the powers and duties of his office, and until he transmits to them a written declaration to the contrary, such powers and duties shall be discharged by the Vice President as Acting President.

Section 4. Whenever the Vice President and a majority of either the principal officers of the executive departments or of such other body as Congress may by law provide, transmit to the President pro tempore of the Senate and the Speaker of the House of Representatives their written declaration that the President is unable to discharge the powers and duties of his office, the Vice President shall immediately assume the powers and duties of the office as Acting President.

Thereafter, when the President transmits to the President pro tempore of the Senate and the Speaker of the House of Representatives his written declaration that no inability exists, he shall resume the powers and duties of his office unless the Vice President and a majority of either the principal officers of the executive department or of such other body as Congress may by law provide, transmit within four days to the President pro tempore of the Senate and the Speaker of the House of Representatives their written declaration that the President is unable to discharge the powers and duties of his office. Thereupon Congress shall decide the issue, assembling within forty-eight hours for that purpose if not in session. If the Congress, within twenty-one days after receipt of the latter written declaration, or, if Congress is not in session, within twenty-one days after Congress is required to assemble, determines by two-thirds vote of both Houses that the President is unable to discharge the powers and duties of his office, the Vice President shall continue to discharge the same as Acting President; otherwise, the President shall resume the powers and duties of his office.

Amendment XXVI

Passed by Congress March 23, 1971. Ratified July 1, 1971.

Section 1. The right of citizens of the United States, who are eighteen years of age or older, to vote shall not be denied or abridged by the United States or by any State on account of age.

Section 2. The Congress shall have power to enforce this article by appropriate legislation.

Amendment XXVII

Originally proposed Sept. 25, 1789. Ratified May 7, 1992.

No law, varying the compensation for the services of the Senators and Representatives, shall take effect, until an election of representatives shall have intervened.

B

Select Jurisdictional Provisions

28 U.S.C. §1330: Actions against foreign states

(a) The district courts shall have original jurisdiction without regard to amount in controversy of any nonjury civil action against a foreign state as defined in section 1603(a) of this title as to any claim for relief in personam with respect to which the foreign state is not entitled to immunity either under sections 1605-1607 of this title or under any applicable international agreement.

(b) Personal jurisdiction over a foreign state shall exist as to every claim for relief over which the district courts have jurisdiction under subsection (a) where service has been made under section 1608 of this title.

(c) For purposes of subsection (b), an appearance by a foreign state does not confer personal jurisdiction with respect to any claim for relief not arising out of any transaction or occurrence enumerated in sections 1605-1607 of this title.

28 U.S.C §1331: Federal question

The district courts shall have original jurisdiction of all civil actions arising under the Constitution, laws, or treaties of the United States.

28 U.S.C. §1332: Diversity of citizenship; amount in controversy; costs

(a) The district courts shall have original jurisdiction of all civil actions where the matter in controversy exceeds the sum or value of $75,000, exclusive of interest and costs, and is between —
    (1) citizens of different States;
    (2) citizens of a State and citizens or subjects of a foreign state;
    (3) citizens of different States and in which citizens or subjects of a foreign state are additional parties; and
    (4) a foreign state, defined in section 1603(a) of this title, as plaintiff and citizens of a State or of different States.

For the purposes of this section, section 1335, and section 1441, an alien admitted to the United States for permanent residence shall be deemed a citizen of the State in which such alien is domiciled.

(b) Except when express provision therefor is otherwise made in a statute of the United States, where the plaintiff who files the case originally in the Federal courts is finally adjudged to be entitled to recover less than the sum or value of $75,000, computed without regard to any setoff or counterclaim to which the defendant may be adjudged to be entitled, and exclusive of interest and costs, the district court may deny costs to the plaintiff and, in addition, may impose costs on the plaintiff.

(c) For the purposes of this section and section 1441 of this title—

(1) a corporation shall be deemed to be a citizen of any State by which it has been incorporated and of the State where it has its principal place of business, except that in any direct action against the insurer of a policy or contract of liability insurance, whether incorporated or unincorporated, to which action the insured is not joined as a party-defendant, such insurer shall be deemed a citizen of the State of which the insured is a citizen, as well as of any State by which the insurer has been incorporated and of the State where it has its principal place of business; and

(2) the legal representative of the estate of a decedent shall be deemed to be a citizen only of the same State as the decedent, and the legal representative of an infant or incompetent shall be deemed to be a citizen only of the same State as the infant or incompetent.

(d) (1) In this subsection—

(A) the term "class" means all of the class members in a class action;

(B) the term "class action" means any civil action filed under rule 23 of the Federal Rules of Civil Procedure or similar State statute or rule of judicial procedure authorizing an action to be brought by 1 or more representative persons as a class action;

(C) the term "class certification order" means an order issued by a court approving the treatment of some or all aspects of a civil action as a class action; and

(D) the term "class members" means the persons (named or unnamed) who fall within the definition of the proposed or certified class in a class action.

(2) The district courts shall have original jurisdiction of any civil action in which the matter in controversy exceeds the sum or value of $5,000,000, exclusive of interest and costs, and is a class action in which—

(A) any member of a class of plaintiffs is a citizen of a State different from any defendant;

(B) any member of a class of plaintiffs is a foreign state or a citizen or subject of a foreign state and any defendant is a citizen of a State; or

(C) any member of a class of plaintiffs is a citizen of a State and any defendant is a foreign state or a citizen or subject of a foreign state.

(3) A district court may, in the interests of justice and looking at the totality of the circumstances, decline to exercise jurisdiction under paragraph (2) over a class action in which greater than one-third but less than two-thirds of the members of all proposed plaintiff classes in the

aggregate and the primary defendants are citizens of the State in which the action was originally filed based on consideration of—

    (A) whether the claims asserted involve matters of national or interstate interest;

    (B) whether the claims asserted will be governed by laws of the State in which the action was originally filed or by the laws of other States;

    (C) whether the class action has been pleaded in a manner that seeks to avoid Federal jurisdiction;

    (D) whether the action was brought in a forum with a distinct nexus with the class members, the alleged harm, or the defendants;

    (E) whether the number of citizens of the State in which the action was originally filed in all proposed plaintiff classes in the aggregate is substantially larger than the number of citizens from any other State, and the citizenship of the other members of the proposed class is dispersed among a substantial number of States; and

    (F) whether, during the 3-year period preceding the filing of that class action, 1 or more other class actions asserting the same or similar claims on behalf of the same or other persons have been filed.

(4) A district court shall decline to exercise jurisdiction under paragraph (2)—

    (A) (i) over a class action in which—

        (I) greater than two-thirds of the members of all proposed plaintiff classes in the aggregate are citizens of the State in which the action was originally filed;

        (II) at least 1 defendant is a defendant—

            (aa) from whom significant relief is sought by members of the plaintiff class;

            (bb) whose alleged conduct forms a significant basis for the claims asserted by the proposed plaintiff class; and

            (cc) who is a citizen of the State in which the action was originally filed; and

        (III) principal injuries resulting from the alleged conduct or any related conduct of each defendant were incurred in the State in which the action was originally filed; and

    (ii) during the 3-year period preceding the filing of that class action, no other class action has been filed asserting the same or similar factual allegations against any of the defendants on behalf of the same or other persons; or

    (B) two-thirds or more of the members of all proposed plaintiff classes in the aggregate, and the primary defendants, are citizens of the State in which the action was originally filed.

(5) Paragraphs (2) through (4) shall not apply to any class action in which—

    (A) the primary defendants are States, State officials, or other governmental entities against whom the district court may be foreclosed from ordering relief; or

(B) the number of members of all proposed plaintiff classes in the aggregate is less than 100.

(6) In any class action, the claims of the individual class members shall be aggregated to determine whether the matter in controversy exceeds the sum or value of $ 5,000,000, exclusive of interest and costs.

(7) Citizenship of the members of the proposed plaintiff classes shall be determined for purposes of paragraphs (2) through (6) as of the date of filing of the complaint or amended complaint, or, if the case stated by the initial pleading is not subject to Federal jurisdiction, as of the date of service by plaintiffs of an amended pleading, motion, or other paper, indicating the existence of Federal jurisdiction.

(8) This subsection shall apply to any class action before or after the entry of a class certification order by the court with respect to that action.

(9) Paragraph (2) shall not apply to any class action that solely involves a claim —

(A) concerning a covered security as defined under 16(f)(3) of the Securities Act of 1933 (15 U.S.C. 78p(f)(3)) and section 28(f)(5)(E) of the Securities Exchange Act of 1934 (15 U.S.C. 78bb(f)(5)(E));

(B) that relates to the internal affairs or governance of a corporation or other form of business enterprise and that arises under or by virtue of the laws of the State in which such corporation or business enterprise is incorporated or organized; or

(C) that relates to the rights, duties (including fiduciary duties), and obligations relating to or created by or pursuant to any security (as defined under section 2(a)(1) of the Securities Act of 1933 (15 U.S.C. 77b(a)(1)) and the regulations issued thereunder).

(10) For purposes of this subsection and section 1453, an unincorporated association shall be deemed to be a citizen of the State where it has its principal place of business and the State under whose laws it is organized.

(11) (A) For purposes of this subsection and section 1453, a mass action shall be deemed to be a class action removable under paragraphs (2) through (10) if it otherwise meets the provisions of those paragraphs.

(B) (i) As used in subparagraph (A), the term "mass action" means any civil action (except a civil action within the scope of section 1711(2)) in which monetary relief claims of 100 or more persons are proposed to be tried jointly on the ground that the plaintiffs' claims involve common questions of law or fact, except that jurisdiction shall exist only over those plaintiffs whose claims in a mass action satisfy the jurisdictional amount requirements under subsection (a).

(ii) As used in subparagraph (A), the term "mass action" shall not include any civil action in which —

(I) all of the claims in the action arise from an event or occurrence in the State in which the action was filed, and that allegedly resulted in injuries in that State or in States contiguous to that State;

(II) the claims are joined upon motion of a defendant;

(III) all of the claims in the action are asserted on behalf of the general public (and not on behalf of individual claimants or members of a purported class) pursuant to a State statute specifically authorizing such action; or

(IV) the claims have been consolidated or coordinated solely for pretrial proceedings.

(C) (i) Any action(s) removed to Federal court pursuant to this subsection shall not thereafter be transferred to any other court pursuant to section 1407, or the rules promulgated thereunder, unless a majority of the plaintiffs in the action request transfer pursuant to section 1407.

(ii) This subparagraph will not apply —

(I) to cases certified pursuant to rule 23 of the Federal Rules of Civil Procedure; or

(II) if plaintiffs propose that the action proceed as a class action pursuant to rule 23 of the Federal Rules of Civil Procedure.

(D) The limitations periods on any claims asserted in a mass action that is removed to Federal court pursuant to this subsection shall be deemed tolled during the period that the action is pending in Federal court.

(e) The word "States", as used in this section, includes the Territories, the District of Columbia, and the Commonwealth of Puerto Rico.

28 U.S.C. §1333: Admiralty, maritime and prize cases

The district courts shall have original jurisdiction, exclusive of the courts of the States, of:

(1) Any civil case of admiralty or maritime jurisdiction, saving to suitors in all cases all other remedies to which they are otherwise entitled.

(2) Any prize brought into the United States and all proceedings for the condemnation of property taken as prize.

28 U.S.C. §1350: Alien's action for tort

The district courts shall have original jurisdiction of any civil action by an alien for a tort only, committed in violation of the law of nations or a treaty of the United States.

28 U.S.C. §1351: Consuls, vice consuls, and members of a diplomatic mission as defendant

The district courts shall have original jurisdiction, exclusive of the courts of the States, of all civil actions and proceedings against—

(1) consuls or vice consuls of foreign states; or

(2) members of a mission or members of their families (as such terms are defined in section 2 of the Diplomatic Relations Act).

28 U.S.C. §1356: Seizures not within admiralty and maritime jurisdiction

The district courts shall have original jurisdiction, exclusive of the courts of the States, of any seizure under any law of the United States on land or upon waters not within admiralty and maritime jurisdiction, except matters within the jurisdiction of the Court of International Trade under section 1582 of this title.

28 U.S.C. §1391: Venue generally

(a) A civil action wherein jurisdiction is founded only on diversity of citizenship may, except as otherwise provided by law, be brought only in (1) a judicial district where any defendant resides, if all defendants reside in the same State, (2) a judicial district in which a substantial part of the events or omissions giving rise to the claim occurred, or a substantial part of property that is the subject of the action is situated, or (3) a judicial district in which any defendant is subject to personal jurisdiction at the time the action is commenced, if there is no district in which the action may otherwise be brought.

(b) A civil action wherein jurisdiction is not founded solely on diversity of citizenship may, except as otherwise provided by law, be brought only in (1) a judicial district where any defendant resides, if all defendants reside in the same State, (2) a judicial district in which a substantial part of the events or omissions giving rise to the claim occurred, or a substantial part of property that is the subject of the action is situated, or (3) a judicial district in which any defendant may be found, if there is no district in which the action may otherwise be brought.

(c) For purposes of venue under this chapter, a defendant that is a corporation shall be deemed to reside in any judicial district in which it is subject to personal jurisdiction at the time the action is commenced. In a State which has more than one judicial district and in which a defendant that is a corporation is subject to personal jurisdiction at the time an action is commenced, such corporation shall be deemed to reside in any district in that State within which its contacts would be sufficient to subject it to personal jurisdiction if that district were a separate State, and, if there is no such district, the corporation shall be deemed to reside in the district within which it has the most significant contacts.

(d) An alien may be sued in any district.

(e) A civil action in which a defendant is an officer or employee of the United States or any agency thereof acting in his official capacity or under color of legal authority, or an agency of the United States, or the United States, may, except as otherwise provided by law, be brought in any judicial district in which (1) a defendant in the action resides, (2) a substantial part of the events or omissions giving rise to the claim occurred or a substantial part of property that is the subject of the action is situated, or (3) the plaintiff resides if no real property is involved in the action. Additional persons may be joined as parties to any such action in accordance with the Federal Rules of Civil Procedure and with such other venue requirements as would be applicable if the United States or one of its officers, employees, or agencies were not a party.

The summons and complaint in such an action shall be served as provided by the Federal Rules of Civil Procedure except that the delivery of the summons and complaint to the officer or agency as required by the rules may be made by certified mail beyond the territorial limits of the district in which the action is brought.

(f) A civil action against a foreign state as defined in section 1603(a) of this title may be brought—

   (1) in any judicial district in which a substantial part of the events or omissions giving rise to the claim occurred, or a substantial part of property that is the subject of the action is situated;

   (2) in any judicial district in which the vessel or cargo of a foreign state is situated, if the claim is asserted under section 1605(b) of this title;

   (3) in any judicial district in which the agency or instrumentality is licensed to do business or is doing business, if the action is brought against an agency or instrumentality of a foreign state as defined in section 1603(b) of this title; or

   (4) in the United States District Court for the District of Columbia if the action is brought against a foreign state or political subdivision thereof.

(g) A civil action in which jurisdiction of the district court is based upon section 1369 of this title [relating to certain mass tort cases] may be brought in any district in which any defendant resides or in which a substantial part of the accident giving rise to the action took place.

28 U.S.C. §1441: Actions removable generally

(a) Except as otherwise expressly provided by Act of Congress, any civil action brought in a State court of which the district courts of the United States have original jurisdiction, may be removed by the defendant or the defendants, to the district court of the United States for the district and division embracing the place where such action is pending. For purposes of removal under this chapter, the citizenship of defendants sued under fictitious names shall be disregarded.

(b) Any civil action of which the district courts have original jurisdiction founded on a claim or right arising under the Constitution, treaties or laws of the United States shall be removable without regard to the citizenship or residence of the parties. Any other such action shall be removable only if none of the parties in interest properly joined and served as defendants is a citizen of the State in which such action is brought.

(c) Whenever a separate and independent claim or cause of action within the jurisdiction conferred by section 1331 of this title is joined with one or more otherwise nonremovable claims or causes of action, the entire case may be removed and the district court may determine all issues therein, or, in its discretion, may remand all matters in which State law predominates.

(d) Any civil action brought in a State court against a foreign state as defined in section 1603(a) of this title may be removed by the foreign state to the district court of the United States for the district and division embracing the place where such action is pending. Upon removal the action shall be tried by the court without jury. Where removal is based upon this subsection, the time limitations of section 1446(b) of this chapter may be enlarged at any time for cause shown.

(e) (1) Notwithstanding the provisions of subsection (b) of this section, a defendant in a civil action in a State court may remove the action to the district court of the United States for the district and division embracing the place where the action is pending if—

(A) the action could have been brought in a United States district court under section 1369 of this title; or

(B) the defendant is a party to an action which is or could have been brought, in whole or in part, under section 1369 in a United States district court and arises from the same accident as the action in State court, even if the action to be removed could not have been brought in a district court as an original matter.

The removal of an action under this subsection shall be made in accordance with section 1446 of this title, except that a notice of removal may also be filed before trial of the action in State court within 30 days after the date on which the defendant first becomes a party to an action under section 1369 in a United States district court that arises from the same accident as the action in State court, or at a later time with leave of the district court.

(2) Whenever an action is removed under this subsection and the district court to which it is removed or transferred under section 1407(j) has made a liability determination requiring further proceedings as to damages, the district court shall remand the action to the State court from which it had been removed for the determination of damages, unless the court finds that, for the convenience of parties and witnesses and in the interest of justice, the action should be retained for the determination of damages.

(3) Any remand under paragraph (2) shall not be effective until 60 days after the district court has issued an order determining liability and has certified its intention to remand the removed action for the determination of damages. An appeal with respect to the liability determination of the district court may be taken during that 60-day period to the court of appeals with appellate jurisdiction over the district court. In the event a party files such an appeal, the remand shall not be effective until the appeal has been finally disposed of. Once the remand has become effective, the liability determination shall not be subject to further review by appeal or otherwise.

(4) Any decision under this subsection concerning remand for the determination of damages shall not be reviewable by appeal or otherwise.

(5) An action removed under this subsection shall be deemed to be an action under section 1369 and an action in which jurisdiction is based on section 1369 of this title for purposes of this section and sections 1407, 1697, and 1785 of this title.

(6) Nothing in this subsection shall restrict the authority of the district court to transfer or dismiss an action on the ground of inconvenient forum.

(f) The court to which such civil action is removed is not precluded from hearing and determining any claim in such civil action because the State court from which such civil action is removed did not have jurisdiction over that claim.

C

Foreign Sovereign Immunities Act

28 U.S.C. §1602: Findings and declaration of purpose

The Congress finds that the determination by United States courts of the claims of foreign states to immunity from the jurisdiction of such courts would serve the interests of justice and would protect the rights of both foreign states and litigants in United States courts. Under international law, states are not immune from the jurisdiction of foreign courts insofar as their commercial activities are concerned, and their commercial property may be levied upon for the satisfaction of judgments rendered against them in connection with their commercial activities. Claims of foreign states to immunity should henceforth be decided by courts of the United States and of the States in conformity with the principles set forth in this chapter.

28 U.S.C. §1603: Definitions

For purposes of this chapter—

(a) A "foreign state," except as used in section 1608 of this title, includes a political subdivision of a foreign state or an agency or instrumentality of a foreign state as defined in subsection (b).

(b) An "agency or instrumentality of a foreign state" means any entity—

(1) which is a separate legal person, corporate or otherwise, and

(2) which is an organ of a foreign state or political subdivision thereof, or a majority of whose shares or other ownership interest is owned by a foreign state or political subdivision thereof, and

(3) which is neither a citizen of a State of the United States as defined in section 1332(c) and (e) of this title nor created under the laws of any third country.

(c) The "United States" includes all territory and waters, continental or insular, subject to the jurisdiction of the United States.

(d) A "commercial activity" means either a regular course of commercial conduct or a particular commercial transaction or act. The commercial character of an activity shall be determined by reference to the nature of the course of conduct or particular transaction or act, rather than by reference to its purpose.

(e) A "commercial activity carried on in the United States by a foreign state" means commercial activity carried on by such state and having substantial contact with the United States.

28 U.S.C. §1604: Immunity of a foreign state from jurisdiction

Subject to existing international agreements to which the United States is a party at the time of enactment of this Act [enacted Oct. 21, 1976] a foreign state shall be immune from the jurisdiction of the courts of the United States and of the States except as provided in sections 1605 to 1607 of this chapter.

28 U.S.C. §1605: General exceptions to the jurisdictional immunity of a foreign state

(a) A foreign state shall not be immune from the jurisdiction of courts of the United States or of the States in any case —

(1) in which the foreign state has waived its immunity either explicitly or by implication, notwithstanding any withdrawal of the waiver which the foreign state may purport to effect except in accordance with the terms of the waiver;

(2) in which the action is based upon a commercial activity carried on in the United States by the foreign state; or upon an act performed in the United States in connection with a commercial activity of the foreign state elsewhere; or upon an act outside the territory of the United States in connection with a commercial activity of the foreign state elsewhere and that act causes a direct effect in the United States;

(3) in which rights in property taken in violation of international law are in issue and that property or any property exchanged for such property is present in the United States in connection with a commercial activity carried on in the United States by the foreign state; or that property or any property exchanged for such property is owned or operated by an agency or instrumentality of the foreign state and that agency or instrumentality is engaged in a commercial activity in the United States;

(4) in which rights in property in the United States acquired by succession or gift or rights in immovable property situated in the United States are in issue;

(5) not otherwise encompassed in paragraph (2) above, in which money damages are sought against a foreign state for personal injury or death, or damage to or loss of property, occurring in the United States and caused by the tortious act or omission of that foreign state or of any official or employee of that foreign state while acting within the scope of his office or employment; except this paragraph shall not apply to —

(A) any claim based upon the exercise or performance or the failure to exercise or perform a discretionary function regardless of whether the discretion be abused, or

(B) any claim arising out of malicious prosecution, abuse of process, libel, slander, misrepresentation, deceit, or interference with contract rights;

(6) in which the action is brought, either to enforce an agreement made by the foreign state with or for the benefit of a private party to

submit to arbitration all or any differences which have arisen or which may arise between the parties with respect to a defined legal relationship, whether contractual or not, concerning a subject matter capable of settlement by arbitration under the laws of the United States, or to confirm an award made pursuant to such an agreement to arbitrate, if (A) the arbitration takes place or is intended to take place in the United States, (B) the agreement or award is or may be governed by a treaty or other international agreement in force for the United States calling for the recognition and enforcement of arbitral awards, (C) the underlying claim, save for the agreement to arbitrate, could have been brought in a United States court under this section or section 1607, or (D) paragraph (1) of this subsection is otherwise applicable; or

(7) not otherwise covered by paragraph (2), in which money damages are sought against a foreign state for personal injury or death that was caused by an act of torture, extrajudicial killing, aircraft sabotage, hostage taking, or the provision of material support or resources (as defined in section 2339A of title 18) for such an act if such act or provision of material support is engaged in by an official, employee, or agent of such foreign state while acting within the scope of his or her office, employment, or agency, except that the court shall decline to hear a claim under this paragraph—

(A) if the foreign state was not designated as a state sponsor of terrorism under section 6(j) of the Export Administration Act of 1979 or section 620A of the Foreign Assistance Act of 1961 at the time the act occurred, unless later so designated as a result of such act or the act is related to Case Number 1:00CV03110(EGS) in the United States District Court for the District of Columbia; and

(B) even if the foreign state is or was so designated, if—

(i) the act occurred in the foreign state against which the claim has been brought and the claimant has not afforded the foreign state a reasonable opportunity to arbitrate the claim in accordance with accepted international rules of arbitration; or

(ii) neither the claimant nor the victim was a national of the United States (as that term is defined in section 101(a)(22) of the Immigration and Nationality Act when the act upon which the claim is based occurred.

(b) A foreign state shall not be immune from the jurisdiction of the courts of the United States in any case in which a suit in admiralty is brought to enforce a maritime lien against a vessel or cargo of the foreign state, which maritime lien is based upon a commercial activity of the foreign state: Provided, That—

(1) notice of the suit is given by delivery of a copy of the summons and of the complaint to the person, or his agent, having possession of the vessel or cargo against which the maritime lien is asserted; and if the vessel or cargo is arrested pursuant to process obtained on behalf of the party bringing the suit, the service of process of arrest shall be deemed to constitute valid delivery of such notice, but the party bringing the suit shall be liable for any damages sustained by the foreign state as a

result of the arrest if the party bringing the suit had actual or constructive knowledge that the vessel or cargo of a foreign state was involved; and

(2) notice to the foreign state of the commencement of suit as provided in section 1608 of this title is initiated within ten days either of the delivery of notice as provided in paragraph (1) of this subsection or, in the case of a party who was unaware that the vessel or cargo of a foreign state was involved, of the date such party determined the existence of the foreign state's interest.

(c) Whenever notice is delivered under subsection (b)(1), the suit to enforce a maritime lien shall thereafter proceed and shall be heard and determined according to the principles of law and rules of practice of suits in rem whenever it appears that, had the vessel been privately owned and possessed, a suit in rem might have been maintained. A decree against the foreign state may include costs of the suit and, if the decree is for a money judgment, interest as ordered by the court, except that the court may not award judgment against the foreign state in an amount greater than the value of the vessel or cargo upon which the maritime lien arose. Such value shall be determined as of the time notice is served under subsection (b)(1). Decrees shall be subject to appeal and revision as provided in other cases of admiralty and maritime jurisdiction. Nothing shall preclude the plaintiff in any proper case from seeking relief in personam in the same action brought to enforce a maritime lien as provided in this section.

(d) A foreign state shall not be immune from the jurisdiction of the courts of the United States in any action brought to foreclose a preferred mortgage, as defined in the Ship Mortgage Act, 1920 and following. Such action shall be brought, heard, and determined in accordance with the provisions of that Act and in accordance with the principles of law and rules of practice of suits in rem, whenever it appears that had the vessel been privately owned and possessed a suit in rem might have been maintained.

(e) For purposes of paragraph (7) of subsection (a)—

(1) the terms "torture" and "extrajudicial killing" have the meaning given those terms in section 3 of the Torture Victim Protection Act of 1991;

(2) the term "hostage taking" has the meaning given that term in Article 1 of the International Convention Against the Taking of Hostages; and

(3) the term "aircraft sabotage" has the meaning given that term in Article 1 of the Convention for the Suppression of Unlawful Acts Against the Safety of Civil Aviation.

(f) No action shall be maintained under subsection (a)(7) unless the action is commenced not later than 10 years after the date on which the cause of action arose. All principles of equitable tolling, including the period during which the foreign state was immune from suit, shall apply in calculating this limitation period.

(g) Limitation on discovery.

(1) In general.

(A) Subject to paragraph (2), if an action is filed that would otherwise be barred by section 1604, but for subsection (a)(7), the court, upon request of the Attorney General, shall stay any request, demand, or order for discovery on the United States that the Attorney General certifies would significantly interfere with a criminal investigation or prosecution, or a national security operation, related to the incident that gave rise to the cause of action, until such time as the Attorney General advises the court that such request, demand, or order will no longer so interfere.

(B) A stay under this paragraph shall be in effect during the 12-month period beginning on the date on which the court issues the order to stay discovery. The court shall renew the order to stay discovery for additional 12-month periods upon motion by the United States if the Attorney General certifies that discovery would significantly interfere with a criminal investigation or prosecution, or a national security operation, related to the incident that gave rise to the cause of action.

(2) Sunset.

(A) Subject to subparagraph (B), no stay shall be granted or continued in effect under paragraph (1) after the date that is 10 years after the date on which the incident that gave rise to the cause of action occurred.

(B) After the period referred to in subparagraph (A), the court, upon request of the Attorney General, may stay any request, demand, or order for discovery on the United States that the court finds a substantial likelihood would —

(i) create a serious threat of death or serious bodily injury to any person;

(ii) adversely affect the ability of the United States to work in cooperation with foreign and international law enforcement agencies in investigating violations of United States law; or

(iii) obstruct the criminal case related to the incident that gave rise to the cause of action or undermine the potential for a conviction in such case.

(3) Evaluation of evidence. The court's evaluation of any request for a stay under this subsection filed by the Attorney General shall be conducted ex parte and in camera.

(4) Bar on motions to dismiss. A stay of discovery under this subsection shall constitute a bar to the granting of a motion to dismiss under rules 12(b)(6) and 56 of the Federal Rules of Civil Procedure.

(5) Construction. Nothing in this subsection shall prevent the United States from seeking protective orders or asserting privileges ordinarily available to the United States.

28 U.S.C. §1606: Extent of liability

As to any claim for relief with respect to which a foreign state is not entitled to immunity under section 1605 or 1607 of this chapter, the foreign state shall be liable in the same manner and to the same extent as a private individual under like circumstances; but a foreign state except for an agency or instrumentality thereof shall not be liable for punitive damages; if, however, in any case wherein death was caused, the law of the place where the action or omission occurred provides, or has been construed to provide, for damages only punitive in nature, the foreign state shall be liable for actual or compensatory damages measured by the pecuniary injuries resulting from such death which were incurred by the persons for whose benefit the action was brought.

28 U.S.C. §1607: Counterclaims

In any action brought by a foreign state, or in which a foreign state intervenes, in a court of the United States or of a State, the foreign state shall not be accorded immunity with respect to any counterclaim —

(a) for which a foreign state would not be entitled to immunity under section 1605 of this chapter had such claim been brought in a separate action against the foreign state; or

(b) arising out of the transaction or occurrence that is the subject matter of the claim of the foreign state; or

(c) to the extent that the counterclaim does not seek relief exceeding in amount or differing in kind from that sought by the foreign state.

28 U.S.C. §1608: Service; time to answer; default

(a) Service in the courts of the United States and of the States shall be made upon a foreign state or political subdivision of a foreign state:

(1) by delivery of a copy of the summons and complaint in accordance with any special arrangement for service between the plaintiff and the foreign state or political subdivision; or

(2) if no special arrangement exists, by delivery of a copy of the summons and complaint in accordance with an applicable international convention on service of judicial documents; or

(3) if service cannot be made under paragraphs (1) or (2), by sending a copy of the summons and complaint and a notice of suit, together with a translation of each into the official language of the foreign state, by any form of mail requiring a signed receipt, to be addressed and dispatched by the clerk of the court to the head of the ministry of foreign affairs of the foreign state concerned, or

(4) if service cannot be made within 30 days under paragraph (3), by sending two copies of the summons and complaint and a notice of suit, together with a translation of each into the official language of the foreign state, by any form of mail requiring a signed receipt, to be addressed and dispatched by the clerk of the court to the Secretary of State in Washington, District of Columbia, to the attention of the Director of Special Consular Services — and the Secretary shall transmit one copy of the papers through diplomatic channels to the foreign state and shall send to the clerk of the court a certified copy of the diplomatic note indicating when the papers were transmitted.

As used in this subsection, a "notice of suit" shall mean a notice addressed to a foreign state and in a form prescribed by the Secretary of State by regulation.

(b) Service in the courts of the United States and of the States shall be made upon an agency or instrumentality of a foreign state:

(1) by delivery of a copy of the summons and complaint in accordance with any special arrangement for service between the plaintiff and the agency or instrumentality; or

(2) if no special arrangement exists, by delivery of a copy of the summons and complaint either to an officer, a managing or general agent, or to any other agent authorized by appointment or by law to receive service of process in the United States; or in accordance with an applicable international convention on service of judicial documents; or

(3) if service cannot be made under paragraphs (1) or (2), and if reasonably calculated to give actual notice, by delivery of a copy of the summons and complaint, together with a translation of each into the official language of the foreign state —

(A) as directed by an authority of the foreign state or political subdivision in response to a letter rogatory or request or

(B) by any form of mail requiring a signed receipt, to be addressed and dispatched by the clerk of the court to the agency or instrumentality to be served, or

(C) as directed by order of the court consistent with the law of the place where service is to be made.

(c) Service shall be deemed to have been made —

(1) in the case of service under subsection (a)(4), as of the date of transmittal indicated in the certified copy of the diplomatic note; and

(2) in any other case under this section, as of the date of receipt indicated in the certification, signed and returned postal receipt, or other proof of service applicable to the method of service employed.

(d) In any action brought in a court of the United States or of a State, a foreign state, a political subdivision thereof, or an agency or instrumentality of a foreign state shall serve an answer or other responsive pleading to the complaint within sixty days after service has been made under this section.

(e) No judgment by default shall be entered by a court of the United States or of a State against a foreign state, a political subdivision thereof, or an agency or instrumentality of a foreign state, unless the claimant establishes his claim or right to relief by evidence satisfactory to the court. A copy of any such default judgment shall be sent to the foreign state or political subdivision in the manner prescribed for service in this section.

28 U.S.C. §1609: Immunity from attachment and execution of property of a foreign state

Subject to existing international agreements to which the United States is a party at the time of enactment of this Act [enacted Oct. 21, 1976] the property in the United States of a foreign state shall be immune from attachment arrest and execution except as provided in sections 1610 and 1611 of this chapter.

28 U.S.C. §1610: Exceptions to the immunity from attachment or execution

(a) The property in the United States of a foreign state, as defined in section 1603(a) of this chapter, used for a commercial activity in the United States, shall not be immune from attachment in aid of execution, or from execution, upon a judgment entered by a court of the United States or of a State after the effective date of this Act, if—

(1) the foreign state has waived its immunity from attachment in aid of execution or from execution either explicitly or by implication, notwithstanding any withdrawal of the waiver the foreign state may purport to effect except in accordance with the terms of the waiver, or

(2) the property is or was used for the commercial activity upon which the claim is based, or

(3) the execution relates to a judgment establishing rights in property which has been taken in violation of international law or which has been exchanged for property taken in violation of international law, or

(4) the execution relates to a judgment establishing rights in property—

(A) which is acquired by succession or gift, or

(B) which is immovable and situated in the United States: Provided, That such property is not used for purposes of maintaining a diplomatic or consular mission or the residence of the Chief of such mission, or

(5) the property consists of any contractual obligation or any proceeds from such a contractual obligation to indemnify or hold harmless the foreign state or its employees under a policy of automobile or other liability or casualty insurance covering the claim which merged into the judgment, or

(6) the judgment is based on an order confirming an arbitral award rendered against the foreign state, provided that attachment in aid of execution, or execution, would not be inconsistent with any provision in the arbitral agreement, or

(7) the judgment relates to a claim for which the foreign state is not immune under section 1605(a)(7), regardless of whether the property is or was involved with the act upon which the claim is based.

(b) In addition to subsection (a), any property in the United States of an agency or instrumentality of a foreign state engaged in commercial activity in the United States shall not be immune from attachment in aid of execution, or from execution, upon a judgment entered by a court of the United States or of a State after the effective date of this Act if—

(1) the agency or instrumentality has waived its immunity from attachment in aid of execution or from execution either explicitly or implicitly, notwithstanding any withdrawal of the waiver the agency or instrumentality may purport to effect except in accordance with the terms of the waiver, or

(2) the judgment relates to a claim for which the agency or instrumentality is not immune by virtue of section 1605(a)(2), (3), (5), or (7), or 1605(b) of this chapter, regardless of whether the property is or was involved in the act upon which the claim is based.

(c) No attachment or execution referred to in subsections (a) and (b) of this section shall be permitted until the court has ordered such attachment and execution after having determined that a reasonable period of time has elapsed following the entry of judgment and the giving of any notice required under section 1608(e) of this chapter.

(d) The property of a foreign state, as defined in section 1603(a) of this chapter, used for a commercial activity in the United States, shall not be immune from attachment prior to the entry of judgment in any action brought in a court of the United States or of a State, or prior to the elapse of the period of time provided in subsection (c) of this section, if

(1) the foreign state has explicitly waived its immunity from attachment prior to judgment, notwithstanding any withdrawal of the waiver the foreign state may purport to effect except in accordance with the terms of the waiver, and

(2) the purpose of the attachment is to secure satisfaction of a judgment that has been or may ultimately be entered against the foreign state, and not to obtain jurisdiction.

(e) The vessels of a foreign state shall not be immune from arrest in rem, interlocutory sale, and execution in actions brought to foreclose a preferred mortgage as provided in section 1605(d).

(f)(1)(A) Notwithstanding any other provision of law, including but not limited to section 208(f) of the Foreign Missions Act, and except as provided in subparagraph (B), any property with respect to which financial transactions are prohibited or regulated pursuant to section 5(b) of the Trading with the Enemy Act, section 620(a) of the Foreign Assistance Act of 1961, sections 202 and 203 of the International Emergency Economic Powers Act, or any other proclamation, order, regulation, or license issued pursuant thereto, shall be subject to execution or attachment in aid of execution of any judgment relating to a claim for which a foreign state (including any agency or instrumentality or such state) claiming such property is not immune under section 1605(a)(7).

(B) Subparagraph (A) shall not apply if, at the time the property is expropriated or seized by the foreign state, the property has been held in title by a natural person or, if held in trust, has been held for the benefit of a natural person or persons.

(2)(A) At the request of any party in whose favor a judgment has been issued with respect to a claim for which the foreign state is not immune under section 1605(a)(7), the Secretary of the Treasury and the Secretary of State should make every effort to fully, promptly, and effectively assist any judgment creditor or any court that has issued any such judgment in identifying, locating, and executing against the property of that foreign state or any agency or instrumentality of such state.

(B) In providing such assistance, the Secretaries —

(i) may provide such information to the court under seal; and

(ii) should make every effort to provide the information in a manner sufficient to allow the court to direct the United States Marshall's office to promptly and effectively execute against that property.

(3) Waiver. The President may waive any provision of paragraph (1) in the interest of national security.

28 U.S.C. §1611: Certain types of property immune from execution

(a) Notwithstanding the provisions of section 1610 of this chapter, the property of those organizations designated by the President as being entitled to enjoy the privileges, exemptions, and immunities provided by the International Organizations Immunities Act shall not be subject to attachment or any other judicial process impeding the disbursement of funds to, or on the order of, a foreign state as the result of an action brought in the courts of the United States or of the States.

(b) Notwithstanding the provisions of section 1610 of this chapter, the property of a foreign state shall be immune from attachment and from execution, if—

(1) the property is that of a foreign central bank or monetary authority held for its own account, unless such bank or authority, or its parent foreign government, has explicitly waived its immunity from attachment in aid of execution, or from execution, notwithstanding any withdrawal of the waiver which the bank, authority or government may purport to effect except in accordance with the terms of the waiver; or

(2) the property is, or is intended to be, used in connection with a military activity and

(A) is of a military character, or

(B) is under the control of a military authority or defense agency.

(c) Notwithstanding the provisions of section 1610 of this chapter, the property of a foreign state shall be immune from attachment and from execution in an action brought under section 302 of the Cuban Liberty and Democratic Solidarity (LIBERTAD) Act of 1996 to the extent that the property is a facility or installation used by an accredited diplomatic mission for official purposes.

Table of Cases

Principal cases are in italics. Cases cited in excerpted materials are not listed here.

Index